مركز بلفاست الإسلامي

Belfast Islamic Centre

38 Wellington Park, Belfast BT9 6DN.

Telephone: 664465

THE
GLORIOUS
QUR'ĀN

TEXT, TRANSLATION & COMMENTARY

'ABDUL MĀJID DARYĀBĀDĪ

THE ISLAMIC FOUNDATION

This publication has been sponsored by
Al-Maktoum Charitable Foundation
United Arab Emirates

Published by

THE ISLAMIC FOUNDATION

Markfield Conference Centre, Ratby Lane,
Markfield, Leicester LE67 9SY, United Kingdom
Tel: (01530) 244944/5, Fax: (01530) 244946
E-mail: i.foundation@islamic-foundation.org.uk
Website: www.islamic-foundation.org.uk

Quran House, P.O. Box 30611, Nairobi, Kenya

P.M.B. 3193, Kano, Nigeria

British Library Cataloguing-in-Publication Data

The Glorious Quran : text, translation and commentary
1. Koran – Commentaries
I. Daryabadi, Abdul Majid
297.1'22

ISBN 0 86037 360 6

Typeset by: Naved Khan
Cover design: Imtiaze A. Manjra

Contents

Contents

Contents

Contents

Contents

Contents

Contents

Contents

Contents

Contents

x

FOREWORD

It is our great pleasure and privilege to bring out Mawlana Abdul Majid Daryabadi's *The Glorious Qur'ān*, containing a selection of his commentary on the Qur'ān, with a special focus on comparative religion.

Mawlana Daryabadi (1892–1977) embarked on his venture in the 1930s when the field of English translations of the Qur'ān was dominated by Orientalists and Qadiyanis. With the onslaught of Westernization in the then colonial British India, he realized the pressing need for an English translation of the Qur'ān which would help the ever-growing number of Western-educated Muslims in the subcontinent gain and renew their faith in Islam. It will persuade them of the superiority of the Qur'ān, its life-giving worldview, its marvellous literary features, its all-embracing guidance, its pronouncements being historically accurate and rationally convincing, its pristine purity in sharp contrast with the corrupted text of the Bible, and its impeccable divine origin. He succeeds, in large measure, in delivering the above message, which was badly needed then and remains so up to this day.

Gifted with his first-hand knowledge of the Bible and Western scholarship on Islam, his critical acumen, his sharp, discerning rational faculty and his firm grounding in both the primary and secondary sources on Islam, and above all, his long and close association with his mentor, Shaykh Ashraf 'Alī Thānwī, an illustrious heir to Shāh Walīullāh's legacy in the then British India, Mawlana Daryabadi demonstrates in his commentary how the Qur'ān stands out and above all else in guiding man to the path which ensures the best for him in both his individual and collective life in this world and the Hereafter.

Some hallmarks of Mawlana Daryabadi's work are:
a.   As a conscientious Muslim scholar he is painstakingly faithful to the Qur'ānic text in his English rendering. He is so particular on this count that in many instances he retains the Arabic syntax and word order in his English translation. In this respect he excels Abdullah Yusuf Ali who offers mostly a loose paraphrase of the Qur'ānic text in his English version. Furthermore, in doing so Mawlana Daryabadi corrects the unpardonable numerous mistakes of omissions, interpolations and distortions of the Qur'ānic text spawned by Orientalists, namely George Sale, J.M. Rodwell, E.H. Palmer, Richard Bell and the Qadiyani translator, Muhammad Ali.

b.   With his enviable familiarity with the Bible and world faiths he extensively quotes earlier Scriptures with a view to demonstrating with clinching evidence how the Qur'ān stands superior to the distorted Scriptures in its moral overview, its historical accuracy and its natural, rational description of things which instantly strikes a chord with the human heart and mind. This remarkable feature of his, with its focus on comparative religion he helped many seekers of truth especially in the West, to appreciate the Qur'ān as the Word of God and Islam as the natural way, guiding man to eternal peace and bliss. It will not be out of place to allude to Sister Maryam Jameelah's observation that Daryabadi's present work greatly helped her in drawing close to and eventually in embracing Islam. We are sure many brothers and Sisters in the West will have no difficulty, like Sister Jameelah, in identifying with the help of this work the eternal truths which the Qur'ān embodies.

c.   Unlike the contemporary English translations of the Qur'ān, namely Abdullah Yusuf Ali and Muhammad Ali, Mawlana Daryabadi states with full conviction and without any hint of apologia the authentic Muslim viewpoint on miracles, angels, the afterlife and all that the Qur'ān describes under the rubric of *al-Ghayb* (the verities lying beyond the reach of human perception). He thus does not depart from the centuries-old traditional position. Yet his interpretation in the current idiom is of special appeal and interest for modern readers of the Qur'ān.

d.   For bringing out in full the import of several Qur'ānic verses, their underlying wisdom and their relevance in our times, Mawlana Daryabadi draws upon the whole range of modern Western scholarship – archaeology, anthropology, mythology, history, geography, psychology, law, ethics, sociology, folklore and travel literature.

He sifts a plethora of evidence for bringing into sharper relief the wisdom and guidance contained in the Qur'ān. An instance in point is the Qur'ānic position on the gender issue which is addressed with reference to the latest psychological, sociological, sexual and anthropological theories. Nonetheless, there is the sparing use of current scientific debates in Mawlana Daryabadi's commentary, denoting as it does that the Qur'ān is essentially a book of guidance *par excellence* for mankind, not a book aimed at elucidating or foretelling scientific facts.

In view of the many distinctions of Daryabadi's work, published earlier from Lahore and Lucknow, the Islamic Foundation decided to re-issue it and sought the permission of the Academy of Islamic Research and Publications, Nadwatul Ulema, Lucknow, for the issue of this edition which comprises the English translation of the entire Qur'ānic text and a selection of Daryabadi's commentary. We are indeed grateful to Shaykh Sayyid Abul Hasan 'Alī Nadwī and Shaykh Muḥammad Rabey Nadwi of the Academy for having generously acceded to our request. I am thankful also to my colleagues at the Foundation who helped in the production of this work.

May Allah enable all of us to reap the benefits accruing from the study of the Qur'ān (*Āmīn*).

Rabī' al-Thānī 1421H
July 2000 CE

Dr. Manazir Ahsan
Director General

In the Name of Allah, the Compassionate, the Merciful

PREFACE

Of all great works the Holy Qur'ān is perhaps the least translatable. Arabic is not at all easy to translate into a language so widely and radically different from it in structure and genius as English, unless it be with the aid of loose periphrasis and lax paraphrase. Even so the fire of the original is quenched, its vivacious perspicuity lost, and the so-called literal translation looks lifeless and dreary. That the language of the Arabs abounds in nuance and that both the noun and the verb are ultimately flexible, is a fact well known to every student of that tongue.

The difficulty is increased hundredfold when one has to render into English, with any degree of accuracy and precision, a work so rich in meaning, so pithy in expression, so vigorous in style and so subtle in its implications as the Holy Qur'ān. To reproduce even partially its exotic beauty, wonderful grandeur and magical vivacity without sacrificing the requirements of the English idiom and usage, is the despair of the translator and an ideal impossible to attain. The result is that every fresh attempt at translating the Holy Writ brings home, in varying degrees, the truth of the old saying that nothing is so unlike an original as its copy.

The impediments confronting an honest translator may be summed up under six main headings and various sub-headings:

1. In the first place comes the comparative poverty of the English language. For instance:

(i) There are a large number of Arabic verbs which cannot be translated into English as verbs, such as etc. امات، طغى، من، ابطل، اسرف، استوى، صدق، بخل and one has perforce to render each of these words not by a single word but by a combination of words. Thus يبخل has to be translated as niggardly, صدق as truthful, يستوي as equal, يسرف as extravagant, يبطل as make vain or render void, من as conferring a benefit, يطغى as exorbitant, and يميت as causes death.

(ii) There is no equivalent for the Arabic مضارع (aorist) in English, or, for that matter, in any other language known to the translator. The Arabic مضارع combines both present and future tenses, whereas in other languages, including English, a tense is either present or future. Thus thousands of Arabic verbs can only be rendered incompletely into English.

(iii) In English grammar there are only two numbers, singular and plural, and there is no single word to convey the sense of the Arabic dual (تثنيه) in nouns as well as verbs, both in the second and third person.

(iv) There is comparative dearth of اسماء الفاعل (nomina agentis) in the English language, whereas they abound in Arabic. مستقدمون، قانتون، معجزون، مفلحون آخرون، صادقون، شاكرون، متقون، مشركون، مستاخرون، and many similar words have to be rendered as adjectives or participles, not as substantives.

(v) Next, the repetition of synonyms, chiefly for the sake of emphasis, is a frequent occurrence in Arabic; in fact, at times it is of considerable literary merit and beauty. In the English language there is no sanction for it. Thus many such expressions as انا نحن نحي الموتى (literally, Verily, We! We! We! quicken the dead) or انا نحن نحي ونميت (literally, Verily, We! surely We! We quicken and cause death) or انا نحن نزلنا الذكر (literally, Verily, We! We! We have revealed the Admonition) remain only partly translated.

3.   Another serious difficulty is caused by the case with which ellipses occur in the best and finest Arabic style and where both words and phrases have to be supplied by the reader to make the sense complete. Sometimes, only the subject is mentioned and the predicate entirely suppressed, whilst on other occasions the reverse is the case. The obvious duty of the translator in all such instances is to supply the omission, although his attempts in many cases must be hazardous.

4.   Yet another perplexity faced by the translator is the abrupt grammatical transition, in one and the same sentence, frequently found in Arabic:

(i) of person, as from the first and second person to the third, or *vice versa*;

(ii) of number, from plural to singular, or *vice versa*.

5.   A further complication is caused by what is known as (انتشار ضمائر) i.e., a personal or relative pronoun having a different antecedent in one and the same sentence. The translator cannot afford to allow such ambiguities; he has to make a choice.

6.   Finally, there is no real equivalence in the import of many Arabic and English words generally held to be synonyms. The Arabic word زنى for instance, has no equivalent in English, both adultery and fornication being of much narrower import. Similarly, English has few words to express such closely related Arabic terms as, ترهيب، اشفاق، خشيت، خوف and, as in the phrase تقوى (as in the phrase تقوى الله). Nor is English perhaps rich enough to clearly indicate the shades of meaning of such sets of words as جان and حية، ثعبان، or رحمن and رحيم، or مقتدر and قدير، قادر .

As to the genius of the Arabic language, it may not be amiss to recall a few observations made by the distinguished Arabists, Arnold and Guillaume: 'Arabic is fitted to express relations with more conciseness than the Aryan languages because of the extraordinary flexibility of the verb and noun. Thus the ideas in break, shatter, try to break, cause to break, allow to be broken, break one another, ask someone to break, are among many variations of the fundamental verbal theme which can, or could, be expressed by vowel changes and consonantal augments without the aid of the supplementary verbs and pronouns which we have to employ in English. The noun, too, has an appropriate form for many diverse things, such as the time and place of an action, bodily defects, diseases, instruments, colours, trades, and so on. One example must suffice. Let us take the root *d-w-r*, which, in its simplest form, means to turn or revolve (intransitive).

dawwara, to turn a thing round.	*dāwara*, to walk about with someone.
	tadawwara
adāra, to make go round, and so to control.	*istadāra* to be round in shape.
dawr, turning (noun).	*dawrah*, one turning.
dawarān, circulation.	*duwār*, vertigo.
dawwār, pedlar or vagrant.	*dawwārah*, mariner's compass.
madār, axis.	*mudārah*, round water-skin.
mudīr, controller.	

None of these forms is fortuitous, but is predetermined by the structural genius of the Arabic language.' Arnold and Guillaume, *The Legacy of Islam*, pp. vi–vii.

To take another instance:

'From the root KTB "write", we have KaTaBnā, "we wrote", naKTuBu, "we will write", KāTiBun, "writing, a writer", KiTāBun, "a book", maKTaBun, "a place of writting, a school," muKTiBun "a teacher of writing." taKāTaBā "they two corresponded with one another", astaKTiBu, "I will ask (him) to write", waKtaTaBa, "and he got his name written down (in the register)," KuTTāBun, "scribes", muKāTaBatun, "correspondence", etc. (*Encyclopaedia Britannica*. 2, p. 192).

Add to these inherent handicaps my own incompetence, my meagre knowledge of English and only a passing acquaintance with Arabic and the audacity of the enterprise becomes apparent. Further, it has been my lot to work almost unaided and single-handed. The outcome of this seven year labour of love is before God and man, and certainly it is not for me to pass any judgement on my own work. Had I been able to foresee at the commencement of the task the amount of labour it would involve and the length of time it would necessitate, my courage would surely have failed me and I would not have undertaken the work at all. If there is any merit discernible in the work it is absolutely owing to the grace and mercy of the Almighty and if there are faults (and undoubtedly they are many and serious), they must be credited to my own incapacity. My constant endeavour has been to give as literal and as faithful a rendering of the Holy Qur'ān as is consistent with tolerable English. Accuracy, rather than literary embellishment, is what I have aimed for throughout. I have also attempted, in my own humble way, to follow closely the style and phraseology of the Authorized Version of the English Bible, though it would be nothing short of temerity to expect that that standard has been even appreciably achieved.

In regard to the arrangement of the commentary, a word or two will suffice:
(i) Comments on lexical, grammatical, historic, geographical, and general exegetic interest are given in the footnotes.
(ii) Where an elucidation seemed necessary in order to complete the sense, it has been placed in parentheses, again in the footnotes. The reader is kindly requested to treat such matter as if it formed an integral part of the text and to read the two side by side.
(iii) Ellipses have been supplied in the text itself.

A few characteristics of my translation and transliteration may here be briefly noted. The word 'Allah' in the monotheistic context has always been retained in translation as Allah, and only rendered as 'God' when the content is distinctly pagan or polytheistic. The words نصراني and نصارى I have invariably translated as Nazarene and Nazarenes, not as Christian. The Holy Qur'ān allows no status to Christianity as such. The religion of the Qur'ān and the Prophet is always referred to as Islam, not as Muhammadanism.

Now remains the pleasant duty of acknowledging obligations and recording thanks. To several of my precursors I am more or less indebted, but in particular to Sale, Lane, Pickthall and Nawab 'Imad-ul-Mulk Bilgrami (whose unfinished and unpublished translation, up to Sūrah Ṭā Hā, I have the good fortune to possess). To Dr. Bell, the latest of the English translators, my debt is especially great. In exegetic and explanatory notes I have found Ashraf 'Alī Thānwi's Urdu *Bayān al-Qur'ān* (12 Vols.) of invaluable help, and I have also drawn largely upon Wherry's Commentary and, in a lesser degree, upon 'Abdullah Yusuf 'Ali's. Many other authors, both ancient and modern, besides those explicitly quoted in the following pages, must, I fear, remain unacknowledged by name. In many cases, they impressed themselves so indelibly on my memory that their very words became part and parcel of my phraseology, but I could not in every instance remember whence they came. This is a general acknowledgment of any unconscious plagiarism that I may have committed. A list of the principal books cited and referred to by me, given at the end of this work, may, however, to some extent, extenuate my crime.

I have been considerably profited by the suggestions of several of my esteemed friends and scholars to whom part of this work was submitted for detailed criticism. To Dr. M.H. Syed and Dr. A.S. Siddiqi, both of Allahabad University, I owe not a few improvements in language and transliteration respectively.

Abdul Majid Daryabadi

Bara Banki (India)
December, 1941 C.E.

In the name of Allah, the Compassionate, the Merciful

INTRODUCTION

The Qur'ānic *i'jāz*, variously interpreted as its inimitable ellipticism, miraculous elegance, grandiose cadence and emotive and evocative force, is so multilateral that Imām Suyūṭī has in his work, enumerated 35 distinctive features of the Divine Scripture, all of which pertain to its literary excellence alone. These, by no means, exhaust the marvellous super-excellence of the Holy Qur'ān: some have been discussed by other writers while others are yet to be expounded, but these are so self-evident that not even the most inveterate enemy of Islam can deny them. One of these is that writers like T. Noldeke, Friedrick Schwally, Charles Francis Potter, Philip K. Hitti and several other Orientalists, none of whom are known for their sympathetic approach to Islam, had to acknowledge the fact that the Qur'ān is 'the most widely read book in existence,'1 and the Prophet to whom it was revealed was 'the most successful of all the Prophets.'2 They had, willy-nilly, to admit this undeniable fact for they had noticed that Christian missionary societies, financed by affluent Western countries, had succeeded in rendering the Christian Bible into about seven hundred languages,3 making finely printed copies of it available to nearly all urban centres or placing it in every high class hotel the world over, yet the numbers who go through these in ten years is just a fraction of those who recite the Qur'ān every day.4

Another notable aspect of the *i'jaz* of the Qur'ān is that notwithstanding the persistent campaign launched against it since the beginning of the thirteenth century A.D. to the present and which sees the Holy Qur'ān as a product of the human mind, drawing the material contained in it indiscriminately from the apocryphal books of Judaism and Christianity, hundreds of its translations, commentaries and glossaries have been brought out, even in Europe. Nor has the political and industrial ascendancy of the West, coupled with its intellectual and educational supremacy and its control over the world's mass media, been able to shake the faith of the Muslims in the Holy Qur'ān as the Word of God. This conviction has increased with the passage of time rather than being eroded by these deliberate misrepresentations: the denigrators of the Qur'ān have, on the other hand, been forced to put themselves on their guard. Professor R.B. Sergeant writes in his introduction to the *Dictionary and Glossary of the Kuran* by John Penrice that readers of the Qur'ān ought to understand the Book directly from it since the Arab and Muslim countries which are now forsaking conservatism in favour of modernism still take the Scripture as a divine revelation and the people are still accustomed to saying, "God Exalted has said" before quoting any passage from it and ending the citation with the words, "God Almighty has truly spoken".

European scholars of Islam, whether they be Sergeant or Sale or contributors to the *Encyclopaedia Britannica*, cannot be expected to express anything beyond their own impressions of the Holy Qur'ān. They, even if not inspired by a malicious prejudice, cannot shake off their mistaken notions about Islam that have become a part of their intangible heritage of thought and feeling. But, for us, Muslims, it is an apparent fact that God Almighty has Himself taken the responsibility of preserving the Holy Qur'ān in its absolute purity. 'Verily We, it is We Who have revealed the Admonition, and verily We are its Guardian'. [15:9].

This prophecy has been strikingly confirmed by the fact that the Qur'ān has remained free from all alterations, accretions and deletions ever since it was sent down to the Holy Prophet (peace be upon him). The purity of the Qur'ānic text, maintained through fourteen centuries, has already been acknowledged by all, friend and foe alike. I should better cite here the comments of the learned author of this exegesis on the above verse. He writes: Islam knows no such thing as "redactions" of its Holy Text. Even those who have most stoutly denied its being the Word of God are unanimous in testifying to its being exactly the same "work of Muhammad" as it was thirteen centuries ago. Let us have the testimony of a few such unwilling witnesses:

(i) "The text of the Qur'an is the purest of all works of a like antiquity". (Wherry: *Commentary on the Koran* I, p. 349).

(ii) "Othman's recension has remained the authorised text, from the time it was made until the present day." (Palmer: *The Quran*, p. liv).

(iii) "The text of this recension substantially corresponds to the actual utterances of Muhammed himself". (Arnold: *Islamic Faith*, p. 9).

(iv) "All sects and parties have the same text of the Qur'an" (Hurgroneje: *Mohammedanism*, p. 18).

(v) "It is an immense merit in the Kuran that there is no doubt as to its genuineness. That very word we can now read with full confidence that it has remained unchanged through nearly thirteen hundred years" (Lane-Poole: *Selections from the Kuran*, p. 3).

(vi) "The recension of 'Othman has been handed down to us unaltered... There is probably in the world no other work which has remained twelve centuries with so pure a text" (Muir: *Life of Muhammad*, pp. xxii–xxiii).

(vii) "In the Koran we have, beyond all reasonable doubt, the exact words of Mohammed without substraction and without addition". (Bosworth Smith: *Mohammed and Mohammedanism*, p. 22).

(viii) "The Koran was his own creation; and it lies before us practically unchanged from the form which he himself gave it". (Torrey: *Jewish Foundations of Islam*, p. 2)."

In addition to these testimonies from European Orientalists about the purity of the text of the Holy Qur'ān, the author goes on to substantiate the claim of the Qur'ān to be a Divine Revelation which is undisputed and unique among all the religious Scriptures. He writes:

'Not only is the meaning of the Holy Book therefore inspired but every word, every letter dictated through the angel Gabriel to the Holy Prophet from an Archetype preserved in the heaven. That is the distinctive claim of the Holy Qur'ān shared by no other "revealed Book" in the world. The Bible, in particular "makes no such claim... The Bible is the work of a large number of poets, prophets, statesmen, and lawgivers, extending over a vast period of time, and incorporates with itself other and earlier, and often conflicting documents'. (Bosworth Smith: *Mohammed and Mohammedanism* p. 19).

The Divine care to preserve the purity of the Holy Qur'ān provided the impulse to put dots on alphabets of similar shape in order to distinguish between their pronunciation, to develop the twin sciences of philology and lexicography, and to lay down the rules of Arabic grammar and the criteria for rhetoric and the style of prose writing. This literary activity has never ceased for a day since the second century of the Islamic era. Additionally, the etymological structure of the Arabic language has saved its dialects, like a strong cementing force, from falling apart into distinct languages and thus, the Divine Revelation has remained intelligible to succeeding generations. The providential arrangement of writing commentaries to the Holy Qur'ān started as early as the third century AH, is also noteworthy. At the outset, exegesis of the Qur'ān formed a part of the science of *ḥadīth* since it was generally thought that Divine Revelation could only be understood in light of the Holy Prophet's Traditions, especially those handed down by 'Abdullāh Ibn 'Abbās. However, the exegesis of the Qur'ān became an independent science with the *Tafsīr al-Ṭabarī* of Abū Ja'far Muḥammad

Ibn Jarīr al-Ṭabarī (d. 310 AH) and it has ever since been vigorously cultivated by Muslim scholars. The commentaries on the Holy Qur'ān written from time to time are in fact a mine of historical information shedding light on the way the Qur'ān was understood during different periods.

Arabists and Orientalists, on the other hand, started to translate the Holy Qur'ān from the thirteenth century AD and rendered it into almost all European languages, of which the largest number of translations have been brought out in French, German and English. A list of such translations is given by Professor Hamidullah in the introduction to his own French rendering of the Holy Qur'ān published in 1961. His other work entitled *Al-Qur'ān fī-Kull Lisān*, now out of print, contains a complete list of all the translations of the Holy Qur'ān brought out up to 1341/1922. The list, I believe, would now be two-fold in volume if Professor Hamidullah were to bring it up-to-date.5

Translations of the Holy Qur'ān in English can be divided into two categories. Firstly, there are those penned either by non-Muslim Orientalists or by those Muslim apologists who were unduly impressed by the political ascendancy and industrial advancement of the West, such as the Qadiyani exegetes, Shaikh Muḥammad 'Abduh of Egypt, Sir Syed Ahmad Khan of India and Muhammad Asad of Austria, but their writings never met with the approval of the Muslims. Secondly, there are Muslim translators and commentators who mostly belong, excepting Marmaduke Pickthall, to the Indo-Pak subcontinent. Pickthall was an English Muslim, a journalist and a literary man of standing but he, too, was commissioned by the then Niẓām of Hyderabad to undertake an explanatory translation of the Holy Qur'ān and he also wrote that work in India.

Among those belonging to the second group, the translation and commentary on the Holy Qur'ān by Abdullah Yusuf Ali was received well. His rendering of the Qur'ānic verses is in blank verse which, according to him, is more suited to conveying something of the Qur'ān's inimitable symphony to its readers. The requirements of prosody, however, made it inevitable that he alter the word order of the sacred text. He had also occasionally to deviate from a literal rendering. Pickthall's explanatory translation, on the other hand, is most readable. Although it too is not free from mistakes, it has an edge over other translations because of its fluency and gracefulness of style.

There was, however, the need for another English translation of the Holy Qur'ān, complete with explanatory notes, which could be recommended with confidence to Muslims and non-Muslims whose mother tongue was English or who found it easy, owing to their cultural background or educational upbringing, to understand it better in the English language. The author of such an exegesis inevitably had to expound the Qur'ānic text in terms acceptable to scholars of the *Ahl al-Sunnah wa al-Jamā'ah*; to avoid putting forward his own views and ideas in the exegesis; to be fully conversant with Arabic lexicon and rules of grammar; to avoid an apologetic approach in expounding Qur'ānic injunctions and institutions; to have an implicit faith in Life-After-Death and the rewards and retributions promised in the Qur'ān as Divine pronouncements instead of taking them merely as symbolical expressions; to have studied all the classical and modern commentaries in depth; to expound the significance of Qur'ānic injunctions in regard to polygamy, slavery, dowry, the execution of apostates, blood-wit etc.; to hold the same belief about the throne (*'arsh* and *kursī*), the preserved tablet (*lawḥ al-Maḥfūẓ*), jinn, angels, prophethood (*nubuwwah*), Revelation (*waḥī*), and the earlier and final Divine Scriptures as entertained by the earliest Muslims; and to have no qualms about the bodily lifting of Jesus Christ to the higher regions. Taking all these factors into account, Abdul Majid Daryabadi's translation and commentary is undoubtedly unique and most acceptable among all the exegetical renderings of the Holy Qur'ān attempted so far in the English language.

The exegesis by Daryabadi throws ample light on all those communities who have been mentioned in the Holy Qur'ān along with their geographical locations and the eras in which they flourished. One can find all the necessary details about the earlier Prophets who find a mention in the Holy Qur'ān, since it provides answers to such questions as what was the time of their advent, who were the peoples to whom they disseminated the Message vouchsafed to them, who were the 'Ādites and Thamūdites and the people of Prophet Ṣāliḥ, where did those people live, where were Babil and Madyan located and similar other questions that arise in one's mind while reading the Holy Qur'ān.

His exegesis also demonstrates, in light of human experience and researches made in the field of anthropology and sociology, the superiority of the Islamic social order and its legislations pertaining to marriage, divorce, inheritance etc., over all other social laws and systems. It shows how Islamic injunctions represent the most refined and elaborate system of social existence known to the civilized world.

In addition to these, a distinguishing feature of Daryabadi's exegesis is that it provides a conclusive answer to those Jewish and Christian critics of Islam who claim that the Holy Qur'ān draws its material from the Scriptures and apocryphal writings of Judaism and Christianity. It demonstrates how these critics are unable to appreciate the fact that the Holy Qur'ān has been revealed to confirm the Scriptures of old and to restate and uphold the spirit of their true teachings, which, by itself, involves refutation of such accretions, alterations and additions as have found a place in the Scriptures of Judaism and Christianity.

'And when there came unto them a Book from before Allah confirming that which was with them – and aforetime they were entreating God for victory over those who disbelieved – then when there came unto them that which they recognised, they disbelieved therein". (2: 89).

That the Qur'ān is a repository of the Divine Message revealed in the earlier Scriptures is an article of faith for Muslims, but it was necessary to bring out those teachings of the Torah and the Gospels which were confirmed by the Holy Qur'ān in order to distinguish them from the spurious matter inserted into these Scriptures by their scribes, translators and commentators. For whatever in these Books finds confirmation by the Holy Qur'ān is undoubtedly correct; everything else is a later addition mixed up with Divine Revelation. The learned author has taken great pains to make a thorough, comparative analysis of Biblical and Qur'ānic teachings and the narratives of events common to both, in order to show how the Holy Qur'ān upholds only the correct and original teachings of the Old and New Testaments. He also provides food for thought to those Orientalists and students of comparative religion who prefer not to talk about the systematic refusal of the Holy Qur'ān to confirm numerous accretions to the existing Bible. The exegesis pinpoints all such differences showing that the Biblical version of many an incident is nothing but a product of human imagination. His treatment of such matters makes it amply clear that if there had been any parallelism in the Bible and the Qur'ān, as asserted by almost all European scholars, there would not have been the differences, indicated by him, in the narration of the same event by these Scriptures. To give an example we may refer to the following verse in the Holy Qur'ān:

O people of the Book; do not exceed the bounds in your Religion, and say not of Allah save what is the truth. The Messiah 'Īsā, son of Maryam, is but a Messenger of Allah and His Word–He cast it upon Maryam and a Spirit from Him. Believe therefore in Allah and His Messengers, and do not say: three". (4: 171).

Commenting on the Christian belief in Trinity, the learned author says:

'Trinity denotes the central doctrine of Christian religion. It means that God is three really distinctive Persons – the Father, the Son, and the Holy Ghost. Each of these persons is truly the same God, and has all His infinite perfections, yet He is really distinct from each of the three Persons. These Persons are co-equal, co-eternal and consubstantial, and deserve co-equal glory and adoration, which the Church expresses in the oft-repeated prayer: "Glory be to the Father, and to the Son, and to the Holy Ghost". (Allen and Wynne: *New Catholic Dictionary*, New York, p. 973.) The book of Islam 'found in the dogma of Trinity what every emancipated thinker finds on impartial reflection – an absurd legend, which is neither reconciliable with first principles of reason, nor of any value whatever for our religious advancement. In the Brahmanic religion the Trimurti is also conceived as a "divine unity" made up of three persons - Brahma (the creator), Vishnu (the sustainer) and Shiva (the destroyer)'. (Haeckal: *Riddle of the Universe*, pp. 226, 233). 'The Divine trinity has been considered a tripersonal trinity, each person being God and Lord. Men's minds have been brought by this into such a state of bewilderment that they do not know whether there is one God or whether there are three; one is on their lips, but three in their thoughts.' (Swedenborg: *The True Christian Religion*, p. 5). The Nicene Creed really teaches three Divine Persons and denies three Gods, and leaves us to guess what else is a Divine Person but a God or a God but a Divine Person". (Newman: *Phases of Faith*, p. 23).

The Jews and Christians generally charge Islam with preaching fanaticism and intolerance, as for example, its prohibition of marriage between a believing and disbelieving couple. The author has, in his commentary on the relevant verse, quoted the other Scriptures to show that the criticism actually applies to these religions rather than to Islam. In like manner, he has demonstrated the superiority of Islamic legislation in regard to divorce and marriage vis-a-vis the ruptured family relationships of the Christian West.

Classical commentators of the Holy Qur'ān occasionally had to take the help of Israelite traditions, though cautiously, for elucidating a certain event of which only a particular aspect of the happening finds a mention in the Qur'ān and this to draw a moral from it. To cite an example here, the Qur'ān says about King Solomon in verse 102 of *Sūrah al-Baqarah*: 'And Sulaimān blasphemed not, but the satans blasphemed; teaching the people magic. And they follow also what was sent unto the two angels in Babil, Hārūt and Mārūt.'

In the absence of any more detail about the incident, one may wonder how the charge of blasphemy came to be levelled against King Solomon, a Prophet of God, and which has been refuted by the Qur'ān. Like earlier exegetes, Daryabadi has also referred to the accusation of idolatry made against King Solomon in 1 Ki. 11: 4, 9, 10. He also mentions how the Jews unblushingly attributed to him the cult of crude occultism and witchcraft, and goes on to cite the findings of modern Biblical researches which support the Qur'ān in stoutly denying these charges. Similarly, he sets forth evidence to show that Babylonia was the strongest citadel of magic and witchcraft in all antiquity.

Another distinctive feature of Daryabadi's rendering of the Qur'ānic text is that he has always kept in view the most appropriate expression in English or the one which is nearest to the interpretation of a word used in the Holy Qur'ān. For example, the words (*ẓāhir*) and (*bāṭin*) in the passage (6: 120) have been translated by him as outside and inside, and this conveys the literal sense of these words. The derived meanings of these two words namely open and secret, which are normally adopted by other translators in rendering this passage into English, are given by him in the footnotes. This approach shows the author's painstaking diligence and reverential regard for the sacred text. Another example of the assiduous care taken by Daryabadi in this regard is to be found in rendering the verse 17: 29. This verse has been translated to read as follows:

'Let not your hand be chained to your neck, nor stretch it forth to the utmost of its extremity, lest you sit down reproached, impoverished.'

The English rendering of the above verse is literal; an idiomatic translation would have better conveyed the sense but it would have meant a deviation from the text of the sacred Scripture. Unlike other translators of the Holy Qur'ān who prefer to give the derived meanings of an Arabic word or phrase, Daryabadi has chosen to give an exact translation of the text and then explained in a footnote that 'let not your hand be chained to your neck' means do not be niggardly. This, however, does not suggest that the renderings of other translators are incorrect, but it nevertheless evinces the regard and attachment of the author, as well as his preference for maintaining the original wordings, to the Divine Revelation. He goes on to explain the correct significance of the words and phrases according to Arabic usage and also points out, at several places, the incorrect renderings given by earlier translators, and thus acquaints the readers with the Arabic idiom.

Every student of the Holy Qur'ān knows that the Divine Scripture has its own distinctive vocabulary. As, for instance, the Qur'ān is not referred to by its proper name at all places; often it is alluded to as (*al-Dhikr*), or (*al-Kitāb*), or (*al-Furqān*). For Doomsday, it uses the words (*Yawm al-Qiyāmah*), (*Yawm al-Ḥisāb*), (*Yawm al-Taghābun*) and (*Yawm al-Ākhirah*). In addition to (*al-Ṣalāt*), Prayers are also referred to as (*al-Dhikr*) and (*Qur'ān al-Fajr*) and similar other epithets. Classical commentators of the Qur'ān have explained the correct purport of each word in the context of particular verses so as to make it clear where a certain word with more than one connotation as, for example, (*al-Dhikr*) denotes the Qur'ān and where it implies Prayer. Legists of Islam have likewise indicated the significance of each word having more than one import in its particular context. In the verse (2: 4) the phrase (اركعوا مع الراكعين) signifies offering congregational prayers as explained by Qurṭubī, Baghawī, al-Nasafī al-Baiḍāwī and al-Zamakhsharī. Instead of rendering this phrase as bow down among those who bow the author has interpreted it as 'bow down with those who bow down', and further elucidated it in the notes with the words, with Muslims in congregational prayer so that the correct significance of the phrase given by classical exegetes becomes clear to readers.

The Holy Qur'ān is, after all, the Word of God, perfect and faultless, while no man can make a claim to finality or impeccability. Every product of the human mind is likely to contain some deficiency, yet, for all that, Abdul Majid Daryabadi has acquitted himself of this onerous task in a laudable manner. Throughout his life he preoccupied himself with the study of the Holy Qur'ān and wrote an exegesis in Urdu in addition to the English one. His translation and commentary is, to my mind, unique and the most reliable among all translations and commentaries of the Qur'ān so far attempted in the English language.

May Allah accept his praiseworthy endeavour and shower His choicest blessings on him.

The Academy of Islamic Research and Publications deems it a favour from the Almighty that the heirs and successors of the late Abdul Majid Daryabadi agreed to transfer the publication rights of this commentary to it. The first edition of this work was brought out by the Taj Company of Lahore, in 1957, after which the author revised his earlier translation. The late author desired that a new edition be brought out with the revised translation but, as God had willed it, his wish could not be fulfilled during his lifetime. Now, the commentary is being published with the revised translation. Muhammad Rabey Nadwi took a keen interest in fulfilling the wishes of the departed author while Syed Mohiuddin, an associate scholar of the Academy, and Sher Mohammed Syed of Lahore took pains to check and correct the mistakes that had crept into the earlier edition by comparing almost all the quotations given in the notes with the original sources. Certain additions made by the author in his manuscript have also been incorporated into this edition. May Allah recompense all of them with goodly returns.

Abul Hasan Ali Nadwi

Lucknow   Rector

15 Shawwāl 1401H   Nadwatul Ulema

16 August 1981

Notes

1. Charles Francis Potter, *The Faith Man Lives By*, Surrey, 1995, p.18; Phillip K. Hitti, *History of the Arabs*, London, 1953, p.426.

2. Lamertime, *Histoire de la Turquie*, Paris, 1854, 2, p. 277; D.G. Hogarth, *A History of Arabia*, Oxford, 1922, p.52.

3. Muḥammad Mubārak, *Khaṣā'iṣ al-Lughat al-'Arabīyah*, Beirut, p.6.

4. John Arnold, 'World Religions and Societies' *Readers Digest* (June 1961).

5. For a comprehensive bibliography of the Qur'ān translations in world languages, see Ekmeleddin Ihsanoglu (ed.), *World Bibliography of Translations of the Meanings of the Holy Quran: Printed Translations 1515-1980*, Istanbul, OIC Research Centre for Islamic History, Art and Culture, 1986, pp. 913.

ABBREVIATIONS

(1) BOOKS OF THE BIBLE

Ac.	=	Acts of the Apostles.
Am.	=	Amos.
1. Ch.	=	The First Book of Chronicles.
2. Ch.	=	The Second Book of Chronicles.
Col.	=	Colossians.
1. Cor.	=	Paul's First Epistle to the Corinthians.
2. Cor.	=	Paul's Second Epistle to the Corinthians.
Dn.	=	The Book of Daniel.
Dt.	=	Deuteronomy: The Fifth Book of Moses.
Eph.	=	Ephesians.
Ex.	=	Exodus: The Second Book of Moses.
Ez.	=	Ezra.
Ezek.	=	The Book of the Prophet Ezekiel.
Gr. Jn.	=	The Epistle General of John.
Ga.	=	Paul's Epistle to the Galatians.
Ge.	=	Genesis: The First Book of Moses.
He.	=	Paul's Epistle to the Hebrews.
Ho.	=	Hosea.
Is.	=	Isaiah.
Ja.	=	The General Epistle of James.
Jn.	=	The Gospel according to St. John.
Jo.	=	Joel.
Job.	=	The Book of Job.
Jon.	=	The Book of Jonah.
Josh.	=	The Book of Joshua.
Judg.	=	The Book of Judges.
Je.	=	The Book of Jeremiah.
1. Ki.	=	The First Book of Kings.
2. Ki.	=	The Second Book of Kings.

La.	=	The Lamentations of Jeremiah.
Lk.	=	The Gospel according to St. Luke.
Le.	=	Leviticus: The Third Book of Moses.
Mi.	=	Micah.
Mk.	=	The Gospel according to St. Mark.
Mt.	=	The Gospel according to St. Matthew.
Na.	=	Nahum.
Ne.	=	The Book of Nehemiah.
Nu.	=	Numbers: The Fourth Book of Moses.
1. Pe.	=	The First Epistle General of Peter.
2. Pe.	=	The Second Epistle General of Peter.
Ph.	=	Paul's Epistle to the Philippians.
Pr.	=	Proverbs.
Ps.	=	Psalms.
Re.	=	The Revelation of St. John.
Ro.	=	Paul's Epistle to the Romans.
1. Sa.	=	The First Book of Samuel.
2. Sa.	=	The Second Book of Samuel.
So.	=	The Song of Solomon.
1. Thes.	=	Paul's First Epistle to the Thessalonians.
2. Thes.	=	Paul's Second Epistle to the Thessalonians.
1. Ti.	=	Paul's First Epistle to Timothy.
2. Ti.	=	Paul's Second Epistle to Timothy.
Tt.	=	Paul's Epistle to Titus.
Ze.	=	Zechariah.

(2) GENERAL

AAM.	=	Abul A'lā Mawdūdī, Urdu translator and commentator of the Holy Qur'ān.
Ant.	=	Josephus' *Antiquities of the Jews* (Routledge, London).
Aq.	=	Shāh 'Abdul Qādir Dihlawi (d. 1241 AH/1826 CE). Urdu translator and commentator of the Holy Qur'ān.
ASB.	=	Asad's English Translation of *Ṣaḥīḥ al-Bukhārī*.
AV.	=	Authorized Version of the Bible.

AYA.	=	Abdullah Yusuf Ali. English translator and commentator of the Holy Qur'ān.
Bdh	=	Nasir-ud-Dīn 'Abdullāh Baidawī (d. 685 AH/1282 CE). Commentator of the Holy Qur'an.
BK.	=	*Book of Knowledge*, 4 Vols. (Educational Book Co., London).
CD.	=	Allen and Wynne, *New Catholic Dictionary* (New York).
CE.	=	McDannall, *Concise Encyclopedia*, 8 Vols. (New York).
CE.	=	Christian Era.
DB.	=	Hasting, *Dictionary of the Bible*, 5 Vols. (Clark, London).
DCA.	=	Smith and Cheetham, *Dictionary of Christian Antiquities*, 2 Vols. (Murray, London).
DCG	=	Hasting, *Dictionary of Christ and the Gospels*, 2 Vols.
DV.	=	*Douay Version of the Bible.*
EBi.	=	Cheyne and Black, *Encyclopedia Biblica*, 4 Vols. (Black, London).
EBr.	=	*Encyclopedia Britannica*, 29 Vols., 11th Edition (London); *Encyclopedia Britannica*, 24 Vols., 14th Edition (London and New York). Where no edition is specified, the reference is to 14th Edition.
EI.	=	Houtsma and Wensink, *Encyclopedia of Islam*, 5 Vols. (Luzac, London).
EMK.	=	Hammerton, *Encyclopedia of Modern Knowledge*, 5 Vols. (Waverly, New York).
ERE	=	Hasting, *Encyclopedia of Religion and Ethics,* 13 Vols. (Clark, London)
ESS.	=	Seligman, *Encyclopedia of the Social Sciences*, 15 Vols. (Macmillan, London).
ET.	=	Cohen, *Everyman's Talmud* (Dent, London).
FWN.	=	Frazer, *Worship of Nature*, 2 Vols. (Macmillan, London).
GB.	=	Ragg, *The Gospel of Barnabas* (Oxford).
GRE.	=	Gibbon, *Decline and Fall of the Roman Empire*, 7 Vols. (Methuen, London).
HHW.	=	*Historians History of the World*, 25 Vols. (The Times, London).
HJ.	=	*The Hibbert Journal* (Constable, London).
IA.	=	'Abdullāh Ibn 'Abbās (d. 68 AH/688 CE). (A Companion and cousin of the Prophet).
IQ.	=	Ibn Qutaibab (d. 276 AH/890 CE). Author of *Arabic Glossary of the Holy Qur'ān.*
JE.	=	*The Jewish Encyclopedia*, 12 Vols. (Funks Wagnalls, New York).

LL.	=	Lane, *Arabic-English Lexicon*, 8 Vols. (Williams Norgate, London).
LSK.	=	Lane-Poole, *Selections from the Kuran* (Trubner, London).
MA.	=	Mawlana Mohammad 'Ali (d. 1349 AH/1931 CE) Indian Muslim leader. (Not to be confused with his namesake of Lahore and a translator of the Qur'an.) The references are to his unpublished work, 'Islam: The Kingdom of God' (since published as *My Life-A Fragment* by Sh. M. Ashraf, Lahore).
NSBD.	=	*A New Standard Bible Dictionary* (Funk & Wagnalls, New York).
NSD.	=	*New Standard Dictionary of the English Language*, 4 Vols. (Funk Wagnalls, New York).
NT.	=	The New Testament.
OT.	=	The Old Testament.
PC.	=	Tylor, *Primitive Culture*, 2 Vols. (Murray, London).
Rgh.	=	Al-Rāghib al-Isfahānī, Ḥusain b. Muḥammad, *al-Mufradāt fi Gharā'ib al-Qur'ān*.
RV.	=	Revised Version of the Bible.
RZ.	=	Imam Fakhruddīn al-Rāzī (d. 659 AH/1209 CE). Well-known commentator of the Holy Qur'an.
SOED.	=	*Shorter Oxford English Dictionary*, 2 Vols. (Oxford).
SPD.	=	Sale, 'Preliminary Discourse to the Translation of the Koran', prefixed as Introduction to Wherry's *Commentary on the Kuran*, 4 Vols. (Trubner, London).
Th.	=	Ashraf 'Alī Thānwī (b. 1280 AH/1864 CE) Urdu translator and commentator of the Holy Qur'an.
UHW.	=	Hammerton, *Universal History of the World*, 8 Vols. (New York).
VJE.	=	Vallentine, *Jewish Encyclopedia* (London).
WGAL	=	Wright, *Grammar of the Arabic Language*, 2 vols. (Cambridge).
Zm.	=	Zamakhsharī (d. 538 AH/1144 CE). Commentator of the Holy Qur'ān.

Sūrah[1] 1

al-Fātiḥah[2]

(Makkan, 7 Verses)

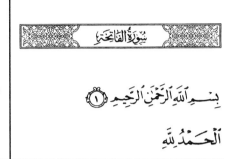

1. In the name of Allah,[3] the Compassionate,[4] the Merciful[5]

2. All praise unto Allah,[6]

---

1. A *Sūrah* is a chapter. There are 114 Chapters in the Qur'ān, each Chapter having been named and assigned its proper place by the Prophet himself under divine instruction.

2. A simple and pithy, yet wonderfully comprehensive prelude to the Word of God. Its beauty, grandeur and self-sufficiency simply defy comparison. 'A vigorous hymn of praise to God. The thoughts are so simple as to need no explanation, and yet the prayer is full of meaning' (*EBr.* XV. p. 903 (11th Ed.)).

3. The word Allah is incapable of translation. It is not a common noun meaning a god or even God. It is a proper noun *par excellence*. No plural can be formed from it, and it is, according to the best authorities on the Arabic language, without derivation. The word connotes all the attributes of perfection and beauty in their infinitude, and denotes none but the One True and Unique God, the Absolute, Supreme, Perfect, Tender, Mighty, Gracious, Benign and Compassionate. The English word God, which is 'the common Teutonic word for a personal object of religious worship. applied to all superhuman beings of heathen mythologies who exercise power over nature and man' (*EBr.* X. p. 460), and which primarily meant only 'what is invoked' and 'what is worshipped by sacrifice' (*SOED.* I. p. 808), is hardly an approximate substitute.

4. In other words, the possessor of the utmost degree of mercy or compassion. The word is only expressive of God's love to man, and not of man's love to man, or to Him. The term is too strong to be used of men. All the *Sūrahs* (with one solitary exception) begin with this headline, which sums up in two fine words God's relation to man, the relation *par excellence* of love, sympathy, concern, solicitude, compassion and mercy. This, in itself, is sufficient to confound those detractors of the Qur'ān, who depict the God of Islam as a cruel, wrathful, and relentless Deity. The God the Muslims adore and worship, whatever else He may be, is above all, the Compassionate and the Merciful.

5. Contrast with this unreservedly monotheistic introductory formula of Islam the glaringly polytheistic introductory formula of Christianity: 'In the name of the Father, and of the Son, and of the Holy Ghost.'

6. Him alone. Note the absolutely monotheistic note of the very first words of the Holy Qur'ān. It is He alone Who is the recipient of all praise; the Praiseworthy; the Praised One. None of His favoured angels and Prophets are to be associated with Him, even by implication.

Lord[7] of the worlds.[8]

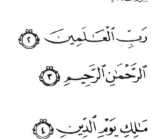

3. The Compassionate, the Merciful.[9]

4. Sovereign of the Day of Reckoning.[10]

---

7. Lord is but a poor substitute for the Arabic '*Rabb*' which signifies not only the Sovereign but also the Sustainer, the Nourisher, the Regulator, and the Perfector. The relation in which the God of Islam stands to all His creation is that of a righteous, benign Ruler, and not that of mere 'father'.

8. In other words, the Universal Patron, the All-in-all Guardian. Not a tribal deity, nor the national god of any specially favoured race of people, nor the narrow Lord of the Hosts or the anthropomorphic our Father in heaven. Unlike many a tribal or national god, embodying the spirit of a particular nation, and perishing with its death, He is the ever-living moral Ruler of the world, the all-embracing and all-comprehensive Godhead. And from the unity of the Creator there naturally follows the essential unity of all creation.

9. Both words, *al-Raḥmān* and *al-Raḥīm*, are derived from *al-Raḥmah* which signifies tenderness, requiring the exercise of beneficence and thus comprising the idea of love and mercy. Both are intensive forms. The former denotes tenderness towards all His creatures in general, and the latter towards His worshippers in particular. The Divine attribute of mercy may, on analysis, be found to have the following as its components: (i) His provision of everything beforehand that could be needed by man in the world; (ii) His concern for the well-being of man, both in life and death; (iii) His tenderness for man's helplessness, and (iv) a disposition on His part to deal kindly and generously with man.

10. When His Sovereignty shall be more evident than ever, and manifest even to the worst scoffers. The general Requital will follow the general Resurrection, wherein all men, good and bad, will be judged according to their faith and works. The verse completely repudiates the Christian doctrine that Christ, not God, would be the judge. Cf. the NT. 'For the Father judgeth no man, but hath committed all judgement unto the Son'. (Jn. 5: 22).

5. You alone we Worship, and of You alone we seek help.[11]

6. Guide us in the straight path,

7. The path of those whom You have favoured.

On whom Your indignation has not befallen, and who have not gone astray.

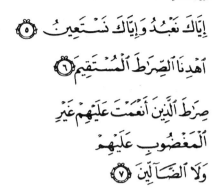

---

11. Note again the strictly monotheistic tone of the Islamic prayer. Not only is there to be no creature-worship but even the invoking of help from any saint, Prophet, angel, Son, Daughter, or Mother is absolutely forbidden. In Him alone perfection dwells. He Alone must be invoked. Contrast with this the doctrine of the Roman Church: 'That the saints who reign with Christ offer to God their prayers for man; that it is good and useful to invoke them by supplication and to have recourse to their aid and assistance in order to obtain from God His benefits through His Son' (*EBr.* XIX. p. 820).

In Hinduism the invocations to Indira, Agni, Soma and many others are too well known to need description.

Sūrah 2

al-Baqarah

(Madinan, 40 Sections, 286 Verses)

In the name of Allah, the Compassionate, the Merciful

Section 1

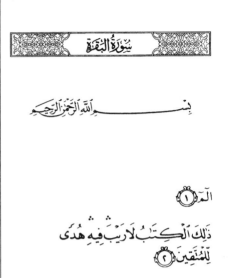

1. *Alif, Lām, Mīm.*[12]

2. This Book whereof there is no doubt,[13] is a guidance[14] to the God fearing,

---

12. Three letters of the Arabic alphabet generally held to be symbolic of some profound and sublime mystic verities. 'God knows best what He means by these letters' (Th.). Some, however, consider the letters to be an abbreviation meaning: 'I am Allah, the best Knower.' Arabic orators sometimes used to open their discourses with similar vocables. Also compare Ps. 119 in the OT, where the Psalmist has arranged his meditations in an elaborate alphabetical form. It has been called the alphabet of Divine Love.

13. That is the immediate, infallible word of God. The Qur'ān differs from all other sacred literatures in claiming to be inspired in the strictest sense, whereby each and every word is the Word of God Himself, and in its being preserved in its original purity. Hence this construct means: This is a Book in which nothing is doubtful but everything is absolutely true and strictly accurate; not changeable like human knowledge.

14. Not a text–book of chronology or of physical science, but a Guidance, showing the right way to right beliefs and right conduct. Not a book meant to be read as most Europeans read it today sitting comfortably in an armchair with their critical faculties ready to carp and cavil at the least provocation. It was not revealed to the Arabs as a literature designed only to please, though it was admitted by the most inveterate enemies of the Prophet to be superior to any existing literature in the language of which they were proud. And yet it was not its literary excellence that had the chief significance for those for whom it was revealed in this fragmentary fashion. To them it was a Holy Writ, God's Commandment, the Law and the Ethics according to which they had to shape their lives (MA.).

3. Who believe in the Unseen[15] and establish prayer, and of what We have provided them expend;

اَلَّذِينَ يُؤْمِنُونَ بِالْغَيْبِ وَيُقِيمُونَ الصَّلَوٰةَ وَمِمَّا رَزَقْنَهُمْ يُنفِقُونَ ٣

4. And who believe in what has been sent down to you, and what has been sent down before you, and of the Hereafter they are convinced.

وَالَّذِينَ يُؤْمِنُونَ بِمَا أُنزِلَ إِلَيْكَ وَمَا أُنزِلَ مِن قَبْلِكَ وَبِالْأَخِرَةِ هُمْ يُوقِنُونَ ٤

5. These are on Guidance from their Lord,[16] and these are the blissful ones.

أُوْلَٰئِكَ عَلَىٰ هُدًى مِّن رَّبِّهِمْ وَأُوْلَٰئِكَ هُمُ الْمُفْلِحُونَ ٥

---

15. In other words, what lies beyond this world of sense and which is indiscernible by mere reason; such things as Resurrection, Paradise, Hell, etc., which are unperceivable; absent from the range, or beyond the reach of by sense perception, or of mental perception: or undiscoverable unless by means of Divine Revelation (LL.). Now this Unseen or Great Beyond is the very breath of Religion. Whoever disbelieves in it, disbelieves in Religion altogether. 'Were one asked', says the eminent Harvard psychologist, William James, 'to characterize the life of religion in the broadest and most general terms possible, one might say that there is an unseen order, and that our supreme good lies in harmoniously adjusting ourselves thereto. This belief and this adjustment are the religious attitude in the soul' (*Varieties of Religious Experience*, p. 53). The reality, the existence, of this Great Beyond, so long ignored or even denied and ridiculed by the materialistic West, is at long last being recognized by modern science. Says a leading British archaeologist of the day: 'The unsound materialistic teaching of the past generation obscured this great fact of existence. Too much emphasis was placed on what was dubbed "Reason," and too little on Intuition' (Marston, *The Bible is True*, p. 214). The recognition by modern science of the reality of the Unseen has dealt a death–blow to materialism' (Marston, *The Bible Comes Alive*, p. 252).

16. To sum up: the rightly-guided and the God-fearing are distinguished by (i) their belief in the Unseen Beyond, (ii) their intense devotion to their Creator (or their steadfastness in prayer), (iii) their benevolence to their fellow-creatures (or the free spending of their possessions), (iv) their belief in the Prophet's Messengership, (v) their belief in all previous Books, and (vi) their firm belief in the Hereafter.

6. Surely those who have disbelieved, it is alike to them whether you have warned them or have not warned them; they will not believe.

إِنَّ ٱلَّذِينَ كَفَرُواْ سَوَآءٌ عَلَيْهِمْ ءَأَنذَرْتَهُمْ أَمْ لَمْ تُنذِرْهُمْ لَا يُؤْمِنُونَ ۝

7. Allah has set a seal on their hearts and on their hearing and on their sight is a covering, and for them shall be a mighty torment.

خَتَمَ ٱللَّهُ عَلَىٰ قُلُوبِهِمْ وَعَلَىٰ سَمْعِهِمْ وَعَلَىٰٓ أَبْصَـٰرِهِمْ غِشَـٰوَةٌ وَلَهُمْ عَذَابٌ عَظِيمٌ ۝

Section 2

8. And of mankind are some who say: 'We believe in Allah and in the Last Day,' yet they are not Believers.[17]

وَمِنَ ٱلنَّاسِ مَن يَقُولُ ءَامَنَّا بِٱللَّهِ وَبِٱلْيَوْمِ ٱلْأَخِرِ وَمَا هُم بِمُؤْمِنِينَ ۝

9. They would deceive Allah and those who believe, whereas they deceive not save themselves, and they perceive not.

يُخَـٰدِعُونَ ٱللَّهَ وَٱلَّذِينَ ءَامَنُواْ وَمَا يَخْدَعُونَ إِلَّآ أَنفُسَهُمْ وَمَا يَشْعُرُونَ ۝

10. In their hearts is a disease, so Allah has increased unto them that disease, and for them shall be an afflictive torment for they have been lying.

فِى قُلُوبِهِم مَّرَضٌ فَزَادَهُمُ ٱللَّهُ مَرَضًا وَلَهُمْ عَذَابٌ أَلِيمٌۢ بِمَا كَانُواْ يَكْذِبُونَ ۝

11. And when it is said to them: 'Make not mischief on the earth,' they say: 'We are but reformists.'

وَإِذَا قِيلَ لَهُمْ لَا تُفْسِدُواْ فِى ٱلْأَرْضِ قَالُوٓاْ إِنَّمَا نَحْنُ مُصْلِحُونَ ۝

---

17. Not believing at heart, and in fact. The preceding section spoke of two classes of people, the Believers and unbelievers. The present section describes another class really a subvariety of the disbelieving class, the hypocrites or the dissemblers who abounded in Madina. This singular class of people professed Islam with their lips and pretended to be good and faithful Muslims, yet were not only infidels at heart but inveterate enemies of the Messenger and the Message he had brought.

12. Surely it is they who are the mischief-makers and yet they realize not.

أَلَآ إِنَّهُمْ هُمُ ٱلْمُفْسِدُونَ وَلَٰكِن لَّا يَشْعُرُونَ ﴿١٢﴾

13. And when it is said to them: 'Believe as people have believed,' they say: 'Shall we believe as fools have believed?' Surely it is they who are the fools, and yet they know not.

وَإِذَا قِيلَ لَهُمْ ءَامِنُوا كَمَآ ءَامَنَ ٱلنَّاسُ قَالُوٓا أَنُؤْمِنُ كَمَآ ءَامَنَ ٱلسُّفَهَآءُ أَلَآ إِنَّهُمْ هُمُ ٱلسُّفَهَآءُ وَلَٰكِن لَّا يَعْلَمُونَ ﴿١٣﴾

14. And when they meet those who have believed they say: 'We believe.' And when they are alone with their devils they say: 'Surely we are with you; we were but mocking.'

وَإِذَا لَقُوا ٱلَّذِينَ ءَامَنُوا قَالُوٓا ءَامَنَّا وَإِذَا خَلَوْا إِلَىٰ شَيَٰطِينِهِمْ قَالُوٓا إِنَّا مَعَكُمْ إِنَّمَا نَحْنُ مُسْتَهْزِءُونَ ﴿١٤﴾

15. Allah mocks back at them, and lets them wander bewildered in their insolence.

ٱللَّهُ يَسْتَهْزِئُ بِهِمْ وَيَمُدُّهُمْ فِي طُغْيَٰنِهِمْ يَعْمَهُونَ ﴿١٥﴾

16. These are they who have purchased error for guidance but their commerce profited them not. Nor have they ever become guided.

أُوْلَٰٓئِكَ ٱلَّذِينَ ٱشْتَرَوُا ٱلضَّلَٰلَةَ بِٱلْهُدَىٰ فَمَا رَبِحَت تِّجَٰرَتُهُمْ وَمَا كَانُوا مُهْتَدِينَ ﴿١٦﴾

17. Their likeness is as the likeness of him who kindled a fire, then when it lit up what was around him, Allah took away their light and left them in darkness where they see not.

مَثَلُهُمْ كَمَثَلِ ٱلَّذِي ٱسْتَوْقَدَ نَارًا فَلَمَّآ أَضَآءَتْ مَا حَوْلَهُ ذَهَبَ ٱللَّهُ بِنُورِهِمْ وَتَرَكَهُمْ فِي ظُلُمَٰتٍ لَّا يُبْصِرُونَ ﴿١٧﴾

18. Deaf, dumb, blind, therefore they will not return to light.

صُمٌّ بُكْمٌ عُمْيٌ فَهُمْ لَا يَرْجِعُونَ ﴿١٨﴾

19. Or,[18] like a rain-laden cloud from heaven, wherein are darkness, thunder and lightning. They put their fingers in their ears because of the thunder-claps, fearful of death, while Allah has encompassed the disbelievers.

أَوْ كَصَيِّبٍ مِّنَ ٱلسَّمَآءِ فِيهِ ظُلُمَٰتٌ وَرَعْدٌ وَبَرْقٌ يَجْعَلُونَ أَصَٰبِعَهُمْ فِىٓ ءَاذَانِهِم مِّنَ ٱلصَّوَٰعِقِ حَذَرَ ٱلْمَوْتِ وَٱللَّهُ مُحِيطٌۢ بِٱلْكَٰفِرِينَ ۝

20. The lightning almost snatches away their sight; whensoever it flashes on them, they walk therein, and when it becomes dark they stand still. And had Allah willed He would assuredly have taken away their hearing and their sight. Surely Allah is Potent over everything.

يَكَادُ ٱلْبَرْقُ يَخْطَفُ أَبْصَٰرَهُمْ كُلَّمَآ أَضَآءَ لَهُم مَّشَوْا۟ فِيهِ وَإِذَآ أَظْلَمَ عَلَيْهِمْ قَامُوا۟ وَلَوْ شَآءَ ٱللَّهُ لَذَهَبَ بِسَمْعِهِمْ وَأَبْصَٰرِهِمْ إِنَّ ٱللَّهَ عَلَىٰ كُلِّ شَىْءٍ قَدِيرٌ ۝

Section 3

21. O mankind![19] Worship your Lord Who has created you[20] and those before you, haply you may become God-fearing.

يَٰٓأَيُّهَا ٱلنَّاسُ ٱعْبُدُوا۟ رَبَّكُمُ ٱلَّذِى خَلَقَكُمْ وَٱلَّذِينَ مِن قَبْلِكُمْ لَعَلَّكُمْ تَتَّقُونَ ۝

---

18. The Madinan hypocrites were of two varieties. One class of them were rejecters of Faith outright and only managed to disguise their views and beliefs. The parable in verses 17 – 18 refers to this class of dissemblers. The other group were not so definite and emphatic in their rejection of Faith. They wavered, swinging to and fro, like some modern sceptics. They are the subject of the parable in verses 19 – 20.

19. The message of the Qur'ān is addressed to the whole of mankind, not to just a section of it, conditioned by race, colour or country. The components of this Message are a belief in the Unity of God, and a belief in the Messengership of Muhammad (on him be peace). And these two grand and central truths are now formally presented in this verse and the three succeeding verses. The Holy Qur'ān commands us as well as persuades us to believe in Him and His unity. In this verse these elements both of command and persuasion are happily blended.

20. Created you out of nothing. Nor does man, as claimed by the pantheists, emanate from God.

22. Who has made the earth for you a carpet and the heaven a canopy and sent down from heaven water[21] and brought forth therewith fruits as a provision for you,[22] set not up compeers to Allah, while you know.

اَلَّذِى جَعَلَ لَكُمُ الْأَرْضَ فِرَٰشًا وَالسَّمَآءَ بِنَآءً وَأَنزَلَ مِنَ السَّمَآءِ مَآءً فَأَخْرَجَ بِهِۦ مِنَ الثَّمَرَٰتِ رِزْقًا لَّكُمْ فَلَا تَجْعَلُوا لِلَّهِ أَندَادًا وَأَنتُمْ تَعْلَمُونَ ۝

23. And if you are in doubt concerning what We have sent down upon Our bondman[23] then bring a chapter like it, and call upon your witnesses, besides Allah, if you are truthful.

وَإِن كُنتُمْ فِى رَيْبٍ مِّمَّا نَزَّلْنَا عَلَىٰ عَبْدِنَا فَأْتُوا بِسُورَةٍ مِّن مِّثْلِهِۦ وَادْعُوا شُهَدَآءَكُم مِّن دُونِ اللَّهِ إِن كُنتُمْ صَٰدِقِينَ ۝

24. But if you do not, and you cannot,[24] then dread the Fire whose fuel is men and stones,[25] prepared for the disbelievers.[26]

فَإِن لَّمْ تَفْعَلُوا وَلَن تَفْعَلُوا فَاتَّقُوا النَّارَ الَّتِى وَقُودُهَا النَّاسُ وَالْحِجَارَةُ أُعِدَّتْ لِلْكَٰفِرِينَ ۝

---

21. This does away with all concepts of a sky – god and a rain – god.

22. The Qur'ān, as already noted, is in no sense a text–book of the ever–changing physical sciences, and makes no mention of astronomical and geographical facts as such. Various phenomena of nature, as they appear to the average layman, clear of scientific bias, are described but this only establishes, strengthens and illustrates its central theme, viz., the undivided and indivisible Sovereignty of the Lord – God, and to uproot the divinity of all minor gods, such as the corn – god, the fruit – god, etc.

23. Namely, the Prophet Muḥammad (on him be peace). Note that the greatest of Messengers and the recipient of the highest honour possible is but a servant, a slave, a bondsman of God, having not the remotest community of nature with Him. Not an avatar, nor an incarnation, nor a son, nor yet an actual embodiment of Godhead; but a mere mortal, who would only convey to his fellow men a fuller knowledge of the Divine mind and will. In the Bible too, the phrase 'servants of Yahwa, is honorific and not disparaging' (*EBi*. e. 4398). Bondage to God really implies emancipation from all other servitudes.

24. Here is a most provoking challenge to the enemies of Islam, both ancient and modern, that has remained unanswered all these centuries, and is a unique standing miracle.

25. These stones, which the polytheists worshipped and from which they carved idols and images, would be placed in Hell alongside their worshippers to increase their mental agony and torture. Polytheism has almost invariably manifested itself in stone-worshipping, and sacred stones are perhaps the commonest type of idols. 'All the world over and at all periods of history, we find among the most common objects of human worship certain blocks of stones' (Allen, *Evolution of the Idea of God*, p. 40). 'The worship of holy stones is one of the oldest forms of religion of which evidence has been preserved to us, and one of the most universal' (*EBi*. c. 2979).

26. The Hell-fire is thus intended, primarily and mainly, for the infidels, the outright rejecters of Faith, and not for mere sinners.

25. And give the glad tiding to those who believe and do righteous work that surely for them shall be Gardens beneath which rivers flow. Whenever they will be provided with fruit therefrom, they shall say: 'This is that with which we were provided before;' and they shall be given things consimilar, and for them shall be therein spouses purified,[27] and therein they shall be abiders.

وَبَشِّرِ ٱلَّذِينَ ءَامَنُوا۟ وَعَمِلُوا۟ ٱلصَّٰلِحَٰتِ أَنَّ لَهُمْ جَنَّٰتٍ تَجْرِى مِن تَحْتِهَا ٱلْأَنْهَٰرُ كُلَّمَا رُزِقُوا۟ مِنْهَا مِن ثَمَرَةٍ رِّزْقًا قَالُوا۟ هَٰذَا ٱلَّذِى رُزِقْنَا مِن قَبْلُ وَأُتُوا۟ بِهِۦ مُتَشَٰبِهًا وَلَهُمْ فِيهَا أَزْوَٰجٌ مُّطَهَّرَةٌ وَهُمْ فِيهَا خَٰلِدُونَ ﴿٢٥﴾

26. Surely Allah is not ashamed to use a similitude, be it of a gnat or of anything above it. Then as to those who believe, they know that is the Truth from their Lord. And as to those who disbelieve, they say: 'What did Allah intend by this similitude?' Many He sends astray thereby and many He guides thereby, and He sends not astray thereby any except the transgressors,

إِنَّ ٱللَّهَ لَا يَسْتَحْىِۦٓ أَن يَضْرِبَ مَثَلًا مَّا بَعُوضَةً فَمَا فَوْقَهَا فَأَمَّا ٱلَّذِينَ ءَامَنُوا۟ فَيَعْلَمُونَ أَنَّهُ ٱلْحَقُّ مِن رَّبِّهِمْ وَأَمَّا ٱلَّذِينَ كَفَرُوا۟ فَيَقُولُونَ مَاذَآ أَرَادَ ٱللَّهُ بِهَٰذَا مَثَلًا يُضِلُّ بِهِۦ كَثِيرًا وَيَهْدِى بِهِۦ كَثِيرًا وَمَا يُضِلُّ بِهِۦٓ إِلَّا ٱلْفَٰسِقِينَ ﴿٢٦﴾

---

27. In other words, 'wives purified from the pollution of the menstrual discharge and other natural evacuations' (LL.). Human personality, once its survival is admitted, survives in its totality, and not in part only. And if there is a blessed, eternal life in Paradise, it must be in its complete fullness. Without loss or diminution of any of the intellectual, emotional, and volitional, even sensual factors that enrich earthly life, excluding, of course, all taint of vice. Lack of conjugal love and happiness would surely be an impoverishment, not an enhancement, of the life to come. The survival of human personality, if at all, must be in its entirety, and not only in its abstract, intellectual parts.

27. Who break the covenant of Allah after its ratification,[28] and cut asunder what Allah has commanded to be joined and make mischief in the land. It is they who are the losers.

ٱلَّذِينَ يَنقُضُونَ عَهْدَ ٱللَّهِ مِنۢ بَعْدِ مِيثَٰقِهِۦ وَيَقْطَعُونَ مَآ أَمَرَ ٱللَّهُ بِهِۦٓ أَن يُوصَلَ وَيُفْسِدُونَ فِى ٱلْأَرْضِ أُوْلَٰٓئِكَ هُمُ ٱلْخَٰسِرُونَ ﴿٢٧﴾

28. How will you disbelieve in Allah whereas you were lifeless and He gave you life; thereafter He will cause you to die, then He will give you life, and then unto Him you shall be returned?

كَيْفَ تَكْفُرُونَ بِٱللَّهِ وَكُنتُمْ أَمْوَٰتًا فَأَحْيَٰكُمْ ثُمَّ يُمِيتُكُمْ ثُمَّ يُحْيِيكُمْ ثُمَّ إِلَيْهِ تُرْجَعُونَ ﴿٢٨﴾

29. He it is Who created for you all that is on the earth, then He turned to the heaven, and formed them seven heavens. And He is of everything the Knower.

هُوَ ٱلَّذِى خَلَقَ لَكُم مَّا فِى ٱلْأَرْضِ جَمِيعًا ثُمَّ ٱسْتَوَىٰٓ إِلَى ٱلسَّمَآءِ فَسَوَّىٰهُنَّ سَبْعَ سَمَٰوَٰتٍ وَهُوَ بِكُلِّ شَىْءٍ عَلِيمٌ ﴿٢٩﴾

Section 4

30. And recall when your Lord said to the angels:[29] 'Surely I am going to place a vicegerent[30] on the earth.'

وَإِذْ قَالَ رَبُّكَ لِلْمَلَٰٓئِكَةِ إِنِّى جَاعِلٌ فِى ٱلْأَرْضِ خَلِيفَةً

---

28. By this are meant the duties and obligations imposed by God towards Himself and towards one's parents, family, neighbours, community, country and fellow – creatures in general.

29. Thereby giving them an opportunity to express themselves. Angels are superterrestrial, incorporeal, real and objective beings, not personified qualities and abstractions. They are faithful servants of God and His trusted Messengers, and as pure spirits absolutely sinless and incorruptible. They are, in Islam, as unmistakably distinct from gods as from men; and Islam knows no such things as fallen angels or degraded gods.

30. Note that this vicegerent is a created being, and, as such entirely and sharply marked off from God, the Creator. Also note that the primary purpose of man in this world is to act as the vicegerent of God, and to establish in His name a complete and perfect way of God.

They said[31]: 'Will You place therein one who will act corruptly therein and shed blood,[32] while we hallow Your praise and glorify You?' Allah said: 'Verily I know what you do not know.'[33]

قَالُوٓاْ أَتَجْعَلُ فِيهَا مَن يُفْسِدُ فِيهَا وَ يَسْفِكُ ٱلدِّمَآءَ وَنَحْنُ نُسَبِّحُ بِحَمْدِكَ وَ نُقَدِّسُ لَكَّ قَالَ إِنِّيٓ أَعْلَمُ مَا لَا تَعْلَمُونَ ۝

31. And He taught Adam[34] the names, all of them, then He set them before the angels, and said: 'Declare to me the names of those, if you are truthful.'

وَعَلَّمَ ءَادَمَ ٱلْأَسْمَآءَ كُلَّهَا ثُمَّ عَرَضَهُمْ عَلَى ٱلْمَلَـٰٓئِكَةِ فَقَالَ أَنۢبِـُٔونِي بِأَسْمَآءِ هَـٰٓؤُلَآءِ إِن كُنتُمْ صَـٰدِقِينَ ۝

32. They said: 'Hallowed be You! No knowledge have we save what You have taught us,[35] surely You alone are the Knower, the Wise.'

قَالُوٓاْ سُبْحَـٰنَكَ لَا عِلْمَ لَنَآ إِلَّا مَا عَلَّمْتَنَآ إِنَّكَ أَنتَ ٱلْعَلِيمُ ٱلْحَكِيمُ ۝

33. Allah said: 'O Adam! Declare to them the names of those objects.' Then when he had declared to them the names of those objects, He said: 'Did I not tell you, surely I know the hidden in the heavens and the earth and know that which you disclose and what you have been concealing?'

قَالَ يَـٰٓـَٔادَمُ أَنۢبِئْهُم بِأَسْمَآئِهِمْ فَلَمَّآ أَنۢبَأَهُم بِأَسْمَآئِهِمْ قَالَ أَلَمْ أَقُل لَّكُمْ إِنِّيٓ أَعْلَمُ غَيْبَ ٱلسَّمَـٰوَٰتِ وَٱلْأَرْضِ وَأَعْلَمُ مَا تُبْدُونَ وَمَا كُنتُمْ تَكْتُمُونَ ۝

---

31. Not by way of protest or complaint but out of excess loyalty and devotion, 'as the most devoted bondsmen who could hardly bear their Beloved Master to employ a new servant besides them, for any of His services' (Th.).

32. This the angels surmised from man's constitution. And this is endorsed by the teaching of modern psychology that man's primary instincts are predatory and individualistic rather than social.

33. Knowledge of man's nature, and his capacities, and of his special aptitude for Divine vicegerency. A corrective angelolatry. Angels are not co – equal with God even in respect of knowledge.

34. The first progenitor of the human race. He was a Prophet.

35. Another death-blow to the doctrine of angelolatry. Angels far from being omnipotent have only very limited knowledge.

34. And recall when We said to the angels: prostrate yourselves before Adam, they prostrated themselves, but not Iblīs,[36] he refused and was stiff-necked, and became one of the disbelievers.

وَإِذْ قُلْنَا لِلْمَلَٰٓئِكَةِ ٱسْجُدُوا۟ لِءَادَمَ فَسَجَدُوٓا۟ إِلَّآ إِبْلِيسَ أَبَىٰ وَٱسْتَكْبَرَ وَكَانَ مِنَ ٱلْكَٰفِرِينَ ٣٤

35. And We said: O Adam! Dwell you and your spouse in the Garden, and eat both of you plentifully thereof as you desire, but do not approach, both of you, that tree, lest you become of the transgressors.

وَقُلْنَا يَٰٓـَٔادَمُ ٱسْكُنْ أَنتَ وَزَوْجُكَ ٱلْجَنَّةَ وَكُلَا مِنْهَا رَغَدًا حَيْثُ شِئْتُمَا وَلَا تَقْرَبَا هَٰذِهِ ٱلشَّجَرَةَ فَتَكُونَا مِنَ ٱلظَّٰلِمِينَ ٣٥

36. Then Satan caused the two to slip[37] therefrom and drove forth the two from what they were in. And We said: 'Get you all down, each of you as enemy of each, and on the earth will be an abode for you and enjoyment for a time.'

فَأَزَلَّهُمَا ٱلشَّيْطَٰنُ عَنْهَا فَأَخْرَجَهُمَا مِمَّا كَانَا فِيهِ وَقُلْنَا ٱهْبِطُوا۟ بَعْضُكُمْ لِبَعْضٍ عَدُوٌّ وَلَكُمْ فِي ٱلْأَرْضِ مُسْتَقَرٌّ وَمَتَٰعٌ إِلَىٰ حِينٍ ٣٦

37. Then Adam learnt certain words from his Lord, and He relented towards him. Surely it is He Who is the Relenting,[38] the Merciful.

فَتَلَقَّىٰٓ ءَادَمُ مِن رَّبِّهِۦ كَلِمَٰتٍ فَتَابَ عَلَيْهِ إِنَّهُۥ هُوَ ٱلتَّوَّابُ ٱلرَّحِيمُ ٣٧

---

36. Iblis, literally, being the disappointed one. He was not an angel but a *jinn*, as expressly mentioned in the Qur'ān (*Surah al-Kahf*, verse 50).

37. This by his cunning and clever stratagem, the nature of which could not be perceived by Adam and his consort. Iblis, it is related in the traditions of the Prophet, went up to Adam and his consort in disguise and affecting his true friendship and fidelity to them, offered to show them the way to the tree of eternity, the fruit of which shall cause them never to separate from Allah's presence, the very thing that they longed for most, and swore to them, by Allah, that he was their most faithful adviser. It was thus that they partook of the forbidden tree. There was none of willful and deliberate disobedience on the part of Adam. He was simply taken in.

38. The Prophet 'was never tired of telling the people how God was Very Forgiving, that His love for men was more tender than of the mother-bird for her young' (*LSK.* Intro., p. LXXX).

38. We said: 'Get down all of you from here, and if there comes to you guidance from Me, then whoso follows My guidance, no fear shall come on them, nor shall they grieve.

قُلْنَا اهْبِطُوا مِنْهَا جَمِيعًا فَإِمَّا يَأْتِيَنَّكُم مِّنِّي هُدًى فَمَن تَبِعَ هُدَايَ فَلَا خَوْفٌ عَلَيْهِمْ وَلَا هُمْ يَحْزَنُونَ ﴿٣٨﴾

39. And those who disbelieve and belie Our signs, they shall be inmates of the Fire; therein they shall abide.'

وَالَّذِينَ كَفَرُوا وَكَذَّبُوا بِآيَاتِنَا أُولَٰئِكَ أَصْحَابُ النَّارِ هُمْ فِيهَا خَالِدُونَ ﴿٣٩﴾

Section 5

40. O Children of Israel![39] Remember My favour wherewith I favoured you, and fulfil My covenant, and I shall fulfil your covenant, and dread Me alone.

يَا بَنِي إِسْرَائِيلَ اذْكُرُوا نِعْمَتِيَ الَّتِي أَنْعَمْتُ عَلَيْكُمْ وَأَوْفُوا بِعَهْدِي أُوفِ بِعَهْدِكُمْ وَإِيَّايَ فَارْهَبُونِ ﴿٤٠﴾

39. Children of Israel is the national designation of the Jews. Israel was the name borne by their ancestor, Jacob, the father of the twelve tribes, a son of Isaac, and a grandson of Abraham (on all of whom be peace). This nation of priests, patriarchs and Prophets, perhaps the most remarkable people in ancient history, blessed of their Lord, were always great in the realm of religion and faith, and mighty and glorious for long periods in the affairs of the world, and had migrated in their thousands, after the capture of Jerusalem by the Romans under Titus, into Arabia, and had settled in and around Madina long before the advent of the Prophet. The whole of north-eastern Arabia was dotted about by their colonies, and many of the Arab pagans, in the course of time, had come to adopt their ways and their Faith. In the third century of the Christian era, an Arabian tribe, living in the remote south of the peninsula adopted the Jewish faith. As proud possessors of the Book and the Divine Law, and even more as adepts in crude occult sciences and magical crafts, these Arab Jews were, in the early days of Islam, in effect the intellectual masters of the country. In matters religious and Divine, they were the trusted advisors of the unlettered pagans and their acknowledged superiors. Jewish legends, Jewish tenets and Jewish feats of exorcism were by now popular knowledge throughout Arabia. The 'idolatry of Arabia', to use the words of Muir, had formed a compromise with Judaism, and had imbibed many of its legends and perhaps many of its tenets. It was the Jews, again, who had long been predicting a new redeemer, and who actively looked for him. This helps to explain the extent of the attention they receive in the Qur'ān, and the long series of admonitions, warnings and exhortations addressed to them. In the domain of religion they were always the foremost; in Arabia, contemporaneous with Islam, their importance stood especially high.

41. And believe in what I have sent down confirming what is with you, and be not the first to disbelieve therein. And barter not My Signs for a small price,[40] and fear Me alone.

وَءَامِنُوۡا بِمَاۤ أَنزَلۡتُ مُصَدِّقًا لِّمَا مَعَكُمۡ وَلَا تَكُوۡنُوۡاۤ أَوَّلَ كَافِرٍۭ بِهِۦ وَلَا تَشۡتَرُوۡا بِـَٔايَـٰتِى ثَمَنًا قَلِيلًا وَإِيَّـٰىَ فَٱتَّقُونِ ﴿٤١﴾

42. And confound not the Truth with falsehood,[41] nor conceal the Truth while you know.

وَلَا تَلۡبِسُوا الۡحَقَّ بِٱلۡبَـٰطِلِ وَتَكۡتُمُوا الۡحَقَّ وَأَنتُمۡ تَعۡلَمُونَ ﴿٤٢﴾

---

40. To reject Truth for monetary considerations for the inducements of this transitory, ephemeral world, is to barter eternal happiness and bliss for a small price. That the Jews had even in ancient times evinced a special weakness for the allurements of lucre, is borne out by the OT itself: 'He is a merchant, the balances of deceit are in his hand; he loveth to oppress' (Ho. 12: 7). Also in Am. 8: 4–5. Again, in NT times, Paul and Peter both bring the same charge against the Jews. 'There are many unruly and vain talkers and deceivers, specially they of circumcision: whose mouths must be stopped, when they subvert whole houses, teaching things which they ought not, for filthy lucre's sake' (Ti. 1: 10–11). 'And many follow their pernicious ways; by reason of whom the way of truth shall be evil spoken of. And through covetousness shall they with feigned words make merchandise of you' (2 Pe. 2: 2–3).

41. In other words, by perverting the text or by handling it deceitfully. Cf. 2 Cor. 4: 2. One such method common with the Jews as well as the Christians, was the method of allegory. 'The Palestinian Jews allegorised the OT. in order to satisfy their conscience for the non–observance of laws that had become impracticable, or to justify traditional and often trivial increment or, generally for homiletical purposes the Hellenistic Jews allegorise the OT to prove that their religion had the same rationale as Greek philosophy, and that Moses had been the teacher, or, at all events, the anticipator, of Pythagoras, Plato, Aristotle, and the Stoics' (*DB*. I. p. 65). Compare *JE*. I, pp. 403–404.

43. And establish prayer, and give the poor – rate[42] and bow down with those who bow.[43]

وَأَقِيمُواْ ٱلصَّلَوٰةَ وَءَاتُواْ ٱلزَّكَوٰةَ وَٱرْكَعُواْ مَعَ ٱلرَّٰكِعِينَ ۝

44. Do you enjoin mankind to piety and forget yourselves while you read the Book? Do you not understand?

أَتَأْمُرُونَ ٱلنَّاسَ بِٱلْبِرِّ وَتَنسَوْنَ أَنفُسَكُمْ وَأَنتُمْ تَتْلُونَ ٱلْكِتَٰبَ أَفَلَا تَعْقِلُونَ ۝

45. And seek help in patience and prayer, and surely it is hard, save to the meek,

وَٱسْتَعِينُواْ بِٱلصَّبْرِ وَٱلصَّلَوٰةِ وَإِنَّهَا لَكَبِيرَةٌ إِلَّا عَلَى ٱلْخَٰشِعِينَ ۝

---

42. As this would cure the mind of avarice and greed (Th.). Literally, purity and purification, in the language of Islamic law means the poor – rate, the portion, or amount, of property that is given therefrom as the due of God, by its possessor to the poor in order that he may purify it thereby (LL.). The payment of this religious tax is obligatory, provided that the property is of a certain amount and has been in possession for one lunar year. The tax varies according to the nature and amount of the property; but generally it is one–fortieth thereof, or of its value, i.e., 2.5 per cent.

43. Those who pray being the Muslims in congregational prayers. This ordered service of Divine worship is one of the most characteristic features of the religious life of Muslim society and its impressive character has frequently been noted by travellers and others in the East. The late Bishop Lefroy thus commented upon it: 'No one who comes in contact for the first time with the Mohammadans can fail to be struck with this aspect of their faith. Wherever one may be, in the open street, one is struck with this aspect of their faith. it is the most ordinary thing to see a man, without the slightest touch of pharisaism or parade, quietly and humbly leave whatever pursuit he may be at the moment engaged in, in order to say his prayer of the appointed hour. The very regularity of the daily call to prayer as it rings out at earliest dawn before light commences or amid all the noises and bustle of business hours or again as evening closes in, is fraught with the same majesty' (Arnold, *Islamic Faith*, p. 29). 'As a disciplinary measure this congregational prayer must have had great value for the proud, individualistic sons of the desert. It developed in them the sense of social equality and the consciousness of solidarity. It promoted that brotherhood of community of believers which the religion of Muḥammad had theoretically substituted for blood relationship. The prayer ground thus became the first drill ground of Islam.' (Hitti, *History of the Arabs,* p. 132).

46. Who know, that surely they are going to meet their Lord, and that surely to Him they are going to return.[44]

اَلَّذِينَ يَظُنُّونَ أَنَّهُم مُّلَٰقُواْ رَبِّهِمْ وَأَنَّهُمْ إِلَيْهِ رَٰجِعُونَ ﴿٤٦﴾

Section 6

47. O Children of Israel! Remember My favour with which I favoured you, and that surely I preferred you[45] above the worlds.

يَٰبَنِيٓ إِسْرَٰٓءِيلَ ٱذْكُرُواْ نِعْمَتِيَ ٱلَّتِيٓ أَنْعَمْتُ عَلَيْكُمْ وَأَنِّي فَضَّلْتُكُمْ عَلَى ٱلْعَٰلَمِينَ ﴿٤٧﴾

48. And fear a Day when not in aught will a soul satisfy for another soul[46] nor will intercession profit it, nor will any compensation be accepted therefore, nor will they be helped.

وَٱتَّقُواْ يَوْمًا لَّا تَجْزِى نَفْسٌ عَن نَّفْسٍ شَيْـًٔا وَلَا يُقْبَلُ مِنْهَا شَفَٰعَةٌ وَلَا يُؤْخَذُ مِنْهَا عَدْلٌ وَلَا هُمْ يُنصَرُونَ ﴿٤٨﴾

---

44. It is this living belief in a future life which makes the greatest hardship and sacrifice easy to Believers.

45. Preferred them as a people, as a race. Now what did this preference of the Israelites consist of ? Was it their commerce, their adventures, their martial glory, their achievements in the arts, or their eminence in science? Nothing of the sort. Their singular glory and peculiar excellence, as a race, lay in their special mission – their tenacious, pure and absolute monotheism–in fact, the only living monotheism that the world knew before the advent of Islam. 'The Hebrews alone of all Semitic people reached the stage of pure monotheism, through the teachings of their prophets ... As long as a man refused allegiance to other gods, he was looked upon as a Jew: whoever denies the existence of other gods is called a Jew. The unity of God was a revealed truth for the Jew, there was no need of proof to establish it; it was the leading tenet of the faith' (*JE*. VIII. pp. 659 and 661).

46. This is to repudiate the Rabbinical doctrine that 'grace is to be given to some because of the merits of their ancestors, to others because of the merits of their descendants' (*JE*. VI. p. 61).

49. And recall when We delivered you from the house of Pharaoh[47] imposing upon you evil chastisement, slaughtering your sons, and sparing your women, and in that was a mighty trial from your Lord.

وَإِذْ نَجَّيْنَاكُم مِّنْ ءَالِ فِرْعَوْنَ يَسُومُونَكُمْ سُوٓءَ ٱلْعَذَابِ يُذَبِّحُونَ أَبْنَآءَكُمْ وَيَسْتَحْيُونَ نِسَآءَكُمْ ۚ وَفِى ذَٰلِكُم بَلَآءٌ مِّن رَّبِّكُمْ عَظِيمٌ ﴿٤٩﴾

50. And recall when We separated for you the sea, and delivered you, and drowned Pharaoh's house, while you looked on.

وَإِذْ فَرَقْنَا بِكُمُ ٱلْبَحْرَ فَأَنجَيْنَاكُمْ وَأَغْرَقْنَآ ءَالَ فِرْعَوْنَ وَأَنتُمْ تَنظُرُونَ ﴿٥٠﴾

51. And recall when We treated with Moses forty nights, then you betook the calf[48] after him, and you were transgressors.

وَإِذْ وَٰعَدْنَا مُوسَىٰٓ أَرْبَعِينَ لَيْلَةً ثُمَّ ٱتَّخَذْتُمُ ٱلْعِجْلَ مِنۢ بَعْدِهِۦ وَأَنتُمْ ظَٰلِمُونَ ﴿٥١﴾

---

47. Pharaoh or its Biblical equivalent. Pharaoh, is the Hebraized title of the ancient kings of Egypt, like the Tsar of Russia, the Sultan of Turkey, or the Khedive of Egypt. The Pharaoh spoken of here, the one contemporaneous with Moses (peace be on him) was, till recently, believed to be Rameses II, in the 13th century BC, or Merenptah, or both. 'Rameses II of the 19th dynasty is generally accounted as the Pharaoh of the Oppression, and his son and successor, Merenptah is considered to be the Pharaoh of the Exodus... The Oppression evidently lasted many years. Rameses II reigned 67 years, and thus the Exodus may have taken place in the short reign of Merenptah, the son and successor of that aged king' (*DB*. III. p. 820). Also *JE*, IX. p. 660. 'Fresh archaeological evidence, however, identifies the Pharaoh of Oppression with Thotmas III and the Pharaoh of the Exodus with Amenhatap II, and postulates the date of the Exodus as falling between 1447 BC and 1417 BC. The Exodus must, therefore, have taken place after Thotmas III's death in 1447 BC, and during the reign of Amenhatap II' (Marston, *The Bible is True*, p. 171).

48. The calf being taken for worship. The Israelites in their impatience during the temporary absence of Moses (peace be on him) had taken to the image–worship of a golden calf. The Bible narrates the story of calf – worship by the Israelites in great detail (Ex. 32: 1–8). The Qur'ān is in substantial agreement with it, except in one very important particular, where the Bible makes the Prophet Aaron (Aaron), him of all people! responsible for this act of outrageous impiety.

52. Then We forgave you there-after, that haply you may return thanks.

ثُمَّ عَفَوْنَا عَنكُم مِّنۢ بَعْدِ ذَٰلِكَ لَعَلَّكُمْ تَشْكُرُونَ ۞

53. And recall when We gave to Moses the Book and the distinction that haply you may be rightly guided.

وَإِذْ ءَاتَيْنَا مُوسَى ٱلْكِتَـٰبَ وَٱلْفُرْقَانَ لَعَلَّكُمْ تَهْتَدُونَ ۞

54. And recall when Moses said to his people: 'O my people! Surely you have wronged yourselves by your taking the calf for worship; so now turn to your Maker and slay one another. That will be right for you with your Maker.' Then He relented towards you. Surely it is He Who is the Relenting, the Merciful.

وَإِذْ قَالَ مُوسَىٰ لِقَوْمِهِ يَـٰقَوْمِ إِنَّكُمْ ظَلَمْتُمْ أَنفُسَكُم بِٱتِّخَاذِكُمُ ٱلْعِجْلَ فَتُوبُوٓا۟ إِلَىٰ بَارِئِكُمْ فَٱقْتُلُوٓا۟ أَنفُسَكُمْ ذَٰلِكُمْ خَيْرٌ لَّكُمْ عِندَ بَارِئِكُمْ فَتَابَ عَلَيْكُمْ إِنَّهُۥ هُوَ ٱلتَّوَّابُ ٱلرَّحِيمُ ۞

55. And recall when you said: 'O Moses! We will not believe in you till we see God openly.' Thereupon a thunderbolt took hold of you, while you looked on.

وَإِذْ قُلْتُمْ يَـٰمُوسَىٰ لَن نُّؤْمِنَ لَكَ حَتَّىٰ نَرَى ٱللَّهَ جَهْرَةً فَأَخَذَتْكُمُ ٱلصَّـٰعِقَةُ وَأَنتُمْ تَنظُرُونَ ۞

56. Then We raised you after your death that haply you may return thanks.

ثُمَّ بَعَثْنَـٰكُم مِّنۢ بَعْدِ مَوْتِكُمْ لَعَلَّكُمْ تَشْكُرُونَ ۞

57. And We overshadowed you with cloud, and We sent down upon you manna and quails: eat of the good things wherewith We have provided you. And they wronged not Us, but themselves they were wont to wrong.

وَظَلَّلْنَا عَلَيْكُمُ ٱلْغَمَامَ وَأَنزَلْنَا عَلَيْكُمُ ٱلْمَنَّ وَٱلسَّلْوَىٰ كُلُوا۟ مِن طَيِّبَـٰتِ مَا رَزَقْنَـٰكُمْ وَمَا ظَلَمُونَا وَلَـٰكِن كَانُوٓا۟ أَنفُسَهُمْ يَظْلِمُونَ ۞

58. And recall when We said: enter this township and eat plentifully of it as you will, and enter the gate prostrating, and say: 'Forgiveness'; We shall forgive you your transgressions, and We shall give increase to the well-doers.[49]

وَإِذۡ قُلۡنَا ٱدۡخُلُواۡ هَٰذِهِ ٱلۡقَرۡيَةَ فَكُلُواۡ مِنۡهَا حَيۡثُ شِئۡتُمۡ رَغَدًا وَٱدۡخُلُواۡ ٱلۡبَابَ سُجَّدًا وَقُولُواۡ حِطَّةٌ نَّغۡفِرۡ لَكُمۡ خَطَٰيَٰكُمۡ وَسَنَزِيدُ ٱلۡمُحۡسِنِينَ ۝

59. Then the evil-doers changed the Word that had been told them for another; so We sent down upon the evil-doers a scourge from heaven, for they were wont to transgress.

فَبَدَّلَ ٱلَّذِينَ ظَلَمُواۡ قَوۡلًا غَيۡرَ ٱلَّذِى قِيلَ لَهُمۡ فَأَنزَلۡنَا عَلَى ٱلَّذِينَ ظَلَمُواۡ رِجۡزًا مِّنَ ٱلسَّمَآءِ بِمَا كَانُواۡ يَفۡسُقُونَ ۝

Section 7

60. And recall when Moses prayed for drink for his people. So We said: 'Smite with your staff the rock.' Then there gushed forth out of it twelve springs; every people already knew their drinking place; eat and drink of the provision of Allah, and make not mischief on the earth as corrupters.

وَإِذِ ٱسۡتَسۡقَىٰ مُوسَىٰ لِقَوۡمِهِۦ فَقُلۡنَا ٱضۡرِب بِّعَصَاكَ ٱلۡحَجَرَ فَٱنفَجَرَتۡ مِنۡهُ ٱثۡنَتَا عَشۡرَةَ عَيۡنًا قَدۡ عَلِمَ كُلُّ أُنَاسٍ مَّشۡرَبَهُمۡ كُلُواۡ وَٱشۡرَبُواۡ مِن رِّزۡقِ ٱللَّهِ وَلَا تَعۡثَوۡاۡ فِى ٱلۡأَرۡضِ مُفۡسِدِينَ ۝

---

49. In the way of favours and rewards. The Bible omits to mention all these significant and important moral aspects of the narrative.

61. And recall when you said: 'O Moses, we will not bear patiently with one sort of food, so supplicate your Lord for us that He bring forth for us of what the earth grows–of its vegetables, and its cucumbers, its wheat, its lentils and its onions.' Moses said: 'Would you take in exchange what is meaner for what is better? Get ye down into a city, as there is surely in it what you ask for.' And stuck upon them were abasement and poverty. And they drew on themselves wrath from Allah. This, because they were ever disbelieving in the signs of Allah[50]

وَإِذْ قُلْتُمْ يَـٰمُوسَىٰ لَن نَّصْبِرَ عَلَىٰ طَعَامٍ وَٰحِدٍ فَٱدْعُ لَنَا رَبَّكَ يُخْرِجْ لَنَا مِمَّا تُنۢبِتُ ٱلْأَرْضُ مِنۢ بَقْلِهَا وَقِثَّآئِهَا وَفُومِهَا وَعَدَسِهَا وَبَصَلِهَا ۖ قَالَ أَتَسْتَبْدِلُونَ ٱلَّذِى هُوَ أَدْنَىٰ بِٱلَّذِى هُوَ خَيْرٌ ۚ ٱهْبِطُوا۟ مِصْرًا فَإِنَّ لَكُم مَّا سَأَلْتُمْ ۗ وَضُرِبَتْ عَلَيْهِمُ ٱلذِّلَّةُ وَٱلْمَسْكَنَةُ وَبَآءُو بِغَضَبٍ مِّنَ ٱللَّهِ ۗ ذَٰلِكَ بِأَنَّهُمْ كَانُوا۟ يَكْفُرُونَ بِـَٔايَـٰتِ ٱللَّهِ

---

50. The Bible abounds in doleful narratives of their rebellion and revolt. To give only a few such extracts out of many: 'Remember and forget not, how you provoked the Lord your God to wrath in the wilderness; from the day you did depart out of the land of Egypt, until you came unto this place, you have been rebellious against the Lord. Also in Horeb you provoked the Lord to wrath, so that the Lord was angry with you to have destroyed you. When I was gone up in the Mount to receive the tablets of stone ... the Lord said unto me: ... your people which you have brought forth out of Egypt have corrupted themselves; they are quickly turned aside out of the way which I commanded them; they have made them a molten image. Furthermore, the Lord spake unto me, saying, I have seen this people, and blot out their name from under heaven,' (Dt. 9: 7–13). 'You rebelled against the commandment of the Lord, your God, and you believed Him not, nor harkened to His voice. You have been rebellious against the Lord from the day that I knew you' (Dt. 9: 23–24). 'I know your rebellion, and your stiff–neck; behold, while I am yet alive with you this day, you have been rebellious against the Lord; and how much more after my death? ... I know that after my death you will utterly corrupt yourselves, and turn aside from the way which I have commanded you; and evil will befall you in the later days; because you will do evil in the sight of the Lord, to provoke him to anger through the work of your hands' (Dt. 31: 27–29).

and slaying the Prophets unjustly[51]. This, because they disobeyed[52] and were ever transgressing.

وَيَقْتُلُونَ ٱلنَّبِيِّنَ بِغَيْرِ ٱلْحَقِّ ذَٰلِكَ بِمَا عَصَوا۟ وَّكَانُوا۟ يَعْتَدُونَ ۝

51. Wrongful and unjust not only in the sight of God, as the murder of a Prophet in any instance is bound to be, but wrongful, unjust and illegal, even according to Israel's own code of law and justice. To take the instance of Jesus: He 'was not condemned, but he was slain. His martyrdom was no miscarriage of justice, it was a murder' (Rosadi, *Trial of Jesus*, p. 301). 'In this trial was a violence done to the forms and rules of Hebrew as well as to the principles of justice' (Innes, *Trial of Jesus Christ*, p. 35). 'Such a process had neither the form nor the fairness of a judicial trial' (Ibid., p. 59).

52. For the uniformly rebellious attitude of Israel towards their greatest leader and benefactor, the Prophet Moses, compare and consult their national historian Josephus: 'They were very angry at their conductor Moses and were zealous in their attempt to stone him as the direct occasion of their present miseries' (*Ant.* III. 1: 3). '... the multitude were irritated and bitterly set against him' (III. 1: 4). 'They again turned their anger against Moses, but he at first avoided the fury of the multitude...' (III. 1: 7). 'The multitude began again to be mutinous and to blame Moses for the misfortunes they had suffered in their travels (III. 13: 1). 'The multitude therefore became still more unruly and more mutinous against Moses than before. And Moses was basely abused by them' (III. 13: 1). 'They again blamed Moses and made clamour against him and his brother Aaron... They passed that night very ill and with contumacious language against them: but in the morning they ran to a congregation intending to stone Moses and Aaron, and so to return to Egypt' (III. 14: 3). '... notwithstanding the indignities they had offered to their legislator and his laws and their disobedience to the commandments which He had sent them by Moses (IV. 2: 1). 'When forty years were completed, Moses gathered the congregation together near Jordan... and all the people being come together, he spoke thus to them; ... 'you know that I have been oftener in danger of death from you than from our enemies' (8: 1–2).

Section 8

62. Surely those who believe and those who are Judaized[53] and Nazarene[54] and Sabaean,[55] whoso

إِنَّ ٱلَّذِينَ ءَامَنُواْ وَٱلَّذِينَ هَادُواْ وَ
ٱلنَّصَـٰرَىٰ وَٱلصَّـٰبِئِينَ

53. The correct rendering of this Qur'ānic expression can only be those who are Judaized or those who have become Jews. 'It is the first time that the Qur'ān speaks of the "Jews" as distinct from the Children of Israel.' The two terms, though frequently used as synonymous, are not exactly coextensive or interchangeable. The Israelites are a race, a nation, a people, a huge family, the sons of a particular progenitor, conscious and proud of their high lineage. The Jews are also a religious community, believers in particular tenets, members of a certain faith. The Holy Qur'ān, regardful of the niceties of expression, has always observed this distinction. When speaking of the religious beliefs and practices of the Hebrews and those who adopted their faith, it uses the term Jews; when alluding to their history and their national traits it uses the term the Children of Israel. The Israelites ceased to exist as a nation with the destruction of the Temple in AD 70 and, thenceforth, they became a purely religious community.

54. Nasara is, in its proper sense, Nazarenes, not Christians. A Nasara is a Nazarene in its original meaning and a Christian only in its secondary application (LL.). Nazarene is derived from Nazareth, the place where Jesus passed his youth. The Nazarenes or the primitive Christians were the followers of the original pre–Pauline Church, quite unlike the present – day Pauline variety of Christianity. Nor is the title 'in itself disparaging' (*EBi.* c. 3356), rather, 'it was a primitive designation for Christians' (*ERE.* III. p. 374).

55. A Sabi is literally 'one who goes forth from one religion to another (LL.). 'The Sabians who are first mentioned in the Koran were a semi – Christian sect of Babylonia, the Elkasaites, closely resembling the Mandeans or so-called "Christians of St. John the Baptist", but not identical with them' (*EBr.* XIX. p. 790). According to another definition, they were a sect in ancient Persia and Chaldea, who believed in the unity of God but also worshipped intelligences supposed to reside in the heavenly bodies. 'The genuine Sabians of Arabic writers were a Judaeo–Christian sect who also called themselves Nasoraie d'Yahya, the Nasoreans (i.e., the observants of St. John), and therefore became erroneously known to the modern world as the Christians of St. John (the Baptist), (Hitti, *History of the Arabs* p. 357). They 'practised the rite of baptism after birth, before marriage and on various other occasions. They inhabited the lower plains of Babylonia, and as a sect they go back to the first century after Christ... Mentioned thrice in the Koran, these Babylonian Sabians acquired a *dhimma* status and were classified by Moslems as a "protected" sect. The community still survives to the number of five thousand in the swampy lands near al-Basrah. Living in the neighbourhood of rivers is necessitated by the fact that immersion in flowing water is an essential, and certainly the most characteristic feature of their religious practice' (Ibid.).

believes in Allah and the Last Day and works righteously – their wage is with their Lord;[56] and no fear shall come on them nor shall they grieve.

مَنْ ءَامَنَ بِاللَّهِ وَالْيَوْمِ الْأَخِرِ وَعَمِلَ صَلِحًا فَلَهُمْ أَجْرُهُمْ عِندَ رَبِّهِمْ وَلَا خَوْفٌ عَلَيْهِمْ وَلَا هُمْ يَحْزَنُونَ ۝

63. And recall when We took your bond and raised over you the Tur,[57] saying: 'Hold fast to what We have given you, and remember what is therein, haply you may become God-fearing.'

وَإِذْ أَخَذْنَا مِيثَقَكُمْ وَرَفَعْنَا فَوْقَكُمُ الطُّورَ خُذُواْ مَا ءَاتَيْنَكُم بِقُوَّةٍ وَاذْكُرُواْ مَا فِيهِ لَعَلَّكُمْ تَتَّقُونَ ۝

---

56. Right belief and right conduct are the only *sine qua non* of salvation which every individual has in his own hands. However grave his misbelief or misconduct in the past, he is not past redemption. If he only accepts God's Truth, and obeys. His laws, however late in life, the blessings both of this world and the Next are his. Not even the Jews with their centuries – old record of crime and corruption, depravity and rebellion, are debarred from Allah's All – embracing Grace and Mercy: provided they mend their ways (Th.). Salvation is not confined to any particular race or nationality.

57. 'And it came to pass – that there were thunders and lightning, and a thick cloud upon the Mount, and the voice of the trumpet exceeding loud; so that all the people that was in the camp trembled, and they stood at the nether part of the mount. And Mount Sinai was altogether on a smoke... and the whole Mount quaked greatly' (Ex. 19: 17–18). That the Mount was actually inverted over the Israelites is what is expressly narrated in the Talmud. 'The Holy One, blessed be He, inverted Mount Sinai over them like a huge vessel and declared, "If you accept the Torah, well and good; if not, here shall be your sepulchre' (*ET.* p. 66). 'God suspended the Mount over them as a bat, and said to them, if you accept the Torah, it is all right; if not, you will find here your tomb' (*JE.* IV. 321). The term is applied to Mount Sinai and to the Mount of Olives, and to several other mountains (LL.). Here it denotes Mount Sinai. There are several summits in the group of mountains collectively known as the Sinai.

64. Then you turned away thereafter, so had not the grace of Allah and His mercy been upon you, you had been of the losers.

ثُمَّ تَوَلَّيْتُم مِّنْ بَعْدِ ذَلِكَ فَلَوْلَا فَضْلُ اللَّهِ عَلَيْكُمْ وَرَحْمَتُهُ لَكُنتُم مِّنَ الْخَاسِرِينَ ﴿٦٤﴾

65. And assuredly you know of those of you who trespassed in the matter of the Sabbath, and We said to them: 'Be you apes despised.'[58]

وَلَقَدْ عَلِمْتُمُ الَّذِينَ اعْتَدَوْا مِنكُمْ فِي السَّبْتِ فَقُلْنَا لَهُمْ كُونُوا قِرَدَةً خَاسِئِينَ ﴿٦٥﴾

66. And We made it a deterrent to those of their day and those after them and an admonition to the God-Fearing.

فَجَعَلْنَاهَا نَكَالًا لِّمَا بَيْنَ يَدَيْهَا وَمَا خَلْفَهَا وَمَوْعِظَةً لِّلْمُتَّقِينَ ﴿٦٦﴾

67. And recall when Moses said to his people: 'Allah commands you that you slaughter a cow.' They said: 'Make you a jest of us?' Moses said: 'I take refuge with Allah that I should be of the pagans.'

وَإِذْ قَالَ مُوسَى لِقَوْمِهِ إِنَّ اللَّهَ يَأْمُرُكُمْ أَن تَذْبَحُوا بَقَرَةً قَالُوا أَتَتَّخِذُنَا هُزُوًا قَالَ أَعُوذُ بِاللَّهِ أَنْ أَكُونَ مِنَ الْجَاهِلِينَ ﴿٦٧﴾

---

58. Despised and driven away. There are several points to note. In the first place, the Qur'ān does not say whether the sentence was actually carried out, or ultimately rescinded on the transgressors' repentance, some commentators adopting the latter suggestion. Secondly, the transformation may have taken place only in manners and morals as held by some early commentators, and not physically. Thirdly, the Qur'ān only argues from the Jews' knowledge of, and their credence to, such an event ('Ye know it perfectly well'), and itself says nothing about its occurrence or otherwise. The usual Qur'ānic way of rehearsing the facts of Jewish history is different; it begins with ('and recall when;'). The commonly accepted view of the commentators is that the transformation took place at Eylah or Ailah, in the time of David (on him be peace) and owing to his curse on the persistent Sabbath-breakers, and that the offenders were changed into apes, who all died after three days. Eylah, or Elath, of the Bible, was a flourishing harbour on the north-east arm of the Red Sea and is the modern town of Aqabah. The scornful epithet strikes at the root of monkey-adoration and the Hanuman-worship of several polytheistic peoples.

68. They said: 'Supplicate your Lord for us that He make clear to us what she may be.' Moses said: 'He says, she should be a cow neither old nor young, but middling between the two: so perform what you are bidden.'

قَالُوا ادْعُ لَنَا رَبَّكَ يُبَيِّن لَّنَا مَا هِىَ قَالَ إِنَّهُۥ يَقُولُ إِنَّهَا بَقَرَةٌ لَّا فَارِضٌ وَلَا بِكْرٌ عَوَانٌۢ بَيْنَ ذَٰلِكَ فَافْعَلُوا مَا تُؤْمَرُونَ ۝

69. They said: 'Supplicate your Lord for us that He make clear to us what her colour may be.' Moses said: 'He says, she should be a yellow cow whose colour is bright, delighting the beholders.'

قَالُوا ادْعُ لَنَا رَبَّكَ يُبَيِّن لَّنَا مَا لَوْنُهَا قَالَ إِنَّهُۥ يَقُولُ إِنَّهَا بَقَرَةٌ صَفْرَاءُ فَاقِعٌ لَّوْنُهَا تَسُرُّ النَّٰظِرِينَ ۝

70. They said: 'Supplicate your Lord for us that He make clear to us what she may be; the cow has become dubious to us, and surely, if God wills, we shall now be guided.'

قَالُوا ادْعُ لَنَا رَبَّكَ يُبَيِّن لَّنَا مَا هِىَ إِنَّ الْبَقَرَ تَشَٰبَهَ عَلَيْنَا وَإِنَّا إِن شَاءَ اللَّهُ لَمُهْتَدُونَ ۝

71. Moses said: 'He says, surely she should be a cow unyoked not broken to till the ground or to water the field, sound, and without blemish in her.' They said: 'You have now brought the Truth.' Then they slaughtered her, and they were almost not doing it.

قَالَ إِنَّهُۥ يَقُولُ إِنَّهَا بَقَرَةٌ لَّا ذَلُولٌ تُثِيرُ الْأَرْضَ وَلَا تَسْقِى الْحَرْثَ مُسَلَّمَةٌ لَّا شِيَةَ فِيهَا قَالُوا الْـَٰٔنَ جِئْتَ بِالْحَقِّ فَذَبَحُوهَا وَمَا كَادُوا يَفْعَلُونَ ۝

Section 9

72. And recall when you slew a person, then quarrelled among yourselves concerning it and Allah was to disclose what you were hiding.

وَإِذْ قَتَلْتُمْ نَفْسًا فَادَّٰرَٰٔتُمْ فِيهَا وَاللَّهُ مُخْرِجٌ مَّا كُنتُمْ تَكْتُمُونَ ۝

73. Then We said: 'Strike him with part of her. Thus will Allah bring to life the dead, and He shows you His signs that haply you may understand.'

فَقُلْنَا اضْرِبُوهُ بِبَعْضِهَا ۚ كَذَٰلِكَ يُحْىِ اللَّهُ الْمَوْتَىٰ وَيُرِيكُمْ ءَايَٰتِهِۦ لَعَلَّكُمْ تَعْقِلُونَ ۝

74. Then your hearts hardened thereafter so they were as stones or even harder; and surely of stones there are some from which rivers gush forth, and surely there are of them some that split and water issues therefrom, and surely there are of them some that fall down in awe of Allah,[59] and Allah is not unmindful of what you do.

ثُمَّ قَسَتْ قُلُوبُكُم مِّنۢ بَعْدِ ذَٰلِكَ فَهِىَ كَالْحِجَارَةِ أَوْ أَشَدُّ قَسْوَةً ۚ وَإِنَّ مِنَ الْحِجَارَةِ لَمَا يَتَفَجَّرُ مِنْهُ الْأَنْهَٰرُ ۚ وَإِنَّ مِنْهَا لَمَا يَشَّقَّقُ فَيَخْرُجُ مِنْهُ الْمَاءُ ۚ وَإِنَّ مِنْهَا لَمَا يَهْبِطُ مِنْ خَشْيَةِ اللَّهِ ۗ وَمَا اللَّهُ بِغَٰفِلٍ عَمَّا تَعْمَلُونَ ۝

75. Do you covet then that they would believe for you whereas surely a section of them has been hearing the Word of Allah, and then perverting it[60] after they have

أَفَتَطْمَعُونَ أَن يُؤْمِنُوا لَكُمْ وَقَدْ كَانَ فَرِيقٌ مِّنْهُمْ يَسْمَعُونَ كَلَٰمَ اللَّهِ ثُمَّ يُحَرِّفُونَهُۥ مِنۢ بَعْدِ

---

59. A beautiful description, in parable, of three grades of righteous people:

> (i) those who do universal good, such as the Prophets (like big rivers in their beneficence), (ii) those whose outlook is not so broad, yet who do immense service within their limited sphere, such as saints and martyrs (like smaller streams and rivulets); and (iii) those who are true and faithful at least to their own selves; – the general community of the faithful (like stones which are impressionable).

60. Islam was not the first to accuse the Jews of deliberate perversion of their Sacred Texts. The charge dates back to Jeremiah, one of their own Prophets: 'Ye have perverted the Words of the living God, of the Lord of Hosts, our God' (Je. 23: 36). In the NT also there are several allusions to the Jews corrupting and perverting the words of God, as in 2 Cor. 2: 17 and 1 Ti. 1: 10. That the books of the OT exist now in their original purity is not the position of anybody today, not even of the most conservative Jew.

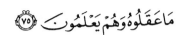

understood it, while they know?[61]

مَاعَقَلُوهُ وَهُمْ يَعۡلَمُونَ ۝

---

61. Very interesting and illuminating are the Jews' own descriptions of the Books of the Bible and their ascription of the authorship to ancient sages and great teachers and never to the Divine Author Himself. 'That the real authority of the Bible is intrinsic rather than prescriptive becomes clear as soon as we think of the circumstances in which the Scriptural canon was formed. The decision by which certain books were included in the Bible and others excluded, was a purely human decision. The great teachers sat in judgement upon the claims of the various works, and decided upon those claims by the light of reason, in other words, by the internal merits of the works themselves. Nor was the decision always easy'. The fate of some books, like Ecclesiastes, and Canticles, and Esther, was, we learn, trembling in the balance even as late as the third century of the present era. The touchstone applied to the various Books was intrinsic worth, and nothing else.' (Joseph, *Judaism as Creed and Life*, p. 18). 'The Bible, being the work of godly men, necessarily contains both a Divine and a human element. But, since everything human is imperfect, we must not expect to find an absolutely perfect representation of Divine Truth even in God's Book. Rays of light, penetrating through a stained–glass window not only part with some of their brilliance but borrow the various colours of the panes. It is so with the Bible ... To think otherwise is to imagine that the authors of the Bible were not human beings but Divine' (Ibid., p. 20). 'Some of the Biblical stories are clearly legends though highly beautiful and instructive ... In regard to scientific matters it reflects only the knowledge of the age in which each writer lived' (Ibid., pp. 22–23). 'The Pentateuch is the work not of one hand but of many hands ... Similar views prevail among scholars with regard to other books of the Bible' (Ibid., p. 24). 'Jewish tradition, while insisting that some Biblical books were composed by the chief actors therein, which is not at all unreasonable, does not hesitate to admit later elaboration and revision of certain books in the Bible' (*VJE*, p. 93). 'As an unimpeachable source of history and chronology the Bible is often disappointing, exhibiting statements and data which seem either vague or contradictory or else fail to agree, with what is known of contemporary oriental history and chronology' (Ibid., p. 95). 'Ancient Jewish traditions attributed the authorship of the Pentateuch (with the exception of the last eight verses describing Moses' death) to Moses himself. But the many inconsistencies and seeming contradictions contained in it attracted the attention of the Rabbis, who exercised their ingenuity in reconciling them' (*JE*. IX. p. 589). 'Spinoza goes so far as to attribute the composition of the Pentateuch not to Moses, but to Ezra, which view appears to have existed then in the time of the Apocrypha' (Ibid., p. 590). The latest analysis, however, has led finally to the definitive attribution of the Pentateuch is contents to no less than 28 different sources.

76. And when they meet those who believe they say: 'We believe,' and when some of them are alone with some others they say: 'Do you tell them of that God has opened to you; so what they may dispute with you therewith before your Lord?' Understand you not then?

وَإِذَا لَقُواْ ٱلَّذِينَ ءَامَنُواْ قَالُواْ ءَامَنَّا وَإِذَا خَلَا بَعْضُهُمْ إِلَىٰ بَعْضٍ قَالُواْ أَتُحَدِّثُونَهُم بِمَا فَتَحَ ٱللَّهُ عَلَيْكُمْ لِيُحَاجُّوكُم بِهِۦ عِندَ رَبِّكُمْ أَفَلَا تَعْقِلُونَ ۝

77. Do they not know that Allah knows what they hide and what they make known?

أَوَلَا يَعْلَمُونَ أَنَّ ٱللَّهَ يَعْلَمُ مَا يُسِرُّونَ وَمَا يُعْلِنُونَ ۝

78. And of them are unlettered ones who do not know the Book but their own vain desires, and they but conjecture.

وَمِنْهُمْ أُمِّيُّونَ لَا يَعْلَمُونَ ٱلْكِتَٰبَ إِلَّآ أَمَانِيَّ وَإِنْ هُمْ إِلَّا يَظُنُّونَ ۝

79. Woe then to them who write out the Book with their own hands and say thereafter: 'This is from God,' that they may barter it for a small price. Woe then to them for what their hands have written, and woe to them for that they earn thereby!

فَوَيْلٌ لِّلَّذِينَ يَكْتُبُونَ ٱلْكِتَٰبَ بِأَيْدِيهِمْ ثُمَّ يَقُولُونَ هَٰذَا مِنْ عِندِ ٱللَّهِ لِيَشْتَرُواْ بِهِۦ ثَمَنًا قَلِيلًا فَوَيْلٌ لَّهُم مِّمَّا كَتَبَتْ أَيْدِيهِمْ وَوَيْلٌ لَّهُم مِّمَّا يَكْسِبُونَ ۝

80. And they say: 'Fire will not touch us save for a few numbered days.' Say: 'Have you taken a covenant with Allah, so that Allah shall not fail His covenant, or do you fabricate against Allah what you have no knowledge of?'

وَقَالُواْ لَن تَمَسَّنَا ٱلنَّارُ إِلَّآ أَيَّامًا مَّعْدُودَةً قُلْ أَتَّخَذْتُمْ عِندَ ٱللَّهِ عَهْدًا فَلَن يُخْلِفَ ٱللَّهُ عَهْدَهُۥ أَمْ تَقُولُونَ عَلَى ٱللَّهِ مَا لَا تَعْلَمُونَ ۝

81. Yea! Whoso earns vice and his sin has encompassed him – these shall be the inmates of the Fire as abiders therein.

بَلَىٰ مَن كَسَبَ سَيِّئَةً وَأَحَٰطَتْ بِهِۦ خَطِيٓـَٔتُهُۥ فَأُوْلَٰٓئِكَ أَصْحَٰبُ ٱلنَّارِ هُمْ فِيهَا خَٰلِدُونَ ۝

82. And they who believe and do righteous works these shall be the inmates of the Garden as abiders therein.

وَٱلَّذِينَ ءَامَنُوا۟ وَعَمِلُوا۟ ٱلصَّٰلِحَٰتِ أُو۟لَٰٓئِكَ أَصْحَٰبُ ٱلْجَنَّةِ هُمْ فِيهَا خَٰلِدُونَ ۝

Section 10

83. And recall when We took a bond with the Children of Israel saying: 'You shall not worship any god save Allah, and show kindness to your parents and also to your kindred and to the orphans and the needy, and speak kindly to mankind and establish prayer and give the poor-rate.' Then you turned away, save a few of you, and you are backsliders.

وَإِذْ أَخَذْنَا مِيثَٰقَ بَنِىٓ إِسْرَٰٓءِيلَ لَا تَعْبُدُونَ إِلَّا ٱللَّهَ وَبِٱلْوَٰلِدَيْنِ إِحْسَانًا وَذِى ٱلْقُرْبَىٰ وَٱلْيَتَٰمَىٰ وَٱلْمَسَٰكِينِ وَقُولُوا۟ لِلنَّاسِ حُسْنًا وَأَقِيمُوا۟ ٱلصَّلَوٰةَ وَءَاتُوا۟ ٱلزَّكَوٰةَ ثُمَّ تَوَلَّيْتُمْ إِلَّا قَلِيلًا مِّنكُمْ وَأَنتُم مُّعْرِضُونَ ۝

84. And recall when We took a bond with you, saying: 'You shall not shed your blood, nor drive one another from your homes,' then you ratified it, and you were witnesses.

وَإِذْ أَخَذْنَا مِيثَٰقَكُمْ لَا تَسْفِكُونَ دِمَآءَكُمْ وَلَا تُخْرِجُونَ أَنفُسَكُم مِّن دِيَٰرِكُمْ ثُمَّ أَقْرَرْتُمْ وَأَنتُمْ تَشْهَدُونَ ۝

85. Thereafter it is you the very ones who slay one another and drive a section of you from their homes; and conspire against them with guilt and inequity; and if they come to you as captives you ransom them; yet forbidden to you was their driving away. Do you believe then in part of the Book and disbelieve in part? What, then, is to be the recompense of

ثُمَّ أَنتُمْ هَٰٓؤُلَآءِ تَقْتُلُونَ أَنفُسَكُمْ وَتُخْرِجُونَ فَرِيقًا مِّنكُم مِّن دِيَٰرِهِمْ تَظَٰهَرُونَ عَلَيْهِم بِٱلْإِثْمِ وَٱلْعُدْوَٰنِ وَإِن يَأْتُوكُمْ أُسَٰرَىٰ تُفَٰدُوهُمْ وَهُوَ مُحَرَّمٌ عَلَيْكُمْ إِخْرَاجُهُمْ أَفَتُؤْمِنُونَ بِبَعْضِ ٱلْكِتَٰبِ وَتَكْفُرُونَ بِبَعْضٍ

those of you who do that, save humiliation in the life of the world? And on the Day of Judgement they shall be brought back to the severest torment;[62] and Allah is not unmindful of what they do.

فَمَا جَزَاءُ مَن يَفْعَلُ ذَٰلِكَ مِنكُمْ إِلَّا خِزْيٌ فِى ٱلْحَيَوٰةِ ٱلدُّنْيَا وَيَوْمَ ٱلْقِيَٰمَةِ يُرَدُّونَ إِلَىٰٓ أَشَدِّ ٱلْعَذَابِ وَمَا ٱللَّهُ بِغَٰفِلٍ عَمَّا تَعْمَلُونَ ٨٥

86. These are they who have purchased the life of the world for the Hereafter; so the torment shall not be lightened for them, nor shall they be helped.

أُوْلَٰٓئِكَ ٱلَّذِينَ ٱشْتَرَوُا۟ ٱلْحَيَوٰةَ ٱلدُّنْيَا بِٱلْءَاخِرَةِ فَلَا يُخَفَّفُ عَنْهُمُ ٱلْعَذَابُ وَلَا هُمْ يُنصَرُونَ ٨٦

Section 11

87. And assuredly We gave to Moses the Book, and We followed him up by Messengers after him; and to Jesus,[63] son of Maryam, We gave the evidence and aided him with the Holy Spirit.[64] Then

وَلَقَدْ ءَاتَيْنَا مُوسَى ٱلْكِتَٰبَ وَقَفَّيْنَا مِنۢ بَعْدِهِۦ بِٱلرُّسُلِ وَءَاتَيْنَا عِيسَى ٱبْنَ مَرْيَمَ ٱلْبَيِّنَٰتِ وَأَيَّدْنَٰهُ بِرُوحِ ٱلْقُدُسِ

---

62. Compare the denunciation of the Jews in the NT: 'Ye serpents, ye generation of vipers, how can ye escape the damnation of Hell?' (Mt. 23: 33).

63. Namely, Jesus, the last Prophet of the house of Israel, who, according to his apostles at Jerusalem, 'was the Christ as the anointed man, not as the incarnate Angel, Messiah born by a virgin, nor as the man united with the celestial Christ by the Holy Spirit' (Bunsen, *Islam or True Christianity*, p. 141). The later -day concepts of so-called Christianity were recognized neither by Jesus himself nor by his 12 apostles (Ibid.).

64. Namely the angel Gabriel, who attended on Jesus (peace be on him) constantly and succoured him in a special way. This Holy Spirit of Islam has nothing, save name, in common with the Holy Ghost of Christianity, who is 'the Third Person of the Blessed Trinity... the Spirit of the Father and of the Son' proceeding 'alike from both as from one common principle' (*CD*. p. 451). Islam does not support the preposterous proposition that 'the Holy Spirit is rightly included in the Godhead, and to be worshipped and glorified with the Father and the Son as divine'. (*ERE*. XI. p. 798). Nor has it any such polytheistic doctrine to promulgate as that the Holy Spirit is 'Sovereign and Life-giving Who proceedeth from the Father, Who with the Father and the Son is together worshipped and glorified'. (*EBr.* XI. p. 635).

whenever there came to you a Messenger with what your hearts desired not, you waxed stiff – necked, and some you denied and others you slew.

أَفَكُلَّمَا جَآءَكُمْ رَسُولٌ بِمَا لَا تَهْوَىٰ أَنفُسُكُمُ ٱسْتَكْبَرْتُمْ فَفَرِيقًا كَذَّبْتُمْ وَفَرِيقًا تَقْتُلُونَ ﴿٨٧﴾

88. And they say: 'Our hearts are in a covering.' Nay! Allah has cursed them because of their infidelity: little therefore is that which they believe.

وَقَالُوا۟ قُلُوبُنَا غُلْفٌۢ بَل لَّعَنَهُمُ ٱللَّهُ بِكُفْرِهِمْ فَقَلِيلًا مَّا يُؤْمِنُونَ ﴿٨٨﴾

89. And when there came to them a Book from Allah confirming what was with them – and aforetime they were entreating God for victory over those who disbelieved – then when there came to them what they recognized, they disbelieved therein; so Allah's curse be on the infidels!

وَلَمَّا جَآءَهُمْ كِتَـٰبٌ مِّنْ عِندِ ٱللَّهِ مُصَدِّقٌ لِّمَا مَعَهُمْ وَكَانُوا۟ مِن قَبْلُ يَسْتَفْتِحُونَ عَلَى ٱلَّذِينَ كَفَرُوا۟ فَلَمَّا جَآءَهُم مَّا عَرَفُوا۟ كَفَرُوا۟ بِهِۦ فَلَعْنَةُ ٱللَّهِ عَلَى ٱلْكَـٰفِرِينَ ﴿٨٩﴾

90. Vile is that for which they have sold themselves, disbelieving in what Allah has sent down,[65] out of envy, that Allah shall reveal, out of His grace, to whomsoever of His bondsmen He will.[66] Therefore they have drawn upon themselves wrath upon wrath, and to the infidels shall be an ignominious torment.

بِئْسَمَا ٱشْتَرَوْا۟ بِهِۦ أَنفُسَهُمْ أَن يَكْفُرُوا۟ بِمَآ أَنزَلَ ٱللَّهُ بَغْيًا أَن يُنَزِّلَ ٱللَّهُ مِن فَضْلِهِۦ عَلَىٰ مَن يَشَآءُ مِنْ عِبَادِهِۦ فَبَآءُو بِغَضَبٍ عَلَىٰ غَضَبٍ وَلِلْكَـٰفِرِينَ عَذَابٌ مُّهِينٌ ﴿٩٠﴾

---

65. This emphasizes the fact that Jewish opposition was not based upon any intellectual misapprehension, but was solely due to chagrin and malice at finding a non–Israelite endowed with the high gift of Prophethood.

66. The Jews, with the superiority complex of their race and their 'election' were smarting under the fact, too real and too patent to be ignored, that the new Messenger had risen not among themselves but among their cousins, the Children of Ismā'īl, whom they had so long held in contempt and derision.

91. And when it is said to them: 'Believe in what Allah has sent down now', they say: 'We believe in what has been sent down to us.' And they disbelieve in what is besides that, while it is the Truth, confirming what is with them.[67] Say: 'Why then did you kill Allah's Prophets aforetime if you have been believers?'

وَإِذَا قِيلَ لَهُمْ ءَامِنُواْ بِمَا أَنزَلَ ٱللَّهُ قَالُواْ نُؤْمِنُ بِمَا أُنزِلَ عَلَيْنَا وَيَكْفُرُونَ بِمَا وَرَاءَهُ وَهُوَ ٱلْحَقُّ مُصَدِّقًا لِّمَا مَعَهُمْ قُلْ فَلِمَ تَقْتُلُونَ أَنۢبِيَاءَ ٱللَّهِ مِن قَبْلُ إِن كُنتُم مُّؤْمِنِينَ ۝

92. And assuredly Moses came to you with evidence, then you took to yourselves the calf after him, and you were transgressors.

وَلَقَدْ جَاءَكُم مُّوسَىٰ بِٱلْبَيِّنَٰتِ ثُمَّ ٱتَّخَذْتُمُ ٱلْعِجْلَ مِنۢ بَعْدِهِ وَأَنتُمْ ظَٰلِمُونَ ۝

93. And recall when We took your bond and raised over you the Tur, saying: hold fast to what We gave you and listen. They said: 'We hear and we deny.' And into their hearts the calf was made to sink because of their infidelity. Say: 'Vile is what your belief commands you, if you are believers at all.'

وَإِذْ أَخَذْنَا مِيثَٰقَكُمْ وَرَفَعْنَا فَوْقَكُمُ ٱلطُّورَ خُذُواْ مَا ءَاتَيْنَٰكُم بِقُوَّةٍ وَٱسْمَعُواْ قَالُواْ سَمِعْنَا وَعَصَيْنَا وَأُشْرِبُواْ فِى قُلُوبِهِمُ ٱلْعِجْلَ بِكُفْرِهِمْ قُلْ بِئْسَمَا يَأْمُرُكُم بِهِ إِيمَٰنُكُمْ إِن كُنتُم مُّؤْمِنِينَ ۝

94. Say: 'If for you alone is the abode of the Hereafter with Allah to the exclusion of mankind, then long for death, if you are truthful.'

قُلْ إِن كَانَتْ لَكُمُ ٱلدَّارُ ٱلْءَاخِرَةُ عِندَ ٱللَّهِ خَالِصَةً مِّن دُونِ ٱلنَّاسِ فَتَمَنَّوُاْ ٱلْمَوْتَ إِن كُنتُمْ صَٰدِقِينَ ۝

95. And they will never long for it, because of what their hands have sent on before, and Allah is the Knower of transgressors.

وَلَن يَتَمَنَّوْهُ أَبَدًۢا بِمَا قَدَّمَتْ أَيْدِيهِمْ وَٱللَّهُ عَلِيمٌۢ بِٱلظَّٰلِمِينَ ۝

---

67. The answer to the Jewish argument is twofold. They ought to believe in the Qur'ān, first, because it is True in itself, supported by independent evidence; and secondly, because it confirms and corroborates and supplements their own Scripture, and does not detract from it.

96. And surely you will find them the greediest of all the people for life, even greedier than those who associate. Every one of them desires life for a thousand years, and yet this will not save him from the torment, even if he has lived so long. And Allah is the Beholder of what they do.

وَلَتَجِدَنَّهُمْ أَحْرَصَ النَّاسِ عَلَىٰ حَيَوٰةٍ وَمِنَ الَّذِينَ أَشْرَكُوا يَوَدُّ أَحَدُهُمْ لَوْ يُعَمَّرُ أَلْفَ سَنَةٍ وَمَا هُوَ بِمُزَحْزِحِهِ مِنَ الْعَذَابِ أَن يُعَمَّرَ وَاللَّهُ بَصِيرٌ بِمَا يَعْمَلُونَ ۝

Section 12

97. Say: 'Whoso is an enemy to Gabriel – then surely it is he who has brought down this revelation, by Allah's command, to your heart confirming what went before, and a guidance and glad tiding to the believers.'

قُلْ مَن كَانَ عَدُوًّا لِّجِبْرِيلَ فَإِنَّهُ نَزَّلَهُ عَلَىٰ قَلْبِكَ بِإِذْنِ اللَّهِ مُصَدِّقًا لِّمَا بَيْنَ يَدَيْهِ وَهُدًى وَبُشْرَىٰ لِلْمُؤْمِنِينَ ۝

98. Whoso is an enemy to Allah and His angels and His Messengers and Gabriel and Michael, then surely Allah is an enemy to the infidels.

مَن كَانَ عَدُوًّا لِّلَّهِ وَمَلَٰئِكَتِهِ وَرُسُلِهِ وَجِبْرِيلَ وَمِيكَٰلَ فَإِنَّ اللَّهَ عَدُوٌّ لِّلْكَٰفِرِينَ ۝

99. And assuredly We have sent down upon you evident signs and none disbelieves in them except the wicked.

وَلَقَدْ أَنزَلْنَا إِلَيْكَ ءَايَٰتٍ بَيِّنَٰتٍ وَمَا يَكْفُرُ بِهَا إِلَّا الْفَٰسِقُونَ ۝

100. Is it that whenever they enter into a covenant some party among them casts it aside? Aye! Most of them do not believe.

أَوَكُلَّمَا عَٰهَدُوا عَهْدًا نَّبَذَهُ فَرِيقٌ مِّنْهُم بَلْ أَكْثَرُهُمْ لَا يُؤْمِنُونَ ۝

101. And whenever there came to them a Messenger from Allah confirming what was with them, a party among those who were given the Book, cast Allah's Book behind their backs as though they did not know.

وَلَمَّا جَاءَهُمْ رَسُولٌ مِّنْ عِندِ اللَّهِ مُصَدِّقٌ لِّمَا مَعَهُمْ نَبَذَ فَرِيقٌ مِّنَ الَّذِينَ أُوتُوا الْكِتَٰبَ كِتَٰبَ اللَّهِ وَرَآءَ ظُهُورِهِمْ كَأَنَّهُمْ لَا يَعْلَمُونَ ۝

102. And they[68] follow what satans recited in the reign of Solomon. And Solomon[69]

وَاتَّبَعُوا مَا تَتْلُوا الشَّيَٰطِينُ عَلَىٰ مُلْكِ سُلَيْمَٰنَ وَمَا كَفَرَ سُلَيْمَٰنُ

68. The Jews of Arabia, who were noted for their feats of exorcism and magic. 'The practice of magic was common throughout ancient Israel... A knowledge of magic was indispensable to a member of the chief council or of the judiciary, and might be acquired even from the heathen. The most profound scholars were adept in the black art and the law did not deny its power. The people who cared little for the views of the learned, were devoted to witchcraft.' 'Adultery and sorcery have destroyed everything; the Majesty of God departed from Israel... Exorcism also flourished. The Greco – Roman world regarded the Jews as a race of magicians' (JE. VIII. p. 255). This reputation of the Jews as skilled magicians and expert exorcists continued right up to the time of the Prophet: 'They were in Arabia at the advent of Islam, adept in magic, and preferred the weapons of the black art to those of open warfare' (Margoliouth, *Mohammed*, p. 189). The Arab Jews were adept in the black magic both of Palestine and Chaldia (Babylonia). They inherited the one and acquired the other. The Chaldeans after they had ceased to be a nation, 'dispersed all over the world, carrying their delusive science with them practising and teaching it, welcomed everywhere by the credulous and superstitious' (Ragozin, *The Chaldea*, p. 255). And no better pupil could they have found than the Jews. 'Babylonia ... continued to be regarded with reverence by the Jews in all parts' (JE. II. pp. 413–414). 'Contact with Babylonia tended to stimulate the angelology and demonology of Israel' (EBr. XIII. p. 187).

69. The King Solomon (373–933 BC) of the Bible, who, according to the teachings of Islam, was not an idolatrous king, but a true Prophet of God and a benevolent and wise ruler. The Jews, true to their traditions of ingratitude and malevolence, have not hesitated to malign their own hero and national benefactor, the Prophet Solomon (on him be peace), and to accuse him of the most heinous of all offences – idolatry! (See 1 Ki. 11: 4, 9, 10). They have also unblushingly attributed to him the cult of crude occultism and witchcraft. The Qur'ān upholds the honour of all Prophets of God, to whatever race or age they may belong, and believes in the saintliness and sinlessness of every one of them. It takes this opportunity to sweep aside all the ugly tales and outrageous imputations about him and says in effect that far from being an unbeliever or a blasphemer, he never practised any such black art as the pagans did.

blasphemed not, but satans blasphemed, teaching the people magic. And they follow also what was sent down[70] unto the two angels in Bābil, Hārūt and Mārūt. To none did the two teach it until they had said: 'We are but a temptation, so blaspheme not.' But they did learn from the two that with which they might separate man from his wife,[71] though they could harm none thereby save by Allah's will. And they have learnt what harms them and does not profit them.

And assuredly they knew that whoso traffics therein, his is no portion in the Hereafter. And surely vile is the price for which they have bartered themselves; would that they knew!

103. And had they believed and feared, surely better had been the reward from Allah; would that they knew!

وَلَٰكِنَّ ٱلشَّيَٰطِينَ كَفَرُواْ يُعَلِّمُونَ ٱلنَّاسَ ٱلسِّحْرَ وَمَآ أُنزِلَ عَلَى ٱلْمَلَكَيْنِ بِبَابِلَ هَٰرُوتَ وَمَٰرُوتَ وَمَا يُعَلِّمَانِ مِنْ أَحَدٍ حَتَّىٰ يَقُولَآ إِنَّمَا نَحْنُ فِتْنَةٌ فَلَا تَكْفُرْ فَيَتَعَلَّمُونَ مِنْهُمَا مَا يُفَرِّقُونَ بِهِۦ بَيْنَ ٱلْمَرْءِ وَزَوْجِهِۦ وَمَا هُم بِضَآرِّينَ بِهِۦ مِنْ أَحَدٍ إِلَّا بِإِذْنِ ٱللَّهِ وَيَتَعَلَّمُونَ مَا يَضُرُّهُمْ وَلَا يَنفَعُهُمْ وَلَقَدْ عَلِمُواْ لَمَنِ ٱشْتَرَىٰهُ مَا لَهُۥ فِي ٱلْأَخِرَةِ مِنْ خَلَٰقٍ وَلَبِئْسَ مَا شَرَوْاْ بِهِۦٓ أَنفُسَهُمْ لَوْ كَانُواْ يَعْلَمُونَ ﴿١٠٢﴾

وَلَوْ أَنَّهُمْ ءَامَنُواْ وَٱتَّقَوْاْ لَمَثُوبَةٌ مِّنْ عِندِ ٱللَّهِ خَيْرٌ لَّوْ كَانُواْ يَعْلَمُونَ ﴿١٠٣﴾

---

70. 'Which was sent down' means that a special and intimate knowledge was given, in order that its nature be explained and its mischief be demonstrated in full, and that people may be weaned from the engulfing superstition, just as a physician acquires an intimate knowledge of diseases, not of course to propagate but to combat them and just again as a police officer familarizes himself with the ways of criminals and law – breakers with the sole purpose to prevent them.

71. 'The commonest form of magic was the love – charm, specially the love – charm required for an illicit amour. Such magic was practised specially by women so that magic and adultery frequently are mentioned together... The context of the passages in Exodus which mention sorcery clearly that it was associated with sexual license and unnatural vices' (*JE*. VIII. p. 255).

Section 13

104. O you who believe! Do not say: 'Ra'inā',[72] but say: 'Unẓurnā', and listen; and to the infidels (shall be) an afflictive torment.

يَـٰٓأَيُّهَا ٱلَّذِينَ ءَامَنُوا۟ لَا تَقُولُوا۟ رَٰعِنَا وَقُولُوا۟ ٱنظُرْنَا وَٱسْمَعُوا۟ وَلِلْكَـٰفِرِينَ عَذَابٌ أَلِيمٌ ﴿١٠٤﴾

105. Those who disbelieve, be they of the People of the Book or of the associators, do not like that aught of good should be sent down upon you from your Lord whereas Allah singles out for His mercy whom He wills, and Allah is the Possessor of mighty grace.

مَّا يَوَدُّ ٱلَّذِينَ كَفَرُوا۟ مِنْ أَهْلِ ٱلْكِتَـٰبِ وَلَا ٱلْمُشْرِكِينَ أَن يُنَزَّلَ عَلَيْكُم مِّنْ خَيْرٍ مِّن رَّبِّكُمْ وَٱللَّهُ يَخْتَصُّ بِرَحْمَتِهِۦ مَن يَشَآءُ وَٱللَّهُ ذُو ٱلْفَضْلِ ٱلْعَظِيمِ ﴿١٠٥﴾

106. Whatsoever verse We abrogate[73] or cause to be forgotten We bring a better one or the like of it; do you not know that Allah is Potent over everything?

مَا نَنسَخْ مِنْ ءَايَةٍ أَوْ نُنسِهَا نَأْتِ بِخَيْرٍ مِّنْهَآ أَوْ مِثْلِهَآ أَلَمْ تَعْلَمْ أَنَّ ٱللَّهَ عَلَىٰ كُلِّ شَىْءٍ قَدِيرٌ ﴿١٠٦﴾

---

72. 'Meaning, listen to us'. The term, innocent in itself, was turned by a little twist in pronunciation into a word of reproach and insult by the Jews when addressing the Prophet — to such depths of pettiness had they descended! The Muslims are forbidden to use this ambiguous expression to call the Prophet's attention.

73. There is nothing to be ashamed of in the doctrine of certain laws, temporary or local, being superseded or abrogated by certain other laws, permanent and universal, and enacted by the same Law – giver, specially during the course of the promulgation of that law. The course of Qur'ānic revelation has been avowedly gradual. It took about 23 years to finish and complete the legislation. Small wonder, then, that certain minor laws, admittedly transitory, were replaced by certain others, lasting and eternal. Even Divine laws may be subject to Divine improvement, just as is every object and phenomenon in the physical universe of His creation. It must, however, be clearly understood that the doctrine of abrogation applies to 'law' only, and even there to instruments of minor or secondary importance. Beliefs, articles of faith, principles of law, narratives, exhortations, moral precepts, and spiritual verities, none of these are subject to abrogation or repeal.

107. Do you not know that surely Allah! His is the dominion of the heavens and the earth? And for you there is, besides Allah, no guardian or helper.

أَلَمْ تَعْلَمْ أَنَّ ٱللَّهَ لَهُۥ مُلْكُ ٱلسَّمَـٰوَٰتِ وَٱلْأَرْضِ ۗ وَمَا لَكُم مِّن دُونِ ٱللَّهِ مِن وَلِيٍّ وَلَا نَصِيرٍ ۝

108. Do you seek to question your Messenger as Moses was questioned before? And whoso exchanges infidelity for belief, he has assuredly strayed from the even way.

أَمْ تُرِيدُونَ أَن تَسْـَٔلُوا۟ رَسُولَكُمْ كَمَا سُئِلَ مُوسَىٰ مِن قَبْلُ ۗ وَمَن يَتَبَدَّلِ ٱلْكُفْرَ بِٱلْإِيمَـٰنِ فَقَدْ ضَلَّ سَوَآءَ ٱلسَّبِيلِ ۝

109. Many of the people of the Book desire that they could turn you away as infidels after you have believed, out of envy from their souls, after the Truth has dawned upon them; so pardon them and pass over, until Allah sends the command. Surely Allah is Potent over everything.

وَدَّ كَثِيرٌ مِّنْ أَهْلِ ٱلْكِتَـٰبِ لَوْ يَرُدُّونَكُم مِّنۢ بَعْدِ إِيمَـٰنِكُمْ كُفَّارًا حَسَدًا مِّنْ عِندِ أَنفُسِهِم مِّنۢ بَعْدِ مَا تَبَيَّنَ لَهُمُ ٱلْحَقُّ ۖ فَٱعْفُوا۟ وَٱصْفَحُوا۟ حَتَّىٰ يَأْتِيَ ٱللَّهُ بِأَمْرِهِۦٓ ۗ إِنَّ ٱللَّهَ عَلَىٰ كُلِّ شَىْءٍ قَدِيرٌ ۝

110. And establish prayer and give the poor-rate, and whatever of good you send forth for your souls you shall find with Allah; surely Allah is the Beholder of what you do.

وَأَقِيمُوا۟ ٱلصَّلَوٰةَ وَءَاتُوا۟ ٱلزَّكَوٰةَ ۚ وَمَا تُقَدِّمُوا۟ لِأَنفُسِكُم مِّنْ خَيْرٍ تَجِدُوهُ عِندَ ٱللَّهِ ۗ إِنَّ ٱللَّهَ بِمَا تَعْمَلُونَ بَصِيرٌ ۝

111. And they say: 'None shall enter the Garden except he be a Jew[74] or a Christian.'[75] Such are their vain desires. Say: 'Forth with your proof if you are truthful.'

وَقَالُوا لَن يَدْخُلَ ٱلْجَنَّةَ إِلَّا مَن كَانَ هُودًا أَوْ نَصَرَىٰ تِلْكَ أَمَانِيُّهُمْ قُلْ هَاتُوا بُرْهَـٰنَكُمْ إِن كُنتُمْ صَـٰدِقِينَ ﴿١١١﴾

112. Aye! Whoso submits himself to Allah and he is a good-doer, his wage is with his Lord. No fear shall come on them nor shall they grieve.

بَلَىٰ مَنْ أَسْلَمَ وَجْهَهُ لِلَّهِ وَهُوَ مُحْسِنٌ فَلَهُ أَجْرُهُ عِندَ رَبِّهِ وَلَا خَوْفٌ عَلَيْهِمْ وَلَا هُمْ يَحْزَنُونَ ﴿١١٢﴾

Section 14

113. And the Jews say: 'The Nazarenes are not grounded on anything', and the Nazarenes say: 'The Jews are not grounded on anything,' while they recite the same Book. Even so they who do not know say the like of their saying. Allah will judge between them on the Day of Judgement regarding what they have been differing in.

وَقَالَتِ ٱلْيَهُودُ لَيْسَتِ ٱلنَّصَرَىٰ عَلَىٰ شَىْءٍ وَقَالَتِ ٱلنَّصَرَىٰ لَيْسَتِ ٱلْيَهُودُ عَلَىٰ شَىْءٍ وَهُمْ يَتْلُونَ ٱلْكِتَـٰبَ كَذَٰلِكَ قَالَ ٱلَّذِينَ لَا يَعْلَمُونَ مِثْلَ قَوْلِهِمْ فَٱللَّهُ يَحْكُمُ بَيْنَهُمْ يَوْمَ ٱلْقِيَـٰمَةِ فِيمَا كَانُوا فِيهِ يَخْتَلِفُونَ ﴿١١٣﴾

---

74. This, at least, is what the Jews believe. 'Salvation is of the Jews'. (Jn. 4: 22). 'Mankind might all enjoy the divine favour, and yet this favour might still be strictly limited to Jews by the simple condition that mankind must become Jew, must receive circumcision, the physical token of Judaism, and adopt its social and religious customs' (*EBi.* c. 1685).

75. This, according to the Christians. 'Unless a man be born again of water and the Holy Ghost, he cannot enter into the Kingdom of God' (Jn. 3: 5, DV.). 'I am the door: by me if any man enters in, he shall be saved, and shall go in and go out, and find pasture' (Jn. 10: 9). 'Neither is there salvation in any other: for there is no other name under heaven given among men, whereby we must be saved' (Ac. 4: 12, DV).

114. And who is more ungodly than he who prevents that His Name being mentioned in the mosques of Allah and strives after their ruin? Those, it is not for them to enter them except in fear. To them shall come humiliation in this world, and to them in the Hereafter shall come a mighty torment.

وَمَنْ أَظْلَمُ مِمَّن مَّنَعَ مَسَاجِدَ اللَّهِ أَن يُذْكَرَ فِيهَا اسْمُهُ وَسَعَىٰ فِى خَرَابِهَآ أُوْلَٰئِكَ مَا كَانَ لَهُمْ أَن يَدْخُلُوهَآ إِلَّا خَآئِفِينَ لَهُمْ فِى الدُّنْيَا خِزْيٌ وَلَهُمْ فِى الْأَخِرَةِ عَذَابٌ عَظِيمٌ ۝

115. And Allah's is the east[76] and the west; so wherever you turn there is the Face of Allah;[77] surely Allah is the Pervading, the Knowing.

وَلِلَّهِ الْمَشْرِقُ وَالْمَغْرِبُ فَأَيْنَمَا تُوَلُّوا فَثَمَّ وَجْهُ اللَّهِ إِنَّ اللَّهَ وَاسِعٌ عَلِيمٌ ۝

76. The direction to which Christians, in common with sun–worshippers and many other polytheists, attach special sanctity. 'From very early times and in more than one ethnic religion, the direction toward which the worshipper made his prayer was considered of great importance... The Essenes prayed in the direction of the rising sun and the Syrian Christians also turned eastward at prayer. The Zoroastrians attached great importance to the points of the compass in their ritual of purification of prayer and in the building of the fire – temples, the Bareshnum, and the towers of silence... In the Anglican Church the import and importance of the eastward position is still a matter of grave discussion' (*The Moslem World*, January, 1937, p. 13).

77. Literally the face or countenance of Allah signifies His presence. He is not located in any particular direction. He is everywhere and on every side, equally. This completely repudiates the pagan and the Christian practice of orientation. 'Many Greek temples were also designed to face the rising sun. In the earliest Christian basilicas in Rome the apse was placed at the west end, so that the priest who served the altar from behind, facing the congregation, himself faced the east and the rising sun... it is more probable that his orientation was due to an underlying tradition whose roots go far back beyond the origin of Christianity' (*EBr.* XVI. p. 889). 'Orientation in ritual observance is perhaps most pronounced in Asia, which may be more or less indirectly the source from which the European observance is derived' (*ERE.* X. p. 85).

116. And they say: 'God has betaken unto Him a son.'[78] Hallowed be He.[79] His is whatever is in the heavens and in the earth;[80] all are unto Him subservient.

وَقَالُواْ ٱتَّخَذَ ٱللَّهُ وَلَدًا ۗ سُبْحَـٰنَهُ ۖ بَل لَّهُۥ مَا فِى ٱلسَّمَـٰوَٰتِ وَٱلۡأَرۡضِ ۖ كُلٌّ لَّهُۥ قَـٰنِتُونَ ﴿١١٦﴾

117. The Originator of the heavens and the earth, and whenever He decrees an affair, He merely says to it, 'Be', and it becomes.

بَدِيعُ ٱلسَّمَـٰوَٰتِ وَٱلۡأَرۡضِ ۖ وَإِذَا قَضَىٰٓ أَمۡرًا فَإِنَّمَا يَقُولُ لَهُۥ كُن فَيَكُونُ ﴿١١٧﴾

118. And those who do not know say: 'Why does not God speak to us direct or why does not a sign of our choice come to us?' Thus have said those before them, the like of their saying being similar to their hearts. We have already manifested signs to the people who would be convinced.

وَقَالَ ٱلَّذِينَ لَا يَعۡلَمُونَ لَوۡلَا يُكَلِّمُنَا ٱللَّهُ أَوۡ تَأۡتِينَآ ءَايَةٌ ۗ كَذَٰلِكَ قَالَ ٱلَّذِينَ مِن قَبۡلِهِم مِّثۡلَ قَوۡلِهِمۡ ۘ تَشَـٰبَهَتۡ قُلُوبُهُمۡ ۗ قَدۡ بَيَّنَّا ٱلۡأَيَـٰتِ لِقَوۡمٍ يُوقِنُونَ ﴿١١٨﴾

---

78. Who is himself a god. According to the Christians, God 'the Son is the second Person of the Blessed Trinity. He is the only begotten and eternal Son of the Father. He is consubstantial with the Father' (*CD*. p. 912). The first two articles of the Apostle's creed run: 'I believe in God, the Father Almighty, Creator of heaven and earth, and in Jesus Christ, His only Son, our Lord.' The form of the word 'hath taken unto him' suggests that the reference is, in particular, to the 'Adoptionist' Christianity which held that Christ as Man was only the adoptive Son of God' (*CD*. p. 13). The Adoptionists hold 'that Christ was mere man, miraculously conceived indeed, but adopted as the Son of God only by the supreme degree in which he had been filled with the divine wisdom and power' (*UHW*. IV. p. 2331). They asserted that 'Jesus was a man imbued with the Holy Spirit's inspiration from his baptism and so attaining such a perfection of holiness that he was adopted by God and exalted to Divine dignity' (*EBr.* I. p. 177).

79. He is far from all these derogatory limitations! Thus this is an exclamation of protest against the degrading implications of the doctrine of 'Sonship'.

80. That is all His creatures, high and low. He is the Creator of all that exists; its sole Maker and Master. This alone describes the correct relationship between Him and the world. To ascribe to Him the grossly materialistic relationship of fatherhood and sonship, in however etherealized a form, is the height of absurdity.

119. Surely We have sent you with the Truth as a bearer of glad tidings and a warner, and you shall not be questioned about inmates of the Flame.

إِنَّآ أَرْسَلْنَاكَ بِالْحَقِّ بَشِيرًا وَنَذِيرًا وَلَا تُسْئَلُ عَنْ أَصْحَابِ الْجَحِيمِ ۝

120. And the Jews will never be pleased with you nor the Nazarenes unless you follow their faith. Say: 'Surely the guidance of Allah, that is the true guidance.' And were you to follow their desires after what has come to you of the knowledge, there will be for you neither a protector nor a helper against Allah.

وَلَن تَرْضَىٰ عَنكَ الْيَهُودُ وَلَا النَّصَارَىٰ حَتَّىٰ تَتَّبِعَ مِلَّتَهُمْ قُلْ إِنَّ هُدَى اللَّهِ هُوَ الْهُدَىٰ وَلَئِنِ اتَّبَعْتَ أَهْوَآءَهُم بَعْدَ الَّذِى جَآءَكَ مِنَ الْعِلْمِ مَا لَكَ مِنَ اللَّهِ مِن وَلِيٍّ وَلَا نَصِيرٍ ۝

121. Those to whom We have given the Book and who recite it as it ought to be recited they shall believe in it and those who disbelieve in it, those alone shall be the losers.

الَّذِينَ ءَاتَيْنَاهُمُ الْكِتَابَ يَتْلُونَهُۥ حَقَّ تِلَاوَتِهِۦٓ أُوْلَٰئِكَ يُؤْمِنُونَ بِهِۦ وَمَن يَكْفُرْ بِهِۦ فَأُوْلَٰئِكَ هُمُ الْخَاسِرُونَ ۝

Section 15

122. O Children of Israel! Remember My favour with which I favoured you and that I preferred you above the worlds.

يَٰبَنِىٓ إِسْرَٰٓءِيلَ اذْكُرُوا نِعْمَتِىَ الَّتِىٓ أَنْعَمْتُ عَلَيْكُمْ وَأَنِّى فَضَّلْتُكُمْ عَلَى الْعَٰلَمِينَ ۝

123. And fear the Day when not in aught will a soul satisfy for another soul nor will compensation be accepted for it, nor will intercession profit it, nor will they be helped.

وَاتَّقُوا يَوْمًا لَّا تَجْزِى نَفْسٌ عَن نَّفْسٍ شَيْئًا وَلَا يُقْبَلُ مِنْهَا عَدْلٌ وَلَا تَنفَعُهَا شَفَٰعَةٌ وَلَا هُمْ يُنصَرُونَ ۝

124. And recall when his Lord tried Abraham[81] with commands; then he fulfilled them. Allah said: 'Surely I am going to make you a leader of mankind.' Abraham[82] said: 'From my progeny too.' Allah said: 'My promise shall not reach the ungodly.'

وَإِذِ ابْتَلَىٰ إِبْرَٰهِـۧمَ رَبُّهُۥ بِكَلِمَٰتٍ فَأَتَمَّهُنَّ قَالَ إِنِّى جَاعِلُكَ لِلنَّاسِ إِمَامًا قَالَ وَمِن ذُرِّيَّتِى قَالَ لَا يَنَالُ عَهْدِى الظَّٰلِمِينَ ۝

125. And recall when We appointed the House[83] a resort to mankind[84] and a place of security and said:

وَإِذْ جَعَلْنَا الْبَيْتَ مَثَابَةً لِّلنَّاسِ وَأَمْنًا

---

81. Abraham (peace and blessings be upon him) was required to demonstrate to the world his absolute devotion to Him. Abraham of the Bible, the great Prophet and patriarch, first of Chaldea and laterly of Syria, Palestine and Arabia, was the common progenitor of the Arabs and the Israelites. The name is personal, not tribal, and the personality is real and historical — a singularly majestic and attractive character — not an ethnological myth. Referring to the patriarchs, Abraham and other founders of the Hebrew race and nation, says a modern authority: 'The modern critical theory that these fathers of the Hebrews are mythical, representing either personified tribes of Canaanite deities has been disproved by recent archaeological discoveries', (*VJE*. p. 505). His dates of birth and death are, according to the latest computation by Sir Charles Marston, 2160 BC, and 1985 BC respectively. His age, according to the Bible, was 175 years (Ge. 25: 7).

82. As regards his faith Abraham (peace and blessings be upon him) was a model, a pattern, in true religion and piety. As a leader of mankind in this sense, he continues to be till this very day the accepted head of the three great peoples of the world, the Muslims, the Christians and the Jews. 'He is not, in the first instance, the progenitor of the people but the founder and leader of a religious movement. Like Mohammad, some 2,000 years later, he stood at the head of a great movement among the Semitic peoples and tribes' (*EBr*. I. p. 60).

83. The House at Makka, i.e., the Ka'bah. 'A shrine of immemorial antiquity, one which Diodorous Siculus, a hundred years before the Christian era, tells us, was even then most ancient, and most exceedingly revered by the whole Arab race' (Bosworth Smith, *Mohammed and Mohammedanism*, p. 166).

84. Imagine the number of pilgrims that have been visiting the House in a reverential spirit, for all these hundreds and thousand of years since the time of Abraham (peace and blessings be upon him)!

'Take the station of Abraham for a place of prayer.' And We covenanted with Abraham and Ishmael saying: 'Purify both of you My House for those who will circumambulate it and those who will stay and those who will bow and prostrate themselves.'

وَٱتَّخِذُوا۟ مِن مَّقَامِ إِبْرَٰهِۦمَ مُصَلًّى وَعَهِدْنَآ إِلَىٰٓ إِبْرَٰهِۦمَ وَإِسْمَٰعِيلَ أَن طَهِّرَا بَيْتِىَ لِلطَّآئِفِينَ وَٱلْعَٰكِفِينَ وَٱلرُّكَّعِ ٱلسُّجُودِ ۝

126. And recall when Abraham said: 'My Lord! Make this city a place of security[85] and provide its inhabitants with fruits[86] such of them as will believe in Allah and the Last Day.' Allah said: 'And whoso will disbelieve, him also I shall give enjoyment for a while; and then I shall drive him to the torment of the Fire, an ill abode.'

وَإِذْ قَالَ إِبْرَٰهِۦمُ رَبِّ ٱجْعَلْ هَٰذَا بَلَدًا ءَامِنًا وَٱرْزُقْ أَهْلَهُۥ مِنَ ٱلثَّمَرَٰتِ مَنْ ءَامَنَ مِنْهُم بِٱللَّهِ وَٱلْيَوْمِ ٱلْءَاخِرِ قَالَ وَمَن كَفَرَ فَأُمَتِّعُهُۥ قَلِيلًا ثُمَّ أَضْطَرُّهُۥٓ إِلَىٰ عَذَابِ ٱلنَّارِ وَبِئْسَ ٱلْمَصِيرُ ۝

127. And recall when Abraham was raising[87] the foundations of the House, and Ishmael also praying: 'Our Lord! Accept this from us,[88] surely You alone are the Hearer, the Knower!

وَإِذْ يَرْفَعُ إِبْرَٰهِۦمُ ٱلْقَوَاعِدَ مِنَ ٱلْبَيْتِ وَإِسْمَٰعِيلُ رَبَّنَا تَقَبَّلْ مِنَّآ إِنَّكَ أَنتَ ٱلسَّمِيعُ ٱلْعَلِيمُ ۝

---

85. The prayer was granted in full. Hence in the law of Islam it is forbidden, within the sacred precincts, to shed any human blood and to hunt or shoot any game, as also to cut or pull out plants.

86. To fully realize the significance of this part of the prayer it is necessary to remember that the territory of Makka was, and is largely even now, almost a desert that is uncultivated and incapable of bearing fruit or vegetation.

87. Note that Abraham (peace and blessings be upon him) was raising, not laying, the foundation. The House existed long before the time of Adam (peace and blessings be upon him). According to traditions Abraham and Ishmael (peace and blessings be upon them) only rebuilt it on its old foundations.

88. They beseeched that Allah accept this building as a humble token of their submission. Remarkable, here, is the note of true humility ringing in the prayer of the two great Prophets.

128. 'Our Lord! Make us submissive to You, and of our progeny a community submissive to You, and show us our rites, and relent towards us. Surely You alone are the Relenting, the Merciful.

رَبَّنَا وَٱجۡعَلۡنَا مُسۡلِمَيۡنِ لَكَ وَمِن ذُرِّيَّتِنَآ أُمَّةً مُّسۡلِمَةً لَّكَ وَأَرِنَا مَنَاسِكَنَا وَتُبۡ عَلَيۡنَآ إِنَّكَ أَنتَ ٱلتَّوَّابُ ٱلرَّحِيمُ ۝

129. Our Lord! Raise up for them a Messenger from among them,[89] who will recite to them Your revelations and will teach them the Book and wisdom, and will cleanse them.[90] Surely You alone are the Mighty, the Wise!'

رَبَّنَا وَٱبۡعَثۡ فِيهِمۡ رَسُولًا مِّنۡهُمۡ يَتۡلُواْ عَلَيۡهِمۡ ءَايَٰتِكَ وَيُعَلِّمُهُمُ ٱلۡكِتَٰبَ وَٱلۡحِكۡمَةَ وَيُزَكِّيهِمۡ إِنَّكَ أَنتَ ٱلۡعَزِيزُ ٱلۡحَكِيمُ ۝

Section 16

130. And who shall be averse from the faith of Abraham save one who befools himself! And assuredly We chose him in this world, and surely he in the Hereafter he shall be among the righteous.

وَمَن يَرۡغَبُ عَن مِّلَّةِ إِبۡرَٰهِـۧمَ إِلَّا مَن سَفِهَ نَفۡسَهُۥ وَلَقَدِ ٱصۡطَفَيۡنَٰهُ فِي ٱلدُّنۡيَا وَإِنَّهُۥ فِي ٱلۡءَاخِرَةِ لَمِنَ ٱلصَّٰلِحِينَ ۝

131. Recall when his Lord said unto him: 'Submit', he said: 'I submit to the Lord of the worlds.'

إِذۡ قَالَ لَهُۥ رَبُّهُۥٓ أَسۡلِمۡ قَالَ أَسۡلَمۡتُ لِرَبِّ ٱلۡعَٰلَمِينَ ۝

---

89. Note the very clear reference in the OT which is reiterated in the NT to the advent of a Prophet from among their brethren of Israel, i.e., the Ismaelites: 'I will raise up a Prophet from among their brethren, like unto thee' (Dt. 18: 18). Moses truly said unto the fathers: 'A Prophet shall the Lord, your God, raise up unto you of your brethren, like unto me' (Ac. 3: 22).

90. Clears them of sin and unbelief. The mission of this Ismaelite Prophet of God was thus to be fourfold:

i.   He would recite and deliver to his people the revelations exactly as he received them, and would, in this sense, be a trusted Divine Messenger.

ii.   He would not only transmit the Message but would also expound, interpret and illustrate the teaching he was commanded to impart, and would, in this phase of his life, be a Divine teacher.

iii.   Besides explaining to the many the injunctions of Divine Law, he would also unravel to the elect of his people the deeper significance of Divine Wisdom, and initiate them in the profundities of Spirit and the subtleties of soul. He would, on this account, be known as an exponent of Divine Wisdom.

iv.   He would, by his words and deeds, present and practise, raise and uplift the moral tone of his people, purge them of vice and immorality, and make them pious and godly. He would in this capacity be called a Divine Reformer and Law–giver. He would thus be a representative of God with men, but be endowed with a personality of his own — a personality so full of wonderful achievements in this respect, as to wrest even from unfriendly observers, the appellation of 'that most successful of all Prophets and religious personalities' (*EBr.* XV. 11th Ed., p. 898).

132. And Abraham enjoined the same to his sons and so did Jacob also saying: 'O my sons: surely Allah has chosen for you the religion; so die not except as Muslims.'[91]

وَوَصَّىٰ بِهَآ إِبْرَٰهِـمُ بَنِيهِ وَيَعْقُوبُ يَٰبَنِىَّ إِنَّ ٱللَّهَ ٱصْطَفَىٰ لَكُمُ ٱلدِّينَ فَلَا تَمُوتُنَّ إِلَّا وَأَنتُم مُّسْلِمُونَ ﴿١٣٢﴾

133. Were you witnesses when death presented itself to Jacob, and when he said to his sons: 'What will you worship after me?' They said: 'We shall worship your God, the God of your fathers, Abraham and Ishmael and Isaac, the one and only God, and to Him we are submissive.'[92]

أَمْ كُنتُمْ شُهَدَآءَ إِذْ حَضَرَ يَعْقُوبَ ٱلْمَوْتُ إِذْ قَالَ لِبَنِيهِ مَا تَعْبُدُونَ مِنۢ بَعْدِى قَالُوا نَعْبُدُ إِلَٰهَكَ وَإِلَٰهَ ءَابَآئِكَ إِبْرَٰهِـمَ وَإِسْمَٰعِيلَ وَإِسْحَٰقَ إِلَٰهًا وَٰحِدًا وَنَحْنُ لَهُۥ مُسْلِمُونَ ﴿١٣٣﴾

134. They are a community who have passed away; to them shall be what they earned, and to you what you earn; and you shall not be questioned as to what they were wont to work.

تِلْكَ أُمَّةٌ قَدْ خَلَتْ لَهَا مَا كَسَبَتْ وَلَكُم مَّا كَسَبْتُمْ وَلَا تُسْـَٔلُونَ عَمَّا كَانُوا يَعْمَلُونَ ﴿١٣٤﴾

135. And they say: 'Become Jews or Nazarenes, and you shall be guided.' Say: 'Aye! We follow the faith of Abraham, the upright, and he was not of the polytheists.'

وَقَالُوا كُونُوا هُودًا أَوْ نَصَٰرَىٰ تَهْتَدُوا قُلْ بَلْ مِلَّةَ إِبْرَٰهِـمَ حَنِيفًا وَمَا كَانَ مِنَ ٱلْمُشْرِكِينَ ﴿١٣٥﴾

---

91. Or, those who submit. Islam, in its essence, is thus not a new religion at all but a continuation and restoration of the old religion of Abraham, Jacob, and other Prophets of old (peace and blessings be upon them).

92. Submissive in the faith of Islam. The basic, cardinal doctrine of Islam is none other than the Unity of God, proclaimed and preached by all the Prophets of old, only restated, reinstated, and restored, not originated by the Prophet of Islam (peace be on him). Cf. the OT: 'And God spoke unto Moses, and said unto him, I am Lord: and I appeared unto Abraham, unto Isaac, and unto Jacob, by the name of God Almighty' (Ex. 6: 2–3).

136. Say: 'We believe in Allah and what has been sent down to us and what was sent down to Abraham and Ishmael and Isaac and Jacob and the tribes and what was given to Moses and 'Isa, and what was given to the Prophets[93] from their Lord! We make no difference between any of them, and to Him we are submissive.'

قُولُوٓاْ ءَامَنَّا بِٱللَّهِ وَمَآ أُنزِلَ إِلَيْنَا وَمَآ أُنزِلَ إِلَىٰٓ إِبْرَٰهِـۧمَ وَإِسْمَٰعِيلَ وَإِسْحَٰقَ وَيَعْقُوبَ وَٱلْأَسْبَاطِ وَمَآ أُوتِيَ مُوسَىٰ وَعِيسَىٰ وَمَآ أُوتِيَ ٱلنَّبِيُّونَ مِن رَّبِّهِمْ لَا نُفَرِّقُ بَيْنَ أَحَدٍ مِّنْهُمْ وَنَحْنُ لَهُۥ مُسْلِمُونَ ﴿١٣٦﴾

137. So if they believe in the like of what you believe in, surely they are guided; but if they turn away, then they are but in schism. So Allah will suffice you against them; and He is the Hearer, the Knower.

فَإِنْ ءَامَنُواْ بِمِثْلِ مَآ ءَامَنتُم بِهِۦ فَقَدِ ٱهْتَدَواْ وَّإِن تَوَلَّوْاْ فَإِنَّمَا هُمْ فِي شِقَاقٍ فَسَيَكْفِيكَهُمُ ٱللَّهُ وَهُوَ ٱلسَّمِيعُ ٱلْعَلِيمُ ﴿١٣٧﴾

138. Ours is the dye of Allah and who is better at dyeing than Allah? And we are His worshippers.

صِبْغَةَ ٱللَّهِ وَمَنْ أَحْسَنُ مِنَ ٱللَّهِ صِبْغَةً وَنَحْنُ لَهُۥ عَٰبِدُونَ ﴿١٣٨﴾

139. Say: 'Do you contend with us regarding Allah whereas He is our Lord even as He is your Lord? And to us our works, and to you your works, and we are His devotees.'

قُلْ أَتُحَآجُّونَنَا فِي ٱللَّهِ وَهُوَ رَبُّنَا وَرَبُّكُمْ وَلَنَآ أَعْمَٰلُنَا وَلَكُمْ أَعْمَٰلُكُمْ وَنَحْنُ لَهُۥ مُخْلِصُونَ ﴿١٣٩﴾

---

93. Given to them in general. Obser ve once again that Islam is, in no sense, an innovation but a mere continuity of the Faith of Abraham, Ishmael, Isaac, Jacob, Moses, Jesus and all other true Prophets (peace and blessings be upon them).

140. Or, do you say that Abraham and Ishmael and Isaac and Jacob and the tribes were Jews or Nazarenes? Say: 'Are you the more knowing or is Allah?' And who is more unjust than he who conceals Allah's testimony that is with him? And Allah is not unmindful of what you do.[94]

أَمْ تَقُولُونَ إِنَّ إِبْرَاهِيمَ وَإِسْمَعِيلَ وَإِسْحَقَ وَيَعْقُوبَ وَٱلْأَسْبَاطَ كَانُوا۟ هُودًا أَوْ نَصَرَىٰ قُلْ ءَأَنتُمْ أَعْلَمُ أَمِ ٱللَّهُ وَمَنْ أَظْلَمُ مِمَّن كَتَمَ شَهَٰدَةً عِندَهُۥ مِنَ ٱللَّهِ وَمَا ٱللَّهُ بِغَٰفِلٍ عَمَّا تَعْمَلُونَ ﴿١٤٠﴾

141. They are a community who have passed away: to them shall be what they earned, and to you what you earn and you will not be questioned as to what they were wont to work.

تِلْكَ أُمَّةٌ قَدْ خَلَتْ لَهَا مَا كَسَبَتْ وَلَكُم مَّا كَسَبْتُمْ وَلَا تُسْـَٔلُونَ عَمَّا كَانُوا۟ يَعْمَلُونَ ﴿١٤١﴾

Section 17

142. Presently will the fools among the people[95] say: 'What has turned them away from this Qibla on which they had been?'[96] Say: 'Allah's is the east and the west; He guides whom He will to the straight path.'

سَيَقُولُ ٱلسُّفَهَآءُ مِنَ ٱلنَّاسِ مَا وَلَّىٰهُمْ عَن قِبْلَتِهِمُ ٱلَّتِى كَانُوا۟ عَلَيْهَا قُل لِّلَّهِ ٱلْمَشْرِقُ وَٱلْمَغْرِبُ يَهْدِى مَن يَشَآءُ إِلَىٰ صِرَٰطٍ مُّسْتَقِيمٍ ﴿١٤٢﴾

---

94. (O Jews and Christians!). Here it is being expressed that a parrot-like repetition of the names of the patriarchs and other illustrious ancestors, without adopting the faith they had and without following their ways, would do no good. Only individual merit not ancestral would be counted upon.

95. The fools being those without a proper understanding of the religious truths. Special reference here is made to the Jews and Christians who took great offence at the Muslims' change in the direction of prayer, from the Temple at Jerusalem to the Ka'bah in Makka.

96. (So far), i.e., the Temple of Solomon at Jerusalem which was the first Qibla of Islam. Sixteen months after his arrival in Madina, the Prophet received the Divine command, as contained in verse 144, to abandon Jerusalem for the Ka'bah in Makka. This mortified the Jews who had hoped that the Prophet would continue praying towards their Qiblah. This was taken as meaning that now the last link that bound Islam to Judaism was broken.

143. And thus We have made you a community justly-balanced,[97] that you might be witnesses to mankind, and that the Messenger might be a witness[98] to you. And We did not appoint the Qiblah you had, save in order that We might know demonstrably him who follows the Messenger from him who turns back upon his heels. And assuredly the change is grievous, save to them whom Allah has guided. And Allah is not to let your faith go wasted; surely Allah is to mankind the Tender, the Merciful.

وَكَذَٰلِكَ جَعَلْنَٰكُمْ أُمَّةً وَسَطًا لِّتَكُونُوا۟ شُهَدَآءَ عَلَى ٱلنَّاسِ وَيَكُونَ ٱلرَّسُولُ عَلَيْكُمْ شَهِيدًا ۗ وَمَا جَعَلْنَا ٱلْقِبْلَةَ ٱلَّتِى كُنتَ عَلَيْهَآ إِلَّا لِنَعْلَمَ مَن يَتَّبِعُ ٱلرَّسُولَ مِمَّن يَنقَلِبُ عَلَىٰ عَقِبَيْهِ ۚ وَإِن كَانَتْ لَكَبِيرَةً إِلَّا عَلَى ٱلَّذِينَ هَدَى ٱللَّهُ ۗ وَمَا كَانَ ٱللَّهُ لِيُضِيعَ إِيمَٰنَكُمْ ۚ إِنَّ ٱللَّهَ بِٱلنَّاسِ لَرَءُوفٌ رَّحِيمٌ ﴿١٤٣﴾

144. Assuredly We have seen you turning your face to the heaven; so We shall surely cause you to turn towards the Qiblah which will please you. Turn then your face towards the Sacred Mosque; and turn, wherever you be, your faces towards it.[99] And surely those who are given the Book know this to be the Truth and from their Lord. Allah is not unmindful of what they work.

قَدْ نَرَىٰ تَقَلُّبَ وَجْهِكَ فِى ٱلسَّمَآءِ ۖ فَلَنُوَلِّيَنَّكَ قِبْلَةً تَرْضَىٰهَا ۚ فَوَلِّ وَجْهَكَ شَطْرَ ٱلْمَسْجِدِ ٱلْحَرَامِ ۚ وَحَيْثُ مَا كُنتُمْ فَوَلُّوا۟ وُجُوهَكُمْ شَطْرَهُۥ ۗ وَإِنَّ ٱلَّذِينَ أُوتُوا۟ ٱلْكِتَٰبَ لَيَعْلَمُونَ أَنَّهُ ٱلْحَقُّ مِن رَّبِّهِمْ ۗ وَمَا ٱللَّهُ بِغَٰفِلٍ عَمَّا يَعْمَلُونَ ﴿١٤٤﴾

97. A people who have hit the golden mean; who are not inclined to either extreme, well-poised in every virtue. 'A nation conforming, or conformable, to the just mean; just; equitable' (LL.).

98. The Prophet's absolutely pure and perfect life will serve as the norm, the standard, by which the Muslims will be judged.

99. (While praying, in whatsoever direction it might happen to be). 'A bird's-eye view of the Moslem world at the hour of prayer would present the spectacle of a series of concentric circles of worships radiating from the Ka'bah at Makka and covering an ever – widening area from Sierra Leone to Conton and from Tobolsk to Cape Town' (Hitti, *History of the Arabs* pp. 130–131).

145. And should you bring to them who are given the Book every Sign, they would not follow your Qiblah: neither are you to be a follower of their Qiblah,[100] nor does one section of them follow the Qiblah of the other. And should you yield to their desires, after what has come to you of the true knowledge, then surely you will become one of the transgressors.

146. Those to whom We have given the Book recognize him even as they recognize their own children,[101] and surely a party of them hide the truth while they know.

147. The Truth is from your Lord; do not then be of the doubters.

وَلَئِنْ أَتَيْتَ ٱلَّذِينَ أُوتُوا۟ ٱلْكِتَٰبَ بِكُلِّ ءَايَةٍ مَّا تَبِعُوا۟ قِبْلَتَكَ وَمَآ أَنتَ بِتَابِعٍ قِبْلَتَهُمْ وَمَا بَعْضُهُم بِتَابِعٍ قِبْلَةَ بَعْضٍ وَلَئِنِ ٱتَّبَعْتَ أَهْوَآءَهُم مِّنۢ بَعْدِ مَا جَآءَكَ مِنَ ٱلْعِلْمِ إِنَّكَ إِذًا لَّمِنَ ٱلظَّٰلِمِينَ ﴿١٤٥﴾

ٱلَّذِينَ ءَاتَيْنَٰهُمُ ٱلْكِتَٰبَ يَعْرِفُونَهُۥ كَمَا يَعْرِفُونَ أَبْنَآءَهُمْ وَإِنَّ فَرِيقًا مِّنْهُمْ لَيَكْتُمُونَ ٱلْحَقَّ وَهُمْ يَعْلَمُونَ ﴿١٤٦﴾

ٱلْحَقُّ مِن رَّبِّكَ فَلَا تَكُونَنَّ مِنَ ٱلْمُمْتَرِينَ ﴿١٤٧﴾

---

100. In other words, you have a distinctive Qiblah for your own community. The Prophet 'desired that the Muslims should have a Qiblah of their own, which would symbolise their unity and their spiritual independence, from the ritual of non-Muslims. In fact, the subsequent command to Muslims to face in their prayers a central point common to them alone, has powerfully contributed to that distinctive feeling of unity which to this day, in spite of so many differences and sectarian dissensions, binds the Muslims together into one single ummah and makes them realise that they are a group of their own, different from the rest of the world. It is impossible to over-estimate this feeling of unity' (*ASB*. I. p. 60).

101. Namely, the Prophets of their own race. The Jews are here charged with denying the Prophet after their recognizing him, on the strength of clear prophecies in their own Books, as clearly as they recognized the Prophets of Israel. The plural pronoun is used in the collective sense, meaning their race, not individuals. 'There is no room to doubt', says a Christian biographer of the Prophet, 'that a section of the Jews not only hinted, before the Prophet, but even affirmed that he was that Prophet whom the Lord their God should raise up unto them of their brethren' (Muir, *The Life of Muhammad*, p. 98).

Section 18

148. For every one is a goal whitherward he turns; so strive to be foremost in virtues. Wherever you may be, Allah shall bring you all together; surely Allah is Potent over everything.

وَلِكُلٍّ وِجۡهَةٌ هُوَ مُوَلِّيهَا ۖ فَاسۡتَبِقُوا الۡخَيۡرَاتِ ۚ أَيۡنَ مَا تَكُونُوا يَأۡتِ بِكُمُ اللّٰهُ جَمِيعًا ۚ إِنَّ اللّٰهَ عَلَىٰ كُلِّ شَيۡءٍ قَدِيرٌ ۝

149. And from wherever you go forth, turn your face towards the Sacred Mosque; and it is surely the very Truth from your Lord; and Allah is not unmindful of what you work.

وَمِنۡ حَيۡثُ خَرَجۡتَ فَوَلِّ وَجۡهَكَ شَطۡرَ الۡمَسۡجِدِ الۡحَرَامِ ۖ وَإِنَّهُ لَلۡحَقُّ مِنۡ رَّبِّكَ ۗ وَمَا اللّٰهُ بِغَافِلٍ عَمَّا تَعۡمَلُونَ ۝

150. And from wherever you go forth, turn your face towards the Sacred Mosque;[102] and wherever you may be, turn your face towards it, lest there should be with people an argument against you except those of them who transgress; so do not fear them, but fear Me, so that I may perfect My favour upon you and that you may remain truly guided.

وَمِنۡ حَيۡثُ خَرَجۡتَ فَوَلِّ وَجۡهَكَ شَطۡرَ الۡمَسۡجِدِ الۡحَرَامِ ۚ وَحَيۡثُ مَا كُنۡتُمۡ فَوَلُّوا وُجُوهَكُمۡ شَطۡرَهُ ۙ لِئَلَّا يَكُونَ لِلنَّاسِ عَلَيۡكُمۡ حُجَّةٌ إِلَّا الَّذِينَ ظَلَمُوا مِنۡهُمۡ فَلَا تَخۡشَوۡهُمۡ وَاخۡشَوۡنِي وَلِأُتِمَّ نِعۡمَتِي عَلَيۡكُمۡ وَلَعَلَّكُمۡ تَهۡتَدُونَ ۝

151. Thus We have sent forth to you a Messenger from amongst you, who recites to you Our revelations and purifies you and teaches you the Book[103] and wisdom, and teaches you what you were not wont to know.

كَمَا أَرۡسَلۡنَا فِيكُمۡ رَسُولًا مِّنكُمۡ يَتۡلُوا عَلَيۡكُمۡ ءَايَاتِنَا وَيُزَكِّيكُمۡ وَيُعَلِّمُكُمُ الۡكِتَابَ وَالۡحِكۡمَةَ وَيُعَلِّمُكُم مَّا لَمۡ تَكُونُوا تَعۡلَمُونَ ۝

---

102. The command is repeated for the sake of emphasis. The value of having one particular Qiblah for the entire community of the faithful, scattered throughout the world, and composed of men and women of every race and country cannot be overemphasized.

103. The Prophet was not a mere faithful transmitter. He was also a teacher, and an interpreter.

152. Remember Me therefore, and I shall remember you, and to Me pay thanks and do not deny Me.

فَٱذۡكُرُونِىٓ أَذۡكُرۡكُمۡ وَٱشۡكُرُوا۟ لِى وَلَا تَكۡفُرُونِ ۝

Section 19

153. O you who believe; seek help in patience and prayer; surely Allah is with the patient.[104]

يَـٰٓأَيُّهَا ٱلَّذِينَ ءَامَنُوا۟ ٱسۡتَعِينُوا۟ بِٱلصَّبۡرِ وَٱلصَّلَوٰةِ إِنَّ ٱللَّهَ مَعَ ٱلصَّـٰبِرِينَ ۝

154. And do not speak of those slain in the way of Allah as dead. Nay, they are alive, but you do not perceive.

وَلَا تَقُولُوا۟ لِمَن يُقۡتَلُ فِى سَبِيلِ ٱللَّهِ أَمۡوَٰتُۢ بَلۡ أَحۡيَآءٌ وَلَـٰكِن لَّا تَشۡعُرُونَ ۝

155. And We shall surely test you with some of fear and hunger and loss in riches and lives and fruits; and bear glad tidings to the patient ones.

وَلَنَبۡلُوَنَّكُم بِشَىۡءٍ مِّنَ ٱلۡخَوۡفِ وَٱلۡجُوعِ وَنَقۡصٍ مِّنَ ٱلۡأَمۡوَٰلِ وَٱلۡأَنفُسِ وَٱلثَّمَرَٰتِ وَبَشِّرِ ٱلصَّـٰبِرِينَ ۝

156. Who, when an affliction afflicts them, say: 'Surely we are Allah's and surely to Him we shall return.'[105]

ٱلَّذِينَ إِذَآ أَصَـٰبَتۡهُم مُّصِيبَةٌ قَالُوٓا۟ إِنَّا لِلَّهِ وَإِنَّآ إِلَيۡهِ رَٰجِعُونَ ۝

157. They are the ones on whom shall be benediction from their Lord and mercy, and they are the ones who are guided.

أُو۟لَـٰٓئِكَ عَلَيۡهِمۡ صَلَوَٰتٌ مِّن رَّبِّهِمۡ وَرَحۡمَةٌ وَأُو۟لَـٰٓئِكَ هُمُ ٱلۡمُهۡتَدُونَ ۝

---

104. This consciousness of the accompaniment of God, this awareness that He is with us, is the greatest comfort that the human mind can have in this world, and the greatest antidote to our sense of loneliness.

105. When and where we shall surely be more than repaid for any amount of loss incurred here and now. Every affliction that befalls a Muslim is cheerfully borne by him in the perfect assurance that either it is to wash him of his sins or to bless him in the Hereafter.

158. Surely Ṣafā and Marwah[106] are of the landmarks of Allah so whosoever makes a pilgrimage to the House, or performs the 'Umra in him is to be no fault if he walks in between the two. And whosoever does good voluntarily, then surely Allah is the Appreciative, the Knowing.

إِنَّ ٱلصَّفَا وَٱلْمَرْوَةَ مِن شَعَآئِرِ ٱللَّهِ فَمَنْ حَجَّ ٱلْبَيْتَ أَوِ ٱعْتَمَرَ فَلَا جُنَاحَ عَلَيْهِ أَن يَطَّوَّفَ بِهِمَا وَمَن تَطَوَّعَ خَيْرًا فَإِنَّ ٱللَّهَ شَاكِرٌ عَلِيمٌ ١٥٨

159. Surely those who conceal what We have sent down of evidence and the guidance after We have expounded it to mankind in the Book, they are the very ones cursed by Allah and cursed by the cursers:[107]

إِنَّ ٱلَّذِينَ يَكْتُمُونَ مَآ أَنزَلْنَا مِنَ ٱلْبَيِّنَتِ وَٱلْهُدَىٰ مِنۢ بَعْدِ مَا بَيَّنَّهُ لِلنَّاسِ فِى ٱلْكِتَبِ أُوْلَٰئِكَ يَلْعَنُهُمُ ٱللَّهُ وَيَلْعَنُهُمُ ٱللَّعِنُونَ ١٥٩

160. Save those who repent and make amends and make known the Truth. Those are the very ones towards whom I relent: and I am the Relenting, the Merciful.[108]

إِلَّا ٱلَّذِينَ تَابُواْ وَأَصْلَحُواْ وَبَيَّنُواْ فَأُوْلَٰئِكَ أَتُوبُ عَلَيْهِمْ وَأَنَا ٱلتَّوَّابُ ٱلرَّحِيمُ ١٦٠

106. Ṣafā and Marwah are two eminences surmounted by arches, in the heart of Makka in the vicinity of the Sacred Mosque, indeed on either side. The distance, 493 paces long, has to be traversed seven times, partly with hasty steps, in the blessed memory of Hagar who ran to and fro in search of water when left alone with her baby, Ishmael, in the waterless desert of Makka.

107. Though among angels, men and genii, i.e., all such as abhor and detest evil. The Christian concept of 'curse' is singularly amusing, if not actually blasphemous. The non-observance of the law, St. Paul teaches, puts men under a curse: from this curse Christ redeems them by becoming Himself a curse on their behalf. The proof that Christ did become a curse is given in the form of a reference to the Crucifixion it is written: 'Cursed is everyone that hangeth on a tree ... In His death on the cross He was identified under God's dispensation with the doom of sin: He became a curse for us: and it is on this our redemption depends' (*DB*. I. p. 535).

108. The God of Islam, unlike the God of so many religions, is neither jealous nor vindictive. This requires frequent reiteration not only in view of the doctrines of the pagans but also of the teachings of the Bible. 'Beware of him, and obey his voice, provoke him not; for he will not pardon your transgressions' (Ex. 23: 21). 'He is a holy God: he is a jealous God; he will not forgive your transgressions nor your sins' (Jo. 24: 19).

161. Surely those who disbelieve and die while they are disbelievers, then it is they on whom shall be the curse of Allah and angels and mankind all!

إِنَّ ٱلَّذِينَ كَفَرُوا۟ وَمَاتُوا۟ وَهُمْ كُفَّارٌ أُو۟لَٰٓئِكَ عَلَيْهِمْ لَعْنَةُ ٱللَّهِ وَٱلْمَلَٰٓئِكَةِ وَٱلنَّاسِ أَجْمَعِينَ ﴿١٦١﴾

162. They shall be abiders therein; the torment on them shall not be lightened, nor shall they be respited.

خَٰلِدِينَ فِيهَا لَا يُخَفَّفُ عَنْهُمُ ٱلْعَذَابُ وَلَا هُمْ يُنظَرُونَ ﴿١٦٢﴾

163. And your God is the One God;[109] there is no god but He, the Compassionate, the Merciful.

وَإِلَٰهُكُمْ إِلَٰهٌ وَٰحِدٌ لَّا إِلَٰهَ إِلَّا هُوَ ٱلرَّحْمَٰنُ ٱلرَّحِيمُ ﴿١٦٣﴾

Section 20

164. Surely in the creation of the heavens and the earth and the alternation of night and day, and the ships that sail upon the ocean laden with what profits mankind; and in what Allah sends down of water from the heavens and revives the earth thereby after its death, and scatters in it of all sorts of moving creatures, and in the veering of winds and clouds subjected for service between the Heavens and earth;

إِنَّ فِى خَلْقِ ٱلسَّمَٰوَٰتِ وَٱلْأَرْضِ وَٱخْتِلَٰفِ ٱلَّيْلِ وَٱلنَّهَارِ وَٱلْفُلْكِ ٱلَّتِى تَجْرِى فِى ٱلْبَحْرِ بِمَا يَنفَعُ ٱلنَّاسَ وَمَا أَنزَلَ ٱللَّهُ مِنَ ٱلسَّمَآءِ مِن مَّآءٍ فَأَحْيَا بِهِ ٱلْأَرْضَ بَعْدَ مَوْتِهَا وَبَثَّ فِيهَا مِن كُلِّ دَآبَّةٍ وَتَصْرِيفِ ٱلرِّيَٰحِ وَٱلسَّحَابِ ٱلْمُسَخَّرِ بَيْنَ ٱلسَّمَآءِ وَٱلْأَرْضِ

---

109. (O mankind! and not many or several). This unequivocally repudiates and condemns the Trinity of Christian godhead, the dualism of the Zoroastrian Divinity, and the multiplicity of gods of polytheistic peoples.

in these are signs[110] to a people who understand.

165. And of mankind are some who set up compeers to Allah; they love them as with the love due to Allah. And those who believe are the strongest in love of Allah.[111] Would that those who are ungodly saw now what they shall see when they see the torment, that surely power belonged wholly to Allah, and that Allah was Severe in requital.

166. Remember when those who were followed shall disown those who followed them,[112] and they all shall behold the torment and cut asunder shall be their cords.

لَّأَيَـٰتٍ لِّقَوْمٍ يَعْقِلُونَ ﴿١٦٤﴾

وَمِنَ ٱلنَّاسِ مَن يَتَّخِذُ مِن دُونِ ٱللَّهِ أَندَادًا يُحِبُّونَهُمْ كَحُبِّ ٱللَّهِ ۖ وَٱلَّذِينَ ءَامَنُوٓا۟ أَشَدُّ حُبًّا لِّلَّهِ ۗ وَلَوْ يَرَى ٱلَّذِينَ ظَلَمُوٓا۟ إِذْ يَرَوْنَ ٱلْعَذَابَ أَنَّ ٱلْقُوَّةَ لِلَّهِ جَمِيعًا وَأَنَّ ٱللَّهَ شَدِيدُ ٱلْعَذَابِ ﴿١٦٥﴾

إِذْ تَبَرَّأَ ٱلَّذِينَ ٱتُّبِعُوا۟ مِنَ ٱلَّذِينَ ٱتَّبَعُوا۟ وَرَأَوُا۟ ٱلْعَذَابَ وَتَقَطَّعَتْ بِهِمُ ٱلْأَسْبَابُ ﴿١٦٦﴾

---

110. Signs of His Unity, Might and Wisdom. It is precisely such phenomena of nature from which have emerged a major part of the gods of polytheism. These grand and beautiful objects of nature striking awe and wonder and exciting admiration in the human mind are in fact but evidence of the unique handiwork of their Creator; and it is absolutely foolish to adore and worship 'a heaven-god', an earth-god, a sun-god, a moon-god, a rain-god, a wind- god, and the like. All such various deities of the polytheistic nations are described at length by the writers on sociology and anthropology. See for example, *PC*. II. pp. 247–304; *FWN*. I and II. The Holy Qur'an leads from the study of nature to the contemplation of the Author of nature.

111. Love of God, then, and not His fear alone, as generally misrepresented by the Christian missionaries, is the spur of Islam. In the ideology of Islam, love of God combines equally with His fear the incentive to do good. And a devout Muslim is one whose love for Allah is supreme, unsurpassed by his love for anything else. It is his love for God that gives a definite and permanent direction to his will and forms the standing motive of his moral and religious life.

112. On the Judgement Day, the leaders of irreligion will forsake and wash their hands of their disciples, as if they were not accomplices in the latter's career of sin and disobedience.

167. And those who had followed shall say: 'Would that for us were a return, then we would disown them as they have disowned us.' Thus will Allah show them their works as anguish; and they shall not be coming forth from the Fire.

وَقَالَ ٱلَّذِينَ ٱتَّبَعُوٓاْ لَوۡ أَنَّ لَنَا كَرَّةً فَنَتَبَرَّأَ مِنۡهُمۡ كَمَا تَبَرَّءُواْ مِنَّاۗ كَذَٰلِكَ يُرِيهِمُ ٱللَّهُ أَعۡمَٰلَهُمۡ حَسَرَٰتٍ عَلَيۡهِمۡۖ وَمَاهُم بِخَٰرِجِينَ مِنَ ٱلنَّارِ ۝

Section 21

168. O mankind! Eat of whatever is on the earth lawful and good, and do not walk in the footsteps of Satan; surely he is to you an enemy manifest.

يَٰٓأَيُّهَا ٱلنَّاسُ كُلُواْ مِمَّا فِي ٱلۡأَرۡضِ حَلَٰلًا طَيِّبًا وَلَا تَتَّبِعُواْ خُطُوَٰتِ ٱلشَّيۡطَٰنِۚ إِنَّهُ لَكُمۡ عَدُوٌّ مُّبِينٌ ۝

169. He only commands you to evil and indecency and that you should say against Allah what you do not know.

إِنَّمَا يَأۡمُرُكُم بِٱلسُّوٓءِ وَٱلۡفَحۡشَآءِ وَأَن تَقُولُواْ عَلَى ٱللَّهِ مَا لَا تَعۡلَمُونَ ۝

170. And when it is said to them: 'Follow what Allah has sent down,' they say: 'Nay, we shall follow that way whereon we found our fathers' [113] – even though their fathers did not understand anything nor were they guided.

وَإِذَا قِيلَ لَهُمُ ٱتَّبِعُواْ مَآ أَنزَلَ ٱللَّهُ قَالُواْ بَلۡ نَتَّبِعُ مَآ أَلۡفَيۡنَا عَلَيۡهِ ءَابَآءَنَاۗ أَوَلَوۡ كَانَ ءَابَآؤُهُمۡ لَا يَعۡقِلُونَ شَيۡـًٔا وَلَا يَهۡتَدُونَ ۝

171. And the likeness of those who disbelieve is as the likeness of him who shouts to that which hears nothing, except the sound of a call and a cry; deaf, dumb, blind; so they do not understand.

وَمَثَلُ ٱلَّذِينَ كَفَرُواْ كَمَثَلِ ٱلَّذِي يَنۡعِقُ بِمَا لَا يَسۡمَعُ إِلَّا دُعَآءً وَنِدَآءًۚ صُمُّۢ بُكۡمٌ عُمۡيٌ فَهُمۡ لَا يَعۡقِلُونَ ۝

---

113. Pagan religions have neither reason nor reasoned beliefs to set by. Their stock-in-trade is ancestral wisdom, old and antiquated traditions and customs transmitted from one generation to another.

172. O you who believe! Eat of the good things with which We have provided you and return thanks to Allah, if Him indeed you are wont to worship.

يَٰٓأَيُّهَا ٱلَّذِينَ ءَامَنُواْ كُلُواْ مِن طَيِّبَٰتِ مَا رَزَقْنَٰكُمْ وَٱشْكُرُواْ لِلَّهِ إِن كُنتُمْ إِيَّاهُ تَعْبُدُونَ ١٧٢

173. He has only forbidden to you the dead animals, and blood, and flesh of swine,[114] and that over which is invoked the name of any other than Allah. But whoso is driven to necessity, neither desiring nor transgressing, on him is no sin; surely Allah is the Forgiving, the Merciful.

إِنَّمَا حَرَّمَ عَلَيْكُمُ ٱلْمَيْتَةَ وَٱلدَّمَ وَلَحْمَ ٱلْخِنزِيرِ وَمَآ أُهِلَّ بِهِۦ لِغَيْرِ ٱللَّهِ فَمَنِ ٱضْطُرَّ غَيْرَ بَاغٍ وَلَا عَادٍ فَلَآ إِثْمَ عَلَيْهِ إِنَّ ٱللَّهَ غَفُورٌ رَّحِيمٌ ١٧٣

---

114. The foul habit and coarse feeding of swine, let alone its liability to leprosy and glandular disease, are sufficient to make its flesh repulsive. Whatever the practice of modern 'Christian' nations in regard to pork, bacon and ham, the Bible's abhorrence of swine is clear. 'And the swine... he is unclean to you' (Le. 11: 7). 'And the swine... it is unclean to you; ye shall not eat of their flesh, nor touch their dead carcass' (Dt. 14: 8). Cf. also Is. 65: 4; Mt. 7: 6; and 2 Pe. 2: 22. 'The eating of swine's flesh is forbidden in Israel... The flesh and blood of swine are described as characteristically heathen and repulsive offerings... The ancient Egyptians and Phoenicians as well as Jews regarded swine as unclean' (*DB.* IV. p. 633). In the English language, hog and its synonyms always imply something that is mean, loathsome or contemptible. Swine, in English, is a low, greedy or vicious person (*NSD*). 'Applied opprobriously to a sexual, degraded, or coarse person; also (in modern use) as a mere term of contempt or abuse' (*SOED.*). And 'swinish', is 'gross specially, in eating or drinking; beastly' (*NSD.*). Sensual, gluttonous; coarse, beastly; (*SOED.*). Pig, again, 'is a person who is like a pig, especially one who is filthy, gluttonous, or grasping' (*NSD.*). Applied opprobriously to a person (*SOED.*). And piggish is greedy; unclean (*NSD.*), 'selfish, mean; unclean, vile' (*SOED.*). Hog, once again, is 'a filthy, gluttonous; or grasping person; also, one selfishly indifferent to the rights of others;' and hoggish means 'like a hog; gluttonous; selfish; filthy; mean' (*NSD.*). Is all this just mere coincidence?

174. Surely those who conceal what Allah has sent down in the Book, and purchase therewith a small gain, these are they who swallow in their bellies nothing but fire. Allah shall not speak to them on the Day of Resurrection, nor purify them, and to them shall be an afflictive torment.

إِنَّ ٱلَّذِينَ يَكۡتُمُونَ مَآ أَنزَلَ ٱللَّهُ مِنَ ٱلۡكِتَٰبِ وَيَشۡتَرُونَ بِهِۦ ثَمَنًا قَلِيلًا أُوْلَٰٓئِكَ مَا يَأۡكُلُونَ فِى بُطُونِهِمۡ إِلَّا ٱلنَّارَ وَلَا يُكَلِّمُهُمُ ٱللَّهُ يَوۡمَ ٱلۡقِيَٰمَةِ وَلَا يُزَكِّيهِمۡ وَلَهُمۡ عَذَابٌ أَلِيمٌ ﴿١٧٤﴾

175. Those are they who have purchased error for guidance and torment for forgiveness. How daring must they be in facing the Fire.

أُوْلَٰٓئِكَ ٱلَّذِينَ ٱشۡتَرَوُاْ ٱلضَّلَٰلَةَ بِٱلۡهُدَىٰ وَٱلۡعَذَابَ بِٱلۡمَغۡفِرَةِ فَمَآ أَصۡبَرَهُمۡ عَلَى ٱلنَّارِ ﴿١٧٥﴾

176. This shall be because Allah has surely sent down the Book with Truth; and surely those who differ respecting the Book are in a wide schism.[115]

ذَٰلِكَ بِأَنَّ ٱللَّهَ نَزَّلَ ٱلۡكِتَٰبَ بِٱلۡحَقِّ وَإِنَّ ٱلَّذِينَ ٱخۡتَلَفُواْ فِى ٱلۡكِتَٰبِ لَفِى شِقَاقٍ بَعِيدٍ ﴿١٧٦﴾

Section 22

177. Virtue is not in this that you turn your faces to the east and the

لَّيۡسَ ٱلۡبِرَّ أَن تُوَلُّواْ وُجُوهَكُمۡ قِبَلَ ٱلۡمَشۡرِقِ

---

115. In other words, at great variance with Truth, and constantly disputing among themselves. The divisions and subdivisions of the Christians are only too well known. Draper, while speaking of the interminable wranglings and bickerings of the Christian sects, refers to 'the incomprehensible jargon of Arians, Nestorians, Entychains, Monothelites, Monophysites, Mariolatrists, and an anarchy of countless disputants' (Draper, *History of the Intellectual Development of Europe*, I, p. 333).

west,[116] but virtue is of him who believes in Allah and the Last Day and the angels and the Book and the Prophet,[117] and gives of his substance, for love of Him,[118] to kindred and orphans and the needy and the wayfarer and the beggars and for redeeming necks;[119] and establishes prayer and gives the poor-rate[120] and is of the

وَٱلۡمَغۡرِبِ وَلَٰكِنَّ ٱلۡبِرَّ مَنۡ ءَامَنَ بِٱللَّهِ وَٱلۡيَوۡمِ ٱلۡأَخِرِ وَٱلۡمَلَٰٓئِكَةِ وَٱلۡكِتَٰبِ وَٱلنَّبِيِّـۧنَ وَءَاتَى ٱلۡمَالَ عَلَىٰ حُبِّهِۦ ذَوِى ٱلۡقُرۡبَىٰ وَٱلۡيَتَٰمَىٰ وَٱلۡمَسَٰكِينَ وَٱبۡنَ ٱلسَّبِيلِ وَٱلسَّآئِلِينَ وَفِى ٱلرِّقَابِ وَأَقَامَ ٱلصَّلَوٰةَ وَءَاتَى ٱلزَّكَوٰةَ

116. Both directions have been held sacred by many pagan nations. In Greek religion, deities were classified as Olympian and Chthonian. The East was the abode of the Olympian gods and the direction to which their temples looked and their worshippers turned when sacrificing to them, 'while the west was the direction which the worshippers of the Chthonian gods faced' (*DB*. V. p. 134). According to the Hindus, the direction of the south -east was sacred to Manu and the performances of *shuddha* faced it during the ceremony (*ERE*. XII. p. 618). It was the belief of the early Church that evil entered from the north. In most early Saxon churches, and in many churches of the Norman period, all over the country, there was a north door. There are few early churches in Shropshire and the border counties that are without their north door; which, in most instances, have been blocked up. The north door is believed to have been used as the entrance to the church on the occasion of baptism, when the child was supposed to have passed from the evil influence of the world and the devil into the care of the Church. The verse strikes at the root of 'direction–worship', and says in effect that there is no merit at all in turning towards any particular direction. Islamic worship, it must be manifest to the reader, is not directed towards any direction as such east, west, north, or south, but towards a particular House, on whatever side of the worshipper it may happen to be.

117. This sums up Islamic belief: belief in God, in His Prophets, in His Books, in the Day of Judgement, and in the Angels.

118. Note the principal motive force, in the Islamic code, to all acts of merit. Not to win the applause of human beings, nor to achieve good name, but to be impelled by the love of one's Creator, Master and Sustainer, and to be moved to win His good–will, a Muslim is truly religious in all his acts of charity and benevolence.

119. Redeeming necks is the freeing of slaves and captives, and is in Islam a primary social duty.

120. Given at regular intervals. A simple and natural, and yet perfectly effective way of solving many an economic problem. This sums up the main aspects of Islamic devotion.

performers of their promises when they have promised; and is of the patient in adversity and affliction and in time of violence; these are they who have proved true,[121] and these are they who are God-fearing.[122]

178. O you who believe! Ordained for you is retaliation in the matter of the slain; the free for the free, and a slave for a slave[123] and a woman for a woman;[124] yet whoso is pardoned anything by his brother,[125] let the service be honourable and payment with kindness. This is an alleviation from your Lord and a mercy; so whoso will transgress hereafter, for him shall be an afflictive torment.

وَٱلْمُوفُونَ بِعَهْدِهِمْ إِذَا عَهَدُواْ وَٱلصَّٰبِرِينَ فِى ٱلْبَأْسَاءِ وَٱلضَّرَّاءِ وَحِينَ ٱلْبَأْسِ أُوْلَٰئِكَ ٱلَّذِينَ صَدَقُواْ وَأُوْلَٰئِكَ هُمُ ٱلْمُتَّقُونَ ۝

يَٰٓأَيُّهَا ٱلَّذِينَ ءَامَنُواْ كُتِبَ عَلَيْكُمُ ٱلْقِصَاصُ فِى ٱلْقَتْلَى ٱلْحُرُّ بِٱلْحُرِّ وَٱلْعَبْدُ بِٱلْعَبْدِ وَٱلْأُنثَىٰ بِٱلْأُنثَىٰ فَمَنْ عُفِىَ لَهُۥ مِنْ أَخِيهِ شَىْءٌ فَٱتِّبَاعٌ بِٱلْمَعْرُوفِ وَأَدَآءٌ إِلَيْهِ بِإِحْسَٰنٍ ذَٰلِكَ تَخْفِيفٌ مِّن رَّبِّكُمْ وَرَحْمَةٌ فَمَنِ ٱعْتَدَىٰ بَعْدَ ذَٰلِكَ فَلَهُۥ عَذَابٌ أَلِيمٌ ۝

---

121. True in their faith: in righteousness. Here is a beautiful resume of the main requirements of the Faith, with the threefold division of: (i) Islamic belief (ii) Islamic devotions, and (iii) The Islamic code of social and moral duties.

122. 'This is one of the noblest verses in the Qur'ān. Faith in God and benevolence towards man is clearly set forth as the essence of religion. It contains a compendium of doctrine to be believed as well as of precepts to be practised in life' (Wherry, *Commentary on the Koran*).

123. 'According to Hanafis the life of a slave stands on an equal footing with that of a free-man, of a woman with that of a man, of a non–Muslim subject with that of a Muslim' (Abdur Raheem, p. 359).

124. The essence of the verse, as is evident, is the insistence on justice, impartial and unalloyed, and a negation of all iniquities. No favour or partiality is to be shown to the murderer if he happens to be a person of wealth and influence, as was customary both with the Jews and the pagan Arabs.

125. Brother being the other party. The law of Islam, unlike the modern law of Europe based on the legal statutes of the pagan Romans, takes into account the civil liability of the murderer even more than his criminal responsibility, and treats murder as an act of injury to the family of the slain rather than an offence against the state. Hence the recognition, in Islamic law, of the rights of relations, and the legality of blood–wit or fine paid to the heirs and kindred of the slain.

179. And for you is life in the Law of retaliation, O men of insight! that haply you will be God-fearing.

وَلَكُمْ فِي الْقِصَاصِ حَيَوٰةٌ يَا أُولِي الْأَلْبَبِ لَعَلَّكُمْ تَتَّقُونَ ۝

180. Ordained for you, when death approaches one of you, if he leaves behind any property, is the making of a bequest for his parents and kindred equitably-a duty on the God-fearing.

كُتِبَ عَلَيْكُمْ إِذَا حَضَرَ أَحَدَكُمُ الْمَوْتُ إِن تَرَكَ خَيْرًا الْوَصِيَّةُ لِلْوَلِدَيْنِ وَ الْأَقْرَبِينَ بِالْمَعْرُوفِ حَقًّا عَلَى الْمُتَّقِينَ ۝

181. Then whoso alters it after he has heard it, the sin thereof shall be only on them who will alter it; surely Allah is the Hearer, the Knower.

فَمَنْ بَدَّلَهُ بَعْدَمَا سَمِعَهُ فَإِنَّمَا إِثْمُهُ عَلَى الَّذِينَ يُبَدِّلُونَهُ إِنَّ اللَّهَ سَمِيعٌ عَلِيمٌ ۝

182. But whoso apprehends from the testator a mistake or a sin and thereupon he makes up the matter between them, on him there shall be no sin; surely Allah is the Forgiver, the Merciful.

فَمَنْ خَافَ مِن مُّوصٍ جَنَفًا أَوْ إِثْمًا فَأَصْلَحَ بَيْنَهُمْ فَلَا إِثْمَ عَلَيْهِ إِنَّ اللَّهَ غَفُورٌ رَّحِيمٌ ۝

Section 23

183. O you who believe! Ordained for you is fasting, even as it was ordained for those before you, that haply you will be God-fearing.[126]

يَا أَيُّهَا الَّذِينَ ءَامَنُوا كُتِبَ عَلَيْكُمُ الصِّيَامُ كَمَا كُتِبَ عَلَى الَّذِينَ مِن قَبْلِكُمْ لَعَلَّكُمْ تَتَّقُونَ ۝

126. The notion being that they attain piety by this regular exercise of self–discipline. It is here that the distinctive characteristic of the Islamic fast comes to the fore. Both the Jews and the Christians took to fasting as a mere mode of expiation or penitence, or for purposes even narrower and strictly formal. 'In olden times fasting was instituted as a sign of mourning, or when danger threatened, or when the seer was preparing himself for a divine revelation', (*JE*. V. p. 347). Islam, however, broadened this outlook considerably, and raised the motive and the purpose of fasting. In Islam it is a voluntary and cheerful renunciation, for a definite period, of all the appetites of flesh lawful in themselves (the unlawful ones being ruled out of course), a salutary exercise of both the body and the spirit. 'Disciplinary fasting', such as the Islamic fasting may be termed, 'is regarded as a reasonable and useful practice, even by those who consider all other forms of fasting to be misconceived and vain. Normally, it is a reasonable part of the soul's preparation for the maintenance of self-control in times of strong temptation' (*EBr*. IX. p. 108).

184. Days numbered.[127] Then whoso among you is ill or journeying, for him is the like number of other days. And those who can keep it with hardship the redemption is the feeding of a poor person; and whoso does good voluntarily it will be better for him,[128] and that you fast will be better for you if you but know.

أَيَّامًا مَّعۡدُودَٰتٍ فَمَن كَانَ مِنكُم مَّرِيضًا أَوۡ عَلَىٰ سَفَرٍ فَعِدَّةٌ مِّنۡ أَيَّامٍ أُخَرَ وَعَلَى ٱلَّذِينَ يُطِيقُونَهُۥ فِدۡيَةٌ طَعَامُ مِسۡكِينٍ فَمَن تَطَوَّعَ خَيۡرًا فَهُوَ خَيۡرٌ لَّهُۥ وَأَن تَصُومُواْ خَيۡرٌ لَّكُمۡ إِن كُنتُمۡ تَعۡلَمُونَ ﴿١٨٤﴾

185. The month of Ramaḍān: in it was sent down the Qur'ān, a guidance to mankind and with evidence; one of the Books of guidance and distinction. So whoso of you witnesses the month, he shall

شَهۡرُ رَمَضَانَ ٱلَّذِىٓ أُنزِلَ فِيهِ ٱلۡقُرۡءَانُ هُدٗى لِّلنَّاسِ وَبَيِّنَٰتٍ مِّنَ ٱلۡهُدَىٰ وَٱلۡفُرۡقَانِ فَمَن شَهِدَ مِنكُمُ ٱلشَّهۡرَ فَلۡيَصُمۡهُ

---

127. The days of fast being 30 or 29. This month supplies the greatest continued test of self-discipline known to the world. So meritorious is this fast in the eyes of the Lord that, according to the sayings of the Prophet, 'the very smell of the mouth of the keeper of a fast is more agreeable to Allah than the smell of musk'. And so sacred is the month that 'with its coming the gates of Paradise are opened and the gates of Hell are closed and devils are chained'.

128. To be munificent and generous is always commendable; it is immeasurably more so in this month of purification, piety and self-denial. Hence it is that the Holy Prophet – the most bountiful of men – was more bountiful than ever in the month of Ramaḍān. The duty to give alms throughout the year becomes that much more during Ramaḍān; and the Holy Prophet declared that until a man has distributed the legal and customary gifts, at the end of the month, before celebrating the Festival of 'Id, his fasts will be kept suspended between heaven and earth.

fast it;[129] and whoso is ill or journeying for him is the like number of other days. Allah desires for you ease and does not desire for you hardship; so you shall complete the number and shall magnify Allah for His having guided you, and haply you may give thanks.

وَمَن كَانَ مَرِيضًا أَوْ عَلَىٰ سَفَرٍ فَعِدَّةٌ مِّنْ أَيَّامٍ أُخَرَ يُرِيدُ ٱللَّهُ بِكُمُ ٱلْيُسْرَ وَلَا يُرِيدُ بِكُمُ ٱلْعُسْرَ وَلِتُكْمِلُوا ٱلْعِدَّةَ وَلِتُكَبِّرُوا ٱللَّهَ عَلَىٰ مَا هَدَىٰكُمْ وَلَعَلَّكُمْ تَشْكُرُونَ ۝

186. And when My bondsmen ask you regarding Me, then surely I am nigh. I answer the call of the caller, when he calls Me; so let them answer Me and believe in Me, haply they may be directed.

وَإِذَا سَأَلَكَ عِبَادِى عَنِّى فَإِنِّى قَرِيبٌ أُجِيبُ دَعْوَةَ ٱلدَّاعِ إِذَا دَعَانِ فَلْيَسْتَجِيبُوا لِى وَلْيُؤْمِنُوا بِى لَعَلَّهُمْ يَرْشُدُونَ ۝

187. Allowed to you, on the night of the fast, is consorting with your women;[130] they are a garment for

أُحِلَّ لَكُمْ لَيْلَةَ ٱلصِّيَامِ ٱلرَّفَثُ إِلَىٰ نِسَآئِكُمْ هُنَّ لِبَاسٌ لَّكُمْ

---

129. Fasting for the whole of the month. The entire month is to be spent in fasting for the whole day, and yet this religion has been accused of attracting men by only pandering to their self-indulgence! Truly has Arnold observed, quoting Carlyle, that the Prophet's 'religion is not an easy one: with rigorous fasts, strict, complex formulas, prayers five times a day, and abstinence from wine, it did not succeed by being an easy religion' (Arnold, *Preaching of Islam*, p. 418).

130. This refers to sexuality and lewd conduct in general 'comprehending everything that a man desires of his wife' (LL.). This permissive commandment is of a later date. Sexual passion, in Islam, is not, as it is in Christianity, the most dreadful of all sins, in fact the original sin which caused the Fall of Man. And normal sexuality can very well co-exist with the sanctity of Ramadan.

you[131] and you are a garment for them.[132] Allah knows that you have been defrauding your-selves,[133] so He has relented towards you and pardoned you.

وَأَنتُمْ لِبَاسٌ لَّهُنَّ عَلِمَ اللَّهُ أَنَّكُمْ كُنتُمْ تَخْتَانُونَ أَنفُسَكُمْ فَتَابَ عَلَيْكُمْ وَعَفَا عَنكُمْ

---

131. So close and intimate, in Islam, are the mutual relations of man and wife. Husband and wife are so called 'because each embraces the other, or because each goes to the other for rest, and consorts with the other' (LL.). The phrase may be paraphrased as saying that men and women use each other as constant and inseparable companions. It emphasizes the fact of their interdependence in life, the one being incomplete without the other. Compare the dictum of a distinguished lady biologist, Dr. Elisabeth Chesser of London: 'A vast amount of energy is wasted in futile argument as to the relative superiority of man and woman... Each sex contains undeveloped organs and functions which are more fully developed in the other... The lesson of biology is that, where sex exists, the two sexes are mutually dependent' (Chesser, *Love, Marriage, Jealousy*, p. 180). Compare with this the attitude of Christianity which holds the woman as an impure creature, perhaps the dirtiest, and regards her as a synonym for the temptress. 'The fathers of Church and the preachers did not cease to utter their thunders against woman, disparaging her, and abusing her as the impure creature, almost devilish' (Letourneau, *Evolution of Marriage*, p. 205). 'In the first few centuries of the Christian era the Western world was inundated with some very remarkable notions about women which came to them from the hills of Tibet... Women were told, with all the weight of a sacred authority, that they should be ashamed of the thought that they were women, and should live in continual penance on account of the curses their sex had brought into the world. The very phrases of Manu used against women were the door of hell, the personification of sin. Some even went so far as to maintain that their bodies were of diabolic origin, but this was decided to be a heresy' (*UHW*. I. p. 379).

132. The metaphor is of exquisite beauty, expressive of close intimacy, identity of interest, mutual comfort and confidence, the mutual upholding of each other's reputation and credit, the mutual respect of one another's secrets, mutual affection, and mutual consolation in misfortune. The whole character of the one becomes an open book to the other. The wedded pair ceases to belong to themselves; they now belong to each other, sharing each other's joys, sorrows, glories and shames. And yet Islam has, in the eyes of 'honest' Christian critics, 'degraded the position of woman!'

133. In respect of the restrictions imposed so far. Earlier, the Muslims were not allowed to lie with their wives even during the night of Ramaḍān. This was relaxed later on. Islam fully recognizes the fact that the sexual instinct is one of the most powerful organic needs.

So now copulate with them[134] and seek what Allah has ordained for you,[135] and eat and drink, until the white thread becomes manifest to you from the black thread of the

فَٱلْـَٔنَ بَٰشِرُوهُنَّ وَٱبْتَغُوا۟ مَا كَتَبَ ٱللَّهُ لَكُمْ وَكُلُوا۟ وَٱشْرَبُوا۟ حَتَّىٰ يَتَبَيَّنَ لَكُمُ ٱلْخَيْطُ ٱلْأَبْيَضُ مِنَ ٱلْخَيْطِ ٱلْأَسْوَدِ مِنَ ٱلْفَجْرِ

---

134. At night during Ramaḍān. The pronoun refers to 'your women'. In Islam, unlike what is in Christianity, sex is not taboo, and sexual intercourse is not an impure act and a disagreeable task imposed on humanity as a punishment for the Fall, and 'to be undertaken in the spirit in which one submits to a surgical operation'. The act of copulation unless coupled with sin, is in itself a perfectly innocent act and, in proper circumstances, it is bodily healthful and mentally pleasurable. 'Failure to enjoy sex', as observed by a modern British social philosopher, 'so far from being virtuous, is a mere physiological or psychological deficiency, like a failure to enjoy food' (Russell, *Marriage and Morals*, p. 111).

135. With regard to offspring. One of the main objects of the union of man and wife is thus seen to be procreation. All forms of contraception are, by implication, interdicted. Birth control, as defeating the primary purpose of the marital act, can find no place in Islam. In individual cases of ill-health or extreme poverty, the remedy lies in marital abstinence, not in the use of artificial contraceptives which, even from a purely materialistic point of view are still far from perfect. 'Contraceptive methods... for the most part, are untrustworthy and frequently even injurious' (Nemilov, *The Biological Tragedy of Woman*, p. 193). 'Nor is the use of some contraceptives free from physical risk. They produce a certain amount of septic absorption and may even cause death' (Scharlieb, *Straight Talks to Women*, p. 140). 'The entirely successful contraceptive, one that would be sure, harmless and simple, has not yet been discovered' (*EBr.* III. p. 650). And fortunately so. 'That there should be no known contraceptive which does not in some way make the complete happiness of marital intercourse, will perhaps be regarded by some as a very wise dispensation of Providence' (Ludovici, *The Woman*, p. 203). One may of course live in abstinence, if he so likes, but there is no sense and no meaning in restricting the act of generation and frustrating its natural outcome. The modern medical expert while recognizing that 'there are women whose health, happiness and efficiency, are being impaired by too frequent pregnancies', is forced to admit that the havoc these artificial practices, so much in vogue, cause is palpable. Dr. Mary Scharlieb, an eminent doctor, after long and elaborate investigations has arrived at the following conclusion: 'From every point of view, the welfare of the individual, the safety of the empire and the purity of our homes, it is evidently most desirable that the use of artificial contraceptives should cease. There is something peculiarly unnatural and nauseous in their use, something essentially destructive of the joy and spontaneity characteristic of wedded love. Great risks to health and happiness are involved in their use' (Scharlieb, *Straight Talks to Women*, pp. 167–168).

دawn; so complete the fast till nightfall. And do not copulate with them while you are retreating in the mosques.[136] These are the bonds of Allah, so do not approach them. Thus Allah expounds His signs to mankind that haply they may fear Him.

188. And do not devour your riches among yourselves in vanity, nor convey them to the judges that you may thereby devour a portion of other people's riches sinfully while you know.[137]

Section 24

189. They ask you of the new moons. Say: 'They are time-marks for mankind and for the season of Ḥajj'. And it is no virtue that you enter your houses by their backs, but the virtue is his who fears God; so enter the houses by their doors, and fear

ثُمَّ أَتِمُّوا۟ ٱلصِّيَامَ إِلَى ٱلَّيْلِ وَلَا تُبَٰشِرُوهُنَّ وَأَنتُمْ عَٰكِفُونَ فِى ٱلْمَسَٰجِدِ تِلْكَ حُدُودُ ٱللَّهِ فَلَا تَقْرَبُوهَا كَذَٰلِكَ يُبَيِّنُ ٱللَّهُ ءَايَٰتِهِۦ لِلنَّاسِ لَعَلَّهُمْ يَتَّقُونَ ۝

وَلَا تَأْكُلُوٓا۟ أَمْوَٰلَكُم بَيْنَكُم بِٱلْبَٰطِلِ وَتُدْلُوا۟ بِهَآ إِلَى ٱلْحُكَّامِ لِتَأْكُلُوا۟ فَرِيقًا مِّنْ أَمْوَٰلِ ٱلنَّاسِ بِٱلْإِثْمِ وَأَنتُمْ تَعْلَمُونَ ۝

يَسْـَٔلُونَكَ عَنِ ٱلْأَهِلَّةِ قُلْ هِىَ مَوَٰقِيتُ لِلنَّاسِ وَٱلْحَجِّ وَلَيْسَ ٱلْبِرُّ بِأَن تَأْتُوا۟ ٱلْبُيُوتَ مِن ظُهُورِهَا وَلَٰكِنَّ ٱلْبِرَّ مَنِ ٱتَّقَىٰ وَأْتُوا۟ ٱلْبُيُوتَ مِنْ أَبْوَٰبِهَا

136. Retreating is a matter of special devotion, nor have anything to do with them lustfully. It is an act of great merit, though not obligatory, following the practice of the Prophet himself, to cut oneself off from all mundane affairs, during the last ten days of Ramadan, which are regarded as specially sacred, while staying day and night in a mosque and being occupied with pious exercises. This is technically known as *I'tikāf*, or retreat, meaning withholding oneself from the customary exercise of freedom of action in the disposal or management of affairs' (LL.).

137. In other words, while you are acting against your conscience. 'In these words we have another example of the way in which Muhammad urged upon his followers the duty of dealing justly with each other' (Roberts, *Social Laws of the Qur'an*, p. 108).

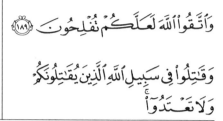

Allah, in order that you may thrive.[138]

190. And fight in the way of Allah those who fight you[139] and do not

---

138. Both in this world and the Next, two entirely distinct, rather mutually destructive, emotions are covered by the same word 'fear'. One is baser, selfish and servile, always arising out of thoughts of danger to self. Fear, in this sense, is removed in the Qur'ān from all righteous and godly persons, in verses like the following, which are reiterated again and again: 'No fear shall come upon them, nor will they grieve.'

But there exists also a noble, higher and disinterested variety of fear, which has its roots not in cowardice or timidity at all but in man's feeling of awe at what his Lord is, and in his contemplating his own utter insignificance and unworthiness. Fear in this sense, attracts; it does not repel. It has the effect of drawing the man closer and closer to his Lord; and he entirely surrenders himself to His will. It is this 'fear of Allah' that is inculcated in a thousand and one ways in the Qur'ān, and is described as the master-key to all success: 'Fear Allah that you may thrive.'

139. Violating the truce they themselves had signed. The Muslims, after having borne untold persecution with almost superhuman fortitude for years and years at the hands of the pagans of Makka, are now for the first time enjoined to take to reprisals. 'For a full thirteen years the Muslims were subjected to relentless persecution in Mecca. The Prophet and his followers fled for life to Medina, but the enemy would not leave them alone in their refuge. They came to attack them within a year, and the first three great battles were fought in the very locality which will show whether the Prophet was an assailant or defendant' (Headley, *The Original Church of Jesus Christ and Islam*, p. 155). The Makkans had signed a truce and were the first to break it. The words 'fight with those who fight against you' clearly show, firstly, that the Muslims were not the aggressors, and secondly, that those of the enemy who were not actual combatants — children, women, monks, hermits, the aged and the infirm, the maimed, and the like — had nothing at all to fear from the Muslim soldiery.

It was in light of this express Divine injunction that the great Abu Bakr, the first Caliph, charged his troops into Syria, 'not to mutilate the dead, nor to slay old men, women, and children, nor to cut down fruit–trees, nor to kill cattle unless they were needed for food; and these humane precepts served like a code of laws of war during the career of Mohammadan conquest.' (Bosworth Smith, *Mohammed and*

Mohammedanism, p. 185). Has not Islam thus, in prescribing war against those who break God's laws, who challenge His righteous authority, and who fill the world with violence and injustice, made every concession short of the impossible? Has any code of military ethics been so chivalrous, so humane, and so tender towards the enemy? 'The moral tone adopted by the Caliph Abū Bakr, in his instructions to the Syrian army, was', says a modern Christian historian, 'so unlike the principles of the Roman government, that it must have commanded profound attention from a subject people. Such a proclamation announced to Jews and Christians' sentiments of justice and principles of toleration which neither Roman emperors nor orthodox bishops had ever adopted as the rule of their conduct' (Finlay, *Greece Under the Romans,* pp. 367 – 368).

trespass;[140] surely Allah does not love the trespassers.

إِنَّ ٱللَّهَ لَا يُحِبُّ ٱلْمُعْتَدِينَ ﴿١٩٠﴾

191. And kill them wherever you come upon them, and drive them out whence they drove you out; and mischief is more grievous[141] than bloodshed. And do not fight them near the Sacred Mosque unless they fight you therein, but if they do fight you there, then kill them. That is the recompense of the infidels.

وَٱقْتُلُوهُمْ حَيْثُ ثَقِفْتُمُوهُمْ وَأَخْرِجُوهُم مِّنْ حَيْثُ أَخْرَجُوكُمْ وَٱلْفِتْنَةُ أَشَدُّ مِنَ ٱلْقَتْلِ وَلَا تُقَٰتِلُوهُمْ عِندَ ٱلْمَسْجِدِ ٱلْحَرَامِ حَتَّىٰ يُقَٰتِلُوكُمْ فِيهِ فَإِن قَٰتَلُوكُمْ فَٱقْتُلُوهُمْ كَذَٰلِكَ جَزَآءُ ٱلْكَٰفِرِينَ ﴿١٩١﴾

192. Then if they desist, then surely Allah is the Forgiver, the Merciful.

فَإِنِ ٱنتَهَوْا۟ فَإِنَّ ٱللَّهَ غَفُورٌ رَّحِيمٌ ﴿١٩٢﴾

193. And fight them until there is no more mischief, and the obedience is to Allah. So if they desist then there is to be no violence save against the ungodly.

وَقَٰتِلُوهُمْ حَتَّىٰ لَا تَكُونَ فِتْنَةٌ وَيَكُونَ ٱلدِّينُ لِلَّهِ فَإِنِ ٱنتَهَوْا۟ فَلَا عُدْوَٰنَ إِلَّا عَلَى ٱلظَّٰلِمِينَ ﴿١٩٣﴾

---

140. In other words, do not violate the truce yourselves; honour your word (Th.); do not step beyond the limits of the law. Compare and contrast the war laws of the Bible: 'And they stopped all the wells of water, and felled all the good trees' (2 Ki. 3: 25). 'For six months did Job remain there with all Israel, until he had cut off every male in Edom' (1. Ki. 11: 16). 'Now go and smite Amalek, and utterly destroy all that they have, and spare them not; but slay both man and woman, infant and suckling, ox and sheep, camel and ass' (1. Sa. 15: 3).

141. Mischief causes greater harm; and leads to graver consequences. There are evils far worse than war; and it is so as to combat manfully these great evils that war is allowed, and sometimes enjoined in Islam. Even the Jains, the religious pacifists of India, to whom all forms of violence are repugnant, hold that 'wars are designed by the Mysterious Unseen for bringing the recalcitrant peoples to book'.

194. A sacred month[142] is in exchange for a sacred month: these are sacredness in return. Whoso therefore offers violence to you, offer violence to him the like of his violence to you and fear Allah, and know that Allah is with the God – fearing.

الشَّهْرُ الْحَرَامُ بِالشَّهْرِ الْحَرَامِ وَالْحُرُمَاتُ قِصَاصٌ فَمَنِ اعْتَدَىٰ عَلَيْكُمْ فَاعْتَدُوا عَلَيْهِ بِمِثْلِ مَا اعْتَدَىٰ عَلَيْكُمْ وَاتَّقُوا اللَّهَ وَاعْلَمُوا أَنَّ اللَّهَ مَعَ الْمُتَّقِينَ ﴿١٩٤﴾

195. And spend in the way of Allah, and do not cast yourselves with your hands in perdition, and do well, surely Allah loves the well – doers.[143]

وَأَنفِقُوا فِى سَبِيلِ اللَّهِ وَلَا تُلْقُوا بِأَيْدِيكُمْ إِلَى التَّهْلُكَةِ وَأَحْسِنُوا إِنَّ اللَّهَ يُحِبُّ الْمُحْسِنِينَ ﴿١٩٥﴾

196. And fulfill the Ḥajj[144] and

وَأَتِمُّوا الْحَجَّ

---

142. A sacred month wherein it is unlawful to make war. The ancient Arabs held four months in the year, Muḥarram, Rajab, Dhū al-Qi'dah and Dhū al-Ḥijjah, as sacred, during which they held it unlawful to wage war.

143. The concept of God in Islam is not that of an inert, passive, First Cause, doing nothing and liking and disliking nothing. The God of Islam actively likes, loves and rewards.

144. 'This great international gathering, attended by thousands of pilgrims every year not only from adjacent countries but from such distant places as China, Senegal, or Cape Town, is an impressive manifestation of the unity of the Muslim world, and serves to keep alive the feeling of brotherhood in Islam. The same thought is impressed upon those Muslims who have been unable themselves to make the pilgrimage, in that on the very same day in which the sacrifices are being performed outside the city of Mecca, the faithful in every other part of the world celebrate the Feast of Sacrifice in a similar fashion, and are thus linked by bonds of sympathy with their more fortunate brethren in the sacred city' (Arnold, *The Islamic Faith*, p. 37). 'The pilgrimage proved in the end a great aid in unification, for the men of every tribe and race met at Mecca with a common purpose, and in a common worship, and a feeling of brotherhood could not but be engendered in the process' (Denison, *Emotion as the Basis of Civilization*, p. 275). 'Down through the ages this institution has continued to serve as the major unifying influence in Islam and the most effective common bond among the diverse believers. It rendered almost every capable Moslem perforce a traveller for once in his life – time. The socializing influence of such a gathering of the brotherhood of believers from the four quarters'othe earth is hard to overestimate. It afforded opportunity for Negroes, Berbers, Chinese, Persians, Syrians, Turks, Arabs – rich and poor, high and low, to fraternize and meet together on the common ground of faith' (Hitti, The *History of the Arabs*, p. 136).

'Umrah[145] for Allah. And if you be besieged, send whatever offering you can afford, and shave not your heads until the offering reaches its destination. Then whoso of you is ill or has hurt in his head for him is an expiation by fasting or alms or a rite. Then when you are secure, whoso combines 'Umrah with Ḥajj for him is whatever offering is easy. And whoso cannot afford them the expiation is a fast of three days during the Ḥajj and of seven when you return; these are ten days complete. This is for him whose family does not dwell near the Sacred Mosque. And fear Allah, and know that surely Allah is Stern in chastising.

Section 25

197. The season of Ḥajj is the months known so whoever enjoins upon himself the Ḥajj therein there is to be no lewdness[146] nor

---

145. 'Umrah is a respectful visit to the Ka'bah that may be performed, unlike Ḥajj, at any time of the year, with fewer rites and ceremonies than Ḥajj proper. While the ajj is obligatory on every Muslim who possesses the means necessary for the journey, 'Umrah is only an act of additional merit.

146. Lewdness in language is forbidden, let alone in deed. The injunction is in striking contrast with the absolutely lewd and obscene rites and practices in the pre-Islamic Ḥajj, and also with the conditions prevailing in modern festivals and large religious gatherings of polytheistic peoples.

wickedness nor disputing during the Ḥajj; and whatever good you do Allah shall know it. And take provision for the journey; surely the best provision is piety, and fear Me, O men of understanding;

وَلَا جِدَالَ فِى الْحَجِّ ۗ وَمَا تَفْعَلُوا مِنْ خَيْرٍ يَعْلَمْهُ اللَّهُ ۗ وَتَزَوَّدُوا فَإِنَّ خَيْرَ الزَّادِ التَّقْوَىٰ ۚ وَاتَّقُونِ يَا أُولِى الْأَلْبَابِ ﴿١٩٧﴾

198. No fault it is in you if you seek grace from your Lord by trading. Then when you press on from 'Arafāt[147] remember Allah near the sacred monument.[148] Remember Him as He has guided you, and you were before of those astray.

لَيْسَ عَلَيْكُمْ جُنَاحٌ أَنْ تَبْتَغُوا فَضْلًا مِنْ رَبِّكُمْ ۚ فَإِذَا أَفَضْتُمْ مِنْ عَرَفَاتٍ فَاذْكُرُوا اللَّهَ عِنْدَ الْمَشْعَرِ الْحَرَامِ ۖ وَاذْكُرُوهُ كَمَا هَدَاكُمْ وَإِنْ كُنْتُمْ مِنْ قَبْلِهِ لَمِنَ الضَّالِّينَ ﴿١٩٨﴾

199. Then press on from where the other people press on, and ask forgiveness of Allah; surely Allah is the Forgiving, the Merciful.

ثُمَّ أَفِيضُوا مِنْ حَيْثُ أَفَاضَ النَّاسُ وَاسْتَغْفِرُوا اللَّهَ ۚ إِنَّ اللَّهَ غَفُورٌ رَحِيمٌ ﴿١٩٩﴾

---

147. Leaving 'Arafāt on the return journey, after making the prescribed stay there. 'Arafat is a plain, miles wide, round a small "Hill of Mercy" rising only about 200 feet above the adjoining plain about 12 miles from Makka on the road to Taif. It is here that the essential ceremony of the Ḥajj, or "standing" has to be performed on the 9th of Dhū al-Ḥijjah, any time from mid-day till evening. The plain of 'Arafāt spreads southward from the hill of 'Arafāt and is bounded on the east by the lofty mountain chain of Taif. It is covered by a low growth of mimosa plants, and is filled with life only on one day of the year (9 Dhū al-Ḥijjah) when the pilgrims pitch their camps for the celebration of the prescribed wukuf' (*EI.* I. p. 418).

148. 'Near the sacred monument' means the ground bordering on it in Muzdalifah, where, immediately after the return from 'Arafāt in the evening of the 9th Dhū al-Ḥijjah night prayer is said, and where the night is spent.

200. And when you have completed your rites,[149] remember Allah as you remember your fathers or with a stronger remembrance.[150] And of mankind there are some who say: 'Our Lord! Give us our portion in the world'; and for such there shall be no portion in the Hereafter.

فَإِذَا قَضَيْتُم مَّنَـٰسِكَكُمْ فَٱذْكُرُواْ ٱللَّهَ كَذِكْرِكُمْ ءَابَآءَكُمْ أَوْ أَشَدَّ ذِكْرًا ۗ فَمِنَ ٱلنَّاسِ مَن يَقُولُ رَبَّنَآ ءَاتِنَا فِى ٱلدُّنْيَا وَمَا لَهُۥ فِى ٱلْأَخِرَةِ مِنْ خَلَـٰقٍ ۝

201. And of them there are some who say: 'Our Lord! Give us good in the world and good in the Hereafter,[151] and save us from the torment of the Fire.'[152]

وَمِنْهُم مَّن يَقُولُ رَبَّنَآ ءَاتِنَا فِى ٱلدُّنْيَا حَسَنَةً وَفِى ٱلْأَخِرَةِ حَسَنَةً وَقِنَا عَذَابَ ٱلنَّارِ ۝

202. These are ones for whom there will be a share for what they have earned, and Allah is Swift at reckoning.

أُوْلَـٰٓئِكَ لَهُمْ نَصِيبٌ مِّمَّا كَسَبُواْ ۚ وَٱللَّهُ سَرِيعُ ٱلْحِسَابِ ۝

---

149. 'The foremost goal of this pilgrimage is the assembling of Muslims from different parts of the world. They shall learn to understand one another and know the needs of Muslim countries other than their own. And this is the practical method of promoting the great Commonwealth of Islam, the brotherhood of men bound together by the same ideal of devotion to God, whose Oneness, as also the unity of all Muslims, are symbolised in the Qibla of Mecca' (*ASB*. I. p. 40).

150. This is how Islam succeeded in effecting far – reaching reforms, and metamorphosed morally and spiritually the entire Arab nation. There is a clear hint in the verse that our association with God should be, at least, as lively and as realistic as with our parents.

151. Note the object desired and sought in prayer is not the world at all, but good, and good only in whatsoever it may be found – whether in this world or in the Next (Th.). Contrast with this the Christian concept embodied in the reported saying of Christ: 'My kingdom is not of this world' (Jn. 18: 36).

152. An ideal prayer, a favourite of the Holy Prophet, combining in two brief sentences all the blessings of this world and the Next. And this has led to the perplexed remark of a Christian writer: 'This is one of the most puzzling paradoxes in Islam. As to recognizing, using and enjoining this world, Islam is a most practical religion, but on its doctrine of salvation, it is absolutely and entirely other – worldly' (McDonald, *The Religious Attitude and Life in Islam*, p. 43).

203. And remember Allah on the days numbered. Then whoso hastens away even in two days, on him is no sin, and whoso stays on, on him is no sin, this for him who fears Allah, and fear Allah, and know that to Him you will be gathered.

وَٱذۡكُرُواْ ٱللَّهَ فِىٓ أَيَّامٍ مَّعۡدُودَٰتٍۚ فَمَن تَعَجَّلَ فِى يَوۡمَيۡنِ فَلَآ إِثۡمَ عَلَيۡهِ وَمَن تَأَخَّرَ فَلَآ إِثۡمَ عَلَيۡهِۚ لِمَنِ ٱتَّقَىٰۗ وَٱتَّقُواْ ٱللَّهَ وَٱعۡلَمُوٓاْ أَنَّكُمۡ إِلَيۡهِ تُحۡشَرُونَ ﴿٢٠٣﴾

204. And of mankind is he whose discourse for the purpose of this world you admire and he takes Allah to witness as to what is in his heart, while he is the most contentious of opponents.

وَمِنَ ٱلنَّاسِ مَن يُعۡجِبُكَ قَوۡلُهُۥ فِى ٱلۡحَيَوٰةِ ٱلدُّنۡيَا وَيُشۡهِدُ ٱللَّهَ عَلَىٰ مَا فِى قَلۡبِهِۦ وَهُوَ أَلَدُّ ٱلۡخِصَامِ ﴿٢٠٤﴾

205. And when he turns away he speeds through the land so that he may make mischief therein and destroy the tillage and the stock. And Allah approves not mischief.

وَإِذَا تَوَلَّىٰ سَعَىٰ فِى ٱلۡأَرۡضِ لِيُفۡسِدَ فِيهَا وَيُهۡلِكَ ٱلۡحَرۡثَ وَٱلنَّسۡلَۚ وَٱللَّهُ لَا يُحِبُّ ٱلۡفَسَادَ ﴿٢٠٥﴾

206. And when he is told: 'Fear Allah', arrogance prompts him to sin. Enough for him is Hell: surely an ill resort!

وَإِذَا قِيلَ لَهُ ٱتَّقِ ٱللَّهَ أَخَذَتۡهُ ٱلۡعِزَّةُ بِٱلۡإِثۡمِۚ فَحَسۡبُهُۥ جَهَنَّمُۚ وَلَبِئۡسَ ٱلۡمِهَادُ ﴿٢٠٦﴾

207. And of mankind is he who sells his life seeking the pleasure of Allah, and Allah is Tender to His servants.

وَمِنَ ٱلنَّاسِ مَن يَشۡرِى نَفۡسَهُ ٱبۡتِغَآءَ مَرۡضَاتِ ٱللَّهِۚ وَٱللَّهُ رَءُوفٌۢ بِٱلۡعِبَادِ ﴿٢٠٧﴾

208. O you who believe! Enter into Islam wholly,[153] and do not follow the foot – steps of Satan; surely he is to you an enemy manifest.

209. Then if you slip after what has come to you of the evidence, know that Allah is the Mighty, the Wise.

210. Do they await only that Allah shall come to them in the shadows of the clouds[154] and also the angels, and the affair is already decreed? And to Allah are all affairs returned.

Section 26

211. Ask you the children of Israel, how many a manifest sign We brought to them. And whoso alters the favour of Allah after it has come to him, then surely Allah is Stern in chastising.

يَـٰٓأَيُّهَا ٱلَّذِينَ ءَامَنُوا۟ ٱدۡخُلُوا۟ فِى ٱلسِّلۡمِ كَآفَّةً وَلَا تَتَّبِعُوا۟ خُطُوَٰتِ ٱلشَّيۡطَـٰنِ إِنَّهُۥ لَكُمۡ عَدُوٌّ مُّبِينٌ ۝

فَإِن زَلَلۡتُم مِّنۢ بَعۡدِ مَا جَآءَتۡكُمُ ٱلۡبَيِّنَـٰتُ فَٱعۡلَمُوٓا۟ أَنَّ ٱللَّهَ عَزِيزٌ حَكِيمٌ ۝

هَلۡ يَنظُرُونَ إِلَّآ أَن يَأۡتِيَهُمُ ٱللَّهُ فِى ظُلَلٍ مِّنَ ٱلۡغَمَامِ وَٱلۡمَلَـٰٓئِكَةُ وَقُضِىَ ٱلۡأَمۡرُ وَإِلَى ٱللَّهِ تُرۡجَعُ ٱلۡأُمُورُ ۝

سَلۡ بَنِىٓ إِسۡرَٰٓءِيلَ كَمۡ ءَاتَيۡنَـٰهُم مِّنۡ ءَايَةٍۭ بَيِّنَةٍ وَمَن يُبَدِّلۡ نِعۡمَةَ ٱللَّهِ مِنۢ بَعۡدِ مَا جَآءَتۡهُ فَإِنَّ ٱللَّهَ شَدِيدُ ٱلۡعِقَابِ ۝

---

153. In other words, accept, and act on, the law of Islam in its every little detail. 'Islam embraces life in its totality. It takes world and Hereafter, soul and body, individual and society, equally into consideration' (Muhammad Asad, *Islam at the Crossroads*, pp. 119–120). It is, to use a word of recent origin, totalitarian. 'By a million roots', says a Christian observer, 'penetrating every phase of life, all of them with religious significance, it is able to maintain its hold upon the life of the Moslem peoples'. The secular and the religious, the material and the spiritual are not separated in the all-inclusive system of Islam. Whatever may be true of other faiths and creeds, in Islam religion is the very breath of life; it matters above everything; it is the mainspring of a Muslim's conduct.

154. The reference is to the anthropomorphic concept of the Jews who held the cloud as the chariot of God. Cf. the Bible: 'Bless the Lord, O my soul. Who layeth the beams of his chambers in the waters; who maketh the clouds his chariot: who walketh upon the wings of the wind' (Ps. 104: 1, 3). 'Behold, the Lord rideth upon a swift cloud, and shall come into Egypt' (Is. 19: 1).

212. Fair-seeming is made the life of this world to those who disbelieve, and they scoff at those who believe, whereas those who fear God shall be above them on the Day of Judgement. And Allah provides for whom He will without measure.[155]

زُيِّنَ لِلَّذِينَ كَفَرُواْ الْحَيَوٰةُ الدُّنْيَا وَيَسْخَرُونَ مِنَ الَّذِينَ ءَامَنُواْ وَالَّذِينَ اتَّقَوْاْ فَوْقَهُمْ يَوْمَ الْقِيَمَةِ وَاللَّهُ يَرْزُقُ مَن يَشَاءُ بِغَيْرِ حِسَابٍ ۝

213. Mankind was one community[156] thereafter Allah raised Prophets as bearers of glad tidings and warners, and He sent down

كَانَ النَّاسُ أُمَّةً وَٰحِدَةً فَبَعَثَ اللَّهُ النَّبِيِّنَ مُبَشِّرِينَ وَمُنذِرِينَ

---

155. So mere material prosperity is no criterion of happiness, and an exuberance of wealth is by no means a measure of moral worth, whether of the individual or of communities or nations.

156. Originally, one community, following the One True religion. This implies that originally there was but one religion in the world — the religion of Monotheism. Contrary to the conclusions arrived at by an older generation of scientists and pseudo–scientists, recent discoveries both in archaeology and anthropology have proved that monotheism, not polytheism, was the religion of the oldest races of mankind. 'The evidence of Anthropology', says a leading archaeologist of the day, Sir Charles Marston, is 'that the original religion of the early races was actually Monotheism or something very like it' (Marston, *The Bible is True*, p. 25). 'The theory of the evolution of religion is contradicted by the evidence of both Archaeology and Anthropology' (Ibid., p. 29). 'This is the very careful and deliberate conclusion of Dr. Langdon, Professor at Oxford, probably the greatest living authority on cuneiform literature... As a result of his excavations at Kish, Dr. Langdon writes: "In my opinion, the history of the oldest religion of man is a rapid decline from monotheism to extreme polytheism and wide–spread belief in evil spirits. It is in a very true sense the history of the fall of man" (Ibid., pp. 58, 61). 'Thus is the evidence, from those most ancient libraries of cuneiform tablets, that Monotheism was the original religion. And there is confirmation of this great fact from other sources, especially from the science of Anthropology. Along with this is the evidence of a universal belief in a Future Life' (Ibid., p. 265). 'I may fail to carry conviction in concluding that, both in Sumerian and Semitic religions, monotheism preceded polytheism and belief in good and evil spirits. The evidence and reasons for this conclusion, so contrary to accepted and current views have been set down with care and with the perception of adverse criticism. It is, I trust, the conclusion of knowledge and not of audacious preconception' (Langdon, *Semitic Mythology*, p. xviii).

with them the Book with Truth so that He may judge between mankind respecting what they disputed. And none disputed thereof save those to whom it was given after the evidence had come to them, out of spite among themselves. Then Allah guided those who believed in the Truth of that respecting which they disputed, by His leave. Allah guides whom He will to a straight path.

وَأَنزَلَ مَعَهُمُ ٱلْكِتَبَ بِٱلْحَقِّ لِيَحْكُمَ بَيْنَ ٱلنَّاسِ فِيمَا ٱخْتَلَفُواْ فِيهِ وَمَا ٱخْتَلَفَ فِيهِ إِلَّا ٱلَّذِينَ أُوتُوهُ مِنۢ بَعْدِ مَا جَآءَتْهُمُ ٱلْبَيِّنَتُ بَغْيًۢا بَيْنَهُمْ فَهَدَى ٱللَّهُ ٱلَّذِينَ ءَامَنُواْ لِمَا ٱخْتَلَفُواْ فِيهِ مِنَ ٱلْحَقِّ بِإِذْنِهِۦ وَٱللَّهُ يَهْدِى مَن يَشَآءُ إِلَى صِرَطٍ مُّسْتَقِيمٍ ۝٢١٣

214. Do you imagine that you will enter the Garden while yet there has not come upon you the like of what came upon those who have passed away before you? There touched them adversity and distress, and so shaken were they, that even their Messenger and those who believed with him said: 'When will come the help of Allah?' Lo! Surely Allah's help is nigh.

أَمْ حَسِبْتُمْ أَن تَدْخُلُواْ ٱلْجَنَّةَ وَلَمَّا يَأْتِكُم مَّثَلُ ٱلَّذِينَ خَلَوْاْ مِن قَبْلِكُم مَّسَّتْهُمُ ٱلْبَأْسَآءُ وَٱلضَّرَّآءُ وَزُلْزِلُواْ حَتَّىٰ يَقُولَ ٱلرَّسُولُ وَٱلَّذِينَ ءَامَنُواْ مَعَهُۥ مَتَىٰ نَصْرُ ٱللَّهِ أَلَآ إِنَّ نَصْرَ ٱللَّهِ قَرِيبٌ ۝٢١٤

215. They ask you as to how they will spend. Say: 'Whatever you spend of wealth, let it be for parents and kindred and orphans and the needy and the wayfarer, and whatever good you do, surely Allah is Knower thereof.'

يَسْـَٔلُونَكَ مَاذَا يُنفِقُونَ قُلْ مَآ أَنفَقْتُم مِّنْ خَيْرٍ فَلِلْوَٰلِدَيْنِ وَٱلْأَقْرَبِينَ وَٱلْيَتَٰمَىٰ وَٱلْمَسَٰكِينِ وَٱبْنِ ٱلسَّبِيلِ وَمَا تَفْعَلُواْ مِنْ خَيْرٍ فَإِنَّ ٱللَّهَ بِهِۦ عَلِيمٌ ۝٢١٥

216. Ordained for you is fighting,[157] abhorrent as it may be to you.[158] Haply you abhor a thing while it is good for you, and haply you desire a thing, while it is bad for you. Allah knows and you do not know.

كُتِبَ عَلَيْكُمُ ٱلْقِتَالُ وَهُوَ كُرْهٌ لَّكُمْ وَعَسَىٰٓ أَن تَكْرَهُواْ شَيْئًا وَهُوَ خَيْرٌ لَّكُمْ وَعَسَىٰٓ أَن تُحِبُّواْ شَيْئًا وَهُوَ شَرٌّ لَّكُمْ وَٱللَّهُ يَعْلَمُ وَأَنتُمْ لَا تَعْلَمُونَ ﴿٢١٦﴾

Section 27

217. They ask you of the sacred month, of fighting therein. Say: 'Fighting therein is grievous; but hindering people from the way of Allah and disbelief in Him and in the sanctity of the Sacred Mosque and driving out its dwellers therefrom are more grievous with Allah, and

يَسْـَٔلُونَكَ عَنِ ٱلشَّهْرِ ٱلْحَرَامِ قِتَالٍ فِيهِ قُلْ قِتَالٌ فِيهِ كَبِيرٌ وَصَدٌّ عَن سَبِيلِ ٱللَّهِ وَكُفْرٌ بِهِۦ وَٱلْمَسْجِدِ ٱلْحَرَامِ وَإِخْرَاجُ أَهْلِهِۦ مِنْهُ أَكْبَرُ عِندَ ٱللَّهِ

---

157. War, it has been truly said, is sanctioned by the law of nature – the constitution of man and the constitution of society – and is at times a biological and sociological necessity. Islam, the ideal practical religion, has allowed it, but only in cases of sheer necessity. In Christianity, 'the coming Day of the Lord is associated with terrible wars... In the Epistles, St. Paul shows in a dozen references to a soldier's career that he looked at it with interest and even with sympathy' (*DB*. IV . p. 895). And speaking historically, the contrast, says a Christian writer, between the Christian and the Muslim warriors 'has not been so sharp as is often supposed. The Saxon wars of Charles the Great were avowedly religious wars, and differed chiefly from the Syrian wars of Omar and of Ali in that they were much more protracted and vastly less successful' (Bosworth Smith, *Mohammed and Mohammedanism*, pp. 184–85).

158. Persecuted, harassed, afflicted, poverty-ridden, exiled, and small in number as the Muslims were at the time of the enactment of warfare, it was but natural that they were none too fond of crossing swords with the mighty forces that had conspired for their extirpation. Nothing short of express and emphatic Divine Command could urge them on to the field of battle. And yet the Islamic Jihads are declared to be 'designed by the Prophet to satisfy his discontented adherents by an accession of plunder!' (Margoliouth). Such is this European scholar's love of veracity! Such is his wonderful reading of history!

mischief is far more grievous than bloodshed. And they will not cease fighting you with a view to making you apostatize[159] from your religion, if they could. And he who among you apostatizes from his faith and dies while he is an infidel, then these are the very ones whose works shall be of no effect in this world and the Hereafter, and they shall be the inmates of the Fire. Therein they shall be abiders.

وَٱلْفِتْنَةُ أَكْبَرُ مِنَ ٱلْقَتْلِ وَلَا يَزَالُونَ يُقَٰتِلُونَكُمْ حَتَّىٰ يَرُدُّوكُمْ عَن دِينِكُمْ إِنِ ٱسْتَطَٰعُوا۟ وَمَن يَرْتَدِدْ مِنكُمْ عَن دِينِهِۦ فَيَمُتْ وَهُوَ كَافِرٌ فَأُو۟لَٰٓئِكَ حَبِطَتْ أَعْمَٰلُهُمْ فِى ٱلدُّنْيَا وَٱلْءَاخِرَةِ وَأُو۟لَٰٓئِكَ أَصْحَٰبُ ٱلنَّارِ هُمْ فِيهَا خَٰلِدُونَ ۝٢١٧

218. Surely those who have believed and those who have emigrated and have striven hard in the way of Allah all these hope for the mercy of Allah. And Allah is the Forgiving, the Merciful.

إِنَّ ٱلَّذِينَ ءَامَنُوا۟ وَٱلَّذِينَ هَاجَرُوا۟ وَجَٰهَدُوا۟ فِى سَبِيلِ ٱللَّهِ أُو۟لَٰٓئِكَ يَرْجُونَ رَحْمَتَ ٱللَّهِ وَٱللَّهُ غَفُورٌ رَّحِيمٌ ۝٢١٨

219. They ask you of wine and gambling say: 'In both is a great sin and some benefit for men, but the sin of them is greater than their benefit.' And they ask you as to what they shall spend. Say: 'the redundant portion.' Thus does Allah expound to you His commandments so that you may ponder –

يَسْـَٔلُونَكَ عَنِ ٱلْخَمْرِ وَٱلْمَيْسِرِ قُلْ فِيهِمَآ إِثْمٌ كَبِيرٌ وَمَنَٰفِعُ لِلنَّاسِ وَإِثْمُهُمَآ أَكْبَرُ مِن نَّفْعِهِمَا وَيَسْـَٔلُونَكَ مَاذَا يُنفِقُونَ قُلِ ٱلْعَفْوَ كَذَٰلِكَ يُبَيِّنُ ٱللَّهُ لَكُمُ ٱلْءَايَٰتِ لَعَلَّكُمْ تَتَفَكَّرُونَ ۝٢١٩

---

159. In the law of Moses, apostasy was punishable with death. 'If thy brother entice thee secretly, saying, Let us go and serve other gods... you shalt surely kill him; And thou shall stone him with stones, that he die' (Dt. 13: 6–10).

220. On this world and the Hereafter. And they ask you of orphans. Say: 'To set right affair for them is best. If you mix with them, then they are your brethren; Allah knows the foul-dealer from the fair-dealer. And had Allah so willed, He could have afflicted you; surely Allah is the Mighty, the Wise.'

فِى ٱلدُّنْيَا وَٱلْأَخِرَةِ وَيَسْـَٔلُونَكَ عَنِ ٱلْيَتَمَىٰ قُلْ إِصْلَاحٌ لَّهُمْ خَيْرٌ وَإِن تُخَالِطُوهُمْ فَإِخْوَٰنُكُمْ وَٱللَّهُ يَعْلَمُ ٱلْمُفْسِدَ مِنَ ٱلْمُصْلِحِ وَلَوْ شَآءَ ٱللَّهُ لَأَعْنَتَكُمْ إِنَّ ٱللَّهَ عَزِيزٌ حَكِيمٌ ﴿٢٢٠﴾

221. And wed not idolatresses until they believe;[160] and assuredly a believing slave girl is better than an idolatress, although she pleases you. And wed not your women to idolaters until they believe; and assuredly a believing slave is better than an idolater, although he pleases you. These call you to the Fire, while Allah calls you to the Garden and to forgive-ness, by His leave. And He expounds His commandments to mankind that perhaps they may be admonished.[161]

وَلَا تَنكِحُوا۟ ٱلْمُشْرِكَٰتِ حَتَّىٰ يُؤْمِنَّ وَلَأَمَةٌ مُّؤْمِنَةٌ خَيْرٌ مِّن مُّشْرِكَةٍ وَلَوْ أَعْجَبَتْكُمْ وَلَا تُنكِحُوا۟ ٱلْمُشْرِكِينَ حَتَّىٰ يُؤْمِنُوا۟ وَلَعَبْدٌ مُّؤْمِنٌ خَيْرٌ مِّن مُّشْرِكٍ وَلَوْ أَعْجَبَكُمْ أُو۟لَٰٓئِكَ يَدْعُونَ إِلَى ٱلنَّارِ وَٱللَّهُ يَدْعُوٓا۟ إِلَى ٱلْجَنَّةِ وَٱلْمَغْفِرَةِ بِإِذْنِهِۦ وَيُبَيِّنُ ءَايَٰتِهِۦ لِلنَّاسِ لَعَلَّهُمْ يَتَذَكَّرُونَ ﴿٢٢١﴾

---

160. Cf. the OT: 'Neither shalt thou make marriages with them; thy daughter thou shalt not give unto his son, nor his daughter shall thou take unto thy son. For they will turn away thy son from following me, that they may serve other gods' (Dt. 7: 3–4). 'And separate yourselves from the people of the land, and from the strange wives' (Ez. 10: 11). 'And in the spirit of Ezra's ordinance, late religious authorities interdicted matrimonial connections between Israelites and all Gentiles. This prohibition is the established law of the Talmud and the Rabbinical codes' (Westermarck, *Short History of Marriage*, pp. 56–57). And the NT: 'Be you not unequally yoked together with unbelievers; for what fellowship hath righteousness with unrighteousness? and what communion hath light with darkness?' (2 Cor. 6: 14).

161. The danger that a Believer, after the intimate relationship of marriage, may be led into the path of infidelity and impiety is ever-present and ever-pressing.

Section 28

222. And they ask you of menstruation. Say: 'It is a pollution, so keep away from women during menstruation, and go not in unto them till they have cleansed themselves. Then when they have thoroughly cleansed themselves go in unto them as Allah has directed you. Surely Allah loves the repentants, and He loves the cleansers of themselves.'

وَيَسۡـَٔلُونَكَ عَنِ ٱلۡمَحِيضِۖ قُلۡ هُوَ أَذٗى فَٱعۡتَزِلُواْ ٱلنِّسَآءَ فِي ٱلۡمَحِيضِۖ وَلَا تَقۡرَبُوهُنَّ حَتَّىٰ يَطۡهُرۡنَۖ فَإِذَا تَطَهَّرۡنَ فَأۡتُوهُنَّ مِنۡ حَيۡثُ أَمَرَكُمُ ٱللَّهُۚ إِنَّ ٱللَّهَ يُحِبُّ ٱلتَّوَّٰبِينَ وَيُحِبُّ ٱلۡمُتَطَهِّرِينَ ۝

223. Your women are a tillage[162] for you, then go in unto your tillage as[163] you will, and provide beforehand for your souls. And fear Allah,[164] and know that you are going to meet Him, and give you glad tidings to the believers.

نِسَآؤُكُمۡ حَرۡثٞ لَّكُمۡ فَأۡتُواْ حَرۡثَكُمۡ أَنَّىٰ شِئۡتُمۡۖ وَقَدِّمُواْ لِأَنفُسِكُمۡۚ وَٱتَّقُواْ ٱللَّهَ وَٱعۡلَمُوٓاْ أَنَّكُم مُّلَٰقُوهُۗ وَبَشِّرِ ٱلۡمُؤۡمِنِينَ ۝

224. And make not Allah a butt of your oaths so that you shall not act piously nor fear Allah nor set things right between men; and Allah is the Hearer, the Knower.

وَلَا تَجۡعَلُواْ ٱللَّهَ عُرۡضَةٗ لِّأَيۡمَٰنِكُمۡ أَن تَبَرُّواْ وَتَتَّقُواْ وَتُصۡلِحُواْ بَيۡنَ ٱلنَّاسِۚ وَٱللَّهُ سَمِيعٌ عَلِيمٞ ۝

---

162. Like the soil which receives the seeds and grows the plant: 'Your wives or women, are unto you things wherein ye sow offspring; they are thus likened to places that are ploughed for sowing' (LL.).

163. Or, when. The word, *annā* signifies 'whence' as well as 'when', and 'how' and has been used in all these senses in the Holy Qur'ān. Here, it can be interpreted by either 'as' or 'when', as has in fact been done by some of the best authorities. Even if understood in the sense of 'whence', it only amounts to saying, whatever posture you may adopt in entering your tilth (and not entering anything else, and cannot be construed by any stretch of the imagination to allow any filthy, unnatural practice).

164. Fear Allah at all times and on all occasions. Fear of God and the full realization of one's responsibility are the keynote of a Muslim's life, of his every action, large or small.

225. Allah shall not take you to task for the vain in your oaths, but He shall take you to task for what your hearts have earned, and He is the Forgiving, the Forbearing.

لَّا يُؤَاخِذُكُمُ ٱللَّهُ بِٱللَّغْوِ فِىٓ أَيْمَـٰنِكُمْ وَلَـٰكِن يُؤَاخِذُكُم بِمَا كَسَبَتْ قُلُوبُكُمْ وَٱللَّهُ غَفُورٌ حَلِيمٌ ۝

226. For those who swear off from their wives is the waiting of four months;[165] then if they go back, surely Allah is the Forgiving, the Merciful.

لِّلَّذِينَ يُؤْلُونَ مِن نِّسَآئِهِمْ تَرَبُّصُ أَرْبَعَةِ أَشْهُرٍ فَإِن فَآءُو فَإِنَّ ٱللَّهَ غَفُورٌ رَّحِيمٌ ۝

227. And if they resolve a divorce, then surely Allah is the Hearer, the Knower.

وَإِنْ عَزَمُوا ٱلطَّلَـٰقَ فَإِنَّ ٱللَّهَ سَمِيعٌ عَلِيمٌ ۝

228. And the divorced[166] women shall keep themselves in waiting for three courses; nor is it allowed to them that they should conceal what Allah has created in their wombs, if they believe in Allah and the Last Day. And their husbands are more

وَٱلْمُطَلَّقَـٰتُ يَتَرَبَّصْنَ بِأَنفُسِهِنَّ ثَلَـٰثَةَ قُرُوٓءٍ وَلَا يَحِلُّ لَهُنَّ أَن يَكْتُمْنَ مَا خَلَقَ ٱللَّهُ فِىٓ أَرْحَامِهِنَّ إِن كُنَّ يُؤْمِنَّ بِٱللَّهِ وَٱلْيَوْمِ ٱلْأَخِرِ وَبُعُولَتُهُنَّ

---

165. This is to prevent so important a step being taken hastily or in the heat of passion, and for cool consideration and deliberation, during which either the husband may re-establish the marital relations, or at the end of which the wife may automatically be released. A wise check on the impulsiveness of the husband.

166. The course of divorce, or the dissolution of the marriage tie, among ancient nations has been erratic, some making it too loose, others making it too tight. Speaking sociologically, every religion has to meet two ends in the sphere of marriage and family – to raise the standard of morality and to sanctify the marriage contract. But in practice some religions have become too lenient, others too rigid. Jewish law allows it as a matter of no great concern. If a husband finds 'some uncleanness in her; then let him write her a bill of divorcement, and give it in her hand, and send her out of his house, and when she is departed out of his house, she may go and be another man's wife' (Dt. 24: 1, 2). Christianity, on the other hand, taking its stand on the reported saying of Jesus: 'What therefore God hath joined together, let not man put asunder... Whosoever shall put away his wife, and marry another, commit adultery against her (Mk. 10: 9, 11), and also upon the dictum of Paul: 'Let not the wife depart

from her husband' (I, Cor. 7: 10), has interdicted divorce altogether. The Catholics hold: 'When the sacrament of matrimony has been received by a man and a woman and ratified by their cohabitation as husband and wife, their union cannot be dissolved except by death' (*CD*. p. 477). The climax was reached in the rules of the Roman Catholic Church which 'treats marriage as a sacrament and demands indissolubility and unchanging fidelity. This in itself is unreasonable. Judaism takes account of the mutability of human feelings, and frees people when the chains of matrimony become fetters; but the Catholic Church refuses to recognize any such change of feeling. The bonds of matrimony become a chain as heavy and galling as iron in which two people must languish for the term of their natural lives' (Bauer, *Woman and Love*, II, p. 291). The Protestants allow it no doubt, but only on such grounds as are of comparatively rare occurrence – fornication, for instance. Islam has steered its course midway between the two, avoiding the extremes of either making divorce too rigid or banning it altogether, or of making it too loose and frivolous. Islam has adopted the only wise course open, that of imposing certain conditions and limitations upon the right of the husband to dissolve the matrimonial bond, the object of which is 'to ensure that the husband was not acting in haste or anger and the separation becomes inevitable in the interests of the husband and the wife and the children' (Abdur Raheem, *Muhammadan Jurisprudence*, p. 336).

entitled to their restoration[167] during the same, if they desire rectification. And to women is due like what is due from women[168] honourably. And for men there is a degree above them. And Allah is the Mighty, the Wise.

أَحَقُّ بِرَدِّهِنَّ فِى ذَٰلِكَ إِنۡ أَرَادُوٓاْ إِصۡلَٰحًا ۚ وَلَهُنَّ مِثۡلُ ٱلَّذِى عَلَيۡهِنَّ بِٱلۡمَعۡرُوفِ ۚ وَلِلرِّجَالِ عَلَيۡهِنَّ دَرَجَةٌ ۗ وَٱللَّهُ عَزِيزٌ حَكِيمٌ ۩ ﴿٢٢٨﴾

Section 29

229. Divorce is twice; thereafter either retaining her honourably or releasing her kindly. And it is not

ٱلطَّلَٰقُ مَرَّتَانِ ۖ فَإِمۡسَاكٌۢ بِمَعۡرُوفٍ أَوۡ تَسۡرِيحٌۢ بِإِحۡسَٰنٍ ۗ وَلَا يَحِلُّ

---

167. Restoration rather than that the divorce be made absolute and irrevocable. Divorce, though perfectly legitimate in itself, is not to be taken too light – heartedly or on flimsy grounds. Verses like the above tend to discourage the practice, unless, of course, there be strong reasons for taking the step, or the incompatibility of temperaments be well established. The Prophet observed: 'Of all the permissible acts, divorce is the most disapproved of by Allah'.

168. Women's rights *vis-a-vis* men. In plainer language: women have rights quite similar to those of men. This bold and explicit declaration of the rights of women centuries and centuries before Mill dreamt of writing on the *Subjection of Women*, has no parallel in the pages of other Divine Scriptures. Contrast with this the attitude of the Bible which as a punishment for Eve makes the wife a subject of her husband who is to rule over her. 'According to the Old Testament, woman is responsible for the fall of man, and this became the cornerstone of Christian teaching. It is a remarkable fact that the Gospel (barring Mt. 19: 9) contains not a word in favour of woman... The Epistles of St. Paul definitely insist that no change can be permitted in the position of woman... St. Jerome has aught but good to say of woman : "Woman is the gate of the devil, the road of evil, the sting of the scorpion." Canon law declares: "Man only is created to the image of God, not woman: therefore woman shall serve him and be his handmaid." The Provincial Council of Macon (sixth century) seriously discussed the question "whether woman had a soul at all" (Kraft–Ebing, *Psychopathia Sexualis*, p. 4, n. 12th Ed.). The effect of the teachings of the Jewish rabbis and Christian fathers was that in the course of history 'woman was represented as the door of hell, as the mother of all human ills. She should be ashamed at the very thought that she is a woman' (Lecky, *History of European Morals*, II, p. 357–58).

Islam grants full dignity to woman as a human being. Each sex is meant to complement the other. Woman is not sub – human. The true relation between the sexes is one of interdependence.

allowed to you to take away anything of what you have given them, except when the two fear that they may not observe the bounds of Allah. Then, if you fear that the two may not observe the bounds of Allah, there is no blame on the two for that with which she redeems herself. These are the bounds of Allah, therefore do not trespass them. And whoso trespasses the bounds of Allah, then it is those who are the ungodly.

230. If he divorces her finally, she is not lawful for him thereafter unless she weds a husband other than he; then if he also divorces her, there is no blame on the two if they return to each other, provided they think that they will now observe the bounds of Allah. And these are the bounds of Allah, He expounds them to a people who know.

231. And when you have divorced your women and they have attained their period, then either retain them honourably or release them kindly:[169] and do not retain them to their hurt so that you may

لَكُمۡ أَن تَأۡخُذُواۡ مِمَّآ ءَاتَيۡتُمُوهُنَّ شَيۡـًٔا إِلَّآ أَن يَخَافَآ أَلَّا يُقِيمَا حُدُودَ ٱللَّهِۖ فَإِنۡ خِفۡتُمۡ أَلَّا يُقِيمَا حُدُودَ ٱللَّهِ فَلَا جُنَاحَ عَلَيۡهِمَا فِيمَا ٱفۡتَدَتۡ بِهِۦۗ تِلۡكَ حُدُودُ ٱللَّهِ فَلَا تَعۡتَدُوهَاۚ وَمَن يَتَعَدَّ حُدُودَ ٱللَّهِ فَأُوۡلَٰٓئِكَ هُمُ ٱلظَّٰلِمُونَ ٢٢٩

فَإِن طَلَّقَهَا فَلَا تَحِلُّ لَهُۥ مِنۢ بَعۡدُ حَتَّىٰ تَنكِحَ زَوۡجًا غَيۡرَهُۥۗ فَإِن طَلَّقَهَا فَلَا جُنَاحَ عَلَيۡهِمَآ أَن يَتَرَاجَعَآ إِن ظَنَّآ أَن يُقِيمَا حُدُودَ ٱللَّهِۗ وَتِلۡكَ حُدُودُ ٱللَّهِ يُبَيِّنُهَا لِقَوۡمٍ يَعۡلَمُونَ ٢٣٠

وَإِذَا طَلَّقۡتُمُ ٱلنِّسَآءَ فَبَلَغۡنَ أَجَلَهُنَّ فَأَمۡسِكُوهُنَّ بِمَعۡرُوفٍ أَوۡ سَرِّحُوهُنَّ بِمَعۡرُوفٍۚ وَلَا تُمۡسِكُوهُنَّ ضِرَارًا لِّتَعۡتَدُواۡ

---

169. This is for the second time that husbands are enjoined to behave towards their wives honourably and generously whether they retain them or divorce them. The duty to be kind, fair, and chivalrous towards wives is not contingent on something else; it is unconditional.

trespass;[170] and whoso does this assuredly wrongs his soul. And do not hold Allah's commandments in mockery, and remember Allah's favour upon you, and that He has sent down upon you the Book and wisdom with which He admonishes you. And fear Allah, and know that surely Allah is the Knower of everything.

وَمَن يَفْعَلْ ذَٰلِكَ فَقَدْ ظَلَمَ نَفْسَهُۥ وَلَا تَتَّخِذُوٓاْ ءَايَٰتِ ٱللَّهِ هُزُوٗاۚ وَٱذْكُرُواْ نِعْمَتَ ٱللَّهِ عَلَيْكُمْ وَمَآ أَنزَلَ عَلَيْكُم مِّنَ ٱلْكِتَٰبِ وَٱلْحِكْمَةِ يَعِظُكُم بِهِۦۚ وَٱتَّقُواْ ٱللَّهَ وَٱعْلَمُوٓاْ أَنَّ ٱللَّهَ بِكُلِّ شَيْءٍ عَلِيمٞ ﴿٢٣١﴾

Section 30

232. And when you have divorced women and they have attained their period, do not straiten them so that they will not rewed their husbands, after they have agreed between themselves honourably. Hereby is admonished he among you who believes in Allah and the Last Day: this is cleaner for you and purer. Allah knows and you do not know.

وَإِذَا طَلَّقْتُمُ ٱلنِّسَآءَ فَبَلَغْنَ أَجَلَهُنَّ فَلَا تَعْضُلُوهُنَّ أَن يَنكِحْنَ أَزْوَٰجَهُنَّ إِذَا تَرَٰضَوْاْ بَيْنَهُم بِٱلْمَعْرُوفِۗ ذَٰلِكَ يُوعَظُ بِهِۦ مَن كَانَ مِنكُمْ يُؤْمِنُ بِٱللَّهِ وَٱلْيَوْمِ ٱلْأٓخِرِۗ ذَٰلِكُمْ أَزْكَىٰ لَكُمْ وَأَطْهَرُۗ وَٱللَّهُ يَعْلَمُ وَأَنتُمْ لَا تَعْلَمُونَ ﴿٢٣٢﴾

233. And mothers shall suckle their children two whole years; this is for him who intends that he shall complete the suckling, and on him to whom the child is born is the mother's provision and clothing honourably – not a soul is tasked

وَٱلْوَٰلِدَٰتُ يُرْضِعْنَ أَوْلَٰدَهُنَّ حَوْلَيْنِ كَامِلَيْنِۖ لِمَنْ أَرَادَ أَن يُتِمَّ ٱلرَّضَاعَةَۚ وَعَلَى ٱلْمَوْلُودِ لَهُۥ رِزْقُهُنَّ وَكِسْوَتُهُنَّ بِٱلْمَعْرُوفِۚ

---

170. Trespass the bounds of law. Observe the emphasis with which the Qur'ān, as the spokesman of the helpless and the weak, defends and safeguards the rights of divorced women. It is certainly not the Holy Qur'ān, but the Bible, which treats of the man as the owner, and the woman as his chattel, his possession (Cf. *EBi.* c. 1498).

لَا تُكَلَّفُ نَفْسٌ إِلَّا وُسْعَهَا لَا تُضَآرَّ
وَالِدَةٌ بِوَلَدِهَا وَلَا مَوْلُودٌ لَّهُ بِوَلَدِهِ
وَعَلَى ٱلْوَارِثِ مِثْلُ ذَٰلِكَ فَإِنْ أَرَادَا فِصَالًا عَن
تَرَاضٍ مِّنْهُمَا وَتَشَاوُرٍ فَلَا جُنَاحَ عَلَيْهِمَا وَإِنْ
أَرَدتُّمْ أَن تَسْتَرْضِعُوٓا۟ أَوْلَٰدَكُمْ فَلَا جُنَاحَ
عَلَيْكُمْ إِذَا سَلَّمْتُم مَّآ ءَاتَيْتُم بِٱلْمَعْرُوفِ وَٱتَّقُوا۟
ٱللَّهَ وَٱعْلَمُوٓا۟ أَنَّ ٱللَّهَ بِمَا تَعْمَلُونَ بَصِيرٌ ﴿٢٣٣﴾

except according to its capacity. Neither shall a mother be hurt because of her child nor shall he to whom the child is born because of his child; and on the heir shall devolve the like thereof. Then if the two desire weaning by agreement between them and mutual counsel, there is no blame on the two. And if you desire to give your children for suckling, there is no blame on you when you hand over whatever you have agreed to give her honourably. And fear Allah, and know that Allah is the Beholder of what you do.

وَٱلَّذِينَ يُتَوَفَّوْنَ مِنكُمْ وَيَذَرُونَ أَزْوَٰجًا
يَتَرَبَّصْنَ بِأَنفُسِهِنَّ أَرْبَعَةَ أَشْهُرٍ وَعَشْرًا
فَإِذَا بَلَغْنَ أَجَلَهُنَّ فَلَا جُنَاحَ عَلَيْكُمْ
فِيمَا فَعَلْنَ فِىٓ أَنفُسِهِنَّ بِٱلْمَعْرُوفِ وَٱللَّهُ
بِمَا تَعْمَلُونَ خَبِيرٌ ﴿٢٣٤﴾

234. And as for those of you who die and leave wives behind, they shall keep themselves in waiting for four months and ten days. Then when they have attained their period, there is no blame on you for what they do with themselves honourably. Allah is Aware of whatever you do.

وَلَا جُنَاحَ عَلَيْكُمْ فِيمَا عَرَّضْتُم بِهِ مِنْ
خِطْبَةِ ٱلنِّسَآءِ أَوْ أَكْنَنتُمْ فِىٓ أَنفُسِكُمْ
عَلِمَ ٱللَّهُ أَنَّكُمْ سَتَذْكُرُونَهُنَّ وَلَٰكِن لَّا
تُوَاعِدُوهُنَّ سِرًّا إِلَّآ أَن تَقُولُوا۟
قَوْلًا مَّعْرُوفًا

235. And there is no blame on you in that you speak indirectly of your troth to the said women or conceal it in your souls! Allah knows that you will soon make mention of these women. But make no promise to them in secret, except that you speak an honourable saying. And

even resolve not on the wedding –
knot until the prescribed term has
attained its end. And know that
Allah knows what is in your souls,
so beware of Him, and know that
Allah is the Forgiving, the
Forbearing.

وَلَا تَعْزِمُواْ عُقْدَةَ ٱلنِّكَاحِ حَتَّىٰ يَبْلُغَ
ٱلْكِتَٰبُ أَجَلَهُۥ وَٱعْلَمُوٓاْ أَنَّ ٱللَّهَ يَعْلَمُ مَا
فِىٓ أَنفُسِكُمْ فَٱحْذَرُوهُ وَٱعْلَمُوٓاْ
أَنَّ ٱللَّهَ غَفُورٌ حَلِيمٌ ﴿٢٣٥﴾

Section 31

236. There is no blame on you if
you divorce women while yet you
have not touched them nor settled
with them a settlement. Benefit
them; on the affluent, is due
according to his means and on the
straitened is due according to his
means: an honourable present –
incumbent on the well-doers.

لَّا جُنَاحَ عَلَيْكُمْ إِن طَلَّقْتُمُ ٱلنِّسَآءَ مَا لَمْ
تَمَسُّوهُنَّ أَوْ تَفْرِضُواْ لَهُنَّ فَرِيضَةً وَ
مَتِّعُوهُنَّ عَلَى ٱلْمُوسِعِ قَدَرُهُۥ وَعَلَى ٱلْمُقْتِرِ
قَدَرُهُۥ مَتَٰعًا بِٱلْمَعْرُوفِ حَقًّا عَلَى ٱلْمُحْسِنِينَ ﴿٢٣٦﴾

237. And if you divorce them
before you have touched them, but
have already settled with them a
settlement, then due from you is
half of what you have settled
unless the wives forgo, or he in
whose hand is the wedding-knot
forgoes: and that you should forgo
is higher to piety. And do not
forget grace among yourselves;
surely Allah is the Beholder of
what you do.

وَإِن طَلَّقْتُمُوهُنَّ مِن قَبْلِ أَن تَمَسُّوهُنَّ وَقَدْ
فَرَضْتُمْ لَهُنَّ فَرِيضَةً فَنِصْفُ مَا فَرَضْتُمْ
إِلَّآ أَن يَعْفُونَ أَوْ يَعْفُوَاْ ٱلَّذِى بِيَدِهِۦ
عُقْدَةُ ٱلنِّكَاحِ وَأَن تَعْفُوٓاْ أَقْرَبُ
لِلتَّقْوَىٰ وَلَا تَنسَوُاْ ٱلْفَضْلَ بَيْنَكُمْ
إِنَّ ٱللَّهَ بِمَا تَعْمَلُونَ بَصِيرٌ ﴿٢٣٧﴾

238. Be watchful over the prayers,
and the middle prayer, and stand up
to Allah truly devout.

حَٰفِظُواْ عَلَى ٱلصَّلَوَٰتِ وَٱلصَّلَوٰةِ
ٱلْوُسْطَىٰ وَقُومُواْ لِلَّهِ قَٰنِتِينَ ﴿٢٣٨﴾

239. And if you fear then pray on foot or riding; then when you are secure, remember Allah in the way He has taught you which you even knew not.

فَإِنْ خِفْتُمْ فَرِجَالًا أَوْ رُكْبَانًا فَإِذَآ أَمِنتُمْ فَٱذْكُرُوا۟ ٱللَّهَ كَمَا عَلَّمَكُم مَّا لَمْ تَكُونُوا۟ تَعْلَمُونَ ﴿٢٣٩﴾

240. And those of you who die and leave wives, they shall make a bequest to their wives a year's maintenance without their having to go out; then if they go out then there is no blame on you for what they may do with themselves honourably, and Allah is the Mighty, the Wise.

وَٱلَّذِينَ يُتَوَفَّوْنَ مِنكُمْ وَيَذَرُونَ أَزْوَٰجًا وَصِيَّةً لِّأَزْوَٰجِهِم مَّتَٰعًا إِلَى ٱلْحَوْلِ غَيْرَ إِخْرَاجٍ فَإِنْ خَرَجْنَ فَلَا جُنَاحَ عَلَيْكُمْ فِي مَا فَعَلْنَ فِىٓ أَنفُسِهِنَّ مِن مَّعْرُوفٍ وَٱللَّهُ عَزِيزٌ حَكِيمٌ ﴿٢٤٠﴾

241. And for the divorced women an honourable present: incumbent on the God-fearing.

وَلِلْمُطَلَّقَٰتِ مَتَٰعٌۢ بِٱلْمَعْرُوفِ حَقًّا عَلَى ٱلْمُتَّقِينَ ﴿٢٤١﴾

242. Thus does Allah expound to you His commandments; haply you may reflect.

كَذَٰلِكَ يُبَيِّنُ ٱللَّهُ لَكُمْ ءَايَٰتِهِۦ لَعَلَّكُمْ تَعْقِلُونَ ﴿٢٤٢﴾

Section 32

243. Have you not looked at those who went forth from their dwellings, and they were in their thousands to escape death? Then Allah said to them: 'Die'; and thereafter revived them. Surely Allah is Gracious to men, although most men do not give thanks.

أَلَمْ تَرَ إِلَى ٱلَّذِينَ خَرَجُوا۟ مِن دِيَٰرِهِمْ وَهُمْ أُلُوفٌ حَذَرَ ٱلْمَوْتِ فَقَالَ لَهُمُ ٱللَّهُ مُوتُوا۟ ثُمَّ أَحْيَٰهُمْ إِنَّ ٱللَّهَ لَذُو فَضْلٍ عَلَى ٱلنَّاسِ وَلَٰكِنَّ أَكْثَرَ ٱلنَّاسِ لَا يَشْكُرُونَ ﴿٢٤٣﴾

244. And fight in the way of Allah, and know that Allah is the Hearer, the Knower.

وَقَٰتِلُوا۟ فِي سَبِيلِ ٱللَّهِ وَٱعْلَمُوٓا۟ أَنَّ ٱللَّهَ سَمِيعٌ عَلِيمٌ ﴿٢٤٤﴾

245. Who is it that will lend to Allah a goodly loan, so that He will multiply it to him manifold? And Allah scants and amplifies, and to Him you all shall be returned.

مَن ذَا ٱلَّذِى يُقْرِضُ ٱللَّهَ قَرْضًا حَسَنًا فَيُضَٰعِفَهُۥ لَهُۥٓ أَضْعَافًا كَثِيرَةً وَٱللَّهُ يَقْبِضُ وَيَبْصُۜطُ وَإِلَيْهِ تُرْجَعُونَ ٢٤٥

246. Have you not looked at the chiefs of the children of Israel after Moses? They said to a Prophet of theirs: 'Raise for us a king that we may fight in the way of God.' He said: 'May be that if the fighting were prescribed for you, you would not fight.' They said: 'Why should we not fight in the way of God, whereas we have been driven away from our dwellings and children?' Yet when the fighting was prescribed for them, they turned away, save a few of them; and Allah is the Knower of the ungodly.

أَلَمْ تَرَ إِلَى ٱلْمَلَإِ مِنۢ بَنِىٓ إِسْرَٰٓءِيلَ مِنۢ بَعْدِ مُوسَىٰٓ إِذْ قَالُوا۟ لِنَبِىٍّ لَّهُمُ ٱبْعَثْ لَنَا مَلِكًا نُّقَٰتِلْ فِى سَبِيلِ ٱللَّهِ قَالَ هَلْ عَسَيْتُمْ إِن كُتِبَ عَلَيْكُمُ ٱلْقِتَالُ أَلَّا تُقَٰتِلُوا۟ قَالُوا۟ وَمَا لَنَآ أَلَّا نُقَٰتِلَ فِى سَبِيلِ ٱللَّهِ وَقَدْ أُخْرِجْنَا مِن دِيَٰرِنَا وَأَبْنَآئِنَا فَلَمَّا كُتِبَ عَلَيْهِمُ ٱلْقِتَالُ تَوَلَّوْا۟ إِلَّا قَلِيلًا مِّنْهُمْ وَٱللَّهُ عَلِيمٌۢ بِٱلظَّٰلِمِينَ ٢٤٦

247. And their Prophet said to them: 'Surely Allah has raised over you Saul as a king'. They said: 'How can there be kingship for him over us, whereas we are worthier of kingship than he? Nor has he been given plenty of riches.' The Prophet said: 'Surely Allah has chosen him over you, and has increased him in knowledge and physique, and Allah grants kingship to whom He will, and Allah is the Bountiful, the Knowing.'

وَقَالَ لَهُمْ نَبِيُّهُمْ إِنَّ ٱللَّهَ قَدْ بَعَثَ لَكُمْ طَالُوتَ مَلِكًا قَالُوٓا۟ أَنَّىٰ يَكُونُ لَهُ ٱلْمُلْكُ عَلَيْنَا وَنَحْنُ أَحَقُّ بِٱلْمُلْكِ مِنْهُ وَلَمْ يُؤْتَ سَعَةً مِّنَ ٱلْمَالِ قَالَ إِنَّ ٱللَّهَ ٱصْطَفَىٰهُ عَلَيْكُمْ وَزَادَهُۥ بَسْطَةً فِى ٱلْعِلْمِ وَٱلْجِسْمِ وَٱللَّهُ يُؤْتِى مُلْكَهُۥ مَن يَشَآءُ وَٱللَّهُ وَٰسِعٌ عَلِيمٌ ٢٤٧

248. And their Prophet said to them: 'Surely the sign of his kingship is that there shall come to you the ark wherein is tranquillity from your Lord and the relic of what the household of Moses and the household of Aaron had left, the angels bearing it; surely, here is a sign for you if you are believers at all.

وَقَالَ لَهُمْ نَبِيُّهُمْ إِنَّ ءَايَةَ مُلۡكِهِۦ أَن يَأۡتِيَكُمُ ٱلتَّابُوتُ فِيهِ سَكِينَةٌ مِّن رَّبِّكُمْ وَبَقِيَّةٌ مِّمَّا تَرَكَ ءَالُ مُوسَىٰ وَءَالُ هَٰرُونَ تَحۡمِلُهُ ٱلۡمَلَٰٓئِكَةُ إِنَّ فِى ذَٰلِكَ لَأَيَةً لَّكُمۡ إِن كُنتُم مُّؤۡمِنِينَ ﴿٢٤٨﴾

Section 33

249. Then when Saul sallied forth with the hosts, he said: 'Surely Allah will test you with a river, then whoso drinks of it shall not be mine, and whoso tastes it not, shall be mine, excepting him who takes a sip with his hand.' Yet they drank of it, save a few of them. Then when he had crossed it, he and those who believed with him, they said: 'We have no strength today against Goliath and his hosts.' But those who believed and reckoned that they were going to meet Allah, said: 'How often has a small group prevailed against a large group by God's command? And Allah is with the steadfast.'

فَلَمَّا فَصَلَ طَالُوتُ بِٱلۡجُنُودِ قَالَ إِنَّ ٱللَّهَ مُبۡتَلِيكُم بِنَهَرٍ فَمَن شَرِبَ مِنۡهُ فَلَيۡسَ مِنِّى وَمَن لَّمۡ يَطۡعَمۡهُ فَإِنَّهُۥ مِنِّىٓ إِلَّا مَنِ ٱغۡتَرَفَ غُرۡفَةً بِيَدِهِۦ فَشَرِبُوا۟ مِنۡهُ إِلَّا قَلِيلًا مِّنۡهُمۡ فَلَمَّا جَاوَزَهُۥ هُوَ وَٱلَّذِينَ ءَامَنُوا۟ مَعَهُۥ قَالُوا۟ لَا طَاقَةَ لَنَا ٱلۡيَوۡمَ بِجَالُوتَ وَجُنُودِهِۦ قَالَ ٱلَّذِينَ يَظُنُّونَ أَنَّهُم مُّلَٰقُوا۟ ٱللَّهِ كَم مِّن فِئَةٍ قَلِيلَةٍ غَلَبَتۡ فِئَةً كَثِيرَةً بِإِذۡنِ ٱللَّهِ وَٱللَّهُ مَعَ ٱلصَّٰبِرِينَ ﴿٢٤٩﴾

250. And when they arranged themselves against Goliath and his hosts, they said: 'Our Lord! Pour forth on us steadfastness and set firm our feet, and make

وَلَمَّا بَرَزُوا۟ لِجَالُوتَ وَجُنُودِهِۦ قَالُوا۟ رَبَّنَآ أَفۡرِغۡ عَلَيۡنَا صَبۡرًا وَثَبِّتۡ أَقۡدَامَنَا

us triumph over the infidel people.'[171]

وَأَنصُرْنَا عَلَى ٱلْقَوْمِ ٱلْكَـٰفِرِينَ ﴿٢٥٠﴾

251. Then they vanquished them, by the command of Allah; and David slew Goliath, and Allah gave him kingdom and wisdom and taught him of what He willed. And had it not been for Allah's repelling some people by means of others, the earth was surely to be corrupted. But Allah is Gracious to the world.

فَهَزَمُوهُم بِإِذْنِ ٱللَّهِ وَقَتَلَ دَاوُۥدُ جَالُوتَ وَءَاتَىٰهُ ٱللَّهُ ٱلْمُلْكَ وَٱلْحِكْمَةَ وَعَلَّمَهُۥ مِمَّا يَشَآءُ وَلَوْ لَا دَفْعُ ٱللَّهِ ٱلنَّاسَ بَعْضَهُم بِبَعْضٍ لَّفَسَدَتِ ٱلْأَرْضُ وَلَـٰكِنَّ ٱللَّهَ ذُو فَضْلٍ عَلَى ٱلْعَـٰلَمِينَ ﴿٢٥١﴾

252. These are the revelations of Allah: We recite them to you, and, surely, you are one of the envoys.[172]

تِلْكَ ءَايَـٰتُ ٱللَّهِ نَتْلُوهَا عَلَيْكَ بِٱلْحَقِّ وَإِنَّكَ لَمِنَ ٱلْمُرْسَلِينَ ﴿٢٥٢﴾

253. These Messengers! We have preferred some of them above others; to some Allah spoke directly; and some He raised in rank.[173] And We gave Jesus, son of Maryam,[174] evidence, and We aided him with the Holy Spirit.[175]

تِلْكَ ٱلرُّسُلُ فَضَّلْنَا بَعْضَهُمْ عَلَىٰ بَعْضٍ مِّنْهُم مَّن كَلَّمَ ٱللَّهُ وَرَفَعَ بَعْضَهُمْ دَرَجَـٰتٍ وَءَاتَيْنَا عِيسَى ٱبْنَ مَرْيَمَ ٱلْبَيِّنَـٰتِ وَأَيَّدْنَـٰهُ بِرُوحِ ٱلْقُدُسِ

---

171. Observe the beautiful order in the prayer. Firstly, it is the firmness of heart that is sought, then the firmness of feet, and then, as a natural sequel, triumph over the adversary.

172. One of the Divine Messengers. Note the significance of the epithet 'sent ones'. Prophets, in Islam, are always the sent ones – sent by God to the peoples – not themselves godlings or god – incarnations.

173. The obvious reference is to the Prophet Muhammad (peace and blessings be upon him), the prophet *par excellence*, the most exalted of all the Prophets.

174. Maryam being Mary. In view of Christian blasphemy, the fact of Jesus, namely Jesus, being the son of a mere woman required a clear pronouncement.

175. The Holy Spirit, in Islam, is not the third Person of Trinity but the Archangel Gabriel, who was in constant attendance upon the Prophet Jesus, and protected him – a mere mortal from the viles of his enemies. There is no trace, either here or elsewhere in the Holy Qur'ān, of any specially high rank being bestowed on Jesus above the Prophets. He simply has his own place – a very honourable one no doubt, in the long list of the Messengers of God.

And had Allah so willed, those who came after them would not have fought one against the other after the clear signs had come to them, but they fell into variance, then, of them, some believed and some disbelieved.[176] And had Allah so willed, they would not have fought one against the other, but Allah does whatever He intends.

وَلَوۡ شَآءَ ٱللَّهُ مَا ٱقۡتَتَلَ ٱلَّذِينَ مِنۢ بَعۡدِهِم مِّنۢ بَعۡدِ مَا جَآءَتۡهُمُ ٱلۡبَيِّنَٰتُ وَلَٰكِنِ ٱخۡتَلَفُواْ فَمِنۡهُم مَّنۡ ءَامَنَ وَمِنۡهُم مَّن كَفَرَ وَلَوۡ شَآءَ ٱللَّهُ مَا ٱقۡتَتَلُواْ وَلَٰكِنَّ ٱللَّهَ يَفۡعَلُ مَا يُرِيدُ ﴿٢٥٣﴾

Section 34

254. O you who believe! Spend of what We have provided you before the Day arrives when there shall be neither trading nor friendship nor intercession.[177] And it is the infidels who are the ungodly.

يَٰٓأَيُّهَا ٱلَّذِينَ ءَامَنُوٓاْ أَنفِقُواْ مِمَّا رَزَقۡنَٰكُم مِّن قَبۡلِ أَن يَأۡتِيَ يَوۡمٞ لَّا بَيۡعٞ فِيهِ وَلَا خُلَّةٞ وَلَا شَفَٰعَةٞ وَٱلۡكَٰفِرُونَ هُمُ ٱلظَّٰلِمُونَ ﴿٢٥٤﴾

---

176. This, in sum, has been the history of the Prophets and their peoples. The moral for the Prophet is to derive comfort by contemplating on this uniform fact of history, and not to expect wholesale conversion (Th.).

177. Both Jews and Christians – the latter even more than the former were wont to presume that intercession would assist them. 'We were saved through the merits of one mediator, our Lord Jesus Christ... Christ is well qualified to be a mediator, i.e., one who brings estranged parties to amicable agreement. Being God and man, He can best restore friendship between God and the human family' (CD. p. 617). 'His (Christ's) action, to some extent, His teaching, more explicitly the apostolic teaching (represented by St. Paul, St. Peter, St. John and the *Epistle to the Hebrews*) present Him as the Mediator with God on behalf of mankind, making intercession in His prayers on earth and in His heavenly life after the resurrection, but chiefly giving His life as a ransom, shedding His blood for the remission of sin, acting as means of propitiation, doing God's will' (DB. III. p. 320). The Jews also believed in the mediation of Angels and 'Logos'. And Philo, while speaking of 'the Word' on the mediation between God and His creation, is quoted as saying: 'The Father who created the universe has given to His archangelic and most ancient Word a pre– eminent gift to stand on the confines of both; while separating the created things from the Creator he pleads before the immortal God on behalf of the mortal race which sins continually, as is the ambassador sent by the Ruler to the subject Race' (JE. VIII. p. 409). Islam, is as evident, sweeps away all such fanciful, and essentially pagan, ideas of mediation, intercession and propitiation.

255. Allah![178] There is no god but He,[179] the Living,[180] the Sustainer,[181] slumber seizes Him not, nor sleep. His is whatever is in the heavens and whatever is on the earth. Who can intercede with Him, save by His

اللّهُ لَا إِلَهَ إِلَّا هُوَ الْحَيُّ الْقَيُّومُ لَا تَأْخُذُهُۥ
سِنَةٌ وَلَا نَوْمٌ لَّهُۥ مَا فِى السَّمَوَتِ وَمَا فِى
الْأَرْضِ مَن ذَا الَّذِى يَشْفَعُ عِندَهُۥٓ

---

178. The verse known as the Throne Verse has often won the admiration of non–Muslims, even of anti-Muslims... 'a magnificent description of the divine majesty and providence; but it must not be supposed the translation comes up to the dignity of the original. The passage is justly admirable by the Mohammadans who recite it in their prayers; and some of them wear it about them' (*SPD.*). 'One of the most admirable passages in the Koran' (LL.). 'One of the grandest verses of the Qur'an' (Wherry, *Commentary on the Koran*).

179. This is the creed of Islam, negating (all false gods, and affirming the Unity of the One True God. 'There is no god but God — are words simply tantamount in English to the negation of any deity save the One alone; and this much they certainly mean in Arabic, but they imply much more also. Their full sense is, not only to deny absolutely and unreservedly all plurality, whether of nature or of person, in the Supreme Being, not only to establish His Unity in all its simple and incommunicable Oneness, but besides this the words, in Arabic and among Arabs, imply that this one Supreme Being is also the only Agent, the only Force, the only Act existing throughout the universe, and leads to all being else, matter or spirit, instinct or intelligence, physical or moral, nothing but pure, unconditional passivenses, alike in movement or in quiescene, in action or in capacity' (*ERE*, XI. p. 757).

180. The Ever-living; the Deathless; the Eternal; His existence having neither beginning nor end. Even a fact so patent as the deathlessness of God has needed a clear affirmation in view of the peculiar sacrifice of heathen gods every spring, as also in view of the Christ-God who suffered death at the hands of his persecutors. 'The putting to death of a public man–god was a common incident of many religions' (G. Allen, *Evolution of the Idea of God*, p. 90).

181. He is Almighty and the Sole Provider. He sustains the existence of everything and is Himself sustained or supported by nobody. By the mere mention of Life and Self -subsistence as His two essential attributes, the possibility of all co-partnership with Him is negated outright. Contrast with this the Christian belief that 'the Father is no more God without the Son than the Son is God without the Father' (*ERE.* VII. p. 536), as also the Hindu belief that certain deities, at any rate, 'are the offspring of others, and that the gods were originally mortal, who have only acquired immortality either by the practice of austerities or by drinking Soma or else by receiving a gift from Agni and Savita' (*ERE.* XII. p. 602). Obviously Islam brushes aside all such absurdities.

leave?[182] He knows whatever was before them and whatever shall be after them. And they encompass nothing of His knowledge, save what He wills. His throne comprehends the heavens and the earth; and the guarding of both wearies Him not,[183] and He is the High, the Supreme.

إِلَّا بِإِذْنِهِ يَعْلَمُ مَا بَيْنَ أَيْدِيهِمْ وَمَا خَلْفَهُمْ وَلَا يُحِيطُونَ بِشَىْءٍ مِّنْ عِلْمِهِ إِلَّا بِمَا شَاءَ وَسِعَ كُرْسِيُّهُ ٱلسَّمَوَاتِ وَٱلْأَرْضَ وَلَا يَئُودُهُ حِفْظُهُمَا وَهُوَ ٱلْعَلِىُّ ٱلْعَظِيمُ ﴿٢٥٥﴾

256. No compulsion is there in religion.[184] Surely rectitude has become distinct from error. Whoso then denies the devil and believes in Allah has of a surety laid hold of the firm cable of which there is no breaking;[185] and Allah is the Hearing, the Knowing.

لَا إِكْرَاهَ فِى ٱلدِّينِ قَد تَّبَيَّنَ ٱلرُّشْدُ مِنَ ٱلْغَىِّ فَمَن يَكْفُرْ بِٱلطَّاغُوتِ وَيُؤْمِن بِٱللَّهِ فَقَدِ ٱسْتَمْسَكَ بِٱلْعُرْوَةِ ٱلْوُثْقَىٰ لَا ٱنفِصَامَ لَهَا وَٱللَّهُ سَمِيعٌ عَلِيمٌ ﴿٢٥٦﴾

---

182. So that there exists none as permanent or independent 'Mediator.' This completely repudiates the 'doctrine of mediation' which is peculiarly Christian. 'It is not only that peace with God, or the forgiveness of sins, or reconciliation, or eternal life for the spiritually dead is mediated through Christ and His redemption; Christ is presented also as the mediator of creation. All that is has come into being through Him' (*ERE*. VII. p. 516).

183. He needs no rest, and is never tired. This repudiates the Jewish and Christian idea of God 'resting' on the seventh day after His great exertion in creating the universe. 'And on the seventh day God ended his work which he had made; and he rested on the seventh day from all his work which he had made. And God blessed the seventh day, and sanctified it; because in it he had rested from all his work which God created and made (Ge. 2: 2, 3).

184. There is no occasion to employ coercion in the matter of adopting and embracing Islam as its excellence is self – evident. This is the doctrine of toleration in Islam. 'Convictions are not things that can be forced. Whatever compulsion there is, is not in religion but out of religion. Once "the way is made distinct from error" and faith and belief have taken a firm grip on the strong handle of the Truth, that service is due only to the Supreme and the Omnipotent Creator, Sustainer, and Developer of all creation: how can mistrust make us waver and hold us back from His service?' (MA.).

185. So breaking either in this world or the Next. True belief in God is our surest passport to safety both in this world and the Next. If we but adhere to faith, God's help will never fail us.

257. Allah is the Patron of those who believe. He brings them forth from darkness into light. And as for them who disbelieve, their patrons are the devils, they bring them forth from light into darkness. These are inmates of the Fire; therein they shall abide.

Section 35

258. Looked you not at him[186] who contended with Abraham regarding his Lord, because Allah had given him dominion? When Abraham said: 'My Lord is He Who gives life and causes death'; he said, 'I give life and I cause death.' Abraham said: 'Surely Allah brings the sun from the east, then bring it you from the

اللَّهُ وَلِيُّ الَّذِينَ ءَامَنُوا يُخْرِجُهُم مِّنَ الظُّلُمَٰتِ إِلَى النُّورِ وَالَّذِينَ كَفَرُوٓا أَوْلِيَآؤُهُمُ الطَّٰغُوتُ يُخْرِجُونَهُم مِّنَ النُّورِ إِلَى الظُّلُمَٰتِ أُوْلَٰٓئِكَ أَصْحَٰبُ النَّارِ هُمْ فِيهَا خَٰلِدُونَ ۝

أَلَمْ تَرَ إِلَى الَّذِى حَآجَّ إِبْرَٰهِـۧمَ فِى رَبِّهِۦٓ أَنْ ءَاتَىٰهُ اللَّهُ الْمُلْكَ إِذْ قَالَ إِبْرَٰهِـۧمُ رَبِّىَ الَّذِى يُحْىِۦ وَيُمِيتُ قَالَ أَنَا۠ أُحْىِۦ وَأُمِيتُ قَالَ إِبْرَٰهِـۧمُ فَإِنَّ اللَّهَ يَأْتِى بِالشَّمْسِ مِنَ الْمَشْرِقِ فَأْتِ بِهَا مِنَ الْمَغْرِبِ

---

186. The allusion is, according to Muslim commentators, to Nimrod, the tyrant of Chaldea and perhaps the first Babylonian hero – god, who persecuted Abraham (peace and blessings be upon him). His greatness as a king finds mention in the Bible: 'A mighty one in the earth' (Ge. 10: 8), 'a mighty hunter before the Lord' (Ge. 10: 9), and 'mighty upon the earth' (1 Ch. 1: 10), 'he ruled over the cities of Babel, Erech, Accad and Caleh, in the land of Shinar' (Ge. 10: 10), 'He was made king over all the people on earth, appointing Terah his minister. It was then, elated by so much glory, that Nimrod changed his behaviour toward Yahweh and became the most flagrant idolator' (*JE.* IX. p. 309). 'Of all the rulers who made themselves masters of lower Mesopotamia, the most famous was Sargon... and he was identified, perhaps rightly, with the Nimrod of the Old Testament who founded Caleh and was a mighty hunter before the Lord. Later documents were found which established the fact of his life and power, and now at Ur we have relics which add something to his history and illustrate the civilization of his time' (Woolley, *Ur of the Chaldees*, p. 107). 'The founder of the Babylonian monarchy. He flourished about 2450 BC, establishing a kingdom in the plain of Shinar' (*CE.* VI. 1609).

west.' Thereupon he who disbelieved was confounded. And Allah guides not wrong-doers.

259. Or such as he who passed by a town, and it lay overturned on its turrets. He said: 'How shall Allah quicken it after its death?' Thereupon Allah made him dead for a hundred years and then raised him up, and said: 'How long have you tarried?' He said, 'I have tarried a day or part of a day.' Allah said: 'Nay! You have tarried a hundred years; look at your food and your drink; they have not rotten; and look at your ass. And this We have done in order that We may make of you a sign unto men; and look you at the bones, how We shall set them up and clothe them with flesh.' Then when it became clear to him, he said: 'I know that surely Allah is Potent over everything.'

260. And recall when Abraham said: 'My Lord! Show me how You will quicken the dead.' He said: 'Do you not believe?' He said: 'Yea, but that my heart may rest at ease.' He said: 'Take four birds, and tame them unto you, and then put a part of them on each hill, and thereafter summon them; they will come to you speeding. And know then that surely Allah is the Mighty, the Wise.'

فَبُهِتَ ٱلَّذِى كَفَرَ وَٱللَّهُ لَا يَهْدِى ٱلْقَوْمَ ٱلظَّٰلِمِينَ ﴿٢٥٨﴾

أَوْ كَٱلَّذِى مَرَّ عَلَىٰ قَرْيَةٍ وَهِىَ خَاوِيَةٌ عَلَىٰ عُرُوشِهَا قَالَ أَنَّىٰ يُحْىِۦ هَٰذِهِ ٱللَّهُ بَعْدَ مَوْتِهَا فَأَمَاتَهُ ٱللَّهُ مِائَةَ عَامٍ ثُمَّ بَعَثَهُۥ قَالَ كَمْ لَبِثْتَ قَالَ لَبِثْتُ يَوْمًا أَوْ بَعْضَ يَوْمٍ قَالَ بَل لَّبِثْتَ مِائَةَ عَامٍ فَٱنظُرْ إِلَىٰ طَعَامِكَ وَشَرَابِكَ لَمْ يَتَسَنَّهْ وَٱنظُرْ إِلَىٰ حِمَارِكَ وَلِنَجْعَلَكَ ءَايَةً لِّلنَّاسِ وَٱنظُرْ إِلَى ٱلْعِظَامِ كَيْفَ نُنشِزُهَا ثُمَّ نَكْسُوهَا لَحْمًا فَلَمَّا تَبَيَّنَ لَهُۥ قَالَ أَعْلَمُ أَنَّ ٱللَّهَ عَلَىٰ كُلِّ شَىْءٍ قَدِيرٌ ﴿٢٥٩﴾

وَإِذْ قَالَ إِبْرَٰهِۦمُ رَبِّ أَرِنِى كَيْفَ تُحْىِ ٱلْمَوْتَىٰ قَالَ أَوَلَمْ تُؤْمِن قَالَ بَلَىٰ وَلَٰكِن لِّيَطْمَئِنَّ قَلْبِى قَالَ فَخُذْ أَرْبَعَةً مِّنَ ٱلطَّيْرِ فَصُرْهُنَّ إِلَيْكَ ثُمَّ ٱجْعَلْ عَلَىٰ كُلِّ جَبَلٍ مِّنْهُنَّ جُزْءًا ثُمَّ ٱدْعُهُنَّ يَأْتِينَكَ سَعْيًا وَٱعْلَمْ أَنَّ ٱللَّهَ عَزِيزٌ حَكِيمٌ ﴿٢٦٠﴾

Section 36

261. The likeness of those who spend their riches in the way of Allah is as the likeness of a grain that grows seven ears and in each ear one hundred grains; and Allah multiplies unto whom He will. And Allah is the Bountiful, the Knowing.

مَّثَلُ الَّذِينَ يُنفِقُونَ أَمْوَالَهُمْ فِى سَبِيلِ اللَّهِ كَمَثَلِ حَبَّةٍ أَنبَتَتْ سَبْعَ سَنَابِلَ فِى كُلِّ سُنبُلَةٍ مِّائَةُ حَبَّةٍ وَاللَّهُ يُضَاعِفُ لِمَن يَشَاءُ وَاللَّهُ وَاسِعٌ عَلِيمٌ ۝

262. Those who spend their riches in the way of Allah and do not follow up what they have spent by taunt or injury, therein is their wage with Allah, on them shall come no fear, nor shall they grieve.

الَّذِينَ يُنفِقُونَ أَمْوَالَهُمْ فِى سَبِيلِ اللَّهِ ثُمَّ لَا يُتْبِعُونَ مَا أَنفَقُوا مَنًّا وَلَا أَذًى لَّهُمْ أَجْرُهُمْ عِندَ رَبِّهِمْ وَلَا خَوْفٌ عَلَيْهِمْ وَلَا هُمْ يَحْزَنُونَ ۝

263. And honourable word and forgiveness are better than alms followed by injury; and Allah is the Self-Suffing, the Forbearing.

قَوْلٌ مَّعْرُوفٌ وَمَغْفِرَةٌ خَيْرٌ مِّن صَدَقَةٍ يَتْبَعُهَا أَذًى وَاللَّهُ غَنِيٌّ حَلِيمٌ ۝

264. O you who believe! Void not your charities by taunt and by harm,[187] like unto him who spends his riches to be seen of men, and does not believe in Allah and the Last Day. The likeness of him is as the likeness of a smooth rock on which is dust; a torrent falls on it and leaves it bare. They shall not have power over aught they have earned. And Allah guides not an infidel people.

يَا أَيُّهَا الَّذِينَ ءَامَنُوا لَا تُبْطِلُوا صَدَقَاتِكُم بِالْمَنِّ وَالْأَذَىٰ كَالَّذِى يُنفِقُ مَالَهُ رِئَاءَ النَّاسِ وَلَا يُؤْمِنُ بِاللَّهِ وَالْيَوْمِ الْآخِرِ فَمَثَلُهُ كَمَثَلِ صَفْوَانٍ عَلَيْهِ تُرَابٌ فَأَصَابَهُ وَابِلٌ فَتَرَكَهُ صَلْدًا لَّا يَقْدِرُونَ عَلَىٰ شَيْءٍ مِّمَّا كَسَبُوا وَاللَّهُ لَا يَهْدِى الْقَوْمَ الْكَافِرِينَ ۝

---

187. Very noticeable is the emphasis which the Holy Qur'ān lays on the standard of charity being kept high. The kindly feeling of the giver is far more valuable than the gift itself.

265. And the parable of them who spend their riches seeking the pleasure of Allah[188] and for the strengthening of their souls is as the parable of a garden on high; a torrent falls on it, and it yields its fruits twofold; and if no torrent falls on it, then even a gentle rain. And Allah is the Beholder of whatever you do.

وَمَثَلُ ٱلَّذِينَ يُنفِقُونَ أَمْوَٰلَهُمُ ٱبْتِغَآءَ مَرْضَاتِ ٱللَّهِ وَتَثْبِيتًا مِّنْ أَنفُسِهِمْ كَمَثَلِ جَنَّةٍ بِرَبْوَةٍ أَصَابَهَا وَابِلٌ فَـَٔاتَتْ أُكُلَهَا ضِعْفَيْنِ فَإِن لَّمْ يُصِبْهَا وَابِلٌ فَطَلٌّ وَٱللَّهُ بِمَا تَعْمَلُونَ بَصِيرٌ ﴿٢٦٥﴾

266. Would any of you have for himself a garden of date-palms and grape-vines beneath which rivers flow and all sorts of fruits therein are for him, then old age should befall him while he has a progeny of weaklings, and that thereafter a whirlwind wherein is fire should smite it, so that all is consumed? Thus does Allah expound to you His signs that haply you may ponder.

أَيَوَدُّ أَحَدُكُمْ أَن تَكُونَ لَهُۥ جَنَّةٌ مِّن نَّخِيلٍ وَأَعْنَابٍ تَجْرِى مِن تَحْتِهَا ٱلْأَنْهَٰرُ لَهُۥ فِيهَا مِن كُلِّ ٱلثَّمَرَٰتِ وَأَصَابَهُ ٱلْكِبَرُ وَلَهُۥ ذُرِّيَّةٌ ضُعَفَآءُ فَأَصَابَهَآ إِعْصَارٌ فِيهِ نَارٌ فَٱحْتَرَقَتْ كَذَٰلِكَ يُبَيِّنُ ٱللَّهُ لَكُمُ ٱلْـَٔايَٰتِ لَعَلَّكُمْ تَتَفَكَّرُونَ ﴿٢٦٦﴾

Section 37

267. O you who believe! Spend out of the good things you have earned and of what We have produced for you from the earth; and seek not the vile of it to spend, whereas you yourselves would not accept such except that you connived at it. And know that Allah is the Self-Sufficing, the Praiseworthy.

يَـٰٓأَيُّهَا ٱلَّذِينَ ءَامَنُوٓا۟ أَنفِقُوا۟ مِن طَيِّبَٰتِ مَا كَسَبْتُمْ وَمِمَّآ أَخْرَجْنَا لَكُم مِّنَ ٱلْأَرْضِ وَلَا تَيَمَّمُوا۟ ٱلْخَبِيثَ مِنْهُ تُنفِقُونَ وَلَسْتُم بِـَٔاخِذِيهِ إِلَّآ أَن تُغْمِضُوا۟ فِيهِ وَٱعْلَمُوٓا۟ أَنَّ ٱللَّهَ غَنِىٌّ حَمِيدٌ ﴿٢٦٧﴾

---

188. This seeking of the goodwill of the Lord is the only real motivating force with all true believers in every action of theirs.

268. Satan threatens you with poverty,[189] and commands you to ungodliness, whereas Allah promises you forgiveness from Himself and abundance; and Allah is the Bountiful, the Knowing.

ٱلشَّيْطَـٰنُ يَعِدُكُمُ ٱلْفَقْرَ وَيَأْمُرُكُم بِٱلْفَحْشَآءِ وَٱللَّهُ يَعِدُكُم مَّغْفِرَةً مِّنْهُ وَفَضْلًا وَٱللَّهُ وَٰسِعٌ عَلِيمٌ ۝

269. He grants wisdom to whom He will, and he who is granted wisdom is indeed granted abundant good, and none receives admonition save men of understanding.

يُؤْتِى ٱلْحِكْمَةَ مَن يَشَآءُ وَمَن يُؤْتَ ٱلْحِكْمَةَ فَقَدْ أُوتِىَ خَيْرًا كَثِيرًا وَمَا يَذَّكَّرُ إِلَّآ أُوْلُوا ٱلْأَلْبَـٰبِ ۝

270. And whatever you spend or whatever you vow, surely Allah knows them, and for the ungodly there will be no helpers.

وَمَآ أَنفَقْتُم مِّن نَّفَقَةٍ أَوْ نَذَرْتُم مِّن نَّذْرٍ فَإِنَّ ٱللَّهَ يَعْلَمُهُ وَمَا لِلظَّـٰلِمِينَ مِنْ أَنصَارٍ ۝

271. If you publish the alms, even so it is well, and if you conceal them and give them to the poor, it will be better for you, and He will expiate some of your misdeeds. Allah is Aware of what you do.

إِن تُبْدُوا ٱلصَّدَقَـٰتِ فَنِعِمَّا هِىَ وَإِن تُخْفُوهَا وَتُؤْتُوهَا ٱلْفُقَرَآءَ فَهُوَ خَيْرٌ لَّكُمْ وَيُكَفِّرُ عَنكُم مِّن سَيِّـَٔاتِكُمْ وَٱللَّهُ بِمَا تَعْمَلُونَ خَبِيرٌ ۝

272. Not on you is their guidance, but Allah guides whom He will.[190] And whatsoever of good you spend, it is for your own souls; and you spend not save to seek

لَّيْسَ عَلَيْكَ هُدَىٰهُمْ وَلَـٰكِنَّ ٱللَّهَ يَهْدِى مَن يَشَآءُ وَمَا تُنفِقُوا مِنْ خَيْرٍ فَلِأَنفُسِكُمْ وَمَا تُنفِقُونَ

---

189. The devil instills the fear in your mind that you shall be reduced to poverty by your contributing liberally to the works of charity and public good.

190. Guides whom He will in accordance with His universal plan. So relief may unhesitatingly be given to anyone in distress whether believing or disbelieving. Nobody is to be denied help on account of his unbelief. Some Muslims in the Prophet's time hesitated to support the infidel paupers. This verse removes such doubts.

Allah's countenance, and whatever of good you spend shall be repaid to you, and you shall not be wronged.

إِلَّا ابْتِغَاءَ وَجْهِ اللَّهِ وَمَا تُنفِقُوا مِنْ خَيْرٍ يُوَفَّ إِلَيْكُمْ وَأَنتُمْ لَا تُظْلَمُونَ ﴿٢٧٢﴾

273. Charities are for the poor who are sustained in the way of Allah, disabled from going about in the land. The unknowing takes them for the affluent because of their modesty, you would recognize them by their mark, they beg not of men because of their modesty. And whatever of good you will spend, surely Allah is the Knower thereof.

لِلْفُقَرَاءِ الَّذِينَ أُحْصِرُوا فِي سَبِيلِ اللَّهِ لَا يَسْتَطِيعُونَ ضَرْبًا فِي الْأَرْضِ يَحْسَبُهُمُ الْجَاهِلُ أَغْنِيَاءَ مِنَ التَّعَفُّفِ تَعْرِفُهُم بِسِيمَاهُمْ لَا يَسْأَلُونَ النَّاسَ إِلْحَافًا وَمَا تُنفِقُوا مِنْ خَيْرٍ فَإِنَّ اللَّهَ بِهِ عَلِيمٌ ﴿٢٧٣﴾

Section 38

274. Those who spend their riches night and day, secretly and openly, their reward shall be therein with their Lord; no fear shall come on them, nor shall they grieve.

الَّذِينَ يُنفِقُونَ أَمْوَالَهُم بِالَّيْلِ وَالنَّهَارِ سِرًّا وَعَلَانِيَةً فَلَهُمْ أَجْرُهُمْ عِندَ رَبِّهِمْ وَلَا خَوْفٌ عَلَيْهِمْ وَلَا هُمْ يَحْزَنُونَ ﴿٢٧٤﴾

275. Those who devour usury[191] shall not be able to stand except as stands he whom Satan has confounded with his touch. This is

الَّذِينَ يَأْكُلُونَ الرِّبَا لَا يَقُومُونَ إِلَّا كَمَا يَقُومُ الَّذِي يَتَخَبَّطُهُ الشَّيْطَانُ مِنَ الْمَسِّ

---

191. The Arabic word is but partially covered by the English word usury which, in modern parlance, signifies only an exorbitant or extortionate interest. The Arabic expression al-Ribā, or the other hand, means any addition, however slight, over and above the principal sum lent, and this includes both usury and interest. In the language of modern socialism, interest is an unjustifiable tax on the labouring classes, the unpaid wage of the labourer. According to socialist writers of today, money is lent by them who have abundance and returns to them to increase that abundance, the increase being the unpaid dues of labour, which is the only source of wealth — the rich are thus made richer and the poor poorer, by every fresh act of taking interest, and the stability of the social organism is thus disturbed.

because they say: 'Trade is but as usury' whereas Allah has allowed trade[192] and has forbidden usury.[193] So he who receives an admonition from his Lord, and has desisted, may keep what is past, and his affair is with Allah, but he who reverts – such shall be the inmates of the Fire, therein they shall abide.

ذَٰلِكَ بِأَنَّهُمْ قَالُوٓا۟ إِنَّمَا ٱلْبَيْعُ مِثْلُ ٱلرِّبَوٰا۟ وَأَحَلَّ ٱللَّهُ ٱلْبَيْعَ وَحَرَّمَ ٱلرِّبَوٰا۟ فَمَن جَآءَهُۥ مَوْعِظَةٌ مِّن رَّبِّهِۦ فَٱنتَهَىٰ فَلَهُۥ مَا سَلَفَ وَأَمْرُهُۥٓ إِلَى ٱللَّهِ وَمَنْ عَادَ فَأُو۟لَٰٓئِكَ أَصْحَٰبُ ٱلنَّارِ هُمْ فِيهَا خَٰلِدُونَ ﴿٢٧٥﴾

---

192. Thus there is a world of difference between the two. The Author of all laws, physical as well as moral, has allowed the one and disallowed the other. What greater difference could there conceivably be between any two things in the world? The one was comparable to light; the other to darkness. Money–lending, it has truly been remarked, is neither a profession nor a trade. It is not a profession since it calls for no special education or technical knowledge. It is not a trade since there is no sale of any kind in it. It is an occupation, and one of the dirtiest since it takes mean advantage of human distress and thrives on it. Those who are engaged in this business, are as a rule callously mean, who find that the easiest way of increasing their riches is by taking advantage of men in distress who may safely be dominated and bullied.

193. The devastating propensities of usury are visible to every eye. The evils attendant on it are neither few nor far between – the callousness it engenders, the profligacy it lets loose, the greed it encourages, the jealousy it breeds, the misery it entails, the abjectness it inculcates, and so on. Yet it is Islam alone that has the unique distinction of declaring this pernicious practice illegal, absolutely and unconditionally. Greece and Rome both groaned heavily under its yoke, but none of their legislators, like the economists of modern Europe, thought of banning it altogether. In Greece, 'the bulk of the population became gradually indebted to the rich to such an extent that they were practically slaves', and 'usury had given all the power of the state to a small plutocracy' (*EBr.* XXVII. p. 812, 11th Ed.). The Romans fared still worse. 'The attempt to regulate the rate of interest utterly failed. In the course of two or three centuries the small free farmers were utterly destroyed. By the pressure of war and taxes they were all driven into debt, and debt ended practically, if not technically, in slavery' (Ibid.). With all these horrors experienced and patiently borne, nobody ventured to eradicate the evil root and branch. The utmost that a Solon among the ancients or a Bacon among the moderns could advise was to 'grind the tooth of usury, that it bite not too much, that is to say, to regulate its rate, without attaching the slightest moral taint to the usurer'. The Bible went no doubt many steps further inasmuch as it forbade the advance of usurious loans to the Israelites (Ex. 22: 25: DT. 23: 19). But even the Biblical prohibition did not include usurious loans to non-Israelites. It is the Holy Qur'ān which, to its everlasting glory, has categorically forbidden usury in all its forms.

276. Allah obliterates usury, and augments charity. And Allah loves not any ungrateful sinner.

يَمْحَقُ ٱللَّهُ ٱلرِّبَوٰا۟ وَيُرْبِى ٱلصَّدَقَٰتِ وَٱللَّهُ لَا يُحِبُّ كُلَّ كَفَّارٍ أَثِيمٍ ﴿٢٧٦﴾

277. Surely those who believe and work righteously and establish prayer and pay the poor-rate, their reward shall be then with their Lord; and no fear shall come on them nor shall they grieve.

إِنَّ ٱلَّذِينَ ءَامَنُوا۟ وَعَمِلُوا۟ ٱلصَّٰلِحَٰتِ وَأَقَامُوا۟ ٱلصَّلَوٰةَ وَءَاتَوُا۟ ٱلزَّكَوٰةَ لَهُمْ أَجْرُهُمْ عِندَ رَبِّهِمْ وَلَا خَوْفٌ عَلَيْهِمْ وَلَا هُمْ يَحْزَنُونَ ﴿٢٧٧﴾

278. O you who believe! Fear Allah and waive what has yet remained of the usury due to you, if you are believers.

يَٰٓأَيُّهَا ٱلَّذِينَ ءَامَنُوا۟ ٱتَّقُوا۟ ٱللَّهَ وَذَرُوا۟ مَا بَقِىَ مِنَ ٱلرِّبَوٰٓا۟ إِن كُنتُم مُّؤْمِنِينَ ﴿٢٧٨﴾

279. But if you do not, then beware of war from Allah and His Messenger. And if you repent, yours shall be your principal sums; neither wrong others nor be wronged yourselves.

فَإِن لَّمْ تَفْعَلُوا۟ فَأْذَنُوا۟ بِحَرْبٍ مِّنَ ٱللَّهِ وَرَسُولِهِۦ وَإِن تُبْتُمْ فَلَكُمْ رُءُوسُ أَمْوَٰلِكُمْ لَا تَظْلِمُونَ وَلَا تُظْلَمُونَ ﴿٢٧٩﴾

280. And if one should be in difficulty, then let there be a respite till easiness. But if you waive the sum, it will be better for you, if you but know.

وَإِن كَانَ ذُو عُسْرَةٍ فَنَظِرَةٌ إِلَىٰ مَيْسَرَةٍ وَأَن تَصَدَّقُوا۟ خَيْرٌ لَّكُمْ إِن كُنتُمْ تَعْلَمُونَ ﴿٢٨٠﴾

281. And fear the Day when you shall be brought back to Allah, then each soul shall be repaid in full what he has earned and they shall not be wronged.

وَٱتَّقُوا۟ يَوْمًا تُرْجَعُونَ فِيهِ إِلَى ٱللَّهِ ثُمَّ تُوَفَّىٰ كُلُّ نَفْسٍ مَّا كَسَبَتْ وَهُمْ لَا يُظْلَمُونَ ﴿٢٨١﴾

Section 39

282. O you who believe! When you borrow one from another for a time stated, write it down, and let a scribe write it down justly between you, and let not the scribe refuse to write according as Allah has taught him. So let him write then, and let the debtor dictate, and let him fear Allah, his Lord, and diminish not aught of it. But if he who owes is witless or infirm or unable to dictate, then let his guardian dictate justly. And call to witness two witnesses of your men, and if the two be not men, then a man and two women[194] of those you agree upon as witnesses, so that if one of the two errs, then the other will remind her. And let not the witnesses refuse when they are called on. And be not loth to write it down, be it small or big, with its term: this is most equitable in the sight of Allah and most upright for testimony, and likelier that you will not be in doubt – unless it be a transaction concluded on the spot between you; for then there shall be no blame on you if you do not write it down. And call witnesses when

يَـٰٓأَيُّهَا ٱلَّذِينَ ءَامَنُوٓاْ إِذَا تَدَايَنتُم بِدَيۡنٍ إِلَىٰٓ أَجَلٍ مُّسَمًّى فَٱكۡتُبُوهُ وَلۡيَكۡتُب بَّيۡنَكُمۡ كَاتِبُۢ بِٱلۡعَدۡلِ وَلَا يَأۡبَ كَاتِبٌ أَن يَكۡتُبَ كَمَا عَلَّمَهُ ٱللَّهُ فَلۡيَكۡتُبۡ وَلۡيُمۡلِلِ ٱلَّذِي عَلَيۡهِ ٱلۡحَقُّ وَلۡيَتَّقِ ٱللَّهَ رَبَّهُۥ وَلَا يَبۡخَسۡ مِنۡهُ شَيۡـًٔا فَإِن كَانَ ٱلَّذِي عَلَيۡهِ ٱلۡحَقُّ سَفِيهًا أَوۡ ضَعِيفًا أَوۡ لَا يَسۡتَطِيعُ أَن يُمِلَّ هُوَ فَلۡيُمۡلِلۡ وَلِيُّهُۥ بِٱلۡعَدۡلِۚ وَٱسۡتَشۡهِدُواْ شَهِيدَيۡنِ مِن رِّجَالِكُمۡۖ فَإِن لَّمۡ يَكُونَا رَجُلَيۡنِ فَرَجُلٌ وَٱمۡرَأَتَانِ مِمَّن تَرۡضَوۡنَ مِنَ ٱلشُّهَدَآءِ أَن تَضِلَّ إِحۡدَىٰهُمَا فَتُذَكِّرَ إِحۡدَىٰهُمَا ٱلۡأُخۡرَىٰۚ وَلَا يَأۡبَ ٱلشُّهَدَآءُ إِذَا مَا دُعُواْۚ وَلَا تَسۡـَٔمُوٓاْ أَن تَكۡتُبُوهُ صَغِيرًا أَوۡ كَبِيرًا إِلَىٰٓ أَجَلِهِۦۚ ذَٰلِكُمۡ أَقۡسَطُ عِندَ ٱللَّهِ وَأَقۡوَمُ لِلشَّهَٰدَةِ وَأَدۡنَىٰٓ أَلَّا تَرۡتَابُوٓاْ إِلَّآ أَن تَكُونَ تِجَٰرَةً حَاضِرَةً تُدِيرُونَهَا بَيۡنَكُمۡ فَلَيۡسَ عَلَيۡكُمۡ جُنَاحٌ أَلَّا تَكۡتُبُوهَاۗ وَأَشۡهِدُوٓاْ إِذَا تَبَايَعۡتُمۡ

---

194. In the Jewish code the testimony of a woman is inadmissible. 'The witnesses must be men, not women or minors' (*ET*. p. 326). 'Let not the testimony of women be admitted, on account of the levity and boldness of their sex' (*Ant*. IV. 8: 15). 'The witness must be a man, not a woman' (JE. V. p. 277).

you are transacting business with one another; and let not the scribe come to harm nor the witness; and if you do, surely it shall be ungodliness in you. Fear Allah: and Allah teaches you;[195] and Allah is the Knower of everything.

وَلَا يُضَآرَّ كَاتِبٌ وَلَا شَهِيدٌ وَإِن تَفْعَلُوا۟ فَإِنَّهُ فُسُوقٌۢ بِكُمْ وَٱتَّقُوا۟ ٱللَّهَ وَ يُعَلِّمُكُمُ ٱللَّهُ وَٱللَّهُ بِكُلِّ شَىْءٍ عَلِيمٌ ﴿٢٨٢﴾

283. And if you be journeying and you do not find a scribe, then let there be a pledge taken; then, if one of you entrusts the other, let the one who is entrusted discharge his trust, and let him fear Allah, his Lord. And do not withhold the testimony; and whoever withholds it, his heart surely is sinful. And Allah is the Knower of what you do.

وَإِن كُنتُمْ عَلَىٰ سَفَرٍ وَلَمْ تَجِدُوا۟ كَاتِبًا فَرِهَٰنٌ مَّقْبُوضَةٌ فَإِنْ أَمِنَ بَعْضُكُم بَعْضًا فَلْيُؤَدِّ ٱلَّذِى ٱؤْتُمِنَ أَمَٰنَتَهُۥ وَلْيَتَّقِ ٱللَّهَ رَبَّهُۥ وَلَا تَكْتُمُوا۟ ٱلشَّهَٰدَةَ وَمَن يَكْتُمْهَا فَإِنَّهُۥٓ ءَاثِمٌ قَلْبُهُۥ وَٱللَّهُ بِمَا تَعْمَلُونَ عَلِيمٌ ﴿٢٨٣﴾

Section 40

284. Allah's is whatever is in the heavens and whatever is in the earth, and whether you reveal what is in your mind or hide it, Allah will reckon with you therefore, then He will forgive whom He will and torment whom He will, and Allah is Potent over everything.

لِّلَّهِ مَا فِى ٱلسَّمَٰوَٰتِ وَمَا فِى ٱلْأَرْضِ وَإِن تُبْدُوا۟ مَا فِىٓ أَنفُسِكُمْ أَوْ تُخْفُوهُ يُحَاسِبْكُم بِهِ ٱللَّهُ فَيَغْفِرُ لِمَن يَشَآءُ وَيُعَذِّبُ مَن يَشَآءُ وَٱللَّهُ عَلَىٰ كُلِّ شَىْءٍ قَدِيرٌ ﴿٢٨٤﴾

---

195. Allah teaches all that is to your good. Commercial morality is here taught on the highest plane and yet in the most practical manner, both as regards the bargains to be made, the evidence to be provided, the doubts to be avoided, and the duties and rights of scribes and witnesses. Probity even in worldly matters is to be not a mere matter of convenience or policy but a matter of conscience and religious duty. Even our everyday transactions are to be carried out as in the presence of God (AYA.).

285. The Messenger believes in what is sent down to him from his Lord, and so do the believers. They all believe in Allah and His angels and His Books and His Messengers, saying: 'We discriminate not against any of His Messengers.' And they say: 'We hear and obey; Your forgiveness, our Lord! And to You is our return.'

آمَنَ ٱلرَّسُولُ بِمَا أُنزِلَ إِلَيْهِ مِن رَّبِّهِۦ وَٱلْمُؤْمِنُونَ ۚ كُلٌّ ءَامَنَ بِٱللَّهِ وَمَلَـٰٓئِكَتِهِۦ وَكُتُبِهِۦ وَرُسُلِهِۦ لَا نُفَرِّقُ بَيْنَ أَحَدٍ مِّن رُّسُلِهِۦ ۚ وَقَالُوا۟ سَمِعْنَا وَأَطَعْنَا ۖ غُفْرَانَكَ رَبَّنَا وَإِلَيْكَ ٱلْمَصِيرُ ﴿٢٨٥﴾

286. Allah charges not a soul except according to its capacity. For it shall be the good it earns,[196] and against it the evil it earns:[197] Our Lord! Reckon with us not if we forget or err. Our Lord! Burden us not like unto those You burdened before us. Our Lord! Impose not on us that for which we have not strength. And pardon us, forgive us, and have mercy on us. You are our Master, so make us triumph over the disbelieving people.

لَا يُكَلِّفُ ٱللَّهُ نَفْسًا إِلَّا وُسْعَهَا ۚ لَهَا مَا كَسَبَتْ وَعَلَيْهَا مَا ٱكْتَسَبَتْ ۗ رَبَّنَا لَا تُؤَاخِذْنَا إِن نَّسِينَا أَوْ أَخْطَأْنَا ۚ رَبَّنَا وَلَا تَحْمِلْ عَلَيْنَا إِصْرًا كَمَا حَمَلْتَهُۥ عَلَى ٱلَّذِينَ مِن قَبْلِنَا ۚ رَبَّنَا وَلَا تُحَمِّلْنَا مَا لَا طَاقَةَ لَنَا بِهِۦ ۖ وَٱعْفُ عَنَّا وَٱغْفِرْ لَنَا وَٱرْحَمْنَا ۚ أَنتَ مَوْلَىٰنَا فَٱنصُرْنَا عَلَى ٱلْقَوْمِ ٱلْكَـٰفِرِينَ ﴿٢٨٦﴾

---

196. That is earns by choice. So no one shall be held answerable for such thoughts and feelings as intrude themselves on one's mind. All non-deliberate, non- voluntary states of mind are excluded from accountability. Each one is responsible for what he acquires, or earns.

197. Similarly, what is earned by choice. So everyone must win his own redemption. In Islam there is neither an original sin nor universal redemption. Every individual must work out the propensities of his soul — his own possibilities of spiritual success or failure.

Sūrah 3

Āl 'Imrān

(Madinan, 20 Sections, 200 Verses)

*In the name of Allah, the
Compassionate, the Merciful.*

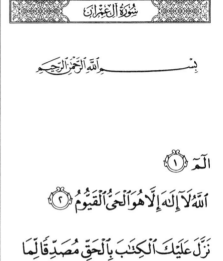

Section 1

1. *Alif, Lām, Mīm.*

2. Allah! There is no god but He,
the Living, the Sustainer.

3. He has revealed the Book to you
with Truth confirming what went
before it and He sent down the
Torah[198] and the Gospel.[199]

---

198. The Torah is certainly not identical with the OT, or even with the Pentateuch,
but is synonymous with the Torah, of which only fragments can at best be found in
the extant Pentateuch. What the Qur'ān commends as a Holy Writ is certainly not
the same book of which it is freely and openly stated that it is 'the work not of God
but of godly men'.

199. The Gospel is not at all identical with the NT or even the Four Gospels of the
Christian Church. The Gospel, according to the teachings of Islam, was a Book
sent down on Jesus (on whom be peace), not a collection of reports and stories
about him compiled at dubious dates by unknown persons, 'an undesigned and
unforeseen product of the apostolic age' (*EBr.* III. p. 513). The NT, according to
Christian belief, far from being the Revealed Word of God, 'was or is no "book" at
all, properly speaking, but a collection of writings, a great many of which were at the
outset not destined for publication and multiplication. Sentences may have been
abbreviated or expressions changed. It is similar with the Gospels. When the first
collection of sayings of Jesus or the first narrative of His deeds was set down in
writing, the next who copied it might feel inclined to enlarge it or to change any
detail according to the form in which he had heard it, without any bad intention ...
It is not possible here to count up all the ways in which errors may originate' (*DB.*
IV. pp. 732–735). In the words of Bishop Gore, 'it was a calamity that verbal infallibility
was ever claimed for them (the Gospel Documents)' (Renan, *Life of Jesus*, p. XII).

4. Aforetime, for a guidance to the people and sent down the criterion. Surely those who deny the signs of Allah, for them shall be a terrible torment, and Allah is the Mighty, the Lord of Retribution.

مِن قَبْلُ هُدًى لِّلنَّاسِ وَأَنزَلَ ٱلْفُرْقَانَّ إِنَّ ٱلَّذِينَ كَفَرُواْ بِـَٔايَٰتِ ٱللَّهِ لَهُمْ عَذَابٌ شَدِيدٌ وَٱللَّهُ عَزِيزٌ ذُو ٱنتِقَامٍ ٤

5. Surely Allah! Nothing is hidden from Him in the earth or in the heaven.

إِنَّ ٱللَّهَ لَا يَخْفَىٰ عَلَيْهِ شَىْءٌ فِى ٱلْأَرْضِ وَلَا فِى ٱلسَّمَآءِ ٥

6. He it is Who fashions you in the wombs as He will; there is no god but He, the Mighty, the Wise!

هُوَ ٱلَّذِى يُصَوِّرُكُمْ فِى ٱلْأَرْحَامِ كَيْفَ يَشَآءُ لَا إِلَٰهَ إِلَّا هُوَ ٱلْعَزِيزُ ٱلْحَكِيمُ ٦

7. He it is Who has sent down to you the Book in which some verses are firmly constructed they are the essence of the Book; and others consimilar. But those in whose hearts is a deviation follow only what is consimilar therein, seeking dissension and seeking to misinterpret the same whereas none knows their interpretation save Allah.[200] And the firmly grounded in knowledge say: 'We believe in it, it is all from our Lord;' and none receives admonition save men of understanding.

هُوَ ٱلَّذِىٓ أَنزَلَ عَلَيْكَ ٱلْكِتَٰبَ مِنْهُ ءَايَٰتٌ مُّحْكَمَٰتٌ هُنَّ أُمُّ ٱلْكِتَٰبِ وَأُخَرُ مُتَشَٰبِهَٰتٌ فَأَمَّا ٱلَّذِينَ فِى قُلُوبِهِمْ زَيْغٌ فَيَتَّبِعُونَ مَا تَشَٰبَهَ مِنْهُ ٱبْتِغَآءَ ٱلْفِتْنَةِ وَٱبْتِغَآءَ تَأْوِيلِهِۦ وَمَا يَعْلَمُ تَأْوِيلَهُۥٓ إِلَّا ٱللَّهُ وَٱلرَّٰسِخُونَ فِى ٱلْعِلْمِ يَقُولُونَ ءَامَنَّا بِهِۦ كُلٌّ مِّنْ عِندِ رَبِّنَا وَمَا يَذَّكَّرُ إِلَّآ أُوْلُواْ ٱلْأَلْبَٰبِ ٧

8. Our Lord! Suffer not our hearts to deviate after that which You have guided us to, and bestow on us from Your presence mercy. Surely it is You Who are the Bestower!

رَبَّنَا لَا تُزِغْ قُلُوبَنَا بَعْدَ إِذْ هَدَيْتَنَا وَهَبْ لَنَا مِن لَّدُنكَ رَحْمَةً إِنَّكَ أَنتَ ٱلْوَهَّابُ ٨

---

200. He can give that true interpretation either in the Qur'ān itself, or through the *Sunnah* of His Prophet. Hence the importance of the *Sunnah* as, next to the Qur'ān, the source of Islamic law.

9. Our Lord! Surely You are the assembler of mankind on a Day of which there is doubt. Surely Allah does not fail His promise.

رَبَّنَا إِنَّكَ جَامِعُ ٱلنَّاسِ لِيَوْمٍ لَّا رَيْبَ فِيهِ إِنَّ ٱللَّهَ لَا يُخْلِفُ ٱلْمِيعَادَ ﴿٩﴾

Section 2

10. Surely those who disbelieve, neither their riches nor their offspring will avail them aught against Allah, and it is they who shall become the fuel of the Fire.

إِنَّ ٱلَّذِينَ كَفَرُوا لَن تُغْنِيَ عَنْهُمْ أَمْوَٰلُهُمْ وَلَا أَوْلَٰدُهُم مِّنَ ٱللَّهِ شَيْـًٔا وَأُوْلَٰٓئِكَ هُمْ وَقُودُ ٱلنَّارِ ﴿١٠﴾

11. Like Pharoah's folk and those before them. They belied Our signs, so Allah seized them for their sins. And Allah is Terrible in chastising.

كَدَأْبِ ءَالِ فِرْعَوْنَ وَٱلَّذِينَ مِن قَبْلِهِمْ كَذَّبُوا بِـَٔايَٰتِنَا فَأَخَذَهُمُ ٱللَّهُ بِذُنُوبِهِمْ وَٱللَّهُ شَدِيدُ ٱلْعِقَابِ ﴿١١﴾

12. Say to them who disbelieve: 'Soon shall you be overcome, and gathered unto Hell, an evil couch.'

قُل لِّلَّذِينَ كَفَرُوا سَتُغْلَبُونَ وَ تُحْشَرُونَ إِلَىٰ جَهَنَّمَ وَبِئْسَ ٱلْمِهَادُ ﴿١٢﴾

13. Indeed there has been for you a sign in the two hosts that met, one host fighting in the way of Allah, and the other disbelieving, beholding themselves with their own eyes, twice as many as they. And Allah aids with His succour whom He will. Surely in this is a lesson for men of insight.

قَدْ كَانَ لَكُمْ ءَايَةٌ فِى فِئَتَيْنِ ٱلْتَقَتَا فِئَةٌ تُقَٰتِلُ فِى سَبِيلِ ٱللَّهِ وَ أُخْرَىٰ كَافِرَةٌ يَرَوْنَهُم مِّثْلَيْهِمْ رَأْىَ ٱلْعَيْنِ وَٱللَّهُ يُؤَيِّدُ بِنَصْرِهِ مَن يَشَآءُ إِنَّ فِى ذَٰلِكَ لَعِبْرَةً لِّأُوْلِى ٱلْأَبْصَٰرِ ﴿١٣﴾

14. Fair-seeming to mankind is made the love of pleasurable things from women and offspring and treasures hoarded of gold and silver and horses branded and cattle and tilth. All that is the enjoyment of the life of this world and with Allah is the best resort.

زُيِّنَ لِلنَّاسِ حُبُّ ٱلشَّهَوَٰتِ مِنَ ٱلنِّسَآءِ وَٱلْبَنِينَ وَٱلْقَنَٰطِيرِ ٱلْمُقَنطَرَةِ مِنَ ٱلذَّهَبِ وَٱلْفِضَّةِ وَٱلْخَيْلِ ٱلْمُسَوَّمَةِ وَٱلْأَنْعَٰمِ وَٱلْحَرْثِ ذَٰلِكَ مَتَٰعُ ٱلْحَيَوٰةِ ٱلدُّنْيَا وَٱللَّهُ عِندَهُۥ حُسْنُ ٱلْمَـَٔابِ ﴿١٤﴾

15. Say: 'Shall I declare to you what is far better than these?' For those who fear Allah are gardens with their Lord beneath which rivers flow where they shall abide, and spouses clean, and the goodwill of Allah. And Allah is the Beholder of His servants.

قُلْ أَؤُنَبِّئُكُم بِخَيْرٍ مِّن ذَٰلِكُمْ لِلَّذِينَ ٱتَّقَوْا۟ عِندَ رَبِّهِمْ جَنَّٰتٌ تَجْرِى مِن تَحْتِهَا ٱلْأَنْهَٰرُ خَٰلِدِينَ فِيهَا وَأَزْوَٰجٌ مُّطَهَّرَةٌ وَرِضْوَٰنٌ مِّنَ ٱللَّهِ وَٱللَّهُ بَصِيرٌۢ بِٱلْعِبَادِ ﴿١٥﴾

16. Who say: 'Our Lord! Surely we have believed so forgive us our sins, and keep us away from the torment of the Fire.'

ٱلَّذِينَ يَقُولُونَ رَبَّنَآ إِنَّنَآ ءَامَنَّا فَٱغْفِرْ لَنَا ذُنُوبَنَا وَقِنَا عَذَابَ ٱلنَّارِ ﴿١٦﴾

17. The steadfast ones and the truthful ones and the devout ones and the spenders in charity, and the ones praying at early dawn for forgiveness.

ٱلصَّٰبِرِينَ وَٱلصَّٰدِقِينَ وَٱلْقَٰنِتِينَ وَٱلْمُنفِقِينَ وَٱلْمُسْتَغْفِرِينَ بِٱلْأَسْحَارِ ﴿١٧﴾

18. Allah bears witness and also the angels and those endowed with knowledge that there is no god but He, the Maintainer of equity; there is no god but He, the Mighty, the Wise.

شَهِدَ ٱللَّهُ أَنَّهُۥ لَآ إِلَٰهَ إِلَّا هُوَ وَٱلْمَلَٰٓئِكَةُ وَأُو۟لُوا۟ ٱلْعِلْمِ قَآئِمًۢا بِٱلْقِسْطِ لَآ إِلَٰهَ إِلَّا هُوَ ٱلْعَزِيزُ ٱلْحَكِيمُ ﴿١٨﴾

19. Surely the true faith with Allah is Islam[201] and those who were given the Book disputed not among themselves save after the knowledge had come to them, out of spite among themselves. And he who disbelieves in the revelations of Allah, then surely Allah is Swift in reckoning.

إِنَّ ٱلدِّينَ عِندَ ٱللَّهِ ٱلْإِسْلَمُ وَمَا ٱخْتَلَفَ ٱلَّذِينَ أُوتُوا ٱلْكِتَبَ إِلَّا مِنۢ بَعْدِ مَا جَآءَهُمُ ٱلْعِلْمُ بَغْيًا بَيْنَهُمْ وَمَن يَكْفُرْ بِـَٔايَتِ ٱللَّهِ فَإِنَّ ٱللَّهَ سَرِيعُ ٱلْحِسَابِ ﴿١٩﴾

20. So if they contend with you, say: 'I have surrendered myself to Allah and also he who follows me.' And say to those who have been given the Book and to the illiterates, 'accept Islam.' Then if they accept Islam they are indeed guided but if they turn away then upon you is only the preaching and Allah is the Beholder of His servants.

فَإِنْ حَآجُّوكَ فَقُلْ أَسْلَمْتُ وَجْهِىَ لِلَّهِ وَمَنِ ٱتَّبَعَنِ وَقُل لِّلَّذِينَ أُوتُوا ٱلْكِتَبَ وَ ٱلْأُمِّيِّنَ ءَأَسْلَمْتُمْ فَإِنْ أَسْلَمُوا فَقَدِ ٱهْتَدَوا وَّإِن تَوَلَّوْا فَإِنَّمَا عَلَيْكَ ٱلْبَلَغُ وَٱللَّهُ بَصِيرٌ بِٱلْعِبَادِ ﴿٢٠﴾

---

201. Islam alone. Islam is the technical name of the creed preached by the Prophet. It has been the Religion of all Prophets in all climes, other religions (so-called) being only so many deviations from it. No Religion is acceptable with God save Islam, which consists in acknowledging the Unity and Soleness of God and embracing the Code which Muhammad (peace be on him) brought. Literally, and in practice, it is 'self-surrender'. 'Submission, absolute surrender to the divine will was a fit designation of the faith revealed to Abraham, Ishmael, and the Arabs' (Torrey, *Jewish Foundations of Islam*, p. 104). Islam, the name applied by Muhammad himself to his religion, means the religion of resignation, submission to the will, the service, the commands of God' (Klein, *The Religion of Islam*, p. 1).

Section 3

21. Surely those who disbelieve in the revelations of Allah and put to death the Prophets without right and kill those among mankind who enjoin equity, announce to them an afflictive torment.

إِنَّ ٱلَّذِينَ يَكۡفُرُونَ بِـَٔايَٰتِ ٱللَّهِ وَ
يَقۡتُلُونَ ٱلنَّبِيِّـۧنَ بِغَيۡرِ حَقٍّ
وَيَقۡتُلُونَ ٱلَّذِينَ يَأۡمُرُونَ
بِٱلۡقِسۡطِ مِنَ ٱلنَّاسِ فَبَشِّرۡهُم
بِعَذَابٍ أَلِيمٍ ۝

22. These are they whose works have come to naught in this world and the Hereafter. Nor shall they have helpers.

أُوْلَٰٓئِكَ ٱلَّذِينَ حَبِطَتۡ أَعۡمَٰلُهُمۡ
فِى ٱلدُّنۡيَا وَٱلۡأٓخِرَةِ وَمَا لَهُم
مِّن نَّٰصِرِينَ ۝

23. Have you not observed those given a portion of the Book called to the Book of Allah, that it may judge between them? Then a party of them turns away unheeding.

أَلَمۡ تَرَ إِلَى ٱلَّذِينَ أُوتُواْ نَصِيبٗا مِّنَ
ٱلۡكِتَٰبِ يُدۡعَوۡنَ إِلَىٰ كِتَٰبِ ٱللَّهِ
لِيَحۡكُمَ بَيۡنَهُمۡ ثُمَّ يَتَوَلَّىٰ فَرِيقٞ مِّنۡهُمۡ
وَهُم مُّعۡرِضُونَ ۝

24. This is because they say: 'The Fire shall not touch us save a few days numbered. And what they have been fabricating has deluded them in their religion.'

ذَٰلِكَ بِأَنَّهُمۡ قَالُواْ لَن تَمَسَّنَا ٱلنَّارُ إِلَّآ
أَيَّامٗا مَّعۡدُودَٰتٖۖ وَغَرَّهُمۡ فِى دِينِهِم مَّا
كَانُواْ يَفۡتَرُونَ ۝

25. How will it be then when He gathers them on the Day about which there is no doubt, and every soul shall be repaid what it has earned; and they shall not be wronged?

فَكَيۡفَ إِذَا جَمَعۡنَٰهُمۡ لِيَوۡمٖ لَّا رَيۡبَ فِيهِ
وَوُفِّيَتۡ كُلُّ نَفۡسٖ مَّا كَسَبَتۡ
وَهُمۡ لَا يُظۡلَمُونَ ۝

26. Say: 'O Allah, Sovereign of the dominion! You give dominion to whom You will,[202] and You take away dominion from whom You will. You exalt whom You will,[203] and You abase whom You will. And in Your hand is the good; and surely You are Potent over everything.

قُلِ ٱللَّهُمَّ مَٰلِكَ ٱلۡمُلۡكِ تُؤۡتِى ٱلۡمُلۡكَ مَن تَشَآءُ وَتَنزِعُ ٱلۡمُلۡكَ مِمَّن تَشَآءُ وَتُعِزُّ مَن تَشَآءُ وَتُذِلُّ مَن تَشَآءُ بِيَدِكَ ٱلۡخَيۡرُ إِنَّكَ عَلَىٰ كُلِّ شَىۡءٍ قَدِيرٌ ۝

27. You plunge night into day and You plunge day into night; and You bring forth the living from the lifeless, and You bring forth the lifeless from the living; and You provide for whom You will without stint.'

تُولِجُ ٱلَّيۡلَ فِى ٱلنَّهَارِ وَتُولِجُ ٱلنَّهَارَ فِى ٱلَّيۡلِ وَتُخۡرِجُ ٱلۡحَىَّ مِنَ ٱلۡمَيِّتِ وَتُخۡرِجُ ٱلۡمَيِّتَ مِنَ ٱلۡحَىِّ وَتَرۡزُقُ مَن تَشَآءُ بِغَيۡرِ حِسَابٍ ۝

---

202. Contrast with this the Hindu idea that the king 'is a great deity in human form' (*ERE.* VII. p. 720), and that among 'eight sacred objects which must be reverenced, worshipped, and circumambulated sun – wise, the eight is a King' (Ibid.). In Islam, a king is a king, a mere man, not a godling. This strikes at the root of 'the Divine right of the king' and all forms of king-worship and emperor-worship, the Pharaoh-worship of the Egyptians and the Mikado-worship of the Japanese.

203. Contrast with this simple Godlike teaching of Islam the amazing theories and grotesque practices of Christian Europe. The principle that kingship is descendible in one sacred family... is not only still that of the British constitution, as that of all monarchical states, but is practically that of kingship from the beginning... The crowning and anointing of the emperors, borrowed from Byzantium and traceable to the influence of the Old Testament, was imitated by lesser potentates: and this 'sacring' by ecclesiastical authority gave to the king a character of special sanctity... In England it is not without significance that sacerdotal vestments... continued to be among the insignia of the sovereign. Moreover, this sacrosanct character he acquired, not by virtue of his 'securing' but by hereditary right; the coronation, anointing and vesting were but the outward and visible symbol of a divine grace adherent to the sovereign by virtue of his title' (*EBr.* XV. p. 3010).

28. Let not the believers take to themselves the infidels as friends besides the believers, and he who does that, does not in aught belong to Allah, unless you indeed fear from them a danger. And Allah warns you of Himself and to Allah is the last return.

لَا يَتَّخِذِ ٱلْمُؤْمِنُونَ ٱلْكَٰفِرِينَ أَوْلِيَآءَ مِن دُونِ ٱلْمُؤْمِنِينَ ۖ وَمَن يَفْعَلْ ذَٰلِكَ فَلَيْسَ مِنَ ٱللَّهِ فِى شَىْءٍ إِلَّآ أَن تَتَّقُوا۟ مِنْهُمْ تُقَىٰةً ۗ وَيُحَذِّرُكُمُ ٱللَّهُ نَفْسَهُۥ ۗ وَإِلَى ٱللَّهِ ٱلْمَصِيرُ ﴿٢٨﴾

29. Say: 'Whether you hide what is in your hearts or publish it Allah knows it;' and He knows what is in the heavens and in the earth; and Allah is Potent over everything.

قُلْ إِن تُخْفُوا۟ مَا فِى صُدُورِكُمْ أَوْ تُبْدُوهُ يَعْلَمْهُ ٱللَّهُ ۗ وَيَعْلَمُ مَا فِى ٱلسَّمَٰوَٰتِ وَمَا فِى ٱلْأَرْضِ ۗ وَٱللَّهُ عَلَىٰ كُلِّ شَىْءٍ قَدِيرٌ ﴿٢٩﴾

30. The Day when each soul shall find presented whatever it has worked of good and whatever it has worked of evil, it would like that there were between it and that Day wide space. And Allah warns you of Himself, Allah is Tender to His servants.

يَوْمَ تَجِدُ كُلُّ نَفْسٍ مَّا عَمِلَتْ مِنْ خَيْرٍ مُّحْضَرًا وَمَا عَمِلَتْ مِن سُوٓءٍ تَوَدُّ لَوْ أَنَّ بَيْنَهَا وَبَيْنَهُۥٓ أَمَدًۢا بَعِيدًا ۗ وَيُحَذِّرُكُمُ ٱللَّهُ نَفْسَهُۥ ۗ وَٱللَّهُ رَءُوفٌۢ بِٱلْعِبَادِ ﴿٣٠﴾

Section 4

31. Say, if you are wont to love Allah, then follow me,[204] and Allah shall love you and forgive you your sins; and Allah is the Forgiving, the Merciful.

قُلْ إِن كُنتُمْ تُحِبُّونَ ٱللَّهَ فَٱتَّبِعُونِى يُحْبِبْكُمُ ٱللَّهُ وَيَغْفِرْ لَكُمْ ذُنُوبَكُمْ ۗ وَٱللَّهُ غَفُورٌ رَّحِيمٌ ﴿٣١﴾

---

204. In other words, perfect your life on my model. The great Prophet is the perfect man; so his life is to serve as a model in every little detail for all true believers.

32. Say: 'Obey Allah and the Messenger', then if they turn away, surely Allah does not love the infidels.

قُلْ أَطِيعُوا اللَّهَ وَالرَّسُولَ فَإِن تَوَلَّوْا فَإِنَّ اللَّهَ لَا يُحِبُّ الْكَافِرِينَ ﴿٣٢﴾

33. Surely did Allah choose Adam and Noah and the house of Abraham and the house of 'Imran above all the worlds.

إِنَّ اللَّهَ اصْطَفَىٰ ءَادَمَ وَنُوحًا وَءَالَ إِبْرَاهِيمَ وَءَالَ عِمْرَانَ عَلَى الْعَالَمِينَ ﴿٣٣﴾

34. The seed of one another, and Allah is the Hearing, the Knowing.

ذُرِّيَّةً بَعْضُهَا مِنۢ بَعْضٍ وَاللَّهُ سَمِيعٌ عَلِيمٌ ﴿٣٤﴾

35. Recall when the wife of 'Imran said: 'My Lord! Surely I have vowed to You what is in my belly to be dedicated; accept this of me. Surely You! Only You are the Hearer, the Knower.'

إِذْ قَالَتِ امْرَأَتُ عِمْرَانَ رَبِّ إِنِّي نَذَرْتُ لَكَ مَا فِي بَطْنِي مُحَرَّرًا فَتَقَبَّلْ مِنِّي إِنَّكَ أَنتَ السَّمِيعُ الْعَلِيمُ ﴿٣٥﴾

36. Then when she bore her, she said: 'My Lord! Surely I bore a female – and Allah knew best what she had borne – and the male is not as the female, and surely I have named her Maryam, and I commit her and her progeny to You for protection from Satan the accursed.'

فَلَمَّا وَضَعَتْهَا قَالَتْ رَبِّ إِنِّي وَضَعْتُهَا أُنثَىٰ وَاللَّهُ أَعْلَمُ بِمَا وَضَعَتْ وَلَيْسَ الذَّكَرُ كَالْأُنثَىٰ وَإِنِّي سَمَّيْتُهَا مَرْيَمَ وَإِنِّي أُعِيذُهَا بِكَ وَذُرِّيَّتَهَا مِنَ الشَّيْطَانِ الرَّجِيمِ ﴿٣٦﴾

37. Then her Lord accepted her with goodly acceptance, and made her grow up with a goodly growth, and He made Zacharia take care of her. Whenever Zacharia entered the apartment to see her, he found provision by her. He said: 'O Maryam! Whence have you this?' She said: 'This is from Allah.' Surely Allah provides for whom He will without stint.

فَتَقَبَّلَهَا رَبُّهَا بِقَبُولٍ حَسَنٍ وَأَنۢبَتَهَا نَبَاتًا حَسَنًا وَكَفَّلَهَا زَكَرِيَّا كُلَّمَا دَخَلَ عَلَيْهَا زَكَرِيَّا الْمِحْرَابَ وَجَدَ عِندَهَا رِزْقًا قَالَ يَٰمَرْيَمُ أَنَّىٰ لَكِ هَٰذَا قَالَتْ هُوَ مِنْ عِندِ اللَّهِ إِنَّ اللَّهَ يَرْزُقُ مَن يَشَاءُ بِغَيْرِ حِسَابٍ ﴿٣٧﴾

38. Immediately did Zacharia pray to His Lord: 'My Lord! Bestow on me from Your presence a goodly offspring, surely You! Only You are the Hearer of prayer.'

هُنَالِكَ دَعَا زَكَرِيَّا رَبَّهُ قَالَ رَبِّ هَبْ لِى مِن لَّدُنكَ ذُرِّيَّةً طَيِّبَةً إِنَّكَ سَمِيعُ الدُّعَآءِ ﴿٣٨﴾

39. Then the angels called him while he stood praying in the apartment: 'Surely Allah announces to you John, confirming the Word from Allah,[205] a leader and chaste, and a Prophet, from among the righteous.'

فَنَادَتْهُ الْمَلَٰٓئِكَةُ وَهُوَ قَآئِمٌ يُصَلِّى فِى الْمِحْرَابِ أَنَّ اللَّهَ يُبَشِّرُكَ بِيَحْيَىٰ مُصَدِّقًا بِكَلِمَةٍ مِّنَ اللَّهِ وَسَيِّدًا وَحَصُورًا وَنَبِيًّا مِّنَ الصَّٰلِحِينَ ﴿٣٩﴾

40. He said: 'My Lord! How will there be unto me a son while old age has overtaken me and my wife is barren?' Allah said: 'So it shall be, Allah does what He will.'

قَالَ رَبِّ أَنَّىٰ يَكُونُ لِى غُلَٰمٌ وَقَدْ بَلَغَنِىَ الْكِبَرُ وَامْرَأَتِى عَاقِرٌ قَالَ كَذَٰلِكَ اللَّهُ يَفْعَلُ مَا يَشَآءُ ﴿٤٠﴾

41. He said: 'My Lord! Appoint to me a sign.' Allah said: 'Your sign is that you shall not speak to anyone for three days save by tokens, and remember your Lord much, and hallow Him in the evening and morning.'

قَالَ رَبِّ اجْعَل لِّىٓ ءَايَةً قَالَ ءَايَتُكَ أَلَّا تُكَلِّمَ النَّاسَ ثَلَٰثَةَ أَيَّامٍ إِلَّا رَمْزًا وَاذْكُر رَّبَّكَ كَثِيرًا وَسَبِّحْ بِالْعَشِىِّ وَالْإِبْكَٰرِ ﴿٤١﴾

Section 5

42. And recall when the angels said, 'O Maryam, surely Allah chose you and cleansed you and chose you above the women of the worlds.

وَإِذْ قَالَتِ الْمَلَٰٓئِكَةُ يَٰمَرْيَمُ إِنَّ اللَّهَ اصْطَفَىٰكِ وَطَهَّرَكِ وَاصْطَفَىٰكِ عَلَىٰ نِسَآءِ الْعَٰلَمِينَ ﴿٤٢﴾

---

205. 'A Word from Allah' is the Prophet Jesus (peace be on him). He is called 'a Word' because he came into existence by His command, without the ordinary instrumentality of a father (Bdh.).

43. O Maryam! Be devout unto your Lord, prostrate yourself and bow down with those who bow down.'[206]

يَـٰمَرْيَمُ اقْنُتِى لِرَبِّكِ وَاسْجُدِى وَارْكَعِى مَعَ الرَّاكِعِينَ ﴿٤٣﴾

44. This is of the tidings of the Unseen which We reveal to you and you were not with them when they cast their reeds as to which of them should have charge of Maryam. Nor were you with them when they disputed.

ذَٰلِكَ مِنْ أَنبَآءِ الْغَيْبِ نُوحِيهِ إِلَيْكَ وَمَا كُنتَ لَدَيْهِمْ إِذْ يُلْقُونَ أَقْلَـٰمَهُمْ أَيُّهُمْ يَكْفُلُ مَرْيَمَ وَمَا كُنتَ لَدَيْهِمْ إِذْ يَخْتَصِمُونَ ﴿٤٤﴾

45. Recall when the angels said: 'O Maryam, surely Allah announces to you a word from Him, his name shall be the Masīḥ,[207] Jesus son of Maryam,[208] illustrious in this world[209] and the Hereafter and one of those brought nigh.'

إِذْ قَالَتِ الْمَلَـٰٓئِكَةُ يَـٰمَرْيَمُ إِنَّ اللَّهَ يُبَشِّرُكِ بِكَلِمَةٍ مِّنْهُ اسْمُهُ الْمَسِيحُ عِيسَى ابْنُ مَرْيَمَ وَجِيهًا فِى الدُّنْيَا وَالْآخِرَةِ وَمِنَ الْمُقَرَّبِينَ ﴿٤٥﴾

206. With all her great gifts, Maryam is a mere mortal, and has no part of Divinity in her whatsoever. She is, like all true and devout servants of God, specially enjoined to pray, and the canons of prayer are mentioned in detail in order to lay stress on their accurate observance. She is neither a goddess, nor a demi-goddess, nor yet a Mother-God!

207. Masih is the Messiah of the Bible. Messiah, the surname of Jesus, or Jesus is a title of honour, literally meaning 'the anointed'. Notice that the Qur'ān fully considers the Messiahship of Jesus; it is only his Divinity, his Son-ship, his God-head that it is so unsparing in its assailing.

208. Himself a mere mortal, Jesus was also the son of a frail, ordinary woman, and not the son of God. The epithet calls attention to, and emphasises, the fact of his humanity. It is one of the miracles of the Qur'ān that in speaking of Jesus it refutes both the Jewish and the Christian misconceptions simultaneously and constantly uses a language that implies answers both to the Christian deification and to the Jewish denunciation.

209. In other words, above the ridicule and vilification of his enemies, the Jews. Wajih, literally is, 'worthy of regard'. The Qur'ān affirms the honour and glory of Jesus (peace be on him), mainly in answer to the calumnies of the Jews who remember him 'as the man who had chiefly brought dissension to Israel', and as one who 'practiced magic and deceived and led astray Israel', with 'coarse allusions to His birth' (*ERE*. VII. p. 551). The few allusions to him contained in the Talmud and the contemporary literature are, for the the most part, contemptuous references to one who deceived Israel, and who owed his birth to the unfaithfulness of his mother; (*ERE*. II. p. 877) but even they have learnt to speak of his person and character in terms of respect and appreciation. Witness recent books on Jesus by Jewish writers.

46. And he shall speak to mankind in the cradle[210] and maturity and be one of the righteous.

وَيُكَلِّمُ ٱلنَّاسَ فِى ٱلْمَهْدِ وَكَهْلًا وَمِنَ ٱلصَّلِحِينَ ﴿٤٦﴾

47. She said: 'My Lord! How will there be a son unto me while no man has touched me?' Allah said: 'So it shall be.' Allah creates what He will. When He decrees a thing, He only says to it, 'Be' and it becomes.

قَالَتْ رَبِّ أَنَّىٰ يَكُونُ لِى وَلَدٌ وَلَمْ يَمْسَسْنِى بَشَرٌ قَالَ كَذَٰلِكِ ٱللَّهُ يَخْلُقُ مَا يَشَآءُ إِذَا قَضَىٰٓ أَمْرًا فَإِنَّمَا يَقُولُ لَهُۥ كُن فَيَكُونُ ﴿٤٧﴾

48. And He shall teach him the Book and wisdom and the Torah and the Gospel.

وَيُعَلِّمُهُ ٱلْكِتَٰبَ وَٱلْحِكْمَةَ وَٱلتَّوْرَىٰةَ وَٱلْإِنجِيلَ ﴿٤٨﴾

49. And a Messenger[211] to the children of Israel with this message, Surely I have come to you with a sign from your Lord. Surely I form for you out of clay the likeness of a bird, and then I breath in it, and a bird it becomes by Allah's leave. And I heal the blind from birth and

وَرَسُولًا إِلَىٰ بَنِىٓ إِسْرَٰٓءِيلَ أَنِّى قَدْ جِئْتُكُم بِـَٔايَةٍ مِّن رَّبِّكُمْ أَنِّىٓ أَخْلُقُ لَكُم مِّنَ ٱلطِّينِ كَهَيْـَٔةِ ٱلطَّيْرِ فَأَنفُخُ فِيهِ فَيَكُونُ طَيْرًا بِإِذْنِ ٱللَّهِ وَأُبْرِئُ ٱلْأَكْمَهَ وَٱلْأَبْرَصَ

---

210. Whilst yet a mere boy. There would be no sense in recording the fact if it meant nothing more than 'the ordinary experience of every child who is not dumb'. A truism like that could hardly merit mention in the Qur'ān. Compare the Gospel of Barnabas: 'Jesus having come to the age of twelve years, went up with Mary and Joseph to Jerusalem... The third Day they found the child in the temple, in the midst of the doctors, disputing with them concerning the law. And every one was amazed at his questions and answers, saying: How can there be such doctrine in him, seeing he is so small and hath not learned to read' (*GB*. p. 15). And also the NT: 'And when he was twelve years old, they went up to Jerusalem... And it came to pass, that after three days they found him in the temple, sitting in the midst of the doctors, both hearing them, and asking them questions. And all that heard him were astonished at his understanding and answers' (Lk. 2: 42, 46, 47).

211. A Messenger of God which is a very different thing on the one hand from God Himself, as misconceived by the Christians, and on the other from a criminal wonder–worker as misjudged by the Jews.

the leper and revive the dead by
Allah's leave. And I declare to you
what you have eaten and what you
have stored in your houses. Surely
in this is a Sign for you, if you be
believers.

وَأُحْيِ ٱلْمَوْتَىٰ بِإِذْنِ ٱللَّهِ وَأُنَبِّئُكُم بِمَا
تَأْكُلُونَ وَمَا تَدَّخِرُونَ فِى بُيُوتِكُمْ
إِنَّ فِى ذَٰلِكَ لَآيَةً لَّكُمْ إِن كُنتُم
مُّؤْمِنِينَ ﴿٤٩﴾

50. And I come confirming the
Torah that was before me, and to
allow to you some of what was
forbidden to you. And I have come
to you with a sign from your Lord;
so fear Allah and obey me.

وَمُصَدِّقًا لِّمَا بَيْنَ يَدَىَّ مِنَ
ٱلتَّوْرَىٰةِ وَلِأُحِلَّ لَكُم بَعْضَ
ٱلَّذِى حُرِّمَ عَلَيْكُمْ وَجِئْتُكُم
بِـَٔايَةٍ مِّن رَّبِّكُمْ فَٱتَّقُوا۟ ٱللَّهَ
وَأَطِيعُونِ ﴿٥٠﴾

51. Surely Allah is my Lord and
your Lord, so worship Him.[212] This
is the straight path.'[213]

إِنَّ ٱللَّهَ رَبِّى وَرَبُّكُمْ فَٱعْبُدُوهُ
هَٰذَا صِرَٰطٌ مُّسْتَقِيمٌ ﴿٥١﴾

---

212. Worship Him only. This, the worship of the One and Only God, is the true
Message of Jesus, the gist of his real teaching. Unity, and pure God – worship; no
trinity, no incarnation, no son-worship, no mother -worship. Cf. the NT: 'Thou shall
worship the Lord thy God, and him only thou shall serve' (Mt. 4: 10). And the
Gospel of Barnabas: 'I confess thee one God alone that hast not had beginning nor
shall ever have end; for by thy mercy gavest thou to all things their beginning and
by thy justice thou shall give to all an end; that hast no likeness among men,
because in thine infinite goodness thou art not subject to motion nor to any
accident. Have mercy on us, for thou has created us, and we are the works of thy
hand' (*EBi*. p. 195).

213. 'There is no indication that He ever acted independently of God, or as an
independent God. Rather does He acknowledge his dependence upon God, by His
habit of prayer and in such words as "this kind goeth not forth save by prayer". He
even repudiated the ascription to himself of godness in the absolute sense in which
it belongs to God alone' (*EBi*. XIII. p. 24). 'There is nothing in these three Gospels
to suggest that their writers thought of Jesus as other than human, a human being
specially endued with spirit of God and standing in an unbroken relation to God
which justified His being spoken of as the "Son of God" (Ibid., p.18).

52. Then when Jesus perceived infidelity in them, he said: 'Who will be my helper unto Allah?' The disciples said: 'We are helpers of Allah, we believe in Allah, and bear you witness that surely we are Muslims.

فَلَمَّا أَحَسَّ عِيسَى مِنْهُمُ الْكُفْرَ قَالَ مَنْ أَنصَارِىٓ إِلَى اللَّهِ قَالَ الْحَوَارِيُّونَ نَحْنُ أَنصَارُ اللَّهِ ءَامَنَّا بِاللَّهِ وَاشْهَدْ بِأَنَّا مُسْلِمُونَ ۝

53. Our Lord! We believe in what You have sent down and we follow the Messenger: write us up therefore with the witnesses.'

رَبَّنَآ ءَامَنَّا بِمَآ أَنزَلْتَ وَاتَّبَعْنَا الرَّسُولَ فَاكْتُبْنَا مَعَ الشَّٰهِدِينَ ۝

54. And they plotted, and Allah plotted and Allah is the Best of plotters.

وَمَكَرُواْ وَمَكَرَ اللَّهُ وَاللَّهُ خَيْرُ الْمَٰكِرِينَ ۝

Section 6

55. Recall when Allah said: 'O Jesus, surely I shall make you die and am lifting you to Me, and am cleansing you from those who disbelieve, and shall place those who follow you above those who deny you till the Day of Resurrection; then to Me shall be the return of you all; then I shall decide between you concerning that in which you have been differing.'

إِذْ قَالَ اللَّهُ يَٰعِيسَىٓ إِنِّى مُتَوَفِّيكَ وَرَافِعُكَ إِلَىَّ وَمُطَهِّرُكَ مِنَ الَّذِينَ كَفَرُواْ وَجَاعِلُ الَّذِينَ اتَّبَعُوكَ فَوْقَ الَّذِينَ كَفَرُوٓاْ إِلَىٰ يَوْمِ الْقِيَٰمَةِ ثُمَّ إِلَىَّ مَرْجِعُكُمْ فَأَحْكُمُ بَيْنَكُمْ فِيمَا كُنتُمْ فِيهِ تَخْتَلِفُونَ ۝

56. Then as for those who disbelieved, I shall torment them with a severe torment in this world and the Hereafter. Nor shall they have any helpers.

فَأَمَّا الَّذِينَ كَفَرُواْ فَأُعَذِّبُهُمْ عَذَابًا شَدِيدًا فِى الدُّنْيَا وَالْأَخِرَةِ وَمَا لَهُم مِّن نَّٰصِرِينَ ۝

57. And as for those who believed and worked righteous works He shall repay them their wages in full, and Allah loves not the ungodly.[214]

وَأَمَّا الَّذِينَ ءَامَنُوا وَعَمِلُوا الصَّلِحَتِ فَيُوَفِّيهِمْ أُجُورَهُمْ وَاللَّهُ لَا يُحِبُّ الظَّلِمِينَ ۝٥٧

58. This We recite unto you of the signs and of the wise admonition.

ذَلِكَ نَتْلُوهُ عَلَيْكَ مِنَ الْآيَتِ وَالذِّكْرِ الْحَكِيمِ ۝٥٨

59. Surely the likeness of Jesus with Allah is as the likeness of Adam;[215] him He created out of dust; then He said to him, 'Be', and he became.

إِنَّ مَثَلَ عِيسَىٰ عِندَ اللَّهِ كَمَثَلِ ءَادَمَ خَلَقَهُ مِن تُرَابٍ ثُمَّ قَالَ لَهُ كُن فَيَكُونُ ۝٥٩

60. This is the Truth from your Lord, so be you not of the doubters.

الْحَقُّ مِن رَّبِّكَ فَلَا تَكُن مِّنَ الْمُمْتَرِينَ ۝٦٠

61. So those who contend with you therein after what has come to you of the knowledge say, 'Come! Let us call our children and your children and our women and your women and ourselves and yourselves, then let us humbly pray, and invoke the curse of Allah upon the liars.'

فَمَنْ حَاجَّكَ فِيهِ مِن بَعْدِ مَا جَاءَكَ مِنَ الْعِلْمِ فَقُلْ تَعَالَوْا نَدْعُ أَبْنَاءَنَا وَأَبْنَاءَكُمْ وَنِسَاءَنَا وَنِسَاءَكُمْ وَأَنفُسَنَا وَأَنفُسَكُمْ ثُمَّ نَبْتَهِلْ فَنَجْعَل لَّعْنَتَ اللَّهِ عَلَى الْكَاذِبِينَ ۝٦١

---

214. Namely, the Jews and Christians both, as both have transgressed the proper limits in the matter of Jesus, the former by slandering him, the latter by their deification of him.

215. Adam (peace and blessings be upon him) being created without a father and a mother. This is the point of comparison and resemblance. Jesus's wonderful nature is like that of Adam (peace and blessings be upon him). He is not consubstantial with God. He is as much a created being as Adam (peace and blessings be upon him). The Divinity of Jesus (peace and blessings be upon him) has been denied by some ancient Christian sects themselves. 'Arius taught that the Son of God was a created being. There was a timing when He did not exist (*EBr.* II. p. 598). Paul of Samosata also held that Jesus Christ, begotten of the Holy Ghost and born of the virgin, was mere man. But the man was 'anointed by the Holy Ghost and for that reason was called Christ... Though the Logos was in Christ, it did not invest him with divinity' (*EBr.* XI. p. 171).

62. Surely this[216] is the true recital; and god there is none save Allah, and surely Allah it is Who is the Mighty, the Wise.

إِنَّ هَٰذَا لَهُوَ ٱلْقَصَصُ ٱلْحَقُّ وَمَا مِنْ إِلَٰهٍ إِلَّا ٱللَّهُ وَإِنَّ ٱللَّهَ لَهُوَ ٱلْعَزِيزُ ٱلْحَكِيمُ ۝

63. But if they turn away, Allah is the Knower of the corrupters.

فَإِن تَوَلَّوْاْ فَإِنَّ ٱللَّهَ عَلِيمٌۢ بِٱلْمُفْسِدِينَ ۝

Section 7

64. Say: 'O People of the Book! Come to a word common to us and you, that we shall worship none save Allah, and that we shall not join anyone with Him, and that none of us shall take others as Lord beside Allah;'[217] then if they turn away; say, bear witness that we are Muslims.

قُلْ يَٰٓأَهْلَ ٱلْكِتَٰبِ تَعَالَوْاْ إِلَىٰ كَلِمَةٍ سَوَآءٍۭ بَيْنَنَا وَبَيْنَكُمْ أَلَّا نَعْبُدَ إِلَّا ٱللَّهَ وَلَا نُشْرِكَ بِهِۦ شَيْـًٔا وَلَا يَتَّخِذَ بَعْضُنَا بَعْضًا أَرْبَابًا مِّن دُونِ ٱللَّهِ فَإِن تَوَلَّوْاْ فَقُولُواْ ٱشْهَدُواْ بِأَنَّا مُسْلِمُونَ ۝

65. O People of the Book! Why do you contend regarding Abraham whereas the Torah and the Gospel were not sent down save after him? Will you not then understand?

يَٰٓأَهْلَ ٱلْكِتَٰبِ لِمَ تُحَآجُّونَ فِىٓ إِبْرَٰهِيمَ وَمَآ أُنزِلَتِ ٱلتَّوْرَىٰةُ وَٱلْإِنجِيلُ إِلَّا مِنۢ بَعْدِهِۦٓ أَفَلَا تَعْقِلُونَ ۝

66. Ah! It is you who fell to contending that of which you had some knowledge; why then should you contend regarding that of which you have no knowledge at all? And Allah knows and you do not know:

هَٰٓأَنتُمْ هَٰٓؤُلَآءِ حَٰجَجْتُمْ فِيمَا لَكُم بِهِۦ عِلْمٌ فَلِمَ تُحَآجُّونَ فِيمَا لَيْسَ لَكُم بِهِۦ عِلْمٌ وَٱللَّهُ يَعْلَمُ وَأَنتُمْ لَا تَعْلَمُونَ ۝

---

216. Namely, the account of Jesus and his mother just given, and the fact that they were nothing more than mere mortals. This then is another instance of the emphatic repudiation of the Christian trinity.

217. This formula of the Oneness of God and of the rejection of all major and minor deities beside Him, the basic principle of Islam, as it is, has always been the common doctrine of all the faiths in their origin. The Jews and the Christians had abandoned, in practice as well as in theory, this simple truth for man-made dogmas of later invention.

67. Abraham was not a Jew, nor a Nazarene, but he was an upright Muslim; nor was he of the polytheists.

مَا كَانَ إِبْرَٰهِيمُ يَهُودِيًّا وَلَا نَصْرَانِيًّا وَلَٰكِن كَانَ حَنِيفًا مُّسْلِمًا وَمَا كَانَ مِنَ ٱلْمُشْرِكِينَ ۝

68. Surely the nearest of mankind to Abraham are those who followed him, and this Prophet and those who believe. And Allah is the Patron of the believers.

إِنَّ أَوْلَى ٱلنَّاسِ بِإِبْرَٰهِيمَ لَلَّذِينَ ٱتَّبَعُوهُ وَهَٰذَا ٱلنَّبِيُّ وَٱلَّذِينَ ءَامَنُوا۟ وَٱللَّهُ وَلِيُّ ٱلْمُؤْمِنِينَ ۝

69. A section of the People of the Book yearns to mislead you, and none they mislead but themselves, and they perceive not.

وَدَّت طَّآئِفَةٌ مِّنْ أَهْلِ ٱلْكِتَٰبِ لَوْ يُضِلُّونَكُمْ وَمَا يُضِلُّونَ إِلَّا أَنفُسَهُمْ وَمَا يَشْعُرُونَ ۝

70. O People of the Book! Why do you deny the Revelations of Allah, while you are witnesses thereof?

يَٰأَهْلَ ٱلْكِتَٰبِ لِمَ تَكْفُرُونَ بِـَٔايَٰتِ ٱللَّهِ وَأَنتُمْ تَشْهَدُونَ ۝

71. O People of the Book! Why do you clothe the Truth with falsehood, and hide the Truth while you know it?

يَٰأَهْلَ ٱلْكِتَٰبِ لِمَ تَلْبِسُونَ ٱلْحَقَّ بِٱلْبَٰطِلِ وَتَكْتُمُونَ ٱلْحَقَّ وَأَنتُمْ تَعْلَمُونَ ۝

Section 8

72. And a section of the People of the Book says: 'believe at day-break in what has been sent down to those who believe and deny at day-end; perhaps they may turn away.'

وَقَالَت طَّآئِفَةٌ مِّنْ أَهْلِ ٱلْكِتَٰبِ ءَامِنُوا۟ بِٱلَّذِىٓ أُنزِلَ عَلَى ٱلَّذِينَ ءَامَنُوا۟ وَجْهَ ٱلنَّهَارِ وَٱكْفُرُوٓا۟ ءَاخِرَهُۥ لَعَلَّهُمْ يَرْجِعُونَ ۝

73. And believe not save one who follows your religion. Say: 'Surely the true guidance is the guidance of Allah.' Do you envy that any one should be given the like of what was given to you; or do you fear, that those others might overcome you in argument before your Lord?' Say: 'Surely the grace is in the hand of Allah. He bestows it on whom He will and Allah is Bountiful, Knowing.'

وَلَا تُؤْمِنُوٓاْ إِلَّا لِمَن تَبِعَ دِينَكُمْ قُلْ إِنَّ الْهُدَىٰ هُدَى اللَّهِ أَن يُؤْتَىٰٓ أَحَدٌ مِّثْلَ مَآ أُوتِيتُمْ أَوْ يُحَآجُّوكُمْ عِندَ رَبِّكُمْ قُلْ إِنَّ الْفَضْلَ بِيَدِ اللَّهِ يُؤْتِيهِ مَن يَشَآءُ وَاللَّهُ وَاسِعٌ عَلِيمٌ ﴿٧٣﴾

74. He singles out for His mercy whom He will, and Allah is the Owner of mighty grace.

يَخْتَصُّ بِرَحْمَتِهِۦ مَن يَشَآءُ وَاللَّهُ ذُو الْفَضْلِ الْعَظِيمِ ﴿٧٤﴾

75. And among the People of the Book is he who, if you trust him with a treasure, will return it to you; and among them is he who, if you trust him with a dinarius, will not restore it to you except you are ever standing over him. This is because they say, there is no way over us in the matter of the illiterates. And they forge a lie against Allah while they know.

وَمِنْ أَهْلِ الْكِتَٰبِ مَنْ إِن تَأْمَنْهُ بِقِنطَارٍ يُؤَدِّهِۦٓ إِلَيْكَ وَمِنْهُم مَّنْ إِن تَأْمَنْهُ بِدِينَارٍ لَّا يُؤَدِّهِۦٓ إِلَيْكَ إِلَّا مَا دُمْتَ عَلَيْهِ قَآئِمًا ذَٰلِكَ بِأَنَّهُمْ قَالُوا لَيْسَ عَلَيْنَا فِي الْأُمِّيِّنَ سَبِيلٌ وَيَقُولُونَ عَلَى اللَّهِ الْكَذِبَ وَهُمْ يَعْلَمُونَ ﴿٧٥﴾

76. Aye! Whoso keeps the covenant and fears Allah, then surely Allah loves the God-fearing.

بَلَىٰ مَنْ أَوْفَىٰ بِعَهْدِهِۦ وَاتَّقَىٰ فَإِنَّ اللَّهَ يُحِبُّ الْمُتَّقِينَ ﴿٧٦﴾

77. Surely those who sell Allah's covenant and their oaths at a small price, no portion is theirs in the Hereafter, nor shall Allah speak to them nor look at them on the Day of Resurrection, nor shall He purify them, and theirs shall be an afflictive torment.

78. And surely among them are some who pervert the Book with their tongues, that you might consider it of the Book yet it is no part of the Book. And they say, it is from God whereas it is not from Allah and they forge a lie against Allah, while they know.

79. It is not possible for a man to whom Allah has given the Book and wisdom and prophethood that he should afterward say to men, be you worshippers of me, beside Allah;[218] but be you faithful servants of the Lord, seeing that you are wont to teach the Book and seeing that you are wont to exercise yourselves therein.

إِنَّ ٱلَّذِينَ يَشْتَرُونَ بِعَهْدِ ٱللَّهِ وَأَيْمَٰنِهِمْ ثَمَنًا قَلِيلًا أُو۟لَٰٓئِكَ لَا خَلَٰقَ لَهُمْ فِى ٱلْأَخِرَةِ وَلَا يُكَلِّمُهُمُ ٱللَّهُ وَلَا يَنظُرُ إِلَيْهِمْ يَوْمَ ٱلْقِيَٰمَةِ وَلَا يُزَكِّيهِمْ وَلَهُمْ عَذَابٌ أَلِيمٌ ۝

وَإِنَّ مِنْهُمْ لَفَرِيقًا يَلْوُونَ أَلْسِنَتَهُم بِٱلْكِتَٰبِ لِتَحْسَبُوهُ مِنَ ٱلْكِتَٰبِ وَمَا هُوَ مِنَ ٱلْكِتَٰبِ وَيَقُولُونَ هُوَ مِنْ عِندِ ٱللَّهِ وَمَا هُوَ مِنْ عِندِ ٱللَّهِ وَيَقُولُونَ عَلَى ٱللَّهِ ٱلْكَذِبَ وَهُمْ يَعْلَمُونَ ۝

مَا كَانَ لِبَشَرٍ أَن يُؤْتِيَهُ ٱللَّهُ ٱلْكِتَٰبَ وَٱلْحُكْمَ وَٱلنُّبُوَّةَ ثُمَّ يَقُولَ لِلنَّاسِ كُونُوا۟ عِبَادًا لِّى مِن دُونِ ٱللَّهِ وَلَٰكِن كُونُوا۟ رَبَّٰنِيِّنَ بِمَا كُنتُمْ تُعَلِّمُونَ ٱلْكِتَٰبَ وَبِمَا كُنتُمْ تَدْرُسُونَ ۝

---

218. All this is said to confute and contradict the trinitarian Christians. Jesus (on him be peace), as a Prophet, could never have taught people to worship him or to make him as co-equal with God in any sense of the word. A Messenger of God invites people to follow him to the obedience of God, and surely not to deify himself.

80. And he would not bid you to take the angels and the Prophets for Lords.[219] Would he bid you to infidelity after you have become Muslims?

وَلَا يَأْمُرَكُمْ أَن تَتَّخِذُوا الْمَلَٰئِكَةَ وَ النَّبِيِّنَ أَرْبَابًا أَيَأْمُرُكُم بِالْكُفْرِ بَعْدَ إِذْ أَنتُم مُّسْلِمُونَ ۝

Section 9

81. And recall when Allah took a bond from the Prophets, whatever of the Book and wisdom I gave you and afterwards there comes to you a Messenger confirming what is with you, you shall surely believe in him and help him. Allah said: 'Do

وَإِذْ أَخَذَ اللَّهُ مِيثَٰقَ النَّبِيِّنَ لَمَآ ءَاتَيْتُكُم مِّن كِتَٰبٍ وَحِكْمَةٍ ثُمَّ جَآءَكُمْ رَسُولٌ مُّصَدِّقٌ لِّمَا مَعَكُمْ لَتُؤْمِنُنَّ بِهِۦ وَلَتَنصُرُنَّهُ ۚ

219. To expatiate on the Christian worship of a Prophet of God would be to underline the obvious; but Christian angelolatry is perhaps not so widely known. It may be well, therefore, to call attention to the fact that 'a certain tendency to angel-worship manifested itself' in the very early Christian Church; in the 4th century the Council of Laodica found 'it necessary to forbid the angel-worship then prevalent in the country. In the next century we find Theodoret referring to this prohibition as necessitated by the spread of this worship through Phrygia and Pisidia' (*DCA*. II. p. 1176). Some of the Apostolic Fathers and the Apologists of the early centuries held and taught that 'God committed the care of men and all things under heaven to angels whom He set over these' (*ERE*. IV. p. 578), and that to the six holy angels 'the Lord delivered all His creation, to increase and to build it and to be members of all creation' (Ibid.). And it was openly averred that along with the Father and the Son 'good angels' also were to be worshipped and adored. 'Both Him and the Son who came forth from Him and taught us true things, and the best of the other good angels, who follow and are made like unto Him, and the prophetic spirit we worship and adore' (Ibid.). Also that 'God has the general providence of the whole; particular parts are assigned to angels' (Ibid.). The Second Council of Nicea, in 787 AD, went so far as to sanction the custom of depicting angels and venerating their images: 'By the action of this Council it would appear that the cults of the angels, which had originated before the beginning of the period under consideration as a private devotion, and had met with considerable opposition from various ecclesiastical writers, formally received the sanction of the Church, and may henceforward be regarded as part of the doctrine publica' (Ibid., p. 581).

you affirm, and do you take My burden thereto?' They said: 'We affirm.' He said: 'Then bear witness, and I am with you among the witnesses.'

82. Now whoso turns away thereafter, it is they who are the ungodly.

83. Do they seek other than the religion of Allah? Yet to Him has submitted whoso is in the heavens and in the earth, willingly or unwillingly,[220] and to Him shall they all be returned.

84. Say: 'We believe in Allah and in what has been sent down to us, and what was sent down to Abraham and Ishmael, and Isaac and Jacob and the tribes, and what was given to Moses and Jesus and other Prophets from their Lord: we discriminate against none of them, and to Him we are submissive.'

85. And whoso seeks a religion other than Islam, it shall not be accepted of him[221] and in the Hereafter he shall be of the lost.

قَالَ ءَأَقْرَرْتُمْ وَأَخَذْتُمْ عَلَىٰ ذَٰلِكُمْ إِصْرِى قَالُوٓا أَقْرَرْنَا قَالَ فَٱشْهَدُوا وَأَنَا۠ مَعَكُم مِّنَ ٱلشَّٰهِدِينَ ۝

فَمَن تَوَلَّىٰ بَعْدَ ذَٰلِكَ فَأُوْلَٰٓئِكَ هُمُ ٱلْفَٰسِقُونَ ۝

أَفَغَيْرَ دِينِ ٱللَّهِ يَبْغُونَ وَلَهُۥٓ أَسْلَمَ مَن فِى ٱلسَّمَٰوَٰتِ وَٱلْأَرْضِ طَوْعًا وَكَرْهًا وَإِلَيْهِ يُرْجَعُونَ ۝

قُلْ ءَامَنَّا بِٱللَّهِ وَمَآ أُنزِلَ عَلَيْنَا وَمَآ أُنزِلَ عَلَىٰٓ إِبْرَٰهِيمَ وَإِسْمَٰعِيلَ وَإِسْحَٰقَ وَيَعْقُوبَ وَٱلْأَسْبَاطِ وَمَآ أُوتِىَ مُوسَىٰ وَعِيسَىٰ وَٱلنَّبِيُّونَ مِن رَّبِّهِمْ لَا نُفَرِّقُ بَيْنَ أَحَدٍ مِّنْهُمْ وَنَحْنُ لَهُۥ مُسْلِمُونَ ۝

وَمَن يَبْتَغِ غَيْرَ ٱلْإِسْلَٰمِ دِينًا فَلَن يُقْبَلَ مِنْهُ وَهُوَ فِى ٱلْءَاخِرَةِ مِنَ ٱلْخَٰسِرِينَ ۝

---

220. All things in nature, whether heavenly or earthly ones bow down to His decrees and have, perforce, to submit to His physical laws — so Exalted is He! His religion alone is worthy of acceptance.

221. This repudiates the comfortable doctrine that all religions are equally good, and that different 'paths' adopted by different nations and different grades of society converge to the same Divinity. There is only one straight line possible between any two points. Even so there is only one True, perfect and sound religion. All other religions are but so many deviations.

86. How will Allah guide a people who disbelieved after their belief and after they bore witness that the Messenger was true and after evidence had come to them? And Allah guides not an ungodly people.

كَيْفَ يَهْدِى اللَّهُ قَوْمًا كَفَرُوا بَعْدَ إِيمَانِهِمْ وَشَهِدُوٓا أَنَّ الرَّسُولَ حَقٌّ وَجَآءَهُمُ الْبَيِّنَتُ وَاللَّهُ لَا يَهْدِى الْقَوْمَ الظَّالِمِينَ ٨٦

87. They are those whose meed is that on them shall be the curse of Allah and of all mankind;

أُوْلَٰٓئِكَ جَزَآؤُهُمْ أَنَّ عَلَيْهِمْ لَعْنَةَ اللَّهِ وَالْمَلَٰٓئِكَةِ وَالنَّاسِ أَجْمَعِينَ ٨٧

88. Abiders therein, their torment shall not be lightened nor shall they be respited.

خَٰلِدِينَ فِيهَا لَا يُخَفَّفُ عَنْهُمُ الْعَذَابُ وَلَا هُمْ يُنظَرُونَ ٨٨

89. Save such as shall repent thereafter and make amends; verily Allah is the Forgiving, the Merciful.

إِلَّا الَّذِينَ تَابُوا مِنۢ بَعْدِ ذَٰلِكَ وَأَصْلَحُوا فَإِنَّ اللَّهَ غَفُورٌ رَّحِيمٌ ٨٩

90. Surely those who disbelieve after they have believed and thereafter wax in infidelity, their repentance shall by no means be accepted. It is those who are astray.

إِنَّ الَّذِينَ كَفَرُوا بَعْدَ إِيمَانِهِمْ ثُمَّ ازْدَادُوا كُفْرًا لَّن تُقْبَلَ تَوْبَتُهُمْ وَأُوْلَٰٓئِكَ هُمُ الضَّآلُّونَ ٩٠

91. Surely those who disbelieve and die while they are infidels, not an earthful of gold shall be accepted from any such, were he to offer it as a ransom. It is they whose torment shall be afflictive; nor shall they have any helpers.

إِنَّ الَّذِينَ كَفَرُوا وَمَاتُوا وَهُمْ كُفَّارٌ فَلَن يُقْبَلَ مِنْ أَحَدِهِم مِّلْءُ الْأَرْضِ ذَهَبًا وَلَوِ افْتَدَىٰ بِهِۦۤ أُوْلَٰٓئِكَ لَهُمْ عَذَابٌ أَلِيمٌ وَمَا لَهُم مِّن نَّٰصِرِينَ ٩١

Section 10

92. You cannot attain virtue unless you spend of what you love and whatever you spend Allah is the Knower thereof.

لَن تَنَالُوا الْبِرَّ حَتَّىٰ تُنفِقُوا مِمَّا تُحِبُّونَ وَمَا تُنفِقُوا مِن شَيْءٍ فَإِنَّ اللَّهَ بِهِۦ عَلِيمٌ ٩٢

93. All food was allowable to the children of Israel, save what Israel had forbidden for himself, before the Torah was revealed. Say, bring you then the Torah and read it, if you are truthful.

كُلُّ ٱلطَّعَامِ كَانَ حِلًّا لِّبَنِىٓ إِسۡرَٰٓءِيلَ إِلَّا مَا حَرَّمَ إِسۡرَٰٓءِيلُ عَلَىٰ نَفۡسِهِۦ مِن قَبۡلِ أَن تُنَزَّلَ ٱلتَّوۡرَٰةُ قُلۡ فَأۡتُواْ بِٱلتَّوۡرَٰةِ فَٱتۡلُوهَآ إِن كُنتُمۡ صَٰدِقِينَ ۝

94. Then he who fabricates a lie after this against Allah, it is those who are the ungodly.

فَمَنِ ٱفۡتَرَىٰ عَلَى ٱللَّهِ ٱلۡكَذِبَ مِنۢ بَعۡدِ ذَٰلِكَ فَأُوْلَٰٓئِكَ هُمُ ٱلظَّٰلِمُونَ ۝

95. Say, Allah has spoken the Truth; follow therefore the faith of Abraham the upright, and he was not of the polytheists.

قُلۡ صَدَقَ ٱللَّهُ فَٱتَّبِعُواْ مِلَّةَ إِبۡرَٰهِيمَ حَنِيفًا وَمَا كَانَ مِنَ ٱلۡمُشۡرِكِينَ ۝

96. Verily the first house set apart for mankind was that at Bakka, blessed and a guidance to the worlds.

إِنَّ أَوَّلَ بَيۡتٍ وُضِعَ لِلنَّاسِ لَلَّذِى بِبَكَّةَ مُبَارَكًا وَهُدًى لِّلۡعَٰلَمِينَ ۝

97. In it are clear signs and the station of Abraham, and he who enters it shall be secure. And incumbent on mankind is pilgrimage to the House for the sake of Allah on him who is able to find a way thereto. And he who disbelieves,[222] then Allah is Independent of all creatures.[223]

فِيهِ ءَايَٰتٌۢ بَيِّنَٰتٌ مَّقَامُ إِبۡرَٰهِيمَ وَمَن دَخَلَهُۥ كَانَ ءَامِنًا وَلِلَّهِ عَلَى ٱلنَّاسِ حِجُّ ٱلۡبَيۡتِ مَنِ ٱسۡتَطَاعَ إِلَيۡهِ سَبِيلًا وَمَن كَفَرَ فَإِنَّ ٱللَّهَ غَنِىٌّ عَنِ ٱلۡعَٰلَمِينَ ۝

---

222. Note the extreme importance of the Pilgrimage. Willful neglect of this commandment of God amounts to the abandonment of His faith.

223. So he who wilfully neglects the pilgrimage does so at his own peril, and not to any possible hurt to his Lord and Creator. The tribal or national god of the polytheistic peoples existed only with and through his tribe or nation. Not so the God of Islam. He is Ever-Living, Self-Sufficient. Whether the whole of mankind served Him or none observed His commandments, it made no difference to Him whatsoever.

98. Say: 'O People of the Book!
Why do you deny the revelations
of Allah, while Allah is a Witness to
what you work?'

قُلْ يَٰٓأَهْلَ ٱلْكِتَٰبِ لِمَ تَكْفُرُونَ بِـَٔايَٰتِ ٱللَّهِ وَٱللَّهُ شَهِيدٌ عَلَىٰ مَا تَعْمَلُونَ ۝

99. Say: 'O People of the Book!
Why do you hinder those who
believe from the way of Allah
seeking to make it crooked, while
you are witnesses? And Allah is not
unmindful of what you work.'

قُلْ يَٰٓأَهْلَ ٱلْكِتَٰبِ لِمَ تَصُدُّونَ عَن سَبِيلِ ٱللَّهِ مَنْ ءَامَنَ تَبْغُونَهَا عِوَجًا وَأَنتُمْ شُهَدَآءُ وَمَا ٱللَّهُ بِغَٰفِلٍ عَمَّا تَعْمَلُونَ ۝

100. O you who believe! Were you
to obey any section of those who
have been given the Book, they
would render you infidels after your
having believed.

يَٰٓأَيُّهَا ٱلَّذِينَ ءَامَنُوٓا۟ إِن تُطِيعُوا۟ فَرِيقًا مِّنَ ٱلَّذِينَ أُوتُوا۟ ٱلْكِتَٰبَ يَرُدُّوكُم بَعْدَ إِيمَٰنِكُمْ كَٰفِرِينَ ۝

101. Yet how can you disbelieve
while to you are recited the
revelations of Allah, and in your
midst is the Messenger of Allah.
And he who holds fast to Allah is
assuredly on a straight path.

وَكَيْفَ تَكْفُرُونَ وَأَنتُمْ تُتْلَىٰ عَلَيْكُمْ ءَايَٰتُ ٱللَّهِ وَفِيكُمْ رَسُولُهُۥ وَمَن يَعْتَصِم بِٱللَّهِ فَقَدْ هُدِىَ إِلَىٰ صِرَٰطٍ مُّسْتَقِيمٍ ۝

Section 11

102. O you who believe! Fear
Allah with fear due to Him,[224] and
do not die except you be Muslims.

يَٰٓأَيُّهَا ٱلَّذِينَ ءَامَنُوا۟ ٱتَّقُوا۟ ٱللَّهَ حَقَّ تُقَاتِهِۦ وَلَا تَمُوتُنَّ إِلَّا وَأَنتُم مُّسْلِمُونَ ۝

---

224. In effect, with as much fear as you are capable of. The verse does not mean: fear
Him with a fear that is worthy of Him, a command impossible to fulfill. The meaning
is: keep clear of sins and transgressions, as you have already kept clear of idolatry
and paganism.

103. And hold fast, all of you to the cord of Allah, and separate not. And remember Allah's favour to you in that you were enemies, and He joined your hearts together,[225] so you became brethren by His favour; and you were on the brink of a pit of Fire and He rescued you from it. Thus does Allah expound to you His revelations that perhaps you may remain guided.

وَٱعْتَصِمُوا بِحَبْلِ ٱللَّهِ جَمِيعًا وَلَا تَفَرَّقُوا ۚ وَٱذْكُرُوا نِعْمَتَ ٱللَّهِ عَلَيْكُمْ إِذْ كُنتُمْ أَعْدَاءً فَأَلَّفَ بَيْنَ قُلُوبِكُمْ فَأَصْبَحْتُم بِنِعْمَتِهِۦٓ إِخْوَٰنًا وَكُنتُمْ عَلَىٰ شَفَا حُفْرَةٍ مِّنَ ٱلنَّارِ فَأَنقَذَكُم مِّنْهَا ۗ كَذَٰلِكَ يُبَيِّنُ ٱللَّهُ لَكُمْ ءَايَٰتِهِۦ لَعَلَّكُمْ تَهْتَدُونَ ﴿١٠٣﴾

104. And let there be among you a community calling others to good and commanding equity and forbidding evil[226]. And it is these who are blissful.

وَلْتَكُن مِّنكُمْ أُمَّةٌ يَدْعُونَ إِلَى ٱلْخَيْرِ وَيَأْمُرُونَ بِٱلْمَعْرُوفِ وَيَنْهَوْنَ عَنِ ٱلْمُنكَرِ ۚ وَأُوْلَٰئِكَ هُمُ ٱلْمُفْلِحُونَ ﴿١٠٤﴾

105. And be not as those who separated and differed among themselves after there had come to them evidence. These are the ones for whom shall be a mighty torment.

وَلَا تَكُونُوا كَٱلَّذِينَ تَفَرَّقُوا وَٱخْتَلَفُوا مِنۢ بَعْدِ مَا جَآءَهُمُ ٱلْبَيِّنَٰتُ ۚ وَأُوْلَٰئِكَ لَهُمْ عَذَابٌ عَظِيمٌ ﴿١٠٥﴾

106. On the Day when some faces will become whitened and other faces will become blackened. Then as for those whose faces shall have become blackened: did you disbelieve after your profession of belief? Taste the torment for you have been disbelieving.

يَوْمَ تَبْيَضُّ وُجُوهٌ وَتَسْوَدُّ وُجُوهٌ ۚ فَأَمَّا ٱلَّذِينَ ٱسْوَدَّتْ وُجُوهُهُمْ أَكَفَرْتُم بَعْدَ إِيمَٰنِكُمْ فَذُوقُوا ٱلْعَذَابَ بِمَا كُنتُمْ تَكْفُرُونَ ﴿١٠٦﴾

---

225. Joined then by means of Islam. 'Within a brief span of mortal life Muhammad called forth out of uncompromising material a nation never united before, in a country that was hitherto but a geographical expression' (Hitti, *History of the Arabs*, pp. 121–122).

226. Since the duty of enjoining right and forbidding wrong entails conditions in which the whole nation cannot share, the Holy Qur'ān, while addressing the entire Muslim people, demands the action of a part of it only.

107. And as for those whose faces shall have become whitened they shall be in Allah's mercy; therein they shall abide.

وَأَمَّا الَّذِينَ ابْيَضَّتْ وُجُوهُهُمْ فَفِى رَحْمَةِ اللَّهِ هُمْ فِيهَا خَالِدُونَ ۝

108. These are revelations of Allah, We rehearse them to you with Truth; and Allah intends no wrong to His creatures.

تِلْكَ ءَايَتُ اللَّهِ نَتْلُوهَا عَلَيْكَ بِالْحَقِّ وَمَا اللَّهُ يُرِيدُ ظُلْمًا لِّلْعَالَمِينَ ۝

109. Allah's is whatever is in the heavens and in the earth; and to Allah are committed all affairs.

وَلِلَّهِ مَا فِى السَّمَوَاتِ وَمَا فِى الْأَرْضِ وَإِلَى اللَّهِ تُرْجَعُ الْأُمُورُ ۝

Section 12

110. You are the best community ever sent forth to mankind; you enjoin good and forbid evil, and you believe in Allah. Now if the People of the Book have faith, it were better for them; among them some are believers, and most of them are ungodly.

كُنتُمْ خَيْرَ أُمَّةٍ أُخْرِجَتْ لِلنَّاسِ تَأْمُرُونَ بِالْمَعْرُوفِ وَتَنْهَوْنَ عَنِ الْمُنكَرِ وَتُؤْمِنُونَ بِاللَّهِ وَلَوْ ءَامَنَ أَهْلُ الْكِتَبِ لَكَانَ خَيْرًا لَّهُم مِّنْهُمُ الْمُؤْمِنُونَ وَأَكْثَرُهُمُ الْفَسِقُونَ ۝

111. They shall not be able to harm you, except with small hurt, and if they fight you, they shall turn their backs upon you; then they will not be helped.

لَن يَضُرُّوكُمْ إِلَّا أَذًى وَإِن يُقَتِلُوكُمْ يُوَلُّوكُمُ الْأَدْبَارَ ثُمَّ لَا يُنصَرُونَ ۝

112. Stuck upon them is abjection wherever they may be, except in a compact with Allah and in a compact with men; and they have drawn upon themselves wrath from

ضُرِبَتْ عَلَيْهِمُ الذِّلَّةُ أَيْنَ مَا ثُقِفُوا إِلَّا بِحَبْلٍ مِّنَ اللَّهِ وَحَبْلٍ مِّنَ النَّاسِ وَبَاءُو بِغَضَبٍ مِّنَ اللَّهِ

Allah, and stuck upon them is poverty. That is because they have been denying the signs of Allah and killing the Prophets of Allah without right. That is because they have disobeyed, and they have been transgressing.

113. Yet were they not all alike. Among the People of the Book there is a community steadfast, reciting the revelations of Allah in the watches of night while they prostrate themselves.

114. And they believe in Allah and the Last Day and enjoin good and forbid evil, and vie with each other in virtues. And these are among the righteous.

115. And whatever of good they do shall not be denied. And Allah is the Knower of the pious.

116. Surely those who disbelieve, neither their riches nor their progeny shall avail themselves aught against Allah. These are the inmates of the Fire; therein they shall abide.

117. The likeness of what they spend in the life of this world is that of a wind in which is intense cold; it befalls the cornfield of a people who have wronged themselves and lays them to waste. Allah wronged them not, but themselves they wrong.

وَضُرِبَتْ عَلَيْهِمُ ٱلْمَسْكَنَةُ ذَٰلِكَ بِأَنَّهُمْ كَانُوا۟ يَكْفُرُونَ بِـَٔايَٰتِ ٱللَّهِ وَيَقْتُلُونَ ٱلْأَنۢبِيَآءَ بِغَيْرِ حَقٍّ ذَٰلِكَ بِمَا عَصَوا۟ وَّكَانُوا۟ يَعْتَدُونَ ۝

لَيْسُوا۟ سَوَآءً مِّنْ أَهْلِ ٱلْكِتَٰبِ أُمَّةٌ قَآئِمَةٌ يَتْلُونَ ءَايَٰتِ ٱللَّهِ ءَانَآءَ ٱلَّيْلِ وَهُمْ يَسْجُدُونَ ۝

يُؤْمِنُونَ بِٱللَّهِ وَٱلْيَوْمِ ٱلْأَخِرِ وَيَأْمُرُونَ بِٱلْمَعْرُوفِ وَيَنْهَوْنَ عَنِ ٱلْمُنكَرِ وَيُسَٰرِعُونَ فِى ٱلْخَيْرَٰتِ وَأُو۟لَٰٓئِكَ مِنَ ٱلصَّٰلِحِينَ ۝

وَمَا يَفْعَلُوا۟ مِنْ خَيْرٍ فَلَن يُكْفَرُوهُ وَٱللَّهُ عَلِيمٌۢ بِٱلْمُتَّقِينَ ۝

إِنَّ ٱلَّذِينَ كَفَرُوا۟ لَن تُغْنِىَ عَنْهُمْ أَمْوَٰلُهُمْ وَلَآ أَوْلَٰدُهُم مِّنَ ٱللَّهِ شَيْـًٔا وَأُو۟لَٰٓئِكَ أَصْحَٰبُ ٱلنَّارِ هُمْ فِيهَا خَٰلِدُونَ ۝

مَثَلُ مَا يُنفِقُونَ فِى هَٰذِهِ ٱلْحَيَوٰةِ ٱلدُّنْيَا كَمَثَلِ رِيحٍ فِيهَا صِرٌّ أَصَابَتْ حَرْثَ قَوْمٍ ظَلَمُوٓا۟ أَنفُسَهُمْ فَأَهْلَكَتْهُ وَمَا ظَلَمَهُمُ ٱللَّهُ وَلَٰكِنْ أَنفُسَهُمْ يَظْلِمُونَ ۝

118. O you who believe! Take not for an intimate anyone besides yourselves for they shall not be remiss in corrupting you. They yearn for what distresses you; surely their malice has shown itself of their own mouths, and what their breasts hide is greater still. Verily We have expounded you the signs, if you will reflect.

يَـٰٓأَيُّهَا ٱلَّذِينَ ءَامَنُوا۟ لَا تَتَّخِذُوا۟ بِطَانَةً مِّن دُونِكُمْ لَا يَأْلُونَكُمْ خَبَالًا وَدُّوا۟ مَا عَنِتُّمْ قَدْ بَدَتِ ٱلْبَغْضَاءُ مِنْ أَفْوَٰهِهِمْ وَمَا تُخْفِى صُدُورُهُمْ أَكْبَرُ قَدْ بَيَّنَّا لَكُمُ ٱلْأَيَـٰتِ إِن كُنتُمْ تَعْقِلُونَ ۝

119. Lo! It is you who love them, while they love you not, and you believe in the Book, all of it. When they meet you, they say, 'we believe.' And when they are alone, they bite their fingers at you in rage. Say, 'perish in your rage. Allah is the Knower of what is in your breasts.'

هَـٰٓأَنتُمْ أُو۟لَآءِ تُحِبُّونَهُمْ وَلَا يُحِبُّونَكُمْ وَتُؤْمِنُونَ بِٱلْكِتَـٰبِ كُلِّهِۦ وَإِذَا لَقُوكُمْ قَالُوٓا۟ ءَامَنَّا وَإِذَا خَلَوْا۟ عَضُّوا۟ عَلَيْكُمُ ٱلْأَنَامِلَ مِنَ ٱلْغَيْظِ قُلْ مُوتُوا۟ بِغَيْظِكُمْ إِنَّ ٱللَّهَ عَلِيمٌۢ بِذَاتِ ٱلصُّدُورِ ۝

120. If there happens to you any good, it grieves them, and if there befalls to you an ill, they rejoice at it. And if you remain persevering and God-fearing their guile shall not harm you at all. Surely Allah is Encompasser of what they work.

إِن تَمْسَسْكُمْ حَسَنَةٌ تَسُؤْهُمْ وَإِن تُصِبْكُمْ سَيِّئَةٌ يَفْرَحُوا۟ بِهَا وَإِن تَصْبِرُوا۟ وَتَتَّقُوا۟ لَا يَضُرُّكُمْ كَيْدُهُمْ شَيْـًٔا إِنَّ ٱللَّهَ بِمَا يَعْمَلُونَ مُحِيطٌ ۝

Section 13

121. And recall when you went forth from your house early to assign position to the believers in the battle. And Allah is the Hearing, the Knowing.

وَإِذْ غَدَوْتَ مِنْ أَهْلِكَ تُبَوِّئُ ٱلْمُؤْمِنِينَ مَقَـٰعِدَ لِلْقِتَالِ وَٱللَّهُ سَمِيعٌ عَلِيمٌ ۝

122. Recall when two sections of you meditated that they should flag, whereas Allah was the Patron of the two. And upon Allah, then, should the believers rely.

إِذْ هَمَّت طَّآئِفَتَانِ مِنكُمْ أَن تَفْشَلَا وَاللَّهُ وَلِيُّهُمَا وَعَلَى اللَّهِ فَلْيَتَوَكَّلِ الْمُؤْمِنُونَ ۝

123. And assuredly Allah succoured you at Badr, while you were humble. So fear Allah that perhaps you may return thanks.

وَلَقَدْ نَصَرَكُمُ اللَّهُ بِبَدْرٍ وَأَنتُمْ أَذِلَّةٌ فَاتَّقُوا اللَّهَ لَعَلَّكُمْ تَشْكُرُونَ ۝

124. Recall when you said to the believers: 'Suffices it not, to you, that your Lord should reinforce you with three thousand angels sent down?'

إِذْ تَقُولُ لِلْمُؤْمِنِينَ أَلَن يَكْفِيَكُمْ أَن يُمِدَّكُمْ رَبُّكُم بِثَلَاثَةِ ءَالَفٍ مِّنَ الْمَلَئِكَةِ مُنزَلِينَ ۝

125. Yea! If you but remain steadfast and God-fearing, and they should come upon you immediately, your Lord shall reinforce you with five thousand angels marked.

بَلَى إِن تَصْبِرُوا وَتَتَّقُوا وَيَأْتُوكُم مِّن فَوْرِهِمْ هَٰذَا يُمْدِدْكُمْ رَبُّكُم بِخَمْسَةِ ءَالَفٍ مِّنَ الْمَلَئِكَةِ مُسَوِّمِينَ ۝

126. And this promise Allah did not make except as a joyful announcement to you, so that thereby your hearts might be set at rest – and no success is there but from Allah, the Mighty, the Wise.

وَمَا جَعَلَهُ اللَّهُ إِلَّا بُشْرَى لَكُمْ وَلِتَطْمَئِنَّ قُلُوبُكُم بِهِ وَمَا النَّصْرُ إِلَّا مِنْ عِندِ اللَّهِ الْعَزِيزِ الْحَكِيمِ ۝

127. In order that He may cut off a portion of those who disbelieve, or abase them so that they may go back frustrated.

لِيَقْطَعَ طَرَفًا مِّنَ الَّذِينَ كَفَرُوا أَوْ يَكْبِتَهُمْ فَيَنقَلِبُوا خَائِبِينَ ۝

128. Naught with you is of the affair; He shall either relent towards them or torment them for they are the ungodly.

لَيْسَ لَكَ مِنَ الْأَمْرِ شَىْءٌ أَوْ يَتُوبَ عَلَيْهِمْ أَوْ يُعَذِّبَهُمْ فَإِنَّهُمْ ظَالِمُونَ ۝

129. Allah's is whatever is in the heavens and whatever is in the earth. He forgives whom He will, and torments whom He will; and Allah is the Forgiving, the Merciful.

وَلِلَّهِ مَا فِى ٱلسَّمَٰوَٰتِ وَمَا فِى ٱلْأَرْضِ يَغْفِرُ لِمَن يَشَآءُ وَيُعَذِّبُ مَن يَشَآءُ وَٱللَّهُ غَفُورٌ رَّحِيمٌ ۝

Section 14

130. O you who believe! Do not devour usury multiplied manifold; and fear Allah, haply ye may thrive.

يَٰٓأَيُّهَا ٱلَّذِينَ ءَامَنُوا۟ لَا تَأْكُلُوا۟ ٱلرِّبَوٰٓا۟ أَضْعَٰفًا مُّضَٰعَفَةً وَٱتَّقُوا۟ ٱللَّهَ لَعَلَّكُمْ تُفْلِحُونَ ۝

131. And beware of the Fire prepared for the infidels[227].

وَٱتَّقُوا۟ ٱلنَّارَ ٱلَّتِىٓ أُعِدَّتْ لِلْكَٰفِرِينَ ۝

132. And obey Allah and the Messenger, haply you may be shown mercy.

وَأَطِيعُوا۟ ٱللَّهَ وَٱلرَّسُولَ لَعَلَّكُمْ تُرْحَمُونَ ۝

133. And hasten to forgiveness from your Lord and towards the Garden as vast as the heavens and the earth, prepared for the God-fearing;[228]

وَسَارِعُوٓا۟ إِلَىٰ مَغْفِرَةٍ مِّن رَّبِّكُمْ وَجَنَّةٍ عَرْضُهَا ٱلسَّمَٰوَٰتُ وَٱلْأَرْضُ أُعِدَّتْ لِلْمُتَّقِينَ ۝

134. Those who spend both in weal and woe, who repress anger and who pardon men; and Allah loves the well-doers.

ٱلَّذِينَ يُنفِقُونَ فِى ٱلسَّرَّآءِ وَٱلضَّرَّآءِ وَٱلْكَٰظِمِينَ ٱلْغَيْظَ وَٱلْعَافِينَ عَنِ ٱلنَّاسِ وَٱللَّهُ يُحِبُّ ٱلْمُحْسِنِينَ ۝

---

227. Essentially and primarily, Hell is intended for the infidels. Muslims are warned to guard themselves against imitating them or practising their actions.

228. Muslims are thus exhorted to acquire positive merits and win the way through to everlasting Bliss and not to rest content with the mere negative aspect of abstaining from evil.

135. And those who, when they have committed a misdeed or wronged themselves, remember Allah and beg forgiveness of their sins – and who forgives sins save Allah?[229] – and do not persist in what they have done while they know.

وَٱلَّذِينَ إِذَا فَعَلُوا۟ فَٰحِشَةً أَوْ ظَلَمُوٓا۟ أَنفُسَهُمْ ذَكَرُوا۟ ٱللَّهَ فَٱسْتَغْفَرُوا۟ لِذُنُوبِهِمْ وَمَن يَغْفِرُ ٱلذُّنُوبَ إِلَّا ٱللَّهُ وَلَمْ يُصِرُّوا۟ عَلَىٰ مَا فَعَلُوا۟ وَهُمْ يَعْلَمُونَ ﴿١٣٥﴾

136. It is those whose recompense is forgiveness from their Lord and Gardens beneath which rivers flow. They shall abide therein. Excellent is the wage of the workers.

أُو۟لَٰٓئِكَ جَزَآؤُهُم مَّغْفِرَةٌ مِّن رَّبِّهِمْ وَجَنَّٰتٌ تَجْرِى مِن تَحْتِهَا ٱلْأَنْهَٰرُ خَٰلِدِينَ فِيهَا ۚ وَنِعْمَ أَجْرُ ٱلْعَٰمِلِينَ ﴿١٣٦﴾

137. Dispensations have gone forth before you; go about them on the earth, and see what has been the end of the beliers!

قَدْ خَلَتْ مِن قَبْلِكُمْ سُنَنٌ فَسِيرُوا۟ فِى ٱلْأَرْضِ فَٱنظُرُوا۟ كَيْفَ كَانَ عَٰقِبَةُ ٱلْمُكَذِّبِينَ ﴿١٣٧﴾

138. This Qur'an is an exposition for mankind and a guidance and admonition for the God-fearing.

هَٰذَا بَيَانٌ لِّلنَّاسِ وَهُدًى وَمَوْعِظَةٌ لِّلْمُتَّقِينَ ﴿١٣٨﴾

---

229. Allah, the God of Mercy and Forgiveness. A staggering blow to the Christian idea that the power to forgive sins is in the hands of Christ and the pastors of his Church. Cf. the NT: 'Then said Jesus to them again... Whosoever sins ye remit, they are remitted unto them; and whosoever sins ye retain, they are retained'. (Jn. 20: 21–23). The unlimited 'power of remitting sin was promised and conferred upon the Apostles and their successors by Jesus Christ. This power is exercised in the Sacrament of Penance' (*CD*. p. 821). And the following is an extract from Dr. Butler's *Catechism* for Roman Catholics:

'Q. By whose power are sins forgiven?

A. By the power of God, which Christ left to the pastors of the Church' (p. 84).

139. And do not faint nor grieve, you shall triumph, if you are believers.

وَلَا تَهِنُوا۟ وَلَا تَحۡزَنُوا۟ وَأَنتُمُ ٱلۡأَعۡلَوۡنَ إِن كُنتُم مُّؤۡمِنِينَ ۝

140. If a distress has come your way, a like distress has surely befallen that people. Such are the haps that We change about among mankind, so that Allah may know those who believe and may take martyrs from among you; and Allah does not love the ungodly.²³⁰

إِن يَمۡسَسۡكُمۡ قَرۡحٌ فَقَدۡ مَسَّ ٱلۡقَوۡمَ قَرۡحٌ مِّثۡلُهُۥ ۚ وَتِلۡكَ ٱلۡأَيَّامُ نُدَاوِلُهَا بَيۡنَ ٱلنَّاسِ وَلِيَعۡلَمَ ٱللَّهُ ٱلَّذِينَ ءَامَنُوا۟ وَيَتَّخِذَ مِنكُمۡ شُهَدَآءَ ۗ وَٱللَّهُ لَا يُحِبُّ ٱلظَّٰلِمِينَ ۝

141. And that Allah may purge those who believe,²³¹ and wipe out the infidels.

وَلِيُمَحِّصَ ٱللَّهُ ٱلَّذِينَ ءَامَنُوا۟ وَيَمۡحَقَ ٱلۡكَٰفِرِينَ ۝

142. Or, do you think that you shall enter the Garden while Allah has not known those who have striven hard, nor yet known the steadfast?

أَمۡ حَسِبۡتُمۡ أَن تَدۡخُلُوا۟ ٱلۡجَنَّةَ وَلَمَّا يَعۡلَمِ ٱللَّهُ ٱلَّذِينَ جَٰهَدُوا۟ مِنكُمۡ وَيَعۡلَمَ ٱلصَّٰبِرِينَ ۝

143. And certainly you were wont to long for death before you had met it. Now you have seen it, even when you are looking on.

وَلَقَدۡ كُنتُمۡ تَمَنَّوۡنَ ٱلۡمَوۡتَ مِن قَبۡلِ أَن تَلۡقَوۡهُ فَقَدۡ رَأَيۡتُمُوهُ وَأَنتُمۡ تَنظُرُونَ ۝

---

230. So that no number of victories on the part of the infidels can prove that they are in the right or are of the loved by God. He allows them occasional success either to tempt them or to test the believers, or with some such other end in view in accordance with His Universal plan.

231. Purge them of any impurities that they might have contracted. Trials and tribulations in the case of true believers have always the effect of purifying their hearts and improving their morals.

Section 15

144. And Muḥammad is naught but a Messenger;[232] and Messengers have surely passed away before him.[233] Will you then, if he dies or is killed, turn round on your heels? And he who turns round on his heels, does not harm Allah at all. And surely Allah will recompense the grateful.

وَمَا مُحَمَّدٌ إِلَّا رَسُولٌ قَدْ خَلَتْ مِن قَبْلِهِ الرُّسُلُ أَفَإِيْن مَّاتَ أَوْ قُتِلَ انقَلَبْتُمْ عَلَىٰ أَعْقَـٰبِكُمْ وَمَن يَنقَلِبْ عَلَىٰ عَقِبَيْهِ فَلَن يَضُرَّ اللَّهَ شَيْئًا وَسَيَجْزِى اللَّهُ الشَّـٰكِرِينَ ﴿١٤٤﴾

145. It is not open to any person to die except by Allah's will at a time recorded. And whoso desires the reward of this world, We grant to him of this, and he who desires the reward of the Hereafter We grant to him of that. And surely We will recompense the grateful.

وَمَا كَانَ لِنَفْسٍ أَن تَمُوتَ إِلَّا بِإِذْنِ اللَّهِ كِتَابًا مُّؤَجَّلًا وَمَن يُرِدْ ثَوَابَ الدُّنْيَا نُؤْتِهِ مِنْهَا وَمَن يُرِدْ ثَوَابَ الْآخِرَةِ نُؤْتِهِ مِنْهَا وَسَنَجْزِى الشَّـٰكِرِينَ ﴿١٤٥﴾

232. Muḥammad (peace and blessings be upon him) therefore is also subject to the law of change; and not an immortal God, beyond the reach of death. 'Mohammed to the end of his life claimed for himself that title only with which he had begun, and which the highest philosophy and the truest Christianity will one day, I venture to believe, agree in yielding to him that of a Prophet, a very Prophet of God' (Bosworth Smith, *Muhammed and Muhammedanism*, p. 344). 'The word "Muḥammad" literally means: A man praised much, or repeatedly, or time after time: endowed with many praiseworthy qualities' (LL.). 'The name was rare among the Arabs' (Muir, *Life of Muhammad*, p. 5). 'No impartial student surveying the career and character of Mohammed can fail to acknowledge his loftiness of purpose, his moral courage, his sincerity, his simplicity, and his kindness. To these qualities must be added unsparing energy and a genius for diplomacy' (Sykes, *History of Persia*, I, p. 520).

233. So he too will pass away at the end of his span of life. 'These verses constitute one of the most moving and impressive portions of the Qur'ān, and the lesson they taught was never forgotten. And yet when seven years later the Prophet lay dead in

the lap of his beloved wife Aysha, the news of his death produced such a consternation among his devoted followers that they expected the heaven to burst open and the earth to cleave asunder and wondered how long it could be for the end of the world to come. The loving Umar was entirely beside himself... It was on a scene of such stormy emotions that the tender–hearted but ever–tranquil Abu Bakr arrived from the suburb of Madina, where he lived... He said to the assembled crowd with that sureness of conviction that had won him the title of Siddiq, "O Men! He who worshipped Muhammad, let him know that verily Muhammad has already passed away; but he who worshipped Allah, let him know that verily Allah is living and shall never die". And then he recited... "And Muhammad is no more than a Messenger..." This allayed all doubts and fears and a great tranquillity ensued. People who had constantly read... the verse that Abu Bakr so appositely quoted, stated that when he recited it on this memorable occasion, it seemed as if it had just been revealed' (MA.). Such is the evergreen freshness of the Holy Qur'ān!

146. And many a Prophet has fought with a number of godly men beside him. For anything that befell them in the way of Allah, they never fainted nor weakened, nor did they abase themselves. And Allah loves the steadfast.

وَكَأَيِّن مِّن نَّبِيّ قَـٰتَلَ مَعَهُۥ رِبِّيُّونَ كَثِيرٌ فَمَا وَهَنُوا لِمَا أَصَابَهُمْ فِى سَبِيلِ اللّٰهِ وَمَا ضَعُفُوا وَمَا اسْتَكَانُوا وَاللّٰهُ يُحِبُّ الصَّـٰبِرِينَ ﴿١٤٦﴾

147. And their speech was nothing but they said: 'Our Lord! Forgive us our sins and our exorbitance in our affairs and make our foothold firm and make us triumph over the disbelieving people.'

وَمَا كَانَ قَوْلَهُمْ إِلَّا أَن قَالُوا رَبَّنَا اغْفِرْ لَنَا ذُنُوبَنَا وَإِسْرَافَنَا فِى أَمْرِنَا وَثَبِّتْ أَقْدَامَنَا وَانصُرْنَا عَلَى الْقَوْمِ الْكَـٰفِرِينَ ﴿١٤٧﴾

148. So Allah granted to them the reward of this world and the excellent reward of the Hereafter. And Allah loves the well-doers.

فَـَٔاتَىٰهُمُ اللّٰهُ ثَوَابَ الدُّنْيَا وَحُسْنَ ثَوَابِ الْءَاخِرَةِ وَاللّٰهُ يُحِبُّ الْمُحْسِنِينَ ﴿١٤٨﴾

Section 16

149. O you who believe! if you obey those who disbelieve, they will send you back on your heels, and you will turn back losers.

يَـٰٓأَيُّهَا الَّذِينَ ءَامَنُوا إِن تُطِيعُوا الَّذِينَ كَفَرُوا يَرُدُّوكُمْ عَلَىٰٓ أَعْقَـٰبِكُمْ فَتَنقَلِبُوا خَـٰسِرِينَ ﴿١٤٩﴾

150. But Allah is your Patron; and He is the Best of helpers.

بَلِ اللّٰهُ مَوْلَـٰكُمْ وَهُوَ خَيْرُ النَّـٰصِرِينَ ﴿١٥٠﴾

151. Soon will We put terror in the hearts of those who disbelieve, for they have joined with Allah that for which Allah has sent down no authority; and their resort is the Fire. Vile is the abode of the wrong-doers.

سَنُلْقِى فِى قُلُوبِ الَّذِينَ كَفَرُوا الرُّعْبَ بِمَا أَشْرَكُوا بِاللّٰهِ مَا لَمْ يُنَزِّلْ بِهِۦ سُلْطَـٰنًا وَمَأْوَىٰهُمُ النَّارُ وَبِئْسَ مَثْوَى الظَّـٰلِمِينَ ﴿١٥١﴾

152. And Allah has assuredly made good His promise to you when you were extirpating them by His will until you flagged and you quarrelled about the command and you disobeyed after He had shown you what you had longed for. Of you some desired this world, and of you some desired the Hereafter, therefore He turned you away from them that He might test you; and verily He has pardoned you, and Allah is Gracious to the believers.

153. And recall you were running off and would not look back on anyone, whilst the Messenger in your rear was calling you. Then He caused grief to overtake you for grief, so that you might not grieve for what you might lose nor for what might befall you. And Allah is Aware of what you work.

154. Then after grief, He sent down to you a secure slumber coming over a section of you while another section concerned themselves with unjust thoughts of Allah: the thought of paganism. They said: 'Have we aught at all of the affairs?' Say: 'The affair is wholly Allah's.' They hide within themselves what they do not disclose to you, saying: 'Had we aught of the affair, we would have not been slain here.' Say: 'Had you stayed in your houses, even then those decreed to be slain would

وَلَقَدْ صَدَقَكُمُ اللَّهُ وَعْدَهُۥٓ
إِذْ تَحُسُّونَهُم بِإِذْنِهِۦ حَتَّىٰٓ إِذَا
فَشِلْتُمْ وَتَنَٰزَعْتُمْ فِى الْأَمْرِ وَ
عَصَيْتُم مِّنۢ بَعْدِ مَآ أَرَىٰكُم مَّا
تُحِبُّونَ مِنكُم مَّن يُرِيدُ الدُّنْيَا
وَمِنكُم مَّن يُرِيدُ الْءَاخِرَةَ ثُمَّ
صَرَفَكُمْ عَنْهُمْ لِيَبْتَلِيَكُمْ وَلَقَدْ
عَفَا عَنكُمْ وَاللَّهُ ذُو فَضْلٍ عَلَى
الْمُؤْمِنِينَ ۝

إِذْ تُصْعِدُونَ وَلَا تَلْوُۥنَ
عَلَىٰٓ أَحَدٍ وَالرَّسُولُ يَدْعُوكُمْ
فِىٓ أُخْرَىٰكُمْ فَأَثَٰبَكُمْ غَمًّۢا بِغَمٍّ
لِّكَيْلَا تَحْزَنُوا۟ عَلَىٰ مَا فَاتَكُمْ
وَلَا مَآ أَصَٰبَكُمْ وَاللَّهُ خَبِيرٌۢ
بِمَا تَعْمَلُونَ ۝

ثُمَّ أَنزَلَ عَلَيْكُم مِّنۢ بَعْدِ الْغَمِّ أَمَنَةً نُّعَاسًا
يَغْشَىٰ طَآئِفَةً مِّنكُمْ وَطَآئِفَةٌ قَدْ
أَهَمَّتْهُمْ أَنفُسُهُمْ يَظُنُّونَ بِاللَّهِ غَيْرَ
الْحَقِّ ظَنَّ الْجَٰهِلِيَّةِ يَقُولُونَ هَل لَّنَا
مِنَ الْأَمْرِ مِن شَىْءٍ قُلْ إِنَّ الْأَمْرَ كُلَّهُۥ لِلَّهِ
يُخْفُونَ فِىٓ أَنفُسِهِم مَّا لَا يُبْدُونَ لَكَ
يَقُولُونَ لَوْ كَانَ لَنَا مِنَ الْأَمْرِ شَىْءٌ مَّا
قُتِلْنَا هَٰهُنَا قُل لَّوْ كُنتُمْ فِى بُيُوتِكُمْ

surely have gone forth to their deathbeds. And this has happened in order that He might test what was in your breasts and purge that which was in your hearts. And Allah is the Knower of what is in the breasts.'

لَبَرَزَ ٱلَّذِينَ كُتِبَ عَلَيْهِمُ ٱلْقَتْلُ إِلَىٰ مَضَاجِعِهِمْ وَلِيَبْتَلِيَ ٱللَّهُ مَا فِى صُدُورِكُمْ وَلِيُمَحِّصَ مَا فِى قُلُوبِكُمْ وَٱللَّهُ عَلِيمٌ بِذَاتِ ٱلصُّدُورِ ﴿١٥٤﴾

155. As for those of you who turned back on the day the two hosts met, it was Satan who made them slip because of something they had earned, and assuredly has Allah pardoned them. Verily Allah is the Forgiving, the Forbearing.

إِنَّ ٱلَّذِينَ تَوَلَّوْا۟ مِنكُمْ يَوْمَ ٱلْتَقَى ٱلْجَمْعَانِ إِنَّمَا ٱسْتَزَلَّهُمُ ٱلشَّيْطَٰنُ بِبَعْضِ مَا كَسَبُوا۟ وَلَقَدْ عَفَا ٱللَّهُ عَنْهُمْ إِنَّ ٱللَّهَ غَفُورٌ حَلِيمٌ ﴿١٥٥﴾

Section 17

156. O you who believe! Be not like those who disbelieve and say of their brethren when they travel in the land or go to religious war: had they been with us, they would not have died nor would have they been slain. This is in order that Allah may cause anguish in their hearts.[234] And it is Allah Who makes alive and causes to die, and Allah is the Beholder of what you work.

يَٰٓأَيُّهَا ٱلَّذِينَ ءَامَنُوا۟ لَا تَكُونُوا۟ كَٱلَّذِينَ كَفَرُوا۟ وَقَالُوا۟ لِإِخْوَٰنِهِمْ إِذَا ضَرَبُوا۟ فِى ٱلْأَرْضِ أَوْ كَانُوا۟ غُزًّى لَّوْ كَانُوا۟ عِندَنَا مَا مَاتُوا۟ وَمَا قُتِلُوا۟ لِيَجْعَلَ ٱللَّهُ ذَٰلِكَ حَسْرَةً فِى قُلُوبِهِمْ وَٱللَّهُ يُحْىِۦ وَيُمِيتُ وَٱللَّهُ بِمَا تَعْمَلُونَ بَصِيرٌ ﴿١٥٦﴾

---

234. The purport of the passage is: Muslims! Do not behave like the hypocrites in uttering such blasphemies and in cherishing such foolish ideas. Whatever is ordained by God in His infinite wisdom is bound to befall them. God is only causing such beliefs as a matter of sighing and lamentation in the hearts of the hypocrites.

157. Surely if you are slain in the way of Allah or die, forgiveness from Allah and mercy are better than what they amass.[235]

وَلَئِن قُتِلۡتُمۡ فِى سَبِيلِ ٱللَّهِ أَوۡ مُتُّمۡ لَمَغۡفِرَةٌ مِّنَ ٱللَّهِ وَرَحۡمَةٌ خَيۡرٌ مِّمَّا يَجۡمَعُونَ ۝

158. And whether you die or are slain, assuredly unto Allah you will be gathered.[236]

وَلَئِن مُّتُّمۡ أَوۡ قُتِلۡتُمۡ لَإِلَى ٱللَّهِ تُحۡشَرُونَ ۝

159. It was then of the mercy of Allah that you have been gentle with them, and were you rough, hard-hearted, they would certainly have dispersed from around you.[237] So pardon them,[238] and ask forgiveness

فَبِمَا رَحۡمَةٍ مِّنَ ٱللَّهِ لِنتَ لَهُمۡ وَلَوۡ كُنتَ فَظًّا غَلِيظَ ٱلۡقَلۡبِ لَٱنفَضُّوا۟ مِنۡ حَوۡلِكَ فَٱعۡفُ عَنۡهُمۡ

---

235. Of this world and its comforts. The meaning is: marching and campaigning is not a thing that can bring about death or hasten the end; but should that occur in the path of the Lord, His Mercy and Forgiveness which you shall obtain by such death are immensely better than what the others amass of this world and its comforts by their life. Everyone journeying or fighting in the cause of God shall be made a partaker of the delights of Paradise.

236. Two things are thus made absolutely plain. Firstly, the hour of death is immutable. It cannot be avoided whether one is at home or abroad, in peace or at war. Secondly, equally inevitable is the return of every soul to God. Why, then, should death in the cause of Faith be feared at all? It ought rather to be courted and welcomed as a sure road to eternal bliss.

237. 'The Prophet was always inclined to mildness...' (*HHW*. VIII, p. 121). 'He never struck anyone in his life... He never first withdrew his hand out of another man's palm, and turned not before the other had turned... He was the most faithful protector of those he protected, the sweetest and most agreeable in conversation; those who saw him were suddenly filled with reverence; those who came near him loved him' (*The Speeches and Table Talk of the Prophet Muhammad*, pp. 27–28). 'Cruelty was no part of Mohammad's nature' (*LSK*. p. LXX). 'Generous and considerate towards his friends, he knew, by well–timed favour and attention, how to gain over even the disaffected and rivet them to his service... He rarely pursued a foe after he had tendered timely submission. His commanding mien inspired the stranger with an undefined and indescribable awe; but on close intimacy, apprehension and fear gave place to confidence and love' (Muir, *Life of Muhammad*, p. 27).

238. Pardon them on your own behalf for their disobeying your commands. It is reported on good authority that the Prophet did not utter a single harsh word to those whose misbehaviour had brought such a disastrous result as at Uhud.

for them and take counsel with them in the affair[239] and when you have resolved, put your trust in Allah. Verily, Allah loves the trustful.

وَاسْتَغْفِرْ لَهُمْ وَشَاوِرْهُمْ فِى الْأَمْرِ فَإِذَا عَزَمْتَ فَتَوَكَّلْ عَلَى اللّٰهِ إِنَّ اللّٰهَ يُحِبُّ الْمُتَوَكِّلِينَ ۝

160. If Allah helps you there is none that can overcome you; and if He forsakes you who is there that can help you after Him? And in Allah let the believers trust.

إِن يَنصُرْكُمُ اللّٰهُ فَلَا غَالِبَ لَكُمْ وَإِن يَخْذُلْكُمْ فَمَن ذَا الَّذِى يَنصُرُكُم مِّنۢ بَعْدِهِ وَعَلَى اللّٰهِ فَلْيَتَوَكَّلِ الْمُؤْمِنُونَ ۝

161. It is not the part of a Prophet to hide anything away; he who hides anything away, he shall bring forth on the Day of Judgement what he had hidden away; then shall each one be repaid in full what he has earned and they shall not be wronged.

وَمَا كَانَ لِنَبِيٍّ أَن يَغُلَّ وَمَن يَغْلُلْ يَأْتِ بِمَا غَلَّ يَوْمَ الْقِيَٰمَةِ ثُمَّ تُوَفَّىٰ كُلُّ نَفْسٍ مَّا كَسَبَتْ وَهُمْ لَا يُظْلَمُونَ ۝

162. Is then he who follows Allah's pleasure[240] like him who has settled under the displeasure of Allah? His resort is Hell, and ill is that destination.

أَفَمَنِ اتَّبَعَ رِضْوَٰنَ اللّٰهِ كَمَنۢ بَآءَ بِسَخَطٍ مِّنَ اللّٰهِ وَمَأْوَىٰهُ جَهَنَّمُ وَبِئْسَ الْمَصِيرُ ۝

163. Of diverse ranks shall be they with Allah, and Allah is the Beholder of what they do.

هُمْ دَرَجَٰتٌ عِندَ اللّٰهِ وَاللّٰهُ بَصِيرٌۢ بِمَا يَعْمَلُونَ ۝

---

239. Take counsel in the important affairs of the community, such as peace and war. Note the essentially democratic character of the commonwealth of Islam. Even the Divinely-guided Prophet is enjoined to establish, by his example, the practice of deliberation in the community.

240. Such as every Prophet is bound to do. The Islamic concept of Prophethood is entirely different from the Biblical description of the Prophets, ascribing to them all manner of evil deeds and acts of the filthiest nature. A Prophet, according to the Qur'ānic sense of the term, is himself sinless and pure before purifying others.

164. Assuredly has Allah conferred a benefit on the believers when He raised up to them a Messenger from amongst themselves, who rehearses to them His revelations and purifies them, and teaches them the Book and wisdom,[241] while they were afore in manifest error.

لَقَدْ مَنَّ ٱللَّهُ عَلَى ٱلْمُؤْمِنِينَ إِذْ بَعَثَ فِيهِمْ رَسُولًا مِّنْ أَنفُسِهِمْ يَتْلُواْ عَلَيْهِمْ ءَايَٰتِهِۦ وَيُزَكِّيهِمْ وَيُعَلِّمُهُمُ ٱلْكِتَٰبَ وَٱلْحِكْمَةَ وَإِن كَانُواْ مِن قَبْلُ لَفِى ضَلَٰلٍ مُّبِينٍ ﴿١٦٤﴾

165. Is it that when a reverse has befallen you, even though you had inflicted twice as much, you say: 'Whence is this?' Say: 'It is but from yourselves.' Surely, Allah is Potent over everything.

أَوَلَمَّا أَصَٰبَتْكُم مُّصِيبَةٌ قَدْ أَصَبْتُم مِّثْلَيْهَا قُلْتُمْ أَنَّىٰ هَٰذَا قُلْ هُوَ مِنْ عِندِ أَنفُسِكُمْ إِنَّ ٱللَّهَ عَلَىٰ كُلِّ شَىْءٍ قَدِيرٌ ﴿١٦٥﴾

166. And what befell you on the day when the two hosts met was by Allah's will, and that He might know the believers.

وَمَآ أَصَٰبَكُمْ يَوْمَ ٱلْتَقَى ٱلْجَمْعَانِ فَبِإِذْنِ ٱللَّهِ وَلِيَعْلَمَ ٱلْمُؤْمِنِينَ ﴿١٦٦﴾

167. And that He might know who played the hypocrite. And it was said to them, come ye, and fight in the way of Allah or defend. They said: 'If we knew it was to be a fair fight we would certainly have followed you.' Nearer were they on that day to infidelity than to faith. They say with their mouths what is not in their hearts; and Allah knows best what they conceal.

وَلِيَعْلَمَ ٱلَّذِينَ نَافَقُواْ وَقِيلَ لَهُمْ تَعَالَوْاْ قَٰتِلُواْ فِى سَبِيلِ ٱللَّهِ أَوِ ٱدْفَعُواْ قَالُواْ لَوْ نَعْلَمُ قِتَالًا لَّٱتَّبَعْنَٰكُمْ هُمْ لِلْكُفْرِ يَوْمَئِذٍ أَقْرَبُ مِنْهُمْ لِلْإِيمَٰنِ يَقُولُونَ بِأَفْوَٰهِهِم مَّا لَيْسَ فِى قُلُوبِهِمْ وَٱللَّهُ أَعْلَمُ بِمَا يَكْتُمُونَ ﴿١٦٧﴾

---

241. In other words, the *Sunnah*. A Prophet, in Islam, is not a mere medium, an inert, mechanical transmitter of divine truths, but a teacher, an interpreter, and an expounder of those profound truths.

168. They say of their brethren, while they themselves stayed at home: 'Had they obeyed us, they would not have been slain' Say: 'Then avert death from yourselves if you are truthful.'

وَٱلَّذِينَ قَالُوا۟ لِإِخْوَٰنِهِمْ وَقَعَدُوا۟ لَوْ أَطَاعُونَا مَا قُتِلُوا۟ قُلْ فَٱدْرَءُوا۟ عَنْ أَنفُسِكُمُ ٱلْمَوْتَ إِن كُنتُمْ صَٰدِقِينَ ۝

169. And reckon you not those slain in the way of Allah as dead. Nay, they are alive and with their Lord, and provided for.

وَلَا تَحْسَبَنَّ ٱلَّذِينَ قُتِلُوا۟ فِى سَبِيلِ ٱللَّهِ أَمْوَٰتًۢا بَلْ أَحْيَآءٌ عِندَ رَبِّهِمْ يُرْزَقُونَ ۝

170. Exulting in what Allah has granted them of His grace. And they rejoice in those who have not yet joined them from behind, in the thought that no fear shall come to them nor shall they grieve.

فَرِحِينَ بِمَآ ءَاتَىٰهُمُ ٱللَّهُ مِن فَضْلِهِۦ وَيَسْتَبْشِرُونَ بِٱلَّذِينَ لَمْ يَلْحَقُوا۟ بِهِم مِّنْ خَلْفِهِمْ أَلَّا خَوْفٌ عَلَيْهِمْ وَلَا هُمْ يَحْزَنُونَ ۝

171. They rejoice at the favour of Allah and His grace and that Allah wastes not the reward of the believers.

يَسْتَبْشِرُونَ بِنِعْمَةٍ مِّنَ ٱللَّهِ وَفَضْلٍ وَأَنَّ ٱللَّهَ لَا يُضِيعُ أَجْرَ ٱلْمُؤْمِنِينَ ۝

Section 18

172. Those who answered to the call of Allah and the Messenger after the wound that befell them, for those who did well among them and feared Allah shall be a mighty wage.

ٱلَّذِينَ ٱسْتَجَابُوا۟ لِلَّهِ وَٱلرَّسُولِ مِنۢ بَعْدِ مَآ أَصَابَهُمُ ٱلْقَرْحُ لِلَّذِينَ أَحْسَنُوا۟ مِنْهُمْ وَٱتَّقَوْا۟ أَجْرٌ عَظِيمٌ ۝

173. And those to whom certain persons said: 'Verily the people have mustered against you, so fear them,' it merely increased them in belief, and they said: 'Suffices us Allah, and an excellent Trustee is He.'

ٱلَّذِينَ قَالَ لَهُمُ ٱلنَّاسُ إِنَّ ٱلنَّاسَ قَدْ جَمَعُوا۟ لَكُمْ فَٱخْشَوْهُمْ فَزَادَهُمْ إِيمَٰنًا وَقَالُوا۟ حَسْبُنَا ٱللَّهُ وَنِعْمَ ٱلْوَكِيلُ ۝

174. They then returned with a favour from Allah and His grace. No evil touched them, and they followed Allah's pleasure, and Allah is the Owner of mighty grace.

175. It is only that Satan affrights you of his friends; so fear them not, but fear Me if you are believers.

176. And let not those grieve you who have turned towards infidelity; verily they shall not harm Allah at all. Allah intends not to provide for them a portion in the Hereafter, and theirs shall be a mighty torment.

177. Of a truth those who have purchased infidelity for belief shall not harm Allah at all and theirs shall be an afflictive torment.

178. And let not those who disbelieve think that We respite them for their good: We respite them only that they increase in sin and theirs shall be an ignominious torment.

179. Allah is not the one to leave the believers in the state wherein you are unless He has discriminated the impure from the pure. And Allah is not to acquaint you with the Unseen but Allah chooses him whom He will of His Messengers. Believe therefore in Allah and His Messengers: and if you believe and fear, yours shall be a mighty reward.

فَٱنقَلَبُواْ بِنِعۡمَةٖ مِّنَ ٱللَّهِ وَفَضۡلٖ لَّمۡ يَمۡسَسۡهُمۡ سُوٓءٞ وَٱتَّبَعُواْ رِضۡوَٰنَ ٱللَّهِۗ وَٱللَّهُ ذُو فَضۡلٍ عَظِيمٍ ۝

إِنَّمَا ذَٰلِكُمُ ٱلشَّيۡطَٰنُ يُخَوِّفُ أَوۡلِيَآءَهُۥ فَلَا تَخَافُوهُمۡ وَخَافُونِ إِن كُنتُم مُّؤۡمِنِينَ ۝

وَلَا يَحۡزُنكَ ٱلَّذِينَ يُسَٰرِعُونَ فِي ٱلۡكُفۡرِۚ إِنَّهُمۡ لَن يَضُرُّواْ ٱللَّهَ شَيۡـًٔاۚ يُرِيدُ ٱللَّهُ أَلَّا يَجۡعَلَ لَهُمۡ حَظّٗا فِي ٱلۡأٓخِرَةِۖ وَلَهُمۡ عَذَابٌ عَظِيمٌ ۝

إِنَّ ٱلَّذِينَ ٱشۡتَرَوُاْ ٱلۡكُفۡرَ بِٱلۡإِيمَٰنِ لَن يَضُرُّواْ ٱللَّهَ شَيۡـًٔاۖ وَلَهُمۡ عَذَابٌ أَلِيمٞ ۝

وَلَا يَحۡسَبَنَّ ٱلَّذِينَ كَفَرُوٓاْ أَنَّمَا نُمۡلِي لَهُمۡ خَيۡرٞ لِّأَنفُسِهِمۡۚ إِنَّمَا نُمۡلِي لَهُمۡ لِيَزۡدَادُوٓاْ إِثۡمٗاۚ وَلَهُمۡ عَذَابٞ مُّهِينٞ ۝

مَّا كَانَ ٱللَّهُ لِيَذَرَ ٱلۡمُؤۡمِنِينَ عَلَىٰ مَآ أَنتُمۡ عَلَيۡهِ حَتَّىٰ يَمِيزَ ٱلۡخَبِيثَ مِنَ ٱلطَّيِّبِۗ وَمَا كَانَ ٱللَّهُ لِيُطۡلِعَكُمۡ عَلَى ٱلۡغَيۡبِ وَلَٰكِنَّ ٱللَّهَ يَجۡتَبِي مِن رُّسُلِهِۦ مَن يَشَآءُۖ فَـَٔامِنُواْ بِٱللَّهِ وَرُسُلِهِۦۚ وَإِن تُؤۡمِنُواْ وَتَتَّقُواْ فَلَكُمۡ أَجۡرٌ عَظِيمٌ ۝

180. And let not those who stint with what Allah has granted them in His grace consider that this is good for them. Nay, it is bad for them, and soon shall that with which they stint be hung round their necks on the Day of Judgement. And Allah's is the heritage of the heavens and the earth. And Allah is Aware of what you do.

وَلَا يَحْسَبَنَّ الَّذِينَ يَبْخَلُونَ بِمَا ءَاتَىٰهُمُ اللَّهُ مِن فَضْلِهِۦ هُوَ خَيْرًا لَّهُم بَلْ هُوَ شَرٌّ لَّهُمْ سَيُطَوَّقُونَ مَا بَخِلُوا۟ بِهِۦ يَوْمَ الْقِيَـٰمَةِ وَلِلَّهِ مِيرَٰثُ السَّمَـٰوَٰتِ وَ الْأَرْضِ وَاللَّهُ بِمَا تَعْمَلُونَ خَبِيرٌ ۝

Section 19

181. Assuredly has Allah heard the words of those who say:[242] 'Surely Allah is poor and we are rich.' Surely We shall write down what they have said and their killing of the Prophets without right, and We shall say: 'Taste the torment of the burning.'

لَّقَدْ سَمِعَ اللَّهُ قَوْلَ الَّذِينَ قَالُوٓا۟ إِنَّ اللَّهَ فَقِيرٌ وَنَحْنُ أَغْنِيَآءُ سَنَكْتُبُ مَا قَالُوا۟ وَقَتْلَهُمُ الْأَنۢبِيَآءَ بِغَيْرِ حَقٍّ وَنَقُولُ ذُوقُوا۟ عَذَابَ الْحَرِيقِ ۝

182. This is for what your hands have sent on before, for verily Allah is no wronger of His slaves.

ذَٰلِكَ بِمَا قَدَّمَتْ أَيْدِيكُمْ وَأَنَّ اللَّهَ لَيْسَ بِظَلَّامٍ لِّلْعَبِيدِ ۝

---

242. They say this by way of ridicule. The reference is to the Jews of the Banū Qaynuqā', a tribe which populated the outskirts of Madina, and followed the money-lending and goldsmith's crafts. They were invited to embrace Islam, and the Prophet wrote to them exhorting, among other things, to lend unto Allah a goodly loan. Phineas Bin Azura, however, a leading Jew, thought it fit to make fun of the expression, and mockingly remarked: 'Surely God is poor, since they seek to borrow for Him.'

183. There are those who say:
'Verily God has covenanted with us
that we should not believe in a
Messenger unless he brings to us
an offering which fire shall devour.'
Say: 'Surely there came to you
Messengers before me with what
you speak of, then why did you kill
them, if you are truthful?'

184. If then they reject you, even
so were Messengers rejected
before you, who came with
evidence and Scripture and the
luminous Book.

185. Every soul shall taste death[243]
and only on the Day of Judgement
will you be repaid your wages in full.
Then he who shall be removed far

ٱلَّذِينَ قَالُوٓاْ إِنَّ ٱللَّهَ عَهِدَ إِلَيْنَآ
أَلَّا نُؤْمِنَ لِرَسُولٍ حَتَّىٰ يَأْتِيَنَا بِقُرْبَانٍ
تَأْكُلُهُ ٱلنَّارُ قُلْ قَدْ جَآءَكُمْ رُسُلٌ
مِّن قَبْلِي بِٱلْبَيِّنَٰتِ وَبِٱلَّذِى قُلْتُمْ فَلِمَ
قَتَلْتُمُوهُمْ إِن كُنتُمْ صَٰدِقِينَ ﴿١٨٣﴾

فَإِن كَذَّبُوكَ فَقَدْ كُذِّبَ رُسُلٌ مِّن
قَبْلِكَ جَآءُو بِٱلْبَيِّنَٰتِ وَٱلزُّبُرِ وَٱلْكِتَٰبِ
ٱلْمُنِيرِ ﴿١٨٤﴾

كُلُّ نَفْسٍ ذَآئِقَةُ ٱلْمَوْتِ وَإِنَّمَا تُوَفَّوْنَ
أُجُورَكُمْ يَوْمَ ٱلْقِيَٰمَةِ فَمَن زُحْزِحَ
عَنِ ٱلنَّارِ

243. Note that, in Islam, death is as natural a phenomenon as life, and a necessary
concomitant of animal life, as the word 'soul' implies. Death, perhaps, had been
known upon the earth long before the human species appeared and it is in no way
connected with the 'original sin' of Adam. This corrects and contradicts the Christian
and Jewish concept of death. Cf. the NT: 'Wherefore, as by one man sin entered
into the world, and death by sin; and so death passed upon all men, for that all have
sinned' (Ro. 5: 12). 'For the wages of sin is death' (5: 23). 'And sin, when it is
finished, bringeth forth death' (Ja. 1: 15). So in Christianity, 'death is a punishment
for sin and though the character of punishment is wiped away in Baptism death
itself remains as an effect of sin' (CD. p. 283). 'Death came through sin; and human
death is the common lot of man, first because of his own personal sin; and, secondly,
because it is part of the inheritance which Adam has transmitted to his descendants'
(DB. I. p. 841). 'And among the Jews death was held to be the consequence of sin
and a sinless person would necessarily be immortal. There is no death without sin'
(ET. p. 78) 'There are different views among Jews concerning the cause of death.
Some assign it to Adam's first sin in partaking of the forbidden fruit. This view is
somewhat modified by the Rabbis, who regard death as the fruit of personal sin;
maintaining that, like Adam, each person dies on account of his own sin' (JE. IV.
p. 483).

away from the Fire and made to enter the Garden, indeed has achieved the goal: and the life of this world is nothing but an illusory enjoyment.

وَأُدْخِلَ ٱلْجَنَّةَ فَقَدْ فَازَّ وَمَا ٱلْحَيَوٰةُ ٱلدُّنْيَا إِلَّا مَتَـٰعُ ٱلْغُرُورِ ﴿١٨٥﴾

186. You shall surely be tried in your riches and in your lives and will surely bear much injury from those who were given the Book before you, and from those who join gods, and if you endure and fear Allah then surely that is of the commandments determined.

لَتُبْلَوُنَّ فِىٓ أَمْوَٰلِكُمْ وَ أَنفُسِكُمْ وَلَتَسْمَعُنَّ مِنَ ٱلَّذِينَ أُوتُوا ٱلْكِتَـٰبَ مِن قَبْلِكُمْ وَمِنَ ٱلَّذِينَ أَشْرَكُوٓا أَذًى كَثِيرًا وَإِن تَصْبِرُوا وَتَتَّقُوا فَإِنَّ ذَٰلِكَ مِنْ عَزْمِ ٱلْأُمُورِ ﴿١٨٦﴾

187. And recall when Allah took a bond from those who were given the Book, you shall surely expound it to the people and you shall not hide it; but thereafter they cast it behind their backs, and sold it for a small price. Vile is that with which they have sold.

وَإِذْ أَخَذَ ٱللَّهُ مِيثَـٰقَ ٱلَّذِينَ أُوتُوا ٱلْكِتَـٰبَ لَتُبَيِّنُنَّهُۥ لِلنَّاسِ وَلَا تَكْتُمُونَهُۥ فَنَبَذُوهُ وَرَآءَ ظُهُورِهِمْ وَٱشْتَرَوْا بِهِۦ ثَمَنًا قَلِيلًا فَبِئْسَ مَا يَشْتَرُونَ ﴿١٨٧﴾

188. Imagine you not that those who exult in what they have brought about and love to be praised for what they have not done, imagine not you that they shall be secure from the torment. And theirs shall be an afflictive torment.

لَا تَحْسَبَنَّ ٱلَّذِينَ يَفْرَحُونَ بِمَآ أَتَوا وَّ يُحِبُّونَ أَن يُحْمَدُوا بِمَا لَمْ يَفْعَلُوا فَلَا تَحْسَبَنَّهُم بِمَفَازَةٍ مِّنَ ٱلْعَذَابِّ وَلَهُمْ عَذَابٌ أَلِيمٌ ﴿١٨٨﴾

189. Allah's is the kingdom of the heavens and the earth and Allah is Potent over everything.

وَلِلَّهِ مُلْكُ ٱلسَّمَـٰوَٰتِ وَٱلْأَرْضِّ وَٱللَّهُ عَلَىٰ كُلِّ شَىْءٍ قَدِيرٌ ﴿١٨٩﴾

Section 20

190. Verily in the creation of the heavens and the earth[244] and in the alternation of the night and the day are signs for men of understanding.

إِنَّ فِى خَلْقِ ٱلسَّمَٰوَٰتِ وَٱلْأَرْضِ وَٱخْتِلَٰفِ ٱلَّيْلِ وَٱلنَّهَارِ لَءَايَٰتٍ لِّأُوْلِى ٱلْأَلْبَٰبِ ﴿١٩٠﴾

191. Whoever remembers Allah standing and sitting and lying on their sides[245] and reflects on the creation of the heavens and the earth, saying: 'Our Lord! You created not all this in vain.[246] Hallowed be You! Save us from the torment of the Fire.

ٱلَّذِينَ يَذْكُرُونَ ٱللَّهَ قِيَٰمًا وَقُعُودًا وَعَلَىٰ جُنُوبِهِمْ وَيَتَفَكَّرُونَ فِى خَلْقِ ٱلسَّمَٰوَٰتِ وَٱلْأَرْضِ رَبَّنَا مَا خَلَقْتَ هَٰذَا بَٰطِلًا سُبْحَٰنَكَ فَقِنَا عَذَابَ ٱلنَّارِ ﴿١٩١﴾

192. Our Lord! Verily he whom You will cast into the Fire, him You have surely humiliated, and for the wrong-doers there shall be no helpers.

رَبَّنَا إِنَّكَ مَن تُدْخِلِ ٱلنَّارَ فَقَدْ أَخْزَيْتَهُۥ وَمَا لِلظَّٰلِمِينَ مِنْ أَنصَارٍ ﴿١٩٢﴾

---

244. As has been stated above the heavens and the earth are all created beings, and there is no such thing as a sky-god or an earth-god, as held by several polytheistic religions. In the Hindu cosmogony, for instance, 'both Heaven and Earth are regarded as gods and as the parents of god even though they are said to have been generated by gods' (*ERE*. IV. p. 156).

245. Constantly remembering Allah and in all attitudes and postures. The thought of God, even according to non-Muslim observers, occupies an abiding place in the mind of every devout Muslim. 'The mere mention of any proposed activity or even of the recurring phenomena of Nature is accompanied with the phrase "If God will"; and pious phrases such as, "God is great" are frequently upon the lips of the devout, and are used to fill up pauses in ordinary conversation' (Arnold, *Islamic Faith*, p. 19).

246. Allah did not create without some wise plan and purpose. *Batil* in this context is 'In play, or sport; acting unprofitably; or aiming at no profit' (LL.). This repudiates the well-known Hindu doctrine of Maya, calling the whole universe an illusion. This also affirms the reality of the external world. The world as we perceive by senses is real, not a phantasm of our imagination.

193. 'Our Lord! Verily we! We have heard a caller calling to belief: believe in your Lord, so we have come to believe. Our Lord, forgive us our sins, and expiate from us misdeeds and let us die along with the pious.

رَّبَّنَا إِنَّنَا سَمِعْنَا مُنَادِيًا يُنَادِى لِلْإِيمَٰنِ أَنْ ءَامِنُوا بِرَبِّكُمْ فَـَٔامَنَّا رَبَّنَا فَٱغْفِرْ لَنَا ذُنُوبَنَا وَكَفِّرْ عَنَّا سَيِّـَٔاتِنَا وَتَوَفَّنَا مَعَ ٱلْأَبْرَارِ ۝١٩٣

194. 'Our Lord! Grant us what You have promised us by Your Messengers, and humiliate us not on the Day of Judgement. Verily You fail not the tryst.'

رَبَّنَا وَءَاتِنَا مَا وَعَدتَّنَا عَلَىٰ رُسُلِكَ وَلَا تُخْزِنَا يَوْمَ ٱلْقِيَٰمَةِ إِنَّكَ لَا تُخْلِفُ ٱلْمِيعَادَ ۝١٩٤

195. Then did their Lord hearken unto them saying: 'I let not the work of a worker amongst you go to waste, man or woman,[247] one of you from the other.'[248] So those who emigrated and were driven forth from their houses and persecuted in My cause, and who fought and were slain,[249] surely I will expiate from their misdeeds and surely I will make them enter into Gardens beneath which rivers flow, a reward from Allah. And Allah! With Him is the excellent reward.

فَٱسْتَجَابَ لَهُمْ رَبُّهُمْ أَنِّى لَا أُضِيعُ عَمَلَ عَٰمِلٍ مِّنكُم مِّن ذَكَرٍ أَوْ أُنثَىٰ بَعْضُكُم مِّنۢ بَعْضٍ فَٱلَّذِينَ هَاجَرُوا وَأُخْرِجُوا مِن دِيَٰرِهِمْ وَأُوذُوا فِى سَبِيلِى وَقَٰتَلُوا وَقُتِلُوا لَأُكَفِّرَنَّ عَنْهُمْ سَيِّـَٔاتِهِمْ وَلَأُدْخِلَنَّهُمْ جَنَّٰتٍ تَجْرِى مِن تَحْتِهَا ٱلْأَنْهَٰرُ ثَوَابًا مِّنْ عِندِ ٱللَّهِ وَٱللَّهُ عِندَهُۥ حُسْنُ ٱلثَّوَابِ ۝١٩٥

---

247. The word 'woman' needed special mention in view of the sub-human status allotted to women in almost all ancient philosophies and religions.

248. The phrase is parenthetical, meaning that man and woman are counterparts to each other and of the same human status. Remember that this Truth was proclaimed to the world not in the twentieth but in the seventh century of the Christian era.

249. The allusion is to the Companions of the Holy Prophet, who in addition to their faith, deep and sound, cheerfully underwent such hard ordeals as are mentioned in the text.

196. Do not be beguiled at the moving to and fro in the cities of those who disbelieve.

لَا يَغُرَّنَّكَ تَقَلُّبُ ٱلَّذِينَ كَفَرُوا۟ فِى ٱلْبِلَٰدِ ۝

197. A brief enjoyment:[250] and then Hell shall be their abode; ill is that resort.

مَتَٰعٌ قَلِيلٌ ثُمَّ مَأْوَىٰهُمْ جَهَنَّمُ ۚ وَبِئْسَ ٱلْمِهَادُ ۝

198. But as to those who fear their Lord, theirs shall be Gardens beneath which rivers flow. They shall abide therein – an entertainment from their Lord, and what is with Allah is still better for the pious.

لَٰكِنِ ٱلَّذِينَ ٱتَّقَوْا۟ رَبَّهُمْ لَهُمْ جَنَّٰتٌ تَجْرِى مِن تَحْتِهَا ٱلْأَنْهَٰرُ خَٰلِدِينَ فِيهَا نُزُلًا مِّنْ عِندِ ٱللَّهِ ۗ وَمَا عِندَ ٱللَّهِ خَيْرٌ لِّلْأَبْرَارِ ۝

199. And among the People of the Book there are some who surely believe in Allah and in what has been sent down to you and what has been sent down to them,[251] humbling themselves before Allah, and they do not sell the revelations of Allah at a small price. These! They shall have their reward with Allah. Verily Allah is Swift at reckoning.

وَإِنَّ مِنْ أَهْلِ ٱلْكِتَٰبِ لَمَن يُؤْمِنُ بِٱللَّهِ وَمَا أُنزِلَ إِلَيْكُمْ وَمَا أُنزِلَ إِلَيْهِمْ خَٰشِعِينَ لِلَّهِ لَا يَشْتَرُونَ بِـَٔايَٰتِ ٱللَّهِ ثَمَنًا قَلِيلًا ۗ أُو۟لَٰئِكَ لَهُمْ أَجْرُهُمْ عِندَ رَبِّهِمْ ۗ إِنَّ ٱللَّهَ سَرِيعُ ٱلْحِسَابِ ۝

200. O you who believe! Persevere and excel in perseverance and be steadfast, and fear Allah, that haply you may thrive.

يَٰٓأَيُّهَا ٱلَّذِينَ ءَامَنُوا۟ ٱصْبِرُوا۟ وَصَابِرُوا۟ وَرَابِطُوا۟ وَٱتَّقُوا۟ ٱللَّهَ لَعَلَّكُمْ تُفْلِحُونَ ۝

---

250. This world is a brief enjoyment. 'This present world in comparison with the Hereafter is like one of you putting his finger in the sea, and let him see how much he brings out.'

251. This refers to the Torah and the Gospel in their genuine and unadulterated states.

Sūrah 4

al-Nisā'

(Madinan, 24 Sections, 176 Verses)

*In the name of Allah, the
Compassionate, the Merciful.*

Section 1

1. O mankind! Fear Allah Who created you[252] of a single soul,[253] and He created from it its mate,[254] and out of the two He spread abroad manifold men and women.

---

252. Allah created us all, the entirety of mankind, irrespective of sex, rank, age, colour, race and nationality. This emphasizes the fact, so obvious and yet so often forgotten, that man is a being created, and therefore stands sharply marked off from his Creator, having nothing in common with Him, and is not joined with Him by a chain of heroes, incarnations, demi-gods and the like. Additionally, evolution, or no evolution, the creation of man is a veritable Truth.

253. We are therefore children of a common ancestor. The single soul referred to is Adam. The Qur'ān here positively asserts the basic unity of mankind and repudiates the doctrine of polygenism ascribing multiple ancestry to mankind, and incidentally also does away with the idea of castes or classes as forming a barrier to the common humanity. Contrast with this the Hindu concept that the Brahman is a caste derived from the gods, and the Sudra from the *Asuras*, or demons' (*ERE.* XI. p. 915).

254. The first woman; Eve, or Hawwa. This implies the essential equality of men and women as human beings. It was not in Islam, but in Christianity, to its eternal shame, that woman was considered 'an inferior, empty-headed moron; for several days in each month she was so unclean as to require secluding like a leper. The Council of Trent, in the sixteenth century, was dubious about her possessing a soul' (Forbath (ed.), *Love, Marriage, Jealousy*, p. 371). This Council, let it be further noted, held from 13th December, 1545 to 4th December, 1563, was of the greatest significance in the history of the Roman Church: 'It would be hard to exaggerate the importance of the Council of Trent' (*CD.* p. 97). For Jewish and Christian accounts of the creation of woman from Adam's rib see Ge. 2: 18, 21–25.

And fear Allah by Whom you importune one another and the wombs.[255] Verily Allah is ever a Watcher over you.

وَاتَّقُوا اللَّهَ الَّذِي تَسَاءَلُونَ بِهِ وَالْأَرْحَامَ إِنَّ اللَّهَ كَانَ عَلَيْكُمْ رَقِيبًا ۝١

2. And give to the orphans their substance, and do not substitute the bad for the good, and do not devour their substance by adding it to your substance. Surely that is a great crime.[256]

وَآتُوا الْيَتَامَىٰ أَمْوَالَهُمْ وَلَا تَتَبَدَّلُوا الْخَبِيثَ بِالطَّيِّبِ وَلَا تَأْكُلُوا أَمْوَالَهُمْ إِلَىٰ أَمْوَالِكُمْ إِنَّهُ كَانَ حُوبًا كَبِيرًا ۝٢

3. And if you apprehend that you will not be able to deal justly with orphan girls, then marry of other women[257] such as please you, by two, or three, or four, but if you apprehend that you shall not be able to act equitably, then marry one only, or what your right hands own. That will be more fit that you may not swerve.

وَإِنْ خِفْتُمْ أَلَّا تُقْسِطُوا فِي الْيَتَامَىٰ فَانكِحُوا مَا طَابَ لَكُم مِّنَ النِّسَاءِ مَثْنَىٰ وَثُلَاثَ وَرُبَاعَ فَإِنْ خِفْتُمْ أَلَّا تَعْدِلُوا فَوَاحِدَةً أَوْ مَا مَلَكَتْ أَيْمَانُكُمْ ذَلِكَ أَدْنَىٰ أَلَّا تَعُولُوا ۝٣

---

255. Meaning kinship. The word has direct reference to the high status of motherhood and wifehood in Islam. Kinship in Islam is regarded as one of the most important social institutions.

256. 'One of the most commendable things which one finds in reading the Qur'an is the solicitude which Muhammad shows for the young, and especially for such as have been deprived of their natural guardians. Again and again he insists upon a kind and just treatment being accorded to children. And working upon his words, the Muhammadan doctors have framed a system of rules concerning the appointment and duties of guardians which is most complete, and extending to the most minute details' (Roberts, *Social Laws of the Qur'an*, pp. 40–41).

257. 'Polygamy was the rule among the Eastern peoples before Mohammad's time' (Ibid., p. 8). 'When we see thousands of miserable women who crowd the streets of Western towns during the night, we must surely feel that it does not lie in Western mouths to reproach Islam for its polygamy. It is better for a woman, happier for a woman, more respectable for a woman, to live in Mohammadan polygamy, united to one man only, with the legitimate child in her arms surrounded with respect than to be seduced, cast out in the streets – perhaps with an illegitimate child outside the pale of law – unsheltered and uncared for to become a victim of any passer–by, night after night, rendered incapable of motherhood, despised of all' (Mrs. Annie Besant).

4. And give to women their dowers as a gift, and if they abandon of themselves anything of it to you, then eat it in pleasure and profit.

5. And do not give to the weak–witted the property which Allah has made for you a means of support, but feed them out of it, and clothe them, and speak to them a word of kind advice.

6. And test the orphans till they attain the age of wedlock, then if you perceive in them discretion, hand over to them their property and do not consume it extravagantly or hastily for fear that they may grow. And whoso is well-to-do, let him abstain, and whoso is needy let him take from it honourably. And when you hand over their property to them, call in witnesses in their presence and Allah suffices as a Reckoner.

7. To males shall be a portion of what their parents and other relations may leave[258] and to females shall be a portion of what their parents and other relations may leave whether it be small or large:[259] a portion allotted.[260]

وَءَاتُوا۟ ٱلنِّسَآءَ صَدُقَٰتِهِنَّ نِحْلَةً فَإِن طِبْنَ لَكُمْ عَن شَىْءٍ مِّنْهُ نَفْسًا فَكُلُوهُ هَنِيٓـًٔا مَّرِيٓـًٔا ۝

وَلَا تُؤْتُوا۟ ٱلسُّفَهَآءَ أَمْوَٰلَكُمُ ٱلَّتِى جَعَلَ ٱللَّهُ لَكُمْ قِيَٰمًا وَٱرْزُقُوهُمْ فِيهَا وَٱكْسُوهُمْ وَقُولُوا۟ لَهُمْ قَوْلًا مَّعْرُوفًا ۝

وَٱبْتَلُوا۟ ٱلْيَتَٰمَىٰ حَتَّىٰٓ إِذَا بَلَغُوا۟ ٱلنِّكَاحَ فَإِنْ ءَانَسْتُم مِّنْهُمْ رُشْدًا فَٱدْفَعُوٓا۟ إِلَيْهِمْ أَمْوَٰلَهُمْ وَلَا تَأْكُلُوهَآ إِسْرَافًا وَبِدَارًا أَن يَكْبَرُوا۟ وَمَن كَانَ غَنِيًّا فَلْيَسْتَعْفِفْ وَمَن كَانَ فَقِيرًا فَلْيَأْكُلْ بِٱلْمَعْرُوفِ فَإِذَا دَفَعْتُمْ إِلَيْهِمْ أَمْوَٰلَهُمْ فَأَشْهِدُوا۟ عَلَيْهِمْ وَكَفَىٰ بِٱللَّهِ حَسِيبًا ۝

لِّلرِّجَالِ نَصِيبٌ مِّمَّا تَرَكَ ٱلْوَٰلِدَانِ وَٱلْأَقْرَبُونَ وَلِلنِّسَآءِ نَصِيبٌ مِّمَّا تَرَكَ ٱلْوَٰلِدَانِ وَٱلْأَقْرَبُونَ مِمَّا قَلَّ مِنْهُ أَوْ كَثُرَ نَصِيبًا مَّفْرُوضًا ۝

---

258. Inheritance upon death. This means that womanhood or childhood or sex or infancy is no bar to inheritance as had once been the case not only in Arabia but in many parts of the ancient world. 'The importance of this reform', says Wherry, 'cannot be overrated. Previous to this women and helpless children could be disinherited by the adult male heirs, and thus be reduced to absolute penury, for no fault but that of being widows and orphans' (Wherry, *Commentary on the Koran*).

8. And when those of kin are present at the division, and the orphans and the needy, provide for them out of it, and speak to them a word of kindness.

9. And let them beware who, should they leave behind them a weak progeny, would be anxious on their account, let them therefore fear Allah and speak to them honourable words.

10. Verily those who devour the property of the orphans wrongfully, only devour fire into their bellies, and soon they shall roast in the Blaze.

وَإِذَا حَضَرَ ٱلْقِسْمَةَ أُوْلُوا ٱلْقُرْبَىٰ وَ ٱلْيَتَـٰمَىٰ وَٱلْمَسَـٰكِينُ فَٱرْزُقُوهُم مِّنْهُ وَقُولُوا لَهُمْ قَوْلًا مَّعْرُوفًا ۝

وَلْيَخْشَ ٱلَّذِينَ لَوْ تَرَكُوا مِنْ خَلْفِهِمْ ذُرِّيَّةً ضِعَـٰفًا خَافُوا عَلَيْهِمْ فَلْيَتَّقُوا ٱللَّهَ وَلْيَقُولُوا قَوْلًا سَدِيدًا ۝

إِنَّ ٱلَّذِينَ يَأْكُلُونَ أَمْوَٰلَ ٱلْيَتَـٰمَىٰ ظُلْمًا إِنَّمَا يَأْكُلُونَ فِى بُطُونِهِمْ نَارًا وَسَيَصْلَوْنَ سَعِيرًا ۝

259. And of this property women shall not be dispossessed when entering on marriage, as was the law in many lands. Even in the much – vaunted Roman law, 'the great majority of women became by marriage, as all women had originally become, the daughters of their husband. The family was based, less upon actual relationship than upon power, and the husband acquired over his wife the same despotic power which the father had over his children. There can be no question that, in strict pursuance of this conception of marriage, all the wife's property passed at first absolutely to the husband, and became fused with the domain of the new family' (Maine, *Early History of Institutions*, p. 312).

260. This Islamic law of inheritance is a landmark in the history of legal and social reform. In the pre–Islamic law of Arabia, women of all ages, and minor boys, had no share in their husbands' and in their fathers' inheritance, on the principle that they alone had the right to inherit who could beat arms. Thus wives, daughters and sisters were excluded altogether, and so were minor sons and brothers. In Islam the cardinal principle of inheritance is to distribute the property among all near relatives, and not to have it centred in the hands of the eldest son — a wise and effective check on capitalism.

Section 2

11. Allah enjoins you in the matter of your children:[261] the male will have as much as the portion of two females,[262] but if they be females more than two, then they will have two – thirds of what he has left, and if only one, she will have a half, and as for his parents, each of the twain will have a sixth of what he has left if he have a child; but if he has no child and his parents be his heirs, then his mother will have a third, but

يُوصِيكُمُ ٱللَّهُ فِي أَوْلَـٰدِكُمْ لِلذَّكَرِ مِثْلُ حَظِّ ٱلْأُنثَيَيْنِ فَإِن كُنَّ نِسَاءً فَوْقَ ٱثْنَتَيْنِ فَلَهُنَّ ثُلُثَا مَا تَرَكَ وَإِن كَانَتْ وَٰحِدَةً فَلَهَا ٱلنِّصْفُ وَلِأَبَوَيْهِ لِكُلِّ وَٰحِدٍ مِّنْهُمَا ٱلسُّدُسُ مِمَّا تَرَكَ إِن كَانَ لَهُۥ وَلَدٌ فَإِن لَّمْ يَكُن لَّهُۥ وَلَدٌ وَوَرِثَهُۥ أَبَوَاهُ فَلِأُمِّهِ ٱلثُّلُثُ

---

261. This concerning their inheriting property. Says Macnaghten, the author of *Principles and Precedents of Mohammedan Law* in his preliminary remarks: 'In these provisions we find ample attention paid to the interest of all those whom nature places in the first rank of our affections; and indeed it is difficult to conceive any system containing rules more strictly just and equitable'. And Rumney, the annotator of *Sirajiyya*, a book on the Muslim law of inheritance, observes: 'The Mohammedan Law of Inheritance comprises beyond question the most refined and elaborate system of rules for the devolution of property that is known to the civilised world' (Mahmudullah, *The Muslim Law of Inheritance*, p. i).

262. The underlying principle almost makes a new departure. Women and minor males were denied inheritance not only in pagan Arabia but also in the law of the Bible, 'women appear to have been universally and in every respect regarded as minors so far as rights of property went... Only sons, not daughters, still less wives, can inherit' (*EBi*, cc. 2728). The inequality between the share of a son and that of a daughter in the law of Islam is more apparent than real. 'The share of the daughter is determined not by any inferiority inherent in her but in view of her economic opportunities, and the place she occupies in the social structure of which she is a part and parcel... While the daughter, according to Mohammedan law, is held to be full owner of the property given to her both by the father and the husband at the time of her marriage; while, further, she absolutely owns her dower money which may be prompt or deferred according to her own choice, and in lieu of which she can hold possession of the whole of her husband's property till payment, the responsibility of maintaining her throughout her life is wholly thrown on the husband' (Iqbal, *Reconstruction of Religious Thought in Islam*, pp. 236–237).

if he have brothers, then his mother will have a sixth; all after paying a bequest he may have bequeathed or a debt. Your fathers and your sons you do not know which of them is nearer to you in benefit; an ordinance this is from Allah. Verily Allah is the Knowing, the Wise.

12. And you will have half of what your wives may leave, if they have no child; but if they have a child then you will have a fourth of what they may leave, after paying a bequest they may have bequeathed or a debt. And they[263] will have a fourth of what you may leave if you have no child, but if you have a child then they will have an eighth of what you may leave, after paying a bequest you may have bequeathed or a debt. And if a man or a woman who leaves an inheritance and has no direct heirs but has a brother or a sister, each of the two will have a sixth; and if more than one, then they will have equal shares in one – third after paying a bequest they may have bequeathed or a debt without prejudice and an ordinance this is from Allah; and Allah is the Knowing, the Forbearing.

---

263. They being the wives. In this point at least, Qur'ānic legislation is acknowledged to be 'in advance of' not only 'the greatest number of barbarous societies but also the Bible'. For, it recognizes 'the right of a widow to inherit from her husband... The Bible was less kind to the widow... It does not place her among her husband's heirs. The Jewish widow was a charge on her children or, if she had none, on her own family' (Letourneau, *Evolution of Marriage*, pp. 259–260).

13. These are the statutes of Allah, and whoever obeys Allah and His Messenger, him He shall admit into the Gardens beneath which rivers flow, as abiders therein; and that is the mighty achievement.

تِلۡكَ حُدُودُ اللّٰهِ وَمَن يُطِعِ اللّٰهَ وَرَسُولَهُ يُدۡخِلۡهُ جَنَّٰتٍ تَجۡرِى مِن تَحۡتِهَا الۡأَنۡهَٰرُ خَٰلِدِينَ فِيهَا وَذَٰلِكَ الۡفَوۡزُ الۡعَظِيمُ ﴿١٣﴾

14. And whoever disobeys Allah and His Messenger, and transgresses His statutes, him He shall cast into the Fire, as an abider therein, and to him shall be an ignominious torment.

وَمَن يَعۡصِ اللّٰهَ وَرَسُولَهُ وَيَتَعَدَّ حُدُودَهُ يُدۡخِلۡهُ نَارًا خَٰلِدًا فِيهَا وَلَهُ عَذَابٌ مُّهِينٌ ﴿١٤﴾

Section 3

15. As for those of your women who may commit whoredom, call against them four witnesses from among you; then if they testify, confine them to their houses, till death completes their term of life, or Allah appoints for them some other way.

وَاللّٰتِى يَأۡتِينَ الۡفَٰحِشَةَ مِن نِّسَآئِكُمۡ فَاسۡتَشۡهِدُواْ عَلَيۡهِنَّ أَرۡبَعَةً مِّنكُمۡ فَإِن شَهِدُواْ فَأَمۡسِكُوهُنَّ فِى الۡبُيُوتِ حَتَّىٰ يَتَوَفَّىٰهُنَّ الۡمَوۡتُ أَوۡ يَجۡعَلَ اللّٰهُ لَهُنَّ سَبِيلًا ﴿١٥﴾

16. And as for those two of you who commit it, hurt them both; then, if they repent and amend, turn away from them, surely Allah is the Relenting, the Merciful.

وَاللّٰذَانِ يَأۡتِيَٰنِهَا مِنكُمۡ فَآذُوهُمَا فَإِن تَابَا وَأَصۡلَحَا فَأَعۡرِضُواْ عَنۡهُمَا إِنَّ اللّٰهَ كَانَ تَوَّابًا رَّحِيمًا ﴿١٦﴾

17. Upon Allah is the repentance of those[264] who do an evil foolishly and then repent speedily; surely it is they to whom Allah shall relent. And Allah is the Knowing, the Wise.

18. And repentance is not for those who go on working evil till death presents itself to one of them, and he says: 'Now I repent'; nor for those who die while they are infidels. These! For them We have prepared an afflictive torment.

19. O you who believe! It is not allowed to you that you inherit the women[265] forcibly, nor shut them up that you may take away from them part of what you had given them,

إِنَّمَا ٱلتَّوْبَةُ عَلَى ٱللَّهِ لِلَّذِينَ يَعْمَلُونَ
ٱلسُّوٓءَ بِجَهَٰلَةٍ ثُمَّ يَتُوبُونَ مِن قَرِيبٍ
فَأُوْلَٰٓئِكَ يَتُوبُ ٱللَّهُ عَلَيْهِمْ وَكَانَ
ٱللَّهُ عَلِيمًا حَكِيمًا ١٧
وَلَيْسَتِ ٱلتَّوْبَةُ لِلَّذِينَ يَعْمَلُونَ
ٱلسَّيِّـَٔاتِ حَتَّىٰٓ إِذَا حَضَرَ أَحَدَهُمُ
ٱلْمَوْتُ قَالَ إِنِّي تُبْتُ ٱلْـَٰٔنَ وَلَا ٱلَّذِينَ
يَمُوتُونَ وَهُمْ كُفَّارٌ أُوْلَٰٓئِكَ
أَعْتَدْنَا لَهُمْ عَذَابًا أَلِيمًا ١٨
يَٰٓأَيُّهَا ٱلَّذِينَ ءَامَنُوا لَا يَحِلُّ لَكُمْ
أَن تَرِثُوا ٱلنِّسَآءَ كَرْهًا وَلَا تَعْضُلُوهُنَّ
لِتَذْهَبُوا بِبَعْضِ مَآ ءَاتَيْتُمُوهُنَّ

264. He promises to accept the repentance of those alone. Repentance has the following elements: (i) enlightenment of the heart, (ii) detestation of the sin, (iii) a resolve to avoid it in the future, and (iv) an earnest crying for God's forgiveness. It thus contains both a negative and a positive aspect — a turning from sin, and a turning to God. A penitent must not be taunted with his past. In the ethics of Islam, the penitent is superior to the sinless.

265. Inheriting women was a practice followed in pre–Islamic days. In pagan Arabia, widows were divided among the heirs of a deceased as goods and chattels. Immediately after a man died, his son or heir would cast a sheet of cloth on each of the widows (except his own mother), and this signified that he had annexed them to himself. Nor was this treatment of the widows confined to Arabia. Even in Greco–Roman civilization, the married woman in Athens 'was part of the paternal patrimony', and 'the dying husband could leave her by will to a friend, with his goods and by the same title', and 'in Rome the wife was bought and subjected to the terrible right of the marital manus' (*The Evolution of Marriage*, p. 261). 'The widows... were regarded as part of the estate, and as such passed ordinarily into the hands of their husbands' heirs'. (*The Social Laws of the Quran*, pp. 62–63). The heirs, in such cases, either married the widow to someone else and kept her dower, or refused to let her marry unless she redeemed herself by paying off handsomely, or else married her himself. One verse of the Qur'ān was sufficient, as by one stroke, to sweep aside all such barbaric customs, a reform of a truly revolutionary character.

except when they are guilty of manifest indecency. And live with them honourably;[266] if you dislike them, perhaps you detest a thing and yet Allah has placed abundant good therein.[267]

20. And if you intend to replace a wife by another, and you have given the one of them a talent, take not back anything of it. Would you take it back by slander and manifest sin?

21. And how can you take back when one of you has gone into the other, and they have obtained from you a rigid bond?

22. And wed not of women those whom your fathers have wedded, except what has already passed. Verily that has been an indecency and an abomination and an evil way.

---

266. This is the basic principle in Islam, of men's relations with their wives. Their faults and foibles are to be tolerated, overlooked, and an attitude of considerateness towards them is to be maintained. To view the same truth biologically: 'Woman will never be able to overcome these handicaps which are deeply rooted in her physical nature... Anyone familiar with the physiology and biology of woman will be less annoyed and irritated at her sudden changes of mood, allegedly unreasonable flares of temper, her unmotivated acts. Understanding this, man will deeply sympathise with the bearers of the egg cells who, having the same aspirations and claims upon life, are burdened with more difficult biological tasks' (Nemilov, *The Biological Tragedy of Woman*, pp. 187–188).

267. Insistence upon justice, goodwill and the fair treatment of the wife will thus be found to be the essence of the matrimonial code of Islam. The law of Islam concerns itself with the happiness and well-being of the wife in a way in which no Christian country does.

Section 4

23. Forbidden to you are your mothers and your daughters and your sisters and your father's sisters and your mother's sisters, and your brother's daughters and your sister's daughters, and your foster-mothers and your foster-sisters, and the mothers of your wives and your step daughters that are your wards, born of your wives to whom you have gone in, but if you have not gone into them, no sin shall be on you, and the wives of your sons that are from your own loins, and also that you should have two sisters together, except what has already passed. Verily Allah is ever the Forgiving, the Merciful.

24. And also forbidden are the wedded among women save those whom your right hands possess; Allah's ordinance for you. And allowed to you is whosoever is beyond that, so that you may seek them with your riches, as properly wedded men, not as fornicators. And for the enjoyment you have received from them, give them their stipulated dowers. And there will be no blame on you in regard to aught on which you mutually agree after the stipulation. Verily Allah is the Knowing, the Wise.

حُرِّمَتْ عَلَيْكُمْ أُمَّهَٰتُكُمْ وَ
بَنَاتُكُمْ وَأَخَوَٰتُكُمْ وَعَمَّٰتُكُمْ وَ
خَٰلَٰتُكُمْ وَبَنَاتُ ٱلْأَخِ وَبَنَاتُ
ٱلْأُخْتِ وَأُمَّهَٰتُكُمُ ٱلَّٰتِىٓ أَرْضَعْنَكُمْ
وَأَخَوَٰتُكُم مِّنَ ٱلرَّضَٰعَةِ وَ
أُمَّهَٰتُ نِسَآئِكُمْ وَرَبَٰٓئِبُكُمُ
ٱلَّٰتِى فِى حُجُورِكُم مِّن نِّسَآئِكُمُ
ٱلَّٰتِى دَخَلْتُم بِهِنَّ فَإِن لَّمْ تَكُونُوا۟
دَخَلْتُم بِهِنَّ فَلَا جُنَاحَ عَلَيْكُمْ
وَحَلَٰٓئِلُ أَبْنَآئِكُمُ ٱلَّذِينَ مِنْ
أَصْلَٰبِكُمْ وَأَن تَجْمَعُوا۟ بَيْنَ
ٱلْأُخْتَيْنِ إِلَّا مَا قَدْ سَلَفَ إِنَّ
ٱللَّهَ كَانَ غَفُورًا رَّحِيمًا ۝

وَٱلْمُحْصَنَٰتُ مِنَ ٱلنِّسَآءِ إِلَّا مَا مَلَكَتْ
أَيْمَٰنُكُمْ كِتَٰبَ ٱللَّهِ عَلَيْكُمْ وَأُحِلَّ
لَكُم مَّا وَرَآءَ ذَٰلِكُمْ أَن تَبْتَغُوا۟
بِأَمْوَٰلِكُم مُّحْصِنِينَ غَيْرَ مُسَٰفِحِينَ
فَمَا ٱسْتَمْتَعْتُم بِهِۦ مِنْهُنَّ فَـَٔاتُوهُنَّ
أُجُورَهُنَّ فَرِيضَةً وَلَا جُنَاحَ عَلَيْكُمْ
فِيمَا تَرَٰضَيْتُم بِهِۦ مِنۢ بَعْدِ ٱلْفَرِيضَةِ
إِنَّ ٱللَّهَ كَانَ عَلِيمًا حَكِيمًا ۝

25. And he among you who has not the affluence so that he may wed believing free women, let him wed such of the believing handmaids as the right hands of people possess. And Allah knows well your belief, the one of you is as the other. You may wed them, then, with the consent of their owners, and give them their dowers as properly wedded women,[268] not as fornicatresses, nor as taking to themselves secret paramours. And when they have been wedded, if they commit an indecency, on them the punishment shall be a half of that for free wedded women. This is for him among you who fears perdition, and that you should abstain is better for you. And Allah is the Forgiving, the Merciful.

وَمَن لَّمۡ يَسۡتَطِعۡ مِنكُمۡ طَوۡلًا أَن يَنكِحَ ٱلۡمُحۡصَنَٰتِ ٱلۡمُؤۡمِنَٰتِ فَمِن مَّا مَلَكَتۡ أَيۡمَٰنُكُم مِّن فَتَيَٰتِكُمُ ٱلۡمُؤۡمِنَٰتِۚ وَٱللَّهُ أَعۡلَمُ بِإِيمَٰنِكُمۚ بَعۡضُكُم مِّنۢ بَعۡضٖۚ فَٱنكِحُوهُنَّ بِإِذۡنِ أَهۡلِهِنَّ وَءَاتُوهُنَّ أُجُورَهُنَّ بِٱلۡمَعۡرُوفِ مُحۡصَنَٰتٍ غَيۡرَ مُسَٰفِحَٰتٖ وَلَا مُتَّخِذَٰتِ أَخۡدَانٖۚ فَإِذَآ أُحۡصِنَّ فَإِنۡ أَتَيۡنَ بِفَٰحِشَةٖ فَعَلَيۡهِنَّ نِصۡفُ مَا عَلَى ٱلۡمُحۡصَنَٰتِ مِنَ ٱلۡعَذَابِۚ ذَٰلِكَ لِمَنۡ خَشِيَ ٱلۡعَنَتَ مِنكُمۚ وَأَن تَصۡبِرُواْ خَيۡرٞ لَّكُمۡۗ وَٱللَّهُ غَفُورٞ رَّحِيمٞ ٢٥

Section 5

26. Allah desires to expound to you and to guide you into the institutions of those before you and relent towards you. And Allah is the Knowing, the Wise.

يُرِيدُ ٱللَّهُ لِيُبَيِّنَ لَكُمۡ وَيَهۡدِيَكُمۡ سُنَنَ ٱلَّذِينَ مِن قَبۡلِكُمۡ وَيَتُوبَ عَلَيۡكُمۚ وَٱللَّهُ عَلِيمٌ حَكِيمٞ ٢٦

27. And Allah desires to relent towards you, and those who follow their lusts desire that you shall incline towards a mighty deviation.

وَٱللَّهُ يُرِيدُ أَن يَتُوبَ عَلَيۡكُمۡ وَيُرِيدُ ٱلَّذِينَ يَتَّبِعُونَ ٱلشَّهَوَٰتِ أَن تَمِيلُواْ مَيۡلًا عَظِيمٗا ٢٧

---

268. Notice the high ideal of chastity and purity pervading the entire system of these enactments.

28. Allah desires that He shall lighten things for you and man has been created a weakling.

يُرِيدُ اللّٰهُ اَنْ يُّخَفِّفَ عَنكُمْ وَخُلِقَ الْإِنسَٰنُ ضَعِيفًا ۝

29. O you who believe! Devour not your property among yourselves[269] unlawfully, but let there be trading among you by mutual agreement; and kill not yourselves.[270] Verily Allah is to you ever Merciful.

يَٰٓأَيُّهَا الَّذِينَ ءَامَنُوا لَا تَأْكُلُوا أَمْوَٰلَكُم بَيْنَكُم بِالْبَٰطِلِ إِلَّا أَن تَكُونَ تِجَٰرَةً عَن تَرَاضٍ مِّنكُمْ وَلَا تَقْتُلُوٓا أَنفُسَكُمْ إِنَّ اللّٰهَ كَانَ بِكُمْ رَحِيمًا ۝

30. And whoever does that in transgression and wrong, him We will soon roast in the Fire, and with Allah that is ever easy.

وَمَن يَفْعَلْ ذَٰلِكَ عُدْوَٰنًا وَظُلْمًا فَسَوْفَ نُصْلِيهِ نَارًا وَكَانَ ذَٰلِكَ عَلَى اللّٰهِ يَسِيرًا ۝

31. If you shun the grievous sins from which you have been prohibited, We will expiate from you your misdeeds, and make you enter a noble entrance.

إِن تَجْتَنِبُوا كَبَآئِرَ مَا تُنْهَوْنَ عَنْهُ نُكَفِّرْ عَنكُمْ سَيِّـَٔاتِكُمْ وَنُدْخِلْكُم مُّدْخَلًا كَرِيمًا ۝

---

269. In other words, do not consume one another's property. Every believer's property is his own. Islam totally rejects the communistic doctrine of the state ownership of all property.

270. This interdicts suicide in all its forms, and has led a famous Christian writer to observe: 'Suicide, which is never expressly condemned in the Bible, is more than once forbidden in the Koran' (Lecky, *History of European Morals*, II, London, p. 56). It may also be taken in a collective sense, the rendering in which case would be: 'And slay not one another.' This would make the life of a believer as intrinsically inviolable as has been made his property in the preceding part of the verse.

32. And do not covet that wherewith Allah has excelled one of you above another.[271] To men shall be the portion of what they earn, and to women shall be the portion of what they earn.[272] And ask Allah for some of His grace. Verily Allah is the Knower of everything.

وَلَا تَتَمَنَّوْا مَا فَضَّلَ اللَّهُ بِهِ بَعْضَكُمْ عَلَىٰ بَعْضٍ لِّلرِّجَالِ نَصِيبٌ مِّمَّا اكْتَسَبُوا وَلِلنِّسَاءِ نَصِيبٌ مِّمَّا اكْتَسَبْنَ وَسْـَٔلُوا اللَّهَ مِن فَضْلِهِ إِنَّ اللَّهَ كَانَ بِكُلِّ شَىْءٍ عَلِيمًا ۞

---

271. This refers to the female sex. That in the scheme of life the role of the male is different in many fundamentals from that of the female is recognized by the modern sciences of biology and psychology alike. 'The desires and conduct of the two sexes are not similar, but are complementary and reciprocal. In courtship the male is active; his role is to court, to pursue, to possess, to control, to protect, to love. The role of the female is passive' (Mercier, *Conduct and its Disorders Biologically Considered*, pp. 289–290). 'Man perhaps even down to the protein molecules of his tissue cells, is biologically different from woman. From the very moment of sex formation in the embryo, the biological dusting of the sexes develops along entirely divergent paths... We must recognize the unquestionable existence of the biological inequality of the sexes. It goes deeper and is of far greater import than it would appear to those not familiar with natural science' (Nemilov, *Biological Tragedy of Woman*, pp. 76–78). 'Will it be possible for woman's emancipation to remove those differences between man and woman which are rooted in their innermost beings. Even the most rabid advocates of woman's rights must accept the undeniable fact that woman bears children, not man; that woman menstruates, not man. It remains equally true that these primitive functions will always be a hindrance to complete emancipation, though they do not preclude advance and improvement in the intellectual and social position of woman, which every fair-minded man willingly recognises as necessary...' According to Mrs. Hawthorne, home is the woman's great arena, and will, she hopes, remain so. 'There she can exercise a sway that no king or emperor can rival. And it is compatible with culture, intellect and earnestness. I should like to cry aloud to the modern woman: Educate yourself; dedicate your time to science; take part in the thoughts and occupations of men, but do not seek to do so as he does. For you will never be his equal, even as he never will be your equal' (Bloch, *Sexual Life in England*, pp. 48–49). 'I venture to prophesy not only that the inherent differences between the sexes will not tend to diminish in the course of evolution but that man will continue, as now and in the past, to emphasise them by custom and convention' (Julian Huxley, *Essays in Popular Science*, p. 63).

272. What women earn through their moral acts. The purport is : in spite of the many and varied differences between men and women in their physical and mental make–up, in matters of spiritual grace and in acts leading to moral perfection, there is no disparity at all between the two sexes. In God's sight as responsible moral agents both are equal.

33. And to everyone We have appointed inheritors of what the parents or relations leave behind, and to them with whom you have made your pledges give them their portion. Verily Allah is ever a Witness over everything.

وَلِكُلٍّ جَعَلْنَا مَوَالِيَ مِمَّا تَرَكَ الْوَالِدَانِ وَالْأَقْرَبُونَ وَالَّذِينَ عَقَدَتْ أَيْمَانُكُمْ فَآتُوهُمْ نَصِيبَهُمْ إِنَّ اللَّهَ كَانَ عَلَى كُلِّ شَيْءٍ شَهِيدًا ۝

Section 6

34. Men are overseers over women,[273] by reason of that wherewith Allah has made one of them excel over another, and by reason of what they spend of their riches. So the righteous women are obedient and watchers in their husbands' absence by the aid and protection of Allah. And those wives whose refractoriness you fear, admonish them and avoid them in

الرِّجَالُ قَوَّامُونَ عَلَى النِّسَاءِ بِمَا فَضَّلَ اللَّهُ بَعْضَهُمْ عَلَى بَعْضٍ وَبِمَا أَنْفَقُوا مِنْ أَمْوَالِهِمْ فَالصَّالِحَاتُ قَانِتَاتٌ حَافِظَاتٌ لِلْغَيْبِ بِمَا حَفِظَ اللَّهُ وَاللَّاتِي تَخَافُونَ نُشُوزَهُنَّ فَعِظُوهُنَّ

273. Compare the attitude of the Bible towards woman: 'Unto the woman he said: thy desire shall be to thy husband, and he shall rule over thee' (Gr. 3: 16). 'Wives, submit yourselves unto your own husbands, as unto the Lord. For the husband is the head of the wife, even as Christ is the head of the church: and he is the saviour of the body. Therefore as the church is subject unto Christ, so let the wives be to their own husbands in every thing' (Eph. 5: 22–24).

A *Qawwām* is, in the parlance of modern sociology, a protector or guardian of the family, and this is a position to which man is by his very nature and constitution entitled. 'A connected result of male superiority in strength, activity and courage is the element of protection in male love, and of trust on the side of the female' (*ERE.* VIII, p. 156). 'That the functions of the husband and father in the family are not merely of the sexual and procreative kind, but involve the duties of supporting and protecting the wife and children, is testified by an array of facts relating to peoples in all quarters of the world and in all stages of civilisation' (Westermarck, *Short History of Marriage*, p. 23). 'Among the lowest savages, as well as the most civilised races of men, we find the family consisting of parents and children, and the father as its protector and supporter' (Ibid., p. 7).

'Until recently women were typically engaged throughout youth and maturity in conceiving, bearing, feeding, and nursing, infants. From girlhood, women were attached to infants. The period of gestation for a human infant is long. Once born, it must be carried upon the back and fed from the breast for a long time, under primitive conditions. Its birth constitutes an ordeal for the mother, in the course of which she may be crippled, at least for enough days to suffice for starvation unless ministered to by others. How to master the uncertain food supply, ravenous wild beasts, hostile tribes, storms and cold is a hard puzzle for a creature carrying heavy children within and upon her body, year in and year out. There is, nevertheless, a way to open this hard cage, that will lead to sustenance and shelter without sacrifice of the child. This way is to get the protection of those who are not cumbered with burdensome generative systems. Thus if men could be induced to supply subsistence women could live without killing or abandoning their infants. At the same time, men were motivated by sex attraction, by the luxury of having routine labours performed for them, and doubtless by pity, to undertake the protection of women and of the helpless offspring to which they were mysteriously subject. Thus men, women and children came to be arranged in family groups, in which men were inevitably lords and masters because they needed the arrangement least' (*EBr.* IX. p. 61). In the words of the German philosopher, E.Von Hartmann, from the moral standpoint, 'the greater number of women pass the whole of their lives in a state of minority, and, therefore, to the end stand in need of supervision and guidance' (Kisch, *Sexual Life of Woman*, p. 153). In the beautiful summing up of D.H. Lawrence, 'Primarily and unprimarily, man is always the pioneer of life, adventuring onward into the unknown, alone with his temerarious, dauntless soul. Woman for him exists only in the twilight by the campfire when day has departed' (Reader, Maxim, *Currents in Modern Science*, p. 192). And according to a modern French writer and thinker: 'Women can direct great business enterprises, and some do with astonishing skill, but the role does not suit them. One of the most successful of these made the following admission: "Do you know that I've always wanted to find a man who could take over my job? Then I would be his assistant, and what a marvellous assistant I could be if I loved him!" It must be recognized that women are excellent assistants rather than original creators. Woman's real creation is her child... Even those who are forced by circumstances to play men's roles play them as women. Queen Victoria was not a great king, but a great Queen acting the king' (Andre Maurois, *Art of Living*, pp. 49–50).

beds and beat them;[274] but if they obey you, do not seek a way against them. Verily Allah is ever Lofty, Grand.

35. And if you fear a break between the pair, set up an arbiter from his family and an arbiter from her family; then if the pair seek amity, Allah shall bring harmony between the two. Verily Allah is ever Knowing, Aware.

36. And worship Allah, and do not join anyone with Him; and to parents show kindness and also to kinsmen and orphans and the needy and the near neighbour and the distant neighbour and the companion by your side and the wayfarer and those whom your right hands possess. Verily Allah does not love the vainglorious and the boastful.

37. Those who are miserly and bid people to miserliness, and conceal what Allah has granted them of His grace; and We have prepared for the infidels an ignominious torment;

38. And those who spend of their wealth to show off to men, and do not believe in Allah nor in the Last Day; and whoso has for him Satan as a companion, a vile companion has he.

وَٱهْجُرُوهُنَّ فِى ٱلْمَضَاجِعِ وَٱضْرِبُوهُنَّ فَإِنْ أَطَعْنَكُمْ فَلَا تَبْغُواْ عَلَيْهِنَّ سَبِيلًا إِنَّ ٱللَّهَ كَانَ عَلِيًّا كَبِيرًا ۝

وَإِنْ خِفْتُمْ شِقَاقَ بَيْنِهِمَا فَٱبْعَثُواْ حَكَمًا مِّنْ أَهْلِهِۦ وَحَكَمًا مِّنْ أَهْلِهَآ إِن يُرِيدَآ إِصْلَٰحًا يُوَفِّقِ ٱللَّهُ بَيْنَهُمَآ إِنَّ ٱللَّهَ كَانَ عَلِيمًا خَبِيرًا ۝

وَٱعْبُدُواْ ٱللَّهَ وَلَا تُشْرِكُواْ بِهِۦ شَيْـًٔا وَبِٱلْوَٰلِدَيْنِ إِحْسَٰنًا وَبِذِى ٱلْقُرْبَىٰ وَٱلْيَتَٰمَىٰ وَٱلْمَسَٰكِينِ وَٱلْجَارِ ذِى ٱلْقُرْبَىٰ وَٱلْجَارِ ٱلْجُنُبِ وَٱلصَّاحِبِ بِٱلْجَنۢبِ وَٱبْنِ ٱلسَّبِيلِ وَمَا مَلَكَتْ أَيْمَٰنُكُمْ إِنَّ ٱللَّهَ لَا يُحِبُّ مَن كَانَ مُخْتَالًا فَخُورًا ۝

ٱلَّذِينَ يَبْخَلُونَ وَيَأْمُرُونَ ٱلنَّاسَ بِٱلْبُخْلِ وَيَكْتُمُونَ مَآ ءَاتَىٰهُمُ ٱللَّهُ مِن فَضْلِهِۦ وَأَعْتَدْنَا لِلْكَٰفِرِينَ عَذَابًا مُّهِينًا ۝

وَٱلَّذِينَ يُنفِقُونَ أَمْوَٰلَهُمْ رِئَآءَ ٱلنَّاسِ وَلَا يُؤْمِنُونَ بِٱللَّهِ وَلَا بِٱلْيَوْمِ ٱلْءَاخِرِ وَمَن يَكُنِ ٱلشَّيْطَٰنُ لَهُۥ قَرِينًا فَسَآءَ قَرِينًا ۝

---

274. The fact must not be lost sight of that the Holy Word is addressed to peoples of all ages and of all grades and stages of social evolution; and it may well be that a remedy that is unthinkable in a particular grade of society is the only feasible and effective corrective in another.

39. And what harm would befall them, were they to believe in Allah and the Last Day and spend out of that wherewith Allah has provided them. And Allah is ever Knower of them.

وَمَاذَا عَلَيْهِمْ لَوْ ءَامَنُوا بِاللّٰهِ وَالْيَوْمِ الْآخِرِ وَأَنفَقُوا مِمَّا رَزَقَهُمُ اللّٰهُ وَكَانَ اللّٰهُ بِهِمْ عَلِيمًا ﴿٣٩﴾

40. Surely Allah does not wrong anyone a grain's weight, and if there is a virtue He will double it and give from His presence a mighty reward.

إِنَّ اللّٰهَ لَا يَظْلِمُ مِثْقَالَ ذَرَّةٍ وَإِن تَكُ حَسَنَةً يُضَٰعِفْهَا وَيُؤْتِ مِن لَّدُنْهُ أَجْرًا عَظِيمًا ﴿٤٠﴾

41. How will it be then, when We bring, out of each community, a witness, and We will bring you against these as a witness?

فَكَيْفَ إِذَا جِئْنَا مِن كُلِّ أُمَّةٍ بِشَهِيدٍ وَجِئْنَا بِكَ عَلَىٰ هَٰٓؤُلَآءِ شَهِيدًا ﴿٤١﴾

42. That Day those who had disbelieved and disobeyed the Messenger would wish that the earth would be levelled over them, and they will not be able to hide any discourse from Allah.

يَوْمَئِذٍ يَوَدُّ الَّذِينَ كَفَرُوا وَعَصَوُا الرَّسُولَ لَوْ تُسَوَّىٰ بِهِمُ الْأَرْضُ وَلَا يَكْتُمُونَ اللّٰهَ حَدِيثًا ﴿٤٢﴾

Section 7

43. O you who believe! Do not approach prayer while you are drunken until you understand what you say, nor yet while you are polluted, save when you are wayfaring, nor until you have washed yourselves. And if you are ailing or on a journey or one of you comes from the privy or you have touched women, and you do not find water then betake yourselves to clean earth and wipe your faces and your hands with it. Verily Allah is ever Pardoning, Forgiving.

يَٰٓأَيُّهَا الَّذِينَ ءَامَنُوا لَا تَقْرَبُوا الصَّلَوٰةَ وَأَنتُمْ سُكَٰرَىٰ حَتَّىٰ تَعْلَمُوا مَا تَقُولُونَ وَلَا جُنُبًا إِلَّا عَابِرِى سَبِيلٍ حَتَّىٰ تَغْتَسِلُوا وَإِن كُنتُم مَّرْضَىٰ أَوْ عَلَىٰ سَفَرٍ أَوْ جَآءَ أَحَدٌ مِّنكُم مِّنَ الْغَآئِطِ أَوْ لَٰمَسْتُمُ النِّسَآءَ فَلَمْ تَجِدُوا مَآءً فَتَيَمَّمُوا صَعِيدًا طَيِّبًا فَامْسَحُوا بِوُجُوهِكُمْ وَأَيْدِيكُمْ إِنَّ اللّٰهَ كَانَ عَفُوًّا غَفُورًا ﴿٤٣﴾

44. Have you not observed those to whom was given a portion of the Book purchasing error, and intending that you would err as regards the way?

أَلَمۡ تَرَ إِلَى ٱلَّذِينَ أُوتُوا۟ نَصِيبًا مِّنَ ٱلۡكِتَٰبِ يَشۡتَرُونَ ٱلضَّلَٰلَةَ وَيُرِيدُونَ أَن تَضِلُّوا۟ ٱلسَّبِيلَ ۝

45. And Allah is the Knower of your enemies; suffices Allah as a Friend, and suffices Allah as a Helper.

وَٱللَّهُ أَعۡلَمُ بِأَعۡدَآئِكُمۡ وَكَفَىٰ بِٱللَّهِ وَلِيًّا وَكَفَىٰ بِٱللَّهِ نَصِيرًا ۝

46. Among those who are Judaized are some who pervert words[275] from their meanings and say; we have heard and we disobey and hear you without being made to hear, and *rā'inā* twisting their tongues and scoffing at the faith.

مِّنَ ٱلَّذِينَ هَادُوا۟ يُحَرِّفُونَ ٱلۡكَلِمَ عَن مَّوَاضِعِهِۦ وَيَقُولُونَ سَمِعۡنَا وَعَصَيۡنَا وَٱسۡمَعۡ غَيۡرَ مُسۡمَعٍ وَرَٰعِنَا لَيًّۢا بِأَلۡسِنَتِهِمۡ وَطَعۡنًا فِى ٱلدِّينِ

---

275. They dislocate and corrupt the very words and passages of the Holy Texts, alter their sense, and twist their rendering. The Holy Qur'ān was not the first to charge the Jews with the falsification of their Scriptures. Even Justin, in the beginning of the second century of the Christian era, charged them 'with immorality and with having expunged from their Bibles much that was favourable to Christianity. These charges were repeated by the succeeding Christian polemicists' (*JE*. X. p. 103). Modern Jewish theology of the Reform School not only admits 'the human origin of the Holy Scriptures' and recognizes that 'the matter recorded is sometimes in contradiction to the proved results of modern historical, physical, and psychological research', but also arrives at the following conclusions:

(i) 'The ancient view of a literal dictation by God must be surrendered.'

(ii) 'The seers and writers of Judea must be regarded as men with human failings, each with his own peculiarity of style and sentiments.'

(iii) And that though 'the prophet and sacred writers were under the influence of the Divine Spirit while revealing, by word or pen, new religious ideas .... the human element in them was not extinguished, and consequently, in regard to their statements, their knowledge, and the form of their communication, they could only have acted as children of their age' (*JE*. VI. pp. 608–609). So the fallibility and the human origins of the Jewish Scriptures are self-confessed.

And had they said : 'We have heard and obey and hear you, and *unzurnā*', it surely had been better for them and more upright. But Allah has cursed them for their infidelity. So they shall not believe, save a few.

وَلَوْ أَنَّهُمْ قَالُوا سَمِعْنَا وَأَطَعْنَا وَاسْمَعْ وَانْظُرْنَا لَكَانَ خَيْرًا لَّهُمْ وَأَقْوَمَ وَلَٰكِن لَّعَنَهُمُ اللَّهُ بِكُفْرِهِمْ فَلَا يُؤْمِنُونَ إِلَّا قَلِيلًا ۝

47. O you who are given the Book, believe in what We have sent down confirming what is with you, before We change faces, and turn them upon their backs, or We might curse them even as We cursed the people of the Sabbath, and Allah's command is ever carried out.

يَٰٓأَيُّهَا الَّذِينَ أُوتُوا الْكِتَٰبَ ءَامِنُوا بِمَا نَزَّلْنَا مُصَدِّقًا لِّمَا مَعَكُم مِّن قَبْلِ أَن نَّطْمِسَ وُجُوهًا فَنَرُدَّهَا عَلَىٰٓ أَدْبَارِهَا أَوْ نَلْعَنَهُمْ كَمَا لَعَنَّا أَصْحَٰبَ السَّبْتِ وَكَانَ أَمْرُ اللَّهِ مَفْعُولًا ۝

48. Surely Allah will not forgive that anyone be joined with Him, and He will forgive all else to whom He will. And whoso joined anyone with Allah, he has certainly fabricated a mighty sin.

إِنَّ اللَّهَ لَا يَغْفِرُ أَن يُشْرَكَ بِهِ وَيَغْفِرُ مَا دُونَ ذَٰلِكَ لِمَن يَشَآءُ وَمَن يُشْرِكْ بِاللَّهِ فَقَدِ افْتَرَىٰٓ إِثْمًا عَظِيمًا ۝

49. Have you not observed those who hold themselves to be pure? Nay, it is Allah Who purifies whom He will, and they shall not be wronged a whit.

أَلَمْ تَرَ إِلَى الَّذِينَ يُزَكُّونَ أَنفُسَهُم بَلِ اللَّهُ يُزَكِّى مَن يَشَآءُ وَلَا يُظْلَمُونَ فَتِيلًا ۝

50. Look! How they fabricate a lie against Allah, and enough is that as a manifest sin.

انظُرْ كَيْفَ يَفْتَرُونَ عَلَى اللَّهِ الْكَذِبَ وَكَفَىٰ بِهِ إِثْمًا مُّبِينًا ۝

Section 8

51. Have you not observed those to whom is given a portion of the Book testifying to idols and devils, and speaking of those who have disbelieved! That these are better guided as regards the way than the believers?

أَلَمْ تَرَ إِلَى ٱلَّذِينَ أُوتُوا نَصِيبًا مِّنَ ٱلْكِتَبِ يُؤْمِنُونَ بِٱلْجِبْتِ وَٱلطَّغُوتِ وَيَقُولُونَ لِلَّذِينَ كَفَرُوا هَؤُلَاءِ أَهْدَىٰ مِنَ ٱلَّذِينَ ءَامَنُوا سَبِيلًا ۞

52. Those are they whom Allah has cursed, and whom Allah curses, for them you shall not find a helper.

أُو۟لَٰٓئِكَ ٱلَّذِينَ لَعَنَهُمُ ٱللَّهُ وَمَن يَلْعَنِ ٱللَّهُ فَلَن تَجِدَ لَهُۥ نَصِيرًا ۞

53. Have they a share in the kingdom? If so, they will not give mankind a speck.

أَمْ لَهُمْ نَصِيبٌ مِّنَ ٱلْمُلْكِ فَإِذًا لَّا يُؤْتُونَ ٱلنَّاسَ نَقِيرًا ۞

54. Or do they envy the people on account of what Allah has granted them out of His grace? So surely We granted the house of Abraham the Book and wisdom and We granted them a mighty kingdom.

أَمْ يَحْسُدُونَ ٱلنَّاسَ عَلَىٰ مَآ ءَاتَىٰهُمُ ٱللَّهُ مِن فَضْلِهِۦ فَقَدْ ءَاتَيْنَآ ءَالَ إِبْرَٰهِيمَ ٱلْكِتَٰبَ وَٱلْحِكْمَةَ وَءَاتَيْنَٰهُم مُّلْكًا عَظِيمًا ۞

55. Then among them were some who believed in it, and among them were others who turned aside from it and enough is Hell as a flame.

فَمِنْهُم مَّنْ ءَامَنَ بِهِۦ وَمِنْهُم مَّن صَدَّ عَنْهُ وَكَفَىٰ بِجَهَنَّمَ سَعِيرًا ۞

56. Verily those who disbelieve in Our revelations, them We will soon cast in the Fire. Whenever their skins are burnt up, We will change them for other skins, to keep up their tasting of the torment. Verily Allah is ever Mighty, Wise.

إِنَّ ٱلَّذِينَ كَفَرُوا بِـَٔايَٰتِنَا سَوْفَ نُصْلِيهِمْ نَارًا كُلَّمَا نَضِجَتْ جُلُودُهُم بَدَّلْنَٰهُمْ جُلُودًا غَيْرَهَا لِيَذُوقُوا ٱلْعَذَابَ إِنَّ ٱللَّهَ كَانَ عَزِيزًا حَكِيمًا ۞

57. And those who believe and do righteous works, soon We will admit them to the Garden beneath which rivers flow abiding there for ever. For them shall be spouses, and We will admit them to a sheltering shade.

وَٱلَّذِينَ ءَامَنُوا۟ وَعَمِلُوا۟ ٱلصَّٰلِحَٰتِ سَنُدۡخِلُهُمۡ جَنَّٰتٍ تَجۡرِى مِن تَحۡتِهَا ٱلۡأَنۡهَٰرُ خَٰلِدِينَ فِيهَآ أَبَدࣰاۖ لَّهُمۡ فِيهَآ أَزۡوَٰجٌ مُّطَهَّرَةࣱۖ وَنُدۡخِلُهُمۡ ظِلࣰّا ظَلِيلًا ٥٧

58. Verily Allah commands that you shall render dues to the owners thereof, and that, when you judge between men, judge with equity. Excellent is that with which Allah exhorts you; verily Allah is ever Hearing, Seeing.

إِنَّ ٱللَّهَ يَأۡمُرُكُمۡ أَن تُؤَدُّوا۟ ٱلۡأَمَٰنَٰتِ إِلَىٰٓ أَهۡلِهَا وَإِذَا حَكَمۡتُم بَيۡنَ ٱلنَّاسِ أَن تَحۡكُمُوا۟ بِٱلۡعَدۡلِۚ إِنَّ ٱللَّهَ نِعِمَّا يَعِظُكُم بِهِۦٓۗ إِنَّ ٱللَّهَ كَانَ سَمِيعَۢا بَصِيرࣰا ٥٨

59. O you who believe! Obey Allah and obey the Messenger and men of authority from amongst you; then if you quarrel in aught, refer it to Allah and the Messenger, if you indeed believe in Allah and the Last Day. That is the best and the fairest interpretation.

يَٰٓأَيُّهَا ٱلَّذِينَ ءَامَنُوٓا۟ أَطِيعُوا۟ ٱللَّهَ وَأَطِيعُوا۟ ٱلرَّسُولَ وَأُو۟لِى ٱلۡأَمۡرِ مِنكُمۡۖ فَإِن تَنَٰزَعۡتُمۡ فِى شَىۡءٍ فَرُدُّوهُ إِلَى ٱللَّهِ وَٱلرَّسُولِ إِن كُنتُمۡ تُؤۡمِنُونَ بِٱللَّهِ وَٱلۡيَوۡمِ ٱلۡأٓخِرِۚ ذَٰلِكَ خَيۡرٌ وَأَحۡسَنُ تَأۡوِيلًا ٥٩

Section 9

60. Have you not observed those who assert that they believe in what has been sent down to you and what has been sent down before you, and yet desire to go to the devil for judgement whereas they have been commanded to deny him; and Satan desires to mislead them far off.

أَلَمۡ تَرَ إِلَى ٱلَّذِينَ يَزۡعُمُونَ أَنَّهُمۡ ءَامَنُوا۟ بِمَآ أُنزِلَ إِلَيۡكَ وَمَآ أُنزِلَ مِن قَبۡلِكَ يُرِيدُونَ أَن يَتَحَاكَمُوٓا۟ إِلَى ٱلطَّٰغُوتِ وَقَدۡ أُمِرُوٓا۟ أَن يَكۡفُرُوا۟ بِهِۦ وَيُرِيدُ ٱلشَّيۡطَٰنُ أَن يُضِلَّهُمۡ ضَلَٰلَۢا بَعِيدࣰا ٦٠

61. And when it is said to them: 'Come to what Allah has sent down and to the Messenger', you will see the hypocrites hang far back from you.

وَإِذَا قِيلَ لَهُمْ تَعَالَوْا إِلَىٰ مَاۤ أَنزَلَ ٱللَّهُ وَإِلَى ٱلرَّسُولِ رَأَيْتَ ٱلْمُنَٰفِقِينَ يَصُدُّونَ عَنكَ صُدُودًا ﴿٦١﴾

62. How then, when some ill befalls them because of what their hands have sent forth and then they came to you swearing by Allah; we meant nothing save kindness and concord.

فَكَيْفَ إِذَاۤ أَصَٰبَتْهُم مُّصِيبَةٌۢ بِمَا قَدَّمَتْ أَيْدِيهِمْ ثُمَّ جَآءُوكَ يَحْلِفُونَ بِٱللَّهِ إِنْ أَرَدْنَاۤ إِلَّاۤ إِحْسَٰنًا وَتَوْفِيقًا ﴿٦٢﴾

63. Those are they of whom Allah knows whatever is in their hearts; so turn from them and admonish them, and speak to them for their souls with effective words.

أُوْلَٰٓئِكَ ٱلَّذِينَ يَعْلَمُ ٱللَّهُ مَا فِى قُلُوبِهِمْ فَأَعْرِضْ عَنْهُمْ وَعِظْهُمْ وَقُل لَّهُمْ فِىٓ أَنفُسِهِمْ قَوْلًۢا بَلِيغًا ﴿٦٣﴾

64. And not a Messenger have We sent but to be obeyed by Allah's will. And if they, when they had wronged their souls, had come to you and begged the forgiveness of Allah and the Messenger and the Messenger had begged forgiveness for them, they would surely have found Allah the Relenting, the Merciful.

وَمَاۤ أَرْسَلْنَا مِن رَّسُولٍ إِلَّا لِيُطَاعَ بِإِذْنِ ٱللَّهِ وَلَوْ أَنَّهُمْ إِذ ظَّلَمُوۤا أَنفُسَهُمْ جَآءُوكَ فَٱسْتَغْفَرُوا ٱللَّهَ وَٱسْتَغْفَرَ لَهُمُ ٱلرَّسُولُ لَوَجَدُوا ٱللَّهَ تَوَّابًا رَّحِيمًا ﴿٦٤﴾

65. Aye! By your Lord, they shall not really believe until they have made you judge of what is disputed among them, and then find no demur in their hearts against what you have decreed and they submit with full submission.

فَلَا وَرَبِّكَ لَا يُؤْمِنُونَ حَتَّىٰ يُحَكِّمُوكَ فِيمَا شَجَرَ بَيْنَهُمْ ثُمَّ لَا يَجِدُوا فِىٓ أَنفُسِهِمْ حَرَجًا مِّمَّا قَضَيْتَ وَيُسَلِّمُوا تَسْلِيمًا ﴿٦٥﴾

66. And had We prescribed to them: kill yourselves or go forth from your dwellings, they would not have done it, save a few of them. And had they performed what they were exhorted to perform, it would have been better for them and more strengthening.

67. And then surely We would have given them from Our presence a mighty reward.

68. And surely We would have guided them to a straight path.

69. And whoso obeys Allah and the Messenger, then those shall be with them whom Allah has blessed from among the Prophets, the saints, the martyrs, and the righteous. Excellent are these as a company!

70. That is the grace from Allah, and Allah suffices as the Knower!

Section 10

71. O you who believe! Be on your guard; then sally forth in detachments or all together.

72. And surely there is among you he who tarries behind, and if an ill befalls you, he says: 'Surely God has been gracious to me in that I was not present with them.'

وَلَوْ أَنَّا كَتَبْنَا عَلَيْهِمْ أَنِ اقْتُلُوٓاْ
أَنفُسَكُمْ أَوِ اخْرُجُواْ مِن دِيَـٰرِكُم مَّا
فَعَلُوهُ إِلَّا قَلِيلٌ مِّنْهُمْ وَلَوْ أَنَّهُمْ فَعَلُواْ
مَا يُوعَظُونَ بِهِۦ لَكَانَ خَيْرًا لَّهُمْ
وَأَشَدَّ تَثْبِيتًا ﴿٦٦﴾

وَإِذًا لَّآتَيْنَـٰهُم مِّن لَّدُنَّآ أَجْرًا عَظِيمًا ﴿٦٧﴾

وَلَهَدَيْنَـٰهُمْ صِرَٰطًا مُّسْتَقِيمًا ﴿٦٨﴾

وَمَن يُطِعِ اللَّهَ وَالرَّسُولَ فَأُوْلَـٰٓئِكَ مَعَ
الَّذِينَ أَنْعَمَ اللَّهُ عَلَيْهِم مِّنَ النَّبِيِّـۧنَ وَ
الصِّدِّيقِينَ وَالشُّهَدَآءِ وَالصَّـٰلِحِينَ
وَحَسُنَ أُوْلَـٰٓئِكَ رَفِيقًا ﴿٦٩﴾

ذَٰلِكَ الْفَضْلُ مِنَ اللَّهِ وَكَفَىٰ
بِاللَّهِ عَلِيمًا ﴿٧٠﴾

يَـٰٓأَيُّهَا الَّذِينَ ءَامَنُواْ خُذُواْ حِذْرَكُمْ
فَانفِرُواْ ثُبَاتٍ أَوِ انفِرُواْ جَمِيعًا ﴿٧١﴾

وَإِنَّ مِنكُمْ لَمَن لَّيُبَطِّئَنَّ فَإِنْ أَصَـٰبَتْكُم
مُّصِيبَةٌ قَالَ قَدْ أَنْعَمَ اللَّهُ عَلَىَّ إِذْ لَمْ
أَكُن مَّعَهُمْ شَهِيدًا ﴿٧٢﴾

73. And if there comes to you a favour from Allah then, as if there had been no affection between you and him, he says: 'Would that I had been with them! Then I would have achieved a mighty achievement.'

74. Let them therefore fight in the way of Allah those who have purchased the life of this world for the Hereafter. And whoso fights in the way of Allah, and is then slain or triumphs, We will in any case give him a mighty reward.

75. And what ails you that you do not fight in the way of Allah and for the oppressed among men and women and children who say: 'Our Lord! Take us from this town the people of which are ungodly, and appoint us from before You a friend and appoint us from before You a helper.'

76. Those who believe, fight in the way of Allah and those who disbelieve fight in the way of the devil. Fight then against the friends of Satan; verily the craft of Satan is ever feeble.[276]

وَلَئِنْ أَصَابَكُمْ فَضْلٌ مِّنَ اللَّهِ لَيَقُولَنَّ كَأَن لَّمْ تَكُن بَيْنَكُمْ وَبَيْنَهُ مَوَدَّةٌ يَلَيْتَنِي كُنتُ مَعَهُمْ فَأَفُوزَ فَوْزًا عَظِيمًا ۝

فَلْيُقَاتِلْ فِي سَبِيلِ اللَّهِ الَّذِينَ يَشْرُونَ الْحَيَوٰةَ الدُّنْيَا بِالْآخِرَةِ وَمَن يُقَاتِلْ فِي سَبِيلِ اللَّهِ فَيُقْتَلْ أَوْ يَغْلِبْ فَسَوْفَ نُؤْتِيهِ أَجْرًا عَظِيمًا ۝

وَمَا لَكُمْ لَا تُقَاتِلُونَ فِي سَبِيلِ اللَّهِ وَالْمُسْتَضْعَفِينَ مِنَ الرِّجَالِ وَالنِّسَاءِ وَالْوِلْدَانِ الَّذِينَ يَقُولُونَ رَبَّنَا أَخْرِجْنَا مِنْ هَذِهِ الْقَرْيَةِ الظَّالِمِ أَهْلُهَا وَاجْعَل لَّنَا مِن لَّدُنكَ وَلِيًّا وَاجْعَل لَّنَا مِن لَّدُنكَ نَصِيرًا ۝

الَّذِينَ آمَنُوا يُقَاتِلُونَ فِي سَبِيلِ اللَّهِ وَالَّذِينَ كَفَرُوا يُقَاتِلُونَ فِي سَبِيلِ الطَّاغُوتِ فَقَاتِلُوا أَوْلِيَاءَ الشَّيْطَانِ إِنَّ كَيْدَ الشَّيْطَانِ كَانَ ضَعِيفًا ۝

---

276. Satan, in Islam, is not a dreadful power, a thing to be afraid of. He is to be despised by true believers, and his hosts are sure to be vanquished in the long run. This teaching deals a death-blow to the concept of Satan as an Evil Deity or sub–deity who has to be propitiated.

Section 11

77. Have you not observed those to whom it was said: 'Withhold your hands, and establish prayer and pay the poor-rate,' but when thereafter fighting was prescribed to them, Lo! There is a party of them dreading men as with the dread of Allah or with even greater dread; and they say: 'Our Lord! Why have You prescribed to us fighting? Would that You had let us tarry till a term nearby!' Say: 'Trifling is the enjoyment of this world, far better is the Hereafter for him who fears Allah; and you shall not be wronged a whit.'

أَلَمْ تَرَ إِلَى ٱلَّذِينَ قِيلَ لَهُمْ كُفُّوٓا أَيْدِيَكُمْ وَ أَقِيمُوا۟ ٱلصَّلَوٰةَ وَءَاتُوا۟ ٱلزَّكَوٰةَ فَلَمَّا كُتِبَ عَلَيْهِمُ ٱلْقِتَالُ إِذَا فَرِيقٌ مِّنْهُمْ يَخْشَوْنَ ٱلنَّاسَ كَخَشْيَةِ ٱللَّهِ أَوْ أَشَدَّ خَشْيَةً وَقَالُوا۟ رَبَّنَا لِمَ كَتَبْتَ عَلَيْنَا ٱلْقِتَالَ لَوْ لَآ أَخَّرْتَنَآ إِلَىٰٓ أَجَلٍ قَرِيبٍ قُلْ مَتَٰعُ ٱلدُّنْيَا قَلِيلٌ وَٱلْأَخِرَةُ خَيْرٌ لِّمَنِ ٱتَّقَىٰ وَلَا تُظْلَمُونَ فَتِيلًا ۝

78. Death shall overtake you wheresoever you may be, even though you are in fortresses plastered. And if there reaches them some good they say: 'This is from Allah;' and if there reaches them some ill, they say this is because of you. Say: 'From Allah is everything.' What ails then this people, that they do not understand any speech?

أَيْنَمَا تَكُونُوا۟ يُدْرِككُّمُ ٱلْمَوْتُ وَلَوْ كُنتُمْ فِى بُرُوجٍ مُّشَيَّدَةٍ وَإِن تُصِبْهُمْ حَسَنَةٌ يَقُولُوا۟ هَٰذِهِۦ مِنْ عِندِ ٱللَّهِ وَإِن تُصِبْهُمْ سَيِّئَةٌ يَقُولُوا۟ هَٰذِهِۦ مِنْ عِندِكَ قُلْ كُلٌّ مِّنْ عِندِ ٱللَّهِ فَمَالِ هَٰٓؤُلَآءِ ٱلْقَوْمِ لَا يَكَادُونَ يَفْقَهُونَ حَدِيثًا ۝

79. Whatsoever of good reaches you is from Allah, and whatsoever of ill reaches you is because of yourself. And We have sent you as a Messenger to mankind, and enough is Allah as a Witness.

مَّآ أَصَابَكَ مِنْ حَسَنَةٍ فَمِنَ ٱللَّهِ وَمَآ أَصَابَكَ مِن سَيِّئَةٍ فَمِن نَّفْسِكَ وَأَرْسَلْنَٰكَ لِلنَّاسِ رَسُولًا وَكَفَىٰ بِٱللَّهِ شَهِيدًا ۝

80. He who obeys the Messenger has indeed obeyed Allah, and he who turns away, We have not sent you over them as a keeper.

81. And they say, 'obedience'. Yet when they go forth from before you, a group of them plan together by night other than they had said; and Allah writes down what they plan by night. So turn you from them and trust in Allah, and enough is Allah as a Trustee.

82. Do they not then ponder on the Qur'ān? Were it from other than Allah they would surely find therein many a contradiction.

83. And when there comes to them aught of security or alarm, they spread it abroad, whereas had they referred it to the Messenger and those in authority among them, those of them who can think it out would have known it. And had there not been Allah's favour with you and His mercy, you would surely have followed Satan, save a few of you.

84. Fight you therefore in the way of Allah; you are not tasked except for your own soul, and persuade the believers; Allah will perchance withhold the might of those who disbelieve. And Allah is Stronger in might and Stronger in chastising.

مَّن يُطِعِ ٱلرَّسُولَ فَقَدۡ أَطَاعَ ٱللَّهَ وَمَن تَوَلَّىٰ فَمَآ أَرۡسَلۡنَٰكَ عَلَيۡهِمۡ حَفِيظًا ۝

وَيَقُولُونَ طَاعَةٌ فَإِذَا بَرَزُواْ مِنۡ عِندِكَ بَيَّتَ طَآئِفَةٌ مِّنۡهُمۡ غَيۡرَ ٱلَّذِى تَقُولُ وَٱللَّهُ يَكۡتُبُ مَا يُبَيِّتُونَ فَأَعۡرِضۡ عَنۡهُمۡ وَتَوَكَّلۡ عَلَى ٱللَّهِ وَكَفَىٰ بِٱللَّهِ وَكِيلًا ۝

أَفَلَا يَتَدَبَّرُونَ ٱلۡقُرۡءَانَ وَلَوۡ كَانَ مِنۡ عِندِ غَيۡرِ ٱللَّهِ لَوَجَدُواْ فِيهِ ٱخۡتِلَٰفًا كَثِيرًا ۝

وَإِذَا جَآءَهُمۡ أَمۡرٌ مِّنَ ٱلۡأَمۡنِ أَوِ ٱلۡخَوۡفِ أَذَاعُواْ بِهِۦ وَلَوۡ رَدُّوهُ إِلَى ٱلرَّسُولِ وَإِلَىٰٓ أُوْلِى ٱلۡأَمۡرِ مِنۡهُمۡ لَعَلِمَهُ ٱلَّذِينَ يَسۡتَنۢبِطُونَهُۥ مِنۡهُمۡ وَلَوۡلَا فَضۡلُ ٱللَّهِ عَلَيۡكُمۡ وَرَحۡمَتُهُۥ لَٱتَّبَعۡتُمُ ٱلشَّيۡطَٰنَ إِلَّا قَلِيلًا ۝

فَقَٰتِلۡ فِى سَبِيلِ ٱللَّهِ لَا تُكَلَّفُ إِلَّا نَفۡسَكَ وَحَرِّضِ ٱلۡمُؤۡمِنِينَ عَسَى ٱللَّهُ أَن يَكُفَّ بَأۡسَ ٱلَّذِينَ كَفَرُواْ وَٱللَّهُ أَشَدُّ بَأۡسًا وَأَشَدُّ تَنكِيلًا ۝

85. He who intercedes with a goodly intercession, his shall be a portion therefrom and he who intercedes with an ill intercession his shall be a responsibility thereof; and Allah is the Controller of everything.

مَّن يَشْفَعْ شَفَعَةً حَسَنَةً يَكُن لَّهُ نَصِيبٌ مِّنْهَا وَمَن يَشْفَعْ شَفَعَةً سَيِّئَةً يَكُن لَّهُ كِفْلٌ مِّنْهَا وَكَانَ ٱللَّهُ عَلَىٰ كُلِّ شَيْءٍ مُّقِيتًا ﴿٨٥﴾

86. And when you are greeted with a greeting, then greet back with one better than that or return that. Verily Allah is the Reckoner of everything.

وَإِذَا حُيِّيتُم بِتَحِيَّةٍ فَحَيُّواْ بِأَحْسَنَ مِنْهَا أَوْ رُدُّوهَآ إِنَّ ٱللَّهَ كَانَ عَلَىٰ كُلِّ شَيْءٍ حَسِيبًا ﴿٨٦﴾

87. Allah! There is no god but He. Surely He will gather you together on the Day of Judgement, of which there is no doubt, and who is more truthful in discourse than Allah?

ٱللَّهُ لَآ إِلَٰهَ إِلَّا هُوَ لَيَجْمَعَنَّكُمْ إِلَىٰ يَوْمِ ٱلْقِيَٰمَةِ لَا رَيْبَ فِيهِ وَمَنْ أَصْدَقُ مِنَ ٱللَّهِ حَدِيثًا ﴿٨٧﴾

Section 12

88. What ails you then that you are two parties regarding the hypocrites, whereas Allah has overthrown them because of what they have earned? Would you lead aright those whom Allah has sent astray? And whoso Allah sends astray, for him you shall not find a way.

فَمَا لَكُمْ فِي ٱلْمُنَٰفِقِينَ فِئَتَيْنِ وَٱللَّهُ أَرْكَسَهُم بِمَا كَسَبُوٓاْ أَتُرِيدُونَ أَن تَهْدُواْ مَنْ أَضَلَّ ٱللَّهُ وَمَن يُضْلِلِ ٱللَّهُ فَلَن تَجِدَ لَهُۥ سَبِيلًا ﴿٨٨﴾

89. They yearn that you disbelieved even as they have disbelieved, so that you may be all alike. So do not take friends from among them unless they migrate for the sake of Allah; and if they turn away then seize them and kill them wherever you find them, and do not take from among them a friend or a helper.

90. Excepting those who join a people between whom and you there is a compact or who came to you with their breasts straitened that they should fight you or fight their own people. And had Allah so willed, He would have surely set them upon you. If then they withdraw from you, and do not fight against you, and offer you peace, then Allah does not assign you a way against them.

91. Surely you will find others desiring that they may be secure from you and may be secure from their people, and yet whenever they are brought back into the temptation they revert to it. Then if they do not withdraw from you, nor offer you peace, nor restrain their hands, seize them and kill them wherever you find them. These! Against them, We have given you clear authority.

وَدُّواْ لَوْ تَكْفُرُونَ كَمَا كَفَرُواْ فَتَكُونُونَ
سَوَآءً فَلَا تَتَّخِذُواْ مِنْهُمْ أَوْلِيَآءَ حَتَّىٰ
يُهَاجِرُواْ فِى سَبِيلِ ٱللَّهِ فَإِن تَوَلَّوْاْ
فَخُذُوهُمْ وَٱقْتُلُوهُمْ حَيْثُ
وَجَدتُّمُوهُمْ وَلَا تَتَّخِذُواْ مِنْهُمْ
وَلِيًّا وَلَا نَصِيرًا ﴿٨٩﴾

إِلَّا ٱلَّذِينَ يَصِلُونَ إِلَىٰ قَوْمٍ بَيْنَكُمْ وَبَيْنَهُم
مِّيثَٰقٌ أَوْ جَآءُوكُمْ حَصِرَتْ صُدُورُهُمْ
أَن يُقَٰتِلُوكُمْ أَوْ يُقَٰتِلُواْ قَوْمَهُمْ وَلَوْ شَآءَ
ٱللَّهُ لَسَلَّطَهُمْ عَلَيْكُمْ فَلَقَٰتَلُوكُمْ فَإِنِ
ٱعْتَزَلُوكُمْ فَلَمْ يُقَٰتِلُوكُمْ وَأَلْقَوْاْ إِلَيْكُمُ
ٱلسَّلَمَ فَمَا جَعَلَ ٱللَّهُ لَكُمْ عَلَيْهِمْ
سَبِيلًا ﴿٩٠﴾

سَتَجِدُونَ ءَاخَرِينَ يُرِيدُونَ أَن يَأْمَنُوكُمْ
وَيَأْمَنُواْ قَوْمَهُمْ كُلَّ مَا رُدُّوٓاْ إِلَى ٱلْفِتْنَةِ
أُرْكِسُواْ فِيهَا فَإِن لَّمْ يَعْتَزِلُوكُمْ وَيُلْقُوٓاْ إِلَيْكُمُ
ٱلسَّلَمَ وَيَكُفُّوٓاْ أَيْدِيَهُمْ فَخُذُوهُمْ
وَٱقْتُلُوهُمْ حَيْثُ ثَقِفْتُمُوهُمْ
وَأُوْلَٰٓئِكُمْ جَعَلْنَا لَكُمْ عَلَيْهِمْ
سُلْطَٰنًا مُّبِينًا ﴿٩١﴾

Section 13

92. It is not for a believer to kill a believer save by mischance; and he who kills a believer by mischance, on him is the setting free of a believing slave and blood wit to be delivered to his family except that they forgo. Then if he is of a people hostile to you and is himself a believer, then the setting free of a believing slave; and if he be of a people between whom and you is a compact then the blood wit to be delivered to his family and the setting free of a believing slave. Then whoso does not find the wherewithal, on him is the fasting for two months in succession; a penance from Allah. And Allah is ever Knowing, Wise.

93. And he who kills a believer wilfully, his requital is Hell as an abider therein, and Allah shall be wroth with him and shall curse him and shall prepare for him a terrible torment.

94. O you who believe! When you march forth in the way of Allah, make things clear and do not say to one who offers you a greeting; 'you are none of a believer, seeking the perishable goods of the life of this world;' for with Allah are abundant spoils. Even thus were

وَمَا كَانَ لِمُؤْمِنٍ أَن يَقْتُلَ مُؤْمِنًا إِلَّا خَطَـًٔا وَمَن قَتَلَ مُؤْمِنًا خَطَـًٔا فَتَحْرِيرُ رَقَبَةٍ مُّؤْمِنَةٍ وَدِيَةٌ مُّسَلَّمَةٌ إِلَىٰٓ أَهْلِهِۦٓ إِلَّآ أَن يَصَّدَّقُوا۟ فَإِن كَانَ مِن قَوْمٍ عَدُوٍّ لَّكُمْ وَهُوَ مُؤْمِنٌ فَتَحْرِيرُ رَقَبَةٍ مُّؤْمِنَةٍ وَإِن كَانَ مِن قَوْمٍ بَيْنَكُمْ وَبَيْنَهُم مِّيثَـٰقٌ فَدِيَةٌ مُّسَلَّمَةٌ إِلَىٰٓ أَهْلِهِۦ وَتَحْرِيرُ رَقَبَةٍ مُّؤْمِنَةٍ فَمَن لَّمْ يَجِدْ فَصِيَامُ شَهْرَيْنِ مُتَتَابِعَيْنِ تَوْبَةً مِّنَ ٱللَّهِ وَكَانَ ٱللَّهُ عَلِيمًا حَكِيمًا ﴿٩٢﴾

وَمَن يَقْتُلْ مُؤْمِنًا مُّتَعَمِّدًا فَجَزَآؤُهُۥ جَهَنَّمُ خَـٰلِدًا فِيهَا وَغَضِبَ ٱللَّهُ عَلَيْهِ وَلَعَنَهُۥ وَأَعَدَّ لَهُۥ عَذَابًا عَظِيمًا ﴿٩٣﴾

يَـٰٓأَيُّهَا ٱلَّذِينَ ءَامَنُوٓا۟ إِذَا ضَرَبْتُمْ فِى سَبِيلِ ٱللَّهِ فَتَبَيَّنُوا۟ وَلَا تَقُولُوا۟ لِمَنْ أَلْقَىٰٓ إِلَيْكُمُ ٱلسَّلَـٰمَ لَسْتَ مُؤْمِنًا تَبْتَغُونَ عَرَضَ ٱلْحَيَوٰةِ ٱلدُّنْيَا فَعِندَ ٱللَّهِ مَغَانِمُ كَثِيرَةٌ

you aforetime, then Allah did a favour to you. So make things clear. Verily Allah is ever Aware of what you do.

95. Not equal are the holders-back among the Believers, save those who are disabled and the strivers in the way of Allah with their riches and their lives. Allah has preferred in rank the strivers with their riches and their lives above the holders-back, and to all Allah has promised good. And Allah has preferred the strivers above the holders-back with a mighty reward.

96. Ranks from Him and forgiveness and mercy; and Allah is ever Forgiving, Merciful.

Section 14

97. Verily to those whom the angels carry off in death while yet they are wronging their souls, they will say: 'What were you in?' They will say: 'Weakened were we in the land.' They will say: 'Was not Allah's land wide so that you could migrate thereto?' These! Their resort is Hell; an evil retreat.

98. Excepting the weak ones among men, women and children, unable to find a stratagem and not guided to the way.

كَذَٰلِكَ كُنتُم مِّن قَبْلُ فَمَنَّ ٱللَّهُ عَلَيْكُمْ فَتَبَيَّنُوٓا۟ إِنَّ ٱللَّهَ كَانَ بِمَا تَعْمَلُونَ خَبِيرًا ۝

لَّا يَسْتَوِى ٱلْقَٰعِدُونَ مِنَ ٱلْمُؤْمِنِينَ غَيْرُ أُو۟لِى ٱلضَّرَرِ وَٱلْمُجَٰهِدُونَ فِى سَبِيلِ ٱللَّهِ بِأَمْوَٰلِهِمْ وَأَنفُسِهِمْ فَضَّلَ ٱللَّهُ ٱلْمُجَٰهِدِينَ بِأَمْوَٰلِهِمْ وَأَنفُسِهِمْ عَلَى ٱلْقَٰعِدِينَ دَرَجَةً وَكُلًّا وَعَدَ ٱللَّهُ ٱلْحُسْنَىٰ وَفَضَّلَ ٱللَّهُ ٱلْمُجَٰهِدِينَ عَلَى ٱلْقَٰعِدِينَ أَجْرًا عَظِيمًا ۝

دَرَجَٰتٍ مِّنْهُ وَمَغْفِرَةً وَرَحْمَةً وَكَانَ ٱللَّهُ غَفُورًا رَّحِيمًا ۝

إِنَّ ٱلَّذِينَ تَوَفَّىٰهُمُ ٱلْمَلَٰٓئِكَةُ ظَالِمِىٓ أَنفُسِهِمْ قَالُوا۟ فِيمَ كُنتُمْ قَالُوا۟ كُنَّا مُسْتَضْعَفِينَ فِى ٱلْأَرْضِ قَالُوٓا۟ أَلَمْ تَكُنْ أَرْضُ ٱللَّهِ وَٰسِعَةً فَتُهَاجِرُوا۟ فِيهَا فَأُو۟لَٰٓئِكَ مَأْوَىٰهُمْ جَهَنَّمُ وَسَآءَتْ مَصِيرًا ۝

إِلَّا ٱلْمُسْتَضْعَفِينَ مِنَ ٱلرِّجَالِ وَٱلنِّسَآءِ وَٱلْوِلْدَٰنِ لَا يَسْتَطِيعُونَ حِيلَةً وَلَا يَهْتَدُونَ سَبِيلًا ۝

99. These are they whom Allah is likely to pardon, and Allah is ever Pardoning, Forgiving.

فَأُوْلَٰٓئِكَ عَسَى ٱللَّهُ أَن يَعْفُوَ عَنْهُمْ وَكَانَ ٱللَّهُ عَفُوًّا غَفُورًا ۝

100. And he who migrates in the way of Allah shall find in the earth plentiful refuge and amplitude; and he who goes forth from his house as a fugitive unto Allah and His Messenger, and death overtakes him, his reward has surely devolved upon Allah, and Allah is ever Forgiving, Merciful.

وَمَن يُهَاجِرْ فِى سَبِيلِ ٱللَّهِ يَجِدْ فِى ٱلْأَرْضِ مُرَٰغَمًا كَثِيرًا وَسَعَةً وَمَن يَخْرُجْ مِنۢ بَيْتِهِۦ مُهَاجِرًا إِلَى ٱللَّهِ وَرَسُولِهِۦ ثُمَّ يُدْرِكْهُ ٱلْمَوْتُ فَقَدْ وَقَعَ أَجْرُهُۥ عَلَى ٱللَّهِ وَكَانَ ٱللَّهُ غَفُورًا رَّحِيمًا ۝

Section 15

101. And when you are journeying in the earth, it will be no fault in you that you shorten the prayer if you apprehend that those who disbelieve will molest you; verily the infidels are ever unto you an avowed enemy.

وَإِذَا ضَرَبْتُمْ فِى ٱلْأَرْضِ فَلَيْسَ عَلَيْكُمْ جُنَاحٌ أَن تَقْصُرُوا۟ مِنَ ٱلصَّلَوٰةِ إِنْ خِفْتُمْ أَن يَفْتِنَكُمُ ٱلَّذِينَ كَفَرُوٓا۟ إِنَّ ٱلْكَٰفِرِينَ كَانُوا۟ لَكُمْ عَدُوًّا مُّبِينًا ۝

102. And when you are amidst them and have set up the prayer for them, then let a party of them stand with you and let them retain their weapons; then when they have prostrated themselves, let them go behind you, and let another party who have not yet prayed come and pray with you; and let them also take their precautions and their weapons. Those who disbelieve

وَإِذَا كُنتَ فِيهِمْ فَأَقَمْتَ لَهُمُ ٱلصَّلَوٰةَ فَلْتَقُمْ طَآئِفَةٌ مِّنْهُم مَّعَكَ وَلْيَأْخُذُوٓا۟ أَسْلِحَتَهُمْ فَإِذَا سَجَدُوا۟ فَلْيَكُونُوا۟ مِن وَرَآئِكُمْ وَلْتَأْتِ طَآئِفَةٌ أُخْرَىٰ لَمْ يُصَلُّوا۟ فَلْيُصَلُّوا۟ مَعَكَ وَلْيَأْخُذُوا۟ حِذْرَهُمْ وَأَسْلِحَتَهُمْ

wish that you neglected your weapons and your baggage, so that they might swoop down upon you in one swoop. No fault there will be in you if there is an injury to you from rain or you are ailing, that you lay down your arms and yet take your caution. Verily Allah has prepared for the infidels an ignominious torment.

وَدَّ ٱلَّذِينَ كَفَرُوا لَوْ تَغْفُلُونَ عَنْ أَسْلِحَتِكُمْ وَأَمْتِعَتِكُمْ فَيَمِيلُونَ عَلَيْكُم مَّيْلَةً وَٰحِدَةً وَلَا جُنَاحَ عَلَيْكُمْ إِن كَانَ بِكُمْ أَذًى مِّن مَّطَرٍ أَوْ كُنتُم مَّرْضَىٰٓ أَن تَضَعُوٓا أَسْلِحَتَكُمْ وَخُذُوا حِذْرَكُمْ إِنَّ ٱللَّهَ أَعَدَّ لِلْكَٰفِرِينَ عَذَابًا مُّهِينًا ۝

103. Then when you have finished the prayer, remember Allah, standing, sitting, and lying on your sides. Then when you are secure, establish prayer; verily the prayer is prescribed to believers at definite times.

فَإِذَا قَضَيْتُمُ ٱلصَّلَوٰةَ فَٱذْكُرُوا ٱللَّهَ قِيَٰمًا وَقُعُودًا وَعَلَىٰ جُنُوبِكُمْ فَإِذَا ٱطْمَأْنَنتُمْ فَأَقِيمُوا ٱلصَّلَوٰةَ إِنَّ ٱلصَّلَوٰةَ كَانَتْ عَلَى ٱلْمُؤْمِنِينَ كِتَٰبًا مَّوْقُوتًا ۝

104. And do not slacken in seeking the enemy people; if you are suffering then they suffer even as you suffer, and you hope from Allah what they hope not. And Allah is ever Knowing, Wise.

وَلَا تَهِنُوا فِى ٱبْتِغَآءِ ٱلْقَوْمِ إِن تَكُونُوا تَأْلَمُونَ فَإِنَّهُمْ يَأْلَمُونَ كَمَا تَأْلَمُونَ وَتَرْجُونَ مِنَ ٱللَّهِ مَا لَا يَرْجُونَ وَكَانَ ٱللَّهُ عَلِيمًا حَكِيمًا ۝

Section 16

105. Verily We; it is We Who have sent down the Book to you with Truth, that you might judge between people by what Allah has shown you; and be not you a pleader on behalf of the deceivers.

إِنَّآ أَنزَلْنَآ إِلَيْكَ ٱلْكِتَٰبَ بِٱلْحَقِّ لِتَحْكُمَ بَيْنَ ٱلنَّاسِ بِمَآ أَرَىٰكَ ٱللَّهُ وَلَا تَكُن لِّلْخَآئِنِينَ خَصِيمًا ۝

106. And beg you forgiveness of Allah; verily Allah is ever Forgiving, Merciful.

وَٱسْتَغْفِرِ ٱللَّهَ إِنَّ ٱللَّهَ كَانَ غَفُورًا رَّحِيمًا ۝

107. And plead not you for those who defraud their souls, verily Allah does not love one who is a defrauder, sinner.

وَلَا تُجَدِلْ عَنِ ٱلَّذِينَ يَخْتَانُونَ أَنفُسَهُمْ إِنَّ ٱللَّهَ لَا يُحِبُّ مَن كَانَ خَوَّانًا أَثِيمًا ۝

108. They feel ashamed of men and do not feel ashamed of Allah, whereas He is present with them when by night they plan together discourses which do not please Him; and Allah is ever an Encompasser of what they do.

يَسْتَخْفُونَ مِنَ ٱلنَّاسِ وَلَا يَسْتَخْفُونَ مِنَ ٱللَّهِ وَهُوَ مَعَهُمْ إِذْ يُبَيِّتُونَ مَا لَا يَرْضَىٰ مِنَ ٱلْقَوْلِ وَكَانَ ٱللَّهُ بِمَا يَعْمَلُونَ مُحِيطًا ۝

109. Lo! It is you who have contended for them in the life of this world; then who will contend for them with Allah on the Day of Judgement, or who will be their champion?

هَٰٓأَنتُمْ هَٰٓؤُلَآءِ جَٰدَلْتُمْ عَنْهُمْ فِى ٱلْحَيَوٰةِ ٱلدُّنْيَا فَمَن يُجَٰدِلُ ٱللَّهَ عَنْهُمْ يَوْمَ ٱلْقِيَٰمَةِ أَم مَّن يَكُونُ عَلَيْهِمْ وَكِيلًا ۝

110. And he who works an evil or wrongs his own soul and thereafter begs forgiveness of Allah, shall find Allah the Forgiving, the Merciful.

وَمَن يَعْمَلْ سُوٓءًا أَوْ يَظْلِمْ نَفْسَهُ ثُمَّ يَسْتَغْفِرِ ٱللَّهَ يَجِدِ ٱللَّهَ غَفُورًا رَّحِيمًا ۝

111. And he who earns a sin, only against his own soul earns it; and Allah is ever Knowing, Wise.

وَمَن يَكْسِبْ إِثْمًا فَإِنَّمَا يَكْسِبُهُ عَلَىٰ نَفْسِهِ وَكَانَ ٱللَّهُ عَلِيمًا حَكِيمًا ۝

112. And he who earns a vice or a sin and thereafter casts it on an innocent one, has certainly borne a calumny[277] and a manifest sin.

Section 17

113. Were not the grace of Allah and His mercy on you, a party of them had surely resolved to mislead you, whereas they mislead none but themselves; and they shall not be able to hurt you in aught. And Allah has sent down to you the Book and wisdom, and has taught you what you know not; and the grace of Allah on you is ever mighty.

114. No good is there in much of their whispers except in him who commands charity or kindness or reconciliation among mankind; and he who does this, seeking the goodwill of Allah, him We will presently give a mighty reward.

115. And he who opposes the Messenger after Truth has become manifest to him and follows another way than that of the believers, him We will let follow that to which he has turned and him We will roast in Hell – an evil retreat!

---

277. Calumny, denoting all the unjust accusations which have the effect of damaging or lowering another's reputation, is always a prominent feature of a depraved society. Islam condemns it in the strongest terms, so that it may not raise its head even in forms too subtle to be reached by the arms of the law.

Section 18

116. Verily Allah shall not forgive that aught be associated with Him, and He shall forgive all else to whom He will, and he who associates aught with Allah has certainly strayed far away.

117. They invoke not beside Him but females, and they also invoke nothing but a Satan rebellious.

118. Allah has accursed him, and he said: 'I will surely take of Your creatures a portion allotted,

119. And surely I will lead them astray, and I will fill them with vain desires, and I will bid them so that they will slit the ears of the cattle, and I will bid them so that they will alter the creation of Allah.' And he who takes Satan instead of Allah, for a friend, shall surely suffer a manifest loss.

120. Satan makes them promises and fills them with vain desires, and Satan promises them but vain desires.

121. These: their resort shall be Hell, and they shall not find an escape therefrom.

إِنَّ ٱللَّهَ لَا يَغْفِرُ أَن يُشْرَكَ بِهِۦ وَيَغْفِرُ مَا دُونَ ذَٰلِكَ لِمَن يَشَآءُ وَمَن يُشْرِكْ بِٱللَّهِ فَقَدْ ضَلَّ ضَلَٰلَۢا بَعِيدًا ﴿١١٦﴾

إِن يَدْعُونَ مِن دُونِهِۦٓ إِلَّآ إِنَٰثًا وَإِن يَدْعُونَ إِلَّا شَيْطَٰنًا مَّرِيدًا ﴿١١٧﴾

لَّعَنَهُ ٱللَّهُ وَقَالَ لَأَتَّخِذَنَّ مِنْ عِبَادِكَ نَصِيبًا مَّفْرُوضًا ﴿١١٨﴾

وَلَأُضِلَّنَّهُمْ وَلَأُمَنِّيَنَّهُمْ وَلَآمُرَنَّهُمْ فَلَيُبَتِّكُنَّ ءَاذَانَ ٱلْأَنْعَٰمِ وَلَآمُرَنَّهُمْ فَلَيُغَيِّرُنَّ خَلْقَ ٱللَّهِ وَمَن يَتَّخِذِ ٱلشَّيْطَٰنَ وَلِيًّا مِّن دُونِ ٱللَّهِ فَقَدْ خَسِرَ خُسْرَانًا مُّبِينًا ﴿١١٩﴾

يَعِدُهُمْ وَيُمَنِّيهِمْ وَمَا يَعِدُهُمُ ٱلشَّيْطَٰنُ إِلَّا غُرُورًا ﴿١٢٠﴾

أُوْلَٰٓئِكَ مَأْوَىٰهُمْ جَهَنَّمُ وَلَا يَجِدُونَ عَنْهَا مَحِيصًا ﴿١٢١﴾

122. And those who believe and work righteous works, soon We shall admit them to Gardens beneath which rivers flow as abiders therein for ever: the promise of Allah, True. And who is more truthful than Allah in speech?

وَٱلَّذِينَ ءَامَنُوا۟ وَعَمِلُوا۟ ٱلصَّٰلِحَٰتِ سَنُدْخِلُهُمْ جَنَّٰتٍ تَجْرِى مِن تَحْتِهَا ٱلْأَنْهَٰرُ خَٰلِدِينَ فِيهَآ أَبَدًا وَعْدَ ٱللَّهِ حَقًّا وَمَنْ أَصْدَقُ مِنَ ٱللَّهِ قِيلًا ۝

123. Not by your vain desires nor by the vain desires of the People of the Book are the promises of Allah to be fulfilled; he who works an evil shall be requited therefore, and he shall not find, beside Allah, a protector nor a helper.

لَّيْسَ بِأَمَانِيِّكُمْ وَلَآ أَمَانِىِّ أَهْلِ ٱلْكِتَٰبِ مَن يَعْمَلْ سُوٓءًا يُجْزَ بِهِ وَلَا يَجِدْ لَهُۥ مِن دُونِ ٱللَّهِ وَلِيًّا وَلَا نَصِيرًا ۝

124. And he who works righteous works, male or female, and is a believer – these shall enter the Garden and shall not be wronged a speck.

وَمَن يَعْمَلْ مِنَ ٱلصَّٰلِحَٰتِ مِن ذَكَرٍ أَوْ أُنثَىٰ وَهُوَ مُؤْمِنٌ فَأُو۟لَٰٓئِكَ يَدْخُلُونَ ٱلْجَنَّةَ وَلَا يُظْلَمُونَ نَقِيرًا ۝

125. And who can be better in religion than he who submits his face to Allah, and is sincere, and follows the faith of Abraham, the upright? And Allah has taken Abraham for a friend.

وَمَنْ أَحْسَنُ دِينًا مِّمَّنْ أَسْلَمَ وَجْهَهُۥ لِلَّهِ وَهُوَ مُحْسِنٌ وَٱتَّبَعَ مِلَّةَ إِبْرَٰهِيمَ حَنِيفًا وَٱتَّخَذَ ٱللَّهُ إِبْرَٰهِيمَ خَلِيلًا ۝

126. And Allah's is whatsoever is in the heavens and whatsoever is in the earth, and Allah is ever an Encompasser of everything.

وَلِلَّهِ مَا فِى ٱلسَّمَٰوَٰتِ وَمَا فِى ٱلْأَرْضِ وَكَانَ ٱللَّهُ بِكُلِّ شَىْءٍ مُّحِيطًا ۝

Section 19

127. And they ask your decree concerning women. Say: 'Allah decrees to you concerning them and so do the revelations that have been recited to you in the Book concerning the orphaned women to whom you do not give what is prescribed for them and yet desire that you will wed them, and concerning the oppressed children, you will deal with the orphans in equity, and whatsoever good you do, then verily Allah is ever Aware of it.

وَيَسْتَفْتُونَكَ فِى ٱلنِّسَآءِ قُلِ ٱللَّهُ يُفْتِيكُمْ فِيهِنَّ وَمَا يُتْلَىٰ عَلَيْكُمْ فِى ٱلْكِتَـٰبِ فِى يَتَـٰمَى ٱلنِّسَآءِ ٱلَّـٰتِى لَا تُؤْتُونَهُنَّ مَا كُتِبَ لَهُنَّ وَتَرْغَبُونَ أَن تَنكِحُوهُنَّ وَٱلْمُسْتَضْعَفِينَ مِنَ ٱلْوِلْدَٰنِ وَأَن تَقُومُوا۟ لِلْيَتَـٰمَىٰ بِٱلْقِسْطِ وَمَا تَفْعَلُوا۟ مِنْ خَيْرٍ فَإِنَّ ٱللَّهَ كَانَ بِهِۦ عَلِيمًا ﴿١٢٧﴾

128. And if a woman apprehends refractoriness or estrangement from her husband, it shall be no blame on the pair if they effect between them a reconciliation, and reconciliation is always good. And souls are ingrained with greed. And if you act kindly and fear Him, then verily Allah is ever Aware of what you do.

وَإِنِ ٱمْرَأَةٌ خَافَتْ مِنۢ بَعْلِهَا نُشُوزًا أَوْ إِعْرَاضًا فَلَا جُنَاحَ عَلَيْهِمَآ أَن يُصْلِحَا بَيْنَهُمَا صُلْحًا وَٱلصُّلْحُ خَيْرٌ وَأُحْضِرَتِ ٱلْأَنفُسُ ٱلشُّحَّ وَإِن تُحْسِنُوا۟ وَتَتَّقُوا۟ فَإِنَّ ٱللَّهَ كَانَ بِمَا تَعْمَلُونَ خَبِيرًا ﴿١٢٨﴾

129. And you are not able to deal equitably between wives, even though you long to do so; but incline not an extreme inclining, so that you leave her as it were suspended.[278] And if you effect reconciliation and fear Allah, then Allah is ever Forgiving, Merciful.

وَلَن تَسْتَطِيعُوٓا۟ أَن تَعْدِلُوا۟ بَيْنَ ٱلنِّسَآءِ وَلَوْ حَرَصْتُمْ فَلَا تَمِيلُوا۟ كُلَّ ٱلْمَيْلِ فَتَذَرُوهَا كَٱلْمُعَلَّقَةِ وَإِن تُصْلِحُوا۟ وَتَتَّقُوا۟ فَإِنَّ ٱللَّهَ كَانَ غَفُورًا رَّحِيمًا ﴿١٢٩﴾

---

278. In other words, like the one neither in wedlock, nor divorced and free to marry someone else. This condemns the Christian institution 'separation from bed and board' which even when perpetual 'does not however give either party the right to remarry during the lifetime of the other' (*EBr.* XVI. p. 952).

130. And if the pair must separate, Allah shall enrich each of them of His bounty; and Allah is ever Bountiful, Wise.

وَإِن يَتَفَرَّقَا يُغۡنِ ٱللَّهُ كُلًّا مِّن سَعَتِهِۦ وَكَانَ ٱللَّهُ وَٰسِعًا حَكِيمٗا ﴿١٣٠﴾

131. And Allah's is whatsoever is in the heavens and whatsoever is in the earth. And assuredly We enjoined those who were given the Book before you and yourselves: fear Allah, and if you disbelieve, then Allah's is whatsoever is in the heavens and whatsoever is in the earth, and Allah is ever Self-Sufficient, Praiseworthy.

وَلِلَّهِ مَا فِى ٱلسَّمَٰوَٰتِ وَمَا فِى ٱلۡأَرۡضِ وَلَقَدۡ وَصَّيۡنَا ٱلَّذِينَ أُوتُواْ ٱلۡكِتَٰبَ مِن قَبۡلِكُمۡ وَإِيَّاكُمۡ أَنِ ٱتَّقُواْ ٱللَّهَ وَإِن تَكۡفُرُواْ فَإِنَّ لِلَّهِ مَا فِى ٱلسَّمَٰوَٰتِ وَمَا فِى ٱلۡأَرۡضِ وَكَانَ ٱللَّهُ غَنِيًّا حَمِيدٗا ﴿١٣١﴾

132. And Allah's is whatsoever is in the heavens and whatsoever is in the earth, and suffices Allah as a Champion.

وَلِلَّهِ مَا فِى ٱلسَّمَٰوَٰتِ وَمَا فِى ٱلۡأَرۡضِ وَكَفَىٰ بِٱللَّهِ وَكِيلًا ﴿١٣٢﴾

133. If He will, He can take you away, O mankind! And bring forward others. And Allah is ever Potent over that.

إِن يَشَأۡ يُذۡهِبۡكُمۡ أَيُّهَا ٱلنَّاسُ وَيَأۡتِ بِـَٔاخَرِينَ وَكَانَ ٱللَّهُ عَلَىٰ ذَٰلِكَ قَدِيرٗا ﴿١٣٣﴾

134. He who seeks the reward of this world, with Allah is the reward of this world and the Hereafter, and Allah is ever Hearing, Seeing.

مَّن كَانَ يُرِيدُ ثَوَابَ ٱلدُّنۡيَا فَعِندَ ٱللَّهِ ثَوَابُ ٱلدُّنۡيَا وَٱلۡأَخِرَةِ وَكَانَ ٱللَّهُ سَمِيعَۢا بَصِيرٗا ﴿١٣٤﴾

Section 20

135. O you who believe! Be you maintainers of equity and bearers of testimony for Allah's sake, though it be against yourselves or your parents or kindred. Be he rich or poor Allah is higher unto either; so follow not the caprice, lest you may deviate. If you incline or turn away, then verily Allah is Aware of what you work.

136. O you who believe! Believe in Allah and His Messenger and the Book He has sent down to His Messenger and the Book He sent down formerly; and he who disbelieves in Allah and His angels and His Books and His Messengers and the Last Day, has strayed far away.

137. Verily those who believed and then disbelieved, and then believed and then disbelieved, and thereafter waxed in infidelity, Allah shall not forgive them nor guide them on the way.

138. Announce to the hypocrites that theirs shall be an afflictive torment.

139. Those who take infidels, instead of the believers, for friends, do they seek honour with them? Verily then honour is Allah's altogether.

يَـٰٓأَيُّهَا ٱلَّذِينَ ءَامَنُوا۟ كُونُوا۟ قَوَّٰمِينَ بِٱلْقِسْطِ شُهَدَآءَ لِلَّهِ وَلَوْ عَلَىٰٓ أَنفُسِكُمْ أَوِ ٱلْوَٰلِدَيْنِ وَٱلْأَقْرَبِينَ إِن يَكُنْ غَنِيًّا أَوْ فَقِيرًا فَٱللَّهُ أَوْلَىٰ بِهِمَا فَلَا تَتَّبِعُوا۟ ٱلْهَوَىٰٓ أَن تَعْدِلُوا۟ وَإِن تَلْوُۥٓا۟ أَوْ تُعْرِضُوا۟ فَإِنَّ ٱللَّهَ كَانَ بِمَا تَعْمَلُونَ خَبِيرًا ﴿١٣٥﴾

يَـٰٓأَيُّهَا ٱلَّذِينَ ءَامَنُوٓا۟ ءَامِنُوا۟ بِٱللَّهِ وَرَسُولِهِۦ وَٱلْكِتَـٰبِ ٱلَّذِى نَزَّلَ عَلَىٰ رَسُولِهِۦ وَٱلْكِتَـٰبِ ٱلَّذِىٓ أَنزَلَ مِن قَبْلُ وَمَن يَكْفُرْ بِٱللَّهِ وَمَلَـٰٓئِكَتِهِۦ وَكُتُبِهِۦ وَرُسُلِهِۦ وَٱلْيَوْمِ ٱلْءَاخِرِ فَقَدْ ضَلَّ ضَلَـٰلًۢا بَعِيدًا ﴿١٣٦﴾

إِنَّ ٱلَّذِينَ ءَامَنُوا۟ ثُمَّ كَفَرُوا۟ ثُمَّ ءَامَنُوا۟ ثُمَّ كَفَرُوا۟ ثُمَّ ٱزْدَادُوا۟ كُفْرًا لَّمْ يَكُنِ ٱللَّهُ لِيَغْفِرَ لَهُمْ وَلَا لِيَهْدِيَهُمْ سَبِيلًۢا ﴿١٣٧﴾

بَشِّرِ ٱلْمُنَـٰفِقِينَ بِأَنَّ لَهُمْ عَذَابًا أَلِيمًا ﴿١٣٨﴾

ٱلَّذِينَ يَتَّخِذُونَ ٱلْكَـٰفِرِينَ أَوْلِيَآءَ مِن دُونِ ٱلْمُؤْمِنِينَ أَيَبْتَغُونَ عِندَهُمُ ٱلْعِزَّةَ فَإِنَّ ٱلْعِزَّةَ لِلَّهِ جَمِيعًا ﴿١٣٩﴾

140. And it has been revealed to you in the Book that when you hear Allah's revelations being disbelieved in and mocked at, do not sit down with them until they plunge into a discourse other than that; for, then, you would surely become like unto them. Verily Allah is about to gather hypocrites and infidels in Hell together.

وَقَدْ نَزَّلَ عَلَيْكُمْ فِي ٱلْكِتَٰبِ أَنْ إِذَا سَمِعْتُمْ ءَايَٰتِ ٱللَّهِ يُكْفَرُ بِهَا وَيُسْتَهْزَأُ بِهَا فَلَا تَقْعُدُوا۟ مَعَهُمْ حَتَّىٰ يَخُوضُوا۟ فِي حَدِيثٍ غَيْرِهِۦٓ إِنَّكُمْ إِذًا مِّثْلُهُمْ إِنَّ ٱللَّهَ جَامِعُ ٱلْمُنَٰفِقِينَ وَٱلْكَٰفِرِينَ فِي جَهَنَّمَ جَمِيعًا ﴿١٤٠﴾

141. Those who wait about you. If then there is victory for you from Allah, they say: 'Were we not with you?' And if there is a portion for the infidels, they say: 'Did we not gain mastery over you and did we not keep you back from the believers?' Allah shall judge between you on the Day of Judgement, and Allah shall not make a way for the infidels against the believers.

ٱلَّذِينَ يَتَرَبَّصُونَ بِكُمْ فَإِن كَانَ لَكُمْ فَتْحٌ مِّنَ ٱللَّهِ قَالُوٓا۟ أَلَمْ نَكُن مَّعَكُمْ وَإِن كَانَ لِلْكَٰفِرِينَ نَصِيبٌ قَالُوٓا۟ أَلَمْ نَسْتَحْوِذْ عَلَيْكُمْ وَنَمْنَعْكُم مِّنَ ٱلْمُؤْمِنِينَ فَٱللَّهُ يَحْكُمُ بَيْنَكُمْ يَوْمَ ٱلْقِيَٰمَةِ وَلَن يَجْعَلَ ٱللَّهُ لِلْكَٰفِرِينَ عَلَى ٱلْمُؤْمِنِينَ سَبِيلًا ﴿١٤١﴾

Section 21

142. Verily the hypocrites would beguile Allah, whereas it is He who beguiles them and when they stand up to prayer, they stand up languidly, making a show to the people, and they remember Allah but little.

إِنَّ ٱلْمُنَٰفِقِينَ يُخَٰدِعُونَ ٱللَّهَ وَهُوَ خَٰدِعُهُمْ وَإِذَا قَامُوٓا۟ إِلَى ٱلصَّلَوٰةِ قَامُوا۟ كُسَالَىٰ يُرَآءُونَ ٱلنَّاسَ وَلَا يَذْكُرُونَ ٱللَّهَ إِلَّا قَلِيلًا ﴿١٤٢﴾

143. Wavering between this and that, neither for this nor for that; and he whom Allah sends astray, for him you will not find a way.

مُّذَبْذَبِينَ بَيْنَ ذَٰلِكَ لَآ إِلَىٰ هَٰٓؤُلَآءِ وَلَآ إِلَىٰ هَٰٓؤُلَآءِ وَمَن يُضْلِلِ ٱللَّهُ فَلَن تَجِدَ لَهُۥ سَبِيلًا ﴿١٤٣﴾

144. O you who believe! Do not take infidels, instead of believers, for friends. Would you give Allah as manifest authority against you?

145. Verily the hypocrites shall be in the lowest abyss of the Fire, and you will not find for them a helper.

146. Except those who will yet repent and amend and hold fast by Allah and make their religion solely for Allah. These then shall be with the believers, and soon shall Allah give the believers a mighty reward.

147. What will Allah do with your torment, if you return thanks and believe? And Allah is ever Appreciative, Knowing.

148. Allah does not approve of the uttering of harsh words, except by one who has been wronged; and Allah is ever Hearing, Knowing.

149. Whether you disclose a good or conceal it, or pardon an evil, surely Allah is ever Pardoning, Potent.

150. Verily those who disbelieve in Allah and His Messengers and would differentiate between Allah and His Messengers and say: 'Some we believe in and others we deny', and who would take a way in between this and that.

يَـٰٓأَيُّهَا ٱلَّذِينَ ءَامَنُوا۟ لَا تَتَّخِذُوا۟ ٱلْكَـٰفِرِينَ أَوْلِيَآءَ مِن دُونِ ٱلْمُؤْمِنِينَ أَتُرِيدُونَ أَن تَجْعَلُوا۟ لِلَّهِ عَلَيْكُمْ سُلْطَـٰنًا مُّبِينًا ﴿١٤٤﴾

إِنَّ ٱلْمُنَـٰفِقِينَ فِى ٱلدَّرْكِ ٱلْأَسْفَلِ مِنَ ٱلنَّارِ وَلَن تَجِدَ لَهُمْ نَصِيرًا ﴿١٤٥﴾

إِلَّا ٱلَّذِينَ تَابُوا۟ وَأَصْلَحُوا۟ وَٱعْتَصَمُوا۟ بِٱللَّهِ وَأَخْلَصُوا۟ دِينَهُمْ لِلَّهِ فَأُو۟لَـٰٓئِكَ مَعَ ٱلْمُؤْمِنِينَ وَسَوْفَ يُؤْتِ ٱللَّهُ ٱلْمُؤْمِنِينَ أَجْرًا عَظِيمًا ﴿١٤٦﴾

مَّا يَفْعَلُ ٱللَّهُ بِعَذَابِكُمْ إِن شَكَرْتُمْ وَءَامَنتُمْ وَكَانَ ٱللَّهُ شَاكِرًا عَلِيمًا ﴿١٤٧﴾

لَّا يُحِبُّ ٱللَّهُ ٱلْجَهْرَ بِٱلسُّوٓءِ مِنَ ٱلْقَوْلِ إِلَّا مَن ظُلِمَ وَكَانَ ٱللَّهُ سَمِيعًا عَلِيمًا ﴿١٤٨﴾

إِن تُبْدُوا۟ خَيْرًا أَوْ تُخْفُوهُ أَوْ تَعْفُوا۟ عَن سُوٓءٍ فَإِنَّ ٱللَّهَ كَانَ عَفُوًّا قَدِيرًا ﴿١٤٩﴾

إِنَّ ٱلَّذِينَ يَكْفُرُونَ بِٱللَّهِ وَرُسُلِهِۦ وَيُرِيدُونَ أَن يُفَرِّقُوا۟ بَيْنَ ٱللَّهِ وَرُسُلِهِۦ وَيَقُولُونَ نُؤْمِنُ بِبَعْضٍ وَنَكْفُرُ بِبَعْضٍ وَيُرِيدُونَ أَن يَتَّخِذُوا۟ بَيْنَ ذَٰلِكَ سَبِيلًا ﴿١٥٠﴾

151. They are the disbelievers in every truth, and We have prepared for the disbelievers an ignominious torment.

أُوْلَٰٓئِكَ هُمُ ٱلْكَٰفِرُونَ حَقًّا ۚ وَأَعْتَدْنَا لِلْكَٰفِرِينَ عَذَابًا مُّهِينًا ۝

152. And as to those who believe in Allah and His Messengers and do not differentiate between any of them, soon We shall give them their wages; and Allah is ever Forgiving, Merciful.

وَٱلَّذِينَ ءَامَنُوا۟ بِٱللَّهِ وَرُسُلِهِۦ وَلَمْ يُفَرِّقُوا۟ بَيْنَ أَحَدٍ مِّنْهُمْ أُوْلَٰٓئِكَ سَوْفَ يُؤْتِيهِمْ أُجُورَهُمْ ۗ وَكَانَ ٱللَّهُ غَفُورًا رَّحِيمًا ۝

Section 22

153. The people of the Book ask you to bring down a Book to them from the heaven. But surely they asked Moses a thing even greater than that; they said: 'Show us God openly.' Thereupon a thunderbolt overtook them for their ungodliness. Then they took a calf after there had come to them the evidence. Even so We pardoned that, and We invested Moses with manifest authority.

يَسْـَٔلُكَ أَهْلُ ٱلْكِتَٰبِ أَن تُنَزِّلَ عَلَيْهِمْ كِتَٰبًا مِّنَ ٱلسَّمَآءِ ۚ فَقَدْ سَأَلُوا۟ مُوسَىٰٓ أَكْبَرَ مِن ذَٰلِكَ فَقَالُوٓا۟ أَرِنَا ٱللَّهَ جَهْرَةً فَأَخَذَتْهُمُ ٱلصَّٰعِقَةُ بِظُلْمِهِمْ ۚ ثُمَّ ٱتَّخَذُوا۟ ٱلْعِجْلَ مِنۢ بَعْدِ مَا جَآءَتْهُمُ ٱلْبَيِّنَٰتُ فَعَفَوْنَا عَن ذَٰلِكَ ۚ وَءَاتَيْنَا مُوسَىٰ سُلْطَٰنًا مُّبِينًا ۝

154. We raised the Tur over them for this bond. And We said to them: 'Enter the gate prostrating yourselves.' And We said to them: 'Do not violate the Sabbath,' and We took from them a firm bond.

وَرَفَعْنَا فَوْقَهُمُ ٱلطُّورَ بِمِيثَٰقِهِمْ وَقُلْنَا لَهُمُ ٱدْخُلُوا۟ ٱلْبَابَ سُجَّدًا وَقُلْنَا لَهُمْ لَا تَعْدُوا۟ فِي ٱلسَّبْتِ وَأَخَذْنَا مِنْهُم مِّيثَٰقًا غَلِيظًا ۝

155. Accursed are they then for their breach of the bond and their rejection of the commandments of Allah and their putting of the Prophets to death without justification, and their saying: 'Our hearts are sealed.' Aye! Allah has set a seal upon them for their disbelief, so they believe not but a little.

فَبِمَا نَقْضِهِم مِّيثَاقَهُمْ وَكُفْرِهِم بِآيَاتِ اللَّهِ وَقَتْلِهِمُ الْأَنبِيَاءَ بِغَيْرِ حَقٍّ وَقَوْلِهِمْ قُلُوبُنَا غُلْفٌ بَلْ طَبَعَ اللَّهُ عَلَيْهَا بِكُفْرِهِمْ فَلَا يُؤْمِنُونَ إِلَّا قَلِيلًا ﴿١٥٥﴾

156. And for their blasphemy and for the uttering against Maryam a grievous calumny.

وَبِكُفْرِهِمْ وَقَوْلِهِمْ عَلَى مَرْيَمَ بُهْتَانًا عَظِيمًا ﴿١٥٦﴾

157. And for their saying: 'We put to death the Messiah Jesus,[279] son of Maryam, a Messenger of Allah.[280] Yet they killed him not, nor did they send him to the cross, but it was made dubious to them.[281]

وَقَوْلِهِمْ إِنَّا قَتَلْنَا الْمَسِيحَ عِيسَى ابْنَ مَرْيَمَ رَسُولَ اللَّهِ وَمَا قَتَلُوهُ وَمَا صَلَبُوهُ وَلَٰكِن شُبِّهَ لَهُمْ

---

279. It was not only the Christians who made the Jews accountable for the 'death' of Jesus, but the Jews themselves spoke with pride and delight of their achievement... 'Then all the men of Jerusalem being well–armed and mailed, captured Jesus. And when his disciples saw that he was captive in their hands, and that it was in vain to fight, they took to their legs, and lifted up their voices and wept bitterly. And the men of Jerusalem waxed stronger and conquered the bastard, the son of a woman in her separation, with his multitude, slaying many of them, while the rest fled to the mountains' (Schonfield, *According to the Hebrews*, p. 46, f.n.).

280. The epithet is appended to emphasize the true rank and status of Jesus, which is in – between the two blasphemous extremes of Judaism and Christianity.

281. It was not Jesus who was executed but another, who was miraculously substituted for him (how and in what way is another question, and is not touched upon in the Qur'ān). This true doctrine regarding Jesus is shared by an early Christian sect. The Basilidians maintained that Jesus 'changed form with Simon of Cyrene who actually suffered in his place' (*EBr.* III. p. 176). 'Irenaeus says that Basilidess account of the crucifixion was that Simon of Cyrene was crucified by mistake, and Jesus himself took the form of Simon, and stood by and laughed at them' (*ERE.* IV. p. 833).

And surely those who differ therein are in doubt about it; they have no true knowledge thereof; they but follow a conjecture;[282] of a surety they killed him not.

وَإِنَّ ٱلَّذِينَ ٱخۡتَلَفُواْ فِيهِ لَفِى شَكٍّ مِّنۡهُ مَا لَهُم بِهِۦ مِنۡ عِلۡمٍ إِلَّا ٱتِّبَاعَ ٱلظَّنِّ وَمَا قَتَلُوهُ يَقِينَۢا ۝

158. But Allah raised him unto Himself, and Allah is ever Mighty, Wise.

بَل رَّفَعَهُ ٱللَّهُ إِلَيۡهِ وَكَانَ ٱللَّهُ عَزِيزًا حَكِيمًا ۝

159. And there is none among the People of the Book but shall surely believe in him before his death, and on the Day of Judgement he shall be a witness against them.

وَإِن مِّنۡ أَهۡلِ ٱلۡكِتَـٰبِ إِلَّا لَيُؤۡمِنَنَّ بِهِۦ قَبۡلَ مَوۡتِهِۦ وَيَوۡمَ ٱلۡقِيَـٰمَةِ يَكُونُ عَلَيۡهِمۡ شَهِيدًا ۝

160. So because of the wrong-doing on the part of those who are Judaized, We forbade to them the good things that had been allowed to them and also because of their keeping away from Allah's way.

فَبِظُلۡمٍ مِّنَ ٱلَّذِينَ هَادُواْ حَرَّمۡنَا عَلَيۡهِمۡ طَيِّبَـٰتٍ أُحِلَّتۡ لَهُمۡ وَبِصَدِّهِمۡ عَن سَبِيلِ ٱللَّهِ كَثِيرًا ۝

---

282. Being reduced to the most slender and precarious of speculations. That there exists a mass of legends, full of discrepancies, regarding Jesus and very little of historical, authentic material about him is also the verdict of the best modern Biblical scholars. 'By their resemblances and differences, arguments and disarguments', says a competent authority, referring to the traditional accounts of Jesus, 'they raise many questions as to the origin, relative dates and literary criticisms, which have called forth a multitude of conflicting hypotheses and a most extensive critical literature... All that one may do with propriety is to indicate what he regards as the most plausible opinion' (*EBi*, c. 2435).

161. And also because of their taking the usury that they were prohibited, and also because of their consuming the riches of men unlawfully. And for the infidels among them We have prepared an afflictive torment.

وَأَخْذِهِمُ الرِّبَوٰا۟ وَقَدْ نُهُوا۟ عَنْهُ وَأَكْلِهِمْ أَمْوَٰلَ ٱلنَّاسِ بِٱلْبَٰطِلِ وَأَعْتَدْنَا لِلْكَٰفِرِينَ مِنْهُمْ عَذَابًا أَلِيمًا ۝

162. But of them the well-grounded in knowledge and the Believers believe in what has been sent down to you and what has been sent down before you and the establishers of prayer and the givers of the poor-rate and the believers in Allah and the Last Day — it is those to whom We shall soon give a mighty wage.

لَّٰكِنِ ٱلرَّٰسِخُونَ فِى ٱلْعِلْمِ مِنْهُمْ وَٱلْمُؤْمِنُونَ يُؤْمِنُونَ بِمَآ أُنزِلَ إِلَيْكَ وَمَآ أُنزِلَ مِن قَبْلِكَ وَٱلْمُقِيمِينَ ٱلصَّلَوٰةَ وَٱلْمُؤْتُونَ ٱلزَّكَوٰةَ وَٱلْمُؤْمِنُونَ بِٱللَّهِ وَٱلْيَوْمِ ٱلْءَاخِرِ أُو۟لَٰٓئِكَ سَنُؤْتِيهِمْ أَجْرًا عَظِيمًا ۝

Section 23

163. Surely We have revealed to you, even as We revealed to Noah and the Prophets after him, and as We revealed to Abraham and Ishmael and Isaac and Jacob and the tribes, and Jesus and Job and Jonah and Aaron and Solomon; and to David We gave a Scripture.

إِنَّآ أَوْحَيْنَآ إِلَيْكَ كَمَآ أَوْحَيْنَآ إِلَىٰ نُوحٍ وَٱلنَّبِيِّـۧنَ مِنۢ بَعْدِهِۦ وَأَوْحَيْنَآ إِلَىٰٓ إِبْرَٰهِيمَ وَإِسْمَٰعِيلَ وَإِسْحَٰقَ وَيَعْقُوبَ وَٱلْأَسْبَاطِ وَعِيسَىٰ وَأَيُّوبَ وَيُونُسَ وَهَٰرُونَ وَسُلَيْمَٰنَ وَءَاتَيْنَا دَاوُۥدَ زَبُورًا ۝

164. And We revealed to you Messengers, some of whom We have narrated to you before and of others of whom We have not narrated to you; and to Moses Allah spoke directly.

وَرُسُلًا قَدْ قَصَصْنَٰهُمْ عَلَيْكَ مِن قَبْلُ وَرُسُلًا لَّمْ نَقْصُصْهُمْ عَلَيْكَ وَكَلَّمَ ٱللَّهُ مُوسَىٰ تَكْلِيمًا ۝

165. We sent all these Messengers as bearers of glad tidings and warners in order that there be no plea for mankind against Allah after the Messengers; and Allah is ever Mighty, Wise.

رُسُلًا مُّبَشِّرِينَ وَمُنذِرِينَ لِئَلَّا يَكُونَ لِلنَّاسِ عَلَى اللَّهِ حُجَّةٌ بَعْدَ الرُّسُلِ ۚ وَكَانَ اللَّهُ عَزِيزًا حَكِيمًا ﴿١٦٥﴾

166. But Allah bears witness by what He has sent down to you. He sent it down with His own Knowledge and the angels also bear witness; and enough is Allah as a Witness.

لَّـٰكِنِ اللَّهُ يَشْهَدُ بِمَا أَنزَلَ إِلَيْكَ ۖ أَنزَلَهُ بِعِلْمِهِ ۖ وَالْمَلَـٰئِكَةُ يَشْهَدُونَ ۚ وَكَفَىٰ بِاللَّهِ شَهِيدًا ﴿١٦٦﴾

167. Surely those who have disbelieved and keep others from the way of Allah have strayed far away.

إِنَّ الَّذِينَ كَفَرُوا وَصَدُّوا عَن سَبِيلِ اللَّهِ قَدْ ضَلُّوا ضَلَالًا بَعِيدًا ﴿١٦٧﴾

168. Surely those who have disbelieved and done wrong, Allah is not one to forgive them nor to guide them to any way.

إِنَّ الَّذِينَ كَفَرُوا وَظَلَمُوا لَمْ يَكُنِ اللَّهُ لِيَغْفِرَ لَهُمْ وَلَا لِيَهْدِيَهُمْ طَرِيقًا ﴿١٦٨﴾

169. Except the way to Hell as abiders therein for ever; and this is ever easy with Allah.

إِلَّا طَرِيقَ جَهَنَّمَ خَالِدِينَ فِيهَا أَبَدًا ۚ وَكَانَ ذَٰلِكَ عَلَى اللَّهِ يَسِيرًا ﴿١٦٩﴾

170. O mankind! Assuredly there has come to you the Messenger with the Truth from your Lord; so believe in him that it may be well for you. And if you disbelieve, then surely Allah's is whatever is in the heavens and the earth; and Allah is ever Knowing, Wise.

يَا أَيُّهَا النَّاسُ قَدْ جَاءَكُمُ الرَّسُولُ بِالْحَقِّ مِن رَّبِّكُمْ فَآمِنُوا خَيْرًا لَّكُمْ ۚ وَإِن تَكْفُرُوا فَإِنَّ لِلَّهِ مَا فِي السَّمَاوَاتِ وَالْأَرْضِ ۚ وَكَانَ اللَّهُ عَلِيمًا حَكِيمًا ﴿١٧٠﴾

171. O People of the Book! Do not exceed the bounds in your Religion, and do not say of Allah save what is the Truth. The Messiah Jesus, son of Maryam, is but a Messenger of Allah and His Word – He cast it upon Maryam – and a Spirit from Him. Believe therefore in Allah and His Messengers, and do not say: 'Three.'[283] Desist that it may be well for you. Allah is but the One God; hallowed be He that there should be up to Him a son! His is whatever is in the heavens and the earth and enough is Allah as a Trustee!

يَـٰٓأَهۡلَ ٱلۡكِتَـٰبِ لَا تَغۡلُواْ فِى دِينِكُمۡ وَلَا تَقُولُواْ عَلَى ٱللَّهِ إِلَّا ٱلۡحَقَّ إِنَّمَا ٱلۡمَسِيحُ عِيسَى ٱبۡنُ مَرۡيَمَ رَسُولُ ٱللَّهِ وَكَلِمَتُهُۥٓ أَلۡقَىٰهَآ إِلَىٰ مَرۡيَمَ وَرُوحٌ مِّنۡهُ فَـَٔامِنُواْ بِٱللَّهِ وَرُسُلِهِۦ وَلَا تَقُولُواْ ثَلَٰثَةٌ ٱنتَهُواْ خَيۡرًا لَّكُمۡ إِنَّمَا ٱللَّهُ إِلَٰهٌ وَٰحِدٌ سُبۡحَـٰنَهُۥٓ أَن يَكُونَ لَهُۥ وَلَدٌ لَّهُۥ مَا فِى ٱلسَّمَـٰوَٰتِ وَمَا فِى ٱلۡأَرۡضِ وَكَفَىٰ بِٱللَّهِ وَكِيلًا ﴿١٧١﴾

283. Trinity denotes the central doctrine of the Christian religion. It means that God 'is three really distinct Persons, the Father, the Son, and the Holy Ghost. Each of these Persons is truly the same God, and has all His infinite perfections, yet He is really distinct from each of the other Persons... These Persons are co – equal, co – eternal and consubstantial, and deserve co – equal glory and adoration, which the Church expresses in the oft – repeated prayer: "Glory be to the Father, and to the Son, and to the Holy Ghost" '(CD. p. 973). The Book of Islam 'found in the dogma of Trinity what every emancipated thinker finds on impartial reflection an absurd legend, which is neither reconcilable with the first principle of reason nor of any value whatever for our religious advancement. In the Brahmanic religion the Trimurti is also conceived as a "divine unity" made up of three persons Brahma (the Creator), Vishnu (the Sustainer), and Shiva (the Destroyer)' (Haeckel, *Riddle of the Universe*, pp. 226, 233). 'They divided the Divine Trinity into three persons, each one of them being God and Lord; and thence a sort of frenzy has gone forth into the whole of theology, and thus into the Church ... It is a frenzy, because the minds of men have been driven by it into such a delirium, that they do not know whether there is one God, or whether there are three: there is one in the speech of lips, but three in the thought of the mind' (Swedenborg, *The True Christian Religion*, p. 5). 'The Nicene Creed really teaches three Divine Persons and denies three Gods, and leaves us to guess what else is a Divine Person but a God or a God but a Divine Person' (Newman, *Phases of Faith*, p. 33).

Section 24

172. The Messiah does not disdain that he should be a servant of Allah[284] nor do the angels brought near[285] to him. And he who disdains serving Him and is stiff-necked, soon He shall gather them all unto Him.

لَن يَسْتَنكِفَ ٱلْمَسِيحُ أَن يَكُونَ عَبْدًا لِّلَّهِ وَلَا ٱلْمَلَٰٓئِكَةُ ٱلْمُقَرَّبُونَ ۚ وَمَن يَسْتَنكِفْ عَنْ عِبَادَتِهِۦ وَيَسْتَكْبِرْ فَسَيَحْشُرُهُمْ إِلَيْهِ جَمِيعًا ١٧٢

284. Namely a true worshipper and obedient servant of God. Cf. Christ's own words as recorded in the Christian Gospels: 'My meat is to do the will of him that sent me, and to finish his work' (Jn. 4: 34). 'If ye keep my commandments, ye shall abide in my love; even as I have kept my Father's commandments, and abide in his love' (15: 10). And Peter, an apostle, has in the course of a long address used the following words: 'Jesus of Nazareth, a man approved of God among you ...' (Ac. 2: 22). These words, according to the best Biblical scholars, describe Jesus as he was known and regarded by his contemporaries. 'He was "found in fashion as a man", that is, in all particulars which presented themselves to outward observation. He appeared and behaved as one of the human race. He "was made man". The Gospels leave no room for doubt as to the completeness with which these statements are to be accepted... He not only made no claim to omniscience: He distinctly waived it... There is still less reason to predicate the omnipotence of Jesus. There is no indication that he ever acted independently of God, or as an independent God. Rather does he acknowledge dependence upon God, by his habit of prayer and in such words as "this kind goeth not forth save by prayer". He even repudiates the ascription to himself of goodness in the absolute sense in which it belongs to God alone' (*EBr.* XIII, p. 24).

285. This knocks the bottom out of Christian angelolatry. In the Catholic Catechism one comes across the following daily prayer addressed to Our Angel Guardian: 'O Angel of God, to whose care I am committed! enlighten and direct me, defend and govern me this day, and during my whole life! Amen'. This adoration of the angels 'can be traced to the earliest ages of the Church. We venerate their excellence and petition their ministrations. The month of October is especially dedicated to them and the feast of all the angels is celebrated in common with that of Michael, on 29th Sept.' (*CD.* p. 44).

173. Then as to those who have believed and worked righteous works, He will give them their wages in full and will give an increase out of His grace. And as to those who disdained and were stiff-necked, He will torment them with an afflictive torment. And they shall not find for themselves, against Allah, a protector or a friend.

فَأَمَّا ٱلَّذِينَ ءَامَنُوا۟ وَعَمِلُوا۟ ٱلصَّٰلِحَٰتِ فَيُوَفِّيهِمْ أُجُورَهُمْ وَيَزِيدُهُم مِّن فَضْلِهِۦ وَأَمَّا ٱلَّذِينَ ٱسْتَنكَفُوا۟ وَٱسْتَكْبَرُوا۟ فَيُعَذِّبُهُمْ عَذَابًا أَلِيمًا وَلَا يَجِدُونَ لَهُم مِّن دُونِ ٱللَّهِ وَلِيًّا وَلَا نَصِيرًا ۝

174. O mankind! There surely has come to you an argument from your Lord and We have sent down to you a manifest light.

يَٰٓأَيُّهَا ٱلنَّاسُ قَدْ جَآءَكُم بُرْهَٰنٌ مِّن رَّبِّكُمْ وَأَنزَلْنَآ إِلَيْكُمْ نُورًا مُّبِينًا ۝

175. Then as to those who believe in Allah and hold fast by Him, soon He will admit them to His mercy and grace and will lead them to Himself by a straight path.

فَأَمَّا ٱلَّذِينَ ءَامَنُوا۟ بِٱللَّهِ وَٱعْتَصَمُوا۟ بِهِۦ فَسَيُدْخِلُهُمْ فِى رَحْمَةٍ مِّنْهُ وَفَضْلٍ وَيَهْدِيهِمْ إِلَيْهِ صِرَٰطًا مُّسْتَقِيمًا ۝

176. They ask you for a pronouncement. Say: 'Allah pronounces thus in the matter of one without father or child; if a person perishes and has no child but has a sister, hers will be the half of what he has left; and he will be her heir if she has no child: if there be two sisters, then theirs shall be two-thirds of what he has left; and if there be both brothers and sisters, then the male will have as much as the portion of two females. Allah explains this to you lest you err, and Allah is the Knower of everything.'

يَسْتَفْتُونَكَ قُلِ ٱللَّهُ يُفْتِيكُمْ فِى ٱلْكَلَٰلَةِ إِنِ ٱمْرُؤٌا۟ هَلَكَ لَيْسَ لَهُۥ وَلَدٌ وَلَهُۥٓ أُخْتٌ فَلَهَا نِصْفُ مَا تَرَكَ وَهُوَ يَرِثُهَآ إِن لَّمْ يَكُن لَّهَا وَلَدٌ فَإِن كَانَتَا ٱثْنَتَيْنِ فَلَهُمَا ٱلثُّلُثَانِ مِمَّا تَرَكَ وَإِن كَانُوٓا۟ إِخْوَةً رِّجَالًا وَنِسَآءً فَلِلذَّكَرِ مِثْلُ حَظِّ ٱلْأُنثَيَيْنِ يُبَيِّنُ ٱللَّهُ لَكُمْ أَن تَضِلُّوا۟ وَٱللَّهُ بِكُلِّ شَىْءٍ عَلِيمٌ ۝

Sūrah 5

al-Mā'idah

(Madinan, 16 Sections, 120 Verses)

In the name of Allah, the Compassionate, the Merciful

♦

Section 1

1. O you who believe! Fulfill your obligations. Allowed to you are all cattle quadrupeds except those announced to you, not allowing game while you are in a state of sanctity: Verily Allah ordains what He will.

2. O you who believe! Do not profane the landmarks of Allah nor any sacred month, nor the offering nor the victims with garlands, nor those repairing to the Sacred House seeking the grace and goodwill of their Lord. And when you have put off the state of sanctity, you may hunt. And let not the detestation for a people, because they kept you from the Sacred Mosque, incite you to trespass. Cooperate with one another in virtue and piety, and do not cooperate in sin and transgression. Fear Allah. Verily Allah is Severe in chastising.

يَـٰٓأَيُّهَا ٱلَّذِينَ ءَامَنُوٓاْ أَوْفُواْ بِٱلْعُقُودِ أُحِلَّتْ لَكُم بَهِيمَةُ ٱلْأَنْعَٰمِ إِلَّا مَا يُتْلَىٰ عَلَيْكُمْ غَيْرَ مُحِلِّى ٱلصَّيْدِ وَأَنتُمْ حُرُمٌ إِنَّ ٱللَّهَ يَحْكُمُ مَا يُرِيدُ ﴿١﴾

يَـٰٓأَيُّهَا ٱلَّذِينَ ءَامَنُواْ لَا تُحِلُّواْ شَعَـٰٓئِرَ ٱللَّهِ وَلَا ٱلشَّهْرَ ٱلْحَرَامَ وَلَا ٱلْهَدْىَ وَلَا ٱلْقَلَـٰٓئِدَ وَلَآ ءَآمِّينَ ٱلْبَيْتَ ٱلْحَرَامَ يَبْتَغُونَ فَضْلًا مِّن رَّبِّهِمْ وَرِضْوَٰنًا وَإِذَا حَلَلْتُمْ فَٱصْطَادُواْ وَلَا يَجْرِمَنَّكُمْ شَنَـَٔانُ قَوْمٍ أَن صَدُّوكُمْ عَنِ ٱلْمَسْجِدِ ٱلْحَرَامِ أَن تَعْتَدُواْ وَتَعَاوَنُواْ عَلَى ٱلْبِرِّ وَٱلتَّقْوَىٰ وَلَا تَعَاوَنُواْ عَلَى ٱلْإِثْمِ وَٱلْعُدْوَٰنِ وَٱتَّقُواْ ٱللَّهَ إِنَّ ٱللَّهَ شَدِيدُ ٱلْعِقَابِ ﴿٢﴾

3. Forbidden to your are dead-meat, blood, swine-flesh, any animal dedicated to other than Allah, the strangled, the felled, the tumbled, the gored, the mangled by beasts of prey, unless you make it clean by giving it the death-stroke yourselves and what has been sacrificed on the altars. Also forbidden to you is partition by divining arrow.[286] All that is an abomination. Those who disbelieve have this day[287] despaired of your

حُرِّمَتْ عَلَيْكُمُ ٱلْمَيْتَةُ وَٱلدَّمُ وَلَحْمُ ٱلْخِنزِيرِ وَمَآ أُهِلَّ لِغَيْرِ ٱللَّهِ بِهِۦ وَ ٱلْمُنْخَنِقَةُ وَٱلْمَوْقُوذَةُ وَٱلْمُتَرَدِّيَةُ وَ ٱلنَّطِيحَةُ وَمَآ أَكَلَ ٱلسَّبُعُ إِلَّا مَا ذَكَّيْتُمْ وَمَا ذُبِحَ عَلَى ٱلنُّصُبِ وَأَن تَسْتَقْسِمُوا بِٱلْأَزْلَٰمِ ذَٰلِكُمْ فِسْقٌ ٱلْيَوْمَ يَئِسَ ٱلَّذِينَ كَفَرُوا مِن دِينِكُمْ فَلَا تَخْشَوْهُمْ وَٱخْشَوْنِ

286. *Zalam* is 'an arrow without a head and without feathers: which was applied to those divining arrows by means of which the Arabs in the time of Ignorance sought to know what was allotted to them and they put them in a receptacle, and when any of them desired to make a journey, or to accomplish a want, or when he desired to perform some affair, he put his hand into that receptacle, and took forth an arrow; and if the arrow upon which was "Command" came forth, he went to accomplish his purpose, but if that upon which was "Prohibition" came forth he refrained; and if the blank came forth, they shuffled them a second time' (*LL.*). 'It was the custom to draw lots for joints of a camel with arrows, some feathered and others unfeathered, kept for this purpose in the temple of Mecca' (Rodwell, *The Koran*).

287. In other words, now. The verse was revealed on Friday, the 9th of Dhū al-Hijjah at 'Arafāt, in itself a festive occasion in the 10th year of the Hijrah when the Holy Prophet performed his valedictory Ḥajj, triumphant at the head of 1,20,000 devoted and faithful followers. Memorable indeed was the address he delivered on this occasion. The following abridged version is by Lane – Poole:

> Ye people! Hearken to my words; for I know not whether after this year I shall ever be among you, here again.

> Your lives and your property are sacred and inviolable among one another until the end of time.

> The Lord has ordained to every man the share of his inheritance: a testament is not lawful to the prejudice of heirs.

> The child belongs to the parent: and the violator of wedlock shall get stoned.

Ye people! Ye have rights demandable of your wives, and they have rights demandable of you. Treat your women well.

And your slaves, see that you feed them with such food as ye eat yourselves, and clothe them with the stuff ye wear. And if they commit a fault which ye are not willing to forgive, then sell them, for they are the servants of the Lord, and are not to be tormented.

Ye people! Hearken unto my speech and comprehend it. Know that every Muslim is the brother of every other Muslim. All of you are on the same equality: ye are one brotherhood.

Then, looking up to heaven, he cried 'O Lord! I have delivered my message and fulfilled my mission'. And all the multitude answered, 'Yea, verily have you'. 'O Lord! I beseech You, bear You witness to it!' and, like Moses, he lifted up his hands and blessed the people' (*LSK*. Intro. pp. LXVIII – LXIX).

religion. So fear them not; fear Me. This day I have perfected[288] your religion for you and have completed My favour upon you, and have chosen for you Islam as your religion. He who is driven to extreme hunger, not inclining to sin, verily then Allah is the Forgiving, the Merciful.

اَلْيَوْمَ أَكْمَلْتُ لَكُمْ دِينَكُمْ وَأَتْمَمْتُ عَلَيْكُمْ نِعْمَتِي وَرَضِيتُ لَكُمُ الْإِسْلَامَ دِينًا فَمَنِ اضْطُرَّ فِي مَخْمَصَةٍ غَيْرَ مُتَجَانِفٍ لِإِثْمٍ فَإِنَّ اللَّهَ غَفُورٌ رَحِيمٌ ٣

4. They ask you, what is allowed to them. Say: 'Allowed to you are all clean foods, and as to the animals of prey which you have trained as Allah has taught you, eat of what they have caught for you, and mention the name of Allah over it, and fear Allah; verily Allah is Swift in reckoning.'

يَسْأَلُونَكَ مَاذَا أُحِلَّ لَهُمْ قُلْ أُحِلَّ لَكُمُ الطَّيِّبَاتُ وَمَا عَلَّمْتُمْ مِنَ الْجَوَارِحِ مُكَلِّبِينَ تُعَلِّمُونَهُنَّ مِمَّا عَلَّمَكُمُ اللَّهُ فَكُلُوا مِمَّا أَمْسَكْنَ عَلَيْكُمْ وَاذْكُرُوا اسْمَ اللَّهِ عَلَيْهِ وَاتَّقُوا اللَّهَ إِنَّ اللَّهَ سَرِيعُ الْحِسَابِ ٤

288. Perfected Religion in every little detail and until the end of time, and which mankind shall never be able to outgrow. The world, says a European convert to Islam, 'has not been able to produce a better system of ethics than that expressed in Islam; it has not been able to put the idea of human brotherhood on a practical footing as Islam did in its supernational conception of "Ummah"; it has not been able to create a social structure in which the conflicts and conflictions between the members are as efficiently reduced to a minimum as in the social plan of Islam; it has not been able to enhance the dignity of man; his feeling of security; his spiritual hope; and last, but surely not least, his happiness. In all these things the present achievements of the human race fall considerably short of the Islamic programme. Where, then, is the justification for saying that Islam is "out of date?"' (Asad, *Islam at the Crossroads*, p. 133).

5. This day allowed to you are all clean foods and the meat of those given the Book is allowable for you and your meat is allowable for them, as also allowed to you are the chaste believing women and the chaste women of those given the Book before you[289] when you have given them their dowers, taking them in wedlock, neither fornicating nor taking them as mistresses. And whoso rejects faith, his work will surely come to nothing, and in the Hereafter he will be of the losers.

اَلْيَوْمَ أُحِلَّ لَكُمُ الطَّيِّبَٰتُ وَطَعَامُ الَّذِينَ أُوتُواْ الْكِتَٰبَ حِلٌّ لَّكُمْ وَطَعَامُكُمْ حِلٌّ لَّهُمْ وَالْمُحْصَنَٰتُ مِنَ الْمُؤْمِنَٰتِ وَالْمُحْصَنَٰتُ مِنَ الَّذِينَ أُوتُواْ الْكِتَٰبَ مِن قَبْلِكُمْ إِذَآ ءَاتَيْتُمُوهُنَّ أُجُورَهُنَّ مُحْصِنِينَ غَيْرَ مُسَٰفِحِينَ وَلَا مُتَّخِذِىٓ أَخْدَانٍ وَمَن يَكْفُرْ بِالْإِيمَٰنِ فَقَدْ حَبِطَ عَمَلُهُ وَهُوَ فِى الْآخِرَةِ مِنَ الْخَٰسِرِينَ ۞

Section 2

6. O you who believe! When you stand up for prayer, wash your faces and your hands up to the elbows, and wipe your heads and wash your feet up to the ankles; and if you are polluted, purify

يَٰٓأَيُّهَا الَّذِينَ ءَامَنُوٓاْ إِذَا قُمْتُمْ إِلَى الصَّلَوٰةِ فَاغْسِلُواْ وُجُوهَكُمْ وَأَيْدِيَكُمْ إِلَى الْمَرَافِقِ وَامْسَحُواْ بِرُءُوسِكُمْ وَأَرْجُلَكُمْ إِلَى الْكَعْبَيْنِ وَإِن كُنتُمْ جُنُبًا فَاطَّهَّرُواْ

---

289. Notice the distinction Islam makes between a marriage with a Jewess or a Christian woman and a marriage with a pagan woman. Note again that the Jewish and Christian wives are not asked to renounce their religion forthwith.

yourselves.[290] And if you are ailing or on a journey or one of you comes from the privy or you have touched women, and you do not find water, betake yourselves to clean earth and wipe your faces and hands with it. Allah does not mean to lay upon you a hardship, but means to purify you and to complete His favour upon you that perhaps you may return thanks.

7. And remember Allah's favour on you and His bond with which He bound you firmly when you said: 'We hear and we obey.' And fear Allah; surely Allah is the Knower of what is in your breasts.

8. O you who believe! Be maintainers of your pact with Allah and witnesses in equity, and let not the detestation for a people incite you not to act fairly;[291] act fairly; that is nigh unto piety. And fear Allah; surely Allah is Aware of what you work.

وَإِن كُنتُم مَّرْضَىٰٓ أَوْ عَلَىٰ سَفَرٍ أَوْ جَآءَ أَحَدٌ مِّنكُم مِّنَ ٱلْغَآئِطِ أَوْ لَٰمَسْتُمُ ٱلنِّسَآءَ فَلَمْ تَجِدُوا۟ مَآءً فَتَيَمَّمُوا۟ صَعِيدًا طَيِّبًا فَٱمْسَحُوا۟ بِوُجُوهِكُمْ وَأَيْدِيكُم مِّنْهُ مَا يُرِيدُ ٱللَّهُ لِيَجْعَلَ عَلَيْكُم مِّنْ حَرَجٍ وَلَٰكِن يُرِيدُ لِيُطَهِّرَكُمْ وَلِيُتِمَّ نِعْمَتَهُۥ عَلَيْكُمْ لَعَلَّكُمْ تَشْكُرُونَ ٦

وَٱذْكُرُوا۟ نِعْمَةَ ٱللَّهِ عَلَيْكُمْ وَمِيثَٰقَهُ ٱلَّذِى وَاثَقَكُم بِهِۦٓ إِذْ قُلْتُمْ سَمِعْنَا وَأَطَعْنَا وَٱتَّقُوا۟ ٱللَّهَ إِنَّ ٱللَّهَ عَلِيمٌۢ بِذَاتِ ٱلصُّدُورِ ٧

يَٰٓأَيُّهَا ٱلَّذِينَ ءَامَنُوا۟ كُونُوا۟ قَوَّٰمِينَ لِلَّهِ شُهَدَآءَ بِٱلْقِسْطِ وَلَا يَجْرِمَنَّكُمْ شَنَـَٔانُ قَوْمٍ عَلَىٰٓ أَلَّا تَعْدِلُوا۟ ٱعْدِلُوا۟ هُوَ أَقْرَبُ لِلتَّقْوَىٰ وَٱتَّقُوا۟ ٱللَّهَ إِنَّ ٱللَّهَ خَبِيرٌۢ بِمَا تَعْمَلُونَ ٨

---

290. Purification by bathing. Contrast this emphasis on physical cleanliness with the Christian view obtaining in the early Christian centuries. 'The cleanliness of the body was regarded as a pollution of the soul, and the saints who were most admired had become one hideous mass of clotted filth. St. Athanasius relates with enthusiasm how St. Anthony, the patriarch of monachism, had never, to extreme old age, been guilty of washing his feet St. Euphraxia joined a convent of one hundred and thirty nuns, who never washed their feet, and who shuddered at the mention of a bath' (Lecky, *History of European Morals,* II, p. 47). A pious pilgrim, in the 4th century, 'boasted that she had not washed her face for 18 years for fear of removing the baptismal chrism' (*EBr.* I. p. 49).

291. They must all act fairly in their affairs, whatever the provocation. The meaning is: be always fair in your dealings with men and let no indignation, howsoever righteous, against any person make you depart from the path of Truth, justice and equity.

9. Allah has promised those who believe and work righteous works that for them shall be forgiveness and a mighty return.

وَعَدَ ٱللَّهُ ٱلَّذِينَ ءَامَنُواْ وَعَمِلُواْ ٱلصَّٰلِحَٰتِ لَهُم مَّغْفِرَةٌ وَأَجْرٌ عَظِيمٌ ۟

10. And those who disbelieve and belie Our signs, they shall be the inmates of the Flame.

وَٱلَّذِينَ كَفَرُواْ وَكَذَّبُواْ بِـَٔايَٰتِنَآ أُوْلَٰٓئِكَ أَصْحَٰبُ ٱلْجَحِيمِ ۟

11. O you who believe! Remember Allah's favour on you when a people determined to stretch forth their hands against you, but He withheld their hands from you. And fear Allah, and on Allah let the believers rely.

يَٰٓأَيُّهَا ٱلَّذِينَ ءَامَنُواْ ٱذْكُرُواْ نِعْمَتَ ٱللَّهِ عَلَيْكُمْ إِذْ هَمَّ قَوْمٌ أَن يَبْسُطُوٓاْ إِلَيْكُمْ أَيْدِيَهُمْ فَكَفَّ أَيْدِيَهُمْ عَنكُمْ وَٱتَّقُواْ ٱللَّهَ وَعَلَى ٱللَّهِ فَلْيَتَوَكَّلِ ٱلْمُؤْمِنُونَ ۟

Section 3

12. Assuredly Allah took a bond from the children of Israel and We raised from amongst them twelve leaders. And Allah said: 'Surely I am with you; if you establish prayer and pay the poor-rate and believe in My Messengers and support them and lend to Allah a goodly loan, I will expiate for you your misdeeds and will admit you to Gardens beneath which rivers flow, then he of you who disbelieves thereafter has surely strayed from the level way.

وَلَقَدْ أَخَذَ ٱللَّهُ مِيثَٰقَ بَنِىٓ إِسْرَٰٓءِيلَ وَبَعَثْنَا مِنْهُمُ ٱثْنَىْ عَشَرَ نَقِيبًا وَقَالَ ٱللَّهُ إِنِّى مَعَكُمْ لَئِنْ أَقَمْتُمُ ٱلصَّلَوٰةَ وَءَاتَيْتُمُ ٱلزَّكَوٰةَ وَءَامَنتُم بِرُسُلِى وَعَزَّرْتُمُوهُمْ وَأَقْرَضْتُمُ ٱللَّهَ قَرْضًا حَسَنًا لَّأُكَفِّرَنَّ عَنكُمْ سَيِّـَٔاتِكُمْ وَلَأُدْخِلَنَّكُمْ جَنَّٰتٍ تَجْرِى مِن تَحْتِهَا ٱلْأَنْهَٰرُ فَمَن كَفَرَ بَعْدَ ذَٰلِكَ مِنكُمْ فَقَدْ ضَلَّ سَوَآءَ ٱلسَّبِيلِ ۟

13. Thus for the breach of their bond, We accursed them and We made their hearts hard. They pervert the words from their meanings and have abandoned a good portion of that with which they were exhorted.[292] And you will not cease to find them bent upon defrauding on their part, save a few of them, yet pardon them and overlook them; surely Allah loves the well-doers.

فَبِمَا نَقْضِهِم مِّيثَاقَهُمْ لَعَنَّهُمْ وَجَعَلْنَا قُلُوبَهُمْ قَاسِيَةً يُحَرِّفُونَ ٱلْكَلِمَ عَن مَّوَاضِعِهِۦ وَنَسُوا۟ حَظًّا مِّمَّا ذُكِّرُوا۟ بِهِۦ وَلَا تَزَالُ تَطَّلِعُ عَلَىٰ خَآئِنَةٍ مِّنْهُمْ إِلَّا قَلِيلًا مِّنْهُمْ فَٱعْفُ عَنْهُمْ وَٱصْفَحْ إِنَّ ٱللَّهَ يُحِبُّ ٱلْمُحْسِنِينَ ١٣

14. And of them who say: 'We are Nazarenes', We took a bond from them,[293] but they have abandoned a good portion of that with which

وَمِنَ ٱلَّذِينَ قَالُوٓا۟ إِنَّا نَصَٰرَىٰٓ أَخَذْنَا مِيثَاقَهُمْ فَنَسُوا۟ حَظًّا مِّمَّا ذُكِّرُوا۟ بِهِۦ

292. Look at the Jews' own estimate for the correctness and accuracy of their Scripture: 'We infer with certainty that the ancient copies of the Torah contained no vowels or accents, and that these have come down to us by oral tradition. For the multiplication of copies, human copyists had to be employed. It is by no means contrary to our faith in the Bible to assume that, as far as the human work of these copyists is concerned, it must have been subject to the fate of all human work, to error and imperfection. And, in fact, there are many copies of the Bible that abound in mistakes; there are passages in the Scripture that vary in different manuscripts; hence numerous *varioe lectiones* met with in the critical editions of the Bible' (Friedlander, *The Jewish Religion,* p. 53).

293. A bond to the effect that they would believe in the Final Prophet. Witness numerous references to him, the well -known and well-recognized 'that Prophet' or 'the Prophet' found even in the garbled text of the modern Gospels: 'And this is the record of John, when the Jews sent priests and Levites from Jerusalem to ask him, Who art thou? Art you that Prophet! And he answered, No And they asked him, and said unto him, Why baptizest thou then, if thou be not that Christ, nor Elijah, neither that Prophet' (Jn. 1: 19, 21, 25). 'Jesus stood and cried, saying, If any man thirst, let him come unto me and drink Many of the people therefore, when they heard this saying, said: Of a truth this is the Prophet' (Jn. 7: 37, 40). 'If ye love me, keep my commandments. And I will pray to the Father, and he shall give you another Comforter, that he may abide with you for ever' (Jn. 14: 15, 16). 'It is expedient for you that I go away: for if I go not away, the Comforter will not come unto you; but if I depart, I will send him unto you. And when he is come, he will reprove the world of sin, and of righteousness, and of judgement' (Jn. 16: 7, 8).

they were exhorted; so We have caused enmity and hatred among them[294] till the Day of Judgement, and soon will Allah declare to them what they have been performing all along.

فَأَغْرَيْنَا بَيْنَهُمُ الْعَدَاوَةَ وَالْبَغْضَاءَ إِلَىٰ يَوْمِ الْقِيَامَةِ وَسَوْفَ يُنَبِّئُهُمُ اللَّهُ بِمَا كَانُوا يَصْنَعُونَ ۝

15. O People of the Book! Surely there has come to you Our Messenger expounding to you much in the Book that you were wont to hide and much he passes over. To be sure, there has come to you from Allah a light and a Book luminous.

يَا أَهْلَ الْكِتَابِ قَدْ جَاءَكُمْ رَسُولُنَا يُبَيِّنُ لَكُمْ كَثِيرًا مِّمَّا كُنْتُمْ تُخْفُونَ مِنَ الْكِتَابِ وَيَعْفُوا عَن كَثِيرٍ قَدْ جَاءَكُم مِّنَ اللَّهِ نُورٌ وَكِتَابٌ مُّبِينٌ ۝

16. With it Allah guides those who follow His goodwill to the ways of safety, and He brings them forth out of darkness into the light by His command, and guides them on to the right path.

يَهْدِي بِهِ اللَّهُ مَنِ اتَّبَعَ رِضْوَانَهُ سُبُلَ السَّلَامِ وَيُخْرِجُهُم مِّنَ الظُّلُمَاتِ إِلَى النُّورِ بِإِذْنِهِ وَيَهْدِيهِمْ إِلَىٰ صِرَاطٍ مُّسْتَقِيمٍ ۝

---

294. This applies to the Christian sects and sub–sects. The reference here is to the permanent and perennial 'war of creeds within the Church' and not the political antagonism between the European states which happen to be Christian — some of them only in name. The Catholics are, from the Protestant standpoint, no better than 'Popish persons, who desire still to keep the people in ignorance and darkness' (See dedication of the AV to King James). In a similar vein, the Catholics point their finger to the amount of 'immorality and corruption prevalent among Luther's followers' (CD. p. 815). And such wordy acrimony has frequently given place to severe religious persecution, and even massacres. In Dean Milman's admirable summing up of Church history: 'Bloodshed, murder, treachery, assassination, even during the public worship of God these are the frightful means by which each party strives to maintain its opinions and to defeat its adversary' (Lecky, History of European Morals, II, p. 82 n.). 'After having been persecuted by the pagans, the Christians persecuted each other over nonsensical follies. They killed, imprisoned or exiled each other over the word homooesiss or the sense of the word pheysis, nature, which the Nestorian school of Antioch understood differently from the Monophysite school of Alexandria' (Dermingham, Life of Mahomet, p.117).

17. Certainly they are disbelievers who assert: the Messiah, son of Maryam,[295] is the very God himself. Say: who can avail in aught against Allah, if He meant to destroy Jesus,

لَقَدْ كَفَرَ الَّذِينَ قَالُوٓا إِنَّ اللَّهَ هُوَ الْمَسِيحُ ابْنُ مَرْيَمَ قُلْ فَمَن يَمْلِكُ مِنَ اللَّهِ شَيْئًا إِنْ أَرَادَ أَن يُهْلِكَ الْمَسِيحَ ابْنَ مَرْيَمَ

295. The reference here is mainly to certain less well-known strands of Christianity, such as Docetism, Monarchianism and Sabellianism, which rest on some such propositions as the following: 'That one and the same God is the Creator and Father of all things; and that when it pleased Him, He appeared.' 'When the Father had not been born, He yet was justly styled Father; and when it pleased Him to undergo generation, having been begotten, He Himself became His own Son, not another's.' Father and Son, so called, are one, but Himself for Himself' (*ERE.* VIII. p. 779). 'Modalistic monarchianism conceiving that the whole fullness of the Godhead, dwelt in Christ maintained that the names Father and son were only different designations of the same subject, the one God' (*EBr.* XV. p. 686). But hardly distinguishable from these 'heresies' and equally bewildering to the Muslim mind is the accepted central doctrine of orthodox Christianity: 'Jesus is very God of very God, who for us men and for our salvation came down from heaven and was made Man'. His nature is 'consubstantial with God'. He is not inferior to the Father, nor posterior, nor merely like unto Him, but identical in substance and in essence with Him. He is truly God, God of very God, consubstantial with the Father, as the Nicene Creed has it, having, or rather, being, the Godhead no less than the Father' (*CD.* p. 252). In short, for all practical purposes the terms, God and Christ are interchangeable. 'As early as twenty years after the Ascension the doctrine of Christ's Deity was already finally established in the Church. It is not argued about or proved, but assumed as one of those fundamental ideas about which Christians are agreed. Thus it is stated that He existed before He was born into the world, and indeed before all creation, in a status of equality with God; that He created the world as the Father's agent that He is actually God, and therefore, to be worshipped with divine honours by angels and men'. (Dummelow, *Commentary on the Holy Bible,* p. cviii). Two references in the NT itself are quite explicit: 'Christ came, who is over all, God blessed for ever. (Ro. 9: 5). 'Looking for that blessed hope, and the glorious appearing of the great God and our Saviour Jesus Christ' (Tt. 2, 13).

son of Maryam, and his mother[296] and those on the earth altogether? And Allah's is the kingdom of the heavens and the earth and what is in between. He creates whatever He will, and Allah is Potent over everything.

وَأُمَّهُۥۖ وَمَن فِى ٱلۡأَرۡضِ جَمِيعًاۗ وَلِلَّهِ مُلۡكُ ٱلسَّمَٰوَٰتِ وَٱلۡأَرۡضِ وَمَا بَيۡنَهُمَاۚ يَخۡلُقُ مَا يَشَآءُۚ وَٱللَّهُ عَلَىٰ كُلِّ شَىۡءٖ قَدِيرٌ ۝

18. And the Jews and the Nazarenes say: 'We are the children of God and His loved ones.' Say: 'Why then does He perish you for your sins?' Aye! You are but men, part of His creation. He forgives whom He will, and chastises whom He will. And Allah's is the kingdom of the heavens and the earth and what is in between. And to Him is the return.

وَقَالَتِ ٱلۡيَهُودُ وَٱلنَّصَٰرَىٰ نَحۡنُ أَبۡنَٰٓؤُاْ ٱللَّهِ وَأَحِبَّٰٓؤُهُۥۚ قُلۡ فَلِمَ يُعَذِّبُكُم بِذُنُوبِكُمۖ بَلۡ أَنتُم بَشَرٌ مِّمَّنۡ خَلَقَۚ يَغۡفِرُ لِمَن يَشَآءُ وَيُعَذِّبُ مَن يَشَآءُۚ وَلِلَّهِ مُلۡكُ ٱلسَّمَٰوَٰتِ وَٱلۡأَرۡضِ وَمَا بَيۡنَهُمَاۖ وَإِلَيۡهِ ٱلۡمَصِيرُ ۝

296. Maryam is also adored and worshipped as a Divinity by a very large number of the Christians. 'In the most widely distributed form of Christianity the "virgin" mother of Christ plays an important part as a fourth deity; in many Catholic countries she is practically taken to be much more powerful and influential than the three male persons of the celestial administration' (Haeckel, *Riddle of the Universe,* p. 323). Even as early as the 3rd century, the titles of Mary as the 'Mother of God' and as the 'Queen of Heaven', 'were demanded by the more fanatical Christians who claimed Divine honours for the ideal and prototype of virginity' (*DB.* III, p. 289). 'Mariolatry is probably now more prevalent in the Church of Rome that at any former time' (Ibid., 291). In the Orient there existed, in the early centuries, certain (Christian) sects who worshipped Mary. The Collyridians, says St. Epiphany, offered little cakes (collyris) as sacrifices to the Virgin like those offered to Ceres by the pagans' (Dermingham, *Life of Mahomet,* p. 111). The title of Thotokos, or 'Mother of God' was enforced on the Virgin Mary by the Ecumenical Council of Ephesus in 431. According to the Roman Catholic Church, 'God, without ceasing to be God, in the characteristic phrase of St. Paul "implied Himself" and was born in human form of Mary's womb and she became Virgin Mother, the Virgin Mother of God' (Ptoserpie, *The Council of Ephesus and the Divine Motherhood,* p. 4). 'To Catholics the council of Ephesus is above all, the Council of "Thotokos", Mother of God. From it dates the rise of that intimate and personal devotion to Our Blessed Lady which ever since has found one of the most beautiful and distinguishing features of the Catholic Church. Mother of God! It is the form and centre and explanation of the worship we pay to her' (Ibid., p. 23).

19. O People of the Book! There has come to you Our Messenger, after a cessation of the Messengers, expounding to you lest you may say: 'There came not to us any bearer of glad tidings or warner.' So now there has surely come to you a bearer of glad tidings and a warner; and Allah is Potent over everything.

يَـٰٓأَهۡلَ ٱلۡكِتَـٰبِ قَدۡ جَآءَكُمۡ رَسُولُنَا يُبَيِّنُ لَكُمۡ عَلَىٰ فَتۡرَةٖ مِّنَ ٱلرُّسُلِ أَن تَقُولُوٓاْ مَا جَآءَنَا مِنۢ بَشِيرٖ وَلَا نَذِيرٖۖ فَقَدۡ جَآءَكُم بَشِيرٞ وَنَذِيرٞۗ وَٱللَّهُ عَلَىٰ كُلِّ شَيۡءٖ قَدِيرٞ ﴿١٩﴾

Section 4

20. And recall when Moses said to his people: 'O my people! Remember the favour of Allah on you when He made among you Messengers and made you princes, and gave to you what He did not give to any people in the world.

وَإِذۡ قَالَ مُوسَىٰ لِقَوۡمِهِۦ يَـٰقَوۡمِ ٱذۡكُرُواْ نِعۡمَةَ ٱللَّهِ عَلَيۡكُمۡ إِذۡ جَعَلَ فِيكُمۡ أَنۢبِيَآءَ وَجَعَلَكُم مُّلُوكٗا وَءَاتَىٰكُم مَّا لَمۡ يُؤۡتِ أَحَدٗا مِّنَ ٱلۡعَـٰلَمِينَ ﴿٢٠﴾

21. O my people! Enter the holy land which Allah has ordained for you, and do not turn back, for then you will become losers.'

يَـٰقَوۡمِ ٱدۡخُلُواْ ٱلۡأَرۡضَ ٱلۡمُقَدَّسَةَ ٱلَّتِي كَتَبَ ٱللَّهُ لَكُمۡ وَلَا تَرۡتَدُّواْ عَلَىٰٓ أَدۡبَارِكُمۡ فَتَنقَلِبُواْ خَـٰسِرِينَ ﴿٢١﴾

22. They said: 'O Moses! Verily therein are a people high – handed and we shall never march to it so long as they do not depart: if they depart, we shall certainly march to it.'

قَالُواْ يَـٰمُوسَىٰٓ إِنَّ فِيهَا قَوۡمٗا جَبَّارِينَ وَإِنَّا لَن نَّدۡخُلَهَا حَتَّىٰ يَخۡرُجُواْ مِنۡهَا فَإِن يَخۡرُجُواْ مِنۡهَا فَإِنَّا دَٰخِلُونَ ﴿٢٢﴾

23. Thereupon spoke a couple of men who feared God and whom Allah had favoured: 'enter the gate against them, then as you enter it you will overcome, and put your trust in God, if you are indeed believers.'

قَالَ رَجُلَانِ مِنَ ٱلَّذِينَ يَخَافُونَ أَنۡعَمَ ٱللَّهُ عَلَيۡهِمَا ٱدۡخُلُواْ عَلَيۡهِمُ ٱلۡبَابَ فَإِذَا دَخَلۡتُمُوهُ فَإِنَّكُمۡ غَـٰلِبُونَۚ وَعَلَى ٱللَّهِ فَتَوَكَّلُوٓاْ إِن كُنتُم مُّؤۡمِنِينَ ﴿٢٣﴾

24. Yet the people said: 'O Moses!
Certainly we shall never march to it
so long as they remain there, go
forth you and your Lord, and fight
you twain, while we remain here
sitting.'

قَالُوْا يَمُوسَىٰٓ إِنَّا لَن نَّدْخُلَهَآ أَبَدًا
مَّا دَامُوْا فِيهَا فَاذْهَبْ أَنتَ وَرَبُّكَ
فَقَتِلَآ إِنَّا هَٰهُنَا قَٰعِدُونَ ﴿٢٤﴾

25. Moses said: 'My Lord! I have
no control over any but myself and
my brother so decide You between
us and this wicked people.'

قَالَ رَبِّ إِنِّى لَآ أَمْلِكُ إِلَّا نَفْسِى وَأَخِىۖ
فَٱفْرُقْ بَيْنَنَا وَبَيْنَ ٱلْقَوْمِ
ٱلْفَٰسِقِينَ ﴿٢٥﴾

26. Allah said: 'Verily then it is
forbidden to them for forty years
while they shall wander about in the
land, so lament not over the fate of
this wicked people.'

قَالَ فَإِنَّهَا مُحَرَّمَةٌ عَلَيْهِمْ أَرْبَعِينَ سَنَةًۚ
يَتِيهُونَ فِى ٱلْأَرْضِ فَلَا تَأْسَ عَلَى
ٱلْقَوْمِ ٱلْفَٰسِقِينَ ﴿٢٦﴾

Section 5

27. And recite you to them with
Truth the tale of the two sons of
Adam, when the two offered an
offering, and it was accepted from
one of them, and was not accepted
from the other. He said: 'I will surely
kill you.' The other said: 'Allah
accepts only from the God-
fearing.[297]

وَٱتْلُ عَلَيْهِمْ نَبَأَ ٱبْنَىْ ءَادَمَ بِٱلْحَقِّ إِذْ
قَرَّبَا قُرْبَانًا فَتُقُبِّلَ مِنْ أَحَدِهِمَا وَلَمْ
يُتَقَبَّلْ مِنَ ٱلْآخَرِ قَالَ لَأَقْتُلَنَّكَۖ
قَالَ إِنَّمَا يَتَقَبَّلُ ٱللَّهُ مِنَ ٱلْمُتَّقِينَ ﴿٢٧﴾

---

297. Compare and contrast the Qur'ānic narrative, replete with moral lessons, with
the insipid and uninspiring Biblical version in Ge. 4: 2–5, 8.

28. If you stretch forth your hand against me to kill me, I shall not be stretching forth my hand against you to kill you, verily I fear Allah, the Lord of the worlds.

29. I would rather that you bear my sin and your own sin, and then you become of the inmates of the Fire. That is the recompense of the wicked.'

30. Then his mind made the killing of his brother pleasant to him, so he killed him and became of the losers.

31. Then Allah sent a raven, scratching in the earth to show how he might cover the corpse of his brother. He said: 'Woe unto me! I am incapable of being even like this raven so that I might cover the corpse of my brother.' And he was of the remorseful.

32. Because of that We prescribed to the children of Israel, that whoso kills a person, except for a person, or for corruption in the land, it shall be as if he had killed all mankind, and whoso brings life to one it shall be as if he had brought life to all mankind. And assuredly there came to them Our Messengers with evidence, yet even after that many of them are acting in the land extravagantly.

لَئِنۢ بَسَطتَ إِلَيَّ يَدَكَ لِتَقْتُلَنِي مَآ أَنَا۠ بِبَاسِطٍ يَدِيَ إِلَيْكَ لِأَقْتُلَكَ إِنِّيٓ أَخَافُ ٱللَّهَ رَبَّ ٱلْعَٰلَمِينَ ۝

إِنِّيٓ أُرِيدُ أَن تَبُوٓأَ بِإِثْمِي وَإِثْمِكَ فَتَكُونَ مِنْ أَصْحَٰبِ ٱلنَّارِ وَذَٰلِكَ جَزَٰٓؤُا۟ ٱلظَّٰلِمِينَ ۝

فَطَوَّعَتْ لَهُۥ نَفْسُهُۥ قَتْلَ أَخِيهِ فَقَتَلَهُۥ فَأَصْبَحَ مِنَ ٱلْخَٰسِرِينَ ۝

فَبَعَثَ ٱللَّهُ غُرَابًا يَبْحَثُ فِي ٱلْأَرْضِ لِيُرِيَهُۥ كَيْفَ يُوَٰرِي سَوْءَةَ أَخِيهِ قَالَ يَٰوَيْلَتَىٰٓ أَعَجَزْتُ أَنْ أَكُونَ مِثْلَ هَٰذَا ٱلْغُرَابِ فَأُوَٰرِيَ سَوْءَةَ أَخِي فَأَصْبَحَ مِنَ ٱلنَّٰدِمِينَ ۝

مِنْ أَجْلِ ذَٰلِكَ كَتَبْنَا عَلَىٰ بَنِيٓ إِسْرَٰٓءِيلَ أَنَّهُۥ مَن قَتَلَ نَفْسًۢا بِغَيْرِ نَفْسٍ أَوْ فَسَادٍ فِي ٱلْأَرْضِ فَكَأَنَّمَا قَتَلَ ٱلنَّاسَ جَمِيعًا وَمَنْ أَحْيَاهَا فَكَأَنَّمَآ أَحْيَا ٱلنَّاسَ جَمِيعًا وَلَقَدْ جَآءَتْهُمْ رُسُلُنَا بِٱلْبَيِّنَٰتِ ثُمَّ إِنَّ كَثِيرًا مِّنْهُم بَعْدَ ذَٰلِكَ فِي ٱلْأَرْضِ لَمُسْرِفُونَ ۝

33. The recompense of those who wage war against Allah and His Messenger, and go about in the land making mischief is only that they shall be slain, or crucified, or their hands and their feet be cut off on opposite sides, or they be banished from the land. Such shall be their humiliation in this world,[298] and in the Hereafter theirs shall be a mighty torment.

إِنَّمَا جَزَٰٓؤُا۟ ٱلَّذِينَ يُحَارِبُونَ ٱللَّهَ وَرَسُولَهُۥ وَيَسْعَوْنَ فِى ٱلْأَرْضِ فَسَادًا أَن يُقَتَّلُوٓا۟ أَوْ يُصَلَّبُوٓا۟ أَوْ تُقَطَّعَ أَيْدِيهِمْ وَأَرْجُلُهُم مِّنْ خِلَٰفٍ أَوْ يُنفَوْا۟ مِنَ ٱلْأَرْضِ ۚ ذَٰلِكَ لَهُمْ خِزْىٌ فِى ٱلدُّنْيَا ۖ وَلَهُمْ فِى ٱلْأَخِرَةِ عَذَابٌ عَظِيمٌ ۝

34. Save those who repent before you overpower them; for know that Allah is the Forgiving, the Merciful.

إِلَّا ٱلَّذِينَ تَابُوا۟ مِن قَبْلِ أَن تَقْدِرُوا۟ عَلَيْهِمْ ۖ فَٱعْلَمُوٓا۟ أَنَّ ٱللَّهَ غَفُورٌ رَّحِيمٌ ۝

Section 6

35. O you who believe; fear Allah and seek approach to Him, and strive hard in His way, that haply you may thrive.

يَٰٓأَيُّهَا ٱلَّذِينَ ءَامَنُوا۟ ٱتَّقُوا۟ ٱللَّهَ وَٱبْتَغُوٓا۟ إِلَيْهِ ٱلْوَسِيلَةَ وَجَٰهِدُوا۟ فِى سَبِيلِهِۦ لَعَلَّكُمْ تُفْلِحُونَ ۝

298. Lest some of these penalties may appear 'barbarous' to some hypersensitive Western reader, let him cast a glance on 'drawing and quartering', a penalty of the English Criminal Code maintained as late as the 18th century, inflicted on those found guilty of high treason touching the king's person or government. The person committed was usually drawn on a sledge to the place of execution; there he was hanged by the neck from a scaffold, being cut down and disembowelled, while still alive; his head then was cut from his body and his corpse divided into four quarters. With the profession of their faith declared as high treason by law many Catholics of England and Ireland suffered this death. 'In the reign of Henry III and Edward I there is abundant evidence that death was the common punishment of felony; and this continued to be the law of the land as to treason and as to all felonies, except petty larceny, down to the year 1826' (Stephen, *History of the Criminal Law of England*, I. p. 458). In contemporary English law, robbery is larceny with violence; and the guilty is liable to penal servitude for life, and, in addition, if a male, to be once privately whipped. The elements of the offence are essentially the same under American law (*EBr.* XIX. p. 346).

36. Surely those who have disbelieved, if they possessed all that is in the earth and with it as much again to ransom themselves thereby from the torment on the Day of Judgement, it shall not be accepted of them, and theirs shall be an afflictive torment.

إِنَّ ٱلَّذِينَ كَفَرُوۤاْ لَوۡ أَنَّ لَهُم مَّا فِى ٱلۡأَرۡضِ جَمِيعًا وَمِثۡلَهُۥ مَعَهُۥ لِيَفۡتَدُواْ بِهِۦ مِنۡ عَذَابِ يَوۡمِ ٱلۡقِيَٰمَةِ مَا نُقُبِّلَ مِنۡهُمۡۖ وَلَهُمۡ عَذَابٌ أَلِيمٌ ٣٦

37. They will long to escape from the Fire, but they shall not be able to escape from it, and theirs shall be a lasting torment.

يُرِيدُونَ أَن يَخۡرُجُواْ مِنَ ٱلنَّارِ وَمَا هُم بِخَٰرِجِينَ مِنۡهَاۖ وَلَهُمۡ عَذَابٌ مُّقِيمٌ ٣٧

38. As for the male thief and the female thief, cut off their hands as a recompense for what they have earned;[299] an exemplary punishment from Allah; and Allah is the Mighty, the Wise.

وَٱلسَّارِقُ وَٱلسَّارِقَةُ فَٱقۡطَعُوۤاْ أَيۡدِيَهُمَا جَزَآءَ بِمَا كَسَبَا نَكَٰلًا مِّنَ ٱللَّهِۗ وَٱللَّهُ عَزِيزٌ حَكِيمٌ ٣٨

---

299. This provided that:

(i) the value of the thing stolen be not less than one dinar or 10 dirhams, and

(ii) two male witnesses of good character give their testimony against the accused, or he himself confesses his guilt.

In addition, there are provisions in Hanafi law to the effect that 'a thief's hands shall not be cut off for the theft of what cannot be guarded, or is not worth–guarding, being found in the lands in great quantity, such as dry wood, hay, grass, reeds, game, fish, lime, etc., also such articles of food as are quickly perishable, as milk, meat, fresh fruit, etc. Finally, a thief's hand shall not be cut off if the thing stolen hath no conventional value, even though it be otherwise regarded as of great worth' (Roberts, *Social Laws of the Qur'an*, p. 93). Cf. the law of the OT: 'If a thief be found breaking up, and be smitten that he die, there shall no blood be shed of him' (Ex. 22: 2). 'If a man be found stealing any of his brethren of the children of Israel, and make merchandise of him, or sell him; then that thief shall die' (Dt. 24: 7). Similarly in the Hammurabi, the Athenian, and the Roman codes, theft is, in certain cases, punishable with death. And in the common law of England, till a comparatively recent date, grand larceny, or theft of goods above the value of one shilling in the house of the owner, was a capital crime (*EBr.* XIII, p. 721).

39. Then whoso repents after his wickedness and makes amends Allah shall certainly relent towards him. Allah is the Forgiving, the Merciful.

40. Do you not know that Allah's is the kingdom of the heavens and the earth? He chastises whom He will, and He forgives whom He will;[300] and Allah is Potent over everything.[301]

41. O Messenger! Let not those grieve you who hasten toward infidelity from among those who say with their mouths: 'We believe', yet their hearts do not believe, and from among those who are Judaized; listeners to falsehoods, listeners to another people who do not come to you; they distort the words from their places, saying: 'If what you are given is this, accept it, and if that is not given you, be on your guard.' And you shall not avail against Allah in aught anyone whom Allah wishes to try. They are those whose hearts He would not purify; to them is humiliation in this world, and to them in the Hereafter there shall be a mighty torment.

---

300. This in exercise of His wisdom and mercy. This refutes the doctrine of Karma as promulgated in some Indian religions, that there is no remission of sins, and that God Himself is powerless to forego and forgive!

301. In other words, He has the will of His own Supreme Will; and He can and does exercise His Judgement in every individual case. He is not a mute, inert, First Cause, enchained by inexorable laws, and powerless to use His will.

42. Listeners are they to falsehood and devourers of the forbidden. So if they come to you, either judge between them or turn away from them. And if you turned away from them, they shall not be able to harm you in aught; and if you judged them, judge between them with equity; verily Allah loves the equitable.

سَمَّـٰعُونَ لِلْكَذِبِ أَكَّـٰلُونَ لِلسُّحْتِ فَإِن جَآءُوكَ فَٱحْكُم بَيْنَهُمْ أَوْ أَعْرِضْ عَنْهُمْ وَإِن تُعْرِضْ عَنْهُمْ فَلَن يَضُرُّوكَ شَيْئًا وَإِنْ حَكَمْتَ فَٱحْكُم بَيْنَهُم بِٱلْقِسْطِ إِنَّ ٱللَّهَ يُحِبُّ ٱلْمُقْسِطِينَ ﴿٤٢﴾

43. And how will they ask you for judgement, while they have the Torah, in which is Allah's judgement? And they turn away thereafter! They are no believers at all.

وَكَيْفَ يُحَكِّمُونَكَ وَعِندَهُمُ ٱلتَّوْرَٰئَةُ فِيهَا حُكْمُ ٱللَّهِ ثُمَّ يَتَوَلَّوْنَ مِنۢ بَعْدِ ذَٰلِكَ وَمَآ أُوْلَـٰٓئِكَ بِٱلْمُؤْمِنِينَ ﴿٤٣﴾

Section 7

44. It is We Who have sent down the Torah in which was guidance and a light. By it the Prophets who submitted themselves judged those who were Judaized, and so did the divines and the rabbis; they judged by what was committed to their keeping of the Book of Allah, and to which they were witnesses. So fear not mankind, but fear Me, and sell not My revelations for a paltry price. And he who does not judge by what Allah has sent down, it is they who are the infidels.

إِنَّآ أَنزَلْنَا ٱلتَّوْرَٰئَةَ فِيهَا هُدًى وَنُورٌ يَحْكُمُ بِهَا ٱلنَّبِيُّونَ ٱلَّذِينَ أَسْلَمُوا۟ لِلَّذِينَ هَادُوا۟ وَٱلرَّبَّـٰنِيُّونَ وَٱلْأَحْبَارُ بِمَا ٱسْتُحْفِظُوا۟ مِن كِتَـٰبِ ٱللَّهِ وَكَانُوا۟ عَلَيْهِ شُهَدَآءَ فَلَا تَخْشَوُا۟ ٱلنَّاسَ وَٱخْشَوْنِ وَلَا تَشْتَرُوا۟ بِـَٔايَـٰتِى ثَمَنًا قَلِيلًا وَمَن لَّمْ يَحْكُم بِمَآ أَنزَلَ ٱللَّهُ فَأُوْلَـٰٓئِكَ هُمُ ٱلْكَـٰفِرُونَ ﴿٤٤﴾

45. And We enjoined for them in it life for life, eye for eye, nose for nose, ear for ear, tooth for tooth, and injuries in reprisal. And whoso forgoes it, this shall be for him an expiation. And he who does not judge according to what Allah has sent down, it is they who are the wrong-doers.

وَكَتَبْنَا عَلَيْهِمْ فِيهَآ أَنَّ النَّفْسَ بِالنَّفْسِ وَالْعَيْنَ بِالْعَيْنِ وَالْأَنفَ بِالْأَنفِ وَالْأُذُنَ بِالْأُذُنِ وَالسِّنَّ بِالسِّنِّ وَالْجُرُوحَ قِصَاصٌ فَمَن تَصَدَّقَ بِهِ فَهُوَ كَفَّارَةٌ لَّهُ وَمَن لَّمْ يَحْكُم بِمَآ أَنزَلَ اللَّهُ فَأُوْلَٰئِكَ هُمُ الظَّٰلِمُونَ ﴿٤٥﴾

46. And in their footsteps We caused Jesus, son of Maryam, to follow, confirming what went afore him, the Torah, and We gave him the Gospel, in which was guidance and light, confirming that the Torah preceded it, and a guidance and an admonition to the God-fearing.

وَقَفَّيْنَا عَلَىٰ ءَاثَٰرِهِم بِعِيسَى ابْنِ مَرْيَمَ مُصَدِّقًا لِّمَا بَيْنَ يَدَيْهِ مِنَ التَّوْرَىٰةِ وَءَاتَيْنَٰهُ الْإِنجِيلَ فِيهِ هُدًى وَنُورٌ وَمُصَدِّقًا لِّمَا بَيْنَ يَدَيْهِ مِنَ التَّوْرَىٰةِ وَهُدًى وَمَوْعِظَةً لِّلْمُتَّقِينَ ﴿٤٦﴾

47. And let the people of the Gospel judge by what Allah has sent down. And he who does not judge according to what Allah has sent down, it is they who are the ungodly.

وَلْيَحْكُمْ أَهْلُ الْإِنجِيلِ بِمَآ أَنزَلَ اللَّهُ فِيهِ وَمَن لَّمْ يَحْكُم بِمَآ أَنزَلَ اللَّهُ فَأُوْلَٰئِكَ هُمُ الْفَٰسِقُونَ ﴿٤٧﴾

48. And We have sent down the Book to you with Truth and confirming what has preceded it of the Book, and as a guardian over it.[302] So judge you between them according to what Allah has sent down, and do not follow their desires, away from what has come to you of the Truth. To every one of you We have ordained a law and a

وَأَنزَلْنَآ إِلَيْكَ الْكِتَٰبَ بِالْحَقِّ مُصَدِّقًا لِّمَا بَيْنَ يَدَيْهِ مِنَ الْكِتَٰبِ وَمُهَيْمِنًا عَلَيْهِ فَاحْكُم بَيْنَهُم بِمَآ أَنزَلَ اللَّهُ وَلَا تَتَّبِعْ أَهْوَآءَهُمْ عَمَّا جَآءَكَ مِنَ الْحَقِّ لِكُلٍّ جَعَلْنَا مِنكُمْ شِرْعَةً وَمِنْهَاجًا

302. Or 'its protector'. That is one of the outstanding merits of the Holy Qur'ān. Not only does it embody within itself all the truths of the old Scriptures, but it also stands to preserve them from corruption, and serves as a text whereby their perversions, interpolations and inaccuracies can be known and corrected. And as

to the very fallible nature of the Bible — well, this is self – confessed. The infallibility of the Bible, says one of its best modern apologists, 'consists of no absolute immunity from errors. Even the Gospels defy the humanist in some details, misquote at least one passage from the OT, and misattribute another passage. The OT, in its cosmogony and in its history, fails again and again to satisfy an exact standard of accuracy and to consist with modern knowledge, while its statistics are not seldom inconsistent in detail. Many of its lapses are covered up by the kindly offices of textual tradition and translation, though every scholar knows them familiarly. Others have been smoothed over by the indulgent resources of an ingenious interpretation. It is now a commonplace of Biblical learning that God has been at no pains to prevent errors of history and knowledge and defect in the text and its transmission from finding an entrance into the scared pages of His Written Word', (*ERE.* VII. pp. 262–263).

way, and had Allah so willed[303], He would have made you all a single community, but He willed it not, in order that He may try you by what He has given you. Hasten therefore to virtues; to Allah is the return of you all; then He shall declare to you regarding what you have been disputing.

وَلَوْ شَاءَ اللَّهُ لَجَعَلَكُمْ أُمَّةً وَاحِدَةً وَلَكِن لِّيَبْلُوَكُمْ فِي مَا ءَاتَنكُمْ فَاسْتَبِقُوا الْخَيْرَاتِ إِلَى اللَّهِ مَرْجِعُكُمْ جَمِيعًا فَيُنَبِّئُكُم بِمَا كُنتُمْ فِيهِ تَخْتَلِفُونَ ﴿٤٨﴾

49. And judge you between them according to what Allah has sent down, and do not follow their desires, and be on guard lest they tempt you away from any part of what Allah has sent down to you. Then if they turn away, know you that Allah wishes to afflict them for some of their sins. And verily many of mankind are transgressors.

وَأَنِ احْكُم بَيْنَهُم بِمَا أَنزَلَ اللَّهُ وَلَا تَتَّبِعْ أَهْوَاءَهُمْ وَاحْذَرْهُمْ أَن يَفْتِنُوكَ عَن بَعْضِ مَا أَنزَلَ اللَّهُ إِلَيْكَ فَإِن تَوَلَّوْا فَاعْلَمْ أَنَّمَا يُرِيدُ اللَّهُ أَن يُصِيبَهُم بِبَعْضِ ذُنُوبِهِمْ وَإِنَّ كَثِيرًا مِّنَ النَّاسِ لَفَاسِقُونَ ﴿٤٩﴾

50. Do they then seek the judgment of paganism? And who is better in judgement than Allah for a people who have firm faith?

أَفَحُكْمَ الْجَاهِلِيَّةِ يَبْغُونَ وَمَنْ أَحْسَنُ مِنَ اللَّهِ حُكْمًا لِّقَوْمٍ يُوقِنُونَ ﴿٥٠﴾

---

303. Willed in conformity with His universal plan. The Will of God, which is the course of His physical law, is not to be confused with the goodwill or pleasure of God, which is the course of His moral law. 'What is' is always very distant from, and at times quite opposed to, 'what ought to be'.

Section 8

51. O you who believe! Do not take the Jews and the Nazarenes for friends; friends they are to each other and if any of you befriends them, verily then he is one of them. Surely Allah does not guide a transgressing people.

يَـٰٓأَيُّهَا ٱلَّذِينَ ءَامَنُوا۟ لَا تَتَّخِذُوا۟ ٱلْيَهُودَ وَٱلنَّصَـٰرَىٰٓ أَوْلِيَآءَ بَعْضُهُمْ أَوْلِيَآءُ بَعْضٍ وَمَن يَتَوَلَّهُم مِّنكُمْ فَإِنَّهُۥ مِنْهُمْ إِنَّ ٱللَّهَ لَا يَهْدِى ٱلْقَوْمَ ٱلظَّـٰلِمِينَ ﴿٥١﴾

52. So you see those in whose hearts is a disease hasten toward them saying: 'We fear lest some misfortune may befall us.' But may be Allah will bring a victory or some other affair from Himself, then they shall find themselves regretful for what they have been keeping secret in their minds.

فَتَرَى ٱلَّذِينَ فِى قُلُوبِهِم مَّرَضٌ يُسَـٰرِعُونَ فِيهِمْ يَقُولُونَ نَخْشَىٰٓ أَن تُصِيبَنَا دَآئِرَةٌ فَعَسَى ٱللَّهُ أَن يَأْتِىَ بِٱلْفَتْحِ أَوْ أَمْرٍ مِّنْ عِندِهِۦ فَيُصْبِحُوا۟ عَلَىٰ مَآ أَسَرُّوا۟ فِىٓ أَنفُسِهِمْ نَـٰدِمِينَ ﴿٥٢﴾

53. And those who believe will say: 'Are they the same who affirmed by solemn oath of Allah that they were with you?' Their works came to nothing and they found themselves losers.

وَيَقُولُ ٱلَّذِينَ ءَامَنُوٓا۟ أَهَـٰٓؤُلَآءِ ٱلَّذِينَ أَقْسَمُوا۟ بِٱللَّهِ جَهْدَ أَيْمَـٰنِهِمْ إِنَّهُمْ لَمَعَكُمْ حَبِطَتْ أَعْمَـٰلُهُمْ فَأَصْبَحُوا۟ خَـٰسِرِينَ ﴿٥٣﴾

54. O you who believe! Whoever of you apostates from his religion, then Allah shall soon bring a people whom He shall love and who shall love Him, gentle towards the believers, stern towards the infidels, striving hard in the way of Allah, and unheeding the reproof of any reprover. This is the grace of Allah; He bestows it on whomso He will. And Allah is the Bountiful, the Knowing.

يَـٰٓأَيُّهَا ٱلَّذِينَ ءَامَنُوا۟ مَن يَرْتَدَّ مِنكُمْ عَن دِينِهِۦ فَسَوْفَ يَأْتِى ٱللَّهُ بِقَوْمٍ يُحِبُّهُمْ وَيُحِبُّونَهُۥٓ أَذِلَّةٍ عَلَى ٱلْمُؤْمِنِينَ أَعِزَّةٍ عَلَى ٱلْكَـٰفِرِينَ يُجَـٰهِدُونَ فِى سَبِيلِ ٱللَّهِ وَلَا يَخَافُونَ لَوْمَةَ لَآئِمٍ ذَٰلِكَ فَضْلُ ٱللَّهِ يُؤْتِيهِ مَن يَشَآءُ وَٱللَّهُ وَٰسِعٌ عَلِيمٌ ﴿٥٤﴾

55. Your friend is but Allah and His Messenger and those who have believed – those who establish the prayer and pay the poor–rate, while they bow down.

إِنَّمَا وَلِيُّكُمُ ٱللَّهُ وَرَسُولُهُۥ وَٱلَّذِينَ ءَامَنُواْ ٱلَّذِينَ يُقِيمُونَ ٱلصَّلَوٰةَ وَيُؤۡتُونَ ٱلزَّكَوٰةَ وَهُمۡ رَٰكِعُونَ ۝

56. And whoever befriends Allah and His Messenger and those who have believed, then the party of Allah! – it is they who will be triumphant.

وَمَن يَتَوَلَّ ٱللَّهَ وَرَسُولَهُۥ وَٱلَّذِينَ ءَامَنُواْ فَإِنَّ حِزۡبَ ٱللَّهِ هُمُ ٱلۡغَٰلِبُونَ ۝

Section 9

57. O you who believe! Do not take as friends those who make a mockery and fun of your religion from among those who have been given the Book before you and other infidels. And fear Allah, if you are believers.

يَٰٓأَيُّهَا ٱلَّذِينَ ءَامَنُواْ لَا تَتَّخِذُواْ ٱلَّذِينَ ٱتَّخَذُواْ دِينَكُمۡ هُزُوًا وَلَعِبًا مِّنَ ٱلَّذِينَ أُوتُواْ ٱلۡكِتَٰبَ مِن قَبۡلِكُمۡ وَٱلۡكُفَّارَ أَوۡلِيَآءَ وَٱتَّقُواْ ٱللَّهَ إِن كُنتُم مُّؤۡمِنِينَ ۝

58. And when you call for the prayer[304] they make a mockery and

وَإِذَا نَادَيۡتُمۡ إِلَى ٱلصَّلَوٰةِ ٱتَّخَذُوهَا هُزُوًا وَلَعِبًا

---

304. The formula of the public call to Prayer (*Adhān*) runs thus:

God is Most Great (repeated four times).

I testify that there is no god but God (repeated twice).

I testify that Muḥammad is the Messenger of God (repeated twice).

Come to the prayer (repeated twice).

Come to the bliss (repeated twice).

Prayer is better than sleep (repeated twice but added only in the morning prayer). God is Most Great (repeated twice). There is no god but God.

fun of it.[305] This, because they are a people who have no understanding.

ذَٰلِكَ بِأَنَّهُمْ قَوْمٌ لَّا يَعْقِلُونَ ٥٨

59. Say: 'O People of the Book! What is that for which you persecute us save that we believe in Allah and in what has been sent down to us and what had been sent down before? And most of you are ungodly.'

قُلْ يَـٰٓأَهْلَ ٱلْكِتَٰبِ هَلْ تَنقِمُونَ مِنَّا إِلَّا أَنْ ءَامَنَّا بِٱللَّهِ وَمَا أُنزِلَ إِلَيْنَا وَمَا أُنزِلَ مِن قَبْلُ وَأَنَّ أَكْثَرَكُمْ فَـٰسِقُونَ ٥٩

60. Say: 'O People of the Book! Shall I declare to you something worse as a way with Allah than that?' It is they whom Allah has accursed and with whom He is angered and whom some He has changed into apes and swine and worshippers of false gods – those are worse in abode and furthest astray from the level way.

قُلْ هَلْ أُنَبِّئُكُم بِشَرٍّ مِّن ذَٰلِكَ مَثُوبَةً عِندَ ٱللَّهِ مَن لَّعَنَهُ ٱللَّهُ وَغَضِبَ عَلَيْهِ وَجَعَلَ مِنْهُمُ ٱلْقِرَدَةَ وَٱلْخَنَازِيرَ وَعَبَدَ ٱلطَّٰغُوتَ أُولَـٰٓئِكَ شَرٌّ مَّكَانًا وَأَضَلُّ عَن سَوَآءِ ٱلسَّبِيلِ ٦٠

61. And when they come to you they say: 'We believe'; yet infidels they came and infidels they departed. Yet Allah is the Knower of what they have been concealing.

وَإِذَا جَآءُوكُمْ قَالُوٓا۟ ءَامَنَّا وَقَد دَّخَلُوا۟ بِٱلْكُفْرِ وَهُمْ قَدْ خَرَجُوا۟ بِهِۦ وَٱللَّهُ أَعْلَمُ بِمَا كَانُوا۟ يَكْتُمُونَ ٦١

---

305. Now, is there anything in the formula quoted above to laugh at or to make fun of? Here is what an English writer has to say: 'The beauty of the Mohammadan Call to prayer', writes Hadland Davis in *Blue Peter* 'is unforgettable. Five times, within twenty – four hours, wherever Islam holds sway that sacred summons is sounded wit sonorous, far – reaching voice. It comes, not from the gateway of a mosque, nor from a house – top, nor from the market–place, but from a lovely minaret that looks like a white, long – stemmed flower rising clear, strong and comely above the traffic of men. Whether it is heard at dawn or sunset, or when the purple bright sky is ablaze with stars, that call moves the infidel as well as the devotee. Someone has happily said that "the Moslem Call is eternally beginning and never terminating", a prayer "that may indeed be suspended yet never finished and adoration that may pause but never end".'

62. And you will see many of them hastening towards sin and wickedness[306] and devouring of the unlawful.[307] Vile indeed is what they have been doing.

وَتَرَىٰ كَثِيرًا مِّنْهُمْ يُسَـٰرِعُونَ فِي ٱلْإِثْمِ وَٱلْعُدْوَٰنِ وَأَكْلِهِمُ ٱلسُّحْتَ لَبِئْسَ مَا كَانُوا۟ يَعْمَلُونَ ۝

63. Why then do their divines and priests forbid not them from blasphemy and from devouring of the unlawful? Vile indeed is what they have been performing!

لَوْلَا يَنْهَىٰهُمُ ٱلرَّبَّـٰنِيُّونَ وَٱلْأَحْبَارُ عَن قَوْلِهِمُ ٱلْإِثْمَ وَأَكْلِهِمُ ٱلسُّحْتَ لَبِئْسَ مَا كَانُوا۟ يَصْنَعُونَ ۝

64. And the Jews say, 'the hand of Allah is fettered.' Fettered be their own hands, and cursed be they for what they have uttered! Aye! His hands are both wide open; He expends howsoever He will, and surely what has been sent down to you from your Lord increases many of them in exorbitance and infidelity. And We have cast among them enmity and spite till the Day of Judgement; whenever they kindle

وَقَالَتِ ٱلْيَهُودُ يَدُ ٱللَّهِ مَغْلُولَةٌ غُلَّتْ أَيْدِيهِمْ وَلُعِنُوا۟ بِمَا قَالُوا۟ بَلْ يَدَاهُ مَبْسُوطَتَانِ يُنفِقُ كَيْفَ يَشَآءُ وَلَيَزِيدَنَّ كَثِيرًا مِّنْهُم مَّآ أُنزِلَ إِلَيْكَ مِن رَّبِّكَ طُغْيَـٰنًا وَكُفْرًا وَأَلْقَيْنَا بَيْنَهُمُ ٱلْعَدَٰوَةَ وَٱلْبَغْضَآءَ إِلَىٰ يَوْمِ ٱلْقِيَـٰمَةِ

---

306. Compare the denunciation in their own Scriptures: 'Their feet run to evil, and make haste to shade blood' (Pr. 1: 16). 'Your iniquities have separated between you and your God, and your sins have hid his face from you. Your hands are defiled with blood, and your fingers with iniquity; your lips have spoken lies, your tongue hath muttered perverseness. None call for justice, nor any plead for truth: they trust in vanity, and speak lies; they conceive mischief, and bring forth iniquity. Their feet run to evil, and they make haste to shed innocent blood; their thoughts are thoughts of iniquity; wasting and destruction are in their paths' (Is. 59: 2–7).

307. Compare the OT: 'They build up Zion with blood, and Jerusalem with iniquity. The heads thereof judge for reward, and the priests thereof teach for hire' (Mi. 3: 10–11). 'Thy princes are rebellious, and companions of thieves: every one loves gifts, and follows after rewards; they judge not the fatherless, neither does the cause of the widow come unto them' (Is. 1: 23). 'Yea, they are greedy dogs which can never have enough' (Is. 56: 11).

the fire of war, Allah puts it out, and they strive after corruption in the land; and Allah approves not the corrupters.

كُلَّمَآ أَوْقَدُواْ نَارًا لِّلْحَرْبِ أَطْفَأَهَا اللَّهُ وَيَسْعَوْنَ فِي الْأَرْضِ فَسَادًا وَاللَّهُ لَا يُحِبُّ الْمُفْسِدِينَ ٦٤

65. And had the People of the Book believed and feared, We would surely have expiated from them their misdeeds and would surely have admitted them to the Garden of Delight.

وَلَوْ أَنَّ أَهْلَ الْكِتَٰبِ ءَامَنُواْ وَاتَّقَوْاْ لَكَفَّرْنَا عَنْهُمْ سَيِّئَاتِهِمْ وَلَأَدْخَلْنَٰهُمْ جَنَّٰتِ النَّعِيمِ ٦٥

66. And had they established the Torah and the Gospel and what has now been sent down to them from their Lord, they would have received abundance from above and from beneath. Among them is a community right-doing; but for many of them vile is what they do!

وَلَوْ أَنَّهُمْ أَقَامُواْ التَّوْرَٮٰةَ وَالْإِنجِيلَ وَمَآ أُنزِلَ إِلَيْهِم مِّن رَّبِّهِمْ لَأَكَلُواْ مِن فَوْقِهِمْ وَمِن تَحْتِ أَرْجُلِهِمْ مِّنْهُمْ أُمَّةٌ مُّقْتَصِدَةٌ وَكَثِيرٌ مِّنْهُمْ سَآءَ مَا يَعْمَلُونَ ٦٦

Section 10

67. O Messenger! Preach you whatever has been sent down to you from your Lord; and if you do it not, then you have not preached His Message. Allah shall protect you from men. Allah does not guide a disbelieving people.

يَٰٓأَيُّهَا الرَّسُولُ بَلِّغْ مَآ أُنزِلَ إِلَيْكَ مِن رَّبِّكَ وَإِن لَّمْ تَفْعَلْ فَمَا بَلَّغْتَ رِسَالَتَهُ وَاللَّهُ يَعْصِمُكَ مِنَ النَّاسِ إِنَّ اللَّهَ لَا يَهْدِي الْقَوْمَ الْكَٰفِرِينَ ٦٧

68. Say: 'O People of the Book!
You rest not on anything unless you
establish the Torah and the Gospel
and what has now been sent down
to you from your Lord. And what
has been sent down to you will surely
increase many of them in
exorbitance and infidelity; so mourn
you not over a disbelieving people.'

قُل يَـٰٓأَهۡلَ ٱلۡكِتَـٰبِ لَسۡتُمۡ عَلَىٰ شَىۡءٍ حَتَّىٰ
تُقِيمُوا۟ ٱلتَّوۡرَىٰةَ وَٱلۡإِنجِيلَ وَمَآ أُنزِلَ
إِلَيۡكُم مِّن رَّبِّكُمۡ وَلَيَزِيدَنَّ كَثِيرًا
مِّنۡهُم مَّآ أُنزِلَ إِلَيۡكَ مِن رَّبِّكَ طُغۡيَـٰنًا
وَكُفۡرًا فَلَا تَأۡسَ عَلَى ٱلۡقَوۡمِ ٱلۡكَـٰفِرِينَ ﴿٦٨﴾

69. Surely those who believe and
those who are Judaized and the
Sabians and the Nazarenes, any of
who believes in Allah and the Last
Day and works righteously no fear
shall come on them, nor shall they
grieve.[308]

إِنَّ ٱلَّذِينَ ءَامَنُوا۟ وَٱلَّذِينَ هَادُوا۟ وَ
ٱلصَّـٰبِـُٔونَ وَٱلنَّصَـٰرَىٰ مَنۡ ءَامَنَ بِٱللَّهِ وَ
ٱلۡيَوۡمِ ٱلۡأَخِرِ وَعَمِلَ صَـٰلِحًا فَلَا خَوۡفٌ
عَلَيۡهِمۡ وَلَا هُمۡ يَحۡزَنُونَ ﴿٦٩﴾

70. Assuredly did We take a bond
from the children of Israel and We
sent Messengers to them.
Whenever there came to them a
Messenger with what their souls did
not like, a party of them they belied
and a party they put to death.

لَقَدۡ أَخَذۡنَا مِيثَـٰقَ بَنِىٓ إِسۡرَٰٓءِيلَ
وَأَرۡسَلۡنَآ إِلَيۡهِمۡ رُسُلًا كُلَّمَا جَآءَهُمۡ
رَسُولٌۢ بِمَا لَا تَهۡوَىٰٓ أَنفُسُهُمۡ فَرِيقًا
كَذَّبُوا۟ وَفَرِيقًا يَقۡتُلُونَ ﴿٧٠﴾

---

308. This refers to the Hereafter. 'It was on the banks of the lower Euphrates
that the Sabians or Christians of St. John the Baptist had settled, whom the
Arabs called Mughtasila (Ablutionists), because they were always washing
in the river; not only were they still living there in the time of Muhammad, but
they are there to this day, under the name of Sabian' (Huart, *Ancient Persia
and Iranian Civilization*, p. 179).

71. And they imagined that no harm would come to them; so they blinded and deafened themselves. Thereafter Allah relented towards them, then they again blinded and deafened themselves. And Allah is the Beholder of what they work.

وَحَسِبُوۤا أَلَّا تَكُونَ فِتۡنَةٌ فَعَمُوۡا وَصَمُّوۡا ثُمَّ تَابَ اللّٰهُ عَلَيۡهِمۡ ثُمَّ عَمُوۡا وَصَمُّوۡا كَثِيۡرٌ مِّنۡهُمۡ وَاللّٰهُ بَصِيۡرٌۢ بِمَا يَعۡمَلُوۡنَ ۝

72. Assuredly they have dis-believed who say: 'The Messiah son of Maryam is the very God;' whereas the Messiah had said: 'O Children of Israel: worship Allah, my Lord and your Lord; he who joins anyone with Allah, Allah shall surely forbid the Garden to him, and his resort is the Fire; and the ungodly shall have no helpers.'

لَقَدۡ كَفَرَ الَّذِيۡنَ قَالُوۤا إِنَّ اللّٰهَ هُوَ الۡمَسِيۡحُ ابۡنُ مَرۡيَمَ وَقَالَ الۡمَسِيۡحُ يٰبَنِيۤ إِسۡرَاۤءِيۡلَ اعۡبُدُوا اللّٰهَ رَبِّيۡ وَرَبَّكُمۡ إِنَّهُ مَنۡ يُّشۡرِكۡ بِاللّٰهِ فَقَدۡ حَرَّمَ اللّٰهُ عَلَيۡهِ الۡجَنَّةَ وَمَأۡوٰىهُ النَّارُ وَمَا لِلظّٰلِمِيۡنَ مِنۡ أَنۡصَارٍ ۝

73. Assuredly those have dis–believed who say: 'God is the third of the three,' whereas there is no god except the One God,[309] Allah. And if they do not desist from what they say, there shall surely befall those of them who have disbelieved an afflictive torment.

لَقَدۡ كَفَرَ الَّذِيۡنَ قَالُوۤا إِنَّ اللّٰهَ ثَالِثُ ثَلٰثَةٍ وَمَا مِنۡ إِلٰهٍ إِلَّاۤ إِلٰهٌ وَاحِدٌ وَإِنۡ لَّمۡ يَنۡتَهُوۡا عَمَّا يَقُوۡلُوۡنَ لَيَمَسَّنَّ الَّذِيۡنَ كَفَرُوۡا مِنۡهُمۡ عَذَابٌ أَلِيۡمٌ ۝

74. Why do they not turn towards Allah and ask His forgiveness? And Allah is the Forgiving, the Merciful.

أَفَلَا يَتُوۡبُوۡنَ إِلَى اللّٰهِ وَيَسۡتَغۡفِرُوۡنَهُ وَاللّٰهُ غَفُوۡرٌ رَّحِيۡمٌ ۝

---

309. There is no divisibility of God's Person. And thus the Christians are as much steeped in polytheism as are the pagans. The Christians 'acknowledged one God indeed with the lips, but in three persons, each of whom simply or by himself was God' (Swedenborg, *The True Christian Religion,* p. 817).

75. The Messiah, son of Maryam, was nothing but a Messenger. Surely there passed away Messengers before him, and his mother was a saintly woman; they both ate earthly food. See how We explain to them Our evidence. Then see whither they are deviating!

مَّا ٱلْمَسِيحُ ٱبْنُ مَرْيَمَ إِلَّا رَسُولٌ قَدْ خَلَتْ مِن قَبْلِهِ ٱلرُّسُلُ وَأُمُّهُ صِدِّيقَةٌ كَانَا يَأْكُلَانِ ٱلطَّعَامَ ٱنظُرْ كَيْفَ نُبَيِّنُ لَهُمُ ٱلْآيَٰتِ ثُمَّ ٱنظُرْ أَنَّىٰ يُؤْفَكُونَ ﴿٧٥﴾

76. Say: 'Do you worship, beside Allah, what does not avail you in harm or good[310], whereas it is Allah Who is the Hearing, the Knowing?'

قُلْ أَتَعْبُدُونَ مِن دُونِ ٱللَّهِ مَا لَا يَمْلِكُ لَكُمْ ضَرًّا وَلَا نَفْعًا وَٱللَّهُ هُوَ ٱلسَّمِيعُ ٱلْعَلِيمُ ﴿٧٦﴾

77. Say: 'O People of the Book! Do not exceed the just bounds in your religion, except with Truth, and do not follow the fancies of a people who strayed before and have led many astray and have strayed from the level way.'[311]

قُلْ يَٰأَهْلَ ٱلْكِتَٰبِ لَا تَغْلُوا۟ فِي دِينِكُمْ غَيْرَ ٱلْحَقِّ وَلَا تَتَّبِعُوٓا۟ أَهْوَآءَ قَوْمٍ قَدْ ضَلُّوا۟ مِن قَبْلُ وَأَضَلُّوا۟ كَثِيرًا وَضَلُّوا۟ عَن سَوَآءِ ٱلسَّبِيلِ ﴿٧٧﴾

310. Christianity gradually 'assumed a form that was quite as polytheistic and quite as idolatrous as the ancient paganism' (Lecky, *History of European Morals,* II, p. 97). 'The polytheist peoples of the world with a variety of gods and goddesses, which enter into its machinery more or less independently. It reaches its highest stage in Hellenic polytheism. At a much lower stage we have Catholic polytheism, in which innumerable "saints" (many of them of very equivocal repute) are venerated as subordinate divinities, and prayed to exert thin mediation with the supreme divinity' (Haeckel, *Riddle of the Universe,* p. 236).

311. Now who exactly are these erring peoples — the prototype of Christian error? The allusion may well be to the 'highly cultured' yet polytheistic and idolatrous nations of Greece and Rome — many of whose superstitions and blasphemies the early Church, inspired by Paul of Tarsus, was only too prone to imbibe. St. Paul, the

founder of the later – day Christianity, 'owed much to the Greek philosophy and thought, gained partly in formal education at Tarsus, partly by assimilation of the knowledge which floated on the surface of a more or less educated society and became insensibly the property of all its members' (*DB*. V. p. 150). 'The Roman Church owes something of the elaboration of its ceremonial, and its care for the little things of life, to the old Roman religion, and the many local and functional saints of present – day Italy are in effect the successors of the ancient spirits' (*UHW*, III. p. 1753). 'And the later – day Greek also through the popularity of the cult of Asklepios 'was becoming habituated to the concept of Man God, who suffered, and was glorified after death (*EMK*. II. p. 1414). Greece 'supplied the philosophy of the Christian religion which, after Plotnus and Prophyry, had a more vigorous life within the Church with the Hellenic world and which led very early to the attempt to interpret the mysteries of the Christian faith in the terms of Greek philosophy. There are traces of this even in the Epistles of St. Paul. The process, however, so far as the books of the New Testament are concerned, is most conspicuous in the fourth Gospel. The writer of this life of Christ, whoever he may have been, was clearly influenced by Platonism' (*UHW*. IV. p. 2330).

Section 11

78. Cursed were those who disbelieved from among the children of Israel by the tongue of David and Jesus, son of Maryam. This, because they disobeyed and were ever-transgressing.

لُعِنَ الَّذِينَ كَفَرُوا مِنۢ بَنِىٓ إِسۡرَٰٓءِيلَ عَلَىٰ لِسَانِ دَاوُۥدَ وَعِيسَى ابۡنِ مَرۡيَمَ ذَٰلِكَ بِمَا عَصَوا وَّكَانُوا يَعۡتَدُونَ ۝

79. They were wont not to desist from the evil they committed. Vile is what they have been doing!

كَانُوا لَا يَتَنَاهَوۡنَ عَن مُّنكَرٍ فَعَلُوهُ لَبِئۡسَ مَا كَانُوا يَفۡعَلُونَ ۝

80. You will see many of them befriending those who disbelieve. Vile surely is what their souls have sent forth for them, so that Allah became incensed against them; and in torment they shall abide.

تَرَىٰ كَثِيرًا مِّنۡهُمۡ يَتَوَلَّوۡنَ الَّذِينَ كَفَرُوا لَبِئۡسَ مَا قَدَّمَتۡ لَهُمۡ أَنفُسُهُمۡ أَن سَخِطَ اللَّهُ عَلَيۡهِمۡ وَفِى الۡعَذَابِ هُمۡ خَٰلِدُونَ ۝

81. And had they believed in Allah and the Prophet and what has been sent down to him, they would not have taken them for friends; but many of them are transgressors.

وَلَوۡ كَانُوا يُؤۡمِنُونَ بِاللَّهِ وَالنَّبِىِّ وَمَآ أُنزِلَ إِلَيۡهِ مَا اتَّخَذُوهُمۡ أَوۡلِيَآءَ وَلَٰكِنَّ كَثِيرًا مِّنۡهُمۡ فَٰسِقُونَ ۝

82. Surely you will find the Jews and polytheists the bitterest of mankind in enmity towards those who believe. And surely you will find the nearest in affection to the believers those who say: 'We are Nazarenes.' This, because among them are priests and monks and because they are not stiff-necked.

لَتَجِدَنَّ أَشَدَّ النَّاسِ عَدَٰوَةً لِّلَّذِينَ ءَامَنُوا الۡيَهُودَ وَالَّذِينَ أَشۡرَكُوا وَلَتَجِدَنَّ أَقۡرَبَهُم مَّوَدَّةً لِّلَّذِينَ ءَامَنُوا الَّذِينَ قَالُوٓا إِنَّا نَصَٰرَىٰ ذَٰلِكَ بِأَنَّ مِنۡهُمۡ قِسِّيسِينَ وَ رُهۡبَانًا وَأَنَّهُمۡ لَا يَسۡتَكۡبِرُونَ ۝

83. And when they hear what has been sent down to the Messenger you see their eyes overflow with tears because of the Truth they have recognized. They say: 'Our Lord! We believe; so write us down with the witnesses.

وَإِذَا سَمِعُوا مَا أُنزِلَ إِلَى ٱلرَّسُولِ تَرَىٰ أَعْيُنَهُمْ تَفِيضُ مِنَ ٱلدَّمْعِ مِمَّا عَرَفُوا مِنَ ٱلْحَقِّ يَقُولُونَ رَبَّنَآ ءَامَنَّا فَٱكْتُبْنَا مَعَ ٱلشَّٰهِدِينَ ﴿٨٣﴾

84. And why should we not believe in Allah and in what has come down to us of the Truth? And we long that our Lord will enter us with the righteous people.'

وَمَا لَنَا لَا نُؤْمِنُ بِٱللَّهِ وَمَا جَآءَنَا مِنَ ٱلْحَقِّ وَنَطْمَعُ أَن يُدْخِلَنَا رَبُّنَا مَعَ ٱلْقَوْمِ ٱلصَّٰلِحِينَ ﴿٨٤﴾

85. Therefore Allah will reward them, for what they said, with Gardens beneath which rivers flow as abiders therein. Such is the recompense of the well-doers.

فَأَثَٰبَهُمُ ٱللَّهُ بِمَا قَالُوا جَنَّٰتٍ تَجْرِى مِن تَحْتِهَا ٱلْأَنْهَٰرُ خَٰلِدِينَ فِيهَا وَذَٰلِكَ جَزَآءُ ٱلْمُحْسِنِينَ ﴿٨٥﴾

86. And those who disbelieved and belied Our signs, they shall be the inmates of the Flaming Fire.

وَٱلَّذِينَ كَفَرُوا وَكَذَّبُوا بِـَٔايَٰتِنَآ أُو۟لَٰٓئِكَ أَصْحَٰبُ ٱلْجَحِيمِ ﴿٨٦﴾

Section 12

87. O you who believe! Forbid not to yourselves the good things Allah has allowed to you, and trespass not; verily Allah does not love the trespassers.

يَٰٓأَيُّهَا ٱلَّذِينَ ءَامَنُوا لَا تُحَرِّمُوا طَيِّبَٰتِ مَآ أَحَلَّ ٱللَّهُ لَكُمْ وَلَا تَعْتَدُوٓا إِنَّ ٱللَّهَ لَا يُحِبُّ ٱلْمُعْتَدِينَ ﴿٨٧﴾

88. And eat of that with which Allah has provided you as lawful and good; and fear Allah, in whom you are believers.

وَكُلُوا مِمَّا رَزَقَكُمُ ٱللَّهُ حَلَٰلًا طَيِّبًا وَٱتَّقُوا ٱللَّهَ ٱلَّذِىٓ أَنتُم بِهِۦ مُؤْمِنُونَ ﴿٨٨﴾

89. Allah shall not take you to task for the vain in your oaths; but He shall take you to task for what your oaths make binding. Its atonement is the feeding of ten poor men with the middle sort of that with which you feed your household, or the clothing of them or the freeing of a slave; but he who cannot afford, for him is a fasting of three days. That is the atonement of your oaths when you have sworn, and bear in mind your oaths. Thus does Allah expound to you His commandments, that haply you may return thanks.

90. O you who believe! Wine and gambling and stone altars and divining arrows are only an abomination, a handiwork of Satan; so shun it, that haply you may thrive.

91. Satan only seeks to breed enmity and spite among you by means of wine[312] and gambling[313] and would keep you from the remembrance of Allah and from prayer; will you not then desist?

لَا يُؤَاخِذُكُمُ ٱللَّهُ بِٱللَّغْوِ فِىٓ أَيْمَٰنِكُمْ وَلَٰكِن يُؤَاخِذُكُم بِمَا عَقَّدتُّمُ ٱلْأَيْمَٰنَ فَكَفَّٰرَتُهُۥٓ إِطْعَامُ عَشَرَةِ مَسَٰكِينَ مِنْ أَوْسَطِ مَا تُطْعِمُونَ أَهْلِيكُمْ أَوْ كِسْوَتُهُمْ أَوْ تَحْرِيرُ رَقَبَةٍ فَمَن لَّمْ يَجِدْ فَصِيَامُ ثَلَٰثَةِ أَيَّامٍ ذَٰلِكَ كَفَّٰرَةُ أَيْمَٰنِكُمْ إِذَا حَلَفْتُمْ وَٱحْفَظُوٓا أَيْمَٰنَكُمْ كَذَٰلِكَ يُبَيِّنُ ٱللَّهُ لَكُمْ ءَايَٰتِهِۦ لَعَلَّكُمْ تَشْكُرُونَ ﴿٨٩﴾

يَٰٓأَيُّهَا ٱلَّذِينَ ءَامَنُوٓا إِنَّمَا ٱلْخَمْرُ وَٱلْمَيْسِرُ وَٱلْأَنصَابُ وَٱلْأَزْلَٰمُ رِجْسٌ مِّنْ عَمَلِ ٱلشَّيْطَٰنِ فَٱجْتَنِبُوهُ لَعَلَّكُمْ تُفْلِحُونَ ﴿٩٠﴾

إِنَّمَا يُرِيدُ ٱلشَّيْطَٰنُ أَن يُوقِعَ بَيْنَكُمُ ٱلْعَدَٰوَةَ وَٱلْبَغْضَآءَ فِى ٱلْخَمْرِ وَٱلْمَيْسِرِ وَيَصُدَّكُمْ عَن ذِكْرِ ٱللَّهِ وَعَنِ ٱلصَّلَوٰةِ فَهَلْ أَنتُم مُّنتَهُونَ ﴿٩١﴾

312. The close relationship of alcoholism and crime is well known. 'There is universal testimony as to the close relationship between excessive drinking and breaches of the moral law and the laws of the state. This is a direct consequence of the paralyses of the higher faculties, intellectual and moral, and the resulting free play given to the lower inclinations' (ERE. I. p. 301). 'Alcohol belongs to a family of poisonous chemicals. Its theoretic food – value is of no use in practical dietetics. It is never a stimulant. It has a sedative drug – action in moderate doses, and a narcotic poison–action in excess. Its use as a beverage is physiologically unsound, economically disastrous, socially disruptive, and materially poisonous!' (Dastur, pp. 108–109).

313. The devastating results of gambling on a large scale are too patent to be dwelt on at length. And as to the ethics, even according to European moralists, gambling is nothing short of robbery by mutual agreement (ERE. VI, p. 166). Gambling houses

are almost everywhere notorious centres of crime and prostitution. 'Sexual activity', as observed by a German writer, 'is often combined with gambling, as is anything which will induce a state of high nervous excitement'. (i) And gambling, remarks another observer, generally 'leads to other excesses, little good comes from the easily–got money; one is in the mood for pleasure, and he who loses seeks to drown his care and so takes refuge in both wine and woman'. (ii) Says an English chronicler speaking of 11th century England: 'Suicide was a thing that happened very often during this extraordinary period as the result of heavy betting; and wild extravagance was not confined to the young, men, for the old gamblers were the most inveterate and the most reckless of the time. Staid statesmen lost as heavily and as madly as the raw striplings; and the insidious disease spread to the women. Among the women gamblers the greatest tragedy was that many of them paid the debts which they could not meet in cash by the sacrifice of their honour' (*EMK*. V. p. 2386). And who has not heard of the ancient Indian king Yudhisthira playing away all his wealth and kingdom, and finally his brothers, himself and his wife Drupidi, in a game of dice? (Cf: *The Mahabharata*).

92. Obey Allah and obey the Messenger, and beware, and if you turn away, then know that upon Our Messenger rests only the plain preaching.

وَأَطِيعُوا۟ ٱللَّهَ وَأَطِيعُوا۟ ٱلرَّسُولَ وَٱحْذَرُوا۟ فَإِن تَوَلَّيْتُمْ فَٱعْلَمُوٓا۟ أَنَّمَا عَلَىٰ رَسُولِنَا ٱلْبَلَٰغُ ٱلْمُبِينُ ﴿٩٢﴾

93. No sin is on those who believe and work righteous works for what they have eaten so long as they abstained and believed and worked righteous works, and shall again abstain and believe, and shall again abstain and do well; and Allah loves the well-doers.

لَيْسَ عَلَى ٱلَّذِينَ ءَامَنُوا۟ وَعَمِلُوا۟ ٱلصَّٰلِحَٰتِ جُنَاحٌ فِيمَا طَعِمُوٓا۟ إِذَا مَا ٱتَّقَوا۟ وَّءَامَنُوا۟ وَعَمِلُوا۟ ٱلصَّٰلِحَٰتِ ثُمَّ ٱتَّقَوا۟ وَّءَامَنُوا۟ ثُمَّ ٱتَّقَوا۟ وَّأَحْسَنُوا۟ وَٱللَّهُ يُحِبُّ ٱلْمُحْسِنِينَ ﴿٩٣﴾

Section 13

94. O you who believe! Allah shall surely test you with aught of the chase which your hands and your lances may reach, in order that Allah may know whoever fears Him Unseen; but he who will trespass thereafter, for him is an afflictive torment.

يَٰٓأَيُّهَا ٱلَّذِينَ ءَامَنُوا۟ لَيَبْلُوَنَّكُمُ ٱللَّهُ بِشَىْءٍ مِّنَ ٱلصَّيْدِ تَنَالُهُۥٓ أَيْدِيكُمْ وَرِمَاحُكُمْ لِيَعْلَمَ ٱللَّهُ مَن يَخَافُهُۥ بِٱلْغَيْبِ فَمَنِ ٱعْتَدَىٰ بَعْدَ ذَٰلِكَ فَلَهُۥ عَذَابٌ أَلِيمٌ ﴿٩٤﴾

95. O you who believe! Do not kill of the chase while you are in a state of sanctity, and he among you who kills it wittingly, his compensation is the like of what he has killed, in domestic flocks, which two equitable persons among you will judge: an offering brought to the Kaʿba; or as an expiation the feeding of the needy or its equivalent in fasts that he may taste the

يَٰٓأَيُّهَا ٱلَّذِينَ ءَامَنُوا۟ لَا تَقْتُلُوا۟ ٱلصَّيْدَ وَأَنتُمْ حُرُمٌ وَمَن قَتَلَهُۥ مِنكُم مُّتَعَمِّدًا فَجَزَآءٌ مِّثْلُ مَا قَتَلَ مِنَ ٱلنَّعَمِ يَحْكُمُ بِهِۦ ذَوَا عَدْلٍ مِّنكُمْ هَدْيًۢا بَٰلِغَ ٱلْكَعْبَةِ أَوْ كَفَّٰرَةٌ طَعَامُ مَسَٰكِينَ أَوْ عَدْلُ ذَٰلِكَ صِيَامًا لِّيَذُوقَ وَبَالَ أَمْرِهِۦ

enormity of his deed. Allah has pardoned what is past, but he who returns, Allah shall take retribution from him; verily Allah is the Mighty, the Lord of Retribution.

عَفَا ٱللَّهُ عَمَّا سَلَفَ وَمَنْ عَادَ فَيَنتَقِمُ ٱللَّهُ مِنْهُ وَٱللَّهُ عَزِيزٌ ذُو ٱنتِقَامٍ ۝

96. Allowed to you is the game of the sea and its eating; a provision for you and for the caravan. And forbidden to you is the game of the land while you are in a state of sanctity. And fear Allah to Whom you shall be gathered.

أُحِلَّ لَكُمْ صَيْدُ ٱلْبَحْرِ وَطَعَامُهُۥ مَتَٰعًا لَّكُمْ وَلِلسَّيَّارَةِ وَحُرِّمَ عَلَيْكُمْ صَيْدُ ٱلْبَرِّ مَا دُمْتُمْ حُرُمًا وَٱتَّقُوا۟ ٱللَّهَ ٱلَّذِىٓ إِلَيْهِ تُحْشَرُونَ ۝

97. Allah has made the Kaʿba, the Sacred House, a maintenance for mankind, and so also the sacred month, and the offering and the victim garlanded. That is in order that you may know that Allah knows all that is in the heavens and all that is in the earth, and that Allah is the Knower of everything.

جَعَلَ ٱللَّهُ ٱلْكَعْبَةَ ٱلْبَيْتَ ٱلْحَرَامَ قِيَٰمًا لِّلنَّاسِ وَٱلشَّهْرَ ٱلْحَرَامَ وَٱلْهَدْىَ وَٱلْقَلَٰئِدَ ذَٰلِكَ لِتَعْلَمُوٓا۟ أَنَّ ٱللَّهَ يَعْلَمُ مَا فِى ٱلسَّمَٰوَٰتِ وَمَا فِى ٱلْأَرْضِ وَأَنَّ ٱللَّهَ بِكُلِّ شَىْءٍ عَلِيمٌ ۝

98. Know that Allah is Severe in chastising and that Allah is Forgiving, Merciful.

ٱعْلَمُوٓا۟ أَنَّ ٱللَّهَ شَدِيدُ ٱلْعِقَابِ وَأَنَّ ٱللَّهَ غَفُورٌ رَّحِيمٌ ۝

99. Nothing rests on the Messenger save the preaching, and Allah knows what you disclose and what you hide.

مَّا عَلَى ٱلرَّسُولِ إِلَّا ٱلْبَلَٰغُ وَٱللَّهُ يَعْلَمُ مَا تُبْدُونَ وَمَا تَكْتُمُونَ ۝

100. Say: 'Equal are not the foul and the pure even though the abundance of the foul may please you. So fear Allah. O men of understanding! That haply you may thrive.'

قُل لَّا يَسْتَوِى ٱلْخَبِيثُ وَٱلطَّيِّبُ وَلَوْ أَعْجَبَكَ كَثْرَةُ ٱلْخَبِيثِ فَٱتَّقُوا۟ ٱللَّهَ يَٰٓأُو۟لِى ٱلْأَلْبَٰبِ لَعَلَّكُمْ تُفْلِحُونَ ۝

Section 14

101. O you who believe! Ask not of things which if disclosed to you, may annoy you, and if you ask of them while the Qur'ān is yet being revealed, they may be disclosed to you. Allah has pardoned that, and Allah is the Forgiving, the Forbearing.

يَـٰٓأَيُّهَا ٱلَّذِينَ ءَامَنُوا۟ لَا تَسْـَٔلُوا۟ عَنْ أَشْيَآءَ إِن تُبْدَ لَكُمْ تَسُؤْكُمْ وَإِن تَسْـَٔلُوا۟ عَنْهَا حِينَ يُنَزَّلُ ٱلْقُرْءَانُ تُبْدَ لَكُمْ عَفَا ٱللَّهُ عَنْهَا وَٱللَّهُ غَفُورٌ حَلِيمٌ ﴿١٠١﴾

102. Surely people have asked questions before you, and were then found disbelieving therein.

قَدْ سَأَلَهَا قَوْمٌ مِّن قَبْلِكُمْ ثُمَّ أَصْبَحُوا۟ بِهَا كَـٰفِرِينَ ﴿١٠٢﴾

103. It is not Allah Who appointed aught of the Baḥīrah[314] or the Sā'ibah[315] or the Waṣīlā[316] or the Ḥām;[317] but it is the disbelievers who have fabricated a lie against Allah, and most of them do not reflect.

مَا جَعَلَ ٱللَّهُ مِنۢ بَحِيرَةٍ وَلَا سَآئِبَةٍ وَلَا وَصِيلَةٍ وَلَا حَامٍ وَلَـٰكِنَّ ٱلَّذِينَ كَفَرُوا۟ يَفْتَرُونَ عَلَى ٱللَّهِ ٱلْكَذِبَ وَأَكْثَرُهُمْ لَا يَعْقِلُونَ ﴿١٠٣﴾

---

314. The mother camel whose milk was dedicated by the pagan Arabs to their gods. 'Bahira was the name given to a camel which had ten young ones, her ear was then slit and she was turned loose to feed. When she died, her flesh was eaten by the men only, the women being forbidden to touch it' (Palmer, *The Qur'an*).

315. A camel, turned loose, as a consecrated animal, to feed and be exempt from common services. 'Saiba signifies merely, a camel turned loose, her being so turned out was generally in fulfillment of a vow' (Ibid.).

316. 'Wasila was a term applied to any cattle, including sheep and goats, and generally meant a beast who had brought forth a male and female at the seventh parturation' (Ibid.).

317. The dedicated stallion. 'Ham was stallion camel which after begetting ten young ones was turned loose' (Ibid.).

104. And when it is said to them: 'Come to what Allah has sent down', and to the Messenger, they say: 'Enough for us is what we found our fathers on.' What! Even though their fathers knew not anything nor were guided.

105. O you who believe! On you rests the case of yourselves[318]; it cannot harm you as to whoso strays so long as you keep yourselves guided. To Allah is the return of you all. Then He will declare to you what you were wont to work.

106. O you who believe! The testimony among you, when you are face to face with death, at the making of a bequest shall be that of two equitable persons from among you, or two others from among those not of you, if you be journeying in the land and death afflicts you. You should detain the twain after the prayer, if you be in doubt, and they should swear by Allah affirming: 'we shall not barter it for a price, even though he be a kinsman, and we shall not hide the testimony of Allah, lest we should be the sinners.'

---

318. We are responsible for ourselves primarily and in the first place. The first and foremost duty of every individual is to save his own soul, and not to be unduly worried over others. Cf. the NT: 'Let every man prove his own work, and then shall he have rejoicing in himself alone, and not in another. For every man shall bear his own burden' (Ga. 6: 4, 5).

107. If then it appears to you that the two had been guilty of a sin, two others should take their place from amongst those who were sinned against, the two nearest of kin, and they should swear by Allah affirming: 'our testimony is worthier of credit than their testimony and we have not trespassed, for then we would have been among the wrong-doers.'

فَإِنْ عُثِرَ عَلَىٰٓ أَنَّهُمَا ٱسْتَحَقَّآ إِثْمًا فَـَٔاخَرَانِ يَقُومَانِ مَقَامَهُمَا مِنَ ٱلَّذِينَ ٱسْتَحَقَّ عَلَيْهِمُ ٱلْأَوْلَيَٰنِ فَيُقْسِمَانِ بِٱللَّهِ لَشَهَٰدَتُنَآ أَحَقُّ مِن شَهَٰدَتِهِمَا وَمَا ٱعْتَدَيْنَآ إِنَّآ إِذًا لَّمِنَ ٱلظَّٰلِمِينَ ﴿١٠٧﴾

108. That should make it more likely that their testimony would be according to the fact thereof, or they shall fear that their oaths would be admitted after their oaths. And fear Allah and hearken and Allah does not guide a wicked people.

ذَٰلِكَ أَدْنَىٰٓ أَن يَأْتُوا۟ بِٱلشَّهَٰدَةِ عَلَىٰ وَجْهِهَآ أَوْ يَخَافُوٓا۟ أَن تُرَدَّ أَيْمَٰنُۢ بَعْدَ أَيْمَٰنِهِمْ وَٱتَّقُوا۟ ٱللَّهَ وَٱسْمَعُوا۟ وَٱللَّهُ لَا يَهْدِى ٱلْقَوْمَ ٱلْفَٰسِقِينَ ﴿١٠٨﴾

Section 15

109. Beware of the Day when Allah will gather the Messengers and say to them: 'How were you answered?' They will say: 'No knowledge have we; verily You only are the Great Knower of things hidden.'

يَوْمَ يَجْمَعُ ٱللَّهُ ٱلرُّسُلَ فَيَقُولُ مَاذَآ أُجِبْتُمْ قَالُوا۟ لَا عِلْمَ لَنَآ إِنَّكَ أَنتَ عَلَّٰمُ ٱلْغُيُوبِ ﴿١٠٩﴾

110. Call to mind when Allah will say: 'O Jesus, son of Maryam, remember My favour upon you and your mother when I aided you with the Holy Spirit, so that you spoke to mankind in the cradle and in maturity, and when I taught you the Book and wisdom and Torah and the Gospel, and when you formed out of clay as though the likeness of a bird by My command; and you breathed into it and it became a bird by My command, and you healed those born blind and the leper by My command; and when you caused the dead to come forth by My command;[319] and when I restrained the children of Israel from you when you came to them with evidence, and those of them who disbelieved said: 'This is but magic manifest.'[320]

إِذْ قَالَ اللَّهُ يَعِيسَى ابْنَ مَرْيَمَ اذْكُرْ نِعْمَتِى عَلَيْكَ وَعَلَى وَالِدَتِكَ إِذْ أَيَّدْتُكَ بِرُوحِ الْقُدُسِ تُكَلِّمُ النَّاسَ فِى الْمَهْدِ وَكَهْلًا وَإِذْ عَلَّمْتُكَ الْكِتَبَ وَالْحِكْمَةَ وَالتَّوْرَنةَ وَالْإِنجِيلَ وَإِذْ تَخْلُقُ مِنَ الطِّينِ كَهَيْئَةِ الطَّيْرِ بِإِذْنِى فَتَنفُخُ فِيهَا فَتَكُونُ طَيْرًا بِإِذْنِى وَتُبْرِئُ الْأَكْمَهَ وَالْأَبْرَصَ بِإِذْنِى وَإِذْ تُخْرِجُ الْمَوْتَى بِإِذْنِى وَإِذْ كَفَفْتُ بَنِى إِسْرَءِيلَ عَنكَ إِذْ جِئْتَهُم بِالْبَيِّنَتِ فَقَالَ الَّذِينَ كَفَرُوا مِنْهُمْ إِنْ هَذَآ إِلَّا سِحْرٌ مُّبِينٌ ۝

---

319. Notice the constant refrain, 'by My command', emphasizing the humanity of Jesus and deliberately combating the Christian idea of his Divinity.

320. According to Jewish sources, 'Jesus learned magic in Egypt and performed his miracles by means of it. The accusation of magic is frequently brought against Jesus' (*JE*. VII. p. 171). 'The nearest approach to a defined opinion about Him in the Talmud is the statement that "he practised magic and deceived and led astray Israel' (*ERE*. VII. p. 551). 'Now when the wise men saw that all were believing in him, straightway they bound him fast and led him before Helene, the Queen, under whose hand was the land of Israel. They said unto her, This man is a sorcerer, and he deceives the world' (Schonfield, *According to the Hebrews*, p. 41).

111. Recall when I revealed to the disciples: 'Believe in Me and My Messenger, they said: "We have believed, and bear you witness that verily we are Muslims.'

وَإِذْ أَوْحَيْتُ إِلَى ٱلْحَوَارِيِّنَ أَنْ ءَامِنُواْ بِي وَبِرَسُولِي قَالُواْ ءَامَنَّا وَٱشْهَدْ بِأَنَّنَا مُسْلِمُونَ ۝

112. Recall when the disciples said: 'O Jesus, son of Maryam[321], can your Lord send down to us some food from the heaven?' He said: 'Fear Allah, if you are indeed believers.'

إِذْ قَالَ ٱلْحَوَارِيُّونَ يَٰعِيسَى ٱبْنَ مَرْيَمَ هَلْ يَسْتَطِيعُ رَبُّكَ أَن يُنَزِّلَ عَلَيْنَا مَآئِدَةً مِّنَ ٱلسَّمَآءِ قَالَ ٱتَّقُواْ ٱللَّهَ إِن كُنتُم مُّؤْمِنِينَ ۝

113. They said: 'We mean that we may eat of it and we may set our hearts at rest and be assured that you have spoken the Truth to us and we should be its witnesses.'

قَالُواْ نُرِيدُ أَن نَّأْكُلَ مِنْهَا وَتَطْمَئِنَّ قُلُوبُنَا وَنَعْلَمَ أَن قَدْ صَدَقْتَنَا وَنَكُونَ عَلَيْهَا مِنَ ٱلشَّٰهِدِينَ ۝

114. Jesus, son of Maryam, said: 'Allah, our Lord! Send down to us some food from the heaven, that it may become an occasion of joy to us – the first of us and the last of us – a sign from You; provide for us as You are the Best of Providers.'

قَالَ عِيسَى ٱبْنُ مَرْيَمَ ٱللَّهُمَّ رَبَّنَآ أَنزِلْ عَلَيْنَا مَآئِدَةً مِّنَ ٱلسَّمَآءِ تَكُونُ لَنَا عِيدًا لِّأَوَّلِنَا وَءَاخِرِنَا وَءَايَةً مِّنكَ وَٱرْزُقْنَا وَأَنتَ خَيْرُ ٱلرَّٰزِقِينَ ۝

115. Allah said: 'Surely I am going to send it down to you, but whoever of you disbelieves afterwards, I shall torment him with a torment which I shall not do to any of My creatures of the worlds.'

قَالَ ٱللَّهُ إِنِّى مُنَزِّلُهَا عَلَيْكُمْ فَمَن يَكْفُرْ بَعْدُ مِنكُمْ فَإِنِّى أُعَذِّبُهُۥ عَذَابًا لَّا أُعَذِّبُهُۥٓ أَحَدًا مِّنَ ٱلْعَٰلَمِينَ ۝

321. This form of address is to indicate that not even the closest associates of Jesus regarded him as anything but a human being born of a woman. 'Apart from the Birth stories at the opening of Matthew and Luke (the exact significance of which in this respect is ambiguous) there is nothing in these three Gospels to suggest that their writers thought of Jesus as other than human' (*EBr.* XIII. p. 16).

Section 16

116. Recall when Allah will say: 'O Jesus, son of Maryam! Was it you who said to the people: "Take me and my mother as two gods[322] besides Allah?' Jesus will say: 'Hallowed be You; it was not for me to say that to which I had no right; had I said it, You were sure to know it. You know what is in my mind, and I do not know what is in Your mind. Verily You, only You are the Great Knower of things hidden.

117. I said not to them aught save what you bade me: worship Allah, Lord of me and Lord of you. I was a witness over them so long as I was among them then when You took me up, You have been the Watcher, and You are a Witness over everything.

118. Should You torment them, then verily they are Your creatures and should You forgive them,[323] then verily You, only You, are the Mighty, the Wise.'

وَإِذْ قَالَ اللَّهُ يَـٰعِيسَى ابْنَ مَرْيَمَ ءَأَنتَ قُلْتَ لِلنَّاسِ اتَّخِذُونِي وَأُمِّيَ إِلَـٰهَيْنِ مِن دُونِ اللَّهِ قَالَ سُبْحَٰنَكَ مَا يَكُونُ لِيٓ أَنْ أَقُولَ مَا لَيْسَ لِي بِحَقٍّ إِن كُنتُ قُلْتُهُ فَقَدْ عَلِمْتَهُ تَعْلَمُ مَا فِي نَفْسِي وَلَآ أَعْلَمُ مَا فِي نَفْسِكَ إِنَّكَ أَنتَ عَلَّـٰمُ الْغُيُوبِ ۝

مَا قُلْتُ لَهُمْ إِلَّا مَآ أَمَرْتَنِي بِهِۦٓ أَنِ اعْبُدُواْ اللَّهَ رَبِّي وَرَبَّكُمْ وَكُنتُ عَلَيْهِمْ شَهِيدًا مَّا دُمْتُ فِيهِمْ فَلَمَّا تَوَفَّيْتَنِي كُنتَ أَنتَ الرَّقِيبَ عَلَيْهِمْ وَأَنتَ عَلَىٰ كُلِّ شَيْءٍ شَهِيدٌ ۝

إِن تُعَذِّبْهُمْ فَإِنَّهُمْ عِبَادُكَ وَإِن تَغْفِرْ لَهُمْ فَإِنَّكَ أَنتَ الْعَزِيزُ الْحَكِيمُ ۝

---

322. In other words as objects of worship and adoration. The reference obviously is to the cult of Mary or Madonna — the Mariolatry common to most Christians.

323. All this is in repudiation of the Christian dogmas of atonement and judgement. It is God alone Who shall be the Judge and Arbiter on the Last Day, and not any of His saints, Prophets or Messengers, nor Christ. Contrast this with the polytheistic doctrine of the Church: 'For as the Father raise up the dead, and quicken them; even so the Son quicken when He will. For the Father judge no man, but has committed all judgment to the Son' (Jn. 5: 22). 'Our Lord, while affirming His filial subordination to the Father yet declares that He exercises the Father's whole power and authority: the power to quicken those dead in sin, the power to raise men from literal death at the Last Day, and the power to judge the world' (Dummelow, *Commentary on the Holy Bible*, p. 783–784).

119. Allah will say: 'This is a Day when their truthfulness will benefit the truthful. Theirs shall be Gardens beneath which rivers flow; they shall abide there for ever. Well-pleased is Allah with them, and well-pleased are they with Allah; this is the supreme achievement.'

قَالَ ٱللَّهُ هَٰذَا يَوۡمُ يَنفَعُ ٱلصَّٰدِقِينَ صِدۡقُهُمۡ لَهُمۡ جَنَّٰتٌ تَجۡرِي مِن تَحۡتِهَا ٱلۡأَنۡهَٰرُ خَٰلِدِينَ فِيهَآ أَبَدًا رَّضِيَ ٱللَّهُ عَنۡهُمۡ وَرَضُواْ عَنۡهُ ذَٰلِكَ ٱلۡفَوۡزُ ٱلۡعَظِيمُ ﴿١١٩﴾

120. Allah's is the kingdom of the heavens and the earth and whatsoever is therein and He is Potent over everything.

لِلَّهِ مُلۡكُ ٱلسَّمَٰوَٰتِ وَٱلۡأَرۡضِ وَمَا فِيهِنَّ وَهُوَ عَلَىٰ كُلِّ شَيۡءٍ قَدِيرُۢ ﴿١٢٠﴾

Sūrah 6

al-An'ām

(Makkan, 20 Sections, 165 Verses)

In the name of Allah, the Compassionate, the Merciful.

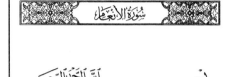

Section 1

1. All praise to Allah, Who created the heavens and the earth[324] and made the darkness and the light,[325] yet those who disbelieve equalize others with their Lord.

2. He it is Who created you of clay, and then decreed a term, a term determined with Him – and yet you waver.

3. He is Allah in the heavens and the earth. He knows your concealing and your revealing and so He knows what you earn.

---

324. Indeed He created all other substances. 'He is the sole Creator, with no intermediate agencies or sub-deities as supposed by certain Greek philosophers. This also completely repudiates the Hindu concept of the universe, in which both heaven and earth are regarded as gods, and as the parents of gods, even though they are said to have been generated by gods. Sometimes one god, Indira, or Agni, or Rudra, or Soma – sometimes all the gods together – are said to have generated or created heaven and earth, the whole world; and the act of creating is metaphorically expressed as building, sacrificing, or weaving' (*ERE*. IV, p. 156).

325. Similarly as He also created all other properties. Both the light and the dark are created beings and God is the source and Creator of both. This strikes at the root of dualism, and repudiates the position of those religions which hold light and darkness as uncreated beings existing from the beginning, and that light is the creation of good gods while darkness is associated with evil spirits.

4. And not a sign comes to them of the signs of their Lord, but that they have been backsliding therefrom.

وَمَا تَأْتِيهِم مِّنْ ءَايَةٍ مِّنْ ءَايَتِ رَبِّهِمْ إِلَّا كَانُوا۟ عَنْهَا مُعْرِضِينَ ﴿٤﴾

5. Assuredly they belied the Truth when it came to them, so now there is coming to them the tidings of what they have been mocking.

فَقَدْ كَذَّبُوا۟ بِٱلْحَقِّ لَمَّا جَآءَهُمْ فَسَوْفَ يَأْتِيهِمْ أَنۢبَٰٓؤُا۟ مَا كَانُوا۟ بِهِۦ يَسْتَهْزِءُونَ ﴿٥﴾

6. Have they not observed how many a generation before them We have destroyed whom We had established on the earth as We have not established you, and upon whom We had poured rains from heaven, and beneath whom We had made the rivers flow; yet We destroyed them for their sins, and We produced after them a generation of others.

أَلَمْ يَرَوْا۟ كَمْ أَهْلَكْنَا مِن قَبْلِهِم مِّن قَرْنٍ مَّكَّنَّٰهُمْ فِى ٱلْأَرْضِ مَا لَمْ نُمَكِّن لَّكُمْ وَأَرْسَلْنَا ٱلسَّمَآءَ عَلَيْهِم مِّدْرَارًا وَجَعَلْنَا ٱلْأَنْهَٰرَ تَجْرِى مِن تَحْتِهِمْ فَأَهْلَكْنَٰهُم بِذُنُوبِهِمْ وَأَنشَأْنَا مِنۢ بَعْدِهِمْ قَرْنًا ءَاخَرِينَ ﴿٦﴾

7. And had We sent down to them a Book written upon parchment which they could have touched with their hands, even then those who disbelieve would have said: 'This is naught but magic manifest.'

وَلَوْ نَزَّلْنَا عَلَيْكَ كِتَٰبًا فِى قِرْطَاسٍ فَلَمَسُوهُ بِأَيْدِيهِمْ لَقَالَ ٱلَّذِينَ كَفَرُوٓا۟ إِنْ هَٰذَآ إِلَّا سِحْرٌ مُّبِينٌ ﴿٧﴾

8. And they say: 'Why has not an angel been sent down to him?' Were We to send down an angel, the affair would have been decreed, and they would not be respited.

وَقَالُوا۟ لَوْلَآ أُنزِلَ عَلَيْهِ مَلَكٌ وَلَوْ أَنزَلْنَا مَلَكًا لَّقُضِىَ ٱلْأَمْرُ ثُمَّ لَا يُنظَرُونَ ﴿٨﴾

9. And had We made him an angel,
We would still have made him a
man, and We would have
confounded for them what you have
now been confounding.

وَلَوۡ جَعَلۡنَٰهُ مَلَكًا لَّجَعَلۡنَٰهُ رَجُلًا وَ
لَّلَبَسۡنَا عَلَيۡهِمۡ مَّا يَلۡبِسُونَ ۝

10. And assuredly mocked were
the Messengers before you; then at
what they scoffed beset those who
had been mocking.

وَلَقَدِ ٱسۡتُهۡزِئَ بِرُسُلٍ مِّن قَبۡلِكَ فَحَاقَ
بِٱلَّذِينَ سَخِرُواۡ مِنۡهُم مَّا كَانُواۡ بِهِۦ
يَسۡتَهۡزِءُونَ ۝

Section 2

11. Say: ʿGo about in the land and
see how has been the end of the
beliers.ʾ

قُلۡ سِيرُواۡ فِى ٱلۡأَرۡضِ ثُمَّ ٱنظُرُواۡ
كَيۡفَ كَانَ عَٰقِبَةُ
ٱلۡمُكَذِّبِينَ ۝

12. Say: ʿWhose is all that is in
the heavens and the earth?ʾ Say:
ʿAllahʾs.ʾ He has prescribed
mercy for Himself. Surely He
shall gather you together on the
Day of Judgement, of which
there is no doubt. Those who
have lost their souls shall not
come to believe.

قُل لِّمَن مَّا فِى ٱلسَّمَٰوَٰتِ وَٱلۡأَرۡضِ قُل لِّلَّهِ
كَتَبَ عَلَىٰ نَفۡسِهِ ٱلرَّحۡمَةَ لَيَجۡمَعَنَّكُمۡ
إِلَىٰ يَوۡمِ ٱلۡقِيَٰمَةِ لَا رَيۡبَ فِيهِ ٱلَّذِينَ
خَسِرُواۡ أَنفُسَهُمۡ فَهُمۡ لَا يُؤۡمِنُونَ ۝

13. His is whatsoever dwells in the
night and the day; and He is the
Hearer, the Knower.

وَلَهُۥ مَا سَكَنَ فِى ٱلَّيۡلِ وَٱلنَّهَارِ وَهُوَ
ٱلسَّمِيعُ ٱلۡعَلِيمُ ۝

14. Say: 'Shall I take for a patron any other than Allah, the Maker of the heavens and the earth.[326] He feeds, and is not fed.'[327] Say: 'I am commanded that I be the first who surrenders himself, and that: be you not of the polytheists.'

قُلۡ أَغَيۡرَ ٱللَّهِ أَتَّخِذُ وَلِيًّا فَاطِرِ ٱلسَّمَٰوَٰتِ وَ ٱلۡأَرۡضِ وَهُوَ يُطۡعِمُ وَلَا يُطۡعَمُ قُلۡ إِنِّيٓ أُمِرۡتُ أَنۡ أَكُونَ أَوَّلَ مَنۡ أَسۡلَمَ وَلَا تَكُونَنَّ مِنَ ٱلۡمُشۡرِكِينَ ۝

15. Say: 'Verily I fear, if I disobey my Lord, the torment of a Mighty Day.'

قُلۡ إِنِّيٓ أَخَافُ إِنۡ عَصَيۡتُ رَبِّي عَذَابَ يَوۡمٍ عَظِيمٍ ۝

---

326. The heavens and the earth being the two most common objects of worship. 'Of all the phenomena of nature the most universal is perhaps the sky. No wonder that a phenomenon so universal and so impressive should at an early date have mystified men with wonder and awe and found a place in their religion.' (*FWN.* I. p. 19). Furthermore, in polytheistic mythology, the earth is the counterpart of the sky. 'In mythology the Earth, regarded as a person, is often conceived of as the wife of the Sky-god. We have seen that among the ancient Aryans of India the Sky and Earth were thus personified as Husband and Wife under the names of Dyaus and Prithivi, the father and mother of all living creatures' (Ibid., p. 316). Frazer, in his voluminous work, gives minute and accurate details of 'Sky-worship' in Vedic India, Iran, Greece, Rome, Babylonia, Egypt, China, Korea, Western Africa, the Congo, Southern Africa, and Eastern Africa, and of 'Earth-worship' in Vedic India, Greece, Rome, Babylonia, Assyria, China, India, and various parts of Africa and America.

327. This because He is Independent of all needs. According to the crudities of the polytheistic peoples, the gods actually consume the food and drink that are offered to them. The Babylonian gods, for instance, 'conceived of in such human wise, knew thirst and hunger as did men, and had to be propitiated by drink and food' (Woolley, *Abraham*, p. 157). (See also *ERE.* VI. p. 63 and *PC.* II. p. 375). Christian nations have gone one better. Leaving the stage of feeding one's gods far behind, they unabashedly proceed to eat their god! What else is their well–known festival of the Eucharist? 'The Catholic Church teaches that in the Eucharist, the Body and Blood of the God–man are really, truly, substantially, and abidingly present together with His Soul and divinity for the nourishment of souls, by reason of the Transubstantiaton of the bread and wine into the Body and Blood of Christ, which takes place in the unbloody sacrifice of the New Testament, i.e., the Mass' (*CD.* p. 345). And this is what is openly taught in the approved and authorized Catholic Catechism.

16. From whom it is averted on that Day, upon him indeed He has had mercy; that is a supreme achievement.

مَن يُصْرَفْ عَنْهُ يَوْمَئِذٍ فَقَدْ رَحِمَهُ وَذَٰلِكَ الْفَوْزُ الْمُبِينُ ۝

17. If Allah touches them with harm, there is none to reverse it but He, and if He touches you with good then He is Potent over everything.

وَإِن يَمْسَسْكَ اللَّهُ بِضُرٍّ فَلَا كَاشِفَ لَهُ إِلَّا هُوَ وَإِن يَمْسَسْكَ بِخَيْرٍ فَهُوَ عَلَىٰ كُلِّ شَيْءٍ قَدِيرٌ ۝

18. He is the Supreme above His creatures, and He is the Wise, the Aware.'

وَهُوَ الْقَاهِرُ فَوْقَ عِبَادِهِ وَهُوَ الْحَكِيمُ الْخَبِيرُ ۝

19. Say: 'What thing is the greatest in testimony?' Say: 'Allah is a witness between me and you, and this Qur'ān has been revealed to me that I may thereby warn you and whomsoever it may reach. Would you indeed testify that there is another god along with Allah?' Say: 'I do not testify.' Say: 'Verily He is the One God, and I am quit of what you join with Him.'

قُلْ أَيُّ شَيْءٍ أَكْبَرُ شَهَادَةً قُلِ اللَّهُ شَهِيدٌ بَيْنِي وَبَيْنَكُمْ وَأُوحِيَ إِلَيَّ هَٰذَا الْقُرْءَانُ لِأُنذِرَكُم بِهِ وَمَن بَلَغَ أَئِنَّكُمْ لَتَشْهَدُونَ أَنَّ مَعَ اللَّهِ ءَالِهَةً أُخْرَىٰ قُل لَّا أَشْهَدُ قُلْ إِنَّمَا هُوَ إِلَٰهٌ وَٰحِدٌ وَإِنَّنِي بَرِيٓءٌ مِّمَّا تُشْرِكُونَ ۝

20. Those to whom We have given the Book recognize him as they recognize their own children; yet those who have lost their souls will not believe.

الَّذِينَ ءَاتَيْنَاهُمُ الْكِتَابَ يَعْرِفُونَهُ كَمَا يَعْرِفُونَ أَبْنَاءَهُمُ الَّذِينَ خَسِرُوٓا أَنفُسَهُمْ فَهُمْ لَا يُؤْمِنُونَ ۝

Section 3

21. And who is a greater wrong-doer than he who fabricates a lie against Allah or belies His signs? Verily the wrong-doers shall not thrive.

وَمَنْ أَظْلَمُ مِمَّنِ افْتَرَىٰ عَلَى اللَّهِ كَذِبًا أَوْ كَذَّبَ بِآيَاتِهِ ۚ إِنَّهُ لَا يُفْلِحُ الظَّالِمُونَ ﴿٢١﴾

22. And let them beware the Day when We shall gather them all together, then We shall say to those who associated: 'Where are your associate-gods whom you have been asserting?'

وَيَوْمَ نَحْشُرُهُمْ جَمِيعًا ثُمَّ نَقُولُ لِلَّذِينَ أَشْرَكُوا أَيْنَ شُرَكَاؤُكُمُ الَّذِينَ كُنتُمْ تَزْعُمُونَ ﴿٢٢﴾

23. Then they will have no excuse but to say: 'By God our Lord, we have not been associaters.'

ثُمَّ لَمْ تَكُن فِتْنَتُهُمْ إِلَّا أَن قَالُوا وَاللَّهِ رَبِّنَا مَا كُنَّا مُشْرِكِينَ ﴿٢٣﴾

24. See! How they lied against themselves! And then these failed them what they had been fabricating.

انظُرْ كَيْفَ كَذَبُوا عَلَىٰ أَنفُسِهِمْ ۚ وَضَلَّ عَنْهُم مَّا كَانُوا يَفْتَرُونَ ﴿٢٤﴾

25. And of them are some who hearken to you, and We have set veils over their hearts so that they understand it not, and in their ears heaviness, and any sign though they may see, they will not believe in it; inasmuch as when they come to you, they dispute with you. Then those

وَمِنْهُم مَّن يَسْتَمِعُ إِلَيْكَ ۖ وَجَعَلْنَا عَلَىٰ قُلُوبِهِمْ أَكِنَّةً أَن يَفْقَهُوهُ وَفِي ءَاذَانِهِمْ وَقْرًا ۚ وَإِن يَرَوْا كُلَّ ءَايَةٍ لَّا يُؤْمِنُوا بِهَا ۚ حَتَّىٰ إِذَا جَاءُوكَ يُجَادِلُونَكَ

who disbelieve say: 'This is nothing but the fables of the ancients.'[328]

يَقُولُ ٱلَّذِينَ كَفَرُوٓاْ إِنْ هَٰذَآ إِلَّآ أَسَٰطِيرُ ٱلْأَوَّلِينَ ﴿٢٥﴾

26. And they prohibit others from it, and they themselves withdraw from it, and they destroy nothing but their own souls, yet they perceive not.

وَهُمْ يَنْهَوْنَ عَنْهُ وَيَنْـَٔوْنَ عَنْهُ وَإِن يُهْلِكُونَ إِلَّآ أَنفُسَهُمْ وَمَا يَشْعُرُونَ ﴿٢٦﴾

27. And could you see when they shall be held over the Fire; and then they will say: 'Would that we were sent back to the world and this time we shall not belie the signs of our Lord and we shall be of the believers.'

وَلَوْ تَرَىٰٓ إِذْ وُقِفُواْ عَلَى ٱلنَّارِ فَقَالُواْ يَٰلَيْتَنَا نُرَدُّ وَلَا نُكَذِّبَ بِـَٔايَٰتِ رَبِّنَا وَنَكُونَ مِنَ ٱلْمُؤْمِنِينَ ﴿٢٧﴾

28. Yea! Manifest has become to them what they had been hiding. And were they sent back they would surely revert to what was prohibited to them, and surely they are perfect liars.

بَلْ بَدَا لَهُم مَّا كَانُواْ يُخْفُونَ مِن قَبْلُ وَلَوْ رُدُّواْ لَعَادُواْ لِمَا نُهُواْ عَنْهُ وَإِنَّهُمْ لَكَٰذِبُونَ ﴿٢٨﴾

29. And they say: 'There is nothing but the life of this world, nor are we to be raised.'

وَقَالُوٓاْ إِنْ هِىَ إِلَّا حَيَاتُنَا ٱلدُّنْيَا وَمَا نَحْنُ بِمَبْعُوثِينَ ﴿٢٩﴾

---

328. Asatir signifies lies; falsehood; fiction; stories having no foundation, or no right tendency or tenor such as we commonly term legends; or wonderful stories of the ancients. A similar charge of borrowing from the ancient Scriptures, based on a list of parallel passages is still hurled at the Holy Qur'ān by a number of learned Jews and Christians of the modern age — as if that could be any proof at all of the falsity of the Qur'ān! But it is something to note that by now some of their own scholars have come to recognize the utter hollowness of this charge. 'Is a religion less true because it recognizes itself in other garbs, because it incorporates in itself all that is best in the system which it expands or supplants? What if we found the whole Sermon on the Mount dispersed about in the writings of the Jewish Rabbis, as we unquestionably find some part of it' (Bosworth Smith, *Mohammed and Mohammedanism*, p. 13).

30. And could you see when they shall be held before their Lord! He will say: 'Is this not real?' They will say: 'Aye! By our Lord!' He will say: 'Taste you then the torment, for you have been disbelieving.'

Section 4

31. Lost surely are those who belie their meeting with Allah until when the Hour comes on them suddenly, and they will exclaim: 'Woe betide us, that we neglected it!', while they will be bearing their burdens on their backs. Lo! Vile is what they will bear.

32. And naught is the life of this world but a play and a sport: and surely the abode of the Hereafter is better for those who fear. Do you not then reflect?

33. We know well that surely what they say grieves you, but it is not you they belie; it is the signs of Allah which the ungodly gainsay.

34. And Messengers have assuredly been belied before you, but they patiently bore of which they were belied, and they were persecuted, till Our succour reached them. And none can alter the decisions of Allah; and surely there has reached you some tidings of the sent ones.

وَلَوۡ تَرَىٰٓ إِذۡ وُقِفُوۡا عَلَىٰ رَبِّهِمۡ قَالَ أَلَيۡسَ هَٰذَا بِالۡحَقِّ قَالُوۡا بَلَىٰ وَرَبِّنَا قَالَ فَذُوۡقُوا الۡعَذَابَ بِمَا كُنۡتُمۡ تَكۡفُرُوۡنَ ۝٣٠

قَدۡ خَسِرَ الَّذِيۡنَ كَذَّبُوۡا بِلِقَآءِ اللّٰهِ حَتّٰىٓ إِذَا جَآءَتۡهُمُ السَّاعَةُ بَغۡتَةً قَالُوۡا يٰحَسۡرَتَنَا عَلَىٰ مَا فَرَّطۡنَا فِيۡهَا وَهُمۡ يَحۡمِلُوۡنَ أَوۡزَارَهُمۡ عَلَىٰ ظُهُوۡرِهِمۡ أَلَا سَآءَ مَا يَزِرُوۡنَ ۝٣١

وَمَا الۡحَيٰوةُ الدُّنۡيَآ إِلَّا لَعِبٌ وَّلَهۡوٌ وَلَلدَّارُ الۡاٰخِرَةُ خَيۡرٌ لِّلَّذِيۡنَ يَتَّقُوۡنَ أَفَلَا تَعۡقِلُوۡنَ ۝٣٢

قَدۡ نَعۡلَمُ إِنَّهُ لَيَحۡزُنُكَ الَّذِيۡ يَقُوۡلُوۡنَ فَإِنَّهُمۡ لَا يُكَذِّبُوۡنَكَ وَلٰكِنَّ الظّٰلِمِيۡنَ بِاٰيٰتِ اللّٰهِ يَجۡحَدُوۡنَ ۝٣٣

وَلَقَدۡ كُذِّبَتۡ رُسُلٌ مِّنۡ قَبۡلِكَ فَصَبَرُوۡا عَلَىٰ مَا كُذِّبُوۡا وَأُوۡذُوۡا حَتّٰىٓ أَتٰهُمۡ نَصۡرُنَا وَلَا مُبَدِّلَ لِكَلِمٰتِ اللّٰهِ وَلَقَدۡ جَآءَكَ مِنۡ نَّبَإِى الۡمُرۡسَلِيۡنَ ۝٣٤

35. And if their aversion is hard upon you, then seek out, if you can, an opening into the earth or a ladder to the heaven so that you may bring to them a sign. And had Allah willed, He would have assembled them one and all into the guidance, so be not then you of the ignorant.

وَإِن كَانَ كَبُرَ عَلَيْكَ إِعْرَاضُهُمْ فَإِنِ
ٱسْتَطَعْتَ أَن تَبْتَغِيَ نَفَقًا فِي ٱلْأَرْضِ أَوْ
سُلَّمًا فِي ٱلسَّمَاءِ فَتَأْتِيَهُم بِآيَةٍ وَلَوْ شَآءَ
ٱللَّهُ لَجَمَعَهُمْ عَلَى ٱلْهُدَىٰ فَلَا تَكُونَنَّ
مِنَ ٱلْجَٰهِلِينَ ۝

36. It is only those who hearken that respond. And as to the dead, Allah will raise them and thereafter to Him they will be returned.

إِنَّمَا يَسْتَجِيبُ ٱلَّذِينَ يَسْمَعُونَ وَٱلْمَوْتَىٰ
يَبْعَثُهُمُ ٱللَّهُ ثُمَّ إِلَيْهِ يُرْجَعُونَ ۝

37. And they say: 'Why is not a sign sent down upon him from his Lord?' Say: 'Verily Allah is able to send down a sign; yet most of them know not.'

وَقَالُوا لَوْلَا نُزِّلَ عَلَيْهِ ءَايَةٌ مِّن رَّبِّهِ قُلْ إِنَّ
ٱللَّهَ قَادِرٌ عَلَىٰ أَن يُنَزِّلَ ءَايَةً وَلَٰكِنَّ
أَكْثَرَهُمْ لَا يَعْلَمُونَ ۝

38. And there is not an animal on the earth or a fowl with its two wings but are communities like you. And We have not been remiss in respect of anything in the Book; then unto their Lord they shall be gathered.

وَمَا مِن دَآبَّةٍ فِي ٱلْأَرْضِ وَلَا طَٰئِرٍ يَطِيرُ
بِجَنَاحَيْهِ إِلَّا أُمَمٌ أَمْثَالُكُم مَّا فَرَّطْنَا فِي
ٱلْكِتَٰبِ مِن شَىْءٍ ثُمَّ إِلَىٰ رَبِّهِمْ
يُحْشَرُونَ ۝

39. And those who belie Our signs are deaf and dumb, in darkness. Allah sends astray whom He will, and He puts on the right path whom He will.

وَٱلَّذِينَ كَذَّبُوا بِآيَٰتِنَا صُمٌّ وَبُكْمٌ فِي
ٱلظُّلُمَٰتِ مَن يَشَإِ ٱللَّهُ يُضْلِلْهُ وَمَن
يَشَأْ يَجْعَلْهُ عَلَىٰ صِرَٰطٍ مُّسْتَقِيمٍ ۝

40. Say: 'Look you now; were Allah's torment to come upon you, or the Hour to come upon you, would you then cry to other than Allah, if you are truthful?

قُلْ أَرَءَيْتَكُمْ إِنْ أَتَىٰكُمْ عَذَابُ ٱللَّهِ أَوْ
أَتَتْكُمُ ٱلسَّاعَةُ أَغَيْرَ ٱللَّهِ تَدْعُونَ إِن
كُنتُمْ صَٰدِقِينَ ۝

41. Aye! To Him alone you would cry, and if He willed He would remove that for which you cried to Him, and you would forget at that time what you now join with Him.'

بَلۡ إِيَّاهُ تَدۡعُوۡنَ فَيَكۡشِفُ مَا تَدۡعُوۡنَ إِلَيۡهِ إِنۡ شَآءَ وَتَنۡسَوۡنَ مَا تُشۡرِكُوۡنَ ۝

Section 5

42. And assuredly We sent Messengers unto communities before you, then We seized them with adversity and distress, that haply they may humble themselves.

وَلَقَدۡ أَرۡسَلۡنَاۤ إِلَىٰۤ أُمَمٍ مِّنۡ قَبۡلِكَ فَأَخَذۡنَٰهُمۡ بِالۡبَأۡسَآءِ وَالضَّرَّآءِ لَعَلَّهُمۡ يَتَضَرَّعُوۡنَ ۝

43. Wherefore did they not, when the affliction upon them came from Us, humble themselves? But their hearts became hardened and Satan made fair-seeming to them what they were wont to do.

فَلَوۡلَاۤ إِذۡ جَآءَهُمۡ بَأۡسُنَا تَضَرَّعُوۡا وَلَٰكِن قَسَتۡ قُلُوۡبُهُمۡ وَزَيَّنَ لَهُمُ الشَّيۡطَٰنُ مَا كَانُوۡا يَعۡمَلُوۡنَ ۝

44. Then when they forgot that of which they were reminded, We opened upon them the doors of everything, until when they boasted of what they were given, We seized them on a sudden, and lo! They were dumbfounded.

فَلَمَّا نَسُوۡا مَا ذُكِّرُوۡا بِهِ فَتَحۡنَا عَلَيۡهِمۡ أَبۡوَٰبَ كُلِّ شَىۡءٍ حَتَّىٰۤ إِذَا فَرِحُوۡا بِمَاۤ أُوۡتُوۡۤا أَخَذۡنَٰهُمۡ بَغۡتَةً فَإِذَا هُمۡ مُّبۡلِسُوۡنَ ۝

45. Then the people who committed wrong were cut off completely. And all praise is to Allah, the Lord of the worlds.

فَقُطِعَ دَابِرُ الۡقَوۡمِ الَّذِيۡنَ ظَلَمُوۡا وَالۡحَمۡدُ لِلَّهِ رَبِّ الۡعَٰلَمِيۡنَ ۝

46. Say: 'Look you now, were Allah to take away your hearing and your sight and seal up your hearts what god, other than Allah, will bring them to you?' See how variously We propound the signs, yet they turn aside.

قُلْ أَرَءَيْتُمْ إِنْ أَخَذَ اللَّهُ سَمْعَكُمْ وَأَبْصَارَكُمْ وَخَتَمَ عَلَىٰ قُلُوبِكُم مَّنْ إِلَٰهٌ غَيْرُ اللَّهِ يَأْتِيكُم بِهِ ۗ انظُرْ كَيْفَ نُصَرِّفُ الْآيَاتِ ثُمَّ هُمْ يَصْدِفُونَ ٤٦

47. Say: 'Look you now, were Allah's chastisement to come upon you suddenly and openly, would there be destroyed any but the wrong-doers?'

قُلْ أَرَءَيْتَكُمْ إِنْ أَتَاكُمْ عَذَابُ اللَّهِ بَغْتَةً أَوْ جَهْرَةً هَلْ يُهْلَكُ إِلَّا الْقَوْمُ الظَّالِمُونَ ٤٧

48. We do not send the Messengers except as bearers of glad tidings and warners. Then to whoever believes and amends on such shall come no fear nor shall they grieve.

وَمَا نُرْسِلُ الْمُرْسَلِينَ إِلَّا مُبَشِّرِينَ وَمُنذِرِينَ ۖ فَمَنْ ءَامَنَ وَأَصْلَحَ فَلَا خَوْفٌ عَلَيْهِمْ وَلَا هُمْ يَحْزَنُونَ ٤٨

49. And then who belies Our signs torment shall overtake them for they have been transgressors.

وَالَّذِينَ كَذَّبُوا بِآيَاتِنَا يَمَسُّهُمُ الْعَذَابُ بِمَا كَانُوا يَفْسُقُونَ ٤٩

50. Say: 'I do not say that with me are the treasures of Allah, nor do I know the Unseen; nor do I say to you that I am an angel, I but follow what has been revealed to me.'[329] Say: 'Are the blind and the seeing equal? Will you not then ponder?'

قُل لَّا أَقُولُ لَكُمْ عِندِي خَزَائِنُ اللَّهِ وَلَا أَعْلَمُ الْغَيْبَ وَلَا أَقُولُ لَكُمْ إِنِّي مَلَكٌ ۖ إِنْ أَتَّبِعُ إِلَّا مَا يُوحَىٰ إِلَيَّ ۚ قُلْ هَلْ يَسْتَوِي الْأَعْمَىٰ وَالْبَصِيرُ ۚ أَفَلَا تَتَفَكَّرُونَ ٥٠

---

329. Contrast with this sublime doctrine of Prophethood in Islam the role of Christ in Christianity: 'The Father loves the Son, and has given all things into his hands' (Jn. 3: 35). 'I and my Father are one' (Jn. 10: 30). 'All things that the Father has are mine' (Jn 16: 15). Surely the polytheists of the grossest variety could hardly go further!

Section 6

51. And warn you therewith those who fear God that they shall be gathered before their Lord, when there shall be no patron nor intercessor besides Him; haply they may become God-fearing.

وَأَنذِرْ بِهِ الَّذِينَ يَخَافُونَ أَن يُحْشَرُوٓاْ إِلَىٰ رَبِّهِمْ لَيْسَ لَهُم مِّن دُونِهِۦ وَلِىٌّ وَلَا شَفِيعٌ لَّعَلَّهُمْ يَتَّقُونَ ۝

52. And do not drive away from before you those who call upon their Lord morning and evening seeking His grace. Not on you is their reckoning, nor on them any of your reckoning, so that you may drive them away and thus become of the wrong-doers.

وَلَا تَطْرُدِ الَّذِينَ يَدْعُونَ رَبَّهُم بِالْغَدَوٰةِ وَالْعَشِىِّ يُرِيدُونَ وَجْهَهُۥ مَا عَلَيْكَ مِنْ حِسَابِهِم مِّن شَىْءٍ وَمَا مِنْ حِسَابِكَ عَلَيْهِم مِّن شَىْءٍ فَتَطْرُدَهُمْ فَتَكُونَ مِنَ الظَّالِمِينَ ۝

53. And thus We have tried some of them by means of others, that they might say: 'Are those they whom Allah has favoured among us?'[330] Is not Allah the Best Knower of the thankful?[331]

وَكَذَٰلِكَ فَتَنَّا بَعْضَهُم بِبَعْضٍ لِّيَقُولُوٓاْ أَهَٰٓؤُلَآءِ مَنَّ اللَّهُ عَلَيْهِم مِّنۢ بَيْنِنَآ أَلَيْسَ اللَّهُ بِأَعْلَمَ بِالشَّٰكِرِينَ ۝

54. And when those who believe in Our signs come to you, say: 'Peace be on you, your Lord has prescribed mercy on Himself; so that any of you who does an evil through ignorance then repents and amends, then verily He is the Forgiving, the Merciful.'

وَإِذَا جَآءَكَ الَّذِينَ يُؤْمِنُونَ بِـَٔايَٰتِنَا فَقُلْ سَلَٰمٌ عَلَيْكُمْ كَتَبَ رَبُّكُمْ عَلَىٰ نَفْسِهِ الرَّحْمَةَ أَنَّهُۥ مَنْ عَمِلَ مِنكُمْ سُوٓءًۢا بِجَهَٰلَةٍ ثُمَّ تَابَ مِنۢ بَعْدِهِۦ وَأَصْلَحَ فَأَنَّهُۥ غَفُورٌ رَّحِيمٌ ۝

---

330. Are they the elect of God? Could these persons with empty purses and no position be said to be the favourites of God? Thus spoke the leaders of the Quraish in derision and scorn.

331. God alone knows best who performs his duty by Him and who does not, and He guides each according to his desert. This moral capacity has nothing to do with poverty and riches.

55. And thus We expound revelations so that the way of the culprits may be shown up.

وَكَذَٰلِكَ نُفَصِّلُ الۡاٰیٰتِ وَلِتَسۡتَبِینَ سَبِیلُ الۡمُجۡرِمِینَ ۝

Section 7

56. Say: 'Verily I am forbidden to worship those whom you call upon besides Allah.' Say: 'I shall not follow your vain desires, for then I shall be gone astray, and shall not remain of the guided.'

قُلۡ اِنِّیۡ نُهِیۡتُ اَنۡ اَعۡبُدَ الَّذِینَ تَدۡعُونَ مِن دُونِ اللّٰهِ قُلۡ لَّاۤ اَتَّبِعُ اَهۡوَاۤءَكُمۡ قَدۡ ضَلَلۡتُ اِذًا وَّمَاۤ اَنَا مِنَ الۡمُهۡتَدِینَ ۝

57. Say: 'I stand upon an evidence from my Lord, and you belie it; not with me is what you would hasten on. Then the decision is but of Allah. He recounts the Truth, and He is the Best of Deciders.'

قُلۡ اِنِّیۡ عَلَیٰ بَیِّنَةٍ مِّن رَّبِّیۡ وَكَذَّبۡتُم بِهِ مَا عِنۡدِی مَا تَسۡتَعۡجِلُونَ بِهِ اِنِ الۡحُكۡمُ اِلَّا لِلّٰهِ یَقُصُّ الۡحَقَّ وَهُوَ خَیۡرُ الۡفَاصِلِینَ ۝

58. Say: 'If what you fain would hasten on is with me, the affair would have been decided between me and you, and Allah is the Best Knower of the ungodly.'

قُلۡ لَّوۡ اَنَّ عِنۡدِی مَا تَسۡتَعۡجِلُونَ بِهِ لَقُضِیَ الۡاَمۡرُ بَیۡنِی وَبَیۡنَكُمۡ وَاللّٰهُ اَعۡلَمُ بِالظّٰلِمِینَ ۝

59. And with Him are the keys of the Unseen; none knows them but He.[332] And He knows whoever is in the land and in the sea. Not a leaf falls but He knows it, nor a seed-grain grows in the darkness of the earth, nor aught of fresh and dry but is in a luminous Book.

وَعِنۡدَهُ مَفَاتِحُ الۡغَیۡبِ لَا یَعۡلَمُهَاۤ اِلَّا هُوَ وَیَعۡلَمُ مَا فِی الۡبَرِّ وَالۡبَحۡرِ وَمَا تَسۡقُطُ مِن وَّرَقَةٍ اِلَّا یَعۡلَمُهَا وَلَا حَبَّةٍ فِی ظُلُمٰتِ الۡاَرۡضِ وَلَا رَطۡبٍ وَّلَا یَابِسٍ اِلَّا فِی كِتٰبٍ مُّبِینٍ ۝

---

332. Far from possessing them, none has even a knowledge of them. He alone is Omniscient, Omnipotent.

60. And He it is Who takes your souls by night and knows what you earn by day. Then He raises you therein that there may be fulfilled the term allotted. Thereafter to Him shall be your return; and then He shall declare to you what you have been working.

وَهُوَ ٱلَّذِي يَتَوَفَّىٰكُم بِٱلَّيْلِ وَيَعْلَمُ مَا جَرَحْتُم بِٱلنَّهَارِ ثُمَّ يَبْعَثُكُمْ فِيهِ لِيُقْضَىٰٓ أَجَلٌ مُّسَمًّى ثُمَّ إِلَيْهِ مَرْجِعُكُمْ ثُمَّ يُنَبِّئُكُم بِمَا كُنتُمْ تَعْمَلُونَ ﴿٦٠﴾

Section 8

61. And He is the Supreme over His creatures and He sends guardians over you until when death comes to one of you. Our Messengers take his soul, and they do not fail.

وَهُوَ ٱلْقَاهِرُ فَوْقَ عِبَادِهِۦ وَيُرْسِلُ عَلَيْكُمْ حَفَظَةً حَتَّىٰٓ إِذَا جَآءَ أَحَدَكُمُ ٱلْمَوْتُ تَوَفَّتْهُ رُسُلُنَا وَهُمْ لَا يُفَرِّطُونَ ﴿٦١﴾

62. Then they all shall be taken back to Allah, their true Master. Lo! His shall be the decision,[333] and He is the Most Swift of reckoners.

ثُمَّ رُدُّوٓا۟ إِلَى ٱللَّهِ مَوْلَىٰهُمُ ٱلْحَقِّ أَلَا لَهُ ٱلْحُكْمُ وَهُوَ أَسْرَعُ ٱلْحَٰسِبِينَ ﴿٦٢﴾

---

333. There is only His decision, no other. This is specially to combat the Christian doctrine representing Christ as Judge. 'The Son of man shall come in the glory of his Father with his angels; and then he shall reward every man according to his works' (Mt. 16: 27). 'When the Son of man shall come in his glory, and all the holy angels with him, then shall he sit upon the throne of his glory; and before him shall be gathered all nations; and he shall separate them one from another, as a shepherd divides his sheep from the goats; and he shall set the sheep on his right hand but the goats on the left. Then shall the king say unto them on his right hand, Come, ye blessed of my Father' (Mt. 25: 31–34). 'That there will be a General Judgment is an article of faith. The judge will be Christ' (*CD.* p. 523). 'In the Gospels, while the Father is spoken of as Judge, Christ's influence at the Judgment is also spoken of and more generally He Himself is Judge, and exercises this function on all men' (*ERE.* V. p. 325).

63. Say : 'Who delivers you from the darkness of the land and the sea, when you cry unto Him in humility and secretly, if He delivers us from this, we will surely be of the thankful.'

قُلْ مَن يُنَجِّيكُم مِّن ظُلُمَـٰتِ ٱلْبَرِّ وَٱلْبَحْرِ تَدْعُونَهُۥ تَضَرُّعًا وَخُفْيَةً لَّئِنْ أَنجَىٰنَا مِنْ هَـٰذِهِۦ لَنَكُونَنَّ مِنَ ٱلشَّـٰكِرِينَ ۝

64. Say: 'Allah delivers you from this and from every pain, yet you join thereafter others with Him.'

قُلِ ٱللَّهُ يُنَجِّيكُم مِّنْهَا وَمِن كُلِّ كَرْبٍ ثُمَّ أَنتُمْ تُشْرِكُونَ ۝

65. Say: 'He is able to stir up chastisement on you from above you or from beneath your feet or to confound you by faction and to make you taste the violence of one another.' Behold! How variously We propound the signs that haply they may understand.

قُلْ هُوَ ٱلْقَادِرُ عَلَىٰٓ أَن يَبْعَثَ عَلَيْكُمْ عَذَابًا مِّن فَوْقِكُمْ أَوْ مِن تَحْتِ أَرْجُلِكُمْ أَوْ يَلْبِسَكُمْ شِيَعًا وَيُذِيقَ بَعْضَكُم بَأْسَ بَعْضٍ ٱنظُرْ كَيْفَ نُصَرِّفُ ٱلْأَيَـٰتِ لَعَلَّهُمْ يَفْقَهُونَ ۝

66. And your people belie it, while it is certain to befall. Say: 'I am not a guardian over you.

وَكَذَّبَ بِهِۦ قَوْمُكَ وَهُوَ ٱلْحَقُّ قُل لَّسْتُ عَلَيْكُم بِوَكِيلٍ ۝

67. For every announcement is a set time, and presently you will know.'

لِّكُلِّ نَبَإٍ مُّسْتَقَرٌّ وَسَوْفَ تَعْلَمُونَ ۝

68. And when you see those who plunge in Our revelations, keep away from them until they plunge in a discourse other than that; and if Satan causes you to forget, than sit not you after recollection with the impious people.

وَإِذَا رَأَيْتَ ٱلَّذِينَ يَخُوضُونَ فِىٓ ءَايَـٰتِنَا فَأَعْرِضْ عَنْهُمْ حَتَّىٰ يَخُوضُوا۟ فِى حَدِيثٍ غَيْرِهِۦ وَإِمَّا يُنسِيَنَّكَ ٱلشَّيْطَـٰنُ فَلَا تَقْعُدْ بَعْدَ ٱلذِّكْرَىٰ مَعَ ٱلْقَوْمِ ٱلظَّـٰلِمِينَ ۝

69. And nothing on their account shall be on those who are God-fearing, but admonition that haply they also may become God-fearing.

وَمَا عَلَى ٱلَّذِينَ يَتَّقُونَ مِنْ حِسَابِهِم مِّن شَىْءٍ وَلَـٰكِن ذِكْرَىٰ لَعَلَّهُمْ يَتَّقُونَ ۝

70. And leave those alone who have taken their religion as a play and a sport, and whom the life of the world has beguiled. And admonish them by verses lest a soul may be given up to perdition for what it has earned, when for him there shall be no friend or intercessor besides Allah, and when if he offers every equivalent it shall not be accepted of him. Those are they who are given up to perdition for what they have earned. For them shall be a drink of boiling water and an afflictive torment, for they were wont to disbelieve.

وَذَرِ الَّذِيْنَ اتَّخَذُوْا دِيْنَهُمْ لَعِبًا وَلَهْوًا وَغَرَّتْهُمُ الْحَيٰوةُ الدُّنْيَا وَذَكِّرْ بِهٖ اَنْ تُبْسَلَ نَفْسٌ بِمَا كَسَبَتْ لَيْسَ لَهَا مِنْ دُوْنِ اللّٰهِ وَلِيٌّ وَلَا شَفِيْعٌ وَاِنْ تَعْدِلْ كُلَّ عَدْلٍ لَّا يُؤْخَذْ مِنْهَا اُولٰٓئِكَ الَّذِيْنَ اُبْسِلُوْا بِمَا كَسَبُوْا لَهُمْ شَرَابٌ مِّنْ حَمِيْمٍ وَعَذَابٌ اَلِيْمٌ بِمَا كَانُوْا يَكْفُرُوْنَ ۝

Section 9

71. Say: 'Shall we call upon, besides Allah, what can neither profit us nor hurt us, and shall we turn our heels after Allah has guided us, like one whom devils have beguiled to wander bewildered in the land, his companions calling him to the right path, come to us?' Say: 'Verily the guidance of Allah is the real guidance, and we are bidden to submit ourselves to the Lord of the worlds:

قُلْ اَنَدْعُوْا مِنْ دُوْنِ اللّٰهِ مَا لَا يَنْفَعُنَا وَلَا يَضُرُّنَا وَنُرَدُّ عَلٰٓى اَعْقَابِنَا بَعْدَ اِذْ هَدٰىنَا اللّٰهُ كَالَّذِى اسْتَهْوَتْهُ الشَّيٰطِيْنُ فِى الْاَرْضِ حَيْرَانَ لَهٗٓ اَصْحٰبٌ يَّدْعُوْنَهٗٓ اِلَى الْهُدَى ائْتِنَا قُلْ اِنَّ هُدَى اللّٰهِ هُوَ الْهُدٰى وَاُمِرْنَا لِنُسْلِمَ لِرَبِّ الْعٰلَمِيْنَ ۝

72. So establish prayer and fear Him, for it is He to Whom you shall be gathered.'

وَاَنْ اَقِيْمُوا الصَّلٰوةَ وَاتَّقُوْهُ وَهُوَ الَّذِىٓ اِلَيْهِ تُحْشَرُوْنَ ۝

73. It is He Who has created the heavens and the earth with a purpose. And the Day when He says: 'Be', it shall become. His saying is the reality. His will be the dominion the Day the trumpet will be blown. Knower of the Unseen and the Seen, He is the Wise, the Aware.

وَهُوَ ٱلَّذِى خَلَقَ ٱلسَّمَٰوَٰتِ وَٱلْأَرْضَ بِٱلْحَقِّ وَيَوْمَ يَقُولُ كُن فَيَكُونُ قَوْلُهُ ٱلْحَقُّ وَلَهُ ٱلْمُلْكُ يَوْمَ يُنفَخُ فِى ٱلصُّورِ عَٰلِمُ ٱلْغَيْبِ وَٱلشَّهَٰدَةِ وَهُوَ ٱلْحَكِيمُ ٱلْخَبِيرُ ﴿٧٣﴾

74. Recall when Abraham said to his father: 'Āzar, take you idols for gods. I see you and your people in manifest error.'

وَإِذْ قَالَ إِبْرَٰهِيمُ لِأَبِيهِ ءَازَرَ أَتَتَّخِذُ أَصْنَامًا ءَالِهَةً إِنِّى أَرَىٰكَ وَقَوْمَكَ فِى ضَلَٰلٍ مُّبِينٍ ﴿٧٤﴾

75. And in like manner did We show Abraham the governance of the heavens and the earth, in order that he might become of the convinced.

وَكَذَٰلِكَ نُرِى إِبْرَٰهِيمَ مَلَكُوتَ ٱلسَّمَٰوَٰتِ وَٱلْأَرْضِ وَلِيَكُونَ مِنَ ٱلْمُوقِنِينَ ﴿٧٥﴾

76. Then when the night darkened on him, he saw a star. He said: 'This is my Lord.' Then when it set, he said: 'I love not the setting ones.'

فَلَمَّا جَنَّ عَلَيْهِ ٱلَّيْلُ رَءَا كَوْكَبًا قَالَ هَٰذَا رَبِّى فَلَمَّا أَفَلَ قَالَ لَا أُحِبُّ ٱلْءَافِلِينَ ﴿٧٦﴾

77. Then when he saw the moon rising up, he said: 'This is my Lord.' Then when it set, he said: 'Were it not that my Lord kept me guiding. I must have been of the erring people.'

فَلَمَّا رَءَا ٱلْقَمَرَ بَازِغًا قَالَ هَٰذَا رَبِّى فَلَمَّا أَفَلَ قَالَ لَئِن لَّمْ يَهْدِنِى رَبِّى لَأَكُونَنَّ مِنَ ٱلْقَوْمِ ٱلضَّآلِّينَ ﴿٧٧﴾

78. Then when he saw the sun rising up, he said: 'This is my Lord! This is the greatest.' Then when it set, he said: 'O my people! I am quit of what you associate with God.

فَلَمَّا رَءَا ٱلشَّمْسَ بَازِغَةً قَالَ هَٰذَا رَبِّى هَٰذَآ أَكْبَرُ فَلَمَّا أَفَلَتْ قَالَ يَٰقَوْمِ إِنِّى بَرِىٓءٌ مِّمَّا تُشْرِكُونَ ﴿٧٨﴾

79. Verily I have set my face towards Him Who has created the heavens and the earth, upright, and I am not of the associaters.'

إِنِّي وَجَّهْتُ وَجْهِيَ لِلَّذِى فَطَرَ السَّمَوَاتِ وَالْأَرْضَ حَنِيفًا وَمَا أَنَا مِنَ الْمُشْرِكِينَ ﴿٧٩﴾

80. And his people contended with him. He said: 'Do you contend with me regarding Allah when He has guided me? I am not at all afraid of what you associate with Him, save anything that my Lord may will. My Lord comprehends everything in His knowledge. Will you not then be admonished?

وَحَآجَّهُ قَوْمُهُ قَالَ أَتُحَاجُّونِّي فِي اللَّهِ وَقَدْ هَدَانِ وَلَا أَخَافُ مَا تُشْرِكُونَ بِهِ إِلَّا أَن يَشَاءَ رَبِّي شَيْئًا وَسِعَ رَبِّي كُلَّ شَيْءٍ عِلْمًا أَفَلَا تَتَذَكَّرُونَ ﴿٨٠﴾

81. And how should I fear what you have associated with Him, while you do not fear to associate with Allah that for which He has sent down to you no authority? Which then of the two parties is worthier of security, if you but knew?

وَكَيْفَ أَخَافُ مَا أَشْرَكْتُمْ وَلَا تَخَافُونَ أَنَّكُمْ أَشْرَكْتُم بِاللَّهِ مَا لَمْ يُنَزِّلْ بِهِ عَلَيْكُمْ سُلْطَانًا فَأَيُّ الْفَرِيقَيْنِ أَحَقُّ بِالْأَمْنِ إِن كُنتُمْ تَعْلَمُونَ ﴿٨١﴾

82. It is those who believe and do not confound their belief with wrong-doing. These! Theirs is the security and they are the guided.'

الَّذِينَ ءَامَنُوا وَلَمْ يَلْبِسُوا إِيمَانَهُم بِظُلْمٍ أُوْلَئِكَ لَهُمُ الْأَمْنُ وَهُم مُّهْتَدُونَ ﴿٨٢﴾

Section 10

83. This was the argument which We gave to Abraham against his people. We raise in degrees whom We please; verily your Lord is the Wise, the Knowing.

وَتِلْكَ حُجَّتُنَا ءَاتَيْنَاهَا إِبْرَاهِيمَ عَلَى قَوْمِهِ نَرْفَعُ دَرَجَاتٍ مَّن نَّشَاءُ إِنَّ رَبَّكَ حَكِيمٌ عَلِيمٌ ﴿٨٣﴾

84. And We bestowed upon him Isaac and Jacob; each one We guided. And Noah We had guided before, and of his progeny David and Solomon and Job and Joseph and Moses and Aaron, and thus We recompense the well-doers.

وَوَهَبْنَا لَهُۥٓ إِسْحَٰقَ وَيَعْقُوبَۚ كُلًّا هَدَيْنَاۚ وَنُوحًا هَدَيْنَا مِن قَبْلُۖ وَمِن ذُرِّيَّتِهِۦ دَاوُۥدَ وَسُلَيْمَٰنَ وَأَيُّوبَ وَيُوسُفَ وَمُوسَىٰ وَهَٰرُونَۚ وَكَذَٰلِكَ نَجْزِى ٱلْمُحْسِنِينَ ۝

85. And also Zacharia and John and 'Īsā and Ilyās; each one was of the righteous.

وَزَكَرِيَّا وَيَحْيَىٰ وَعِيسَىٰ وَإِلْيَاسَۖ كُلٌّ مِّنَ ٱلصَّٰلِحِينَ ۝

86. And also Ishmael and al-Yasa', and Jonah and Lot; each of them We preferred above the worlds.

وَإِسْمَٰعِيلَ وَٱلْيَسَعَ وَيُونُسَ وَلُوطًاۚ وَكُلًّا فَضَّلْنَا عَلَى ٱلْعَٰلَمِينَ ۝

87. And also some of their fathers and their progeny and their brethren; We chose them and guided them on the right path.

وَمِنْ ءَابَآئِهِمْ وَذُرِّيَّٰتِهِمْ وَإِخْوَٰنِهِمْۖ وَٱجْتَبَيْنَٰهُمْ وَهَدَيْنَٰهُمْ إِلَىٰ صِرَٰطٍ مُّسْتَقِيمٍ ۝

88. This is the guidance of Allah with which He guides whomsoever of His creatures He wills. And if they had associated, to nothing would have come all that they were wont to do.

ذَٰلِكَ هُدَى ٱللَّهِ يَهْدِى بِهِۦ مَن يَشَآءُ مِنْ عِبَادِهِۦۚ وَلَوْ أَشْرَكُوا۟ لَحَبِطَ عَنْهُم مَّا كَانُوا۟ يَعْمَلُونَ ۝

89. Those are they to whom We gave the Book and judgement and prophethood. Wherefore if those disbelieve therein, We have surely entrusted it to a people who are not disbelievers therein.

أُو۟لَٰٓئِكَ ٱلَّذِينَ ءَاتَيْنَٰهُمُ ٱلْكِتَٰبَ وَٱلْحُكْمَ وَٱلنُّبُوَّةَۚ فَإِن يَكْفُرْ بِهَا هَٰٓؤُلَآءِ فَقَدْ وَكَّلْنَا بِهَا قَوْمًا لَّيْسُوا۟ بِهَا بِكَٰفِرِينَ ۝

90. Those are they whom Allah had guided; so follow you their guidance. Say: 'I ask no wage for it. It is but an admonition to the worlds.'[334]

أُوْلَٰٓئِكَ ٱلَّذِينَ هَدَى ٱللَّهُ فَبِهُدَىٰهُمُ ٱقۡتَدِهۡ قُل لَّآ أَسۡـَٔلُكُمۡ عَلَيۡهِ أَجۡرًا إِنۡ هُوَ إِلَّا ذِكۡرَىٰ لِلۡعَٰلَمِينَ ٩٠

Section 11

91. They did not estimate Allah with an estimation due to Him, when they said: 'On no human being has God sent down anything at all.' Say: 'Who sent down the Book with which Moses came, a light and guidance to mankind, which you have made into separate parchments. Some of it you disclose and much of it you conceal. And you were taught what you know not, neither you nor your fathers.' Say: 'Allah', and leave them alone sporting in their vain discourse.

وَمَا قَدَرُواْ ٱللَّهَ حَقَّ قَدۡرِهِۦٓ إِذۡ قَالُواْ مَآ أَنزَلَ ٱللَّهُ عَلَىٰ بَشَرٍ مِّن شَيۡءٍ قُلۡ مَنۡ أَنزَلَ ٱلۡكِتَٰبَ ٱلَّذِي جَآءَ بِهِۦ مُوسَىٰ نُورًا وَهُدًى لِّلنَّاسِ تَجۡعَلُونَهُۥ قَرَاطِيسَ تُبۡدُونَهَا وَتُخۡفُونَ كَثِيرًا وَعُلِّمۡتُم مَّا لَمۡ تَعۡلَمُوٓاْ أَنتُمۡ وَلَآ ءَابَآؤُكُمۡ قُلِ ٱللَّهُ ثُمَّ ذَرۡهُمۡ فِي خَوۡضِهِمۡ يَلۡعَبُونَ ٩١

---

334. This for their own benefit. Note the universality of the Qur'ānic message. It addresses itself not to the Arabs, but to the world at large. The Holy Book, even according to the testimony of the non–Muslim observers, 'has exercised a great control over the destinies of mankind, and still serves as a rule of life to a very large portion of our race' (Draper, *History of the Intellectual Development of Europe*, I, p. 340). And to them it is a matter of wonder, 'how deeply to this book Asia and America are indebted for daily guidance, how deeply Europe and America for the light of science' (Ibid., p. 345). According to a distinguished European scholar 'though the youngest of the epoch–making books, the Koran is the most widely read book ever written' (Hitti, *History of the Arabs*, p. 126).

92. And this is a Book We have sent down, blessed and confirming what has been before it. And it is sent that you may warn with it the mother of towns and those around it. And those who believe in the Hereafter believe in it and they guard the prayer.

وَهَٰذَا كِتَٰبٌ أَنزَلْنَٰهُ مُبَارَكٌ مُّصَدِّقُ ٱلَّذِى بَيْنَ يَدَيْهِ وَلِتُنذِرَ أُمَّ ٱلْقُرَىٰ وَمَنْ حَوْلَهَا ۚ وَٱلَّذِينَ يُؤْمِنُونَ بِٱلْءَاخِرَةِ يُؤْمِنُونَ بِهِۦ ۖ وَهُمْ عَلَىٰ صَلَاتِهِمْ يُحَافِظُونَ ﴿٩٢﴾

93. And who is a greater wrong-doer than one who fabricates a lie against Allah or says: 'A revelation has come to me whereas no revelation has come to him in aught', and one who says: 'I shall send down the like of what Allah has sent down.' Would that you see when the wrong-doers are in the pangs of death while the angels are stretching forth their hands saying: 'Yield up your souls; today you will be awarded a torment of ignominy for what you have been saying of Allah other than the Truth, and against His signs you were wont to be stiff-necked.'

وَمَنْ أَظْلَمُ مِمَّنِ ٱفْتَرَىٰ عَلَى ٱللَّهِ كَذِبًا أَوْ قَالَ أُوحِىَ إِلَىَّ وَلَمْ يُوحَ إِلَيْهِ شَىْءٌ ۗ وَمَن قَالَ سَأُنزِلُ مِثْلَ مَا أَنزَلَ ٱللَّهُ ۗ وَلَوْ تَرَىٰ إِذِ ٱلظَّٰلِمُونَ فِى غَمَرَٰتِ ٱلْمَوْتِ وَٱلْمَلَٰئِكَةُ بَاسِطُوٓا۟ أَيْدِيهِمْ أَخْرِجُوٓا۟ أَنفُسَكُمُ ٱلْيَوْمَ تُجْزَوْنَ عَذَابَ ٱلْهُونِ بِمَا كُنتُمْ تَقُولُونَ عَلَى ٱللَّهِ غَيْرَ ٱلْحَقِّ وَكُنتُمْ عَنْ ءَايَٰتِهِۦ تَسْتَكْبِرُونَ ﴿٩٣﴾

94. And now ye are come to Us singly even as We created you for the first time, and you have left behind your backs what We had granted to you; and We do not see along with you your intercessors whom you fancied were Our associates in respect of you as you asserted. Now are the ties between you severed, and strayed from you is what you were wont to assert.

وَلَقَدْ جِئْتُمُونَا فُرَٰدَىٰ كَمَا خَلَقْنَٰكُمْ أَوَّلَ مَرَّةٍ وَتَرَكْتُم مَّا خَوَّلْنَٰكُمْ وَرَآءَ ظُهُورِكُمْ ۖ وَمَا نَرَىٰ مَعَكُمْ شُفَعَآءَكُمُ ٱلَّذِينَ زَعَمْتُمْ أَنَّهُمْ فِيكُمْ شُرَكَٰٓؤُا۟ ۚ لَقَد تَّقَطَّعَ بَيْنَكُمْ وَضَلَّ عَنكُم مَّا كُنتُمْ تَزْعُمُونَ ﴿٩٤﴾

Section 12

95. Allah is the Cleaver of seed-grain and the date-stone, He brings forth the living from the lifeless and He is the bringer forth of the lifeless from the living. Such is Allah, so why, then, are you deviating?

إِنَّ ٱللَّهَ فَالِقُ ٱلۡحَبِّ وَٱلنَّوَىٰ يُخۡرِجُ ٱلۡحَيَّ مِنَ ٱلۡمَيِّتِ وَمُخۡرِجُ ٱلۡمَيِّتِ مِنَ ٱلۡحَيِّ ذَٰلِكُمُ ٱللَّهُ فَأَنَّىٰ تُؤۡفَكُونَ ۝

96. Cleaver of the dawn. He has appointed the night as a repose and appointed the sun and the moon according to a reckoning. That is the disposition of the Mighty, the Knowing.

فَالِقُ ٱلۡإِصۡبَاحِ وَجَعَلَ ٱلَّيۡلَ سَكَنًا وَٱلشَّمۡسَ وَٱلۡقَمَرَ حُسۡبَانًا ذَٰلِكَ تَقۡدِيرُ ٱلۡعَزِيزِ ٱلۡعَلِيمِ ۝

97. It is He Who has made for you the stars that you may be guided with them in the darkness of the land and the sea. Surely We have expounded the signs[335] for a people who know.

وَهُوَ ٱلَّذِى جَعَلَ لَكُمُ ٱلنُّجُومَ لِتَهۡتَدُواْ بِهَا فِى ظُلُمَٰتِ ٱلۡبَرِّ وَٱلۡبَحۡرِ قَدۡ فَصَّلۡنَا ٱلۡأَيَٰتِ لِقَوۡمٍ يَعۡلَمُونَ ۝

98. It is He Who has produced you from one person,[336] and provided for you an abode and a depository. Surely We have expounded the signs for a people who understand.

وَهُوَ ٱلَّذِىٓ أَنشَأَكُم مِّن نَّفۡسٍ وَٰحِدَةٍ فَمُسۡتَقَرٌّ وَمُسۡتَوۡدَعٌ قَدۡ فَصَّلۡنَا ٱلۡأَيَٰتِ لِقَوۡمٍ يَفۡقَهُونَ ۝

---

335. i.e. 'Signs of Our might, favour and uniqueness.' They demonstrate that these heavenly bodies are as much subject to His will and control as any of the humblest objects in the universe.

336. (O mankind!) i.e., from one single person, Adam. This clearly enunciates the unity of the human race. Races of men, however diverse they may be and however divergent in their characteristics, have nevertheless a common origin and have sprung from the same ancestry.

99. It is He Who has sent down water from the heaven and We have thereby brought forth growth of every kind, and out of it We have brought forth green stalks from which We produce close-growing seed-grain. And from the date-stone; from the spathe thereof come forth clusters of dates low-hanging; and gardens of grapes, and the olive, and the pomegranate, like unto one another and unlike. Look at the fruit thereof when it fruits and the reforming thereof. Verily in them are signs for a people who believe.

وَهُوَ ٱلَّذِىٓ أَنزَلَ مِنَ ٱلسَّمَآءِ مَآءً فَأَخْرَجْنَا بِهِۦ نَبَاتَ كُلِّ شَىْءٍ فَأَخْرَجْنَا مِنْهُ خَضِرًا نُّخْرِجُ مِنْهُ حَبًّا مُّتَرَاكِبًا وَمِنَ ٱلنَّخْلِ مِن طَلْعِهَا قِنْوَانٌ دَانِيَةٌ وَجَنَّٰتٍ مِّنْ أَعْنَابٍ وَٱلزَّيْتُونَ وَٱلرُّمَّانَ مُشْتَبِهًا وَغَيْرَ مُتَشَٰبِهٍ ۗ ٱنظُرُوٓا۟ إِلَىٰ ثَمَرِهِۦٓ إِذَآ أَثْمَرَ وَيَنْعِهِۦٓ ۚ إِنَّ فِى ذَٰلِكُمْ لَءَايَٰتٍ لِّقَوْمٍ يُؤْمِنُونَ ۝

100. And they have set up genii[337] as associates of Allah, whereas He has created them, and they impute to Him falsely without knowledge, sons and daughters. Hallowed be He and far above what they ascribe!

وَجَعَلُوا۟ لِلَّهِ شُرَكَآءَ ٱلْجِنَّ وَخَلَقَهُمْ ۖ وَخَرَقُوا۟ لَهُۥ بَنِينَ وَبَنَٰتٍ بِغَيْرِ عِلْمٍ ۚ سُبْحَٰنَهُۥ وَتَعَٰلَىٰ عَمَّا يَصِفُونَ ۝

---

337. *Jinn* are a definite order of conscious beings, intelligent, corporeal and usually invisible, made of smokeless flame, as men are of clay, created before Adam. They eat and drink, and propagate their species, and are subject to death, much in the same way as human beings are, though as a rule invisible to the human eye. They manifest themselves to men at will, mostly in animal form.

Section – 13

101. Originator of the heavens and the earth! How should He have a son when there is for Him no spouse?[338] He has created everything and He is the Knower of everything.

بَدِيعُ ٱلسَّمَوَٰتِ وَٱلْأَرْضِ أَنَّىٰ يَكُونُ لَهُۥ وَلَدٌ وَلَمْ تَكُن لَّهُۥ صَٰحِبَةٌ وَخَلَقَ كُلَّ شَيْءٍ وَهُوَ بِكُلِّ شَيْءٍ عَلِيمٌ ﴿١٠١﴾

102. Such is Allah, your Lord! There is no god but He,[339] the Creator of everything; so worship Him. And He is of everything a Guardian.

ذَٰلِكُمُ ٱللَّهُ رَبُّكُمْ لَا إِلَٰهَ إِلَّا هُوَ خَٰلِقُ كُلِّ شَيْءٍ فَٱعْبُدُوهُ وَهُوَ عَلَىٰ كُلِّ شَيْءٍ وَكِيلٌ ﴿١٠٢﴾

103. Sights comprehend Him not, He comprehends all sights; and He is the Subtle, the Aware.

لَّا تُدْرِكُهُ ٱلْأَبْصَٰرُ وَهُوَ يُدْرِكُ ٱلْأَبْصَٰرَ وَهُوَ ٱللَّطِيفُ ٱلْخَبِيرُ ﴿١٠٣﴾

104. Surely there has come to you enlightenment from your Lord. Whoever then will see, will do so for his own soul, and whosoever blinds himself, will do so to his own hurt. And say you: 'I am not over you an overseer.'

قَدْ جَاءَكُم بَصَائِرُ مِن رَّبِّكُمْ فَمَنْ أَبْصَرَ فَلِنَفْسِهِ وَمَنْ عَمِيَ فَعَلَيْهَا وَمَا أَنَا عَلَيْكُم بِحَفِيظٍ ﴿١٠٤﴾

---

338. This refutes the polytheism of several peoples such as the Hindus, the Babylonians, and the Egyptians, who maintained that each god had a female companion or consort. Indian polytheism went still further. 'Even God', according to the Upanishads, 'had a desire for progeny and wanted a wife unto himself for propagation' (Indira, *Status of Women in Ancient India*, pp. 129–133).

339. This is not monolatry, but the highest, the purest and the most uncompromising monotheism ever found in the religious literature of the world.

105. And thus We variously propound the revelation, and this is in order that they may say, 'you have studied', and that We may expound it to a people who know.

وَكَذَٰلِكَ نُصَرِّفُ ٱلْءَايَٰتِ وَلِيَقُولُواْ دَرَسْتَ وَلِنُبَيِّنَهُۥ لِقَوْمٍ يَعْلَمُونَ ﴿١٠٥﴾

106. Follow you what has been revealed to you by your Lord; no god is there but He, and turn you away from the polytheists.

ٱتَّبِعْ مَآ أُوحِىَ إِلَيْكَ مِن رَّبِّكَ لَآ إِلَٰهَ إِلَّا هُوَ وَأَعْرِضْ عَنِ ٱلْمُشْرِكِينَ ﴿١٠٦﴾

107. Had Allah willed, they would not have joined others with Him; and We have not made you a watcher over them. Nor are you an overseer unto them.

وَلَوْ شَآءَ ٱللَّهُ مَآ أَشْرَكُواْ وَمَا جَعَلْنَٰكَ عَلَيْهِمْ حَفِيظًا وَمَآ أَنتَ عَلَيْهِم بِوَكِيلٍ ﴿١٠٧﴾

108. Revile not those whom they invoke besides Allah, lest they may revile Allah spitefully without knowledge. Thus fair-seeming to every community We have made their work; then to their Lord is their return, and then He will declare to them what they were wont to work.

وَلَا تَسُبُّواْ ٱلَّذِينَ يَدْعُونَ مِن دُونِ ٱللَّهِ فَيَسُبُّواْ ٱللَّهَ عَدْوًۢا بِغَيْرِ عِلْمٍ كَذَٰلِكَ زَيَّنَّا لِكُلِّ أُمَّةٍ عَمَلَهُمْ ثُمَّ إِلَىٰ رَبِّهِم مَّرْجِعُهُمْ فَيُنَبِّئُهُم بِمَا كَانُواْ يَعْمَلُونَ ﴿١٠٨﴾

109. And they swore by God with you their solemn oaths: if there came to them a sign they would surely believe therein. Say: 'signs are but with Allah,[340] and what will make you perceive that even if it came they will not believe.'

وَأَقْسَمُواْ بِٱللَّهِ جَهْدَ أَيْمَٰنِهِمْ لَئِن جَآءَتْهُمْ ءَايَةٌ لَّيُؤْمِنُنَّ بِهَا قُلْ إِنَّمَا ٱلْءَايَٰتُ عِندَ ٱللَّهِ وَمَا يُشْعِرُكُمْ أَنَّهَآ إِذَا جَآءَتْ لَا يُؤْمِنُونَ ﴿١٠٩﴾

---

340. Here is one of the most important teachings of Islam. Miracles, signs, wonders, portents, or whatever they might be called, do not occur by any action of the Messenger of God, but by the power of God Himself. No miracle, however clear its evidentiary value, is ever an act of a mortal. The Prophet has no hand in its causation; he only uses it, by the command of God, as an evidence of the veracity of his claim. A miracle is nothing but an invasion of the order of nature, as known to us in common experience, by the command of the Creator of nature, to exhibit the veracity of the claims of His Messenger.

110. And We shall turn aside their hearts and their eye-sight, even as they disbelieved therein for the first time, and We shall let them wander in their exorbitance perplexed.

وَنُقَلِّبُ أَفْئِدَتَهُمْ وَأَبْصَـٰرَهُمْ كَمَا لَرْ يُؤْمِنُوا بِهِ أَوَّلَ مَرَّةٍ وَنَذَرُهُمْ فِى طُغْيَـٰنِهِمْ يَعْمَهُونَ ۝

Section 14

111. And even though We had sent down angels to them, and the dead had spoken to them, and We had gathered together about them everything face to face, they were not such as would believe, unless Allah willed; but most of them speak ignorantly.

وَلَوْ أَنَّنَا نَزَّلْنَا إِلَيْهِمُ الْمَلَـٰئِكَةَ وَكَلَّمَهُمُ الْمَوْتَىٰ وَحَشَرْنَا عَلَيْهِمْ كُلَّ شَىْءٍ قُبُلًا مَّا كَانُوا لِيُؤْمِنُوا إِلَّا أَن يَشَاءَ اللَّهُ وَلَـٰكِنَّ أَكْثَرَهُمْ يَجْهَلُونَ ۝

112. In this way We have appointed to every Prophet an enemy – devils among men and *jinn* – inspiring to each other gilded speech as a delusion. And had your Lord willed, they could not have done so. So leave them alone to their fabrication.

وَكَذَٰلِكَ جَعَلْنَا لِكُلِّ نَبِيٍّ عَدُوًّا شَيَـٰطِينَ الْإِنسِ وَالْجِنِّ يُوحِى بَعْضُهُمْ إِلَىٰ بَعْضٍ زُخْرُفَ الْقَوْلِ غُرُورًا وَلَوْ شَاءَ رَبُّكَ مَا فَعَلُوهُ فَذَرْهُمْ وَمَا يَفْتَرُونَ ۝

113. And this is in order that the hearts of those who do not believe in the Hereafter may incline to it, and that they may remain pleased with it, and that they may do what they are doing.

وَلِتَصْغَىٰ إِلَيْهِ أَفْئِدَةُ الَّذِينَ لَا يُؤْمِنُونَ بِالْآخِرَةِ وَلِيَرْضَوْهُ وَلِيَقْتَرِفُوا مَا هُم مُّقْتَرِفُونَ ۝

114. Say: 'Shall I then seek as judge other than Allah, when it is He Who has sent down toward you the Book[341] detailed.' And those whom We have vouchsafed the Book know that it has been sent down by your Lord in truth; so be not you of the doubters.

أَفَغَيْرَ ٱللَّهِ أَبْتَغِى حَكَمًا وَهُوَ ٱلَّذِىٓ أَنزَلَ إِلَيْكُمُ ٱلْكِتَٰبَ مُفَصَّلًا وَٱلَّذِينَ ءَاتَيْنَٰهُمُ ٱلْكِتَٰبَ يَعْلَمُونَ أَنَّهُۥ مُنَزَّلٌ مِّن رَّبِّكَ بِٱلْحَقِّ فَلَا تَكُونَنَّ مِنَ ٱلْمُمْتَرِينَ ۝

115. Perfected is the Word of your Lord in veracity and justice, and none can change His Word. And He is the Hearer, the Knower.

وَتَمَّتْ كَلِمَتُ رَبِّكَ صِدْقًا وَعَدْلًا لَّا مُبَدِّلَ لِكَلِمَٰتِهِۦ وَهُوَ ٱلسَّمِيعُ ٱلْعَلِيمُ ۝

116. If you obey most of them on earth, they would lead you away from the way of Allah, they follow only their fancy and that but conjecture.

وَإِن تُطِعْ أَكْثَرَ مَن فِى ٱلْأَرْضِ يُضِلُّوكَ عَن سَبِيلِ ٱللَّهِ إِن يَتَّبِعُونَ إِلَّا ٱلظَّنَّ وَإِنْ هُمْ إِلَّا يَخْرُصُونَ ۝

117. Surely your Lord! He knows best who strays and He knows best the guided ones.

إِنَّ رَبَّكَ هُوَ أَعْلَمُ مَن يَضِلُّ عَن سَبِيلِهِۦ وَهُوَ أَعْلَمُ بِٱلْمُهْتَدِينَ ۝

118. Eat of that flesh over which the name of Allah has been pronounced, if you are believers in His revelations.

فَكُلُواْ مِمَّا ذُكِرَ ٱسْمُ ٱللَّهِ عَلَيْهِ إِن كُنتُم بِـَٔايَٰتِهِۦ مُؤْمِنِينَ ۝

119. And why should you not eat that flesh over which the name of Allah has been pronounced, while He has surely detailed for you what He has forbidden you, unless you are driven thereto? Surely many lead others astray by their desires without knowledge. Surely your Lord! He knows best the transgressors.

وَمَا لَكُمْ أَلَّا تَأْكُلُواْ مِمَّا ذُكِرَ ٱسْمُ ٱللَّهِ عَلَيْهِ وَقَدْ فَصَّلَ لَكُم مَّا حَرَّمَ عَلَيْكُمْ إِلَّا مَا ٱضْطُرِرْتُمْ إِلَيْهِ وَإِنَّ كَثِيرًا لَّيُضِلُّونَ بِأَهْوَآئِهِم بِغَيْرِ عِلْمٍ إِنَّ رَبَّكَ هُوَ أَعْلَمُ بِٱلْمُعْتَدِينَ ۝

341. Unique in the whole class of religious Scriptures, and miraculous in its excellences both literary and spiritual.

120. Leave the outside sin and its inside. Surely those who earn sin shall be requited for what they have earned.

121. And do not eat of that over which the name of Allah has not been pronounced; that is sinful. Surely the devils are ever inspiring their friends to wrangle with you. If you obey them, then you will become associaters indeed.

Section 15

122. Is he who was dead and We quickened him, and appointed for him a light with which he walks among mankind, like him who is in darkness from which he cannot emerge? Even so is made fair-seeming to the infidels what they are wont to do.

123. And even so We set up in every town great ones as sinners that they may plot therein; and they plot not save against themselves and they do not perceive.

124. And when there comes to them a sign, they say: 'We shall not believe until we are vouchsafed the like of what is vouchsafed to the Messengers of Allah.' Allah knows best where to place His Messengership. Surely vileness before Allah and severe chastisement shall befall those who have sinned for what they were wont to plot.

وَذَرُوْا ظَاهِرَ الْإِثْمِ وَبَاطِنَهُ ۚ إِنَّ الَّذِيْنَ يَكْسِبُوْنَ الْإِثْمَ سَيُجْزَوْنَ بِمَا كَانُوْا يَقْتَرِفُوْنَ ۝

وَلَا تَأْكُلُوْا مِمَّا لَمْ يُذْكَرِ اسْمُ اللّٰهِ عَلَيْهِ وَإِنَّهُ لَفِسْقٌ ۗ وَإِنَّ الشَّيَاطِيْنَ لَيُوْحُوْنَ إِلَىٰٓ أَوْلِيَآئِهِمْ لِيُجَادِلُوْكُمْ ۚ وَإِنْ أَطَعْتُمُوْهُمْ إِنَّكُمْ لَمُشْرِكُوْنَ ۝

أَوَمَنْ كَانَ مَيْتًا فَأَحْيَيْنَاهُ وَجَعَلْنَا لَهُ نُوْرًا يَمْشِيْ بِهِ فِي النَّاسِ كَمَنْ مَثَلُهُ فِي الظُّلُمَاتِ لَيْسَ بِخَارِجٍ مِنْهَا ۚ كَذَلِكَ زُيِّنَ لِلْكَافِرِيْنَ مَا كَانُوْا يَعْمَلُوْنَ ۝

وَكَذَلِكَ جَعَلْنَا فِيْ كُلِّ قَرْيَةٍ أَكَابِرَ مُجْرِمِيْهَا لِيَمْكُرُوْا فِيْهَا ۖ وَمَا يَمْكُرُوْنَ إِلَّا بِأَنْفُسِهِمْ وَمَا يَشْعُرُوْنَ ۝

وَإِذَا جَآءَتْهُمْ ءَايَةٌ قَالُوْا لَنْ نُّؤْمِنَ حَتَّىٰ نُؤْتَىٰ مِثْلَ مَآ أُوْتِيَ رُسُلُ اللّٰهِ ۘ اللّٰهُ أَعْلَمُ حَيْثُ يَجْعَلُ رِسَالَتَهُ ۗ سَيُصِيْبُ الَّذِيْنَ أَجْرَمُوْا صَغَارٌ عِنْدَ اللّٰهِ وَعَذَابٌ شَدِيْدٌ بِمَا كَانُوْا يَمْكُرُوْنَ ۝

125. So whom Allah wills that He shall guide, He expands his breast for Islam; and whom He wills that He shall send astray, He makes his breast strait, narrow, as if he was mounting up to the heaven. Thus Allah lays the abomination on those who believe not.

فَمَن يُرِدِ اللَّهُ أَن يَهْدِيَهُ يَشْرَحْ صَدْرَهُ لِلْإِسْلَامِ وَمَن يُرِدْ أَن يُضِلَّهُ يَجْعَلْ صَدْرَهُ ضَيِّقًا حَرَجًا كَأَنَّمَا يَصَّعَّدُ فِي السَّمَاءِ كَذَٰلِكَ يَجْعَلُ اللَّهُ الرِّجْسَ عَلَى الَّذِينَ لَا يُؤْمِنُونَ ۝

126. And this is the straight path of your Lord. Certainly We have explained the revelation to a people who would be admonished.

وَهَٰذَا صِرَاطُ رَبِّكَ مُسْتَقِيمًا قَدْ فَصَّلْنَا الْآيَاتِ لِقَوْمٍ يَذَّكَّرُونَ ۝

127. Theirs is an abode of peace with their Lord; and He shall be their patron for what they have been doing.

لَهُمْ دَارُ السَّلَامِ عِندَ رَبِّهِمْ وَهُوَ وَلِيُّهُم بِمَا كَانُوا يَعْمَلُونَ ۝

128. On the day when He will gather them all together: 'O company of *jinn*! You have made much of mankind.' And their friends among mankind will say: 'Our Lord! Much use some of us made of others, and now we have reached the appointed term which You appointed for us.' He will say: 'The Fire shall be your abode where you shall be as abiders, save as Allah may will. Surely your Lord is the Wise, the Knowing.'

وَيَوْمَ يَحْشُرُهُمْ جَمِيعًا يَامَعْشَرَ الْجِنِّ قَدِ اسْتَكْثَرْتُم مِّنَ الْإِنسِ وَقَالَ أَوْلِيَاؤُهُم مِّنَ الْإِنسِ رَبَّنَا اسْتَمْتَعَ بَعْضُنَا بِبَعْضٍ وَبَلَغْنَا أَجَلَنَا الَّذِي أَجَّلْتَ لَنَا قَالَ النَّارُ مَثْوَاكُمْ خَالِدِينَ فِيهَا إِلَّا مَا شَاءَ اللَّهُ إِنَّ رَبَّكَ حَكِيمٌ عَلِيمٌ ۝

129. And thus We shall keep some of the wrong-doers close to others for what they were wont to earn.

وَكَذَٰلِكَ نُوَلِّي بَعْضَ الظَّالِمِينَ بَعْضًا بِمَا كَانُوا يَكْسِبُونَ ۝

Section 16

130. 'O company of *jinn* and mankind! Did not there come to you Messengers from amongst you, recounting to you My signs and warning you of your meeting of this Day?' They shall say: 'We witness against ourselves.' Indeed the life of the world had deluded them, and they shall bear witness against themselves that they had been infidels.

يَـٰمَعْشَرَ الْجِنِّ وَالْإِنسِ أَلَمْ يَأْتِكُمْ رُسُلٌ مِّنكُمْ يَقُصُّونَ عَلَيْكُمْ ءَايَـٰتِى وَيُنذِرُونَكُمْ لِقَآءَ يَوْمِكُمْ هَـٰذَا قَالُوا۟ شَهِدْنَا عَلَىٰٓ أَنفُسِنَا وَغَرَّتْهُمُ الْحَيَوٰةُ الدُّنْيَا وَشَهِدُوا۟ عَلَىٰٓ أَنفُسِهِمْ أَنَّهُمْ كَانُوا۟ كَـٰفِرِينَ ﴿١٣٠﴾

131. This is because your Lord is not one to destroy a township arbitrarily for its wrong-doing while its people are unaware.

ذَٰلِكَ أَن لَّمْ يَكُن رَّبُّكَ مُهْلِكَ الْقُرَىٰ بِظُلْمٍ وَأَهْلُهَا غَـٰفِلُونَ ﴿١٣١﴾

132. For all there will be degrees in accordance with what they did and your Lord is not unaware of what they do.

وَلِكُلٍّ دَرَجَـٰتٌ مِّمَّا عَمِلُوا۟ وَمَا رَبُّكَ بِغَـٰفِلٍ عَمَّا يَعْمَلُونَ ﴿١٣٢﴾

133. And your Lord is Self-Sufficient, the Owner of Mercy. If He wills he can take you away, and make those succeed you, after you, whom He pleases, even as He raised you from the seed of another people.

وَرَبُّكَ الْغَنِىُّ ذُو الرَّحْمَةِ إِن يَشَأْ يُذْهِبْكُمْ وَيَسْتَخْلِفْ مِنۢ بَعْدِكُم مَّا يَشَآءُ كَمَآ أَنشَأَكُم مِّن ذُرِّيَّةِ قَوْمٍ ءَاخَرِينَ ﴿١٣٣﴾

134. Certainly what you are promised is sure to arrive, and you cannot escape.

إِنَّ مَا تُوعَدُونَ لَءَاتٍ وَمَآ أَنتُم بِمُعْجِزِينَ ﴿١٣٤﴾

135. Say: 'O my people! Go on acting in your way; indeed I am going to act in my way; presently you shall know what will be the happy end of the abode; and surely the wrong-doers shall not fare well.'

قُل يَٰقَوْمِ ٱعْمَلُوا۟ عَلَىٰ مَكَانَتِكُمْ إِنِّي عَامِلٌ فَسَوْفَ تَعْلَمُونَ مَن تَكُونُ لَهُۥ عَٰقِبَةُ ٱلدَّارِ إِنَّهُۥ لَا يُفْلِحُ ٱلظَّٰلِمُونَ ۝

136. And they set aside for Allah a portion of the tilth and cattle He had produced, and they say according to their fancy: 'This is for Allah, and this is for our associate-gods.' Then what is for their associate-gods does not reach Allah, while what is for Allah reaches their associate-gods; vile is the way they judge!

وَجَعَلُوا۟ لِلَّهِ مِمَّا ذَرَأَ مِنَ ٱلْحَرْثِ وَٱلْأَنْعَٰمِ نَصِيبًا فَقَالُوا۟ هَٰذَا لِلَّهِ بِزَعْمِهِمْ وَهَٰذَا لِشُرَكَآئِنَا فَمَا كَانَ لِشُرَكَآئِهِمْ فَلَا يَصِلُ إِلَى ٱللَّهِ وَمَا كَانَ لِلَّهِ فَهُوَ يَصِلُ إِلَىٰ شُرَكَآئِهِمْ سَآءَ مَا يَحْكُمُونَ ۝

137. And even so their associate-gods have made fair-seeming to many of the idolaters the killing of their offspring so that they may cause them to perish and that they may confuse them in their faith. And had Allah so willed they would have not done it. Therefore leave them alone and what they fabricate.

وَكَذَٰلِكَ زَيَّنَ لِكَثِيرٍ مِّنَ ٱلْمُشْرِكِينَ قَتْلَ أَوْلَٰدِهِمْ شُرَكَآؤُهُمْ لِيُرْدُوهُمْ وَلِيَلْبِسُوا۟ عَلَيْهِمْ دِينَهُمْ وَلَوْ شَآءَ ٱللَّهُ مَا فَعَلُوهُ فَذَرْهُمْ وَمَا يَفْتَرُونَ ۝

138. And they say according to their fancy: 'Such cattle and tilth are ta-boo; none shall eat of them save whom we allow.' And there are camels whose backs are forbidden, and cattle over which they do not pronounce the name of Allah: a fabrication against Him. Accordingly He shall requite them for what they were wont to fabricate.

وَقَالُوا۟ هَٰذِهِۦ أَنْعَٰمٌ وَحَرْثٌ حِجْرٌ لَّا يَطْعَمُهَآ إِلَّا مَن نَّشَآءُ بِزَعْمِهِمْ وَأَنْعَٰمٌ حُرِّمَتْ ظُهُورُهَا وَأَنْعَٰمٌ لَّا يَذْكُرُونَ ٱسْمَ ٱللَّهِ عَلَيْهَا ٱفْتِرَآءً عَلَيْهِ سَيَجْزِيهِم بِمَا كَانُوا۟ يَفْتَرُونَ ۝

139. And they say: 'What is in the bellies of such cattle is for our males alone, and is forbidden to our wives, and if it be born dead, then they all are partakers of it.' 'Surely He shall requite them for their attribution; He is the Wise, the Knowing.

وَقَالُوا۟ مَا فِى بُطُونِ هَٰذِهِ ٱلْأَنْعَٰمِ خَالِصَةٌ لِّذُكُورِنَا وَمُحَرَّمٌ عَلَىٰٓ أَزْوَٰجِنَا ۖ وَإِن يَكُن مَّيْتَةً فَهُمْ فِيهِ شُرَكَآءُ ۚ سَيَجْزِيهِمْ وَصْفَهُمْ ۚ إِنَّهُۥ حَكِيمٌ عَلِيمٌ ﴿١٣٩﴾

140. Assuredly lost are they who slay their offspring[342] foolishly and without knowledge; and have forbidden what Allah had provided for them: a fabrication against Allah: surely they have strayed and have not become the guided ones.

قَدْ خَسِرَ ٱلَّذِينَ قَتَلُوٓا۟ أَوْلَٰدَهُمْ سَفَهًۢا بِغَيْرِ عِلْمٍ وَحَرَّمُوا۟ مَا رَزَقَهُمُ ٱللَّهُ ٱفْتِرَآءً عَلَى ٱللَّهِ ۚ قَدْ ضَلُّوا۟ وَمَا كَانُوا۟ مُهْتَدِينَ ﴿١٤٠﴾

Section 17

141. And it is He Who has produced gardens, trellised and untrellised, and the date-palm and the corn of varied produce, and the olives and the pomegranates, alike and unlike. Eat of the fruits when they ripen and give what is due of them on the day of harvesting; and waste not; He does not approve the wasters.

وَهُوَ ٱلَّذِىٓ أَنشَأَ جَنَّٰتٍ مَّعْرُوشَٰتٍ وَغَيْرَ مَعْرُوشَٰتٍ وَٱلنَّخْلَ وَٱلزَّرْعَ مُخْتَلِفًا أُكُلُهُۥ وَٱلزَّيْتُونَ وَٱلرُّمَّانَ مُتَشَٰبِهًا وَغَيْرَ مُتَشَٰبِهٍ ۚ كُلُوا۟ مِن ثَمَرِهِۦٓ إِذَآ أَثْمَرَ وَءَاتُوا۟ حَقَّهُۥ يَوْمَ حَصَادِهِۦ ۖ وَلَا تُسْرِفُوٓا۟ ۚ إِنَّهُۥ لَا يُحِبُّ ٱلْمُسْرِفِينَ ﴿١٤١﴾

---

342. The practice of infanticide has been almost universal, neither Greece nor Rome being immune. So the reform effected by Islam was a world reform. 'In sharp contrast to the modern anxiety to lessen child mortality' is the extent in the ancient civilizations 'of the practice of infanticide or of putting new born infants to death or of allowing them to die' (*EBr.* XII. p. 322). The reference may also be to the practice of coitus interruption and other methods of birth control.

142. And of the cattle He has created beasts of burden and small ones. Eat of what Allah has provided for you and follow not the footsteps of Satan, for he is a manifest foe to you.

وَمِنَ ٱلْأَنْعَمِ حَمُولَةً وَفَرْشًا كُلُوا۟ مِمَّا رَزَقَكُمُ ٱللَّهُ وَلَا تَتَّبِعُوا۟ خُطُوَٰتِ ٱلشَّيْطَٰنِ إِنَّهُۥ لَكُمْ عَدُوٌّ مُّبِينٌ ۝

143. Allah has created eight pairs; of the sheep a twain, of the goats a twain. Say: 'Is it the two males He has forbidden or the two females, or what the wombs of the females contain? Declare to me with knowledge, if you are truth-tellers.'

ثَمَٰنِيَةَ أَزْوَٰجٍ مِّنَ ٱلضَّأْنِ ٱثْنَيْنِ وَمِنَ ٱلْمَعْزِ ٱثْنَيْنِ قُلْ ءَآلذَّكَرَيْنِ حَرَّمَ أَمِ ٱلْأُنثَيَيْنِ أَمَّا ٱشْتَمَلَتْ عَلَيْهِ أَرْحَامُ ٱلْأُنثَيَيْنِ نَبِّـُٔونِي بِعِلْمٍ إِن كُنتُمْ صَٰدِقِينَ ۝

144. Of the camels He has created a twain and of the oxen a twain. Say: 'Is it the two males He has forbidden or the two females, or what the wombs of the females contain? Were you present when Allah enjoined this on you? Who then does greater wrong than he who fabricates a lie against Allah that he may lead people astray; surely Allah does not guide a wrong-doing people.'

وَمِنَ ٱلْإِبِلِ ٱثْنَيْنِ وَمِنَ ٱلْبَقَرِ ٱثْنَيْنِ قُلْ ءَآلذَّكَرَيْنِ حَرَّمَ أَمِ ٱلْأُنثَيَيْنِ أَمَّا ٱشْتَمَلَتْ عَلَيْهِ أَرْحَامُ ٱلْأُنثَيَيْنِ أَمْ كُنتُمْ شُهَدَآءَ إِذْ وَصَّىٰكُمُ ٱللَّهُ بِهَٰذَا فَمَنْ أَظْلَمُ مِمَّنِ ٱفْتَرَىٰ عَلَى ٱللَّهِ كَذِبًا لِّيُضِلَّ ٱلنَّاسَ بِغَيْرِ عِلْمٍ إِنَّ ٱللَّهَ لَا يَهْدِى ٱلْقَوْمَ ٱلظَّٰلِمِينَ ۝

Section 18

145. Say: 'I do not find in what has been revealed to me anything forbidden to an eater who eats thereof except it be carcass, running blood or swine-flesh, for that indeed is foul, or an abomination over which is invoked the name of other

قُل لَّآ أَجِدُ فِى مَآ أُوحِىَ إِلَىَّ مُحَرَّمًا عَلَىٰ طَاعِمٍ يَطْعَمُهُۥٓ إِلَّآ أَن يَكُونَ مَيْتَةً أَوْ دَمًا مَّسْفُوحًا أَوْ لَحْمَ خِنزِيرٍ فَإِنَّهُۥ رِجْسٌ أَوْ فِسْقًا أُهِلَّ لِغَيْرِ ٱللَّهِ بِهِۦ

than that of Allah. Then whosoever is driven thereto neither lusting nor transgressing, your Lord is indeed the Forgiving, the Merciful.

فَمَنِ اضْطُرَّ غَيْرَ بَاغٍ وَلَا عَادٍ فَإِنَّ رَبَّكَ غَفُورٌ رَّحِيمٌ ﴿١٤٥﴾

146. And to them who are Judaized We forbade every animal with cloven hoof; and of the bullock and the goats We forbade to them the fat thereof, save what is borne on their backs or entrails or what sticks to the bones. Thus We requited them for their rebellion and We are the Truthful.

وَعَلَى الَّذِينَ هَادُوا حَرَّمْنَا كُلَّ ذِي ظُفُرٍ وَمِنَ الْبَقَرِ وَالْغَنَمِ حَرَّمْنَا عَلَيْهِمْ شُحُومَهُمَا إِلَّا مَا حَمَلَتْ ظُهُورُهُمَا أَوِ الْحَوَايَا أَوْ مَا اخْتَلَطَ بِعَظْمٍ ذَلِكَ جَزَيْنَاهُم بِبَغْيِهِمْ وَإِنَّا لَصَادِقُونَ ﴿١٤٦﴾

147. Now if they belie you, say you: 'Your Lord is the Owner of extensive mercy, and His wrath shall not be turned aside from the guilty people.'

فَإِن كَذَّبُوكَ فَقُل رَّبُّكُمْ ذُو رَحْمَةٍ وَاسِعَةٍ وَلَا يُرَدُّ بَأْسُهُ عَنِ الْقَوْمِ الْمُجْرِمِينَ ﴿١٤٧﴾

148. Soon will those who associate say: 'Had Allah willed we would not have associated, nor our fathers,[343] neither could we have forbidden aught.' Likewise belied those before them, until they tasted Our wrath. Say: 'Is there with you any authority that you may bring it forth to us? You are following only your fancy and only conjecturing.'

سَيَقُولُ الَّذِينَ أَشْرَكُوا لَوْ شَاءَ اللَّهُ مَا أَشْرَكْنَا وَلَا آبَاؤُنَا وَلَا حَرَّمْنَا مِن شَيْءٍ كَذَلِكَ كَذَّبَ الَّذِينَ مِن قَبْلِهِم حَتَّى ذَاقُوا بَأْسَنَا قُلْ هَلْ عِندَكُم مِّنْ عِلْمٍ فَتُخْرِجُوهُ لَنَا إِن تَتَّبِعُونَ إِلَّا الظَّنَّ وَإِنْ أَنتُمْ إِلَّا تَخْرُصُونَ ﴿١٤٨﴾

---

343. The pagans used the word willed in the sense of pleased or approved — they confused the former with the latter and therein lay the fallacy. Their meaning was: if God really approved of the faith of Islam and disapproved of idolatry, He would not let us go on with our worship of false gods. Thus they confused the power and ability bestowed by God on everyone to do whatever he chose with the approval of every course of action. Surely it is God the Creator Who has brought into being the deadliest of poisons; does it follow that He approves of the business of professional poisoners?

149. Say: 'With Allah rests the argument evident. Therefore had He so willed, He would have guided you all.'

قُل فَلِلَّهِ الۡحُجَّةُ الۡبَالِغَةُ فَلَوۡ شَاۤءَ لَهَدٰىكُمۡ أَجۡمَعِيۡنَ ﴿١٤٩﴾

150. Say: Here with your witnesses those who will testify that He has forbidden all this.' Then even if they testify, testify you not with them. And follow you not caprices of those who belie Our signs and those who believe not in the Hereafter while they ascribe equals to their Lord.

قُلۡ هَلُمَّ شُهَدَاۤءَكُمُ الَّذِيۡنَ يَشۡهَدُوۡنَ أَنَّ اللَّهَ حَرَّمَ هٰذَا فَإِن شَهِدُوۡا فَلَا تَشۡهَدۡ مَعَهُمۡ وَلَا تَتَّبِعۡ أَهۡوَاۤءَ الَّذِيۡنَ كَذَّبُوۡا بِاٰيَاتِنَا وَالَّذِيۡنَ لَا يُؤۡمِنُوۡنَ بِالۡاٰخِرَةِ وَهُم بِرَبِّهِمۡ يَعۡدِلُوۡنَ ﴿١٥٠﴾

Section 19

151. Say: 'Come, I shall recite what your Lord has forbidden to you: Associate not anyone with Him and show kindness to your parents, and kill not your offspring for fear of want – We it is Who shall provide for you and them[344] – and approach not indecencies, whether openly or in secret, and slay not anyone whom Allah has forbidden, except for a just cause. In this wise He exhorts you that perhaps you may reflect.

قُلۡ تَعَالَوۡا أَتۡلُ مَا حَرَّمَ رَبُّكُمۡ عَلَيۡكُمۡ أَلَّا تُشۡرِكُوۡا بِهِ شَيۡئًا وَبِالۡوَالِدَيۡنِ إِحۡسَانًا وَلَا تَقۡتُلُوۡا أَوۡلَادَكُم مِّنۡ إِمۡلَاقٍ نَّحۡنُ نَرۡزُقُكُمۡ وَإِيَّاهُمۡ وَلَا تَقۡرَبُوا الۡفَوَاحِشَ مَا ظَهَرَ مِنۡهَا وَمَا بَطَنَ وَلَا تَقۡتُلُوا النَّفۡسَ الَّتِى حَرَّمَ اللَّهُ إِلَّا بِالۡحَقِّ ذٰلِكُمۡ وَصَّاكُمۡ بِهِ لَعَلَّكُمۡ تَعۡقِلُوۡنَ ﴿١٥١﴾

---

344. It is in consonance with this Divine guarantee that, contrary to what Malthus and his disciples calculated, the population has not outrun the means of subsistence, and the truth of the old economic adage has been completely vindicated that 'while every addition to the population means another mouth to feed, it also implies another pair of hands'.

152. And do not approach the substance of an orphan save with what is best until he reaches maturity, and fill up the measure and balance with equity. We burden not a soul except according to its capacity. And when you speak, be fair, even though it be against a kinsman: and fulfill the covenant of Allah. In this wise He enjoins you that perhaps you may be admonished.'

وَلَا تَقْرَبُوا مَالَ الْيَتِيمِ إِلَّا بِالَّتِي هِيَ أَحْسَنُ حَتَّىٰ يَبْلُغَ أَشُدَّهُ وَأَوْفُوا الْكَيْلَ وَالْمِيزَانَ بِالْقِسْطِ لَا نُكَلِّفُ نَفْسًا إِلَّا وُسْعَهَا وَإِذَا قُلْتُمْ فَاعْدِلُوا وَلَوْ كَانَ ذَا قُرْبَىٰ وَبِعَهْدِ اللَّهِ أَوْفُوا ذَٰلِكُمْ وَصَّىٰكُم بِهِ لَعَلَّكُمْ تَذَكَّرُونَ ۝

153. And also that: 'This is My path, straight; follow it then, and do not follow other ways; that will deviate you from His way. In this wise He enjoins you that perhaps you fear Allah.'

وَأَنَّ هَٰذَا صِرَاطِي مُسْتَقِيمًا فَاتَّبِعُوهُ وَلَا تَتَّبِعُوا السُّبُلَ فَتَفَرَّقَ بِكُمْ عَن سَبِيلِهِ ذَٰلِكُمْ وَصَّىٰكُم بِهِ لَعَلَّكُمْ تَتَّقُونَ ۝

154. To Moses We gave the Book, perfect for him who would do good and detailing everything and a guidance and a blessing that perhaps in the meeting of their Lord they would believe.

ثُمَّ ءَاتَيْنَا مُوسَى الْكِتَابَ تَمَامًا عَلَى الَّذِي أَحْسَنَ وَتَفْصِيلًا لِكُلِّ شَيْءٍ وَهُدًى وَرَحْمَةً لَّعَلَّهُم بِلِقَاءِ رَبِّهِمْ يُؤْمِنُونَ ۝

Section 20

155. And this is a Book We have sent down, blest, follow it then and fear Allah, that you may be shown mercy.

وَهَٰذَا كِتَابٌ أَنزَلْنَاهُ مُبَارَكٌ فَاتَّبِعُوهُ وَاتَّقُوا لَعَلَّكُمْ تُرْحَمُونَ ۝

156. Lest you should say: 'The Book was only sent down to the two sects before us, and we were in fact unaware of their readings.'

أَن تَقُولُوا إِنَّمَا أُنزِلَ الْكِتَابُ عَلَىٰ طَائِفَتَيْنِ مِن قَبْلِنَا وَإِن كُنَّا عَن دِرَاسَتِهِمْ لَغَافِلِينَ ۝

157. Or lest you should say: 'If only the Book had been sent down to us, we should surely have been better guided than they.' So now surely there has come to you an evidence from your Lord and a guidance and a mercy. Who then does a greater wrong than he who belies the signs of Allah and shuns them? Soon We will requite those who shun Our signs with an evil chastisement inasmuch as they were wont to shun them.

أَوْ تَقُوْلُوْۤا لَوْ أَنَّاۤ أُنْزِلَ عَلَيْنَا الْكِتٰبُ لَكُنَّاۤ أَهْدٰى مِنْهُمْ فَقَدْ جَآءَكُمْ بَيِّنَةٌ مِّنْ رَّبِّكُمْ وَهُدًى وَّرَحْمَةٌ فَمَنْ أَظْلَمُ مِمَّنْ كَذَّبَ بِاٰيٰتِ اللّٰهِ وَصَدَفَ عَنْهَا سَنَجْزِى الَّذِيْنَ يَصْدِفُوْنَ عَنْ اٰيٰتِنَا سُوْٓءَ الْعَذَابِ بِمَا كَانُوْا يَصْدِفُوْنَ ۝

158. They await indeed that the angels should come to them or that your Lord should come, or that certain of the signs of your Lord should come. On the Day when certain of the signs of your Lord will come, belief will not avail any person who had not believed before or had not earned any good by his belief. Say: 'Well, wait and we also are waiting.'

هَلْ يَنْظُرُوْنَ إِلَّاۤ أَنْ تَأْتِيَهُمُ الْمَلٰٓئِكَةُ أَوْ يَأْتِيَ رَبُّكَ أَوْ يَأْتِيَ بَعْضُ اٰيٰتِ رَبِّكَ يَوْمَ يَأْتِيْ بَعْضُ اٰيٰتِ رَبِّكَ لَا يَنْفَعُ نَفْسًا إِيْمَانُهَا لَمْ تَكُنْ اٰمَنَتْ مِنْ قَبْلُ أَوْ كَسَبَتْ فِيْ إِيْمَانِهَا خَيْرًا قُلِ انْتَظِرُوْۤا إِنَّا مُنْتَظِرُوْنَ ۝

159. Assuredly, those who have split their religion and become sects,[345] you are not amongst them in aught; their affair is only with Allah. Then He will declare to them what they had been wont to do.

إِنَّ الَّذِيْنَ فَرَّقُوْا دِيْنَهُمْ وَكَانُوْا شِيَعًا لَّسْتَ مِنْهُمْ فِيْ شَيْءٍ إِنَّمَاۤ أَمْرُهُمْ إِلَى اللّٰهِ ثُمَّ يُنَبِّئُهُمْ بِمَا كَانُوْا يَفْعَلُوْنَ ۝

---

345. Having done so by schisms. The allusion seems to made in particular, to the interminable schisms and endless squabbles, divisions and subdivisions of the Church, as it existed in the time of the Holy Prophet. The Church, at this time, writes an American Christian, 'through the ambition and wickedness of its clergy, had been brought into a condition of anarchy. In the East the Church had been torn in pieces by contentions and schisms. Among a countless host of disputants may be mentioned Arians, Basilidians, Carpocratians, Collyridians, Eutychians, Gnostics, Jacobites, Marcionites, Marionites, Nestorians, Sabellians, Valentinians. Of these, the Marionites regarded the Trinity as consisting of God the Father, God the Son, and God the Virgin Mary, the Collyridians worshipped the Virgin as a divinity, offering her sacrifices of cakes' (Draper, *History of the Conflict Between Religion and Science*, pp. 78–79).

160. Whoso will come with a virtue, for him there shall be ten like thereof, and whoever will come with vice shall not be requited save with the like thereof, and they shall not be wronged.

مَن جَآءَ بِٱلْحَسَنَةِ فَلَهُ عَشْرُ أَمْثَالِهَا وَمَن جَآءَ بِٱلسَّيِّئَةِ فَلَا يُجْزَىٰ إِلَّا مِثْلَهَا وَهُمْ لَا يُظْلَمُونَ ۝

161. Say: 'As for me, my Lord has guided me to a straight path, a right religion, the faith of Abraham, the upright, and he was not of the polytheists.'

قُلْ إِنَّنِي هَدَىٰنِي رَبِّي إِلَىٰ صِرَٰطٍ مُّسْتَقِيمٍ دِينًا قِيَمًا مِّلَّةَ إِبْرَٰهِيمَ حَنِيفًا وَمَا كَانَ مِنَ ٱلْمُشْرِكِينَ ۝

162. Say: 'Surely my prayer and my rites and my life and my death are all for Allah, Lord of the worlds.

قُلْ إِنَّ صَلَاتِي وَنُسُكِي وَمَحْيَايَ وَمَمَاتِي لِلَّهِ رَبِّ ٱلْعَٰلَمِينَ ۝

163. No associate has He. To this I am bidden, and I am the first of the Muslims.'

لَا شَرِيكَ لَهُۥ وَبِذَٰلِكَ أُمِرْتُ وَأَنَا۠ أَوَّلُ ٱلْمُسْلِمِينَ ۝

164. Say: 'Shall I seek a Lord, other than Allah, while He is the Lord of everything? And no person earns anything save against himself, and no bearer of burden shall bear another's burden.' Thereafter, to your Lord shall be your return and He shall declare to you that concerning which you have been disputing.

قُلْ أَغَيْرَ ٱللَّهِ أَبْغِي رَبًّا وَهُوَ رَبُّ كُلِّ شَيْءٍ وَلَا تَكْسِبُ كُلُّ نَفْسٍ إِلَّا عَلَيْهَا وَلَا تَزِرُ وَازِرَةٌ وِزْرَ أُخْرَىٰ ثُمَّ إِلَىٰ رَبِّكُم مَّرْجِعُكُمْ فَيُنَبِّئُكُم بِمَا كُنتُمْ فِيهِ تَخْتَلِفُونَ ۝

165. And He it is Who has made you vicegerents on the earth, and has raised some of you over others in degrees, that He might try you in what He has bestowed on you. Surely Swift is your Lord in retribution, and surely He is the Forgiving, the Merciful.

وَهُوَ ٱلَّذِي جَعَلَكُمْ خَلَٰٓئِفَ ٱلْأَرْضِ وَرَفَعَ بَعْضَكُمْ فَوْقَ بَعْضٍ دَرَجَٰتٍ لِّيَبْلُوَكُمْ فِي مَآ ءَاتَىٰكُمْ إِنَّ رَبَّكَ سَرِيعُ ٱلْعِقَابِ وَإِنَّهُۥ لَغَفُورٌ رَّحِيمٌ ۝

Sūrah 7

al-A'rāf

(Makkan, 24 Sections, 206 Verses)

In the name of Allah, the Compassionate, the Merciful.

Section 1

1. *Alif, Lām, Mīm, Ṣād.*

2. This is a Book sent down to you; so let there be no straitness in your breast therefor; that you may warn, and this is an admonition to the faithful.

3. Follow what has been brought down to you from your Lord, and do not follow any patrons beside Him; yet little are you admonished.

4. And many a town We have destroyed; upon them Our scourge came at night or while they were taking their midday rest.

5. Then naught was their cry when Our scourge came upon them save that they said: 'Indeed we have been the wrong-doers.'

6. Then We will surely question those to whom Our Messengers were sent, and We will surely question the sent ones.

7. Then We will surely recount to them with knowledge, and We have not been absent.

فَلَنَقُصَّنَّ عَلَيْهِم بِعِلْمٍ وَمَا كُنَّا غَآئِبِينَ ۝

8. And the weighing on that Day is certain; then those whose scales will be heavy shall fare well.

وَٱلْوَزْنُ يَوْمَئِذٍ ٱلْحَقُّ فَمَن ثَقُلَتْ مَوَٰزِينُهُ فَأُوْلَٰٓئِكَ هُمُ ٱلْمُفْلِحُونَ ۝

9. And those whose scales will be light, they are those who lost themselves in respect of Our signs.

وَمَنْ خَفَّتْ مَوَٰزِينُهُ فَأُوْلَٰٓئِكَ ٱلَّذِينَ خَسِرُوٓاْ أَنفُسَهُم بِمَا كَانُواْ بِـَٔايَٰتِنَا يَظْلِمُونَ ۝

10. And assuredly We established you in the earth and appointed for you your livelihood therein; yet little thanks do you return.

وَلَقَدْ مَكَّنَّٰكُمْ فِى ٱلْأَرْضِ وَجَعَلْنَا لَكُمْ فِيهَا مَعَٰيِشَ قَلِيلًا مَّا تَشْكُرُونَ ۝

Section 2

11. And assuredly We created you, then We fashioned you, and thereafter We said to the angels; make obeisance to Adam, then they made obeisance; not so Iblis: he was not of those who made obeisance.

وَلَقَدْ خَلَقْنَٰكُمْ ثُمَّ صَوَّرْنَٰكُمْ ثُمَّ قُلْنَا لِلْمَلَٰٓئِكَةِ ٱسْجُدُواْ لِأَدَمَ فَسَجَدُوٓاْ إِلَّآ إِبْلِيسَ لَمْ يَكُن مِّنَ ٱلسَّٰجِدِينَ ۝

12. Allah said: 'What prevented you, that you should not make obeisance, when I commanded you?' Iblis said: 'I am better than he; me You have created of fire and him You have created of clay.'

قَالَ مَا مَنَعَكَ أَلَّا تَسْجُدَ إِذْ أَمَرْتُكَ قَالَ أَنَا۠ خَيْرٌ مِّنْهُ خَلَقْتَنِى مِن نَّارٍ وَخَلَقْتَهُ مِن طِينٍ ۝

13. Allah said: 'Then get you down from hence, not for you is it to be stiff-necked herein; so go forth; surely you are of the abject ones.'[346]

قَالَ فَٱهۡبِطۡ مِنۡهَا فَمَا يَكُونُ لَكَ أَن تَتَكَبَّرَ فِيهَا فَٱخۡرُجۡ إِنَّكَ مِنَ ٱلصَّٰغِرِينَ ۝

14. Iblis said: 'Respite me till the Day they will be raised up.'

قَالَ أَنظِرۡنِىٓ إِلَىٰ يَوۡمِ يُبۡعَثُونَ ۝

15. Allah said: 'Surely you are of the respited.'

قَالَ إِنَّكَ مِنَ ٱلۡمُنظَرِينَ ۝

16. Iblis said: 'Because You have seduced me I will beset for them Your straight path.

قَالَ فَبِمَآ أَغۡوَيۡتَنِى لَأَقۡعُدَنَّ لَهُمۡ صِرَٰطَكَ ٱلۡمُسۡتَقِيمَ ۝

17. Then surely I will come upon them from before them and from behind them and from their right and from their left, and You shall not find most of them thankful.'

ثُمَّ لَأَتِيَنَّهُم مِّنۢ بَيۡنِ أَيۡدِيهِمۡ وَمِنۡ خَلۡفِهِمۡ وَعَنۡ أَيۡمَٰنِهِمۡ وَعَن شَمَآئِلِهِمۡ وَلَا تَجِدُ أَكۡثَرَهُمۡ شَٰكِرِينَ ۝

18. Allah said: 'Go forth from this, scorned, driven away; whoever of them follows you, then of a surety I will fill Hell with you all.

قَالَ ٱخۡرُجۡ مِنۡهَا مَذۡءُومٗا مَّدۡحُورٗاۖ لَّمَن تَبِعَكَ مِنۡهُمۡ لَأَمۡلَأَنَّ جَهَنَّمَ مِنكُمۡ أَجۡمَعِينَ ۝

19. And O Adam! Dwell you and your spouse in the Garden, and eat you two thereof what you will, and also do not approach that tree, lest you become of the wrong doers.'

وَيَٰٓـَٔادَمُ ٱسۡكُنۡ أَنتَ وَزَوۡجُكَ ٱلۡجَنَّةَ فَكُلَا مِنۡ حَيۡثُ شِئۡتُمَا وَلَا تَقۡرَبَا هَٰذِهِ ٱلشَّجَرَةَ فَتَكُونَا مِنَ ٱلظَّٰلِمِينَ ۝

---

346. The heavens are only meant for the honourable ones. Satan, in Islam, is the most contemptible being conceivable, and has nothing in common with the Miltonic phantasmagory of wars in heaven and the great revenge by the expelled archangel.

20. Then Satan whispered to the two in order that he might show to them what lay hidden from them of their shame, and said: 'Your Lord did not forbid you that tree but lest you should become angels or become of the immortals.'

فَوَسْوَسَ لَهُمَا الشَّيْطَانُ لِيُبْدِىَ لَهُمَا مَا وُرِىَ عَنْهُمَا مِن سَوْءَتِهِمَا وَقَالَ مَا نَهَىٰكُمَا رَبُّكُمَا عَنْ هَٰذِهِ الشَّجَرَةِ إِلَّا أَن تَكُونَا مَلَكَيْنِ أَوْ تَكُونَا مِنَ الْخَٰلِدِينَ ﴿٢٠﴾

21. And he swore to them both: 'I am of your good counsellors.'

وَقَاسَمَهُمَا إِنِّى لَكُمَا لَمِنَ النَّٰصِحِينَ ﴿٢١﴾

22. In this wise with guile he caused the two to fall[347]. Then when they tasted of the tree, their shame became manifest to them, and they began to cover themselves with leaves from the Garden, and their Lord called out to them: 'Did I not forbid you that tree, and did I not tell you Satan is to you a manifest foe?'

فَدَلَّىٰهُمَا بِغُرُورٍ فَلَمَّا ذَاقَا الشَّجَرَةَ بَدَتْ لَهُمَا سَوْءَٰتُهُمَا وَطَفِقَا يَخْصِفَانِ عَلَيْهِمَا مِن وَرَقِ الْجَنَّةِ وَنَادَىٰهُمَا رَبُّهُمَا أَلَمْ أَنْهَكُمَا عَن تِلْكُمَا الشَّجَرَةِ وَأَقُل لَّكُمَا إِنَّ الشَّيْطَٰنَ لَكُمَا عَدُوٌّ مُّبِينٌ ﴿٢٢﴾

23. The two said: 'Our Lord! We have wronged our souls, and if You do not forgive us, we shall of a surety be of the losers.'

قَالَا رَبَّنَا ظَلَمْنَا أَنفُسَنَا وَإِن لَّمْ تَغْفِرْ لَنَا وَتَرْحَمْنَا لَنَكُونَنَّ مِنَ الْخَٰسِرِينَ ﴿٢٣﴾

24. Allah said: 'Get you down, one of you an enemy to another; and for you there shall be on the earth a dwelling and provision for a time.'

قَالَ اهْبِطُوا بَعْضُكُمْ لِبَعْضٍ عَدُوٌّ وَلَكُمْ فِى الْأَرْضِ مُسْتَقَرٌّ وَمَتَٰعٌ إِلَىٰ حِينٍ ﴿٢٤﴾

25. Allah said: 'On it you shall live and on it you shall die, and from it you shall be raised up.'

قَالَ فِيهَا تَحْيَوْنَ وَفِيهَا تَمُوتُونَ وَمِنْهَا تُخْرَجُونَ ﴿٢٥﴾

---

347. Thus the Qur'ān exonerates completely and in a language that is unmistakable and unequivocal Adam and his consort of all deliberate sin.

Section 3

26. O Children of Adam! Surely We have sent down to you a garment covering your shame and as an adornment; and the garment of piety that is the best. This is of the signs of Allah, that perhaps they may be admonished.

يَـٰبَنِىٓ ءَادَمَ قَدۡ أَنزَلۡنَا عَلَيۡكُمۡ لِبَاسًا يُوَٰرِى سَوۡءَٰتِكُمۡ وَرِيشًاۖ وَلِبَاسُ ٱلتَّقۡوَىٰ ذَٰلِكَ خَيۡرٌۚ ذَٰلِكَ مِنۡ ءَايَـٰتِ ٱللَّهِ لَعَلَّهُمۡ يَذَّكَّرُونَ ﴿٢٦﴾

27. O children of Adam! Let not Satan tempt you, as he has driven forth your parents from the Garden, divesting the two of the garment, that he might show to them their shame, Surely he beholds you, he and his tribe, in a way that you do not behold them. Certainly We have made Satans patrons of only those who are not believers.

يَـٰبَنِىٓ ءَادَمَ لَا يَفۡتِنَنَّكُمُ ٱلشَّيۡطَـٰنُ كَمَآ أَخۡرَجَ أَبَوَيۡكُم مِّنَ ٱلۡجَنَّةِ يَنزِعُ عَنۡهُمَا لِبَاسَهُمَا لِيُرِيَهُمَا سَوۡءَٰتِهِمَآۗ إِنَّهُۥ يَرَىٰكُمۡ هُوَ وَقَبِيلُهُۥ مِنۡ حَيۡثُ لَا تَرَوۡنَهُمۡۗ إِنَّا جَعَلۡنَا ٱلشَّيَـٰطِينَ أَوۡلِيَآءَ لِلَّذِينَ لَا يُؤۡمِنُونَ ﴿٢٧﴾

28. And when they commit an indecency they say: 'We found our fathers on it and Allah has enjoined it on us.' Say: 'Certainly Allah does not enjoin an indecency, you say falsely of Allah what you do not know.'

وَإِذَا فَعَلُوا۟ فَـٰحِشَةً قَالُوا۟ وَجَدۡنَا عَلَيۡهَآ ءَابَآءَنَا وَٱللَّهُ أَمَرَنَا بِهَاۗ قُلۡ إِنَّ ٱللَّهَ لَا يَأۡمُرُ بِٱلۡفَحۡشَآءِۖ أَتَقُولُونَ عَلَى ٱللَّهِ مَا لَا تَعۡلَمُونَ ﴿٢٨﴾

29. Say: 'My Lord has enjoined equity, and that you shall set your faces aright at every prostration, and call on Him, making faith pure for Him. Even as He has begun you, you shall be brought back.'

قُلۡ أَمَرَ رَبِّى بِٱلۡقِسۡطِۖ وَأَقِيمُوا۟ وُجُوهَكُمۡ عِندَ كُلِّ مَسۡجِدٍ وَٱدۡعُوهُ مُخۡلِصِينَ لَهُ ٱلدِّينَۚ كَمَا بَدَأَكُمۡ تَعُودُونَ ﴿٢٩﴾

30. A party He has guided, and upon a party straying has been justified. Assuredly they have taken Satans as patrons instead of Allah and they fancy that they are guided ones.

فَرِيقًا هَدَىٰ وَفَرِيقًا حَقَّ عَلَيۡهِمُ الضَّلَـٰلَةُ إِنَّهُمُ اتَّخَذُوا الشَّيَـٰطِينَ أَوۡلِيَآءَ مِن دُونِ اللَّهِ وَيَحۡسَبُونَ أَنَّهُم مُّهۡتَدُونَ ﴿٣٠﴾

31. O children of Adam! Take your adornment at every worship; and eat and drink, and be not extravagant; surely He does not approve of the extravagant ones.

يَـٰبَنِىٓ ءَادَمَ خُذُوا زِينَتَكُمۡ عِندَ كُلِّ مَسۡجِدٍ وَكُلُوا وَاشۡرَبُوا وَلَا تُسۡرِفُوٓا إِنَّهُۥ لَا يُحِبُّ الۡمُسۡرِفِينَ ﴿٣١﴾

Section 4

32. Say: 'Who has forbidden the adornment that Allah has produced for His servants and the clean things of food?' Say: 'On the Day of Resurrection these shall belong to them alone who in the life of this world were believers.' Thus We expound the signs to a people who know.

قُلۡ مَنۡ حَرَّمَ زِينَةَ اللَّهِ الَّتِىٓ أَخۡرَجَ لِعِبَادِهِۦ وَالطَّيِّبَـٰتِ مِنَ الرِّزۡقِ قُلۡ هِىَ لِلَّذِينَ ءَامَنُوا فِى الۡحَيَوٰةِ الدُّنۡيَا خَالِصَةً يَوۡمَ الۡقِيَـٰمَةِ كَذَٰلِكَ نُفَصِّلُ الۡءَايَـٰتِ لِقَوۡمٍ يَعۡلَمُونَ ﴿٣٢﴾

33. Say: 'My Lord has forbidden the indecencies, the open thereof and the hidden thereof, and sin and high – handedness without justice and that you associate anyone with Allah that for which He has sent down no warranty and that you speak of Allah what you know not.'

قُلۡ إِنَّمَا حَرَّمَ رَبِّىَ الۡفَوَٰحِشَ مَا ظَهَرَ مِنۡهَا وَمَا بَطَنَ وَالۡإِثۡمَ وَالۡبَغۡىَ بِغَيۡرِ الۡحَقِّ وَأَن تُشۡرِكُوا بِاللَّهِ مَا لَمۡ يُنَزِّلۡ بِهِۦ سُلۡطَـٰنًا وَأَن تَقُولُوا عَلَى اللَّهِ مَا لَا تَعۡلَمُونَ ﴿٣٣﴾

34. For every community there is a doom; then when its doom is come, not an hour will they stay behind nor go in advance.

وَلِكُلِّ أُمَّةٍ أَجَلٌ فَإِذَا جَآءَ أَجَلُهُمۡ لَا يَسۡتَأۡخِرُونَ سَاعَةً وَلَا يَسۡتَقۡدِمُونَ ﴿٣٤﴾

35. O children of Adam! If there came to you Messengers from among you, recounting My signs to you, then whoever shall fear Allah and act right, on them shall come no fear, nor shall they grieve.

يَبَنِىٓ ءَادَمَ إِمَّا يَأْتِيَنَّكُمْ رُسُلٌ مِّنكُمْ يَقُصُّونَ عَلَيْكُمْ ءَايَتِى فَمَنِ ٱتَّقَىٰ وَأَصْلَحَ فَلَا خَوْفٌ عَلَيْهِمْ وَلَا هُمْ يَحْزَنُونَ ﴿٣٥﴾

36. And those who belie Our Signs and are stiff-necked, against them – they shall be fellows of the Fire and therein they shall be abiders.

وَٱلَّذِينَ كَذَّبُوا بِـَٔايَتِنَا وَٱسْتَكْبَرُوا عَنْهَآ أُوْلَٰٓئِكَ أَصْحَٰبُ ٱلنَّارِ هُمْ فِيهَا خَٰلِدُونَ ﴿٣٦﴾

37. Who does greater wrong than he who fabricates a lie against Allah or belies His signs? For these! Their full portion from the Book shall reach them until when Our Messengers come to them causing them to die, and say: 'Where is that which you were wont to call upon beside Allah?' These will say: 'They have strayed from us.' And they will testify against themselves that they have been infidels.

فَمَنْ أَظْلَمُ مِمَّنِ ٱفْتَرَىٰ عَلَى ٱللَّهِ كَذِبًا أَوْ كَذَّبَ بِـَٔايَٰتِهِۦٓ أُوْلَٰٓئِكَ يَنَالُهُمْ نَصِيبُهُم مِّنَ ٱلْكِتَٰبِ حَتَّىٰٓ إِذَا جَآءَتْهُمْ رُسُلُنَا يَتَوَفَّوْنَهُمْ قَالُوٓا أَيْنَ مَا كُنتُمْ تَدْعُونَ مِن دُونِ ٱللَّهِ قَالُوا ضَلُّوا عَنَّا وَشَهِدُوا عَلَىٰٓ أَنفُسِهِمْ أَنَّهُمْ كَانُوا كَٰفِرِينَ ﴿٣٧﴾

38. Allah will say: 'Enter the Fire among the communities of those who have passed before you, of jinn and mankind.' So oft as a community enters it, it shall curse its sister, until, when all have arrived one after another therein, the last of them will say of the first of them; our Lord; these led us astray; so mete out to them a double torment of the Fire. Allah will say; to each, 'double' but you know not.

قَالَ ٱدْخُلُوا فِىٓ أُمَمٍ قَدْ خَلَتْ مِن قَبْلِكُم مِّنَ ٱلْجِنِّ وَٱلْإِنسِ فِى ٱلنَّارِ كُلَّمَا دَخَلَتْ أُمَّةٌ لَّعَنَتْ أُخْتَهَا حَتَّىٰٓ إِذَا ٱدَّارَكُوا فِيهَا جَمِيعًا قَالَتْ أُخْرَىٰهُمْ لِأُولَىٰهُمْ رَبَّنَا هَٰٓؤُلَآءِ أَضَلُّونَا فَـَٔاتِهِمْ عَذَابًا ضِعْفًا مِّنَ ٱلنَّارِ قَالَ لِكُلٍّ ضِعْفٌ وَلَٰكِن لَّا تَعْلَمُونَ ﴿٣٨﴾

39. The first of them will say to the last of them you have then no preference over us. Taste then you all the torment for what you were wont to earn.

وَقَالَتْ أُولَىٰهُمْ لِأُخْرَىٰهُمْ فَمَا كَانَ لَكُمْ عَلَيْنَا مِن فَضْلٍ فَذُوقُوا۟ ٱلْعَذَابَ بِمَا كُنتُمْ تَكْسِبُونَ ﴿٣٩﴾

Section 5

40. Assuredly those who belie Our signs and are stiff-necked against them, for them will not be opened the portals of heaven nor will they enter the Garden until a camel passes through the eye of a needle. Thus do We requite the culprits.

إِنَّ ٱلَّذِينَ كَذَّبُوا۟ بِـَٔايَٰتِنَا وَٱسْتَكْبَرُوا۟ عَنْهَا لَا تُفَتَّحُ لَهُمْ أَبْوَٰبُ ٱلسَّمَآءِ وَلَا يَدْخُلُونَ ٱلْجَنَّةَ حَتَّىٰ يَلِجَ ٱلْجَمَلُ فِى سَمِّ ٱلْخِيَاطِ ۚ وَكَذَٰلِكَ نَجْزِى ٱلْمُجْرِمِينَ ﴿٤٠﴾

41. Theirs will be a bed in Hell, and over them coverings. Thus do We requite the wrong doers.

لَهُم مِّن جَهَنَّمَ مِهَادٌ وَمِن فَوْقِهِمْ غَوَاشٍ ۚ وَكَذَٰلِكَ نَجْزِى ٱلظَّٰلِمِينَ ﴿٤١﴾

42. And those who believed and worked righteous works, We burden not a soul except according to its capacity. They are the fellows of the Garden; therein they shall be abiders.

وَٱلَّذِينَ ءَامَنُوا۟ وَعَمِلُوا۟ ٱلصَّٰلِحَٰتِ لَا نُكَلِّفُ نَفْسًا إِلَّا وُسْعَهَآ أُو۟لَٰٓئِكَ أَصْحَٰبُ ٱلْجَنَّةِ ۖ هُمْ فِيهَا خَٰلِدُونَ ﴿٤٢﴾

43. And We shall recover whatever of rancour may be in their breasts, rivers flowing beneath them, and they will say: 'All measure of praise be to Allah Who has guided us on to this, we were not such as to find guidance, were it not that Allah had guided us; the Messengers of our Lord came with truth.' And this shall be cried out to them: 'This is the Garden; it you inherit for what you have been working.'

وَنَزَعْنَا مَا فِى صُدُورِهِم مِّنْ غِلٍّ تَجْرِى مِن تَحْتِهِمُ ٱلْأَنْهَٰرُ ۖ وَقَالُوا۟ ٱلْحَمْدُ لِلَّهِ ٱلَّذِى هَدَىٰنَا لِهَٰذَا وَمَا كُنَّا لِنَهْتَدِىَ لَوْلَآ أَنْ هَدَىٰنَا ٱللَّهُ ۖ لَقَدْ جَآءَتْ رُسُلُ رَبِّنَا بِٱلْحَقِّ ۖ وَنُودُوٓا۟ أَن تِلْكُمُ ٱلْجَنَّةُ أُورِثْتُمُوهَا بِمَا كُنتُمْ تَعْمَلُونَ ﴿٤٣﴾

44. And the fellows of the Garden shall cry out to the fellows of the Fire: 'Surely we have found true what our Lord had promised us. Have you found true what your Lord had promised you?' They shall say, 'yea!' Then a crier in between them shall cry, 'the curse of Allah be upon the wrong doers.'

وَنَادَىٰٓ أَصْحَٰبُ ٱلْجَنَّةِ أَصْحَٰبَ ٱلنَّارِ أَن قَدْ وَجَدْنَا مَا وَعَدَنَا رَبُّنَا حَقًّا فَهَلْ وَجَدتُّم مَّا وَعَدَ رَبُّكُمْ حَقًّا ۖ قَالُوا۟ نَعَمْ ۚ فَأَذَّنَ مُؤَذِّنٌۢ بَيْنَهُمْ أَن لَّعْنَةُ ٱللَّهِ عَلَى ٱلظَّٰلِمِينَ ﴿٤٤﴾

45. Those who turned away from the way of Allah and would seek to render it crooked and in the Hereafter they were disbelievers.

ٱلَّذِينَ يَصُدُّونَ عَن سَبِيلِ ٱللَّهِ وَيَبْغُونَهَا عِوَجًا وَهُم بِٱلْءَاخِرَةِ كَٰفِرُونَ ﴿٤٥﴾

46. And between the two there will be a veil, and on the heights[348] will be men recognizing them all by their marks; and they will cry to the fellows of the Garden; peace be on you! They will not have yet entered it while they will be longing.[349]

وَبَيْنَهُمَا حِجَابٌ ۚ وَعَلَى ٱلْأَعْرَافِ رِجَالٌ يَعْرِفُونَ كُلًّۢا بِسِيمَٰهُمْ ۚ وَنَادَوْا۟ أَصْحَٰبَ ٱلْجَنَّةِ أَن سَلَٰمٌ عَلَيْكُمْ ۚ لَمْ يَدْخُلُوهَا وَهُمْ يَطْمَعُونَ ﴿٤٦﴾

47. And when their eyes will be turned to the fellows of the Fire, they will cry: 'Our Lord! Place us not with these wrong-doing people.'

وَإِذَا صُرِفَتْ أَبْصَٰرُهُمْ تِلْقَآءَ أَصْحَٰبِ ٱلنَّارِ قَالُوا۟ رَبَّنَا لَا تَجْعَلْنَا مَعَ ٱلْقَوْمِ ٱلظَّٰلِمِينَ ﴿٤٧﴾

---

348. The heights thereof. A'rāf literally is an elevated place or an elevated portion of the earth or ground; and is applied to a wall between Paradise and Hell, or its upper parts (LL.).

349. They will long to enter it. They will be the people whose good and bad deeds are equal, and who, though eventually due to be received in Paradise are not immediately fit for admittance thereinto.

Section 6

48. The fellows of the heights will cry to the men whom they recognize by their marks, and say: 'Your multitude availed you naught nor that over which you were wont to be stiff-necked.

وَنَادَىٰٓ أَصْحَـٰبُ ٱلْأَعْرَافِ رِجَالًا يَعْرِفُونَهُم بِسِيمَىٰهُمْ قَالُوا مَآ أَغْنَىٰ عَنكُمْ جَمْعُكُمْ وَمَا كُنتُمْ تَسْتَكْبِرُونَ ٤٨

49. Are these the men of whom you swore that Allah would not reach them with His mercy? Enter the Garden, on you shall come no fear, nor shall you grieve.'

أَهَـٰٓؤُلَآءِ ٱلَّذِينَ أَقْسَمْتُمْ لَا يَنَالُهُمُ ٱللَّهُ بِرَحْمَةٍ ٱدْخُلُوا ٱلْجَنَّةَ لَا خَوْفٌ عَلَيْكُمْ وَلَآ أَنتُمْ تَحْزَنُونَ ٤٩

50. And the fellows of the Fire will cry to the fellows of the Garden: 'Pour out on us some water or something what Allah has provided you with.' They will say: 'Surely Allah has forbidden them both to the infidels.

وَنَادَىٰٓ أَصْحَـٰبُ ٱلنَّارِ أَصْحَـٰبَ ٱلْجَنَّةِ أَنْ أَفِيضُوا عَلَيْنَا مِنَ ٱلْمَآءِ أَوْ مِمَّا رَزَقَكُمُ ٱللَّهُ قَالُوٓا إِنَّ ٱللَّهَ حَرَّمَهُمَا عَلَى ٱلْكَـٰفِرِينَ ٥٠

51. Who took their religion as an idle sport and a play and whom the life of the world beguiled.' So today We shall forget them even as they neglected the meeting of this Day of theirs and as they were ever gainsaying Our signs.

ٱلَّذِينَ ٱتَّخَذُوا دِينَهُمْ لَهْوًا وَلَعِبًا وَغَرَّتْهُمُ ٱلْحَيَوٰةُ ٱلدُّنْيَا فَٱلْيَوْمَ نَنسَىٰهُمْ كَمَا نَسُوا لِقَآءَ يَوْمِهِمْ هَـٰذَا وَمَا كَانُوا بِـَٔايَـٰتِنَا يَجْحَدُونَ ٥١

52. And surely We have brought to them a Book which We have detailed according to knowledge, a guidance and a mercy to a people who believe.

وَلَقَدْ جِئْنَـٰهُم بِكِتَـٰبٍ فَصَّلْنَـٰهُ عَلَىٰ عِلْمٍ هُدًى وَرَحْمَةً لِّقَوْمٍ يُؤْمِنُونَ ٥٢

53. They await only its fulfilment, the Day whereon its fulfilment arrives those who had been negligent of it will say: 'Surely the Messengers of our Lord brought the Truth. Are there no intercessors for us that they might intercede for us or could we be sent back that we might work otherwise than we were wont to work?' Surely they have lost themselves, and there has strayed from them what they were wont to fabricate.

هَلْ يَنظُرُونَ إِلَّا تَأْوِيلَهُ يَوْمَ يَأْتِى تَأْوِيلُهُ يَقُولُ الَّذِينَ نَسُوهُ مِن قَبْلُ قَدْ جَآءَتْ رُسُلُ رَبِّنَا بِالْحَقِّ فَهَل لَّنَا مِن شُفَعَآءَ فَيَشْفَعُوا لَنَا أَوْ نُرَدُّ فَنَعْمَلَ غَيْرَ الَّذِى كُنَّا نَعْمَلُ قَدْ خَسِرُوا أَنفُسَهُمْ وَضَلَّ عَنْهُم مَّا كَانُوا يَفْتَرُونَ ۝

Section 7

54. In Truth your Lord is Allah Who created the heavens and the earth in six days, then established Himself on the throne, making the night cover the day, seeking it swiftly, and created the sun and the moon and the stars subjected to His command. Lo! His is the creation and the command[350]; Blessed is Allah, the Lord of the worlds.

إِنَّ رَبَّكُمُ اللَّهُ الَّذِى خَلَقَ السَّمَٰوَٰتِ وَالْأَرْضَ فِى سِتَّةِ أَيَّامٍ ثُمَّ اسْتَوَىٰ عَلَى الْعَرْشِ يُغْشِى الَّيْلَ النَّهَارَ يَطْلُبُهُ حَثِيثًا وَالشَّمْسَ وَالْقَمَرَ وَالنُّجُومَ مُسَخَّرَٰتٍ بِأَمْرِهِ أَلَا لَهُ الْخَلْقُ وَالْأَمْرُ تَبَارَكَ اللَّهُ رَبُّ الْعَٰلَمِينَ ۝

---

350. God is the Sole Ruler, the Sole Sovereign, the Sole Maintainer of the universe. It is not, as the Hindus believe, that He 'having performed His legitimate part in the mundane evolution by His original creation of the universe, has retired into the background' (*EBr.* XI. p. 577), leaving the governance of the world to minor local deities. Nor is His Divine activity, as the deists imagine, 'confined to the creation of the world and the fixation of its primary collocation' (*EBr.* VII. p. 144), the world-process being determined by these alone.

55. Call on your Lord in humility and in secrecy. Surely, He approves not the trespassers.[351]

ادْعُوْا رَبَّكُمْ تَضَرُّعًا وَخُفْيَةً ۚ إِنَّهُ لَا يُحِبُّ الْمُعْتَدِيْنَ ۝

56. Act not corruptly on the earth after its good ordering, and call on Him in fearing and longing, surely the Mercy of Allah is nigh to the well-doers.

وَلَا تُفْسِدُوْا فِي الْأَرْضِ بَعْدَ إِصْلَاحِهَا وَادْعُوْهُ خَوْفًا وَّطَمَعًا ۚ إِنَّ رَحْمَتَ اللّٰهِ قَرِيْبٌ مِّنَ الْمُحْسِنِيْنَ ۝

57. He it is Who sends forth heralding winds before His mercy, until when they have gathered up heavy-laden cloud, We drive it on to a dead land and send down rain thereby, bringing forth with it all manner of fruit. In this wise, We raise the dead; perchance, you may take heed.

وَهُوَ الَّذِيْ يُرْسِلُ الرِّيَاحَ بُشْرًا بَيْنَ يَدَيْ رَحْمَتِهِ ۚ حَتّٰى إِذَا أَقَلَّتْ سَحَابًا ثِقَالًا سُقْنَاهُ لِبَلَدٍ مَّيِّتٍ فَأَنْزَلْنَا بِهِ الْمَاءَ فَأَخْرَجْنَا بِهِ مِنْ كُلِّ الثَّمَرَاتِ ۚ كَذَٰلِكَ نُخْرِجُ الْمَوْتٰى لَعَلَّكُمْ تَذَكَّرُوْنَ ۝

58. A good soil! Its herbage comes forth by the will of the Lord, and that which is barren brings forth scantily. In this wise, We vary the signs for a people who return thanks.

وَالْبَلَدُ الطَّيِّبُ يَخْرُجُ نَبَاتُهُ بِإِذْنِ رَبِّهِ ۚ وَالَّذِيْ خَبُثَ لَا يَخْرُجُ إِلَّا نَكِدًا ۚ كَذَٰلِكَ نُصَرِّفُ الْآيَاتِ لِقَوْمٍ يَّشْكُرُوْنَ ۝

---

351. Namely, those who go beyond the proper limits in prayer, and are either vain, vociferous or frivolous in their prayers. The Hindus believe that mantras, or magical formulae, if enchanted punctiliously by a Brahman, 'will constrain the gods to gratify the worshipper's wishes' (*EBr.* III. p. 1012). And prayer in the Hindu sense of the term, 'denotes a compulsory, not a devotional attitude in the officiant'. Clearly Islam repudiates all this.

Section 8

59. Assuredly We sent Noah[352] to his people, and he said: 'O my people! Worship Allah, no god you have other than He; verily I fear for you the torment of a Mighty Day.'

لَقَدْ أَرْسَلْنَا نُوحًا إِلَى قَوْمِهِ فَقَالَ يَقَوْمِ اعْبُدُوا اللَّهَ مَا لَكُمْ مِنْ إِلَهٍ غَيْرُهُ إِنِّى أَخَافُ عَلَيْكُمْ عَذَابَ يَوْمٍ عَظِيمٍ ۝

60. The chiefs of his people said: 'Surely we see you in error manifest.'

قَالَ الْمَلَأُ مِنْ قَوْمِهِ إِنَّا لَنَرَىكَ فِى ضَلَالٍ مُّبِينٍ ۝

61. Noah said: 'O my people! Not with me is error, but I am a Messenger from the Lord of the worlds.

قَالَ يَقَوْمِ لَيْسَ بِى ضَلَالَةٌ وَلَكِنِّى رَسُولٌ مِّن رَّبِّ الْعَلَمِينَ ۝

62. I preach to you the Messages of my Lord and I counsel you good, and I know from Allah what you do not know.

أُبَلِّغُكُمْ رِسَلَتِ رَبِّى وَأَنصَحُ لَكُمْ وَأَعْلَمُ مِنَ اللَّهِ مَا لَا تَعْلَمُونَ ۝

63. Do you marvel that an admonition from your Lord should come to you through a man from amongst you, so that he may warn you, and that you may fear God, and that perchance you may be shown mercy?'[353]

أَوَعِجِبْتُمْ أَن جَآءَكُمْ ذِكْرٌ مِّن رَّبِّكُمْ عَلَى رَجُلٍ مِّنكُمْ لِيُنذِرَكُمْ وَلِتَتَّقُوا وَلَعَلَّكُمْ تُرْحَمُونَ ۝

---

352. Sent Noah as a Prophet. He is the Prophet Noah (probably 2948–1998 BC) of the Bible, but unlike the Biblical character, he is a True Messenger of God, an embodiment of piety and virtue, and has nothing about him of the shameless drunkenness so brazenly imputed to him in the Bible: 'And he drank of the wine, and was drunken; and he was uncovered within his tent' (Ge. 9: 21).

353. The idea of Messengership is directly opposed by the theory of Incarnation. To polytheistic peoples it is always a matter of utmost amazement that a mere man should be Divinely commissioned with the reform of his fellow–beings. It must be, according to their concept, the very God who should incarnate himself in human form to redeem humanity, and all mortals laying claim to Messengership are *ipso facto* impostors and must be condemned unheard.

64. Then they disbelieved him; thereupon We delivered him and those with him in the ark, and drowned those who disbelieved Our signs. Certainly they were a people blind.

فَكَذَّبُوهُ فَأَنجَيۡنَٰهُ وَٱلَّذِينَ مَعَهُۥ فِي ٱلۡفُلۡكِ وَأَغۡرَقۡنَا ٱلَّذِينَ كَذَّبُواۡ بِـَٔايَٰتِنَآ إِنَّهُمۡ كَانُواۡ قَوۡمًا عَمِينَ ۝

Section 9

65. And to the 'Ād[354], We sent their brother, Hūd. He said: 'O my people! Worship Allah, no god you have other then He. Do you not fear?'

وَإِلَىٰ عَادٍ أَخَاهُمۡ هُودًا قَالَ يَٰقَوۡمِ ٱعۡبُدُواۡ ٱللَّهَ مَا لَكُم مِّنۡ إِلَٰهٍ غَيۡرُهُۥٓ أَفَلَا تَتَّقُونَ ۝

66. The chiefs of those who disbelieved among his people said: 'In Truth, we see you in folly and in Truth we deem you to be of the liars.'

قَالَ ٱلۡمَلَأُ ٱلَّذِينَ كَفَرُواۡ مِن قَوۡمِهِۦٓ إِنَّا لَنَرَىٰكَ فِي سَفَاهَةٍ وَإِنَّا لَنَظُنُّكَ مِنَ ٱلۡكَٰذِبِينَ ۝

67. Hūd said: 'O my people! Not with me is folly, but I am a Messenger from the Lord of the worlds.

قَالَ يَٰقَوۡمِ لَيۡسَ بِي سَفَاهَةٌ وَلَٰكِنِّي رَسُولٌ مِّن رَّبِّ ٱلۡعَٰلَمِينَ ۝

68. I preach to you the messages from my Lord; and I am to you a faithful counsellor.

أُبَلِّغُكُمۡ رِسَٰلَٰتِ رَبِّي وَأَنَا۠ لَكُمۡ نَاصِحٌ أَمِينٌ ۝

---

354. An Arab people, flourishing in the south of the Arabian peninsula, with their dominion extended from the north of the Persian Gulf in the east to the southern end of the Red Sea in the west. Their story was well known to the Arabs of the Holy Prophet's time. 'The ancient poets knew' the Ad as an ancient nation that had perished, hence the expression 'since the time of Ad'. Their kings are mentioned in the Dīwān of the Hudhailites and their prudence in that of Nābigha (*EI.* I. p. 121). They were zealous idolaters.

69. 'Do you marvel that an admonition from your Lord should come to you upon a man from amongst you so that he may warn you? Remember that time when He made you successors after the people of Noah[355] and increased you amply in stature. Remember the bounties of Allah, that perchance you may fare well.'

أَوَعَجِبْتُمْ أَن جَآءَكُمْ ذِكْرٌ مِّن رَّبِّكُمْ عَلَىٰ رَجُلٍ مِّنكُمْ لِيُنذِرَكُمْ وَاذْكُرُوٓاْ إِذْ جَعَلَكُمْ خُلَفَآءَ مِنۢ بَعْدِ قَوْمِ نُوحٍ وَزَادَكُمْ فِي ٱلْخَلْقِ بَصْۜطَةً فَاذْكُرُوٓاْ ءَالَآءَ ٱللَّهِ لَعَلَّكُمْ تُفْلِحُونَ ٦٩

70. They said: 'Have you come to us that we should worship Allah alone and leave what our fathers were wont to worship? Bring you then upon us that wherewith you have threatened us, if you speak truth.'

قَالُوٓاْ أَجِئْتَنَا لِنَعْبُدَ ٱللَّهَ وَحْدَهُۥ وَنَذَرَ مَا كَانَ يَعْبُدُ ءَابَآؤُنَا فَأْتِنَا بِمَا تَعِدُنَآ إِن كُنتَ مِنَ ٱلصَّٰدِقِينَ ٧٠

71. Hud said: 'Surely there have befallen you wrath and indignation from your Lord. Do you dispute with me over the names you have named, you and your fathers, for which Allah has sent down no warranty? Wait then; I also will be of those who wait.'

قَالَ قَدْ وَقَعَ عَلَيْكُم مِّن رَّبِّكُمْ رِجْسٌ وَغَضَبٌ أَتُجَٰدِلُونَنِي فِيٓ أَسْمَآءٍ سَمَّيْتُمُوهَآ أَنتُمْ وَءَابَآؤُكُم مَّا نَزَّلَ ٱللَّهُ بِهَا مِن سُلْطَٰنٍ فَٱنتَظِرُوٓاْ إِنِّي مَعَكُم مِّنَ ٱلْمُنتَظِرِينَ ٧١

72. Then We delivered him and those with him by a mercy from Us, and We utterly cut off those who belied Our signs, and would not be believers.

فَأَنجَيْنَٰهُ وَٱلَّذِينَ مَعَهُۥ بِرَحْمَةٍ مِّنَّا وَقَطَعْنَا دَابِرَ ٱلَّذِينَ كَذَّبُواْ بِـَٔايَٰتِنَا وَمَا كَانُواْ مُؤْمِنِينَ ٧٢

---

355. The 'Adites were separated only by a few generations from the people of Noah. 'The tribe of Ad, the son of Aws, the son of Aram, the son of Sem, the son of Noah, who after the confusion of tongues, settled in al-Ahqaf, or the winding sands in the province of Hadhramaut, where his posterity greatly multiplied' (*SPD*. p. 20).

Section 10

73. To the Thamūd[356] We sent their brother Ṣāliḥ. He said: 'O my people! Worship Allah, no god you have but He; surely there has come to you evidence from your Lord, that is the she-camel of Allah, a sign to you; so leave her alone, pasturing on Allah's earth, and do not touch her with evil, lest there seize you an afflictive torment.

وَإِلَىٰ ثَمُودَ أَخَاهُمْ صَـٰلِحًا قَالَ يَـٰقَوْمِ اعْبُدُوا اللَّهَ مَا لَكُم مِّنْ إِلَـٰهٍ غَيْرُهُۥ قَدْ جَآءَتْكُم بَيِّنَةٌ مِّن رَّبِّكُمْ هَـٰذِهِۦ نَاقَةُ اللَّهِ لَكُمْ ءَايَةً فَذَرُوهَا تَأْكُلْ فِىٓ أَرْضِ اللَّهِ وَلَا تَمَسُّوهَا بِسُوٓءٍ فَيَأْخُذَكُمْ عَذَابٌ أَلِيمٌ ﴿٧٣﴾

74. And remember the time when He made you successors of the 'Ād, and inherited you in the earth; you take for yourselves palaces in the plains, and you hew out the mountains as houses. Remember the bounties of Allah and commit not evil on the earth as corrupters.'

وَاذْكُرُوٓا إِذْ جَعَلَكُمْ خُلَفَآءَ مِنۢ بَعْدِ عَادٍ وَبَوَّأَكُمْ فِى الْأَرْضِ تَتَّخِذُونَ مِن سُهُولِهَا قُصُورًا وَتَنْحِتُونَ الْجِبَالَ بُيُوتًا فَاذْكُرُوٓا ءَالَآءَ اللَّهِ وَلَا تَعْثَوْا فِى الْأَرْضِ مُفْسِدِينَ ﴿٧٤﴾

75. The chiefs of those who were stiff-necked amongst his people said to those who were counted weak to such of them as believed: 'Do you know that Ṣāliḥ is a sent one of his Lord?' They said: 'Indeed we are believers in that with which he has been sent.'

قَالَ الْمَلَأُ الَّذِينَ اسْتَكْبَرُوا مِن قَوْمِهِۦ لِلَّذِينَ اسْتُضْعِفُوا لِمَنْ ءَامَنَ مِنْهُمْ أَتَعْلَمُونَ أَنَّ صَـٰلِحًا مُّرْسَلٌ مِّن رَّبِّهِۦ قَالُوٓا إِنَّا بِمَآ أُرْسِلَ بِهِۦ مُؤْمِنُونَ ﴿٧٥﴾

---

356. Another ancient and powerful people of Arabia, closely related to the 'Adites and heirs to their civilization and culture, with their seat in the north–west corner of Arabia, forming the southern boundary of Syria. 'Unlike the 'Adites, of whom we find no trace in historical times, the Thamudites are mentioned as still existing by Diodorus Siculus and Ptolemy; and they survived down to the fifth century AD in the corps of equities Thamudeni attached to the army of the Byzantine emperors' (Nicholson, *Literary History of the Arabs*, p. 3). The recently excavated rocky city of Petra, near Ma'an, may go back to Thamud' (AYA).

76. Those who were stiff-necked said: 'Surely we are disbelievers in what you believe.'

قَالَ الَّذِينَ اسۡتَكۡبَرُوٓا إِنَّا بِالَّذِىٓ ءَامَنتُم بِهِۦ كَفِرُونَ ﴿٧٦﴾

77. Then they hamstrung the she camel and disdained the command of their Lord, and said: 'O Ṣāliḥ, bring upon us that with which you have threatened us, if you are in truth of the sent ones.'

فَعَقَرُوا النَّاقَةَ وَعَتَوۡا عَنۡ أَمۡرِ رَبِّهِمۡ وَقَالُوا يَٰصَٰلِحُ ٱئۡتِنَا بِمَا تَعِدُنَآ إِن كُنتَ مِنَ ٱلۡمُرۡسَلِينَ ﴿٧٧﴾

78. Thereupon an earthquake seized them so that they lay prone in their dwellings.

فَأَخَذَتۡهُمُ ٱلرَّجۡفَةُ فَأَصۡبَحُوا فِى دَارِهِمۡ جَٰثِمِينَ ﴿٧٨﴾

79. Then he turned from them, and said: 'O my people! Assuredly I did deliver to you the messages of my Lord, and counselled you good, but you do not approve the good counsellors.'

فَتَوَلَّىٰ عَنۡهُمۡ وَقَالَ يَٰقَوۡمِ لَقَدۡ أَبۡلَغۡتُكُمۡ رِسَالَةَ رَبِّى وَنَصَحۡتُ لَكُمۡ وَلَٰكِن لَّا تُحِبُّونَ ٱلنَّٰصِحِينَ ﴿٧٩﴾

80. And We sent Lot,[357] when he said to his people: 'Do you commit an indecency with which none has preceded you in the worlds?[358]

وَلُوطًا إِذۡ قَالَ لِقَوۡمِهِۦٓ أَتَأۡتُونَ ٱلۡفَٰحِشَةَ مَا سَبَقَكُم بِهَا مِنۡ أَحَدٍ مِّنَ ٱلۡعَٰلَمِينَ ﴿٨٠﴾

---

357. Lot equates to the Lot of the Bible. (Ge. 19: 1–38). The story is Biblical, 'but freed from some shameful features which are a blot on the biblical narrative' (AYA).

358. Mark the implication of the word preceded. Of course, there have been nations and nations since the time of Lot, not before it, revelling in sodomy, and calling it euphemistically homosexual practices. That 'in Greek society of the fifth and fourth centuries homosexualism, was frankly recognized' (*ESS*. I. p. 25), that among the ancient Greeks 'it was idealized not merely in association with military virtues but with intellectual, aesthetic, and even ethical qualities' (Ellis, *Psychology of Sex*, p. 219), that in the Middle Ages it 'flourished not only in camps but also in cloisters' (Ibid., p. 220), and that it plays a conspicuous part in the modern civilized world are almost truisms.

81. Verily you go in lustfully to men instead of women! Aye! You are a people extravagant.'

إِنَّكُمْ لَتَأْتُونَ الرِّجَالَ شَهْوَةً مِّن دُونِ النِّسَاءِ بَلْ أَنتُمْ قَوْمٌ مُّسْرِفُونَ ۝

82. Naught was the answer of his people save that they said: 'Drive them forth from your city; indeed they are a people who would be pure!'

وَمَا كَانَ جَوَابَ قَوْمِهِ إِلَّا أَن قَالُوا أَخْرِجُوهُم مِّن قَرْيَتِكُمْ إِنَّهُمْ أُنَاسٌ يَتَطَهَّرُونَ ۝

83. Then We delivered him and his family, save his wife, she was among the lingerers.

فَأَنجَيْنَاهُ وَأَهْلَهُ إِلَّا امْرَأَتَهُ كَانَتْ مِنَ الْغَابِرِينَ ۝

84. And We poured down upon them a rain. So behold! What the end of the culprits was!

وَأَمْطَرْنَا عَلَيْهِم مَّطَرًا فَانظُرْ كَيْفَ كَانَ عَاقِبَةُ الْمُجْرِمِينَ ۝

Section 11

85. To the Madain, We sent their brother Shu'ayb. He said: 'O my people! Worship Allah, no god you have but He. Surely there has come to you evidence from your Lord; so give full weight and measure, and do not defraud people of their things, and do not act corruptly on the earth after its ordering; that is the best for you, if you be believers.

وَإِلَى مَدْيَنَ أَخَاهُمْ شُعَيْبًا قَالَ يَا قَوْمِ اعْبُدُوا اللَّهَ مَا لَكُم مِّنْ إِلَهٍ غَيْرُهُ قَدْ جَاءَتْكُم بَيِّنَةٌ مِّن رَّبِّكُمْ فَأَوْفُوا الْكَيْلَ وَالْمِيزَانَ وَلَا تَبْخَسُوا النَّاسَ أَشْيَاءَهُمْ وَلَا تُفْسِدُوا فِي الْأَرْضِ بَعْدَ إِصْلَاحِهَا ذَلِكُمْ خَيْرٌ لَّكُمْ إِن كُنتُم مُّؤْمِنِينَ ۝

86. And do not beset every highway menacing and turning aside from the path of Allah those who believe in Him and seeking to render it crooked. And remember when you were small, and He thereafter multiplied you; and behold! What the end of the corrupters was like!

وَلَا تَقْعُدُوا بِكُلِّ صِرَاطٍ تُوعِدُونَ وَتَصُدُّونَ عَن سَبِيلِ اللَّهِ مَنْ آمَنَ بِهِ وَتَبْغُونَهَا عِوَجًا وَاذْكُرُوا إِذْ كُنتُمْ قَلِيلًا فَكَثَّرَكُمْ وَانظُرُوا كَيْفَ كَانَ عَاقِبَةُ الْمُفْسِدِينَ ۝

87. And if there is a party of you who believe in that with which I am sent and a party who do not believe, then have patience until Allah judges between us and He is the Best of Judges.'

88. The chiefs of those who were stiff-necked among his people said: 'Surely we will drive you forth, O Shu'ayb and those who have believed with you from our city, or else you shall return to our faith.' He said: 'What! Even though we abhor it.

89. We must have been fabricating a lie against Allah, if we returned to your faith after Allah has delivered us from it. And it is not for us to return thereto except that Allah, our Lord, so willed; everything our Lord comprehends in His knowledge, in Allah we place our trust. O our Lord! Decide between us and our people with Truth; You are the Best of the Deciders.'

90. And the chiefs of those who disbelieved among his people said: 'Should you follow Shu'ayb, lo! Verily you shall be the losers.'

91. An earthquake thereupon felled them; so that they lay prone in their dwellings.

وَإِن كَانَ طَآئِفَةٌ مِّنكُمْ ءَامَنُوا۟ بِٱلَّذِىٓ أُرْسِلْتُ بِهِۦ وَطَآئِفَةٌ لَّمْ يُؤْمِنُوا۟ فَٱصْبِرُوا۟ حَتَّىٰ يَحْكُمَ ٱللَّهُ بَيْنَنَا ۚ وَهُوَ خَيْرُ ٱلْحَٰكِمِينَ ۝

قَالَ ٱلْمَلَأُ ٱلَّذِينَ ٱسْتَكْبَرُوا۟ مِن قَوْمِهِۦ لَنُخْرِجَنَّكَ يَٰشُعَيْبُ وَٱلَّذِينَ ءَامَنُوا۟ مَعَكَ مِن قَرْيَتِنَآ أَوْ لَتَعُودُنَّ فِى مِلَّتِنَا ۚ قَالَ أَوَلَوْ كُنَّا كَٰرِهِينَ ۝

قَدِ ٱفْتَرَيْنَا عَلَى ٱللَّهِ كَذِبًا إِنْ عُدْنَا فِى مِلَّتِكُم بَعْدَ إِذْ نَجَّىٰنَا ٱللَّهُ مِنْهَا ۚ وَمَا يَكُونُ لَنَآ أَن نَّعُودَ فِيهَآ إِلَّآ أَن يَشَآءَ ٱللَّهُ رَبُّنَا ۚ وَسِعَ رَبُّنَا كُلَّ شَىْءٍ عِلْمًا ۚ عَلَى ٱللَّهِ تَوَكَّلْنَا ۚ رَبَّنَا ٱفْتَحْ بَيْنَنَا وَبَيْنَ قَوْمِنَا بِٱلْحَقِّ وَأَنتَ خَيْرُ ٱلْفَٰتِحِينَ ۝

وَقَالَ ٱلْمَلَأُ ٱلَّذِينَ كَفَرُوا۟ مِن قَوْمِهِۦ لَئِنِ ٱتَّبَعْتُمْ شُعَيْبًا إِنَّكُمْ إِذًا لَّخَٰسِرُونَ ۝

فَأَخَذَتْهُمُ ٱلرَّجْفَةُ فَأَصْبَحُوا۟ فِى دَارِهِمْ جَٰثِمِينَ ۝

92. Those who had belied Shu'ayb became as though they had not dwelt therein; those who had belied Shu'ayb, it was they who were the losers.

اَلَّذِينَ كَذَّبُواْ شُعَيْبًا كَأَن لَّمْ يَغْنَوْاْ فِيهَا ۚ اَلَّذِينَ كَذَّبُواْ شُعَيْبًا كَانُواْ هُمُ الْخَسِرِينَ ۝

93. Then he turned from them and said: 'O my people! Assuredly I delivered to you the messages of my Lord and counselled you good; how then should I lament over a disbelieving people?'

فَتَوَلَّىٰ عَنْهُمْ وَقَالَ يَٰقَوْمِ لَقَدْ أَبْلَغْتُكُمْ رِسَٰلَٰتِ رَبِّى وَنَصَحْتُ لَكُمْ ۖ فَكَيْفَ ءَاسَىٰ عَلَىٰ قَوْمٍ كَٰفِرِينَ ۝

Section 12

94. We did not send a Prophet to any town but We afflicted its people with calamities and disasters that perchance they might humble themselves.

وَمَآ أَرْسَلْنَا فِى قَرْيَةٍ مِّن نَّبِىٍّ إِلَّآ أَخَذْنَآ أَهْلَهَا بِالْبَأْسَآءِ وَالضَّرَّآءِ لَعَلَّهُمْ يَضَّرَّعُونَ ۝

95. Thereafter We changed ease for adversity until they abounded and said: 'Even thus did tribulation and prosperity touch our fathers.' Then We laid hold of them of a sudden while they perceived not.

ثُمَّ بَدَّلْنَا مَكَانَ السَّيِّئَةِ الْحَسَنَةَ حَتَّىٰ عَفَوْاْ وَقَالُواْ قَدْ مَسَّ ءَابَآءَنَا الضَّرَّآءُ وَالسَّرَّآءُ فَأَخَذْنَٰهُم بَغْتَةً وَهُمْ لَا يَشْعُرُونَ ۝

96. And had the people of those towns believed and feared Allah, We would of a surety have opened up to them blessings from the heavens and the earth; but they belied, so We seized them for what they had been earning.

وَلَوْ أَنَّ أَهْلَ الْقُرَىٰٓ ءَامَنُواْ وَاتَّقَوْاْ لَفَتَحْنَا عَلَيْهِم بَرَكَٰتٍ مِّنَ السَّمَآءِ وَالْأَرْضِ وَلَٰكِن كَذَّبُواْ فَأَخَذْنَٰهُم بِمَا كَانُواْ يَكْسِبُونَ ۝

97. Are the people of towns then secure that Our wrath would not visit them at night while they are slumbering?

أَفَأَمِنَ أَهْلُ ٱلْقُرَىٰٓ أَن يَأْتِيَهُم بَأْسُنَا بَيَـٰتًا وَهُمْ نَآئِمُونَ ۝

98. Or, are the people of towns then secure that Our wrath would not visit them by daylight while they are disporting themselves?

أَوَأَمِنَ أَهْلُ ٱلْقُرَىٰٓ أَن يَأْتِيَهُم بَأْسُنَا ضُحًى وَهُمْ يَلْعَبُونَ ۝

99. Are they then secure against the contrivance of Allah? None feels secure against Allah's contrivance except the people who are lost.

أَفَأَمِنُوا۟ مَكْرَ ٱللَّهِ فَلَا يَأْمَنُ مَكْرَ ٱللَّهِ إِلَّا ٱلْقَوْمُ ٱلْخَـٰسِرُونَ ۝

Section 13

100. Does it not guide the people who inherit the land thereafter, that had We willed, We would have afflicted them for their sins? And We have put a seal upon their hearts, so that they are bereft of hearing.

أَوَلَمْ يَهْدِ لِلَّذِينَ يَرِثُونَ ٱلْأَرْضَ مِنۢ بَعْدِ أَهْلِهَآ أَن لَّوْ نَشَآءُ أَصَبْنَـٰهُم بِذُنُوبِهِمْ وَنَطْبَعُ عَلَىٰ قُلُوبِهِمْ فَهُمْ لَا يَسْمَعُونَ ۝

101. Of those towns We have recounted to you some of their tidings: 'Assuredly there came to them their Messengers with evidence, but they were not such as to believe what they had first rejected.' Thus Allah put a seal upon the hearts of the infidels.

تِلْكَ ٱلْقُرَىٰ نَقُصُّ عَلَيْكَ مِنْ أَنۢبَآئِهَا ۚ وَلَقَدْ جَآءَتْهُمْ رُسُلُهُم بِٱلْبَيِّنَـٰتِ فَمَا كَانُوا۟ لِيُؤْمِنُوا۟ بِمَا كَذَّبُوا۟ مِن قَبْلُ ۚ كَذَٰلِكَ يَطْبَعُ ٱللَّهُ عَلَىٰ قُلُوبِ ٱلْكَـٰفِرِينَ ۝

102. We found no regard for covenant in most of them; and most of them We found ungodly.

وَمَا وَجَدْنَا لِأَكْثَرِهِم مِّنْ عَهْدٍ ۖ وَإِن وَجَدْنَآ أَكْثَرَهُمْ لَفَـٰسِقِينَ ۝

103. Then We sent after them Moses with Our signs to Pharaoh and his chiefs, but they wronged them. Behold then what the end of the corrupters was like.

ثُمَّ بَعَثْنَا مِنْ بَعْدِهِم مُّوسَىٰ بِآيَٰتِنَآ إِلَىٰ فِرْعَوْنَ وَمَلَإِيْهِ فَظَلَمُواْ بِهَا فَانظُرْ كَيْفَ كَانَ عَٰقِبَةُ ٱلْمُفْسِدِينَ ﴿١٠٣﴾

104. And Moses said: 'O Pharaoh! I am a Messenger from the Lord of the worlds.

وَقَالَ مُوسَىٰ يَٰفِرْعَوْنُ إِنِّى رَسُولٌ مِّن رَّبِّ ٱلْعَٰلَمِينَ ﴿١٠٤﴾

105. Incumbent it is upon me that I speak nothing concerning Allah except the Truth; surely I have brought to you evidence from your Lord[359]; so let the children of Israel depart with me.'

حَقِيقٌ عَلَىٰٓ أَن لَّآ أَقُولَ عَلَى ٱللَّهِ إِلَّا ٱلْحَقَّ قَدْ جِئْتُكُم بِبَيِّنَةٍ مِّن رَّبِّكُمْ فَأَرْسِلْ مَعِىَ بَنِىٓ إِسْرَٰٓءِيلَ ﴿١٠٥﴾

106. Pharaoh said: 'If you have brought a sign, come forth with it if you are of the truth-tellers.'

قَالَ إِن كُنتَ جِئْتَ بِآيَةٍ فَأْتِ بِهَآ إِن كُنتَ مِنَ ٱلصَّٰدِقِينَ ﴿١٠٦﴾

107. Then Moses threw his rod, when, lo! It was a serpent manifest.

فَأَلْقَىٰ عَصَاهُ فَإِذَا هِىَ ثُعْبَانٌ مُّبِينٌ ﴿١٠٧﴾

108. And he drew forth his hand, it was white to the beholders.

وَنَزَعَ يَدَهُۥ فَإِذَا هِىَ بَيْضَآءُ لِلنَّٰظِرِينَ ﴿١٠٨﴾

Section 14

109. The chiefs of the people of Pharaoh said: 'This is indeed a magician knowing.

قَالَ ٱلْمَلَأُ مِن قَوْمِ فِرْعَوْنَ إِنَّ هَٰذَا لَسَٰحِرٌ عَلِيمٌ ﴿١٠٩﴾

---

359. Mark the words 'your Lord'. The Qur'ānic God is the Universal God of the Egyptians as well as of the Israelites, and not the Biblical God 'the Lord God of the Hebrews'.

110. He will banish you from your land; so what is it that you now propose?'

111. They said: 'Put him and his brother off, and send callers to the cities.

112 That they may bring to you every magician knowing.'

113. And the magicians came to Pharaoh. They said: 'Certainly there is a reward for us, if we are the victors.'

114. Pharaoh said: 'Yea! And you shall be of those brought nigh.'

115. They said: 'O Moses! Either you cast down, or we shall be the ones to cast down first.'

116. Moses said: 'Cast down yours.' Then when they cast down, they enchanted the eyes of the people[360] and frightened them and brought mighty magic to bear.

يُرِيدُ أَن يُخْرِجَكُم مِّنْ أَرْضِكُمْ فَمَاذَا تَأْمُرُونَ ۝

قَالُوٓاْ أَرْجِهْ وَأَخَاهُ وَأَرْسِلْ فِي ٱلْمَدَآئِنِ حَٰشِرِينَ ۝

يَأْتُوكَ بِكُلِّ سَٰحِرٍ عَلِيمٍ ۝

وَجَآءَ ٱلسَّحَرَةُ فِرْعَوْنَ قَالُوٓاْ إِنَّ لَنَا لَأَجْرًا إِن كُنَّا نَحْنُ ٱلْغَٰلِبِينَ ۝

قَالَ نَعَمْ وَإِنَّكُمْ لَمِنَ ٱلْمُقَرَّبِينَ ۝

قَالُوٓاْ يَٰمُوسَىٰٓ إِمَّآ أَن تُلْقِىَ وَإِمَّآ أَن نَّكُونَ نَحْنُ ٱلْمُلْقِينَ ۝

قَالَ أَلْقُواْ فَلَمَّآ أَلْقَوْاْ سَحَرُوٓاْ أَعْيُنَ ٱلنَّاسِ وَٱسْتَرْهَبُوهُمْ وَجَآءُو بِسِحْرٍ عَظِيمٍ ۝

---

360. According to the Bible, the Egyptian magicians cast down their rods 'and they became serpents' (Ex. 7: 12). Note that the Holy Qur'ān lends no support to the view that the rods and cords of the magicians actually 'became serpents'. It only affirms that the magicians enchanted the eyes of the people. This is for the hundredth time that the Qur'ān is correcting an inaccuracy of the Bible. Indeed, the findings of modern European scholars agree with the Qur'ān rather than with the Bible. 'It would be quite wrong', says a modern authority, 'to ascribe the miracles performed by the Pharaoh's magicians to anything else than jugglery' (EBi. c. 1221). 'What was done on this occasion was probably a clever piece of sleight of hand' (Dummelow, *Commentary on the Holy Bible*, p. 55). 'Most modern critics are of the opinion that the magicians bore in their hands real snakes, rendered torpid and stiffy, so as to look like rods, which, on being thrown to the ground, were disenchanted, and resumed their natural character. Another explanation is that they were mere clever jugglers, adept in sleight of hand, and that the snakes were substituted for the rods, which were skillfully hidden away' (Rawlinson, *Moses: His Life and Times*, p. 93).

117. And We revealed to Moses: 'Cast your rod.' And lo! It swallowed up what they had feigned.

وَأَوْحَيْنَا إِلَى مُوسَى أَنْ أَلْقِ عَصَاكَ فَإِذَا هِيَ تَلْقَفُ مَا يَأْفِكُونَ ۝

118. Thus the Truth prevailed, and what they had prepared vanished.

فَوَقَعَ الْحَقُّ وَبَطَلَ مَا كَانُوا يَعْمَلُونَ ۝

119. Thus were they overcome and made to look abject.

فَغُلِبُوا هُنَالِكَ وَانْقَلَبُوا صَاغِرِينَ ۝

120. And the magicians flung themselves prostrate.

وَأُلْقِيَ السَّحَرَةُ سَاجِدِينَ ۝

121. They said: 'We believe in the Lord of the worlds.

قَالُوا آمَنَّا بِرَبِّ الْعَالَمِينَ ۝

122. The Lord of Moses and Aaron.'

رَبِّ مُوسَى وَهَارُونَ ۝

123. Pharaoh said:[361] 'Did you believe before I gave you leave? Assuredly this is a plot you have crafted in the city that you drive forth its people. So now you shall know.

قَالَ فِرْعَوْنُ آمَنْتُمْ بِهِ قَبْلَ أَنْ آذَنَ لَكُمْ إِنَّ هَذَا لَمَكْرٌ مَّكَرْتُمُوهُ فِي الْمَدِينَةِ لِتُخْرِجُوا مِنْهَا أَهْلَهَا فَسَوْفَ تَعْلَمُونَ ۝

124. Surely I will cut off your hands and feet on opposite sides and thereafter I will crucify you all.'

لَأُقَطِّعَنَّ أَيْدِيَكُمْ وَأَرْجُلَكُمْ مِّنْ خِلَافٍ ثُمَّ لَأُصَلِّبَنَّكُمْ أَجْمَعِينَ ۝

125. They said: 'Verily to our Lord we are turning,

قَالُوا إِنَّا إِلَى رَبِّنَا مُنقَلِبُونَ ۝

---

361. Saying thus in his extreme discomfiture. The triumph of Moses and Aaron was complete. The supreme magic of Egypt had been vanquished and humbled by the Divine Messengers, and yet Pharaoh cold-bloodedly hardened his heart and deliberately shut his eyes against the light.

126. And what is it that for which you take vengeance on us save that we believed in the signs of our Lord when they came to us. Our Lord! Pour out on us perseverance and cause us to die as Muslims.'

وَمَا تَنقِمُ مِنَّا إِلَّا أَنْ ءَامَنَّا بِـَٔايَٰتِ رَبِّنَا لَمَّا جَآءَتْنَا رَبَّنَآ أَفْرِغْ عَلَيْنَا صَبْرًا وَتَوَفَّنَا مُسْلِمِينَ ۝

Section 15

127. And the chiefs of the people of Pharaoh said: 'Will you leave alone Moses and his people to act corruptly in the land and to abandon you and the gods?' Pharaoh said: 'Soon we shall slay their sons and let live their women; we are masters over them.'

وَقَالَ ٱلْمَلَأُ مِن قَوْمِ فِرْعَوْنَ أَتَذَرُ مُوسَىٰ وَقَوْمَهُۥ لِيُفْسِدُوا۟ فِي ٱلْأَرْضِ وَيَذَرَكَ وَءَالِهَتَكَ قَالَ سَنُقَتِّلُ أَبْنَآءَهُمْ وَنَسْتَحْىِۦ نِسَآءَهُمْ وَإِنَّا فَوْقَهُمْ قَٰهِرُونَ ۝

128. Moses said to his people: 'Seek help in Allah and perseverance; verily the earth is Allah's; He makes whomsoever of His bondsmen He wills inherit it; and the happy end is of the God-fearing.'

قَالَ مُوسَىٰ لِقَوْمِهِ ٱسْتَعِينُوا۟ بِٱللَّهِ وَٱصْبِرُوٓا۟ إِنَّ ٱلْأَرْضَ لِلَّهِ يُورِثُهَا مَن يَشَآءُ مِنْ عِبَادِهِۦ وَٱلْعَٰقِبَةُ لِلْمُتَّقِينَ ۝

129. They said: 'Oppressed we have been before you came to us and since you have come to us.' He said: 'Belike your Lord will destroy your foe and establish you in their stead in the land, that He may see how you act.'

قَالُوٓا۟ أُوذِينَا مِن قَبْلِ أَن تَأْتِيَنَا وَمِنۢ بَعْدِ مَا جِئْتَنَا قَالَ عَسَىٰ رَبُّكُمْ أَن يُهْلِكَ عَدُوَّكُمْ وَيَسْتَخْلِفَكُمْ فِي ٱلْأَرْضِ فَيَنظُرَ كَيْفَ تَعْمَلُونَ ۝

Section 16

130. Assuredly, We afflicted the people of Pharaoh with lean years and lack of fruits, that they might take heed.

وَلَقَدْ أَخَذْنَا ءَالَ فِرْعَوْنَ بِالسِّنِينَ وَ نَقْصٍ مِّنَ الثَّمَرَٰتِ لَعَلَّهُمْ يَذَّكَّرُونَ ۝

131. So whenever good came their way, they would say, 'ours is this.' And if evil afflicted them, they would lay it to the ill augury of Moses and those with him. Lo! Their ill augury was only with Allah; but most of them knew not.

فَإِذَا جَآءَتْهُمُ الْحَسَنَةُ قَالُوا لَنَا هَٰذِهِۦ وَإِن تُصِبْهُمْ سَيِّئَةٌ يَطَّيَّرُوا بِمُوسَىٰ وَمَن مَّعَهُۥٓ أَلَآ إِنَّمَا طَٰٓئِرُهُمْ عِندَ اللَّهِ وَلَٰكِنَّ أَكْثَرَهُمْ لَا يَعْلَمُونَ ۝

132. They said: 'Whatever the nature of a sign you may bring to us with which to enchant us, in you we are not going to be believers.'

وَقَالُوا مَهْمَا تَأْتِنَا بِهِۦ مِنْ ءَايَةٍ لِّتَسْحَرَنَا بِهَا فَمَا نَحْنُ لَكَ بِمُؤْمِنِينَ ۝

133. Thereafter We sent upon them the flood and the locusts, and the lice, and the frogs and the blood: signs detailed; yet they remained stiff-necked and they were a people sinful.

فَأَرْسَلْنَا عَلَيْهِمُ الطُّوفَانَ وَالْجَرَادَ وَالْقُمَّلَ وَالضَّفَادِعَ وَالدَّمَ ءَايَٰتٍ مُّفَصَّلَٰتٍ فَاسْتَكْبَرُوا وَكَانُوا قَوْمًا مُّجْرِمِينَ ۝

134. Whenever a plague fell on them they said: 'O Moses! Supplicate your Lord for us by what your Lord has covenanted with you; if you remove the plague from us, we will believe in you, and we will send with you the children of Israel.'

وَلَمَّا وَقَعَ عَلَيْهِمُ الرِّجْزُ قَالُوا يَٰمُوسَى ادْعُ لَنَا رَبَّكَ بِمَا عَهِدَ عِندَكَ لَئِن كَشَفْتَ عَنَّا الرِّجْزَ لَنُؤْمِنَنَّ لَكَ وَ لَنُرْسِلَنَّ مَعَكَ بَنِي إِسْرَٰٓءِيلَ ۝

135. Then whenever We removed the plague from them till a term which they were to reach, lo! They were breaking faith.

فَلَمَّا كَشَفْنَا عَنْهُمُ الرِّجْزَ إِلَىٰ أَجَلٍ هُم بَالِغُوهُ إِذَا هُمْ يَنكُثُونَ ۝

136. Therefore, We took vengeance on them and drowned them in the sea: for they belied Our signs and were neglectful of them.

فَانتَقَمْنَا مِنْهُمْ فَأَغْرَقْنَاهُمْ فِي الْيَمِّ بِأَنَّهُمْ كَذَّبُوا بِآيَاتِنَا وَكَانُوا عَنْهَا غَافِلِينَ ۝

137. And We caused the people who had been oppressed to inherit the land, the eastern and western parts of it, which We had blessed. And fulfilled was the good word of your Lord to the children of Israel for they were long-suffering, and We annihilated what Pharaoh and his people had built and what they had raised.

وَأَوْرَثْنَا الْقَوْمَ الَّذِينَ كَانُوا يُسْتَضْعَفُونَ مَشَارِقَ الْأَرْضِ وَمَغَارِبَهَا الَّتِي بَارَكْنَا فِيهَا وَتَمَّتْ كَلِمَتُ رَبِّكَ الْحُسْنَىٰ عَلَىٰ بَنِي إِسْرَائِيلَ بِمَا صَبَرُوا وَدَمَّرْنَا مَا كَانَ يَصْنَعُ فِرْعَوْنُ وَقَوْمُهُ وَمَا كَانُوا يَعْرِشُونَ ۝

138. And We led the children of Israel across the sea. Then they came upon a people clinging to the idols they had. They said: 'O Moses! Make for us a god, even as they have gods.' He said: 'Verily you are a people given to paganism.'

وَجَاوَزْنَا بِبَنِي إِسْرَائِيلَ الْبَحْرَ فَأَتَوْا عَلَىٰ قَوْمٍ يَعْكُفُونَ عَلَىٰ أَصْنَامٍ لَّهُمْ قَالُوا يَامُوسَى اجْعَل لَّنَا إِلَٰهًا كَمَا لَهُمْ ءَالِهَةٌ قَالَ إِنَّكُمْ قَوْمٌ تَجْهَلُونَ ۝

139. Verily those! Vain is that in which they were engaged and vain became what they had been doing.

إِنَّ هَٰؤُلَاءِ مُتَبَّرٌ مَّا هُمْ فِيهِ وَبَاطِلٌ مَّا كَانُوا يَعْمَلُونَ ۝

140. He said: 'Shall I seek for you a god other than Allah whereas He has raised you above the world?'

قَالَ أَغَيْرَ اللَّهِ أَبْغِيكُمْ إِلَٰهًا وَهُوَ فَضَّلَكُمْ عَلَى الْعَالَمِينَ ۝

141. Recall that time We delivered you from the house of Pharaoh who was perpetrating upon your terrible torment, slaying your sons and letting your women live; and in that was a tremendous trial from your Lord.

وَإِذْ أَنجَيْنَكُم مِّنْ ءَالِ فِرْعَوْنَ يَسُومُونَكُمْ سُوٓءَ ٱلْعَذَابِ يُقَتِّلُونَ أَبْنَآءَكُمْ وَيَسْتَحْيُونَ نِسَآءَكُمْ وَفِى ذَٰلِكُم بَلَآءٌ مِّن رَّبِّكُمْ عَظِيمٌ ۝

Section 17

142. And We treated with Moses thirty nights, and We completed them with ten; so the appointment of his Lord was completed by forty nights. And Moses said to his brother Aaron: 'Act you in my place among my people and rectify, and do not follow the way of the corrupters.'

وَوَٰعَدْنَا مُوسَىٰ ثَلَٰثِينَ لَيْلَةً وَأَتْمَمْنَٰهَا بِعَشْرٍ فَتَمَّ مِيقَٰتُ رَبِّهِۦٓ أَرْبَعِينَ لَيْلَةً وَقَالَ مُوسَىٰ لِأَخِيهِ هَٰرُونَ ٱخْلُفْنِى فِى قَوْمِى وَأَصْلِحْ وَلَا تَتَّبِعْ سَبِيلَ ٱلْمُفْسِدِينَ ۝

143. And when Moses came at Our appointment, his Lord spoke to him. He said: 'Lord! Show Yourself to me, that I may look at You!' Allah said: 'You cannot see Me. But look at this mount; if it stands in its place, then you will see Me.' Then when his Lord unveiled His glory to the mount, it turned it to dust, and Moses fell down thunder struck. Then when he recovered, he said: 'Hallowed be You! I turn to You repentant, and I am the first of the believers.'

وَلَمَّا جَآءَ مُوسَىٰ لِمِيقَٰتِنَا وَكَلَّمَهُۥ رَبُّهُۥ قَالَ رَبِّ أَرِنِىٓ أَنظُرْ إِلَيْكَ قَالَ لَن تَرَىٰنِى وَلَٰكِنِ ٱنظُرْ إِلَى ٱلْجَبَلِ فَإِنِ ٱسْتَقَرَّ مَكَانَهُۥ فَسَوْفَ تَرَىٰنِى فَلَمَّا تَجَلَّىٰ رَبُّهُۥ لِلْجَبَلِ جَعَلَهُۥ دَكًّا وَخَرَّ مُوسَىٰ صَعِقًا فَلَمَّآ أَفَاقَ قَالَ سُبْحَٰنَكَ تُبْتُ إِلَيْكَ وَأَنَا۠ أَوَّلُ ٱلْمُؤْمِنِينَ ۝

144. Allah said: 'O Moses I have chosen you indeed above mankind by My messages and by My speaking, so hold fast what I have given you, and be of the grateful.'

قَالَ يَٰمُوسَىٰٓ إِنِّى ٱصْطَفَيْتُكَ عَلَى ٱلنَّاسِ بِرِسَٰلَٰتِى وَبِكَلَٰمِى فَخُذْ مَآ ءَاتَيْتُكَ وَكُن مِّنَ ٱلشَّٰكِرِينَ ﴿١٤٤﴾

145. And in the tablets We wrote for him of everything an exhortation, and a detail of everything. So hold you fast with firmness, and bid your people follow the best of it; soon I shall show you the abode of the ungodly people.

وَكَتَبْنَا لَهُۥ فِى ٱلْأَلْوَاحِ مِن كُلِّ شَىْءٍ مَّوْعِظَةً وَتَفْصِيلًا لِّكُلِّ شَىْءٍ فَخُذْهَا بِقُوَّةٍ وَأْمُرْ قَوْمَكَ يَأْخُذُواْ بِأَحْسَنِهَا سَأُوْرِيكُمْ دَارَ ٱلْفَٰسِقِينَ ﴿١٤٥﴾

146. I will turn away from My signs those who are big with pride on the earth unjustly, and even though they may see every sign they will not believe; and if they see the path of rectitude they will take it as their path, and if they see the path of error they will take it as their path. This is because they belied Our signs and they were ever neglectful of them.

سَأَصْرِفُ عَنْ ءَايَٰتِىَ ٱلَّذِينَ يَتَكَبَّرُونَ فِى ٱلْأَرْضِ بِغَيْرِ ٱلْحَقِّ وَإِن يَرَوْاْ كُلَّ ءَايَةٍ لَّا يُؤْمِنُواْ بِهَا وَإِن يَرَوْاْ سَبِيلَ ٱلرُّشْدِ لَا يَتَّخِذُوهُ سَبِيلًا وَإِن يَرَوْاْ سَبِيلَ ٱلْغَىِّ يَتَّخِذُوهُ سَبِيلًا ذَٰلِكَ بِأَنَّهُمْ كَذَّبُواْ بِـَٔايَٰتِنَا وَكَانُواْ عَنْهَا غَٰفِلِينَ ﴿١٤٦﴾

147. Those who belie Our signs and the meeting of the Hereafter, vain shall be their works. They shall be requited only for what they wrought.

وَٱلَّذِينَ كَذَّبُواْ بِـَٔايَٰتِنَا وَلِقَآءِ ٱلْأَخِرَةِ حَبِطَتْ أَعْمَٰلُهُمْ هَلْ يُجْزَوْنَ إِلَّا مَا كَانُواْ يَعْمَلُونَ ﴿١٤٧﴾

Section 18

148. And the people of Moses after him, made of their trinkets a calf; a body with a low. Did they not see that it neither spoke to them nor could it guide them to a way? They took it for their god, and they became evil-doers.

وَاتَّخَذَ قَوۡمُ مُوۡسٰى مِنۢ بَعۡدِهٖ مِنۡ حُلِيِّهِمۡ عِجۡلًا جَسَدًا لَّهٗ خُوَارٌ‌ اَلَمۡ يَرَوۡا اَنَّهٗ لَا يُكَلِّمُهُمۡ وَلَا يَهۡدِيۡهِمۡ سَبِيۡلًا اتَّخَذُوۡهُ وَكَانُوۡا ظٰلِمِيۡنَ ۞

149. And when they repented and saw they had strayed, they said: 'If our Lord does not have mercy on us and does not forgive us, we shall surely be of the losers.'

وَلَمَّا سُقِطَ فِىۡۤ اَيۡدِيۡهِمۡ وَرَاَوۡا اَنَّهُمۡ قَدۡ ضَلُّوۡا قَالُوۡا لَئِنۡ لَّمۡ يَرۡحَمۡنَا رَبُّنَا وَيَغۡفِرۡ لَنَا لَنَكُوۡنَنَّ مِنَ الۡخٰسِرِيۡنَ ۞

150. When Moses returned to his people indignant and sorrowing he said: 'Ill is that which you have acted as my successor, in my absence! Did you outstrip your Lord's commandment?' And he cast the tablets and seized the head of his brother dragging him to himself. Aaron said: 'Son of my mother: the people held me weak, and well nigh slew me, so do not cause the enemies to rejoice over me and do not place me with the wrongdoing people.'[362]

وَلَمَّا رَجَعَ مُوۡسٰۤى اِلٰى قَوۡمِهٖ غَضۡبَانَ اَسِفًا قَالَ بِئۡسَمَا خَلَفۡتُمُوۡنِىۡ مِنۢ بَعۡدِىۡ اَعَجِلۡتُمۡ اَمۡرَ رَبِّكُمۡ‌ وَاَلۡقَى الۡاَلۡوَاحَ وَاَخَذَ بِرَاۡسِ اَخِيۡهِ يَجُرُّهٗۤ اِلَيۡهِ‌ قَالَ ابۡنَ اُمَّ اِنَّ الۡقَوۡمَ اسۡتَضۡعَفُوۡنِىۡ وَكَادُوۡا يَقۡتُلُوۡنَنِىۡ فَلَا تُشۡمِتۡ بِىَ الۡاَعۡدَآءَ وَلَا تَجۡعَلۡنِىۡ مَعَ الۡقَوۡمِ الظّٰلِمِيۡنَ ۞

---

362. Contrast this highly meritorious attitude displayed by Aaron as depicted by the Qur'an with the Biblical version which fathers the very responsibility of calf–worship on Aaron, i.e., Aaron. See Ex. 32: 2–6. According to Biblical scholars, a clue to the contradictory delineation of Aaron in the Old Testament is found in the documentary analysis which shows that the 'narrative is the result of combining two distinct accounts' (*NSD*. pp. 15. 121).

151. Moses said: 'O Lord: Forgive me and my brother, and cause us twain to enter into Your Mercy, and You are the most Merciful of the merciful.'

Section 19

152. Those who took to themselves the calf will presently be overtaken with wrath from their Lord and abasement in the life of this world. Thus do We requite the forgers.

153. And those who committed evils, and thereafter repented and believed, verily your Lord is thereafter the Forgiving, the Merciful.

154. And when the anger of Moses was allayed, he took up the tablets, and in the inscription thereon were guidance and mercy unto those who are in awe of their Lord.

155. And Moses singled out of his people seventy men for Our appointment then when the earthquake seized them, he said: 'Lord: Had You willed, You would have killed them afore and me also. Wilt you kill us for what the fools among us have done? It is only Your trial by which You send astray whom You will and keep guided whom You will. You are the Patron. So forgive us and have mercy on us; and You are the Best of the forgivers.

قَالَ رَبِّ اغْفِرْ لِي وَلِأَخِي وَأَدْخِلْنَا فِي رَحْمَتِكَ وَأَنتَ أَرْحَمُ الرَّاحِمِينَ ۝

إِنَّ الَّذِينَ اتَّخَذُوا الْعِجْلَ سَيَنَالُهُمْ غَضَبٌ مِّن رَّبِّهِمْ وَذِلَّةٌ فِي الْحَيَوٰةِ الدُّنْيَا ۚ وَكَذَٰلِكَ نَجْزِي الْمُفْتَرِينَ ۝

وَالَّذِينَ عَمِلُوا السَّيِّئَاتِ ثُمَّ تَابُوا مِنۢ بَعْدِهَا وَءَامَنُوا إِنَّ رَبَّكَ مِنۢ بَعْدِهَا لَغَفُورٌ رَّحِيمٌ ۝

وَلَمَّا سَكَتَ عَن مُّوسَى الْغَضَبُ أَخَذَ الْأَلْوَاحَ ۖ وَفِي نُسْخَتِهَا هُدًى وَرَحْمَةٌ لِّلَّذِينَ هُمْ لِرَبِّهِمْ يَرْهَبُونَ ۝

وَاخْتَارَ مُوسَىٰ قَوْمَهُ سَبْعِينَ رَجُلًا لِّمِيقَاتِنَا ۖ فَلَمَّا أَخَذَتْهُمُ الرَّجْفَةُ قَالَ رَبِّ لَوْ شِئْتَ أَهْلَكْتَهُم مِّن قَبْلُ وَإِيَّايَ ۖ أَتُهْلِكُنَا بِمَا فَعَلَ السُّفَهَاءُ مِنَّا ۖ إِنْ هِيَ إِلَّا فِتْنَتُكَ تُضِلُّ بِهَا مَن تَشَاءُ وَتَهْدِي مَن تَشَاءُ ۚ أَنتَ وَلِيُّنَا فَاغْفِرْ لَنَا وَارْحَمْنَا ۖ وَأَنتَ خَيْرُ الْغَافِرِينَ ۝

156. And ordain for us good in the world and in the Hereafter; surely we have been guided to You.' Allah said: 'As to My chastisement, I afflict therewith whom I will, and as to My mercy, it comprehends everything. I will therefore ordain it for those who fear God and pay the poor-rate and those who believe in Our signs.'

157. Those who follow the Messenger, the unlettered Prophet, whom they find described in the Torah[363] and

وَاكْتُبْ لَنَا فِيْ هٰذِهِ الدُّنْيَا حَسَنَةً وَّفِي الْاٰخِرَةِ اِنَّا هُدْنَآ اِلَيْكَ قَالَ عَذَابِيْٓ اُصِيْبُ بِهٖ مَنْ اَشَآءُ وَرَحْمَتِيْ وَسِعَتْ كُلَّ شَيْءٍ فَسَاكْتُبُهَا لِلَّذِيْنَ يَتَّقُوْنَ وَيُؤْتُوْنَ الزَّكٰوةَ وَالَّذِيْنَ هُمْ بِاٰيٰتِنَا يُؤْمِنُوْنَ ۞

اَلَّذِيْنَ يَتَّبِعُوْنَ الرَّسُوْلَ النَّبِيَّ الْاُمِّيَّ الَّذِيْ يَجِدُوْنَهٗ مَكْتُوْبًا عِنْدَهُمْ فِي التَّوْرٰىةِ وَالْاِنْجِيْلِ

363. Here are a few references with a running commentary:

(i) 'I will raise them up a Prophet from among their brethren, like unto thee, and will put my words in his mouth; and he shall speak unto them all that I shall command him' (Dt. 18: 18).

'Their' referring to the Israelites, 'their brethren', must clearly be the Ishmaelites; and thus the promised Prophet must be an Ishmaelite. 'Like unto thee' obviously means 'like unto Moses' in having a Law of his own. The description will put my words shall command him' is also alluded to in Jn. 16: 13.

(ii) 'The Lord came from Sinai, and rose up from Seir unto them; he shined forth from Mount Paran, and he came with ten thousands of saints: from his right hand went a fiery law for them' (Dt. 33: 2). Coming after Moses ('from Sinai') and Jesus ('from Seir') the allusion 'from Mount Paran', which is in Makka, is clearly to the Prophet born in Makka. It was he who entered that city as a victor at the head of 10,000 saintly companions and holding in his hand 'a fiery law'.

(iii) 'And as for Ishmael, I have heard thee: Behold, I have blessed him and will make him fruitful, and will multiply him exceedingly; twelve princes shall he beget, and I will make him a great nation' (Ge. 17: 20). This promise from God to bless Ishmael found its complete fulfilment in the person of Muḥammad (on him be peace!) – an Ishmaelite being appointed the Prophet for the entire world.

(iv) 'The sceptre shall not be taken away from Judah, not a ruler from his thigh, till he come that is to be sent: and he shall be the expectation of nations' (Ge. 49: 10. *DV.*). It was at the advent of this Ishmaelite 'sent one' that prophecy in Israel ceased, and it was he under whom the nations of the world gathered.

(v) 'I will make thy name to be remembered in all generations: therefore shall the people praise thee for ever and ever' (Ps. 45: 17). 'Muḥammad' literally means 'the praised one'. And it is his name coupled with that of his Creator, which is being proclaimed from the mosque minarets five times every day throughout the world.

(vi) 'Behold my servant, whom I uphold; mine elect, in whom my soul delighteth; I have put my Spirit upon him; he shall bring forth judgment to the Gentiles. And the isles shall wait for his law'. (Is. 42: 1, 4).

It is precisely Muḥammad, the 'servant of God' and His 'elect' (Muṣṭafā) who brought judgement to the Gentiles, and whose law has been awaited by the distant 'isles'.

(vii) 'Yea, he is altogether lovely. This is my beloved, and this is my friend' (So. 5: 16).

The word 'lovely' used in the English Bible is a substitute for the Hebrew one, 'Muhammadin'. As this name of our Prophet is a noun adjective, the sacred poet uses it in a manner answering both the interpretation of a proper noun and an adjective' (Syed Ahmad Khan, *Essays on the Life of Mohammed*, X. p. 16).

As further references, the following may be cited: Hab. 3: 3; Hag 2: 7–9; Mal. 3: 1.

Gospel[364] which are with them; he bids them to the seemly and forbids them the unseemly, allows to them things clean, and prohibits them things unclean, and relieves them of their burdens and the shackles which have been upon them. Then those who believe in him and side with him and succour him and follow the light which has been sent down with him, those are the prosperous.'

يَأْمُرُهُم بِٱلْمَعْرُوفِ وَيَنْهَىٰهُمْ عَنِ ٱلْمُنكَرِ وَيُحِلُّ لَهُمُ ٱلطَّيِّبَـٰتِ وَيُحَرِّمُ عَلَيْهِمُ ٱلْخَبَـٰٓئِثَ وَيَضَعُ عَنْهُمْ إِصْرَهُمْ وَٱلْأَغْلَـٰلَ ٱلَّتِى كَانَتْ عَلَيْهِمْ ۚ فَٱلَّذِينَ ءَامَنُوا۟ بِهِۦ وَعَزَّرُوهُ وَنَصَرُوهُ وَٱتَّبَعُوا۟ ٱلنُّورَ ٱلَّذِىٓ أُنزِلَ مَعَهُۥٓ ۙ أُو۟لَـٰٓئِكَ هُمُ ٱلْمُفْلِحُونَ ۝

---

364. Even in the manipulated and mutilated NT of the present – day the allusions are neither too scanty nor too enigmatical:

(i)   'Did ye never read in the Scriptures, the stone which the builders rejected, the same is become the head of the corner; this is the Lord's doing, and it is marvellous in our eyes? Therefore say I unto you, the kingdom of God shall be taken from you, and given to a nation bringing forth the fruits thereof. And whosoever it shall fall, it will grind him to powder' (Mt. 21: 42–44).

It was the progeny of Ishmael that was so long rejected and looked down upon by the Jews and also by the Christians. It was one of those very Ishmaelites who at long last was raised to the highest honour. The announcement that this Prophet's opponents shall be smashed is even more clear.

(ii)   'Tarry in the city of Jerusalem until ye be endued with power from on high' (Lk. 24: 49).

It was after the advent of the Prophet Muhammad (peace and blessings be upon him) that the reverence paid to Jerusalem was transferred to the Kaʿba.

(iii)   'Who are you? And he confessed, and denied not; but confesses, I am not the Christ. And they asked him, what then? Are You Elijah? And he said, I am not. Are you that Prophet? And he answered, No. And they asked him, and said unto him, Why baptizest you then, if thou be not Christ, nor Elijah, neither that Prophet? (Jn. 1: 19–21, 25). The questions were put by the learned among the Jews to John the Baptist, which clearly indicates that besides Christ and Elijah (Elias in the Authorized King James' Version of 1611), they expected another Prophet, who was so well known that instead of designating him by name, a mere pronoun, 'that Prophet' was deemed quite sufficient.

(iv)   'Many of the people therefore, when they heard this saying, said, of a truth this is the Prophet, others said, this is the Christ'. (Jn. 7: 40–41). Another very clear reference to the advent of the well-known Prophet, 'the Prophet'.

(v)   'And I will pray the Father, and he shall give you another Comforter that he may abide with you for ever' (Jn. 14:16).

(vi)   'But when the Comforter is come, whom I shall send unto you from the Father, even the Spirit of truth, which proceed from the Father, he shall testify of me' (Jn. 15: 26).

(vii)   'And when he is come, he will reprove the world of sin, and of righteousness, and of judgment. Howbeit when he, the Spirit of truth, is come, he will guide you into all truth: for he shall not speak of himself, but whatsoever he shall hear, that shall he speak: and he will shew you things to come' (Jn. 16: 8–13).

All these descriptions of the Comforter exactly fit the Prophet Muḥammad (peace and blessings be upon him). He it is who, as the final Prophet, brought an abiding Message ('abiding with you for ever'), who testified to the Truth of Jesus ('he shall testify of me'), and who 'reproved the world of sin, and of righteousness, and of judgement', And he, above all, was the Divine mouthpiece, reproducing the Words of God precisely as he received them ('he shall not speak of himself, but whosoever he shall hear, that shall he speak').

This also accords with the 'Gospels', accepted as they are as canonical by the Christian Church. When we come to the Gospel of St. Barnabas we find the references as plain as they could possibly be — the Prophet is not only delineated in full but also prophesied by name. See Ragg, *The Gospel of St. Barnabas*, pp. 33, 99, 101, 103, 109, 167, 169, 223, 381.

Section 20

158. Say: 'O mankind! Verily I am Allah's Messenger to you all. Of Him whose is the dominion of the heavens and the earth. No god is there but He; He gives life and causes death. Believe then in Allah and His Messenger, the unlettered Prophet, who believes in Allah and His Word; and follow him that haply you may be guided.'

قُلْ يَـٰٓأَيُّهَا ٱلنَّاسُ إِنِّى رَسُولُ ٱللَّهِ إِلَيْكُمْ جَمِيعًا ٱلَّذِى لَهُۥ مُلْكُ ٱلسَّمَـٰوَٰتِ وَٱلْأَرْضِ لَآ إِلَـٰهَ إِلَّا هُوَ يُحْىِۦ وَيُمِيتُ فَـَٔامِنُوا۟ بِٱللَّهِ وَرَسُولِهِ ٱلنَّبِىِّ ٱلْأُمِّىِّ ٱلَّذِى يُؤْمِنُ بِٱللَّهِ وَ كَلِمَـٰتِهِۦ وَٱتَّبِعُوهُ لَعَلَّكُمْ تَهْتَدُونَ ۝

159. And of the people of Moses there is a community guiding others by the Truth and judging thereby.

وَمِن قَوْمِ مُوسَىٰٓ أُمَّةٌ يَهْدُونَ بِٱلْحَقِّ وَبِهِۦ يَعْدِلُونَ ۝

160. And We divided them into twelve tribes as nations. And We revealed to Moses, when his people asked him for water: 'Smite the rock with your rod.' Then gushed forth from it twelve springs; each people already knew their drinking-place. And We shaded them with thick clouds; and We sent down upon them the manna and the quail, saying: eat of the pure things with which We have provided you. And they wronged Us not, but themselves they were wont to wrong.

وَقَطَّعْنَـٰهُمُ ٱثْنَتَىْ عَشْرَةَ أَسْبَاطًا أُمَمًا وَأَوْحَيْنَآ إِلَىٰ مُوسَىٰٓ إِذِ ٱسْتَسْقَىٰهُ قَوْمُهُۥٓ أَنِ ٱضْرِب بِّعَصَاكَ ٱلْحَجَرَ فَٱنۢبَجَسَتْ مِنْهُ ٱثْنَتَا عَشْرَةَ عَيْنًا قَدْ عَلِمَ كُلُّ أُنَاسٍ مَّشْرَبَهُمْ وَظَلَّلْنَا عَلَيْهِمُ ٱلْغَمَـٰمَ وَ أَنزَلْنَا عَلَيْهِمُ ٱلْمَنَّ وَٱلسَّلْوَىٰ كُلُوا۟ مِن طَيِّبَـٰتِ مَا رَزَقْنَـٰكُمْ وَمَا ظَلَمُونَا وَلَـٰكِن كَانُوٓا۟ أَنفُسَهُمْ يَظْلِمُونَ ۝

161. Recall the time it was said to them: 'Reside in this town and eat from it wherever you wish, and say forgive us and enter the gate bowing;' and We shall forgive you your trespasses. We give abundance to the well doers.

162. Then those of them who did wrong changed the Word that had been told them for another; thereupon We sent a scourge upon them from the heaven, for they were wont to transgress.

Section 21

163. And ask you them about the town that stood by the sea when they transgressed in the matter of the Sabbath, when their fish came to them openly on the Sabbath day and did not come to them on the day they did not observe the Sabbath. Thus We tested them for they were wont to act wickedly.

164. And recall what time a community of them said: 'Why do you exhort a people whom Allah is going to kill or chastise with a severe chastisement?' They said: 'To justify us before your Lord and that haply you may fear God.'

وَإِذْ قِيلَ لَهُمُ اسْكُنُوا هَٰذِهِ الْقَرْيَةَ وَكُلُوا مِنْهَا حَيْثُ شِئْتُمْ وَقُولُوا حِطَّةٌ وَادْخُلُوا الْبَابَ سُجَّدًا نَّغْفِرْ لَكُمْ خَطِيئَاتِكُمْ ۚ سَنَزِيدُ الْمُحْسِنِينَ ۝

فَبَدَّلَ الَّذِينَ ظَلَمُوا مِنْهُمْ قَوْلًا غَيْرَ الَّذِي قِيلَ لَهُمْ فَأَرْسَلْنَا عَلَيْهِمْ رِجْزًا مِّنَ السَّمَاءِ بِمَا كَانُوا يَظْلِمُونَ ۝

وَسْئَلْهُمْ عَنِ الْقَرْيَةِ الَّتِي كَانَتْ حَاضِرَةَ الْبَحْرِ إِذْ يَعْدُونَ فِي السَّبْتِ إِذْ تَأْتِيهِمْ حِيتَانُهُمْ يَوْمَ سَبْتِهِمْ شُرَّعًا وَيَوْمَ لَا يَسْبِتُونَ ۙ لَا تَأْتِيهِمْ ۚ كَذَٰلِكَ نَبْلُوهُم بِمَا كَانُوا يَفْسُقُونَ ۝

وَإِذْ قَالَتْ أُمَّةٌ مِّنْهُمْ لِمَ تَعِظُونَ قَوْمًا ۙ اللَّهُ مُهْلِكُهُمْ أَوْ مُعَذِّبُهُمْ عَذَابًا شَدِيدًا ۖ قَالُوا مَعْذِرَةً إِلَىٰ رَبِّكُمْ وَلَعَلَّهُمْ يَتَّقُونَ ۝

165. Then when they forgot what they had been exhorted with, We delivered those who restrained others from evil and We seized those who did wrong with a distressing torment for they were wont to transgress.

فَلَمَّا نَسُوۡا مَا ذُكِّرُوۡا بِهٖۤ اَنۡجَيۡنَا الَّذِيۡنَ يَنۡهَوۡنَ عَنِ السُّوۡٓءِ وَاَخَذۡنَا الَّذِيۡنَ ظَلَمُوۡا بِعَذَابٍۭ بَئِيۡسٍۭ بِمَا كَانُوۡا يَفۡسُقُوۡنَ ﴿١٦٥﴾

166. So when they exceeded the limits of what they were prohibited, We said to them: 'Be ye apes despised.'

فَلَمَّا عَتَوۡا عَنۡ مَّا نُهُوۡا عَنۡهُ قُلۡنَا لَهُمۡ كُوۡنُوۡا قِرَدَةً خَاسِئِيۡنَ ﴿١٦٦﴾

167. And recall when your Lord proclaimed that He would surely raise upon them, till the Day of Resurrection, someone perpetrating upon them the worst oppression. Verily your Lord is Swift in retribution; and verily He is the Forgiving, the Merciful.

وَاِذۡ تَاَذَّنَ رَبُّكَ لَيَبۡعَثَنَّ عَلَيۡهِمۡ اِلَى يَوۡمِ الۡقِيٰمَةِ مَنۡ يَّسُوۡمُهُمۡ سُوۡٓءَ الۡعَذَابِ اِنَّ رَبَّكَ لَسَرِيۡعُ الۡعِقَابِ وَاِنَّهٗ لَغَفُوۡرٌ رَّحِيۡمٌ ﴿١٦٧﴾

168. And We cut them up into communities on the earth; some of them righteous and some of them otherwise; and We tempted them with good and evil that perchance they may return.

وَقَطَّعۡنٰهُمۡ فِى الۡاَرۡضِ اُمَمًا مِّنۡهُمُ الصّٰلِحُوۡنَ وَمِنۡهُمۡ دُوۡنَ ذٰلِكَ وَ بَلَوۡنٰهُمۡ بِالۡحَسَنٰتِ وَالسَّيِّاٰتِ لَعَلَّهُمۡ يَرۡجِعُوۡنَ ﴿١٦٨﴾

169. Then succeeded them a posterity who inherited the Book but who took the things of this world,[365] saying: 'Assuredly it will be forgiven us.' And if there comes to them other things like it, they shall take it. Has there not

فَخَلَفَ مِنۡۢ بَعۡدِهِمۡ خَلۡفٌ وَّرِثُوا الۡكِتٰبَ يَاۡخُذُوۡنَ عَرَضَ هٰذَا الۡاَدۡنٰى وَيَقُوۡلُوۡنَ سَيُغۡفَرُ لَنَا وَاِنۡ يَّاۡتِهِمۡ عَرَضٌ مِّثۡلُهٗ يَاۡخُذُوۡهُ اَلَمۡ يُؤۡخَذۡ عَلَيۡهِمۡ

---

365. The reference is to the Jews' acceptance of bribes for wresting judgement and corrupting the text of their Books and to their extortion of money.

lain upon them the bond of the
Book that shall say of God
anything but truth? And they have
read what is in it, and the abode
of the Hereafter is better for those
who fear. Do you not then
understand?

170.   And those who stand fast
by the Book and establish prayer
verily We will not waste the return
of rectifiers.

171.   And recall when We shook
the mountain over them as though
it was a canopy and they imagined
that it was going to fall upon them
and We said: 'Hold firmly to what
We have given you and remember
what is in that, that haply you may
fear.'

Section 22

172.   And recall when your Lord
brought forth from the children of
Adam their posterity from their
backs and made them testify as to
themselves saying: 'Am I not your
Lord?' They said: 'Yea!366 We
testify.' That was lest you should
say on the Day of Resurrection:
'Verily of this we have been
unaware.'

مِّيثَقُ ٱلْكِتَبِ أَن لَّا يَقُولُواْ عَلَى ٱللَّهِ إِلَّا
ٱلْحَقَّ وَدَرَسُواْ مَا فِيهِ وَٱلدَّارُ ٱلْأَخِرَةُ
خَيْرٌ لِّلَّذِينَ يَتَّقُونَ أَفَلَا تَعْقِلُونَ ﴿١٦٩﴾

وَٱلَّذِينَ يُمَسِّكُونَ بِٱلْكِتَبِ وَأَقَامُواْ
ٱلصَّلَوٰةَ إِنَّا لَا نُضِيعُ أَجْرَ ٱلْمُصْلِحِينَ ﴿١٧٠﴾

وَإِذْ نَتَقْنَا ٱلْجَبَلَ فَوْقَهُمْ كَأَنَّهُ ظُلَّةٌ
وَظَنُّواْ أَنَّهُ وَاقِعٌ بِهِمْ خُذُواْ مَا ءَاتَيْنَكُم
بِقُوَّةٍ وَٱذْكُرُواْ مَا فِيهِ لَعَلَّكُمْ تَتَّقُونَ ﴿١٧١﴾

وَإِذْ أَخَذَ رَبُّكَ مِنۢ بَنِىٓ ءَادَمَ مِن ظُهُورِهِمْ
ذُرِّيَّتَهُمْ وَأَشْهَدَهُمْ عَلَىٰٓ أَنفُسِهِمْ أَلَسْتُ
بِرَبِّكُمْ قَالُواْ بَلَىٰ شَهِدْنَآ أَن تَقُولُواْ يَوْمَ
ٱلْقِيَمَةِ إِنَّا كُنَّا عَنْ هَذَا غَفِلِينَ ﴿١٧٢﴾

366. You are our Lord. Thus was the covenant of Monotheism inscribed, not like
the covenant of Israel upon the tablets of stone but impressed upon the heart,
the soul, of man. That this will to acknowledge and obey the One God forms part

of man's rational nature has at long last been recognized by anthropologists who have now come to believe that instead of monotheism being a development of primitive polytheism, the latter itself is a degeneration of the former. 'The earliest conception of deity is really monotheistic' (Marston, *The Bible Comes Alive*, p. 273). 'Evolutionary ethnologists and anthropologists of the nineteenth century presupposed the primeval human culture as utterly barbaric and bewilderingly polytheistic or animistic. Later ethnological researches have however, completely reversed this conclusion'. 'The startling reports of Andrew Lang on the original monotheism of these Pygmies and related tribes, belonging, like them, to Primeval culture, marked a new epoch in ethnological research. The Viennese ethnologist, Professor Father W. Schmidt collected all data and reports, referring to the subject. The result of this undertaking supported Andrew Lang's ideas on the broadest basis. Monotheism appears to be really at the very beginning of religious thought. The point which mostly concerns us in these studies is the fact that monotheism is found to have been the original form of religion' (Ehrenfels, *The Islamic Culture*, October 1946, pp. 436–37).

173. Or lest you should say: 'It was only our fathers who associated before, and we have been a posterity after them, will You destroy us then for what the followers of falsehood did?'

أَوَنَقُولُوٓاْ إِنَّمَآ أَشْرَكَ ءَابَآؤُنَا مِن قَبْلُ وَكُنَّا ذُرِّيَّةً مِّنۢ بَعْدِهِمْ أَفَتُهْلِكُنَا بِمَا فَعَلَ ٱلْمُبْطِلُونَ ۝

174. And thus do We detail the revelations, that haply they might return.

وَكَذَٰلِكَ نُفَصِّلُ ٱلْأَيَٰتِ وَلَعَلَّهُمْ يَرْجِعُونَ ۝

175. And recite to them the story of one to whom We gave Our signs, but he sloughed them off; so Satan followed him, and he became of the perverted.

وَٱتْلُ عَلَيْهِمْ نَبَأَ ٱلَّذِىٓ ءَاتَيْنَٰهُ ءَايَٰتِنَا فَٱنسَلَخَ مِنْهَا فَأَتْبَعَهُ ٱلشَّيْطَٰنُ فَكَانَ مِنَ ٱلْغَاوِينَ ۝

176. And had We willed We would surely have lifted him thereby, but he clung to the earth and pursued his desire, so his parable is the parable of a dog,[367] who, if you assail him lolls out his tongue and if you leave him alone, then also lolls out his tongue. Such is the parable of the people who belie Our signs, so recount you the story that haply they may reflect.

وَلَوْ شِئْنَا لَرَفَعْنَٰهُ بِهَا وَلَٰكِنَّهُۥٓ أَخْلَدَ إِلَى ٱلْأَرْضِ وَٱتَّبَعَ هَوَىٰهُ فَمَثَلُهُۥ كَمَثَلِ ٱلْكَلْبِ إِن تَحْمِلْ عَلَيْهِ يَلْهَثْ أَوْ تَتْرُكْهُ يَلْهَث ذَّٰلِكَ مَثَلُ ٱلْقَوْمِ ٱلَّذِينَ كَذَّبُواْ بِـَٔايَٰتِنَا فَٱقْصُصِ ٱلْقَصَصَ لَعَلَّهُمْ يَتَفَكَّرُونَ ۝

---

367. Dog is, with many nations and people, a term of abuse. In the Bible it is mentioned in many places, but almost 'always with contempt' (*DB*. I. p. 616). The word is in English, synonymous, in a secondary and derived sense, with 'worthless, surly, or cowardly fellow'. Though admired and even worshipped by some, it has been execrated by most others. The Hindus denounce it as unclean. Certain other nations, on the other hand, have venerated and worshipped the dog. 'In ancient Egypt, dogs were commonly respected and mummified, in particular at Cynopolis. In ancient Persia the dog was held in the highest esteem, and most rigorous penalties were exacted for killing it'. (*ERE*. I. p. 512). In ancient Syria, 'the dog was sacred among the Harranians. They offered sacrificial gifts to it, and in certain mysteries dogs were solemnly declared to be the brothers of the mystics' (Smith, *Religion of the Semites*, p. 291).

177. Vile is the likeness of the people who belie Our signs, and their own souls they are wont to wrong.

سَآءَ مَثَلًا ٱلۡقَوۡمُ ٱلَّذِينَ كَذَّبُواْ بِـَٔايَٰتِنَا وَأَنفُسَهُمۡ كَانُواْ يَظۡلِمُونَ ﴿١٧٧﴾

178. Whomso Allah guides, he is the rightly guided, and whomso He sends astray, those! They are the losers.

مَن يَهۡدِ ٱللَّهُ فَهُوَ ٱلۡمُهۡتَدِى وَمَن يُضۡلِلۡ فَأُوْلَٰٓئِكَ هُمُ ٱلۡخَٰسِرُونَ ﴿١٧٨﴾

179. Assuredly, We have created for Hell many of the jinn and mankind. They have hearts, yet do not understand with them; they have eyes yet do not see with them; and they have ears yet do not hear with them. They are like cattle; nay, even further astray. Those! They are the heedless ones.

وَلَقَدۡ ذَرَأۡنَا لِجَهَنَّمَ كَثِيرًا مِّنَ ٱلۡجِنِّ وَٱلۡإِنسِۖ لَهُمۡ قُلُوبٌ لَّا يَفۡقَهُونَ بِهَا وَلَهُمۡ أَعۡيُنٌ لَّا يُبۡصِرُونَ بِهَا وَلَهُمۡ ءَاذَانٌ لَّا يَسۡمَعُونَ بِهَآۚ أُوْلَٰٓئِكَ كَٱلۡأَنۡعَٰمِ بَلۡ هُمۡ أَضَلُّۚ أُوْلَٰٓئِكَ هُمُ ٱلۡغَٰفِلُونَ ﴿١٧٩﴾

180. Allah's are the excellent names;[368] so call Him by them, and leave alone those who profane His names. Presently will they be requited for what they have been doing.

وَلِلَّهِ ٱلۡأَسۡمَآءُ ٱلۡحُسۡنَىٰ فَٱدۡعُوهُ بِهَاۖ وَذَرُواْ ٱلَّذِينَ يُلۡحِدُونَ فِىٓ أَسۡمَٰٓئِهِۦۚ سَيُجۡزَوۡنَ مَا كَانُواْ يَعۡمَلُونَ ﴿١٨٠﴾

181. And of those who We have created, there is a community guiding others with Truth as by it they act justly.

وَمِمَّنۡ خَلَقۡنَآ أُمَّةٌ يَهۡدُونَ بِٱلۡحَقِّ وَبِهِۦ يَعۡدِلُونَ ﴿١٨١﴾

---

368. These in turn convey His excellent Attributes and Functions. This repudiates the queer doctrine of the namelessness of God, characteristic of the Alexandrian schools of philosophy and also, to some extent, of Jewish thought: 'Philo taught that God was without qualities and incomprehensible in His essence. He was the Nameless Existing. So to Plotinus God as the One could be described only negatively', (*ERE*. IX. p. 172).

Section 23

182. And those who belie Our signs, We lead them on, step by step, in a way they do not know.

وَالَّذِيْنَ كَذَّبُوْا بِاٰيٰتِنَا سَنَسْتَدْرِجُهُمْ مِّنْ حَيْثُ لَا يَعْلَمُوْنَ ۞

183. I respite them; My contrivance is severe.

وَأُمْلِىْ لَهُمْ ۚ إِنَّ كَيْدِىْ مَتِيْنٌ ۞

184. Do they not reflect that there is no madness[369] in their compatriot? He is none but a manifest warner.

أَوَلَمْ يَتَفَكَّرُوْا مَا بِصَاحِبِهِمْ مِّنْ جِنَّةٍ ۚ إِنْ هُوَ إِلَّا نَذِيْرٌ مُّبِيْنٌ ۞

185. Do they not look at the governance of the heavens and the earth and whatever Allah has created of aught and at the fact that their own term might be drawn nigh? In what discourse will then they believe thereafter?

أَوَلَمْ يَنْظُرُوْا فِىْ مَلَكُوْتِ السَّمٰوٰتِ وَالْأَرْضِ وَمَا خَلَقَ اللّٰهُ مِنْ شَيْءٍ وَأَنْ عَسٰى أَنْ يَكُوْنَ قَدِ اقْتَرَبَ أَجَلُهُمْ ۚ فَبِأَىِّ حَدِيْثٍ بَعْدَهُ يُؤْمِنُوْنَ ۞

186. Whoso Allah sends astray, no guide is then for him and He lets them wander perplexed in their exorbitance.

مَنْ يُّضْلِلِ اللّٰهُ فَلَا هَادِىَ لَهُ ۚ وَيَذَرُهُمْ فِىْ طُغْيَانِهِمْ يَعْمَهُوْنَ ۞

---

369. The Prophet's almost incredible achievements are still the wonder and admiration of an unbelieving world. 'The success of Mohammad as a law-giver and the stability of his institutions during a long series of generations, and in every condition of social polity, prove that this extraordinary man was formed by a rare combination of the qualities both of a Lycurgus and an Alexander' (Finlay, *Greece Under the Romans,* p. 446). 'Endowed with a refined mind and delicate taste, reserved and meditative, he lived much within himself The fair character and honourable bearing of the unobtrusive youth was the approbations of his fellow–citizens; and he received the title, by common consent, of al-Amin, the Faithful' (Muir, *Life of Muhammad,* pp. 19–20). Savary, who, as an enlightened Westerner,' of course, refused 'to call Mohammad a prophet', is 'nevertheless forced to recognize him as one of the greatest men who ever lived', and finds himself bound to concede that 'his political and military ability and his capacity for governing men were extraordinary', and to regard him 'as one of those unusual personalities occasionally appearing in history, who remake their environment and enlist men in their triumphant train'. (Andrae, *Mohammed,* pp. 244 and 245).

187. They ask you concerning the Hour and when it is to come. Say: 'Its knowledge is with my Lord alone; none can disclose its time but He; heavy it is in the heavens and the earth; it shall not come upon you except of a sudden.'[370] They ask you as if you were familiar with it. Say: 'Knowledge of it is with Allah; but most of them know not.'

يَسْئَلُوْنَكَ عَنِ السَّاعَةِ أَيَّانَ مُرْسَىٰهَا قُلْ إِنَّمَا عِلْمُهَا عِنْدَ رَبِّى لَا يُجَلِّيْهَا لِوَقْتِهَآ إِلَّا هُوَ ثَقُلَتْ فِى السَّمَٰوَٰتِ وَالْأَرْضِ لَا تَأْتِيْكُمْ إِلَّا بَغْتَةً يَسْئَلُوْنَكَ كَأَنَّكَ حَفِىٌّ عَنْهَا قُلْ إِنَّمَا عِلْمُهَا عِنْدَ اللّٰهِ وَلَٰكِنَّ أَكْثَرَ النَّاسِ لَا يَعْلَمُوْنَ ۝

188. Say: 'I possess no power of benefit or hurt to myself save as Allah wills;[371] and had I knowledge of the Unseen, I would have amassed ample good, and evil would not have touched me. I am naught but a warner and bringer of good tidings to a people who believe.'

قُلْ لَّا أَمْلِكُ لِنَفْسِى نَفْعًا وَّلَا ضَرًّا إِلَّا مَا شَآءَ اللّٰهُ وَلَوْ كُنْتُ أَعْلَمُ الْغَيْبَ لَاسْتَكْثَرْتُ مِنَ الْخَيْرِ وَمَا مَسَّنِىَ السُّوْءُ إِنْ أَنَا إِلَّا نَذِيْرٌ وَّبَشِيْرٌ لِّقَوْمٍ يُّؤْمِنُوْنَ ۝

---

370. It has often been held that the NT 'contains indications of the signs of the approaching End, and from time to time enthusiasts have identified the approaching End, with their own time or that immediately ahead. Nevertheless the End has not arrived; and even if it did come, now it would not be a real fulfillment of what is written in the New Testament' (*EBr.* III. p. 523).

371. Note the unparalleled monotheistic note ringing in this verse and the preceding ones. Every power, large or small, is God's; and the greatest and holiest of the Prophets is nothing before Him. Contrast this with the doctrines of sonship, consubstantiation, incarnation and coequality with God, common to so many religions.

Section 24

189. He it is Who created you from a single soul,[372] and He created of him his mate that he might find comfort in her.[373] Then when he covers her, she bears a light burden and passes by with it; then when she grows heavy they call upon Allah their Lord: 'If You grant us a goodly child we shall surely be of the grateful.'

190. But when He bestowed upon them a goodly child, they set up to Him associates in respect of what He has bestowed upon them. Exalted be Allah far from what they associate!

هُوَ ٱلَّذِى خَلَقَكُم مِّن نَّفْسٍ وَٰحِدَةٍ وَ جَعَلَ مِنْهَا زَوْجَهَا لِيَسْكُنَ إِلَيْهَا فَلَمَّا تَغَشَّىٰهَا حَمَلَتْ حَمْلًا خَفِيفًا فَمَرَّتْ بِهِۦ فَلَمَّآ أَثْقَلَت دَّعَوَا ٱللَّهَ رَبَّهُمَا لَئِنْ ءَاتَيْتَنَا صَٰلِحًا لَّنَكُونَنَّ مِنَ ٱلشَّٰكِرِينَ ۝

فَلَمَّآ ءَاتَىٰهُمَا صَٰلِحًا جَعَلَا لَهُۥ شُرَكَآءَ فِيمَآ ءَاتَىٰهُمَا فَتَعَٰلَى ٱللَّهُ عَمَّا يُشْرِكُونَ ۝

---

372. That single soul being Adam. The implication of which fact is that all men belong to one species, and that racial variations notwithstanding, there is no essential difference between man and man. If the modern world had only kept this elementary truth in mind, there would have been no occasion for it to lament that 'the progress of civilization is threatened by the serious danger of racial conflict and the still more serious evil, the demoralization caused by inter–racial and colour prejudice' (*EBr.* VI. p. 571). 'The time must come when it will seem absurd that French and Germans, Americans and Japanese, French and English, can even have been divided by imaginary barriers no less absurd than the recollection that the people of Burgundy and Artoris, of Mechlanbourg and Hanover, of Wessex and Northumberland were once taught to believe themselves natural enemies' (Fyfe, *The Illusion of National Character,* p. 23).

373. The word 'repose' meaning comfort, describes in a nutshell the various attitudes the two sexes can adopt towards each other, of love in youth, of companionship in middle age, and of care and attendance in infirmity. Contrast with this the status of woman in Christianity. 'Woman was represented as the door of hell, as the mother of all human ills. Women were even forbidden by a provincial council, in the sixth century, on account of their impurity, to receive the Eucharist into their naked hands. Their essentially subordinate position was continually maintained' (Lecky, *History of European Morals,* II, 1869 ed., pp. 357–358).

191. Do they associate those who cannot create anything, and are created,

192. And who cannot succour them, nor can succour themselves?

193. And if you call them towards guidance they do not follow you. It is the same to you whether you call them or be silent.

194. Verily those whom you call upon besides Allah are creatures like you; so call on them and let them answer you, if you say sooth.

195. Have they feet with which they walk? Have they hands with which they grip? Have they eyes with which they see? Have they ears with which they hear? Say: call upon your associate gods and then plot against me and give no respite.

196. My protector surely is Allah Who has revealed the Book, and Who protects the righteous.

197. And those whom you call upon beside Allah cannot succour you nor themselves can they succour.'

198. And if you call them towards guidance, they will not hear, and you will behold them looking at you, yet they do not see.

أَيُشْرِكُونَ مَا لَا يَخْلُقُ شَيْئًا وَهُمْ يُخْلَقُونَ ۝

وَلَا يَسْتَطِيعُونَ لَهُمْ نَصْرًا وَلَا أَنفُسَهُمْ يَنصُرُونَ ۝

وَإِن تَدْعُوهُمْ إِلَى الْهُدَىٰ لَا يَتَّبِعُوكُمْ سَوَآءٌ عَلَيْكُمْ أَدَعَوْتُمُوهُمْ أَمْ أَنتُمْ صَامِتُونَ ۝

إِنَّ الَّذِينَ تَدْعُونَ مِن دُونِ اللَّهِ عِبَادٌ أَمْثَالُكُمْ فَادْعُوهُمْ فَلْيَسْتَجِيبُوا لَكُمْ إِن كُنتُمْ صَادِقِينَ ۝

أَلَهُمْ أَرْجُلٌ يَمْشُونَ بِهَا أَمْ لَهُمْ أَيْدٍ يَبْطِشُونَ بِهَا أَمْ لَهُمْ أَعْيُنٌ يُبْصِرُونَ بِهَا أَمْ لَهُمْ ءَاذَانٌ يَسْمَعُونَ بِهَا قُلِ ادْعُوا شُرَكَآءَكُمْ ثُمَّ كِيدُونِ فَلَا تُنظِرُونِ ۝

إِنَّ وَلِيِّيَ اللَّهُ الَّذِي نَزَّلَ الْكِتَابَ وَهُوَ يَتَوَلَّى الصَّالِحِينَ ۝

وَالَّذِينَ تَدْعُونَ مِن دُونِهِ لَا يَسْتَطِيعُونَ نَصْرَكُمْ وَلَا أَنفُسَهُمْ يَنصُرُونَ ۝

وَإِن تَدْعُوهُمْ إِلَى الْهُدَىٰ لَا يَسْمَعُوا وَتَرَاهُمْ يَنظُرُونَ إِلَيْكَ وَهُمْ لَا يُبْصِرُونَ ۝

199. Show forgiveness and enjoin what is honourable and turn away from the ignorant.

خُذِ ٱلْعَفْوَ وَأْمُرْ بِٱلْعُرْفِ وَأَعْرِضْ عَنِ ٱلْجَٰهِلِينَ ﴿١٩٩﴾

200. And if there comes to you a prompting from Satan, seek then refuge in Allah, verily He is the Hearing, the Knowing.

وَإِمَّا يَنزَغَنَّكَ مِنَ ٱلشَّيْطَٰنِ نَزْغٌ فَٱسْتَعِذْ بِٱللَّهِ إِنَّهُۥ سَمِيعٌ عَلِيمٌ ﴿٢٠٠﴾

201. Verily those who fear God when an instigation from Satan touches them, they call to mind Allah, and lo! They are enlightened.

إِنَّ ٱلَّذِينَ ٱتَّقَوْا۟ إِذَا مَسَّهُمْ طَٰٓئِفٌ مِّنَ ٱلشَّيْطَٰنِ تَذَكَّرُوا۟ فَإِذَا هُم مُّبْصِرُونَ ﴿٢٠١﴾

202. And their brethren drag them on towards error, so they stop not short.

وَإِخْوَٰنُهُمْ يَمُدُّونَهُمْ فِى ٱلْغَىِّ ثُمَّ لَا يُقْصِرُونَ ﴿٢٠٢﴾

203. And whence you bring them not a particular sign they say; why have you not brought it? Say: 'I follow only what has been revealed to me by my Lord[374]. This is an enlightenment from your Lord and a guidance and a mercy to people who believe.'

وَإِذَا لَمْ تَأْتِهِم بِـَٔايَةٍ قَالُوا۟ لَوْلَا ٱجْتَبَيْتَهَا قُلْ إِنَّمَآ أَتَّبِعُ مَا يُوحَىٰٓ إِلَىَّ مِن رَّبِّى هَٰذَا بَصَآئِرُ مِن رَّبِّكُمْ وَهُدًى وَرَحْمَةٌ لِّقَوْمٍ يُؤْمِنُونَ ﴿٢٠٣﴾

---

374. That is the gist of Prophethood in Islam. Prophets are only the faithful Messengers of God. No Prophet is empowered to perform miracles on his own accord in order to please the infidels. It is only God Who, in His infinite wisdom and power, can, and does sometimes, alter the working of His usual, ordinary, normal laws, and bring about what to the limited, finite, intelligence of men appears miraculous. He Alone is the Author, equally with the ordinary, everyday events, of natural, extraordinary, and 'super' natural events, known in human languages as miracles. To conceive of men as being of God, even the greatest and holiest of them as authors, habitual or occasional, of any happenings in the universe, is to ascribe to them attributes of Divinity.

204. So when the Qur'ān is recited, listen to it and keep silence; haply you may be shown mercy.

وَإِذَا قُرِئَ ٱلۡقُرۡءَانُ فَٱسۡتَمِعُوا۟ لَهُۥ وَأَنصِتُوا۟ لَعَلَّكُمۡ تُرۡحَمُونَ ۝

205. Remember your Lord within yourself with humility and reverence, without loudness in word, morning and evening, and be you not of the heedless.

وَٱذۡكُر رَّبَّكَ فِى نَفۡسِكَ تَضَرُّعًا وَخِيفَةً وَدُونَ ٱلۡجَهۡرِ مِنَ ٱلۡقَوۡلِ بِٱلۡغُدُوِّ وَٱلۡءَاصَالِ وَلَا تَكُن مِّنَ ٱلۡغَٰفِلِينَ ۝

206. Assuredly those who are with your Lord do not disclaim against His service, they hallow Him and before Him they prostrate themselves.

إِنَّ ٱلَّذِينَ عِندَ رَبِّكَ لَا يَسۡتَكۡبِرُونَ عَنۡ عِبَادَتِهِۦ وَيُسَبِّحُونَهُۥ وَلَهُۥ يَسۡجُدُونَ ۝

Sūrah 8

al-Anfāl

(Madinan, 10 Sections, 75 Verses)

*In the name of Allah, the
Compassionate, the Merciful.*

Section 1

1. They ask you concerning the spoils; you; the spoils are Allah's and the Messenger's. So fear Allah, and set right the matter among you, and obey Allah and His Messenger, if you are believers.

2. The believers are only those whose hearts quake with awe when Allah is mentioned, and when His revelations are rehearsed to them, it increases their faith and they put trust in their Lord,

3. Who establish prayer and who spend of what We have provided them.

4. These are they who are the true believers. For them are degrees with their Lord and forgiveness and a provision honourable.

5. As your Lord had caused you to go forth from your houses for a right cause, while a party of the faithful were reluctant.

6. Disputing with you respecting the right cause after it had become manifest, as though they were led forth to death while they looked on.

يُجَدِلُونَكَ فِي ٱلْحَقِّ بَعْدَ مَا تَبَيَّنَ كَأَنَّمَا يُسَاقُونَ إِلَى ٱلْمَوْتِ وَهُمْ يَنظُرُونَ ٦

7. And recall when Allah was promising you one of the two parties that it should be yours and you wished that the one not armed should be yours; while Allah sought to justify the Truth by His words and to cut off the root of the infidels.[375]

وَإِذْ يَعِدُكُمُ ٱللَّهُ إِحْدَى ٱلطَّآئِفَتَيْنِ أَنَّهَا لَكُمْ وَتَوَدُّونَ أَنَّ غَيْرَ ذَاتِ ٱلشَّوْكَةِ تَكُونُ لَكُمْ وَيُرِيدُ ٱللَّهُ أَن يُحِقَّ ٱلْحَقَّ بِكَلِمَٰتِهِۦ وَيَقْطَعَ دَابِرَ ٱلْكَٰفِرِينَ ٧

8. In order that He might justify the Truth and falsify the false, though the guilty ones were averse to it.

لِيُحِقَّ ٱلْحَقَّ وَيُبْطِلَ ٱلْبَٰطِلَ وَلَوْ كَرِهَ ٱلْمُجْرِمُونَ ٨

9. And recall when you implored your Lord[376] and He answered you: 'Surely I am about to succour you with a thousand angels, rank on rank.'

إِذْ تَسْتَغِيثُونَ رَبَّكُمْ فَٱسْتَجَابَ لَكُمْ أَنِّي مُمِدُّكُم بِأَلْفٍ مِّنَ ٱلْمَلَٰٓئِكَةِ مُرْدِفِينَ ٩

---

375. Muir's description of the pagan debacle is both vivid and faithful. 'Before the onset of the brave three hundred, they began to waver. Their movements were impeded by the heavy sands on which they stood; and, when the ranks gave way, their numbers added but confusion. The Muslims followed eagerly their retreating steps, slaying or taking captive all that fell within their reach. Retreat soon turned into ignominious rout; and the flying host casting away their armour, abandoned beasts of burden, camp and equipage. Many of the principal men of Mecca, and some of Mohammed's bitterest opponents were amongst the slain. Chief of these was Abu Jahl'. (Muir, *Life of Muhammad*, p. 226).

376. Imploring Him for succour. The Prophet's supplication on this occasion, a noble specimen of the earnestness of his soul will bear reproduction. Raising his hands aloft, he poured forth his soul thus: 'O Lord! I beseech You forget not Your promise of assistance and of victory. O Lord! If this little band be vanquished, idolatry will prevail; and the pure worship of You cease from off the earth!' And he continued to repeat these words till his cloak fell off from his back.

10. And Allah did not make this promise save as a glad tiding and that your minds might be assured; and victory comes only from Allah. Verily Allah is the Mighty, the Wise.

وَمَا جَعَلَهُ اللّٰهُ اِلَّا بُشۡرٰى وَلِتَطۡمَئِنَّ بِهٖ قُلُوۡبُكُمۡ وَمَا النَّصۡرُ اِلَّا مِنۡ عِنۡدِ اللّٰهِ اِنَّ اللّٰهَ عَزِيۡزٌ حَكِيۡمٌ ﴿١٠﴾

Section 2

11. Recall when He caused a slumber to cover you as a security from Himself, and He sent down water on you from heaven that He might cleanse you thereby and take away from you the defilement of Satan, and that He might gird up your hearts and make your feet firm thereby.

اِذۡ يُغَشِّيۡكُمُ النُّعَاسَ اَمَنَةً مِّنۡهُ وَيُنَزِّلُ عَلَيۡكُمۡ مِّنَ السَّمَاءِ مَاءً لِّيُطَهِّرَكُمۡ بِهٖ وَيُذۡهِبَ عَنۡكُمۡ رِجۡزَ الشَّيۡطٰنِ وَلِيَرۡبِطَ عَلٰى قُلُوۡبِكُمۡ وَيُثَبِّتَ بِهِ الۡاَقۡدَامَ ﴿١١﴾

12. And recall when your Lord inspired the angels: 'Verily I am with you, so keep firm those who have believed; I will cast terror into the hearts of those who have disbelieved; so strike them above the necks and smite of them every fingertip.'

اِذۡ يُوۡحِىۡ رَبُّكَ اِلَى الۡمَلٰئِكَةِ اَنِّىۡ مَعَكُمۡ فَثَبِّتُوا الَّذِيۡنَ اٰمَنُوۡا سَاُلۡقِىۡ فِىۡ قُلُوۡبِ الَّذِيۡنَ كَفَرُوا الرُّعۡبَ فَاضۡرِبُوۡا فَوۡقَ الۡاَعۡنَاقِ وَاضۡرِبُوۡا مِنۡهُمۡ كُلَّ بَنَانٍ ﴿١٢﴾

13. This, because they defied Allah and His Messenger and whoever defies Allah and His Messenger, then surely Allah is Severe in chastisement.

ذٰلِكَ بِاَنَّهُمۡ شَاۤقُّوا اللّٰهَ وَرَسُوۡلَهٗ وَمَنۡ يُّشَاقِقِ اللّٰهَ وَرَسُوۡلَهٗ فَاِنَّ اللّٰهَ شَدِيۡدُ الۡعِقَابِ ﴿١٣﴾

14. This! Taste it then, and know that for the infidels is the torment of the Fire.

ذٰلِكُمۡ فَذُوۡقُوۡهُ وَاَنَّ لِلۡكٰفِرِيۡنَ عَذَابَ النَّارِ ﴿١٤﴾

15. O you who believe! When you face those who disbelieve marching to battle, do not turn your backs to them.

يَـٰٓأَيُّهَا ٱلَّذِينَ ءَامَنُوٓاْ إِذَا لَقِيتُمُ ٱلَّذِينَ كَفَرُواْ زَحۡفٗا فَلَا تُوَلُّوهُمُ ٱلۡأَدۡبَارَ ﴿١٥﴾

16. And whosoever turns his back to them on such a day, unless it be swerving to a fight or wriggling round to another company, he has surely drawn upon himself wrath from Allah, and his resort is Hell, an evil destination.

وَمَن يُوَلِّهِمۡ يَوۡمَئِذٖ دُبُرَهُۥٓ إِلَّا مُتَحَرِّفٗا لِّقِتَالٍ أَوۡ مُتَحَيِّزًا إِلَىٰ فِئَةٖ فَقَدۡ بَآءَ بِغَضَبٖ مِّنَ ٱللَّهِ وَمَأۡوَىٰهُ جَهَنَّمُۖ وَبِئۡسَ ٱلۡمَصِيرُ ﴿١٦﴾

17. You therefore slew them not, but Allah slew them; threw you not when you threw, but Allah threw; in order that He might try the believers with a goodly trial from Him. Surely Allah is the Hearing, the Knowing.

فَلَمۡ تَقۡتُلُوهُمۡ وَلَٰكِنَّ ٱللَّهَ قَتَلَهُمۡۚ وَمَا رَمَيۡتَ إِذۡ رَمَيۡتَ وَلَٰكِنَّ ٱللَّهَ رَمَىٰۚ وَلِيُبۡلِيَ ٱلۡمُؤۡمِنِينَ مِنۡهُ بَلَآءً حَسَنًاۚ إِنَّ ٱللَّهَ سَمِيعٌ عَلِيمٞ ﴿١٧﴾

18. Thus! And know that Allah weakens the plot of the infidels.

ذَٰلِكُمۡ وَأَنَّ ٱللَّهَ مُوهِنُ كَيۡدِ ٱلۡكَٰفِرِينَ ﴿١٨﴾

19. If you beseech a judgement then surely a judgement has come to you. If you desist, better it will be for you, and if you revert, We will also revert; and your host shall avail you not, numerous though it might be, and know that surely Allah is with the believers.

إِن تَسۡتَفۡتِحُواْ فَقَدۡ جَآءَكُمُ ٱلۡفَتۡحُۖ وَإِن تَنتَهُواْ فَهُوَ خَيۡرٞ لَّكُمۡۖ وَإِن تَعُودُواْ نَعُدۡ وَلَن تُغۡنِيَ عَنكُمۡ فِئَتُكُمۡ شَيۡـٔٗا وَلَوۡ كَثُرَتۡ وَأَنَّ ٱللَّهَ مَعَ ٱلۡمُؤۡمِنِينَ ﴿١٩﴾

Section 3

20. O you who believe! Obey Allah and His Messenger, and do not turn away while you are hearing.

يَـٰٓأَيُّهَا ٱلَّذِينَ ءَامَنُوٓاْ أَطِيعُواْ ٱللَّهَ وَرَسُولَهُۥ وَلَا تَوَلَّوۡاْ عَنۡهُ وَأَنتُمۡ تَسۡمَعُونَ ﴿٢٠﴾

21. And do not be like those who say: 'We hear'; whereas they do not hear.

وَلَا تَكُونُوا كَالَّذِينَ قَالُوا سَمِعْنَا وَهُمْ لَا يَسْمَعُونَ ۝

22. Verily the vilest of beasts in Allah's sight are the deaf and the dumb who do not understand.

إِنَّ شَرَّ الدَّوَابِّ عِندَ اللَّهِ الصُّمُّ الْبُكْمُ الَّذِينَ لَا يَعْقِلُونَ ۝

23. And had Allah known in them any good He would surely have made them hear; and even if He had made them hear, they would have surely turned away as backsliders.

وَلَوْ عَلِمَ اللَّهُ فِيهِمْ خَيْرًا لَّأَسْمَعَهُمْ وَلَوْ أَسْمَعَهُمْ لَتَوَلَّوا وَّهُم مُّعْرِضُونَ ۝

24. O you who believe! Answer Allah and the Messenger when He calls on you to what gives you life; and know that Allah interposes between man and his heart, and know that verily to Him you all shall be gathered.

يَا أَيُّهَا الَّذِينَ ءَامَنُوا اسْتَجِيبُوا لِلَّهِ وَلِلرَّسُولِ إِذَا دَعَاكُمْ لِمَا يُحْيِيكُمْ وَاعْلَمُوا أَنَّ اللَّهَ يَحُولُ بَيْنَ الْمَرْءِ وَقَلْبِهِ وَأَنَّهُ إِلَيْهِ تُحْشَرُونَ ۝

25. And fear the tribulation that shall afflict not those alone who among you do wrong;[377] and know verily that Allah is Severe in chastising.

وَاتَّقُوا فِتْنَةً لَّا تُصِيبَنَّ الَّذِينَ ظَلَمُوا مِنكُمْ خَاصَّةً وَاعْلَمُوا أَنَّ اللَّهَ شَدِيدُ الْعِقَابِ ۝

26. And remember when you were few and downtrodden in the land and fearing that the people would snatch you away; then He gave you refuge and strengthened you with His help and provided you with good things that haply you might be grateful.

وَاذْكُرُوا إِذْ أَنتُمْ قَلِيلٌ مُّسْتَضْعَفُونَ فِي الْأَرْضِ تَخَافُونَ أَن يَتَخَطَّفَكُمُ النَّاسُ فَآوَاكُمْ وَأَيَّدَكُم بِنَصْرِهِ وَرَزَقَكُم مِّنَ الطَّيِّبَاتِ لَعَلَّكُمْ تَشْكُرُونَ ۝

---

377. The Divine chastisement visits not only those who are the actual perpetrators of crime but it falls on those also who remain indifferent to the sin and vice around them, and do not admonish the wicked. Islam does not expect of its followers to be passive spectators of guilt and crime; it requires them to be active opponents, so far as in their power, to all forms of irreligion and impiety.

27. O you who believe! Do not defraud Allah and the Messenger, and do not defraud your trusts while you know.

يَـٰٓأَيُّهَا ٱلَّذِينَ ءَامَنُوا۟ لَا تَخُونُوا۟ ٱللَّهَ وَٱلرَّسُولَ وَتَخُونُوٓا۟ أَمَـٰنَـٰتِكُمْ وَأَنتُمْ تَعْلَمُونَ ۝

28. And know that your riches and your offspring are but a temptation[378], and that verily with Him is a mighty reward.

وَٱعْلَمُوٓا۟ أَنَّمَآ أَمْوَٰلُكُمْ وَأَوْلَـٰدُكُمْ فِتْنَةٌ وَأَنَّ ٱللَّهَ عِندَهُۥٓ أَجْرٌ عَظِيمٌ ۝

Section 4

29. O you who believe! If you fear Allah, He will make for you a distinction and will expiate for you your misdeeds and forgive you; and Allah is the Owner of mighty grace.

يَـٰٓأَيُّهَا ٱلَّذِينَ ءَامَنُوٓا۟ إِن تَتَّقُوا۟ ٱللَّهَ يَجْعَل لَّكُمْ فُرْقَانًا وَيُكَفِّرْ عَنكُمْ سَيِّـَٔاتِكُمْ وَيَغْفِرْ لَكُمْ وَٱللَّهُ ذُو ٱلْفَضْلِ ٱلْعَظِيمِ ۝

30. And recall when those who disbelieved were plotting against you to confine you or to slay you or to drive you forth; they were plotting and Allah was plotting, and Allah is the Best of plotters.

وَإِذْ يَمْكُرُ بِكَ ٱلَّذِينَ كَفَرُوا۟ لِيُثْبِتُوكَ أَوْ يَقْتُلُوكَ أَوْ يُخْرِجُوكَ وَيَمْكُرُونَ وَيَمْكُرُ ٱللَّهُ وَٱللَّهُ خَيْرُ ٱلْمَـٰكِرِينَ ۝

31. And when Our revelations are rehearsed to them, they say: 'We have heard, we could, if only we willed, say the like of this; nothing is this but fables of the ancients'.

وَإِذَا تُتْلَىٰ عَلَيْهِمْ ءَايَـٰتُنَا قَالُوا۟ قَدْ سَمِعْنَا لَوْ نَشَآءُ لَقُلْنَا مِثْلَ هَـٰذَآ إِنْ هَـٰذَآ إِلَّآ أَسَـٰطِيرُ ٱلْأَوَّلِينَ ۝

---

378. These are a trial, a test, to find out who mishandles these gifts of God and who uses them in a proper and legitimate way. Note that temptation is not synonymous with sin, nor is love of children or fondness for wealth, in itself, sinful. Such emotions, appetites, instincts, etc., are part of man, as it has pleased God to make him so. It is only human will that can shape them into sins.

32. And recall when they said: 'O Allah, if this be indeed the Truth from you, rain down stones upon us from the heaven or bring on us a torment afflictive.'

وَإِذْ قَالُوا اللَّهُمَّ إِن كَانَ هَذَا هُوَ الْحَقَّ مِنْ عِندِكَ فَأَمْطِرْ عَلَيْنَا حِجَارَةً مِّنَ السَّمَاءِ أَوِ ائْتِنَا بِعَذَابٍ أَلِيمٍ ۝

33. And Allah is not the One to chastise them while you are in their midst; nor was Allah going to chastise them while they were asking forgiveness.

وَمَا كَانَ اللَّهُ لِيُعَذِّبَهُمْ وَأَنتَ فِيهِمْ وَمَا كَانَ اللَّهُ مُعَذِّبَهُمْ وَهُمْ يَسْتَغْفِرُونَ ۝

34. And what ails them that Allah should not chastise them when they are hindering people from the Sacred Mosque, whereas they are not even its guardians – its guardians are none but the God–fearing yet most of them do not know.

وَمَا لَهُمْ أَلَّا يُعَذِّبَهُمُ اللَّهُ وَهُمْ يَصُدُّونَ عَنِ الْمَسْجِدِ الْحَرَامِ وَمَا كَانُوا أَوْلِيَاءَهُ إِنْ أَوْلِيَاؤُهُ إِلَّا الْمُتَّقُونَ وَلَكِنَّ أَكْثَرَهُمْ لَا يَعْلَمُونَ ۝

35. And naught was their prayer at the house but whistling and hand-clapping[379]. Taste then the torment for you were wont to disbelieve.

وَمَا كَانَ صَلَاتُهُمْ عِندَ الْبَيْتِ إِلَّا مُكَاءً وَتَصْدِيَةً فَذُوقُوا الْعَذَابَ بِمَا كُنتُمْ تَكْفُرُونَ ۝

---

379. 'They used to go round the Caaba naked, both men and women, whistling at the same time through their fingers, and clapping their hands' (*SPD*.). Witness also the present-day practices of many a creed which not only allow but prescribe the use of musical instruments at public worship. Worse still, dancing has formed part and even now forms part of the chief acts of devotion and worship in many religions. 'Religious processions went with song and dance to the Egyptian temples, and Plato said that all dancing ought to be thus an act of religion. In fact, it was so to a great extent in Greece, as were the Cretan chorus, moving in measured pace, sang hymns to Apollo, and in Rome, where the Salian priests sang and danced, beating their shields, along the streets at the yearly festival of Mars. Remnants of such ceremonies, come down from the religion of England before Christian times, are still sometimes to be seen in the dances of boys and girls round the Midsummer bonfire, or of the mummers of Yuletide' (Tylor, *Anthropology*, Vol. II, p. 53).

36. Those who disbelieve are spending their riches in order to hinder people from the way of Allah; so they will go on spending them. Thereafter, they will become an anguish to them; then they shall be overcome. And those who disbelieve shall be gathered for Hell.

إِنَّ الَّذِينَ كَفَرُوا يُنفِقُونَ أَمْوَلَهُمْ لِيَصُدُّوا عَن سَبِيلِ اللَّهِ فَسَيُنفِقُونَهَا ثُمَّ تَكُونُ عَلَيْهِمْ حَسْرَةً ثُمَّ يُغْلَبُونَ وَالَّذِينَ كَفَرُوا إِلَىٰ جَهَنَّمَ يُحْشَرُونَ ﴿٣٦﴾

37. In order that Allah may distinguish the vile from the good, and the vile He shall put one upon another, and shall pile them all together, and shall place them into Hell. Those; it is they who are the losers.

لِيَمِيزَ اللَّهُ الْخَبِيثَ مِنَ الطَّيِّبِ وَيَجْعَلَ الْخَبِيثَ بَعْضَهُ عَلَىٰ بَعْضٍ فَيَرْكُمَهُ جَمِيعًا فَيَجْعَلَهُ فِي جَهَنَّمَ أُوْلَٰئِكَ هُمُ الْخَسِرُونَ ﴿٣٧﴾

Section 5

38. Say to those who have believed; if they desist now, what is past will be forgiven them, and if they revert, then already has gone forth the dispensation of the ancients.

قُل لِّلَّذِينَ كَفَرُوا إِن يَنتَهُوا يُغْفَرْ لَهُم مَّا قَدْ سَلَفَ وَإِن يَعُودُوا فَقَدْ مَضَتْ سُنَّتُ الْأَوَّلِينَ ﴿٣٨﴾

39. Fight them until there be no persecution and religion be wholly Allah's. So if they now desist, then Allah is the Beholder of what they are doing.

وَقَاتِلُوهُمْ حَتَّىٰ لَا تَكُونَ فِتْنَةٌ وَيَكُونَ الدِّينُ كُلُّهُ لِلَّهِ فَإِنِ انتَهَوْا فَإِنَّ اللَّهَ بِمَا يَعْمَلُونَ بَصِيرٌ ﴿٣٩﴾

40. And if they turn away, then know that Allah is your Patron, Excellent Patron, and Excellent Helper!

وَإِن تَوَلَّوْا فَاعْلَمُوا أَنَّ اللَّهَ مَوْلَٰكُمْ نِعْمَ الْمَوْلَىٰ وَنِعْمَ النَّصِيرُ ﴿٤٠﴾

41. And know that whatever of the spoils you get then verily to Allah belongs one – fifth thereof and to the Messenger and to his kindred and the orphans and the needy and the wayfarer, if you have believed in Allah and what We sent down upon Our bondsmen on the day of distinction, the day when the two hosts met. And Allah is Potent over everything.

وَٱعْلَمُوٓاْ أَنَّمَا غَنِمْتُم مِّن شَىْءٍ فَأَنَّ لِلَّهِ خُمُسَهُۥ وَلِلرَّسُولِ وَلِذِى ٱلْقُرْبَىٰ وَٱلْيَتَٰمَىٰ وَٱلْمَسَٰكِينِ وَٱبْنِ ٱلسَّبِيلِ إِن كُنتُمْ ءَامَنتُم بِٱللَّهِ وَمَآ أَنزَلْنَا عَلَىٰ عَبْدِنَا يَوْمَ ٱلْفُرْقَانِ يَوْمَ ٱلْتَقَى ٱلْجَمْعَانِ ۗ وَٱللَّهُ عَلَىٰ كُلِّ شَىْءٍ قَدِيرٌ ٤١

42. And recall when you were on this side and they were on that side and the caravan below you. And if you were mutually to make the appointment you would have surely failed the appointment. But the action was so brought about in order that Allah may accomplish a decree already ordered, so that he who was to perish might perish after evidence and he who was to survive might survive after evidence. And verily Allah is the Hearing, the Knowing.

إِذْ أَنتُم بِٱلْعُدْوَةِ ٱلدُّنْيَا وَهُم بِٱلْعُدْوَةِ ٱلْقُصْوَىٰ وَٱلرَّكْبُ أَسْفَلَ مِنكُمْ ۚ وَلَوْ تَوَاعَدتُّمْ لَٱخْتَلَفْتُمْ فِى ٱلْمِيعَٰدِ ۙ وَلَٰكِن لِّيَقْضِىَ ٱللَّهُ أَمْرًا كَانَ مَفْعُولًا لِّيَهْلِكَ مَنْ هَلَكَ عَن بَيِّنَةٍ وَيَحْيَىٰ مَنْ حَىَّ عَنۢ بَيِّنَةٍ ۗ وَإِنَّ ٱللَّهَ لَسَمِيعٌ عَلِيمٌ ٤٢

43. And recall when Allah showed them as but a few to you in your dream. Had He shown them as numerous to you, surely you would have flagged and surely you would have wrangled over the affair, but Allah spared you. Verily He is the Knower of what is in the breasts.

إِذْ يُرِيكَهُمُ ٱللَّهُ فِى مَنَامِكَ قَلِيلًا ۖ وَلَوْ أَرَىٰكَهُمْ كَثِيرًا لَّفَشِلْتُمْ وَلَتَنَٰزَعْتُمْ فِى ٱلْأَمْرِ وَلَٰكِنَّ ٱللَّهَ سَلَّمَ ۗ إِنَّهُۥ عَلِيمٌۢ بِذَاتِ ٱلصُّدُورِ ٤٣

44. And recall when He showed them as few in your eyes when you met, and lessened you in their eyes in order that Allah might accomplish an affair already ordained, and to Allah are all affairs returned.

وَإِذْ يُرِيكُمُوهُمْ إِذِ الْتَقَيْتُمْ فِىٓ أَعْيُنِكُمْ قَلِيلًا وَيُقَلِّلُكُمْ فِىٓ أَعْيُنِهِمْ لِيَقْضِىَ اللَّهُ أَمْرًا كَانَ مَفْعُولًا ۗ وَإِلَى اللَّهِ تُرْجَعُ الْأُمُورُ ﴿٤٤﴾

Section 6

45. O you who believe! When you encounter a party, stand firm and remember Allah fervently[380], that haply you may fare well.

يَـٰٓأَيُّهَا الَّذِينَ ءَامَنُوٓا إِذَا لَقِيتُمْ فِئَةً فَاثْبُتُوا وَاذْكُرُوا اللَّهَ كَثِيرًا لَّعَلَّكُمْ تُفْلِحُونَ ﴿٤٥﴾

46. And obey Allah and His Messenger, and do not dispute, with an emotion, lest you flag and your predominance depart, and be steadfast. Verily Allah is with the steadfast.

وَأَطِيعُوا اللَّهَ وَرَسُولَهُ وَلَا تَنَـٰزَعُوا فَتَفْشَلُوا وَتَذْهَبَ رِيحُكُمْ ۖ وَاصْبِرُوٓا ۚ إِنَّ اللَّهَ مَعَ الصَّـٰبِرِينَ ﴿٤٦﴾

47. And do not be like those who came forth from their homes vaunting and to be seen of men and debarring others from the way of Allah. Allah is the Encompasser of what they work.

وَلَا تَكُونُوا كَالَّذِينَ خَرَجُوا مِن دِيَـٰرِهِم بَطَرًا وَرِئَآءَ النَّاسِ وَيَصُدُّونَ عَن سَبِيلِ اللَّهِ ۚ وَاللَّهُ بِمَا يَعْمَلُونَ مُحِيطٌ ﴿٤٧﴾

---

380. Remember Him and often, as that would make hearts firm. Mark the high place assigned in Islam to the remembrance of God. A Muslim even when face to face with death, is directed not to defer his devotions, but is on the contrary exhorted to remember his Lord God even more and often. This attitude of devotion and prayerfulness is the second condition of success.

48. And recall when Satan made their works fair seeming to them, and said: 'There is none of mankind to overcome you today, and surely I am your neighbour.' Then when the two parties faced each other, he turned on his heels, and said: 'Verily I am quit of you, verily I can see what you cannot; verily I fear Allah; and Allah is Severe in chastising.'

وَإِذْ زَيَّنَ لَهُمُ ٱلشَّيْطَٰنُ أَعْمَٰلَهُمْ وَقَالَ لَا غَالِبَ لَكُمُ ٱلْيَوْمَ مِنَ ٱلنَّاسِ وَإِنِّي جَارٌ لَّكُمْ فَلَمَّا تَرَآءَتِ ٱلْفِئَتَانِ نَكَصَ عَلَىٰ عَقِبَيْهِ وَقَالَ إِنِّي بَرِيٓءٌ مِّنكُمْ إِنِّيٓ أَرَىٰ مَا لَا تَرَوْنَ إِنِّيٓ أَخَافُ ٱللَّهَ وَٱللَّهُ شَدِيدُ ٱلْعِقَابِ ﴿٤٨﴾

Section 7

49. And recall when the hypocrites and those in whose hearts was a disease said: 'Their religion has deluded them.' And whoever relies on Allah, then verily Allah is the Mighty, the Wise.

إِذْ يَقُولُ ٱلْمُنَٰفِقُونَ وَٱلَّذِينَ فِي قُلُوبِهِم مَّرَضٌ غَرَّ هَٰٓؤُلَآءِ دِينُهُمْ وَمَن يَتَوَكَّلْ عَلَى ٱللَّهِ فَإِنَّ ٱللَّهَ عَزِيزٌ حَكِيمٌ ﴿٤٩﴾

50. And could you see when the angels take away the life of those who disbelieve striking their faces and their backs; taste the torment of burning.

وَلَوْ تَرَىٰٓ إِذْ يَتَوَفَّى ٱلَّذِينَ كَفَرُوا۟ ٱلْمَلَٰٓئِكَةُ يَضْرِبُونَ وُجُوهَهُمْ وَأَدْبَٰرَهُمْ وَذُوقُوا۟ عَذَابَ ٱلْحَرِيقِ ﴿٥٠﴾

51. This, because of what your hands had forwarded and Allah is never unjust to His creatures.[381]

ذَٰلِكَ بِمَا قَدَّمَتْ أَيْدِيكُمْ وَأَنَّ ٱللَّهَ لَيْسَ بِظَلَّٰمٍ لِّلْعَبِيدِ ﴿٥١﴾

---

381. This marks out the Just God of Islam from the capricious gods of polytheism and also from the 'jealous' God of the Bible. Cf. the OT: 'I the Lord thy God am a jealous God, visiting the iniquity of the fathers upon the children unto the third and fourth generation of them that hate me' (Ex. 20: 5).

52. Like the wont of the house of Pharaoh and those before them, they disbelieved in the signs of Allah; so Allah seized them for their sins. Verily Allah is the Strong, the Severe in chastising.

كَدَأْبِ ءَالِ فِرْعَوْنَ وَالَّذِينَ مِن قَبْلِهِمْ كَفَرُوا بِعَايَتِ اللَّهِ فَأَخَذَهُمُ اللَّهُ بِذُنُوبِهِمْ إِنَّ اللَّهَ قَوِيٌّ شَدِيدُ الْعِقَابِ ۝

53. This, because Allah is not the One to change His favour once conferred on a people until they changed what was in themselves. Verily Allah is the Hearing, the Knowing.

ذَلِكَ بِأَنَّ اللَّهَ لَمْ يَكُ مُغَيِّرًا نِّعْمَةً أَنْعَمَهَا عَلَى قَوْمٍ حَتَّى يُغَيِّرُوا مَا بِأَنفُسِهِمْ وَأَنَّ اللَّهَ سَمِيعٌ عَلِيمٌ ۝

54. Like the wont of the house of Pharaoh and those before them, they belied the Signs of their Lord, so We destroyed them for their sins, and drowned the house of Pharaoh and all of them were wrong-doers.

كَدَأْبِ ءَالِ فِرْعَوْنَ وَالَّذِينَ مِن قَبْلِهِمْ كَذَّبُوا بِعَايَتِ رَبِّهِمْ فَأَهْلَكْنَهُم بِذُنُوبِهِمْ وَأَغْرَقْنَا ءَالَ فِرْعَوْنَ وَكُلٌّ كَانُوا ظَلِمِينَ ۝

55. Verily the vilest of moving creatures with Allah are those who disbelieve wherefore they shall not believe.

إِنَّ شَرَّ الدَّوَابِّ عِندَ اللَّهِ الَّذِينَ كَفَرُوا فَهُمْ لَا يُؤْمِنُونَ ۝

56. They with whom you covenanted, then they break their covenant every time, and they do not fear.

الَّذِينَ عَهَدتَّ مِنْهُمْ ثُمَّ يَنقُضُونَ عَهْدَهُمْ فِي كُلِّ مَرَّةٍ وَهُمْ لَا يَتَّقُونَ ۝

57. Wherefore if you come upon them in war, deal with them so as to scatter them, and then who are behind them haply they may be admonished.

فَإِمَّا تَثْقَفَنَّهُمْ فِي الْحَرْبِ فَشَرِّدْ بِهِم مَّنْ خَلْفَهُمْ لَعَلَّهُمْ يَذَّكَّرُونَ ۝

58.   And should you fear treachery from any people cast back to them their covenant[382] so as to be equal. Verily Allah does not approve the treacherous.[383]

وَإِمَّا تَخَافَنَّ مِن قَوْمٍ خِيَانَةً فَانْبِذْ إِلَيْهِمْ عَلَى سَوَآءٍ إِنَّ ٱللَّهَ لَا يُحِبُّ ٱلْخَآئِنِينَ ﴿٥٨﴾

Section 8

59.   Let not those who disbelieve deem that they have escaped Me; assuredly they cannot frustrate Allah's purpose.

وَلَا يَحْسَبَنَّ ٱلَّذِينَ كَفَرُوٓاْ سَبَقُوٓاْ إِنَّهُمْ لَا يُعْجِزُونَ ﴿٥٩﴾

60.   And get ready against them whatever you can of force and well-fed horses with which you may overpower Allah's enemy and your enemy and others besides them whom you do not know; Allah knows them. And whatever you spend in the way of Allah shall be repaid to you in full, and you shall not be wronged.

وَأَعِدُّواْ لَهُم مَّا ٱسْتَطَعْتُم مِّن قُوَّةٍ وَمِن رِّبَاطِ ٱلْخَيْلِ تُرْهِبُونَ بِهِۦ عَدُوَّ ٱللَّهِ وَعَدُوَّكُمْ وَءَاخَرِينَ مِن دُونِهِمْ لَا تَعْلَمُونَهُمُ ٱللَّهُ يَعْلَمُهُمْ وَمَا تُنفِقُواْ مِن شَىْءٍ فِى سَبِيلِ ٱللَّهِ يُوَفَّ إِلَيْكُمْ وَأَنتُمْ لَا تُظْلَمُونَ ﴿٦٠﴾

61.   And if they incline to peace, then do you incline to it; and rely you on Allah. Verily He! He is the Hearing, the Knowing.

وَإِن جَنَحُواْ لِلسَّلْمِ فَٱجْنَحْ لَهَا وَتَوَكَّلْ عَلَى ٱللَّهِ إِنَّهُۥ هُوَ ٱلسَّمِيعُ ٱلْعَلِيمُ ﴿٦١﴾

---

382. This at your discretion, but inform them accordingly. It is obligatory on the part of the Muslim head of government to apprise the enemy beforehand of the non-existence of compacts and treaties. Fighting without this previous notice is unlawful. Could a course of action be more chivalrous or honourable?

383. All this implies disapproval of counter-treachery even in self-defence as justified and approved by some other religions.

62. And if they seek to deceive you, then Allah is sufficient for them. He it is Who has confirmed you with His help and with the believers.

وَإِن يُرِيدُوٓاْ أَن يَخۡدَعُوكَ فَإِنَّ حَسۡبَكَ ٱللَّهُ هُوَ ٱلَّذِىٓ أَيَّدَكَ بِنَصۡرِهِۦ وَبِٱلۡمُؤۡمِنِينَ ۝

63. And He united their hearts. Had you spent all that is on the earth you could not have united their hearts, but Allah united them; Verily He is the Mighty, the Wise.

وَأَلَّفَ بَيۡنَ قُلُوبِهِمۡ لَوۡ أَنفَقۡتَ مَا فِى ٱلۡأَرۡضِ جَمِيعًا مَّآ أَلَّفۡتَ بَيۡنَ قُلُوبِهِمۡ وَلَٰكِنَّ ٱللَّهَ أَلَّفَ بَيۡنَهُمۡۚ إِنَّهُۥ عَزِيزٌ حَكِيمٌ ۝

64. O Prophet! Sufficient for you is Allah and those who follow you of the believers.

يَٰٓأَيُّهَا ٱلنَّبِىُّ حَسۡبُكَ ٱللَّهُ وَمَنِ ٱتَّبَعَكَ مِنَ ٱلۡمُؤۡمِنِينَ ۝

Section 9

65. O Prophet! Urge the believers unto fighting. If there be twenty of you steadfast, they will overcome two hundred and if there be of you a hundred, they will overcome a thousand of those who disbelieve, for they are a people who do not understand.

يَٰٓأَيُّهَا ٱلنَّبِىُّ حَرِّضِ ٱلۡمُؤۡمِنِينَ عَلَى ٱلۡقِتَالِۚ إِن يَكُن مِّنكُمۡ عِشۡرُونَ صَٰبِرُونَ يَغۡلِبُواْ مِاْئَتَيۡنِۚ وَإِن يَكُن مِّنكُم مِّائَةٌ يَغۡلِبُوٓاْ أَلۡفًا مِّنَ ٱلَّذِينَ كَفَرُواْ بِأَنَّهُمۡ قَوۡمٌ لَّا يَفۡقَهُونَ ۝

66. Now Allah has lightened your burden, and He knows that there is in you a weakness. So if there be a hundred of you steadfast, they will overcome two hundred, and if there be a thousand of you they will overcome two thousand by the will of Allah; and Allah is with the steadfast.

ٱلۡـَٰٔنَ خَفَّفَ ٱللَّهُ عَنكُمۡ وَعَلِمَ أَنَّ فِيكُمۡ ضَعۡفًاۚ فَإِن يَكُن مِّنكُم مِّائَةٌ صَابِرَةٌ يَغۡلِبُواْ مِاْئَتَيۡنِۚ وَإِن يَكُن مِّنكُمۡ أَلۡفٌ يَغۡلِبُوٓاْ أَلۡفَيۡنِ بِإِذۡنِ ٱللَّهِۗ وَٱللَّهُ مَعَ ٱلصَّٰبِرِينَ ۝

67. It does not behove a Prophet that he should have captives until he has greatly slaughtered in the land. You seek the gains of this world, while Allah seeks the Hereafter; and Allah is the Mighty, the Wise.

مَا كَانَ لِنَبِيٍّ أَن يَكُونَ لَهُ أَسْرَىٰ حَتَّىٰ يُثْخِنَ فِي الْأَرْضِ تُرِيدُونَ عَرَضَ الدُّنْيَا وَاللَّهُ يُرِيدُ الْآخِرَةَ وَاللَّهُ عَزِيزٌ حَكِيمٌ ۝

68. Were it not that a Writ had already gone forth from Allah, a mighty torment would surely have touched you for what you took.

لَّوْلَا كِتَابٌ مِّنَ اللَّهِ سَبَقَ لَمَسَّكُمْ فِيمَا أَخَذْتُمْ عَذَابٌ عَظِيمٌ ۝

69. Enjoy you then of what you have obtained of spoil, lawful and clean, and fear Allah. Verily Allah is the Forgiving, the Merciful.

فَكُلُوا مِمَّا غَنِمْتُمْ حَلَالًا طَيِّبًا وَاتَّقُوا اللَّهَ إِنَّ اللَّهَ غَفُورٌ رَّحِيمٌ ۝

Section 10

70. O Prophet! Say to the captives that are in your hands; if Allah knows any good in your hearts He shall give you better than what has been taken away from you, and shall forgive you; and Allah is the Forgiving, the Merciful.

يَا أَيُّهَا النَّبِيُّ قُل لِّمَن فِي أَيْدِيكُم مِّنَ الْأَسْرَىٰ إِن يَعْلَمِ اللَّهُ فِي قُلُوبِكُمْ خَيْرًا يُؤْتِكُمْ خَيْرًا مِّمَّا أُخِذَ مِنكُمْ وَيَغْفِرْ لَكُمْ وَاللَّهُ غَفُورٌ رَّحِيمٌ ۝

71. And if they seek to trick you, they have tricked Allah before, yet Allah gave you power over them; and Allah is the Knowing, the Wise.

وَإِن يُرِيدُوا خِيَانَتَكَ فَقَدْ خَانُوا اللَّهَ مِن قَبْلُ فَأَمْكَنَ مِنْهُمْ وَاللَّهُ عَلِيمٌ حَكِيمٌ ۝

72. Surely those who believed and emigrated and strove hard in the way of Allah with their riches and lives; and those who gave refuge and succoured; those shall be heirs one unto another. And those who believed and did not emigrate, you have naught of inheritance to do with them unless they emigrate. And should they seek succour from you in the matter of religion, then incumbent on you is their succour except against a people with whom you have a treaty. And Allah is the Beholder of what you work.

إِنَّ ٱلَّذِينَ ءَامَنُواْ وَهَاجَرُواْ وَجَٰهَدُواْ بِأَمۡوَٰلِهِمۡ وَأَنفُسِهِمۡ فِى سَبِيلِ ٱللَّهِ وَٱلَّذِينَ ءَاوَواْ وَّنَصَرُوٓاْ أُوْلَٰٓئِكَ بَعۡضُهُمۡ أَوۡلِيَآءُ بَعۡضٍ وَٱلَّذِينَ ءَامَنُواْ وَلَمۡ يُهَاجِرُواْ مَا لَكُم مِّن وَلَٰيَتِهِم مِّن شَىۡءٍ حَتَّىٰ يُهَاجِرُواْ وَإِنِ ٱسۡتَنصَرُوكُمۡ فِى ٱلدِّينِ فَعَلَيۡكُمُ ٱلنَّصۡرُ إِلَّا عَلَىٰ قَوۡمِۭ بَيۡنَكُمۡ وَبَيۡنَهُم مِّيثَٰقٌ وَٱللَّهُ بِمَا تَعۡمَلُونَ بَصِيرٌ ﴿٧٢﴾

73. And those who disbelieve; they shall be heirs one unto another. If you do not do this, persecution and great corruption there will be in the land.

وَٱلَّذِينَ كَفَرُواْ بَعۡضُهُمۡ أَوۡلِيَآءُ بَعۡضٍ إِلَّا تَفۡعَلُوهُ تَكُن فِتۡنَةٌ فِى ٱلۡأَرۡضِ وَفَسَادٌ كَبِيرٌ ﴿٧٣﴾

74. And those who have believed and emigrated and striven hard in the way of Allah, and those who gave refuge and succoured these! They are the believers in very truth; for them shall be forgiveness and an honourable provision.

وَٱلَّذِينَ ءَامَنُواْ وَهَاجَرُواْ وَجَٰهَدُواْ فِى سَبِيلِ ٱللَّهِ وَٱلَّذِينَ ءَاوَواْ وَّنَصَرُوٓاْ أُوْلَٰٓئِكَ هُمُ ٱلۡمُؤۡمِنُونَ حَقًّا لَّهُم مَّغۡفِرَةٌ وَرِزۡقٌ كَرِيمٌ ﴿٧٤﴾

75. And those who believed afterwards and emigrated and strove hard along with you; these also are of you; and the kindred by blood are nearer unto one another in Allah's decree. Verily Allah is the Knower of everything.

وَٱلَّذِينَ ءَامَنُواْ مِنۢ بَعۡدُ وَهَاجَرُواْ وَجَٰهَدُواْ مَعَكُمۡ فَأُوْلَٰٓئِكَ مِنكُمۡ وَأُوْلُواْ ٱلۡأَرۡحَامِ بَعۡضُهُمۡ أَوۡلَىٰ بِبَعۡضٍ فِى كِتَٰبِ ٱللَّهِ إِنَّ ٱللَّهَ بِكُلِّ شَىۡءٍ عَلِيمٌ ﴿٧٥﴾

Sūrah 9

al-Tawbah

(Madinan, 16 Sections, 129 Verses)

Section 1

1. Freedom from obligation is from Allah and His Messenger to the associators with whom you had covenanted.

بَرَآءَةٌ مِّنَ ٱللَّهِ وَرَسُولِهِۦٓ إِلَى ٱلَّذِينَ عَٰهَدتُّم مِّنَ ٱلۡمُشۡرِكِينَ ﴿١﴾

2. Go about then, in the land for four months, and know that you cannot escape Allah, and that verily Allah is the humiliator of the infidels.

فَسِيحُوا۟ فِي ٱلۡأَرۡضِ أَرۡبَعَةَ أَشۡهُرٍ وَٱعۡلَمُوٓا۟ أَنَّكُمۡ غَيۡرُ مُعۡجِزِى ٱللَّهِ وَأَنَّ ٱللَّهَ مُخۡزِى ٱلۡكَٰفِرِينَ ﴿٢﴾

3. And a proclamation is this from Allah and His Messenger to mankind on the day of the greater pilgrimage that Allah is quit of the associators and so is His Messenger. Therefore if you repent, it shall be better for you, but if you turn away, then know that you cannot escape Allah. And announce to those who disbelieve an afflictive torment.

وَأَذَٰنٌ مِّنَ ٱللَّهِ وَرَسُولِهِۦٓ إِلَى ٱلنَّاسِ يَوۡمَ ٱلۡحَجِّ ٱلۡأَكۡبَرِ أَنَّ ٱللَّهَ بَرِىٓءٌ مِّنَ ٱلۡمُشۡرِكِينَ وَرَسُولُهُۥ فَإِن تُبۡتُمۡ فَهُوَ خَيۡرٌ لَّكُمۡ وَإِن تَوَلَّيۡتُمۡ فَٱعۡلَمُوٓا۟ أَنَّكُمۡ غَيۡرُ مُعۡجِزِى ٱللَّهِ وَبَشِّرِ ٱلَّذِينَ كَفَرُوا۟ بِعَذَابٍ أَلِيمٍ ﴿٣﴾

4.　Except those of the associators with whom you covenanted and they have not failed you in anything, nor have they backed up any one against you; so fulfil to them their covenant till their full period. Assuredly Allah loves the God-fearing.

إِلَّا ٱلَّذِينَ عَـٰهَدتُّم مِّنَ ٱلْمُشْرِكِينَ ثُمَّ لَمْ يَنقُصُوكُمْ شَيْئًا وَلَمْ يُظَـٰهِرُوا۟ عَلَيْكُمْ أَحَدًا فَأَتِمُّوٓا۟ إِلَيْهِمْ عَهْدَهُمْ إِلَىٰ مُدَّتِهِمْ ۚ إِنَّ ٱللَّهَ يُحِبُّ ٱلْمُتَّقِينَ ﴿٤﴾

5.　When, therefore, the sacred months have slipped away, slay the associators wherever you find them and capture them and confine them and lie in wait for them at every ambush. Then should they repent and establish prayer and give the poor-rate, leave them alone, verily Allah is the Forgiving, the Merciful.

فَإِذَا ٱنسَلَخَ ٱلْأَشْهُرُ ٱلْحُرُمُ فَٱقْتُلُوا۟ ٱلْمُشْرِكِينَ حَيْثُ وَجَدتُّمُوهُمْ وَخُذُوهُمْ وَٱحْصُرُوهُمْ وَٱقْعُدُوا۟ لَهُمْ كُلَّ مَرْصَدٍ ۚ فَإِن تَابُوا۟ وَأَقَامُوا۟ ٱلصَّلَوٰةَ وَءَاتَوُا۟ ٱلزَّكَوٰةَ فَخَلُّوا۟ سَبِيلَهُمْ ۚ إِنَّ ٱللَّهَ غَفُورٌ رَّحِيمٌ ﴿٥﴾

6.　And should any of the associators seek your protection, grant him protection, that he may hear the Word of Allah, then let him reach his place of security. That is because they are a people who do not know.

وَإِنْ أَحَدٌ مِّنَ ٱلْمُشْرِكِينَ ٱسْتَجَارَكَ فَأَجِرْهُ حَتَّىٰ يَسْمَعَ كَلَـٰمَ ٱللَّهِ ثُمَّ أَبْلِغْهُ مَأْمَنَهُ ۚ ذَٰلِكَ بِأَنَّهُمْ قَوْمٌ لَّا يَعْلَمُونَ ﴿٦﴾

Section 2

7.　How can there be for the associators a covenant with Allah and His Messenger save for those with whom you covenanted near the Sacred Mosque? Act straight with them so long as they act straight with you. Verily Allah loves the God-fearing.

كَيْفَ يَكُونُ لِلْمُشْرِكِينَ عَهْدٌ عِندَ ٱللَّهِ وَعِندَ رَسُولِهِۦٓ إِلَّا ٱلَّذِينَ عَـٰهَدتُّمْ عِندَ ٱلْمَسْجِدِ ٱلْحَرَامِ ۖ فَمَا ٱسْتَقَـٰمُوا۟ لَكُمْ فَٱسْتَقِيمُوا۟ لَهُمْ ۚ إِنَّ ٱللَّهَ يُحِبُّ ٱلْمُتَّقِينَ ﴿٧﴾

8. How indeed? When if they get the better of you, they respect you not regarding either kinship or agreement. They flatter you with their mouths, the while their hearts refuse; and most of them are ungodly.

كَيۡفَ وَإِن يَظۡهَرُواْ عَلَيۡكُمۡ لَا يَرۡقُبُواْ فِيكُمۡ إِلَّا وَلَا ذِمَّةً يُرۡضُونَكُم بِأَفۡوَٰهِهِمۡ وَتَأۡبَىٰ قُلُوبُهُمۡ وَأَكۡثَرُهُمۡ فَٰسِقُونَ ٨

9. They have sold the revelations of Allah for a small price, so they keep back them from His path. Vile is that which they are working.

ٱشۡتَرَوۡاْ بِـَٔايَٰتِ ٱللَّهِ ثَمَنًا قَلِيلًا فَصَدُّواْ عَن سَبِيلِهِۦ إِنَّهُمۡ سَآءَ مَا كَانُواْ يَعۡمَلُونَ ٩

10. They respect no kinship or agreement in a believer: those! They are the transgressors.

لَا يَرۡقُبُونَ فِى مُؤۡمِنٍ إِلًّا وَلَا ذِمَّةً وَأُوْلَٰٓئِكَ هُمُ ٱلۡمُعۡتَدُونَ ١٠

11. If they repent and establish prayer and give the poor-rate they are your brethren-in-faith. And We expound the revelations for a people who know.

فَإِن تَابُواْ وَأَقَامُواْ ٱلصَّلَوٰةَ وَءَاتَوُاْ ٱلزَّكَوٰةَ فَإِخۡوَٰنُكُمۡ فِى ٱلدِّينِ وَ نُفَصِّلُ ٱلۡأَيَٰتِ لِقَوۡمٍ يَعۡلَمُونَ ١١

12. And if they violate their oaths after their covenant and revile your religion[384], fight those leaders of infidelity–verily, no oaths shall hold in their case. Haply they may desist.

وَإِن نَّكَثُوٓاْ أَيۡمَٰنَهُم مِّنۢ بَعۡدِ عَهۡدِهِمۡ وَطَعَنُواْ فِى دِينِكُمۡ فَقَٰتِلُوٓاْ أَئِمَّةَ ٱلۡكُفۡرِ إِنَّهُمۡ لَآ أَيۡمَٰنَ لَهُمۡ لَعَلَّهُمۡ يَنتَهُونَ ١٢

---

384. This conveys more than anything else the idea of defiance. Reviling God's Religion is blasphemy in its worst form, and blasphemy, both in the Jewish and Christian religions, is punishable with death. 'And he that blasphemeth the name of the Lord, he shall surely be put to death, and all the congregation shall certainly stone him' (Le. 24: 16). It also stood, till recently, in the secular laws of Europe as an indictable offence with the capital sentence. 'By the law of Scotland, as it originally stood, the punishment of blasphemy was death. In France the punishment was death in various forms, burning alive, mutilation, torture, or corporal punishment' (*EBr.* IV. p. 44).

13. Will you not fight a people who have violated their oaths and conspired the banishment of the Messenger and who have therefore begun against you first? Are you afraid of them? Allah is worthier that you should fear Him, if you are believers at all.

أَلَا تُقَاتِلُونَ قَوْمًا نَّكَثُوٓا أَيْمَنَهُمْ وَهَمُّوا بِإِخْرَاجِ ٱلرَّسُولِ وَهُم بَدَءُوكُمْ أَوَّلَ مَرَّةٍ أَتَخْشَوْنَهُمْ فَٱللَّهُ أَحَقُّ أَن تَخْشَوْهُ إِن كُنتُم مُّؤْمِنِينَ ١٣

14. Fight them; Allah will chastise them at your hands, and humble them and give you victory over them and heal the spirit of the believing people.

قَـٰتِلُوهُمْ يُعَذِّبْهُمُ ٱللَّهُ بِأَيْدِيكُمْ وَيُخْزِهِمْ وَيَنصُرْكُمْ عَلَيْهِمْ وَيَشْفِ صُدُورَ قَوْمٍ مُّؤْمِنِينَ ١٤

15. And He shall take away the rage from their hearts. And Allah shall relent towards whom He pleases; and Allah is the Knowing, the Wise.

وَيُذْهِبْ غَيْظَ قُلُوبِهِمْ وَيَتُوبُ ٱللَّهُ عَلَىٰ مَن يَشَآءُ وَٱللَّهُ عَلِيمٌ حَكِيمٌ ١٥

16. Do you think that you would be left alone while Allah has not known those of you who have striven hard and have not taken an ally besides Him and His Messenger and the faithful? Allah is Aware of what you do.

أَمْ حَسِبْتُمْ أَن تُتْرَكُوا وَلَمَّا يَعْلَمِ ٱللَّهُ ٱلَّذِينَ جَهَدُوا مِنكُمْ وَلَمْ يَتَّخِذُوا مِن دُونِ ٱللَّهِ وَلَا رَسُولِهِ وَلَا ٱلْمُؤْمِنِينَ وَلِيجَةً وَٱللَّهُ خَبِيرٌ بِمَا تَعْمَلُونَ ١٦

Section 3

17. It is not for the associators that they will tend Allah's mosques, while giving evidence of infidelity against themselves. Those! Vain shall be their works, and in the Fire they shall abide.

مَا كَانَ لِلْمُشْرِكِينَ أَن يَعْمُرُوا مَسَٰجِدَ ٱللَّهِ شَٰهِدِينَ عَلَىٰٓ أَنفُسِهِم بِٱلْكُفْرِ أُو۟لَـٰٓئِكَ حَبِطَتْ أَعْمَٰلُهُمْ وَفِي ٱلنَّارِ هُمْ خَٰلِدُونَ ١٧

18. They only shall tend Allah's mosques who believe in Allah and the Last Day and establish prayer and give the poor-rate and fear none save Allah. They may be among the guided ones.

إِنَّمَا يَعْمُرُ مَسَاجِدَ اللَّهِ مَنْ ءَامَنَ بِاللَّهِ وَالْيَوْمِ الْءَاخِرِ وَأَقَامَ الصَّلَوٰةَ وَءَاتَى الزَّكَوٰةَ وَلَمْ يَخْشَ إِلَّا اللَّهَ فَعَسَىٰٓ أُوْلَٰٓئِكَ أَن يَكُونُوا مِنَ الْمُهْتَدِينَ ۝

19. Do you think the giving of drinks to pilgrims and the tendance of the Sacred Mosque is like the conduct of one who believes in Allah and the Last Day and strives hard in the way of Allah? Equal they are not in Allah's sight, and Allah does not guide the wrong-doing people.

أَجَعَلْتُمْ سِقَايَةَ الْحَاجِّ وَعِمَارَةَ الْمَسْجِدِ الْحَرَامِ كَمَنْ ءَامَنَ بِاللَّهِ وَالْيَوْمِ الْءَاخِرِ وَجَٰهَدَ فِى سَبِيلِ اللَّهِ لَا يَسْتَوُۥنَ عِندَ اللَّهِ وَاللَّهُ لَا يَهْدِى الْقَوْمَ الظَّٰلِمِينَ ۝

20. Those who have believed and have emigrated and have striven hard in the way of Allah with their riches and their lives are far higher in degree with Allah. Those! They are the achievers.

الَّذِينَ ءَامَنُوا وَهَاجَرُوا وَجَٰهَدُوا فِى سَبِيلِ اللَّهِ بِأَمْوَٰلِهِمْ وَأَنفُسِهِمْ أَعْظَمُ دَرَجَةً عِندَ اللَّهِ وَأُوْلَٰٓئِكَ هُمُ الْفَآئِزُونَ ۝

21. Their Lord gives them glad tidings of a mercy from Him and of goodwill and of the Gardens wherein theirs will be a lasting delight.

يُبَشِّرُهُمْ رَبُّهُم بِرَحْمَةٍ مِّنْهُ وَرِضْوَٰنٍ وَجَنَّٰتٍ لَّهُمْ فِيهَا نَعِيمٌ مُّقِيمٌ ۝

22. As abiders there for ever. Verily, with Allah is a reward mighty.

خَٰلِدِينَ فِيهَا أَبَدًا إِنَّ اللَّهَ عِندَهُۥٓ أَجْرٌ عَظِيمٌ ۝

23. O you who believe! Do not take your fathers and brothers for friends if they love infidelity above faith. Whoever of you then befriends them; then those! They are the wrong-doers.

يَٰٓأَيُّهَا الَّذِينَ ءَامَنُوا لَا تَتَّخِذُوٓا ءَابَآءَكُمْ وَإِخْوَٰنَكُمْ أَوْلِيَآءَ إِنِ اسْتَحَبُّوا الْكُفْرَ عَلَى الْإِيمَٰنِ وَمَن يَتَوَلَّهُم مِّنكُمْ فَأُوْلَٰٓئِكَ هُمُ الظَّٰلِمُونَ ۝

24. Say; if your fathers and your sons and your brothers and your wives and your family and the riches you have acquired and the trade in which you fear a slackening and the dwellings which please you are dearer to you than Allah and His Messenger and striving in His cause, then wait until He brings about His decree; and Allah does not guide the ungodly people.

Section 4

25. Assuredly Allah has succoured you on many fields and on the day of Hunain, when your number elated you; then it availed you not, and the earth, wide as it is, straitened unto you; then you turned away in retreat.

26. Thereafter, did Allah send down His calm upon His Messenger and upon the believers; and He sent down the hosts that you did not see, and chastised them who disbelieved: such is the recompense of the infidels.

27. Thereafter, Allah will relent towards whom He pleases, and Allah is the Forgiving, the Merciful.

28. O you who believe! The associators are simply filthy; so let them not approach the Sacred

قُل إِن كَانَ ءَابَآؤُكُمْ وَأَبْنَآؤُكُمْ وَ
إِخْوَانُكُمْ وَأَزْوَاجُكُمْ وَعَشِيرَتُكُمْ وَأَمْوَالٌ
ٱقْتَرَفْتُمُوهَا وَتِجَارَةٌ تَخْشَوْنَ كَسَادَهَا
وَمَسَاكِنُ تَرْضَوْنَهَآ أَحَبَّ إِلَيْكُم
مِّنَ ٱللَّهِ وَرَسُولِهِ وَجِهَادٍ فِى سَبِيلِهِ
فَتَرَبَّصُوا حَتَّىٰ يَأْتِىَ ٱللَّهُ بِأَمْرِهِ وَٱللَّهُ
لَا يَهْدِى ٱلْقَوْمَ ٱلْفَٰسِقِينَ ﴿٢٤﴾

لَقَدْ نَصَرَكُمُ ٱللَّهُ فِى مَوَاطِنَ كَثِيرَةٍ
وَيَوْمَ حُنَيْنٍ إِذْ أَعْجَبَتْكُمْ
كَثْرَتُكُمْ فَلَمْ تُغْنِ عَنكُمْ شَيْـًٔا
وَضَاقَتْ عَلَيْكُمُ ٱلْأَرْضُ
بِمَا رَحُبَتْ ثُمَّ وَلَّيْتُم مُّدْبِرِينَ ﴿٢٥﴾

ثُمَّ أَنزَلَ ٱللَّهُ سَكِينَتَهُ عَلَىٰ رَسُولِهِ وَعَلَى
ٱلْمُؤْمِنِينَ وَأَنزَلَ جُنُودًا لَّمْ تَرَوْهَا
وَعَذَّبَ ٱلَّذِينَ كَفَرُوا وَذَٰلِكَ
جَزَآءُ ٱلْكَٰفِرِينَ ﴿٢٦﴾

ثُمَّ يَتُوبُ ٱللَّهُ مِنۢ بَعْدِ ذَٰلِكَ عَلَىٰ مَن
يَشَآءُ وَٱللَّهُ غَفُورٌ رَّحِيمٌ ﴿٢٧﴾

يَٰٓأَيُّهَا ٱلَّذِينَ ءَامَنُوا إِنَّمَا
ٱلْمُشْرِكُونَ نَجَسٌ فَلَا يَقْرَبُوا

Mosque after this year; and if you fear poverty, Allah shall presently enrich you out of His bounty if He pleases. Verily Allah is the Knowing, the Wise.

29. Fight them who do not believe in Allah or in the Last Day, and hold not that as forbidden which Allah and His Messenger have forbidden, and do not observe the true faith of those who have been given the Book, until they pay the tribute[385] out of their hands, and they are subdued.

اَلْمَسْجِدَ الْحَرَامَ بَعْدَ عَامِهِمْ هَـٰذَا وَإِنْ خِفْتُمْ عَيْلَةً فَسَوْفَ يُغْنِيكُمُ اللّٰهُ مِن فَضْلِهِ إِن شَآءَ إِنَّ اللّٰهَ عَلِيمٌ حَكِيمٌ ۝

قَتِلُوا الَّذِينَ لَا يُؤْمِنُونَ بِاللّٰهِ وَلَا بِالْيَوْمِ الْأَخِرِ وَلَا يُحَرِّمُونَ مَا حَرَّمَ اللّٰهُ وَرَسُولُهُ وَلَا يَدِينُونَ دِينَ الْحَقِّ مِنَ الَّذِينَ أُوتُوا الْكِتَبَ حَتَّىٰ يُعْطُوا الْجِزْيَةَ عَن يَدٍ وَهُمْ صَغِرُونَ ۝

---

385. *Jizyah*, the root meaning of which is compensation, signifies, 'the tax that is taken from the fee non-Muslim subjects of a Muslim government pay, whereby they ratify the compact that assures them protection' (*LL.*). In effect it was a tax levied on able-bodied males of military age as a substitute for compulsory military service, the exemption being the destitute, females, children, slaves, monks and hermits. Non-Muslims under the Muslim state were exempted from compulsory military service, and it was only just and equitable that they should pay some little amount in return for the protection afforded by Muslim soldiery' How rigidly the Muslims observed the condition of this ability to afford protection is well evidenced by an incident in the reign of the second Caliph. The Emperor Heraclius had raised an enormous army with which to drive back the invading forces of the Muslims, who had in consequence to concentrate all their energies on the impending encounter. The Arab general, Abū 'Ubaydah, accordingly, wrote to the governors of the conquered cities of Syria, ordering them to pay back all the *jizyah*, that had been collected from the cities, and wrote to the people, saying 'The agreement between us was that we should protect you, and as this is not now in our power, we return you all that we took'. In accordance with this order enormous sums were paid back out of the state treasury, and the Christians called down blessings on the heads of the Muslims, saying: 'May God give you rule over us again and make you victorious over the Romans: had it been they, they would not have given us back anything, but would have taken all that remained with us' (Arnold, *Preaching of Islam*, pp. 60–61). 'It is very noticeable that when any Christian people served in the Muslim army, they were exempted from the payment of this tax' (Ibid., p. 61). 'The collectors of the *Jizyah* were particularly instructed to show leniency, and refrain from all harsh treatment of the infliction of corporal punishment, in case of non–payment' (Ibid., p. 60).

Section 5

30. And the Jews say, Ezra is a child of God;[386] and the Nazarenes say, the Messiah is a child of God. That is their saying with their mouths, resembling the saying of those who disbelieved aforetime. Allah confound them! Whither are they turning away.

وَقَالَتِ الْيَهُودُ عُزَيْرُ ابْنُ اللَّهِ وَقَالَتِ النَّصَارَى الْمَسِيحُ ابْنُ اللَّهِ ذَلِكَ قَوْلُهُم بِأَفْوَاهِهِمْ يُضَاهِئُونَ قَوْلَ الَّذِينَ كَفَرُوا مِن قَبْلُ قَاتَلَهُمُ اللَّهُ أَنَّى يُؤْفَكُونَ ﴿٣٠﴾

---

386. 'Uzair is Ezra of the Bible, whose official title in the Jewish tradition is the 'Scribe of the words of the commandments of the Lord and His statutes for Israel' (Friedlander, *The Jewish Religion*, p. 125), and whose work constitutes a landmark in the history of Judaism. 'One of the most important personages of his day, and of far–reaching influence upon the development of Judaism' (*JE*. V. p. 32). Spinoza 'goes so far as to attribute the composition of the Pentateuch, not to Moses, but to Ezra, which view appears to have existed even in the time of the Apocrypha' (IX. p. 590). 'He is said to have restored not only the law, which had been burnt, but also all the other Hebrew Scriptures which had been destroyed, and seventy apocryphal works in addition' (*EBr.* IX. p. 14). 'With the Return', i.e., since the era of Ezra 'began the codification of the Torah and Scriptures, their translation and exegesis, and the development of their intensive teaching. From now onwards Judaism can be spoken of as distinct from the religion of Israel'. (*VJE*. p. 339). 'He succeeded in reviving with increased strength the old Jewish national religious ideal; and because he did so he is called the father of Judaism' (*The Columbia Encyclopedia*, p. 599). He was the first of the scribes or *soferin*. But who exactly were they? and what standing had they in Jewish theology? Not only were they 'the great authorities on the text of the Scriptures and on its interpretation' but it was they who first 'fixed the norm of Jewish religious practice', and they were considered competent to effect whatever changes they liked even in the Scripture. In fact they did introduce 'eighteen changes into the text of the Pentateuch, chiefly in order to soften expressions which were considered too harsh by a later age. They also modified some of the precepts of the Pentateuch in order to meet the spirit of the age and the needs of the times. These modifications are called in the Talmud *dibre soferin*, "the words of the Scribes", and were accepted as binding by later generation'. (*VJE*. pp. 585–586). 'Uzair's traditionary tomb is on the Tigris, near its junction with the Euphrates, (Layard, *Ninevah and Babylon*, p. 501 f.n.).

31. They have taken their priests and their monks for their Lords, besides Allah, and also the Masīḥ, son of Maryam; whereas they were enjoined that they should worship but One God; no god is there but He. Hallowed be He from that which they associate.

اِتَّخَذُوْٓا اَحْبَارَهُمْ وَرُهْبَانَهُمْ اَرْبَابًا مِّنْ دُوْنِ اللّٰهِ وَالْمَسِيْحَ ابْنَ مَرْيَمَ ۚ وَمَآ اُمِرُوْٓا اِلَّا لِيَعْبُدُوْٓا اِلٰهًا وَّاحِدًا ۚ لَّآ اِلٰهَ اِلَّا هُوَ ۚ سُبْحٰنَهُ عَمَّا يُشْرِكُوْنَ ۞

32. They seek to extinguish the light of Allah with their mouths; and Allah refuses to do otherwise than perfect His light[387], although the infidels may detest it.

يُرِيْدُوْنَ اَنْ يُّطْفِـُٔوْا نُوْرَ اللّٰهِ بِاَفْوَاهِهِمْ وَيَاْبَى اللّٰهُ اِلَّآ اَنْ يُّتِمَّ نُوْرَهُ وَلَوْ كَرِهَ الْكٰفِرُوْنَ ۞

33. He it is who has sent down His Messenger with guidance and the true faith, that He may make it prevail[388] over all religions[389], although the associators may detest it.

هُوَ الَّذِيْٓ اَرْسَلَ رَسُوْلَهُ بِالْهُدٰى وَدِيْنِ الْحَقِّ لِيُظْهِرَهُ عَلَى الدِّيْنِ كُلِّهِ ۚ وَلَوْ كَرِهَ الْمُشْرِكُوْنَ ۞

---

387. By spreading His religion far and wide and making it a signal success, a prophecy that has stood the test of fourteen centuries. Witness the admission of Sale, that the success achieved by Islam is 'unexampled in the world' (*SPD*). And the still more recent admission of a competent European scholar, that the Prophet Muhammad is 'the most successful of all prophets and religious personalities' (*EBr.* XV. p. 898).

388. That it prevail by means of solid achievement and clear argument. Note that it is the religion of Islam, as such, that is to outshine and outlive all other religions; and there is no necessary connection between the religious superiority of Islam and the political supremacy of the Muslim states.

389. Witness the confession of failure on the part of Christian missionaries with all their vast resources: 'The solid mass of experience due to the efforts of numerous missionaries is not of an encouraging nature. There is no reasonable hope of the conversion of important numbers of Mohammadans to any Christian denomination', (Hurgronje, *Mohammadanism*, p. 174).

34. O you who believe! Surely many of the priests and monks devour the substance of men in falsehood, and hinder people from the way of Allah. And those who hoard up gold and silver and do not spend them in the way of Allah, announce you to them an afflictive torment.

35. On a Day when they shall be heated in Hellfire, and with it shall be branded their foreheads and their sides and their backs: 'this is what you have treasured up for yourselves, so taste now what you have been treasuring up.'

36. Verily, the number of months with Allah is twelve months ordained in the Writ of Allah on the Day when He created the heavens and the earth; and of these, four are sacred; that is the right religion. Wherefore wrong not yourselves in this respect. And fight the associators, all of them, as they fight all of you, and know that Allah is with the God-fearing.

37. The postponement is but an addition to infidelity, with which the infidels are led astray, allowing it one year and forbidding it another year, that they may make up the number which Allah has sanctified, and then they allow what Allah has forbidden. Fair-seeming to them are made their foul acts; and Allah does not guide an infidel people.

يَـٰٓأَيُّهَا ٱلَّذِينَ ءَامَنُوٓاْ إِنَّ كَثِيرًا مِّنَ ٱلْأَحْبَارِ وَٱلرُّهْبَانِ لَيَأْكُلُونَ أَمْوَٰلَ ٱلنَّاسِ بِٱلْبَٰطِلِ وَيَصُدُّونَ عَن سَبِيلِ ٱللَّهِ ۗ وَٱلَّذِينَ يَكْنِزُونَ ٱلذَّهَبَ وَٱلْفِضَّةَ وَلَا يُنفِقُونَهَا فِى سَبِيلِ ٱللَّهِ فَبَشِّرْهُم بِعَذَابٍ أَلِيمٍ ﴿٣٤﴾

يَوْمَ يُحْمَىٰ عَلَيْهَا فِى نَارِ جَهَنَّمَ فَتُكْوَىٰ بِهَا جِبَاهُهُمْ وَجُنُوبُهُمْ وَظُهُورُهُمْ ۖ هَٰذَا مَا كَنَزْتُمْ لِأَنفُسِكُمْ فَذُوقُواْ مَا كُنتُمْ تَكْنِزُونَ ﴿٣٥﴾

إِنَّ عِدَّةَ ٱلشُّهُورِ عِندَ ٱللَّهِ ٱثْنَا عَشَرَ شَهْرًا فِى كِتَٰبِ ٱللَّهِ يَوْمَ خَلَقَ ٱلسَّمَٰوَٰتِ وَٱلْأَرْضَ مِنْهَآ أَرْبَعَةٌ حُرُمٌ ۚ ذَٰلِكَ ٱلدِّينُ ٱلْقَيِّمُ ۚ فَلَا تَظْلِمُواْ فِيهِنَّ أَنفُسَكُمْ ۚ وَقَٰتِلُواْ ٱلْمُشْرِكِينَ كَآفَّةً كَمَا يُقَٰتِلُونَكُمْ كَآفَّةً ۚ وَٱعْلَمُوٓاْ أَنَّ ٱللَّهَ مَعَ ٱلْمُتَّقِينَ ﴿٣٦﴾

إِنَّمَا ٱلنَّسِىٓءُ زِيَادَةٌ فِى ٱلْكُفْرِ ۖ يُضَلُّ بِهِ ٱلَّذِينَ كَفَرُواْ يُحِلُّونَهُۥ عَامًا وَيُحَرِّمُونَهُۥ عَامًا لِّيُوَاطِـُٔواْ عِدَّةَ مَا حَرَّمَ ٱللَّهُ فَيُحِلُّواْ مَا حَرَّمَ ٱللَّهُ ۚ زُيِّنَ لَهُمْ سُوٓءُ أَعْمَٰلِهِمْ ۗ وَٱللَّهُ لَا يَهْدِى ٱلْقَوْمَ ٱلْكَٰفِرِينَ ﴿٣٧﴾

Section 6

38. O you who believe! Why is it with you that when it is said to you march forth in the way of Allah, you linger slothfully earthward? Are you pleased with the life of the world rather than the Hereafter? Whereas the enjoyment of the life of the world by the side of the Hereafter is but little.

يَـٰٓأَيُّهَا ٱلَّذِينَ ءَامَنُوا۟ مَا لَكُمْ إِذَا قِيلَ لَكُمُ ٱنفِرُوا۟ فِى سَبِيلِ ٱللَّهِ ٱثَّاقَلْتُمْ إِلَى ٱلْأَرْضِ أَرَضِيتُم بِٱلْحَيَوٰةِ ٱلدُّنْيَا مِنَ ٱلْءَاخِرَةِ فَمَا مَتَٰعُ ٱلْحَيَوٰةِ ٱلدُّنْيَا فِى ٱلْءَاخِرَةِ إِلَّا قَلِيلٌ ﴿٣٨﴾

39. If you do not march forth, He will torment you with an affliction, and will replace you by another people, and Him you cannot harm in any way; and Allah is Potent over everything.

إِلَّا تَنفِرُوا۟ يُعَذِّبْكُمْ عَذَابًا أَلِيمًا وَيَسْتَبْدِلْ قَوْمًا غَيْرَكُمْ وَلَا تَضُرُّوهُ شَيْـًٔا وَٱللَّهُ عَلَىٰ كُلِّ شَىْءٍ قَدِيرٌ ﴿٣٩﴾

40. If you do not succour him, then surely Allah has succoured him when those who disbelieved banished him; the second of the two; when the two were in a cave, and when he said to his companion: 'Do not grieve, verily Allah is with us.' Then Allah sent down His peace on him and supported him with hosts which you did not see, and made the word of those who disbelieved the lowest and the Word of Allah is the uppermost. And Allah is the Mighty, the Wise.

إِلَّا تَنصُرُوهُ فَقَدْ نَصَرَهُ ٱللَّهُ إِذْ أَخْرَجَهُ ٱلَّذِينَ كَفَرُوا۟ ثَانِىَ ٱثْنَيْنِ إِذْ هُمَا فِى ٱلْغَارِ إِذْ يَقُولُ لِصَٰحِبِهِۦ لَا تَحْزَنْ إِنَّ ٱللَّهَ مَعَنَا فَأَنزَلَ ٱللَّهُ سَكِينَتَهُۥ عَلَيْهِ وَأَيَّدَهُۥ بِجُنُودٍ لَّمْ تَرَوْهَا وَجَعَلَ كَلِمَةَ ٱلَّذِينَ كَفَرُوا۟ ٱلسُّفْلَىٰ وَكَلِمَةُ ٱللَّهِ هِىَ ٱلْعُلْيَا وَٱللَّهُ عَزِيزٌ حَكِيمٌ ﴿٤٠﴾

41. March forth, light and heavy, and strive hard with your riches and lives in the way of Allah; that is the best for you, if you have knowledge.

انفِرُواْ خِفَافًا وَثِقَالًا وَجَٰهِدُواْ بِأَمۡوَٰلِكُمۡ وَأَنفُسِكُمۡ فِي سَبِيلِ ٱللَّهِ ذَٰلِكُمۡ خَيۡرٌ لَّكُمۡ إِن كُنتُمۡ تَعۡلَمُونَ ۝

42. Were there a gain nigh and a journey easy, they would have followed you, but the distance was too far to them. Still they will swear by Allah saying; if only we could, we would surely have come forth with you. They kill their own souls and Allah knows that verily they are liars.

لَوۡ كَانَ عَرَضًا قَرِيبًا وَسَفَرًا قَاصِدًا لَّٱتَّبَعُوكَ وَلَٰكِنۢ بَعُدَتۡ عَلَيۡهِمُ ٱلشُّقَّةُ وَسَيَحۡلِفُونَ بِٱللَّهِ لَوِ ٱسۡتَطَعۡنَا لَخَرَجۡنَا مَعَكُمۡ يُهۡلِكُونَ أَنفُسَهُمۡ وَٱللَّهُ يَعۡلَمُ إِنَّهُمۡ لَكَٰذِبُونَ ۝

Section 7

43. Allah pardon you! Why did you give them leave before it was clear unto you as to who told the truth and you had known the liars?

عَفَا ٱللَّهُ عَنكَ لِمَ أَذِنتَ لَهُمۡ حَتَّىٰ يَتَبَيَّنَ لَكَ ٱلَّذِينَ صَدَقُواْ وَتَعۡلَمَ ٱلۡكَٰذِبِينَ ۝

44. Those who believe in Allah and the Last Day would not ask your leave to be excused from striving hard with their riches and their lives, and Allah is the Knower of the God-fearing.

لَا يَسۡتَٔۡذِنُكَ ٱلَّذِينَ يُؤۡمِنُونَ بِٱللَّهِ وَٱلۡيَوۡمِ ٱلۡأَخِرِ أَن يُجَٰهِدُواْ بِأَمۡوَٰلِهِمۡ وَأَنفُسِهِمۡ وَٱللَّهُ عَلِيمٌ بِٱلۡمُتَّقِينَ ۝

45. It is only those who do not believe in Allah and the Last Day and whose hearts doubt who ask your leave; so in their doubt they are tossed to and fro.

إِنَّمَا يَسۡتَٔۡذِنُكَ ٱلَّذِينَ لَا يُؤۡمِنُونَ بِٱللَّهِ وَٱلۡيَوۡمِ ٱلۡأَخِرِ وَٱرۡتَابَتۡ قُلُوبُهُمۡ فَهُمۡ فِي رَيۡبِهِمۡ يَتَرَدَّدُونَ ۝

46. Had they intended the marching forth, they would have made some preparation for it; but Allah was averse to their wending, so He withheld them and the word was passed; stay at home with the stay-at-homes.

وَلَوۡ أَرَادُواْ ٱلۡخُرُوجَ لَأَعَدُّواْ لَهُۥ عُدَّةً وَلَٰكِن كَرِهَ ٱللَّهُ ٱنۢبِعَاثَهُمۡ فَثَبَّطَهُمۡ وَقِيلَ ٱقۡعُدُواْ مَعَ ٱلۡقَٰعِدِينَ ﴿٤٦﴾

47. Had they marched forth with you, they would have added to you nothing save unsoundness, and they would have hurried about in your midst seeking sedition unto you; and there are among you listeners to them; and Allah is the Knower of the wrong-doers.

لَوۡ خَرَجُواْ فِيكُم مَّا زَادُوكُمۡ إِلَّا خَبَالًا وَلَأَوۡضَعُواْ خِلَٰلَكُمۡ يَبۡغُونَكُمُ ٱلۡفِتۡنَةَ وَفِيكُمۡ سَمَّٰعُونَ لَهُمۡۗ وَٱللَّهُ عَلِيمٌۢ بِٱلظَّٰلِمِينَ ﴿٤٧﴾

48. Assuredly they sought confusion before and turned the affairs upside down for you until the Truth arrived and the decree of Allah prevailed, averse though they were.

لَقَدِ ٱبۡتَغَوُاْ ٱلۡفِتۡنَةَ مِن قَبۡلُ وَقَلَّبُواْ لَكَ ٱلۡأُمُورَ حَتَّىٰ جَآءَ ٱلۡحَقُّ وَظَهَرَ أَمۡرُ ٱللَّهِ وَهُمۡ كَٰرِهُونَ ﴿٤٨﴾

49. And among them there is he who says: 'Give me leave and tempt me not.' Lo! Into temptation they are already fallen; and verily Hell is the encompasser of the infidels.

وَمِنۡهُم مَّن يَقُولُ ٱئۡذَن لِّي وَلَا تَفۡتِنِّيٓۚ أَلَا فِي ٱلۡفِتۡنَةِ سَقَطُواْۗ وَإِنَّ جَهَنَّمَ لَمُحِيطَةٌۢ بِٱلۡكَٰفِرِينَ ﴿٤٩﴾

50. If good happens to you it annoys them and if an affliction befalls you, they say: 'We surely took hold of our affairs before.' And they turn away while they are exulting.

إِن تُصِبۡكَ حَسَنَةٌ تَسُؤۡهُمۡۖ وَإِن تُصِبۡكَ مُصِيبَةٌ يَقُولُواْ قَدۡ أَخَذۡنَآ أَمۡرَنَا مِن قَبۡلُ وَيَتَوَلَّواْ وَّهُمۡ فَرِحُونَ ﴿٥٠﴾

51. Say: 'Nothing shall ever befall us save what Allah has ordained for us; He is our Patron and on Allah let the believers rely.'

قُل لَّن يُصِيبَنَا إِلَّا مَا كَتَبَ ٱللَّهُ لَنَا هُوَ مَوْلَىٰنَا وَعَلَى ٱللَّهِ فَلْيَتَوَكَّلِ ٱلْمُؤْمِنُونَ ﴿٥١﴾

52. Say: 'Do you await for us anything save one of the two excellences, while for you we wait that Allah shall afflict you with a torment from Himself, or at our hands? Await then, we also are with you awaiting.'

قُلْ هَلْ تَرَبَّصُونَ بِنَا إِلَّا إِحْدَى ٱلْحُسْنَيَيْنِ وَنَحْنُ نَتَرَبَّصُ بِكُمْ أَن يُصِيبَكُمُ ٱللَّهُ بِعَذَابٍ مِّنْ عِندِهِ أَوْ بِأَيْدِينَا فَتَرَبَّصُوٓا إِنَّا مَعَكُم مُّتَرَبِّصُونَ ﴿٥٢﴾

53. Say: 'Spend willingly or unwillingly it will not be accepted from you; verily you are a people ever ungodly.'

قُلْ أَنفِقُوا طَوْعًا أَوْ كَرْهًا لَّن يُتَقَبَّلَ مِنكُمْ إِنَّكُمْ كُنتُمْ قَوْمًا فَٰسِقِينَ ﴿٥٣﴾

54. And nothing does prevent their spendings from being accepted except that they have disbelieved in Allah and His Messenger, and that they perform not prayer except as sluggards and spend not save as those averse.

وَمَا مَنَعَهُمْ أَن تُقْبَلَ مِنْهُمْ نَفَقَٰتُهُمْ إِلَّا أَنَّهُمْ كَفَرُوا بِٱللَّهِ وَبِرَسُولِهِ وَلَا يَأْتُونَ ٱلصَّلَوٰةَ إِلَّا وَهُمْ كُسَالَىٰ وَلَا يُنفِقُونَ إِلَّا وَهُمْ كَٰرِهُونَ ﴿٥٤﴾

55. Let not therefore their riches and their children amaze you, Allah only intends to chastise them therewith in the life of the world and that their souls should depart while they are infidels.

فَلَا تُعْجِبْكَ أَمْوَٰلُهُمْ وَلَآ أَوْلَٰدُهُمْ إِنَّمَا يُرِيدُ ٱللَّهُ لِيُعَذِّبَهُم بِهَا فِي ٱلْحَيَوٰةِ ٱلدُّنْيَا وَتَزْهَقَ أَنفُسُهُمْ وَهُمْ كَٰفِرُونَ ﴿٥٥﴾

56. They swear by Allah that they are surely of you, while they are not of you; but they are a people who dread.

وَيَحْلِفُونَ بِٱللَّهِ إِنَّهُمْ لَمِنكُمْ وَمَا هُم مِّنكُمْ وَلَٰكِنَّهُمْ قَوْمٌ يَفْرَقُونَ ﴿٥٦﴾

57. Could they find a place of shelter or caverns or a retreating hole, they would turn round to it, rushing headlong.

لَوۡ يَجِدُونَ مَلۡجَأً أَوۡ مَغَـٰرَتٍ أَوۡ مُدَّخَلًا لَّوَلَّوۡاۡ إِلَيۡهِ وَهُمۡ يَجۡمَحُونَ ۞

58. And of them are some who traduce you in respect of alms. Then if they are given a share of these, they are pleased, and if they are given none, lo! They are enraged.

وَمِنۡهُم مَّن يَلۡمِزُكَ فِى ٱلصَّدَقَـٰتِ فَإِنۡ أُعۡطُواۡ مِنۡهَا رَضُواۡ وَإِن لَّمۡ يُعۡطَوۡاۡ مِنۡهَاۤ إِذَا هُمۡ يَسۡخَطُونَ ۞

59. Would that they were content with what Allah and His Messenger had given them and were to say: 'sufficient to us is Allah, soon will Allah give us out of His Grace, and so will His Messenger, verily to Allah we lean.'

وَلَوۡ أَنَّهُمۡ رَضُواۡ مَاۤ ءَاتَىٰهُمُ ٱللَّهُ وَرَسُولُهُۥ وَقَالُواۡ حَسۡبُنَا ٱللَّهُ سَيُؤۡتِينَا ٱللَّهُ مِن فَضۡلِهِۦ وَرَسُولُهُۥۤ إِنَّاۤ إِلَى ٱللَّهِ رَٰغِبُونَ ۞

Section 8

60. The obligatory alms are only for the poor and the needy and the agents employed therein and those whose hearts are conciliated and those in bondage and debtors and for expenditure in the way of Allah and for the wayfarer; an ordinance from Allah, and Allah is the Knowing, the Wise.

إِنَّمَا ٱلصَّدَقَـٰتُ لِلۡفُقَرَآءِ وَٱلۡمَسَـٰكِينِ وَٱلۡعَـٰمِلِينَ عَلَيۡهَا وَٱلۡمُؤَلَّفَةِ قُلُوبُهُمۡ وَفِى ٱلرِّقَابِ وَٱلۡغَـٰرِمِينَ وَفِى سَبِيلِ ٱللَّهِ وَٱبۡنِ ٱلسَّبِيلِ فَرِيضَةً مِّنَ ٱللَّهِ وَٱللَّهُ عَلِيمٌ حَكِيمٌ ۞

61. And of them are some who vex the Messenger and say he is all ears. Say: 'He is all ears unto what is good for you, believing in Allah and giving credence to the believers and a mercy to those of you who believe.' And those who vex the Messenger of Allah, for them shall be a painful chastisement.

وَمِنۡهُمُ ٱلَّذِينَ يُؤۡذُونَ ٱلنَّبِىَّ وَيَقُولُونَ هُوَ أُذُنٌ قُلۡ أُذُنُ خَيۡرٍ لَّكُمۡ يُؤۡمِنُ بِٱللَّهِ وَيُؤۡمِنُ لِلۡمُؤۡمِنِينَ وَرَحۡمَةٌ لِّلَّذِينَ ءَامَنُواۡ مِنكُمۡ وَٱلَّذِينَ يُؤۡذُونَ رَسُولَ ٱللَّهِ لَهُمۡ عَذَابٌ أَلِيمٌ ۞

62. They swear to you by Allah in order that you may be pleased, while worthier are Allah and His Messenger that they should please Him, if they be believers indeed.

يَحْلِفُونَ بِٱللَّهِ لَكُمْ لِيُرْضُوكُمْ وَٱللَّهُ وَرَسُولُهُۥٓ أَحَقُّ أَن يُرْضُوهُ إِن كَانُوا۟ مُؤْمِنِينَ ۝

63. Do they not know that anyone who opposes Allah and His Messenger, verily for him shall be Hell fire in which he shall abide: a mighty humiliation?

أَلَمْ يَعْلَمُوٓا۟ أَنَّهُۥ مَن يُحَادِدِ ٱللَّهَ وَرَسُولَهُۥ فَأَنَّ لَهُۥ نَارَ جَهَنَّمَ خَالِدًا فِيهَا ذَٰلِكَ ٱلْخِزْىُ ٱلْعَظِيمُ ۝

64. The hypocrites fear lest a Surah should be revealed to them declaring to them what is in their hearts. Say: 'Mock ye: truly Allah is about to bring out what you apprehend.'

يَحْذَرُ ٱلْمُنَٰفِقُونَ أَن تُنَزَّلَ عَلَيْهِمْ سُورَةٌ تُنَبِّئُهُم بِمَا فِى قُلُوبِهِمْ قُلِ ٱسْتَهْزِءُوٓا۟ إِنَّ ٱللَّهَ مُخْرِجٌ مَّا تَحْذَرُونَ ۝

65. Should you question them, they will surely say, 'We were only plunging about and playing.' Say: 'Was it Allah and His signs and His Messenger that you have been mocking?'

وَلَئِن سَأَلْتَهُمْ لَيَقُولُنَّ إِنَّمَا كُنَّا نَخُوضُ وَنَلْعَبُ قُلْ أَبِٱللَّهِ وَءَايَٰتِهِۦ وَرَسُولِهِۦ كُنتُمْ تَسْتَهْزِءُونَ ۝

66. Make no excuse. Of a surety you are disbelieving after declaring your faith. If a section of you We will pardon, another section We will chastise, for they have remained sinners.

لَا تَعْتَذِرُوا۟ قَدْ كَفَرْتُم بَعْدَ إِيمَٰنِكُمْ إِن نَّعْفُ عَن طَآئِفَةٍ مِّنكُمْ نُعَذِّبْ طَآئِفَةًۢ بِأَنَّهُمْ كَانُوا۟ مُجْرِمِينَ ۝

Section 9

67. The hypocrites, men and women, are all of a piece, they bid what is disreputable and prohibit what is reputable, and they tighten their hands. They neglected Allah and so He has neglected them. Verily, the hypocrites are the ungodly ones.

ٱلْمُنَٰفِقُونَ وَٱلْمُنَٰفِقَٰتُ بَعْضُهُم مِّنۢ بَعْضٍ يَأْمُرُونَ بِٱلْمُنكَرِ وَيَنْهَوْنَ عَنِ ٱلْمَعْرُوفِ وَيَقْبِضُونَ أَيْدِيَهُمْ نَسُوا۟ ٱللَّهَ فَنَسِيَهُمْ إِنَّ ٱلْمُنَٰفِقِينَ هُمُ ٱلْفَٰسِقُونَ ۝

68. Allah has promised the hypocritical men and women and the infidels Hell fire wherein they shall abide; sufficient is that unto them. And Allah shall accurse them and theirs shall be a lasting chastisement.

وَعَدَ ٱللَّهُ ٱلۡمُنَٰفِقِينَ وَٱلۡمُنَٰفِقَٰتِ وَٱلۡكُفَّارَ نَارَ جَهَنَّمَ خَٰلِدِينَ فِيهَا هِيَ حَسۡبُهُمۡ وَلَعَنَهُمُ ٱللَّهُ وَلَهُمۡ عَذَابٌ مُّقِيمٌ ۝

69. You are like those before you; mightier than you were they in prowess and more abundant in riches and children. They enjoyed their portion awhile, so enjoy your portion awhile even as those before you enjoyed their portion awhile, and you plunged about even as they plunged about. Their works have come to nothing in the world and the Hereafter, and they are the losers!

كَٱلَّذِينَ مِن قَبۡلِكُمۡ كَانُوٓاْ أَشَدَّ مِنكُمۡ قُوَّةً وَأَكۡثَرَ أَمۡوَٰلًا وَأَوۡلَٰدًا فَٱسۡتَمۡتَعُواْ بِخَلَٰقِهِمۡ فَٱسۡتَمۡتَعۡتُم بِخَلَٰقِكُمۡ كَمَا ٱسۡتَمۡتَعَ ٱلَّذِينَ مِن قَبۡلِكُم بِخَلَٰقِهِمۡ وَخُضۡتُمۡ كَٱلَّذِي خَاضُوٓاْ أُوْلَٰٓئِكَ حَبِطَتۡ أَعۡمَٰلُهُمۡ فِي ٱلدُّنۡيَا وَٱلۡأٓخِرَةِ وَأُوْلَٰٓئِكَ هُمُ ٱلۡخَٰسِرُونَ ۝

70. Have the tidings not come to them of those before them; the people of Nuh and 'Ad and the Thamud and the people of Abraham and the dwellers of Madyan and of the overturned towns? There came to them each their Messenger with evidence. So Allah was not the One to wrong them, but themselves they were wont to wrong.

أَلَمۡ يَأۡتِهِمۡ نَبَأُ ٱلَّذِينَ مِن قَبۡلِهِمۡ قَوۡمِ نُوحٍ وَعَادٍ وَثَمُودَ وَقَوۡمِ إِبۡرَٰهِيمَ وَأَصۡحَٰبِ مَدۡيَنَ وَٱلۡمُؤۡتَفِكَٰتِ أَتَتۡهُمۡ رُسُلُهُم بِٱلۡبَيِّنَٰتِ فَمَا كَانَ ٱللَّهُ لِيَظۡلِمَهُمۡ وَلَٰكِن كَانُوٓاْ أَنفُسَهُمۡ يَظۡلِمُونَ ۝

71. And the believing men and women are friends to one another; they bid each other what is reputable and prohibit what is disreputable, and establish prayer and pay the poor-rate and obey Allah and His Messenger. Those! Allah will surely show mercy to them; verily, Allah is the Mighty, the Wise.

وَٱلۡمُؤۡمِنُونَ وَٱلۡمُؤۡمِنَٰتُ بَعۡضُهُمۡ أَوۡلِيَآءُ بَعۡضٍ يَأۡمُرُونَ بِٱلۡمَعۡرُوفِ وَيَنۡهَوۡنَ عَنِ ٱلۡمُنكَرِ وَيُقِيمُونَ ٱلصَّلَوٰةَ وَيُؤۡتُونَ ٱلزَّكَوٰةَ وَيُطِيعُونَ ٱللَّهَ وَرَسُولَهُۥٓ أُوْلَٰٓئِكَ سَيَرۡحَمُهُمُ ٱللَّهُ إِنَّ ٱللَّهَ عَزِيزٌ حَكِيمٌ ۝

72. Allah has promised the believing men and women Gardens under which rivers flow, wherein they shall abide, and goodly dwellings in the everlasting Gardens and goodwill from Allah is the greatest of all, that is the supreme achievement.

وَعَدَاللَّهُ الْمُؤْمِنِينَ وَالْمُؤْمِنَٰتِ جَنَّٰتٍ تَجْرِي مِن تَحْتِهَا الْأَنْهَٰرُ خَٰلِدِينَ فِيهَا وَمَسَٰكِنَ طَيِّبَةً فِي جَنَّٰتِ عَدْنٍ وَرِضْوَٰنٌ مِّنَ اللَّهِ أَكْبَرُ ذَٰلِكَ هُوَ الْفَوْزُ الْعَظِيمُ ﴿٧٢﴾

Section 10

73. O Prophet! Strive hard against the infidels and the hypocrites, and be stern with them. And their resort is Hell, a helpless destination.

يَٰٓأَيُّهَا النَّبِيُّ جَٰهِدِ الْكُفَّارَ وَالْمُنَٰفِقِينَ وَاغْلُظْ عَلَيْهِمْ وَمَأْوَىٰهُمْ جَهَنَّمُ وَبِئْسَ الْمَصِيرُ ﴿٧٣﴾

74. They swear by Allah that they said it not, but assuredly they uttered the word of infidelity and disbelieved after their profession of Islam and they resolved that to which they could not attain. And they avenged not except this that Allah and His Messenger had enriched them out of His grace. If then they repent, it will be better for them, and if they turn away, Allah shall chastise them with an afflictive torment in the world and the Hereafter, and on the earth theirs shall be no friend or helper.

يَحْلِفُونَ بِاللَّهِ مَا قَالُوا۟ وَلَقَدْ قَالُوا۟ كَلِمَةَ الْكُفْرِ وَكَفَرُوا۟ بَعْدَ إِسْلَٰمِهِمْ وَهَمُّوا۟ بِمَا لَمْ يَنَالُوا۟ وَمَا نَقَمُوٓا۟ إِلَّآ أَنْ أَغْنَٰهُمُ اللَّهُ وَرَسُولُهُۥ مِن فَضْلِهِۦ فَإِن يَتُوبُوا۟ يَكُ خَيْرًا لَّهُمْ وَإِن يَتَوَلَّوْا۟ يُعَذِّبْهُمُ اللَّهُ عَذَابًا أَلِيمًا فِي الدُّنْيَا وَالْأَخِرَةِ وَمَا لَهُمْ فِي الْأَرْضِ مِن وَلِيٍّ وَلَا نَصِيرٍ ﴿٧٤﴾

75. And of them are some who covenanted with Allah saying, 'If He gives us of His grace, we shall surely pay the poor-rate and shall become of the righteous.'

وَمِنْهُم مَّنْ عَٰهَدَ اللَّهَ لَئِنْ ءَاتَٰنَا مِن فَضْلِهِۦ لَنَصَّدَّقَنَّ وَلَنَكُونَنَّ مِنَ الصَّٰلِحِينَ ﴿٧٥﴾

76. Then when He gave them out of His grace, they became niggardly therewith and turned away as backsliders.

فَلَمَّآ ءَاتَىٰهُم مِّن فَضۡلِهِۦ بَخِلُواْ بِهِۦ وَتَوَلَّواْ وَّهُم مُّعۡرِضُونَ ۝

77. So He chastised them by setting hypocrisy in their hearts until the Day they will meet Him, because they kept back from Allah what they had promised Him, and because they were wont to lie.

فَأَعۡقَبَهُمۡ نِفَاقًا فِى قُلُوبِهِمۡ إِلَىٰ يَوۡمِ يَلۡقَوۡنَهُۥ بِمَآ أَخۡلَفُواْ ٱللَّهَ مَا وَعَدُوهُ وَبِمَا كَانُواْ يَكۡذِبُونَ ۝

78. Know they not that Allah knows their secret and their whisper, and that Allah is the Knower of things Unseen?

أَلَمۡ يَعۡلَمُوٓاْ أَنَّ ٱللَّهَ يَعۡلَمُ سِرَّهُمۡ وَنَجۡوَىٰهُمۡ وَأَنَّ ٱللَّهَ عَلَّٰمُ ٱلۡغُيُوبِ ۝

79. These are they who traduce those who give alms cheerfully, from among the believers, and those who do not have anything to give but their hard earnings. At them they scoff; Allah shall scoff back at them and theirs shall be an afflictive torment.

ٱلَّذِينَ يَلۡمِزُونَ ٱلۡمُطَّوِّعِينَ مِنَ ٱلۡمُؤۡمِنِينَ فِى ٱلصَّدَقَٰتِ وَٱلَّذِينَ لَا يَجِدُونَ إِلَّا جُهۡدَهُمۡ فَيَسۡخَرُونَ مِنۡهُمۡ سَخِرَ ٱللَّهُ مِنۡهُمۡ وَلَهُمۡ عَذَابٌ أَلِيمٌ ۝

80. Ask forgiveness for them or ask not forgiveness for them; if you ask for forgiveness for them seventy times, Allah will not forgive them. This, because they disbelieved in Allah and His Messenger, and Allah does not guide the ungodly people.

ٱسۡتَغۡفِرۡ لَهُمۡ أَوۡ لَا تَسۡتَغۡفِرۡ لَهُمۡ إِن تَسۡتَغۡفِرۡ لَهُمۡ سَبۡعِينَ مَرَّةً فَلَن يَغۡفِرَ ٱللَّهُ لَهُمۡ ذَٰلِكَ بِأَنَّهُمۡ كَفَرُواْ بِٱللَّهِ وَرَسُولِهِۦ وَٱللَّهُ لَا يَهۡدِى ٱلۡقَوۡمَ ٱلۡفَٰسِقِينَ ۝

Section 11

81. Those who were left rejoiced at their staying behind the Messenger of Allah, and they detested to strive hard with riches and their lives in the way of Allah, and they said: 'do not march forth in the heat.' Say: 'Hotter still is Hell fire.' Would that they understood!'

فَرِحَ ٱلْمُخَلَّفُونَ بِمَقْعَدِهِمْ خِلَٰفَ رَسُولِ ٱللَّهِ وَكَرِهُوٓاْ أَن يُجَٰهِدُواْ بِأَمْوَٰلِهِمْ وَأَنفُسِهِمْ فِى سَبِيلِ ٱللَّهِ وَقَالُواْ لَا تَنفِرُواْ فِى ٱلْحَرِّ قُلْ نَارُ جَهَنَّمَ أَشَدُّ حَرًّا لَّوْ كَانُواْ يَفْقَهُونَ ۝

82. Little then let them laugh, and much shall they weep; this is the recompense of what they have been earning.

فَلْيَضْحَكُواْ قَلِيلًا وَلْيَبْكُواْ كَثِيرًا جَزَآءَۢ بِمَا كَانُواْ يَكْسِبُونَ ۝

83. If, then, Allah brings you back to a party of them, and they ask leave of you for marching forth, say: 'Never shall you march forth with me, nor ever fight an enemy with me; verily, you were well-pleased to tarry at home the first time, so stay now with the stay-at-homes.'

فَإِن رَّجَعَكَ ٱللَّهُ إِلَىٰ طَآئِفَةٍ مِّنْهُمْ فَٱسْتَـْٔذَنُوكَ لِلْخُرُوجِ فَقُل لَّن تَخْرُجُواْ مَعِىَ أَبَدًا وَلَن تُقَٰتِلُواْ مَعِىَ عَدُوًّا إِنَّكُمْ رَضِيتُم بِٱلْقُعُودِ أَوَّلَ مَرَّةٍ فَٱقْعُدُواْ مَعَ ٱلْخَٰلِفِينَ ۝

84. And pray you not ever over any of them when he is dead, nor stand you over his grave. Surely they have denied Allah and His Messenger and died while they were rejecters.

وَلَا تُصَلِّ عَلَىٰٓ أَحَدٍ مِّنْهُم مَّاتَ أَبَدًا وَلَا تَقُمْ عَلَىٰ قَبْرِهِۦٓ إِنَّهُمْ كَفَرُواْ بِٱللَّهِ وَرَسُولِهِۦ وَمَاتُواْ وَهُمْ فَٰسِقُونَ ۝

85. And let not their riches and their children amaze you. Allah intends only to chastise them therewith in the world, and that their souls may depart while they are infidels.

وَلَا تُعْجِبْكَ أَمْوَٰلُهُمْ وَأَوْلَٰدُهُمْ إِنَّمَا يُرِيدُ ٱللَّهُ أَن يُعَذِّبَهُم بِهَا فِى ٱلدُّنْيَا وَتَزْهَقَ أَنفُسُهُمْ وَهُمْ كَٰفِرُونَ ۝

86. And whenever any Surah is sent down commanding belief in Allah and striving hard in the company of His Messenger, the opulent among them ask leave of you, and say: 'Leave us, we shall be with those who stay.'

وَإِذَآ أُنزِلَتْ سُورَةٌ أَنْ ءَامِنُوا بِاللَّهِ وَجَٰهِدُوا مَعَ رَسُولِهِ ٱسْتَـْٔذَنَكَ أُولُوا ٱلطَّوْلِ مِنْهُمْ وَقَالُوا ذَرْنَا نَكُن مَّعَ ٱلْقَٰعِدِينَ ۝

87. Well pleased are they to be with the women sitters-at-home, and their hearts are sealed up, so they are bereft of understanding.

رَضُوا بِأَن يَكُونُوا مَعَ ٱلْخَوَالِفِ وَطُبِعَ عَلَىٰ قُلُوبِهِمْ فَهُمْ لَا يَفْقَهُونَ ۝

88. But the Messenger and those who believed in his company strive hard with their riches and their lives. These are they for whom are goods, and these are the blissful.

لَٰكِنِ ٱلرَّسُولُ وَٱلَّذِينَ ءَامَنُوا مَعَهُ جَٰهَدُوا بِأَمْوَٰلِهِمْ وَأَنفُسِهِمْ وَأُولَٰٓئِكَ لَهُمُ ٱلْخَيْرَٰتُ وَأُولَٰٓئِكَ هُمُ ٱلْمُفْلِحُونَ ۝

89. For them Allah has got ready Gardens under which rivers flow; therein they shall abide; that is a supreme achievement.

أَعَدَّ ٱللَّهُ لَهُمْ جَنَّٰتٍ تَجْرِي مِن تَحْتِهَا ٱلْأَنْهَٰرُ خَٰلِدِينَ فِيهَا ذَٰلِكَ ٱلْفَوْزُ ٱلْعَظِيمُ ۝

Section 12

90. And there came the apologists from the dwellers of the desert praying that leave may be granted to them, and those who had lied to Allah and His Messenger sat at home. An afflictive torment shall pain those of them who disbelieve.

وَجَآءَ ٱلْمُعَذِّرُونَ مِنَ ٱلْأَعْرَابِ لِيُؤْذَنَ لَهُمْ وَقَعَدَ ٱلَّذِينَ كَذَبُوا ٱللَّهَ وَرَسُولَهُ سَيُصِيبُ ٱلَّذِينَ كَفَرُوا مِنْهُمْ عَذَابٌ أَلِيمٌ ۝

91. Not on the feeble and the ailing nor on those who do not find the wherewithal to spend is there any blame, when they are true to Allah and His Messenger. No way of reproach is there against the well-doers; and Allah is the Forgiving, the Merciful.

لَيْسَ عَلَى الضُّعَفَآءِ وَلَا عَلَى الْمَرْضَى وَلَا عَلَى الَّذِينَ لَا يَجِدُونَ مَا يُنفِقُونَ حَرَجٌ إِذَا نَصَحُوا لِلَّهِ وَرَسُولِهِۦ مَا عَلَى الْمُحْسِنِينَ مِن سَبِيلٍ وَاللَّهُ غَفُورٌ رَّحِيمٌ ۝

92. Nor on those who, when they came to you that you might mount them and you said, 'I do not find any animal to mount you on,' turned back while their eyes overflowed with tears of grief that they could not find aught to spend.

وَلَا عَلَى الَّذِينَ إِذَا مَا أَتَوْكَ لِتَحْمِلَهُمْ قُلْتَ لَا أَجِدُ مَا أَحْمِلُكُمْ عَلَيْهِ تَوَلَّوا وَّأَعْيُنُهُمْ تَفِيضُ مِنَ الدَّمْعِ حَزَنًا أَلَّا يَجِدُوا مَا يُنفِقُونَ ۝

93. The way is only against those who ask leave of you while they are rich. They are pleased to be with the women sitters-at-home. Allah has sealed up their hearts, so they do not know.

إِنَّمَا السَّبِيلُ عَلَى الَّذِينَ يَسْتَـٔذِنُونَكَ وَهُمْ أَغْنِيَآءُ رَضُوا بِأَن يَكُونُوا مَعَ الْخَوَالِفِ وَطَبَعَ اللَّهُ عَلَى قُلُوبِهِمْ فَهُمْ لَا يَعْلَمُونَ ۝

94. They will apologize to you when you return to them. Say: 'Make no excuse; we shall by no means believe you; Allah has already declared to us some tidings about you, and Allah will behold your work, and so will His Messenger, and thereafter you will be brought back to Him Who knows the hidden and the manifest, and who will declare to you what you have been working.'

يَعْتَذِرُونَ إِلَيْكُمْ إِذَا رَجَعْتُمْ إِلَيْهِمْ قُل لَّا تَعْتَذِرُوا لَن نُّؤْمِنَ لَكُمْ قَدْ نَبَّأَنَا اللَّهُ مِنْ أَخْبَارِكُمْ وَسَيَرَى اللَّهُ عَمَلَكُمْ وَرَسُولُهُ ثُمَّ تُرَدُّونَ إِلَى عَالِمِ الْغَيْبِ وَالشَّهَادَةِ فَيُنَبِّئُكُم بِمَا كُنتُمْ تَعْمَلُونَ ۝

95. When you return to them they will indeed swear to you by Allah that you may turn aside from them. So turn aside from them; verily, they are an abomination and their resort is Hell; a recompense for what they have been earning.

سَيَحْلِفُونَ بِاللَّهِ لَكُمْ إِذَا انقَلَبْتُمْ إِلَيْهِمْ لِتُعْرِضُوا عَنْهُمْ فَأَعْرِضُوا عَنْهُمْ إِنَّهُمْ رِجْسٌ وَمَأْوَاهُمْ جَهَنَّمُ جَزَاءً بِمَا كَانُوا يَكْسِبُونَ ٩٥

96. They will swear to you in order that you may be reconciled with them. Then even if you are reconciled with them, Allah is not to be reconciled with a people who are ungodly.

يَحْلِفُونَ لَكُمْ لِتَرْضَوْا عَنْهُمْ فَإِن تَرْضَوْا عَنْهُمْ فَإِنَّ اللَّهَ لَا يَرْضَىٰ عَنِ الْقَوْمِ الْفَاسِقِينَ ٩٦

97. The desert-dwellers are the hardest in infidelity and hypocrisy and they are likeliest not to know the ordinances which Allah has imposed upon His Messenger. And Allah is the Knowing, the Wise.

الْأَعْرَابُ أَشَدُّ كُفْرًا وَنِفَاقًا وَأَجْدَرُ أَلَّا يَعْلَمُوا حُدُودَ مَا أَنزَلَ اللَّهُ عَلَىٰ رَسُولِهِ وَاللَّهُ عَلِيمٌ حَكِيمٌ ٩٧

98. And among the desert-dwellers is one who takes what he spends as a fine, and waits for evil turns of fortune for you. Theirs shall be the evil turn. And Allah is the Hearing, the Knowing.

وَمِنَ الْأَعْرَابِ مَن يَتَّخِذُ مَا يُنفِقُ مَغْرَمًا وَيَتَرَبَّصُ بِكُمُ الدَّوَائِرَ عَلَيْهِمْ دَائِرَةُ السَّوْءِ وَاللَّهُ سَمِيعٌ عَلِيمٌ ٩٨

99. And among the desert-dwellers is one who believes in Allah and the Last Day and takes what he spends as approaches to Allah and the blessings of His Messenger. Lo! Verily these are an approach for them; and soon will Allah enter them into His mercy. Surely Allah is the Forgiving, the Merciful.

وَمِنَ الْأَعْرَابِ مَن يُؤْمِنُ بِاللَّهِ وَالْيَوْمِ الْآخِرِ وَيَتَّخِذُ مَا يُنفِقُ قُرُبَاتٍ عِندَ اللَّهِ وَصَلَوَاتِ الرَّسُولِ أَلَا إِنَّهَا قُرْبَةٌ لَّهُمْ سَيُدْخِلُهُمُ اللَّهُ فِي رَحْمَتِهِ إِنَّ اللَّهَ غَفُورٌ رَّحِيمٌ ٩٩

Section 13

100. And the emigrants and the helpers, the leaders and the pioneers and those who followed them in well-doing, well-pleased is Allah with them and well-pleased are they with Him, and He has prepared for them Gardens under which rivers flow as abiders there for ever. That is the supreme achievement.

وَٱلسَّـٰبِقُونَ ٱلْأَوَّلُونَ مِنَ ٱلْمُهَـٰجِرِينَ وَٱلْأَنصَارِ وَٱلَّذِينَ ٱتَّبَعُوهُم بِإِحْسَـٰنٍ رَّضِىَ ٱللَّهُ عَنْهُمْ وَرَضُوا۟ عَنْهُ وَأَعَدَّ لَهُمْ جَنَّـٰتٍ تَجْرِى تَحْتَهَا ٱلْأَنْهَـٰرُ خَـٰلِدِينَ فِيهَآ أَبَدًا ذَٰلِكَ ٱلْفَوْزُ ٱلْعَظِيمُ ۝

101. And among the desert-dwellers around you some are hypocrites and so are some of the dwellers of Madina, they have become inured to hypocrisy. You did not know them; We know them. We will chastise them twice, and thereafter they shall be brought back to a terrible torment.

وَمِمَّنْ حَوْلَكُم مِّنَ ٱلْأَعْرَابِ مُنَـٰفِقُونَ وَمِنْ أَهْلِ ٱلْمَدِينَةِ مَرَدُوا۟ عَلَى ٱلنِّفَاقِ لَا تَعْلَمُهُمْ نَحْنُ نَعْلَمُهُمْ سَنُعَذِّبُهُم مَّرَّتَيْنِ ثُمَّ يُرَدُّونَ إِلَىٰ عَذَابٍ عَظِيمٍ ۝

102. And others[390] have confessed their sins,[391] they have mixed up a righteous deed with another that was vicious. Perchance Allah is to relent towards them: verily, Allah is the Forgiving, the Merciful.[392]

وَءَاخَرُونَ ٱعْتَرَفُوا۟ بِذُنُوبِهِمْ خَلَطُوا۟ عَمَلًا صَـٰلِحًا وَءَاخَرَ سَيِّئًا عَسَى ٱللَّهُ أَن يَتُوبَ عَلَيْهِمْ إِنَّ ٱللَّهَ غَفُورٌ رَّحِيمٌ ۝

---

390. Now the reference is to the weak-spirited Muslim stay-at-homes, not to the hypocrites. Certainly they lacked the strength to accompany the Prophet on the expedition, yet they were of the faithful all the same.

391. Those Muslim stay-at-homes in their extreme remorse had of their own accord, bound themselves to the pillars of the mosque and had vowed that they would not free themselves until they were set free by the Prophet himself.

392. The Prophet, after this verse was revealed, set those men free and blessed them.

103. Take alms of their riches; thereby you will cleanse them and purify them[393], and pray for them. Verily, your prayer is a solace for them, and Allah is the Hearing, the Knowing.

خُذْ مِنْ أَمْوَٰلِهِمْ صَدَقَةً تُطَهِّرُهُمْ وَتُزَكِّيهِم بِهَا وَصَلِّ عَلَيْهِمْ إِنَّ صَلَوٰتَكَ سَكَنٌ لَّهُمْ وَٱللَّهُ سَمِيعٌ عَلِيمٌ ١٠٣

104. Do they not know that it is Allah Who accepts the repentance of His bondsmen and takes the alms and that it is Allah Who is the Relenting, the Merciful?[394]

أَلَمْ يَعْلَمُوٓا۟ أَنَّ ٱللَّهَ هُوَ يَقْبَلُ ٱلتَّوْبَةَ عَنْ عِبَادِهِۦ وَيَأْخُذُ ٱلصَّدَقَٰتِ وَأَنَّ ٱللَّهَ هُوَ ٱلتَّوَّابُ ٱلرَّحِيمُ ١٠٤

105. And say: 'Work on! Allah holds your work, and so does His Messenger and the believers, and soon you will be brought back to the Knower of the hidden and the manifest. He will then declare to you what you have been working.'

وَقُلِ ٱعْمَلُوا۟ فَسَيَرَى ٱللَّهُ عَمَلَكُمْ وَرَسُولُهُۥ وَٱلْمُؤْمِنُونَ وَسَتُرَدُّونَ إِلَىٰ عَٰلِمِ ٱلْغَيْبِ وَٱلشَّهَٰدَةِ فَيُنَبِّئُكُم بِمَا كُنتُمْ تَعْمَلُونَ ١٠٥

106. And others are awaiting the decree of Allah whether He is to chastise them or relent towards them, and Allah is the Knowing, the Wise.

وَءَاخَرُونَ مُرْجَوْنَ لِأَمْرِ ٱللَّهِ إِمَّا يُعَذِّبُهُمْ وَإِمَّا يَتُوبُ عَلَيْهِمْ وَٱللَّهُ عَلِيمٌ حَكِيمٌ ١٠٦

---

393. Cleanse them of the ill-effects of their wrongdoing. Those three persons on being pardoned presented the Holy Prophet with charitable gifts which he refused saying that he had no orders to accept anything from them. Thereupon the present verse was revealed.

394. So it is to Him that one must always turn in repentance and to obtain His Mercy. The expiation of sins, in Islam, let it be noted once again, entirely rests, next to the repentance of the sinner himself, on the Forgiving and Merciful nature of God.

107. And as for those who have set up a mosque for hurting and blaspheming and the causing of division among the believers and as a lurking–place for one who has warred against Allah and His Messenger before, surely they will swear, 'we meant only good', while Allah testifies that they are truly liars.

وَٱلَّذِينَ ٱتَّخَذُوا۟ مَسۡجِدًا ضِرَارًا وَكُفۡرًا وَتَفۡرِيقَۢا بَيۡنَ ٱلۡمُؤۡمِنِينَ وَإِرۡصَادًا لِّمَنۡ حَارَبَ ٱللَّهَ وَرَسُولَهُۥ مِن قَبۡلُ وَلَيَحۡلِفُنَّ إِنۡ أَرَدۡنَآ إِلَّا ٱلۡحُسۡنَىٰ وَٱللَّهُ يَشۡهَدُ إِنَّهُمۡ لَكَٰذِبُونَ ۝

108. You shall never stand therein. Surely a mosque built from the first day on piety is worthier that you should stand therein.[395] In it are men who love to purify themselves, and Allah approves the pure.[396]

لَا تَقُمۡ فِيهِ أَبَدًا ۚ لَّمَسۡجِدٌ أُسِّسَ عَلَى ٱلتَّقۡوَىٰ مِنۡ أَوَّلِ يَوۡمٍ أَحَقُّ أَن تَقُومَ فِيهِ ۚ فِيهِ رِجَالٌ يُحِبُّونَ أَن يَتَطَهَّرُوا۟ ۚ وَٱللَّهُ يُحِبُّ ٱلۡمُطَّهِّرِينَ ۝

109. Is he, then, who has founded his building upon piety towards Allah and His goodwill better or he who has founded his building on the brink of a crumbling bank, so that it crumbles with him into the Hell fire? And Allah does not guide a wrong-doing people.

أَفَمَنۡ أَسَّسَ بُنۡيَٰنَهُۥ عَلَىٰ تَقۡوَىٰ مِنَ ٱللَّهِ وَرِضۡوَٰنٍ خَيۡرٌ أَم مَّنۡ أَسَّسَ بُنۡيَٰنَهُۥ عَلَىٰ شَفَا جُرُفٍ هَارٍ فَٱنۡهَارَ بِهِۦ فِي نَارِ جَهَنَّمَ ۗ وَٱللَّهُ لَا يَهۡدِى ٱلۡقَوۡمَ ٱلظَّٰلِمِينَ ۝

110. And their building which they have built will not cease to be a cause of doubt in their hearts unless it be that their hearts are cut asunder; and Allah is the Knowing, the Wise.

لَا يَزَالُ بُنۡيَٰنُهُمُ ٱلَّذِى بَنَوۡا۟ رِيبَةً فِى قُلُوبِهِمۡ إِلَّآ أَن تَقَطَّعَ قُلُوبُهُمۡ ۗ وَٱللَّهُ عَلِيمٌ حَكِيمٌ ۝

---

395. The allusion is to the Mosque at Qubā, a place about 3 miles to the south – east of Madina, where the Prophet had rested for four days before entering the city on his emigration from Makka, and where he had laid the foundation of the Mosque.

396. Contrast with this position of importance assigned to cleanliness in Islam, the theory and practice of the Christian 'fathers' and 'saints' in the early Middle Ages. 'Dirt and disease became' in Christendom from CE 373 onward, 'the honourable insignia of saintship; loathsome fakirs exhibited their filth and their sores for the veneration of the faithful' (*UHW*. IV. p. 2333).

Section 14

111. Surely Allah has purchased of the faithful their lives and their riches for the price that theirs shall be the Garden: they fight in the way of Allah and slay and are slain, a promise due thereon in the Torah and the Gospel and the Qur'ān. And who is more true to His covenant than Allah? Rejoice therefore in your bargain which you have made, and that is a mighty achievement.

112. They are those who repent, who worship, who praise, who fast constantly, who bow down, who prostrate themselves, who bid the reputable and forbid the disreputable, and who keep the ordinances of Allah and bear glad tidings to the believers.

113. It is not for the Prophet and those who believe to ask for the forgiveness of the associators, even though they be relatives after it has become clear to them that they are the fellows of the Flaming Fire.

114. And Abraham's asking for the forgiveness of his father was only in pursuance of a promise which He had made to him. Then, when it became clear to him that he was an enemy of Allah, he declared himself quit of him. Verily, Abraham was long-suffering, forbearing.

إِنَّ ٱللَّهَ ٱشْتَرَىٰ مِنَ ٱلْمُؤْمِنِينَ أَنفُسَهُمْ وَأَمْوَٰلَهُم بِأَنَّ لَهُمُ ٱلْجَنَّةَ يُقَـٰتِلُونَ فِى سَبِيلِ ٱللَّهِ فَيَقْتُلُونَ وَيُقْتَلُونَ وَعْدًا عَلَيْهِ حَقًّا فِى ٱلتَّوْرَٮٰةِ وَٱلْإِنجِيلِ وَٱلْقُرْءَانِ وَمَنْ أَوْفَىٰ بِعَهْدِهِۦ مِنَ ٱللَّهِ فَٱسْتَبْشِرُوا۟ بِبَيْعِكُمُ ٱلَّذِى بَايَعْتُم بِهِۦ وَذَٰلِكَ هُوَ ٱلْفَوْزُ ٱلْعَظِيمُ ۝١١١

ٱلتَّـٰٓئِبُونَ ٱلْعَـٰبِدُونَ ٱلْحَـٰمِدُونَ ٱلسَّـٰٓئِحُونَ ٱلرَّٰكِعُونَ ٱلسَّـٰجِدُونَ ٱلْأَمِرُونَ بِٱلْمَعْرُوفِ وَٱلنَّاهُونَ عَنِ ٱلْمُنكَرِ وَٱلْحَـٰفِظُونَ لِحُدُودِ ٱللَّهِ وَبَشِّرِ ٱلْمُؤْمِنِينَ ۝١١٢

مَا كَانَ لِلنَّبِىِّ وَٱلَّذِينَ ءَامَنُوٓا۟ أَن يَسْتَغْفِرُوا۟ لِلْمُشْرِكِينَ وَلَوْ كَانُوٓا۟ أُو۟لِى قُرْبَىٰ مِنۢ بَعْدِ مَا تَبَيَّنَ لَهُمْ أَنَّهُمْ أَصْحَـٰبُ ٱلْجَحِيمِ ۝١١٣

وَمَا كَانَ ٱسْتِغْفَارُ إِبْرَٰهِيمَ لِأَبِيهِ إِلَّا عَن مَّوْعِدَةٍ وَعَدَهَآ إِيَّاهُ فَلَمَّا تَبَيَّنَ لَهُۥٓ أَنَّهُۥ عَدُوٌّ لِّلَّهِ تَبَرَّأَ مِنْهُ إِنَّ إِبْرَٰهِيمَ لَأَوَّٰهٌ حَلِيمٌ ۝١١٤

115. Allah is not the One to lead a people astray after He has guided them until He makes clear to them as to what they should guard against. Verily, Allah is the Knower of everything.

وَمَا كَانَ ٱللَّهُ لِيُضِلَّ قَوۡمًۢا بَعۡدَ إِذۡ هَدَىٰهُمۡ حَتَّىٰ يُبَيِّنَ لَهُم مَّا يَتَّقُونَّ إِنَّ ٱللَّهَ بِكُلِّ شَيۡءٍ عَلِيمٌ ۝

116. Assuredly Allah's is the dominion of the heavens and the earth. He gives life and He causes to die; and for you there is, besides Allah, no protector or helper.

إِنَّ ٱللَّهَ لَهُۥ مُلۡكُ ٱلسَّمَٰوَٰتِ وَٱلۡأَرۡضِ يُحۡىِۦ وَيُمِيتُّ وَمَا لَكُم مِّن دُونِ ٱللَّهِ مِن وَلِيٍّ وَلَا نَصِيرٍ ۝

117. Assuredly has Allah relented towards the Prophet and the emigrants and the helpers who followed him in the hour of distress after the hearts of a part of them had nearly swerved aside when He relented towards them, He is to them the Clement, the Merciful.

لَّقَد تَّابَ ٱللَّهُ عَلَى ٱلنَّبِيِّ وَٱلۡمُهَٰجِرِينَ وَٱلۡأَنصَارِ ٱلَّذِينَ ٱتَّبَعُوهُ فِى سَاعَةِ ٱلۡعُسۡرَةِ مِنۢ بَعۡدِ مَا كَادَ يَزِيغُ قُلُوبُ فَرِيقٍ مِّنۡهُمۡ ثُمَّ تَابَ عَلَيۡهِمۡ إِنَّهُۥ بِهِمۡ رَءُوفٌ رَّحِيمٌ ۝

118. And He relented toward the three who were left behind until when the earth, vast as it is, became straitened unto them, and their own lives became straitened unto them, and they imagined that there was no refuge from Allah except in Him. Thereafter He relented towards them, so that they might repent. Verily, Allah is the Relenting, the Merciful.

وَعَلَى ٱلثَّلَٰثَةِ ٱلَّذِينَ خُلِّفُوا۟ حَتَّىٰ إِذَا ضَاقَتۡ عَلَيۡهِمُ ٱلۡأَرۡضُ بِمَا رَحُبَتۡ وَضَاقَتۡ عَلَيۡهِمۡ أَنفُسُهُمۡ وَظَنُّوٓا۟ أَن لَّا مَلۡجَأَ مِنَ ٱللَّهِ إِلَّآ إِلَيۡهِ ثُمَّ تَابَ عَلَيۡهِمۡ لِيَتُوبُوٓا۟ إِنَّ ٱللَّهَ هُوَ ٱلتَّوَّابُ ٱلرَّحِيمُ ۝

Section 15

119. O you who believe! Fear Allah and be with the truthful.

يَـٰٓأَيُّهَا ٱلَّذِينَ ءَامَنُوا۟ ٱتَّقُوا۟ ٱللَّهَ وَكُونُوا۟ مَعَ ٱلصَّـٰدِقِينَ ﴿١١٩﴾

120. It was not for the people of Madina and those around them of the desert-dwellers that they should forsake the Messenger of Allah, nor that they should prefer themselves before him. That is because they are neither smitten with thirst or fatigue or hunger in the way of Allah, nor do they tread any step enraging the infidels, nor do they accomplish an attainment from the enemy, but a good deed is thereby written down unto them. Allah surely leaves not to waste the reward to the well-doers.

مَا كَانَ لِأَهْلِ ٱلْمَدِينَةِ وَمَنْ حَوْلَهُم مِّنَ ٱلْأَعْرَابِ أَن يَتَخَلَّفُوا۟ عَن رَّسُولِ ٱللَّهِ وَلَا يَرْغَبُوا۟ بِأَنفُسِهِمْ عَن نَّفْسِهِۦ ۚ ذَٰلِكَ بِأَنَّهُمْ لَا يُصِيبُهُمْ ظَمَأٌ وَلَا نَصَبٌ وَلَا مَخْمَصَةٌ فِى سَبِيلِ ٱللَّهِ وَلَا يَطَـُٔونَ مَوْطِئًا يَغِيظُ ٱلْكُفَّارَ وَلَا يَنَالُونَ مِنْ عَدُوٍّ نَّيْلًا إِلَّا كُتِبَ لَهُم بِهِۦ عَمَلٌ صَـٰلِحٌ ۚ إِنَّ ٱللَّهَ لَا يُضِيعُ أَجْرَ ٱلْمُحْسِنِينَ ﴿١٢٠﴾

121. And they do not spend any sum, small or great, or traverse a valley but it is written down unto them, so that Allah may recompense them with the best for what they have been working.

وَلَا يُنفِقُونَ نَفَقَةً صَغِيرَةً وَلَا كَبِيرَةً وَلَا يَقْطَعُونَ وَادِيًا إِلَّا كُتِبَ لَهُمْ لِيَجْزِيَهُمُ ٱللَّهُ أَحْسَنَ مَا كَانُوا۟ يَعْمَلُونَ ﴿١٢١﴾

122. And it is not for the faithful to march forth all together. So why should not a band from each party of them march forth, and the rest get instruction in religion, and to warn their people when they return to them? Perchance they may beware.

وَمَا كَانَ ٱلْمُؤْمِنُونَ لِيَنفِرُوا۟ كَآفَّةً ۚ فَلَوْلَا نَفَرَ مِن كُلِّ فِرْقَةٍ مِّنْهُمْ طَآئِفَةٌ لِّيَتَفَقَّهُوا۟ فِى ٱلدِّينِ وَلِيُنذِرُوا۟ قَوْمَهُمْ إِذَا رَجَعُوٓا۟ إِلَيْهِمْ لَعَلَّهُمْ يَحْذَرُونَ ﴿١٢٢﴾

Section 16

123. O you who believe! Fight the infidels who are close to you, and surely let them find in you sternness, and know that Allah is with the God-fearing.

يَـٰٓأَيُّهَا ٱلَّذِينَ ءَامَنُوا۟ قَـٰتِلُوا۟ ٱلَّذِينَ يَلُونَكُم مِّنَ ٱلْكُفَّارِ وَلْيَجِدُوا۟ فِيكُمْ غِلْظَةً وَٱعْلَمُوٓا۟ أَنَّ ٱللَّهَ مَعَ ٱلْمُتَّقِينَ ۝

124. And whenever a Surah is sent down, there are some of them who say: 'Which of you has this increased in faith?' As for the faithful it has increased them in faith and they rejoice.

وَإِذَا مَآ أُنزِلَتْ سُورَةٌ فَمِنْهُم مَّن يَقُولُ أَيُّكُمْ زَادَتْهُ هَـٰذِهِۦٓ إِيمَـٰنًا فَأَمَّا ٱلَّذِينَ ءَامَنُوا۟ فَزَادَتْهُمْ إِيمَـٰنًا وَهُمْ يَسْتَبْشِرُونَ ۝

125. And as for those in whose heart is a disease unto them it has increased pollution to their pollution, and they die while they are infidels.

وَأَمَّا ٱلَّذِينَ فِى قُلُوبِهِم مَّرَضٌ فَزَادَتْهُمْ رِجْسًا إِلَىٰ رِجْسِهِمْ وَمَاتُوا۟ وَهُمْ كَـٰفِرُونَ ۝

126. Do they not observe that they are tested every year once or twice? Yet they neither repent nor are they admonished.

أَوَلَا يَرَوْنَ أَنَّهُمْ يُفْتَنُونَ فِى كُلِّ عَامٍ مَّرَّةً أَوْ مَرَّتَيْنِ ثُمَّ لَا يَتُوبُونَ وَلَا هُمْ يَذَّكَّرُونَ ۝

127. And whenever a *Sūrah* is sent down they look on at each other, as though saying, 'does anyone watch you?' Then they turn to go. Allah has turned away their hearts, for verily they are a people who do not want to understand.

وَإِذَا مَآ أُنزِلَتْ سُورَةٌ نَّظَرَ بَعْضُهُمْ إِلَىٰ بَعْضٍ هَلْ يَرَىٰكُم مِّنْ أَحَدٍ ثُمَّ ٱنصَرَفُوا۟ صَرَفَ ٱللَّهُ قُلُوبَهُم بِأَنَّهُمْ قَوْمٌ لَّا يَفْقَهُونَ ۝

128. Assuredly there has come to you a Messenger from among yourselves; heavy upon him is whatever harasses you, and who is solicitous for you and is unto the faithful tender and merciful.

لَقَدْ جَآءَكُمْ رَسُولٌ مِّنْ أَنفُسِكُمْ عَزِيزٌ عَلَيْهِ مَا عَنِتُّمْ حَرِيصٌ عَلَيْكُم بِالْمُؤْمِنِينَ رَءُوفٌ رَّحِيمٌ ۝

129. If then, they turn away, say: 'Sufficing unto me is Allah, there is no god but He; in Him I put my trust, and He is the Lord of the mighty throne.'

فَإِن تَوَلَّوْاْ فَقُلْ حَسْبِيَ اللَّهُ لَآ إِلَٰهَ إِلَّا هُوَ عَلَيْهِ تَوَكَّلْتُ وَهُوَ رَبُّ الْعَرْشِ الْعَظِيمِ ۝

Sūrah 10

Yūnus

(Makkan, 11 Sections, 109 Verses)

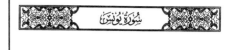

*In the name of Allah, the
Compassionate, the Merciful.*

Section 1

1. *Alif, Lām, Rā.* These are the verses of the wise Book.

2. Is it a matter of wonder to mankind that We should reveal to a man among them saying: 'Warn you mankind, and bear the faithful the glad tidings that theirs shall be a sure footing with their Lord?' The infidels say that this is a plain sorcerer.[397]

3. Verily, your Lord is Allah Who has created the heavens and earth in six days, then established Himself on the throne[398]

---

397. The pagans of Arabia, like the pagans elsewhere, had no concept of Prophethood and Revelation at all. They would understand incarnation — God becoming man — or else explain the fact of Messengership by attributing it to magic and sorcery. In idolatrous communities it is the sorcerers or magicians who are credited with supernatural powers, the principal of which is the power of foretelling the future.

398. The Throne of authority and majesty. The God of Islam being above matter and spirit cannot possibly have an abode or a seat of His Own. His Throne cannot in any sense of the word be described as His dwelling–place. It is of course, supermundane above the firmament and all created things; and thus it connotes the ideas of Authority, Glory, Majesty and Holiness.

disposing the affair,[399] no intercessor is there except after His leave.[400] That is Allah, your Lord; so worship Him. Would you not then be admonished?

4. To Him is the return of you all. The promise of Allah is true. He begins the creation, then He shall repeat it, that He may requite with equity those who believed and did righteous deeds. And those who disbelieved for those shall be a draught of boiling water and an afflictive torment, for they were wont to disbelieve.

5. He it is Who has made the sun a glow and the moon a light, and has determined mansions for her that you may know the number of the years and the reckoning. Allah has not created all this except with a purpose. He expounds these signs to those who know.

6. Verily in the alternation of night and day and in what Allah has created in the heavens and the earth are surely signs to a people who fear God.

يُدَبِّرُ الْأَمْرَ مَا مِن شَفِيعٍ إِلَّا مِنۢ بَعْدِ إِذْنِهِۦ ذَٰلِكُمُ اللَّهُ رَبُّكُمْ فَاعْبُدُوهُ أَفَلَا تَذَكَّرُونَ ۝٣

إِلَيْهِ مَرْجِعُكُمْ جَمِيعًا وَعْدَ اللَّهِ حَقًّا إِنَّهُۥ يَبْدَؤُا۟ الْخَلْقَ ثُمَّ يُعِيدُهُۥ لِيَجْزِىَ الَّذِينَ ءَامَنُوا۟ وَعَمِلُوا۟ الصَّٰلِحَٰتِ بِالْقِسْطِ وَالَّذِينَ كَفَرُوا۟ لَهُمْ شَرَابٌ مِّنْ حَمِيمٍ وَعَذَابٌ أَلِيمٌۢ بِمَا كَانُوا۟ يَكْفُرُونَ ۝٤

هُوَ الَّذِى جَعَلَ الشَّمْسَ ضِيَآءً وَالْقَمَرَ نُورًا وَقَدَّرَهُۥ مَنَازِلَ لِتَعْلَمُوا۟ عَدَدَ السِّنِينَ وَالْحِسَابَ مَا خَلَقَ اللَّهُ ذَٰلِكَ إِلَّا بِالْحَقِّ يُفَصِّلُ الْءَايَٰتِ لِقَوْمٍ يَعْلَمُونَ ۝٥

إِنَّ فِى اخْتِلَٰفِ الَّيْلِ وَالنَّهَارِ وَمَا خَلَقَ اللَّهُ فِى السَّمَٰوَٰتِ وَالْأَرْضِ لَءَايَٰتٍ لِّقَوْمٍ يَتَّقُونَ ۝٦

399. The affair of all His creation, i.e. governing all things with supreme justice and wisdom. He is not only the Creator but also the constant Ruler and the continuous Disposer of affairs.

400. In other words, and there is no saving through the merits of a mediator. This refutes not only the doctrine of the pagans who imagined that their gods were intercessors with the Great God for them but also the Christian dogma of mediation. The Christian position, briefly, is this: 'God and man have been estranged. The relation which normally subsists between them has been destroyed and the work of the mediation is to restore it. There is one mediator between God and man, Himself man, Jesus Christ, who gave Himself a ransom for all' (*EBr.* VIII. p. 856).

7. Verily those who hope not for meeting with Us, and are well pleased with the life of the world, and are satisfied with it, and those who are heedless of Our signs.

8. These! Their abode shall be the Fire for what they have been earning.

9. Verily those who believe and do righteous deeds, their Lord will guide them through their Faith; beneath them will flow rivers in the Gardens of delight.

10. Their call therein will be: 'Hallowed be you, O Allah!', and their greeting therein, 'peace!' And the end of their call will be: 'All praise to Allah, the Lord of the worlds.'

Section 2

11. And were Allah to hasten the ill to mankind as their desire of hastening the good, their fate would surely have been sealed to them. So We let alone those who hope not for meeting with Us, wandering in their exorbitance perplexed.

12. And when harm touches man, he calls Us on his side, or sitting or standing, when We have removed his harm from him, he passes on as though he had never called Us because of the harm that touched him. In this wise is made fair-seeming to the extravagant what they have been working.

إِنَّ ٱلَّذِينَ لَا يَرْجُونَ لِقَآءَنَا وَرَضُوا۟ بِٱلْحَيَوٰةِ ٱلدُّنْيَا وَٱطْمَأَنُّوا۟ بِهَا وَٱلَّذِينَ هُمْ عَنْ ءَايَٰتِنَا غَٰفِلُونَ ۝

أُو۟لَٰٓئِكَ مَأْوَىٰهُمُ ٱلنَّارُ بِمَا كَانُوا۟ يَكْسِبُونَ ۝

إِنَّ ٱلَّذِينَ ءَامَنُوا۟ وَعَمِلُوا۟ ٱلصَّٰلِحَٰتِ يَهْدِيهِمْ رَبُّهُم بِإِيمَٰنِهِمْ تَجْرِى مِن تَحْتِهِمُ ٱلْأَنْهَٰرُ فِى جَنَّٰتِ ٱلنَّعِيمِ ۝

دَعْوَىٰهُمْ فِيهَا سُبْحَٰنَكَ ٱللَّهُمَّ وَتَحِيَّتُهُمْ فِيهَا سَلَٰمٌ وَءَاخِرُ دَعْوَىٰهُمْ أَنِ ٱلْحَمْدُ لِلَّهِ رَبِّ ٱلْعَٰلَمِينَ ۝

وَلَوْ يُعَجِّلُ ٱللَّهُ لِلنَّاسِ ٱلشَّرَّ ٱسْتِعْجَالَهُم بِٱلْخَيْرِ لَقُضِىَ إِلَيْهِمْ أَجَلُهُمْ فَنَذَرُ ٱلَّذِينَ لَا يَرْجُونَ لِقَآءَنَا فِى طُغْيَٰنِهِمْ يَعْمَهُونَ ۝

وَإِذَا مَسَّ ٱلْإِنسَٰنَ ٱلضُّرُّ دَعَانَا لِجَنۢبِهِۦ أَوْ قَاعِدًا أَوْ قَآئِمًا فَلَمَّا كَشَفْنَا عَنْهُ ضُرَّهُۥ مَرَّ كَأَن لَّمْ يَدْعُنَآ إِلَىٰ ضُرٍّ مَّسَّهُۥ كَذَٰلِكَ زُيِّنَ لِلْمُسْرِفِينَ مَا كَانُوا۟ يَعْمَلُونَ ۝

13. And assuredly We have destroyed generations before you when they did wrong, while their Messengers came to them with the evidence, and they were not such as to believe. In this wise, We requite the sinning people.

وَلَقَدْ أَهْلَكْنَا الْقُرُونَ مِن قَبْلِكُمْ لَمَّا ظَلَمُوا وَجَاءَتْهُمْ رُسُلُهُم بِالْبَيِّنَاتِ وَمَا كَانُوا لِيُؤْمِنُوا كَذَٰلِكَ نَجْزِي الْقَوْمَ الْمُجْرِمِينَ ﴿١٣﴾

14. Then We appointed you in the land as successors after them, that We might see how you would work.

ثُمَّ جَعَلْنَاكُمْ خَلَائِفَ فِي الْأَرْضِ مِن بَعْدِهِم لِنَنظُرَ كَيْفَ تَعْمَلُونَ ﴿١٤﴾

15. And whenever Our clear revelations are rehearsed to them, those who hope not for the meeting with Us, say: 'Bring us a Qur'ān other than this or change it.' Say: 'It does not lie with me to change it of my own accord; I only follow what is revealed to me;[401] verily I fear, if I disobey my Lord, the torment of an awful Day.'

وَإِذَا تُتْلَىٰ عَلَيْهِمْ ءَايَاتُنَا بَيِّنَاتٍ قَالَ الَّذِينَ لَا يَرْجُونَ لِقَاءَنَا ائْتِ بِقُرْءَانٍ غَيْرِ هَٰذَا أَوْ بَدِّلْهُ قُلْ مَا يَكُونُ لِيَ أَنْ أُبَدِّلَهُ مِن تِلْقَاءِ نَفْسِي إِنْ أَتَّبِعُ إِلَّا مَا يُوحَىٰ إِلَيَّ إِنِّي أَخَافُ إِنْ عَصَيْتُ رَبِّي عَذَابَ يَوْمٍ عَظِيمٍ ﴿١٥﴾

16. Say: 'Had Allah so willed, I would not have rehearsed it to you, nor would He have acquainted you therewith. Of a surety, I have tarried with you a life time before it.[402] Would you not then reflect?'

قُل لَّوْ شَاءَ اللَّهُ مَا تَلَوْتُهُ عَلَيْكُمْ وَلَا أَدْرَاكُم بِهِ فَقَدْ لَبِثْتُ فِيكُمْ عُمُرًا مِّن قَبْلِهِ أَفَلَا تَعْقِلُونَ ﴿١٦﴾

---

401. I am but an instrument; a mere mouthpiece. Note that in Islam a Prophet, whether he wills it or not, is impelled to announce whatever descends on Him from Above — nothing more, nothing less, nothing else. Far from constraining the Revelation to come to him, he cannot make the slightest alteration in it at his choice.

402. In this sense before it came to me. The Prophet's veracity was almost a by-word in Makka.

17. Who then is a greater wrong-doer than he who forges a lie against Allah or belies His revelations? Surely the culprits shall not prosper.

فَمَنْ أَظْلَمُ مِمَّنِ افْتَرَىٰ عَلَى اللّٰهِ كَذِبًا أَوْ كَذَّبَ بِآيَاتِهِ إِنَّهُ لَا يُفْلِحُ الْمُجْرِمُونَ ۝

18. And they worship, besides Allah, what neither harms them nor profits them, and they say: 'These are our intercessors with Allah.' Say: 'Do you presume to apprise Allah of what He knows not in the heavens nor the earth? Hallowed be He and Exalted far above what you associate!'

وَيَعْبُدُونَ مِن دُونِ اللّٰهِ مَا لَا يَضُرُّهُمْ وَلَا يَنفَعُهُمْ وَيَقُولُونَ هَٰؤُلَاءِ شُفَعَاؤُنَا عِندَ اللّٰهِ قُلْ أَتُنَبِّئُونَ اللّٰهَ بِمَا لَا يَعْلَمُ فِي السَّمَاوَاتِ وَلَا فِي الْأَرْضِ سُبْحَانَهُ وَتَعَالَىٰ عَمَّا يُشْرِكُونَ ۝

19. And mankind were but a single community;[403] then they differed. And had not a word from your Lord gone forth, it would have been decreed between them regarding what they differed.

وَمَا كَانَ النَّاسُ إِلَّا أُمَّةً وَاحِدَةً فَاخْتَلَفُوا وَلَوْلَا كَلِمَةٌ سَبَقَتْ مِن رَّبِّكَ لَقُضِيَ بَيْنَهُمْ فِيمَا فِيهِ يَخْتَلِفُونَ ۝

20. And they say: how is it that not a sign is sent down on him from his lord? Say: 'The hidden belongs to Allah alone; so wait, verily I am with you among those who wait.'[404]

وَيَقُولُونَ لَوْلَا أُنزِلَ عَلَيْهِ آيَةٌ مِّن رَّبِّهِ فَقُلْ إِنَّمَا الْغَيْبُ لِلّٰهِ فَانتَظِرُوا إِنِّي مَعَكُم مِّنَ الْمُنتَظِرِينَ ۝

---

403. Possessors of one religion only, the True religion of the Unity of God. The Holy Qur'ān frankly repudiates and negates the current opinion that monotheism has been evolved out of polytheism. It openly proclaims that monotheism was the original, universal religion of mankind gradually debased into polytheism.

404. The passage does not imply that the Prophet wrought no miracle, but it only amounts to saying; the matter rests entirely with God; it lies with Him alone whether He allows a particular miracle or not; and performance of this or that miracle has clearly nothing to do with the true functions of a Messenger of God.

Section 3

21. And when We let mankind taste of Our mercy after an adversity has touched them, forthwith they have a scheme in regard to Our signs. Say: 'Allah is Swifter in scheming. Verily Our Messengers write down what you plot.'

وَإِذَآ أَذَقْنَا ٱلنَّاسَ رَحْمَةً مِّنۢ بَعْدِ ضَرَّآءَ مَسَّتْهُمْ إِذَا لَهُم مَّكْرٌ فِىٓ ءَايَاتِنَا قُلِ ٱللَّهُ أَسْرَعُ مَكْرًا إِنَّ رُسُلَنَا يَكْتُبُونَ مَا تَمْكُرُونَ ۝

22. He it is Who enables you to travel by land and sea until when you are in ships and they run away with them with a goodly wind and they rejoice thereat, there comes upon them a tempestuous wind and there comes upon them a billow from every side, and they imagine that they are encircled therein, they cry to Allah making their Faith pure for Him: 'if you deliver us from this, we would surely be of those who are grateful.'

هُوَ ٱلَّذِى يُسَيِّرُكُمْ فِى ٱلْبَرِّ وَٱلْبَحْرِ حَتَّىٰٓ إِذَا كُنتُمْ فِى ٱلْفُلْكِ وَجَرَيْنَ بِهِم بِرِيحٍ طَيِّبَةٍ وَفَرِحُوا بِهَا جَآءَتْهَا رِيحٌ عَاصِفٌ وَجَآءَهُمُ ٱلْمَوْجُ مِن كُلِّ مَكَانٍ وَظَنُّوٓا أَنَّهُمْ أُحِيطَ بِهِمْ دَعَوُا ٱللَّهَ مُخْلِصِينَ لَهُ ٱلدِّينَ لَئِنْ أَنجَيْتَنَا مِنْ هَٰذِهِ لَنَكُونَنَّ مِنَ ٱلشَّاكِرِينَ ۝

23. Yet when He delivers them, they forthwith rebel in the earth without justice. O men! Your rebellion is only against yourselves a brief enjoyment of the life of the world; thereafter unto Us is your return; then We will declare to you what you have been working.

فَلَمَّآ أَنجَىٰهُمْ إِذَا هُمْ يَبْغُونَ فِى ٱلْأَرْضِ بِغَيْرِ ٱلْحَقِّ يَٰٓأَيُّهَا ٱلنَّاسُ إِنَّمَا بَغْيُكُمْ عَلَىٰٓ أَنفُسِكُم مَّتَٰعَ ٱلْحَيَوٰةِ ٱلدُّنْيَا ثُمَّ إِلَيْنَا مَرْجِعُكُمْ فَنُنَبِّئُكُم بِمَا كُنتُمْ تَعْمَلُونَ ۝

24. The likeness of the life of the world is only as the rain which We send down from the sky, with which mingles the growth of the earth, of which men and cattle eat, until, when the earth puts on her ornament and is adorned and its inhabitants imagine that they are potent over it, there comes to it Our decree by night or by day, then We make it stubble as though it had not flourished yesterday. This is how We detail the signs to a people who ponder.

إِنَّمَا مَثَلُ ٱلْحَيَوٰةِ ٱلدُّنْيَا كَمَآءٍ أَنزَلْنَٰهُ مِنَ ٱلسَّمَآءِ فَٱخْتَلَطَ بِهِۦ نَبَاتُ ٱلْأَرْضِ مِمَّا يَأْكُلُ ٱلنَّاسُ وَٱلْأَنْعَٰمُ حَتَّىٰٓ إِذَآ أَخَذَتِ ٱلْأَرْضُ زُخْرُفَهَا وَٱزَّيَّنَتْ وَظَنَّ أَهْلُهَآ أَنَّهُمْ قَٰدِرُونَ عَلَيْهَآ أَتَىٰهَآ أَمْرُنَا لَيْلًا أَوْ نَهَارًا فَجَعَلْنَٰهَا حَصِيدًا كَأَن لَّمْ تَغْنَ بِٱلْأَمْسِ كَذَٰلِكَ نُفَصِّلُ ٱلْءَايَٰتِ لِقَوْمٍ يَتَفَكَّرُونَ ﴿٢٤﴾

25. And Allah calls to the abode of peace and guides whomsoever He will to the straight path.

وَٱللَّهُ يَدْعُوٓاْ إِلَىٰ دَارِ ٱلسَّلَٰمِ وَيَهْدِى مَن يَشَآءُ إِلَىٰ صِرَٰطٍ مُّسْتَقِيمٍ ﴿٢٥﴾

26. To those who have done good is the good reward and an increase; neither darkness nor abjection will cover their faces. These are the inhabitants of the Garden; therein they shall abide.

لِّلَّذِينَ أَحْسَنُواْ ٱلْحُسْنَىٰ وَزِيَادَةٌ وَلَا يَرْهَقُ وُجُوهَهُمْ قَتَرٌ وَلَا ذِلَّةٌ أُوْلَٰٓئِكَ أَصْحَٰبُ ٱلْجَنَّةِ هُمْ فِيهَا خَٰلِدُونَ ﴿٢٦﴾

27. And to those who have earned misdeeds, the requital of a misdeed is the like thereof[405], and abjection will cover them; no defender they shall have from Allah, as though their faces were overcast with pieces of night, pitch-dark. These are the inhabitants of the Fire; therein they shall abide.

وَٱلَّذِينَ كَسَبُواْ ٱلسَّيِّـَٔاتِ جَزَآءُ سَيِّئَةٍ بِمِثْلِهَا وَتَرْهَقُهُمْ ذِلَّةٌ مَّا لَهُم مِّنَ ٱللَّهِ مِنْ عَاصِمٍ كَأَنَّمَآ أُغْشِيَتْ وُجُوهُهُمْ قِطَعًا مِّنَ ٱلَّيْلِ مُظْلِمًا أُوْلَٰٓئِكَ أَصْحَٰبُ ٱلنَّارِ هُمْ فِيهَا خَٰلِدُونَ ﴿٢٧﴾

---

405. In other words, a punishment equal thereunto. Observe that while the blessed will be rewarded beyond their merits and in fact beyond all measure, the condemned will receive their punishment only with exact justice.

28. Remember the Day whereon We shall muster them together, then We shall say to those who associated; keep your place, you and your associate gods. Then We shall cause a split between them; and their associate-gods will say, 'It was not us that you were worshipping.'

وَيَوۡمَ نَحۡشُرُهُمۡ جَمِيعًا ثُمَّ نَقُولُ لِلَّذِينَ أَشۡرَكُواْ مَكَانَكُمۡ أَنتُمۡ وَشُرَكَآؤُكُمۡ فَزَيَّلۡنَا بَيۡنَهُمۡ وَقَالَ شُرَكَآؤُهُم مَّا كُنتُمۡ إِيَّانَا تَعۡبُدُونَ ۝

29. 'God suffices as witness between you and us; of your worship we have been even unaware.'

فَكَفَىٰ بِٱللَّهِ شَهِيدَۢا بَيۡنَنَا وَبَيۡنَكُمۡ إِن كُنَّا عَنۡ عِبَادَتِكُمۡ لَغَٰفِلِينَ ۝

30. Therein every soul will know what it sent before, and they shall be brought back to Allah, their rightful Owner, and there shall stray from them that which they have been wont to forge.

هُنَالِكَ تَبۡلُواْ كُلُّ نَفۡسٍ مَّآ أَسۡلَفَتۡۚ وَرُدُّواْ إِلَى ٱللَّهِ مَوۡلَٰهُمُ ٱلۡحَقِّۖ وَضَلَّ عَنۡهُم مَّا كَانُواْ يَفۡتَرُونَ ۝

Section 4

31. Say: 'Who does provide for you from the heaven and the earth, or who owns the ear and the eye, and who brings forth the living from the lifeless and brings forth the lifeless from the living and who disposes the affair?' They will then surely say, 'Allah'. Say: 'Will you not then fear Him?'

قُلۡ مَن يَرۡزُقُكُم مِّنَ ٱلسَّمَآءِ وَٱلۡأَرۡضِ أَمَّن يَمۡلِكُ ٱلسَّمۡعَ وَٱلۡأَبۡصَٰرَ وَمَن يُخۡرِجُ ٱلۡحَىَّ مِنَ ٱلۡمَيِّتِ وَيُخۡرِجُ ٱلۡمَيِّتَ مِنَ ٱلۡحَىِّ وَمَن يُدَبِّرُ ٱلۡأَمۡرَۚ فَسَيَقُولُونَ ٱللَّهُۚ فَقُلۡ أَفَلَا تَتَّقُونَ ۝

32. Such is Allah, your rightful Lord. What then is after the Truth except the error? Whither then are you drifting?

فَذَٰلِكُمُ ٱللَّهُ رَبُّكُمُ ٱلۡحَقُّۖ فَمَاذَا بَعۡدَ ٱلۡحَقِّ إِلَّا ٱلضَّلَٰلُۖ فَأَنَّىٰ تُصۡرَفُونَ ۝

33. In this wise is the Word of your Lord justified on those who transgress; they shall not come to believe.

كَذَٰلِكَ حَقَّتۡ كَلِمَتُ رَبِّكَ عَلَى ٱلَّذِينَ فَسَقُوٓاْ أَنَّهُمۡ لَا يُؤۡمِنُونَ ﴿٣٣﴾

34. Say: 'Who is there among any of your associate gods who originates the creation and then repeats it?' Say: 'Allah originates the creation and then shall repeat it. Whither then are you deviating?'

قُلۡ هَلۡ مِن شُرَكَآئِكُم مَّن يَبۡدَؤُاْ ٱلۡخَلۡقَ ثُمَّ يُعِيدُهُۥ قُلِ ٱللَّهُ يَبۡدَؤُاْ ٱلۡخَلۡقَ ثُمَّ يُعِيدُهُۥ فَأَنَّىٰ تُؤۡفَكُونَ ﴿٣٤﴾

35. Say: 'Is there any of your associate gods who guides you to the Truth?' Say: 'Allah guides to the Truth. Is He, then, who guides to the Truth worthier to be followed, or one who finds not the guidance unless he is himself guided? What ails you then? How ill you judge!'

قُلۡ هَلۡ مِن شُرَكَآئِكُم مَّن يَهۡدِىٓ إِلَى ٱلۡحَقِّ قُلِ ٱللَّهُ يَهۡدِى لِلۡحَقِّ أَفَمَن يَهۡدِىٓ إِلَى ٱلۡحَقِّ أَحَقُّ أَن يُتَّبَعَ أَمَّن لَّا يَهِدِّىٓ إِلَّآ أَن يُهۡدَىٰ فَمَا لَكُمۡ كَيۡفَ تَحۡكُمُونَ ﴿٣٥﴾

36. And most of them follow conjecture: verily, conjecture does not avail against the Truth. Verily, Allah is the Knower of what they do.

وَمَا يَتَّبِعُ أَكۡثَرُهُمۡ إِلَّا ظَنًّا إِنَّ ٱلظَّنَّ لَا يُغۡنِى مِنَ ٱلۡحَقِّ شَيۡـًٔا إِنَّ ٱللَّهَ عَلِيمٌۢ بِمَا يَفۡعَلُونَ ﴿٣٦﴾

37. And this Qur'ān is not such as could be fabricated against Allah; it is but a confirmation of what is before it, and an expounding of the decree of which there is no doubt, from the Lord of the worlds.

وَمَا كَانَ هَٰذَا ٱلۡقُرۡءَانُ أَن يُفۡتَرَىٰ مِن دُونِ ٱللَّهِ وَلَٰكِن تَصۡدِيقَ ٱلَّذِى بَيۡنَ يَدَيۡهِ وَتَفۡصِيلَ ٱلۡكِتَٰبِ لَا رَيۡبَ فِيهِ مِن رَّبِّ ٱلۡعَٰلَمِينَ ﴿٣٧﴾

38. Do they say, 'he has fabricated it?' Say: 'Then bring a *Sūrah* like it[406] and call upon whomsoever you can beside Allah, if you speak truth.'

أَمْ يَقُولُونَ افْتَرَىٰهُ قُلْ فَأْتُواْ بِسُورَةٍ مِّثْلِهِ وَادْعُواْ مَنِ اسْتَطَعْتُم مِّن دُونِ اللَّهِ إِن كُنتُمْ صَادِقِينَ ٣٨

39. Aye! They have belied what their knowledge could not comprehend and what has not yet been fulfilled. Even so have belied those who were before them; behold then how has been the end of the wrongdoers.

بَلْ كَذَّبُواْ بِمَا لَمْ يُحِيطُواْ بِعِلْمِهِ وَلَمَّا يَأْتِهِمْ تَأْوِيلُهُ كَذَٰلِكَ كَذَّبَ الَّذِينَ مِن قَبْلِهِمْ فَانظُرْ كَيْفَ كَانَ عَٰقِبَةُ الظَّٰلِمِينَ ٣٩

40. And of them are some who will believe therein and of them are some who will not believe therein, and thy Lord is the Best Knower of the corrupters.

وَمِنْهُم مَّن يُؤْمِنُ بِهِ وَمِنْهُم مَّن لَّا يُؤْمِنُ بِهِ وَرَبُّكَ أَعْلَمُ بِالْمُفْسِدِينَ ٤٠

Section 5

41. And if they belie you, then say: 'My deeds are mine, and your deeds are yours; you are quit of what I do, and I am quit of what you do.'

وَإِن كَذَّبُوكَ فَقُل لِّى عَمَلِى وَلَكُمْ عَمَلُكُمْ أَنتُم بَرِيٓـُٔونَ مِمَّآ أَعْمَلُ وَأَنَا۠ بَرِىٓءٌ مِّمَّا تَعْمَلُونَ ٤١

---

406. A chapter surpassing the excellence of its contents or even grander in its use of language and more beautiful in style. 'The best of Arab writers', says Palmer, 'has never succeeded in producing anything equal in merit to the Quran' (Palmer, *The Qur'an*, p. lv). 'Typical Semites, the Arabians created or developed no great art of their own. Their artistic nature found expression through one medium only: speech. If the Greek gloried primarily in his statues and architecture, the Arabian found in his ode a finer mode of self–expression. "The beauty of man", declares an Arabic adage, "lies in the eloquence of his tongue". By virtue of its peculiar structure Arabic lent itself admirably to a terse, trenchant, epigrammatic manner of speech. Islam made full use of this feature of the language and of this psychological peculiarity of its people. Hence the "miraculous character", *'ijaz*, of the style and composition of the Koran, adduced by Muslims as the strongest argument in favour of the genuineness of their faith' (Hitti, *History of the Arabs*, pp. 90–91).

42. And of them are some who give an ear to you, so can you make the deaf hear, while they do not apprehend?

وَمِنْهُم مَّن يَسْتَمِعُونَ إِلَيْكَ أَفَأَنتَ تُسْمِعُ الصُّمَّ وَلَوْ كَانُواْ لَا يَعْقِلُونَ ﴿٤٢﴾

43. And of them are some who look at you, so can you guide the blind, while they do not see?

وَمِنْهُم مَّن يَنظُرُ إِلَيْكَ أَفَأَنتَ تَهْدِى الْعُمْىَ وَلَوْ كَانُواْ لَا يُبْصِرُونَ ﴿٤٣﴾

44. Verily, Allah does not wrong in aught, but mankind wrong themselves[407].

إِنَّ اللَّهَ لَا يَظْلِمُ النَّاسَ شَيْئًا وَلَكِنَّ النَّاسَ أَنفُسَهُمْ يَظْلِمُونَ ﴿٤٤﴾

45. And on the Day when He shall gather them, as though they had not tarried save an hour of the day, they shall mutually recognize. Lost surely are those who belie the meeting with Allah and they were not such as to be guided.

وَيَوْمَ يَحْشُرُهُمْ كَأَن لَّمْ يَلْبَثُواْ إِلَّا سَاعَةً مِّنَ النَّهَارِ يَتَعَارَفُونَ بَيْنَهُمْ قَدْ خَسِرَ الَّذِينَ كَذَّبُواْ بِلِقَاءِ اللَّهِ وَمَا كَانُواْ مُهْتَدِينَ ﴿٤٥﴾

46. Whether We show you some of the signs We have provided them, or We cause you to die, to Us is their return, and Allah is a Witness of what they do.

وَإِمَّا نُرِيَنَّكَ بَعْضَ الَّذِى نَعِدُهُمْ أَوْ نَتَوَفَّيَنَّكَ فَإِلَيْنَا مَرْجِعُهُمْ ثُمَّ اللَّهُ شَهِيدٌ عَلَى مَا يَفْعَلُونَ ﴿٤٦﴾

47. For each community there has been sent a Messenger, and when their Messenger has arrived, the affair between them is decreed in equity, and they are not wronged.

وَلِكُلِّ أُمَّةٍ رَّسُولٌ فَإِذَا جَاءَ رَسُولُهُمْ قُضِىَ بَيْنَهُم بِالْقِسْطِ وَهُمْ لَا يُظْلَمُونَ ﴿٤٧﴾

48. And they say: 'When is coming that promise, if you speak truth?'

وَيَقُولُونَ مَتَى هَذَا الْوَعْدُ إِن كُنتُمْ صَادِقِينَ ﴿٤٨﴾

---

407. It is not He Who wantonly deprives anyone of his sight, or hearing, or understanding, but rather perverse people themselves make ill use of their senses and understanding.

49. Say: 'I do not own any power of hurt or benefit to myself, save what Allah may will. For each community is a term; when their term arrives, not an hour can they stay behind nor can they advance.'

قُل لَّآ أَمْلِكُ لِنَفْسِى ضَرًّا وَلَا نَفْعًا إِلَّا مَا شَآءَ ٱللَّهُ لِكُلِّ أُمَّةٍ أَجَلٌ إِذَا جَآءَ أَجَلُهُمْ فَلَا يَسْتَـْٔخِرُونَ سَاعَةً وَلَا يَسْتَقْدِمُونَ ۝

50. Say: 'Bethink you, if His chastisement come on you by night or by day, which portion thereof would the culprits hasten on?

قُلْ أَرَءَيْتُمْ إِنْ أَتَىٰكُمْ عَذَابُهُۥ بَيَـٰتًا أَوْ نَهَارًا مَّاذَا يَسْتَعْجِلُ مِنْهُ ٱلْمُجْرِمُونَ ۝

51. Is it, then, that when it has actually befallen that you will believe therein? Now! Whereas you have been hastening it on all along.'

أَثُمَّ إِذَا مَا وَقَعَ ءَامَنتُم بِهِۦٓ ءَآلْـَٰٔنَ وَقَدْ كُنتُم بِهِۦ تَسْتَعْجِلُونَ ۝

52. Thereafter it will be said to them who wronged themselves; taste the torment everlasting; you are requited not save for what you have been earning.

ثُمَّ قِيلَ لِلَّذِينَ ظَلَمُواْ ذُوقُواْ عَذَابَ ٱلْخُلْدِ هَلْ تُجْزَوْنَ إِلَّا بِمَا كُنتُمْ تَكْسِبُونَ ۝

53. They ask you to tell them if it be true. Say: 'Yea! By my Lord, it is the very Truth, and you shall not be able to escape.'

وَيَسْتَنۢبِـُٔونَكَ أَحَقٌّ هُوَ قُلْ إِى وَرَبِّىٓ إِنَّهُۥ لَحَقٌّ وَمَآ أَنتُم بِمُعْجِزِينَ ۝

Section 6

54. And if everyone who has wronged had all that is in the earth, surely he would ransom himself therewith. And they shall conceal the remorse when they are to face the torment, and the matter will be decreed between them in equity, and they shall not be wronged.

وَلَوْ أَنَّ لِكُلِّ نَفْسٍ ظَلَمَتْ مَا فِى ٱلْأَرْضِ لَٱفْتَدَتْ بِهِۦ وَأَسَرُّواْ ٱلنَّدَامَةَ لَمَّا رَأَوُاْ ٱلْعَذَابَ وَقُضِىَ بَيْنَهُم بِٱلْقِسْطِ وَهُمْ لَا يُظْلَمُونَ ۝

55.   Lo! Verily Allah's is whatsoever is in the heavens and the earth. Lo! Verily Allah's promise is true; but most of the people do not know.

أَلَا إِنَّ لِلَّهِ مَا فِى ٱلسَّمَـٰوَٰتِ وَٱلْأَرْضِ ۗ أَلَا إِنَّ وَعْدَ ٱللَّهِ حَقٌّ وَلَـٰكِنَّ أَكْثَرَهُمْ لَا يَعْلَمُونَ ۝

56.   He gives life and causes to die, and to Him you shall be returned.

هُوَ يُحْىِۦ وَيُمِيتُ وَإِلَيْهِ تُرْجَعُونَ ۝

57.   O mankind! There has come to you an exhortation from your Lord and a healing for what is in your breasts, and a guidance and a mercy for the believers.

يَـٰٓأَيُّهَا ٱلنَّاسُ قَدْ جَآءَتْكُم مَّوْعِظَةٌ مِّن رَّبِّكُمْ وَشِفَآءٌ لِّمَا فِى ٱلصُّدُورِ وَهُدًى وَرَحْمَةٌ لِّلْمُؤْمِنِينَ ۝

58.   Say you: 'In the grace of Allah and in His mercy let them therefore rejoice; far better it is than what they amass.'

قُلْ بِفَضْلِ ٱللَّهِ وَبِرَحْمَتِهِۦ فَبِذَٰلِكَ فَلْيَفْرَحُوا۟ هُوَ خَيْرٌ مِّمَّا يَجْمَعُونَ ۝

59.   Say: 'Bethink of what Allah has sent down to you of provision, and you have then made thereof allowable and forbidden?' Say: 'Is it that Allah has given you leave, or do you fabricate a lie against Allah?'

قُلْ أَرَءَيْتُم مَّآ أَنزَلَ ٱللَّهُ لَكُم مِّن رِّزْقٍ فَجَعَلْتُم مِّنْهُ حَرَامًا وَحَلَـٰلًا قُلْ ءَآللَّهُ أَذِنَ لَكُمْ ۖ أَمْ عَلَى ٱللَّهِ تَفْتَرُونَ ۝

60.   And what do they imagine those who fabricate a lie against Allah on the Day of Resurrection? Verily, Allah is the Owner of grace unto mankind; but most of them do not return thanks.

وَمَا ظَنُّ ٱلَّذِينَ يَفْتَرُونَ عَلَى ٱللَّهِ ٱلْكَذِبَ يَوْمَ ٱلْقِيَـٰمَةِ ۗ إِنَّ ٱللَّهَ لَذُو فَضْلٍ عَلَى ٱلنَّاسِ وَلَـٰكِنَّ أَكْثَرَهُمْ لَا يَشْكُرُونَ ۝

Section 7

61. You are not engaged in any business nor do you recite any part of the Qur'ān nor do you work, but We are witnesses over you when you are engaged therein. And there escapes not your Lord the weight of an ant in the earth or the heavens, nor less than that nor greater, but it is in a luminous Book.[408]

وَمَا تَكُونُ فِى شَأْنٍ وَمَا تَتْلُواْ مِنْهُ مِن قُرْءَانٍ وَلَا تَعْمَلُونَ مِنْ عَمَلٍ إِلَّا كُنَّا عَلَيْكُمْ شُهُودًا إِذْ تُفِيضُونَ فِيهِ وَمَا يَعْزُبُ عَن رَّبِّكَ مِن مِّثْقَالِ ذَرَّةٍ فِى ٱلْأَرْضِ وَلَا فِى ٱلسَّمَاءِ وَلَآ أَصْغَرَ مِن ذَٰلِكَ وَلَآ أَكْبَرَ إِلَّا فِى كِتَٰبٍ مُّبِينٍ ۝

62. Lo! Verily the friends of Allah! No fear shall come upon them nor shall they grieve.

أَلَآ إِنَّ أَوْلِيَآءَ ٱللَّهِ لَا خَوْفٌ عَلَيْهِمْ وَلَا هُمْ يَحْزَنُونَ ۝

63. They who believed and have been fearing Allah.

ٱلَّذِينَ ءَامَنُواْ وَكَانُواْ يَتَّقُونَ ۝

64. For them is glad tidings in the life of the world and in the Hereafter. There is no changing in the words of Allah. That is a mighty achievement.

لَهُمُ ٱلْبُشْرَىٰ فِى ٱلْحَيَوٰةِ ٱلدُّنْيَا وَفِى ٱلْأَخِرَةِ لَا تَبْدِيلَ لِكَلِمَٰتِ ٱللَّهِ ذَٰلِكَ هُوَ ٱلْفَوْزُ ٱلْعَظِيمُ ۝

65. And let not their saying grieve you. Verily honour is wholly Allah's. He is the Hearer, the Knower.

وَلَا يَحْزُنكَ قَوْلُهُمْ إِنَّ ٱلْعِزَّةَ لِلَّهِ جَمِيعًا هُوَ ٱلسَّمِيعُ ٱلْعَلِيمُ ۝

66. Lo! Indeed Allah's is whosoever is in the heavens and whosoever is on the earth. What is it that they follow who call associate gods besides Allah? They follow but a guess and they are but conjecturing.

أَلَآ إِنَّ لِلَّهِ مَن فِى ٱلسَّمَٰوَٰتِ وَمَن فِى ٱلْأَرْضِ وَمَا يَتَّبِعُ ٱلَّذِينَ يَدْعُونَ مِن دُونِ ٱللَّهِ شُرَكَآءَ إِن يَتَّبِعُونَ إِلَّا ٱلظَّنَّ وَإِنْ هُمْ إِلَّا يَخْرُصُونَ ۝

---

408. Namely, the Preserved Tablets whereon all God's decrees are recorded and registered. He is thus not only Omnipresent but also Omniscient. This repudiates the foolish doctrine of certain philosophers that God has knowledge of universals only, and not of particulars.

67. He it is Who has appointed for you the night that you may repose therein and the day enlightening. Surely in that are signs for a people who listen.

هُوَالَّذِی جَعَلَ لَكُمُ الَّيۡلَ لِتَسۡكُنُوۡا فِيۡهِ وَالنَّهَارَ مُبۡصِرًا اِنَّ فِیۡ ذٰلِكَ لَاٰيٰتٍ لِّقَوۡمٍ يَّسۡمَعُوۡنَ ۞

68. They say: 'God has taken a son.'[409] Hallowed be He, the Self–Sufficient! His is whatever is in the heavens and whatever is in the earth. No warranty is there with you for this. Do you ascribe falsely to Allah what you know not?

قَالُوا اتَّخَذَ اللّٰهُ وَلَدًا سُبۡحٰنَهٗ ۚ هُوَالۡغَنِیُّ لَهٗ مَا فِی السَّمٰوٰتِ وَمَا فِی الۡاَرۡضِ اِنۡ عِنۡدَكُمۡ مِّنۡ سُلۡطٰنٍ بِهٰذَا اَتَقُوۡلُوۡنَ عَلَی اللّٰهِ مَا لَا تَعۡلَمُوۡنَ ۞

69. Say: 'Verily those who forge a lie against Allah shall not prosper.'

قُلۡ اِنَّ الَّذِیۡنَ یَفۡتَرُوۡنَ عَلَی اللّٰهِ الۡكَذِبَ لَا يُفۡلِحُوۡنَ ۞

70. A brief enjoyment in the world; then to Us is their return. Then We will make them taste a severe torment in that they have been disbelieving.

مَتَاعٌ فِی الدُّنۡيَا ثُمَّ اِلَيۡنَا مَرۡجِعُهُمۡ ثُمَّ نُذِيۡقُهُمُ الۡعَذَابَ الشَّدِيۡدَ بِمَا كَانُوۡا يَكۡفُرُوۡنَ ۞

Section 8

71. Recite you to them the story of Noah when he said to his people: 'O my people! If my standing forth and my admonishing with the commands of Allah offends you then, on Allah I rely. So devise your affair, you and your associate gods and let not your affair be dubious for you; have it decreed against me, and give me no respite.

وَاتۡلُ عَلَيۡهِمۡ نَبَاَ نُوۡحٍ ۘ اِذۡ قَالَ لِقَوۡمِهٖ يٰقَوۡمِ اِنۡ كَانَ كَبُرَ عَلَيۡكُمۡ مَّقَامِیۡ وَتَذۡكِيۡرِیۡ بِاٰيٰتِ اللّٰهِ فَعَلَی اللّٰهِ تَوَكَّلۡتُ فَاَجۡمِعُوۡا اَمۡرَكُمۡ وَشُرَكَاۤءَكُمۡ ثُمَّ لَا يَكُنۡ اَمۡرُكُمۡ عَلَيۡكُمۡ غُمَّةً ثُمَّ اقۡضُوۡا اِلَیَّ وَلَا تُنۡظِرُوۡنِ ۞

409. The reference here is not to Christ, but to the various son–gods of the polytheistic nations. The doctrine of the sonship of God is not peculiarly Christian. Pagan mythologies and polytheistic theologies teem with such notions, and Arab mythology at that time was no exception.

72. So then if you turn away, I have asked of you no wage, my reward is only with Allah, and I am commanded to be of those who submit.'

فَإِن تَوَلَّيۡتُمۡ فَمَا سَأَلۡتُكُم مِّنۡ أَجۡرٍ إِنۡ أَجۡرِيَ إِلَّا عَلَى ٱللَّهِ وَأُمِرۡتُ أَنۡ أَكُونَ مِنَ ٱلۡمُسۡلِمِينَ ۝

73. Then they denied him; We delivered him and those with him in the ark, and We made them successors; while We drowned them who belied Our signs.[410] Behold then how was the end of those who had been warned.

فَكَذَّبُوهُ فَنَجَّيۡنَٰهُ وَمَن مَّعَهُۥ فِى ٱلۡفُلۡكِ وَجَعَلۡنَٰهُمۡ خَلَٰٓئِفَ وَأَغۡرَقۡنَا ٱلَّذِينَ كَذَّبُوا۟ بِـَٔايَٰتِنَا فَٱنظُرۡ كَيۡفَ كَانَ عَٰقِبَةُ ٱلۡمُنذَرِينَ ۝

74. Then We sent other Messengers after him to their people, and they brought the evidence, but they were not such as to believe what they had once rejected. Thus We seal the hearts of the transgressors.

ثُمَّ بَعَثۡنَا مِنۢ بَعۡدِهِۦ رُسُلًا إِلَىٰ قَوۡمِهِمۡ فَجَآءُوهُم بِٱلۡبَيِّنَٰتِ فَمَا كَانُوا۟ لِيُؤۡمِنُوا۟ بِمَا كَذَّبُوا۟ بِهِۦ مِن قَبۡلُ كَذَٰلِكَ نَطۡبَعُ عَلَىٰ قُلُوبِ ٱلۡمُعۡتَدِينَ ۝

75. After them We sent Moses and Aaron to Pharaoh and his chiefs with Our signs, but they grew stiff-necked and they were a culprit people.[411]

ثُمَّ بَعَثۡنَا مِنۢ بَعۡدِهِم مُّوسَىٰ وَهَٰرُونَ إِلَىٰ فِرۡعَوۡنَ وَمَلَإِيْهِۦ بِـَٔايَٰتِنَا فَٱسۡتَكۡبَرُوا۟ وَكَانُوا۟ قَوۡمًا مُّجۡرِمِينَ ۝

76. Then when there came to them the Truth from Us, they said, 'this is clear magic.'

فَلَمَّا جَآءَهُمُ ٱلۡحَقُّ مِنۡ عِندِنَا قَالُوٓا۟ إِنَّ هَٰذَا لَسِحۡرٌ مُّبِينٌ ۝

---

410. Note that the Holy Qur'ān makes no claim of a universal deluge. It only says that those who rejected Noah's mission were drowned. It is not the Qur'ān but the Bible that asserts the universal character of the deluge. 'And the Lord said: I will destroy man whom I have created from the face of the earth'. (Ge. 6: 7).

411. Note that the Bible makes no mention of Moses and Aaron having been sent to the Egyptians as Messengers of God for their conversion to the True Faith. It is the Holy Qur'ān that makes good this serious omission. In fact it is inconceivable that Moses, being a Messenger of God, should leave the gross irreligion of Egypt untouched.

77. Moses said: 'Do you say this of the Truth after it has come to you? Is this magic? And the magicians do not fare well.'

قَالَ مُوسَىٰٓ أَتَقُولُونَ لِلْحَقِّ لَمَّا جَآءَكُمْ أَسِحْرٌ هَٰذَا وَلَا يُفْلِحُ ٱلسَّٰحِرُونَ ﴿٧٧﴾

78. They said: 'Have you come to turn us aside from that faith we found our fathers thereon, and that the greatness in the land shall be for you two? For the sake of you two we are not going to be believers.'

قَالُوٓا۟ أَجِئْتَنَا لِتَلْفِتَنَا عَمَّا وَجَدْنَا عَلَيْهِ ءَابَآءَنَا وَتَكُونَ لَكُمَا ٱلْكِبْرِيَآءُ فِى ٱلْأَرْضِ وَمَا نَحْنُ لَكُمَا بِمُؤْمِنِينَ ﴿٧٨﴾

79. And Pharaoh said, 'bring to me every magician knowing.'

وَقَالَ فِرْعَوْنُ ٱئْتُونِى بِكُلِّ سَٰحِرٍ عَلِيمٍ ﴿٧٩﴾

80. Then when the magicians were come, Moses said to them: 'Cast down what you are going to cast down.'

فَلَمَّا جَآءَ ٱلسَّحَرَةُ قَالَ لَهُم مُّوسَىٰٓ أَلْقُوا۟ مَآ أَنتُم مُّلْقُونَ ﴿٨٠﴾

81. Then when they had cast down, Moses said: 'What you have brought is magic; verily Allah will soon make it vain'; Allah does not set right the work of the corrupters.

فَلَمَّآ أَلْقَوْا۟ قَالَ مُوسَىٰ مَا جِئْتُم بِهِ ٱلسِّحْرُ إِنَّ ٱللَّهَ سَيُبْطِلُهُۥٓ إِنَّ ٱللَّهَ لَا يُصْلِحُ عَمَلَ ٱلْمُفْسِدِينَ ﴿٨١﴾

82. And Allah justifies the Truth according to His words, much as the culprits may detest it.

وَيُحِقُّ ٱللَّهُ ٱلْحَقَّ بِكَلِمَٰتِهِۦ وَلَوْ كَرِهَ ٱلْمُجْرِمُونَ ﴿٨٢﴾

Section 9

83. Then none believed in Moses save a posterity of his people, through the fear of Pharaoh and their chiefs, lest he should persecute them. And truly Pharaoh was lofty in the land and of the extravagant.

فَمَآ ءَامَنَ لِمُوسَىٰٓ إِلَّا ذُرِّيَّةٌ مِّن قَوْمِهِۦ عَلَىٰ خَوْفٍ مِّن فِرْعَوْنَ وَمَلَإِيْهِمْ أَن يَفْتِنَهُمْ وَإِنَّ فِرْعَوْنَ لَعَالٍ فِى ٱلْأَرْضِ وَإِنَّهُۥ لَمِنَ ٱلْمُسْرِفِينَ ﴿٨٣﴾

84. Moses said: 'My people! If you have been believers in Allah, then on Him rely, if you are Muslims.'

85. So they said: 'On Allah we rely. Our Lord! Make us not a temptation to the wrong doing people.

86. And deliver us in Your Mercy from the disbelieving people.'

87. And We revealed to Moses and his brother; inhabit houses for your people in Egypt, and make your houses a place of worship, establish prayer and give glad tidings to the believers.

88. And Moses said: 'Our Lord! Verily You have given to Pharaoh and his chiefs adornment and riches in the life of world, Our Lord, that they may lead astray men from Your way. Our Lord! Wipe out their riches, and harden their hearts, so that they may not believe until they face the afflictive torment.'

89. Allah said: 'Surely the petition of you two is granted; so keep straight on, and do not follow the path of those who are bereft of knowledge.'

90. And We led the children of Israel across the sea; then Pharaoh and their hosts pursued them in rebellion and enmity, until, when the drowning overtook him, he said: 'I believe that He! There is no god but He, in whom the children of Israel believe, and I am of the Muslims.'

وَقَالَ مُوسَىٰ يَٰقَوْمِ إِن كُنتُمْ ءَامَنتُم بِٱللَّهِ فَعَلَيْهِ تَوَكَّلُوٓا۟ إِن كُنتُم مُّسْلِمِينَ ﴿٨٤﴾

فَقَالُوا۟ عَلَى ٱللَّهِ تَوَكَّلْنَا رَبَّنَا لَا تَجْعَلْنَا فِتْنَةً لِّلْقَوْمِ ٱلظَّٰلِمِينَ ﴿٨٥﴾

وَنَجِّنَا بِرَحْمَتِكَ مِنَ ٱلْقَوْمِ ٱلْكَٰفِرِينَ ﴿٨٦﴾

وَأَوْحَيْنَآ إِلَىٰ مُوسَىٰ وَأَخِيهِ أَن تَبَوَّءَا لِقَوْمِكُمَا بِمِصْرَ بُيُوتًا وَٱجْعَلُوا۟ بُيُوتَكُمْ قِبْلَةً وَأَقِيمُوا۟ ٱلصَّلَوٰةَ وَبَشِّرِ ٱلْمُؤْمِنِينَ ﴿٨٧﴾

وَقَالَ مُوسَىٰ رَبَّنَآ إِنَّكَ ءَاتَيْتَ فِرْعَوْنَ وَمَلَأَهُۥ زِينَةً وَأَمْوَٰلًا فِى ٱلْحَيَوٰةِ ٱلدُّنْيَا رَبَّنَا لِيُضِلُّوا۟ عَن سَبِيلِكَ رَبَّنَا ٱطْمِسْ عَلَىٰٓ أَمْوَٰلِهِمْ وَٱشْدُدْ عَلَىٰ قُلُوبِهِمْ فَلَا يُؤْمِنُوا۟ حَتَّىٰ يَرَوُا۟ ٱلْعَذَابَ ٱلْأَلِيمَ ﴿٨٨﴾

قَالَ قَدْ أُجِيبَت دَّعْوَتُكُمَا فَٱسْتَقِيمَا وَلَا تَتَّبِعَآنِّ سَبِيلَ ٱلَّذِينَ لَا يَعْلَمُونَ ﴿٨٩﴾

وَجَٰوَزْنَا بِبَنِىٓ إِسْرَٰٓءِيلَ ٱلْبَحْرَ فَأَتْبَعَهُمْ فِرْعَوْنُ وَجُنُودُهُۥ بَغْيًا وَعَدْوًا حَتَّىٰٓ إِذَآ أَدْرَكَهُ ٱلْغَرَقُ قَالَ ءَامَنتُ أَنَّهُۥ لَآ إِلَٰهَ إِلَّا ٱلَّذِىٓ ءَامَنَتْ بِهِۦ بَنُوٓا۟ إِسْرَٰٓءِيلَ وَأَنَا۠ مِنَ ٱلْمُسْلِمِينَ ﴿٩٠﴾

91. Now indeed! While you have rebelled afore, and was of the corrupters!

ءَآلْـَٰنَ وَقَدْ عَصَيْتَ قَبْلُ وَكُنتَ مِنَ ٱلْمُفْسِدِينَ ۝

92. So this day We deliver you in your body that you may be a sign to those after you; and verily many of mankind are heedless of Our signs.

فَٱلْيَوْمَ نُنَجِّيكَ بِبَدَنِكَ لِتَكُونَ لِمَنْ خَلْفَكَ ءَايَةً وَإِنَّ كَثِيرًا مِّنَ ٱلنَّاسِ عَنْ ءَايَٰتِنَا لَغَٰفِلُونَ ۝

Section 10

93. And assuredly We settled the children of Israel into a secure settlement, and We provided them with good things, and they did not differ until there had come to them knowledge. Verily your Lord shall judge between them on the Day of Resurrection as to what they had been differing in.

وَلَقَدْ بَوَّأْنَا بَنِىٓ إِسْرَٰٓءِيلَ مُبَوَّأَ صِدْقٍ وَرَزَقْنَٰهُم مِّنَ ٱلطَّيِّبَٰتِ فَمَا ٱخْتَلَفُوا۟ حَتَّىٰ جَآءَهُمُ ٱلْعِلْمُ إِنَّ رَبَّكَ يَقْضِى بَيْنَهُمْ يَوْمَ ٱلْقِيَٰمَةِ فِيمَا كَانُوا۟ فِيهِ يَخْتَلِفُونَ ۝

94. If you be in doubt concerning what We have sent down to you, ask then those who have read the Book before you. Assuredly the Truth has come to you from your Lord, so be not then of the doubters.

فَإِن كُنتَ فِى شَكٍّ مِّمَّآ أَنزَلْنَآ إِلَيْكَ فَسْـَٔلِ ٱلَّذِينَ يَقْرَءُونَ ٱلْكِتَٰبَ مِن قَبْلِكَ لَقَدْ جَآءَكَ ٱلْحَقُّ مِن رَّبِّكَ فَلَا تَكُونَنَّ مِنَ ٱلْمُمْتَرِينَ ۝

95. And be not of those who belie Allah's signs, lest you be of the losers.

وَلَا تَكُونَنَّ مِنَ ٱلَّذِينَ كَذَّبُوا۟ بِـَٔايَٰتِ ٱللَّهِ فَتَكُونَ مِنَ ٱلْخَٰسِرِينَ ۝

96. Surely those on whom the Word of your Lord has been justified shall not believe.

إِنَّ ٱلَّذِينَ حَقَّتْ عَلَيْهِمْ كَلِمَتُ رَبِّكَ لَا يُؤْمِنُونَ ۝

97. Even though every sign should come to them, until they face an afflictive torment.

وَلَوْ جَآءَتْهُمْ كُلُّ ءَايَةٍ حَتَّىٰ يَرَوُاْ ٱلْعَذَابَ ٱلْأَلِيمَ ۝

98. Why then was there not a town which believed, so that its faith might have profited, except the people of Jonah?[412] When they believed, We removed from them the chastisement of abjection in the life of the world, and We let them enjoy for a season.

فَلَوْلَا كَانَتْ قَرْيَةٌ ءَامَنَتْ فَنَفَعَهَآ إِيمَٰنُهَآ إِلَّا قَوْمَ يُونُسَ لَمَّآ ءَامَنُواْ كَشَفْنَا عَنْهُمْ عَذَابَ ٱلْخِزْيِ فِى ٱلْحَيَوٰةِ ٱلدُّنْيَا وَمَتَّعْنَٰهُمْ إِلَىٰ حِينٍ ۝

99. And had your Lord willed, those on the earth would have believed, all of them, together; can you then compel mankind that they become believers?

وَلَوْ شَآءَ رَبُّكَ لَأَمَنَ مَن فِى ٱلْأَرْضِ كُلُّهُمْ جَمِيعًا أَفَأَنتَ تُكْرِهُ ٱلنَّاسَ حَتَّىٰ يَكُونُواْ مُؤْمِنِينَ ۝

100. It is not for any soul that it should believe save with Allah's will, and He lays an abomination upon those who do not reflect.

وَمَا كَانَ لِنَفْسٍ أَن تُؤْمِنَ إِلَّا بِإِذْنِ ٱللَّهِ وَيَجْعَلُ ٱلرِّجْسَ عَلَى ٱلَّذِينَ لَا يَعْقِلُونَ ۝

101. Say: 'Behold what is in the heavens and the earth; and signs and warnings do not avail those who do not believe.'

قُلِ ٱنظُرُواْ مَاذَا فِى ٱلسَّمَٰوَٰتِ وَٱلْأَرْضِ وَمَا تُغْنِى ٱلْءَايَٰتُ وَٱلنُّذُرُ عَن قَوْمٍ لَّا يُؤْمِنُونَ ۝

---

412. Jonah equates to the Jonah of the Bible; a Prophet of God. He was sent to the idolatrous people of Nineveh, the Assyrian capital, which stood near the place where Mosul now stands in Iraq. They saved themselves by timely repentance at the very first and rather distant Signs of Divine wrath, when the Prophet had left them after threatening them with the impending doom. Son of Amittai, he lived probably in the first half of the 8th century BC. 'He spake by the hand of his servant Jonah, the son of Amittai, the prophet, which was of Gath-hepher' (2 Ki. 14: 25). 'The story presupposes a pre–exilic date, when Assyria was at the height of its power and Nineveh was the metropolis of the world' (*VJE*. p. 325). That he lived in the time of Jeroboam II is clearly affirmed in the Bible, and the reign of this King is generally believed to have lasted from 781 to 741 BC.

102. Do they not await aught but the days of those who have passed away before them? Say: 'Wait then, I am with you among those who wait.'

فَهَلۡ يَنتَظِرُونَ إِلَّا مِثۡلَ أَيَّامِ ٱلَّذِينَ خَلَوۡا۟ مِن قَبۡلِهِمۡ قُلۡ فَٱنتَظِرُوٓا۟ إِنِّى مَعَكُم مِّنَ ٱلۡمُنتَظِرِينَ ۝

103. Thereafter, We rescued Our Messengers and those who believed. Even so, as is incumbent upon Us, We deliver the believers.

ثُمَّ نُنَجِّى رُسُلَنَا وَٱلَّذِينَ ءَامَنُوا۟ كَذَٰلِكَ حَقًّا عَلَيۡنَا نُنجِ ٱلۡمُؤۡمِنِينَ ۝

Section 11

104. Say: 'O men! If you are in doubt concerning my religion, then I worship not those you worship besides Allah, but I worship Allah Who causes you to die, and I am commanded that I should be of the believers;

قُلۡ يَٰٓأَيُّهَا ٱلنَّاسُ إِن كُنتُمۡ فِى شَكٍّ مِّن دِينِى فَلَا أَعۡبُدُ ٱلَّذِينَ تَعۡبُدُونَ مِن دُونِ ٱللَّهِ وَلَٰكِنۡ أَعۡبُدُ ٱللَّهَ ٱلَّذِى يَتَوَفَّىٰكُمۡ وَأُمِرۡتُ أَنۡ أَكُونَ مِنَ ٱلۡمُؤۡمِنِينَ ۝

105. And that; keep your face straight toward the religion, upright; and by no means be of the polytheists.

وَأَنۡ أَقِمۡ وَجۡهَكَ لِلدِّينِ حَنِيفًا وَلَا تَكُونَنَّ مِنَ ٱلۡمُشۡرِكِينَ ۝

106. And do not invoke besides Allah what can neither profit you nor hurt you, then if you do so, you are forthwith of the wrong-doers.'

وَلَا تَدۡعُ مِن دُونِ ٱللَّهِ مَا لَا يَنفَعُكَ وَلَا يَضُرُّكَ فَإِن فَعَلۡتَ فَإِنَّكَ إِذًا مِّنَ ٱلظَّٰلِمِينَ ۝

107. And if Allah touches you with hurt there is no remover thereof but He, and if He intends any good, there is no averter of His grace. He lets it befall on whomsoever of His bondsmen He will; and He is the Forgiving, the Merciful.[413]

وَإِن يَمْسَسْكَ ٱللَّهُ بِضُرٍّ فَلَا كَاشِفَ لَهُۥ إِلَّا هُوَ وَإِن يُرِدْكَ بِخَيْرٍ فَلَا رَآدَّ لِفَضْلِهِۦ يُصِيبُ بِهِۦ مَن يَشَآءُ مِنْ عِبَادِهِۦ وَهُوَ ٱلْغَفُورُ ٱلرَّحِيمُ ﴿١٠٧﴾

108. Say: 'O mankind! The Truth has surely come to you from your Lord; any one who is guided is only guided for himself, and any one who strays, strays only against himself; and I am not your keeper.'

قُلْ يَـٰٓأَيُّهَا ٱلنَّاسُ قَدْ جَآءَكُمُ ٱلْحَقُّ مِن رَّبِّكُمْ فَمَنِ ٱهْتَدَىٰ فَإِنَّمَا يَهْتَدِى لِنَفْسِهِۦ وَمَن ضَلَّ فَإِنَّمَا يَضِلُّ عَلَيْهَا وَمَآ أَنَا۠ عَلَيْكُم بِوَكِيلٍ ﴿١٠٨﴾

109. And follow you whatever is revealed to you and endure until Allah decides, and He is the Best of deciders.

وَٱتَّبِعْ مَا يُوحَىٰٓ إِلَيْكَ وَٱصْبِرْ حَتَّىٰ يَحْكُمَ ٱللَّهُ وَهُوَ خَيْرُ ٱلْحَٰكِمِينَ ﴿١٠٩﴾

---

413. The passage is at once a vigorous denunciation of idolatry and a passionate exhortation for belief in the One True God.

Sūrah 11

Hūd

(Makkan, 10 Sections, 123 Verses)

In the name of Allah, the Compassionate, the Merciful.

Section 1

1. *Alif, Lām, Rā.* This is a Book, verses of which are guarded, and then detailed, from the Wise, the Aware.

2. Saying: 'You shall not worship except Allah. Verily I am unto you a warner from Him, and a bearer of glad tidings.

3. And that; ask forgiveness of your Lord, then turn to Him in repentance. He will let you enjoy a goodly enjoyment until a term appointed and will grant His grace to every owner of grace. And if you turn away, I fear for you the torment of a Great Day.

4. To Allah is your return and He is Potent over everything.'

5. Lo! They fold their breasts that they may hide from Him. Lo! When they cover themselves with their garments, He knows what they conceal and what they reveal. Verily, He is the Knower of the innermost secrets.

6. No moving creature is there on the earth but upon Allah is its provision, and He knows its dwelling and resting place, everything is in a Book luminous.

وَمَا مِن دَآبَّةٍ فِى ٱلۡأَرۡضِ إِلَّا عَلَى ٱللَّهِ رِزۡقُهَا وَيَعۡلَمُ مُسۡتَقَرَّهَا وَمُسۡتَوۡدَعَهَا كُلٌّ فِى كِتَٰبٍ مُّبِينٍ ٦

7. He it is Who has created the heavens and the earth in six days and His throne was on the water that He might test you, as to which of you is excellent in work.[414] And if you say, 'you shall be certainly raised after death,' those who disbelieve are sure to say, 'naught is this but magic manifest.'

وَهُوَ ٱلَّذِى خَلَقَ ٱلسَّمَٰوَٰتِ وَٱلۡأَرۡضَ فِى سِتَّةِ أَيَّامٍ وَكَانَ عَرۡشُهُۥ عَلَى ٱلۡمَآءِ لِيَبۡلُوَكُمۡ أَيُّكُمۡ أَحۡسَنُ عَمَلًا وَلَئِن قُلۡتَ إِنَّكُم مَّبۡعُوثُونَ مِنۢ بَعۡدِ ٱلۡمَوۡتِ لَيَقُولَنَّ ٱلَّذِينَ كَفَرُوٓا۟ إِنۡ هَٰذَآ إِلَّا سِحۡرٌ مُّبِينٌ ٧

8. And if We defer from them the chastisement till a determined period, they say, 'what does withhold it?' Lo! the day it befalls them it shall not be averted from them and there shall encompass them what they have been mocking at.

وَلَئِنۡ أَخَّرۡنَا عَنۡهُمُ ٱلۡعَذَابَ إِلَىٰٓ أُمَّةٍ مَّعۡدُودَةٍ لَّيَقُولُنَّ مَا يَحۡبِسُهُۥٓ أَلَا يَوۡمَ يَأۡتِيهِمۡ لَيۡسَ مَصۡرُوفًا عَنۡهُمۡ وَحَاقَ بِهِم مَّا كَانُوا۟ بِهِۦ يَسۡتَهۡزِءُونَ ٨

---

414. In other words, before the creation of the heavens and the earth. This is only a restatement of the well – known scientific fact that a universal sea preceded the birth of the land. Cf. the Bible. 'And the earth was without form, and void: and darkness was upon the face to the deep. And the spirit of God moved upon the face of the waters'. (Ge. 1: 2). According to another rendering, adopted by Ewald, Dillmann, and Schrader: 'and the earth was waste and void, and darkness was over the watery abyss, and the breath of God was brooding over the waters' *DB*. I. 502). It is, however, to be noted that unlike the Bible, which lays down a sequence of the creation of the heavens and earth and which has been disproved by modern scientific researches, the Qur'ān does not describe their origin in any particular sequence.

Section 2

9. And if We let man taste mercy from Us, and then withdraw it from him, surely he is despairing, blaspheming.

وَلَئِنۡ أَذَقۡنَا ٱلۡإِنسَـٰنَ مِنَّا رَحۡمَةً ثُمَّ نَزَعۡنَـٰهَا مِنۡهُ إِنَّهُۥ لَيَـُٔوسٌ كَفُورٌ ۝

10. And if We let him taste favour after harm has touched him, he says, 'ills have departed from me' and he becomes elated, boastful.

وَلَئِنۡ أَذَقۡنَـٰهُ نَعۡمَآءَ بَعۡدَ ضَرَّآءَ مَسَّتۡهُ لَيَقُولَنَّ ذَهَبَ ٱلسَّيِّئَاتُ عَنِّیۤ إِنَّهُۥ لَفَرِحٌ فَخُورٌ ۝

11. Not so are those who persevere and do righteous works. Those; theirs shall be forgiveness and a great reward.

إِلَّا ٱلَّذِينَ صَبَرُواْ وَعَمِلُواْ ٱلصَّـٰلِحَـٰتِ أُوْلَـٰٓئِكَ لَهُم مَّغۡفِرَةٌ وَأَجۡرٌ كَبِيرٌ ۝

12. So perchance you may abandon part of what has been revealed to you, and your breast is straitened thereby, because they say, 'why has not a treasure been sent down on him or an angel come with him?' You are but a warner, and of everything Allah is a Trustee.

فَلَعَلَّكَ تَارِكُۢ بَعۡضَ مَا يُوحَىٰٓ إِلَيۡكَ وَضَآئِقُۢ بِهِۦ صَدۡرُكَ أَن يَقُولُواْ لَوۡلَآ أُنزِلَ عَلَيۡهِ كَنزٌ أَوۡ جَآءَ مَعَهُۥ مَلَكٌ إِنَّمَآ أَنتَ نَذِيرٌ وَٱللَّهُ عَلَىٰ كُلِّ شَیۡءٍ وَكِيلٌ ۝

13. Or do they say, 'he has fabricated it?' Say: 'Bring you then ten Surahs the like of it, fabricated, and call whom you can besides Allah, if you speak truth.'

أَمۡ يَقُولُونَ ٱفۡتَرَىٰهُ قُلۡ فَأۡتُواْ بِعَشۡرِ سُوَرٍ مِّثۡلِهِۦ مُفۡتَرَيَـٰتٍ وَٱدۡعُواْ مَنِ ٱسۡتَطَعۡتُم مِّن دُونِ ٱللَّهِ إِن كُنتُمۡ صَـٰدِقِينَ ۝

14. Then if they do not respond[415], you know that it has been sent down with the knowledge of Allah, and that there is no god but He; are you Muslims then?

فَإِلَّمۡ يَسۡتَجِيبُواْ لَكُمۡ فَٱعۡلَمُوٓاْ أَنَّمَآ أُنزِلَ بِعِلۡمِ ٱللَّهِ وَأَن لَّآ إِلَٰهَ إِلَّا هُوَۖ فَهَلۡ أَنتُم مُّسۡلِمُونَ ﴿١٤﴾

15. Anyone who desires the life of the world and its embellishment, We shall repay them in full their works therein, and in it they shall not be defrauded.

مَن كَانَ يُرِيدُ ٱلۡحَيَوٰةَ ٱلدُّنۡيَا وَزِينَتَهَا نُوَفِّ إِلَيۡهِمۡ أَعۡمَٰلَهُمۡ فِيهَا وَهُمۡ فِيهَا لَا يُبۡخَسُونَ ﴿١٥﴾

16. These are they for whom there is nothing in the Hereafter except the Fire; to nothing shall come what they have performed, and vain is what they have been working.

أُوْلَٰٓئِكَ ٱلَّذِينَ لَيۡسَ لَهُمۡ فِي ٱلۡأَخِرَةِ إِلَّا ٱلنَّارُۖ وَحَبِطَ مَا صَنَعُواْ فِيهَا وَبَٰطِلٞ مَّا كَانُواْ يَعۡمَلُونَ ﴿١٦﴾

17. Is he like him who rests upon evidence from His Lord, and there recites it a witness from Him?[416] And before it was the Book of Moses, a pattern and a mercy; these believe therein; and whoever of the sects disbelieves therein, the Fire is his promised resort. Be then you not in doubt thereof, verily it is the Truth from your Lord, yet most of mankind do not believe.

أَفَمَن كَانَ عَلَىٰ بَيِّنَةٖ مِّن رَّبِّهِۦ وَيَتۡلُوهُ شَاهِدٞ مِّنۡهُ وَمِن قَبۡلِهِۦ كِتَٰبُ مُوسَىٰٓ إِمَامٗا وَرَحۡمَةًۚ أُوْلَٰٓئِكَ يُؤۡمِنُونَ بِهِۦۚ وَمَن يَكۡفُرۡ بِهِۦ مِنَ ٱلۡأَحۡزَابِ فَٱلنَّارُ مَوۡعِدُهُۥ فَلَا تَكُ فِي مِرۡيَةٖ مِّنۡهُۚ إِنَّهُ ٱلۡحَقُّ مِن رَّبِّكَ وَلَٰكِنَّ أَكۡثَرَ ٱلنَّاسِ لَا يُؤۡمِنُونَ ﴿١٧﴾

---

415. If they fail to produce anything like the Qur'ān. 'The best of Arab writers has never succeeded in producing anything equal in merit to the Qur'ān' (Palmer, *The Qur'an*, p. lv). 'We find even so bigoted an opponent of Islam acknowledging that the Qur'an was composed in such eloquent and beautiful language that even Christians could not help reading and admiring it' (Arnold, *Preaching of Islam*, p. 138).

416. The whole life of the Prophet was that of a living witness of God and a witness to the truths of the Holy Qur'ān.

18. And who does a greater wrong than he who fabricates a lie against Allah? These shall be set before their Lord, and the witnesses shall say; these are they who lied against their Lord. Lo! The curse of Allah shall fall on the wrong-doers.

وَمَنْ أَظْلَمُ مِمَّنِ افْتَرَىٰ عَلَى اللَّهِ كَذِبًا أُوْلَـٰٓئِكَ يُعْرَضُونَ عَلَىٰ رَبِّهِمْ وَيَقُولُ الْأَشْهَٰدُ هَـٰٓؤُلَآءِ الَّذِينَ كَذَبُواْ عَلَىٰ رَبِّهِمْ أَلَا لَعْنَةُ اللَّهِ عَلَى الظَّٰلِمِينَ ۝

19. Who hinder others from the path of Allah and seek crookedness therein, they, in the Hereafter are disbelievers.

الَّذِينَ يَصُدُّونَ عَن سَبِيلِ اللَّهِ وَيَبْغُونَهَا عِوَجًا وَهُم بِالْأَخِرَةِ هُمْ كَٰفِرُونَ ۝

20. These could not escape on the earth, nor could there be for them protectors against Allah; doubled shall be the torment for them; they were not able to hearken nor be clear sighted.

أُوْلَـٰٓئِكَ لَمْ يَكُونُواْ مُعْجِزِينَ فِي الْأَرْضِ وَمَا كَانَ لَهُم مِّن دُونِ اللَّهِ مِنْ أَوْلِيَآءَ يُضَٰعَفُ لَهُمُ الْعَذَابُ مَا كَانُواْ يَسْتَطِيعُونَ السَّمْعَ وَمَا كَانُواْ يُبْصِرُونَ ۝

21. These are they who have lost their souls, and what has strayed from them is what they had been fabricating.

أُوْلَـٰٓئِكَ الَّذِينَ خَسِرُواْ أَنفُسَهُمْ وَضَلَّ عَنْهُم مَّا كَانُواْ يَفْتَرُونَ ۝

22. Undoubtedly they! They, in the Hereafter shall be the greatest losers.

لَا جَرَمَ أَنَّهُمْ فِي الْأَخِرَةِ هُمُ الْأَخْسَرُونَ ۝

23. Surely those who believed and worked righteous works and humbled themselves before their Lord – they shall be the inhabitants of the Garden; therein shall they abide.

إِنَّ الَّذِينَ ءَامَنُواْ وَعَمِلُواْ الصَّٰلِحَٰتِ وَأَخْبَتُوٓاْ إِلَىٰ رَبِّهِمْ أُوْلَـٰٓئِكَ أَصْحَٰبُ الْجَنَّةِ هُمْ فِيهَا خَٰلِدُونَ ۝

24. The likeness of the two parties is as the blind and deaf, and the seeing and hearing. Are the two equal in likeness? Are you not admonished then?

مَثَلُ الْفَرِيقَيْنِ كَالْأَعْمَىٰ وَالْأَصَمِّ وَالْبَصِيرِ وَالسَّمِيعِ هَلْ يَسْتَوِيَانِ مَثَلًا أَفَلَا تَذَكَّرُونَ ۝

Section 3

25. And assuredly We sent Noah
to his people saying: 'I am to you
a plain warner.

وَلَقَدْ أَرْسَلْنَا نُوحًا إِلَىٰ قَوْمِهِ إِنِّي لَكُمْ
نَذِيرٌ مُّبِينٌ ﴿٢٥﴾

26. That you shall worship none
except Allah; verily I fear for you
the torment of a Day afflictive.'

أَن لَّا تَعْبُدُوٓا۟ إِلَّا ٱللَّهَ إِنِّيٓ أَخَافُ عَلَيْكُمْ
عَذَابَ يَوْمٍ أَلِيمٍ ﴿٢٦﴾

27. The chiefs of those who
disbelieved among his people
said: 'We find you nothing more
than a human being like
ourselves,[417] and we find no one
except the meanest of us following
you by an immature opinion; nor
do we find in you any superiority
over us; nay! We deem that you
are all liars.'

فَقَالَ ٱلْمَلَأُ ٱلَّذِينَ كَفَرُوا۟ مِن قَوْمِهِ مَا
نَرَىٰكَ إِلَّا بَشَرًا مِّثْلَنَا وَمَا نَرَىٰكَ
ٱتَّبَعَكَ إِلَّا ٱلَّذِينَ هُمْ أَرَاذِلُنَا بَادِىَ
ٱلرَّأْىِ وَمَا نَرَىٰ لَكُمْ عَلَيْنَا مِن فَضْلٍ بَلْ
نَظُنُّكُمْ كَٰذِبِينَ ﴿٢٧﴾

28. He said: 'Bethink O my
people; if I rested upon evidence
from my Lord, and a mercy has
come to me from Him, and that
has been obscured to you, can we
make you adhere to it, while you
are averse thereto?

قَالَ يَٰقَوْمِ أَرَءَيْتُمْ إِن كُنتُ عَلَىٰ بَيِّنَةٍ مِّن رَّبِّى
وَءَاتَىٰنِى رَحْمَةً مِّنْ عِندِهِ فَعُمِّيَتْ عَلَيْكُمْ
أَنُلْزِمُكُمُوهَا وَأَنتُمْ لَهَا كَٰرِهُونَ ﴿٢٨﴾

29. 'And O my people: I do not
ask of you any riches therefor; my
reward is only with Allah.[418] And I
am not going to drive away those

وَيَٰقَوْمِ لَآ أَسْـَٔلُكُمْ عَلَيْهِ مَالًا إِنْ أَجْرِىَ
إِلَّا عَلَى ٱللَّهِ وَمَآ أَنَا۠ بِطَارِدِ ٱلَّذِينَ ءَامَنُوٓا۟

---

417. Their notion being that no mere mortal can be a Messenger of God. This has
been the ever – recurring argument of polytheistic nations. A god–man, according
to them, must be above humanity and must partake of His Divine nature.

418. This is one of the distinguishing features of the Prophets of God. They
have no ends of their own to serve; they work absolutely disinterestedly.

who have believed; they are going to meet their Lord, but I find you a people steeped in ignorance.

30. 'O my people! Who will support me against Allah, if I drove them away? Are you not admonished then?

31. And I do not say to you that with me are the treasures of Allah, nor that I know the Unseen, nor do I say; I am an angel. And I do not speak of them whom your eyes despise as those on whom Allah will not bestow any good. Allah knows best what is in their souls. Verily in that case I should be of the wrong-doers.'

32. They said: O Noah! Surely you have disputed with us and multiplied the dispute with us; now bring us that with which you threaten us, if you be of the truth-tellers.'

33. He said: 'Only Allah will bring it on you if He will, and you will not escape.

34. Nor would my good counsel profit you even if I wished to give you good counsel, if Allah wished to keep you astray. He is your Lord, and to Him you shall be returned.'

إِنَّهُم مُّلَٰقُوا۟ رَبِّهِمْ وَلَٰكِنِّىٓ أَرَىٰكُمْ قَوْمًا تَجْهَلُونَ ﴿٢٩﴾

وَيَٰقَوْمِ مَن يَنصُرُنِى مِنَ ٱللَّهِ إِن طَرَدتُّهُمْ أَفَلَا تَذَكَّرُونَ ﴿٣٠﴾

وَلَآ أَقُولُ لَكُمْ عِندِى خَزَآئِنُ ٱللَّهِ وَلَآ أَعْلَمُ ٱلْغَيْبَ وَلَآ أَقُولُ إِنِّى مَلَكٌ وَلَآ أَقُولُ لِلَّذِينَ تَزْدَرِىٓ أَعْيُنُكُمْ لَن يُؤْتِيَهُمُ ٱللَّهُ خَيْرًا ٱللَّهُ أَعْلَمُ بِمَا فِىٓ أَنفُسِهِمْ إِنِّىٓ إِذًا لَّمِنَ ٱلظَّٰلِمِينَ ﴿٣١﴾

قَالُوا۟ يَٰنُوحُ قَدْ جَٰدَلْتَنَا فَأَكْثَرْتَ جِدَٰلَنَا فَأْتِنَا بِمَا تَعِدُنَآ إِن كُنتَ مِنَ ٱلصَّٰدِقِينَ ﴿٣٢﴾

قَالَ إِنَّمَا يَأْتِيكُم بِهِ ٱللَّهُ إِن شَآءَ وَمَآ أَنتُم بِمُعْجِزِينَ ﴿٣٣﴾

وَلَا يَنفَعُكُمْ نُصْحِىٓ إِنْ أَرَدتُّ أَنْ أَنصَحَ لَكُمْ إِن كَانَ ٱللَّهُ يُرِيدُ أَن يُغْوِيَكُمْ هُوَ رَبُّكُمْ وَإِلَيْهِ تُرْجَعُونَ ﴿٣٤﴾

35. Or do they say, 'he has fabricated it?' Say: 'On me be my guilt, and I am quit of that of which you are guilty.'

Section 4

36. And to Noah it was revealed; verily none of your people will believe save those who have believed already, so do not be distressed at what they have been doing.

37. And make you the ark under Our eyes and Our revelation; and do not address Me regarding those who have done wrong; they are surely to be drowned.

38. And as he was making the ark, and whenever the chiefs of the people passed by him they scoffed at him. He said: 'If you scoff at us, we also shall scoff at you, as you scoff at us.

39. So presently you shall know on whom comes a torment that humiliates him, and on whom is let loose the torment lasting.'

40. Thus were they employed when Our decree came and the oven boiled over. We said: 'Carry thereon of every kind two, and your household, save him thereof against whom the Word has already gone forth, and the faithful.' And these had not believed with him save a few.

أَمْ يَقُولُونَ ٱفْتَرَىٰهُ قُلْ إِنِ ٱفْتَرَيْتُهُۥ فَعَلَىَّ إِجْرَامِى وَأَنَا۠ بَرِىٓءٌ مِّمَّا تُجْرِمُونَ ﴿٣٥﴾

وَأُوحِىَ إِلَىٰ نُوحٍ أَنَّهُۥ لَن يُؤْمِنَ مِن قَوْمِكَ إِلَّا مَن قَدْ ءَامَنَ فَلَا تَبْتَئِسْ بِمَا كَانُوا۟ يَفْعَلُونَ ﴿٣٦﴾

وَٱصْنَعِ ٱلْفُلْكَ بِأَعْيُنِنَا وَوَحْيِنَا وَلَا تُخَٰطِبْنِى فِى ٱلَّذِينَ ظَلَمُوٓا۟ إِنَّهُم مُّغْرَقُونَ ﴿٣٧﴾

وَيَصْنَعُ ٱلْفُلْكَ وَكُلَّمَا مَرَّ عَلَيْهِ مَلَأٌ مِّن قَوْمِهِۦ سَخِرُوا۟ مِنْهُ قَالَ إِن تَسْخَرُوا۟ مِنَّا فَإِنَّا نَسْخَرُ مِنكُمْ كَمَا تَسْخَرُونَ ﴿٣٨﴾

فَسَوْفَ تَعْلَمُونَ مَن يَأْتِيهِ عَذَابٌ يُخْزِيهِ وَيَحِلُّ عَلَيْهِ عَذَابٌ مُّقِيمٌ ﴿٣٩﴾

حَتَّىٰٓ إِذَا جَآءَ أَمْرُنَا وَفَارَ ٱلتَّنُّورُ قُلْنَا ٱحْمِلْ فِيهَا مِن كُلٍّ زَوْجَيْنِ ٱثْنَيْنِ وَأَهْلَكَ إِلَّا مَن سَبَقَ عَلَيْهِ ٱلْقَوْلُ وَمَنْ ءَامَنَ وَمَآ ءَامَنَ مَعَهُۥٓ إِلَّا قَلِيلٌ ﴿٤٠﴾

41. And he said: 'Embark therein; in the name of Allah be its course and its anchorage; verily my Lord is the Forgiving, the Merciful.'

وَقَالَ ٱرْكَبُوا۟ فِيهَا بِسْمِ ٱللَّهِ مَجْرٜىٰهَا وَمُرْسَىٰهَآ إِنَّ رَبِّى لَغَفُورٌ رَّحِيمٌ ﴿٤١﴾

42. And it moved on with them amidst waves like mountains, and Noah called out to his son, and he was apart; my son! Embark with us, and be not with the infidels.'

وَهِىَ تَجْرِى بِهِمْ فِى مَوْجٍ كَٱلْجِبَالِ وَنَادَىٰ نُوحٌ ٱبْنَهُۥ وَكَانَ فِى مَعْزِلٍ يَٰبُنَىَّ ٱرْكَب مَّعَنَا وَلَا تَكُن مَّعَ ٱلْكَٰفِرِينَ ﴿٤٢﴾

43. He said: 'I shall betake me to a mountain which will shield me from the water.' Noah said: 'There is no protector today from the decree of Allah save for one on whom He has mercy.' And a wave intervened between the two; so he was of the drowned.

قَالَ سَـَٔاوِىٓ إِلَىٰ جَبَلٍ يَعْصِمُنِى مِنَ ٱلْمَآءِ قَالَ لَا عَاصِمَ ٱلْيَوْمَ مِنْ أَمْرِ ٱللَّهِ إِلَّا مَن رَّحِمَ وَحَالَ بَيْنَهُمَا ٱلْمَوْجُ فَكَانَ مِنَ ٱلْمُغْرَقِينَ ﴿٤٣﴾

44. And it was said: 'O earth, swallow up your water, and cease, O heaven;' And the water abated; and fulfilled was the decree. And it rested upon the Judi, and it was said; away with the wrong – doing people.

وَقِيلَ يَٰٓأَرْضُ ٱبْلَعِى مَآءَكِ وَيَٰسَمَآءُ أَقْلِعِى وَغِيضَ ٱلْمَآءُ وَقُضِىَ ٱلْأَمْرُ وَٱسْتَوَتْ عَلَى ٱلْجُودِىِّ وَقِيلَ بُعْدًا لِّلْقَوْمِ ٱلظَّٰلِمِينَ ﴿٤٤﴾

45. And Noah cried to his Lord, and said: 'Lord! Verily my son is of my household, and Your promise is the Truth, and You are the Greatest of rulers.'

وَنَادَىٰ نُوحٌ رَّبَّهُۥ فَقَالَ رَبِّ إِنَّ ٱبْنِى مِنْ أَهْلِى وَإِنَّ وَعْدَكَ ٱلْحَقُّ وَأَنتَ أَحْكَمُ ٱلْحَٰكِمِينَ ﴿٤٥﴾

46. He said: 'O Noah! Verily he is not of your household! Verily, he is of the unrighteous conduct; so do not ask Me that of which you have no knowledge. I exhort you to be not of the ignorant.'

قَالَ يَٰنُوحُ إِنَّهُۥ لَيْسَ مِنْ أَهْلِكَ إِنَّهُۥ عَمَلٌ غَيْرُ صَٰلِحٍ فَلَا تَسْـَٔلْنِ مَا لَيْسَ لَكَ بِهِۦ عِلْمٌ إِنِّىٓ أَعِظُكَ أَن تَكُونَ مِنَ ٱلْجَٰهِلِينَ ﴿٤٦﴾

47. Noah said: 'Lord! I take refuge with You lest I may ask You that of which I have no knowledge. And if You forgive me not and have no mercy on me, I shall be among the losers.'

قَالَ رَبِّ إِنِّيٓ أَعُوذُ بِكَ أَنْ أَسْـَٔلَكَ مَا لَيْسَ لِي بِهِۦ عِلْمٌ وَإِلَّا تَغْفِرْ لِي وَتَرْحَمْنِىٓ أَكُن مِّنَ ٱلْخَٰسِرِينَ ۝

48. It was said: 'O Noah! Get you down with peace from Us and blessings upon you and the communities with you. And there shall be communities whom We shall let enjoy themselves, and afterwards there shall befall them from Us an afflictive torment.'

قِيلَ يَٰنُوحُ ٱهْبِطْ بِسَلَٰمٍ مِّنَّا وَبَرَكَٰتٍ عَلَيْكَ وَعَلَىٰٓ أُمَمٍ مِّمَّن مَّعَكَ وَأُمَمٌ سَنُمَتِّعُهُمْ ثُمَّ يَمَسُّهُم مِّنَّا عَذَابٌ أَلِيمٌ ۝

49. That is of the stories of the Unseen! We reveal it to you; you knew it not, nor did your nation know it ere this. So be you steadfast; verily the happy end is for the God-fearing.

تِلْكَ مِنْ أَنۢبَآءِ ٱلْغَيْبِ نُوحِيهَآ إِلَيْكَ مَا كُنتَ تَعْلَمُهَآ أَنتَ وَلَا قَوْمُكَ مِن قَبْلِ هَٰذَا فَٱصْبِرْ إِنَّ ٱلْعَٰقِبَةَ لِلْمُتَّقِينَ ۝

Section 5

50. And We sent to the 'Ad their brother, Hūd. He said: 'O my people! Worship Allah, there is no god but He; you are but fabricators.

وَإِلَىٰ عَادٍ أَخَاهُمْ هُودًا قَالَ يَٰقَوْمِ ٱعْبُدُوا۟ ٱللَّهَ مَا لَكُم مِّنْ إِلَٰهٍ غَيْرُهُۥٓ إِنْ أَنتُمْ إِلَّا مُفْتَرُونَ ۝

51. O my people! I ask of you no wage therefor; my reward is only on Him Who created me, will you not then reflect?

يَٰقَوْمِ لَآ أَسْـَٔلُكُمْ عَلَيْهِ أَجْرًا إِنْ أَجْرِىَ إِلَّا عَلَى ٱلَّذِى فَطَرَنِىٓ أَفَلَا تَعْقِلُونَ ۝

52. O my people, ask forgiveness of your Lord, then repent to Him; He will send upon you the heavens pouring, and He will add strength upon your strength and turn not away as guilty ones.'

وَيَٰقَوْمِ ٱسْتَغْفِرُوا۟ رَبَّكُمْ ثُمَّ تُوبُوٓا۟ إِلَيْهِ يُرْسِلِ ٱلسَّمَآءَ عَلَيْكُم مِّدْرَارًا وَيَزِدْكُمْ قُوَّةً إِلَىٰ قُوَّتِكُمْ وَلَا تَتَوَلَّوْا۟ مُجْرِمِينَ ﴿٥٢﴾

53. They said: 'O Hūd! You have not brought us evidence and we are not going to abandon our gods for your saying, nor are we going to be believers in you.

قَالُوا۟ يَٰهُودُ مَا جِئْتَنَا بِبَيِّنَةٍ وَمَا نَحْنُ بِتَارِكِىٓ ءَالِهَتِنَا عَن قَوْلِكَ وَمَا نَحْنُ لَكَ بِمُؤْمِنِينَ ﴿٥٣﴾

54. All that we say is that some of our gods have stuck you with evil.' He said: 'Verily I call Allah to witness, and bear you witness, that I am quit of what you associate,

إِن نَّقُولُ إِلَّا ٱعْتَرَىٰكَ بَعْضُ ءَالِهَتِنَا بِسُوٓءٍ قَالَ إِنِّىٓ أُشْهِدُ ٱللَّهَ وَٱشْهَدُوٓا۟ أَنِّى بَرِىٓءٌ مِّمَّا تُشْرِكُونَ ﴿٥٤﴾

55. With Him. So plot against me all together and do not respite me.

مِن دُونِهِۦ فَكِيدُونِى جَمِيعًا ثُمَّ لَا تُنظِرُونِ ﴿٥٥﴾

56. I rely on Allah, my Lord; no moving creature is there whose destiny He does not control,[419] verily my Lord is on the straight path.

إِنِّى تَوَكَّلْتُ عَلَى ٱللَّهِ رَبِّى وَرَبِّكُم مَّا مِن دَآبَّةٍ إِلَّا هُوَ ءَاخِذٌۢ بِنَاصِيَتِهَآ إِنَّ رَبِّى عَلَىٰ صِرَٰطٍ مُّسْتَقِيمٍ ﴿٥٦﴾

---

419. Literally, He holds it by its forelock, i.e. He exercises absolute power over it. The idiom, in Arabic, refers to a horse's forelock; the animal held in this manner being considered to be reduced to the lowest subjection. The moral is: everything, large or small, is in the firm grasp of God.

57. If then you turn away, I have preached to you that with which I was sent to you. And my Lord will set up in succession a people other than you, and you shall not be able to harm Him at all, verily my Lord is over everything a Guardian.'

فَإِن تَوَلَّوْا فَقَدْ أَبْلَغْتُكُم مَّآ أُرْسِلْتُ بِهِۦ إِلَيْكُمْ وَيَسْتَخْلِفُ رَبِّى قَوْمًا غَيْرَكُمْ وَلَا تَضُرُّونَهُۥ شَيْـًٔا إِنَّ رَبِّى عَلَىٰ كُلِّ شَىْءٍ حَفِيظٌ ۝

58. And then when Our decree came to pass, We delivered Hud and those who believed with him by a mercy from Us, and We delivered them from a rough torment.

وَلَمَّا جَآءَ أَمْرُنَا نَجَّيْنَا هُودًا وَٱلَّذِينَ ءَامَنُوا مَعَهُۥ بِرَحْمَةٍ مِّنَّا وَنَجَّيْنَٰهُم مِّنْ عَذَابٍ غَلِيظٍ ۝

59. Such were the 'Ād. They opposed the signs of their Lord and denied His Messengers and followed the bidding of any tyrant.

وَتِلْكَ عَادٌ جَحَدُوا بِـَٔايَٰتِ رَبِّهِمْ وَعَصَوْا رُسُلَهُۥ وَٱتَّبَعُوٓا أَمْرَ كُلِّ جَبَّارٍ عَنِيدٍ ۝

60. And they were followed in this world by a curse, and so will they be on Judgement Day. Lo; verily the 'Ad disbelieved in the Lord. Lo! Away with 'Ad, the people of Hud.

وَأُتْبِعُوا فِى هَٰذِهِ ٱلدُّنْيَا لَعْنَةً وَيَوْمَ ٱلْقِيَٰمَةِ أَلَآ إِنَّ عَادًا كَفَرُوا رَبَّهُمْ أَلَا بُعْدًا لِّعَادٍ قَوْمِ هُودٍ ۝

Section 6

61. And to the Thamūd We sent their brother Ṣāliḥ. He said: 'O my people! Worship Allah, there is no god for you but He. He has made you spring out from the earth and has made you dwell therein. Therefore ask forgiveness of Him, then turn to Him in repentance; verily my Lord is the Nigh, the Responsive.'

وَإِلَىٰ ثَمُودَ أَخَاهُمْ صَٰلِحًا قَالَ يَٰقَوْمِ ٱعْبُدُوا ٱللَّهَ مَا لَكُم مِّنْ إِلَٰهٍ غَيْرُهُۥ هُوَ أَنشَأَكُم مِّنَ ٱلْأَرْضِ وَٱسْتَعْمَرَكُمْ فِيهَا فَٱسْتَغْفِرُوهُ ثُمَّ تُوبُوٓا إِلَيْهِ إِنَّ رَبِّى قَرِيبٌ مُّجِيبٌ ۝

62. They said: 'O Ṣāliḥ! Hitherto you were amongst us as one hoped for. Do you forbid us to worship what our fathers have worshipped? We are in disquieting doubt regarding that to which you call us.'

قَالُوۡا يَـٰصَـٰلِحُ قَدۡ كُنۡتَ فِيۡنَا مَرۡجُوًّا قَبۡلَ هَـٰذَآ أَتَنۡهَـٰنَآ أَن نَّعۡبُدَ مَا يَعۡبُدُ ءَابَآؤُنَا وَإِنَّنَا لَفِىۡ شَكٍّ مِّمَّا تَدۡعُوۡنَآ إِلَيۡهِ مُرِيۡبٍ ۝

63. He said: 'O my people! Think! If I stand upon evidence from my Lord, and there has come to me from Him a mercy, then who will succour me against Allah, if I disobey Him? You then increase me not save in loss.

قَالَ يَـٰقَوۡمِ أَرَءَيۡتُمۡ إِن كُنۡتُ عَلَىٰ بَيِّنَةٍ مِّن رَّبِّىۡ وَءَاتَىٰنِىۡ مِنۡهُ رَحۡمَةً فَمَن يَنصُرُنِىۡ مِنَ اللَّهِ إِنۡ عَصَيۡتُهُ فَمَا تَزِيۡدُوۡنَنِىۡ غَيۡرَ تَخۡسِيۡرٍ ۝

64. And O my people! Here is the she-camel of Allah, a sign to you; so leave her to graze at will in Allah's land, and do not touch her with evil, lest there may overtake you an instant chastisement.'

وَيَـٰقَوۡمِ هَـٰذِهِۦ نَاقَةُ اللَّهِ لَكُمۡ ءَايَةً فَذَرُوۡهَا تَأۡكُلۡ فِىۡ أَرۡضِ اللَّهِ وَلَا تَمَسُّوۡهَا بِسُوۤءٍ فَيَأۡخُذَكُمۡ عَذَابٌ قَرِيۡبٌ ۝

65. Yet they hamstrung her. Then he said: 'Enjoy yourselves in your dwellings only for three days, a prophecy sure to be fulfilled.'

فَعَقَرُوۡهَا فَقَالَ تَمَتَّعُوۡا فِىۡ دَارِكُمۡ ثَلَـٰثَةَ أَيَّامٍ ذَٰلِكَ وَعۡدٌ غَيۡرُ مَكۡذُوۡبٍ ۝

66. Then when Our decree came to pass, We delivered Salih and those who believed with him, by a mercy from Us and from the humiliation of that day. Verily your Lord! He is the Strong, the Mighty.

فَلَمَّا جَآءَ أَمۡرُنَا نَجَّيۡنَا صَـٰلِحًا وَالَّذِيۡنَ ءَامَنُوۡا مَعَهُۥ بِرَحۡمَةٍ مِّنَّا وَمِنۡ خِزۡىِ يَوۡمِئِذٍ إِنَّ رَبَّكَ هُوَ الۡقَوِىُّ الۡعَزِيۡزُ ۝

67. And the shout overtook those who had done wrong, so they lay in their dwellings crouching,

وَأَخَذَ الَّذِيۡنَ ظَلَمُوا الصَّيۡحَةُ فَأَصۡبَحُوۡا فِىۡ دِيَارِهِمۡ جَـٰثِمِيۡنَ ۝

68. As though they had never lived at ease therein. Lo! Verily the Thamūd disbelieved in their Lord. Lo! Away with the Thamūd.

كَأَن لَّمۡ يَغۡنَوۡا۟ فِيهَآ أَلَآ إِنَّ ثَمُودَا۟ كَفَرُوا۟ رَبَّهُمۡ أَلَا بُعۡدًا لِّلثَّمُودِ ۝

Section 7

69. And assuredly Our Messengers came to Abraham with glad tidings. They said: 'Peace!' He said: 'Peace!' And soon he brought a calf roasted.

وَلَقَدۡ جَآءَتۡ رُسُلُنَآ إِبۡرَٰهِيمَ بِالۡبُشۡرَىٰ قَالُوا۟ سَلَٰمًا قَالَ سَلَٰمٌ فَمَا لَبِثَ أَن جَآءَ بِعِجۡلٍ حَنِيذٍ ۝

70. And when he saw that their hands did not touch it he mistrusted them, and conceived a fear of them. They said: 'Do not fear; verily we are sent to the people of Lot.'

فَلَمَّا رَءَآ أَيۡدِيَهُمۡ لَا تَصِلُ إِلَيۡهِ نَكِرَهُمۡ وَأَوۡجَسَ مِنۡهُمۡ خِيفَةً قَالُوا۟ لَا تَخَفۡ إِنَّآ أُرۡسِلۡنَآ إِلَىٰ قَوۡمِ لُوطٍ ۝

71. And his wife was standing by; she laughed. And We gave her the glad tidings of Isaac and after Isaac, Jacob.

وَامۡرَأَتُهُۥ قَآئِمَةٌ فَضَحِكَتۡ فَبَشَّرۡنَٰهَا بِإِسۡحَٰقَ وَمِن وَرَآءِ إِسۡحَٰقَ يَعۡقُوبَ ۝

72. She said: 'O for me! Shall I bear a child when I am old? And this my husband is advanced in years! A marvellous thing is this!'

قَالَتۡ يَٰوَيۡلَتَىٰٓ ءَأَلِدُ وَأَنَا۠ عَجُوزٌ وَهَٰذَا بَعۡلِي شَيۡخًا إِنَّ هَٰذَا لَشَىۡءٌ عَجِيبٌ ۝

73. They said: 'Marvel you the decree of Allah? The mercy of Allah and His blessings be upon you. O people of the house, verily He is the Praiseworthy, the Glorious.'

قَالُوٓا۟ أَتَعۡجَبِينَ مِنۡ أَمۡرِ اللَّهِ رَحۡمَتُ اللَّهِ وَبَرَكَٰتُهُۥ عَلَيۡكُمۡ أَهۡلَ الۡبَيۡتِ إِنَّهُۥ حَمِيدٌ مَّجِيدٌ ۝

74. Then when alarm had left Abraham and the glad tidings had come home to him, he took to disputing with Us for the people of Lot.

فَلَمَّا ذَهَبَ عَنْ إِبْرَٰهِيمَ ٱلرَّوْعُ وَجَآءَتْهُ ٱلْبُشْرَىٰ يُجَٰدِلُنَا فِى قَوْمِ لُوطٍ ۝

75. Verily Abraham was forbearing, long suffering, penitent.

إِنَّ إِبْرَٰهِيمَ لَحَلِيمٌ أَوَّٰهٌ مُّنِيبٌ ۝

76. Abraham! Leave off this; the decree from your Lord has already come, and verily upon them an approaching torment is unavoidable.

يَٰٓإِبْرَٰهِيمُ أَعْرِضْ عَنْ هَٰذَآ إِنَّهُۥ قَدْ جَآءَ أَمْرُ رَبِّكَ وَإِنَّهُمْ ءَاتِيهِمْ عَذَابٌ غَيْرُ مَرْدُودٍ ۝

77. And when Our envoys came to Lot, he was distressed on their account, and he felt straitened for them, and he said, 'this is a dreadful day.'

وَلَمَّا جَآءَتْ رُسُلُنَا لُوطًا سِىٓءَ بِهِمْ وَضَاقَ بِهِمْ ذَرْعًا وَقَالَ هَٰذَا يَوْمٌ عَصِيبٌ ۝

78. And his people came to him rushing on towards him, and they were wont to work vices before he said: 'O my people! Here are my daughters; clean are they for you, so fear Allah and do not disgrace me in the face of my guests; is there among you no man right-minded?'

وَجَآءَهُۥ قَوْمُهُۥ يُهْرَعُونَ إِلَيْهِ وَمِن قَبْلُ كَانُوا۟ يَعْمَلُونَ ٱلسَّيِّـَٔاتِ قَالَ يَٰقَوْمِ هَٰٓؤُلَآءِ بَنَاتِى هُنَّ أَطْهَرُ لَكُمْ فَٱتَّقُوا۟ ٱللَّهَ وَلَا تُخْزُونِ فِى ضَيْفِىٓ أَلَيْسَ مِنكُمْ رَجُلٌ رَّشِيدٌ ۝

79. They said: 'Assuredly you know that we have no right to your daughters, and verily you know what we would have.'

قَالُوا۟ لَقَدْ عَلِمْتَ مَا لَنَا فِى بَنَاتِكَ مِنْ حَقٍّ وَإِنَّكَ لَتَعْلَمُ مَا نُرِيدُ ۝

80. He said: 'Would that I had strength against you or could betake me to a powerful support!'

قَالَ لَوْ أَنَّ لِى بِكُمْ قُوَّةً أَوْ ءَاوِىٓ إِلَىٰ رُكْنٍ شَدِيدٍ ۝

81. They said: 'O Lot! Verily we are envoys of your Lord; they shall by no means reach you. Go forth you with your household in a part of the night, and let none of you look back save your wife. Certainly what happens to them will happen to her also, this appointment is for the morning; is not morning nigh?'

قَالُوا۟ يَٰلُوطُ إِنَّا رُسُلُ رَبِّكَ لَن يَصِلُوٓا۟ إِلَيْكَ فَأَسْرِ بِأَهْلِكَ بِقِطْعٍ مِّنَ ٱلَّيْلِ وَلَا يَلْتَفِتْ مِنكُمْ أَحَدٌ إِلَّا ٱمْرَأَتَكَ إِنَّهُۥ مُصِيبُهَا مَآ أَصَابَهُمْ إِنَّ مَوْعِدَهُمُ ٱلصُّبْحُ أَلَيْسَ ٱلصُّبْحُ بِقَرِيبٍ ﴿٨١﴾

82. Then when Our decree came to pass, We turned the upside thereof downward, and We rained thereon stones of baked clay, piled up,

فَلَمَّا جَآءَ أَمْرُنَا جَعَلْنَا عَٰلِيَهَا سَافِلَهَا وَأَمْطَرْنَا عَلَيْهَا حِجَارَةً مِّن سِجِّيلٍ مَّنضُودٍ ﴿٨٢﴾

83. Marked from before your Lord. Nor are they far away from those wrong-doers.

مُّسَوَّمَةً عِندَ رَبِّكَ وَمَا هِىَ مِنَ ٱلظَّٰلِمِينَ بِبَعِيدٍ ﴿٨٣﴾

Section 8

84. And to the Madyan We sent their brother Shu'ayb. He said: 'O my people! Worship Allah; there is no god for you but He. Do not give short measure and weight. I find you in prosperity, and verily I fear for you the torment of an encompassing Day.

وَإِلَىٰ مَدْيَنَ أَخَاهُمْ شُعَيْبًا قَالَ يَٰقَوْمِ ٱعْبُدُوا۟ ٱللَّهَ مَا لَكُم مِّنْ إِلَٰهٍ غَيْرُهُۥ وَلَا تَنقُصُوا۟ ٱلْمِكْيَالَ وَٱلْمِيزَانَ إِنِّىٓ أَرَىٰكُم بِخَيْرٍ وَإِنِّىٓ أَخَافُ عَلَيْكُمْ عَذَابَ يَوْمٍ مُّحِيطٍ ﴿٨٤﴾

85. O my people! Give full measure and weight with equity, and do not defraud the people of their things, and do not commit mischief on the earth as corrupters.

وَيَٰقَوْمِ أَوْفُوا۟ ٱلْمِكْيَالَ وَٱلْمِيزَانَ بِٱلْقِسْطِ وَلَا تَبْخَسُوا۟ ٱلنَّاسَ أَشْيَآءَهُمْ وَلَا تَعْثَوْا۟ فِى ٱلْأَرْضِ مُفْسِدِينَ ﴿٨٥﴾

86. Allah's remainder is better for you, if you are believers, and I am not over you a guardian.'

بَقِيَّتُ اللّٰهِ خَيْرٌ لَّكُمْ إِن كُنتُم مُّؤْمِنِينَ ۚ وَمَآ أَنَا۠ عَلَيْكُم بِحَفِيظٍ ۝

87. They said: 'O Shu‘ayb! Does your prayer bid you that we should abandon what our fathers worshipped; or that we should not do with our riches whatsoever we will? You, indeed! You certainly are mild, right-minded!'

قَالُوا۟ يَٰشُعَيْبُ أَصَلَوٰتُكَ تَأْمُرُكَ أَن نَّتْرُكَ مَا يَعْبُدُ ءَابَآؤُنَآ أَوْ أَن نَّفْعَلَ فِىٓ أَمْوَٰلِنَا مَا نَشَٰٓؤُا۟ ۖ إِنَّكَ لَأَنتَ ٱلْحَلِيمُ ٱلرَّشِيدُ ۝

88. He said: 'O my people think, if I rested upon evidence from my Lord, and He has provided me with a goodly provision from Himself, shall I fail to deliver His Message? I do not desire, in order to oppose you, to do what I forbid you. I desire only reformation so far as I am able, and my hope is not a success save with Allah; in Him I rely and to Him I turn in repentance.

قَالَ يَٰقَوْمِ أَرَءَيْتُمْ إِن كُنتُ عَلَىٰ بَيِّنَةٍ مِّن رَّبِّى وَرَزَقَنِى مِنْهُ رِزْقًا حَسَنًا ۚ وَمَآ أُرِيدُ أَنْ أُخَالِفَكُمْ إِلَىٰ مَآ أَنْهَىٰكُمْ عَنْهُ ۚ إِنْ أُرِيدُ إِلَّا ٱلْإِصْلَٰحَ مَا ٱسْتَطَعْتُ ۚ وَمَا تَوْفِيقِىٓ إِلَّا بِٱللّٰهِ ۚ عَلَيْهِ تَوَكَّلْتُ وَإِلَيْهِ أُنِيبُ ۝

89. O my people! Let not the cleavage with me incite you so that there befall you the like of what befell the people of Noah and the people of Hūd and the people of Ṣāliḥ and the people of Lot are not far away from you.

وَيَٰقَوْمِ لَا يَجْرِمَنَّكُمْ شِقَاقِىٓ أَن يُصِيبَكُم مِّثْلُ مَآ أَصَابَ قَوْمَ نُوحٍ أَوْ قَوْمَ هُودٍ أَوْ قَوْمَ صَٰلِحٍ ۚ وَمَا قَوْمُ لُوطٍ مِّنكُم بِبَعِيدٍ ۝

90. Ask forgiveness of your Lord, and turn to Him in repentance; verily my Lord is Merciful, Loving.'

وَٱسْتَغْفِرُوا۟ رَبَّكُمْ ثُمَّ تُوبُوٓا۟ إِلَيْهِ ۚ إِنَّ رَبِّى رَحِيمٌ وَدُودٌ ۝

91. They said: 'O Shu'ayb! We do not understand much of what you say, and verily we see you weak among us; and were it not for your tribe we would surely have stoned you, and you are not mighty among us.'

قَالُوا يَٰشُعَيۡبُ مَا نَفۡقَهُ كَثِيرًا مِّمَّا تَقُولُ وَإِنَّا لَنَرَىٰكَ فِينَا ضَعِيفًا وَلَوۡلَا رَهۡطُكَ لَرَجَمۡنَٰكَ وَمَآ أَنتَ عَلَيۡنَا بِعَزِيزٍ ۝

92. He said: 'O my people! Is my tribe then stronger with you than Allah? Him you have cast behind your back, neglected; verily my Lord is the Encompasser of what you do.

قَالَ يَٰقَوۡمِ أَرَهۡطِىٓ أَعَزُّ عَلَيۡكُم مِّنَ ٱللَّهِ وَٱتَّخَذۡتُمُوهُ وَرَآءَكُمۡ ظِهۡرِيًّا إِنَّ رَبِّى بِمَا تَعۡمَلُونَ مُحِيطٌ ۝

93. 'O my people! Act according to your station, verily I am going to work in my way; presently you will know on whom comes a chastisement, humiliating him and who is a liar. And watch; I am also with you a watcher.'

وَيَٰقَوۡمِ ٱعۡمَلُوا عَلَىٰ مَكَانَتِكُمۡ إِنِّى عَٰمِلٌ سَوۡفَ تَعۡلَمُونَ مَن يَأۡتِيهِ عَذَابٌ يُخۡزِيهِ وَمَنۡ هُوَ كَٰذِبٌ وَٱرۡتَقِبُوٓا إِنِّى مَعَكُمۡ رَقِيبٌ ۝

94. And when Our decree came to pass, We delivered Shu'ayb and those who believed with him by a mercy from Us, and the shout overtook them who did wrong, so they lay in their dwellings crouching;

وَلَمَّا جَآءَ أَمۡرُنَا نَجَّيۡنَا شُعَيۡبًا وَٱلَّذِينَ ءَامَنُوا مَعَهُۥ بِرَحۡمَةٍ مِّنَّا وَأَخَذَتِ ٱلَّذِينَ ظَلَمُوا ٱلصَّيۡحَةُ فَأَصۡبَحُوا فِى دِيَٰرِهِمۡ جَٰثِمِينَ ۝

95. As though they had never lived at ease therein. Lo! A far removal for the Madyan, even as the Thamūd were removed afar!

كَأَن لَّمۡ يَغۡنَوۡا فِيهَآ أَلَا بُعۡدًا لِّمَدۡيَنَ كَمَا بَعِدَتۡ ثَمُودُ ۝

Section 9

96. And assuredly We sent Moses with Our signs and a clear authority;

وَلَقَدْ أَرْسَلْنَا مُوسَىٰ بِآيَٰتِنَا وَسُلْطَٰنٍ مُّبِينٍ ﴿٩٦﴾

97. To Pharaoh, and his chiefs. They followed the commandment of Pharaoh, and the commandment of Pharaoh was not rightly-directed.

إِلَىٰ فِرْعَوْنَ وَمَلَإِيْهِ فَٱتَّبَعُوٓاْ أَمْرَ فِرْعَوْنَ وَمَآ أَمْرُ فِرْعَوْنَ بِرَشِيدٍ ﴿٩٧﴾

98. He shall head his people on the Day of Resurrection and cause them to descend into the Fire, ill is the descent so descended!

يَقْدُمُ قَوْمَهُ يَوْمَ ٱلْقِيَٰمَةِ فَأَوْرَدَهُمُ ٱلنَّارَ وَبِئْسَ ٱلْوِرْدُ ٱلْمَوْرُودُ ﴿٩٨﴾

99. And they were followed in this world by a curse, and so they will be on the Day of Resurrection, ill is the present so presented!

وَأُتْبِعُواْ فِى هَٰذِهِ لَعْنَةً وَيَوْمَ ٱلْقِيَٰمَةِ بِئْسَ ٱلرِّفْدُ ٱلْمَرْفُودُ ﴿٩٩﴾

100. That is from the stories of the cities which We recount to you; of them some are standing and some mown down.

ذَٰلِكَ مِنْ أَنۢبَآءِ ٱلْقُرَىٰ نَقُصُّهُ عَلَيْكَ مِنْهَا قَآئِمٌ وَحَصِيدٌ ﴿١٠٠﴾

101. And We wronged them not, but they wronged themselves. So their gods whom they called upon besides Allah did not avail them in any way, when there came the decree of your Lord, they added to them nothing save perdition.

وَمَا ظَلَمْنَٰهُمْ وَلَٰكِن ظَلَمُوٓاْ أَنفُسَهُمْ فَمَآ أَغْنَتْ عَنْهُمْ ءَالِهَتُهُمُ ٱلَّتِى يَدْعُونَ مِن دُونِ ٱللَّهِ مِن شَىْءٍ لَّمَّا جَآءَ أَمْرُ رَبِّكَ وَمَا زَادُوهُمْ غَيْرَ تَتْبِيبٍ ﴿١٠١﴾

102. Such is the overtaking of your Lord when He overtakes the cities while they are wrong-doers; verily His overtaking is afflictive, severe.

وَكَذَٰلِكَ أَخْذُ رَبِّكَ إِذَآ أَخَذَ ٱلْقُرَىٰ وَهِىَ ظَـٰلِمَةٌ إِنَّ أَخْذَهُۥ أَلِيمٌ شَدِيدٌ ۝

103. Verily, herein is a sign to him who fears the torment of the Hereafter. That is a Day whereon mankind shall be gathered together, and that is a Day to be witnessed.

إِنَّ فِى ذَٰلِكَ لَءَايَةً لِّمَنْ خَافَ عَذَابَ ٱلْءَاخِرَةِ ذَٰلِكَ يَوْمٌ مَّجْمُوعٌ لَّهُ ٱلنَّاسُ وَذَٰلِكَ يَوْمٌ مَّشْهُودٌ ۝

104. And We defer it not but to a term determined.

وَمَا نُؤَخِّرُهُۥٓ إِلَّا لِأَجَلٍ مَّعْدُودٍ ۝

105. The day it comes, no soul shall speak save by His leave; then of them some shall be wretched and some blest.

يَوْمَ يَأْتِ لَا تَكَلَّمُ نَفْسٌ إِلَّا بِإِذْنِهِۦ فَمِنْهُمْ شَقِىٌّ وَسَعِيدٌ ۝

106. As for those who shall be wretched, they shall be in the Fire, there for them shall be panting and roaring.

فَأَمَّا ٱلَّذِينَ شَقُوا۟ فَفِى ٱلنَّارِ لَهُمْ فِيهَا زَفِيرٌ وَشَهِيقٌ ۝

107. They shall abide there so long as the heavens and the earth remain, save as your Lord may will. Verily your Lord is the doer of whatever He intends.[420]

خَـٰلِدِينَ فِيهَا مَا دَامَتِ ٱلسَّمَـٰوَٰتُ وَ ٱلْأَرْضُ إِلَّا مَا شَآءَ رَبُّكَ إِنَّ رَبَّكَ فَعَّالٌ لِّمَا يُرِيدُ ۝

---

420. He is without any let or hindrance on the part of anyone. His power is All-in-All. He can do anything, and is not bound by any conditions or by any co-equal entities. This refutes *in toto* the position of deists and others who have restricted Divine activity to the creation of the world and the fixation of its primary collocations, and also the doctrine of those who like the Arya Samaj, conceive of God as no other than 'a great Cosmic Executive, whose business is to preside over the inexorable processes of transmigration and Karma' (*ERE*. II. p. 60). In Greece, the power even of the highest god was limited, and overruling fate then became an inexorable law, before which even he must bow.' (*DB*. V. p. 147). The God of Islam rules and sways the world and man, subordinates the laws of nature to His will, and is not governed by them. It is His will which is Supreme and All-Powerful, and not any abstract cosmic law.

108. And as for those who shall be blest, they shall be in the Garden, abiding therein so long as the heavens and the earth remain, save as your Lord may will, a gift unending.

وَأَمَّا ٱلَّذِينَ سُعِدُواْ فَفِى ٱلْجَنَّةِ خَٰلِدِينَ فِيهَا مَا دَامَتِ ٱلسَّمَٰوَٰتُ وَٱلْأَرْضُ إِلَّا مَا شَآءَ رَبُّكَ عَطَآءً غَيْرَ مَجْذُوذٍ ۝

109. So be not you in doubt concerning what these people worship. They worship only as their fathers worshipped before; and verily We will repay them their portion in full, undiminished.

فَلَا تَكُ فِى مِرْيَةٍ مِّمَّا يَعْبُدُ هَٰٓؤُلَآءِ مَا يَعْبُدُونَ إِلَّا كَمَا يَعْبُدُ ءَابَآؤُهُم مِّن قَبْلُ وَإِنَّا لَمُوَفُّوهُمْ نَصِيبَهُمْ غَيْرَ مَنقُوصٍ ۝

Section 10

110. And assuredly We gave the Book to Moses, and disputation arose thereabout; and had not a word preceded from your Lord, it would have been decreed between them. And verily they are concerning that in disquieting doubt.

وَلَقَدْ ءَاتَيْنَا مُوسَى ٱلْكِتَٰبَ فَٱخْتُلِفَ فِيهِ وَلَوْلَا كَلِمَةٌ سَبَقَتْ مِن رَّبِّكَ لَقُضِىَ بَيْنَهُمْ وَإِنَّهُمْ لَفِى شَكٍّ مِّنْهُ مُرِيبٍ ۝

111. And to each of them your Lord will repay their works in full; verily He is aware of what they work.

وَإِنَّ كُلًّا لَّمَّا لَيُوَفِّيَنَّهُمْ رَبُّكَ أَعْمَٰلَهُمْ إِنَّهُۥ بِمَا يَعْمَلُونَ خَبِيرٌ ۝

112. So stand you straight as you have been bidden, you and whoever repented with you, and do not be arrogant; verily He is the beholder of what you work.

فَٱسْتَقِمْ كَمَآ أُمِرْتَ وَمَن تَابَ مَعَكَ وَلَا تَطْغَوْاْ إِنَّهُۥ بِمَا تَعْمَلُونَ بَصِيرٌ ۝

113. And do not lean towards those who do wrong, lest the Fire should touch you, and you have no protector besides Allah nor you would then be succoured.

وَلَا تَرۡكَنُوٓاۡ إِلَى ٱلَّذِينَ ظَلَمُواۡ فَتَمَسَّكُمُ ٱلنَّارُ وَمَا لَكُم مِّن دُونِ ٱللَّهِ مِنۡ أَوۡلِيَآءَ ثُمَّ لَا تُنصَرُونَ ۝

114. Establish you prayer at the two ends of the day, and in some watches of the night. Verily virtues obliterate vices. That is a reminder to the mindful.

وَأَقِمِ ٱلصَّلَوٰةَ طَرَفِيِ ٱلنَّهَارِ وَزُلَفًا مِّنَ ٱلَّيۡلِ إِنَّ ٱلۡحَسَنَٰتِ يُذۡهِبۡنَ ٱلسَّيِّئَاتِ ذَٰلِكَ ذِكۡرَىٰ لِلذَّٰكِرِينَ ۝

115. And be patient you; verily Allah does not waste the reward of the well-doers.

وَٱصۡبِرۡ فَإِنَّ ٱللَّهَ لَا يُضِيعُ أَجۡرَ ٱلۡمُحۡسِنِينَ ۝

116. Why were there not among the generations before you owners of wisdom restraining others from corruption on the earth, except a few of those whom We delivered from among them? And those who did wrong followed that in which they luxuriated, and they had been sinners.

فَلَوۡلَا كَانَ مِنَ ٱلۡقُرُونِ مِن قَبۡلِكُمۡ أُوۡلُواۡ بَقِيَّةٍ يَنۡهَوۡنَ عَنِ ٱلۡفَسَادِ فِي ٱلۡأَرۡضِ إِلَّا قَلِيلًا مِّمَّنۡ أَنجَيۡنَا مِنۡهُمۡ وَٱتَّبَعَ ٱلَّذِينَ ظَلَمُواۡ مَآ أُتۡرِفُواۡ فِيهِ وَكَانُواۡ مُجۡرِمِينَ ۝

117. And your Lord is not the One to destroy cities wrongfully while their inhabitants were men of rectitude.

وَمَا كَانَ رَبُّكَ لِيُهۡلِكَ ٱلۡقُرَىٰ بِظُلۡمٍ وَأَهۡلُهَا مُصۡلِحُونَ ۝

118. And had your Lord willed He would surely have made mankind of a single community; and they will not cease differing.

وَلَوۡ شَآءَ رَبُّكَ لَجَعَلَ ٱلنَّاسَ أُمَّةً وَٰحِدَةً وَلَا يَزَالُونَ مُخۡتَلِفِينَ ۝

119. Save those on whom your Lord has mercy; and for that He has created them. And fulfilled will be the Word of your Lord: surely I will fill Hell with the *jinn* and mankind together.

إِلَّا مَن رَّحِمَ رَبُّكَ وَلِذَٰلِكَ خَلَقَهُمۡ وَتَمَّتۡ كَلِمَةُ رَبِّكَ لَأَمۡلَأَنَّ جَهَنَّمَ مِنَ ٱلۡجِنَّةِ وَٱلنَّاسِ أَجۡمَعِينَ ۝

120. And all that We recount to you of the stories of the Messengers is in order that We make your heart firm thereby. And in this there has come to you Truth and an exhortation and an admonition to the believers.

وَكُلًّا نَّقُصُّ عَلَيْكَ مِنْ أَنۢبَآءِ ٱلرُّسُلِ مَا نُثَبِّتُ بِهِۦ فُؤَادَكَ ۚ وَجَآءَكَ فِى هَٰذِهِ ٱلْحَقُّ وَمَوْعِظَةٌ وَذِكْرَىٰ لِلْمُؤْمِنِينَ ۝

121. And say to those who do not believe: 'Act according to your station, verily we are going to work in our way.

وَقُل لِّلَّذِينَ لَا يُؤْمِنُونَ ٱعْمَلُوا۟ عَلَىٰ مَكَانَتِكُمْ إِنَّا عَٰمِلُونَ ۝

122. Await; as verily we are awaiting.

وَٱنتَظِرُوٓا۟ إِنَّا مُنتَظِرُونَ ۝

123. Allah's is the Unseen of the heavens and the earth. And to Him will that whole affair be brought back. So worship Him and rely on Him; and your Lord is not heedless of what you work.'

وَلِلَّهِ غَيْبُ ٱلسَّمَٰوَٰتِ وَٱلْأَرْضِ وَإِلَيْهِ يُرْجَعُ ٱلْأَمْرُ كُلُّهُۥ فَٱعْبُدْهُ وَتَوَكَّلْ عَلَيْهِ ۚ وَمَا رَبُّكَ بِغَٰفِلٍ عَمَّا تَعْمَلُونَ ۝

Sūrah 12

Yūsuf

(Makkan, 12 Sections, 111 Verses)

*In the name of Allah, the
Compassionate, the Merciful.*

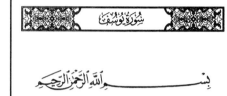

Section 1

1.   *Alif, Lām, Rā.* These are the
verses of a Book luminous.

2.   Verily We! We have sent it
down, an Arabic recitation, that
perchance you may reflect.

3.   We! We recount to you the
best of stories,[421] by revealing to
you, this Qur'ān, though you have
been hitherto among the unaware
ones.

4.   Recall when Joseph said to
his father: 'O my father! I have
seen eleven stars and the sun and
the moon; I have seen them
prostrating themselves before
me.'

---

421. The story of Joseph as given in the Qur'ān 'is similar to but not identical with
the Biblical story'; but the atmosphere is wholly different. 'The Biblical story is like
a folk – tale in which morality has no place. Its tendency is to exalt the clever and
financially – minded Jew against the Egyptian, and to explain certain ethnic and
tribal peculiarities in later Jewish history. Joseph is shown as buying up all the
cattle and the land of the poor Egyptians for the state under the stress of famine
conditions, and making the Israelites "rulers over Pharaoh's cattle". The Qur'ānic
story, on the other hand, is less a narrative than a highly spiritual sermon explaining
the seeming contradictions in life, the enduring nature of virtue in a world full of flex
and change, and the marvellous working of God's eternal purpose in His Plan is
unfolded to us on the wide canvas of history' (AYA.).

5. He said: 'O my son! Do not recount your vision to your brethren, lest they may scheme a plot against you. Verily Satan is to men a manifest enemy.'

قَالَ يَبُنَيَّ لَا تَقۡصُصۡ رُءۡيَاكَ عَلَىٰٓ إِخۡوَتِكَ فَيَكِيدُوۡا لَكَ كَيۡدًا إِنَّ الشَّيۡطَٰنَ لِلۡإِنسَٰنِ عَدُوٌّ مُّبِينٌ ۝

6. And thus will your Lord choose you and teach you of the interpretation of discourses, and will fulfill His favour upon you and upon the house of Jacob, as He has fulfilled it upon your fathers, Abraham and Isaac formerly. Verily your Lord is the Knowing, the Wise.

وَكَذَٰلِكَ يَجۡتَبِيكَ رَبُّكَ وَيُعَلِّمُكَ مِن تَأۡوِيلِ الۡأَحَادِيثِ وَيُتِمُّ نِعۡمَتَهُۥ عَلَيۡكَ وَعَلَىٰٓ ءَالِ يَعۡقُوبَ كَمَآ أَتَمَّهَا عَلَىٰٓ أَبَوَيۡكَ مِن قَبۡلُ إِبۡرَٰهِيمَ وَإِسۡحَٰقَ إِنَّ رَبَّكَ عَلِيمٌ حَكِيمٌ ۝

Section 2

7. Assuredly in Joseph and his brethren there have been signs for the inquirers.

لَّقَدۡ كَانَ فِى يُوۡسُفَ وَإِخۡوَتِهِۦٓ ءَايَٰتٌ لِّلسَّآئِلِينَ ۝

8. Recall when they said: 'Surely Joseph and his brother are dearer to our father than we, whereas we are a band; our father is in a manifest error indeed.

إِذۡ قَالُوۡا لَيُوۡسُفُ وَأَخُوهُ أَحَبُّ إِلَىٰٓ أَبِينَا مِنَّا وَنَحۡنُ عُصۡبَةٌ إِنَّ أَبَانَا لَفِى ضَلَٰلٍ مُّبِينٍ ۝

9. Slay Joseph or cast him away to some land; your father's solicitude will be free for you and you will be thereafter a people favoured.'

اقۡتُلُوۡا يُوۡسُفَ أَوِ اطۡرَحُوهُ أَرۡضًا يَخۡلُ لَكُمۡ وَجۡهُ أَبِيكُمۡ وَتَكُونُوۡا مِنۢ بَعۡدِهِۦ قَوۡمًا صَٰلِحِينَ ۝

10. Said a speaker from among them: 'Do not slay Joseph, but cast him into the bottom of a well, some of the caravan will take him up, if you must be doing.'

قَالَ قَآئِلٌ مِّنۡهُمۡ لَا تَقۡتُلُوۡا يُوۡسُفَ وَأَلۡقُوهُ فِى غَيَٰبَتِ الۡجُبِّ يَلۡتَقِطۡهُ بَعۡضُ السَّيَّارَةِ إِن كُنتُمۡ فَٰعِلِينَ ۝

11. They said: 'O our father! Why is it that you do not trust us with Joseph, whereas we are his well-wishers?

قَالُوۡا یٰۤاَبَانَا مَا لَكَ لَا تَاۡمَنَّا عَلٰی یُوۡسُفَ وَ اِنَّا لَهٗ لَنٰصِحُوۡنَ ۝

12. Send him with us tomorrow, that he may refresh himself and play, and we are to be his guards.'

اَرۡسِلۡهُ مَعَنَا غَدًا یَّرۡتَعۡ وَ یَلۡعَبۡ وَ اِنَّا لَهٗ لَحٰفِظُوۡنَ ۝

13. He said: 'Verily it grieves me that you should take him away, and I fear lest a wolf may devour him, while you are negligent of him.'

قَالَ اِنِّیۡ لَیَحۡزُنُنِیۡۤ اَنۡ تَذۡهَبُوۡا بِهٖ وَ اَخَافُ اَنۡ یَّاۡكُلَهُ الذِّئۡبُ وَ اَنۡتُمۡ عَنۡهُ غٰفِلُوۡنَ ۝

14. They said: 'If the wolf devoured him despite our numbers, we shall surely be lost.'

قَالُوۡا لَئِنۡ اَكَلَهُ الذِّئۡبُ وَ نَحۡنُ عُصۡبَةٌ اِنَّاۤ اِذًا لَّخٰسِرُوۡنَ ۝

15. So when they took him away and resolved to place him in the bottom of the well, We revealed to him: 'Surely you will declare to them their affair, while they perceive it not.'

فَلَمَّا ذَهَبُوۡا بِهٖ وَ اَجۡمَعُوۡۤا اَنۡ یَّجۡعَلُوۡهُ فِیۡ غَیٰبَتِ الۡجُبِّ وَ اَوۡحَیۡنَاۤ اِلَیۡهِ لَتُنَبِّئَنَّهُمۡ بِاَمۡرِهِمۡ هٰذَا وَ هُمۡ لَا یَشۡعُرُوۡنَ ۝

16. And they came to their father at nightfall, weeping.

وَ جَآءُوۡۤ اَبَاهُمۡ عِشَآءً یَّبۡكُوۡنَ ۝

17. They said: 'Father! We went off competing and left Joseph by our stuff, so a wolf devoured him; and you will not put credence in us; though we are the truth-tellers.'

قَالُوۡا یٰۤاَبَانَاۤ اِنَّا ذَهَبۡنَا نَسۡتَبِقُ وَ تَرَكۡنَا یُوۡسُفَ عِنۡدَ مَتَاعِنَا فَاَكَلَهُ الذِّئۡبُ وَ مَاۤ اَنۡتَ بِمُؤۡمِنٍ لَّنَا وَ لَوۡ كُنَّا صٰدِقِیۡنَ ۝

18. And they brought his shirt with false blood. He said: 'Nay! You have embellished for yourself an affair; so patience is seemly. And Allah is to be implored for help in what you ascribe.'

وَجَآءُوْ عَلَىٰ قَمِيصِهِ بِدَمٍ كَذِبٍ قَالَ بَلْ سَوَّلَتْ لَكُمْ أَنْفُسُكُمْ أَمْرًا فَصَبْرٌ جَمِيلٌ وَاللّٰهُ الْمُسْتَعَانُ عَلَىٰ مَا تَصِفُوْنَ ۝

19. And there came a caravan, and they sent their water-drawer, and he let down his bucket. He said: 'O glad tidings! Here is a youth.' They hid him as merchandise. And Allah was the knower of what they did.

وَجَآءَتْ سَيَّارَةٌ فَأَرْسَلُوْا وَارِدَهُمْ فَأَدْلَىٰ دَلْوَهُ قَالَ يَا بُشْرَىٰ هٰذَا غُلَامٌ وَأَسَرُّوْهُ بِضَاعَةً وَاللّٰهُ عَلِيْمٌ بِمَا يَعْمَلُوْنَ ۝

20. And they sold him for a mean price, a few counted dirhams; and they were in regard to him indifferent.

وَشَرَوْهُ بِثَمَنٍ بَخْسٍ دَرَاهِمَ مَعْدُوْدَةٍ وَكَانُوْا فِيْهِ مِنَ الزَّاهِدِيْنَ ۝

Section 3

21. And he who bought him in Egypt said to his wife: 'make his lodging goodly; perchance he may profit us or we may take him as a son.' And thus We made a place for Joseph in the land, and it was in order that We may instruct him in the interpretation of discourses. And Allah is dominant in His purpose, but most men know not.

وَقَالَ الَّذِي اشْتَرَىٰهُ مِنْ مِّصْرَ لِامْرَأَتِهِ أَكْرِمِيْ مَثْوَاهُ عَسَىٰ أَنْ يَنْفَعَنَا أَوْ نَتَّخِذَهُ وَلَدًا وَكَذَلِكَ مَكَّنَّا لِيُوْسُفَ فِي الْأَرْضِ وَلِنُعَلِّمَهُ مِنْ تَأْوِيْلِ الْأَحَادِيْثِ وَاللّٰهُ غَالِبٌ عَلَىٰ أَمْرِهِ وَلٰكِنَّ أَكْثَرَ النَّاسِ لَا يَعْلَمُوْنَ ۝

22. And when he reached his maturity, We endowed him with judgement and knowledge; and thus We recompose the well-doers.

وَلَمَّا بَلَغَ أَشُدَّهُ ءَاتَيْنَاهُ حُكْمًا وَعِلْمًا وَكَذَلِكَ نَجْزِي الْمُحْسِنِيْنَ ۝

23. And she in whose house he was solicited him and she closed the doors and said: 'Come on, O you!' He said: 'Allah be my refuge: Verily he is my Master, He has made me a goodly dwelling, verily the wrong-doers do not prosper.'

وَرَٰوَدَتْهُ ٱلَّتِى هُوَ فِى بَيْتِهَا عَن نَّفْسِهِۦ وَغَلَّقَتِ ٱلْأَبْوَٰبَ وَقَالَتْ هَيْتَ لَكَ قَالَ مَعَاذَ ٱللَّهِ إِنَّهُۥ رَبِّىٓ أَحْسَنَ مَثْوَاىَ إِنَّهُۥ لَا يُفْلِحُ ٱلظَّٰلِمُونَ ﴿٢٣﴾

24. And assuredly she besought him, and he would have besought her were it not that he had seen the argument of his Lord. Thus We did, in order that We might avert from him all evil and indecency; verily he was a single-hearted bondman of Ours.

وَلَقَدْ هَمَّتْ بِهِۦ وَهَمَّ بِهَا لَوْلَآ أَن رَّءَا بُرْهَٰنَ رَبِّهِۦ كَذَٰلِكَ لِنَصْرِفَ عَنْهُ ٱلسُّوٓءَ وَٱلْفَحْشَآءَ إِنَّهُۥ مِنْ عِبَادِنَا ٱلْمُخْلَصِينَ ﴿٢٤﴾

25. And the two raced to the door, and she rent his shirt from behind. And the two met her master at the door. She said: 'What is the recompense of him who intended evil towards your household except that he be imprisoned, or an afflictive chastisement?'

وَٱسْتَبَقَا ٱلْبَابَ وَقَدَّتْ قَمِيصَهُۥ مِن دُبُرٍ وَأَلْفَيَا سَيِّدَهَا لَدَا ٱلْبَابِ قَالَتْ مَا جَزَآءُ مَنْ أَرَادَ بِأَهْلِكَ سُوٓءًا إِلَّآ أَن يُسْجَنَ أَوْ عَذَابٌ أَلِيمٌ ﴿٢٥﴾

26. He said, 'it is she who solicited me.' And a witness from her own household bore witness; if his shirt is rent in front, she speaks truth and he is a liar.

قَالَ هِىَ رَٰوَدَتْنِى عَن نَّفْسِى وَشَهِدَ شَاهِدٌ مِّنْ أَهْلِهَآ إِن كَانَ قَمِيصُهُۥ قُدَّ مِن قُبُلٍ فَصَدَقَتْ وَهُوَ مِنَ ٱلْكَٰذِبِينَ ﴿٢٦﴾

27. But if his shirt is rent from behind, she lies and he is a truth-teller.

وَإِن كَانَ قَمِيصُهُۥ قُدَّ مِن دُبُرٍ فَكَذَبَتْ وَهُوَ مِنَ ٱلصَّٰدِقِينَ ﴿٢٧﴾

28. So when he saw his shirt rent from behind, he said: 'Verily it is the guile of you women; the guile of you women is mighty.[422]

فَلَمَّا رَءَا قَمِيصَهُ قُدَّ مِن دُبُرٍ قَالَ إِنَّهُ مِن كَيْدِكُنَّ إِنَّ كَيْدَكُنَّ عَظِيمٌ ۝

29. 'Joseph! Turn away therefrom; and you woman! Ask forgiveness for your sin; verily you have been guilty.'

يُوسُفُ أَعْرِضْ عَنْ هَذَا وَٱسْتَغْفِرِى لِذَنبِكِ إِنَّكِ كُنتِ مِنَ ٱلْخَاطِئِينَ ۝

Section 4

30. And women in the town said: 'The wife of the 'Azīz has solicited her page, he has inflamed her with love, verily we see her in manifest error.'

وَقَالَ نِسْوَةٌ فِى ٱلْمَدِينَةِ ٱمْرَأَتُ ٱلْعَزِيزِ تُرَٰوِدُ فَتَىٰهَا عَن نَّفْسِهِ قَدْ شَغَفَهَا حُبًّا إِنَّا لَنَرَىٰهَا فِى ضَلَٰلٍ مُّبِينٍ ۝

---

422. Notice that this is not the dictum of Islam, but an observation of Potiphar – a view that has found favour with many non-Muslim savants and writers. 'Nature has not destined them, as the weaker sex, to be dependent on strength, but on cunning; that is why they are instinctively crafty, and have an ineradicable tendency to lie' (Schopenhauer, *Essays*, p. 66). Compare the following Buddhist aphorism: 'Inscrutable as the way of a fish in water is the nature of women, those thieves of many devices, with whom truth is hard to find' (*ERE*. V. p. 271). Compare also the observations of modern scientific writers: 'Everyone is acquainted with instances from life or from the history of women whose quick and cunning ruses have saved lover or husband or child. It is inevitable, and results from the constitution of women, acting in the conditions under which they are generally placed' (Havelock Ellis, *Man and Woman*, p. 196), From folklore and myth, from national proverbs and traditions, and from the text–books of the oldest religions, therefore, we learn that woman is two–faced, or false, or treacherous, or disloyal' (Ludovici, *The Woman*, p. 304). 'Woman's tendency to ruse and deception is a constant, positive and life–promoting instinct'. (Ibid., p. 307, n.). 'Finally among the great thinkers of Europe who have held the view that women are indifferent to truth, and incapable of rectitude. I would further mention Rousseau, Diderot, La Bruyere, and that great genius Kant'. (Ibid., p. 320, n.).

31. Then when she heard of their cunning talk, she sent to them a messenger and prepared for them a repose, and provided each with a knife. And she said: 'Come forth to them.' Then when they saw him, they were astonished at him, and they made a cut in their hands, and said: 'How perfect is God! No man is he; he is no one but a noble angel.'

فَلَمَّا سَمِعَتۡ بِمَكۡرِهِنَّ أَرۡسَلَتۡ إِلَیۡهِنَّ وَ أَعۡتَدَتۡ لَهُنَّ مُتَّكَأً وَءَاتَتۡ كُلَّ وَٰحِدَةٍ مِّنۡهُنَّ سِكِّینًا وَقَالَتِ اخۡرُجۡ عَلَیۡهِنَّ فَلَمَّا رَأَیۡنَهُۥۤ أَكۡبَرۡنَهُۥ وَقَطَّعۡنَ أَیۡدِیَهُنَّ وَقُلۡنَ حَٰشَ لِلَّهِ مَا هَٰذَا بَشَرًا إِنۡ هَٰذَاۤ إِلَّا مَلَكٌ كَرِیمٌ ۝

32. She said: 'This is he whom you reproached me for. Assuredly I solicited him, but he abstained. Yet if he does not what I wish him to do, he is sure to be imprisoned and sure to be humbled.'

قَالَتۡ فَذَٰلِكُنَّ الَّذِی لُمۡتُنَّنِی فِیهِۖ وَلَقَدۡ رَٰوَدتُّهُۥ عَن نَّفۡسِهِۦ فَاسۡتَعۡصَمَۖ وَلَئِن لَّمۡ یَفۡعَلۡ مَاۤ ءَامُرُهُۥ لَیُسۡجَنَنَّ وَلَیَكُونًا مِّنَ الصَّٰغِرِینَ ۝

33. He said: 'My Lord! Prison is dearer to me than that these women call me to; and if You do not avert their guile from me I should incline to them and become of the ignorant.'[423]

قَالَ رَبِّ السِّجۡنُ أَحَبُّ إِلَیَّ مِمَّا یَدۡعُونَنِیۤ إِلَیۡهِۖ وَإِلَّا تَصۡرِفۡ عَنِّی كَیۡدَهُنَّ أَصۡبُ إِلَیۡهِنَّ وَأَكُن مِّنَ الۡجَٰهِلِینَ ۝

34. Then his Lord answered to him and averted their guile from him. Verily He! He is the Hearer, the Knower!

فَاسۡتَجَابَ لَهُۥ رَبُّهُۥ فَصَرَفَ عَنۡهُ كَیۡدَهُنَّ إِنَّهُۥ هُوَ السَّمِیعُ الۡعَلِیمُ ۝

35. Thereafter it occurred to them, even after they had seen the signs, to imprison him for a season.

ثُمَّ بَدَا لَهُم مِّنۢ بَعۡدِ مَا رَأَوُا الۡءَایَٰتِ لَیَسۡجُنُنَّهُۥ حَتَّىٰ حِینٍ ۝

---

423. Note the entire dependence of God's Prophets on His protection.

Section 5

36. And there entered with him two pages in the prison. One of them said: 'Verily I saw myself pressing wine'; and the other said: 'Verily I saw myself carrying upon my head bread whereof the birds were eating.' Declare to us the interpretation thereof, verily we see you of the well-doers.'[424]

وَدَخَلَ مَعَهُ ٱلسِّجْنَ فَتَيَانِ قَالَ أَحَدُهُمَا إِنِّي أَرَىٰنِي أَعْصِرُ خَمْرًا وَقَالَ ٱلْآخَرُ إِنِّي أَرَىٰنِي أَحْمِلُ فَوْقَ رَأْسِي خُبْزًا تَأْكُلُ ٱلطَّيْرُ مِنْهُ نَبِّئْنَا بِتَأْوِيلِهِ إِنَّا نَرَىٰكَ مِنَ ٱلْمُحْسِنِينَ ﴿٣٦﴾

37. He said: 'No food will come to you for your sustenance but before it comes to you I shall have declared to you the interpretation thereof. That is of what my Lord has taught me.[425] Verily I have abandoned the creed of a people who do not believe in Allah and who are disbelievers in the Hereafter.[426]

قَالَ لَا يَأْتِيكُمَا طَعَامٌ تُرْزَقَانِهِ إِلَّا نَبَّأْتُكُمَا بِتَأْوِيلِهِ قَبْلَ أَن يَأْتِيَكُمَا ذَٰلِكُمَا مِمَّا عَلَّمَنِي رَبِّي إِنِّي تَرَكْتُ مِلَّةَ قَوْمٍ لَّا يُؤْمِنُونَ بِٱللَّهِ وَهُم بِٱلْآخِرَةِ هُمْ كَٰفِرُونَ ﴿٣٧﴾

---

424. Joseph's fellow-prisoners had evidently perceived his marks of wisdom, piety and beneficence, features characteristic of a Prophet of God.

425. In other words, that there is no personal credit to me; all this is God's free gift and blessing. Further, by making a distinct reference to God's gift, Joseph distinguishes his power of true interpretation of dreams from the crudities of magicians and soothsayers.

426. The Egyptians were of course ignorant of the Unity of God, and were for all practical purposes deniers of Resurrection. 'Presumably, this world appeared to the ancient Egyptian in a light so fine that in general he was unable to conceive of a time when it should be no more, and when no Egyptian should dwell any more on the banks of the Nile' (*DB*. V. p. 181). Note that it is the Qur'ān, not the Bible, that credits Joseph, as befits the character of a Prophet, with this excellent discourse on True Religion.

38. 'And I have followed the creed of my fathers, Abraham and Isaac and Jacob; it is not for us to associate anything with Allah. That is of Allah's grace upon us and mankind, but most of mankind thank not.

39. 'O my two fellow prisoners! Are sundry lords better or Allah the One, the Subduer?

40. You do not worship besides Him, but only names you have forged, you and your fathers. Allah has not sent down for them any authority. Judgement is but Allah's;[427] He has commanded that you should worship none except Him. That is the right religion, but most of mankind know not.

41. O my two fellow prisoners! As for one of you he will pour out wine for his master, and as for the other, he will be crucified, and the birds will eat off his head; thus is decreed the affair, of which you two inquired.'

42. And he said to one of them, who he imagined would be saved: 'Mention me before your master.' But Satan caused him to forget to mention him to his lord. So that he stayed in the prison for several years.

427. His alone is the all-inclusive Sovereignty. In the theocracy of Islam, God is the only Sovereign, the only Law-giver. And this has a direct bearing on the political theory of the Islamic State.

Section 6

43. And the king said: 'I saw seven fat cows, which seven lean ones are devouring and seven green corn-ears and seven other dry. O chiefs! Give me an answer in regard to my vision, if a vision you are at all able to interpret.'

وَقَالَ ٱلْمَلِكُ إِنِّى أَرَىٰ سَبْعَ بَقَرَٰتٍ سِمَانٍ يَأْكُلُهُنَّ سَبْعٌ عِجَافٌ وَسَبْعَ سُنۢبُلَٰتٍ خُضْرٍ وَأُخَرَ يَابِسَٰتٍ يَٰٓأَيُّهَا ٱلْمَلَأُ أَفْتُونِى فِى رُءْيَٰىَ إِن كُنتُمْ لِلرُّءْيَا تَعْبُرُونَ ﴿٤٣﴾

44. They said: 'Medleys of a nightmare! And in the interpretation of a nightmare we are not skilled.'

قَالُوٓاْ أَضْغَٰثُ أَحْلَٰمٍ وَمَا نَحْنُ بِتَأْوِيلِ ٱلْأَحْلَٰمِ بِعَٰلِمِينَ ﴿٤٤﴾

45. Then the one of the two who was saved, now at length remembered and said: 'I shall declare to you interpretation thereof; so send me forth.'

وَقَالَ ٱلَّذِى نَجَا مِنْهُمَا وَٱدَّكَرَ بَعْدَ أُمَّةٍ أَنَا۠ أُنَبِّئُكُم بِتَأْوِيلِهِۦ فَأَرْسِلُونِ ﴿٤٥﴾

46. 'Joseph, O saint! Give an answer to us in regard to seven fat cows, which seven lean ones are devouring and seven green corn-ears and seven others dry. Perchance I may return to the people; perchance they may learn.'

يُوسُفُ أَيُّهَا ٱلصِّدِّيقُ أَفْتِنَا فِى سَبْعِ بَقَرَٰتٍ سِمَانٍ يَأْكُلُهُنَّ سَبْعٌ عِجَافٌ وَسَبْعِ سُنۢبُلَٰتٍ خُضْرٍ وَأُخَرَ يَابِسَٰتٍ لَّعَلِّىٓ أَرْجِعُ إِلَى ٱلنَّاسِ لَعَلَّهُمْ يَعْلَمُونَ ﴿٤٦﴾

47. He said: 'You shall sow seven years as is your wont, and what you reap leave in its ears, except a little of it which you may eat.

قَالَ تَزْرَعُونَ سَبْعَ سِنِينَ دَأَبًا فَمَا حَصَدتُّمْ فَذَرُوهُ فِى سُنۢبُلِهِۦٓ إِلَّا قَلِيلًا مِّمَّا تَأْكُلُونَ ﴿٤٧﴾

48. Thereafter will come seven hard years which will devour what you have laid up beforehand for them, except a little which you shall preserve.

ثُمَّ يَأْتِى مِنۢ بَعْدِ ذَٰلِكَ سَبْعٌ شِدَادٌ يَأْكُلْنَ مَا قَدَّمْتُمْ لَهُنَّ إِلَّا قَلِيلًا مِّمَّا تُحْصِنُونَ ﴿٤٨﴾

49. Thereafter will come another year when people will have rain and when they will press grapes.'

ثُمَّ يَأْتِى مِنْ بَعْدِ ذَلِكَ عَامٌ فِيهِ يُغَاثُ النَّاسُ وَفِيهِ يَعْصِرُونَ ۝

Section 7

50. And the king said: 'Bring him to me.' Then when the messenger came to him, he said: 'Return to your lord, and ask him, what about the women who cut their hands? Verily my Lord is the knower of their guile.'

وَقَالَ الْمَلِكُ ائْتُونِي بِهِ فَلَمَّا جَاءَهُ الرَّسُولُ قَالَ ارْجِعْ إِلَى رَبِّكَ فَسْئَلْهُ مَا بَالُ النِّسْوَةِ اللَّاتِي قَطَّعْنَ أَيْدِيَهُنَّ إِنَّ رَبِّي بِكَيْدِهِنَّ عَلِيمٌ ۝

51. He said: 'What was the matter with you when you solicited Joseph?' They said: 'How perfect is God! We know not of any evil against him.' The wife of 'Azīz said: 'Now has the truth come to light. It was I who sought to seduce him, and he is of the truth-tellers.'

قَالَ مَا خَطْبُكُنَّ إِذْ رَاوَدْتُنَّ يُوسُفَ عَن نَّفْسِهِ قُلْنَ حَاشَ لِلَّهِ مَا عَلِمْنَا عَلَيْهِ مِن سُوءٍ قَالَتِ امْرَأَتُ الْعَزِيزِ الْآنَ حَصْحَصَ الْحَقُّ أَنَا رَاوَدتُّهُ عَن نَّفْسِهِ وَإِنَّهُ لَمِنَ الصَّادِقِينَ ۝

52. He said: 'That I did in order that he may know that I did not betray him in secret, and that Allah guides not the guile of betrayers.

ذَلِكَ لِيَعْلَمَ أَنِّي لَمْ أَخُنْهُ بِالْغَيْبِ وَأَنَّ اللَّهَ لَا يَهْدِي كَيْدَ الْخَائِنِينَ ۝

53. Nor do I acquit myself. Verily the self ever urges to evil save that self on whom my Lord has mercy; verily my Lord is the Forgiving, the Merciful.'

وَمَا أُبَرِّئُ نَفْسِي إِنَّ النَّفْسَ لَأَمَّارَةٌ بِالسُّوءِ إِلَّا مَا رَحِمَ رَبِّي إِنَّ رَبِّي غَفُورٌ رَّحِيمٌ ۝

54. And the king said: 'Bring him to me. I shall single him out for myself.' Then when he spoke to him, he said: 'You are today with us high-placed, entrusted.'

وَقَالَ ٱلْمَلِكُ ٱئْتُونِي بِهِ أَسْتَخْلِصْهُ لِنَفْسِى فَلَمَّا كَلَّمَهُ قَالَ إِنَّكَ ٱلْيَوْمَ لَدَيْنَا مَكِينٌ أَمِينٌ ۝

55. He said: 'Set me over the store houses of the land; I shall be a knowing keeper.'

قَالَ ٱجْعَلْنِي عَلَىٰ خَزَآئِنِ ٱلْأَرْضِ إِنِّي حَفِيظٌ عَلِيمٌ ۝

56. In this wise We established Joseph in the land so that he might settle therein wherever he wished. We bestow of Our mercy on whom We will, and We are not to waste the reward of the well-doers.

وَكَذَٰلِكَ مَكَّنَّا لِيُوسُفَ فِي ٱلْأَرْضِ يَتَبَوَّأُ مِنْهَا حَيْثُ يَشَآءُ نُصِيبُ بِرَحْمَتِنَا مَن نَّشَآءُ وَلَا نُضِيعُ أَجْرَ ٱلْمُحْسِنِينَ ۝

57. And surely the reward of the Hereafter is better for those who believe and ever fear.

وَلَأَجْرُ ٱلْآخِرَةِ خَيْرٌ لِّلَّذِينَ ءَامَنُوا۟ وَكَانُوا۟ يَتَّقُونَ ۝

Section 8

58. And the brethren of Joseph came and entered unto him, and he recognized them, while they did not recognize him.

وَجَآءَ إِخْوَةُ يُوسُفَ فَدَخَلُوا۟ عَلَيْهِ فَعَرَفَهُمْ وَهُمْ لَهُ مُنكِرُونَ ۝

59. And when he had furnished them with their furnishing, he said: 'Bring to me a brother of yours from your father; do you not see that I give full measure and that I am the best of hosts?

وَلَمَّا جَهَّزَهُم بِجَهَازِهِمْ قَالَ ٱئْتُونِي بِأَخٍ لَّكُم مِّنْ أَبِيكُمْ أَلَا تَرَوْنَ أَنِّي أُوفِي ٱلْكَيْلَ وَأَنَا۠ خَيْرُ ٱلْمُنزِلِينَ ۝

60. But if you do not bring him to me there shall be no measuring for you from me and you shall not approach me.'

فَإِن لَّمْ تَأْتُونِي بِهِ فَلَا كَيْلَ لَكُمْ عِندِى وَلَا تَقْرَبُونِ ۝

61. They said: 'We will certainly solicit him of his father and certainly we will do it.'

قَالُوا سَنُرَوِدُ عَنْهُ أَبَاهُ وَإِنَّا لَفَاعِلُونَ ۝

62. And he said to his pages: 'Put their merchandise into their packs; they will find it when they reach back to their household; perchance they may return.'

وَقَالَ لِفِتْيَٰنِهِ اجْعَلُوا بِضَٰعَتَهُمْ فِي رِحَالِهِمْ لَعَلَّهُمْ يَعْرِفُونَهَا إِذَا انقَلَبُوٓا إِلَىٰٓ أَهْلِهِمْ لَعَلَّهُمْ يَرْجِعُونَ ۝

63. Then when they returned to their father, they said: 'Father, the measuring has been denied us, so send you with us our brother, and we shall get our measure; and certainly we shall be his guards.'

فَلَمَّا رَجَعُوٓا إِلَىٰٓ أَبِيهِمْ قَالُوا يَٰٓأَبَانَا مُنِعَ مِنَّا الْكَيْلُ فَأَرْسِلْ مَعَنَآ أَخَانَا نَكْتَلْ وَإِنَّا لَهُۥ لَحَٰفِظُونَ ۝

64. He said: 'I can trust you with him only as I trusted you with his brother before; Allah is the best Guard. He is the Most Merciful of the merciful.'

قَالَ هَلْ ءَامَنُكُمْ عَلَيْهِ إِلَّا كَمَآ أَمِنتُكُمْ عَلَىٰٓ أَخِيهِ مِن قَبْلُ فَاللَّهُ خَيْرٌ حَٰفِظًا وَهُوَ أَرْحَمُ الرَّٰحِمِينَ ۝

65. And when they opened their pack they found their merchandise returned to them; they said: 'Father! What more can we desire? Here is our merchandise returned to us, we shall have portions for our family and shall guard our brother and shall add another measure of a camel-load; this is only an easy measure.'

وَلَمَّا فَتَحُوا مَتَٰعَهُمْ وَجَدُوا بِضَٰعَتَهُمْ رُدَّتْ إِلَيْهِمْ قَالُوا يَٰٓأَبَانَا مَا نَبْغِى هَٰذِهِ بِضَٰعَتُنَا رُدَّتْ إِلَيْنَا وَنَمِيرُ أَهْلَنَا وَنَحْفَظُ أَخَانَا وَنَزْدَادُ كَيْلَ بَعِيرٍ ذَٰلِكَ كَيْلٌ يَسِيرٌ ۝

66. He said: 'I will by no means send him with you until you give me an assurance by Allah that you will bring him back to me, unless it be that you are prevented.' Then when they gave him their assurance, he said: 'Allah is a Witness over what we have said.'

قَالَ لَنْ أُرْسِلَهُ مَعَكُمْ حَتَّىٰ تُؤْتُونِ مَوْثِقًا مِّنَ اللَّهِ لَتَأْتُنَّنِى بِهِ إِلَّا أَن يُحَاطَ بِكُمْ فَلَمَّا ءَاتَوْهُ مَوْثِقَهُمْ قَالَ اللَّهُ عَلَىٰ مَا نَقُولُ وَكِيلٌ ۝

67. And he said: 'My sons! Do not enter by one gate, but enter by different gates, and I cannot avail you against Allah at all; judgement is but Allah's. On Him I rely, and on Him let the relying rely.'

وَقَالَ يَٰبَنِىَّ لَا تَدْخُلُوا۟ مِنۢ بَابٍ وَٰحِدٍ وَ ادْخُلُوا۟ مِنْ أَبْوَٰبٍ مُّتَفَرِّقَةٍ وَمَا أُغْنِى عَنكُم مِّنَ اللَّهِ مِن شَىْءٍ إِنِ الْحُكْمُ إِلَّا لِلَّهِ عَلَيْهِ تَوَكَّلْتُ وَعَلَيْهِ فَلْيَتَوَكَّلِ الْمُتَوَكِّلُونَ ۝

68. And when they entered as their father had enjoined them to enter, it did not avail them against Allah at all. It was only a craving in the heart of Jacob that he satisfied, verily he was endued with knowledge, for We had taught him;[428] but most people know not.

وَلَمَّا دَخَلُوا۟ مِنْ حَيْثُ أَمَرَهُمْ أَبُوهُم مَّا كَانَ يُغْنِى عَنْهُم مِّنَ اللَّهِ مِن شَىْءٍ إِلَّا حَاجَةً فِى نَفْسِ يَعْقُوبَ قَضَىٰهَا وَإِنَّهُ لَذُو عِلْمٍ لِّمَا عَلَّمْنَٰهُ وَلَٰكِنَّ أَكْثَرَ النَّاسِ لَا يَعْلَمُونَ ۝

Section 9

69. And when they entered unto Joseph, he betook his full brother to himself and said: 'I am your own brother Joseph, so do not grieve over what they have been doing.'

وَلَمَّا دَخَلُوا۟ عَلَىٰ يُوسُفَ ءَاوَىٰٓ إِلَيْهِ أَخَاهُ قَالَ إِنِّىٓ أَنَا۠ أَخُوكَ فَلَا تَبْتَئِسْ بِمَا كَانُوا۟ يَعْمَلُونَ ۝

---

428. So He knew and understood perfectly well that no human prudence could be really effective unless willed by God.

70. And when he had furnished them with their furnishing he placed the drinking-cup in his brother's pack. Thereafter a crier cried, 'Caravan men! You are thieves.'

فَلَمَّا جَهَّزَهُم بِجَهَازِهِمْ جَعَلَ ٱلسِّقَايَةَ فِى رَحْلِ أَخِيهِ ثُمَّ أَذَّنَ مُؤَذِّنٌ أَيَّتُهَا ٱلْعِيرُ إِنَّكُمْ لَسَٰرِقُونَ ٧٠

71. They said, as they turned to them: 'What is it that you are missing?'

قَالُوا۟ وَأَقْبَلُوا۟ عَلَيْهِم مَّاذَا تَفْقِدُونَ ٧١

72. They said: 'We miss the royal cup and for him who brings it shall be a camel-load, and of him I am a guarantor.'

قَالُوا۟ نَفْقِدُ صُوَاعَ ٱلْمَلِكِ وَلِمَن جَآءَ بِهِۦ حِمْلُ بَعِيرٍ وَأَنَا۠ بِهِۦ زَعِيمٌ ٧٢

73. They said: 'By God! Assuredly you know that we have not come to work corruption in the land, nor have we been thieves.'

قَالُوا۟ تَٱللَّهِ لَقَدْ عَلِمْتُم مَّا جِئْنَا لِنُفْسِدَ فِى ٱلْأَرْضِ وَمَا كُنَّا سَٰرِقِينَ ٧٣

74. They said: 'What shall be the penalty of him, if you are found liars?'

قَالُوا۟ فَمَا جَزَٰٓؤُهُۥ إِن كُنتُمْ كَٰذِبِينَ ٧٤

75. They said: 'His penalty is that he in whose pack it is found shall himself be the recompense thereof; thus we recompense the wrong-doers.'

قَالُوا۟ جَزَٰٓؤُهُۥ مَن وُجِدَ فِى رَحْلِهِۦ فَهُوَ جَزَٰٓؤُهُۥ كَذَٰلِكَ نَجْزِى ٱلظَّٰلِمِينَ ٧٥

76. Then he began with their sacks before the bag of his brother; then he brought it forth from the bag of his brother. In this wise We contrived for Joseph. He was not to get his brother by the law of the king, except that Allah willed. We exalt in degrees whom

فَبَدَأَ بِأَوْعِيَتِهِمْ قَبْلَ وِعَآءِ أَخِيهِ ثُمَّ ٱسْتَخْرَجَهَا مِن وِعَآءِ أَخِيهِ كَذَٰلِكَ كِدْنَا لِيُوسُفَ مَا كَانَ لِيَأْخُذَ أَخَاهُ فِى دِينِ ٱلْمَلِكِ إِلَّآ أَن يَشَآءَ ٱللَّهُ

We will, and above every knowing one is a knower.[429]

نَرْفَعُ دَرَجَتٍ مَّن نَّشَاءُ وَفَوْقَ كُلِّ ذِى عِلْمٍ عَلِيمٌ ۝

77. They said: 'If he steals, then a brother of his has stolen afore.' But Joseph concealed it in himself, and disclosed it not to them. He said: 'You are in evil plight, and Allah is the Best Knower of what you ascribe.'

قَالُوا إِن يَسْرِقْ فَقَدْ سَرَقَ أَخٌ لَّهُ مِن قَبْلُ فَأَسَرَّهَا يُوسُفُ فِى نَفْسِهِ وَلَمْ يُبْدِهَا لَهُمْ قَالَ أَنتُمْ شَرٌّ مَّكَانًا وَاللَّهُ أَعْلَمُ بِمَا تَصِفُونَ ۝

78. They said: 'O 'Azīz, verily he has a father, an old man very aged; so take one of us in his stead; verily we perceive you to be of the well-doers.'

قَالُوا يَأَيُّهَا الْعَزِيزُ إِنَّ لَهُ أَبًا شَيْخًا كَبِيرًا فَخُذْ أَحَدَنَا مَكَانَهُ إِنَّا نَرَٰكَ مِنَ الْمُحْسِنِينَ ۝

79. He said: 'God forbid that we should take anyone but him with whom we found our stuff; verily we then should be the wrong-doers.'

قَالَ مَعَاذَ اللَّهِ أَن نَّأْخُذَ إِلَّا مَن وَجَدْنَا مَتَٰعَنَا عِندَهُ إِنَّا إِذًا لَّظَٰلِمُونَ ۝

Section 10

80. Then when they despaired of him they counselled together privately. The eldest of them said: 'Do you not remember that your father has taken an assurance from you before Allah? And earlier you have been remiss in your duty in respect of Joseph; so I will by no means go forth from the land until my father gives me leave or Allah judges for me, and He is the Best of Judges.

فَلَمَّا اسْتَيْـَٔسُوا مِنْهُ خَلَصُوا نَجِيًّا قَالَ كَبِيرُهُمْ أَلَمْ تَعْلَمُوا أَنَّ أَبَاكُمْ قَدْ أَخَذَ عَلَيْكُم مَّوْثِقًا مِّنَ اللَّهِ وَمِن قَبْلُ مَا فَرَّطتُمْ فِى يُوسُفَ فَلَنْ أَبْرَحَ الْأَرْضَ حَتَّىٰ يَأْذَنَ لِى أَبِى أَوْ يَحْكُمَ اللَّهُ لِى وَهُوَ خَيْرُ الْحَٰكِمِينَ ۝

---

429. Human knowledge, however profound, is after all relative; in God Alone does perfection dwell. The passage is introduced as a corrective to human conceit.

81. Return to your father and say: 'Father! Verily your son has stolen, and we testify not save according to what we know, and of the unseen we could not be watchers.

وَارْجِعُوٓاْ إِلَىٰٓ أَبِيكُمْ فَقُولُواْ يَٰٓأَبَانَآ إِنَّ ٱبْنَكَ سَرَقَ وَمَا شَهِدْنَآ إِلَّا بِمَا عَلِمْنَا وَمَا كُنَّا لِلْغَيْبِ حَٰفِظِينَ ۝

82. And inquire of the people of the city where we have been and of the caravan with whom we have travelled there; and verily we speak truth.'

وَسْـَٔلِ ٱلْقَرْيَةَ ٱلَّتِي كُنَّا فِيهَا وَٱلْعِيرَ ٱلَّتِيٓ أَقْبَلْنَا فِيهَا وَإِنَّا لَصَٰدِقُونَ ۝

83. He said: 'Nay! Your minds have embellished for you an affair. So patience is comely. Perchance Allah may bring them all to me; verily He! Only He is the Knowing, the Wise.'

قَالَ بَلْ سَوَّلَتْ لَكُمْ أَنفُسُكُمْ أَمْرًا فَصَبْرٌ جَمِيلٌ عَسَى ٱللَّهُ أَن يَأْتِيَنِي بِهِمْ جَمِيعًا إِنَّهُۥ هُوَ ٱلْعَلِيمُ ٱلْحَكِيمُ ۝

84. And he turned away from them, and said: 'O my grief for Joseph!' and his eyes were whitened with grief, and he was choked with sorrow.

وَتَوَلَّىٰ عَنْهُمْ وَقَالَ يَٰٓأَسَفَىٰ عَلَىٰ يُوسُفَ وَٱبْيَضَّتْ عَيْنَاهُ مِنَ ٱلْحُزْنِ فَهُوَ كَظِيمٌ ۝

85. They said: 'By Allah, you will not cease remembering Joseph until you are wizened or you be of the dead.'

قَالُواْ تَٱللَّهِ تَفْتَؤُاْ تَذْكُرُ يُوسُفَ حَتَّىٰ تَكُونَ حَرَضًا أَوْ تَكُونَ مِنَ ٱلْهَٰلِكِينَ ۝

86. He said: 'I only bewail my anguish and sorrow unto Allah, and I know from Allah what you know not.

قَالَ إِنَّمَآ أَشْكُواْ بَثِّي وَحُزْنِيٓ إِلَى ٱللَّهِ وَأَعْلَمُ مِنَ ٱللَّهِ مَا لَا تَعْلَمُونَ ۝

87. My sons! Go and ascertain about Joseph and his brother, and despair not of the mercy of Allah; none despair of the mercy of Allah except a people disbelieving.'

يَٰبَنِيَّ ٱذْهَبُواْ فَتَحَسَّسُواْ مِن يُوسُفَ وَأَخِيهِ وَلَا تَايْـَٔسُواْ مِن رَّوْحِ ٱللَّهِ إِنَّهُۥ لَا يَايْـَٔسُ مِن رَّوْحِ ٱللَّهِ إِلَّا ٱلْقَوْمُ ٱلْكَٰفِرُونَ ۝

88. And when they entered unto him, they said: 'O 'Azīz! Distress has seized us and our family and we have brought scant goods, so give us full measure and be charitable to us; verily Allah rewards the charitable.'

فَلَمَّا دَخَلُوا عَلَيْهِ قَالُوا يَا أَيُّهَا الْعَزِيزُ مَسَّنَا وَأَهْلَنَا الضُّرُّ وَجِئْنَا بِبِضَاعَةٍ مُّزْجَاةٍ فَأَوْفِ لَنَا الْكَيْلَ وَتَصَدَّقْ عَلَيْنَا إِنَّ اللَّهَ يَجْزِي الْمُتَصَدِّقِينَ ۝

89. He said: 'Remember what you did to Joseph and his brother while you were ignorant?'

قَالَ هَلْ عَلِمْتُم مَّا فَعَلْتُم بِيُوسُفَ وَ أَخِيهِ إِذْ أَنتُمْ جَاهِلُونَ ۝

90. They said: 'Are you Joseph?' He said: 'I am Joseph and this is my brother; Allah has surely been gracious to us; verily he who fears God and endures affliction, then Allah leaves not the reward of well-doers to waste.'

قَالُوا أَإِنَّكَ لَأَنتَ يُوسُفُ قَالَ أَنَا يُوسُفُ وَهَـٰذَا أَخِي قَدْ مَنَّ اللَّهُ عَلَيْنَا إِنَّهُ مَن يَتَّقِ وَيَصْبِرْ فَإِنَّ اللَّهَ لَا يُضِيعُ أَجْرَ الْمُحْسِنِينَ ۝

91. They said: 'Verily Allah has chosen you above us, and we have been sinners indeed.'

قَالُوا تَاللَّهِ لَقَدْ آثَرَكَ اللَّهُ عَلَيْنَا وَإِن كُنَّا لَخَاطِئِينَ ۝

92. He said: 'No reproach on you today;[430] may Allah forgive you, and He is the Most Merciful of the merciful.

قَالَ لَا تَثْرِيبَ عَلَيْكُمُ الْيَوْمَ يَغْفِرُ اللَّهُ لَكُمْ وَهُوَ أَرْحَمُ الرَّاحِمِينَ ۝

93. Go with this shirt of mine and cast it upon my father's face; he shall become clear-sighted; and bring to me all your family.'

اذْهَبُوا بِقَمِيصِي هَـٰذَا فَأَلْقُوهُ عَلَى وَجْهِ أَبِي يَأْتِ بَصِيرًا وَأْتُونِي بِأَهْلِكُمْ أَجْمَعِينَ ۝

---

430. Joseph does not himself reproach his brothers. In identical language, the Holy Prophet freely forgives a whole population of his worst foes who were entirely at his mercy when he entered Makka as a conqueror at the head of a powerful army.

Section 11

94. And when the caravan had departed their father said: 'Surely I feel the breath of Joseph, if you do not think I am doting.'

وَلَمَّا فَصَلَتِ ٱلْعِيرُ قَالَ أَبُوهُمْ إِنِّى لَأَجِدُ رِيحَ يُوسُفَ لَوْلَا أَن تُفَنِّدُونِ ۝

95. They said: 'By Allah! You are in your old-time illusion.'

قَالُوا۟ تَٱللَّهِ إِنَّكَ لَفِى ضَلَٰلِكَ ٱلْقَدِيمِ ۝

96. Then when the bringer of the glad tidings arrived, he cast it upon his face and he became clear-sighted. He said: 'Did not I tell you, that I knew from Allah what you knew not?'

فَلَمَّا أَن جَآءَ ٱلْبَشِيرُ أَلْقَىٰهُ عَلَىٰ وَجْهِهِۦ فَٱرْتَدَّ بَصِيرًا قَالَ أَلَمْ أَقُل لَّكُمْ إِنِّى أَعْلَمُ مِنَ ٱللَّهِ مَا لَا تَعْلَمُونَ ۝

97. They said: 'Father! Pray for us the forgiveness of our sins, verily we have been sinners.'

قَالُوا۟ يَٰٓأَبَانَا ٱسْتَغْفِرْ لَنَا ذُنُوبَنَآ إِنَّا كُنَّا خَٰطِـِٔينَ ۝

98. He said: 'Presently I shall pray to my Lord for forgiveness for you, verily He! Only He is the Forgiving, the Merciful.'

قَالَ سَوْفَ أَسْتَغْفِرُ لَكُمْ رَبِّىٓ إِنَّهُۥ هُوَ ٱلْغَفُورُ ٱلرَّحِيمُ ۝

99. Then when they entered unto Joseph, he betook his parents to himself and said: 'Enter Egypt, Allah willing, in security.'

فَلَمَّا دَخَلُوا۟ عَلَىٰ يُوسُفَ ءَاوَىٰٓ إِلَيْهِ أَبَوَيْهِ وَقَالَ ٱدْخُلُوا۟ مِصْرَ إِن شَآءَ ٱللَّهُ ءَامِنِينَ ۝

100. And he raised his parents to the throne, and they fell down before him prostrate. And he said: 'Father! This is the interpretation of my dream aforetime, my Lord has now made it come true;[431] and surely He did well by me

وَرَفَعَ أَبَوَيْهِ عَلَى ٱلْعَرْشِ وَخَرُّوا۟ لَهُۥ سُجَّدًا وَقَالَ يَٰٓأَبَتِ هَٰذَا تَأْوِيلُ رُءْيَٰىَ مِن قَبْلُ قَدْ جَعَلَهَا رَبِّى حَقًّا

---

431. Note that Joseph in keeping with his character as a Prophet of God is all humility, and attributes everything good and worthy not to himself but to the Grace of God.

when he took me forth from the prison, and has brought you from the desert after Satan had stirred strife between me and my brethren; verily my Lord is Subtle to whom He will. Verily He, only He, is the Knowing, the Wise.

وَقَدۡ أَحۡسَنَ بِىٓ إِذۡ أَخۡرَجَنِى مِنَ ٱلسِّجۡنِ وَجَآءَ بِكُم مِّنَ ٱلۡبَدۡوِ مِنۢ بَعۡدِ أَن نَّزَغَ ٱلشَّيۡطَٰنُ بَيۡنِى وَبَيۡنَ إِخۡوَتِىٓ إِنَّ رَبِّى لَطِيفٞ لِّمَا يَشَآءُ إِنَّهُۥ هُوَ ٱلۡعَلِيمُ ٱلۡحَكِيمُ ﴿١٠٠﴾

101. My Lord You have given me of the dominion, and taught me of the interpretation of discourse, Creator of the heavens and the earth! You are my Patron in the world and the Hereafter. Make me die a Muslim and join me with the righteous.'

رَبِّ قَدۡ ءَاتَيۡتَنِى مِنَ ٱلۡمُلۡكِ وَعَلَّمۡتَنِى مِن تَأۡوِيلِ ٱلۡأَحَادِيثِ فَاطِرَ ٱلسَّمَٰوَٰتِ وَٱلۡأَرۡضِ أَنتَ وَلِيِّۦ فِى ٱلدُّنۡيَا وَٱلۡأَخِرَةِ تَوَفَّنِى مُسۡلِمٗا وَأَلۡحِقۡنِى بِٱلصَّٰلِحِينَ ﴿١٠١﴾

102. This is of the tidings of the Unseen, which We reveal to you; nor were you with them when they resolved on their affair while they were plotting.

ذَٰلِكَ مِنۡ أَنۢبَآءِ ٱلۡغَيۡبِ نُوحِيهِ إِلَيۡكَ وَمَا كُنتَ لَدَيۡهِمۡ إِذۡ أَجۡمَعُوٓاۡ أَمۡرَهُمۡ وَهُمۡ يَمۡكُرُونَ ﴿١٠٢﴾

103. And most of the people, though you desire ardently, are not going to be believers.

وَمَآ أَكۡثَرُ ٱلنَّاسِ وَلَوۡ حَرَصۡتَ بِمُؤۡمِنِينَ ﴿١٠٣﴾

104. And you did not ask of them any wage for it, it is but an admonition[432] to the worlds.

وَمَا تَسۡـَٔلُهُمۡ عَلَيۡهِ مِنۡ أَجۡرٍ إِنۡ هُوَ إِلَّا ذِكۡرٞ لِّلۡعَٰلَمِينَ ﴿١٠٤﴾

Section 12

105. And how many a sign in the heavens and the earth they pass by, while they are averse therefrom.

وَكَأَيِّن مِّنۡ ءَايَةٖ فِى ٱلسَّمَٰوَٰتِ وَٱلۡأَرۡضِ يَمُرُّونَ عَلَيۡهَا وَهُمۡ عَنۡهَا مُعۡرِضُونَ ﴿١٠٥﴾

---

432. So whoever denies it, does so at his own peril. The mission of Islam is thus unequivocally universal. The True Faith is to be preached to all nations, and the whole of the human race is to be summoned to the belief in the One God.

106. And most of them do not believe in Allah except as associators.[433]

وَمَا يُؤْمِنُ أَكْثَرُهُم بِٱللَّهِ إِلَّا وَهُم مُّشْرِكُونَ ﴿١٠٦﴾

107. Are they then secure against this, that there may come upon them an overwhelming of Allah's torment, or that there may come upon them the Hour of a sudden while they perceive not?

أَفَأَمِنُوٓا۟ أَن تَأْتِيَهُمْ غَٰشِيَةٌ مِّنْ عَذَابِ ٱللَّهِ أَوْ تَأْتِيَهُمُ ٱلسَّاعَةُ بَغْتَةً وَهُمْ لَا يَشْعُرُونَ ﴿١٠٧﴾

108. Say you: 'This is my way; I call to Allah resting upon an insight, I, and whoso follows me. Hallowed be Allah! And I am not of the associators.'

قُلْ هَٰذِهِۦ سَبِيلِىٓ أَدْعُوٓا۟ إِلَى ٱللَّهِ عَلَىٰ بَصِيرَةٍ أَنَا۠ وَمَنِ ٱتَّبَعَنِى وَسُبْحَٰنَ ٱللَّهِ وَمَآ أَنَا۠ مِنَ ٱلْمُشْرِكِينَ ﴿١٠٨﴾

109. And we sent not before you any save men unto whom We revealed from among the people of the towns. Have then they not travelled about in the land? Have they observed how has been the end of those before them? And surely the abode of the Hereafter is best for the God-fearing. Do you not then reflect?

وَمَآ أَرْسَلْنَا مِن قَبْلِكَ إِلَّا رِجَالًا نُّوحِىٓ إِلَيْهِم مِّنْ أَهْلِ ٱلْقُرَىٰٓ أَفَلَمْ يَسِيرُوا۟ فِى ٱلْأَرْضِ فَيَنظُرُوا۟ كَيْفَ كَانَ عَٰقِبَةُ ٱلَّذِينَ مِن قَبْلِهِمْ وَلَدَارُ ٱلْءَاخِرَةِ خَيْرٌ لِّلَّذِينَ ٱتَّقَوْا۟ أَفَلَا تَعْقِلُونَ ﴿١٠٩﴾

---

433. They attribute partners to Him in spite of their profession of monotheism. The description covers not only the open idolatry of polytheistic peoples but also its veiled forms such as Christolatry, Mariolatry, the worship of heroes, the adoration of saints and the deification of Reason. The phrase may also contain a reference to the pseudo – monotheism of the Greek philosophers, especially of Plato, who in common with others was never fully monotheistic, even if he shows a strong tendency in that direction now and again His divinity is and remains God and yet gods at the same time, and he continues to use the singular and the plural with an indifference which seems to us thoroughly perverse' (Guchi, *Plato's Thought*, p. 178).

حَتَّىٰٓ إِذَا ٱسْتَيْـَٔسَ ٱلرُّسُلُ وَظَنُّوٓا۟ أَنَّهُمْ قَدْ كُذِبُوا۟ جَآءَهُمْ نَصْرُنَا فَنُجِّىَ مَن نَّشَآءُ ۖ وَلَا يُرَدُّ بَأْسُنَا عَنِ ٱلْقَوْمِ ٱلْمُجْرِمِينَ ﴿١١٠﴾

لَقَدْ كَانَ فِى قَصَصِهِمْ عِبْرَةٌ لِّأُو۟لِى ٱلْأَلْبَـٰبِ ۗ مَا كَانَ حَدِيثًا يُفْتَرَىٰ وَلَـٰكِن تَصْدِيقَ ٱلَّذِى بَيْنَ يَدَيْهِ وَتَفْصِيلَ كُلِّ شَىْءٍ وَهُدًى وَرَحْمَةً لِّقَوْمٍ يُؤْمِنُونَ ﴿١١١﴾

110. Respited were they until when the Messengers had despaired and imagined that they were deluded, there came unto them Our succour; and whosoever We willed was delivered. And Our wrath is not warded off from a sinning people.

111. Assuredly in their stories is a lesson[434] for men of understanding. It is not a discourse concocted but a confirmation of what went before it, and a detailing of everything, and a guidance and a mercy to a people who believe.

---

434. These stories provide lessons by which one may take warning or example. Narratives in the Qur'ān invariably point to a moral, teaching that God always finally rewards the righteous and punishes the wicked.

Sūrah 13

al-Ra'd

(Makkan, 6 Sections, 43 Verses)

In the name of Allah, the Compassionate, the Merciful.

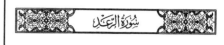

Section 1

1. *Alif, Lām, Mīm, Rā.* These are the verses of the Book. And what is sent down to you from your Lord is the Truth, but most of the people believe not.

2. Allah it is Who has raised the heavens without pillars you can see, then He established Himself on the Throne and subjected the sun and the moon to Himself, each running to a determined period. He directs the affairs and details the signs, that haply you may be convinced of the meeting with your Lord.

3. And He it is Who has stretched the earth, and placed therein firm mountains and rivers, and of every fruit He has placed therein two in pairs. He covers the night with the day; verily in that are signs for a people who ponder.

4. And in the earth are regions adjoining and gardens of vines and corn fields, and palm trees, clustered and single, watered by the same water; yet some We make excel others in food. Verily in that are signs for a people who reflect.

وَفِى ٱلْأَرْضِ قِطَعٌ مُّتَجَٰوِرَٰتٌ وَجَنَّٰتٌ مِّنْ أَعْنَٰبٍ وَزَرْعٌ وَنَخِيلٌ صِنْوَانٌ وَغَيْرُ صِنْوَانٍ يُسْقَىٰ بِمَآءٍ وَٰحِدٍ وَنُفَضِّلُ بَعْضَهَا عَلَىٰ بَعْضٍ فِى ٱلْأُكُلِ إِنَّ فِى ذَٰلِكَ لَءَايَٰتٍ لِّقَوْمٍ يَعْقِلُونَ ۝

5. And should you marvel, then marvellous is their saying: 'When we have become dust, shall we be in a new creation?' These are they who disbelieved in their Lord; and these! Shackles round their necks; and these shall be the fellows of the Fire as abiders therein.

وَإِن تَعْجَبْ فَعَجَبٌ قَوْلُهُمْ أَءِذَا كُنَّا تُرَٰبًا أَءِنَّا لَفِى خَلْقٍ جَدِيدٍ أُوْلَٰٓئِكَ ٱلَّذِينَ كَفَرُوا بِرَبِّهِمْ وَأُوْلَٰٓئِكَ ٱلْأَغْلَٰلُ فِىٓ أَعْنَاقِهِمْ وَأُوْلَٰٓئِكَ أَصْحَٰبُ ٱلنَّارِ هُمْ فِيهَا خَٰلِدُونَ ۝

6. And they ask you to hasten the evil before the good, while examples have already gone forth before them. And your Lord is the Owner of forgiveness to mankind despite their wrong-doing; and verily your Lord is Severe in requital.

وَيَسْتَعْجِلُونَكَ بِٱلسَّيِّئَةِ قَبْلَ ٱلْحَسَنَةِ وَقَدْ خَلَتْ مِن قَبْلِهِمُ ٱلْمَثُلَٰتُ وَإِنَّ رَبَّكَ لَذُو مَغْفِرَةٍ لِّلنَّاسِ عَلَىٰ ظُلْمِهِمْ وَإِنَّ رَبَّكَ لَشَدِيدُ ٱلْعِقَابِ ۝

7. And those who disbelieve say: 'Why is not a sign[435] sent down to him from his Lord?' You are but a warner, and to every people there is a guide.

وَيَقُولُ ٱلَّذِينَ كَفَرُوا لَوْلَآ أُنزِلَ عَلَيْهِ ءَايَةٌ مِّن رَّبِّهِۦ إِنَّمَآ أَنتَ مُنذِرٌ وَلِكُلِّ قَوْمٍ هَادٍ ۝

---

435. In other words, a miracle such as we desire. A miracle, in Islamic phraseology, is an event deviating from the usual course of events, appearing at the hands of him who claims to be a Prophet, as a challenge to those who deny this, and of such a nature that it makes it impossible for them to produce the like of it. It is God's testimony to the Truth of his Prophet, as a challenge to those who deny this, and it is of such a nature that it makes it impossible for them to produce the like of it. It is God's testimony to the Truth of His Prophets, but clearly an act of God, not of the Prophet.

Section 2

8.　Allah knows what every female bears and what the wombs want and what they exceed, and with Him everything is in due measure.

9.　Knower of the hidden and the manifest! The Great, the Exalted!

10.　Alike to Him is he among you who hides the Word and he who proclaims it, and he who hides himself in the night and he who goes about freely in the day.

11.　For each one are attendant angels, before him and behind him. They guard him with Allah's command. Verily Allah alters not what is with a people, until you alter what is within them. And when Allah intends evil to a people, there is no turning it back, nor is there for them any patron, beside Him.

12.　He it is Who shows lightning to you[436] for inspiring fear and hope, and brings up the heavy clouds.

اَللّٰهُ يَعْلَمُ مَا تَحْمِلُ كُلُّ أُنْثَىٰ وَمَا تَغِيضُ الْأَرْحَامُ وَمَا تَزْدَادُ وَكُلُّ شَيْءٍ عِنْدَهُ بِمِقْدَارٍ ۝

عَالِمُ الْغَيْبِ وَالشَّهَادَةِ الْكَبِيرُ الْمُتَعَالِ ۝

سَوَاءٌ مِنْكُمْ مَنْ أَسَرَّ الْقَوْلَ وَمَنْ جَهَرَ بِهِ وَمَنْ هُوَ مُسْتَخْفٍ بِاللَّيْلِ وَسَارِبٌ بِالنَّهَارِ ۝

لَهُ مُعَقِّبَاتٌ مِنْ بَيْنِ يَدَيْهِ وَمِنْ خَلْفِهِ يَحْفَظُونَهُ مِنْ أَمْرِ اللّٰهِ إِنَّ اللّٰهَ لَا يُغَيِّرُ مَا بِقَوْمٍ حَتَّىٰ يُغَيِّرُوا مَا بِأَنْفُسِهِمْ وَإِذَا أَرَادَ اللّٰهُ بِقَوْمٍ سُوءًا فَلَا مَرَدَّ لَهُ وَمَا لَهُمْ مِنْ دُونِهِ مِنْ وَالٍ ۝

هُوَ الَّذِي يُرِيكُمُ الْبَرْقَ خَوْفًا وَطَمَعًا وَيُنْشِئُ السَّحَابَ الثِّقَالَ ۝

---

436. So lightning, as a created, natural force, like all other natural forces, is a mere inanimate instrument in God's hands; and the thunderstorm is not a semi–divine being who, as taught by certain superstitious religions, could harm anybody.

13. And the thunder hallows His glory,[437] and so do the angels, in awe of Him, and He sends the thunderbolts and smites with them whomsoever He will.[438] They dispute concerning Allah, and He is Strong in prowess.[439]

وَيُسَبِّحُ الرَّعْدُ بِحَمْدِهِ وَالْمَلَـٰئِكَةُ مِنْ خِيفَتِهِ وَيُرْسِلُ الصَّوَاعِقَ فَيُصِيبُ بِهَا مَن يَشَاءُ وَهُمْ يُجَـٰدِلُونَ فِى اللَّهِ وَهُوَ شَدِيدُ الْمِحَالِ ﴿١٣﴾

14. To Him alone is the true call; and those whom they call upon beside Him answer them not at all, save as is answered one stretching out his palms to water that it may reach his mouth, while it will reach him not. And the supplication of infidels goes only astray.

لَهُ دَعْوَةُ الْحَقِّ وَالَّذِينَ يَدْعُونَ مِن دُونِهِ لَا يَسْتَجِيبُونَ لَهُم بِشَىْءٍ إِلَّا كَبَـٰسِطِ كَفَّيْهِ إِلَى الْمَاءِ لِيَبْلُغَ فَاهُ وَمَا هُوَ بِبَـٰلِغِهِ وَمَا دُعَاءُ الْكَـٰفِرِينَ إِلَّا فِى ضَلَـٰلٍ ﴿١٤﴾

15. And to Allah bows whosoever is in the heavens and the earth, willingly or unwillingly,[440] and also their shadows in the mornings and the evenings.

وَلِلَّهِ يَسْجُدُ مَن فِى السَّمَـٰوَٰتِ وَالْأَرْضِ طَوْعًا وَكَرْهًا وَظِلَـٰلُهُم بِالْغُدُوِّ وَالْآصَالِ ۩ ﴿١٥﴾

---

437. As do countless others celebrate His praise. Compare and contrast the attitude of various polytheistic peoples. 'Thunder was one of the great gods of the Germans.' (Menzies, *History of Religion*, p. 29). 'The place of the Thunder-god in polytheistic religion is similar to that of the Rain-god, in many cases even to entire coincidence. But his character is rather of wrath than of beneficence' (*PC*. II. p. 262). According to the Greeks, 'the thunderbolt was cast by Zeus' (*ERE*. X. p. 370). 'The Mandans attributed thunder to the flapping of the wings of a huge bird' (Ibid.).

438. It is He, the All-Powerful One, Who does all this, and not any minor 'thunder-god' such as Zeus (of the Greeks), Jupiter (of the Romans) or Indra (of the Hindus). See *PC*. II. pp. 262–265.

439. It was not beneficence but wrath and prowess that the polytheists attributed to their thunder-gods; hence it is this particular misconception that is noted here, and the All-Sufficiency of God is pointed out in this respect.

440. Everything, high or low is after all a created being, and must as such submit to the laws of the Creator, whether willingly, as in the case of good believers and inanimate objects, or unwillingly, as in the case of devils and rebels.

16. Say you: 'Who is the Lord of the heavens and the earth?' Say: 'Allah.' Say: 'Have you then taken beside Him, patrons who own neither benefit nor hurt to themselves?' Say you: 'Are the blind and the seeing alike or are darkness and light alike?' Or have they set up associates with Allah, who have created as He has created, so that the Creation has become dubious to them? Say: 'Allah is the Creator of everything; and He is the One, the Subduer.'

قُلْ مَن رَّبُّ ٱلسَّمَٰوَٰتِ وَٱلْأَرْضِ قُلِ ٱللَّهُ قُلْ أَفَٱتَّخَذْتُم مِّن دُونِهِۦٓ أَوْلِيَآءَ لَا يَمْلِكُونَ لِأَنفُسِهِمْ نَفْعًا وَلَا ضَرًّا قُلْ هَلْ يَسْتَوِى ٱلْأَعْمَىٰ وَٱلْبَصِيرُ أَمْ هَلْ تَسْتَوِى ٱلظُّلُمَٰتُ وَٱلنُّورُ أَمْ جَعَلُوا۟ لِلَّهِ شُرَكَآءَ خَلَقُوا۟ كَخَلْقِهِۦ فَتَشَٰبَهَ ٱلْخَلْقُ عَلَيْهِمْ قُلِ ٱللَّهُ خَٰلِقُ كُلِّ شَىْءٍ وَهُوَ ٱلْوَٰحِدُ ٱلْقَهَّٰرُ ﴿١٦﴾

17. He sends down water from the heaven, so that the valleys flow according to their measure; then the torrent bears the scum on top; and from that over which they kindle a fire seeking ornaments or goods arises a scum like thereto: thus Allah propounds the truth and falsehood. Then as for the scum, it departs as rubbish, and as for that which benefits mankind, it lasts on the earth; thus does Allah propound similitudes.

أَنزَلَ مِنَ ٱلسَّمَآءِ مَآءً فَسَالَتْ أَوْدِيَةٌۢ بِقَدَرِهَا فَٱحْتَمَلَ ٱلسَّيْلُ زَبَدًا رَّابِيًا وَمِمَّا يُوقِدُونَ عَلَيْهِ فِى ٱلنَّارِ ٱبْتِغَآءَ حِلْيَةٍ أَوْ مَتَٰعٍ زَبَدٌ مِّثْلُهُۥ كَذَٰلِكَ يَضْرِبُ ٱللَّهُ ٱلْحَقَّ وَٱلْبَٰطِلَ فَأَمَّا ٱلزَّبَدُ فَيَذْهَبُ جُفَآءً وَأَمَّا مَا يَنفَعُ ٱلنَّاسَ فَيَمْكُثُ فِى ٱلْأَرْضِ كَذَٰلِكَ يَضْرِبُ ٱللَّهُ ٱلْأَمْثَالَ ﴿١٧﴾

18. For those who answer their Lord is ordained good. And as for those who do not answer their Lord, if they had all that is in the earth together with its like, they would ransom themselves with that. These! For them shall be an evil reckoning; and their resort is Hell, a hapless bed!

لِلَّذِينَ ٱسْتَجَابُوا۟ لِرَبِّهِمُ ٱلْحُسْنَىٰ وَٱلَّذِينَ لَمْ يَسْتَجِيبُوا۟ لَهُۥ لَوْ أَنَّ لَهُم مَّا فِى ٱلْأَرْضِ جَمِيعًا وَمِثْلَهُۥ مَعَهُۥ لَٱفْتَدَوْا۟ بِهِۦٓ أُو۟لَٰٓئِكَ لَهُمْ سُوٓءُ ٱلْحِسَابِ وَمَأْوَىٰهُمْ جَهَنَّمُ وَبِئْسَ ٱلْمِهَادُ ﴿١٨﴾

Section 3

19. Shall he then who knows that what has been sent down upon you is the truth be like him who is blind? Only men of understanding are admonished.

أَفَمَن يَعْلَمُ أَنَّمَا أُنزِلَ إِلَيْكَ مِن رَّبِّكَ الْحَقُّ كَمَنْ هُوَ أَعْمَىٰٓ إِنَّمَا يَتَذَكَّرُ أُوْلُواْ الْأَلْبَٰبِ ۝

20. Those who fulfill the covenant of Allah, and do not violate the bond;

الَّذِينَ يُوفُونَ بِعَهْدِ اللَّهِ وَلَا يَنقُضُونَ الْمِيثَٰقَ ۝

21. And those who enjoin what Allah has commanded to be enjoined and fear their Lord, and dread the evil-reckoning;

وَالَّذِينَ يَصِلُونَ مَآ أَمَرَ اللَّهُ بِهِۦٓ أَن يُوصَلَ وَيَخْشَوْنَ رَبَّهُمْ وَيَخَافُونَ سُوٓءَ الْحِسَابِ ۝

22. And those who preserve seeking the pleasure of their Lord and establish prayer and spend, privately and publicly, out of what We have provided them, and combat evil with good. These: for them is the happy end in the abode:

وَالَّذِينَ صَبَرُواْ ابْتِغَآءَ وَجْهِ رَبِّهِمْ وَأَقَامُواْ الصَّلَوٰةَ وَأَنفَقُواْ مِمَّا رَزَقْنَٰهُمْ سِرًّا وَعَلَانِيَةً وَيَدْرَءُونَ بِالْحَسَنَةِ السَّيِّئَةَ أُوْلَٰٓئِكَ لَهُمْ عُقْبَى الدَّارِ ۝

23. Gardens everlasting; they shall enter them, and also whosoever would have acted righteously from among their fathers and spouses and progeny. And angels shall enter unto them from every portal, saying:

جَنَّٰتُ عَدْنٍ يَدْخُلُونَهَا وَمَن صَلَحَ مِنْ ءَابَآئِهِمْ وَأَزْوَٰجِهِمْ وَذُرِّيَّٰتِهِمْ وَالْمَلَٰٓئِكَةُ يَدْخُلُونَ عَلَيْهِم مِّن كُلِّ بَابٍ ۝

24. 'Peace be upon you, for you patiently persevered.' Excellent then is the happy end in the abode!

سَلَٰمٌ عَلَيْكُم بِمَا صَبَرْتُمْ فَنِعْمَ عُقْبَى الدَّارِ ۝

25. And those who violate the covenant of Allah after its ratification and sunder what Allah has commenced to be conjoined and act corruptly in the earth upon them is a curse, and for them shall be the evil abode.

وَٱلَّذِينَ يَنقُضُونَ عَهْدَ ٱللَّهِ مِنۢ بَعْدِ مِيثَٰقِهِۦ وَيَقْطَعُونَ مَآ أَمَرَ ٱللَّهُ بِهِۦٓ أَن يُوصَلَ وَيُفْسِدُونَ فِى ٱلْأَرْضِ أُوْلَٰٓئِكَ لَهُمُ ٱللَّعْنَةُ وَلَهُمْ سُوٓءُ ٱلدَّارِ ﴿٢٥﴾

26. Allah increases the provision for whom He will and also He stints. They exult in the life of this world, whereas the life of this world, by the side of the Hereafter, is only a passing enjoyment.

ٱللَّهُ يَبْسُطُ ٱلرِّزْقَ لِمَن يَشَآءُ وَيَقْدِرُ وَفَرِحُواْ بِٱلْحَيَوٰةِ ٱلدُّنْيَا وَمَا ٱلْحَيَوٰةُ ٱلدُّنْيَا فِى ٱلْأَخِرَةِ إِلَّا مَتَٰعٌ ﴿٢٦﴾

Section 4

27. And those who disbelieve say: 'Why is it that a sign is not sent down to him from his Lord?' Say you: 'Verily Allah sends astray whom He will, and guides to Himself whoso turns in penitence.

وَيَقُولُ ٱلَّذِينَ كَفَرُواْ لَوْلَآ أُنزِلَ عَلَيْهِ ءَايَةٌ مِّن رَّبِّهِۦ قُلْ إِنَّ ٱللَّهَ يُضِلُّ مَن يَشَآءُ وَيَهْدِىٓ إِلَيْهِ مَنْ أَنَابَ ﴿٢٧﴾

28. They are those who believe and whose hearts find comfort in the remembrance of Allah. Lo! In the remembrance of Allah hearts do find comfort.

ٱلَّذِينَ ءَامَنُواْ وَتَطْمَئِنُّ قُلُوبُهُم بِذِكْرِ ٱللَّهِ أَلَا بِذِكْرِ ٱللَّهِ تَطْمَئِنُّ ٱلْقُلُوبُ ﴿٢٨﴾

29. Those who believe and work righteous works, for them is bliss and a happy resort.'

ٱلَّذِينَ ءَامَنُواْ وَعَمِلُواْ ٱلصَّٰلِحَٰتِ طُوبَىٰ لَهُمْ وَحُسْنُ مَـَٔابٍ ﴿٢٩﴾

30. Thus We have sent you to a community before whom other communities have passed away, in order that you may recite to them what We have revealed to you; yet they deny the Compassionate. Say: 'He is my Lord, there is no god but He; on Him I rely, and to Him is my return in penitence.'

كَذَٰلِكَ أَرۡسَلۡنَٰكَ فِىٓ أُمَّةٍ قَدۡ خَلَتۡ مِن قَبۡلِهَآ أُمَمٌ لِّتَتۡلُوَاْ عَلَيۡهِمُ ٱلَّذِىٓ أَوۡحَيۡنَآ إِلَيۡكَ وَهُمۡ يَكۡفُرُونَ بِٱلرَّحۡمَٰنِ قُلۡ هُوَ رَبِّى لَآ إِلَٰهَ إِلَّا هُوَ عَلَيۡهِ تَوَكَّلۡتُ وَإِلَيۡهِ مَتَابِ ۝

31. And if there were a Qur'ān whereby mountains could be moved or the earth could be traversed or the dead could be spoken to, it would be in vain. Aye! The affair belongs to Allah entirely. Have not then those who believe yet known that had Allah willed, He would have guided all mankind? And a rattling adversity does not cease to befall those who disbelieve, for what they have wrought or to alight near their dwelling, until Allah's promise comes; verily Allah does not fail His tryst.

وَلَوۡ أَنَّ قُرۡءَانًا سُيِّرَتۡ بِهِ ٱلۡجِبَالُ أَوۡ قُطِّعَتۡ بِهِ ٱلۡأَرۡضُ أَوۡ كُلِّمَ بِهِ ٱلۡمَوۡتَىٰ بَل لِّلَّهِ ٱلۡأَمۡرُ جَمِيعًا أَفَلَمۡ يَاْيۡـَٔسِ ٱلَّذِينَ ءَامَنُوٓاْ أَن لَّوۡ يَشَآءُ ٱللَّهُ لَهَدَى ٱلنَّاسَ جَمِيعًا وَلَا يَزَالُ ٱلَّذِينَ كَفَرُواْ تُصِيبُهُم بِمَا صَنَعُواْ قَارِعَةٌ أَوۡ تَحُلُّ قَرِيبًا مِّن دَارِهِمۡ حَتَّىٰ يَأۡتِىَ وَعۡدُ ٱللَّهِ إِنَّ ٱللَّهَ لَا يُخۡلِفُ ٱلۡمِيعَادَ ۝

Section 5

32. And assuredly mocked were the Messengers before you; then I respited those who disbelieved; thereafter I seized them, so how terrible has been My requital.

وَلَقَدِ ٱسۡتُهۡزِئَ بِرُسُلٍ مِّن قَبۡلِكَ فَأَمۡلَيۡتُ لِلَّذِينَ كَفَرُواْ ثُمَّ أَخَذۡتُهُمۡ فَكَيۡفَ كَانَ عِقَابِ ۝

33. Is He, then, who is ever standing over every soul with what he earns, like unto another? And yet they have set up associates unto Allah. Say: 'Name them. Would you inform Him of what He knows not on the earth. Or is it by way of outward enquiry.' Aye! Fair-seeming to those who disbelieve is made their plotting, and they have been hindered from the way. And whom Allah sends astray, for him there is no guide.

أَفَمَنْ هُوَ قَآئِمٌ عَلَىٰ كُلِّ نَفْسٍ بِمَا كَسَبَتْ وَ جَعَلُوا۟ لِلَّهِ شُرَكَآءَ قُلْ سَمُّوهُمْ أَمْ تُنَبِّئُونَهُۥ بِمَا لَا يَعْلَمُ فِى ٱلْأَرْضِ أَم بِظَٰهِرٍ مِّنَ ٱلْقَوْلِ بَلْ زُيِّنَ لِلَّذِينَ كَفَرُوا۟ مَكْرُهُمْ وَ صُدُّوا۟ عَنِ ٱلسَّبِيلِ وَمَن يُضْلِلِ ٱللَّهُ فَمَا لَهُۥ مِنْ هَادٍ ۩٣٣

34. For them is chastisement in the life of this world, and surely the chastisement of the Hereafter is harder. None can protect them from Allah.

لَهُمْ عَذَابٌ فِى ٱلْحَيَوٰةِ ٱلدُّنْيَا وَلَعَذَابُ ٱلْآخِرَةِ أَشَقُّ وَمَا لَهُم مِّنَ ٱللَّهِ مِن وَاقٍ ۩٣٤

35. The likeness of the Garden which has been promised to the God-fearing is of running streams underneath, its fruit eternal, and so is its shade. This is the ending of those who fear Allah, and the ending of the infidels is the Fire.

مَّثَلُ ٱلْجَنَّةِ ٱلَّتِى وُعِدَ ٱلْمُتَّقُونَ تَجْرِى مِن تَحْتِهَا ٱلْأَنْهَٰرُ أُكُلُهَا دَآئِمٌ وَظِلُّهَا تِلْكَ عُقْبَى ٱلَّذِينَ ٱتَّقَوا۟ وَّعُقْبَى ٱلْكَٰفِرِينَ ٱلنَّارُ ۩٣٥

36. They to whom the Book has been given rejoice at what has been sent down to you, and of their bands are some who reject part of it. Say: 'I have only been bidden that I should worship Allah and should not associate aught with Him. To Him I call, and to Him is my return.'

وَٱلَّذِينَ ءَاتَيْنَٰهُمُ ٱلْكِتَٰبَ يَفْرَحُونَ بِمَآ أُنزِلَ إِلَيْكَ وَمِنَ ٱلْأَحْزَابِ مَن يُنكِرُ بَعْضَهُۥ قُلْ إِنَّمَآ أُمِرْتُ أَنْ أَعْبُدَ ٱللَّهَ وَلَا أُشْرِكَ بِهِۦ إِلَيْهِ أَدْعُوا۟ وَإِلَيْهِ مَـَٔابِ ۩٣٦

37. And thus We have sent it down as a judgement in Arabic. And were you to follow their vain desires, after what has come to you of knowledge, you will not have any patron or protector against Allah.

وَكَذَٰلِكَ أَنزَلْنَٰهُ حُكْمًا عَرَبِيًّا وَلَئِنِ ٱتَّبَعْتَ أَهْوَآءَهُم بَعْدَ مَا جَآءَكَ مِنَ ٱلْعِلْمِ مَا لَكَ مِنَ ٱللَّهِ مِن وَلِيٍّ وَلَا وَاقٍ ۝

Section 6

38. Assuredly We have sent Messengers before you and We made for them wives and progeny;[441] and it is not for a Messenger to produce a verse, except by the command of Allah;[442] for every term there is a Book.[443]

وَلَقَدْ أَرْسَلْنَا رُسُلًا مِّن قَبْلِكَ وَجَعَلْنَا لَهُمْ أَزْوَٰجًا وَذُرِّيَّةً وَمَا كَانَ لِرَسُولٍ أَن يَأْتِيَ بِـَٔايَةٍ إِلَّا بِإِذْنِ ٱللَّهِ لِكُلِّ أَجَلٍ كِتَابٌ ۝

441. Therefore, there is no reproach on you if you are blessed with wives and children. There is absolutely no contradiction between a family life and the dignity of Prophetic office; and there is nothing unholy or unclean about marriage and married life. This refutes the position of the Nazarenes/Christians and others who have held that women and the begetting of children were repugnant to spirituality. Influenced by the teachings of Paul, 'the celibate life was exalted above that of marriage, on the ground that there was in marriage and its relations something impure and defiling'. In the language of some Gnostic sects, 'it belonged to the kingdom of Demiurgus, the creator of the material universe and of the human body as a part of it, not to that of the higher Christ-Acon, who was Lord of the kingdom' (*DCA*. I. p. 324). Orders of celibates are found in many religious systems, especially in Buddhism and Christianity, and marriage and marital relations have been considered very low by these two religions.

442. This is said in answer to the Jews and Christians who objected to the Qur'ān on the grounds of its deviation from the ancient Scriptures. They are told that the Omniscient God alone legislates in consonance with the time and place, and it is not in the hands of any mortal Prophet to promulgate of his own accord any particular Divine Law or Commandment.

443. A Book with Laws and Ordinances suited to that particular age. So there is no force in the objection that the Qur'ān differed in certain of its commandments with previous revelations.

39. Allah abolishes what He will, and keeps; and with Him is the mother of the Book.

يَمْحُوا۟ ٱللَّهُ مَا يَشَآءُ وَيُثْبِتُ ۖ وَعِندَهُۥٓ أُمُّ ٱلْكِتَٰبِ ۝

40. Whether We show you part of what We have promised them, or We take you away, on you is only the preaching, and on Us is the reckoning.

وَإِن مَّا نُرِيَنَّكَ بَعْضَ ٱلَّذِى نَعِدُهُمْ أَوْ نَتَوَفَّيَنَّكَ فَإِنَّمَا عَلَيْكَ ٱلْبَلَٰغُ وَعَلَيْنَا ٱلْحِسَابُ ۝

41. Do they not see that We visit the land diminishing it by its borders? Allah judges and there is no reviser of His Judgement; and He is Swift in reckoning.

أَوَلَمْ يَرَوْا۟ أَنَّا نَأْتِى ٱلْأَرْضَ نَنقُصُهَا مِنْ أَطْرَافِهَا ۚ وَٱللَّهُ يَحْكُمُ لَا مُعَقِّبَ لِحُكْمِهِۦ ۚ وَهُوَ سَرِيعُ ٱلْحِسَابِ ۝

42. And of a surety there plotted those before them, but to Allah belongs the plotting entirely. He knows what each soul earns. And soon will the infidels know for whom is the happy ending of the abode.

وَقَدْ مَكَرَ ٱلَّذِينَ مِن قَبْلِهِمْ فَلِلَّهِ ٱلْمَكْرُ جَمِيعًا ۖ يَعْلَمُ مَا تَكْسِبُ كُلُّ نَفْسٍ ۗ وَسَيَعْلَمُ ٱلْكُفَّٰرُ لِمَنْ عُقْبَى ٱلدَّارِ ۝

43. And those who disbelieve say: 'You are not a sent one.' Say you: 'Allah is a sufficient witness between me and you, and also he with whom is the knowledge of the Book.'

وَيَقُولُ ٱلَّذِينَ كَفَرُوا۟ لَسْتَ مُرْسَلًا ۚ قُلْ كَفَىٰ بِٱللَّهِ شَهِيدًۢا بَيْنِى وَبَيْنَكُمْ وَمَنْ عِندَهُۥ عِلْمُ ٱلْكِتَٰبِ ۝

Surah 14

Ibrāhīm

(Makkan, 7 Sections, 52 Verses)

In the name of Allah, the Compassionate, the Merciful.

Section 1

1. *Alif, Lām, Rā.* This is a Book which We have sent down to you that you may bring forth mankind from darkness to light, by the command of their Lord, to the path of the Mighty, the Praiseworthy.

2. Allah, Whose is whatever is in the heavens and whatever is in the earth, and woe be to the infidels because of a severe torment.

3. Those who prefer the life of this world to the Hereafter, and hinder people from the way of Allah and seek crookedness therein, these are in far-off error.

4. And We sent not a Messenger but with the speech of his people that he might expound the Message to them. Then Allah sends astray whom He will and guides whom He will. He is the Mighty, the Wise.

الٓرۚ كِتَٰبٌ أَنزَلۡنَٰهُ إِلَيۡكَ لِتُخۡرِجَ ٱلنَّاسَ مِنَ ٱلظُّلُمَٰتِ إِلَى ٱلنُّورِ بِإِذۡنِ رَبِّهِمۡ إِلَىٰ صِرَٰطِ ٱلۡعَزِيزِ ٱلۡحَمِيدِ ۝١

ٱللَّهِ ٱلَّذِي لَهُۥ مَا فِي ٱلسَّمَٰوَٰتِ وَمَا فِي ٱلۡأَرۡضِۗ وَوَيۡلٌ لِّلۡكَٰفِرِينَ مِنۡ عَذَابٍ شَدِيدٍ ۝٢

ٱلَّذِينَ يَسۡتَحِبُّونَ ٱلۡحَيَوٰةَ ٱلدُّنۡيَا عَلَى ٱلۡأٓخِرَةِ وَيَصُدُّونَ عَن سَبِيلِ ٱللَّهِ وَيَبۡغُونَهَا عِوَجًاۚ أُوْلَٰٓئِكَ فِي ضَلَٰلٍ بَعِيدٍ ۝٣

وَمَآ أَرۡسَلۡنَا مِن رَّسُولٍ إِلَّا بِلِسَانِ قَوۡمِهِۦ لِيُبَيِّنَ لَهُمۡۖ فَيُضِلُّ ٱللَّهُ مَن يَشَآءُ وَيَهۡدِي مَن يَشَآءُۚ وَهُوَ ٱلۡعَزِيزُ ٱلۡحَكِيمُ ۝٤

5. And assuredly We sent Moses with Our signs saying: 'Bring forth your people from darkness into light, and remind them of the annals of Allah.' Verily therein are signs for everyone patient and thankful.

6. And recall when Moses said to his people: 'Remember the favour of Allah upon you when He delivered you from the house of Pharaoh who were imposing upon you evil torment, slaying your sons and letting your women live, and in it was a terrible trial from your Lord.'

Section 2

7. And recall when your Lord proclaimed: 'If you give thanks I will increase you, and if you disbelieve, My torment is severe.'

8. And Moses said: 'If you disbelieve, you and all those on the earth, then verily Allah is the Self-Sufficient, the Praiseworthy.'

9. Have not the tidings come to you of those before you; the people of Noah and the 'Ād and the Thamūd and those after them? None knows them save Allah. There came to them their Messengers with evidence, but they put their hands to their mouths, and said, 'Verily we disbelieve in that with which you have been sent, and regarding that to which you call us we are in doubt disquieting.'

وَلَقَدْ أَرْسَلْنَا مُوسَىٰ بِـَٔايَٰتِنَآ أَنْ أَخْرِجْ قَوْمَكَ مِنَ ٱلظُّلُمَٰتِ إِلَى ٱلنُّورِ وَذَكِّرْهُم بِأَيَّىٰمِ ٱللَّهِ إِنَّ فِى ذَٰلِكَ لَءَايَٰتٍ لِّكُلِّ صَبَّارٍ شَكُورٍ ۝

وَإِذْ قَالَ مُوسَىٰ لِقَوْمِهِ ٱذْكُرُوا۟ نِعْمَةَ ٱللَّهِ عَلَيْكُمْ إِذْ أَنجَىٰكُم مِّنْ ءَالِ فِرْعَوْنَ يَسُومُونَكُمْ سُوٓءَ ٱلْعَذَابِ وَيُذَبِّحُونَ أَبْنَآءَكُمْ وَيَسْتَحْيُونَ نِسَآءَكُمْ وَفِى ذَٰلِكُم بَلَآءٌ مِّن رَّبِّكُمْ عَظِيمٌ ۝

وَإِذْ تَأَذَّنَ رَبُّكُمْ لَئِن شَكَرْتُمْ لَأَزِيدَنَّكُمْ وَلَئِن كَفَرْتُمْ إِنَّ عَذَابِى لَشَدِيدٌ ۝

وَقَالَ مُوسَىٰ إِن تَكْفُرُوٓا۟ أَنتُمْ وَمَن فِى ٱلْأَرْضِ جَمِيعًا فَإِنَّ ٱللَّهَ لَغَنِىٌّ حَمِيدٌ ۝

أَلَمْ يَأْتِكُمْ نَبَؤُا۟ ٱلَّذِينَ مِن قَبْلِكُمْ قَوْمِ نُوحٍ وَعَادٍ وَثَمُودَ وَٱلَّذِينَ مِنۢ بَعْدِهِمْ لَا يَعْلَمُهُمْ إِلَّا ٱللَّهُ جَآءَتْهُمْ رُسُلُهُم بِٱلْبَيِّنَٰتِ فَرَدُّوٓا۟ أَيْدِيَهُمْ فِىٓ أَفْوَٰهِهِمْ وَقَالُوٓا۟ إِنَّا كَفَرْنَا بِمَآ أُرْسِلْتُم بِهِۦ وَإِنَّا لَفِى شَكٍّ مِّمَّا تَدْعُونَنَآ إِلَيْهِ مُرِيبٍ ۝

10. Their Messengers said: 'What! Is there doubt about Allah, the Maker of the heavens and the earth? He calls you that He may forgive you of your sins and retain you till a term fixed.' They said: 'You are but like us; you mean to turn us aside from what our fathers have been worshipping; so bring us a manifest authority.'

قَالَتْ رُسُلُهُمْ أَفِى اللَّهِ شَكٌّ فَاطِرِ السَّمَوَاتِ وَالْأَرْضِ يَدْعُوكُمْ لِيَغْفِرَ لَكُم مِّن ذُنُوبِكُمْ وَيُؤَخِّرَكُمْ إِلَىٰٓ أَجَلٍ مُّسَمًّى قَالُوٓاْ إِنْ أَنتُمْ إِلَّا بَشَرٌ مِّثْلُنَا تُرِيدُونَ أَن تَصُدُّونَا عَمَّا كَانَ يَعْبُدُ ءَابَآؤُنَا فَأْتُونَا بِسُلْطَانٍ مُّبِينٍ ۝

11. Their Messengers said to them: 'We are nothing but human beings like you, but Allah bestows favour on whom He will of His bondsmen, and it is not for us to bring you a miracle except by the command of Allah. On Allah then let the believers rely.

قَالَتْ لَهُمْ رُسُلُهُمْ إِن نَّحْنُ إِلَّا بَشَرٌ مِّثْلُكُمْ وَلَكِنَّ اللَّهَ يَمُنُّ عَلَىٰ مَن يَشَآءُ مِنْ عِبَادِهِ وَمَا كَانَ لَنَآ أَن نَّأْتِيَكُم بِسُلْطَانٍ إِلَّا بِإِذْنِ اللَّهِ وَعَلَى اللَّهِ فَلْيَتَوَكَّلِ الْمُؤْمِنُونَ ۝

12. And why should we not rely on Allah when He surely has guided us on our ways? And we shall surely bear with patience that with which you afflict us; and in Allah then let the trustful put their trust.'

وَمَا لَنَآ أَلَّا نَتَوَكَّلَ عَلَى اللَّهِ وَقَدْ هَدَىٰنَا سُبُلَنَا وَلَنَصْبِرَنَّ عَلَىٰ مَآ ءَاذَيْتُمُونَا وَعَلَى اللَّهِ فَلْيَتَوَكَّلِ الْمُتَوَكِّلُونَ ۝

Section 3

13. And those who disbelieved said to their Messengers: 'We will surely drive you forth from our land, or else you shall have to return to our faith.' Then their Lord revealed to them: 'We will surely destroy the wrong-doers.

وَقَالَ الَّذِينَ كَفَرُواْ لِرُسُلِهِمْ لَنُخْرِجَنَّكُم مِّنْ أَرْضِنَآ أَوْ لَتَعُودُنَّ فِى مِلَّتِنَا فَأَوْحَىٰٓ إِلَيْهِمْ رَبُّهُمْ لَنُهْلِكَنَّ الظَّالِمِينَ ۝

14. And We will surely cause you to dwell in the land after them; that is for him who fears standing before Me, and fears My threat.'

وَلَنُسۡكِنَنَّكُمُ ٱلۡأَرۡضَ مِنۢ بَعۡدِهِمۡ ذَٰلِكَ لِمَنۡ خَافَ مَقَامِى وَخَافَ وَعِيدِ ۝

15. And they besought judgement, and disappointed was every obstinate tyrant.

وَٱسۡتَفۡتَحُوا۟ وَخَابَ كُلُّ جَبَّارٍ عَنِيدٍ ۝

16. Behind him is Hell, and he shall be made to drink of fetid water;

مِّن وَرَآئِهِۦ جَهَنَّمُ وَيُسۡقَىٰ مِن مَّآءٍ صَدِيدٍ ۝

17. Which he gulps, but can scarce swallow. And death comes upon him from every side, and yet he is not dead, and behind him is a torment terrible.

يَتَجَرَّعُهُۥ وَلَا يَكَادُ يُسِيغُهُۥ وَيَأۡتِيهِ ٱلۡمَوۡتُ مِن كُلِّ مَكَانٍ وَمَا هُوَ بِمَيِّتٍ وَمِن وَرَآئِهِۦ عَذَابٌ غَلِيظٌ ۝

18. The likeness of those who disbelieve in their Lord is that their works are like ashes upon which the wind blows hard on a stormy day; they shall not be able to get aught of what they have earned. That is a straying far off.

مَّثَلُ ٱلَّذِينَ كَفَرُوا۟ بِرَبِّهِمۡ أَعۡمَٰلُهُمۡ كَرَمَادٍ ٱشۡتَدَّتۡ بِهِ ٱلرِّيحُ فِى يَوۡمٍ عَاصِفٍ لَّا يَقۡدِرُونَ مِمَّا كَسَبُوا۟ عَلَىٰ شَىۡءٍ ذَٰلِكَ هُوَ ٱلضَّلَٰلُ ٱلۡبَعِيدُ ۝

19. Do you not see that Allah has created the heavens and the earth with a purpose? If He willed He would make you pass away and bring a creation new.

أَلَمۡ تَرَ أَنَّ ٱللَّهَ خَلَقَ ٱلسَّمَٰوَٰتِ وَٱلۡأَرۡضَ بِٱلۡحَقِّ إِن يَشَأۡ يُذۡهِبۡكُمۡ وَيَأۡتِ بِخَلۡقٍ جَدِيدٍ ۝

20. And for Allah that is not hard.

وَمَا ذَٰلِكَ عَلَى ٱللَّهِ بِعَزِيزٍ ۝

21. They all shall appear before Allah; then those who were counted weak shall say to those who were stiff-necked: 'Verily we were unto you a following, are you going to avail us at all against the torment of Allah?' They will say: 'Had Allah guided us we would have guided you too; it is now equal to us whether we become impatient or bear patiently; for us there is no place of escape.'

وَبَرَزُوا۟ لِلَّهِ جَمِيعًا فَقَالَ ٱلضُّعَفَٰٓؤُا۟ لِلَّذِينَ ٱسْتَكْبَرُوٓا۟ إِنَّا كُنَّا لَكُمْ تَبَعًا فَهَلْ أَنتُم مُّغْنُونَ عَنَّا مِنْ عَذَابِ ٱللَّهِ مِن شَىْءٍ قَالُوا۟ لَوْ هَدَىٰنَا ٱللَّهُ لَهَدَيْنَٰكُمْ سَوَآءٌ عَلَيْنَآ أَجَزِعْنَآ أَمْ صَبَرْنَا مَا لَنَا مِن مَّحِيصٍ ۝

Section 4

22. And Satan will say, after the affair has been decreed: 'Verily Allah promised you a promise of Truth, and I also promised you, then I failed you[444]; and I had over you no authority, save that I called you and you responded to me, so do not reproach me but reproach yourself; I am not going to help you nor are you going to help me; surely I deny your having associated me with God before. Verily for the wrong-doers there is an afflictive torment.'

وَقَالَ ٱلشَّيْطَٰنُ لَمَّا قُضِىَ ٱلْأَمْرُ إِنَّ ٱللَّهَ وَعَدَكُمْ وَعْدَ ٱلْحَقِّ وَوَعَدتُّكُمْ فَأَخْلَفْتُكُمْ وَمَا كَانَ لِىَ عَلَيْكُم مِّن سُلْطَٰنٍ إِلَّآ أَن دَعَوْتُكُمْ فَٱسْتَجَبْتُمْ لِى فَلَا تَلُومُونِى وَلُومُوٓا۟ أَنفُسَكُم مَّآ أَنَا۠ بِمُصْرِخِكُمْ وَمَآ أَنتُم بِمُصْرِخِىَّ إِنِّى كَفَرْتُ بِمَآ أَشْرَكْتُمُونِ مِن قَبْلُ إِنَّ ٱلظَّٰلِمِينَ لَهُمْ عَذَابٌ أَلِيمٌ ۝

---

444. Failed you of your own accord. The principle involved here is a most important one. In Islam, there is no such thing as the inheritance of a sinful nature, or a predisposition to a life of sin and disobedience. Sin is only a habit formed because of one's weakness, and no man who is alert need ever be overcome by evil or the devil. It is an overrating of the devil's strength to say that he is, in the main, responsible for anybody's fall, when, as a matter of fact, he has no power at all except of evil suggestion. A man of Faith, if he asserts his will, is always sure to come out successful in his struggles against evil.

23. And those who believed and worked righteous works shall be made to enter Gardens with running streams, abiding therein by the command of their Lord, their greeting there will be, 'peace!'

وَأُدْخِلَ ٱلَّذِينَ ءَامَنُوا۟ وَعَمِلُوا۟ ٱلصَّـٰلِحَـٰتِ جَنَّـٰتٍ تَجْرِى مِن تَحْتِهَا ٱلْأَنْهَـٰرُ خَـٰلِدِينَ فِيهَا بِإِذْنِ رَبِّهِمْ ۖ تَحِيَّتُهُمْ فِيهَا سَلَـٰمٌ ۝

24. Do you not see how Allah has propounded the similitude of the clean word? It is like a clean tree, its roots firmly fixed, and its branches reaching the heaven;

أَلَمْ تَرَ كَيْفَ ضَرَبَ ٱللَّهُ مَثَلًا كَلِمَةً طَيِّبَةً كَشَجَرَةٍ طَيِّبَةٍ أَصْلُهَا ثَابِتٌ وَفَرْعُهَا فِى ٱلسَّمَآءِ ۝

25. Giving its fruit at every season by the command of its Lord. And Allah propounds similitudes for mankind that haply they may be admonished.

تُؤْتِى أُكُلَهَا كُلَّ حِينٍ بِإِذْنِ رَبِّهَا ۗ وَيَضْرِبُ ٱللَّهُ ٱلْأَمْثَالَ لِلنَّاسِ لَعَلَّهُمْ يَتَذَكَّرُونَ ۝

26. And the similitude of a foul word is a foul tree, uprooted from upon the earth, there is for it no stability.

وَمَثَلُ كَلِمَةٍ خَبِيثَةٍ كَشَجَرَةٍ خَبِيثَةٍ ٱجْتُثَّتْ مِن فَوْقِ ٱلْأَرْضِ مَا لَهَا مِن قَرَارٍ ۝

27. Allah keeps firm those who believe by the firm word in the life of the world and the Hereafter, and Allah sends astray the wrong-doers, Allah does whatever He will.

يُثَبِّتُ ٱللَّهُ ٱلَّذِينَ ءَامَنُوا۟ بِٱلْقَوْلِ ٱلثَّابِتِ فِى ٱلْحَيَوٰةِ ٱلدُّنْيَا وَفِى ٱلْأَخِرَةِ ۖ وَيُضِلُّ ٱللَّهُ ٱلظَّـٰلِمِينَ ۚ وَيَفْعَلُ ٱللَّهُ مَا يَشَآءُ ۝

Section 5

28. Do you not see those who returned the favour of Allah with infidelity and caused their people to alight in the dwelling of perdition?

أَلَمْ تَرَ إِلَى ٱلَّذِينَ بَدَّلُوا۟ نِعْمَتَ ٱللَّهِ كُفْرًا وَأَحَلُّوا۟ قَوْمَهُمْ دَارَ ٱلْبَوَارِ ۝

29. Hell, in which they will roast. How ill is the settlement!

جَهَنَّمَ يَصْلَوْنَهَا ۖ وَبِئْسَ ٱلْقَرَارُ ﴿٢٩﴾

30. They have set up compeers to Allah, that they may lead men astray from His path. Say: 'Enjoy, then verily your making is to the Fire.'

وَجَعَلُوا۟ لِلَّهِ أَندَادًا لِّيُضِلُّوا۟ عَن سَبِيلِهِۦ ۗ قُلْ تَمَتَّعُوا۟ فَإِنَّ مَصِيرَكُمْ إِلَى ٱلنَّارِ ﴿٣٠﴾

31. Say to those of My bondsmen who have believed, that they may establish prayer and spend privately and publicly of that with which We have provided them before the Day arrives when there will be no bargaining or befriending.

قُل لِّعِبَادِىَ ٱلَّذِينَ ءَامَنُوا۟ يُقِيمُوا۟ ٱلصَّلَوٰةَ وَيُنفِقُوا۟ مِمَّا رَزَقْنَٰهُمْ سِرًّا وَعَلَانِيَةً مِّن قَبْلِ أَن يَأْتِىَ يَوْمٌ لَّا بَيْعٌ فِيهِ وَلَا خِلَٰلٌ ﴿٣١﴾

32. Allah it is Who has created the heavens and the earth, and sent down from the heavens water and has thereby brought forth fruits as a provision for you and He has subjected the ships for you that they may run in the sea by His command; and He has subjected the rivers for you.

ٱللَّهُ ٱلَّذِى خَلَقَ ٱلسَّمَٰوَٰتِ وَٱلْأَرْضَ وَأَنزَلَ مِنَ ٱلسَّمَاءِ مَاءً فَأَخْرَجَ بِهِۦ مِنَ ٱلثَّمَرَٰتِ رِزْقًا لَّكُمْ ۖ وَسَخَّرَ لَكُمُ ٱلْفُلْكَ لِتَجْرِىَ فِى ٱلْبَحْرِ بِأَمْرِهِۦ ۖ وَسَخَّرَ لَكُمُ ٱلْأَنْهَٰرَ ﴿٣٢﴾

33. And He has subjected for you the sun and the moon, both in constant toil; and He has subjected for you the night and the day.

وَسَخَّرَ لَكُمُ ٱلشَّمْسَ وَٱلْقَمَرَ دَائِبَيْنِ ۖ وَسَخَّرَ لَكُمُ ٱلَّيْلَ وَٱلنَّهَارَ ﴿٣٣﴾

34. And He has granted to you some of everything you asked Him. And if you count Allah's favours, you cannot compute them. Verily man is a great wrong-doer, highly ungrateful.

وَءَاتَىٰكُم مِّن كُلِّ مَا سَأَلْتُمُوهُ ۚ وَإِن تَعُدُّوا۟ نِعْمَتَ ٱللَّهِ لَا تُحْصُوهَا ۗ إِنَّ ٱلْإِنسَٰنَ لَظَلُومٌ كَفَّارٌ ﴿٣٤﴾

Section 6

35. And recall when Abraham said: 'Lord! Make this city secure, and keep me and my sons away from worshipping the idols.

وَإِذْ قَالَ إِبْرَٰهِيمُ رَبِّ ٱجْعَلْ هَٰذَا ٱلْبَلَدَ ءَامِنًا وَٱجْنُبْنِى وَبَنِىَّ أَن نَّعْبُدَ ٱلْأَصْنَامَ ﴿٣٥﴾

36. Lord! They have sent astray many among mankind; whosoever follows me is of me, and whoever disobeys me then verily You are the Forgiving, the Merciful.

رَبِّ إِنَّهُنَّ أَضْلَلْنَ كَثِيرًا مِّنَ ٱلنَّاسِ فَمَن تَبِعَنِى فَإِنَّهُ مِنِّى وَمَنْ عَصَانِى فَإِنَّكَ غَفُورٌ رَّحِيمٌ ﴿٣٦﴾

37. Our Lord! Verily I have caused some of my progeny to dwell in a valley where is no sown land by Your Sacred House, our Lord, in order that they might establish prayer; make You therefore the hearts of some of mankind to yearn towards them, and provide them You with fruits,[445] haply they may give thanks.

رَّبَّنَا إِنِّى أَسْكَنتُ مِن ذُرِّيَّتِى بِوَادٍ غَيْرِ ذِى زَرْعٍ عِندَ بَيْتِكَ ٱلْمُحَرَّمِ رَبَّنَا لِيُقِيمُوا۟ ٱلصَّلَوٰةَ فَٱجْعَلْ أَفْئِدَةً مِّنَ ٱلنَّاسِ تَهْوِىٓ إِلَيْهِمْ وَٱرْزُقْهُم مِّنَ ٱلثَّمَرَٰتِ لَعَلَّهُمْ يَشْكُرُونَ ﴿٣٧﴾

38. Our Lord! Verily You know what we conceal and what we disclose, and naught is concealed from Allah in the earth or the heavens.

رَبَّنَا إِنَّكَ تَعْلَمُ مَا نُخْفِى وَمَا نُعْلِنُ وَمَا يَخْفَىٰ عَلَى ٱللَّهِ مِن شَىْءٍ فِى ٱلْأَرْضِ وَلَا فِى ٱلسَّمَآءِ ﴿٣٨﴾

39. All praise be to Allah Who has bestowed on me, despite old age, Ishmael and Isaac. Verily my Lord is the Hearer of supplication.

ٱلْحَمْدُ لِلَّهِ ٱلَّذِى وَهَبَ لِى عَلَى ٱلْكِبَرِ إِسْمَٰعِيلَ وَإِسْحَٰقَ إِنَّ رَبِّى لَسَمِيعُ ٱلدُّعَآءِ ﴿٣٩﴾

---

445. The way in which this prayer has been granted is most striking. The city of Makka, absolutely barren and unproductive, is supplied throughout the year with all sorts of fresh fruit; and at the pilgrimage season the abundance of this supply is simply amazing.

40. Lord! Make me established of prayer and also from my progeny, our Lord! And accept You my supplication!

رَبِّ اجْعَلْنِى مُقِيمَ الصَّلَوٰةِ وَمِن ذُرِّيَّتِى ۚ رَبَّنَا وَتَقَبَّلْ دُعَاءِ ۝

41. Our Lord! Forgive me and my parents and the believers on the Day when will be set up the reckoning.'

رَبَّنَا اغْفِرْ لِى وَلِوَٰلِدَىَّ وَلِلْمُؤْمِنِينَ يَوْمَ يَقُومُ الْحِسَابُ ۝

Section 7

42. Do not consider Allah heedless of what the wrong-doers do: He only defers them to a Day when eyes shall remain staring.

وَلَا تَحْسَبَنَّ اللَّهَ غَٰفِلًا عَمَّا يَعْمَلُ الظَّٰلِمُونَ ۚ إِنَّمَا يُؤَخِّرُهُمْ لِيَوْمٍ تَشْخَصُ فِيهِ الْأَبْصَٰرُ ۝

43. They will be hastening forward, their heads upraised, staring but seeing nothing and their hearts vacant.

مُهْطِعِينَ مُقْنِعِى رُءُوسِهِمْ لَا يَرْتَدُّ إِلَيْهِمْ طَرْفُهُمْ ۖ وَأَفْـِٔدَتُهُمْ هَوَآءٌ ۝

44. And warn you mankind of the Day when the torment shall come unto them; then the wrong-doers shall say: 'Our Lord! Defer us to a term near at hand; we will answer to Your call and we will follow the Messengers.' Were you not wont to swear before that for you there was to be no decline?

وَأَنذِرِ النَّاسَ يَوْمَ يَأْتِيهِمُ الْعَذَابُ فَيَقُولُ الَّذِينَ ظَلَمُوا رَبَّنَا أَخِّرْنَا إِلَىٰ أَجَلٍ قَرِيبٍ نُّجِبْ دَعْوَتَكَ وَنَتَّبِعِ الرُّسُلَ ۗ أَوَلَمْ تَكُونُوا أَقْسَمْتُم مِّن قَبْلُ مَا لَكُم مِّن زَوَالٍ ۝

45. 'You dwell in the dwellings of those who have wronged themselves and it was clear to you how We had dealt with them, and We had propounded for you similitudes.'

وَسَكَنتُمْ فِى مَسَٰكِنِ الَّذِينَ ظَلَمُوا أَنفُسَهُمْ وَتَبَيَّنَ لَكُمْ كَيْفَ فَعَلْنَا بِهِمْ وَضَرَبْنَا لَكُمُ الْأَمْثَالَ ۝

46. Of a surety they plotted their plot, and with Allah was their plot, though their plot was such as to remove mountains thereby.

47. So imagine not you that Allah is going to fail His promise to His Messengers. Verily Allah is the Mighty, the Lord of vengeance.[446]

48. On the Day when the earth will be changed into another earth, and the heavens also; and all creatures will appear before Allah, the One,[447] the Subduer.

49. And you will see the guilty on that Day bound in fetters.

50. Their trousers shall be of pitch, and the Fire shall cover their faces.

51. All this in order that Allah may requite each soul according to what he has earned; verily Allah is Swift in reckoning.

52. This is a preaching for mankind, that they may be warned thereby, and that they may know that there is only One God, and that the men of understanding may be admonished.

وَقَدْ مَكَرُوا مَكْرَهُمْ وَعِنْدَ اللّٰهِ مَكْرُهُمْ وَإِنْ كَانَ مَكْرُهُمْ لِتَزُوْلَ مِنْهُ الْجِبَالُ ﴿٤٦﴾

فَلَا تَحْسَبَنَّ اللّٰهَ مُخْلِفَ وَعْدِهِ رُسُلَهُ ۚ إِنَّ اللّٰهَ عَزِيْزٌ ذُو انْتِقَامٍ ﴿٤٧﴾

يَوْمَ تُبَدَّلُ الْأَرْضُ غَيْرَ الْأَرْضِ وَالسَّمٰوٰتُ وَبَرَزُوا لِلّٰهِ الْوَاحِدِ الْقَهَّارِ ﴿٤٨﴾

وَتَرَى الْمُجْرِمِيْنَ يَوْمَئِذٍ مُقَرَّنِيْنَ فِي الْأَصْفَادِ ﴿٤٩﴾

سَرَابِيْلُهُمْ مِّنْ قَطِرَانٍ وَتَغْشٰى وُجُوْهَهُمُ النَّارُ ﴿٥٠﴾

لِيَجْزِيَ اللّٰهُ كُلَّ نَفْسٍ مَّا كَسَبَتْ ۚ إِنَّ اللّٰهَ سَرِيْعُ الْحِسَابِ ﴿٥١﴾

هٰذَا بَلَاغٌ لِّلنَّاسِ وَلِيُنْذَرُوا بِهِ وَلِيَعْلَمُوا أَنَّمَا هُوَ إِلٰهٌ وَاحِدٌ وَلِيَذَّكَّرَ أُولُوا الْأَلْبَابِ ﴿٥٢﴾

---

446. The God of Islam is not an abstraction, an impersonal and inert something. He is a living Personality, Just, Awful, Awarder of punishment to the guilty.

447. This refutes the grossly polytheistic notion of Christianity that not before God, but before 'the Son of man' 'shall be gathered all nations: and he shall separate them one from another' (Mt. 25: 32).

Sūrah 15

al-Ḥijr

(Makkan, 6 Sections, 99 Verses)

In the name of Allah, the Compassionate, the Merciful.

Section 1

1. *Alif, Lām, Rā.* These are the verses of a Book and a Qur'ān luminous.

2. Often would those who disbelieved desire that they had been Muslims.

3. Leave them you to eat and enjoy, and let vain hopes divert them; presently they will come to know.

4. Not a town We have destroyed but there was for it a decree known.

5. No community can precede its term nor can it fall behind.

6. And they say: 'O you to whom the admonition has been sent down! Verily you are possessed;

7. Why do you not bring angels to us if you are of the truth-tellers?'

8. We send not down the angels save with judgement; and then they would not be respited.

9. Verily We! It is We Who have revealed the admonition,[448] and We are its Guardian.[449]

إِنَّا نَحْنُ نَزَّلْنَا الذِّكْرَ وَإِنَّا لَهُ لَحَافِظُونَ ۝

10. And assuredly We have sent Messengers before you among the sects of the ancients.

وَلَقَدْ أَرْسَلْنَا مِن قَبْلِكَ فِي شِيَعِ الْأَوَّلِينَ ۝

11. And not a Messenger came to them but at him they were wont to mock.

وَمَا يَأْتِيهِم مِّن رَّسُولٍ إِلَّا كَانُوا بِهِ يَسْتَهْزِءُونَ ۝

12. Even so We make a way for it in the hearts of the culprits.

كَذَلِكَ نَسْلُكُهُ فِي قُلُوبِ الْمُجْرِمِينَ ۝

13. They do not believe in it, and already the example of the ancients has gone forth.

لَا يُؤْمِنُونَ بِهِ وَقَدْ خَلَتْ سُنَّةُ الْأَوَّلِينَ ۝

14. And if We opened upon them a door of the heaven, and they passed the day mounting thereto,

وَلَوْ فَتَحْنَا عَلَيْهِم بَابًا مِّنَ السَّمَاءِ فَظَلُّوا فِيهِ يَعْرُجُونَ ۝

15. They would surely say: 'Our eyes have been dazzled; aye! We must have been enchanted.'

لَقَالُوا إِنَّمَا سُكِّرَتْ أَبْصَارُنَا بَلْ نَحْنُ قَوْمٌ مَّسْحُورُونَ ۝

---

448. Revealed it verbally and literally, with no human element therein whatever, the Prophet being merely the unerring mouthpiece of God. Not only is the meaning of the Holy Book therefore inspired but every word, every letter dictated — through the angel Gabriel to the Prophet from an Archetype preserved in the heavens. This is the distinctive claim of the Holy Qur'ān shared by no other 'revealed Books' in the world. 'The Bible, in particular, makes no such claims. The Bible is the work of a large number of poets/prophets, statesmen and lawgivers, extending over a vast period of time, and incorporates with itself other and earlier, and often conflicting documents' (Bosworth Smith, *Mohammed and Mohammedanism*, p. 19).

449. Guardians of its absolute purity, against all corruption, accretion and mutilation. Islam knows no such thing as 'redactions' to its Holy Text. Even those who have most stoutly denied its being the Word of God are unanimous in testifying to its being exactly the same 'work of Muḥammad' as it was fourteen centuries ago. Let us have the testimony of a few such unwilling witnesses:

(i)   'This text of the Qur'an is the purest of all the works of alike antiquity' (Wherry, *Commentary on the Koran*, I. p. 349).

(ii)   'Othman's recension has remained the authorised text from the time it was made until the present day' (Palmer, *The Quran*, p. lix).

(iii)   'The text of this recension substantially corresponds to the actual utterances of Muhammad himself' (Arnold, *Islamic Faith*, p. 9).

(iv)   'All sects and parties have the same text of the Qur'an' (Hurgronje, *Mohammedanism*, p.18).

(v)   'It is an immense merit in the Kuran that there is no doubt as to its genuineness... That very word we can now read with full confidence that it has remained unchanged through nearly thirteen hundred years' (*LSK.*, p. 3).

(vi)   'The recension of 'Othman has been handed down to us unaltered. There is probably in the world no other work which has remained twelve centuries with so pure a text' (Muir, *Life of Muhammad*, pp. XXII–XXIII).

(vii)   'In the Kuran we have, beyond all reasonable doubt, the exact words of Mohammad without substraction and without addition' (Bosworth Smith, *Mohammed and Mohammedanism*, p. 22).

(viii)   'The Koran was his own creation; and it lies before us practically unchanged from the form which he himself gave it' (Torrey, *Jewish Foundations of Islam*, p. 2).

(ix)   'Modern critics agree that the copies current today are almost exact replicas of the original mother text as complied by Zayd, and that, on the whole, the text of the Koran today is as Muhammad produced it. As some Semitic scholar has remarked, there are probably more variations in the reading of one chapter of Genesis in Hebrew than there are in the entire Koran' (Hitti, *History of the Arabs*, p. 123).

Section 2

16. And assuredly We have set constellations in the heavens and made it fairseeming to the onlookers.

وَلَقَدْ جَعَلْنَا فِي السَّمَاءِ بُرُوجًا وَزَيَّنَّـٰهَا لِلنَّـٰظِرِينَ ﴿١٦﴾

17. And We have guarded it from every Satan damned;

وَحَفِظْنَـٰهَا مِن كُلِّ شَيْطَـٰنٍ رَّجِيمٍ ﴿١٧﴾

18. Save him who steals the hearing, and him who pursues a flame gleaming.

إِلَّا مَنِ اسْتَرَقَ السَّمْعَ فَأَتْبَعَهُ شِهَابٌ مُّبِينٌ ﴿١٨﴾

19. And the earth! We have stretched it out and have cast on it firm mountains, and We have caused to spring up on it everything in due measure.

وَالْأَرْضَ مَدَدْنَـٰهَا وَأَلْقَيْنَا فِيهَا رَوَاسِيَ وَأَنبَتْنَا فِيهَا مِن كُلِّ شَيْءٍ مَّوْزُونٍ ﴿١٩﴾

20. And We have appointed on it your means of living and also for those of whom you are not the providers.

وَجَعَلْنَا لَكُمْ فِيهَا مَعَـٰيِشَ وَمَن لَّسْتُمْ لَهُ بِرَٰزِقِينَ ﴿٢٠﴾

21. And there is nothing of which there are not with Us the treasurers, and We do not send it down, save in a known measure.

وَإِن مِّن شَيْءٍ إِلَّا عِندَنَا خَزَائِنُهُ وَمَا نُنَزِّلُهُ إِلَّا بِقَدَرٍ مَّعْلُومٍ ﴿٢١﴾

22. And We send the winds fertilizing, then We send down water from the heaven, and We give it to you to drink, and of it you could not be the treasurers.

وَأَرْسَلْنَا الرِّيَـٰحَ لَوَٰقِحَ فَأَنزَلْنَا مِنَ السَّمَاءِ مَاءً فَأَسْقَيْنَـٰكُمُوهُ وَمَا أَنتُمْ لَهُ بِخَـٰزِنِينَ ﴿٢٢﴾

23. And verily We! We it is who give life and death, and We shall be the survivors.

وَإِنَّا لَنَحْنُ نُحْيِ وَنُمِيتُ وَنَحْنُ الْوَٰرِثُونَ ﴿٢٣﴾

24. And assuredly We know those of you who have gone before and those who will come here after.

وَلَقَدۡ عَلِمۡنَا الۡمُسۡتَقۡدِمِينَ مِنكُمۡ وَلَقَدۡ عَلِمۡنَا الۡمُسۡتَـٔۡخِرِينَ ﴿٢٤﴾

25. And verily your Lord! He will gather them and verily He is the Wise, the Knowing.

وَإِنَّ رَبَّكَ هُوَ يَحۡشُرُهُمۡ إِنَّهُۥ حَكِيمٌ عَلِيمٌ ﴿٢٥﴾

Section 3

26. And assuredly We have created human beings from ringing clay of moulded loam.

وَلَقَدۡ خَلَقۡنَا الۡإِنسَـٰنَ مِن صَلۡصَـٰلٍ مِّنۡ حَمَإٍ مَّسۡنُونٍ ﴿٢٦﴾

27. And the *jinn*, We had created them afore of the fire of the scorching wind.[450]

وَالۡجَآنَّ خَلَقۡنَـٰهُ مِن قَبۡلُ مِن نَّارِ السَّمُومِ ﴿٢٧﴾

28. And recall when your Lord said to the angels: 'I am about to create a man from ringing clay of moulded loam.

وَإِذۡ قَالَ رَبُّكَ لِلۡمَلَـٰٓئِكَةِ إِنِّي خَـٰلِقٌۢ بَشَرًا مِّن صَلۡصَـٰلٍ مِّنۡ حَمَإٍ مَّسۡنُونٍ ﴿٢٨﴾

29. Then when I have formed him and breathed into him of My spirit[451], fall down unto him prostrate.'

فَإِذَا سَوَّيۡتُهُۥ وَنَفَخۡتُ فِيهِ مِن رُّوحِي فَقَعُوا۟ لَهُۥ سَـٰجِدِينَ ﴿٢٩﴾

30. So the angels prostrated themselves, all of them together.

فَسَجَدَ الۡمَلَـٰٓئِكَةُ كُلُّهُمۡ أَجۡمَعُونَ ﴿٣٠﴾

---

450. The genii are therefore neither gods nor demi-gods, but ordinary created beings, and mortal like men, only made of a different substance. The Bible while narrating this period of the world's history speaks of the 'Sons of God' and 'giants' as inhabiting the earth. (Ge. 6: 2, 4).

451. Note that this spirit was at no time withdrawn. This strikes at the root of Pauline Christianity which proceeds on the assumption that in consequence of the fall of Adam and Eve, the Spirit which God breathed into the nostrils of Adam was withdrawn.

31. But Iblīs did not, he refused to be with the prostrate.

إِلَّا إِبْلِيسَ أَبَىٰ أَن يَكُونَ مَعَ ٱلسَّٰجِدِينَ ﴿٣١﴾

32. Allah said: 'O Iblīs! How is it that you are not with the prostrate?'

قَالَ يَـٰٓإِبْلِيسُ مَا لَكَ أَلَّا تَكُونَ مَعَ ٱلسَّٰجِدِينَ ﴿٣٢﴾

33. He said: 'It was not for me that I should prostrate myself before a human being whom You have created from ringing clay of moulded loam.'

قَالَ لَمْ أَكُن لِّأَسْجُدَ لِبَشَرٍ خَلَقْتَهُۥ مِن صَلْصَٰلٍ مِّنْ حَمَإٍ مَّسْنُونٍ ﴿٣٣﴾

34. Allah said: 'Then get you forth from here, verily you are one damned.

قَالَ فَٱخْرُجْ مِنْهَا فَإِنَّكَ رَجِيمٌ ﴿٣٤﴾

35. And on you shall be the curse of all on the Day of Judgement.'

وَإِنَّ عَلَيْكَ ٱللَّعْنَةَ إِلَىٰ يَوْمِ ٱلدِّينِ ﴿٣٥﴾

36. He said: 'Lord! Respite me then till the Day on which people will be raised up.'

قَالَ رَبِّ فَأَنظِرْنِىٓ إِلَىٰ يَوْمِ يُبْعَثُونَ ﴿٣٦﴾

37. Allah said: 'Well, then you are of the respited.

قَالَ فَإِنَّكَ مِنَ ٱلْمُنظَرِينَ ﴿٣٧﴾

38. Till the Day of the time known.'

إِلَىٰ يَوْمِ ٱلْوَقْتِ ٱلْمَعْلُومِ ﴿٣٨﴾

39. He said: 'Lord! Because You have led me to err, I will surely make things alluring to them on the earth, and I will surely seduce them all;

قَالَ رَبِّ بِمَآ أَغْوَيْتَنِى لَأُزَيِّنَنَّ لَهُمْ فِى ٱلْأَرْضِ وَلَأُغْوِيَنَّهُمْ أَجْمَعِينَ ﴿٣٩﴾

40. But not such of them as are Your sincere bondsmen.'

إِلَّا عِبَادَكَ مِنْهُمُ ٱلْمُخْلَصِينَ ﴿٤٠﴾

41. Allah said: 'This is the path leading to Me straight;

قَالَ هَذَا صِرَاطٌ عَلَيَّ مُسْتَقِيمٌ ۝

42. Verily as for My bondsmen, no authority shall you have over them,[452] except over erring ones who follow you.'

إِنَّ عِبَادِي لَيْسَ لَكَ عَلَيْهِمْ سُلْطَانٌ إِلَّا مَنِ اتَّبَعَكَ مِنَ الْغَاوِينَ ۝

43. And verily Hell is the place promised to them all.

وَإِنَّ جَهَنَّمَ لَمَوْعِدُهُمْ أَجْمَعِينَ ۝

44. To it are seven portals; to each portal is a portion of them assigned.

لَهَا سَبْعَةُ أَبْوَابٍ لِكُلِّ بَابٍ مِّنْهُمْ جُزْءٌ مَّقْسُومٌ ۝

Section 4

45. The God-fearing shall be amidst Gardens and springs.

إِنَّ الْمُتَّقِينَ فِي جَنَّاتٍ وَعُيُونٍ ۝

46. Enter there in peace, secure.

ادْخُلُوهَا بِسَلَامٍ آمِنِينَ ۝

47. And We will remove what-soever of rancour may be in their hearts; brethren they, sitting upon couches facing each other.

وَنَزَعْنَا مَا فِي صُدُورِهِم مِّنْ غِلٍّ إِخْوَانًا عَلَى سُرُرٍ مُّتَقَابِلِينَ ۝

48. There shall touch them no toil there, nor shall they be ever driven forth from there.

لَا يَمَسُّهُمْ فِيهَا نَصَبٌ وَمَا هُم مِّنْهَا بِمُخْرَجِينَ ۝

49. Declare you to My bondsmen; verily I!, I am the Forgiving, the Merciful.

نَبِّئْ عِبَادِي أَنِّي أَنَا الْغَفُورُ الرَّحِيمُ ۝

50. And verily My torment! That is the torment afflictive!

وَأَنَّ عَذَابِي هُوَ الْعَذَابُ الْأَلِيمُ ۝

---

452. Thus Satan is in no sense a deity or sub–deity, nor is he 'the lord of the material world' as held by several peoples. The real source of evil lies, not in any outside agency, but in the voluntary action of man himself in the apostasy of human will and intelligence from God.

51. And tell you them of Abraham's guests.

وَنَبِّئْهُمْ عَن ضَيْفِ إِبْرَٰهِيمَ ۝

52. When they entered unto him, and said, 'peace!' He said: 'We are afraid of you.'

إِذْ دَخَلُوا عَلَيْهِ فَقَالُوا سَلَٰمًا قَالَ إِنَّا مِنكُمْ وَجِلُونَ ۝

53. They said: 'Do not be afraid; we bear you the glad tidings of a boy knowing.'

قَالُوا لَا تَوْجَلْ إِنَّا نُبَشِّرُكَ بِغُلَٰمٍ عَلِيمٍ ۝

54. He said: 'Do you bear me that glad tiding when old age has touched me? Of what then do you give me the glad tidings?'

قَالَ أَبَشَّرْتُمُونِي عَلَىٰ أَن مَّسَّنِيَ الْكِبَرُ فَبِمَ تُبَشِّرُونَ ۝

55. They said: 'We bear you the glad tidings of a truth; do not be you of the desponding.'

قَالُوا بَشَّرْنَٰكَ بِالْحَقِّ فَلَا تَكُن مِّنَ الْقَٰنِطِينَ ۝

56. He said: 'And who desponds of the mercy of his Lord except the astray?'

قَالَ وَمَن يَقْنَطُ مِن رَّحْمَةِ رَبِّهِ إِلَّا الضَّالُّونَ ۝

57. He said: 'What is your errand, O sent ones?'

قَالَ فَمَا خَطْبُكُمْ أَيُّهَا الْمُرْسَلُونَ ۝

58. They said: 'Verily we have been sent to a people guilty,

قَالُوا إِنَّا أُرْسِلْنَا إِلَىٰ قَوْمٍ مُّجْرِمِينَ ۝

59. All except the household of Lot; surely we are going to deliver all of them;

إِلَّا ءَالَ لُوطٍ إِنَّا لَمُنَجُّوهُمْ أَجْمَعِينَ ۝

60. But not his wife; we have decreed that she will be of them who tarry.'

إِلَّا امْرَأَتَهُ قَدَّرْنَا إِنَّهَا لَمِنَ الْغَٰبِرِينَ ۝

Section 5

61. Then when the sent ones entered into the household of Lot;

فَلَمَّا جَآءَ ءَالَ لُوطٍ الْمُرْسَلُونَ ﴿٦١﴾

62. He said: 'Verily you are a people stranger.'

قَالَ إِنَّكُمْ قَوْمٌ مُّنكَرُونَ ﴿٦٢﴾

63. They said: 'Nay! We have come to you with that of which they have been doubting;

قَالُوا بَلْ جِئْنَكَ بِمَا كَانُوا فِيهِ يَمْتَرُونَ ﴿٦٣﴾

64. And we have brought to you the Truth, and verily we speak truth.

وَأَتَيْنَكَ بِالْحَقِّ وَإِنَّا لَصَدِقُونَ ﴿٦٤﴾

65. So set forth you with your household in a portion of the night, and follow you behind them, and let not one of you look back, and pass wither you are commanded.'

فَأَسْرِ بِأَهْلِكَ بِقِطْعٍ مِّنَ الَّيْلِ وَاتَّبِعْ أَدْبَرَهُمْ وَلَا يَلْتَفِتْ مِنكُمْ أَحَدٌ وَامْضُوا حَيْثُ تُؤْمَرُونَ ﴿٦٥﴾

66. And We decreed to him this commandment because the last of those was to be cut off in the early morning.

وَقَضَيْنَا إِلَيْهِ ذَلِكَ الْأَمْرَ أَنَّ دَابِرَ هَؤُلَاءِ مَقْطُوعٌ مُّصْبِحِينَ ﴿٦٦﴾

67. And there came the people of the city rejoicing.

وَجَآءَ أَهْلُ الْمَدِينَةِ يَسْتَبْشِرُونَ ﴿٦٧﴾

68. He said: 'Verily these are my guests, so humiliate me not;

قَالَ إِنَّ هَؤُلَاءِ ضَيْفِى فَلَا تَفْضَحُونِ ﴿٦٨﴾

69. And fear Allah, and disgrace me not.'

وَاتَّقُوا اللَّهَ وَلَا تُخْزُونِ ﴿٦٩﴾

70. They said: 'Had we not forbidden you against the outside world?'

قَالُوا أَوَلَمْ نَنْهَكَ عَنِ الْعَلَمِينَ ﴿٧٠﴾

71.   He said: 'These are my daughters, if act you must.'

قَالَ هَـٰؤُلَآءِ بَنَاتِیٓ إِن كُنتُمْ فَـٰعِلِینَ ۝

72.   By your life, in their intoxication; they were wandering bewildered.

لَعَمْرُكَ إِنَّهُمْ لَفِی سَكْرَتِهِمْ یَعْمَهُونَ ۝

73.   Then the shout took hold of them at sunrise.

فَأَخَذَتْهُمُ ٱلصَّیْحَةُ مُشْرِقِینَ ۝

74.   And We made the upside thereof downwards, and We rained on them stones of baked clay.

فَجَعَلْنَا عَـٰلِیَهَا سَافِلَهَا وَأَمْطَرْنَا عَلَیْهِمْ حِجَارَةً مِّن سِجِّیلٍ ۝

75.   Verily in that are signs for men of sagacity.

إِنَّ فِی ذَٰلِكَ لَـَٔایَـٰتٍ لِّلْمُتَوَسِّمِینَ ۝

76.   And verily they are on a lasting pathway.

وَإِنَّهَا لَبِسَبِیلٍ مُّقِیمٍ ۝

77.   Verily in that is a sign for the believers.

إِنَّ فِی ذَٰلِكَ لَـَٔایَةً لِّلْمُؤْمِنِینَ ۝

78.   And the dwellers of the wood surely were wrong-doers.

وَإِن كَانَ أَصْحَـٰبُ ٱلْأَیْكَةِ لَظَـٰلِمِینَ ۝

79.   So We took vengeance on them. And verily both are on an open high road.

فَٱنتَقَمْنَا مِنْهُمْ وَإِنَّهُمَا لَبِإِمَامٍ مُّبِینٍ ۝

Section 6

80. And assuredly the dwellers of Ḥijr belied the sent ones.

وَلَقَدْ كَذَّبَ أَصْحَـٰبُ ٱلْحِجْرِ ٱلْمُرْسَلِینَ ۝

81. And We brought Our signs to them, but they turned away from them.

وَءَاتَیْنَـٰهُمْ ءَایَـٰتِنَا فَكَانُوا۟ عَنْهَا مُعْرِضِینَ ۝

82. And they were hewing out houses from mountains, feeling secure.

وَكَانُوا يَنْحِتُونَ مِنَ ٱلْجِبَالِ بُيُوتًا ءَامِنِينَ ﴿٨٢﴾

83. Then the shout took hold of them in the early morn.

فَأَخَذَتْهُمُ ٱلصَّيْحَةُ مُصْبِحِينَ ﴿٨٣﴾

84. Then it availed them not what they had been earning.

فَمَآ أَغْنَىٰ عَنْهُم مَّا كَانُوا يَكْسِبُونَ ﴿٨٤﴾

85. We have not created the heavens and the earth and what is in-between save with a purpose. And the Hour is surely coming. So overlook them you with a seemly overlooking.

وَمَا خَلَقْنَا ٱلسَّمَٰوَٰتِ وَٱلْأَرْضَ وَمَا بَيْنَهُمَآ إِلَّا بِٱلْحَقِّ وَإِنَّ ٱلسَّاعَةَ لَآتِيَةٌ فَٱصْفَحِ ٱلصَّفْحَ ٱلْجَمِيلَ ﴿٨٥﴾

86. Verily your Lord! He is the Great Creator, the Knower.

إِنَّ رَبَّكَ هُوَ ٱلْخَلَّٰقُ ٱلْعَلِيمُ ﴿٨٦﴾

87. And assuredly We have given you seven of the repetitions[453] and the Mighty Qur'ān.[454]

وَلَقَدْ ءَاتَيْنَٰكَ سَبْعًا مِّنَ ٱلْمَثَانِي وَٱلْقُرْءَانَ ٱلْعَظِيمَ ﴿٨٧﴾

88. Do not cast your eyes towards what We have let the classes of infidels enjoy, and grieve not over them; and lower your wings to the believers.

لَا تَمُدَّنَّ عَيْنَيْكَ إِلَىٰ مَا مَتَّعْنَا بِهِۦٓ أَزْوَٰجًا مِّنْهُمْ وَلَا تَحْزَنْ عَلَيْهِمْ وَٱخْفِضْ جَنَاحَكَ لِلْمُؤْمِنِينَ ﴿٨٨﴾

---

453. In other words, of the oft-repeated verses: Sūrah al-Fātiḥah, or the first chapter of the Qur'ān, which consists of seven verses and has to be repeated in every prayer. 'The simple and meaningful Fatihah, often likened to the Lord's Prayer, is reiterated by the faithful Moslem about twenty times a day. This makes it one of the most often repeated formulas ever devised' (Hitti, *History of the Arabs*, p. 131).

454. The Qur'ān itself; so look at these incomparable and invaluable gifts, and overlook the ridicule and persecution of the infidels. That the Qur'ān is one of the mightiest works in existence is acknowledged even by unfriendly Christians. 'The Kuran is undoubtedly the most influential book in the world after the Bible' (*The Columbia Encyclopedia*, p. 983).

89. And say you: 'Verily I! I am a plain warner.'

وَقُلْ إِنِّى أَنَا ٱلنَّذِيرُ ٱلْمُبِينُ ﴿٨٩﴾

90. Even as We have sent down on the dividers,

كَمَآ أَنزَلْنَا عَلَى ٱلْمُقْتَسِمِينَ ﴿٩٠﴾

91. Those who made the Scriptures bits.

ٱلَّذِينَ جَعَلُوا ٱلْقُرْءَانَ عِضِينَ ﴿٩١﴾

92. By your Lord, We will question them all;

فَوَرَبِّكَ لَنَسْـَٔلَنَّهُمْ أَجْمَعِينَ ﴿٩٢﴾

93. For what they have been doing.

عَمَّا كَانُوا يَعْمَلُونَ ﴿٩٣﴾

94. Promulgate you what you are commanded, and turn away from the associators.

فَٱصْدَعْ بِمَا تُؤْمَرُ وَأَعْرِضْ عَنِ ٱلْمُشْرِكِينَ ﴿٩٤﴾

95. Verily We will suffice you against the mockers,

إِنَّا كَفَيْنَٰكَ ٱلْمُسْتَهْزِءِينَ ﴿٩٥﴾

96. Who set up along with Allah another god; presently they shall know.

ٱلَّذِينَ يَجْعَلُونَ مَعَ ٱللَّهِ إِلَٰهًا ءَاخَرَ فَسَوْفَ يَعْلَمُونَ ﴿٩٦﴾

97. And assuredly We know that you straiten your breast by what they say.

وَلَقَدْ نَعْلَمُ أَنَّكَ يَضِيقُ صَدْرُكَ بِمَا يَقُولُونَ ﴿٩٧﴾

98. So hallow you the praise of your Lord, and be you of the prostrate.

فَسَبِّحْ بِحَمْدِ رَبِّكَ وَكُن مِّنَ ٱلسَّٰجِدِينَ ﴿٩٨﴾

99. And worship your Lord until there comes to you the certainty.

وَٱعْبُدْ رَبَّكَ حَتَّىٰ يَأْتِيَكَ ٱلْيَقِينُ ﴿٩٩﴾

Sūrah 16

al-Naḥl

(Makkan, 16 Sections, 128 Verses)

In the name of Allah, the Compassionate, the Merciful.

Section 1

1. The affair of Allah comes, so do not seek to hasten it. Hallowed be He and Exalted above what they associate.

2. He sends down the angels with the Spirit by His command upon whosoever of His bondsmen He wills; warn that there is no god but I, so fear Me.

3. He has created the heavens and the earth with a purpose. Exalted is He above what they associate.

4. He has created man from a drop, and lo! He is a disputant open.

5. And the cattle! He has created them. For you in them there is warmth and other profits and of them you eat.[455]

---

455. This reminds us once more that cattle are meant for human use, not for veneration and worship, as practised by various polytheistic peoples in India, Egypt and Babylonia. The early Semites too 'like other pastoral peoples paid great reverence to cattle, their kinship with whom they had long continued to recognise' (*EBi.* c. 715).

6. And for you there is a beauty in them as you drive them at the eventide and as you drive them out to pasture.

وَلَكُمۡ فِيهَا جَمَالٌ حِيۡنَ تُرِيۡحُوۡنَ وَ حِيۡنَ تَسۡرَحُوۡنَ ۞

7. And they bear your loads to a city which you could not reach except with the travail of your souls; verily your Lord is the Kind, the Merciful.

وَتَحۡمِلُ أَثۡقَالَكُمۡ إِلَى بَلَدٍ لَّمۡ تَكُوۡنُوۡا بَالِغِيۡهِ إِلَّا بِشِقِّ الۡأَنۡفُسِ إِنَّ رَبَّكُمۡ لَرَءُوۡفٌ رَّحِيۡمٌ ۞

8. And He has created horses and mules and asses that you may ride them, and as an adornment;[456] and He creates what you do not know.

وَالۡخَيۡلَ وَالۡبِغَالَ وَالۡحَمِيۡرَ لِتَرۡكَبُوۡهَا وَزِيۡنَةً وَيَخۡلُقُ مَا لَا تَعۡلَمُوۡنَ ۞

9. And upon Allah is the direction of the way, and of that is some crooked, and had He willed, He would have guided you all.

وَعَلَى اللّٰهِ قَصۡدُ السَّبِيۡلِ وَمِنۡهَا جَآئِرٌ وَلَوۡ شَآءَ لَهَدَىٰكُمۡ أَجۡمَعِيۡنَ ۞

Section 2

10. He it is Who sends down from the heaven water for you, from which is drinking and from which is vegetation from which you pasture your herds.

هُوَ الَّذِىٓ أَنۡزَلَ مِنَ السَّمَآءِ مَآءً لَّكُمۡ مِّنۡهُ شَرَابٌ وَمِنۡهُ شَجَرٌ فِيۡهِ تُسِيۡمُوۡنَ ۞

---

456. The proper relation of man with all these creatures is not of adoring them but of understanding and using them. They are neither the incarnation of a deity, nor the receptacle of any indwelling Divine soul; they are merely a means of transport and a source of power and wealth to man. The phenomena of zoolatry have been assigned three distinct motives by anthropologists (*PC*. II. p. 237 ff.):

(i) direct worship of the animal for itself,

(ii) indirect worship of it as a fetish acted through by a deity, and

(iii) veneration for it as a totem or representative of a tribe–ancestor. Clearly all these notions are false and fanciful and an insult to human intelligence. The horse has been invariably an especially holy animal (*ERE*. I. p. 519), while the ass cult too has not been unknown (*ERE*. I. pp. 501–502).

11. He grows thereby the corn and olive and date palms and grapes and all manner of fruit. Verily in that is a sign for a people who ponder.[457]

يُنْبِتُ لَكُمْ بِهِ الزَّرْعَ وَالزَّيْتُوْنَ وَالنَّخِيْلَ وَالْأَعْنَابَ وَمِنْ كُلِّ الثَّمَرَاتِ إِنَّ فِي ذَلِكَ لَآيَةً لِّقَوْمٍ يَتَفَكَّرُوْنَ ۞

12. And He has subjected to you the night and the day and the sun and the moon, and the stars are subjected by His command. Verily in that are signs for a people who understand.

وَسَخَّرَ لَكُمُ الَّيْلَ وَالنَّهَارَ وَالشَّمْسَ وَالْقَمَرَ وَالنُّجُوْمُ مُسَخَّرَاتٌ بِأَمْرِهِ إِنَّ فِي ذَلِكَ لَآيَاتٍ لِّقَوْمٍ يَعْقِلُوْنَ ۞

13. And He has subjected to you what He has multiplied for you on the earth of various kinds. Verily in that is a sign for a people who receive admonition.

وَمَا ذَرَأَ لَكُمْ فِي الْأَرْضِ مُخْتَلِفًا أَلْوَانُهُ إِنَّ فِي ذَلِكَ لَآيَةً لِّقَوْمٍ يَذَّكَّرُوْنَ ۞

14. And He it is who has subjected to you the sea[458] that you may eat of it fresh flesh, and bring forth out of it ornaments you wear. And you see ships ploughing therein, and it is in order that you may seek of His grace and that haply you may be grateful.

وَهُوَ الَّذِي سَخَّرَ الْبَحْرَ لِتَأْكُلُوْا مِنْهُ لَحْمًا طَرِيًّا وَتَسْتَخْرِجُوْا مِنْهُ حِلْيَةً تَلْبَسُوْنَهَا وَتَرَى الْفُلْكَ مَوَاخِرَ فِيْهِ وَلِتَبْتَغُوْا مِنْ فَضْلِهِ وَلَعَلَّكُمْ تَشْكُرُوْنَ ۞

---

457. This strikes at the root of Nature-worship and the cult of Nature-gods. There are no such curiosities in Nature as a God of agriculture, a Patron of husbandry, etc. In civilized Greece, annual festivals, known as Adonia, were held in honour of Adonis, the Vegetation Spirit. The cults of Apollo, as the protector of the fruits of the earth and the lower animals, of Aphrodite, as the bestower of all animal and vegetable fruitfulness, and of Attis, as the god of vegetation, are also well known to students of Greek and Roman history.

458. Subjected the sea to His service. There have been peoples worshipping both rivers and seas. 'Rivers are often worshipped as divine or as fertile mothers, while in Egypt the Nile was worshipped as a man. More usually, however, the cult developed into one paid to gods or spirits of rivers' (*ERE*. IX. p. 204). 'Like the earth, the sea has a double aspect. There are sea-gods, but the sea itself is a great being, feared by men yet also beneficent and worshipped, while even the personified sea-god is sometimes spoken of as the sea itself' (Ibid.).

15. And He has cast firm mountains on the earth lest it move away with you, and rivers and paths that haply you may be directed.

وَأَلْقَىٰ فِى ٱلْأَرْضِ رَوَٰسِىَ أَن تَمِيدَ بِكُمْ وَأَنْهَٰرًا وَسُبُلًا لَّعَلَّكُمْ تَهْتَدُونَ ۝

16. And also landmarks; and by the stars they are guided.

وَعَلَٰمَٰتٍ وَبِٱلنَّجْمِ هُمْ يَهْتَدُونَ ۝

17. Is the One Who creates as one who cannot create? Will you not be admonished?

أَفَمَن يَخْلُقُ كَمَن لَّا يَخْلُقُ أَفَلَا تَذَكَّرُونَ ۝

18. And if you would count the favours of Allah you could not compute them; verily Allah is the Forgiving, the Merciful.

وَإِن تَعُدُّوا۟ نِعْمَةَ ٱللَّهِ لَا تُحْصُوهَآ إِنَّ ٱللَّهَ لَغَفُورٌ رَّحِيمٌ ۝

19. And Allah knows what you keep secret and what you want to make known.

وَٱللَّهُ يَعْلَمُ مَا تُسِرُّونَ وَمَا تُعْلِنُونَ ۝

20. Those upon whom they call besides Allah have not created aught and are themselves created.

وَٱلَّذِينَ يَدْعُونَ مِن دُونِ ٱللَّهِ لَا يَخْلُقُونَ شَيْـًٔا وَهُمْ يُخْلَقُونَ ۝

21. Lifeless are they, not alive, they know not when they will be raised up.

أَمْوَٰتٌ غَيْرُ أَحْيَآءٍ وَمَا يَشْعُرُونَ أَيَّانَ يُبْعَثُونَ ۝

Section 3

22. God of you all is the One God; so those who do not believe in the Hereafter their hearts are perverse and they are stiff-necked.

إِلَٰهُكُمْ إِلَٰهٌ وَٰحِدٌ فَٱلَّذِينَ لَا يُؤْمِنُونَ بِٱلْءَاخِرَةِ قُلُوبُهُم مُّنكِرَةٌ وَهُم مُّسْتَكْبِرُونَ ۝

23. Allah undoubtedly knows what they keep secret and what they want to make known; verily He loves not the stiff-necked.

لَا جَرَمَ أَنَّ ٱللَّهَ يَعْلَمُ مَا يُسِرُّونَ وَمَا يُعْلِنُونَ إِنَّهُۥ لَا يُحِبُّ ٱلْمُسْتَكْبِرِينَ ۝

24. And when it is said to them: 'What is it that your Lord has sent down?' they say: 'Fables of the ancients.'

وَإِذَا قِيلَ لَهُم مَّاذَا أَنزَلَ رَبُّكُمْ قَالُوٓاْ أَسَٰطِيرُ ٱلْأَوَّلِينَ ﴿٢٤﴾

25. As a result they will bear their loads in full on the Day of Judgement and some of the loads of those whom they have led astray without any knowledge. Lo! Vile is the load they shall bear!

لِيَحْمِلُوٓاْ أَوْزَارَهُمْ كَامِلَةً يَوْمَ ٱلْقِيَٰمَةِ وَمِنْ أَوْزَارِ ٱلَّذِينَ يُضِلُّونَهُم بِغَيْرِ عِلْمٍ أَلَا سَآءَ مَا يَزِرُونَ ﴿٢٥﴾

Section 4

26. Surely there plotted those before them, but Allah came upon their structures from their foundations, so the roof fell upon them from above them, and the torment came to them whence they perceived not.

قَدْ مَكَرَ ٱلَّذِينَ مِن قَبْلِهِمْ فَأَتَى ٱللَّهُ بُنْيَٰنَهُم مِّنَ ٱلْقَوَاعِدِ فَخَرَّ عَلَيْهِمُ ٱلسَّقْفُ مِن فَوْقِهِمْ وَأَتَىٰهُمُ ٱلْعَذَابُ مِنْ حَيْثُ لَا يَشْعُرُونَ ﴿٢٦﴾

27. Then on the Day of Judgement He will disgrace them and say: 'Where are My associates regarding whom you used to cause cleavage?' Those who are given knowledge will say: 'Verily the disgrace and ill-hap today are upon the infidels.'

ثُمَّ يَوْمَ ٱلْقِيَٰمَةِ يُخْزِيهِمْ وَيَقُولُ أَيْنَ شُرَكَآءِىَ ٱلَّذِينَ كُنتُمْ تُشَٰقُّونَ فِيهِمْ قَالَ ٱلَّذِينَ أُوتُواْ ٱلْعِلْمَ إِنَّ ٱلْخِزْىَ ٱلْيَوْمَ وَٱلسُّوٓءَ عَلَى ٱلْكَٰفِرِينَ ﴿٢٧﴾

28. Those whom the angels cause to die while they are wronging themselves, and only then they proffer submission; we have not been working any evil. Yea! Allah is the Knower of what they have been doing.

ٱلَّذِينَ تَتَوَفَّىٰهُمُ ٱلْمَلَٰٓئِكَةُ ظَالِمِىٓ أَنفُسِهِمْ فَأَلْقَوُاْ ٱلسَّلَمَ مَا كُنَّا نَعْمَلُ مِن سُوٓءٍ بَلَىٰٓ إِنَّ ٱللَّهَ عَلِيمٌۢ بِمَا كُنتُمْ تَعْمَلُونَ ﴿٢٨﴾

29. So enter the portals of Hell as abiders therein. Vile is the abode of the arrogant.

فَادْخُلُوٓا أَبْوَٰبَ جَهَنَّمَ خَٰلِدِينَ فِيهَا فَلَبِئْسَ مَثْوَى ٱلْمُتَكَبِّرِينَ ﴿٢٩﴾

30. And when it is said to the God-fearing, 'what is it that your Lord has sent down?' They say: 'That which is good.' For those who do good is good in the world, and better still is the dwelling in the Hereafter; Excellent is the dwelling of the God-fearing.

وَقِيلَ لِلَّذِينَ ٱتَّقَوْا مَاذَآ أَنزَلَ رَبُّكُمْ قَالُوا خَيْرًا لِّلَّذِينَ أَحْسَنُوا فِى هَٰذِهِ ٱلدُّنْيَا حَسَنَةٌ وَلَدَارُ ٱلْأَخِرَةِ خَيْرٌ وَلَنِعْمَ دَارُ ٱلْمُتَّقِينَ ﴿٣٠﴾

31. Gardens everlasting which they shall enter, streams running beneath, theirs then shall be whatsoever they will. Thus does Allah recompense the God-fearing.

جَنَّٰتُ عَدْنٍ يَدْخُلُونَهَا تَجْرِى مِن تَحْتِهَا ٱلْأَنْهَٰرُ لَهُمْ فِيهَا مَا يَشَآءُونَ كَذَٰلِكَ يَجْزِى ٱللَّهُ ٱلْمُتَّقِينَ ﴿٣١﴾

32. Those whom the angels take away while they are goodly, saying: 'Peace be upon you, enter the Garden for what you have been working.'

ٱلَّذِينَ تَتَوَفَّىٰهُمُ ٱلْمَلَٰٓئِكَةُ طَيِّبِينَ يَقُولُونَ سَلَٰمٌ عَلَيْكُمُ ٱدْخُلُوا ٱلْجَنَّةَ بِمَا كُنتُمْ تَعْمَلُونَ ﴿٣٢﴾

33. Do they await that the angels should come to them or that the command of your Lord should come? Thus did those before them; Allah wronged them not, but they were wont to wrong themselves.

هَلْ يَنظُرُونَ إِلَّآ أَن تَأْتِيَهُمُ ٱلْمَلَٰٓئِكَةُ أَوْ يَأْتِىَ أَمْرُ رَبِّكَ كَذَٰلِكَ فَعَلَ ٱلَّذِينَ مِن قَبْلِهِمْ وَمَا ظَلَمَهُمُ ٱللَّهُ وَلَٰكِن كَانُوٓا أَنفُسَهُمْ يَظْلِمُونَ ﴿٣٣﴾

34. Then there befell them the vices of what they had worked, and then surrounded them that at which they had been mocking.

فَأَصَابَهُمْ سَيِّئَاتُ مَا عَمِلُوا وَحَاقَ بِهِم مَّا كَانُوا بِهِ يَسْتَهْزِءُونَ ﴿٣٤﴾

Section 5

35. And those who associate say: 'Had God willed we would not have worshipped aught besides Him, neither our fathers; nor would we have forbidden aught apart from Him.[459] Thus did those before them; naught is then on the Messengers excepting a plain preaching.

وَقَالَ الَّذِينَ أَشْرَكُوا لَوْ شَاءَ اللَّهُ مَا عَبَدْنَا مِن دُونِهِ مِن شَيْءٍ نَّحْنُ وَلَا ءَابَآؤُنَا وَلَا حَرَّمْنَا مِن دُونِهِ مِن شَيْءٍ كَذَٰلِكَ فَعَلَ الَّذِينَ مِن قَبْلِهِمْ فَهَلْ عَلَى الرُّسُلِ إِلَّا الْبَلَٰغُ الْمُبِينُ ﴿٣٥﴾

36. And assuredly We have raised in every community a Messenger saying: 'Worship Allah and avoid the devil.' Then of them were some whom Allah guided, and of them were some upon whom the straying was justified. So travel about the land and behold how has been the end of the liars.

وَلَقَدْ بَعَثْنَا فِي كُلِّ أُمَّةٍ رَّسُولًا أَنِ اعْبُدُوا اللَّهَ وَاجْتَنِبُوا الطَّٰغُوتَ فَمِنْهُم مَّنْ هَدَى اللَّهُ وَمِنْهُم مَّنْ حَقَّتْ عَلَيْهِ الضَّلَٰلَةُ فَسِيرُوا فِي الْأَرْضِ فَانظُرُوا كَيْفَ كَانَ عَٰقِبَةُ الْمُكَذِّبِينَ ﴿٣٦﴾

37. If you are solicitous for their guidance, then verily Allah does not guide whom He sends astray and for them there are no helpers.

إِن تَحْرِصْ عَلَىٰ هُدَىٰهُمْ فَإِنَّ اللَّهَ لَا يَهْدِي مَن يُضِلُّ وَمَا لَهُم مِّن نَّٰصِرِينَ ﴿٣٧﴾

38. They swear by God the most solemn of oaths that God would not raise him who dies. Yea! It is a promise on Him incumbent, but most men know not.

وَأَقْسَمُوا بِاللَّهِ جَهْدَ أَيْمَٰنِهِمْ لَا يَبْعَثُ اللَّهُ مَن يَمُوتُ بَلَىٰ وَعْدًا عَلَيْهِ حَقًّا وَلَٰكِنَّ أَكْثَرَ النَّاسِ لَا يَعْلَمُونَ ﴿٣٨﴾

---

459. In other words, without His command. The fallacy, which the pagans' argument involved, lay in their confusion of the 'will' of God and the liberty He has allowed mankind in the choice of their actions — with His pleasure or command; in not distinguishing between the physical laws of God's universe from His moral law. Because He has a universal Plan, and has created venomous reptiles it does not follow that He approves of men being bitten by snakes. Because He has endowed men with the power to steal and the capacity to kill, it does not follow that He is pleased with house–breaking and murder.

39. This will be in order that He may manifest to them that wherein they differ, and that those who disbelieved should come to know that they had been liars.

لِيُبَيِّنَ لَهُمُ الَّذِى يَخْتَلِفُونَ فِيهِ وَلِيَعْلَمَ الَّذِينَ كَفَرُوٓا أَنَّهُمْ كَانُوا كَٰذِبِينَ ۝

40. Our only saying unto a thing, when We intend it, is that We say to it, 'Be'; and it becomes.

إِنَّمَا قَوْلُنَا لِشَىْءٍ إِذَآ أَرَدْنَٰهُ أَن نَّقُولَ لَهُۥ كُن فَيَكُونُ ۝

Section 6

41. And those who have emigrated for the sake of Allah after they had been wronged, We will surely settle them well in the world, and the reward of the Hereafter is greater, if they but knew.

وَالَّذِينَ هَاجَرُوا فِى اللَّهِ مِنۢ بَعْدِ مَا ظُلِمُوا لَنُبَوِّئَنَّهُمْ فِى الدُّنْيَا حَسَنَةً وَلَأَجْرُ الْءَاخِرَةِ أَكْبَرُ لَوْ كَانُوا يَعْلَمُونَ ۝

42. They are those who bear in patience, and in their Lord they trust.

الَّذِينَ صَبَرُوا وَعَلَىٰ رَبِّهِمْ يَتَوَكَّلُونَ ۝

43. And We sent not before you any but men to whom We revealed; so ask the people of the admonition if you know not.

وَمَآ أَرْسَلْنَا مِن قَبْلِكَ إِلَّا رِجَالًا نُّوحِىٓ إِلَيْهِمْ فَسْـَٔلُوٓا أَهْلَ الذِّكْرِ إِن كُنتُمْ لَا تَعْلَمُونَ ۝

44. We sent them with evidence and the Scriptures, and We have sent down unto you the admonition that you may expound unto mankind what has been revealed toward them, and that haply they may reflect.

بِالْبَيِّنَٰتِ وَالزُّبُرِ وَأَنزَلْنَآ إِلَيْكَ الذِّكْرَ لِتُبَيِّنَ لِلنَّاسِ مَا نُزِّلَ إِلَيْهِمْ وَلَعَلَّهُمْ يَتَفَكَّرُونَ ۝

45. Do then those who have plotted vices feel secure that Allah will not sink them into the earth or that the torment may come from whence they know not?

أَفَأَمِنَ ٱلَّذِينَ مَكَرُوا۟ ٱلسَّيِّئَاتِ أَن يَخْسِفَ ٱللَّهُ بِهِمُ ٱلْأَرْضَ أَوْ يَأْتِيَهُمُ ٱلْعَذَابُ مِنْ حَيْثُ لَا يَشْعُرُونَ ﴿٤٥﴾

46. Or, that He will not seize them in their going to and fro? So that they cannot escape.

أَوْ يَأْخُذَهُمْ فِى تَقَلُّبِهِمْ فَمَا هُم بِمُعْجِزِينَ ﴿٤٦﴾

47. Or, that He will not seize them by giving them a fright? Verily your Lord is the Kind, the Merciful.

أَوْ يَأْخُذَهُمْ عَلَىٰ تَخَوُّفٍ فَإِنَّ رَبَّكُمْ لَرَءُوفٌ رَّحِيمٌ ﴿٤٧﴾

48. Have they not observed the things Allah has created? Shadows thereof turn themselves on the right at the left bowing themselves before Allah, and they are lowly.

أَوَلَمْ يَرَوْا۟ إِلَىٰ مَا خَلَقَ ٱللَّهُ مِن شَىْءٍ يَتَفَيَّؤُا۟ ظِلَٰلُهُۥ عَنِ ٱلْيَمِينِ وَٱلشَّمَآئِلِ سُجَّدًا لِّلَّهِ وَهُمْ دَٰخِرُونَ ﴿٤٨﴾

49. And before Allah bows whatever is in the heavens and whatever is in the earth of the living creatures and also the angels; and they are not stiff-necked.

وَلِلَّهِ يَسْجُدُ مَا فِى ٱلسَّمَٰوَٰتِ وَمَا فِى ٱلْأَرْضِ مِن دَآبَّةٍ وَٱلْمَلَٰٓئِكَةُ وَهُمْ لَا يَسْتَكْبِرُونَ ﴿٤٩﴾

50. They fear their Lord above them and do what they are commanded.[460]

يَخَافُونَ رَبَّهُم مِّن فَوْقِهِمْ وَيَفْعَلُونَ مَا يُؤْمَرُونَ ۩ ﴿٥٠﴾

---

460. That is the true position of angels; neither gods, nor demi-gods, they are but His absolutely obedient servants.

Section 7

51. Allah has said: 'Take not to you two gods;[461] He is only One God.[462] So dread Me, Me alone.

وَقَالَ اللَّهُ لَا تَتَّخِذُوٓا إِلَٰهَيْنِ اثْنَيْنِ إِنَّمَا هُوَ إِلَٰهٌ وَٰحِدٌ فَإِيَّٰيَ فَٱرْهَبُونِ ۝

52. His is whatsoever is in the heavens and the earth, and unto Him obedience is due perpetually; will you then fear any other than Allah?'

وَلَهُۥ مَا فِى ٱلسَّمَٰوَٰتِ وَٱلْأَرْضِ وَلَهُ ٱلدِّينُ وَاصِبًا أَفَغَيْرَ ٱللَّهِ تَتَّقُونَ ۝

53. And whatsoever of favours is with you is from Allah; then when distress afflicts you, to Him you cry out.

وَمَا بِكُم مِّن نِّعْمَةٍ فَمِنَ ٱللَّهِ ثُمَّ إِذَا مَسَّكُمُ ٱلضُّرُّ فَإِلَيْهِ تَجْـَٔرُونَ ۝

461. This repudiates 'dualism' in all its forms and shades, especially the Zoroastrian doctrine of two gods or two ultimate principles, Ahriman and Ormazd. 'At the beginning of things there existed the two spirits who represented good and evil. Both spirits possess creative power, which manifest itself positively in the one and negatively in the other' (*EBr.* XXII. p. 988). Dualism, however, is not confined to the Zoroastrian religion. In its 'rudimentary forms the antagonism of a Good and Evil Deity are well known among the lower races of mankind' (PC. II. p. 316). 'Now, in earlier ages mankind has been found believing in many gods, or in two original spiritual principles or gods, the one good and the other evil, which are at conflict in the universe. This latter belief, which we call dualism, is so congruous with part of our experience, both within ourselves and without ourselves, that it is always reviving. Nevertheless I think that, like polytheism properly so–called, it is rationally impossible for us today. The science of nature has demonstrated the absolute unity of nature. Good and evil, as we know them in experience, mind and matter the world of moral purpose and the world of material things, are not the product of two separate original forces. They are knit into one another as phases in one while, results of one force, one system of interconnected law. The universe, material and spiritual, is as Spinoza said, one and (in some sense) of one substance; and God, if there be a God, in part manifest and in part concealed in nature, is one only' (Gore, *Belief in God*, p. 46).

462. One God in Person as well as Attributes, and there is no other Being, good or evil, co-ordinate and co-eternal with Him. Islam gives no quarter to henotheism, which recognizes a plurality of gods as existing but allows the worship of only One God; the Qur'ān is insistent on denying their very existence.

54. Then when He removes the distress from you, forthwith a party of you associates others with their Lord,

ثُمَّ إِذَا كَشَفَ الضُّرَّ عَنكُمْ إِذَا فَرِيقٌ مِّنكُم بِرَبِّهِمْ يُشْرِكُونَ ۝

55. That they may show ingratitude for what We have bestowed upon them. Enjoy then, presently you shall know.

لِيَكْفُرُوا بِمَا آتَيْنَاهُمْ فَتَمَتَّعُوا فَسَوْفَ تَعْلَمُونَ ۝

56. And they appoint for what they know not a portion of what We have provided them. By Allah! You shall surely be questioned regarding what you have been fabricating.

وَيَجْعَلُونَ لِمَا لَا يَعْلَمُونَ نَصِيبًا مِّمَّا رَزَقْنَاهُمْ تَاللَّهِ لَتُسْأَلُنَّ عَمَّا كُنتُمْ تَفْتَرُونَ ۝

57. And they appoint for Allah daughters, Hallowed be He!, and for themselves what they desire.

وَيَجْعَلُونَ لِلَّهِ الْبَنَاتِ سُبْحَانَهُ وَلَهُم مَّا يَشْتَهُونَ ۝

58. And when there is announced unto any of them a female, his face remains darkened the whole day and is wroth inwardly,

وَإِذَا بُشِّرَ أَحَدُهُم بِالْأُنثَى ظَلَّ وَجْهُهُ مُسْوَدًّا وَهُوَ كَظِيمٌ ۝

59. Sulking from the people because of the evil of what has been announced unto him; shall he keep it with ignomy or bury it in the dust?[463] Lo! Vile is what they judge!

يَتَوَارَىٰ مِنَ الْقَوْمِ مِن سُوءِ مَا بُشِّرَ بِهِ أَيُمْسِكُهُ عَلَىٰ هُونٍ أَمْ يَدُسُّهُ فِي التُّرَابِ أَلَا سَاءَ مَا يَحْكُمُونَ ۝

---

463. 'The practice of burying newborn daughters alive was very general' (*HHW*. VIII. p. 8). 'That certain Arab tribes, especially the Tamim, practiced female infanticide is well known' (Robertson-Smith, *Kinship and Marriage in Early Arabia*, p. 129).

60. For those who are disbelievers in the Hereafter is an evil similitude[464], and for Allah is the sublime similitude, and He is the Mighty, the Wise.

لِلَّذِينَ لَا يُؤْمِنُونَ بِالْآخِرَةِ مَثَلُ السَّوْءِ وَلِلَّهِ الْمَثَلُ الْأَعْلَىٰ وَهُوَ الْعَزِيزُ الْحَكِيمُ ۝

Section 8

61. And if Allah were to seize mankind for their wrong doing, not a living creature He would leave on it, but He defers them to a term appointed; then when their term comes, they can neither put it off by an hour nor anticipate it.

وَلَوْ يُؤَاخِذُ اللَّهُ النَّاسَ بِظُلْمِهِم مَّا تَرَكَ عَلَيْهَا مِن دَآبَّةٍ وَلَٰكِن يُؤَخِّرُهُمْ إِلَىٰ أَجَلٍ مُّسَمًّى فَإِذَا جَآءَ أَجَلُهُمْ لَا يَسْتَخْخِرُونَ سَاعَةً وَلَا يَسْتَقْدِمُونَ ۝

62. They ascribe to Allah what they detest, and their tongues utter the falsehood that unto them shall be good; undoubtedly unto them shall be the Fire, and they shall be hastened thereto.

وَيَجْعَلُونَ لِلَّهِ مَا يَكْرَهُونَ وَتَصِفُ أَلْسِنَتُهُمُ الْكَذِبَ أَنَّ لَهُمُ الْحُسْنَىٰ لَا جَرَمَ أَنَّ لَهُمُ النَّارَ وَأَنَّهُم مُّفْرَطُونَ ۝

63. By Allah! We have sent Messengers to communities before you, then Satan made their own works fairseeming unto them, so he is their patron today and to them shall be an afflictive torment.

تَاللَّهِ لَقَدْ أَرْسَلْنَا إِلَىٰ أُمَمٍ مِّن قَبْلِكَ فَزَيَّنَ لَهُمُ الشَّيْطَانُ أَعْمَالَهُمْ فَهُوَ وَلِيُّهُمُ الْيَوْمَ وَلَهُمْ عَذَابٌ أَلِيمٌ ۝

---

464. To Him are to be ascribed the highest and noblest of Attributes. He is the acme of the Attributes of Perfection. This explicitly repudiates the Aristotelian doctrine of a 'limited' God. 'God, as conceived by Aristotle, has a knowledge which is not the knowledge of the universe, and an influence on the universe which does not flow from His knowledge; an influence which can hardly be called an activity since it is the sort of influence that one person may unconsciously have on another, or that even a statue or a picture may have on its admirer' (Ross, *Aristotle*, p. 183).

64. And We have not sent down the Book to you save in order that you may expound to them that whereon they differ and as a guidance and mercy to a people who believe.

وَمَاۤ أَنزَلۡنَا عَلَیۡكَ ٱلۡكِتَـٰبَ إِلَّا لِتُبَیِّنَ لَهُمُ ٱلَّذِی ٱخۡتَلَفُوا۟ فِیهِ وَهُدࣰى وَرَحۡمَةࣰ لِّقَوۡمࣲ یُؤۡمِنُونَ ۝٦٤

65. Allah has sent down from the heaven water, then He revives the earth by it after its death; verily in that is a sign for a people who listen.

وَٱللَّهُ أَنزَلَ مِنَ ٱلسَّمَاۤءِ مَاۤءࣰ فَأَحۡیَا بِهِ ٱلۡأَرۡضَ بَعۡدَ مَوۡتِهَاۤ إِنَّ فِی ذَ ٰلِكَ لَءَایَةࣰ لِّقَوۡمࣲ یَسۡمَعُونَ ۝٦٥

Section 9

66. Verily there is a lesson for you in the cattle; We give you to drink of what is in their bellies, between the dung and blood; milk, pure and pleasant to swallow for the drinkers.

وَإِنَّ لَكُمۡ فِی ٱلۡأَنۡعَـٰمِ لَعِبۡرَةࣰ نُّسۡقِیكُم مِّمَّا فِی بُطُونِهِۦ مِنۢ بَیۡنِ فَرۡثࣲ وَدَمࣲ لَّبَنًا خَالِصࣰا سَاۤئِغࣰا لِّلشَّـٰرِبِینَ ۝٦٦

67. And also a lesson is for you in the fruits of date palms and the grapes of which you take a liquor and a goodly provision, verily in that is a sign for a people who understand.

وَمِن ثَمَرَ ٰتِ ٱلنَّخِیلِ وَٱلۡأَعۡنَـٰبِ تَتَّخِذُونَ مِنۡهُ سَكَرࣰا وَرِزۡقًا حَسَنًاۚ إِنَّ فِی ذَ ٰلِكَ لَءَایَةࣰ لِّقَوۡمࣲ یَعۡقِلُونَ ۝٦٧

68. And your Lord inspired the bee saying: 'Take you for yourself houses of hills, of trees, and of what they erect.

وَأَوۡحَىٰ رَبُّكَ إِلَى ٱلنَّحۡلِ أَنِ ٱتَّخِذِی مِنَ ٱلۡجِبَالِ بُیُوتࣰا وَمِنَ ٱلشَّجَرِ وَمِمَّا یَعۡرِشُونَ ۝٦٨

69. Then eat you of all manner of fruits and tread the ways of your Lord made easy.' There springs forth from their bellies a drink varied in colours; in it is a healing for mankind; verily in that is a sign for a people who reflect.

ثُمَّ كُلِی مِن كُلِّ ٱلثَّمَرَ ٰتِ فَٱسۡلُكِی سُبُلَ رَبِّكِ ذُلُلࣰاۚ یَخۡرُجُ مِنۢ بُطُونِهَا شَرَابࣱ مُّخۡتَلِفٌ أَلۡوَ ٰنُهُۥ فِیهِ شِفَاۤءࣱ لِّلنَّاسِۚ إِنَّ فِی ذَ ٰلِكَ لَءَایَةࣰ لِّقَوۡمࣲ یَتَفَكَّرُونَ ۝٦٩

70. Allah has created you; then He takes your souls. Of you are some who are brought back to the meanest of age, so that they know not aught after having knowledge; verily Allah is the Knowing, the Wise.

وَٱللَّهُ خَلَقَكُمۡ ثُمَّ يَتَوَفَّىٰكُمۡ وَمِنكُم مَّن يُرَدُّ إِلَىٰٓ أَرۡذَلِ ٱلۡعُمُرِ لِكَىۡ لَا يَعۡلَمَ بَعۡدَ عِلۡمٍ شَيۡـًٔا إِنَّ ٱللَّهَ عَلِيمٌ قَدِيرٌ ۝

Section 10

71. And Allah has preferred some of you over some others in provision; then those who are preferred are not going to hand over their provision on those whom their right hands possess, so as to be their equal in that respect. Do they then gainsay the favour of Allah?

وَٱللَّهُ فَضَّلَ بَعۡضَكُمۡ عَلَىٰ بَعۡضٍ فِى ٱلرِّزۡقِ فَمَا ٱلَّذِينَ فُضِّلُوا۟ بِرَآدِّي رِزۡقِهِمۡ عَلَىٰ مَا مَلَكَتۡ أَيۡمَٰنُهُمۡ فَهُمۡ فِيهِ سَوَآءٌ أَفَبِنِعۡمَةِ ٱللَّهِ يَجۡحَدُونَ ۝

72. Allah has made for you of yourselves spouses, and from your spouses He has made for you sons and grandsons; and He has provided you with clean food. Do they then believe in falsehood and disbelieve in Allah's favour?

وَٱللَّهُ جَعَلَ لَكُم مِّنۡ أَنفُسِكُمۡ أَزۡوَٰجًا وَجَعَلَ لَكُم مِّنۡ أَزۡوَٰجِكُم بَنِينَ وَحَفَدَةً وَرَزَقَكُم مِّنَ ٱلطَّيِّبَٰتِ أَفَبِٱلۡبَٰطِلِ يُؤۡمِنُونَ وَبِنِعۡمَتِ ٱللَّهِ هُمۡ يَكۡفُرُونَ ۝

73. And they worship, besides Allah, what does not and cannot own for them any provision from the heavens and the earth.

وَيَعۡبُدُونَ مِن دُونِ ٱللَّهِ مَا لَا يَمۡلِكُ لَهُمۡ رِزۡقًا مِّنَ ٱلسَّمَٰوَٰتِ وَٱلۡأَرۡضِ شَيۡـًٔا وَلَا يَسۡتَطِيعُونَ ۝

74. Do not propound then similitudes for Allah; verily Allah knows and you do not.

فَلَا تَضۡرِبُوا۟ لِلَّهِ ٱلۡأَمۡثَالَ إِنَّ ٱللَّهَ يَعۡلَمُ وَأَنتُمۡ لَا تَعۡلَمُونَ ۝

75. Allah propounds a similitude; there is a bondman enslaved who has not power over aught, and there is one whom We have provided from Ourselves with goodly provision and he spends out of it in private and public; can they be equal? Praise be to Allah. But most of them do not know.

ضَرَبَ ٱللَّهُ مَثَلًا عَبْدًا مَّمْلُوكًا لَّا يَقْدِرُ عَلَىٰ شَىْءٍ وَمَن رَّزَقْنَـٰهُ مِنَّا رِزْقًا حَسَنًا فَهُوَ يُنفِقُ مِنْهُ سِرًّا وَجَهْرًا هَلْ يَسْتَوُۥنَ ٱلْحَمْدُ لِلَّهِ بَلْ أَكْثَرُهُمْ لَا يَعْلَمُونَ ﴿٧٥﴾

76. And Allah propounds a similitude; there are two men, one of them dumb who has not power over aught, and is a burden to his master, wherever he dispatches him he brings to him no good; is he equal to him who commands justice and is himself on the straight path?

وَضَرَبَ ٱللَّهُ مَثَلًا رَّجُلَيْنِ أَحَدُهُمَآ أَبْكَمُ لَا يَقْدِرُ عَلَىٰ شَىْءٍ وَهُوَ كَلٌّ عَلَىٰ مَوْلَىٰهُ أَيْنَمَا يُوَجِّههُّ لَا يَأْتِ بِخَيْرٍ هَلْ يَسْتَوِى هُوَ وَمَن يَأْمُرُ بِٱلْعَدْلِ وَهُوَ عَلَىٰ صِرَٰطٍ مُّسْتَقِيمٍ ﴿٧٦﴾

Section 11

77. Allah's is the Unseen of the heavens and the earth, and the affair of the Hour will be not but as a flash of the eye. Or it is even nearer, verily Allah is Potent over everything.

وَلِلَّهِ غَيْبُ ٱلسَّمَـٰوَٰتِ وَٱلْأَرْضِ وَمَآ أَمْرُ ٱلسَّاعَةِ إِلَّا كَلَمْحِ ٱلْبَصَرِ أَوْ هُوَ أَقْرَبُ إِنَّ ٱللَّهَ عَلَىٰ كُلِّ شَىْءٍ قَدِيرٌ ﴿٧٧﴾

78. And Allah has brought you forth from the bellies of your mothers while you knew not anything, and He appointed for you hearing and sight and hearts that haply you might give thanks.

وَٱللَّهُ أَخْرَجَكُم مِّنۢ بُطُونِ أُمَّهَـٰتِكُمْ لَا تَعْلَمُونَ شَيْـًٔا وَجَعَلَ لَكُمُ ٱلسَّمْعَ وَٱلْأَبْصَـٰرَ وَٱلْأَفْـِٔدَةَ لَعَلَّكُمْ تَشْكُرُونَ ﴿٧٨﴾

79. Do they not see the birds subjected in the firmament of the heaven? None supports them save Allah; verily there are signs in that for a people who believe.

أَلَمْ يَرَوْا إِلَى الطَّيْرِ مُسَخَّرَاتٍ فِي جَوِّ السَّمَاءِ مَا يُمْسِكُهُنَّ إِلَّا اللَّهُ إِنَّ فِي ذَٰلِكَ لَآيَاتٍ لِقَوْمٍ يُؤْمِنُونَ ﴿٧٩﴾

80. Allah has made for you from your houses a repose, and He has made for you from the skins of your cattle houses which you find light on the day of your flitting and on the day of your stopping, and from their wools and their furs and their hair a furnishing and an enjoyment for a season.

وَاللَّهُ جَعَلَ لَكُمْ مِنْ بُيُوتِكُمْ سَكَنًا وَجَعَلَ لَكُمْ مِنْ جُلُودِ الْأَنْعَامِ بُيُوتًا تَسْتَخِفُّونَهَا يَوْمَ ظَعْنِكُمْ وَيَوْمَ إِقَامَتِكُمْ وَمِنْ أَصْوَافِهَا وَأَوْبَارِهَا وَأَشْعَارِهَا أَثَاثًا وَمَتَاعًا إِلَى حِينٍ ﴿٨٠﴾

81. And Allah has made for you of what He has created shades; and He has made for you from the mountains places of retreat, and He has made for you coats protecting you from the heat and coats protecting from violence. Thus He perfects His favour on you that haply you may submit.

وَاللَّهُ جَعَلَ لَكُمْ مِمَّا خَلَقَ ظِلَالًا وَجَعَلَ لَكُمْ مِنَ الْجِبَالِ أَكْنَانًا وَجَعَلَ لَكُمْ سَرَابِيلَ تَقِيكُمُ الْحَرَّ وَسَرَابِيلَ تَقِيكُمْ بَأْسَكُمْ كَذَٰلِكَ يُتِمُّ نِعْمَتَهُ عَلَيْكُمْ لَعَلَّكُمْ تُسْلِمُونَ ﴿٨١﴾

82. Then if they turn away from you, on you is only a plain preaching.

فَإِنْ تَوَلَّوْا فَإِنَّمَا عَلَيْكَ الْبَلَاغُ الْمُبِينُ ﴿٨٢﴾

83. They recognize the favour of Allah, yet they deny it, and most of them are infidels.

يَعْرِفُونَ نِعْمَتَ اللَّهِ ثُمَّ يُنْكِرُونَهَا وَأَكْثَرُهُمُ الْكَافِرُونَ ﴿٨٣﴾

Section 12

84. Beware a Day whereon We will raise up from each community a witness, then those who have disbelieved shall not be given leave, nor shall they be permitted to please Allah.

وَيَوْمَ نَبْعَثُ مِنْ كُلِّ أُمَّةٍ شَهِيدًا ثُمَّ لَا يُؤْذَنُ لِلَّذِينَ كَفَرُوا وَلَا هُمْ يُسْتَعْتَبُونَ ﴿٨٤﴾

سُوۡرَةُ النَّحۡلِ

85. And when those who have done wrong will see the torment, it shall not be lightened unto them, nor shall they be respited.

وَإِذَا رَءَا الَّذِينَ ظَلَمُوا الْعَذَابَ فَلَا يُخَفَّفُ عَنْهُمْ وَلَا هُمْ يُنظَرُونَ ۝

86. And when those who have associated will see their associate-gods, they will say: 'O our Lord! Where are our associate-gods upon whom we have been calling besides You?' They will proffer them the saying: 'Verily you are liars.'

وَإِذَا رَءَا الَّذِينَ أَشْرَكُوا شُرَكَآءَهُمْ قَالُوا رَبَّنَا هَٰؤُلَآءِ شُرَكَآؤُنَا الَّذِينَ كُنَّا نَدْعُوا مِن دُونِكَ فَأَلْقَوْا إِلَيْهِمُ الْقَوْلَ إِنَّكُمْ لَكَٰذِبُونَ ۝

87. And they will proffer submission to Allah on that Day, and there will stray from them what they have been fabricating.

وَأَلْقَوْا إِلَى اللَّهِ يَوْمَئِذٍ السَّلَمَ وَضَلَّ عَنْهُم مَّا كَانُوا يَفْتَرُونَ ۝

88. Those who disbelieved and hindered others from the way of Allah; We will increase for them torment upon torment for they have been spreading corruption.

الَّذِينَ كَفَرُوا وَصَدُّوا عَن سَبِيلِ اللَّهِ زِدْنَٰهُمْ عَذَابًا فَوْقَ الْعَذَابِ بِمَا كَانُوا يُفْسِدُونَ ۝

89. And beware a Day whereon We shall raise up in every community a witness from amongst themselves regarding them, and We shall bring you as a witness regarding these. And We have revealed unto you the Book as an exposition of everything, and as a guidance and mercy and glad tidings to the Muslims.

وَيَوْمَ نَبْعَثُ فِي كُلِّ أُمَّةٍ شَهِيدًا عَلَيْهِم مِّنْ أَنفُسِهِمْ وَجِئْنَا بِكَ شَهِيدًا عَلَىٰ هَٰؤُلَآءِ وَنَزَّلْنَا عَلَيْكَ الْكِتَٰبَ تِبْيَٰنًا لِّكُلِّ شَيْءٍ وَهُدًى وَرَحْمَةً وَبُشْرَىٰ لِلْمُسْلِمِينَ ۝

Section 13

90. Verily Allah commands justice and well-doing and giving to kindred; and He prohibits lewdness and wickedness and oppression. He exhorts you that haply you may be admonished.

إِنَّ ٱللَّهَ يَأْمُرُ بِٱلْعَدْلِ وَٱلْإِحْسَنِ وَ
إِيتَآيِ ذِى ٱلْقُرْبَىٰ وَيَنْهَىٰ عَنِ ٱلْفَحْشَآءِ
وَٱلْمُنكَرِ وَٱلْبَغْىِ يَعِظُكُمْ لَعَلَّكُمْ
تَذَكَّرُونَ ۝

91. Fulfill the covenant of Allah when you have covenanted, and do not break oaths after their confirmation and surely you have appointed Allah your surety. Surely Allah knows whatever you do.

وَأَوْفُوا۟ بِعَهْدِ ٱللَّهِ إِذَا عَهَدتُّمْ وَلَا
تَنقُضُوا۟ ٱلْأَيْمَنَ بَعْدَ تَوْكِيدِهَا وَقَدْ
جَعَلْتُمُ ٱللَّهَ عَلَيْكُمْ كَفِيلًا إِنَّ
ٱللَّهَ يَعْلَمُ مَا تَفْعَلُونَ ۝

92. And do not be like her who unravels her yarn into strands after its strength, holding your oaths a means of discord amongst you that a community may be more numerous than another community. Allah only tests you thereby, and He will surely show to you on the Day of Judgement that wherein you have been differing.

وَلَا تَكُونُوا۟ كَٱلَّتِى نَقَضَتْ غَزْلَهَا مِنۢ
بَعْدِ قُوَّةٍ أَنكَٰثًا تَتَّخِذُونَ أَيْمَنَكُمْ
دَخَلًۢا بَيْنَكُمْ أَن تَكُونَ أُمَّةٌ هِىَ
أَرْبَىٰ مِنْ أُمَّةٍ إِنَّمَا يَبْلُوكُمُ ٱللَّهُ بِهِۦ
وَلَيُبَيِّنَنَّ لَكُمْ يَوْمَ ٱلْقِيَٰمَةِ مَا كُنتُمْ فِيهِ
تَخْتَلِفُونَ ۝

93. Had Allah so willed, He would have made you all one community, but He sends astray whom He will and guides whom He will; and certainly you will be questioned about what you have been working.

وَلَوْ شَآءَ ٱللَّهُ لَجَعَلَكُمْ أُمَّةً وَٰحِدَةً
وَلَٰكِن يُضِلُّ مَن يَشَآءُ وَيَهْدِى مَن
يَشَآءُ وَلَتُسْـَٔلُنَّ عَمَّا كُنتُمْ تَعْمَلُونَ ۝

94. And do not make your oaths a means of discord against you lest a foot may slip after its fixture, and you may taste evil for having hindered others from the way of Allah, and for you there shall be a mighty torment.

وَلَا تَتَّخِذُوۤاْ أَيْمَـٰنَكُمْ دَخَلًا بَيْنَكُمْ فَتَزِلَّ قَدَمٌۢ بَعْدَ ثُبُوتِهَا وَتَذُوقُواْ ٱلسُّوٓءَ بِمَا صَدَدتُّمْ عَن سَبِيلِ ٱللَّهِ وَلَكُمْ عَذَابٌ عَظِيمٌ ﴿٩٤﴾

95. And do not barter the covenant of Allah for a small price; verily what is with Allah is better for you, if you only know.

وَلَا تَشْتَرُواْ بِعَهْدِ ٱللَّهِ ثَمَنًا قَلِيلًا إِنَّمَا عِندَ ٱللَّهِ هُوَ خَيْرٌ لَّكُمْ إِن كُنتُمْ تَعْلَمُونَ ﴿٩٥﴾

96. Whatever is with you is exhaustible, and whatever is with Allah is lasting; and We will surely recompense those who have been patient, their reward for the best of what they have been working.

مَا عِندَكُمْ يَنفَدُ وَمَا عِندَ ٱللَّهِ بَاقٍ وَ لَنَجْزِيَنَّ ٱلَّذِينَ صَبَرُوۤاْ أَجْرَهُم بِأَحْسَنِ مَا كَانُواْ يَعْمَلُونَ ﴿٩٦﴾

97. Whosoever works righteously, male or female,[465] and is a believer,[466] We will surely quicken him to a clean life, and will surely recompense them their reward for the best of what they have been working.

مَنْ عَمِلَ صَـٰلِحًا مِّن ذَكَرٍ أَوْ أُنثَىٰ وَهُوَ مُؤْمِنٌ فَلَنُحْيِيَنَّهُۥ حَيَوٰةً طَيِّبَةً وَ لَنَجْزِيَنَّهُمْ أَجْرَهُم بِأَحْسَنِ مَا كَانُواْ يَعْمَلُونَ ﴿٩٧﴾

98. And when you read the Qur'an, seek refuge with Allah from Satan, the damned.

فَإِذَا قَرَأْتَ ٱلْقُرْءَانَ فَٱسْتَعِذْ بِٱللَّهِ مِنَ ٱلشَّيْطَـٰنِ ٱلرَّجِيمِ ﴿٩٨﴾

99. Verily he has no authority over those who believe and have trust in their Lord.

إِنَّهُۥ لَيْسَ لَهُۥ سُلْطَـٰنٌ عَلَى ٱلَّذِينَ ءَامَنُواْ وَعَلَىٰ رَبِّهِمْ يَتَوَكَّلُونَ ﴿٩٩﴾

---

465. This is to emphasize that in the sight of God there is no difference, so far as good works are concerned, between male and female.

466. The promise is important. Right belief, the *sine qua non* of all virtues and piety, must precede right action.

100. His authority is only over those who befriend him and those who are in respect of Him associators.

إِنَّمَا سُلْطَنُهُ, عَلَى ٱلَّذِينَ يَتَوَلَّوْنَهُ, وَٱلَّذِينَ هُم بِهِۦ مُشْرِكُونَ ١٠٠

Section 14

101. Whenever We change a verse in place of another verse and Allah is the Best Knower of what He sends down, they say: 'You are but an impostor.' Aye! Most of them know not.

وَإِذَا بَدَّلْنَآ ءَايَةً مَّكَانَ ءَايَةٍ وَٱللَّهُ أَعْلَمُ بِمَا يُنَزِّلُ قَالُوٓاْ إِنَّمَآ أَنتَ مُفْتَرٍ بَلْ أَكْثَرُهُمْ لَا يَعْلَمُونَ ١٠١

102. Say you: 'The Holy Spirit has brought it down from your Lord with Truth, that it may establish those who believe, and as a guidance and glad tiding to the Muslims.

قُلْ نَزَّلَهُۥ رُوحُ ٱلْقُدُسِ مِن رَّبِّكَ بِٱلْحَقِّ لِيُثَبِّتَ ٱلَّذِينَ ءَامَنُواْ وَهُدًى وَبُشْرَىٰ لِلْمُسْلِمِينَ ١٠٢

103. And assuredly We know that they say: 'it is only a human being who teaches him.' The speech of him to whom they incline is foreign, while this is plain Arabic speech.

وَلَقَدْ نَعْلَمُ أَنَّهُمْ يَقُولُونَ إِنَّمَا يُعَلِّمُهُۥ بَشَرٌ لِّسَانُ ٱلَّذِى يُلْحِدُونَ إِلَيْهِ أَعْجَمِىٌّ وَهَٰذَا لِسَانٌ عَرَبِىٌّ مُّبِينٌ ١٠٣

104. Verily those who do not believe in the signs of Allah, Allah shall not guide them, and to them there shall be an afflictive torment.

إِنَّ ٱلَّذِينَ لَا يُؤْمِنُونَ بِـَٔايَٰتِ ٱللَّهِ لَا يَهْدِيهِمُ ٱللَّهُ وَلَهُمْ عَذَابٌ أَلِيمٌ ١٠٤

105. It is only those who do not believe in the signs of Allah who fabricate a lie, and those! They are the liars.

إِنَّمَا يَفْتَرِى ٱلْكَذِبَ ٱلَّذِينَ لَا يُؤْمِنُونَ بِـَٔايَٰتِ ٱللَّهِ وَأُوْلَٰٓئِكَ هُمُ ٱلْكَٰذِبُونَ ١٠٥

106. Whosoever disbelieves in Allah after his belief, save him who is constrained and his heart is at rest with the belief but whosoever expands his breast to unbelief, upon them shall be wrath from Allah and to them shall be a mighty torment.

مَن كَفَرَ بِٱللَّهِ مِنۢ بَعْدِ إِيمَٰنِهِۦٓ إِلَّا مَنْ أُكْرِهَ وَقَلْبُهُۥ مُطْمَئِنٌّۢ بِٱلْإِيمَٰنِ وَلَٰكِن مَّن شَرَحَ بِٱلْكُفْرِ صَدْرًا فَعَلَيْهِمْ غَضَبٌ مِّنَ ٱللَّهِ وَلَهُمْ عَذَابٌ عَظِيمٌ ۝

107. That is because they loved the life of the world above the Hereafter, and because Allah does not guide an infidel people.

ذَٰلِكَ بِأَنَّهُمُ ٱسْتَحَبُّوا۟ ٱلْحَيَوٰةَ ٱلدُّنْيَا عَلَى ٱلْءَاخِرَةِ وَأَنَّ ٱللَّهَ لَا يَهْدِى ٱلْقَوْمَ ٱلْكَٰفِرِينَ ۝

108. These are they upon whose hearts and hearing and sight Allah has set a seal; and these! They are the heedless!

أُو۟لَٰٓئِكَ ٱلَّذِينَ طَبَعَ ٱللَّهُ عَلَىٰ قُلُوبِهِمْ وَسَمْعِهِمْ وَأَبْصَٰرِهِمْ وَأُو۟لَٰٓئِكَ هُمُ ٱلْغَٰفِلُونَ ۝

109. Undoubtedly in the Hereafter they shall be the losers.

لَا جَرَمَ أَنَّهُمْ فِى ٱلْءَاخِرَةِ هُمُ ٱلْخَٰسِرُونَ ۝

110. Then, verily, your Lord unto those who emigrated after they had been persuaded, and have thereafter striven hard and endured, your Lord is thereafter, the Forgiving, the Merciful.

ثُمَّ إِنَّ رَبَّكَ لِلَّذِينَ هَاجَرُوا۟ مِنۢ بَعْدِ مَا فُتِنُوا۟ ثُمَّ جَٰهَدُوا۟ وَصَبَرُوٓا۟ إِنَّ رَبَّكَ مِنۢ بَعْدِهَا لَغَفُورٌ رَّحِيمٌ ۝

Section 15

111. Beware a Day whereon every soul will come pleading for itself, and every soul will be paid in full what it has wrought, and they shall not be wronged.

يَوْمَ تَأْتِى كُلُّ نَفْسٍ تُجَٰدِلُ عَن نَّفْسِهَا وَتُوَفَّىٰ كُلُّ نَفْسٍ مَّا عَمِلَتْ وَهُمْ لَا يُظْلَمُونَ ۝

112. Allah propounds a similitude; a town which was secure and at rest, to which came its provision abundantly from every place; then it denied ungratefully the favours of Allah; therefore Allah made it taste the extreme of hunger and fear, because of what they were wont to perform.

وَضَرَبَ ٱللَّهُ مَثَلًا قَرۡيَةً كَانَتۡ ءَامِنَةً مُّطۡمَئِنَّةً يَأۡتِيهَا رِزۡقُهَا رَغَدًا مِّن كُلِّ مَكَانٍ فَكَفَرَتۡ بِأَنۡعُمِ ٱللَّهِ فَأَذَٰقَهَا ٱللَّهُ لِبَاسَ ٱلۡجُوعِ وَٱلۡخَوۡفِ بِمَا كَانُوا۟ يَصۡنَعُونَ ﴿١١٢﴾

113. And assuredly there came to them a Messenger from amongst them, but they belied him wherefore Our torment seized them, while yet they were wrong-doers.

وَلَقَدۡ جَآءَهُمۡ رَسُولٌ مِّنۡهُمۡ فَكَذَّبُوهُ فَأَخَذَهُمُ ٱلۡعَذَابُ وَهُمۡ ظَٰلِمُونَ ﴿١١٣﴾

114. So eat of what Allah has provided you of lawful and clean things, and give thanks for Allah's favour, if it is He Whom you are wont to worship.

فَكُلُوا۟ مِمَّا رَزَقَكُمُ ٱللَّهُ حَلَٰلًا طَيِّبًا وَٱشۡكُرُوا۟ نِعۡمَتَ ٱللَّهِ إِن كُنتُمۡ إِيَّاهُ تَعۡبُدُونَ ﴿١١٤﴾

115. He has disallowed to you only the dead meat and blood and swine-flesh and that over which is invoked the name of other than Allah; then whosoever is driven by necessity, not lusting nor transgressing, verily Allah is the Forgiving, the Merciful.

إِنَّمَا حَرَّمَ عَلَيۡكُمُ ٱلۡمَيۡتَةَ وَٱلدَّمَ وَلَحۡمَ ٱلۡخِنزِيرِ وَمَآ أُهِلَّ لِغَيۡرِ ٱللَّهِ بِهِۦ فَمَنِ ٱضۡطُرَّ غَيۡرَ بَاغٍ وَلَا عَادٍ فَإِنَّ ٱللَّهَ غَفُورٌ رَّحِيمٌ ﴿١١٥﴾

116. And do not say concerning that wherein your tongues utter a lie, this is allowed and this is forbidden that you may forge a lie against Allah; those who forge a lie against Allah shall not prosper.

وَلَا تَقُولُوا۟ لِمَا تَصِفُ أَلۡسِنَتُكُمُ ٱلۡكَذِبَ هَٰذَا حَلَٰلٌ وَهَٰذَا حَرَامٌ لِّتَفۡتَرُوا۟ عَلَى ٱللَّهِ ٱلۡكَذِبَ إِنَّ ٱلَّذِينَ يَفۡتَرُونَ عَلَى ٱللَّهِ ٱلۡكَذِبَ لَا يُفۡلِحُونَ ﴿١١٦﴾

117. A passing enjoyment; and then unto them shall be an afflictive torment.

مَتَـٰعٌ قَلِيلٌ وَلَهُمْ عَذَابٌ أَلِيمٌ ۝

118. To those who are Judaized We have forbidden what We have already recounted unto you; and We wronged them not, but themselves they were wont to wrong.

وَعَلَى ٱلَّذِينَ هَادُوا۟ حَرَّمْنَا مَا قَصَصْنَا عَلَيْكَ مِن قَبْلُ وَمَا ظَلَمْنَـٰهُمْ وَلَـٰكِن كَانُوٓا۟ أَنفُسَهُمْ يَظْلِمُونَ ۝

119. Then, verily, your Lord unto those who work evil from ignorance and repent and amend, your Lord thereafter is to them the Forgiving, the Merciful.

ثُمَّ إِنَّ رَبَّكَ لِلَّذِينَ عَمِلُوا۟ ٱلسُّوٓءَ بِجَهَـٰلَةٍ ثُمَّ تَابُوا۟ مِنۢ بَعْدِ ذَٰلِكَ وَأَصْلَحُوٓا۟ إِنَّ رَبَّكَ مِنۢ بَعْدِهَا لَغَفُورٌ رَّحِيمٌ ۝

Section 16

120. Verily Abraham was a pattern of piety, devout unto Allah, upright, and was not of the associators.

إِنَّ إِبْرَٰهِيمَ كَانَ أُمَّةً قَانِتًا لِّلَّهِ حَنِيفًا وَلَمْ يَكُ مِنَ ٱلْمُشْرِكِينَ ۝

121. Grateful for His favours; He chose him and guided him to a straight path.

شَاكِرًا لِّأَنْعُمِهِ ٱجْتَبَـٰهُ وَهَدَىٰهُ إِلَىٰ صِرَٰطٍ مُّسْتَقِيمٍ ۝

122. And We granted to him good in this world, and in the Hereafter he shall be of the righteous.

وَءَاتَيْنَـٰهُ فِى ٱلدُّنْيَا حَسَنَةً وَإِنَّهُ فِى ٱلْءَاخِرَةِ لَمِنَ ٱلصَّـٰلِحِينَ ۝

123. We revealed afterwards unto you; follow you the faith of Abraham the upright; and he was not of the associators.

ثُمَّ أَوْحَيْنَآ إِلَيْكَ أَنِ ٱتَّبِعْ مِلَّةَ إِبْرَٰهِيمَ حَنِيفًا وَمَا كَانَ مِنَ ٱلْمُشْرِكِينَ ۝

124. The Sabbath was prescribed only for those who differed thereon, and your Lord will decide between them on the Judgement Day concerning that wherein they have been differing.

إِنَّمَا جُعِلَ السَّبْتُ عَلَى الَّذِينَ اخْتَلَفُوا فِيهِ وَإِنَّ رَبَّكَ لَيَحْكُمُ بَيْنَهُمْ يَوْمَ الْقِيَمَةِ فِيمَا كَانُوا فِيهِ يَخْتَلِفُونَ ۝

125. Call you them to the way of your Lord with wisdom and goodly exhortation, and argue with them with what is best. Verily your Lord! He is the Best knower of him who has strayed from His way, and He is the Best Knower of the guided ones.

ادْعُ إِلَى سَبِيلِ رَبِّكَ بِالْحِكْمَةِ وَالْمَوْعِظَةِ الْحَسَنَةِ وَجَادِلْهُمْ بِالَّتِي هِيَ أَحْسَنُ إِنَّ رَبَّكَ هُوَ أَعْلَمُ بِمَنْ ضَلَّ عَنْ سَبِيلِهِ وَهُوَ أَعْلَمُ بِالْمُهْتَدِينَ ۝

126. And if you chastise, then chastise with the like of what you were chastised with, and if you endure patiently then surely it is better for the patient.

وَإِنْ عَاقَبْتُمْ فَعَاقِبُوا بِمِثْلِ مَا عُوقِبْتُمْ بِهِ وَلَئِنْ صَبَرْتُمْ لَهُوَ خَيْرٌ لِلصَّابِرِينَ ۝

127. And endure them patiently, and your patience is not but from Allah; and do not grieve over them, and do not you be in straitness because of what they plot.

وَاصْبِرْ وَمَا صَبْرُكَ إِلَّا بِاللَّهِ وَلَا تَحْزَنْ عَلَيْهِمْ وَلَا تَكُ فِي ضَيْقٍ مِّمَّا يَمْكُرُونَ ۝

128. Allah is with those who are in awe of Him and those who are well-doers.

إِنَّ اللَّهَ مَعَ الَّذِينَ اتَّقَوْا وَالَّذِينَ هُمْ مُحْسِنُونَ ۝

Sūrah 17

al-Isrā'

(Makkan, 12 Sections, 111 Verses)

In the name of Allah, the Compassionate, the Merciful.

Section 1

1. Hallowed be He Who took for a journey His bondsman in a night from the Sacred Mosque to the farther Mosque,[467] the environs of which We have blessed, that We might show him of Our signs.[468] Verily He! He is the Hearer, the Beholder.

2. And We gave Moses the Book and made it a guidance to the Children of Israel: 'Take not beside Me a guardian,

---

467. The farther Mosque being at Jerusalem; from whence he was carried through the seven heavens to the presence of God, and brought back again to Makka the same night. The details of this Ascension are frequently found in the *aḥādīth* of the Prophet. 'Asin, the Spanish professor of Arabic, has traced the great influence this Islamic literature had on Dante and other Christians of the Middle Ages. 'Embellished by later accretions, this miraculous trip still forms a favourite theme in mystic circles in Persia and Turkey, and a Spanish scholar considers it the original source of Dante's Divine Comedy' (Hitti, *History of the Arabs*, p. 114). See also *EI*. III. p. 567. 'Masjid' properly denotes the site, not the building, of a mosque; hence there arises no question of the existence or not of the actual Temple at the time. It is called 'Farther' because it was, at the time, the farthest place of the worship of one God from Makka.

468. Our signs and wonder. The well-known Mi'rāj or Ascension of the Prophet is generally believed to be corporal; but even allowing with some that it was merely a vision, does the reducing of a Prophet's immediate experience to a vision detract, in the least, from its reality or its authority?

3. 'O progeny of those whom We bore with Noah!', verily he was a bondsman grateful.

ذُرِّيَّةَ مَنْ حَمَلْنَا مَعَ نُوحٍ إِنَّهُ كَانَ عَبْدًا شَكُورًا ۝

4. And We decreed for the children of Israel in the Book: you shall surely commit evil twice[469] in the land and you shall rise very high.[470]

وَقَضَيْنَا إِلَىٰ بَنِي إِسْرَاءِيلَ فِي الْكِتَابِ لَتُفْسِدُنَّ فِي الْأَرْضِ مَرَّتَيْنِ وَلَتَعْلُنَّ عُلُوًّا كَبِيرًا ۝

5. Then when the promise came for the first of the two, We raised against you bondsmen of Ours endued with great violence, so they entered the dwellings; and it was a promise fulfilled.

فَإِذَا جَاءَ وَعْدُ أُولَاهُمَا بَعَثْنَا عَلَيْكُمْ عِبَادًا لَنَا أُولِي بَأْسٍ شَدِيدٍ فَجَاسُوا خِلَالَ الدِّيَارِ وَكَانَ وَعْدًا مَفْعُولًا ۝

6. Thereafter We gave you a return of victory over them and We supported you with riches and children, and We made you a numerous concourse.

ثُمَّ رَدَدْنَا لَكُمُ الْكَرَّةَ عَلَيْهِمْ وَأَمْدَدْنَاكُم بِأَمْوَالٍ وَبَنِينَ وَجَعَلْنَاكُمْ أَكْثَرَ نَفِيرًا ۝

---

469. The allusion may be to the well-known destruction of Jerusalem first by Nebuchadnezzar in 586 BC when the Jews were carried off to Babylonia in captivity, and next by the Romans under Titus in 70 CE.

470. Rise high in rebellion, and thereby sin against God and man. The Book of Jeremiah in the Bible is full of forebodings consequent on the rebellious disposition of the Jews and their deeds of impiety. 'The followers of Nebuchadnezzar massacred the inhabitants of Jerusalem, the priests and the people, old and young, women and children who were attending school, even babies in the cradle. The feast of blood at last shocked even the leader of the hostile heathens, who ordered a stay of this wholesale murder' (Polano, *The Talmudic Selections*, p. 320). The rabbis have assigned various causes for the Babylonian exile. 'Some authorities mention general unworthiness; others give specific sins, as idolatry, licentiousness, and bloodshed, incontinency in the drinking of wine, too great indulgence to one another and failure to reprove those who sinned and neglecting the study of the Torah' (*JE*. III. p. 566).

7. If you will do well, you do well for yourselves; and if you will do evil, you shall sin against your own selves. Then when the second promise came, We raised up a people that they may disgrace your faces and may enter the Mosque even as they entered it the first time, and that they may destroy with utter destruction whatsoever may fall under their power.

إِنْ أَحْسَنتُمْ أَحْسَنتُمْ لِأَنفُسِكُمْ وَإِنْ أَسَأْتُمْ فَلَهَا فَإِذَا جَاءَ وَعْدُ الْآخِرَةِ لِيَسُوءُوا وُجُوهَكُمْ وَلِيَدْخُلُوا الْمَسْجِدَ كَمَا دَخَلُوهُ أَوَّلَ مَرَّةٍ وَلِيُتَبِّرُوا مَا عَلَوْا تَتْبِيرًا ۝

8. Perchance your Lord may yet have mercy on you; and if you still revert, We will revert likewise. And We have appointed Hell a prison for the infidels.

عَسَىٰ رَبُّكُمْ أَن يَرْحَمَكُمْ وَإِنْ عُدتُّمْ عُدْنَا وَجَعَلْنَا جَهَنَّمَ لِلْكَافِرِينَ حَصِيرًا ۝

9. Verily this Qur'ān guides unto that path which is straight and bears glad tidings to the believers who work righteous deeds that theirs shall be a great reward.

إِنَّ هَٰذَا الْقُرْآنَ يَهْدِي لِلَّتِي هِيَ أَقْوَمُ وَيُبَشِّرُ الْمُؤْمِنِينَ الَّذِينَ يَعْمَلُونَ الصَّالِحَاتِ أَنَّ لَهُمْ أَجْرًا كَبِيرًا ۝

10. And that those who do not believe in the Hereafter — for them We have prepared an afflictive torment.

وَأَنَّ الَّذِينَ لَا يُؤْمِنُونَ بِالْآخِرَةِ أَعْتَدْنَا لَهُمْ عَذَابًا أَلِيمًا ۝

Section 2

11. And man prays for evil as he should pray for good, and man is ever hasty.

وَيَدْعُ الْإِنسَانُ بِالشَّرِّ دُعَاءَهُ بِالْخَيْرِ وَكَانَ الْإِنسَانُ عَجُولًا ۝

12. And We have appointed the night and the day as two signs; then We blurred the sign of the night and made the sign of the day illuminating that you may seek grace from your Lord, and that you may know the number of years and the Reckoning; and everything We have detailed in full detail.

وَجَعَلۡنَا ٱلَّيۡلَ وَٱلنَّهَارَ ءَايَتَيۡنِ فَمَحَوۡنَآ ءَايَةَ ٱلَّيۡلِ وَجَعَلۡنَآ ءَايَةَ ٱلنَّهَارِ مُبۡصِرَةً لِّتَبۡتَغُواۡ فَضۡلًا مِّن رَّبِّكُمۡ وَلِتَعۡلَمُواۡ عَدَدَ ٱلسِّنِينَ وَٱلۡحِسَابَۚ وَكُلَّ شَىۡءٍ فَصَّلۡنَهُ تَفۡصِيلًا ﴿١٢﴾

13. And every man: We have fastened his actions round his neck, and We shall bring forth unto him on the Day of Judgement a book proffered him open.

وَكُلَّ إِنسَنٍ أَلۡزَمۡنَهُ طَٰٓئِرَهُۥ فِى عُنُقِهِۦۖ وَنُخۡرِجُ لَهُۥ يَوۡمَ ٱلۡقِيَٰمَةِ كِتَٰبًا يَلۡقَىٰهُ مَنشُورًا ﴿١٣﴾

14. Read your book; suffice today your soul against you as a reckoner.

ٱقۡرَأۡ كِتَٰبَكَ كَفَىٰ بِنَفۡسِكَ ٱلۡيَوۡمَ عَلَيۡكَ حَسِيبًا ﴿١٤﴾

15. Whoso is guided, it is only for himself that he is guided, and whoso strays it is only against his soul that he strays; and not one laden bears the load of another.[471] And We do not chastise until We have raised a Messenger.

مَّنِ ٱهۡتَدَىٰ فَإِنَّمَا يَهۡتَدِى لِنَفۡسِهِۦۖ وَمَن ضَلَّ فَإِنَّمَا يَضِلُّ عَلَيۡهَاۚ وَلَا تَزِرُ وَازِرَةٌ وِزۡرَ أُخۡرَىٰۗ وَمَا كُنَّا مُعَذِّبِينَ حَتَّىٰ نَبۡعَثَ رَسُولًا ﴿١٥﴾

16. And when We intend that We shall destroy a town We command its affluent inhabitants, then they transgress therein, and thus the Word is justified on them. Then We annihilate it completely.

وَإِذَآ أَرَدۡنَآ أَن نُّهۡلِكَ قَرۡيَةً أَمَرۡنَا مُتۡرَفِيهَا فَفَسَقُواۡ فِيهَا فَحَقَّ عَلَيۡهَا ٱلۡقَوۡلُ فَدَمَّرۡنَٰهَا تَدۡمِيرًا ﴿١٦﴾

---

471. This establishes and emphasizes once more the principle of personal responsibility, so completely violated and negated by the Jewish and Christian concept of 'mediation', 'satisfaction' and 'atonement'. Curiously enough, in the early days of Pauline Christianity it was held that 'Christ by His sufferings made a payment to Satan to have him relinquish his might to man' (*CD*. p. 77).

17. And many a generation We have destroyed after Noah. And suffices your Lord, the Aware, the Beholder, for the offences of his bondsmen.

وَكَمْ أَهْلَكْنَا مِنَ ٱلْقُرُونِ مِنْ بَعْدِ نُوحٍ وَكَفَىٰ بِرَبِّكَ بِذُنُوبِ عِبَادِهِ خَبِيرَۢا بَصِيرًا ۝١٧

18. Whoso intends the quick-passing world We hasten to him therein whatever We please to whom We intend; thereafter We shall appoint for him Hell where he shall roast, reproved, damned.

مَّن كَانَ يُرِيدُ ٱلْعَاجِلَةَ عَجَّلْنَا لَهُۥ فِيهَا مَا نَشَآءُ لِمَن نُّرِيدُ ثُمَّ جَعَلْنَا لَهُۥ جَهَنَّمَ يَصْلَىٰهَا مَذْمُومًا مَّدْحُورًا ۝١٨

19. And whoso intends the Hereafter and strives therefor with due striving while he is a believer, then those! Their striving shall be appreciated.

وَمَنْ أَرَادَ ٱلْءَاخِرَةَ وَسَعَىٰ لَهَا سَعْيَهَا وَهُوَ مُؤْمِنٌ فَأُوْلَٰٓئِكَ كَانَ سَعْيُهُم مَّشْكُورًا ۝١٩

20. To each – these and those – We extend the bestowal of your Lord, and the bestowal of your Lord is never restrained.

كُلًّا نُّمِدُّ هَٰٓؤُلَآءِ وَهَٰٓؤُلَآءِ مِنْ عَطَآءِ رَبِّكَ وَمَا كَانَ عَطَآءُ رَبِّكَ مَحْظُورًا ۝٢٠

21. See you! How We have preferred some of them over some others; and surely the Hereafter is greater in degrees and greater in preference.

ٱنظُرْ كَيْفَ فَضَّلْنَا بَعْضَهُمْ عَلَىٰ بَعْضٍ وَلَلْءَاخِرَةُ أَكْبَرُ دَرَجَٰتٍ وَأَكْبَرُ تَفْضِيلًا ۝٢١

22. Set not up along with Allah another god, lest you sit down reproved, renounced.

لَّا تَجْعَلْ مَعَ ٱللَّهِ إِلَٰهًا ءَاخَرَ فَتَقْعُدَ مَذْمُومًا مَّخْذُولًا ۝٢٢

Section 3

23. And your Lord has decreed that you should worship none but Him, and show kindness to parents; and if either of them or both of them attain old age with you, say not unto them: 'pooh!', and brow beat them not, and speak to them a respectful speech.

وَقَضَىٰ رَبُّكَ أَلَّا تَعْبُدُوٓاْ إِلَّآ إِيَّاهُ وَبِٱلْوَٰلِدَيْنِ إِحْسَٰنًا إِمَّا يَبْلُغَنَّ عِندَكَ ٱلْكِبَرَ أَحَدُهُمَآ أَوْ كِلَاهُمَا فَلَا تَقُل لَّهُمَآ أُفٍّ وَلَا تَنْهَرْهُمَا وَقُل لَّهُمَا قَوْلًا كَرِيمًا ۝٢٣

24. And lower unto them the wing of meekness out of mercy, and say: Lord! Have mercy on the them as they brought me up when young.

وَٱخْفِضْ لَهُمَا جَنَاحَ ٱلذُّلِّ مِنَ ٱلرَّحْمَةِ وَقُل رَّبِّ ٱرْحَمْهُمَا كَمَا رَبَّيَانِي صَغِيرًا ۝

25. Your Lord is the Best Knower of what is in your souls; if you have been righteous, then He is unto you the Penitent, the Forgiving.

رَّبُّكُمْ أَعْلَمُ بِمَا فِي نُفُوسِكُمْ إِن تَكُونُوا۟ صَٰلِحِينَ فَإِنَّهُۥ كَانَ لِلْأَوَّٰبِينَ غَفُورًا ۝

26. And give you to the kinsman his due, and also to the needy and wayfarer; and squander not in squandering.

وَءَاتِ ذَا ٱلْقُرْبَىٰ حَقَّهُۥ وَٱلْمِسْكِينَ وَٱبْنَ ٱلسَّبِيلِ وَلَا تُبَذِّرْ تَبْذِيرًا ۝

27. Truly the squanderers are the brethren of the devils, and the devil is ever ungrateful to his Lord.

إِنَّ ٱلْمُبَذِّرِينَ كَانُوٓا۟ إِخْوَٰنَ ٱلشَّيَٰطِينِ وَكَانَ ٱلشَّيْطَٰنُ لِرَبِّهِۦ كَفُورًا ۝

28. And if you turn away from them awaiting a mercy from your Lord which you hope, then speak to them a gentle word.

وَإِمَّا تُعْرِضَنَّ عَنْهُمُ ٱبْتِغَآءَ رَحْمَةٍ مِّن رَّبِّكَ تَرْجُوهَا فَقُل لَّهُمْ قَوْلًا مَّيْسُورًا ۝

29. Let not your hand be chained to your neck, nor stretch it forth to its extremity, lest you sit down reproached, impoverished.

وَلَا تَجْعَلْ يَدَكَ مَغْلُولَةً إِلَىٰ عُنُقِكَ وَلَا تَبْسُطْهَا كُلَّ ٱلْبَسْطِ فَتَقْعُدَ مَلُومًا مَّحْسُورًا ۝

30. Verily your Lord extends the provision for whom He will, and measures it out, He is in respect of His creatures the Aware, the Beholder.

إِنَّ رَبَّكَ يَبْسُطُ ٱلرِّزْقَ لِمَن يَشَآءُ وَيَقْدِرُ إِنَّهُۥ كَانَ بِعِبَادِهِۦ خَبِيرًا بَصِيرًا ۝

Section 4

31. Kill not your offspring for fear of want. We provide for them and for yourselves; their killing is a great crime.

وَلَا تَقْتُلُوٓا۟ أَوْلَٰدَكُمْ خَشْيَةَ إِمْلَٰقٍ نَّحْنُ نَرْزُقُهُمْ وَإِيَّاكُمْ إِنَّ قَتْلَهُمْ كَانَ خِطْـًٔا كَبِيرًا ۝

32. And do not approach adultery;[472] it is ever an abomination[473] and vile as a pathway.

وَلَا تَقْرَبُوا۟ ٱلزِّنَىٰٓ إِنَّهُۥ كَانَ فَٰحِشَةً وَسَآءَ سَبِيلًا ۝

33. And do not kill anyone whom Allah has forbidden except by right, and whoever is killed wrongfully. We have surely given his next of kin authority; so let him not exceed killing; verily he is ever succoured.

وَلَا تَقْتُلُوا۟ ٱلنَّفْسَ ٱلَّتِى حَرَّمَ ٱللَّهُ إِلَّا بِٱلْحَقِّ وَمَن قُتِلَ مَظْلُومًا فَقَدْ جَعَلْنَا لِوَلِيِّهِۦ سُلْطَٰنًا فَلَا يُسْرِف فِّى ٱلْقَتْلِ إِنَّهُۥ كَانَ مَنصُورًا ۝

---

472. The Arabic word al-Zinā is much more comprehensive than either fornication, which is restricted to the illicit sexual intercourse of an unmarried person, or adultery which also denotes the sexual intercourse of two persons either of whom is married to a third person. The Arabic term, denotes the sexual intercourse between any man and woman, whether married or not, who do not stand to each other in the relation of husband and wife. Note the very great importance attached by the Qur'ān to this crime. The words are not 'not to commit adultery', but 'approach not adultery', or 'go not nigh unto adultery', thus impeding all the ways and paths that could lead to it. Compare this austere attitude of Islam with the sordid morality of the present-day West. 'Sexual fidelity and discipline are quickly becoming a thing of the past in the modern West' (Asad, *Islam at the Crossroads*, p. 47). Adultery 'has become fashionable in both England and America during the past few years' (Scott, *History of Prostitution*, p. 226). 'The old type prostitute who pranced about gaudily and drunkenly in the Strand, Leicester Square, Piccadilly, and Regent Street, is a thing of the past. There has been a huge increase in promiscuity among men and an ever greater increase among women. The results are that more and more every year is man turning to so-called girls of respectability in order to satisfy his sexual appetite' (Ibid., pp. 224–225). 'Virginity among women is becoming something to sneer at' (Ibid., p. 225). 'Where all are practising what is virtually prostitution there can be no such thing as prostitution' (Ibid., p. 228).

473. That is abominable in itself; impure and debasing for the soul. Islam condemns Zina, or promiscuous unchastity in any and every form outright, whereas it has flourished in all civilized countries, and even prostitution has been recognized by them subject only to regulation by law or by custom. 'In Egypt, Phoenicia, Assyria, Chaldea, Canaan and Persia, the worship of Isis, Moloch, Baal, Astrate, Mylitta and other deities consisted of the most extravagant sensual orgies, and the temples were merely centres of vice. In Babylon some degree of prostitution appears to have been even compulsory and imposed upon all women in honour of the goddess Mylitta. In India the ancient connection between religion and prostitution still survives' (*EBr*. XVIII. p. 58).

34. And do not approach the substance of an orphan save with what is best, until he reaches the age of strength. And fulfil the covenant; verily the covenant shall be questioned.

وَلَا تَقْرَبُواْ مَالَ ٱلْيَتِيمِ إِلَّا بِٱلَّتِي هِىَ أَحْسَنُ حَتَّىٰ يَبْلُغَ أَشُدَّهُۥ وَأَوْفُواْ بِٱلْعَهْدِ إِنَّ ٱلْعَهْدَ كَانَ مَسْـُٔولًا ٣٤

35. And give full measure when you measure, and weigh with an even balance, that is good, and the best interpretation.

وَأَوْفُواْ ٱلْكَيْلَ إِذَا كِلْتُمْ وَزِنُواْ بِٱلْقِسْطَاسِ ٱلْمُسْتَقِيمِ ذَٰلِكَ خَيْرٌ وَأَحْسَنُ تَأْوِيلًا ٣٥

36. And do not you go after that of which you have no knowledge; verily the hearing and the sight and the hearts, each of them shall be questioned about.

وَلَا تَقْفُ مَا لَيْسَ لَكَ بِهِۦ عِلْمٌ إِنَّ ٱلسَّمْعَ وَٱلْبَصَرَ وَٱلْفُؤَادَ كُلُّ أُوْلَٰٓئِكَ كَانَ عَنْهُ مَسْـُٔولًا ٣٦

37. And do not you walk on earth struttingly; verily you will not by any means rend the earth, nor can you attain the mountains in stature.

وَلَا تَمْشِ فِى ٱلْأَرْضِ مَرَحًا إِنَّكَ لَن تَخْرِقَ ٱلْأَرْضَ وَلَن تَبْلُغَ ٱلْجِبَالَ طُولًا ٣٧

38. Each of these! Their vice is to your Lord ever detestable.

كُلُّ ذَٰلِكَ كَانَ سَيِّئُهُۥ عِندَ رَبِّكَ مَكْرُوهًا ٣٨

39. That is part of that wisdom which your Lord has revealed to you, and set not up you along with Allah another god, lest you be cast into Hell reproved, damned.

ذَٰلِكَ مِمَّآ أَوْحَىٰٓ إِلَيْكَ رَبُّكَ مِنَ ٱلْحِكْمَةِ وَلَا تَجْعَلْ مَعَ ٱللَّهِ إِلَٰهًا ءَاخَرَ فَتُلْقَىٰ فِى جَهَنَّمَ مَلُومًا مَّدْحُورًا ٣٩

40. Has then your Lord distinguished yourselves with sons and taken for Himself the females from amongst the angels? Verily you say a mighty saying.

أَفَأَصْفَىٰكُمْ رَبُّكُم بِٱلْبَنِينَ وَٱتَّخَذَ مِنَ ٱلْمَلَٰٓئِكَةِ إِنَٰثًا إِنَّكُمْ لَتَقُولُونَ قَوْلًا عَظِيمًا ٤٠

Section 5

41. Assuredly We have propounded it variously in this Qur'ān so that they might be admonished; but it adds only to their aversion.

وَلَقَدْ صَرَّفْنَا فِي هَٰذَا ٱلْقُرْءَانِ لِيَذَّكَّرُوا۟ وَمَا يَزِيدُهُمْ إِلَّا نُفُورًا ٤١

42. Say: Were there along with Him other gods, as they assert, then they would have brought a way to the Owner of the throne.

قُل لَّوْ كَانَ مَعَهُۥٓ ءَالِهَةٌ كَمَا يَقُولُونَ إِذًا لَّٱبْتَغَوْا۟ إِلَىٰ ذِى ٱلْعَرْشِ سَبِيلًا ٤٢

43. Hallowed be He, and exalted be He above what they say – a great height!

سُبْحَٰنَهُۥ وَتَعَٰلَىٰ عَمَّا يَقُولُونَ عُلُوًّا كَبِيرًا ٤٣

44. There hallow Him the seven heavens and the earth and whosoever is therein.[474] And naught there is but hallows His praise, but you do not understand their hallowing. Verily, He is ever Forbearing, Forgiving.

تُسَبِّحُ لَهُ ٱلسَّمَٰوَٰتُ ٱلسَّبْعُ وَٱلْأَرْضُ وَمَن فِيهِنَّ وَإِن مِّن شَىْءٍ إِلَّا يُسَبِّحُ بِحَمْدِهِۦ وَلَٰكِن لَّا تَفْقَهُونَ تَسْبِيحَهُمْ إِنَّهُۥ كَانَ حَلِيمًا غَفُورًا ٤٤

45. And when you recite the Qur'ān, We set up between you and those who do not believe in the Hereafter a curtain drawn down.

وَإِذَا قَرَأْتَ ٱلْقُرْءَانَ جَعَلْنَا بَيْنَكَ وَبَيْنَ ٱلَّذِينَ لَا يُؤْمِنُونَ بِٱلْءَاخِرَةِ حِجَابًا مَّسْتُورًا ٤٥

---

474. This leaves no room for heaven-gods, earth-gods or any other minor gods. However strange it may sound to us, the fact remains that an earth-god and a heaven-god have found a distinguished place in the pantheon of the mythologies of Babylon, Egypt, India, Greece and Rome; and 'the ever-arching Heaven and the all- producing Earth' have also been conceived of as 'a Father and a Mother of the world, whose offspring are the living creatures, men and beasts and plants' (*PC*. I. p. 322).

46. And We set up veils over their hearts lest they understand it, and in their ears heaviness; and when you mention your Lord alone in reciting the Qur'ān, they turn back as averters.

وَجَعَلْنَا عَلَىٰ قُلُوبِهِمْ أَكِنَّةً أَن يَفْقَهُوهُ وَفِىٓ ءَاذَانِهِمْ وَقْرًا وَإِذَا ذَكَرْتَ رَبَّكَ فِى ٱلْقُرْءَانِ وَحْدَهُۥ وَلَّوْا۟ عَلَىٰٓ أَدْبَٰرِهِمْ نُفُورًا ﴿٤٦﴾

47. We are the Best Knower of that motive with which they listen to you and whenever they counsel together in secret, when the wrong-doers say, you but follow a man enchanted.

نَّحْنُ أَعْلَمُ بِمَا يَسْتَمِعُونَ بِهِۦٓ إِذْ يَسْتَمِعُونَ إِلَيْكَ وَإِذْ هُمْ نَجْوَىٰٓ إِذْ يَقُولُ ٱلظَّٰلِمُونَ إِن تَتَّبِعُونَ إِلَّا رَجُلًا مَّسْحُورًا ﴿٤٧﴾

48. See! How they propound similitudes for you. They have strayed away and cannot find a way.

ٱنظُرْ كَيْفَ ضَرَبُوا۟ لَكَ ٱلْأَمْثَٰلَ فَضَلُّوا۟ فَلَا يَسْتَطِيعُونَ سَبِيلًا ﴿٤٨﴾

49. See! How they say: 'When we shall have become bones and fragments, shall we in truth be raised as new creation?'

وَقَالُوٓا۟ أَءِذَا كُنَّا عِظَٰمًا وَرُفَٰتًا أَءِنَّا لَمَبْعُوثُونَ خَلْقًا جَدِيدًا ﴿٤٩﴾

50. Say: 'Become you stone or iron.

قُلْ كُونُوا۟ حِجَارَةً أَوْ حَدِيدًا ﴿٥٠﴾

51. Or anything created of the things more remote in your breasts.' Then they will say: 'Who will restore us?' Say: 'He Who created you the first time.' Then they will wag their heads at you, and say: 'When will it be?' Say: 'Perhaps it is nigh.'

أَوْ خَلْقًا مِّمَّا يَكْبُرُ فِى صُدُورِكُمْ فَسَيَقُولُونَ مَن يُعِيدُنَا قُلِ ٱلَّذِى فَطَرَكُمْ أَوَّلَ مَرَّةٍ فَسَيُنْغِضُونَ إِلَيْكَ رُءُوسَهُمْ وَيَقُولُونَ مَتَىٰ هُوَ قُلْ عَسَىٰٓ أَن يَكُونَ قَرِيبًا ﴿٥١﴾

52. The Day whereon He will call you, and you will answer with His praise, and you will imagine that you had tarried but little.

يَوْمَ يَدْعُوكُمْ فَتَسْتَجِيبُونَ بِحَمْدِهِۦ وَتَظُنُّونَ إِن لَّبِثْتُمْ إِلَّا قَلِيلًا ﴿٥٢﴾

Section 6

53. Tell you My servants that they should say only what is best. Satan would stir up strife among them; Satan is to man ever an open foe.

وَقُل لِّعِبَادِى يَقُولُوا۟ ٱلَّتِى هِىَ أَحْسَنُ إِنَّ ٱلشَّيْطَٰنَ يَنزَغُ بَيْنَهُمْ إِنَّ ٱلشَّيْطَٰنَ كَانَ لِلْإِنسَٰنِ عَدُوًّا مُّبِينًا ٥٣

54. Your Lord is the Best Knower of you, He will have mercy upon you if He wills, or He will chastise you if He wills. And We have not sent you over them as a trustee.

رَّبُّكُمْ أَعْلَمُ بِكُمْ إِن يَشَأْ يَرْحَمْكُمْ أَوْ إِن يَشَأْ يُعَذِّبْكُمْ وَمَآ أَرْسَلْنَٰكَ عَلَيْهِمْ وَكِيلًا ٥٤

55. And your Lord is the Best Knower of those who are in the heavens and the earth. And assuredly We have preferred some Prophets over others, and We gave David a Scripture.

وَرَبُّكَ أَعْلَمُ بِمَن فِى ٱلسَّمَٰوَٰتِ وَٱلْأَرْضِ وَلَقَدْ فَضَّلْنَا بَعْضَ ٱلنَّبِيِّۦنَ عَلَىٰ بَعْضٍ وَءَاتَيْنَا دَاوُۥدَ زَبُورًا ٥٥

56. Say: 'Call upon those whom you fancy besides Him; they are able neither to remove the distress from you nor to change it off.'

قُلِ ٱدْعُوا۟ ٱلَّذِينَ زَعَمْتُم مِّن دُونِهِۦ فَلَا يَمْلِكُونَ كَشْفَ ٱلضُّرِّ عَنكُمْ وَلَا تَحْوِيلًا ٥٦

57. Those whom they call upon seek access themselves to their Lord, striving which of them shall be the nearest; and they hope for His mercy and fear His chastisement; the chastisement of your Lord is indeed ever to be guarded against.

أُو۟لَٰٓئِكَ ٱلَّذِينَ يَدْعُونَ يَبْتَغُونَ إِلَىٰ رَبِّهِمُ ٱلْوَسِيلَةَ أَيُّهُمْ أَقْرَبُ وَيَرْجُونَ رَحْمَتَهُۥ وَيَخَافُونَ عَذَابَهُۥٓ إِنَّ عَذَابَ رَبِّكَ كَانَ مَحْذُورًا ٥٧

58. Not a town is there but We are going to destroy it before the Day of Judgement, or to chastise it with a severe chastising; that is inscribed in the Book.

وَإِن مِّن قَرْيَةٍ إِلَّا نَحْنُ مُهْلِكُوهَا قَبْلَ يَوْمِ ٱلْقِيَٰمَةِ أَوْ مُعَذِّبُوهَا عَذَابًا شَدِيدًا كَانَ ذَٰلِكَ فِى ٱلْكِتَٰبِ مَسْطُورًا ٥٨

59. And nothing hinders Us from sending the signs except that the ancients belied them. And We gave to Thamūd a she-camel as an illumination, but they did her wrong. And We send not signs but to warn.

وَمَا مَنَعَنَا أَن نُّرْسِلَ بِٱلْآيَـٰتِ إِلَّا أَن كَذَّبَ بِهَا ٱلْأَوَّلُونَ ۚ وَءَاتَيْنَا ثَمُودَ ٱلنَّاقَةَ مُبْصِرَةً فَظَلَمُواْ بِهَا ۚ وَمَا نُرْسِلُ بِٱلْآيَـٰتِ إِلَّا تَخْوِيفًا ۝

60. Recall when We said to you: 'Your Lord has encompassed mankind.' And We made the vision We showed you but a temptation for man, and likewise the tree accursed in the Qur'ān. And We warn them, but it only increases their exorbitance greatly.

وَإِذْ قُلْنَا لَكَ إِنَّ رَبَّكَ أَحَاطَ بِٱلنَّاسِ ۚ وَمَا جَعَلْنَا ٱلرُّءْيَا ٱلَّتِىٓ أَرَيْنَـٰكَ إِلَّا فِتْنَةً لِّلنَّاسِ وَٱلشَّجَرَةَ ٱلْمَلْعُونَةَ فِى ٱلْقُرْءَانِ ۚ وَنُخَوِّفُهُمْ فَمَا يَزِيدُهُمْ إِلَّا طُغْيَـٰنًا كَبِيرًا ۝

Section 7

61. And recall when We said to the angels: 'Bow down before Adam.' So they bowed, but Iblis did not; he said: 'Shall I bow to one whom You have created of clay?'

وَإِذْ قُلْنَا لِلْمَلَـٰٓئِكَةِ ٱسْجُدُواْ لِآدَمَ فَسَجَدُوٓاْ إِلَّآ إِبْلِيسَ قَالَ ءَأَسْجُدُ لِمَنْ خَلَقْتَ طِينًا ۝

62. Iblis said: 'Bethink You: this one whom You have honoured above me? — If You defer me till the Day of Judgement, I will surely seize his progeny, save a few.'

قَالَ أَرَءَيْتَكَ هَـٰذَا ٱلَّذِى كَرَّمْتَ عَلَىَّ لَئِنْ أَخَّرْتَنِ إِلَىٰ يَوْمِ ٱلْقِيَـٰمَةِ لَأَحْتَنِكَنَّ ذُرِّيَّتَهُۥٓ إِلَّا قَلِيلًا ۝

63. Allah said: 'Be you gone; whosoever of them follows you, Hell is your recompense, an ample recompense.'

قَالَ ٱذْهَبْ فَمَن تَبِعَكَ مِنْهُمْ فَإِنَّ جَهَنَّمَ جَزَآؤُكُمْ جَزَآءً مَّوْفُورًا ۝

64. 'And unsettle them whosoever of them you can with your voice, and summon against them your horse and your foot, share with them riches and children and make promise to them,' and Satan promises not but to delude.

65. 'Over My bondsmen you have no authority,'[475] and your Lord suffices as a Guardian.

66. Your Lord is He Who speeds for you the ship in the sea that you may seek His grace, verily He is to you ever Merciful.

67. And when there touches you a distress on the sea, those you call upon fall away except He alone, then when He delivers you on the land you turn away, and man is ever ungrateful.

68. Are you then secure that He will not cause a side of land to swallow you up, or send over you a sand storm, and then you will not find for yourselves a protector?

وَٱسْتَفْزِزْ مَنِ ٱسْتَطَعْتَ مِنْهُم بِصَوْتِكَ وَأَجْلِبْ عَلَيْهِم بِخَيْلِكَ وَرَجِلِكَ وَشَارِكْهُمْ فِى ٱلْأَمْوَٰلِ وَٱلْأَوْلَٰدِ وَعِدْهُمْ وَمَا يَعِدُهُمُ ٱلشَّيْطَٰنُ إِلَّا غُرُورًا ۝

إِنَّ عِبَادِى لَيْسَ لَكَ عَلَيْهِمْ سُلْطَٰنٌ وَكَفَىٰ بِرَبِّكَ وَكِيلًا ۝

رَّبُّكُمُ ٱلَّذِى يُزْجِى لَكُمُ ٱلْفُلْكَ فِى ٱلْبَحْرِ لِتَبْتَغُوا۟ مِن فَضْلِهِۦٓ إِنَّهُۥ كَانَ بِكُمْ رَحِيمًا ۝

وَإِذَا مَسَّكُمُ ٱلضُّرُّ فِى ٱلْبَحْرِ ضَلَّ مَن تَدْعُونَ إِلَّآ إِيَّاهُ فَلَمَّا نَجَّىٰكُمْ إِلَى ٱلْبَرِّ أَعْرَضْتُمْ وَكَانَ ٱلْإِنسَٰنُ كَفُورًا ۝

أَفَأَمِنتُمْ أَن يَخْسِفَ بِكُمْ جَانِبَ ٱلْبَرِّ أَوْ يُرْسِلَ عَلَيْكُمْ حَاصِبًا ثُمَّ لَا تَجِدُوا۟ لَكُمْ وَكِيلًا ۝

---

475. This makes it clear once more that Satan in Islam is not a sort of evil deity. All through the Qur'ān the message is that man himself acquires the habit of sin through his own weakness. The devil is not endowed with any power at all, his influence being confined to suggestion and persuasion only.

69. Or, are you secure that He will not send you back therein another time and send upon a gale of wind and drown you for your having disbelieved, so that you will not find for yourselves an avenger against Us?

أَمۡ أَمِنتُمۡ أَن يُعِيدَكُمۡ فِيهِ تَارَةً أُخۡرَىٰ فَيُرۡسِلَ عَلَيۡكُمۡ قَاصِفًا مِّنَ ٱلرِّيحِ فَيُغۡرِقَكُم بِمَا كَفَرۡتُمۡ ثُمَّ لَا تَجِدُواْ لَكُمۡ عَلَيۡنَا بِهِۦ تَبِيعًا ﴿٦٩﴾

70. And assuredly We have honoured the children of Adam,[476] and have borne them on the land and the sea, and We have provided them with clean things, and We have preferred them with a preference over many of them whom We have created.

وَلَقَدۡ كَرَّمۡنَا بَنِىٓ ءَادَمَ وَحَمَلۡنَٰهُمۡ فِى ٱلۡبَرِّ وَ ٱلۡبَحۡرِ وَرَزَقۡنَٰهُم مِّنَ ٱلطَّيِّبَٰتِ وَ فَضَّلۡنَٰهُمۡ عَلَىٰ كَثِيرٍ مِّمَّنۡ خَلَقۡنَا تَفۡضِيلًا ﴿٧٠﴾

Section 8

71. Remember the Day when We shall call all mankind with their record; then whoever will be given the book in his right hand — those will read their book, and they shall not be wronged a whit.

يَوۡمَ نَدۡعُواْ كُلَّ أُنَاسٍ بِإِمَٰمِهِمۡ فَمَنۡ أُوتِىَ كِتَٰبَهُۥ بِيَمِينِهِۦ فَأُوْلَٰٓئِكَ يَقۡرَءُونَ كِتَٰبَهُمۡ وَلَا يُظۡلَمُونَ فَتِيلًا ﴿٧١﴾

72. And whoever has been blind in this world will be blind in the Hereafter and far astray from the path.

وَمَن كَانَ فِى هَٰذِهِۦ أَعۡمَىٰ فَهُوَ فِى ٱلۡأَخِرَةِ أَعۡمَىٰ وَأَضَلُّ سَبِيلًا ﴿٧٢﴾

73. And surely they had nearly tempted you away from what We have revealed to you, that you should fabricate regarding Us something else, and then surely they would have taken you as a friend!

وَإِن كَادُواْ لَيَفۡتِنُونَكَ عَنِ ٱلَّذِىٓ أَوۡحَيۡنَآ إِلَيۡكَ لِتَفۡتَرِىَ عَلَيۡنَا غَيۡرَهُۥ وَإِذًا لَّٱتَّخَذُوكَ خَلِيلًا ﴿٧٣﴾

---

476. In other words, mankind. The obvious meaning is that man is a creature honoured and honourable, and this completely contradicts the Biblical attitude towards man: 'And it repented the Lord that he had made man on the earth, and it grieved him at his heart' (Ge. 6: 6).

74. And were it not that We had confirmed you, you had almost leaned towards them a little.

وَلَوْلَآ أَن ثَبَّتْنَكَ لَقَدْ كِدتَّ تَرْكَنُ إِلَيْهِمْ شَيْئًا قَلِيلًا ۝

75. In that case, We would have surely made you taste the double of the torment of life and the double of the torment of death and then you would not have found a helper against Us.

إِذًا لَّأَذَقْنَكَ ضِعْفَ ٱلْحَيَوٰةِ وَضِعْفَ ٱلْمَمَاتِ ثُمَّ لَا تَجِدُ لَكَ عَلَيْنَا نَصِيرًا ۝

76. And surely they had almost unsettled you from the land that they might drive you forth from hence. And in that case they would not have tarried after you but a little while.

وَإِن كَادُوا لَيَسْتَفِزُّونَكَ مِنَ ٱلْأَرْضِ لِيُخْرِجُوكَ مِنْهَا ۖ وَإِذًا لَّا يَلْبَثُونَ خِلَفَكَ إِلَّا قَلِيلًا ۝

77. This was Our dispensation with those whom We sent before you of Our Messengers and you will not find a change in this Our dispensation.

سُنَّةَ مَن قَدْ أَرْسَلْنَا قَبْلَكَ مِن رُّسُلِنَا ۖ وَلَا تَجِدُ لِسُنَّتِنَا تَحْوِيلًا ۝

Section 9

78. Establish you the prayer from the decline of the sun to the darkening of the night and the recitation at the dawn; verily the recitation at the dawn is ever borne witness to.

أَقِمِ ٱلصَّلَوٰةَ لِدُلُوكِ ٱلشَّمْسِ إِلَىٰ غَسَقِ ٱلَّيْلِ وَقُرْءَانَ ٱلْفَجْرِ ۖ إِنَّ قُرْءَانَ ٱلْفَجْرِ كَانَ مَشْهُودًا ۝

79. And of the night keep the vigil therein as an act of supererogation for you; perchance your Lord will raise you up in a station praised.

وَمِنَ ٱلَّيۡلِ فَتَهَجَّدۡ بِهِۦ نَافِلَةً لَّكَ عَسَىٰٓ أَن يَبۡعَثَكَ رَبُّكَ مَقَامًا مَّحۡمُودًا ۝

80. And say you: 'Lord! Cause me to enter a rightful entrance and cause to go forth a rightful outgoing, and appoint for me from before You a helpful authority.'

وَقُل رَّبِّ أَدۡخِلۡنِي مُدۡخَلَ صِدۡقٍ وَأَخۡرِجۡنِي مُخۡرَجَ صِدۡقٍ وَٱجۡعَل لِّي مِن لَّدُنكَ سُلۡطَٰنًا نَّصِيرًا ۝

81. And say you: 'The Truth is come and falsehood is vanished:' verily falsehood is ever vanishing.

وَقُلۡ جَآءَ ٱلۡحَقُّ وَزَهَقَ ٱلۡبَٰطِلُ إِنَّ ٱلۡبَٰطِلَ كَانَ زَهُوقًا ۝

82. And We reveal by means of the Qur'ān what is a healing and a mercy to the believers; and it only increases the ungodly in loss.

وَنُنَزِّلُ مِنَ ٱلۡقُرۡءَانِ مَا هُوَ شِفَآءٌ وَرَحۡمَةٌ لِّلۡمُؤۡمِنِينَ وَلَا يَزِيدُ ٱلظَّٰلِمِينَ إِلَّا خَسَارًا ۝

83. And when We show favour to man, he turns away and withdraws on his side; and when evil touches him, he is ever despairing.

وَإِذَآ أَنۡعَمۡنَا عَلَى ٱلۡإِنسَٰنِ أَعۡرَضَ وَنَـَٔا بِجَانِبِهِۦ وَإِذَا مَسَّهُ ٱلشَّرُّ كَانَ يَـُٔوسًا ۝

84. Say: 'Everyone works after his disposition, and your Lord is the Best Knower of him who is best guided on the path.'

قُلۡ كُلٌّ يَعۡمَلُ عَلَىٰ شَاكِلَتِهِۦ فَرَبُّكُمۡ أَعۡلَمُ بِمَنۡ هُوَ أَهۡدَىٰ سَبِيلًا ۝

Section 10

85. And they ask you regarding the Spirit. Say: 'It is only the command of my Lord,[477] and of knowledge you have been given only a little.'[478]

وَيَسْـَٔلُونَكَ عَنِ ٱلرُّوحِ قُلِ ٱلرُّوحُ مِنْ أَمْرِ رَبِّي وَمَآ أُوتِيتُم مِّنَ ٱلْعِلْمِ إِلَّا قَلِيلًا ۝

86. And if We willed, We could surely take away what We have revealed to you, then you will not find against Us any protector.

وَلَئِن شِئْنَا لَنَذْهَبَنَّ بِٱلَّذِىٓ أَوْحَيْنَآ إِلَيْكَ ثُمَّ لَا تَجِدُ لَكَ بِهِۦ عَلَيْنَا وَكِيلًا ۝

477. That it is created, like other beings. This repudiates the position of those polytheistic religions which hold the spirit or soul of man to be an independent, self–subsisting entity, co-eternal with God. In several Indian creeds the fundamental principle is 'the dualism of prakrati and purusa, "matter" and "soul" The result is a kind of trinity consisting of God, soul (or souls) and matter, each category of being having independent self-existence. God is eternal; so is each soul; so also is matter' (*ERE*. II. p. 60). The Greeks, and as their disciples, the early Christian Fathers, also shared the belief in the uncreated nature of the soul. 'Belief in the pre–existence of the soul prevailed widely among the Greeks from an early date, and at a later time became a theory of their philosophers. The influence of Greek thought in this respect was strongly felt in the early Christian Church, and is still apparent to some extent throughout the whole of Western civilization (*ERE*. II. X. p. 236).

478. This refers to mankind which has been granted 'little' as compared with Divine Knowledge. Man is endowed with only as much knowledge as he is capable of understanding and utilizing; and a knowledge of the nature of the soul does not lie within his purview. Even the physical nature of life is not easy for modern science to explain, and this is admitted by leading biologists themselves (See J.A. Thomson's *Science of Life*, p. 83). Furthermore, a materialist philosopher has been led to confess: 'The more we learn about nature, the more do we become aware of our own ignorance. Every problem that is solved, opens up a fresh series of problems not hitherto thought of. The sphere of the Unknown is infinite: the sphere of the Known may be expanding but is always finite. We are no nearer to ultimate solutions than Thales or Pythagoras; the quest for ultimate solutions is merely the symptom of a disordered mind' (*UHW*. VIII. p. 5012).

87. Except as a mercy from the Lord, verily, His grace unto you is ever great.

إِلَّا رَحْمَةً مِّن رَّبِّكَ إِنَّ فَضْلَهُ كَانَ عَلَيْكَ كَبِيرًا ۝

88. Say: 'If the mankind and the jinn leagued together that they might produce the like of this Qur'ān, they could not produce its like,[479] though one to the other were a backer.'

قُل لَّئِنِ ٱجْتَمَعَتِ ٱلْإِنسُ وَٱلْجِنُّ عَلَىٰٓ أَن يَأْتُوا۟ بِمِثْلِ هَٰذَا ٱلْقُرْءَانِ لَا يَأْتُونَ بِمِثْلِهِۦ وَلَوْ كَانَ بَعْضُهُمْ لِبَعْضٍ ظَهِيرًا ۝

89. And assuredly We have variously propounded all manner of similitudes in this Qur'ān for mankind, yet most men have refused everything except disbelief.

وَلَقَدْ صَرَّفْنَا لِلنَّاسِ فِي هَٰذَا ٱلْقُرْءَانِ مِن كُلِّ مَثَلٍ فَأَبَىٰٓ أَكْثَرُ ٱلنَّاسِ إِلَّا كُفُورًا ۝

90. And they say: 'We will by no means believe in you until you cause a fountain to gush forth for us from the earth;

وَقَالُوا۟ لَن نُّؤْمِنَ لَكَ حَتَّىٰ تَفْجُرَ لَنَا مِنَ ٱلْأَرْضِ يَنبُوعًا ۝

91. Or there be for you a garden of palms and vines and you cause rivers to gush forth in their midst;

أَوْ تَكُونَ لَكَ جَنَّةٌ مِّن نَّخِيلٍ وَعِنَبٍ فَتُفَجِّرَ ٱلْأَنْهَٰرَ خِلَٰلَهَا تَفْجِيرًا ۝

92. Or you cause the sky to fall upon us, as you assert, in pieces, or you bring Allah and the angels face to face with us;

أَوْ تُسْقِطَ ٱلسَّمَاءَ كَمَا زَعَمْتَ عَلَيْنَا كِسَفًا أَوْ تَأْتِيَ بِٱللَّهِ وَٱلْمَلَٰٓئِكَةِ قَبِيلًا ۝

93. Or there be for you a house of God, or you mount to the sky, and we will by no means believe even in your mounting until you cause a book to be sent down to us which we may read.' Say: 'Hallowed by my Lord! I am nothing but a human being sent as a Messenger?'

أَوْ يَكُونَ لَكَ بَيْتٌ مِّن زُخْرُفٍ أَوْ تَرْقَىٰ فِي ٱلسَّمَاءِ وَلَن نُّؤْمِنَ لِرُقِيِّكَ حَتَّىٰ تُنَزِّلَ عَلَيْنَا كِتَٰبًا نَّقْرَؤُهُ قُلْ سُبْحَانَ رَبِّي هَلْ كُنتُ إِلَّا بَشَرًا رَّسُولًا ۝

---

479. No code of law and ethics, no system of sociology could ever be a match to the Holy Qur'ān.

Section 11

94. And nothing has prevented men from believing when the guidance came to them except that they said: 'Has Allah sent forth a human being as a Messenger?'

وَمَا مَنَعَ ٱلنَّاسَ أَن يُؤْمِنُوٓا۟ إِذْ جَآءَهُمُ ٱلْهُدَىٰٓ إِلَّآ أَن قَالُوٓا۟ أَبَعَثَ ٱللَّهُ بَشَرًا رَّسُولًا ۝

95. Say: 'Were there on the earth angels walking about contentedly. We would certainly have sent down to them an angel from the heaven as a Messenger.'

قُل لَّوْ كَانَ فِى ٱلْأَرْضِ مَلَـٰٓئِكَةٌ يَمْشُونَ مُطْمَئِنِّينَ لَنَزَّلْنَا عَلَيْهِم مِّنَ ٱلسَّمَآءِ مَلَكًا رَّسُولًا ۝

96. Say: 'Allah suffices as a witness between me and you; verily He is in respect of His creatures, ever Aware, Beholder.

قُلْ كَفَىٰ بِٱللَّهِ شَهِيدًۢا بَيْنِى وَبَيْنَكُمْ إِنَّهُۥ كَانَ بِعِبَادِهِۦ خَبِيرًۢا بَصِيرًا ۝

97. And whom Allah guides he is the rightly-guided, and whom He sends astray — for such you will by no means find friends beside Him. And We shall muster them on the Day of the Judgement lying prone, blind, deaf and dumb, their abode being Hell. As soon as it grows dull, We will increase the Flame for them.

وَمَن يَهْدِ ٱللَّهُ فَهُوَ ٱلْمُهْتَدِ وَمَن يُضْلِلْ فَلَن تَجِدَ لَهُمْ أَوْلِيَآءَ مِن دُونِهِۦ وَنَحْشُرُهُمْ يَوْمَ ٱلْقِيَـٰمَةِ عَلَىٰ وُجُوهِهِمْ عُمْيًا وَبُكْمًا وَصُمًّا مَّأْوَىٰهُمْ جَهَنَّمُ كُلَّمَا خَبَتْ زِدْنَـٰهُمْ سَعِيرًا ۝

98. This shall be their recompense because they disbelieved in Our signs and said: When once we have become bones and fragments, shall we in truth be raised up a new creation?'

ذَٰلِكَ جَزَآؤُهُم بِأَنَّهُمْ كَفَرُوا۟ بِـَٔايَـٰتِنَا وَقَالُوٓا۟ أَءِذَا كُنَّا عِظَـٰمًا وَرُفَـٰتًا أَءِنَّا لَمَبْعُوثُونَ خَلْقًا جَدِيدًا ۝

99. Do they not see that Allah Who created the heavens and the earth is able to create their likes? And He has appointed for them a term of which there is no doubt; yet the ungodly have rejected everything except infidelity.

100. Say: 'If it were you who owned the treasures of the mercy of my Lord, you would surely refrain from spending for fear'; and man is ever miserly.

Section 12

101. And assuredly We gave Moses nine manifest signs — ask you the children of Israel — so when he came to them, Pharaoh said to him: 'I imagine you to be enchanted, O Moses!'

102. Moses said: 'Assuredly you know that none has sent down these things save the Lord of the heavens and the earth as an enlightenment, and verily I imagine you doomed, O Pharaoh.'

103. Then he sought to scan them out of the land; therefore We drowned him and those with him, all together.

104. And after him, We said to the children of Israel: 'Dwell on the earth;' then when comes the promise of the Hereafter, We shall assemble you all together.'

أَوَلَمْ يَرَوْا أَنَّ ٱللَّهَ ٱلَّذِى خَلَقَ ٱلسَّمَٰوَٰتِ وَٱلْأَرْضَ قَادِرٌ عَلَىٰٓ أَن يَخْلُقَ مِثْلَهُمْ وَجَعَلَ لَهُمْ أَجَلًا لَّا رَيْبَ فِيهِ فَأَبَى ٱلظَّٰلِمُونَ إِلَّا كُفُورًا ۝

قُل لَّوْ أَنتُمْ تَمْلِكُونَ خَزَآئِنَ رَحْمَةِ رَبِّىٓ إِذًا لَّأَمْسَكْتُمْ خَشْيَةَ ٱلْإِنفَاقِ وَكَانَ ٱلْإِنسَٰنُ قَتُورًا ۝

وَلَقَدْ ءَاتَيْنَا مُوسَىٰ تِسْعَ ءَايَٰتٍۭ بَيِّنَٰتٍ فَسْـَٔلْ بَنِىٓ إِسْرَٰٓءِيلَ إِذْ جَآءَهُمْ فَقَالَ لَهُۥ فِرْعَوْنُ إِنِّى لَأَظُنُّكَ يَٰمُوسَىٰ مَسْحُورًا ۝

قَالَ لَقَدْ عَلِمْتَ مَآ أَنزَلَ هَٰٓؤُلَآءِ إِلَّا رَبُّ ٱلسَّمَٰوَٰتِ وَٱلْأَرْضِ بَصَآئِرَ وَإِنِّى لَأَظُنُّكَ يَٰفِرْعَوْنُ مَثْبُورًا ۝

فَأَرَادَ أَن يَسْتَفِزَّهُم مِّنَ ٱلْأَرْضِ فَأَغْرَقْنَٰهُ وَمَن مَّعَهُۥ جَمِيعًا ۝

وَقُلْنَا مِنۢ بَعْدِهِۦ لِبَنِىٓ إِسْرَٰٓءِيلَ ٱسْكُنُوا۟ ٱلْأَرْضَ فَإِذَا جَآءَ وَعْدُ ٱلْءَاخِرَةِ جِئْنَا بِكُمْ لَفِيفًا ۝

105. And with Truth We have sent down the Qur'ān, and with Truth it has come down, and We have not sent you but as a bringer of glad tidings and a warner.

وَبِٱلْحَقِّ أَنزَلْنَٰهُ وَبِٱلْحَقِّ نَزَلَ وَمَآ أَرْسَلْنَٰكَ إِلَّا مُبَشِّرًا وَنَذِيرًا ﴿١٠٥﴾

106. And this is a recitation which We have made distinct that you may recite it to mankind with slow deliberation, and We have revealed it at intervals.

وَقُرْءَانًا فَرَقْنَٰهُ لِتَقْرَأَهُۥ عَلَى ٱلنَّاسِ عَلَىٰ مُكْثٍ وَنَزَّلْنَٰهُ تَنزِيلًا ﴿١٠٦﴾

107. Say: 'Whether you believe it or believe it not, verily those who were given knowledge before it, when it is recited to them, fall down on their chins, prostrating.'

قُلْ ءَامِنُوا۟ بِهِۦٓ أَوْ لَا تُؤْمِنُوٓا۟ إِنَّ ٱلَّذِينَ أُوتُوا۟ ٱلْعِلْمَ مِن قَبْلِهِۦٓ إِذَا يُتْلَىٰ عَلَيْهِمْ يَخِرُّونَ لِلْأَذْقَانِ سُجَّدًا ﴿١٠٧﴾

108. And they say: 'Hallowed be our Lord! The promise of our Lord was ever to have been fulfilled.'

وَيَقُولُونَ سُبْحَٰنَ رَبِّنَآ إِن كَانَ وَعْدُ رَبِّنَا لَمَفْعُولًا ﴿١٠٨﴾

109. And they fall down on their chins weeping, and it adds to their humility.

وَيَخِرُّونَ لِلْأَذْقَانِ يَبْكُونَ وَيَزِيدُهُمْ خُشُوعًا ۩ ﴿١٠٩﴾

110. Say: 'Call upon Allah or call upon Rahman, by whichsoever name you call, His are the excellent names. And shout not your prayer, nor speak it low, but seek a midway.'

قُلِ ٱدْعُوا۟ ٱللَّهَ أَوِ ٱدْعُوا۟ ٱلرَّحْمَٰنَ أَيًّا مَّا تَدْعُوا۟ فَلَهُ ٱلْأَسْمَآءُ ٱلْحُسْنَىٰ وَلَا تَجْهَرْ بِصَلَاتِكَ وَلَا تُخَافِتْ بِهَا وَٱبْتَغِ بَيْنَ ذَٰلِكَ سَبِيلًا ﴿١١٠﴾

111. And say: 'All praise to Allah Who has not taken a son, and Whose is no associate in the dominion, nor has He a protector through weakness, and magnify Him with all magnificence.'

وَقُلِ ٱلْحَمْدُ لِلَّهِ ٱلَّذِى لَمْ يَتَّخِذْ وَلَدًا وَلَمْ يَكُن لَّهُ شَرِيكٌ فِى ٱلْمُلْكِ وَلَمْ يَكُن لَّهُۥ وَلِىٌّ مِّنَ ٱلذُّلِّ وَكَبِّرْهُ تَكْبِيرًا ﴿١١١﴾

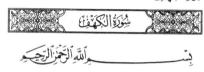

Sūrah 18

al-Kahf

(Makkan, 12 Sections and 110 Verses)

In the name of Allah, the
Compassionate, the Merciful.

Section 1

1. All praise to Allah Who has sent down to His bondman the Book, and allowed no crookedness therein.[480]

2. Straightforward, that it may warn of a severe violence from before Him, and bring glad tidings to the believers who work righteous works that theirs shall be a goodly reward.

3. They will abide there for ever.

4. And that it may warn those who say: 'God has taken a son.'[481]

5. No knowledge they have of it, nor had their fathers. Odious is the word that comes from their mouths; they utter not but a lie.

---

480. The religion of Islam, says an eminent Christian writer, 'is pre-eminently a practical one reflecting the practical and efficient mind of its originator. It offers no unattainable ideal, no theological complications and perplexities, no mystical sacraments and no priestly hierarchy involving ordination, consecration and 'apostolic succession.' (Hitti, *History of the Arabs*, p. 129.)

481. The reference is clearly to the Christians, especially the Adoptionists, 'who held that Christ was a mere man, miraculously conceived indeed, but adopted as the Son of God only by the supreme degree in which he had been filled with the divine wisdom and power'. (*EMK*. IV. p. 1998.)

6. You are, as if going to kill yourself over their footsteps out of sorrow, for they do not believe in this discourse.

فَلَعَلَّكَ بَاخِعٌ نَّفْسَكَ عَلَىٰٓ ءَاثَـٰرِهِمْ إِن لَّمْ يُؤْمِنُوا۟ بِهَـٰذَا ٱلْحَدِيثِ أَسَفًا ﴿٦﴾

7. We have made whatever is on the earth as an adornment of it, that We test them — which of them is best in work.

إِنَّا جَعَلْنَا مَا عَلَى ٱلْأَرْضِ زِينَةً لَّهَا لِنَبْلُوَهُمْ أَيُّهُمْ أَحْسَنُ عَمَلًا ﴿٧﴾

8. And We are going to make whatsoever is on it bare soil.

وَإِنَّا لَجَـٰعِلُونَ مَا عَلَيْهَا صَعِيدًا جُرُزًا ﴿٨﴾

9. Do you think that the people of the cave and the Inscription were of Our signs a marvel?[482]

أَمْ حَسِبْتَ أَنَّ أَصْحَـٰبَ ٱلْكَهْفِ وَٱلرَّقِيمِ كَانُوا۟ مِنْ ءَايَـٰتِنَا عَجَبًا ﴿٩﴾

10. Recall when the youths took themselves to the cave and said: 'O our Lord! Grant us mercy from before You and prepare for us in our affair a right course.'

إِذْ أَوَى ٱلْفِتْيَةُ إِلَى ٱلْكَهْفِ فَقَالُوا۟ رَبَّنَآ ءَاتِنَا مِن لَّدُنكَ رَحْمَةً وَهَيِّئْ لَنَا مِنْ أَمْرِنَا رَشَدًا ﴿١٠﴾

11. Therefore We put a covering over their ears in the cave for a number of years.

فَضَرَبْنَا عَلَىٰٓ ءَاذَانِهِمْ فِى ٱلْكَهْفِ سِنِينَ عَدَدًا ﴿١١﴾

---

482. Who were they? The Holy Qur'ān, as usual, lays stress on the moral lessons of the story, and not on the identification of the persons concerned. The general opinion among Muslim scholars favours the view that they were Christian — 'Christian' in the original, pre-Pauline sense of the word — youths of a good family in Ephesus, who, to avoid the cruel and relentless persecution of the Roman Emperor Decius (250. C.E.), shut themselves up in a cave, and remained there asleep for over three centuries. 'Two Christians, Theodore and Rufinus, write the story of the young martyrs on metal plates, which they placed under the stones closing the cave.' (*ERE.* XI. p. 428.) For the Christian version of the narrative, see *EBr.* XX. p. 383. Ephesus, now Ayasoluk and about 36 miles from Smyrna on the railroad to Aidin, was a Greek city in Asia Minor, and about 6 miles from the sea, nearly opposite the island of Samos. The city is mentioned several times in the NT. al-Raqim means a tablet of lead, whereon were inscribed, or engraved, the names of the People of the Cave, commonly called the Seven Sleepers, and their ancestry, and their story, and their religion, and what it was from which they fled... and which was put upon the entrance of the cave.' (LL.)

12. Thereafter We raised them up that We might know which of the two parties was best at reckoning the time that they had tarried.

ثُمَّ بَعَثْنَاهُمْ لِنَعْلَمَ أَيُّ الْحِزْبَيْنِ أَحْصَىٰ لِمَا لَبِثُوٓا أَمَدًا ﴿١٢﴾

Section 2

13. We recount to you their tidings with Truth. They were certain youths who believed in their Lord, and We increased them in guidance.

نَّحْنُ نَقُصُّ عَلَيْكَ نَبَأَهُم بِالْحَقِّ إِنَّهُمْ فِتْيَةٌ ءَامَنُوا بِرَبِّهِمْ وَزِدْنَاهُمْ هُدًى ﴿١٣﴾

14. We braced their hearts when they stood forth and said: 'Our Lord is the Lord of the heavens and the earth; never shall we call upon a god besides Him, for then we shall be saying an abomination.[483]

وَرَبَطْنَا عَلَىٰ قُلُوبِهِمْ إِذْ قَامُوا فَقَالُوا رَبُّنَا رَبُّ السَّمَٰوَٰتِ وَالْأَرْضِ لَن نَّدْعُوَا۟ مِن دُونِهِۦٓ إِلَٰهًا لَّقَدْ قُلْنَآ إِذًا شَطَطًا ﴿١٤﴾

15. These, our people, have taken for themselves gods beside Him — why then do they not bring for them a clear authority? — Who does a greater wrong than he who fabricates a lie against Allah?'

هَٰٓؤُلَآءِ قَوْمُنَا اتَّخَذُوا مِن دُونِهِۦٓ ءَالِهَةً لَّوْلَا يَأْتُونَ عَلَيْهِم بِسُلْطَٰنٍ بَيِّنٍ فَمَنْ أَظْلَمُ مِمَّنِ افْتَرَىٰ عَلَى اللَّهِ كَذِبًا ﴿١٥﴾

16. And now when you have withdrawn yourselves from them and what they worship, except God, take yourselves to the cave; your Lord will unfold for you some of His mercy, and will prepare an easy arrangement of your affair for you.

وَإِذِ اعْتَزَلْتُمُوهُمْ وَمَا يَعْبُدُونَ إِلَّا اللَّهَ فَأْوُۥٓا إِلَى الْكَهْفِ يَنشُرْ لَكُمْ رَبُّكُم مِّن رَّحْمَتِهِۦ وَيُهَيِّئْ لَكُم مِّنْ أَمْرِكُم مِّرْفَقًا ﴿١٦﴾

---

483. All this shows that the persecuted youths were monotheists and true followers of the Prophet Jesus and not Christ-worshippers of the Pauline variety.

17. And you would see the rising sun veering away from their cave on the right, and the setting sun passing them on the left, while they were in the spacious part of the cave, that is of the signs of Allah. Whom Allah guides, he is the guided indeed, and whom He sends astray, for him you will never find a directing friend.

وَتَرَى ٱلشَّمْسَ إِذَا طَلَعَت تَّزَٰوَرُ عَن كَهْفِهِمْ ذَاتَ ٱلْيَمِينِ وَإِذَا غَرَبَت تَّقْرِضُهُمْ ذَاتَ ٱلشِّمَالِ وَهُمْ فِي فَجْوَةٍ مِّنْهُ ذَٰلِكَ مِنْ ءَايَٰتِ ٱللَّهِ مَن يَهْدِ ٱللَّهُ فَهُوَ ٱلْمُهْتَدِ وَمَن يُضْلِلْ فَلَن تَجِدَ لَهُۥ وَلِيًّا مُّرْشِدًا ۝

Section 3

18. And you would have deemed them awake whereas they were asleep, and We turned them over on the right and the left, while their dog stretched forth his two fore-legs on the threshold. Had you looked at them you would have surely turned away from them in fright and would have been filled with awe of them.

وَتَحْسَبُهُمْ أَيْقَاظًا وَهُمْ رُقُودٌ وَنُقَلِّبُهُمْ ذَاتَ ٱلْيَمِينِ وَذَاتَ ٱلشِّمَالِ وَكَلْبُهُم بَٰسِطٌ ذِرَاعَيْهِ بِٱلْوَصِيدِ لَوِ ٱطَّلَعْتَ عَلَيْهِمْ لَوَلَّيْتَ مِنْهُمْ فِرَارًا وَلَمُلِئْتَ مِنْهُمْ رُعْبًا ۝

19. Likewise, We raised them up that they might question among themselves. There spoke a speaker from amongst them: 'How long have you stayed?' They said: 'We have stayed a day or part of a day.' They said: 'Your Lord knows best how long you have stayed; now send one of you with this your money in the city, and let him find which food is the cleaner there, and let him bring you a provision for that, and let him be circumspect, and let him by no means discover you to anyone.

وَكَذَٰلِكَ بَعَثْنَٰهُمْ لِيَتَسَآءَلُوا۟ بَيْنَهُمْ قَالَ قَآئِلٌ مِّنْهُمْ كَمْ لَبِثْتُمْ قَالُوا۟ لَبِثْنَا يَوْمًا أَوْ بَعْضَ يَوْمٍ قَالُوا۟ رَبُّكُمْ أَعْلَمُ بِمَا لَبِثْتُمْ فَٱبْعَثُوٓا۟ أَحَدَكُم بِوَرِقِكُمْ هَٰذِهِۦٓ إِلَى ٱلْمَدِينَةِ فَلْيَنظُرْ أَيُّهَآ أَزْكَىٰ طَعَامًا فَلْيَأْتِكُم بِرِزْقٍ مِّنْهُ وَلْيَتَلَطَّفْ وَلَا يُشْعِرَنَّ بِكُمْ أَحَدًا ۝

20. Verily they, if they come to know of you, would stone you or make you revert to their faith, and lo! Then you shall never fare well.'

إِنَّهُمْ إِن يَظْهَرُواْ عَلَيْكُمْ يَرْجُمُوكُمْ أَوْ يُعِيدُوكُمْ فِى مِلَّتِهِمْ وَلَن تُفْلِحُوٓاْ إِذًا أَبَدًا ۝

21. And likewise We caused their affair to be lit upon that they might realise[484] that Allah's promise is true, and that of the Hour! There is no doubt about it.[485] Recall when they were disputing among themselves regarding their affair, and they said: 'Build over them a building' — their Lord is the Best Knower about them — then those who prevailed in their affair said: 'Surely we shall raise over them a place of worship.'[486]

وَكَذَٰلِكَ أَعْثَرْنَا عَلَيْهِمْ لِيَعْلَمُوٓاْ أَنَّ وَعْدَ ٱللَّهِ حَقٌّ وَأَنَّ ٱلسَّاعَةَ لَا رَيْبَ فِيهَآ إِذْ يَتَنَـٰزَعُونَ بَيْنَهُمْ أَمْرَهُمْ فَقَالُواْ ٱبْنُواْ عَلَيْهِم بُنْيَـٰنًا رَّبُّهُمْ أَعْلَمُ بِهِمْ قَالَ ٱلَّذِينَ غَلَبُواْ عَلَىٰٓ أَمْرِهِمْ لَنَتَّخِذَنَّ عَلَيْهِم مَّسْجِدًا ۝

---

484. That they might realise with the greater certainty. The astonishingly long sleep of these youths, and their waking after so long a time is clearly reminiscent of the state of the dead being raised to life.

485. This happened precisely at a time when the Christians, seized by a new heresy, had begun to doubt and deny the fact of resurrection. 'After 307 years, in the reign of the emperor Theodosius II, a heresy breaks out, led by a bishop Theodore, denying the resurrection of the dead, and the emperor is greatly perturbed. Then God suggests to Adolius, the proprietor of the field where the cave is to build a sheepfold for his flock; for this purpose the workmen use stones which close the entrance of the cave, and thus the cave is reopened. God awakens the youths, who think that they have slept only one night... Theodosius is informed of what has happened and comes to Ephesus to the cave. One of the youths... tells him that in order to demonstrate the truth of the resurrection, God had caused them to fall asleep and then resuscitated them before the Judgment Day.' (*ERE*. XI. p. 428.)

486. There still stands 'on the eastern side of Mount Pion, overhanging the road that leads from the temple of Diana to the Magnesian gate of the city.... a rock-hewn church, close to a cave in which the "Seven Sleepers of Ephesus" were, according to the legend, saved from the Roman persecution by a slumber of some centuries' duration.' (*DB*. I. p. 725.)

22. Presently they will say: there were three, the fourth being their dog, And they will say: they were five, the sixth being their dog — guessing at the unknown — and they will say: 'They were seven, the eight being their dog.' Say: 'My Lord is the Best Knower of their number; none knows that except only a few; so debate not you regarding their number except an outward debating, and ask not anyone regarding them.'

سَيَقُولُونَ ثَلَاثَةٌ رَّابِعُهُمْ كَلْبُهُمْ وَ يَقُولُونَ خَمْسَةٌ سَادِسُهُمْ كَلْبُهُم رَّجْمًا بِالْغَيْبِ وَيَقُولُونَ سَبْعَةٌ وَثَامِنُهُمْ كَلْبُهُمْ قُل رَّبِّي أَعْلَمُ بِعِدَّتِهِم مَّا يَعْلَمُهُمْ إِلَّا قَلِيلٌ فَلَا تُمَارِ فِيهِمْ إِلَّا مِرَآءً ظَاهِرًا وَلَا تَسْتَفْتِ فِيهِم مِّنْهُمْ أَحَدًا ۝

Section 4

23. And never say you of a thing: 'I am going to do that in the morning;'

وَلَا تَقُولَنَّ لِشَاْىْءٍ إِنِّي فَاعِلٌ ذَٰلِكَ غَدًا ۝

24. Except with this reservation that Allah so will. And remember your Lord when you forget, and say you: 'Perchance my Lord will guide me to something nearer to right direction than this.'

إِلَّا أَن يَشَاءَ اللَّهُ وَاذْكُر رَّبَّكَ إِذَا نَسِيتَ وَقُلْ عَسَىٰ أَن يَهْدِيَنِ رَبِّي لِأَقْرَبَ مِنْ هَٰذَا رَشَدًا ۝

25. And they stayed in their cave three hundred years and added nine.

وَلَبِثُوا فِي كَهْفِهِمْ ثَلَاثَ مِائَةٍ سِنِينَ وَازْدَادُوا تِسْعًا ۝

26. Say: Allah knows best how long they stayed; His alone is the hidden knowledge of the heavens and the earth. How well He sees and hears! They have no patron beside Him, nor in His rule He associates anyone.

قُلِ اللَّهُ أَعْلَمُ بِمَا لَبِثُوا لَهُ غَيْبُ السَّمَٰوَٰتِ وَالْأَرْضِ أَبْصِرْ بِهِ وَ أَسْمِعْ مَا لَهُم مِّن دُونِهِ مِن وَلِيٍّ وَلَا يُشْرِكُ فِي حُكْمِهِ أَحَدًا ۝

سُورَةُ الْكَهْفِ

27. And recite what has been revealed to you of the Book of your Lord; and none may alter His words; and never will you find besides Him a covert.

وَٱتْلُ مَآ أُوحِىَ إِلَيْكَ مِن كِتَابِ رَبِّكَ لَا مُبَدِّلَ لِكَلِمَٰتِهِۦ وَلَن تَجِدَ مِن دُونِهِۦ مُلْتَحَدًا ۝

28. And endure yourself in the company of those who call upon their Lord in the morning and evening, seeking His countenance; and let not your eyes rove from them seeking the adornment of the life of this world; and obey you not him whose heart We have made to neglect of Our remembrance, and who follows his lust, and whose affair is exceeding the bound.

وَٱصْبِرْ نَفْسَكَ مَعَ ٱلَّذِينَ يَدْعُونَ رَبَّهُم بِٱلْغَدَوٰةِ وَٱلْعَشِىِّ يُرِيدُونَ وَجْهَهُۥ وَلَا تَعْدُ عَيْنَاكَ عَنْهُمْ تُرِيدُ زِينَةَ ٱلْحَيَوٰةِ ٱلدُّنْيَا وَلَا تُطِعْ مَنْ أَغْفَلْنَا قَلْبَهُۥ عَن ذِكْرِنَا وَٱتَّبَعَ هَوَىٰهُ وَكَانَ أَمْرُهُۥ فُرُطًا ۝

29. Say: 'The Truth is from your Lord, let him therefore believe who will and let him disbelieve who will.' Verily We have prepared for the wrong-doers a Fire the awnings of which shall encompass them; and if they cry for relief they shall be relieved with water like the dregs of oil scalding their faces. Ill the drink, and vile the resort!

وَقُلِ ٱلْحَقُّ مِن رَّبِّكُمْ فَمَن شَآءَ فَلْيُؤْمِن وَمَن شَآءَ فَلْيَكْفُرْ إِنَّآ أَعْتَدْنَا لِلظَّٰلِمِينَ نَارًا أَحَاطَ بِهِمْ سُرَادِقُهَا وَإِن يَسْتَغِيثُوا۟ يُغَاثُوا۟ بِمَآءٍ كَٱلْمُهْلِ يَشْوِى ٱلْوُجُوهَ بِئْسَ ٱلشَّرَابُ وَسَآءَتْ مُرْتَفَقًا ۝

30. Verily those who believe and work righteous works — We do not waste the reward of him who does well in regard to his work,

إِنَّ ٱلَّذِينَ ءَامَنُوا۟ وَعَمِلُوا۟ ٱلصَّٰلِحَٰتِ إِنَّا لَا نُضِيعُ أَجْرَ مَنْ أَحْسَنَ عَمَلًا ۝

31. These! For them are the Gardens everlasting with running streams. Bedecked they shall be therein with bracelets of gold and they shall wear green robes of satin and brocade, reclining therein on couches. Excellent the reward, and goodly the resort!

أُوْلَـٰٓئِكَ لَهُمۡ جَنَّـٰتُ عَدۡنٍ تَجۡرِى مِن تَحۡتِهِمُ ٱلۡأَنۡهَـٰرُ يُحَلَّوۡنَ فِيهَا مِنۡ أَسَاوِرَ مِن ذَهَبٍ وَيَلۡبَسُونَ ثِيَابًا خُضۡرًا مِّن سُندُسٍ وَإِسۡتَبۡرَقٍ مُّتَّكِـِٔينَ فِيهَا عَلَى ٱلۡأَرَآئِكِ نِعۡمَ ٱلثَّوَابُ وَحَسُنَتۡ مُرۡتَفَقًا ۩

Section 5

32. Proclaim to them the similitude of two men. We made for one of them two gardens of vines and hedged both with palms, and We placed tillage in between.

وَٱضۡرِبۡ لَهُم مَّثَلًا رَّجُلَيۡنِ جَعَلۡنَا لِأَحَدِهِمَا جَنَّتَيۡنِ مِنۡ أَعۡنَـٰبٍ وَحَفَفۡنَـٰهُمَا بِنَخۡلٍ وَجَعَلۡنَا بَيۡنَهُمَا زَرۡعًا ۩

33. Each of the two gardens brought forth the produce, and stinted not anything thereof, and We made a stream to gush forth in the midst of the two.

كِلۡتَا ٱلۡجَنَّتَيۡنِ ءَاتَتۡ أُكُلَهَا وَلَمۡ تَظۡلِم مِّنۡهُ شَيۡـًٔا وَفَجَّرۡنَا خِلَـٰلَهُمَا نَهَرًا ۩

34. And he had property. Then he said to his companion as he spoke to him: 'I am better than you in substance and mightier in respect of retinue.'

وَكَانَ لَهُ ثَمَرٌ فَقَالَ لِصَـٰحِبِهِۦ وَهُوَ يُحَاوِرُهُۥ أَنَا۠ أَكۡثَرُ مِنكَ مَالًا وَأَعَزُّ نَفَرًا ۩

35. And he entered his garden, while he was a wrong-doer in respect of his own soul, and he said: 'I do not consider that it will ever perish;

وَدَخَلَ جَنَّتَهُۥ وَهُوَ ظَالِمٌ لِّنَفۡسِهِۦ قَالَ مَآ أَظُنُّ أَن تَبِيدَ هَـٰذِهِۦٓ أَبَدًا ۩

36. Nor do I consider that the Hour is going to happen; and if I am brought back to my Lord, surely I shall find something better than this as a retreat.'

وَمَآ أَظُنُّ ٱلسَّاعَةَ قَآئِمَةً وَلَئِن رُّدِدتُّ إِلَىٰ رَبِّى لَأَجِدَنَّ خَيۡرًا مِّنۡهَا مُنقَلَبًا ۩

37. His companion said to him, as he spoke to him: 'Are you a disbeliever in Him Who created you of dust; then of a sperm, and formed you a man?

قَالَ لَهُ صَاحِبُهُ وَهُوَ يُحَاوِرُهُۥٓ أَكَفَرْتَ بِالَّذِى خَلَقَكَ مِن تُرَابٍ ثُمَّ مِن نُّطْفَةٍ ثُمَّ سَوَّىٰكَ رَجُلًا ۝

38. But, He is Allah, my Lord, and with my Lord I do not join anyone.

لَّٰكِنَّا۠ هُوَ ٱللَّهُ رَبِّى وَلَآ أُشْرِكُ بِرَبِّىٓ أَحَدًا ۝

39. Why then did you not say when you entered your garden: 'Whatever Allah may will, there is no power save in Allah;' if you see then that I am inferior to you in substance and offspring;

وَلَوْلَآ إِذْ دَخَلْتَ جَنَّتَكَ قُلْتَ مَا شَآءَ ٱللَّهُ لَا قُوَّةَ إِلَّا بِٱللَّهِ إِن تَرَنِ أَنَا۠ أَقَلَّ مِنكَ مَالًا وَوَلَدًا ۝

40. Then perchance my Lord will give me something better than your garden and send on it a bolt from the heaven so that it becomes a slippery plane;

فَعَسَىٰ رَبِّىٓ أَن يُؤْتِيَنِ خَيْرًا مِّن جَنَّتِكَ وَيُرْسِلَ عَلَيْهَا حُسْبَانًا مِّنَ ٱلسَّمَآءِ فَتُصْبِحَ صَعِيدًا زَلَقًا ۝

41. Or the water thereof becomes deep-sunken, so that you can make a search therefor.'

أَوْ يُصْبِحَ مَآؤُهَا غَوْرًا فَلَن تَسْتَطِيعَ لَهُۥ طَلَبًا ۝

42. And his property was encompassed, and lo! He was wringing the palm of his hands over what he had spent on it, so it lay fallen down on its trellises, saying: 'Oh! Would that I had not joined anyone with my Lord!'

وَأُحِيطَ بِثَمَرِهِۦ فَأَصْبَحَ يُقَلِّبُ كَفَّيْهِ عَلَىٰ مَآ أَنفَقَ فِيهَا وَهِىَ خَاوِيَةٌ عَلَىٰ عُرُوشِهَا وَيَقُولُ يَٰلَيْتَنِى لَمْ أُشْرِكْ بِرَبِّىٓ أَحَدًا ۝

43. And there could be no party helping him as against Allah, nor could he be an avenger himself.

وَلَمْ تَكُن لَّهُۥ فِئَةٌ يَنصُرُونَهُۥ مِن دُونِ ٱللَّهِ وَمَا كَانَ مُنتَصِرًا ۝

44. Herein is all protection from Allah the True; excellent is He as to the reward and excellent to the final end!

هُنَالِكَ ٱلْوَلَٰيَةُ لِلَّهِ ٱلْحَقِّ هُوَ خَيْرٌ ثَوَابًا وَخَيْرٌ عُقْبًا ۝

Section 6

45. Propound to them the similitude of the life of this world. It is as water which We send down from the heaven, then there mingles with the vegetation of the earth, and lo! It becomes dry stubble which the winds scatter. And Allah is the Potent over everything .

وَٱضۡرِبۡ لَهُم مَّثَلَ ٱلۡحَيَوٰةِ ٱلدُّنۡيَا كَمَآءٍ أَنزَلۡنَٰهُ مِنَ ٱلسَّمَآءِ فَٱخۡتَلَطَ بِهِۦ نَبَاتُ ٱلۡأَرۡضِ فَأَصۡبَحَ هَشِيمًا تَذۡرُوهُ ٱلرِّيَٰحُ وَكَانَ ٱللَّهُ عَلَىٰ كُلِّ شَىۡءٍ مُّقۡتَدِرًا ﴿٤٥﴾

46. Riches and sons are the adornment of the life of the world, and the righteous works that last are excellent with your Lord in respect of reward and excellent in respect of hope.

ٱلۡمَالُ وَٱلۡبَنُونَ زِينَةُ ٱلۡحَيَوٰةِ ٱلدُّنۡيَا وَ ٱلۡبَٰقِيَٰتُ ٱلصَّٰلِحَٰتُ خَيۡرٌ عِندَ رَبِّكَ ثَوَابًا وَخَيۡرٌ أَمَلًا ﴿٤٦﴾

47. And beware of a Day when We will cause the mountains to pass away, and you will see the earth plain, and We will gather them, and We will leave of them not one.

وَيَوۡمَ نُسَيِّرُ ٱلۡجِبَالَ وَتَرَى ٱلۡأَرۡضَ بَارِزَةً وَحَشَرۡنَٰهُمۡ فَلَمۡ نُغَادِرۡ مِنۡهُمۡ أَحَدًا ﴿٤٧﴾

48. And they shall be sent before your Lord in ranks. Now you are come to Us as We had created you the first time. Aye! You fancied that We had appointed for you no tryst.

وَعُرِضُواْ عَلَىٰ رَبِّكَ صَفًّا لَّقَدۡ جِئۡتُمُونَا كَمَا خَلَقۡنَٰكُمۡ أَوَّلَ مَرَّةٍ بَلۡ زَعَمۡتُمۡ أَلَّن نَّجۡعَلَ لَكُم مَّوۡعِدًا ﴿٤٨﴾

49. And the Book shall be placed, and you will see the culprits alarmed at what is therein, and they will say: 'Ah! Woe to us! What ails this Book that it leaves not any misdeed, small or great, but it has comprehended it!' And they shall find present all that they had wrought; and your Lord wrongs not anyone.

وَوُضِعَ ٱلۡكِتَٰبُ فَتَرَى ٱلۡمُجۡرِمِينَ مُشۡفِقِينَ مِمَّا فِيهِ وَيَقُولُونَ يَٰوَيۡلَتَنَا مَالِ هَٰذَا ٱلۡكِتَٰبِ لَا يُغَادِرُ صَغِيرَةً وَلَا كَبِيرَةً إِلَّا أَحۡصَىٰهَا وَوَجَدُواْ مَا عَمِلُواْ حَاضِرًا وَلَا يَظۡلِمُ رَبُّكَ أَحَدًا ﴿٤٩﴾

Section 7

50. And recall when We said to the angels: 'Make obeisance to Adam,' and they made obeisance, but Iblīs did not. He was of the jinn,[487] so he trespassed the command of his Lord. Would you then take him and his progeny as patrons instead of Me, whereas they are unto you an enemy? Ill is this exchange for the wrong-doers.

وَإِذۡ قُلۡنَا لِلۡمَلَٰٓئِكَةِ ٱسۡجُدُوا۟ لِأٓدَمَ فَسَجَدُوٓا۟ إِلَّآ إِبۡلِيسَ كَانَ مِنَ ٱلۡجِنِّ فَفَسَقَ عَنۡ أَمۡرِ رَبِّهِۦٓ أَفَتَتَّخِذُونَهُۥ وَذُرِّيَّتَهُۥٓ أَوۡلِيَآءَ مِن دُونِى وَهُمۡ لَكُمۡ عَدُوٌّۢ بِئۡسَ لِلظَّٰلِمِينَ بَدَلًا ۝

51. I made them not present at the creation of the heavens and the earth, nor at the creation of themselves; nor was I to take the seducers as supporters.

مَّآ أَشۡهَدتُّهُمۡ خَلۡقَ ٱلسَّمَٰوَٰتِ وَٱلۡأَرۡضِ وَلَا خَلۡقَ أَنفُسِهِمۡ وَمَا كُنتُ مُتَّخِذَ ٱلۡمُضِلِّينَ عَضُدًا ۝

52. And beware a Day whereon I shall say: 'Cry unto My associates whom you fancied.' So they will call upon them and they will answer them not, We shall place between them a barrier.

وَيَوۡمَ يَقُولُ نَادُوا۟ شُرَكَآءِىَ ٱلَّذِينَ زَعَمۡتُمۡ فَدَعَوۡهُمۡ فَلَمۡ يَسۡتَجِيبُوا۟ لَهُمۡ وَجَعَلۡنَا بَيۡنَهُم مَّوۡبِقًا ۝

53. And the culprits will see the Fire and imagine they are about to fall therein; and they shall not find therefrom a way to escape.

وَرَءَا ٱلۡمُجۡرِمُونَ ٱلنَّارَ فَظَنُّوٓا۟ أَنَّهُم مُّوَاقِعُوهَا وَلَمۡ يَجِدُوا۟ عَنۡهَا مَصۡرِفًا ۝

---

487. This categorically denies the myth of Satan being an 'angel' fallen or otherwise. The genii are made of fire, not of light as are angels, and like human beings, can freely choose for themselves the path of right or wrong.

Section 8

54. And assuredly We have set forth all manner of parables in this Qur'ān for mankind, but man is of all things the most contending.

وَلَقَدْ صَرَّفْنَا فِى هٰذَا الْقُرْءَانِ لِلنَّاسِ مِن كُلِّ مَثَلٍ وَكَانَ الْإِنسَٰنُ أَكْثَرَ شَىْءٍ جَدَلًا ﴿٥٤﴾

55. And nothing prevents mankind from believing now when the guidance has come to them and for asking forgiveness of their Lord, except that there may come to them the dispensation of the ancients or that the chastisement may come to them face to face.

وَمَا مَنَعَ النَّاسَ أَن يُؤْمِنُوٓا إِذْ جَآءَهُمُ الْهُدَىٰ وَيَسْتَغْفِرُوا رَبَّهُمْ إِلَّآ أَن تَأْتِيَهُمْ سُنَّةُ الْأَوَّلِينَ أَوْ يَأْتِيَهُمُ الْعَذَابُ قُبُلًا ﴿٥٥﴾

56. And We do not send Messengers save as bringers of glad tidings and warners, and those who disbelieve dispute with falsehood that they may rebut thereby the Truth; and they take My signs and what they are warned of as a mockery.

وَمَا نُرْسِلُ الْمُرْسَلِينَ إِلَّا مُبَشِّرِينَ وَمُنذِرِينَ وَيُجَٰدِلُ الَّذِينَ كَفَرُوا بِالْبَٰطِلِ لِيُدْحِضُوا بِهِ الْحَقَّ وَاتَّخَذُوٓا ءَايَٰتِى وَمَآ أُنذِرُوا هُزُوًا ﴿٥٦﴾

57. And who does greater wrong than he who is admonished with the signs of his Lord and yet turns away from them and forgets what his hands had sent forth? We have set up veils over their hearts last they should understand it, and in their ears a heaviness; and if you call them to the guidance, lo! They will not let themselves be ever guided.

وَمَنْ أَظْلَمُ مِمَّن ذُكِّرَ بِـَٔايَٰتِ رَبِّهِ فَأَعْرَضَ عَنْهَا وَنَسِىَ مَا قَدَّمَتْ يَدَاهُ إِنَّا جَعَلْنَا عَلَىٰ قُلُوبِهِمْ أَكِنَّةً أَن يَفْقَهُوهُ وَفِىٓ ءَاذَانِهِمْ وَقْرًا وَإِن تَدْعُهُمْ إِلَى الْهُدَىٰ فَلَن يَهْتَدُوٓا إِذًا أَبَدًا ﴿٥٧﴾

58. And your Lord is the Forgiver, the Owner of Mercy. Were He to call them to account for what they have earned, He would have hastened torment for them, but for them there is a tryst, and beside it they cannot find a place to take themselves to.

وَرَبُّكَ ٱلۡغَفُورُ ذُو ٱلرَّحۡمَةِ لَوۡ يُؤَاخِذُهُم بِمَا كَسَبُواْ لَعَجَّلَ لَهُمُ ٱلۡعَذَابَ بَل لَّهُم مَّوۡعِدٌ لَّن يَجِدُواْ مِن دُونِهِۦ مَوۡئِلًا ٥٨

59. And these cities! We destroyed them when they did wrong, and We had appointed a tryst for their destruction.

وَتِلۡكَ ٱلۡقُرَىٰٓ أَهۡلَكۡنَٰهُمۡ لَمَّا ظَلَمُواْ وَجَعَلۡنَا لِمَهۡلِكِهِم مَّوۡعِدًا ٥٩

Section 9

60. And recall when Moses said to his page: 'I shall not cease journeying until I reach the confluence of the two seas, or I shall go on for ages.'

وَإِذۡ قَالَ مُوسَىٰ لِفَتَىٰهُ لَآ أَبۡرَحُ حَتَّىٰٓ أَبۡلُغَ مَجۡمَعَ ٱلۡبَحۡرَيۡنِ أَوۡ أَمۡضِيَ حُقُبًا ٦٠

61. And when the two reached the confluence of the two, they forgot their fish, and it found its way into the sea freely.

فَلَمَّا بَلَغَا مَجۡمَعَ بَيۡنِهِمَا نَسِيَا حُوتَهُمَا فَٱتَّخَذَ سَبِيلَهُۥ فِي ٱلۡبَحۡرِ سَرَبًا ٦١

62. And when the two had passed by, he said to his page: 'Bring to us our breakfast. We have indeed got to toil from this journey of ours.'

فَلَمَّا جَاوَزَا قَالَ لِفَتَىٰهُ ءَاتِنَا غَدَآءَنَا لَقَدۡ لَقِينَا مِن سَفَرِنَا هَٰذَا نَصَبًا ٦٢

63. He said: 'Look here! As we were proceeding to the rock I became unmindful of the fish, and nothing but Satan made me forget to mention it to you, and it took marvellously its way into the sea.'

قَالَ أَرَءَيۡتَ إِذۡ أَوَيۡنَآ إِلَى ٱلصَّخۡرَةِ فَإِنِّي نَسِيتُ ٱلۡحُوتَ وَمَآ أَنسَىٰنِيهُ إِلَّا ٱلشَّيۡطَٰنُ أَنۡ أَذۡكُرَهُۥ وَٱتَّخَذَ سَبِيلَهُۥ فِي ٱلۡبَحۡرِ عَجَبًا ٦٣

64. Moses said: 'That is exactly what we have been seeking.' Then they turned back on their footsteps, retracing.

قَالَ ذَلِكَ مَا كُنَّا نَبْغِ فَأَرْتَدَّا عَلَىٰ ءَاثَارِهِمَا قَصَصًا ﴿٦٤﴾

65. Then the two found a bondman from Our own bondman,[488] on him We had bestowed a mercy from before Us and him We had taught a knowledge[489] from Our presence.

فَوَجَدَا عَبْدًا مِّنْ عِبَادِنَا ءَاتَيْنَهُ رَحْمَةً مِّنْ عِندِنَا وَعَلَّمْنَهُ مِن لَّدُنَّا عِلْمًا ﴿٦٥﴾

66. Moses said to him: 'Shall I follow you that you may teach me of what you have been taught, a directive knowledge.'

قَالَ لَهُۥ مُوسَىٰ هَلْ أَتَّبِعُكَ عَلَىٰ أَن تُعَلِّمَنِ مِمَّا عُلِّمْتَ رُشْدًا ﴿٦٦﴾

67. He said: 'Verily you will not be able to have patience with me;

قَالَ إِنَّكَ لَن تَسْتَطِيعَ مَعِىَ صَبْرًا ﴿٦٧﴾

68. And how can you have patience over that which your knowledge does not encompass?'

وَكَيْفَ تَصْبِرُ عَلَىٰ مَا لَمْ تُحِطْ بِهِۦ خُبْرًا ﴿٦٨﴾

69. Moses said: 'You will find me, if Allah will, patient, and I shall not disobey you in any affair.'

قَالَ سَتَجِدُنِى إِن شَآءَ ٱللَّهُ صَابِرًا وَلَآ أَعْصِى لَكَ أَمْرًا ﴿٦٩﴾

70. He said: 'Well, if you would follow me, then do not question me of anything, until I begin to mention it myself.'

قَالَ فَإِنِ ٱتَّبَعْتَنِى فَلَا تَسْـَٔلْنِى عَن شَىْءٍ حَتَّىٰ أُحْدِثَ لَكَ مِنْهُ ذِكْرًا ﴿٧٠﴾

---

488. The Qur'ān does not mention this servant of God by name. In one *hadīth*, he is called Khiḍr, and is reported to have had a life of hundreds of years.

489. This special knowledge consisted mainly of a pre-vision of the events of this world, and was different from the Knowledge of Divine truths imparted to Moses, though by no means superior to it.

Section 10

71. Then the two journeyed together until when they embarked in a boat, he scuttled it. Moses said: 'Have you scuttled it that you may drown the people thereof? Assuredly you have committed a thing grievous.'

فَٱنطَلَقَا حَتَّىٰٓ إِذَا رَكِبَا فِى ٱلسَّفِينَةِ خَرَقَهَا قَالَ أَخَرَقْتَهَا لِتُغْرِقَ أَهْلَهَا لَقَدْ جِئْتَ شَيْـًٔا إِمْرًا ۝

72. He said: 'Did I not tell you that you would not be able to have patience with me?'

قَالَ أَلَمْ أَقُلْ إِنَّكَ لَن تَسْتَطِيعَ مَعِىَ صَبْرًا ۝

73. Moses said: 'Do not take me to task for what I forgot and do not impose hardship in my affair.'

قَالَ لَا تُؤَاخِذْنِى بِمَا نَسِيتُ وَلَا تُرْهِقْنِى مِنْ أَمْرِى عُسْرًا ۝

74. Then the two journeyed till when they met a boy, and he killed him. Moses said: 'Have you killed an innocent person not in return for a person? Assuredly you have committed a thing formidable.'

فَٱنطَلَقَا حَتَّىٰٓ إِذَا لَقِيَا غُلَٰمًا فَقَتَلَهُۥ قَالَ أَقَتَلْتَ نَفْسًا زَكِيَّةًۢ بِغَيْرِ نَفْسٍ لَّقَدْ جِئْتَ شَيْـًٔا نُّكْرًا ۝

75. He said: 'Did I not tell you that you would not be able to have patience with me?'

قَالَ أَلَمْ أَقُل لَّكَ إِنَّكَ لَن تَسْتَطِيعَ مَعِىَ صَبْرًا ۝

76. Moses said: 'If I question you regarding anything after this, abandon me; surely there has reached you an excuse from my side.'

قَالَ إِن سَأَلْتُكَ عَن شَىْءٍۭ بَعْدَهَا فَلَا تُصَٰحِبْنِى قَدْ بَلَغْتَ مِن لَّدُنِّى عُذْرًا ۝

77. Then the two departed, until when they came to the people of a city, they begged food from the citizens; but they refused to entertain the two. Then they, found therein a wall about to collapse and he set it upright. Moses said: 'Had you wished you could have taken a wage therefor.'

فَٱنطَلَقَا حَتَّىٰٓ إِذَآ أَتَيَآ أَهْلَ قَرْيَةٍ ٱسْتَطْعَمَآ أَهْلَهَا فَأَبَوْا أَن يُضَيِّفُوهُمَا فَوَجَدَا فِيهَا جِدَارًا يُرِيدُ أَن يَنقَضَّ فَأَقَامَهُۥ قَالَ لَوْ شِئْتَ لَتَّخَذْتَ عَلَيْهِ أَجْرًا ۝

78. He said: 'This shall be the parting between me and you. Now I shall declare to you the interpretation of that over which you could have no patience.

قَالَ هَٰذَا فِرَاقُ بَيۡنِى وَبَيۡنِكَ سَأُنَبِّئُكَ بِتَأۡوِيلِ مَا لَمۡ تَسۡتَطِع عَّلَيۡهِ صَبۡرًا ۞

79. As for the boat, it belonged to poor men working in the sea. I wanted to damage it, as there was before them a prince confiscating every boat.

أَمَّا ٱلسَّفِينَةُ فَكَانَتۡ لِمَسَٰكِينَ يَعۡمَلُونَ فِى ٱلۡبَحۡرِ فَأَرَدتُّ أَنۡ أَعِيبَهَا وَكَانَ وَرَآءَهُم مَّلِكٌ يَأۡخُذُ كُلَّ سَفِينَةٍ غَصۡبًا ۞

80. And as for the boy his parents were believers, and we apprehended that he might impose upon them exorbitance and infidelity;

وَأَمَّا ٱلۡغُلَٰمُ فَكَانَ أَبَوَاهُ مُؤۡمِنَيۡنِ فَخَشِينَآ أَن يُرۡهِقَهُمَا طُغۡيَٰنًا وَكُفۡرًا ۞

81. So we intended that their Lord should change them with one better than he in piety and closer in affection.

فَأَرَدۡنَآ أَن يُبۡدِلَهُمَا رَبُّهُمَا خَيۡرًا مِّنۡهُ زَكَوٰةً وَأَقۡرَبَ رُحۡمًا ۞

82. And as for the wall, it belonged to two orphan boys in the town and underneath it was a treasure belonging to them, and their father was righteous. So your Lord intended that the twain should attain their maturity and bring forth for themselves their treasure as a mercy from their Lord; and I did it not of my own bidding. That is the interpretation of what you could not bear patiently.'

وَأَمَّا ٱلۡجِدَارُ فَكَانَ لِغُلَٰمَيۡنِ يَتِيمَيۡنِ فِى ٱلۡمَدِينَةِ وَكَانَ تَحۡتَهُ كَنزٌ لَّهُمَا وَكَانَ أَبُوهُمَا صَٰلِحًا فَأَرَادَ رَبُّكَ أَن يَبۡلُغَآ أَشُدَّهُمَا وَيَسۡتَخۡرِجَا كَنزَهُمَا رَحۡمَةً مِّن رَّبِّكَ وَمَا فَعَلۡتُهُ عَنۡ أَمۡرِى ذَٰلِكَ تَأۡوِيلُ مَا لَمۡ تَسۡطِع عَّلَيۡهِ صَبۡرًا ۞

Section 11

83. And they question you of Dhū al-Qarnayn.[490] Say: 'I shall recite to you some mention of him.'

وَيَسْـَٔلُونَكَ عَن ذِى ٱلْقَرْنَيْنِ قُلْ سَأَتْلُوا۟ عَلَيْكُم مِّنْهُ ذِكْرًا ﴿٨٣﴾

84. Verily We! We established him in the earth, and gave him the means of everything.

إِنَّا مَكَّنَّا لَهُۥ فِى ٱلْأَرْضِ وَءَاتَيْنَٰهُ مِن كُلِّ شَىْءٍ سَبَبًا ﴿٨٤﴾

85. Thereafter he followed a way;

فَأَتْبَعَ سَبَبًا ﴿٨٥﴾

86. Until when he reached the setting-place of the sun, he perceived it setting in a miry spring, and he found a nation nearby it. We said: 'O Dhū al-Qarnayn! Either chastise them or take the way of kindness in respect of them.'

حَتَّىٰٓ إِذَا بَلَغَ مَغْرِبَ ٱلشَّمْسِ وَجَدَهَا تَغْرُبُ فِى عَيْنٍ حَمِئَةٍ وَوَجَدَ عِندَهَا قَوْمًا قُلْنَا يَٰذَا ٱلْقَرْنَيْنِ إِمَّآ أَن تُعَذِّبَ وَإِمَّآ أَن تَتَّخِذَ فِيهِمْ حُسْنًا ﴿٨٦﴾

87. He said: 'As for him who does wrong presently we shall chastise him, and then he shall be brought back to his Lord, and He shall torment him with a formidable torment.

قَالَ أَمَّا مَن ظَلَمَ فَسَوْفَ نُعَذِّبُهُۥ ثُمَّ يُرَدُّ إِلَىٰ رَبِّهِۦ فَيُعَذِّبُهُۥ عَذَابًا نُّكْرًا ﴿٨٧﴾

---

490. Literally 'the two-horned'; identified by the majority of commentators with Alexander the Great; so named from his expeditions to the East and West. He was actually represented on his coins with two horns. The horn in the Bible is 'a symbol of strength', and 'is frequently mentioned to signify power and glory' (CD. p. 457). In Hebrew usage 'raising the horn of a people or an individual' signifies victory or pride, breaking signifies 'defeat'. (ERE. VI. p. 792.) Even Moses (peace be on him!) was represented with horns. 'It has become a widespread belief that Moses, when he came down from Mount Sinai with the tables of the Law, had two horns on his forehead.' (JE. VI. p. 463. See also EBi. c. 2111).

88. And as for him who believes and works righteously, for him will be a goodly reward, and anon we shall speak to him some thing easy of our affair.'[491]

وَأَمَّا مَنْ ءَامَنَ وَعَمِلَ صَلِحًا فَلَهُۥ جَزَآءً ٱلْحُسْنَىٰ وَسَنَقُولُ لَهُۥ مِنْ أَمْرِنَا يُسْرًا ﴿٨٨﴾

89. Thereafter he followed a way,

ثُمَّ أَتْبَعَ سَبَبًا ﴿٨٩﴾

90. Until when he reached the rising place of the sun, he perceived it rising upon a nation for whom We had not sent a veil against it.

حَتَّىٰٓ إِذَا بَلَغَ مَطْلِعَ ٱلشَّمْسِ وَجَدَهَا تَطْلُعُ عَلَىٰ قَوْمٍ لَّمْ نَجْعَل لَّهُم مِّن دُونِهَا سِتْرًا ﴿٩٠﴾

91. Thus it was, and surely We have encompassed in knowledge all that was with him.

كَذَٰلِكَ وَقَدْ أَحَطْنَا بِمَا لَدَيْهِ خُبْرًا ﴿٩١﴾

92. Thereafter he followed a way;

ثُمَّ أَتْبَعَ سَبَبًا ﴿٩٢﴾

93. Until when he arrived between the two mountains, he found beside them a people who almost did not understand a word.

حَتَّىٰٓ إِذَا بَلَغَ بَيْنَ ٱلسَّدَّيْنِ وَجَدَ مِن دُونِهِمَا قَوْمًا لَّا يَكَادُونَ يَفْقَهُونَ قَوْلًا ﴿٩٣﴾

---

491. That the King Dhū al-Qarnayn was a man of God is implied throughout his story in the Qur'ān; and if his identification with Alexander the Great be correct, the fact accords well with a reference in the Bible. (Dn. 11:3.) 'It is supposed that the Book of Daniel alludes to Alexander when it refers to a mighty king that "shall stand up, that shall rule with greater dominion" whose kingdom shall be destroyed after his death.' (JE. I. p. 341.) The Jews, the only monotheistic people of his time, were even ready to recognise him as the promised Messiah. 'The Jewish contemporaries of Alexander the Great, dazzled by his glorious achievements, hailed him as the divinely appointed deliverer, the inaugurator of the period of universal peace promised by the Prophets. (*Ibid.*, VIII p. 507) Josephus has described in some detail Alexander's visit to Jerusalem, and the trend of his remarks shows that Alexander was a monotheist. 'When he went up into the temple, he offered sacrifice to God, according to the high priest's direction: and magnificently treated both the high priest and the priests. And when the Book of Daniel was showed him, wherein Daniel declared that one of the Greeks should destroy the empire of the Persians, he supposed that he himself was the person intended.' (*Ant.* XI,8).

94. They said: 'O Dhū al-Qarnayn! Gog and Magog are doing mischief in the land; should we then pay you tribute so that you place between us and them a barrier?'

قَالُوا يَـٰذَا الْقَرْنَيْنِ إِنَّ يَأْجُوجَ وَمَأْجُوجَ مُفْسِدُونَ فِى الْأَرْضِ فَهَلْ نَجْعَلُ لَكَ خَرْجًا عَلَىٰ أَن تَجْعَلَ بَيْنَنَا وَبَيْنَهُمْ سَدًّا ۝

95. He said: 'Better than your tribute is that wherein my Lord has established me[492]; so help me with your labour, and I shall place between you and them a rampart.

قَالَ مَا مَكَّنِّى فِيهِ رَبِّى خَيْرٌ فَأَعِينُونِى بِقُوَّةٍ أَجْعَلْ بَيْنَكُمْ وَبَيْنَهُمْ رَدْمًا ۝

96. Bring me lumps of iron.' Then when he evened up the two mountain sides he said: 'Blow!' Then when he had made it a fire, he said: 'Bring me molten copper and I shall pour it thereon.'

ءَاتُونِى زُبَرَ الْحَدِيدِ حَتَّىٰ إِذَا سَاوَىٰ بَيْنَ الصَّدَفَيْنِ قَالَ انفُخُوا حَتَّىٰ إِذَا جَعَلَهُ نَارًا قَالَ ءَاتُونِى أُفْرِغْ عَلَيْهِ قِطْرًا ۝

97. In this wise they were not able to scale it, nor were they able to burrow through it.

فَمَا اسْطَـٰعُوا أَن يَظْهَرُوهُ وَمَا اسْتَطَـٰعُوا لَهُ نَقْبًا ۝

98. He said: 'This is a mercy from my Lord; then when the promise of my Lord comes, He shall make it powder, and the promise of my Lord is ever true.'

قَالَ هَـٰذَا رَحْمَةٌ مِّن رَّبِّى فَإِذَا جَآءَ وَعْدُ رَبِّى جَعَلَهُ دَكَّآءَ وَكَانَ وَعْدُ رَبِّى حَقًّا ۝

99. And We will let them on that day surge some of them against others, and the Trumpet shall be blown, and then We will muster together.

وَتَرَكْنَا بَعْضَهُمْ يَوْمَئِذٍ يَمُوجُ فِى بَعْضٍ وَنُفِخَ فِى الصُّورِ فَجَمَعْنَاهُمْ جَمْعًا ۝

---

492. Therefore, I do not need any monetary help or subsidy from you. Note that Dhū al-Qarnayn ascribed all his glory to God, and not to his own skill and ability.

100. And We will set Hell on that Day unto the infidels with a setting,

وَعَرَضْنَا جَهَنَّمَ يَوْمَئِذٍ لِّلْكَفِرِينَ عَرْضًا ۞

101. Unto those whose eyes had been under a covering from My remembrance, nor had they been able to hear.

ٱلَّذِينَ كَانَتْ أَعْيُنُهُمْ فِى غِطَآءٍ عَن ذِكْرِى وَكَانُوا۟ لَا يَسْتَطِيعُونَ سَمْعًا ۞

Section 12

102. Do then who disbelieve think that they may take My bondsmen instead of Me, as patrons? We have prepared Hell as an entertainment for the infidels.

أَفَحَسِبَ ٱلَّذِينَ كَفَرُوٓا۟ أَن يَتَّخِذُوا۟ عِبَادِى مِن دُونِىٓ أَوْلِيَآءَ إِنَّآ أَعْتَدْنَا جَهَنَّمَ لِلْكَفِرِينَ نُزُلًا ۞

103. Say: 'Shall We declare to you the greatest losers in respect of works?

قُلْ هَلْ نُنَبِّئُكُم بِٱلْأَخْسَرِينَ أَعْمَلًا ۞

104. They are those whose effort is wasted in the life of the world, and they imagine that they are doing well in action?'

ٱلَّذِينَ ضَلَّ سَعْيُهُمْ فِى ٱلْحَيَوٰةِ ٱلدُّنْيَا وَهُمْ يَحْسَبُونَ أَنَّهُمْ يُحْسِنُونَ صُنْعًا ۞

105. They are those who disbelieve in the signs of their Lord and their meeting with Him, vain shall be made all their works, and We will not allow them any weight on the Day of Judgement.

أُو۟لَٰٓئِكَ ٱلَّذِينَ كَفَرُوا۟ بِـَٔايَٰتِ رَبِّهِمْ وَلِقَآئِهِۦ فَحَبِطَتْ أَعْمَٰلُهُمْ فَلَا نُقِيمُ لَهُمْ يَوْمَ ٱلْقِيَٰمَةِ وَزْنًا ۞

106. That shall be their recompense: Hell; for they disbelieved and held My signs and My Messengers in mockery.

ذَٰلِكَ جَزَآؤُهُمْ جَهَنَّمُ بِمَا كَفَرُوا۟ وَٱتَّخَذُوٓا۟ ءَايَٰتِى وَرُسُلِى هُزُوًا ۞

107. Verily those who believe and do righteous works, theirs shall be Gardens of Paradise for an entertainment;

إِنَّ الَّذِينَ ءَامَنُوا وَعَمِلُوا الصَّلِحَتِ كَانَتْ لَهُمْ جَنَّتُ الْفِرْدَوْسِ نُزُلًا ۝

108. Abiding therein, they shall not seek any removal out of them.

خَلِدِينَ فِيهَا لَا يَبْغُونَ عَنْهَا حِوَلًا ۝

109. Say: 'Were the oceans to become ink for the words of my Lord, the ocean would surely exhaust before the words of my Lord exhausted, even though We brought another ocean for support.'

قُل لَّوْ كَانَ الْبَحْرُ مِدَادًا لِّكَلِمَتِ رَبِّى لَنَفِدَ الْبَحْرُ قَبْلَ أَن تَنفَدَ كَلِمَتُ رَبِّى وَلَوْ جِئْنَا بِمِثْلِهِ مَدَدًا ۝

110. Say: 'I am but a human being like yourselves; revealed unto me is that your God is One God.[493] Whoso then hopes the meeting with his Lord, let him do righteous deeds, and let him not join anyone in the worship of his Lord.'[494]

قُلْ إِنَّمَا أَنَا بَشَرٌ مِّثْلُكُمْ يُوحَى إِلَىَّ أَنَّمَا إِلَهُكُمْ إِلَهٌ وَحِدٌ فَمَن كَانَ يَرْجُوا لِقَآءَ رَبِّهِ فَلْيَعْمَلْ عَمَلًا صَلِحًا وَلَا يُشْرِكْ بِعِبَادَةِ رَبِّهِ أَحَدًا ۝

---

493. Which is the quintessence and central Truth of Islam as opposed to polytheism, trinitarianism, and dualism.

494. So it is not a mere belief in monotheism that matters; all forms of worship and adoration also are due to Him alone.

Sūrah 19

Maryam

(Makkan, 6 Sections, 98 Verses)

In the name of Allah, the Compassionate, the Merciful.

Section 1

1. *Kāf, Hā, Yā, 'Ayn, Ṣād.*

2. This is a mention of the mercy of your Lord to His bondsman, Zacharia.

3. Recall when he cried unto his Lord with a low tone.

4. He said: 'Lord! My bones have waxen feeble and the head is glistening with hoariness, and I have not yet been in my prayer to You, my Lord, unblessed.

5. And I fear my kindred after me, and my wife has been barren; so bestow on me from before You an heir.

6. Inheriting me and inheriting the children of Jacob, and make him, Lord, acceptable.'

7. O Zacharia! We give you the glad tidings of a boy, and his name shall be John, We have not so far made his namesake in your family.'

8. He said: 'Lord! In what wise shall there be a boy for me? My wife has been barren, and I have reached the extreme age.'

9. Allah said: 'Even so! Your Lord says: it is to Me easy. Surely I have created you before, when you were not anything.'

قَالَ كَذَٰلِكَ قَالَ رَبُّكَ هُوَ عَلَىَّ هَيِّنٌ وَقَدۡ خَلَقۡتُكَ مِن قَبۡلُ وَلَمۡ تَكُ شَيۡئًا ۝

10. He said: 'Lord! Appoint me a sign.' Allah said: 'Your sign is that you shall not speak to mankind for three nights, while sound.'

قَالَ رَبِّ ٱجۡعَل لِّىٓ ءَايَةً قَالَ ءَايَتُكَ أَلَّا تُكَلِّمَ ٱلنَّاسَ ثَلَٰثَ لَيَالٍ سَوِيًّا ۝

11. Then he came forth to his people from the sanctuary and he beckoned to them: 'Hallow your Lord morning and evening.'

فَخَرَجَ عَلَىٰ قَوۡمِهِۦ مِنَ ٱلۡمِحۡرَابِ فَأَوۡحَىٰٓ إِلَيۡهِمۡ أَن سَبِّحُواْ بُكۡرَةً وَعَشِيًّا ۝

12. 'O John hold fast the Book. And We granted him wisdom, while yet a child;

يَٰيَحۡيَىٰ خُذِ ٱلۡكِتَٰبَ بِقُوَّةٍ وَءَاتَيۡنَٰهُ ٱلۡحُكۡمَ صَبِيًّا ۝

13. And tenderness from Our presence and purity, and he was pious;

وَحَنَانًا مِّن لَّدُنَّا وَزَكَوٰةً وَكَانَ تَقِيًّا ۝

14. And dutiful to his parents, and was not a high-handed rebel.[495]

وَبَرًّۢا بِوَٰلِدَيۡهِ وَلَمۡ يَكُن جَبَّارًا عَصِيًّا ۝

15. And peace be to him on the day of his birth and death and on the day he will be raised up.

وَسَلَٰمٌ عَلَيۡهِ يَوۡمَ وُلِدَ وَيَوۡمَ يَمُوتُ وَيَوۡمَ يُبۡعَثُ حَيًّا ۝

Section 2

16. And mention you in the Book Maryam, when she retired from her people to a place eastward.

وَٱذۡكُرۡ فِى ٱلۡكِتَٰبِ مَرۡيَمَ إِذِ ٱنتَبَذَتۡ مِنۡ أَهۡلِهَا مَكَانًا شَرۡقِيًّا ۝

---

495. This is here to refute the false accusation of sedition and rebellion brought against John by the state under Herod.

17. Then she took beside them a curtain. Then We sent unto her Our spirit, and he appeared to her in the form of a sound human being.

فَٱتَّخَذَتۡ مِن دُونِهِمۡ حِجَابًا فَأَرۡسَلۡنَآ إِلَيۡهَا رُوحَنَا فَتَمَثَّلَ لَهَا بَشَرًا سَوِيًّا ۝

18. She said: 'Verily I take refuge with the Compassionate from you if you are God-fearing.'

قَالَتۡ إِنِّيٓ أَعُوذُ بِٱلرَّحۡمَٰنِ مِنكَ إِن كُنتَ تَقِيًّا ۝

19. He said: 'I am but an envoy of your Lord, and have come to bestow on you a boy, faultless.'

قَالَ إِنَّمَآ أَنَا۠ رَسُولُ رَبِّكِ لِأَهَبَ لَكِ غُلَٰمًا زَكِيًّا ۝

20. She said: 'How can there be a boy unto me, whereas no human being has touched me, nor I have been a harlot?'[496]

قَالَتۡ أَنَّىٰ يَكُونُ لِي غُلَٰمٌ وَلَمۡ يَمۡسَسۡنِي بَشَرٌ وَلَمۡ أَكُ بَغِيًّا ۝

21. He said: 'Even so! Your Lord says: easy it is with Me, and it is in order that We make him a sign to mankind, and it is a mercy from Us; and it is an affair decreed.'

قَالَ كَذَٰلِكِ قَالَ رَبُّكِ هُوَ عَلَىَّ هَيِّنٌ وَلِنَجۡعَلَهُ ءَايَةً لِّلنَّاسِ وَرَحۡمَةً مِّنَّا وَكَانَ أَمۡرًا مَّقۡضِيًّا ۝

22. Then she conceived him and she retired with him to a place far-off.

فَحَمَلَتۡهُ فَٱنتَبَذَتۡ بِهِۦ مَكَانًا قَصِيًّا ۝

23. Then the birth-pangs drove her to the trunk of a palm-tree. She said: 'Would that I had died before this and had become forgotten, lost in oblivion.'

فَأَجَآءَهَا ٱلۡمَخَاضُ إِلَىٰ جِذۡعِ ٱلنَّخۡلَةِ قَالَتۡ يَٰلَيۡتَنِي مِتُّ قَبۡلَ هَٰذَا وَكُنتُ نَسۡيًا مَّنسِيًّا ۝

24. Then one called from underneath her: 'Grieve not, your Lord has placed underneath you a rivulet;

فَنَادَىٰهَا مِن تَحۡتِهَآ أَلَّا تَحۡزَنِي قَدۡ جَعَلَ رَبُّكِ تَحۡتَكِ سَرِيًّا ۝

---

496. Nor unchaste. This is to refute the most vulgar charge of the Jews that Mary led an immoral life. See Schonfield's *According to the Hebrews*, p. 35.

25. And shake towards you the trunk of the palm-tree, dates will drop on you fresh and ripe;

وَهُزِّيٓ إِلَيْكِ بِجِذْعِ ٱلنَّخْلَةِ تُسَٰقِطْ عَلَيْكِ رُطَبًا جَنِيًّا ﴿٢٥﴾

26. So eat and drink you, and cool your eyes, and if you see of humans anyone say: 'Verily I have vowed to the Compassionate a fast, so I shall not speak to anyone today.'

فَكُلِى وَٱشْرَبِى وَقَرِّى عَيْنًا فَإِمَّا تَرَيِنَّ مِنَ ٱلْبَشَرِ أَحَدًا فَقُولِىٓ إِنِّى نَذَرْتُ لِلرَّحْمَٰنِ صَوْمًا فَلَنْ أُكَلِّمَ ٱلْيَوْمَ إِنسِيًّا ﴿٢٦﴾

27. Then she brought the baby to her people, carrying him. They said: 'O Maryam! You have brought a thing unheard of;

فَأَتَتْ بِهِۦ قَوْمَهَا تَحْمِلُهُۥ قَالُوا۟ يَٰمَرْيَمُ لَقَدْ جِئْتِ شَيْـًٔا فَرِيًّا ﴿٢٧﴾

28. O sister of Aaron: your father was not a man of evil, nor was your mother unchaste.'

يَٰٓأُخْتَ هَٰرُونَ مَا كَانَ أَبُوكِ ٱمْرَأَ سَوْءٍ وَمَا كَانَتْ أُمُّكِ بَغِيًّا ﴿٢٨﴾

29. Then she pointed to him. They said: 'How can we speak to one who is in the cradle, a mere child?'

فَأَشَارَتْ إِلَيْهِ قَالُوا۟ كَيْفَ نُكَلِّمُ مَن كَانَ فِى ٱلْمَهْدِ صَبِيًّا ﴿٢٩﴾

30. He said: 'Verily I am a bondman of Allah. He has given me the Book and made me a Prophet,

قَالَ إِنِّى عَبْدُ ٱللَّهِ ءَاتَٰنِىَ ٱلْكِتَٰبَ وَجَعَلَنِى نَبِيًّا ﴿٣٠﴾

31. And He has made me blessed wherever I may be and enjoined on me prayer and purity as long as I am alive;[497]

وَجَعَلَنِى مُبَارَكًا أَيْنَ مَا كُنتُ وَأَوْصَٰنِى بِٱلصَّلَوٰةِ وَٱلزَّكَوٰةِ مَا دُمْتُ حَيًّا ﴿٣١﴾

---

497. 'I am Jesus, son of Mary, of the seed of David, a man that is mortal and feareth God, and I seek that to God be given honour and glory' (GB. p. 221).

32. And dutiful to my mother,[498] and not made me high-handed and unblest;[499]

وَبَرًّا بِوَالِدَتِى وَلَمْ يَجْعَلْنِى جَبَّارًا شَقِيًّا ۝

33. And peace be on me the day I was born and the day I die and the day I am raised up.'

وَالسَّلَـٰمُ عَلَىَّ يَوْمَ وُلِدتُّ وَيَوْمَ أَمُوتُ وَيَوْمَ أُبْعَثُ حَيًّا ۝

34. Such is Jesus, son of Maryam; this is the word of Truth, wherein they are doubting.

ذَٰلِكَ عِيسَى ابْنُ مَرْيَمَ قَوْلَ الْحَقِّ الَّذِى فِيهِ يَمْتَرُونَ ۝

35. Allah is not the One to take to Himself a son. Hallowed be He. Whensoever He decrees an affair, He only says to it: 'Be', and it becomes.

مَا كَانَ لِلَّهِ أَن يَتَّخِذَ مِن وَلَدٍ سُبْحَـٰنَهُ إِذَا قَضَىٰ أَمْرًا فَإِنَّمَا يَقُولُ لَهُ كُن فَيَكُونُ ۝

36. And verily Allah is my Lord and your Lord, so worship Him, and this is a way straight.

وَإِنَّ اللَّهَ رَبِّى وَرَبُّكُمْ فَاعْبُدُوهُ هَـٰذَا صِرَٰطٌ مُّسْتَقِيمٌ ۝

37. Then the sects have differed among themselves. Woe to those who deny the witness of a mighty Day.

فَاخْتَلَفَ الْأَحْزَابُ مِنۢ بَيْنِهِمْ فَوَيْلٌ لِّلَّذِينَ كَفَرُوا مِن مَّشْهَدِ يَوْمٍ عَظِيمٍ ۝

38. How wonderful in their hearing and in their sight will they be the Day they come to Us! But today the wrong-doers are in manifest error.

أَسْمِعْ بِهِمْ وَأَبْصِرْ يَوْمَ يَأْتُونَنَا لَـٰكِنِ الظَّـٰلِمُونَ الْيَوْمَ فِى ضَلَـٰلٍ مُّبِينٍ ۝

---

498. This refutes and contradicts the position implied in various passages of the NT that the attitude of Jesus towards his mother was cold and indifferent. See Mt. 12: 46–50; Mk. 3: 31–35; Lk. 8: 19–21.

499. 'I am meek and lowly in heart' (Mt. 11 : 29). It is one of the matchless beauties of the Holy Qur'ān that in a few, select words, it demolishes an entire edifice of falsehoods and untruths. By use of the two words *Jabbār* and *Shaqī* it denies exactly the two charges of sedition and blasphemy brought against Jesus by the Jews. 'The charges were two in number, one sedition, the other blasphemy' (Rosadi, *Trial of Jesus*, p. 178).

39. And warn you them of the Day of Sighing when the affair shall have been decreed while yet they are heedless and are not believing.

وَأَنذِرْهُمْ يَوْمَ ٱلْحَسْرَةِ إِذْ قُضِىَ ٱلْأَمْرُ وَهُمْ فِى غَفْلَةٍ وَهُمْ لَا يُؤْمِنُونَ ۝

40. Verily We! We shall inherit the earth and whatever is thereon; and unto Us they shall be returned.

إِنَّا نَحْنُ نَرِثُ ٱلْأَرْضَ وَمَنْ عَلَيْهَا وَإِلَيْنَا يُرْجَعُونَ ۝

Section 3

41. And mention you in the Book of Abraham. He was a man of truth, a Prophet.

وَٱذْكُرْ فِى ٱلْكِتَٰبِ إِبْرَٰهِيمَ إِنَّهُۥ كَانَ صِدِّيقًا نَّبِيًّا ۝

42. Recall when he said to his father: 'Father! Why do you worship that which neither sees nor hears, nor yet avails you at all?

إِذْ قَالَ لِأَبِيهِ يَٰٓأَبَتِ لِمَ تَعْبُدُ مَا لَا يَسْمَعُ وَلَا يُبْصِرُ وَلَا يُغْنِى عَنكَ شَيْـًٔا ۝

43. Father! Verily there has come to me of knowledge what has not come to you. So follow me and I shall guide you to an even path.

يَٰٓأَبَتِ إِنِّى قَدْ جَآءَنِى مِنَ ٱلْعِلْمِ مَا لَمْ يَأْتِكَ فَٱتَّبِعْنِىٓ أَهْدِكَ صِرَٰطًا سَوِيًّا ۝

44. Father! Serve not Satan; surely Satan has been a rebel against the Compassionate.

يَٰٓأَبَتِ لَا تَعْبُدِ ٱلشَّيْطَٰنَ إِنَّ ٱلشَّيْطَٰنَ كَانَ لِلرَّحْمَٰنِ عَصِيًّا ۝

45. Father! Verily I fear there may touch you a torment from the Compassionate, as that you become a companion to Satan.'

يَٰٓأَبَتِ إِنِّىٓ أَخَافُ أَن يَمَسَّكَ عَذَابٌ مِّنَ ٱلرَّحْمَٰنِ فَتَكُونَ لِلشَّيْطَٰنِ وَلِيًّا ۝

46. He said: 'Abraham! Are you averse to my gods? If you desist not, surely I will stone you, and depart you from me for ever so long.'

قَالَ أَرَاغِبٌ أَنتَ عَنْ ءَالِهَتِى يَٰٓإِبْرَٰهِيمُ لَئِن لَّمْ تَنتَهِ لَأَرْجُمَنَّكَ وَٱهْجُرْنِى مَلِيًّا ۝

47. Abraham said: 'Peace be on you, presently I shall ask forgiveness for you from my Lord; verily He is unto me ever solicitous;

قَالَ سَلَـٰمٌ عَلَيْكَ سَأَسْتَغْفِرُ لَكَ رَبِّيٓ إِنَّهُۥ كَانَ بِي حَفِيًّا ۝

48. And I renounce you and all that you serve besides Allah, and I shall call unto my Lord, and I hope in calling unto my Lord I shall not be unblessed.'

وَأَعْتَزِلُكُمْ وَمَا تَدْعُونَ مِن دُونِ ٱللَّهِ وَأَدْعُوٓا۟ رَبِّي عَسَىٰٓ أَلَّآ أَكُونَ بِدُعَآءِ رَبِّي شَقِيًّا ۝

49. Then when he had renounced them and all that they served besides Allah, We bestowed on him Isaac and Jacob and each one We made a Prophet.

فَلَمَّا ٱعْتَزَلَهُمْ وَمَا يَعْبُدُونَ مِن دُونِ ٱللَّهِ وَهَبْنَا لَهُۥٓ إِسْحَـٰقَ وَيَعْقُوبَ وَكُلًّا جَعَلْنَا نَبِيًّا ۝

50. And We bestowed on them of Our mercy, and We made for them a lofty renown.

وَوَهَبْنَا لَهُم مِّن رَّحْمَتِنَا وَجَعَلْنَا لَهُمْ لِسَانَ صِدْقٍ عَلِيًّا ۝

Section 4

51. And mention you in the Book Moses; he was single-hearted, and was a Messenger, Prophet.[500]

وَٱذْكُرْ فِى ٱلْكِتَـٰبِ مُوسَىٰٓ إِنَّهُۥ كَانَ مُخْلَصًا وَكَانَ رَسُولًا نَّبِيًّا ۝

52. And We cried unto him from the right side of the Mount, and We drew him nigh for whispering.

وَنَـٰدَيْنَـٰهُ مِن جَانِبِ ٱلطُّورِ ٱلْأَيْمَنِ وَقَرَّبْنَـٰهُ نَجِيًّا ۝

53. We bestowed on him, out of Our mercy, his brother Aaron, a Prophet.

وَوَهَبْنَا لَهُۥ مِن رَّحْمَتِنَآ أَخَاهُ هَـٰرُونَ نَبِيًّا ۝

---

500. A Prophet in Islam is not a mere 'foreteller'; he is a direct recipient of the Revelation of God and is charged with the duty of acquainting others with things respecting God and things Beyond. A Messenger is one who has a Message; an envoy. Angels also are Messengers in this sense.

54. And mention you in the Book Ishmael; he was true in promise, and was a Messenger, a Prophet.

وَاذْكُرْ فِى ٱلْكِتَٰبِ إِسْمَٰعِيلَ إِنَّهُ كَانَ صَادِقَ ٱلْوَعْدِ وَكَانَ رَسُولًا نَّبِيًّا ۝

55. And he was wont to bid his household to prayer and purity and he was with his Lord an approved one.

وَكَانَ يَأْمُرُ أَهْلَهُ بِٱلصَّلَوٰةِ وَٱلزَّكَوٰةِ وَكَانَ عِندَ رَبِّهِۦ مَرْضِيًّا ۝

56. And mention you in the Book Enoch. He was a man of truth, a Prophet.

وَاذْكُرْ فِى ٱلْكِتَٰبِ إِدْرِيسَ إِنَّهُۥ كَانَ صِدِّيقًا نَّبِيًّا ۝

57. And We exalted him to a lofty position.

وَرَفَعْنَٰهُ مَكَانًا عَلِيًّا ۝

58. These are they whom Allah has favoured from among the Prophets, of the progeny of Adam and of them whom We bore with Noah, and of the progeny of Abraham and Israel, and of them whom We have guided and chosen. Whenever the revelations of the Compassionate were rehearsed to them, they fell down prostrating themselves and weeping.

أُو۟لَٰٓئِكَ ٱلَّذِينَ أَنْعَمَ ٱللَّهُ عَلَيْهِم مِّنَ ٱلنَّبِيِّـۧنَ مِن ذُرِّيَّةِ ءَادَمَ وَمِمَّنْ حَمَلْنَا مَعَ نُوحٍ وَمِن ذُرِّيَّةِ إِبْرَٰهِيمَ وَإِسْرَٰٓءِيلَ وَمِمَّنْ هَدَيْنَا وَٱجْتَبَيْنَآ إِذَا تُتْلَىٰ عَلَيْهِمْ ءَايَٰتُ ٱلرَّحْمَٰنِ خَرُّوا۟ سُجَّدًا وَبُكِيًّا ۩ ۝

59. Then there succeeded them a posterity who neglected prayers and followed lusts; so they shall meet presently with the perdition,

فَخَلَفَ مِنۢ بَعْدِهِمْ خَلْفٌ أَضَاعُوا۟ ٱلصَّلَوٰةَ وَٱتَّبَعُوا۟ ٱلشَّهَوَٰتِ فَسَوْفَ يَلْقَوْنَ غَيًّا ۝

60. Excepting those who may repent and believe and work righteously. These shall enter the Garden and shall not be wronged at all.

إِلَّا مَن تَابَ وَءَامَنَ وَعَمِلَ صَٰلِحًا فَأُو۟لَٰٓئِكَ يَدْخُلُونَ ٱلْجَنَّةَ وَلَا يُظْلَمُونَ شَيْـًٔا ۝

61. Gardens everlasting which the Compassionate has promised to His bondsmen, though yet unseen; verily, His promise is ever to be fulfilled.

جَنّٰتِ عَدْنِ ِالَّتِيْ وَعَدَ الرَّحْمٰنُ عِبَادَهُ بِالْغَيْبِ ۚ اِنَّهُ كَانَ وَعْدُهُ مَأْتِيًّا ۝

62. They shall not hear therein any vain word, but they shall hear only peace; and they shall have therein their provision morning and evening.

لَا يَسْمَعُوْنَ فِيْهَا لَغْوًا اِلَّا سَلٰمًا ۚ وَلَهُمْ رِزْقُهُمْ فِيْهَا بُكْرَةً وَّعَشِيًّا ۝

63. Such is the Garden which We shall cause Our bondsmen to inherit who have been God-fearing.

تِلْكَ الْجَنَّةُ الَّتِيْ نُوْرِثُ مِنْ عِبَادِنَا مَنْ كَانَ تَقِيًّا ۝

64. And we, the angels, do not descend, except by the command of your Lord. His is whatsoever is behind us and whatsoever is in-between; and the Lord is never forgetful.

وَمَا نَتَنَزَّلُ اِلَّا بِاَمْرِ رَبِّكَ ۚ لَهُ مَا بَيْنَ اَيْدِيْنَا وَمَا خَلْفَنَا وَمَا بَيْنَ ذٰلِكَ ۚ وَمَا كَانَ رَبُّكَ نَسِيًّا ۝

65. Lord of the heavens and the earth and what is in-between; so worship Him, and endure patiently in His worship; do you know anyone as His compeer?

رَبُّ السَّمٰوٰتِ وَالْاَرْضِ وَمَا بَيْنَهُمَا فَاعْبُدْهُ وَاصْطَبِرْ لِعِبَادَتِهِ ۚ هَلْ تَعْلَمُ لَهُ سَمِيًّا ۝

Section 5

66. And man says: 'When I am dead, shall I be raised alive?'

وَيَقُوْلُ الْاِنْسَانُ ءَاِذَا مَا مِتُّ لَسَوْفَ اُخْرَجُ حَيًّا ۝

67. Does not man remember that We created him before he was anything?

اَوَلَا يَذْكُرُ الْاِنْسَانُ اَنَّا خَلَقْنٰهُ مِنْ قَبْلُ وَلَمْ يَكُ شَيْئًا ۝

68. By your Lord, then, We will surely gather them and the devils; thereafter We will surely bring them around Hell, kneeling.

فَوَرَبِّكَ لَنَحْشُرَنَّهُمْ وَالشَّيَاطِينَ ثُمَّ لَنُحْضِرَنَّهُمْ حَوْلَ جَهَنَّمَ جِثِيًّا ۝

69. Then, We will surely draw aside from each sect those who were most rebellious against the Compassionate.

ثُمَّ لَنَنزِعَنَّ مِن كُلِّ شِيعَةٍ أَيُّهُمْ أَشَدُّ عَلَى الرَّحْمَٰنِ عِتِيًّا ۝

70. Then surely it is We Who knows best as to which of them were the worthiest of being roasted therein.

ثُمَّ لَنَحْنُ أَعْلَمُ بِالَّذِينَ هُمْ أَوْلَىٰ بِهَا صِلِيًّا ۝

71. And there is not one of you but shall pass over it – an ordinance decreed by your Lord.

وَإِن مِّنكُمْ إِلَّا وَارِدُهَا كَانَ عَلَىٰ رَبِّكَ حَتْمًا مَّقْضِيًّا ۝

72. Then We will deliver them who have feared God and will leave the wrong-doers kneeling therein.

ثُمَّ نُنَجِّي الَّذِينَ اتَّقَوا وَّنَذَرُ الظَّالِمِينَ فِيهَا جِثِيًّا ۝

73. And when Our clear revelations are rehearsed to them, the infidels say to the faithful: 'Which of the two portions is better in station and goodlier in company?'

وَإِذَا تُتْلَىٰ عَلَيْهِمْ ءَايَٰتُنَا بَيِّنَٰتٍ قَالَ الَّذِينَ كَفَرُوا لِلَّذِينَ ءَامَنُوا أَيُّ الْفَرِيقَيْنِ خَيْرٌ مَّقَامًا وَأَحْسَنُ نَدِيًّا ۝

74. And how many a generation We have destroyed before them, who were goodlier in goods and outward appearance?

وَكَمْ أَهْلَكْنَا قَبْلَهُم مِّن قَرْنٍ هُمْ أَحْسَنُ أَثَٰثًا وَرِءْيًا ۝

75. Say: 'Whosoever is in error — surely unto him the Compassionate lengthens a length, until when they behold that with which they were threatened, either the torment or the Hour: then they shall have to know whosoever is worse in position and weaker in hosts.

قُلْ مَن كَانَ فِي الضَّلَٰلَةِ فَلْيَمْدُدْ لَهُ الرَّحْمَٰنُ مَدًّا حَتَّىٰ إِذَا رَأَوْا مَا يُوعَدُونَ إِمَّا الْعَذَابَ وَإِمَّا السَّاعَةَ فَسَيَعْلَمُونَ مَنْ هُوَ شَرٌّ مَّكَانًا وَأَضْعَفُ جُندًا ۝

76. Allah increases in guidance those who let themselves be guided; and with your Lord the righteous works that last are excellent in respect of reward and in respect of return.

وَيَزِيدُ اللَّهُ الَّذِينَ اهْتَدَوْا هُدًى وَالْبَاقِيَاتُ الصَّالِحَاتُ خَيْرٌ عِندَ رَبِّكَ ثَوَابًا وَخَيْرٌ مَّرَدًّا ﴿٧٦﴾

77. Have you observed him who disbelieves in Our signs and says: 'Surely I will be given riches and children?'

أَفَرَءَيْتَ الَّذِي كَفَرَ بِآيَاتِنَا وَقَالَ لَأُوتَيَنَّ مَالًا وَوَلَدًا ﴿٧٧﴾

78. Has he looked unto the Unseen, or has he taken a covenant with the Compassionate?

أَطَّلَعَ الْغَيْبَ أَمِ اتَّخَذَ عِندَ الرَّحْمَٰنِ عَهْدًا ﴿٧٨﴾

79. By no means! We will write down what he says; and We will prolong for him the torment a length.

كَلَّا سَنَكْتُبُ مَا يَقُولُ وَنَمُدُّ لَهُ مِنَ الْعَذَابِ مَدًّا ﴿٧٩﴾

80. And We will inherit from him that of which he spoke and he shall come to Us alone.

وَنَرِثُهُ مَا يَقُولُ وَيَأْتِينَا فَرْدًا ﴿٨٠﴾

81. And they have taken gods besides Allah that they might be a glory for them.

وَاتَّخَذُوا مِن دُونِ اللَّهِ آلِهَةً لِّيَكُونُوا لَهُمْ عِزًّا ﴿٨١﴾

82. By no means! Presently they will deny their worship, and become an adversary unto them.

كَلَّا سَيَكْفُرُونَ بِعِبَادَتِهِمْ وَيَكُونُونَ عَلَيْهِمْ ضِدًّا ﴿٨٢﴾

Section 6

83. Do you not see that We have set the devils upon infidels inciting them by an incitement?

أَلَمْ تَرَ أَنَّا أَرْسَلْنَا الشَّيَاطِينَ عَلَى الْكَافِرِينَ تَؤُزُّهُمْ أَزًّا ﴿٨٣﴾

84. So hasten you not against them; We are only counting against them a counting.

فَلَا تَعْجَلْ عَلَيْهِمْ إِنَّمَا نَعُدُّ لَهُمْ عَدًّا ﴿٨٤﴾

85. On the day whereon We shall gather the pious unto the Compassionate as an embassy;

يَوْمَ نَحْشُرُ الْمُتَّقِينَ إِلَى الرَّحْمَنِ وَفْدًا ﴿٨٥﴾

86. And shall drive the culprits to Hell as a herd;

وَنَسُوقُ الْمُجْرِمِينَ إِلَى جَهَنَّمَ وِرْدًا ﴿٨٦﴾

87. They shall not own intercession, excepting those who have taken with the Compassionate a covenant.[501]

لَا يَمْلِكُونَ الشَّفَاعَةَ إِلَّا مَنِ اتَّخَذَ عِندَ الرَّحْمَنِ عَهْدًا ﴿٨٧﴾

88. And they say: 'The Compassionate has taken a son.'[502]

وَقَالُوا اتَّخَذَ الرَّحْمَنُ وَلَدًا ﴿٨٨﴾

89. Assuredly you have brought a thing monstrous.

لَقَدْ جِئْتُمْ شَيْئًا إِدًّا ﴿٨٩﴾

90. The heavens are well-nigh rent thereat and the earth cleft and the mountains well-nigh fell down;[503]

تَكَادُ السَّمَوَاتُ يَتَفَطَّرْنَ مِنْهُ وَتَنشَقُّ الْأَرْضُ وَتَخِرُّ الْجِبَالُ هَدًّا ﴿٩٠﴾

---

501. Or 'permission'. There is no special mediator in Islam. The God of Islam has not been estranged from mankind, and no special mediator is needed to effect reconciliation.

502. 'God the Son is the Second Person of the Blessed Trinity. He is the only begotten and eternal Son of the Father. He is consubstantial with the Father' (*CD*. p. 912).

503. So staggering is the blasphemy you utter! Compare a saying of Jesus (peace and blessings be upon him) himself, one left unrecorded in the canonical Gospels. 'The crowd drew nigh, and when they knew him, they began to cry out; Welcome to thee, O our God! and they began to do him reverence, as unto God. Whereupon Jesus gave a great groan, and said: Get ye from before me, O mad men, for I fear lest the earth should open and devour me with you for abominable words' (*GB*. p. 213).

91. That they should ascribe to the Compassionate a son.[504]

أَن دَعَوْا لِلرَّحْمَٰنِ وَلَدًا ۝

92. It behoves not the Compassionate that He should take a son.

وَمَا يَنۢبَغِى لِلرَّحْمَٰنِ أَن يَتَّخِذَ وَلَدًا ۝

93. None there is in the heavens and the earth but must come to the Compassionate as a bondsman.

إِن كُلُّ مَن فِى السَّمَٰوَٰتِ وَالْأَرْضِ إِلَّآ ءَاتِى الرَّحْمَٰنِ عَبْدًا ۝

94. Assuredly He has comprehended them and counted them a full counting.[505]

لَّقَدْ أَحْصَىٰهُمْ وَعَدَّهُمْ عَدًّا ۝

95. And every one of them is to come to Him on the Day of Judgement alone.

وَكُلُّهُمْ ءَاتِيهِ يَوْمَ الْقِيَٰمَةِ فَرْدًا ۝

96. Verily those who believe and do righteous works, the Compassionate will assign for them affection.

إِنَّ الَّذِينَ ءَامَنُوا وَعَمِلُوا الصَّٰلِحَٰتِ سَيَجْعَلُ لَهُمُ الرَّحْمَٰنُ وُدًّا ۝

97. So We have made it easy in your tongue in order that you may thereby give glad tidings to the pious and warn thereby a people contentious.

فَإِنَّمَا يَسَّرْنَٰهُ بِلِسَانِكَ لِتُبَشِّرَ بِهِ الْمُتَّقِينَ وَتُنذِرَ بِهِ قَوْمًا لُّدًّا ۝

98. And how many a generation We destroyed before them. But can you perceive anyone of them or hear of them even a whisper?

وَكَمْ أَهْلَكْنَا قَبْلَهُم مِّن قَرْنٍ هَلْ تُحِسُّ مِنْهُم مِّنْ أَحَدٍ أَوْ تَسْمَعُ لَهُمْ رِكْزًا ۝

---

504. Even to the early Christians 'the doctrine of the Trinity appeared inconsistent with the unity of God which is emphasized in the Scriptures. They therefore denied it, and accepted Jesus Christ, not as incarnate God, but as God's highest creature by whom all else was created, or as the perfect man who taught the true doctrine of God' (*EBr.* V. p. 634).

505. He has full and complete knowledge of all of them and of every little detail concerning them.

Sūrah 20

Ṭā Hā

(Makkan, 8 Sections and 135 Verses)

*In the name of Allah, the
Compassionate, the Merciful.*

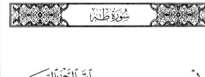

Section 1

1. *Ṭā. Hā.*

2. We have not sent down the
Qur'an on you that you should be
distressed,

3. But only as an admonition to
him who fears God,

4. A Revelation—sent from Him
Who has created the earth and
high heavens,

5. The Compassionate Who is
established on the throne.

6. His is whatsoever is in the
heavens and whatsoever is on the
earth and whatsoever is in
between and whatsoever is
underneath the earth.

7. And if you speak the word
aloud, then He knows the secret
and the most hidden.

8. Allah! No god is there but He.
His are the excellent names.

9. Has there come to you the
story of Moses?

10. Recall when he saw a fire and said to his family: 'Stay, I have perceived a fire! Haply I may bring a brand from it for you, or I may find a guidance at the fire.'

إِذْ رَءَا نَارًا فَقَالَ لِأَهْلِهِ ٱمْكُثُوٓا۟ إِنِّىٓ ءَانَسْتُ نَارًا لَّعَلِّىٓ ءَاتِيكُم مِّنْهَا بِقَبَسٍ أَوْ أَجِدُ عَلَى ٱلنَّارِ هُدًى ﴿١٠﴾

11. Then when he was come thereto, he was cried unto: 'O Moses!

فَلَمَّآ أَتَىٰهَا نُودِىَ يَٰمُوسَىٰٓ ﴿١١﴾

12. Verily I! I am your Lord , so take off your shoes; you are in the Holy valley, Ṭuwā!

إِنِّىٓ أَنَا۠ رَبُّكَ فَٱخْلَعْ نَعْلَيْكَ إِنَّكَ بِٱلْوَادِ ٱلْمُقَدَّسِ طُوًى ﴿١٢﴾

13. And I! I have chosen you. So listen to what will be revealed.

وَأَنَا ٱخْتَرْتُكَ فَٱسْتَمِعْ لِمَا يُوحَىٰٓ ﴿١٣﴾

14. And I! I am Allah. No god is there but I, so worship Me and establish prayer for My remembrance.

إِنَّنِىٓ أَنَا ٱللَّهُ لَآ إِلَٰهَ إِلَّآ أَنَا۠ فَٱعْبُدْنِى وَأَقِمِ ٱلصَّلَوٰةَ لِذِكْرِىٓ ﴿١٤﴾

15. Verily the Hour is coming – I wish to conceal it – in order that everyone may be recompensed according to what he has endeavoured.

إِنَّ ٱلسَّاعَةَ ءَاتِيَةٌ أَكَادُ أُخْفِيهَا لِتُجْزَىٰ كُلُّ نَفْسٍ بِمَا تَسْعَىٰ ﴿١٥﴾

16. So let him not who disbelieves in it and follows his own desire keep you away from it lest you perish.

فَلَا يَصُدَّنَّكَ عَنْهَا مَن لَّا يُؤْمِنُ بِهَا وَٱتَّبَعَ هَوَىٰهُ فَتَرْدَىٰ ﴿١٦﴾

17. And what is in your right hand, O Moses?'

وَمَا تِلْكَ بِيَمِينِكَ يَٰمُوسَىٰ ﴿١٧﴾

18. He said: 'It is my staff. I lean on it, and with it I beat down fodder for my sheep and for me there are other purposes in it.'

قَالَ هِىَ عَصَاىَ أَتَوَكَّؤُا۟ عَلَيْهَا وَأَهُشُّ بِهَا عَلَىٰ غَنَمِى وَلِىَ فِيهَا مَـَٔارِبُ أُخْرَىٰ ﴿١٨﴾

19. Allah said: 'Cast it down, O Moses!'

قَالَ أَلْقِهَا يَمُوسَىٰ ۝

20. So he cast it down, and lo! It was a serpent running along.

فَأَلْقَىٰهَا فَإِذَا هِىَ حَيَّةٌ تَسْعَىٰ ۝

21. Allah said: 'Seize it and have no fear.[506] We shall restore it to its former state.

قَالَ خُذْهَا وَلَا تَخَفْ سَنُعِيدُهَا سِيرَتَهَا الْأُولَىٰ ۝

22. And press your hand to your side, it will come forth white, without hurt,[507] as another Sign;

وَاضْمُمْ يَدَكَ إِلَىٰ جَنَاحِكَ تَخْرُجْ بَيْضَآءَ مِنْ غَيْرِ سُوٓءٍ ءَايَةً أُخْرَىٰ ۝

23. That We may show you of our signs the greatest.

لِنُرِيَكَ مِنْ ءَايَٰتِنَا الْكُبْرَى ۝

24. Go you to Pharaoh, he has grown exorbitant.'

اذْهَبْ إِلَىٰ فِرْعَوْنَ إِنَّهُۥ طَغَىٰ ۝

Section 2

25. He said: 'Lord! Expand for me my breast;

قَالَ رَبِّ اشْرَحْ لِى صَدْرِى ۝

26. And ease for me my affair;

وَيَسِّرْ لِىٓ أَمْرِى ۝

27. And loosen a knot from my tongue;

وَاحْلُلْ عُقْدَةً مِّن لِّسَانِى ۝

---

506. Moses (peace and blessings be upon him) was subject to the primary human emotion of fear as much as any other mortal, and there is absolutely nothing derogatory as regards him that he became frightened at the wonderful 'freak of nature'. Cf. the OT: 'And the Lord said unto him, what is that in thine hand? And he said, a rod. And He said, cast it on the ground. And he cast it on the ground, and it became a serpent; and Moses fled from before it' (Ex. 4: 2–3).

507. In other words, not betokening any disease, but rather glorifying You. The import of the Qur'ānic phrase, 'without hurt', is to correct the derogatory mis-statement of the Bible that 'Moses's hand was leprous as snow' (Ex. 4: 6) and also a story quoted by Josephus, that 'Moses was a leper, and was expelled from Heliopolis on this account' (DB. III. p. 96).

28. That they may understand my speech;

يَفْقَهُوا قَوْلِي ۝

29. And appoint for me a minister from my household,

وَاجْعَل لِّي وَزِيرًا مِّنْ أَهْلِي ۝

30. Aaron, my brother.

هَٰرُونَ أَخِي ۝

31. Strengthen me through him;

اشْدُدْ بِهِ أَزْرِي ۝

32. And associate him in my affair;

وَأَشْرِكْهُ فِي أَمْرِي ۝

33. That we may hallow You oft,

كَيْ نُسَبِّحَكَ كَثِيرًا ۝

34. And may make mention of You oft.

وَنَذْكُرَكَ كَثِيرًا ۝

35. Verily You! You are of us ever a Beholder.'

إِنَّكَ كُنتَ بِنَا بَصِيرًا ۝

36. Allah said: 'Surely you are granted your petition, O Moses!'

قَالَ قَدْ أُوتِيتَ سُؤْلَكَ يَٰمُوسَىٰ ۝

37. And assuredly We conferred a benefit on you another time;

وَلَقَدْ مَنَنَّا عَلَيْكَ مَرَّةً أُخْرَىٰ ۝

38. When We inspired to your mother what We inspired;

إِذْ أَوْحَيْنَا إِلَىٰ أُمِّكَ مَا يُوحَىٰ ۝

39. Saying: 'Cast him in the ark, and cast him in the river, and the river will throw him on the bank, and then an enemy of Mine and an enemy of his will take him up.' And I cast on you love for Me, in order that you may be formed under My eye.

أَنِ اقْذِفِيهِ فِي التَّابُوتِ فَاقْذِفِيهِ فِي الْيَمِّ فَلْيُلْقِهِ الْيَمُّ بِالسَّاحِلِ يَأْخُذْهُ عَدُوٌّ لِّي وَعَدُوٌّ لَّهُۥ وَأَلْقَيْتُ عَلَيْكَ مَحَبَّةً مِّنِّي وَلِتُصْنَعَ عَلَىٰ عَيْنِي ۝

إِذْ تَمْشِىٓ أُخْتُكَ فَتَقُولُ هَلْ أَدُلُّكُمْ عَلَى مَن يَكْفُلُهُۥ ۖ فَرَجَعْنَٰكَ إِلَىٰٓ أُمِّكَ كَىْ تَقَرَّ عَيْنُهَا وَلَا تَحْزَنَ ۚ وَقَتَلْتَ نَفْسًا فَنَجَّيْنَٰكَ مِنَ ٱلْغَمِّ وَفَتَنَّٰكَ فُتُونًا ۚ فَلَبِثْتَ سِنِينَ فِىٓ أَهْلِ مَدْيَنَ ثُمَّ جِئْتَ عَلَىٰ قَدَرٍ يَٰمُوسَىٰ ﴿٤٠﴾

40. Recall your sister was walking along and saying: 'Shall I direct you to one who will take care of him?' Thus We returned you to your mother that she might cool her eyes and she might not grieve. And you slew a person, but We delivered you from sorrow, and We tried you with several trials. Then you tarried for years among the people of Madyan, then you came according to fate, O Moses!

وَٱصْطَنَعْتُكَ لِنَفْسِى ﴿٤١﴾

41. And! Formed you for Myself.

ٱذْهَبْ أَنتَ وَأَخُوكَ بِـَٔايَٰتِى وَلَا تَنِيَا فِى ذِكْرِى ﴿٤٢﴾

42. Go then and your brother with My signs and do not slacken in My remembrance.

ٱذْهَبَآ إِلَىٰ فِرْعَوْنَ إِنَّهُۥ طَغَىٰ ﴿٤٣﴾

43. Go you two to Pharaoh: verily he has waxed insolent.

فَقُولَا لَهُۥ قَوْلًا لَّيِّنًا لَّعَلَّهُۥ يَتَذَكَّرُ أَوْ يَخْشَىٰ ﴿٤٤﴾

44. Then say to him a gentle saying: 'Haply he may be admonished, or he may fear.'

قَالَا رَبَّنَآ إِنَّنَا نَخَافُ أَن يَفْرُطَ عَلَيْنَآ أَوْ أَن يَطْغَىٰ ﴿٤٥﴾

45. The two said: 'Lord! We fear that he may hasten against us, or may wax insolent.'

قَالَ لَا تَخَافَآ ۖ إِنَّنِى مَعَكُمَآ أَسْمَعُ وَأَرَىٰ ﴿٤٦﴾

46. Allah said: 'Fear not; verily I shall be with you both, hearing and seeing.'

فَأْتِيَاهُ فَقُولَآ إِنَّا رَسُولَا رَبِّكَ فَأَرْسِلْ مَعَنَا بَنِىٓ إِسْرَٰٓءِيلَ وَلَا تُعَذِّبْهُمْ ۖ قَدْ جِئْنَٰكَ بِـَٔايَةٍ مِّن رَّبِّكَ ۖ وَٱلسَّلَٰمُ عَلَىٰ مَنِ ٱتَّبَعَ ٱلْهُدَىٰٓ ﴿٤٧﴾

47. So go to him, and say: 'We are envoys of your Lord, so let the children of Israel go with us, and do not chastise them; surely we have come to you with a sign from your Lord; and peace be upon him who follows the guidance.'

48. Verily we! It has been revealed to us that the torment will be for him who denies and turns away.

اِنَّا قَدۡ اُوۡحِیَ اِلَیۡنَاۤ اَنَّ الۡعَذَابَ عَلٰی مَنۡ کَذَّبَ وَتَوَلّٰی ۝

49. Pharaoh said; 'Who is the Lord of you two, O Moses?'

قَالَ فَمَنۡ رَّبُّکُمَا یٰمُوۡسٰی ۝

50. Moses said: 'Our Lord is He Who gave everything its existence, then guided it.'

قَالَ رَبُّنَا الَّذِیۤ اَعۡطٰی کُلَّ شَیۡءٍ خَلۡقَهٗ ثُمَّ هَدٰی ۝

51. He said: 'Then what did happen to the former generations?'

قَالَ فَمَا بَالُ الۡقُرُوۡنِ الۡاُوۡلٰی ۝

52. Moses said: 'That knowledge is with my Lord in the Book; my Lord neither errs nor forgets —

قَالَ عِلۡمُهَا عِنۡدَ رَبِّیۡ فِیۡ کِتٰبٍ لَّا یَضِلُّ رَبِّیۡ وَلَا یَنۡسٰی ۝

53. Who has appointed for you the earth as a bed, and has opened for you the pathways in it, and has sent down from the sky water, and thereby We have brought forth all manner of plants.

اَلَّذِیۡ جَعَلَ لَکُمُ الۡاَرۡضَ مَهۡدًا وَّسَلَکَ لَکُمۡ فِیۡهَا سُبُلًا وَّاَنۡزَلَ مِنَ السَّمَآءِ مَآءً فَاَخۡرَجۡنَا بِهٖۤ اَزۡوَاجًا مِّنۡ نَّبَاتٍ شَتّٰی ۝

54. Eat and pasture your cattle; therein are signs for men of sagacity.

کُلُوۡا وَارۡعَوۡا اَنۡعَامَکُمۡ اِنَّ فِیۡ ذٰلِکَ لَاٰیٰتٍ لِّاُولِی النُّهٰی ۝

Section 3

55. Of it We created you and to it We return you and from it We bring you forth once again.[508]

مِنۡهَا خَلَقۡنٰکُمۡ وَفِیۡهَا نُعِیۡدُکُمۡ وَمِنۡهَا نُخۡرِجُکُمۡ تَارَةً اُخۡرٰی ۝

---

508. O mankind ! The law is universal and immutable. This life is only a prelude to eternity, where we are to face a new life and a new state of things. This verse is publicly recited as a Muslim is lowered into his grave. Note that the Biblical verse 'dust thou art and unto dust shall thou return' makes no mention of resurrection.

56. And assuredly We showed him Our signs, all of them, but he denied and rejected.

وَلَقَدْ أَرَيْنَهُ ءَايَتِنَا كُلَّهَا فَكَذَّبَ وَأَبَىٰ ۝

57. He said: 'Are you come to us that you may drive us out of our land by your magic, O Moses?

قَالَ أَجِئْتَنَا لِتُخْرِجَنَا مِنْ أَرْضِنَا بِسِحْرِكَ يَٰمُوسَىٰ ۝

58. So we shall confront you with a like magic; so make between us and you an appointment in an open space, which we shall not fail, neither you.'

فَلَنَأْتِيَنَّكَ بِسِحْرٍ مِّثْلِهِ فَاجْعَلْ بَيْنَنَا وَبَيْنَكَ مَوْعِدًا لَّا نُخْلِفُهُ نَحْنُ وَلَآ أَنتَ مَكَانًا سُوًى ۝

59. Moses said: 'Your appointment is the gala day, and that the people be gathered in the forenoon.'

قَالَ مَوْعِدُكُمْ يَوْمُ الزِّينَةِ وَأَن يُحْشَرَ النَّاسُ ضُحًى ۝

60. Then Pharaoh turned away, devised his stratagem and then he came.

فَتَوَلَّىٰ فِرْعَوْنُ فَجَمَعَ كَيْدَهُ ثُمَّ أَتَىٰ ۝

61. Moses said to them: 'Woe unto you! Fabricate not a lie against Allah, lest He extirpate you with a torment, and surely he who fabricates loses.'

قَالَ لَهُم مُّوسَىٰ وَيْلَكُمْ لَا تَفْتَرُواْ عَلَى اللَّهِ كَذِبًا فَيُسْحِتَكُم بِعَذَابٍ وَقَدْ خَابَ مَنِ افْتَرَىٰ ۝

62. Then they wrangled about their affair among themselves and kept secret their private counsel.

فَتَنَٰزَعُواْ أَمْرَهُم بَيْنَهُمْ وَأَسَرُّواْ النَّجْوَىٰ ۝

63. They said: 'Verily these two are magicians, intending to drive you forth from your land by their magic and to do away with your superior way.

قَالُواْ إِنْ هَٰذَٰنِ لَسَٰحِرَٰنِ يُرِيدَانِ أَن يُخْرِجَاكُم مِّنْ أَرْضِكُم بِسِحْرِهِمَا وَيَذْهَبَا بِطَرِيقَتِكُمُ الْمُثْلَىٰ ۝

64. 'So devise your stratagem and then come in a row. Fortunate today is he who overcomes.'

فَأَجْمِعُواْ كَيْدَكُمْ ثُمَّ ائْتُواْ صَفًّا وَقَدْ أَفْلَحَ الْيَوْمَ مَنِ اسْتَعْلَىٰ ۝

65. They said: 'Either you cast, or we shall be the first to cast.'

قَالُوا۟ يَٰمُوسَىٰٓ إِمَّآ أَن تُلْقِىَ وَإِمَّآ أَن نَّكُونَ أَوَّلَ مَنْ أَلْقَىٰ ﴿٦٥﴾

66. They said: 'Nay, cast you down.' And lo! Their ropes and their staves, by the magic, made to appear to him as though they were running.

قَالَ بَلْ أَلْقُوا۟ فَإِذَا حِبَالُهُمْ وَعِصِيُّهُمْ يُخَيَّلُ إِلَيْهِ مِن سِحْرِهِمْ أَنَّهَا تَسْعَىٰ ﴿٦٦﴾

67. Then Moses felt a sort of fear in his mind.

فَأَوْجَسَ فِى نَفْسِهِۦ خِيفَةً مُّوسَىٰ ﴿٦٧﴾

68. We said: 'Have no fear; verily you, you shall be superior,

قُلْنَا لَا تَخَفْ إِنَّكَ أَنتَ الْأَعْلَىٰ ﴿٦٨﴾

69. And cast you down what is in your right hand; it shall swallow up what they have wrought. They have only wrought a magician's stratagem, and a magician does not prosper wherever he comes.'

وَأَلْقِ مَا فِى يَمِينِكَ تَلْقَفْ مَا صَنَعُوٓا۟ إِنَّمَا صَنَعُوا۟ كَيْدُ سَٰحِرٍ وَلَا يُفْلِحُ السَّاحِرُ حَيْثُ أَتَىٰ ﴿٦٩﴾

70. Then the magicians were cast down prostrate. They said: 'Now we believe in the Lord of Moses and Aaron.'

فَأُلْقِىَ السَّحَرَةُ سُجَّدًا قَالُوٓا۟ ءَامَنَّا بِرَبِّ هَٰرُونَ وَمُوسَىٰ ﴿٧٠﴾

71. Pharaoh said: 'What! Did you believe in Him before I gave you leave? Surely he is your chief who taught you magic. So I will surely cut off your hands and feet on the opposite sides; and surely crucify you on the trunks of palm-trees; and you will surely know which of us is sterner in torment and more lasting.'

قَالَ ءَامَنتُمْ لَهُۥ قَبْلَ أَنْ ءَاذَنَ لَكُمْ إِنَّهُۥ لَكَبِيرُكُمُ الَّذِى عَلَّمَكُمُ السِّحْرَ فَلَأُقَطِّعَنَّ أَيْدِيَكُمْ وَأَرْجُلَكُم مِّنْ خِلَٰفٍ وَلَأُصَلِّبَنَّكُمْ فِى جُذُوعِ النَّخْلِ وَلَتَعْلَمُنَّ أَيُّنَآ أَشَدُّ عَذَابًا وَأَبْقَىٰ ﴿٧١﴾

72. They said: 'We shall by no means prefer you over what has come to us of the evidence, and over Him Who has created us. So do decree you whatever you shall decree; you can decree only in respect of the life of this world.[509]

قَالُوا لَن نُّؤْثِرَكَ عَلَىٰ مَا جَآءَنَا مِنَ ٱلْبَيِّنَٰتِ وَٱلَّذِى فَطَرَنَا فَٱقْضِ مَآ أَنتَ قَاضٍ إِنَّمَا تَقْضِى هَٰذِهِ ٱلْحَيَوٰةَ ٱلدُّنْيَآ ۝

73. 'Verily we! We have believed in our Lord, that He may forgive us our affairs, and also that to which you have constrained us in the way of magic. And Allah is the Best and Most Lasting.'

إِنَّآ ءَامَنَّا بِرَبِّنَا لِيَغْفِرَ لَنَا خَطَٰيَٰنَا وَمَآ أَكْرَهْتَنَا عَلَيْهِ مِنَ ٱلسِّحْرِ وَٱللَّهُ خَيْرٌ وَأَبْقَىٰ ۝

74. Verily he who comes to his Lord as a culprit, for him is Hell, in which he shall neither die nor live.

إِنَّهُۥ مَن يَأْتِ رَبَّهُۥ مُجْرِمًا فَإِنَّ لَهُۥ جَهَنَّمَ لَا يَمُوتُ فِيهَا وَلَا يَحْيَىٰ ۝

75. And he who comes to Him as a believer, and has done righteous deeds, then for them are high ranks,

وَمَن يَأْتِهِۦ مُؤْمِنًا قَدْ عَمِلَ ٱلصَّٰلِحَٰتِ فَأُوْلَٰٓئِكَ لَهُمُ ٱلدَّرَجَٰتُ ٱلْعُلَىٰ ۝

76. Gardens everlasting with running streams, abiding therein; that is the reward for him who has purified himself.

جَنَّٰتُ عَدْنٍ تَجْرِى مِن تَحْتِهَا ٱلْأَنْهَٰرُ خَٰلِدِينَ فِيهَا وَذَٰلِكَ جَزَآءُ مَن تَزَكَّىٰ ۝

---

509. Note the immediate moral change brought about in the magicians by their conversion to the True Faith. A firm hold upon religious reality has immediately transformed a wordly, materialistic self into a consciously right, superior and blissful self, utterly heedless of the consequences of imperial wrath.

Section 4

77. And assuredly We revealed to Moses saying: 'Depart with My bondsmen in the night, and strike for them in the sea a dry path; you shall fear neither overtaking nor shall you be afraid.'

وَلَقَدۡ أَوۡحَيۡنَآ إِلَىٰ مُوسَىٰٓ أَنۡ أَسۡرِ بِعِبَادِى فَاضۡرِبۡ لَهُمۡ طَرِيقًا فِى ٱلۡبَحۡرِ يَبَسًا لَّا تَخَٰفُ دَرَكًا وَلَا تَخۡشَىٰ ۝

78. Then Pharaoh followed them with his hosts, and there came upon them of the sea what came upon them.

فَأَتۡبَعَهُمۡ فِرۡعَوۡنُ بِجُنُودِهِۦ فَغَشِيَهُم مِّنَ ٱلۡيَمِّ مَا غَشِيَهُمۡ ۝

79. And Pharaoh led his nation astray, and guided them not .

وَأَضَلَّ فِرۡعَوۡنُ قَوۡمَهُۥ وَمَا هَدَىٰ ۝

80. O children of Israel! We delivered you from your enemy, and treated with you on the right side of the mount and sent down on you manna and quails,

يَٰبَنِىٓ إِسۡرَٰٓءِيلَ قَدۡ أَنجَيۡنَٰكُم مِّنۡ عَدُوِّكُمۡ وَوَٰعَدۡنَٰكُمۡ جَانِبَ ٱلطُّورِ ٱلۡأَيۡمَنَ وَنَزَّلۡنَا عَلَيۡكُمُ ٱلۡمَنَّ وَٱلسَّلۡوَىٰ ۝

81. Saying: 'Eat of the clean things with which We have provided you, and wax not insolent thereabout, lest My wrath may come down upon you; and upon whom My wrath comes down, he surely perishes.

كُلُوا۟ مِن طَيِّبَٰتِ مَا رَزَقۡنَٰكُمۡ وَلَا تَطۡغَوۡا۟ فِيهِ فَيَحِلَّ عَلَيۡكُمۡ غَضَبِى وَمَن يَحۡلِلۡ عَلَيۡهِ غَضَبِى فَقَدۡ هَوَىٰ ۝

82. And verily I am the Most Forgiving to him who repents and believes and works righteously and lets himself remain guided.

وَإِنِّى لَغَفَّارٌ لِّمَن تَابَ وَءَامَنَ وَعَمِلَ صَٰلِحًا ثُمَّ ٱهۡتَدَىٰ ۝

83. And what has made you hasten from your people, O Moses?'

وَمَآ أَعۡجَلَكَ عَن قَوۡمِكَ يَٰمُوسَىٰ ۝

84. Moses said: 'Why, they are close on my footsteps, and I hasten to You, Lord! That You might be well-pleased.'

قَالَ هُمْ أُوْلَآءِ عَلَىٰٓ أَثَرِى وَعَجِلْتُ إِلَيْكَ رَبِّ لِتَرْضَىٰ ۞

85. Allah said: 'Verily We have tempted your people after you, and the Sāmirī has led them astray.'⁵¹⁰

قَالَ فَإِنَّا قَدْ فَتَنَّا قَوْمَكَ مِنۢ بَعْدِكَ وَأَضَلَّهُمُ ٱلسَّامِرِيُّ ۞

86. Therefore Moses returned to his people, indignant and sorrowful. He said: 'O my people! Did not my Lord make to you an excellent promise? Did then the promise seem to you too long in coming? Or did you desire that the wrath of your Lord should come upon you, so that you failed to keep my appointment?'

فَرَجَعَ مُوسَىٰٓ إِلَىٰ قَوْمِهِۦ غَضْبَٰنَ أَسِفًا قَالَ يَٰقَوْمِ أَلَمْ يَعِدْكُمْ رَبُّكُمْ وَعْدًا حَسَنًا أَفَطَالَ عَلَيْكُمُ ٱلْعَهْدُ أَمْ أَرَدتُّمْ أَن يَحِلَّ عَلَيْكُمْ غَضَبٌ مِّن رَّبِّكُمْ فَأَخْلَفْتُم مَّوْعِدِى ۞

87. They said: 'We did not fail to keep your appointment of our own will, but we were laden with the load of the people's trinket, so we threw them, as did the Sāmirī into the fire.'

قَالُوا۟ مَآ أَخْلَفْنَا مَوْعِدَكَ بِمَلْكِنَا وَلَٰكِنَّا حُمِّلْنَآ أَوْزَارًا مِّن زِينَةِ ٱلْقَوْمِ فَقَذَفْنَٰهَا فَكَذَٰلِكَ أَلْقَى ٱلسَّامِرِيُّ ۞

88. And he produced for them a calf, a body with a low. Then they said: 'This is your god and the god of Moses, and him he has forgotten.'

فَأَخْرَجَ لَهُمْ عِجْلًا جَسَدًا لَّهُۥ خُوَارٌ فَقَالُوا۟ هَٰذَآ إِلَٰهُكُمْ وَإِلَٰهُ مُوسَىٰ فَنَسِىَ ۞

---

510. By making for them a golden calf for worship. Note once again that it is not the Prophet Aaron (peace and blessings be upon him) but someone else, whom the Qur'ān makes responsible for the abomination, but which is so openly ascribed to him in the Bible.

89. Did they not see that it did not return a word to them, and owned for them neither hurt nor profit?

أَفَلَا يَرَوْنَ أَلَّا يَرْجِعُ إِلَيْهِمْ قَوْلًا وَلَا يَمْلِكُ لَهُمْ ضَرًّا وَلَا نَفْعًا ۟۝

Section 5

90. And assuredly Aaron had said to them afore: 'O my people! You are only being tempted with it, and verily your Lord is the Compassionate, so follow me and obey my command.'⁵¹¹

وَلَقَدْ قَالَ لَهُمْ هَرُونُ مِن قَبْلُ يَقَوْمِ إِنَّمَا فُتِنتُم بِهِ ۖ وَإِنَّ رَبَّكُمُ الرَّحْمَنُ فَاتَّبِعُونِي وَأَطِيعُوٓا أَمْرِى ۝

91. They said: 'We shall by no means cease to be assiduous to it until Moses comes back to us.'

قَالُوا لَن نَّبْرَحَ عَلَيْهِ عَكِفِينَ حَتَّى يَرْجِعَ إِلَيْنَا مُوسَى ۝

92. Moses said: 'O Aaron! What prevented you when you saw them going astray;

قَالَ يَهَرُونُ مَا مَنَعَكَ إِذْ رَأَيْتَهُمْ ضَلُّوٓا ۝

93. That you followed me not? Have you disobeyed my command?'

أَلَّا تَتَّبِعَنِ ۖ أَفَعَصَيْتَ أَمْرِى ۝

94. Aaron said: 'My own brother! Hold me not by my beard nor by my head; really I feared that you would say you caused a division among the children of Israel and had not kept my word.'

قَالَ يَبْنَؤُمَّ لَا تَأْخُذْ بِلِحْيَتِى وَلَا بِرَأْسِىٓ إِنِّى خَشِيتُ أَن تَقُولَ فَرَّقْتَ بَيْنَ بَنِى إِسْرَٰٓءِيلَ وَلَمْ تَرْقُبْ قَوْلِى ۝

95. Moses said: 'What was your object, O Sāmirī?'

قَالَ فَمَا خَطْبُكَ يَسَمِرِىُّ ۝

---

511. This more than vindicates Aaron's unflinching monotheism against the aspersions of the Bible.

96. He said: 'I saw what the people did not see. So I seized a handful of dust from the footstep of the angel, and then I cast it into the fire; thus my mind embellished the affair to me.'

قَالَ بَصُرْتُ بِمَا لَمْ يَبْصُرُوْا بِهٖ فَقَبَضْتُ قَبْضَةً مِّنْ أَثَرِ الرَّسُوْلِ فَنَبَذْتُهَا وَكَذٰلِكَ سَوَّلَتْ لِيْ نَفْسِيْ ۝

97. Moses said: 'Begone you! Verily it shall be for you in life to say, "no contact", and verily yours is a tryst which you shall not fail. And look you at your god to which you have been devoted; we shall surely burn it, and scatter it in the sea in your presence.'

قَالَ فَاذْهَبْ فَإِنَّ لَكَ فِي الْحَيٰوةِ أَنْ تَقُوْلَ لَا مِسَاسَ ۖ وَإِنَّ لَكَ مَوْعِدًا لَّنْ تُخْلَفَهٗ ۖ وَانْظُرْ إِلٰى إِلٰهِكَ الَّذِيْ ظَلْتَ عَلَيْهِ عَاكِفًا ۖ لَّنُحَرِّقَنَّهٗ ثُمَّ لَنَنْسِفَنَّهٗ فِي الْيَمِّ نَسْفًا ۝

98. Your God is only Allah, the One; other than Him there is no god. He comprehends everything in knowledge.

إِنَّمَا إِلٰهُكُمُ اللهُ الَّذِيْ لَا إِلٰهَ إِلَّا هُوَ ۚ وَسِعَ كُلَّ شَيْءٍ عِلْمًا ۝

99. Thus We recount to you some tidings of what has preceded; and surely We have given to you an admonition from before Us.[512]

كَذٰلِكَ نَقُصُّ عَلَيْكَ مِنْ أَنْبَاءِ مَا قَدْ سَبَقَ ۚ وَقَدْ ءَاتَيْنٰكَ مِنْ لَّدُنَّا ذِكْرًا ۝

100. Whosoever turns away from it – verily they shall bear a burden on the Day of Judgement;

مَنْ أَعْرَضَ عَنْهُ فَإِنَّهٗ يَحْمِلُ يَوْمَ الْقِيٰمَةِ وِزْرًا ۝

101. And they shall abide therein. Vile will it be for them on the Day of Judgement as a load,

خٰلِدِيْنَ فِيْهِ ۖ وَسَآءَ لَهُمْ يَوْمَ الْقِيٰمَةِ حِمْلًا ۝

---

512. In other words, the Qur'ān. A true and accurate presentation of ancient and, in many cases, little known facts of history by an unlettered Prophet is in itself strong evidence of his being aided and taught by the Omniscient.

102. The Day when the Trumpet will be blown into, and We shall, on that Day, gather the culprits blear-eyed;

يَوۡمَ يُنفَخُ فِى ٱلصُّورِ وَنَحۡشُرُ ٱلۡمُجۡرِمِينَ يَوۡمَئِذٍ زُرۡقًا ﴿١٠٢﴾

103. Muttering among themselves: you did not tarry save ten days.

يَتَخَٰفَتُونَ بَيۡنَهُمۡ إِن لَّبِثۡتُمۡ إِلَّا عَشۡرًا ﴿١٠٣﴾

104. We very well know what they will say when the best of them in judgement will say: 'You did not tarry save for a day.'

نَّحۡنُ أَعۡلَمُ بِمَا يَقُولُونَ إِذۡ يَقُولُ أَمۡثَلُهُمۡ طَرِيقَةً إِن لَّبِثۡتُمۡ إِلَّا يَوۡمًا ﴿١٠٤﴾

Section 6

105. And they question you regarding the mountains. Say: 'My Lord will scatter them with a total scattering.

وَيَسۡـَٔلُونَكَ عَنِ ٱلۡجِبَالِ فَقُلۡ يَنسِفُهَا رَبِّى نَسۡفًا ﴿١٠٥﴾

106. Then He shall leave it a level plain;

فَيَذَرُهَا قَاعًا صَفۡصَفًا ﴿١٠٦﴾

107. In which you shall not find any crookedness or ruggedness.'

لَّا تَرَىٰ فِيهَا عِوَجًا وَلَآ أَمۡتًا ﴿١٠٧﴾

108. That Day they shall follow the caller for whom there shall be no crookedness, and voices shall be humbled for the Compassionate; so that you shall hear but muttering.[513]

يَوۡمَئِذٍ يَتَّبِعُونَ ٱلدَّاعِىَ لَا عِوَجَ لَهُۥ وَخَشَعَتِ ٱلۡأَصۡوَاتُ لِلرَّحۡمَٰنِ فَلَا تَسۡمَعُ إِلَّا هَمۡسًا ﴿١٠٨﴾

---

513. This repudiates, root and branch, the Christian dogma of Saviourhood. There is no 'saviour' save God; while, according to the Christians, 'the central theme of the apostolic preaching is the proclamation of Jesus as Saviour Jesus is not only Saviour; He is the only Saviour' (DB. IV. p. 365).

109. That Day intercession will not avail except him for whom the Compassionate gives leave, and of whom He approves the Word.

يَوْمَئِذٍ لَّا تَنفَعُ ٱلشَّفَٰعَةُ إِلَّا مَنْ أَذِنَ لَهُ ٱلرَّحْمَٰنُ وَرَضِىَ لَهُۥ قَوْلًا ۝

110. He alone knows what is before them and what is behind them, and they cannot encompass it with their knowledge.

يَعْلَمُ مَا بَيْنَ أَيْدِيهِمْ وَمَا خَلْفَهُمْ وَلَا يُحِيطُونَ بِهِۦ عِلْمًا ۝

111. Downcast will be faces before the Living, the Self-Subsisting, and disappointed will be he who bears a wrong.

وَعَنَتِ ٱلْوُجُوهُ لِلْحَىِّ ٱلْقَيُّومِ وَقَدْ خَابَ مَنْ حَمَلَ ظُلْمًا ۝

112. Whosoever works of righteous deeds and is a believer — he will not fear wrong or begrudging.

وَمَن يَعْمَلْ مِنَ ٱلصَّٰلِحَٰتِ وَهُوَ مُؤْمِنٌ فَلَا يَخَافُ ظُلْمًا وَلَا هَضْمًا ۝

113. And thus We have sent it down, an Arabic recitation, and propounded variously therein of the threats, that haply they may fear God, or that it may generate in them some admonition.

وَكَذَٰلِكَ أَنزَلْنَٰهُ قُرْءَانًا عَرَبِيًّا وَصَرَّفْنَا فِيهِ مِنَ ٱلْوَعِيدِ لَعَلَّهُمْ يَتَّقُونَ أَوْ يُحْدِثُ لَهُمْ ذِكْرًا ۝

114. Exalted is Allah, the True King! Hasten you not with the Qur'an before its revelation to you is finished, and say: 'Lord, give me increase in knowledge.'

فَتَعَٰلَى ٱللَّهُ ٱلْمَلِكُ ٱلْحَقُّ وَلَا تَعْجَلْ بِٱلْقُرْءَانِ مِن قَبْلِ أَن يُقْضَىٰٓ إِلَيْكَ وَحْيُهُۥ وَقُل رَّبِّ زِدْنِى عِلْمًا ۝

115. And assuredly We covenanted with Adam before, then he forgot. Indeed We did not find steadiness in him.

وَلَقَدْ عَهِدْنَآ إِلَىٰٓ ءَادَمَ مِن قَبْلُ فَنَسِىَ وَلَمْ نَجِدْ لَهُۥ عَزْمًا ۝

Section 7

116. Recall when We said to the angels: 'Seek obeisance to Adam.' They sought obeisance, except Iblīs; he refused.

وَإِذْ قُلْنَا لِلْمَلَٰٓئِكَةِ ٱسْجُدُوا۟ لِءَادَمَ فَسَجَدُوٓا۟ إِلَّآ إِبْلِيسَ أَبَىٰ ﴿١١٦﴾

117. Then We said: 'O Adam! Verily he is an enemy to you and your spouse, so let him not expel you two from the Garden, lest you be distressed.

فَقُلْنَا يَٰٓـَٔادَمُ إِنَّ هَٰذَا عَدُوٌّ لَّكَ وَلِزَوْجِكَ فَلَا يُخْرِجَنَّكُمَا مِنَ ٱلْجَنَّةِ فَتَشْقَىٰٓ ﴿١١٧﴾

118. It is for you that you shall not hunger here nor go naked.

إِنَّ لَكَ أَلَّا تَجُوعَ فِيهَا وَلَا تَعْرَىٰ ﴿١١٨﴾

119. Nor that you shall thirst here nor shall you suffer from the sun.'

وَأَنَّكَ لَا تَظْمَؤُا۟ فِيهَا وَلَا تَضْحَىٰ ﴿١١٩﴾

120. Then did Satan whisper to him, saying: 'O Adam! Shall I direct you to a tree of eternity and a dominion that ages not?'

فَوَسْوَسَ إِلَيْهِ ٱلشَّيْطَٰنُ قَالَ يَٰٓـَٔادَمُ هَلْ أَدُلُّكَ عَلَىٰ شَجَرَةِ ٱلْخُلْدِ وَمُلْكٍ لَّا يَبْلَىٰ ﴿١٢٠﴾

121. Then the two ate of that tree, so they beheld their nakedness, and they took to stitching upon themselves with leaves of the Garden.[514] Thus did Adam disobey his Lord, and erred.

فَأَكَلَا مِنْهَا فَبَدَتْ لَهُمَا سَوْءَٰتُهُمَا وَطَفِقَا يَخْصِفَانِ عَلَيْهِمَا مِن وَرَقِ ٱلْجَنَّةِ وَعَصَىٰٓ ءَادَمُ رَبَّهُۥ فَغَوَىٰ ﴿١٢١﴾

122. Thereafter his Lord accepted him, and relented toward him and guided him.

ثُمَّ ٱجْتَبَٰهُ رَبُّهُۥ فَتَابَ عَلَيْهِ وَهَدَىٰ ﴿١٢٢﴾

---

514. So as to conceal their nakedness. This exalts the sense of modesty in human beings, and strikes at the root of phallicism which forms an integral part of pagan art and religion.

123. Allah said: 'Get down you two herefrom together. Some of you are an enemy to some others. Then if there comes to you guidance from Me, whoever follows My guidance, shall neither go astray nor he be distressed.

قَالَ اهْبِطَا مِنْهَا جَمِيعًا بَعْضُكُمْ لِبَعْضٍ عَدُوٌّ فَإِمَّا يَأْتِيَنَّكُم مِّنِّي هُدًى فَمَنِ اتَّبَعَ هُدَايَ فَلَا يَضِلُّ وَلَا يَشْقَى ۝

124. And whoever turns away from My guidance, verily for him will be shrunken livelihood, and We shall raise him up sightless on the Day of Judgement.'

وَمَنْ أَعْرَضَ عَن ذِكْرِي فَإِنَّ لَهُ مَعِيشَةً ضَنكًا وَنَحْشُرُهُ يَوْمَ الْقِيَامَةِ أَعْمَى ۝

125. And he will say: 'Lord! Why have You raised me sightless whereas I have been able to see.'

قَالَ رَبِّ لِمَ حَشَرْتَنِي أَعْمَى وَقَدْ كُنتُ بَصِيرًا ۝

126. Allah will say: 'In a like way did Our signs come to you, and you ignored them, so you too shall be ignored this day.'

قَالَ كَذَلِكَ أَتَتْكَ ءَايَاتُنَا فَنَسِيتَهَا وَكَذَلِكَ الْيَوْمَ تُنسَى ۝

127. We thus requite him who transgresses and does not believe in the signs of your Lord; and surely the torment of the Hereafter is most severe and most lasting.

وَكَذَلِكَ نَجْزِي مَنْ أَسْرَفَ وَلَمْ يُؤْمِن بِآيَاتِ رَبِّهِ وَلَعَذَابُ الْآخِرَةِ أَشَدُّ وَأَبْقَى ۝

128. Has it not served as a guidance to them how many a generation We have destroyed before them, in whose dwellings they walk. Verily therein are signs for men of reason.

أَفَلَمْ يَهْدِ لَهُمْ كَمْ أَهْلَكْنَا قَبْلَهُم مِّنَ الْقُرُونِ يَمْشُونَ فِي مَسَاكِنِهِمْ إِنَّ فِي ذَلِكَ لَآيَاتٍ لِّأُولِي النُّهَى ۝

Section 8

129. And had not a word gone forth from your Lord and a term determined, it must necessarily have come.

وَلَوْلَا كَلِمَةٌ سَبَقَتْ مِن رَّبِّكَ لَكَانَ لِزَامًا وَأَجَلٌ مُّسَمًّى ۝

130. So bear you patiently with what they say, and hallow the praise of your Lord before sunrise and before sunset; and hallow Him in parts of the night and the ends of the day, haply you will be pleased.

فَاصْبِرْ عَلَىٰ مَا يَقُولُونَ وَسَبِّحْ بِحَمْدِ رَبِّكَ قَبْلَ طُلُوعِ الشَّمْسِ وَقَبْلَ غُرُوبِهَا وَمِنْ ءَانَآءِ الَّيْلِ فَسَبِّحْ وَأَطْرَافَ النَّهَارِ لَعَلَّكَ تَرْضَىٰ ۝

131. And do not strain your eyes after what We have given pairs of them to enjoy: the splendour of the life of this world, that We might try them therein; and the provision of your Lord is the best and most lasting.

وَلَا تَمُدَّنَّ عَيْنَيْكَ إِلَىٰ مَا مَتَّعْنَا بِهِ أَزْوَاجًا مِّنْهُمْ زَهْرَةَ الْحَيَوٰةِ الدُّنْيَا لِنَفْتِنَهُمْ فِيهِ وَرِزْقُ رَبِّكَ خَيْرٌ وَأَبْقَىٰ ۝

132. And bid your household for prayer, and persevere you therein. We do not ask any provision of you: it is We Who provided you. The happy end is for piety.

وَأْمُرْ أَهْلَكَ بِالصَّلَوٰةِ وَاصْطَبِرْ عَلَيْهَا لَا نَسْـَٔلُكَ رِزْقًا نَّحْنُ نَرْزُقُكَ وَالْعَٰقِبَةُ لِلتَّقْوَىٰ ۝

133. And they say: 'Why does he not bring us a sign from his Lord? Has not there come to them the fulfilment of what is in the former Scriptures?'

وَقَالُوا لَوْلَا يَأْتِينَا بِـَٔايَةٍ مِّن رَّبِّهِ أَوَلَمْ تَأْتِهِم بَيِّنَةُ مَا فِي الصُّحُفِ الْأُولَىٰ ۝

134. And had We destroyed them with a torment before it, they would have said: 'O our Lord! Why did You not send us a Messenger that we might have followed Your signs before we were disgraced and humiliated.'

وَلَوْ أَنَّآ أَهْلَكْنَٰهُم بِعَذَابٍ مِّن قَبْلِهِۦ لَقَالُوا۟ رَبَّنَا لَوْلَآ أَرْسَلْتَ إِلَيْنَا رَسُولًا فَنَتَّبِعَ ءَايَٰتِكَ مِن قَبْلِ أَن نَّذِلَّ وَنَخْزَىٰ ۝

135. Say: 'Everyone is on the watch; so watch on, and soon you shall know who are the fellows of the even path and who has let himself be guided.'

قُلْ كُلٌّ مُّتَرَبِّصٌ فَتَرَبَّصُوا۟ فَسَتَعْلَمُونَ مَنْ أَصْحَٰبُ ٱلصِّرَٰطِ ٱلسَّوِيِّ وَمَنِ ٱهْتَدَىٰ ۝

Sūrah 21

al-Anbiyā'

(Makkan, 7 Sections, 112 Verses)

In the name of Allah, the Compassionate, the Merciful.

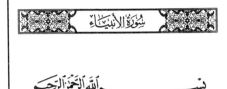

Section 1

1. Their reckoning has approached mankind, while they are turning away unheedingly.

2. No fresh admonition from their Lord comes to them but they listen to it while they are sporting,

3. Their hearts being in a light mood. The wrong-doers keep secret their whispers among themselves: 'This is but a mortal like yourselves; what! Will you be affected by magic while you know?'515

4. The Prophet said: 'My Lord knows the Word in the heavens and the earth; and He is the Hearer, the Knower.'

5. Aye! They say: 'A medley of dreams; aye! He has fabricated it, aye! He is a poet, so let him bring us a sign, as the ancients were sent with.'

---

515. That was the pagan view of the Qur'ān. Its effectiveness they found themselves unable to ignore and they could only explain it away by calling it an enchanted word.

6. Not a town which We destroyed before them came to believe: will these believe?

مَآءَامَنَتْ قَبْلَهُمْ مِّن قَرْيَةٍ أَهْلَكْنَهَا ۖ أَفَهُمْ يُؤْمِنُونَ ۝

7. And We sent not before you but human beings to whom We revealed; so ask the people of admonition, if you do not know.

وَمَآ أَرْسَلْنَا قَبْلَكَ إِلَّا رِجَالًا نُّوحِىٓ إِلَيْهِمْ ۖ فَسْـَٔلُوٓا۟ أَهْلَ الذِّكْرِ إِن كُنتُمْ لَا تَعْلَمُونَ ۝

8. And We made them not bodies requiring no food, nor were they immortals.

وَمَا جَعَلْنَهُمْ جَسَدًا لَّا يَأْكُلُونَ الطَّعَامَ وَمَا كَانُوا۟ خَلِدِينَ ۝

9. Then We fulfilled to them the promise, so We delivered them and those whom We willed, and destroyed the extravagant.

ثُمَّ صَدَقْنَهُمُ الْوَعْدَ فَأَنجَيْنَهُمْ وَمَن نَّشَآءُ وَأَهْلَكْنَا الْمُسْرِفِينَ ۝

10. And assuredly We have sent down to you a Book in which is admonition for you; will you then not reflect?

لَقَدْ أَنزَلْنَآ إِلَيْكُمْ كِتَبًا فِيهِ ذِكْرُكُمْ ۖ أَفَلَا تَعْقِلُونَ ۝

Section 2

11. How many a town did We overthrow which were doing wrong, and We caused to grow up thereafter another nation!

وَكَمْ قَصَمْنَا مِن قَرْيَةٍ كَانَتْ ظَالِمَةً وَأَنشَأْنَا بَعْدَهَا قَوْمًا ءَاخَرِينَ ۝

12. Then when they perceived Our revenge, lo! They were from it fleeing.

فَلَمَّآ أَحَسُّوا۟ بَأْسَنَآ إِذَا هُم مِّنْهَا يَرْكُضُونَ ۝

13. Flee not, and return to that wherein you luxuriated and your dwellings, haply you will be questioned.

لَا تَرْكُضُوا۟ وَارْجِعُوٓا۟ إِلَىٰ مَآ أُتْرِفْتُمْ فِيهِ وَمَسَكِنِكُمْ لَعَلَّكُمْ تُسْـَٔلُونَ ۝

14. They said: 'Woe be to us! Surely we have been wrong-doers.'

قَالُواْ يَٰوَيۡلَنَآ إِنَّا كُنَّا ظَٰلِمِينَ ﴿١٤﴾

15. And this ceased not to be their cry, until We made them a harvest reaped, extinguished.

فَمَا زَالَت تِّلۡكَ دَعۡوَىٰهُمۡ حَتَّىٰ جَعَلۡنَٰهُمۡ حَصِيدًا خَٰمِدِينَ ﴿١٥﴾

16. And We created not the heavens and the earth and what is in-between in play.

وَمَا خَلَقۡنَا ٱلسَّمَآءَ وَٱلۡأَرۡضَ وَمَا بَيۡنَهُمَا لَٰعِبِينَ ﴿١٦﴾

17. Had We intended that We should choose a sport, surely We would choose it from before Us – if We were going to do that.

لَوۡ أَرَدۡنَآ أَن نَّتَّخِذَ لَهۡوًا لَّٱتَّخَذۡنَٰهُ مِن لَّدُنَّآ إِن كُنَّا فَٰعِلِينَ ﴿١٧﴾

18. Aye! We hurl Truth against falsehood, so that it knocks out its brain, and lo! It vanishes, and woe to you for what you utter!

بَلۡ نَقۡذِفُ بِٱلۡحَقِّ عَلَى ٱلۡبَٰطِلِ فَيَدۡمَغُهُۥ فَإِذَا هُوَ زَاهِقٌۚ وَلَكُمُ ٱلۡوَيۡلُ مِمَّا تَصِفُونَ ﴿١٨﴾

19. His is whosoever is in the heavens and the earth and those near Him are not too proud to pay Him homage nor are they ever weary.

وَلَهُۥ مَن فِي ٱلسَّمَٰوَٰتِ وَٱلۡأَرۡضِۚ وَمَنۡ عِندَهُۥ لَا يَسۡتَكۡبِرُونَ عَنۡ عِبَادَتِهِۦ وَلَا يَسۡتَحۡسِرُونَ ﴿١٩﴾

20. And they hallow Him night and day, they do not flag.

يُسَبِّحُونَ ٱلَّيۡلَ وَٱلنَّهَارَ لَا يَفۡتُرُونَ ﴿٢٠﴾

21. Have they taken gods from the earth, who raise up the dead?

أَمِ ٱتَّخَذُوٓاْ ءَالِهَةً مِّنَ ٱلۡأَرۡضِ هُمۡ يُنشِرُونَ ﴿٢١﴾

22. Had there been gods, beside Allah, in between the two, surely the two would have gone to ruin. Hallowed be Allah, the Lord of the throne, from what they utter!

لَوۡ كَانَ فِيهِمَآ ءَالِهَةٌ إِلَّا ٱللَّهُ لَفَسَدَتَاۚ فَسُبۡحَٰنَ ٱللَّهِ رَبِّ ٱلۡعَرۡشِ عَمَّا يَصِفُونَ ﴿٢٢﴾

23. Questioned He shall be not as to what He does, while they shall be questioned.

لَا يُسْـَٔلُ عَمَّا يَفْعَلُ وَهُمْ يُسْـَٔلُونَ ۝

24. Have they taken gods beside Him? Say: 'Forth with your proof! This is an admonition to them with me and an admonition to those before me.' But most of them know not the truth, so they are averters.

أَمِ اتَّخَذُوٓا مِن دُونِهِۦٓ ءَالِهَةً قُلْ هَاتُواْ بُرْهَٰنَكُمْ هَٰذَا ذِكْرُ مَن مَّعِىَ وَذِكْرُ مَن قَبْلِى بَلْ أَكْثَرُهُمْ لَا يَعْلَمُونَ ٱلْحَقَّ فَهُم مُّعْرِضُونَ ۝

25. And We did not send any Messenger before you but We revealed to him: there is no god but I, so worship Me.

وَمَآ أَرْسَلْنَا مِن قَبْلِكَ مِن رَّسُولٍ إِلَّا نُوحِىٓ إِلَيْهِ أَنَّهُۥ لَآ إِلَٰهَ إِلَّآ أَنَا۠ فَٱعْبُدُونِ ۝

26. And they say: 'The Compassionate has taken a son.'[516] Hallowed be He! Aye! They are bondsmen honoured!

وَقَالُواْ ٱتَّخَذَ ٱلرَّحْمَٰنُ وَلَدًا سُبْحَٰنَهُۥ بَلْ عِبَادٌ مُّكْرَمُونَ ۝

27. They precede Him not in word, and by His command they work.

لَا يَسْبِقُونَهُۥ بِٱلْقَوْلِ وَهُم بِأَمْرِهِۦ يَعْمَلُونَ ۝

28. He knows whatsoever is before them and whatsoever is behind them, and they intercede not except for him whom He approves. And in awe of Him they are fearful.

يَعْلَمُ مَا بَيْنَ أَيْدِيهِمْ وَمَا خَلْفَهُمْ وَلَا يَشْفَعُونَ إِلَّا لِمَنِ ٱرْتَضَىٰ وَهُم مِّنْ خَشْيَتِهِۦ مُشْفِقُونَ ۝

29. And whosoever of them should say: 'Verily I am a god beside Him', such a one We will requite with Hell. Thus We requite the ungodly.

وَمَن يَقُلْ مِنْهُمْ إِنِّىٓ إِلَٰهٌ مِّن دُونِهِۦ فَذَٰلِكَ نَجْزِيهِ جَهَنَّمَ كَذَٰلِكَ نَجْزِى ٱلظَّٰلِمِينَ ۝

---

516. Thereby they also mean some of His angels. This particular blasphemy has been world-wide, the Semitics being no exception. 'That the angels, as "sons of God", form part of the old Semitic mythology, is clear from Gen. VI. 2, 4' (Robertson-Smith, *Religion of the Semites*, p. 446).

Section 3

30. Have not those who disbelieved considered that the heavens and the earth were closed up, then We rent them? And We have made of water everything living, will they not then believe?

أَوَلَمْ يَرَ الَّذِينَ كَفَرُوٓا أَنَّ السَّمَٰوَٰتِ وَالْأَرْضَ كَانَتَا رَتْقًا فَفَتَقْنَٰهُمَا وَجَعَلْنَا مِنَ الْمَآءِ كُلَّ شَىْءٍ حَىٍّ أَفَلَا يُؤْمِنُونَ ﴿٣٠﴾

31. And We have placed in the earth firm mountains lest it should move away with them, and We placed therein passages for paths, that haply they may be guided.

وَجَعَلْنَا فِى الْأَرْضِ رَوَٰسِىَ أَن تَمِيدَ بِهِمْ وَجَعَلْنَا فِيهَا فِجَاجًا سُبُلًا لَّعَلَّهُمْ يَهْتَدُونَ ﴿٣١﴾

32. And We have made the heaven a roof, safe; and from the signs thereof they are averters.

وَجَعَلْنَا السَّمَآءَ سَقْفًا مَّحْفُوظًا وَهُمْ عَنْ ءَايَٰتِهَا مُعْرِضُونَ ﴿٣٢﴾

33. And He it is Who has created the night and the day, the sun and the moon, each in an orb floating.

وَهُوَ الَّذِى خَلَقَ الَّيْلَ وَالنَّهَارَ وَالشَّمْسَ وَالْقَمَرَ كُلٌّ فِى فَلَكٍ يَسْبَحُونَ ﴿٣٣﴾

34. And We have not, before you, granted immortality to any human being, so if you die, are they to be immortals?

وَمَا جَعَلْنَا لِبَشَرٍ مِّن قَبْلِكَ الْخُلْدَ أَفَإِيْن مِّتَّ فَهُمُ الْخَٰلِدُونَ ﴿٣٤﴾

35. Every one is going to taste of death, and We shall try you with evil and good as a temptation, and to Us you will be returned.

كُلُّ نَفْسٍ ذَآئِقَةُ الْمَوْتِ وَنَبْلُوكُم بِالشَّرِّ وَالْخَيْرِ فِتْنَةً وَإِلَيْنَا تُرْجَعُونَ ﴿٣٥﴾

36. And when the infidels look at you, they only take you up for mockery: is this the one who mentions your gods with contempt? While in the mention of the Compassionate they are themselves blasphemers.

وَإِذَا رَءَاكَ الَّذِينَ كَفَرُوٓا إِن يَتَّخِذُونَكَ إِلَّا هُزُوًا أَهَٰذَا الَّذِى يَذْكُرُ ءَالِهَتَكُمْ وَهُم بِذِكْرِ الرَّحْمَٰنِ هُمْ كَٰفِرُونَ ﴿٣٦﴾

37. Man was created of haste. I shall surely show you My signs, so ask Me not to hasten.

خَلَقَ ٱلْإِنسَـٰنُ مِنْ عَجَلٍ سَأُوْرِيكُمْ ءَايَـٰتِى فَلَا تَسْتَعْجِلُونِ ۝

38. And they say: 'When is this torment coming, if you speak truth?'

وَيَقُولُونَ مَتَىٰ هَـٰذَا ٱلْوَعْدُ إِن كُنتُمْ صَـٰدِقِينَ ۝

39. If the disbelievers only know of the time when they shall not be able to ward off the Fire from their faces nor from their backs nor shall they be succoured!

لَوْ يَعْلَمُ ٱلَّذِينَ كَفَرُواْ حِينَ لَا يَكُفُّونَ عَن وُجُوهِهِمُ ٱلنَّارَ وَلَا عَن ظُهُورِهِمْ وَلَا هُمْ يُنصَرُونَ ۝

40. Aye! It would come upon them on a sudden and will dumbfound them; they shall not be able to avert it, nor shall they be respited.

بَلْ تَأْتِيهِم بَغْتَةً فَتَبْهَتُهُمْ فَلَا يَسْتَطِيعُونَ رَدَّهَا وَلَا هُمْ يُنظَرُونَ ۝

41. And assuredly mocked were the Messengers before you, then there surrounded the scoffers what they had been mocking at.

وَلَقَدِ ٱسْتُهْزِئَ بِرُسُلٍ مِّن قَبْلِكَ فَحَاقَ بِٱلَّذِينَ سَخِرُواْ مِنْهُم مَّا كَانُواْ بِهِۦ يَسْتَهْزِءُونَ ۝

Section 4

42. Say: 'Who guards you from the Compassionate by night and day?' And yet they avert themselves from the remembrance of their Lord.

قُلْ مَن يَكْلَؤُكُم بِٱلَّيْلِ وَٱلنَّهَارِ مِنَ ٱلرَّحْمَـٰنِ بَلْ هُمْ عَن ذِكْرِ رَبِّهِم مُّعْرِضُونَ ۝

43. Have they gods who defend them against Us? They have no power to succour themselves; and against Us they cannot be kept company with.

أَمْ لَهُمْ ءَالِهَةٌ تَمْنَعُهُم مِّن دُونِنَا لَا يَسْتَطِيعُونَ نَصْرَ أَنفُسِهِمْ وَلَا هُم مِّنَّا يُصْحَبُونَ ۝

44. Aye! We let these people and their fathers enjoy until there grow long upon them the life. Observe they not that We come upon their land, diminishing it by its borders? Will they then triumph?

بَلۡ مَتَّعۡنَا هَٰٓؤُلَآءِ وَءَابَآءَهُمۡ حَتَّىٰ طَالَ عَلَيۡهِمُ ٱلۡعُمُرُۗ أَفَلَا يَرَوۡنَ أَنَّا نَأۡتِى ٱلۡأَرۡضَ نَنقُصُهَا مِنۡ أَطۡرَافِهَآۚ أَفَهُمُ ٱلۡغَٰلِبُونَ ﴿٤٤﴾

45. Say: 'I only warn you by the revelation'; and the deaf do not hear the call when they are warned.

قُلۡ إِنَّمَآ أُنذِرُكُم بِٱلۡوَحۡىِۚ وَلَا يَسۡمَعُ ٱلصُّمُّ ٱلدُّعَآءَ إِذَا مَا يُنذَرُونَ ﴿٤٥﴾

46. And if only a breath of the torment of your Lord were to touch them, they will cry: 'Woe to us! We have been the wrong-doers.'

وَلَئِن مَّسَّتۡهُمۡ نَفۡحَةٌ مِّنۡ عَذَابِ رَبِّكَ لَيَقُولُنَّ يَٰوَيۡلَنَآ إِنَّا كُنَّا ظَٰلِمِينَ ﴿٤٦﴾

47. And We shall set balances of justice for the Day of Judgement. Then no one will be wronged at all if it be but the weight of a grain of mustard-seed, We shall bring it; and suffice We as reckoners.[517]

وَنَضَعُ ٱلۡمَوَٰزِينَ ٱلۡقِسۡطَ لِيَوۡمِ ٱلۡقِيَٰمَةِ فَلَا تُظۡلَمُ نَفۡسٌ شَيۡـًٔاۖ وَإِن كَانَ مِثۡقَالَ حَبَّةٍ مِّنۡ خَرۡدَلٍ أَتَيۡنَا بِهَاۗ وَكَفَىٰ بِنَا حَٰسِبِينَ ﴿٤٧﴾

48. And assuredly We gave to Moses and Aaron the distinction and illumination and an admonition for the God-fearing,

وَلَقَدۡ ءَاتَيۡنَا مُوسَىٰ وَهَٰرُونَ ٱلۡفُرۡقَانَ وَضِيَآءً وَذِكۡرًا لِّلۡمُتَّقِينَ ﴿٤٨﴾

49. Those who fear their Lord, Unseen, and who are fearful of the Hour.

ٱلَّذِينَ يَخۡشَوۡنَ رَبَّهُم بِٱلۡغَيۡبِ وَهُم مِّنَ ٱلسَّاعَةِ مُشۡفِقُونَ ﴿٤٩﴾

---

517. This without the aid of balances. This strikes at the root of the pagan concept requiring a special god of knowledge. The Egyptians, for instance, worshipped Thoth as the divine measurer of celestial seasons and earthly years.

50. And this is an admonition blessed, which We have sent down; will you then be its rejectors?

Section 5

وَهَذَا ذِكْرٌ مُّبَارَكٌ أَنزَلْنَهُ أَفَأَنتُمْ لَهُ مُنكِرُونَ ۝

51. And assuredly We gave rectitude to Abraham aforetime, and him We had ever known.

وَلَقَدْ ءَاتَيْنَا إِبْرَهِيمَ رُشْدَهُ مِن قَبْلُ وَكُنَّا بِهِ عَلِمِينَ ۝

52. Recall when he said to his father and his people: 'What are these images which you are cleaving to?'

إِذْ قَالَ لِأَبِيهِ وَقَوْمِهِ مَا هَذِهِ التَّمَاثِيلُ الَّتِيَ أَنتُمْ لَهَا عَكِفُونَ ۝

53. They said: 'We found our fathers their worshippers.'

قَالُوا وَجَدْنَا ءَابَاءَنَا لَهَا عَبِدِينَ ۝

54. He said: 'Assuredly you, you and your fathers, have been in error manifest.'

قَالَ لَقَدْ كُنتُمْ أَنتُمْ وَءَابَاؤُكُمْ فِي ضَلَلٍ مُّبِينٍ ۝

55. They said: 'Have you come to us in seriousness, or are you among those who sport?'

قَالُوا أَجِئْتَنَا بِالْحَقِّ أَمْ أَنتَ مِنَ اللَّعِبِينَ ۝

56. He said: 'Aye! Your Lord is the Lord of the heavens and the earth. Who created them; and of that I am among the witnesses.

قَالَ بَل رَّبُّكُمْ رَبُّ السَّمَوَتِ وَالْأَرْضِ الَّذِي فَطَرَهُنَّ وَأَنَا عَلَى ذَلِكُم مِّنَ الشَّهِدِينَ ۝

57. And by Allah, I am surely going to devise a plot against your idols, after you have turned your backs.'

وَتَاللَّهِ لَأَكِيدَنَّ أَصْنَمَكُم بَعْدَ أَن تُوَلُّوا مُدْبِرِينَ ۝

58. Then he made them fragments, all except the big one of them, that haply to it they may return.

فَجَعَلَهُمْ جُذَذًا إِلَّا كَبِيرًا لَّهُمْ لَعَلَّهُمْ إِلَيْهِ يَرْجِعُونَ ۝

59. They said: 'Who has done this to our gods? Surely he is of the evil-doers.'

60. They said: 'Among themselves we heard a youth, called Abraham, speak of them with disrespect.'

61. They said: 'Bring him then before the eyes of the people, haply they may bear witness.'

62. They said: 'Are you the one who has done this to our gods, O Abraham?'

63. He said: 'Rather he has done it: the big one of them: so question them, if they ever speak.'

64. They then turned to themselves and said: 'You it is who are the evil-doers.'

65. Thereafter they were put to utter confusion, saying: 'Certainly you know that they speak not.'

66. He said: 'Do you worship them besides Allah what can neither profit you nor hurt you.'

67. 'Fie upon you and upon what you worship besides Allah, will you not then reflect?'

68. They said: 'Burn him and succour your gods, if you will be doing.'

69. We said: 'O Fire! Be you cool-ness and safety for Abraham.'

قَالُوا مَن فَعَلَ هَذَا بِـَالِهَتِنَا إِنَّهُ لَمِنَ الظَّالِمِينَ ٥٩

قَالُوا سَمِعْنَا فَتًى يَذْكُرُهُمْ يُقَالُ لَهُۥٓ إِبْرَٰهِيمُ ٦٠

قَالُوا فَأْتُوا بِهِۦ عَلَىٰٓ أَعْيُنِ النَّاسِ لَعَلَّهُمْ يَشْهَدُونَ ٦١

قَالُوٓا ءَأَنتَ فَعَلْتَ هَذَا بِـَالِهَتِنَا يَـٰٓإِبْرَٰهِيمُ ٦٢

قَالَ بَلْ فَعَلَهُۥ كَبِيرُهُمْ هَذَا فَسْـَٔلُوهُمْ إِن كَانُوا يَنطِقُونَ ٦٣

فَرَجَعُوٓا إِلَىٰٓ أَنفُسِهِمْ فَقَالُوٓا إِنَّكُمْ أَنتُمُ الظَّالِمُونَ ٦٤

ثُمَّ نُكِسُوا عَلَىٰ رُءُوسِهِمْ لَقَدْ عَلِمْتَ مَا هَـٰٓؤُلَآءِ يَنطِقُونَ ٦٥

قَالَ أَفَتَعْبُدُونَ مِن دُونِ اللَّهِ مَا لَا يَنفَعُكُمْ شَيْـًٔا وَلَا يَضُرُّكُمْ ٦٦

أُفٍّ لَّكُمْ وَلِمَا تَعْبُدُونَ مِن دُونِ اللَّهِ أَفَلَا تَعْقِلُونَ ٦٧

قَالُوا حَرِّقُوهُ وَانصُرُوٓا ءَالِهَتَكُمْ إِن كُنتُمْ فَـٰعِلِينَ ٦٨

قُلْنَا يَـٰنَارُ كُونِي بَرْدًا وَسَلَـٰمًا عَلَىٰٓ إِبْرَٰهِيمَ ٦٩

70. And they wanted to do him harm but We made themselves the worst losers.

وَأَرَادُوا بِهِ كَيْدًا فَجَعَلْنَٰهُمُ الْأَخْسَرِينَ ۝

71. And We delivered him and Lot, to the land in which We had placed the blessings for the worlds.

وَنَجَّيْنَٰهُ وَلُوطًا إِلَى الْأَرْضِ الَّتِي بَٰرَكْنَا فِيهَا لِلْعَٰلَمِينَ ۝

72. And We bestowed upon him Isaac and Jacob as a grandson, and each one We made righteous.[518]

وَوَهَبْنَا لَهُ إِسْحَٰقَ وَيَعْقُوبَ نَافِلَةً وَكُلًّا جَعَلْنَا صَٰلِحِينَ ۝

73. And We made them leaders,[519] guiding by Our command, and We revealed to them the doing of good deeds and the establishment of prayers, and the giving of the poor-rate; and of Us they were the worshippers.[520]

وَجَعَلْنَٰهُمْ أَئِمَّةً يَهْدُونَ بِأَمْرِنَا وَأَوْحَيْنَا إِلَيْهِمْ فِعْلَ الْخَيْرَٰتِ وَإِقَامَ الصَّلَوٰةِ وَإِيتَاءَ الزَّكَوٰةِ وَكَانُوا لَنَا عَٰبِدِينَ ۝

74. And as for Lot; We gave him judgement and knowledge, and We delivered him out of the city which had been working foul deeds; verily they were a people evil, wicked.

وَلُوطًا ءَاتَيْنَٰهُ حُكْمًا وَعِلْمًا وَنَجَّيْنَٰهُ مِنَ الْقَرْيَةِ الَّتِي كَانَت تَّعْمَلُ الْخَبَٰئِثَ إِنَّهُمْ كَانُوا قَوْمَ سَوْءٍ فَٰسِقِينَ ۝

---

518. As every Prophet of God is bound to be. This truth, obvious to every Muslim reader needed express affirmation in view of the extremely grave charges of immorality brought against these Israelite Prophets of the Bible.

519. Meaning exemplars; objects of imitation to a people. So these Prophets of God were, the Qur'ān expressly and repeatedly affirms, models of religion and piety, and pre-eminently virtuous and holy, not mere diviners or interpreters of the Law to their people.

520. Thus, in Islam, the role of the Prophet is two-fold. As an organ of Revelation, he is the preceptor of his people in true doctrines and right practices, and, in himself, he is a living embodiment of communion with God.

75. And We caused him to enter Our Mercy; verily he was of the righteous.[521]

وَأَدْخَلْنَـٰهُ فِى رَحْمَتِنَآ إِنَّهُۥ مِنَ ٱلصَّـٰلِحِينَ ﴿٧٥﴾

Section 6

76. And as for Noah, recall when he cried aforetime, We answered him and delivered him and his household from a mighty disaster.

وَنُوحًا إِذْ نَادَىٰ مِن قَبْلُ فَٱسْتَجَبْنَا لَهُۥ فَنَجَّيْنَـٰهُ وَأَهْلَهُۥ مِنَ ٱلْكَرْبِ ٱلْعَظِيمِ ﴿٧٦﴾

77. We succoured him against a people who belied Our signs; verily they were a people evil, so We drowned them all.

وَنَصَرْنَـٰهُ مِنَ ٱلْقَوْمِ ٱلَّذِينَ كَذَّبُوا بِـَٔايَـٰتِنَآ إِنَّهُمْ كَانُوا قَوْمَ سَوْءٍ فَأَغْرَقْنَـٰهُمْ أَجْمَعِينَ ﴿٧٧﴾

78. And as to David and Solomon, recall when they gave judgement regarding the tillage when certain people's sheep had pastured therein at night, and of the judgement concerning them. We were the witnesses.

وَدَاوُۥدَ وَسُلَيْمَـٰنَ إِذْ يَحْكُمَانِ فِى ٱلْحَرْثِ إِذْ نَفَشَتْ فِيهِ غَنَمُ ٱلْقَوْمِ وَكُنَّا لِحُكْمِهِمْ شَـٰهِدِينَ ﴿٧٨﴾

79. So We gave insight into it to Solomon, and to each of the two We gave judgement and knowledge. And We so subjected the mountains that they should hallow Us along with David, and also the birds; and We were the doers.

فَفَهَّمْنَـٰهَا سُلَيْمَـٰنَ وَكُلًّا ءَاتَيْنَا حُكْمًا وَعِلْمًا وَسَخَّرْنَا مَعَ دَاوُۥدَ ٱلْجِبَالَ يُسَبِّحْنَ وَٱلطَّيْرَ وَكُنَّا فَـٰعِلِينَ ﴿٧٩﴾

---

521. This clear, powerful vindication of Lot's saintly character was all the more necessary so as to contradict and repudiate the most atrocious charge of incest brought against him in the Bible (Ge. 19: 30–38). The rabbis, not to be outdone by the Bible, maintained that 'he was given over to lust; therefore he chose Sodom as his residence' (*JE.* VIII. p. 186).

80. And We taught him the art of making the coats of mail for you that it may protect you in your violence; are you then thankful?

81. And to Solomon We subjected the wind, strongly raging, running at his command towards the land, wherein We had placed Our blessing; and of everything We are the Knower.

82. And of the devils were some who dived for him, and worked a work besides that; and of them We were the Watcher.

83. And as to Job, recall when he cried to the Lord: 'Verily affliction has touched me, and You are the Most Merciful of the mercifuls.'

84. So We answered him, and We removed from him what was with him of the affliction, and We gave restoration to him and his household and along with them the like thereof as a mercy from Us and as a remembrance to the devotees.

85. And as for Ishmael and Enoch and Dhū al-Kifl! Each was steadfast.

86. And We caused them to enter Our mercy, verily they were of the righteous.

وَعَلَّمْنَٰهُ صَنْعَةَ لَبُوسٍ لَّكُمْ لِتُحْصِنَكُم مِّنۢ بَأْسِكُمْ فَهَلْ أَنتُمْ شَٰكِرُونَ ۝

وَلِسُلَيْمَٰنَ ٱلرِّيحَ عَاصِفَةً تَجْرِى بِأَمْرِهِۦٓ إِلَى ٱلْأَرْضِ ٱلَّتِى بَٰرَكْنَا فِيهَا وَكُنَّا بِكُلِّ شَىْءٍ عَٰلِمِينَ ۝

وَمِنَ ٱلشَّيَٰطِينِ مَن يَغُوصُونَ لَهُۥ وَيَعْمَلُونَ عَمَلًا دُونَ ذَٰلِكَ وَكُنَّا لَهُمْ حَٰفِظِينَ ۝

وَأَيُّوبَ إِذْ نَادَىٰ رَبَّهُۥٓ أَنِّى مَسَّنِىَ ٱلضُّرُّ وَأَنتَ أَرْحَمُ ٱلرَّٰحِمِينَ ۝

فَٱسْتَجَبْنَا لَهُۥ فَكَشَفْنَا مَا بِهِۦ مِن ضُرٍّ وَءَاتَيْنَٰهُ أَهْلَهُۥ وَمِثْلَهُم مَّعَهُمْ رَحْمَةً مِّنْ عِندِنَا وَذِكْرَىٰ لِلْعَٰبِدِينَ ۝

وَإِسْمَٰعِيلَ وَإِدْرِيسَ وَذَا ٱلْكِفْلِ كُلٌّ مِّنَ ٱلصَّٰبِرِينَ ۝

وَأَدْخَلْنَٰهُمْ فِى رَحْمَتِنَآ إِنَّهُم مِّنَ ٱلصَّٰلِحِينَ ۝

87. And as to Dhū al-Nūn, recall when he departed with anger and imagined that We could have no power over him, and then he cried in the layer of darknesses: 'There is no god but You! Hallowed be You! Verily I have been of the wrong-doers.'522

وَذَا ٱلنُّونِ إِذ ذَّهَبَ مُغَـٰضِبًا فَظَنَّ أَن لَّن نَّقْدِرَ عَلَيْهِ فَنَادَىٰ فِى ٱلظُّلُمَـٰتِ أَن لَّآ إِلَـٰهَ إِلَّآ أَنتَ سُبْحَـٰنَكَ إِنِّى كُنتُ مِنَ ٱلظَّـٰلِمِينَ ۝

88. So We answered him and We delivered him from the distress; and thus do We deliver the believers.

فَٱسْتَجَبْنَا لَهُۥ وَنَجَّيْنَـٰهُ مِنَ ٱلْغَمِّ وَكَذَٰلِكَ نُـۨجِى ٱلْمُؤْمِنِينَ ۝

89. And as for Zacharia, recall when he cried to his Lord: 'Lord! Leave me not heirless though You are the best of inheritors.'

وَزَكَرِيَّآ إِذْ نَادَىٰ رَبَّهُۥ رَبِّ لَا تَذَرْنِى فَرْدًا وَأَنتَ خَيْرُ ٱلْوَٰرِثِينَ ۝

90. So We answered him and bestowed on him John and We made sound for him his spouse. Verily all of them were wont to vie with one another in good deeds and to call upon Us with longing and dread and they were before Us meek.

فَٱسْتَجَبْنَا لَهُۥ وَوَهَبْنَا لَهُۥ يَحْيَىٰ وَأَصْلَحْنَا لَهُۥ زَوْجَهُۥٓ إِنَّهُمْ كَانُوا۟ يُسَـٰرِعُونَ فِى ٱلْخَيْرَٰتِ وَيَدْعُونَنَا رَغَبًا وَرَهَبًا وَكَانُوا۟ لَنَا خَـٰشِعِينَ ۝

91. And as to she who guarded her chastity, We breathed into her of Our Spirit, and made her and her son a sign unto the worlds.

وَٱلَّتِىٓ أَحْصَنَتْ فَرْجَهَا فَنَفَخْنَا فِيهَا مِن رُّوحِنَا وَجَعَلْنَـٰهَا وَٱبْنَهَآ ءَايَةً لِّلْعَـٰلَمِينَ ۝

---

522. So forgive me, my Lord! The forgiveness he craves is for the error of judgement, and not for any sin. The Prophets of God are the very first to own up and acknowledge their mistakes, however unintentional or trivial they may have been.

92. Verily this community of yours is a single community,[523] and I am your Lord; so worship Me.

إِنَّ هَـٰذِهِۦٓ أُمَّتُكُمْ أُمَّةً وَٰحِدَةً وَأَنَا۠ رَبُّكُمْ فَٱعْبُدُونِ ۝

93. And they split up their affair among them, all shall return to Us.

وَتَقَطَّعُوٓا۟ أَمْرَهُم بَيْنَهُمْ كُلٌّ إِلَيْنَا رَٰجِعُونَ ۝

Section 7

94. Whosoever works righteous deeds, and he is a believer, there shall be no denial of his endeavour; and We are for him the writers.

فَمَن يَعْمَلْ مِنَ ٱلصَّـٰلِحَـٰتِ وَهُوَ مُؤْمِنٌ فَلَا كُفْرَانَ لِسَعْيِهِۦ وَإِنَّا لَهُۥ كَـٰتِبُونَ ۝

95. And a ban is laid on every town which We have destroyed that they shall not return.

وَحَرَٰمٌ عَلَىٰ قَرْيَةٍ أَهْلَكْنَـٰهَآ أَنَّهُمْ لَا يَرْجِعُونَ ۝

96. Until when Gog and Magog are let out and from every mount they are trickling down.

حَتَّىٰٓ إِذَا فُتِحَتْ يَأْجُوجُ وَمَأْجُوجُ وَهُم مِّن كُلِّ حَدَبٍ يَنسِلُونَ ۝

97. And there shall approach the true promise, and lo! The eyes of the disbelieving shall be staring. 'Woe to us! Surely we have been unheeding: aye! We have been the wrong-doers.'

وَٱقْتَرَبَ ٱلْوَعْدُ ٱلْحَقُّ فَإِذَا هِىَ شَـٰخِصَةٌ أَبْصَـٰرُ ٱلَّذِينَ كَفَرُوا۟ يَـٰوَيْلَنَا قَدْ كُنَّا فِى غَفْلَةٍ مِّنْ هَـٰذَا بَلْ كُنَّا ظَـٰلِمِينَ ۝

98. Verily you and whatever you worship besides Allah shall be firewood for Hell: you shall go down to it.

إِنَّكُمْ وَمَا تَعْبُدُونَ مِن دُونِ ٱللَّهِ حَصَبُ جَهَنَّمَ أَنتُمْ لَهَا وَٰرِدُونَ ۝

---

523. O Muslims! i.e., this way of life which is prescribed for you is the same as has been preached and practised by all the Prophets and holy men and women, however widely divided by time and space; Islam is only a continuation of that old Religion.

99. Had these been gods, they would not have gone down to it, and all of them, shall abide therein.

لَوْكَانَ هَٰؤُلَاءِ ءَالِهَةً مَّا وَرَدُوهَا وَكُلٌّ فِيهَا خَٰلِدُونَ ۝

100. Theirs shall be roaring therein, and therein they shall hear not.

لَهُمْ فِيهَا زَفِيرٌ وَهُمْ فِيهَا لَا يَسْمَعُونَ ۝

101. Verily those for whom good reward has preceded from Us, they shall be kept far away therefrom.

إِنَّ ٱلَّذِينَ سَبَقَتْ لَهُم مِّنَّا ٱلْحُسْنَىٰ أُوْلَٰٓئِكَ عَنْهَا مُبْعَدُونَ ۝

102. They shall not hear a whisper of it, and they shall abide in that felicity for which there souls long.

لَا يَسْمَعُونَ حَسِيسَهَا وَهُمْ فِي مَا ٱشْتَهَتْ أَنفُسُهُمْ خَٰلِدُونَ ۝

103. Them, the great terror shall not grieve, and angels shall meet them: this is your Day which you were ever promised,

لَا يَحْزُنُهُمُ ٱلْفَزَعُ ٱلْأَكْبَرُ وَتَتَلَقَّىٰهُمُ ٱلْمَلَٰٓئِكَةُ هَٰذَا يَوْمُكُمُ ٱلَّذِى كُنتُمْ تُوعَدُونَ ۝

104. The Day when We shall roll up the heavens like as the rolling up of a scroll for books. Even as We began the first creation, We shall restore it: a promise binding upon Us; verily We are the doers.

يَوْمَ نَطْوِى ٱلسَّمَاءَ كَطَيِّ ٱلسِّجِلِّ لِلْكُتُبِ كَمَا بَدَأْنَا أَوَّلَ خَلْقٍ نُّعِيدُهُ وَعْدًا عَلَيْنَا إِنَّا كُنَّا فَٰعِلِينَ ۝

105. Assuredly We have pre-scribed in the Scripture after the admonition that the land! My righteous bondsmen will inherit it.

وَلَقَدْ كَتَبْنَا فِى ٱلزَّبُورِ مِنۢ بَعْدِ ٱلذِّكْرِ أَنَّ ٱلْأَرْضَ يَرِثُهَا عِبَادِىَ ٱلصَّٰلِحُونَ ۝

106. Verily in this is a preaching for a people who are true worshippers.

إِنَّ فِى هَٰذَا لَبَلَٰغًا لِّقَوْمٍ عَٰبِدِينَ ۝

107. And We have not sent you except as a mercy to the worlds.

وَمَا أَرْسَلْنَٰكَ إِلَّا رَحْمَةً لِّلْعَٰلَمِينَ ۝

108. Say: 'This only has been revealed to me: your God is only One God; do you submit then?'

قُلْ إِنَّمَا يُوحَىٰ إِلَيَّ أَنَّمَا إِلَٰهُكُمْ إِلَٰهٌ وَٰحِدٌ فَهَلْ أَنتُم مُّسْلِمُونَ ۝

109. Then if they turn away, say: 'I have proclaimed to you all alike; and I do not know whether nigh or far is what you are promised.

فَإِن تَوَلَّوْا فَقُلْ ءَاذَنتُكُمْ عَلَىٰ سَوَآءٍ وَإِنْ أَدْرِىٓ أَقَرِيبٌ أَم بَعِيدٌ مَّا تُوعَدُونَ ۝

110. He knows what is spoken aloud, and He knows what you hide.

إِنَّهُۥ يَعْلَمُ ٱلْجَهْرَ مِنَ ٱلْقَوْلِ وَيَعْلَمُ مَا تَكْتُمُونَ ۝

111. I do not know: haply it may be a trial for you, and an enjoyment for a season.'

وَإِنْ أَدْرِى لَعَلَّهُۥ فِتْنَةٌ لَّكُمْ وَمَتَٰعٌ إِلَىٰ حِينٍ ۝

112. He says: 'Lord! Judge you with truth. And Our Lord is the Compassionate Whose help is sought against what you utter.'

قَٰلَ رَبِّ ٱحْكُم بِٱلْحَقِّ وَرَبُّنَا ٱلرَّحْمَٰنُ ٱلْمُسْتَعَانُ عَلَىٰ مَا تَصِفُونَ ۝

Sūrah 22

al-Ḥajj

(Madinan, 10 Sections, 78 Verses)

In the name of Allah, the Compassionate, The Merciful.

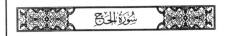

Section 1

1. O mankind! Fear your Lord, the quake of the Hour is to be a mighty thing.

2. The Day when you behold it every suckling woman shall forsake what she suckles, and every pregnant woman shall lay down her burden; and you shall perceive mankind as drunk; whereas drunk they will be not, but the torment of Allah shall be terrible.

3. And of mankind is he who disputes respecting Allah without knowledge, and follows any devil forward:

4. Against whom it is prescribed; whosoever befriends him, him he shall lead astray and shall guide him on to the torment of the flame.

5. O mankind! If you be in doubt respecting the Resurrection, then know We have created you of the dust, then of a drop, then of a clot, then of a piece of flesh, fashioned and unfashioned, that We might manifest to you Our power. And We settle into the wombs what We will for a term determined. Then We bring you forth as babies, then We let you reach your maturity. And of you is he who dies early, and of you he who is brought back to the most abject age, so that after knowing he knows nothing. And you see the earth withered up, and when We send down on it water, it stirs and swells and grows all manner of luxuriant growth.

يَٰٓأَيُّهَا ٱلنَّاسُ إِن كُنتُمۡ فِي رَيۡبٖ مِّنَ ٱلۡبَعۡثِ فَإِنَّا خَلَقۡنَٰكُم مِّن تُرَابٖ ثُمَّ مِن نُّطۡفَةٖ ثُمَّ مِنۡ عَلَقَةٖ ثُمَّ مِن مُّضۡغَةٖ مُّخَلَّقَةٖ وَغَيۡرِ مُخَلَّقَةٖ لِّنُبَيِّنَ لَكُمۡۚ وَنُقِرُّ فِي ٱلۡأَرۡحَامِ مَا نَشَآءُ إِلَىٰٓ أَجَلٖ مُّسَمّٗى ثُمَّ نُخۡرِجُكُمۡ طِفۡلٗا ثُمَّ لِتَبۡلُغُوٓاْ أَشُدَّكُمۡۖ وَمِنكُم مَّن يُتَوَفَّىٰ وَمِنكُم مَّن يُرَدُّ إِلَىٰٓ أَرۡذَلِ ٱلۡعُمُرِ لِكَيۡلَا يَعۡلَمَ مِنۢ بَعۡدِ عِلۡمٖ شَيۡـًٔاۚ وَتَرَى ٱلۡأَرۡضَ هَامِدَةٗ فَإِذَآ أَنزَلۡنَا عَلَيۡهَا ٱلۡمَآءَ ٱهۡتَزَّتۡ وَرَبَتۡ وَأَنۢبَتَتۡ مِن كُلِّ زَوۡجِۭ بَهِيجٖ ٥

6. That is so,[524] because Allah! He is the Truth, and He quickens the dead, and verily He is Potent over everything,

ذَٰلِكَ بِأَنَّ ٱللَّهَ هُوَ ٱلۡحَقُّ وَأَنَّهُۥ يُحۡيِ ٱلۡمَوۡتَىٰ وَأَنَّهُۥ عَلَىٰ كُلِّ شَيۡءٖ قَدِيرٞ ٦

7. And because the Hour is coming – there is no doubt about it – and because Allah will raise up those who are in the graves.[525]

وَأَنَّ ٱلسَّاعَةَ ءَاتِيَةٞ لَّا رَيۡبَ فِيهَا وَأَنَّ ٱللَّهَ يَبۡعَثُ مَن فِي ٱلۡقُبُورِ ٧

---

524. The argument in brief is: cannot the God Who created man and nature, out of nothing, as easily raise the dead?

525. The doctrine of Resurrection had come to be ignored, when not actually denied, by the Jews and the Christians of the Prophet's time, and was of course openly ridiculed by the pagans. 'The Resurrection of the body was denied by his fellow-citizens as an idle imagination'; and the Prophet was denounced 'as a sorcerer or magician, who would pretend that a living body could be reproduced from dust and dead man's bones' (Muir, *Life of Muhammad*, p. 78). Among the Jews, 'the Seducers denied the resurrection' (*JE*. X. p. 383).

8. And of mankind is he who disputes respecting Allah without knowledge or guidance or an illuminating Book,

وَمِنَ ٱلنَّاسِ مَن يُجَـٰدِلُ فِى ٱللَّهِ بِغَيْرِ عِلْمٍ وَلَا هُدًى وَلَا كِتَـٰبٍ مُّنِيرٍ ۝

9. Magnifying himself that he may lead others astray from the way of Allah; for him shall be humiliation in this world, and on the Day of Judgement We will make him taste the torment of burning.

ثَانِىَ عِطْفِهِ لِيُضِلَّ عَن سَبِيلِ ٱللَّهِ لَهُ فِى ٱلدُّنْيَا خِزْىٌ وَنُذِيقُهُ يَوْمَ ٱلْقِيَـٰمَةِ عَذَابَ ٱلْحَرِيقِ ۝

10. That is because of what your hands have sent forth, and verily Allah never wrongs His creatures.

ذَٰلِكَ بِمَا قَدَّمَتْ يَدَاكَ وَأَنَّ ٱللَّهَ لَيْسَ بِظَلَّـٰمٍ لِّلْعَبِيدِ ۝

Section 2

11. And of mankind is he who worships Allah upon the very edge; if there happens to him any good he is contented with it, but if there befalls him a trial, he turns round on his face. He loses both this world and the Hereafter, that indeed is a manifest loss.

وَمِنَ ٱلنَّاسِ مَن يَعْبُدُ ٱللَّهَ عَلَىٰ حَرْفٍ فَإِنْ أَصَابَهُ خَيْرٌ ٱطْمَأَنَّ بِهِ وَإِنْ أَصَابَتْهُ فِتْنَةٌ ٱنقَلَبَ عَلَىٰ وَجْهِهِ خَسِرَ ٱلدُّنْيَا وَٱلْـَٔاخِرَةَ ذَٰلِكَ هُوَ ٱلْخُسْرَانُ ٱلْمُبِينُ ۝

12. He calls upon that, besides Allah, what can neither hurt nor profit him. That indeed is a straying far off.

يَدْعُوا۟ مِن دُونِ ٱللَّهِ مَا لَا يَضُرُّهُ وَمَا لَا يَنفَعُهُ ذَٰلِكَ هُوَ ٱلضَّلَـٰلُ ٱلْبَعِيدُ ۝

13. He calls upon him from whom harm is much nearer than benefit;[526] surely ill is the patron! Ill the comrade!

يَدْعُواْ لَمَن ضَرُّهُۥٓ أَقْرَبُ مِن نَّفْعِهِۦ لَبِئْسَ ٱلْمَوْلَىٰ وَلَبِئْسَ ٱلْعَشِيرُ ﴿١٣﴾

14. Verily Allah shall make those who believe and work righteous deeds enter Gardens with running streams. Verily Allah performs whatsoever He intends.

إِنَّ ٱللَّهَ يُدْخِلُ ٱلَّذِينَ ءَامَنُواْ وَعَمِلُواْ ٱلصَّـٰلِحَـٰتِ جَنَّـٰتٍ تَجْرِى مِن تَحْتِهَا ٱلْأَنْهَـٰرُ إِنَّ ٱللَّهَ يَفْعَلُ مَا يُرِيدُ ﴿١٤﴾

15. Whosoever has been imagining that Allah will not make him triumphant in this world and the Hereafter, let him stretch a cord up to the heavens and let him cut it, and let him look if his guile can do away with that at what he enrages.

مَن كَانَ يَظُنُّ أَن لَّن يَنصُرَهُ ٱللَّهُ فِى ٱلدُّنْيَا وَٱلْأَخِرَةِ فَلْيَمْدُدْ بِسَبَبٍ إِلَى ٱلسَّمَآءِ ثُمَّ لْيَقْطَعْ فَلْيَنظُرْ هَلْ يُذْهِبَنَّ كَيْدُهُۥ مَا يَغِيظُ ﴿١٥﴾

16. And thus We have sent it down as evidence, and verily Allah guides whom He intends.

وَكَذَٰلِكَ أَنزَلْنَـٰهُ ءَايَـٰتٍ بَيِّنَـٰتٍ وَأَنَّ ٱللَّهَ يَهْدِى مَن يُرِيدُ ﴿١٦﴾

17. Verily those who believe and those who are Judaized and the Sabians and the Nazarenes and the Magians and those who associate – verily Allah will decide between them on the Day of Judgement; verily Allah is a Witness over everything.

إِنَّ ٱلَّذِينَ ءَامَنُواْ وَٱلَّذِينَ هَادُواْ وَٱلصَّـٰبِـِٔينَ وَٱلنَّصَـٰرَىٰ وَٱلْمَجُوسَ وَٱلَّذِينَ أَشْرَكُوٓاْ إِنَّ ٱللَّهَ يَفْصِلُ بَيْنَهُمْ يَوْمَ ٱلْقِيَـٰمَةِ إِنَّ ٱللَّهَ عَلَىٰ كُلِّ شَىْءٍ شَهِيدٌ ﴿١٧﴾

---

526. He calls to the worshipper. The meaning being that the harm of idol-worship is sure and patent, while any advantage accruing from them is only imaginary.

18. See you not that Allah! Him adore whosoever is in the heavens and on the earth, and the sun and the moon and the mountains and the trees and the beasts and many of mankind? And there are many of them on whom torment is justified. And whom Allah despises, none can honour and Allah does whatsoever He wills.

أَلَمۡ تَرَ أَنَّ ٱللَّهَ يَسۡجُدُ لَهُۥ مَن فِى ٱلسَّمَٰوَٰتِ وَمَن فِى ٱلۡأَرۡضِ وَٱلشَّمۡسُ وَٱلۡقَمَرُ وَٱلنُّجُومُ وَٱلۡجِبَالُ وَٱلشَّجَرُ وَٱلدَّوَآبُّ وَكَثِيرٌ مِّنَ ٱلنَّاسِۖ وَكَثِيرٌ حَقَّ عَلَيۡهِ ٱلۡعَذَابُۗ وَمَن يُهِنِ ٱللَّهُ فَمَا لَهُۥ مِن مُّكۡرِمٍۚ إِنَّ ٱللَّهَ يَفۡعَلُ مَا يَشَآءُ ۩ ﴿١٨﴾

19. These two are opponents who contended respecting their Lord; then as for those who disbelieved, raiments of fire shall be cut out for them, and hot water shall be poured over their heads.

۞ هَٰذَانِ خَصۡمَانِ ٱخۡتَصَمُواْ فِى رَبِّهِمۡۖ فَٱلَّذِينَ كَفَرُواْ قُطِّعَتۡ لَهُمۡ ثِيَابٌ مِّن نَّارٍ يُصَبُّ مِن فَوۡقِ رُءُوسِهِمُ ٱلۡحَمِيمُ ﴿١٩﴾

20. Melted thereby shall be what is in their bellies and also their skins.

يُصۡهَرُ بِهِۦ مَا فِى بُطُونِهِمۡ وَٱلۡجُلُودُ ﴿٢٠﴾

21. And for them shall be maces of iron.

وَلَهُم مَّقَٰمِعُ مِنۡ حَدِيدٍ ﴿٢١﴾

22. So oft as they, because of anguish, would seek to go forth, they shall be sent back to it: taste the torment of burning.

كُلَّمَآ أَرَادُوٓاْ أَن يَخۡرُجُواْ مِنۡهَا مِنۡ غَمٍّ أُعِيدُواْ فِيهَا وَذُوقُواْ عَذَابَ ٱلۡحَرِيقِ ﴿٢٢﴾

Section 3

23. Verily Allah will make those who believe and work righteous deeds enter Gardens with running streams, where they will be bedecked with bracelets of gold, and with pearls, and their garments therein will be of silk.

إِنَّ ٱللَّهَ يُدۡخِلُ ٱلَّذِينَ ءَامَنُواْ وَعَمِلُواْ ٱلصَّٰلِحَٰتِ جَنَّٰتٍ تَجۡرِى مِن تَحۡتِهَا ٱلۡأَنۡهَٰرُ يُحَلَّوۡنَ فِيهَا مِنۡ أَسَاوِرَ مِن ذَهَبٍ وَلُؤۡلُؤًاۖ وَلِبَاسُهُمۡ فِيهَا حَرِيرٌ ﴿٢٣﴾

24. Guided they have been unto goodly speech and guided they have been to the path of the Praiseworthy.

وَهُدُوٓاْ إِلَى ٱلطَّيِّبِ مِنَ ٱلْقَوْلِ وَهُدُوٓاْ إِلَىٰ صِرَٰطِ ٱلْحَمِيدِ ٢٤

25. Verily those who disbelieve and hinder others from the path of Allah and from the Sacred Mosque which We have made for mankind, equal in respect of which are the dweller therein and the stranger.527 Whosoever will seek profanity therein wrongfully, We shall make him taste of an afflictive torment.

إِنَّ ٱلَّذِينَ كَفَرُواْ وَيَصُدُّونَ عَن سَبِيلِ ٱللَّهِ وَٱلْمَسْجِدِ ٱلْحَرَامِ ٱلَّذِى جَعَلْنَٰهُ لِلنَّاسِ سَوَآءً ٱلْعَٰكِفُ فِيهِ وَٱلْبَادِ وَمَن يُرِدْ فِيهِ بِإِلْحَادٍ بِظُلْمٍ نُّذِقْهُ مِنْ عَذَابٍ أَلِيمٍ ٢٥

Section 4

26. Recall when We settled for Abraham the place of the house, saying: 'Associate not then with Me anyone, and keep pure My house for those who circumambulate and those who stand up and those who bow and prostrate themselves.528

وَإِذْ بَوَّأْنَا لِإِبْرَٰهِيمَ مَكَانَ ٱلْبَيْتِ أَن لَّا تُشْرِكْ بِى شَيْئًا وَطَهِّرْ بَيْتِىَ لِلطَّآئِفِينَ وَٱلْقَآئِمِينَ وَٱلرُّكَّعِ ٱلسُّجُودِ ٢٦

---

527. Note the universal character of the central mosque of Islam; its doors must remain open equally to all worshippers of the One, Universal God.

528. The House is always to be kept perfectly clean both in a literal and a figurative sense, clear of all material and spiritual filth — for all true worshippers of the One Universal God. Furthermore, the House, itself, is not to be taken as an object of worship; it is simply a place for worshipping the One.

27. And proclaim you among mankind the pilgrimage[529]; they shall come to you on foot and on any lean mount, coming from every deep distant point.

28. That they may witness the benefits to them and may mention the name of Allah on the days known over the beast cattle with which He has provided them. So eat of it, and feed the hungry poor.

29. Thereafter let them tidy themselves up and fulfill their vows and circumambulate the ancient house.'

30. Thus it is. And whosoever respects the ordinances of Allah it will be better for him with His Lord. And allowed to you are the cattle, save what have been rehearsed unto you; so avoid the pollution of the idols, and avoid the falsehood.

31. Turning unto Allah, not associating anyone with Him. And whosoever associates anyone with Allah, it is as though he had fallen from the sky and birds had snatched him away, or the wind had swept him to a remote place.

وَأَذِّن فِى ٱلنَّاسِ بِٱلْحَجِّ يَأْتُوكَ رِجَالًا وَعَلَىٰ كُلِّ ضَامِرٍ يَأْتِينَ مِن كُلِّ فَجٍّ عَمِيقٍ ۝

لِّيَشْهَدُوا۟ مَنَٰفِعَ لَهُمْ وَيَذْكُرُوا۟ ٱسْمَ ٱللَّهِ فِىٓ أَيَّامٍ مَّعْلُومَٰتٍ عَلَىٰ مَا رَزَقَهُم مِّنۢ بَهِيمَةِ ٱلْأَنْعَٰمِ فَكُلُوا۟ مِنْهَا وَأَطْعِمُوا۟ ٱلْبَآئِسَ ٱلْفَقِيرَ ۝

ثُمَّ لْيَقْضُوا۟ تَفَثَهُمْ وَلْيُوفُوا۟ نُذُورَهُمْ وَلْيَطَّوَّفُوا۟ بِٱلْبَيْتِ ٱلْعَتِيقِ ۝

ذَٰلِكَ وَمَن يُعَظِّمْ حُرُمَٰتِ ٱللَّهِ فَهُوَ خَيْرٌ لَّهُۥ عِندَ رَبِّهِۦ وَأُحِلَّتْ لَكُمُ ٱلْأَنْعَٰمُ إِلَّا مَا يُتْلَىٰ عَلَيْكُمْ فَٱجْتَنِبُوا۟ ٱلرِّجْسَ مِنَ ٱلْأَوْثَٰنِ وَٱجْتَنِبُوا۟ قَوْلَ ٱلزُّورِ ۝

حُنَفَآءَ لِلَّهِ غَيْرَ مُشْرِكِينَ بِهِۦ وَمَن يُشْرِكْ بِٱللَّهِ فَكَأَنَّمَا خَرَّ مِنَ ٱلسَّمَآءِ فَتَخْطَفُهُ ٱلطَّيْرُ أَوْ تَهْوِى بِهِ ٱلرِّيحُ فِى مَكَانٍ سَحِيقٍ ۝

---

529. It is to this proclamation made by Abraham (peace and blessings be upon him) thousands of years ago, before the era of the press, the post, the telegraph, the wireless, the radio, television, and other such paraphernalia of modern publicity and propaganda that mankind has been responding during all these centuries, by performing the pilgrimage in their tens and hundreds of thousands every year!

32. Thus it is. And whosoever venerates the rites of Allah, then it is from the piety of the hearts.

ذَٰلِكَ ۖ وَمَن يُعَظِّمْ شَعَائِرَ اللَّهِ فَإِنَّهَا مِن تَقْوَى الْقُلُوبِ ﴿٣٢﴾

33. In them there are benefits for you for an appointed term, and thereafter the destination is toward the ancient house.

لَكُمْ فِيهَا مَنَافِعُ إِلَىٰ أَجَلٍ مُّسَمًّى ثُمَّ مَحِلُّهَا إِلَى الْبَيْتِ الْعَتِيقِ ﴿٣٣﴾

Section 5

34. And in every community We have appointed a ritual, so that they may mention the name of Allah over the beast cattle with which He has provided them, and your God is One God, so unto Him submit. And bear you glad tidings to the humble,

وَلِكُلِّ أُمَّةٍ جَعَلْنَا مَنسَكًا لِّيَذْكُرُوا اسْمَ اللَّهِ عَلَىٰ مَا رَزَقَهُم مِّن بَهِيمَةِ الْأَنْعَامِ ۗ فَإِلَٰهُكُمْ إِلَٰهٌ وَاحِدٌ فَلَهُ أَسْلِمُوا ۗ وَبَشِّرِ الْمُخْبِتِينَ ﴿٣٤﴾

35. Those, whose hearts, when Allah is mentioned, are filled with awe, and who patiently endure what befalls them, and those who establish the prayer, and spend of what We have provided them.

الَّذِينَ إِذَا ذُكِرَ اللَّهُ وَجِلَتْ قُلُوبُهُمْ وَالصَّابِرِينَ عَلَىٰ مَا أَصَابَهُمْ وَالْمُقِيمِي الصَّلَاةِ وَمِمَّا رَزَقْنَاهُمْ يُنفِقُونَ ﴿٣٥﴾

36. And camels! We have appointed them for you among the land marks of Allah; for you is good in them. So mention over them the name of Allah, standing in rows. Then when they fall down on their sides, eat of them, and feed the contented and the suppliant. Thus We have subjected them to you that haply you may return thanks.

وَالْبُدْنَ جَعَلْنَاهَا لَكُم مِّن شَعَائِرِ اللَّهِ لَكُمْ فِيهَا خَيْرٌ ۖ فَاذْكُرُوا اسْمَ اللَّهِ عَلَيْهَا صَوَافَّ ۖ فَإِذَا وَجَبَتْ جُنُوبُهَا فَكُلُوا مِنْهَا وَأَطْعِمُوا الْقَانِعَ وَالْمُعْتَرَّ ۚ كَذَٰلِكَ سَخَّرْنَاهَا لَكُمْ لَعَلَّكُمْ تَشْكُرُونَ ﴿٣٦﴾

37. It is neither their flesh nor their blood[530] that reaches Allah, but it is piety from you that reaches Him. He has subjected them to you that you may magnify Allah for He has guided you, and bear you glad tidings to the well-doers.

لَن يَنَالَ ٱللَّهَ لُحُومُهَا وَلَا دِمَآؤُهَا وَلَٰكِن يَنَالُهُ ٱلتَّقۡوَىٰ مِنكُمۡ كَذَٰلِكَ سَخَّرَهَا لَكُمۡ لِتُكَبِّرُوا۟ ٱللَّهَ عَلَىٰ مَا هَدَىٰكُمۡ وَبَشِّرِ ٱلۡمُحۡسِنِينَ ۝

38. Verily Allah will repel infidels from those who believe, verily Allah loves not any treacherous, ungrateful person.

إِنَّ ٱللَّهَ يُدَٰفِعُ عَنِ ٱلَّذِينَ ءَامَنُوٓا۟ إِنَّ ٱللَّهَ لَا يُحِبُّ كُلَّ خَوَّانٍ كَفُورٍ ۝

Section 6

39. Permission to fight is given to those who are fought against, because they have been oppressed,[531] and verily Allah is Potent over their succour,

أُذِنَ لِلَّذِينَ يُقَٰتَلُونَ بِأَنَّهُمۡ ظُلِمُوا۟ وَإِنَّ ٱللَّهَ عَلَىٰ نَصۡرِهِمۡ لَقَدِيرٌ ۝

---

530. In other words, sacrifice is not a sort of meal served before God. Such truths, looking self-evident to the Muslim reader, needed a clear and emphatic enunciation in view of the horrible misconceptions and superstitions prevalent among many nations, not excluding the Jews and Christians. For we read in the OT: 'It is the blood that maketh an atonement for the soul' (Le. 17: 11). And in the NT: 'Without shedding of blood is no remission' (He. 9: 22). Among the Babylonians, 'the gods feast in heaven they eat the offering the gods scent the sweet savour; like flies do they gather themselves together about the offerer' (*EBi.* c. 4119). 'Throughout the Semitic field the fundamental idea of sacrifice was that of communion between the god and his worshippers by joint participation in the living flesh and blood of a sacred victim' (Robertson-Smith, *Religion of the Semites*, p. 345).

531. Oppressed for so long by the infidels, and they have borne all those injuries with patience. This is chronologically the first passage in the Qur'ān allowing the Muslims to take up arms in self-defence, revealed only a little before the Prophet's migration to Madina.

40. Those who have been banished from their abodes without justice except because they say: 'Our Lord is Allah.' And were it not for Allah's repelling of some by means of others, cloisters and churches, synagogues and mosques wherein the name of Allah is mentioned much, would have been pulled down. Surely Allah shall succour him who succours Him; surely Allah is the Strong, the Mighty.

اَلَّذِينَ أُخْرِجُوا مِن دِيَٰرِهِم بِغَيْرِ حَقٍّ إِلَّا أَن يَقُولُوا رَبُّنَا ٱللَّهُ وَلَوْلَا دَفْعُ ٱللَّهِ ٱلنَّاسَ بَعْضَهُم بِبَعْضٍ لَّهُدِّمَتْ صَوَٰمِعُ وَبِيَعٌ وَصَلَوَٰتٌ وَمَسَٰجِدُ يُذْكَرُ فِيهَا ٱسْمُ ٱللَّهِ كَثِيرًا وَلَيَنصُرَنَّ ٱللَّهُ مَن يَنصُرُهُ إِنَّ ٱللَّهَ لَقَوِيٌّ عَزِيزٌ ۝

41. Those who, if We establish them in the land, will establish the prayer and pay the poor-rate and command what is reputable and restrain what is disreputable; and unto Allah is the end of all affairs.

ٱلَّذِينَ إِن مَّكَّنَّٰهُمْ فِي ٱلْأَرْضِ أَقَامُوا ٱلصَّلَوٰةَ وَءَاتَوُا ٱلزَّكَوٰةَ وَأَمَرُوا بِٱلْمَعْرُوفِ وَنَهَوْا عَنِ ٱلْمُنكَرِ وَلِلَّهِ عَٰقِبَةُ ٱلْأُمُورِ ۝

42. And if they belie you, surely there have belied before them the people of Noah and the 'Ad, and the Thamud,

وَإِن يُكَذِّبُوكَ فَقَدْ كَذَّبَتْ قَبْلَهُمْ قَوْمُ نُوحٍ وَعَادٌ وَثَمُودُ ۝

43. And the people of Abraham and the people of Lot,

وَقَوْمُ إِبْرَٰهِيمَ وَقَوْمُ لُوطٍ ۝

44. And the inhabitants of Madyan; and belied was Moses. I gave rein to the infidels, then I seized them, so how has been My wrath!

وَأَصْحَٰبُ مَدْيَنَ وَكُذِّبَ مُوسَىٰ فَأَمْلَيْتُ لِلْكَٰفِرِينَ ثُمَّ أَخَذْتُهُمْ فَكَيْفَ كَانَ نَكِيرِ ۝

45. How many a town have We destroyed, while it was a wrong-doer, and it lies outward on its roofs, and how many a well abandoned and how many a castle fortified!

فَكَأَيِّن مِّن قَرْيَةٍ أَهْلَكْنَٰهَا وَهِيَ ظَالِمَةٌ فَهِيَ خَاوِيَةٌ عَلَىٰ عُرُوشِهَا وَبِئْرٍ مُّعَطَّلَةٍ وَقَصْرٍ مَّشِيدٍ ۝

46. Have they not journeyed in the earth, so that there might become unto them hearts to understand with, or ears to hear with? Surely it is not the sights that are blinded, but blinded are the hearts that are in the breasts.

أَفَلَمْ يَسِيرُوا فِي الْأَرْضِ فَتَكُونَ لَهُمْ قُلُوبٌ يَعْقِلُونَ بِهَا أَوْ ءَاذَانٌ يَسْمَعُونَ بِهَا فَإِنَّهَا لَا تَعْمَى الْأَبْصَرُ وَلَكِن تَعْمَى الْقُلُوبُ الَّتِي فِي الصُّدُورِ ۝

47. And they ask you to hasten on the chastisement, whereas Allah shall not fail His promise. And a day with the Lord is a thousand years of what you compute.

وَيَسْتَعْجِلُونَكَ بِالْعَذَابِ وَلَن يُخْلِفَ اللَّهُ وَعْدَهُ وَإِنَّ يَوْمًا عِندَ رَبِّكَ كَأَلْفِ سَنَةٍ مِّمَّا تَعُدُّونَ ۝

48. And how many a town did I give reins to, while it wronged itself? then I seized it. And unto Me is the return.

وَكَأَيِّن مِّن قَرْيَةٍ أَمْلَيْتُ لَهَا وَهِيَ ظَالِمَةٌ ثُمَّ أَخَذْتُهَا وَإِلَى الْمَصِيرُ ۝

Section 7

49. Say: 'O mankind! I am to you only a manifest warner.'

قُلْ يَا أَيُّهَا النَّاسُ إِنَّمَا أَنَا لَكُمْ نَذِيرٌ مُّبِينٌ ۝

50. Then those who believe and work righteous deeds - for them is forgiveness and an honourable provision.

فَالَّذِينَ ءَامَنُوا وَعَمِلُوا الصَّلِحَتِ لَهُم مَّغْفِرَةٌ وَرِزْقٌ كَرِيمٌ ۝

51. And those who endeavour in respect of Our signs to frustrate them - those shall be the inmates of the Flaming Fire.

وَالَّذِينَ سَعَوْا فِي ءَايَتِنَا مُعَجِزِينَ أُوْلَئِكَ أَصْحَبُ الْجَحِيمِ ۝

52. And We have sent before you no Messenger or Prophet but as he recited Satan cast forth suggestions in respect of the recital. Then Allah abolishes what Satan casts forth, and Allah continues His revelations; and Allah is the Knowing, the Wise -

وَمَا أَرْسَلْنَا مِن قَبْلِكَ مِن رَّسُولٍ وَلَا نَبِيٍّ إِلَّا إِذَا تَمَنَّى أَلْقَى الشَّيْطَنُ فِي أُمْنِيَّتِهِ فَيَنسَخُ اللَّهُ مَا يُلْقِي الشَّيْطَنُ ثُمَّ يُحْكِمُ اللَّهُ ءَايَتِهِ وَاللَّهُ عَلِيمٌ حَكِيمٌ ۝

53. That He may make what Satan casts forth a temptation for those in whose hearts is a disease and whose hearts are hardened – and the ungodly are in divergence far – off —

لِّيَجْعَلَ مَا يُلْقِى ٱلشَّيْطَـٰنُ فِتْنَةً لِّلَّذِينَ فِى قُلُوبِهِم مَّرَضٌ وَٱلْقَاسِيَةِ قُلُوبُهُمْ ۗ وَإِنَّ ٱلظَّـٰلِمِينَ لَفِى شِقَاقٍ بَعِيدٍ ﴿٥٣﴾

54. And that those who have been given knowledge may know that it is the truth from your Lord and may believe therein, and so their hearts may submit to it; and verily Allah is the Guide of those who believe in a straight path.

وَلِيَعْلَمَ ٱلَّذِينَ أُوتُوا۟ ٱلْعِلْمَ أَنَّهُ ٱلْحَقُّ مِن رَّبِّكَ فَيُؤْمِنُوا۟ بِهِۦ فَتُخْبِتَ لَهُۥ قُلُوبُهُمْ ۗ وَإِنَّ ٱللَّهَ لَهَادِ ٱلَّذِينَ ءَامَنُوٓا۟ إِلَىٰ صِرَٰطٍ مُّسْتَقِيمٍ ﴿٥٤﴾

55. And who disbelieve will not cease to be in doubt concerning it until the Hour comes upon them on a sudden, or there comes upon them the torment of the Barren Day.

وَلَا يَزَالُ ٱلَّذِينَ كَفَرُوا۟ فِى مِرْيَةٍ مِّنْهُ حَتَّىٰ تَأْتِيَهُمُ ٱلسَّاعَةُ بَغْتَةً أَوْ يَأْتِيَهُمْ عَذَابُ يَوْمٍ عَقِيمٍ ﴿٥٥﴾

56. The dominion on that Day will be Allah's; He shall decide between them. Then those who believed and worked righteous deeds shall be in the Gardens of Delight.

ٱلْمُلْكُ يَوْمَئِذٍ لِّلَّهِ يَحْكُمُ بَيْنَهُمْ ۚ فَٱلَّذِينَ ءَامَنُوا۟ وَعَمِلُوا۟ ٱلصَّـٰلِحَـٰتِ فِى جَنَّـٰتِ ٱلنَّعِيمِ ﴿٥٦﴾

57. And those who disbelieved and belied Our signs – then these! For them shall be an ignominious torment.

وَٱلَّذِينَ كَفَرُوا۟ وَكَذَّبُوا۟ بِـَٔايَـٰتِنَا فَأُو۟لَـٰٓئِكَ لَهُمْ عَذَابٌ مُّهِينٌ ﴿٥٧﴾

Section 8

58. And those who emigrated in the way of Allah, and then they were slain or they died – surely Allah will provide them with a goodly provision; and surely Allah! He is the best Provider.

59. Of a surety He will make them enter an entrance with which they will be well pleased, and Allah is the Knowing, the Forbearing.

60. That is so. And whoever chastises the like of what he was injured and then he has again been oppressed, surely Allah will succour him: verily Allah is the Pardoning, the Forgiving.

61. That is to be because Allah plunges night into day and plunges day into night, and because He is the Hearing, the Beholding.

62. That is because Allah! He is the Truth, and what they call upon besides Him – it is false. Verily Allah! He is the High, the Great.

63. Do you not see that Allah sends down water from the sky, and the earth becomes green. Verily Allah is the Subtle, the Aware.

64. His is whatever is in the heavens and on the earth; and verily Allah! He is the Self-Sufficient, the Praiseworthy.

وَالَّذِينَ هَاجَرُوا۟ فِى سَبِيلِ اللَّهِ ثُمَّ قُتِلُوٓا۟ أَوۡ مَاتُوا۟ لَيَرۡزُقَنَّهُمُ اللَّهُ رِزۡقًا حَسَنًا ۚ وَإِنَّ اللَّهَ لَهُوَ خَيۡرُ الرَّٰزِقِينَ ﴿٥٨﴾

لَيُدۡخِلَنَّهُم مُّدۡخَلًا يَرۡضَوۡنَهُۥ ۗ وَإِنَّ اللَّهَ لَعَلِيمٌ حَلِيمٌ ﴿٥٩﴾

ذَٰلِكَ وَمَنۡ عَاقَبَ بِمِثۡلِ مَا عُوقِبَ بِهِۦ ثُمَّ بُغِىَ عَلَيۡهِ لَيَنصُرَنَّهُ اللَّهُ ۗ إِنَّ اللَّهَ لَعَفُوٌّ غَفُورٌ ﴿٦٠﴾

ذَٰلِكَ بِأَنَّ اللَّهَ يُولِجُ الَّيۡلَ فِى النَّهَارِ وَيُولِجُ النَّهَارَ فِى الَّيۡلِ وَأَنَّ اللَّهَ سَمِيعٌ بَصِيرٌ ﴿٦١﴾

ذَٰلِكَ بِأَنَّ اللَّهَ هُوَ الۡحَقُّ وَأَنَّ مَا يَدۡعُونَ مِن دُونِهِ هُوَ الۡبَٰطِلُ وَأَنَّ اللَّهَ هُوَ الۡعَلِىُّ الۡكَبِيرُ ﴿٦٢﴾

أَلَمۡ تَرَ أَنَّ اللَّهَ أَنزَلَ مِنَ السَّمَآءِ مَآءً فَتُصۡبِحُ الۡأَرۡضُ مُخۡضَرَّةً ۗ إِنَّ اللَّهَ لَطِيفٌ خَبِيرٌ ﴿٦٣﴾

لَّهُۥ مَا فِى السَّمَٰوَٰتِ وَمَا فِى الۡأَرۡضِ ۗ وَإِنَّ اللَّهَ لَهُوَ الۡغَنِىُّ الۡحَمِيدُ ﴿٦٤﴾

Section 9

65. Do you not see that Allah has subjected to you whatsoever is on the earth and the ships running in the sea by His command? And He withholds the heaven that it fall not on the earth save by His leave. Verily Allah is unto mankind, the Clement, the Merciful.

أَلَمْ تَرَ أَنَّ ٱللَّهَ سَخَّرَ لَكُم مَّا فِى ٱلْأَرْضِ وَٱلْفُلْكَ تَجْرِى فِى ٱلْبَحْرِ بِأَمْرِهِ وَيُمْسِكُ ٱلسَّمَآءَ أَن تَقَعَ عَلَى ٱلْأَرْضِ إِلَّا بِإِذْنِهِ إِنَّ ٱللَّهَ بِٱلنَّاسِ لَرَءُوفٌ رَّحِيمٌ ٦٥

66. He it is Who gave you life and will thereafter cause you to die, and will thereafter give you life again, verily man is ingrateful.

وَهُوَ ٱلَّذِىٓ أَحْيَاكُمْ ثُمَّ يُمِيتُكُمْ ثُمَّ يُحْيِيكُمْ إِنَّ ٱلْإِنسَٰنَ لَكَفُورٌ ٦٦

67. For every community We have ordained a ritual which they observe. Let them not therefore contend with you in the affair; and call them you to your Lord; verily you have true guidance.

لِّكُلِّ أُمَّةٍ جَعَلْنَا مَنسَكًا هُمْ نَاسِكُوهُ فَلَا يُنَٰزِعُنَّكَ فِى ٱلْأَمْرِ وَٱدْعُ إِلَىٰ رَبِّكَ إِنَّكَ لَعَلَىٰ هُدًى مُّسْتَقِيمٍ ٦٧

68. And if they dispute with you, say: 'Allah knows best what you do.

وَإِن جَٰدَلُوكَ فَقُلِ ٱللَّهُ أَعْلَمُ بِمَا تَعْمَلُونَ ٦٨

69. Allah will judge between you on the Day of Judgement concerning that wherein you have been differing.

ٱللَّهُ يَحْكُمُ بَيْنَكُمْ يَوْمَ ٱلْقِيَٰمَةِ فِيمَا كُنتُمْ فِيهِ تَخْتَلِفُونَ ٦٩

70. Do you not know that Allah knows whatsoever is in the heavens and the earth? Verily that is in the Book, and verily that is easy for Allah.'

أَلَمْ تَعْلَمْ أَنَّ ٱللَّهَ يَعْلَمُ مَا فِى ٱلسَّمَآءِ وَٱلْأَرْضِ إِنَّ ذَٰلِكَ فِى كِتَٰبٍ إِنَّ ذَٰلِكَ عَلَى ٱللَّهِ يَسِيرٌ ٧٠

71. They worship besides Allah, that for which He has sent down no authority and that of which they have no knowledge, and for the ungodly there shall not be any helper.

72. And when Our manifest verses are rehearsed unto them, you find repugnance on the faces of those who disbelieve; they seem to spring upon them who rehearse Our verses to them. Say: 'Shall I declare to you something more grievous than that – the Fire? Allah has indeed promised to those who disbelieve an evil destination.

Section 10

73. O mankind! A similitude is propounded; listen to it. Verily those whom you call upon beside Allah can by no means create a single fly, even though all of them assembled for that; and if a fly were to snatch away aught from them, they cannot retain it. Feeble indeed are the seeker and the sought!

74. They have not estimated Allah His rightful estimate; verily Allah is the Strong, the Mighty.

75. Allah chooses Messengers from the angels and mankind; Verily Allah is the Hearing, the Beholding.

وَيَعْبُدُونَ مِن دُونِ ٱللَّهِ مَا لَمْ يُنَزِّلْ بِهِۦ سُلْطَـٰنًا وَمَا لَيْسَ لَهُم بِهِۦ عِلْمٌ وَمَا لِلظَّـٰلِمِينَ مِن نَّصِيرٍ ﴿٧١﴾

وَإِذَا تُتْلَىٰ عَلَيْهِمْ ءَايَـٰتُنَا بَيِّنَـٰتٍ تَعْرِفُ فِى وُجُوهِ ٱلَّذِينَ كَفَرُوا۟ ٱلْمُنكَرَ يَكَادُونَ يَسْطُونَ بِٱلَّذِينَ يَتْلُونَ عَلَيْهِمْ ءَايَـٰتِنَا قُلْ أَفَأُنَبِّئُكُم بِشَرٍّ مِّن ذَٰلِكُمُ ٱلنَّارُ وَعَدَهَا ٱللَّهُ ٱلَّذِينَ كَفَرُوا۟ وَبِئْسَ ٱلْمَصِيرُ ﴿٧٢﴾

يَـٰٓأَيُّهَا ٱلنَّاسُ ضُرِبَ مَثَلٌ فَٱسْتَمِعُوا۟ لَهُۥ إِنَّ ٱلَّذِينَ تَدْعُونَ مِن دُونِ ٱللَّهِ لَن يَخْلُقُوا۟ ذُبَابًا وَلَوِ ٱجْتَمَعُوا۟ لَهُۥ وَإِن يَسْلُبْهُمُ ٱلذُّبَابُ شَيْـًٔا لَّا يَسْتَنقِذُوهُ مِنْهُ ضَعُفَ ٱلطَّالِبُ وَٱلْمَطْلُوبُ ﴿٧٣﴾

مَا قَدَرُوا۟ ٱللَّهَ حَقَّ قَدْرِهِۦٓ إِنَّ ٱللَّهَ لَقَوِىٌّ عَزِيزٌ ﴿٧٤﴾

ٱللَّهُ يَصْطَفِى مِنَ ٱلْمَلَـٰٓئِكَةِ رُسُلًا وَمِنَ ٱلنَّاسِ إِنَّ ٱللَّهَ سَمِيعٌ بَصِيرٌ ﴿٧٥﴾

76. He knows what is before them and what is behind them, and to Allah are returned all affairs.

يَعْلَمُ مَا بَيْنَ أَيْدِيهِمْ وَمَا خَلْفَهُمْ وَإِلَى ٱللَّهِ تُرْجَعُ ٱلْأُمُورُ ۝

77. O you who believe! Bow down and prostrate yourselves and worship your Lord, and do good; haply you may thrive.

يَٰٓأَيُّهَا ٱلَّذِينَ ءَامَنُوا ٱرْكَعُوا وَٱسْجُدُوا وَٱعْبُدُوا رَبَّكُمْ وَٱفْعَلُوا ٱلْخَيْرَ لَعَلَّكُمْ تُفْلِحُونَ ۩ ۝

78. And strive hard for Allah as is due unto him hard striving. He has distinguished you, and has not laid upon you any narrowness in religion: the Faith of your father Abraham. He has named you Muslim before, and in this, that the Messenger may be witness against you and that you may be witnesses against mankind. So establish the prayer and pay the poor-rate, and hold fast by prayer to Allah. He is your Patron – an Excellent Patron and an Excellent Helper!

وَجَٰهِدُوا فِي ٱللَّهِ حَقَّ جِهَادِهِۦ هُوَ ٱجْتَبَىٰكُمْ وَمَا جَعَلَ عَلَيْكُمْ فِي ٱلدِّينِ مِنْ حَرَجٍ مِّلَّةَ أَبِيكُمْ إِبْرَٰهِيمَ هُوَ سَمَّىٰكُمُ ٱلْمُسْلِمِينَ مِن قَبْلُ وَفِي هَٰذَا لِيَكُونَ ٱلرَّسُولُ شَهِيدًا عَلَيْكُمْ وَتَكُونُوا شُهَدَآءَ عَلَى ٱلنَّاسِ فَأَقِيمُوا ٱلصَّلَوٰةَ وَءَاتُوا ٱلزَّكَوٰةَ وَٱعْتَصِمُوا بِٱللَّهِ هُوَ مَوْلَىٰكُمْ فَنِعْمَ ٱلْمَوْلَىٰ وَنِعْمَ ٱلنَّصِيرُ ۝

Sūrah 23

al-Mu'minūn

(Makkan, 6 Sections, 118 Verses)

In the name of Allah, the Compassionate, the Merciful.

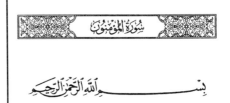

Section 1

1. Blissful are the believers,[532]

2. Those who in their prayers are lowly;

3. And those who turn away from everything vain;

4. And those who are doers for the sake of purification;

5. And those who are guards of their private parts;

6. Save in regard to their wives and those whom their right hands own[533] – so they are not blameworthy.[534]

---

532. This emphasizes the importance of right belief which alone is the spring of right conduct.

533. Such as slave girls, i.e., women taken as captives in war and raised to the status of wives. In the Bible, slavery as an institution is not only recognized but definite laws and ordinances are provided for the purchase, sale and transfer of slaves, both male and female. 'Wherever possible', remarks an English sociologist, 'the man should, of course, have a concubine of some sort' (Ludovici, *The Woman*, p. 172).

534. Regular exercise of sexual functions on the part of men, like all other natural functions, within lawful bounds and in relation to women whose rights and dues they duly observe, is in Islam absolutely above reproach; and wanton abstinence is viewed not as a sign of spirituality but as an aberration. In fact it is the primary purpose of marriage, biologically viewed. Compare and contrast with this the attitude of Christianity which holds that sexual intercourse, even in wedlock, is something of a handicap in the scheme of salvation, and implies that even permitted sexual behaviour is not altogether approved. See Mt. 22: 30, I Cor. 7: 32–34. 'Christianity', writes an English student of sociology, 'being an advocate of eternal life, very logically preaches that sex is to be deplored, to be avoided, and, if possible, negatived. And the Puritan, who may be regarded as the extreme Christian, is notorious for his implacable loathing of sex' (Ludovici, *The Woman*, p. 5).

7. And those who seek beyond that, then it is they who are the transgressors;[535]

فَمَنِ ٱبْتَغَىٰ وَرَآءَ ذَٰلِكَ فَأُوْلَٰٓئِكَ هُمُ ٱلْعَادُونَ ۝

8. And those who are keepers of their trusts and covenant;

وَٱلَّذِينَ هُمْ لِأَمَٰنَٰتِهِمْ وَعَهْدِهِمْ رَٰعُونَ ۝

9. And those who are observant of their prayers:

وَٱلَّذِينَ هُمْ عَلَىٰ صَلَوَٰتِهِمْ يُحَافِظُونَ ۝

10. These! They are indeed the inheritors;

أُوْلَٰٓئِكَ هُمُ ٱلْوَٰرِثُونَ ۝

11. Who shall inherit Paradise; therein they shall abide.

ٱلَّذِينَ يَرِثُونَ ٱلْفِرْدَوْسَ هُمْ فِيهَا خَٰلِدُونَ ۝

12. Assuredly We created man out of an extract of clay.

وَلَقَدْ خَلَقْنَا ٱلْإِنسَٰنَ مِن سُلَٰلَةٍ مِّن طِينٍ ۝

13. Thereafter We made him a sperm in a safe receptacle.

ثُمَّ جَعَلْنَٰهُ نُطْفَةً فِى قَرَارٍ مَّكِينٍ ۝

---

535. Thus every other form of gratifying sexual passion is criminal, and the law of Islam categorically interdicts all forms of extra – marital sexual relations, whether of a normal or abnormal variety, relations which have been so rampant both in ancient and modern nations, often even under the cloak of respectability and approval. Cf. Paul who hints at both male and female excesses: 'Wherefore God also gave them up to uncleanness, through the lusts of their own hearts, to dishonour their own bodies between themselves. For this cause God gave them up unto vile affections; for even their women did change the natural use into that which is against nature. And likewise also the men, leaving the natural use of the woman, burned in their lust toward another' (Ro. 1: 24–27). 'In ancient Rome and Greece homo – sexualism was rampant... Sodomy, pederasty, and tribalism were all practised extensively and openly. Similarly in ancient Egypt, Persia, India and China. The rise of civilisation saw a great extension in the practice and development of sexual vice; and likewise the appearance of new forms and old vices elaborated and given new names. These abnormalities have been restricted to no one country and class' (Forbath (ed.), *Love, Marriage, Jealousy*, p. 110).

14. Thereafter We made the sperm a clot; then We made the clot a lump of flesh; then We made the lump of flesh bones; then We clothed the bones with flesh; thereafter We brought him forth as another creature. Blessed be then Allah, the Best of Creators.

ثُمَّ خَلَقْنَا النُّطْفَةَ عَلَقَةً فَخَلَقْنَا الْعَلَقَةَ مُضْغَةً فَخَلَقْنَا الْمُضْغَةَ عِظَامًا فَكَسَوْنَا الْعِظَامَ لَحْمًا ثُمَّ أَنشَأْنَاهُ خَلْقًا ءَاخَرَ فَتَبَارَكَ اللَّهُ أَحْسَنُ الْخَالِقِينَ ۝

15. Then thereafter you are sure to die.

ثُمَّ إِنَّكُم بَعْدَ ذَلِكَ لَمَيِّتُونَ ۝

16. Then verily on the Day of Judgement you shall be raised up.

ثُمَّ إِنَّكُمْ يَوْمَ الْقِيَامَةِ تُبْعَثُونَ ۝

17. And assuredly We created above you seven paths; and of the creation We have not been neglectful.

وَلَقَدْ خَلَقْنَا فَوْقَكُمْ سَبْعَ طَرَائِقَ وَمَا كُنَّا عَنِ الْخَلْقِ غَافِلِينَ ۝

18. And We sent down from the heaven water in measure, and We command it to settle in the earth; and verily We are able to take it away.

وَأَنزَلْنَا مِنَ السَّمَاءِ مَاءً بِقَدَرٍ فَأَسْكَنَّاهُ فِي الْأَرْضِ وَإِنَّا عَلَى ذَهَابٍ بِهِ لَقَادِرُونَ ۝

19. Then for you, We brought forth with it the gardens of palms and vines; for you therein are many fruits, and thereof you eat;

فَأَنشَأْنَا لَكُم بِهِ جَنَّاتٍ مِّن نَّخِيلٍ وَأَعْنَابٍ لَّكُمْ فِيهَا فَوَاكِهُ كَثِيرَةٌ وَمِنْهَا تَأْكُلُونَ ۝

20. And also a tree that springs forth from the mount of Sinai, that grows oil and is a sauce of the eaters.

وَشَجَرَةً تَخْرُجُ مِن طُورِ سَيْنَاءَ تَنبُتُ بِالدُّهْنِ وَصِبْغٍ لِّلْآكِلِينَ ۝

21. And verily in the cattle there is a lesson for you. We give you to drink of what is in their bellies, and for you in them are many advantages, and of them you eat.

وَإِنَّ لَكُمْ فِي الْأَنْعَامِ لَعِبْرَةً نُّسْقِيكُم مِّمَّا فِي بُطُونِهَا وَلَكُمْ فِيهَا مَنَافِعُ كَثِيرَةٌ وَمِنْهَا تَأْكُلُونَ ۝

22. And you are borne on them and on the ship.

Section 2

وَعَلَيْهَا وَعَلَى ٱلْفُلْكِ تُحْمَلُونَ ۝

23. Assuredly We sent Noah to his people, and he said: 'O my people! Worship Allah: for you there is no god but He; will you then not be God-fearing?'

وَلَقَدْ أَرْسَلْنَا نُوحًا إِلَىٰ قَوْمِهِ فَقَالَ يَٰقَوْمِ
ٱعْبُدُوا۟ ٱللَّهَ مَا لَكُم مِّنْ إِلَٰهٍ غَيْرُهُۥٓ
أَفَلَا تَتَّقُونَ ۝

24. Then the chiefs of them who disbelieved among his people said: 'This is no other human being like you; he seeks to make himself superior to you; and if God had willed He would have sent down angels; we have not heard of this among our ancient fathers.

فَقَالَ ٱلْمَلَؤُا۟ ٱلَّذِينَ كَفَرُوا۟ مِن قَوْمِهِ مَا هَٰذَآ
إِلَّا بَشَرٌ مِّثْلُكُمْ يُرِيدُ أَن يَتَفَضَّلَ عَلَيْكُمْ
وَلَوْ شَآءَ ٱللَّهُ لَأَنزَلَ مَلَٰٓئِكَةً مَّا سَمِعْنَا
بِهَٰذَا فِىٓ ءَابَآئِنَا ٱلْأَوَّلِينَ ۝

25. He is only a man in whom is madness, so wait for him a season.'

إِنْ هُوَ إِلَّا رَجُلٌۢ بِهِۦ جِنَّةٌ فَتَرَبَّصُوا۟
بِهِۦ حَتَّىٰ حِينٍ ۝

26. Noah said: 'Lord! Vindicate me, for they are denying me.'

قَالَ رَبِّ ٱنصُرْنِى بِمَا كَذَّبُونِ ۝

27. Then We revealed unto him saying: 'Build an ark under Our eyes and under Our revelation; then when Our command comes and the oven boils over, make way therein for every pair, two, and your household save him thereof against whom the word has already gone forth, and do not petition Me regarding those who have done wrong; they are certain to be drowned.

فَأَوْحَيْنَآ إِلَيْهِ أَنِ ٱصْنَعِ ٱلْفُلْكَ بِأَعْيُنِنَا
وَوَحْيِنَا فَإِذَا جَآءَ أَمْرُنَا وَفَارَ ٱلتَّنُّورُ
فَٱسْلُكْ فِيهَا مِن كُلِّ زَوْجَيْنِ ٱثْنَيْنِ وَ
أَهْلَكَ إِلَّا مَن سَبَقَ عَلَيْهِ ٱلْقَوْلُ
مِنْهُمْ وَلَا تُخَٰطِبْنِى فِى ٱلَّذِينَ ظَلَمُوٓا۟
إِنَّهُم مُّغْرَقُونَ ۝

28. And when you are settled in the ark, you and those with you, say: "Praise to Allah Who has delivered us from the wrong-doing people.'

فَإِذَا اسْتَوَيْتَ أَنتَ وَمَن مَّعَكَ عَلَى الْفُلْكِ فَقُلِ الْحَمْدُ لِلَّهِ الَّذِي نَجَّانَا مِنَ الْقَوْمِ الظَّالِمِينَ ﴿٢٨﴾

29. And say: 'Lord! Cause me to land at a landing blessed; and You are the best of those who bring to land.'

وَقُل رَّبِّ أَنزِلْنِي مُنزَلًا مُّبَارَكًا وَأَنتَ خَيْرُ الْمُنزِلِينَ ﴿٢٩﴾

30. Verily in that are signs; verily We have ever been testing.

إِنَّ فِي ذَلِكَ لَآيَاتٍ وَإِن كُنَّا لَمُبْتَلِينَ ﴿٣٠﴾

31. Then after them We produced another generation.

ثُمَّ أَنشَأْنَا مِن بَعْدِهِمْ قَرْنًا آخَرِينَ ﴿٣١﴾

32. Then We sent among them a Messenger from among themselves, saying: 'Worship Allah; for you there is no god but He; will you not fear Him?'

فَأَرْسَلْنَا فِيهِمْ رَسُولًا مِّنْهُمْ أَنِ اعْبُدُوا اللَّهَ مَا لَكُم مِّنْ إِلَهٍ غَيْرُهُ أَفَلَا تَتَّقُونَ ﴿٣٢﴾

Section 3

33. The chiefs of them who disbelieved among the people and denied the meeting of the Hereafter and whom We had luxuriated in the life of the world, said: 'This is no other than a human being like you, he eats of what you eat and he drinks of what you drink.

وَقَالَ الْمَلَأُ مِن قَوْمِهِ الَّذِينَ كَفَرُوا وَكَذَّبُوا بِلِقَاءِ الْآخِرَةِ وَأَتْرَفْنَاهُمْ فِي الْحَيَاةِ الدُّنْيَا مَا هَذَا إِلَّا بَشَرٌ مِّثْلُكُمْ يَأْكُلُ مِمَّا تَأْكُلُونَ مِنْهُ وَيَشْرَبُ مِمَّا تَشْرَبُونَ ﴿٣٣﴾

34. And were you to obey a human being like you, you are forthwith to be losers.

وَلَئِنْ أَطَعْتُم بَشَرًا مِّثْلَكُمْ إِنَّكُمْ إِذًا لَّخَاسِرُونَ ﴿٣٤﴾

35. Does he make promise to you that when you have died and have become dust and bones, you are to be brought forth?

أَيَعِدُكُمْ أَنَّكُمْ إِذَا مِتُّمْ وَكُنتُمْ تُرَابًا وَعِظَٰمًا أَنَّكُم مُّخْرَجُونَ ﴿٣٥﴾

36. Away! Away with what you are promised:

هَيْهَاتَ هَيْهَاتَ لِمَا تُوعَدُونَ ﴿٣٦﴾

37. Naught there is but our life of the world; we die and we live, and we are not going to be raised up.

إِنْ هِىَ إِلَّا حَيَاتُنَا ٱلدُّنْيَا نَمُوتُ وَنَحْيَا وَمَا نَحْنُ بِمَبْعُوثِينَ ﴿٣٧﴾

38. He is but a man who has forged a lie against God, and in him we are not going to believe.'

إِنْ هُوَ إِلَّا رَجُلٌ ٱفْتَرَىٰ عَلَى ٱللَّهِ كَذِبًا وَمَا نَحْنُ لَهُ بِمُؤْمِنِينَ ﴿٣٨﴾

39. The Messenger said: 'Lord! Vindicate me, for they are denying me.'

قَالَ رَبِّ ٱنصُرْنِى بِمَا كَذَّبُونِ ﴿٣٩﴾

40. Allah said: 'After a while they will be remorseful.'

قَالَ عَمَّا قَلِيلٍ لَّيُصْبِحُنَّ نَٰدِمِينَ ﴿٤٠﴾

41. Then, a shout laid hold of them in truth, and We made them a refuse; so away with the ungodly people!

فَأَخَذَتْهُمُ ٱلصَّيْحَةُ بِٱلْحَقِّ فَجَعَلْنَٰهُمْ غُثَآءً فَبُعْدًا لِّلْقَوْمِ ٱلظَّٰلِمِينَ ﴿٤١﴾

42. Then after them, We brought forth another generation.

ثُمَّ أَنشَأْنَا مِنۢ بَعْدِهِمْ قُرُونًا ءَاخَرِينَ ﴿٤٢﴾

43. No community can anticipate their term; nor can they lay behind.

مَا تَسْبِقُ مِنْ أُمَّةٍ أَجَلَهَا وَمَا يَسْتَـْٔخِرُونَ ﴿٤٣﴾

44. Then after them We sent Our Messengers successively. But no sooner did there come to a community their Messenger than they belied him. So We made them follow one another, and We made them bywords. So away with a people who do not believe.

ثُمَّ أَرْسَلْنَا رُسُلَنَا تَتْرَا كُلَّ مَا جَآءَ أُمَّةً رَّسُولُهَا كَذَّبُوهُ فَأَتْبَعْنَا بَعْضَهُم بَعْضًا وَجَعَلْنَٰهُمْ أَحَادِيثَ فَبُعْدًا لِّقَوْمٍ لَّا يُؤْمِنُونَ ﴿٤٤﴾

45. Thereafter, We sent Moses and his brother Aaron with Our signs and a manifest authority;

ثُمَّ أَرْسَلْنَا مُوسَىٰ وَأَخَاهُ هَـٰرُونَ بِـَٔايَـٰتِنَا وَسُلْطَـٰنٍ مُّبِينٍ ۝

46. To Pharaoh and his chiefs, but they waxed proud and they were a people self-exalting.

إِلَىٰ فِرْعَوْنَ وَمَلَإِيْهِ فَٱسْتَكْبَرُوا۟ وَكَانُوا۟ قَوْمًا عَالِينَ ۝

47. So they said: 'Shall we believe in two human beings like us, while their community is a subject to us?'

فَقَالُوٓا۟ أَنُؤْمِنُ لِبَشَرَيْنِ مِثْلِنَا وَقَوْمُهُمَا لَنَا عَـٰبِدُونَ ۝

48. Then they belied the two; and so they became of the destroyed.

فَكَذَّبُوهُمَا فَكَانُوا۟ مِنَ ٱلْمُهْلَكِينَ ۝

49. And of a surety We gave Moses the Book that perchance they may be guided.

وَلَقَدْ ءَاتَيْنَا مُوسَى ٱلْكِتَـٰبَ لَعَلَّهُمْ يَهْتَدُونَ ۝

50. And We made the son of Maryam and his mother a sign, and We sheltered them on a height: a quiet abode and running water.

وَجَعَلْنَا ٱبْنَ مَرْيَمَ وَأُمَّهُۥ ءَايَةً وَءَاوَيْنَـٰهُمَآ إِلَىٰ رَبْوَةٍ ذَاتِ قَرَارٍ وَمَعِينٍ ۝

Section 4

51. O you Messengers! Eat of the good things[536] and work righteous deeds, I am the knower of what you do.

يَـٰٓأَيُّهَا ٱلرُّسُلُ كُلُوا۟ مِنَ ٱلطَّيِّبَـٰتِ وَٱعْمَلُوا۟ صَـٰلِحًا إِنِّى بِمَا تَعْمَلُونَ عَلِيمٌ ۝

52. And verily this religion of yours is one religion, and I am your Lord; so fear Me.

وَإِنَّ هَـٰذِهِۦٓ أُمَّتُكُمْ أُمَّةً وَٰحِدَةً وَأَنَا۠ رَبُّكُمْ فَٱتَّقُونِ ۝

---

536. Both you and your peoples. God's Messengership is not at all identical with asceticism. The passage may well imply condemnation of the abstemious practices of Christian monks.

53. Then they cut their affair among them in regard to the Scripture, each sect rejoicing in what is with it.

فَتَقَطَّعُوٓاْ أَمْرَهُم بَيْنَهُمْ زُبُرًا كُلُّ حِزْبٍۭ بِمَا لَدَيْهِمْ فَرِحُونَ ﴿٥٣﴾

54. So leave them in their bewilderment for a season.

فَذَرْهُمْ فِى غَمْرَتِهِمْ حَتَّىٰ حِينٍ ﴿٥٤﴾

55. Do they imagine that in the wealth and children with which We enlarge them,

أَيَحْسَبُونَ أَنَّمَا نُمِدُّهُم بِهِۦ مِن مَّالٍ وَبَنِينَ ﴿٥٥﴾

56. We are hastening them on to good things? Aye! They perceive not.

نُسَارِعُ لَهُمْ فِى الْخَيْرَٰتِ بَل لَّا يَشْعُرُونَ ﴿٥٦﴾

57. Verily those who go in awe for fear of their Lord;

إِنَّ الَّذِينَ هُم مِّنْ خَشْيَةِ رَبِّهِم مُّشْفِقُونَ ﴿٥٧﴾

58. And those who believe in the signs of their Lord;

وَالَّذِينَ هُم بِـَٔايَٰتِ رَبِّهِمْ يُؤْمِنُونَ ﴿٥٨﴾

59. And those who do not join anyone with their Lord;

وَالَّذِينَ هُم بِرَبِّهِمْ لَا يُشْرِكُونَ ﴿٥٩﴾

60. And those who give whatsoever they give while their hearts are anxious that to their Lord they are to be returned.[537]

وَالَّذِينَ يُؤْتُونَ مَآ ءَاتَوا۟ وَّقُلُوبُهُمْ وَجِلَةٌ أَنَّهُمْ إِلَىٰ رَبِّهِمْ رَٰجِعُونَ ﴿٦٠﴾

61. These are hastening on to good, and they are foremost therein.

أُو۟لَٰٓئِكَ يُسَٰرِعُونَ فِى الْخَيْرَٰتِ وَهُمْ لَهَا سَٰبِقُونَ ﴿٦١﴾

62. We do not tax any soul except according to its capacity and with Us is a Book speaking with truth, and wronged they will be not.

وَلَا نُكَلِّفُ نَفْسًا إِلَّا وُسْعَهَا وَلَدَيْنَا كِتَٰبٌ يَنطِقُ بِالْحَقِّ وَهُمْ لَا يُظْلَمُونَ ﴿٦٢﴾

---

537. Filled with self-deprecation a good and devout Muslim is never boastful or presumptuous, and is always skeptical of his good deeds – whether or not they shall be found worthy of acceptance on Judgement Day. Hopeful always of God's mercy, he is never sure of his own virtues.

63. Aye! Their hearts are in bewilderment in respect of this, and they have, besides that, works of which they are the workers,

بَلْ قُلُوبُهُمْ فِى غَمْرَةٍ مِّنْ هَٰذَا وَلَهُمْ أَعْمَٰلٌ مِّن دُونِ ذَٰلِكَ هُمْ لَهَا عَٰمِلُونَ ۝٦٣

64. Until when We lay hold of the luxurious ones of them with the chastisement, and lo! They are imploring!

حَتَّىٰ إِذَآ أَخَذْنَا مُتْرَفِيهِم بِالْعَذَابِ إِذَا هُمْ يَجْـَٔرُونَ ۝٦٤

65. Implore not today, verily you are not to be succoured against Us.

لَا تَجْـَٔرُوا الْيَوْمَ إِنَّكُم مِّنَّا لَا تُنصَرُونَ ۝٦٥

66. Surely My signs have been rehearsed to you, and you were wont to draw back upon your heels;

قَدْ كَانَتْ ءَايَٰتِى تُتْلَىٰ عَلَيْكُمْ فَكُنتُمْ عَلَىٰ أَعْقَٰبِكُمْ تَنكِصُونَ ۝٦٦

67. Stiff-necked, discoursing of it by night, reviling.

مُسْتَكْبِرِينَ بِهِۦ سَٰمِرًا تَهْجُرُونَ ۝٦٧

68. Did they never ponder over the Word? Or did there come to them what had not come to their forefathers?

أَفَلَمْ يَدَّبَّرُوا الْقَوْلَ أَمْ جَآءَهُم مَّا لَمْ يَأْتِ ءَابَآءَهُمُ الْأَوَّلِينَ ۝٦٨

69. Or, is it that they did not recognize their Divine Messenger, so they became his deniers?

أَمْ لَمْ يَعْرِفُوا۟ رَسُولَهُمْ فَهُمْ لَهُۥ مُنكِرُونَ ۝٦٩

70. Or, do they say: 'In him is madness?' Aye! He brought them the truth, yet most of them are averse to the truth.

أَمْ يَقُولُونَ بِهِۦ جِنَّةٌۢ بَلْ جَآءَهُم بِالْحَقِّ وَأَكْثَرُهُمْ لِلْحَقِّ كَٰرِهُونَ ۝٧٠

71. And were the truth to follow their desires, the heavens and the earth and whatsoever is therein would have been corrupted. Aye! We have come to them with their admonition; so it is from their admonition that they turn away.

وَلَوِ اتَّبَعَ الْحَقُّ أَهْوَآءَهُمْ لَفَسَدَتِ السَّمَٰوَٰتُ وَالْأَرْضُ وَمَن فِيهِنَّ بَلْ أَتَيْنَٰهُم بِذِكْرِهِمْ فَهُمْ عَن ذِكْرِهِم مُّعْرِضُونَ ۝٧١

72. Or, is it that you ask of them any maintenance? Better is the maintenance of your Lord, and He is the best of Providers.

أَمْ تَسْئَلُهُمْ خَرْجًا فَخَرَاجُ رَبِّكَ خَيْرٌ وَهُوَ خَيْرُ الرَّازِقِينَ ۞

73. Verily you! Call them to a path straight.

وَإِنَّكَ لَتَدْعُوهُمْ إِلَىٰ صِرَٰطٍ مُّسْتَقِيمٍ ۞

74. And verily those who do not believe in the Hereafter are deviating from the path.

وَإِنَّ الَّذِينَ لَا يُؤْمِنُونَ بِالْآخِرَةِ عَنِ الصِّرَٰطِ لَنَٰكِبُونَ ۞

75. And though We may have mercy on them and may remove whatsoever is of hurt with them, surely they would persist in their exorbitance, wandering perplexed.

وَلَوْ رَحِمْنَٰهُمْ وَكَشَفْنَا مَا بِهِم مِّن ضُرٍّ لَّلَجُّوا فِي طُغْيَٰنِهِمْ يَعْمَهُونَ ۞

76. And assuredly We seized them with chastisement, but they did not humble themselves to their Lord, nor did they entreat,

وَلَقَدْ أَخَذْنَٰهُم بِالْعَذَابِ فَمَا اسْتَكَانُوا لِرَبِّهِمْ وَمَا يَتَضَرَّعُونَ ۞

77. Until when We shall open upon them a portal of severe torment, and lo! They at that are despairing.

حَتَّىٰ إِذَا فَتَحْنَا عَلَيْهِم بَابًا ذَا عَذَابٍ شَدِيدٍ إِذَا هُمْ فِيهِ مُبْلِسُونَ ۞

Section 5

78. And He it is Who brought forth for you hearing and sights and hearts; little thanks you return!

وَهُوَ الَّذِي أَنشَأَ لَكُمُ السَّمْعَ وَالْأَبْصَٰرَ وَالْأَفْئِدَةَ قَلِيلًا مَّا تَشْكُرُونَ ۞

79. And He it is Who spread you on the earth and to Him you will be gathered.

وَهُوَ الَّذِي ذَرَأَكُمْ فِي الْأَرْضِ وَإِلَيْهِ تُحْشَرُونَ ۞

80. And He it is Who gives life and cause to die; and His is the alternation of night and day; will you not then reflect?

وَهُوَ الَّذِیۡ یُحۡیٖ وَیُمِیۡتُ وَلَهُ اخۡتِلَافُ الَّیۡلِ وَالنَّهَارِ اَفَلَا تَعۡقِلُوۡنَ ۞

81. Aye! They say the like of what the ancients said.

بَلۡ قَالُوۡا مِثۡلَ مَا قَالَ الۡاَوَّلُوۡنَ ۞

82. They say: 'When we are dead and have become dust and bones, shall we be raised up indeed?

قَالُوۡۤا ءَاِذَا مِتۡنَا وَكُنَّا تُرَابًا وَّعِظَامًا ءَاِنَّا لَمَبۡعُوۡثُوۡنَ ۞

83. Certainly this we have been promised, we and our fathers, before; but nothing is this but the fables of the ancients.'

لَقَدۡ وُعِدۡنَا نَحۡنُ وَاٰبَآؤُنَا هٰذَا مِنۡ قَبۡلُ اِنۡ هٰذَاۤ اِلَّاۤ اَسَاطِیۡرُ الۡاَوَّلِیۡنَ ۞

84. Say: 'Whose is the earth and whosoever is therein, if you know?'

قُلۡ لِّمَنِ الۡاَرۡضُ وَمَنۡ فِیۡهَاۤ اِنۡ كُنۡتُمۡ تَعۡلَمُوۡنَ ۞

85. They will surely say: 'Allah's.' Say: 'Will you not then heed?'

سَیَقُوۡلُوۡنَ لِلّٰهِ قُلۡ اَفَلَا تَذَكَّرُوۡنَ ۞

86. Say: 'Who is the Lord of the seven heavens and Lord of the mighty throne?'

قُلۡ مَنۡ رَّبُّ السَّمٰوٰتِ السَّبۡعِ وَرَبُّ الۡعَرۡشِ الۡعَظِیۡمِ ۞

87. They will certainly say: 'Allah.' Say: 'Will you not then be God-fearing?'

سَیَقُوۡلُوۡنَ لِلّٰهِ قُلۡ اَفَلَا تَتَّقُوۡنَ ۞

88. Say: 'In whose hand is the sovereignty of everything and who protects all, but against whom there is no protector, if you know?'

قُلۡ مَنۡ بِیَدِهٖ مَلَكُوۡتُ كُلِّ شَیۡءٍ وَّهُوَ یُجِیۡرُ وَلَا یُجَارُ عَلَیۡهِ اِنۡ كُنۡتُمۡ تَعۡلَمُوۡنَ ۞

89. They will certainly say: 'Allah's.' Say: 'How then are you turned away?'

سَیَقُوۡلُوۡنَ لِلّٰهِ قُلۡ فَاَنّٰی تُسۡحَرُوۡنَ ۞

90. Aye! We have brought them the truth, and verily they are the liars.

بَلْ أَتَيْنٰهُمْ بِالْحَقِّ وَ إِنَّهُمْ لَكٰذِبُوْنَ ۝

91. Allah has not taken to Himself any son, and there is no god along with Him; else each god would have gone off with what he had created and one of them would have exalted himself above others. Hallowed be Allah above what they describe.

مَا اتَّخَذَ اللهُ مِنْ وَلَدٍ وَّمَا كَانَ مَعَهٗ مِنْ إِلٰهٍ إِذًا لَّذَهَبَ كُلُّ إِلٰهٍ بِمَا خَلَقَ وَلَعَلَا بَعْضُهُمْ عَلٰى بَعْضٍ سُبْحٰنَ اللهِ عَمَّا يَصِفُوْنَ ۝

92. Knower of the Unseen and the seen, Exalted is He above what they associate.

عٰلِمِ الْغَيْبِ وَالشَّهٰدَةِ فَتَعٰلٰى عَمَّا يُشْرِكُوْنَ ۝

Section 6

93. Say: 'Lord! If You will show me that with which they are threatened;

قُلْ رَّبِّ إِمَّا تُرِيَنِّي مَا يُوْعَدُوْنَ ۝

94. Lord! Then place me not among the wrong-doing people.'

رَبِّ فَلَا تَجْعَلْنِي فِي الْقَوْمِ الظّٰلِمِيْنَ ۝

95. And surely We are able to show you that with which We threaten them.

وَإِنَّا عَلٰى أَنْ نُّرِيَكَ مَا نَعِدُهُمْ لَقٰدِرُوْنَ ۝

96. Repel you the evil with what is the best; We are the best Knower of what they utter.

اِدْفَعْ بِالَّتِي هِيَ أَحْسَنُ السَّيِّئَةَ نَحْنُ أَعْلَمُ بِمَا يَصِفُوْنَ ۝

97. And say: 'Lord! I seek refuge with You from the whisperings of the devils;

وَقُلْ رَّبِّ أَعُوْذُ بِكَ مِنْ هَمَزٰتِ الشَّيٰطِيْنِ ۝

98. And Lord! I seek refuge with You lest they may attend me.'

وَأَعُوْذُ بِكَ رَبِّ أَنْ يَّحْضُرُوْنِ ۝

99. It ceases not until when death comes to one of them and he says: 'Lord! Send me back;

حَتَّىٰٓ إِذَا جَآءَ أَحَدَهُمُ ٱلْمَوْتُ قَالَ رَبِّ ٱرْجِعُونِ ۝

100. That I may work righteously in what I have left'. By no means it is but a word he utters, and in front of them is a barrier[538] until the Day when they shall be raised.

لَعَلِّىٓ أَعْمَلُ صَٰلِحًا فِيمَا تَرَكْتُ كَلَّآ إِنَّهَا كَلِمَةٌ هُوَ قَآئِلُهَا وَمِن وَرَآئِهِم بَرْزَخٌ إِلَىٰ يَوْمِ يُبْعَثُونَ ۝

101. Then when the Trumpet is blown, there will be no kinship among them that Day, nor will they be able to ask of each other.

فَإِذَا نُفِخَ فِى ٱلصُّورِ فَلَآ أَنسَابَ بَيْنَهُمْ يَوْمَئِذٍ وَلَا يَتَسَآءَلُونَ ۝

102. Then he whose scales will be heavy – these! They are the blissful ones.

فَمَن ثَقُلَتْ مَوَٰزِينُهُۥ فَأُوْلَٰٓئِكَ هُمُ ٱلْمُفْلِحُونَ ۝

103. And he whose scales will be light – these are they who have hurt themselves; in Hell they shall abide.

وَمَنْ خَفَّتْ مَوَٰزِينُهُۥ فَأُوْلَٰٓئِكَ ٱلَّذِينَ خَسِرُوٓاْ أَنفُسَهُمْ فِى جَهَنَّمَ خَٰلِدُونَ ۝

104. Their faces the Fire shall scorch, and therein they shall be grinning.

تَلْفَحُ وُجُوهَهُمُ ٱلنَّارُ وَهُمْ فِيهَا كَٰلِحُونَ ۝

105. Have not My revelations been rehearsed to you, and them you have been belying?

أَلَمْ تَكُنْ ءَايَٰتِى تُتْلَىٰ عَلَيْكُمْ فَكُنتُم بِهَا تُكَذِّبُونَ ۝

---

538. Literally 'a thing that intervenes between any two things', in the Qur'anic sense, is 'the interval between the present life and that which is to come, from the period of death to the resurrection, upon which he who dies enters' (LL.). It involves 'a state of consciousness characterised by a change in the ego's attitude towards time and space a state in which the ego catches a glimpse of fresh aspects of Reality, and prepares himself of adjustment to these aspects' (Iqbal, *Reconstruction of Religious Thought in Islam*, pp. 166–167).

106. They will say: 'Our Lord! Our wretchedness overcame us and We have been an erring people.

قَالُوْا رَبَّنَا غَلَبَتْ عَلَيْنَا شِقْوَتُنَا وَكُنَّا قَوْمًا ضَآلِّيْنَ ۝

107. O Our Lord! Take us forth from it; then if we revert, we shall be wrong-doers indeed.'

رَبَّنَا أَخْرِجْنَا مِنْهَا فَإِنْ عُدْنَا فَإِنَّا ظَـٰلِمُوْنَ ۝

108. Allah will say: 'Slink away in it, and speak not to Me.'

قَالَ اخْسَـُٔوْا فِيْهَا وَلَا تُكَلِّمُوْنِ ۝

109. Verily there was a band of My bondsmen who said: 'Our Lord! We have believed, forgive us and have mercy upon us, and You are the best of the merciful ones.'

إِنَّهُ كَانَ فَرِيْقٌ مِّنْ عِبَادِيْ يَقُوْلُوْنَ رَبَّنَا ءَامَنَّا فَاغْفِرْ لَنَا وَارْحَمْنَا وَأَنْتَ خَيْرُ الرَّاحِمِيْنَ ۝

110. Then you took them mockingly, so that they caused you to forget remembrance of Me, and at them you were wont to laugh .

فَاتَّخَذْتُمُوْهُمْ سِخْرِيًّا حَتَّىٰ أَنْسَوْكُمْ ذِكْرِيْ وَ كُنْتُمْ مِّنْهُمْ تَضْحَكُوْنَ ۝

111. Verily I have recompensed them today for they bore patiently; verily they are the achievers.

إِنِّيْ جَزَيْتُهُمُ الْيَوْمَ بِمَا صَبَرُوْا أَنَّهُمْ هُمُ الْفَآئِزُوْنَ ۝

112. Allah will say: 'How long did you tarry on the earth in numbers of years?'

قَالَ كَمْ لَبِثْتُمْ فِي الْأَرْضِ عَدَدَ سِنِيْنَ ۝

113. They will say: 'We tarried a day or part of a day; question them who keep count.'

قَالُوْا لَبِثْنَا يَوْمًا أَوْ بَعْضَ يَوْمٍ فَسْئَلِ الْعَآدِّيْنَ ۝

114. Allah will say: 'You tarried a little indeed would that you had known that in your life-time.

قَالَ إِنْ لَبِثْتُمْ إِلَّا قَلِيْلًا لَّوْ أَنَّكُمْ كُنْتُمْ تَعْلَمُوْنَ ۝

115. 'Do you consider that We have created you in vain and that to Us you are not to return?'[539]

أَفَحَسِبْتُمْ أَنَّمَا خَلَقْنَكُمْ عَبَثًا وَأَنَّكُمْ إِلَيْنَا لَا تُرْجَعُونَ ﴿١١٥﴾

116. So exalted be Allah, the True King! There is no god but He! Lord Of the honoured throne.

فَتَعَلَى اللَّهُ الْمَلِكُ الْحَقُّ لَا إِلَهَ إِلَّا هُوَ رَبُّ الْعَرْشِ الْكَرِيمِ ﴿١١٦﴾

117. And whosoever calls along with Allah unto another god, of whom he has no proof, then his reckoning is only with his Lord; surely the infidels will not thrive.

وَمَن يَدْعُ مَعَ اللَّهِ إِلَهًا ءَاخَرَ لَا بُرْهَنَ لَهُ بِهِ فَإِنَّمَا حِسَابُهُ عِندَ رَبِّهِ إِنَّهُ لَا يُفْلِحُ الْكَفِرُونَ ﴿١١٧﴾

118. And say: 'Lord! Forgive and have mercy, You are the best of the merciful ones.'

وَقُل رَّبِّ اغْفِرْ وَارْحَمْ وَأَنتَ خَيْرُ الرَّحِمِينَ ﴿١١٨﴾

539. To account for yourselves. This contradicts both the Christian doctrine of annihilation and the Buddhist notion of extinction. The end of every human soul is a return to God for final reckoning, not a deliverance from all existence, or a termination of all consciousness, like the blowing out of the flame of a lamp.

Sūrah 24

al-Nūr

(Madinan, 9 Sections, 64 Verses)

In the name of Allah, the Compassionate, the Merciful.

Section 1

1. This is a *Sūrah* We have sent down and which We have ordained, and therein We have sent down revelations manifest, that haply you may be admonished.

2. The adulteress and the adulterer:[540] scourge each of the two with a hundred stripes. And let not tenderness in the law of

---

540. The Arabic word *Zinā* denotes sexual intercourse between any man and woman, whether married or not, who do not stand to each other in the relation of husband and wife, and, as such, has no single word equivalent in the English language. It includes both adultery (i.e., the illicit sexual intercourse of two persons either of whom is married to a third person) and fornication (i.e., the illicit sexual intercourse of unmarried persons). Islam condemns *Zinā* in all its forms outright. Islamic jurisprudence, in this respect, stands 'in splendid isolation from the laws of many other nations'. Among the Greeks, and also in early Rome, illicit sexual intercourse was no crime at all unless a married woman was involved. Even 'in Great Britain it was reckoned a spiritual offence, that is cognizable by the spiritual courts only. Common law took no further notice of it than to allow the party aggrieved an action of damages' (*EBr.* I. p. 234).

Allah[541] take hold of you in regard to the two, if you have come to believe in Allah and the Last Day. And let a band of the believers witness this chastisement.[542]

إِن كُنتُمْ تُؤْمِنُونَ بِٱللَّهِ وَٱلْيَوْمِ ٱلْآخِرِ ۗ وَلْيَشْهَدْ عَذَابَهُمَا طَآئِفَةٌ مِّنَ ٱلْمُؤْمِنِينَ ﴿٢﴾

3. The adulterer weds not but an adulteress or an associatoress: and the adulteress! – None weds her save an adulterer or an associator; and that is forbidden to the believers.

ٱلزَّانِى لَا يَنكِحُ إِلَّا زَانِيَةً أَوْ مُشْرِكَةً وَٱلزَّانِيَةُ لَا يَنكِحُهَآ إِلَّا زَانٍ أَوْ مُشْرِكٌ ۚ وَحُرِّمَ ذَٰلِكَ عَلَى ٱلْمُؤْمِنِينَ ﴿٣﴾

4. And those who accuse clean women and then bring not four eye witnesses,[543] scourge them with eighty stripes[544] and accept not their testimony for ever. And these! They are the transgressors,

وَٱلَّذِينَ يَرْمُونَ ٱلْمُحْصَنَاتِ ثُمَّ لَمْ يَأْتُوا۟ بِأَرْبَعَةِ شُهَدَآءَ فَٱجْلِدُوهُمْ ثَمَانِينَ جَلْدَةً وَلَا تَقْبَلُوا۟ لَهُمْ شَهَادَةً أَبَدًا ۚ وَأُو۟لَٰٓئِكَ هُمُ ٱلْفَاسِقُونَ ﴿٤﴾

5. Excepting those who shall repent thereafter and make amends. Verily Allah is the Forgiving, the Merciful.

إِلَّا ٱلَّذِينَ تَابُوا۟ مِنۢ بَعْدِ ذَٰلِكَ وَأَصْلَحُوا۟ فَإِنَّ ٱللَّهَ غَفُورٌ رَّحِيمٌ ﴿٥﴾

541. A sentiment of tenderness for such culprits is utterly misplaced; and the accumulated experience of mankind is that temperate and calculated severity on such occasions is most effective. Tenderness for the criminal and misplaced clemency has been the besetting sin of the Jews in rabbinical times. 'Capital punishment was, however, of such rare occurrence as to be practically abrogated. In fact many a judge declared openly for its abolition, and a court which had pronounced one sentence of death in seven years was called the court of murderers' (Polano, *The Talmudic Selections*, p. 331).

542. The execution, in order to be a deterrent for others and more humiliating for the offenders, must take place in public, not in private, and they should justify and gratify their natural desire for vengeance upon such criminals.

543. Eye-witnesses to substantiate the charge. Note that the number of witnesses where the honour of a believing woman is involved is double that of the usual number required.

544. Notice the very serious view the Qur'ān takes of slandering chaste women.

6. And as for those who accuse their wives and there are not witnesses for them except themselves, the testimony of one of them shall be to aver four times by Allah that he is of the truthful.

وَٱلَّذِينَ يَرْمُونَ أَزْوَٰجَهُمْ وَلَمْ يَكُن لَّهُمْ شُهَدَآءُ إِلَّا أَنفُسُهُمْ فَشَهَٰدَةُ أَحَدِهِمْ أَرْبَعُ شَهَٰدَٰتٍ بِٱللَّهِ إِنَّهُۥ لَمِنَ ٱلصَّٰدِقِينَ ٦

7. And for the fifth time that the curse of Allah be upon him, if he be of the liars.

وَٱلْخَٰمِسَةُ أَنَّ لَعْنَتَ ٱللَّهِ عَلَيْهِ إِن كَانَ مِنَ ٱلْكَٰذِبِينَ ٧

8. And it will avert the chastisement from her if she swears by Allah four times that he is of the liars;

وَيَدْرَؤُاْ عَنْهَا ٱلْعَذَابَ أَن تَشْهَدَ أَرْبَعَ شَهَٰدَٰتٍ بِٱللَّهِ إِنَّهُۥ لَمِنَ ٱلْكَٰذِبِينَ ٨

9. And for the fifth time that Allah's wrath be upon her if he is of the truth-tellers.

وَٱلْخَٰمِسَةَ أَنَّ غَضَبَ ٱللَّهِ عَلَيْهَآ إِن كَانَ مِنَ ٱلصَّٰدِقِينَ ٩

10. And had it not been for the grace of Allah and His mercy upon you, and that Allah is the Relenting, the Wise, you had been lost.

وَلَوْلَا فَضْلُ ٱللَّهِ عَلَيْكُمْ وَرَحْمَتُهُۥ وَأَنَّ ٱللَّهَ تَوَّابٌ حَكِيمٌ ١٠

Section 2

11. Verily those who brought forward the calumny[545] were a small band among you. Do not consider it an evil for you; nay, it was good for you. Unto everyone of them shall be what he has

إِنَّ ٱلَّذِينَ جَآءُو بِٱلْإِفْكِ عُصْبَةٌ مِّنكُمْ لَا تَحْسَبُوهُ شَرًّا لَّكُم بَلْ هُوَ خَيْرٌ لَّكُمْ لِكُلِّ ٱمْرِئٍ مِّنْهُم مَّا ٱكْتَسَبَ مِنَ ٱلْإِثْمِ

---

545. This against 'Āishah, the Prophet's wife. Literally *ifk* is a lie or falsehood. The verse alludes to a particular incident in 'Āishah's life. In the sixth year of the Hijri era, when the Prophet was returning from the campaign against the Banū Muṣṭaliq,

she was travelling, as usual, in a litter borne on a camel. At one of the halts, not very far from Madina, she dismounted and withdrew from the camp in order to perform her ablutions. When she came back to her litter she discovered that she had forgotten her necklace of Yemen shells, and went back to fetch it, leaving the curtains of the chair closed. The march was in the meantime ordered. Her retinue, seeing the curtain closed, concluded that she was in the chair. They loaded the litter on the camel and started on their journey. She herself says that her weight was next to nothing. Finding herself stranded, she could do nothing but to sit on the ground and to wait until someone should come to fetch her. And there she was found by Ṣafwān ibn al-Muʿaṭṭal whose duty it was to follow the caravan. He let her mount his camel with all the respect and decorum due to the Prophet's wife, turning his face away so as not even to have a look at her, and himself, on foot, led the camel by the halter. This very ordinary and innocent episode furnished some malicious enemies of Islam – the notorious hypocrites of Madina – with an opportunity to raise a scandalous storm.

earned of the sin, and he among them who took the bulk of it, for him shall be a mighty torment.[546]

وَٱلَّذِى تَوَلَّىٰ كِبۡرَهُۥ مِنۡهُمۡ لَهُۥ عَذَابٌ عَظِيمٞ ۝١١

12. Why, therefore did not the faithful men and women, when you heard the slander, think well of their own people and say: 'This is an evident calumny?'

لَّوۡلَآ إِذۡ سَمِعۡتُمُوهُ ظَنَّ ٱلۡمُؤۡمِنُونَ وَٱلۡمُؤۡمِنَٰتُ بِأَنفُسِهِمۡ خَيۡرٗا وَقَالُوا۟ هَٰذَآ إِفۡكٞ مُّبِينٞ ۝١٢

13. Why did not they produce four witnesses thereof? And since they could not produce four witnesses, those! With Allah, they are the very liars!

لَّوۡلَا جَآءُو عَلَيۡهِ بِأَرۡبَعَةِ شُهَدَآءَ فَإِذۡ لَمۡ يَأۡتُوا۟ بِٱلشُّهَدَآءِ فَأُو۟لَٰٓئِكَ عِندَ ٱللَّهِ هُمُ ٱلۡكَٰذِبُونَ ۝١٣

14. Had there not been Allah's grace upon you and His mercy in the world and the Hereafter, surely there would have visited you a severe chastisement for that wherein you had rushed,

وَلَوۡلَا فَضۡلُ ٱللَّهِ عَلَيۡكُمۡ وَرَحۡمَتُهُۥ فِى ٱلدُّنۡيَا وَٱلۡأٓخِرَةِ لَمَسَّكُمۡ فِى مَآ أَفَضۡتُمۡ فِيهِ عَذَابٌ عَظِيمٌ ۝١٤

15. When you were spreading it with your tongues and saying with your mouths that of which you had no knowledge, you consider it light but with Allah it was great.

إِذۡ تَلَقَّوۡنَهُۥ بِأَلۡسِنَتِكُمۡ وَتَقُولُونَ بِأَفۡوَاهِكُم مَّا لَيۡسَ لَكُم بِهِۦ عِلۡمٞ وَتَحۡسَبُونَهُۥ هَيِّنٗا وَهُوَ عِندَ ٱللَّهِ عَظِيمٞ ۝١٥

16. And why, when you heard it, did you not say: 'It is not for us to speak thereof, hallowed be You!, that is a slander mighty?'

وَلَوۡلَآ إِذۡ سَمِعۡتُمُوهُ قُلۡتُم مَّا يَكُونُ لَنَآ أَن نَّتَكَلَّمَ بِهَٰذَا سُبۡحَٰنَكَ هَٰذَا بُهۡتَٰنٌ عَظِيمٞ ۝١٦

17. Allah exhorts you not to repeat the like of it, if you are believers indeed.

يَعِظُكُمُ ٱللَّهُ أَن تَعُودُوا۟ لِمِثۡلِهِۦٓ أَبَدًا إِن كُنتُم مُّؤۡمِنِينَ ۝١٧

---

546. The allusion is to 'Abdullāh ibn Ubayy, the notorious leader of the Madina hypocrites and the originator of this wicked slander.

18. And Allah expounds to you His revelations; and Allah is the Knowing, the Wise.

وَيُبَيِّنُ ٱللَّهُ لَكُمُ ٱلْآيَٰتِ ۚ وَٱللَّهُ عَلِيمٌ حَكِيمٌ ۝

19. Verily those who desire that indecency should be propagated among the faithful for them shall be an afflictive chastisement in the world and the Hereafter.[547] Allah knows and you know not.

إِنَّ ٱلَّذِينَ يُحِبُّونَ أَن تَشِيعَ ٱلْفَٰحِشَةُ فِى ٱلَّذِينَ ءَامَنُوا۟ لَهُمْ عَذَابٌ أَلِيمٌ فِى ٱلدُّنْيَا وَٱلْآخِرَةِ ۚ وَٱللَّهُ يَعْلَمُ وَأَنتُمْ لَا تَعْلَمُونَ ۝

20. And had there not been Allah's grace upon you and His mercy, and that Allah was the Tender and the Merciful, you could have perished.

وَلَوْلَا فَضْلُ ٱللَّهِ عَلَيْكُمْ وَرَحْمَتُهُۥ وَأَنَّ ٱللَّهَ رَءُوفٌ رَّحِيمٌ ۝

Section 3

21. O you who believe! Do not follow the footsteps of Satan. And whoever follows his footsteps, then Satan only bids to indecency and abomination. And had there not been Allah's grace upon you and His mercy, not one of you could have ever been cleansed, but Allah cleanses whomsoever He will. And Allah is the Hearing, the Knowing.

يَٰٓأَيُّهَا ٱلَّذِينَ ءَامَنُوا۟ لَا تَتَّبِعُوا۟ خُطُوَٰتِ ٱلشَّيْطَٰنِ ۚ وَمَن يَتَّبِعْ خُطُوَٰتِ ٱلشَّيْطَٰنِ فَإِنَّهُۥ يَأْمُرُ بِٱلْفَحْشَآءِ وَٱلْمُنكَرِ ۚ وَلَوْلَا فَضْلُ ٱللَّهِ عَلَيْكُمْ وَرَحْمَتُهُۥ مَا زَكَىٰ مِنكُم مِّنْ أَحَدٍ أَبَدًا وَلَٰكِنَّ ٱللَّهَ يُزَكِّى مَن يَشَآءُ ۗ وَٱللَّهُ سَمِيعٌ عَلِيمٌ ۝

---

547. Compare and contrast this exceptionally high tone of the Islamic society with the grossly lewd character of the Christian nations both modern and ancient – the necking and the petting of the moderns, and the kissing habits of the ancients. 'The kiss, the instinctive token of amity and affection from the earliest time found a place in the life and the worship of the Christian Church' (*DCA*. II. p. 902). 'The shameless use' of which 'made the churches resound, occasioning suspicious and evil reports' (Ibid.).

22. And let not the men of affluence and plenty among you swear off from giving to the kindred and the needy and the emigrants in the way of Allah; let them pardon and overlook[548]. Do you not love that Allah should forgive you? And Allah is the Forgiving, the Merciful?

23. Verily those who accuse chaste, unknowing, believing women, shall be cursed in the world and the Hereafter, and for them shall be a mighty chastisement;

24. On the Day when their tongues and hands and feet will bear witness against them for what they were wont to work.

25. On that Day Allah shall pay them their recompense in full and they shall know that Allah is manifestly True.

26. Vile women are for vile men, and vile men are for vile women, and clean women are for clean men and clean men are for clean women; these are quit of what the people say: and for them is forgiveness and an honoured provision.

وَلَا يَأْتَلِ أُوْلُوا۟ الْفَضْلِ مِنكُمْ وَالسَّعَةِ أَن يُؤْتُوٓا۟ أُو۟لِى الْقُرْبَىٰ وَالْمَسَٰكِينَ وَالْمُهَٰجِرِينَ فِى سَبِيلِ اللَّهِ وَلْيَعْفُوا۟ وَلْيَصْفَحُوٓا۟ أَلَا تُحِبُّونَ أَن يَغْفِرَ اللَّهُ لَكُمْ وَاللَّهُ غَفُورٌ رَّحِيمٌ ﴿٢٢﴾

إِنَّ الَّذِينَ يَرْمُونَ الْمُحْصَنَٰتِ الْغَٰفِلَٰتِ الْمُؤْمِنَٰتِ لُعِنُوا۟ فِى الدُّنْيَا وَالْءَاخِرَةِ وَلَهُمْ عَذَابٌ عَظِيمٌ ﴿٢٣﴾

يَوْمَ تَشْهَدُ عَلَيْهِمْ أَلْسِنَتُهُمْ وَأَيْدِيهِمْ وَأَرْجُلُهُم بِمَا كَانُوا۟ يَعْمَلُونَ ﴿٢٤﴾

يَوْمَئِذٍ يُوَفِّيهِمُ اللَّهُ دِينَهُمُ الْحَقَّ وَيَعْلَمُونَ أَنَّ اللَّهَ هُوَ الْحَقُّ الْمُبِينُ ﴿٢٥﴾

الْخَبِيثَٰتُ لِلْخَبِيثِينَ وَالْخَبِيثُونَ لِلْخَبِيثَٰتِ وَالطَّيِّبَٰتُ لِلطَّيِّبِينَ وَالطَّيِّبُونَ لِلطَّيِّبَٰتِ أُو۟لَٰٓئِكَ مُبَرَّءُونَ مِمَّا يَقُولُونَ لَهُم مَّغْفِرَةٌ وَرِزْقٌ كَرِيمٌ ﴿٢٦﴾

---

548. Miṣṭaḥ was an indigent relative of the Prophet's great companion Abū Bakr and was supported by him. In his simplicity of mind he also became a tool in the hypocrites' campaign to scandalize 'Āishah. It was natural for her father, the great Abū Bakr, now to stop his pension but even this small punishment he is not allowed to inflict, and he is exhorted to act up to the highest standard of Islamic ethics and to continue his benevolence.

Section 4

27. O you who believe! Do not enter houses other than your own until you have asked leave and invoked peace on their inmates. That is better for you; haply you may take heed.

28. That if you find no one therein, do not enter until leave has been given you. And if you are told: 'Go back', then go back. It is cleaner for you, and Allah is the Knower of what you do.

29. No fault it is with you that you enter a house uninhabited in which there is some property for you; Allah knows what you disclose and what you conceal.

30. Say to the faithful that they lower their sights[549] and guard their private parts;[550] that is cleaner for them. Verily Allah is Aware of what they perform.

---

549. Thereby not look freely at the faces of the women who are not their sisters, daughters, mothers or wives. Here is a law of inward purity of the strictest kind and a piece of very sound advice to the tempted. This injunction puts a full and complete stop on lusting eyes, and the maxim, if acted upon, does and must serve as a most powerful agency for the prevention and control of sexual crimes. Islam is not at all enamoured of the free and unrestricted intermingling of the sexes and of the mixed gatherings at bridge tables and supper tables, nor in schools, colleges, clubs, cinemas, and public parks. It insists upon segregation of the sexes and altogether bans lewd literature, lewd pictures and lewd cinema. Cf. the Bible: 'But I say unto you. That whosoever look on a woman to lust after her hath committed adultery with her already in his heart' (Mt. 5: 28).

550. Guard them in their entirety. This altogether bans every form of nudity whether under cover of naturism or in the name of health and efficiency.

31. And say to the believing women that they shall lower their sights and guard their private parts and shall not disclose their adornment except what appears of it: and they shall draw their scarves over their bosoms, and shall not disclose their adornment save to their husbands or their fathers or their husband's father or their sons or their husband's sons or their brothers or their brothers' sons or their sisters' sons or their women or what their right hands own or male followers wanting in sex desire or children not acquainted with the privy parts of women. And they shall not strike their feet so that there be known what they hide of their adornment.[551] And turn penitently to Allah you all, O you faithful; haply you may thrive.

32. And wed the single among you and the fit ones among your male and female slaves. If they are poor, Allah will enrich them of His bounty. Allah is the Ample, the Knowing.

---

551. So much so that the Muslim woman is not allowed to tinkle of the ornament of her feet lest it may be suggestive of her sex appeal. Even such remote stimulants to sexual passions are interdicted in Islam! Compare and contrast with this the open lewdness and solicitations of modern dancing-halls and night-clubs. For a similar Biblical condemnation see Is. 3: 16–18.

33. And those who do not find means to marry shall restrain themselves until Allah enriches them of His bounty. And from among those whom your right hands own those who seek a writing write it for them if you find any good in them, and give them of the wealth of Allah which He has given you. And do not constrain your handmaids to harlotry if they would live chastely, in order that you may seek the chance gain of this world. And whosoever will constrain them, then verily Allah is, after their constraint, the Forgiving, the Merciful.

34. And assuredly We have sent down to you revelations illuminating and a similitude for those who passed away before you and an exhortation to the God-fearing.

Section 5

35. Allah is the Light of the heavens and the earth;[552] the likeness of His light is as a niche

وَلْيَسْتَعْفِفِ ٱلَّذِينَ لَا يَجِدُونَ نِكَاحًا حَتَّىٰ يُغْنِيَهُمُ ٱللَّهُ مِن فَضْلِهِ ۗ وَٱلَّذِينَ يَبْتَغُونَ ٱلْكِتَـٰبَ مِمَّا مَلَكَتْ أَيْمَـٰنُكُمْ فَكَاتِبُوهُمْ إِنْ عَلِمْتُمْ فِيهِمْ خَيْرًا ۖ وَءَاتُوهُم مِّن مَّالِ ٱللَّهِ ٱلَّذِىٓ ءَاتَىٰكُمْ ۚ وَلَا تُكْرِهُوا۟ فَتَيَـٰتِكُمْ عَلَى ٱلْبِغَآءِ إِنْ أَرَدْنَ تَحَصُّنًا لِّتَبْتَغُوا۟ عَرَضَ ٱلْحَيَوٰةِ ٱلدُّنْيَا ۚ وَمَن يُكْرِههُّنَّ فَإِنَّ ٱللَّهَ مِنۢ بَعْدِ إِكْرَٰهِهِنَّ غَفُورٌ رَّحِيمٌ ۞

وَلَقَدْ أَنزَلْنَآ إِلَيْكُمْ ءَايَـٰتٍ مُّبَيِّنَـٰتٍ وَمَثَلًا مِّنَ ٱلَّذِينَ خَلَوْا۟ مِن قَبْلِكُمْ وَمَوْعِظَةً لِّلْمُتَّقِينَ ۞

ٱللَّهُ نُورُ ٱلسَّمَـٰوَٰتِ وَٱلْأَرْضِ ۚ مَثَلُ نُورِهِۦ

---

552. He illumines the hearts and homes of all Believers. Or, 'He illumines those in the heavens and on the earth by His light. Cf. the NT: 'God is light, and in Him is no darkness at all' (1 Jn. 1: 5).

wherein is a lamp;[553] the lamp is in a glass; the glass is as though it is a star brilliant; lit from a tree blest, an olive, neither of the east nor of the west; its very oil will shine forth, even though no fire touched it; light upon light. Allah guides unto His light whom He will. Allah propounds similitudes for mankind;[554] and verily Allah is the Knower of everything.

كَمِشۡكَوٰةٍ فِيۡهَا مِصۡبَاحٌ ۖ الۡمِصۡبَاحُ فِىۡ زُجَاجَةٍ ۖ الزُّجَاجَةُ كَأَنَّهَا كَوۡكَبٌ دُرِّىٌّ يُّوۡقَدُ مِنۡ شَجَرَةٍ مُّبَـٰرَكَةٍ زَيۡتُوۡنَةٍ لَّا شَرۡقِيَّةٍ وَّلَا غَرۡبِيَّةٍ يَّكَادُ زَيۡتُهَا يُضِىۡٓءُ وَلَوۡ لَمۡ تَمۡسَسۡهُ نَارٌ ۗ نُوۡرٌ عَلَىٰ نُوۡرٍ ۗ يَهۡدِى اللّٰهُ لِنُوۡرِهٖ مَنۡ يَّشَآءُ ۚ وَيَضۡرِبُ اللّٰهُ الۡأَمۡثَالَ لِلنَّاسِ ۗ وَاللّٰهُ بِكُلِّ شَىۡءٍ عَلِيۡمٌ ۙ ٣٥

36. They worship in houses which Allah has bidden to be exalted and His name to be remembered therein; they hallow Him therein in mornings and evenings,

فِىۡ بُيُوۡتٍ أَذِنَ اللّٰهُ أَنۡ تُرۡفَعَ وَيُذۡكَرَ فِيۡهَا اسۡمُهٗ يُسَبِّحُ لَهٗ فِيۡهَا بِالۡغُدُوِّ وَالۡآصَالِ ۙ ٣٦

37. Men whom neither trade nor business diverts from the remembrance of Allah and the establishment of the prayer and the payment of the poor-rate, in awe of a Day whereon heart and sights will be upset;

رِجَالٌ لَّا تُلۡهِيۡهِمۡ تِجَارَةٌ وَّلَا بَيۡعٌ عَنۡ ذِكۡرِ اللّٰهِ وَإِقَامِ الصَّلَوٰةِ وَإِيۡتَآءِ الزَّكَوٰةِ ۙ يَخَافُوۡنَ يَوۡمًا تَتَقَلَّبُ فِيۡهِ الۡقُلُوۡبُ وَالۡأَبۡصَارُ ۙ ٣٧

---

553. A lamp diffusing its light all round. 'The teaching of modern physics is that the velocity of light cannot be exceeded and is the same for all observers whatever their own system of movement. Thus in the world of change, light is the nearest approach to the Absolute. The metaphor of light as applied to God, therefore, must in view of modern knowledge, be taken to suggest the Absoluteness of God' (Iqbal, *Reconstruction of Religious Thought in Islam*, p. 89).

554. Speaking of the literary charm of the Holy Qur'ān, and taking this particular verse as a specimen says an English lady now happily a Muslim: 'It is impossible to give a translation that can convey the poetry, the subtle meaning that floods the soul when read in the original. To me the simple grandeur of the diction, the variety of the imageries, the splendour of the word-painting differentiates the Koran from all other Scriptures' (Lady Cobbold, *Pilgrimage to Mecca*, p. 240).

38. That Allah may recompense them the best for what they worked and may increase to them of His grace. And Allah propounds for whom He will without measure.

لِيَجْزِيَهُمُ اللَّهُ أَحْسَنَ مَا عَمِلُوا وَيَزِيدَهُم مِّن فَضْلِهِ وَاللَّهُ يَرْزُقُ مَن يَشَاءُ بِغَيْرِ حِسَابٍ ﴿٣٨﴾

39. And those who disbelieve – their works are like a mirage in a desert which the thirsty deems to be water until when he comes thereto, he finds not anything, and finds Allah with himself, and He pays him his account in full; and Allah is Swift in reckoning.

وَالَّذِينَ كَفَرُوا أَعْمَالُهُمْ كَسَرَابٍ بِقِيعَةٍ يَحْسَبُهُ الظَّمْآنُ مَاءً حَتَّى إِذَا جَاءَهُ لَمْ يَجِدْهُ شَيْئًا وَوَجَدَ اللَّهَ عِندَهُ فَوَفَّاهُ حِسَابَهُ وَاللَّهُ سَرِيعُ الْحِسَابِ ﴿٣٩﴾

40. Or, like darkness in a bottomless sea; there covers him a wave from above it, a wave overcast with a cloud; layers upon layers of darkness. When he puts out his hand he can scarcely see it. And to whom Allah does not appoint a light his shall be no light.

أَوْ كَظُلُمَاتٍ فِي بَحْرٍ لُّجِّيٍّ يَغْشَاهُ مَوْجٌ مِّن فَوْقِهِ مَوْجٌ مِّن فَوْقِهِ سَحَابٌ ظُلُمَاتٌ بَعْضُهَا فَوْقَ بَعْضٍ إِذَا أَخْرَجَ يَدَهُ لَمْ يَكَدْ يَرَاهَا وَمَن لَّمْ يَجْعَلِ اللَّهُ لَهُ نُورًا فَمَا لَهُ مِن نُّورٍ ﴿٤٠﴾

Section 6

41. Do you not see that Allah – hallow Him, whosoever is in the heavens and the earth and the birds with wings out-spread?[555] Surely everyone knows his prayer and his hallowing; and Allah is the Knower of what they do.

أَلَمْ تَرَ أَنَّ اللَّهَ يُسَبِّحُ لَهُ مَن فِي السَّمَاوَاتِ وَالْأَرْضِ وَالطَّيْرُ صَافَّاتٍ كُلٌّ قَدْ عَلِمَ صَلَاتَهُ وَتَسْبِيحَهُ وَاللَّهُ عَلِيمٌ بِمَا يَفْعَلُونَ ﴿٤١﴾

---

555. Birds have very frequently been adored, by polytheistic peoples, as vehicles of the great gods, and have themselves been the objects of special cults. The goose, the hawk, the parrot, the vulture, and the wagtail are a few conspicuous representatives of their class. (For Indian and Egyptian bird-cults see *ERE*. IX. p. 232; V. p. 245).

42. Allah's is the sovereignty of the heavens and the earth and to Allah is the return.

وَلِلَّهِ مُلْكُ ٱلسَّمَوَٰتِ وَٱلْأَرْضِ وَإِلَى ٱللَّهِ ٱلْمَصِيرُ ۝

43. Do you not see that Allah drives a cloud along, then compresses it, and then makes it a mass, and you then see fine water come forth from the interstices thereof? And He sends down from the sky mountains in which is hail; then smites with it whom He will and spares whom He will. The flash of His lightning almost takes away the sight.

أَلَمْ تَرَ أَنَّ ٱللَّهَ يُزْجِى سَحَابًا ثُمَّ يُؤَلِّفُ بَيْنَهُۥ ثُمَّ يَجْعَلُهُۥ رُكَامًا فَتَرَى ٱلْوَدْقَ يَخْرُجُ مِنْ خِلَٰلِهِۦ وَيُنَزِّلُ مِنَ ٱلسَّمَآءِ مِن جِبَالٍ فِيهَا مِنۢ بَرَدٍ فَيُصِيبُ بِهِۦ مَن يَشَآءُ وَيَصْرِفُهُۥ عَن مَّن يَشَآءُ يَكَادُ سَنَا بَرْقِهِۦ يَذْهَبُ بِٱلْأَبْصَٰرِ ۝

44. Allah turns away the night and the day over and over; verily in this is a lesson for men of insight.

يُقَلِّبُ ٱللَّهُ ٱلَّيْلَ وَٱلنَّهَارَ إِنَّ فِى ذَٰلِكَ لَعِبْرَةً لِّأُوْلِى ٱلْأَبْصَٰرِ ۝

45. Every moving thing Allah has created of water; of them is one that walks upon his belly, and of them is one that walks upon his two feet, and of them is one that walks upon his four. Allah creates whatsoever He wishes; Allah is Potent over everything.

وَٱللَّهُ خَلَقَ كُلَّ دَآبَّةٍ مِّن مَّآءٍ فَمِنْهُم مَّن يَمْشِى عَلَىٰ بَطْنِهِۦ وَمِنْهُم مَّن يَمْشِى عَلَىٰ رِجْلَيْنِ وَمِنْهُم مَّن يَمْشِى عَلَىٰٓ أَرْبَعٍ يَخْلُقُ ٱللَّهُ مَا يَشَآءُ إِنَّ ٱللَّهَ عَلَىٰ كُلِّ شَىْءٍ قَدِيرٌ ۝

46. Assuredly We have sent down revelations illuminating: and Allah guides whom He wishes to a straight path.

لَّقَدْ أَنزَلْنَآ ءَايَٰتٍ مُّبَيِّنَٰتٍ وَٱللَّهُ يَهْدِى مَن يَشَآءُ إِلَىٰ صِرَٰطٍ مُّسْتَقِيمٍ ۝

47. And they say: 'we have believed in Allah and the Messenger, and we obeyed,' then a party of them backslides thereafter, and believers they are not.

وَيَقُولُونَ ءَامَنَّا بِٱللَّهِ وَبِٱلرَّسُولِ وَأَطَعْنَا ثُمَّ يَتَوَلَّىٰ فَرِيقٌ مِّنْهُم مِّنۢ بَعْدِ ذَٰلِكَ وَمَآ أُوْلَٰٓئِكَ بِٱلْمُؤْمِنِينَ ۝

48. And when they are called to Allah and His Messenger that he may judge between them, lo: a party of them turns aside;

وَإِذَا دُعُوٓا إِلَى ٱللَّهِ وَرَسُولِهِۦ لِيَحْكُمَ بَيْنَهُمْ إِذَا فَرِيقٌ مِّنْهُم مُّعْرِضُونَ ۝

49. And if they had a cause, they would have come to him readily.

وَإِن يَكُن لَّهُمُ ٱلْحَقُّ يَأْتُوٓا إِلَيْهِ مُذْعِنِينَ ۝

50. Is there a disease in their hearts? Or do they doubt? Or do they fear that Allah shall misjudge them, as also His Messenger? Aye! These are the very wrong-doers.

أَفِى قُلُوبِهِم مَّرَضٌ أَمِ ٱرْتَابُوٓا أَمْ يَخَافُونَ أَن يَحِيفَ ٱللَّهُ عَلَيْهِمْ وَرَسُولُهُۥ بَلْ أُوْلَٰٓئِكَ هُمُ ٱلظَّٰلِمُونَ ۝

Section 7

51. The only saying of the faithful, when they were called to Allah and His Messenger that he might adjudge between them, was that they said: 'We hear and we obey.' And these! They are the blissful.

إِنَّمَا كَانَ قَوْلَ ٱلْمُؤْمِنِينَ إِذَا دُعُوٓا إِلَى ٱللَّهِ وَرَسُولِهِۦ لِيَحْكُمَ بَيْنَهُمْ أَن يَقُولُوٓا سَمِعْنَا وَأَطَعْنَا وَأُوْلَٰٓئِكَ هُمُ ٱلْمُفْلِحُونَ ۝

52. And whosoever obeys Allah and his Messenger, and is in awe of Allah and fears Him - these! They are the triumphant.

وَمَن يُطِعِ ٱللَّهَ وَرَسُولَهُۥ وَيَخْشَ ٱللَّهَ وَيَتَّقْهِ فَأُوْلَٰٓئِكَ هُمُ ٱلْفَآئِزُونَ ۝

53. And they swear by Allah with their solemn oaths that if you command them they will surely go forth. Say: 'Do not swear, your obedience is well-known. Verily Allah is Aware of what you do'.

وَأَقْسَمُوا بِٱللَّهِ جَهْدَ أَيْمَٰنِهِمْ لَئِنْ أَمَرْتَهُمْ لَيَخْرُجُنَّ قُل لَّا تُقْسِمُوٓا طَاعَةٌ مَّعْرُوفَةٌ إِنَّ ٱللَّهَ خَبِيرٌۢ بِمَا تَعْمَلُونَ ۝

54. Say: 'Obey Allah and obey the Messenger; then if you turn away, upon him is only that which has been laid upon him, and upon you is that which has been laid upon you. If you obey him you will be guided, and naught is upon the Prophet except the plain preaching.'

قُلْ أَطِيعُوا ٱللَّهَ وَأَطِيعُوا ٱلرَّسُولَ فَإِن تَوَلَّوْا فَإِنَّمَا عَلَيْهِ مَا حُمِّلَ وَعَلَيْكُم مَّا حُمِّلْتُمْ وَإِن تُطِيعُوهُ تَهْتَدُوا وَمَا عَلَى ٱلرَّسُولِ إِلَّا ٱلْبَلَٰغُ ٱلْمُبِينُ ۝

55. Allah has promised those of you who believe and work righteous deeds that He shall make them successors, on the earth even as He made those who were before them successors, and that He shall certainly establish for them their religion which He has approved for them, and that He shall certainly exchange unto them after fear a security, provided they worship Me, joining not aught with Me;[556] and whosoever will disbelieve thereafter, then those! They are the ungodly.

وَعَدَ اللَّهُ الَّذِينَ ءَامَنُوا مِنكُمْ وَعَمِلُوا الصَّٰلِحَٰتِ لَيَسْتَخْلِفَنَّهُمْ فِى الْأَرْضِ كَمَا اسْتَخْلَفَ الَّذِينَ مِن قَبْلِهِمْ وَلَيُمَكِّنَنَّ لَهُمْ دِينَهُمُ الَّذِى ارْتَضَىٰ لَهُمْ وَلَيُبَدِّلَنَّهُم مِّنۢ بَعْدِ خَوْفِهِمْ أَمْنًا يَعْبُدُونَنِى لَا يُشْرِكُونَ بِى شَيْـًٔا وَمَن كَفَرَ بَعْدَ ذَٰلِكَ فَأُولَٰٓئِكَ هُمُ الْفَٰسِقُونَ ۝

56. And establish the prayer, and pay the poor-rate and obey the Messenger, haply you may be shown mercy.

وَأَقِيمُوا الصَّلَوٰةَ وَءَاتُوا الزَّكَوٰةَ وَأَطِيعُوا الرَّسُولَ لَعَلَّكُمْ تُرْحَمُونَ ۝

57. Do not consider them who disbelieve able to frustrate His purpose on the earth, and their abode shall be the Fire – an ill retreat!

لَا تَحْسَبَنَّ الَّذِينَ كَفَرُوا مُعْجِزِينَ فِى الْأَرْضِ وَمَأْوَىٰهُمُ النَّارُ وَلَبِئْسَ الْمَصِيرُ ۝

---

556. Exclusively and whole-heartedly joining nothing with Him. The proviso is important; a mere service paid to Islam is utterly inadequate for the realization of these promises.

Section 8

58. O ye who believe! Let those whom your right hands own and those of you who have not attained puberty ask leave of you three times: before the dawn-prayer, and when you lay aside your garments at noon-day and after the night prayer: three times of privacy for you. No fault is there upon you and upon them beyond these times going round upon you, some of you upon some others. In this way does Allah expound His commandments, and Allah is the Knowing, the Wise.

يَـٰٓأَيُّهَا ٱلَّذِينَ ءَامَنُوا لِيَسْتَـْٔذِنكُمُ ٱلَّذِينَ مَلَكَتْ أَيْمَـٰنُكُمْ وَٱلَّذِينَ لَمْ يَبْلُغُوا ٱلْحُلُمَ مِنكُمْ ثَلَـٰثَ مَرَّٰتٍ مِّن قَبْلِ صَلَوٰةِ ٱلْفَجْرِ وَحِينَ تَضَعُونَ ثِيَابَكُم مِّنَ ٱلظَّهِيرَةِ وَمِنۢ بَعْدِ صَلَوٰةِ ٱلْعِشَآءِ ثَلَـٰثُ عَوْرَٰتٍ لَّكُمْ لَيْسَ عَلَيْكُمْ وَلَا عَلَيْهِمْ جُنَاحٌ بَعْدَهُنَّ طَوَّٰفُونَ عَلَيْكُم بَعْضُكُمْ عَلَىٰ بَعْضٍ كَذَٰلِكَ يُبَيِّنُ ٱللَّهُ لَكُمُ ٱلْأَيَـٰتِ وَٱللَّهُ عَلِيمٌ حَكِيمٌ ٥٨

59. And when the children among you attain puberty then let them also ask leave as those before them asked leave. In this way Allah expounds His commandments; and Allah is the Knowing, the Wise.

وَإِذَا بَلَغَ ٱلْأَطْفَـٰلُ مِنكُمُ ٱلْحُلُمَ فَلْيَسْتَـْٔذِنُوا كَمَا ٱسْتَـْٔذَنَ ٱلَّذِينَ مِن قَبْلِهِمْ كَذَٰلِكَ يُبَيِّنُ ٱللَّهُ لَكُمْ ءَايَـٰتِهِۦ وَٱللَّهُ عَلِيمٌ حَكِيمٌ ٥٩

60. And past child-bearing women who do not expect wedlock – upon them it is no fault that lay aside their outer garments, not flaunting their adornment. And that they should restrain themselves is better for them; and Allah is the Hearing, the Knowing.

وَٱلْقَوَٰعِدُ مِنَ ٱلنِّسَآءِ ٱلَّـٰتِي لَا يَرْجُونَ نِكَاحًا فَلَيْسَ عَلَيْهِنَّ جُنَاحٌ أَن يَضَعْنَ ثِيَابَهُنَّ غَيْرَ مُتَبَرِّجَـٰتٍۭ بِزِينَةٍ وَأَن يَسْتَعْفِفْنَ خَيْرٌ لَّهُنَّ وَٱللَّهُ سَمِيعٌ عَلِيمٌ ٦٠

61. No restriction is there on the blind, nor is there a restriction on the lame, nor is there a restriction on the sick, nor on yourselves that you eat in the houses of your fathers or the houses of your mothers or the houses of your brothers or the houses of your sisters or the houses of your uncles or the houses of your paternal aunts or the houses of your maternal uncles or the houses of your maternal aunts or from that house of which you own the keys or from the house of a friend. No fault is there upon you whether you eat together or eat in separate groups.[557] Then when you enter houses, salute each other with greetings from Allah, blessed and good. Thus Allah expounds to you His revelation, haply you may reflect.

لَّيْسَ عَلَى ٱلْأَعْمَىٰ حَرَجٌ وَلَا عَلَى ٱلْأَعْرَجِ حَرَجٌ وَلَا عَلَى ٱلْمَرِيضِ حَرَجٌ وَلَا عَلَىٰ أَنفُسِكُمْ أَن تَأْكُلُوا۟ مِنۢ بُيُوتِكُمْ أَوْ بُيُوتِ ءَابَآئِكُمْ أَوْ بُيُوتِ أُمَّهَٰتِكُمْ أَوْ بُيُوتِ إِخْوَٰنِكُمْ أَوْ بُيُوتِ أَخَوَٰتِكُمْ أَوْ بُيُوتِ أَعْمَٰمِكُمْ أَوْ بُيُوتِ عَمَّٰتِكُمْ أَوْ بُيُوتِ أَخْوَٰلِكُمْ أَوْ بُيُوتِ خَٰلَٰتِكُمْ أَوْ مَا مَلَكْتُم مَّفَاتِحَهُۥٓ أَوْ صَدِيقِكُمْ لَيْسَ عَلَيْكُمْ جُنَاحٌ أَن تَأْكُلُوا۟ جَمِيعًا أَوْ أَشْتَاتًا فَإِذَا دَخَلْتُم بُيُوتًا فَسَلِّمُوا۟ عَلَىٰٓ أَنفُسِكُمْ تَحِيَّةً مِّنْ عِندِ ٱللَّهِ مُبَٰرَكَةً طَيِّبَةً كَذَٰلِكَ يُبَيِّنُ ٱللَّهُ لَكُمُ ٱلْءَايَٰتِ لَعَلَّكُمْ تَعْقِلُونَ ۝

---

557. This strikes at the root of the Hindu caste system which insists that each one shall eat separately or at most in the company of those belonging to his caste. A similar custom prevailed in Egypt. 'The great lords would not eat with foreigners, nor with their own countrymen who were of lower rank than themselves' (*EMK*. II. p. 855).

Section 9

62. The faithful are those who have believed in Allah and His Messenger, and when they are with him on some affair collecting people together, they do not depart till they have begged his leave. Verily those who ask your leave those are they who really believe in Allah and His Messenger so if they ask your leave for some business of theirs, give leave to whom you will, and implore Allah for their forgiveness. Verily Allah is the Forgiving, the Merciful.

إِنَّمَا ٱلْمُؤْمِنُونَ ٱلَّذِينَ ءَامَنُوا۟ بِٱللَّهِ وَرَسُولِهِۦ وَإِذَا كَانُوا۟ مَعَهُۥ عَلَىٰٓ أَمْرٍ جَامِعٍ لَّمْ يَذْهَبُوا۟ حَتَّىٰ يَسْتَـْٔذِنُوهُ إِنَّ ٱلَّذِينَ يَسْتَـْٔذِنُونَكَ أُو۟لَـٰٓئِكَ ٱلَّذِينَ يُؤْمِنُونَ بِٱللَّهِ وَرَسُولِهِۦ فَإِذَا ٱسْتَـْٔذَنُوكَ لِبَعْضِ شَأْنِهِمْ فَأْذَن لِّمَن شِئْتَ مِنْهُمْ وَٱسْتَغْفِرْ لَهُمُ ٱللَّهَ إِنَّ ٱللَّهَ غَفُورٌ رَّحِيمٌ ۝

63. Do not place the Messenger's calling of you on the same footing as your calling of each other. Of a surety Allah knows them who slip away privately. Let therefore those who oppose His commandment beware lest there befall them a trial or there befall them an afflictive torment.

لَّا تَجْعَلُوا۟ دُعَآءَ ٱلرَّسُولِ بَيْنَكُمْ كَدُعَآءِ بَعْضِكُم بَعْضًا قَدْ يَعْلَمُ ٱللَّهُ ٱلَّذِينَ يَتَسَلَّلُونَ مِنكُمْ لِوَاذًا فَلْيَحْذَرِ ٱلَّذِينَ يُخَالِفُونَ عَنْ أَمْرِهِۦٓ أَن تُصِيبَهُمْ فِتْنَةٌ أَوْ يُصِيبَهُمْ عَذَابٌ أَلِيمٌ ۝

64. Lo! Verily Allah's is whatsoever is in the heavens and the earth. Surely He knows what you are about, and the Day whereon they shall be made to return to Him; then He will declare to them what they worked. And Allah is the Knower of everything.

أَلَآ إِنَّ لِلَّهِ مَا فِى ٱلسَّمَـٰوَٰتِ وَٱلْأَرْضِ قَدْ يَعْلَمُ مَآ أَنتُمْ عَلَيْهِ وَيَوْمَ يُرْجَعُونَ إِلَيْهِ فَيُنَبِّئُهُم بِمَا عَمِلُوا۟ وَٱللَّهُ بِكُلِّ شَىْءٍ عَلِيمٌ ۝

Sūrah 25

al-Furqān

(Makkan, 6 Sections, 77 Verses)

In the name of Allah, the Compassionate, the Merciful.

Section 1

1. Blessed be He Who has sent down the criterion to His bondsman that he may be a warner to the worlds.

2. He it is Whose is the dominion of the heavens and the earth, and Who has not taken a son, and for Whom there is not an associate in the dominion,[558] and Who has created everything and measured it according to a measurement.[559]

---

558. The verse especially aims at the demolition of the two principal forms of Christian polytheism.

559. Several pagan philosophers, such as Epicures, denied *in toto* the Divine superintendence of human affairs, and this human self-sufficiency was echoed by the later-day Jews. The Sadducees among them held that there was no such thing as 'fate', and that 'human actions are not directed according to it, but all actions are in our own power, so that we are ourselves the causes of what is good' (*DB*. IV. p. 53). The Qur'ān corrects all such misconceptions and makes it clear that every event, large or small, that comes to pass in the universe, is the direct outcome of the All-Wise, All-Righteous, All-Powerful God, and not subject either to chance or to necessity, and that the governing hand of God is visible through every process of nature, through the march of history, and through the fortunes of every individual life, steadily working out His preconceived plan.

3. And they have taken gods, besides Him, creating not aught and are themselves created, can neither hurt nor benefit themselves, and have no power of life or death or resurrection.

وَٱتَّخَذُوا۟ مِن دُونِهِۦٓ ءَالِهَةً لَّا يَخْلُقُونَ شَيْـًٔا وَهُمْ يُخْلَقُونَ وَلَا يَمْلِكُونَ لِأَنفُسِهِمْ ضَرًّا وَلَا نَفْعًا وَلَا يَمْلِكُونَ مَوْتًا وَلَا حَيَوٰةً وَلَا نُشُورًا ۝

4. And those who disbelieve say: 'This is naught but falsehood that he has fabricated and other people have associated themselves in it.' Surely they have brought a wrong and falsehood.

وَقَالَ ٱلَّذِينَ كَفَرُوٓا۟ إِنْ هَٰذَآ إِلَّآ إِفْكٌ ٱفْتَرَىٰهُ وَأَعَانَهُۥ عَلَيْهِ قَوْمٌ ءَاخَرُونَ فَقَدْ جَآءُو ظُلْمًا وَزُورًا ۝

5. And they say: 'Fables of the ancients which he has had written down and they are dictated to him morning and evening.'

وَقَالُوٓا۟ أَسَٰطِيرُ ٱلْأَوَّلِينَ ٱكْتَتَبَهَا فَهِىَ تُمْلَىٰ عَلَيْهِ بُكْرَةً وَأَصِيلًا ۝

6. Say: 'He has sent it down Who knows the secret of the heavens and the earth; verily He is ever-Forgiving, Merciful.'

قُلْ أَنزَلَهُ ٱلَّذِى يَعْلَمُ ٱلسِّرَّ فِى ٱلسَّمَٰوَٰتِ وَٱلْأَرْضِ إِنَّهُۥ كَانَ غَفُورًا رَّحِيمًا ۝

7. And they say: 'What is the matter with this Messenger; he eats food and walks about in the market! Why is not an angel sent down on him that there may be along with him a warner?

وَقَالُوا۟ مَالِ هَٰذَا ٱلرَّسُولِ يَأْكُلُ ٱلطَّعَامَ وَيَمْشِى فِى ٱلْأَسْوَاقِ لَوْلَآ أُنزِلَ إِلَيْهِ مَلَكٌ فَيَكُونَ مَعَهُۥ نَذِيرًا ۝

8. Or why is not cast down unto him a treasure or unto him a garden whereof he may eat?' And the wrongdoers say: 'You follow merely a man bewitched.'

أَوْ يُلْقَىٰٓ إِلَيْهِ كَنزٌ أَوْ تَكُونُ لَهُۥ جَنَّةٌ يَأْكُلُ مِنْهَا وَقَالَ ٱلظَّٰلِمُونَ إِن تَتَّبِعُونَ إِلَّا رَجُلًا مَّسْحُورًا ۝

9. See how they propound similitudes for you! So they have strayed and cannot find a way.

ٱنظُرْ كَيْفَ ضَرَبُوا۟ لَكَ ٱلْأَمْثَٰلَ فَضَلُّوا۟ فَلَا يَسْتَطِيعُونَ سَبِيلًا ۝

Section 2

10. Blessed be He Who, if He willed, will assign to you something better than that; Gardens with running water, and assigned palaces to you.

تَبَارَكَ ٱلَّذِىٓ إِن شَآءَ جَعَلَ لَكَ خَيْرًا مِّن ذَٰلِكَ جَنَّٰتٍ تَجْرِى مِن تَحْتِهَا ٱلْأَنْهَٰرُ وَيَجْعَل لَّكَ قُصُورًا ﴿١٠﴾

11. Aye! They belie the Hour, and for him who belies the Hour We have prepared the Flame.

بَلْ كَذَّبُوا۟ بِٱلسَّاعَةِ ۖ وَأَعْتَدْنَا لِمَن كَذَّبَ بِٱلسَّاعَةِ سَعِيرًا ﴿١١﴾

12. When it sees them from afar, they will hear it raging and roaring.

إِذَا رَأَتْهُم مِّن مَّكَانٍ بَعِيدٍ سَمِعُوا۟ لَهَا تَغَيُّظًا وَزَفِيرًا ﴿١٢﴾

13. And when they shall be flung into a strait place thereof, bound up, they shall call therein for death.

وَإِذَآ أُلْقُوا۟ مِنْهَا مَكَانًا ضَيِّقًا مُّقَرَّنِينَ دَعَوْا۟ هُنَالِكَ ثُبُورًا ﴿١٣﴾

14. Call not today for a single death, but call for death manifold.

لَّا تَدْعُوا۟ ٱلْيَوْمَ ثُبُورًا وَٰحِدًا وَٱدْعُوا۟ ثُبُورًا كَثِيرًا ﴿١٤﴾

15. Say: 'Is that better or the Garden of abidance promised to the God-fearing? It shall be theirs as a recompense and as a retreat.

قُلْ أَذَٰلِكَ خَيْرٌ أَمْ جَنَّةُ ٱلْخُلْدِ ٱلَّتِى وُعِدَ ٱلْمُتَّقُونَ ۚ كَانَتْ لَهُمْ جَزَآءً وَمَصِيرًا ﴿١٥﴾

16. Theirs therein shall be all that they wish for, as abiders: a promise from your Lord to be asked for'.

لَّهُمْ فِيهَا مَا يَشَآءُونَ خَٰلِدِينَ ۚ كَانَ عَلَىٰ رَبِّكَ وَعْدًا مَّسْـُٔولًا ﴿١٦﴾

17. And on the Day when He will gather them and what they worship besides Allah and will say: 'Are you the ones who sent these My bondsmen astray or strayed they themselves from the way?'

وَيَوْمَ يَحْشُرُهُمْ وَمَا يَعْبُدُونَ مِن دُونِ ٱللَّهِ فَيَقُولُ ءَأَنتُمْ أَضْلَلْتُمْ عِبَادِى هَٰٓؤُلَآءِ أَمْ هُمْ ضَلُّوا۟ ٱلسَّبِيلَ ﴿١٧﴾

18. They will say: 'Hallowed be You! It behoved us not that we should take besides You any patron, but You allowed them and their fathers enjoyment until they forgot the admonition and they were a people doomed.

قَالُوا۟ سُبْحَٰنَكَ مَا كَانَ يَنۢبَغِى لَنَآ أَن نَّتَّخِذَ مِن دُونِكَ مِنْ أَوْلِيَآءَ وَلَٰكِن مَّتَّعْتَهُمْ وَءَابَآءَهُمْ حَتَّىٰ نَسُوا۟ ٱلذِّكْرَ وَكَانُوا۟ قَوْمًۢا بُورًا ﴿١٨﴾

19. So now they belie you in regard to what you said'; so now you are not able to obtain diversion nor help. And whosoever of you does wrong, him We shall cause to taste a great torment.

فَقَدْ كَذَّبُوكُم بِمَا تَقُولُونَ فَمَا تَسْتَطِيعُونَ صَرْفًا وَلَا نَصْرًا وَمَن يَظْلِم مِّنكُمْ نُذِقْهُ عَذَابًا كَبِيرًا ﴿١٩﴾

20. And We have not sent before you any of the Messengers but they did eat food and did walk about in the market-places. And We have made some of you a temptation to some others; will you have patience? And your Lord is the Beholder.

وَمَآ أَرْسَلْنَا قَبْلَكَ مِنَ ٱلْمُرْسَلِينَ إِلَّآ إِنَّهُمْ لَيَأْكُلُونَ ٱلطَّعَامَ وَ يَمْشُونَ فِى ٱلْأَسْوَاقِ وَجَعَلْنَا بَعْضَكُمْ لِبَعْضٍ فِتْنَةً أَتَصْبِرُونَ وَكَانَ رَبُّكَ بَصِيرًا ﴿٢٠﴾

Section 3

21. And those who look not to their meeting with Us say: 'Why are not angels sent down to us, or why do we see not our Lord?' Assuredly they have proved stiff-necked in their souls and have exceeded the bounds with great excess.

وَقَالَ ٱلَّذِينَ لَا يَرْجُونَ لِقَآءَنَا لَوْلَآ أُنزِلَ عَلَيْنَا ٱلْمَلَٰٓئِكَةُ أَوْ نَرَىٰ رَبَّنَا لَقَدِ ٱسْتَكْبَرُوا۟ فِىٓ أَنفُسِهِمْ وَعَتَوْ عُتُوًّا كَبِيرًا ﴿٢١﴾

22. The Day they will see the angels there will be no joy for the culprits on that day, and they will say: 'Away! away!'

يَوْمَ يَرَوْنَ ٱلْمَلَـٰٓئِكَةَ لَا بُشْرَىٰ يَوْمَئِذٍ لِّلْمُجْرِمِينَ وَيَقُولُونَ حِجْرًا مَّحْجُورًا ۝

23. And We shall set upon what they worked, and shall make it as dust, wind-scattered.

وَقَدِمْنَآ إِلَىٰ مَا عَمِلُوا۟ مِنْ عَمَلٍ فَجَعَلْنَـٰهُ هَبَآءً مَّنثُورًا ۝

24. Fellows of the Garden shall be on that Day in a goodly abode and a goodly repose.

أَصْحَـٰبُ ٱلْجَنَّةِ يَوْمَئِذٍ خَيْرٌ مُّسْتَقَرًّا وَأَحْسَنُ مَقِيلًا ۝

25. And on that Day when the sky shall be rent asunder from the clouds and the angels shall be sent down with a great descending;

وَيَوْمَ تَشَقَّقُ ٱلسَّمَآءُ بِٱلْغَمَـٰمِ وَنُزِّلَ ٱلْمَلَـٰٓئِكَةُ تَنزِيلًا ۝

26. The dominion on that Day shall be the true dominion of the Compassionate, and it shall be a day hard on the infidels.

ٱلْمُلْكُ يَوْمَئِذٍ ٱلْحَقُّ لِلرَّحْمَـٰنِ وَكَانَ يَوْمًا عَلَى ٱلْكَـٰفِرِينَ عَسِيرًا ۝

27. On the Day when the wrong-doer shall gnaw his hands saying: 'Would that I had taken a way with the Messenger!

وَيَوْمَ يَعَضُّ ٱلظَّالِمُ عَلَىٰ يَدَيْهِ يَقُولُ يَـٰلَيْتَنِى ٱتَّخَذْتُ مَعَ ٱلرَّسُولِ سَبِيلًا ۝

28. Ah! Woe unto me! Would that I had not taken such a one for a friend!

يَـٰوَيْلَتَىٰ لَيْتَنِى لَمْ أَتَّخِذْ فُلَانًا خَلِيلًا ۝

29. Assuredly he led me away from the admonition after it had come to me; verily Satan is to man ever a betrayer.'

لَّقَدْ أَضَلَّنِى عَنِ ٱلذِّكْرِ بَعْدَ إِذْ جَآءَنِى وَكَانَ ٱلشَّيْطَـٰنُ لِلْإِنسَـٰنِ خَذُولًا ۝

30. And the Messenger will say: 'Lord! Verily my people took this Qur'ān as a thing to be shunned.'

وَقَالَ ٱلرَّسُولُ يَـٰرَبِّ إِنَّ قَوْمِى ٱتَّخَذُوا۟ هَـٰذَا ٱلْقُرْءَانَ مَهْجُورًا ۝

31. And even so We appointed to every Messenger an enemy from among the culprits. And suffices your Lord as the Guide and the Helper.

وَكَذَٰلِكَ جَعَلْنَا لِكُلِّ نَبِيٍّ عَدُوًّا مِّنَ ٱلْمُجْرِمِينَ ۗ وَكَفَىٰ بِرَبِّكَ هَادِيًا وَنَصِيرًا ﴿٣١﴾

32. And those who disbelieve say: 'Why is the Qur'ān not revealed to him entire at once?' We revealed it thus that we may strengthen your heart with it[560] and We have repeated it with a repetition.[561]

وَقَالَ ٱلَّذِينَ كَفَرُوا لَوْلَا نُزِّلَ عَلَيْهِ ٱلْقُرْءَانُ جُمْلَةً وَٰحِدَةً ۚ كَذَٰلِكَ لِنُثَبِّتَ بِهِۦ فُؤَادَكَ ۖ وَرَتَّلْنَٰهُ تَرْتِيلًا ﴿٣٢﴾

33. And they come not to you with a similitude but We bring you the truth and an excellent interpretation.[562]

وَلَا يَأْتُونَكَ بِمَثَلٍ إِلَّا جِئْنَٰكَ بِٱلْحَقِّ وَأَحْسَنَ تَفْسِيرًا ﴿٣٣﴾

---

560. Both to infuse courage and constancy into the Prophet's mind, and to strengthen his memory and understanding. This is the first of the reasons for the gradual revelation of the Qur'ān. 'The tremendous task of winning the Arab nation, and through them, the whole world, to Islam, required superhuman patience, constancy, and firmness; and they were engendered and developed by a process of gradual revelation. Finally, for the Prophet himself these revelations coming as they did from time to time provided as Prophet's sustenance the spiritual food that strengthened his heart and supplied the necessary stimulus throughout a long and arduous mission. At the most trying moment in his prophetic career it comforted and consoled him, and at no time did it take on a surer tone in predicting ultimate triumph than when to all outward appearances the Prophet's condition was hopeless' (MA, p. 8).

561. Repeated it slowly and in a perfect arrangement for the gradual revelation. Here is another reason. Although the stages were so structured that completion took about 23 years, the whole nonetheless emerged, in the end, as a well-arranged Book.

562. This is the third reason for the long-drawn out stages. The Qur'ān answers all the hostile questions put to the Prophet from time to time.

34. They who shall be gathered prone on their faces into Hell – those shall be the worst in respect of place and the most astray in respect of path.

الَّذِينَ يُحۡشَرُونَ عَلَىٰ وُجُوهِهِمۡ إِلَىٰ جَهَنَّمَ أُوْلَٰٓئِكَ شَرٌّ مَّكَانًا وَأَضَلُّ سَبِيلًا ۝

Section 4

35. And assuredly We gave the Book to Moses and We placed his brother Aaron with him as a minister.

وَلَقَدۡ ءَاتَيۡنَا مُوسَى ٱلۡكِتَٰبَ وَجَعَلۡنَا مَعَهُۥٓ أَخَاهُ هَٰرُونَ وَزِيرًا ۝

36. Then We said: 'Go you two to a people who have belied Our signs.' Then We annihilated them utterly.

فَقُلۡنَا ٱذۡهَبَآ إِلَى ٱلۡقَوۡمِ ٱلَّذِينَ كَذَّبُواْ بِـَٔايَٰتِنَا فَدَمَّرۡنَٰهُمۡ تَدۡمِيرًا ۝

37. And the people of Noah! When they belied Our Messengers[563] We drowned them and made them an example to mankind. And We have prepared for the ungodly an afflictive torment.

وَقَوۡمَ نُوحٍ لَّمَّا كَذَّبُواْ ٱلرُّسُلَ أَغۡرَقۡنَٰهُمۡ وَجَعَلۡنَٰهُمۡ لِلنَّاسِ ءَايَةً وَأَعۡتَدۡنَا لِلظَّٰلِمِينَ عَذَابًا أَلِيمًا ۝

38. And the 'Ād and the Thamūd and the dwellers of the Rass, and many a generation in between.

وَعَادًا وَثَمُودَا۟ وَأَصۡحَٰبَ ٱلرَّسِّ وَقُرُونًا بَيۡنَ ذَٰلِكَ كَثِيرًا ۝

39. And for each of them We propounded a similitude and each We ruined completely.

وَكُلًّا ضَرَبۡنَا لَهُ ٱلۡأَمۡثَٰلَ وَكُلًّا تَبَّرۡنَا تَتۡبِيرًا ۝

---

563. To reject one Messenger of God is tantamount to the rejection of all Prophets; this because since they preach what is fundamentally one and the same doctrine.

40. Assuredly they have passed by the town on which was rained the evil rain. Are they not wont to see it? Aye! They expect not the Resurrection.

وَلَقَدۡ أَتَوۡاْ عَلَى ٱلۡقَرۡيَةِ ٱلَّتِىٓ أُمۡطِرَتۡ مَطَرَ ٱلسَّوۡءِ ۚ أَفَلَمۡ يَكُونُواْ يَرَوۡنَهَا ۚ بَلۡ كَانُواْ لَا يَرۡجُونَ نُشُورًا ﴿٤٠﴾

41. And when they see you, they hold you up for mockery: 'Is he the one whom Allah has sent as an envoy?

وَإِذَا رَأَوۡكَ إِن يَتَّخِذُونَكَ إِلَّا هُزُوًا أَهَـٰذَا ٱلَّذِى بَعَثَ ٱللَّهُ رَسُولًا ﴿٤١﴾

42. Well-nigh he had led us astray from our gods if we had not persevered towards them.' Presently they shall know, when they see the torment, who was more astray in respect of My path?

إِن كَادَ لَيُضِلُّنَا عَنۡ ءَالِهَتِنَا لَوۡلَآ أَن صَبَرۡنَا عَلَيۡهَا ۚ وَسَوۡفَ يَعۡلَمُونَ حِينَ يَرَوۡنَ ٱلۡعَذَابَ مَنۡ أَضَلُّ سَبِيلًا ﴿٤٢﴾

43. Have you seen him who has taken as his god his own desire? Will you over him be a trustee.

أَرَءَيۡتَ مَنِ ٱتَّخَذَ إِلَـٰهَهُۥ هَوَىٰهُ أَفَأَنتَ تَكُونُ عَلَيۡهِ وَكِيلًا ﴿٤٣﴾

44. Do you think that most of them hear or understand? They are but like the cattle; nay, they are even farther astray from the path.

أَمۡ تَحۡسَبُ أَنَّ أَكۡثَرَهُمۡ يَسۡمَعُونَ أَوۡ يَعۡقِلُونَ ۚ إِنۡ هُمۡ إِلَّا كَٱلۡأَنۡعَـٰمِ ۖ بَلۡ هُمۡ أَضَلُّ سَبِيلًا ﴿٤٤﴾

Section 5

45. Have you not observed your Lord – how He has stretched out the shadow? And if He had willed, He would have made it still. Then We have made the sun for it an indication.

أَلَمۡ تَرَ إِلَىٰ رَبِّكَ كَيۡفَ مَدَّ ٱلظِّلَّ وَلَوۡ شَآءَ لَجَعَلَهُۥ سَاكِنًا ثُمَّ جَعَلۡنَا ٱلشَّمۡسَ عَلَيۡهِ دَلِيلًا ﴿٤٥﴾

46. Then We draw it towards Us[564] with an easy drawing.

ثُمَّ قَبَضْنَٰهُ إِلَيْنَا قَبْضًا يَسِيرًا ۝

47. And it is He Who has made for you the night a covering, and the sleep a repose, and has made the day a resurrection.

وَهُوَ ٱلَّذِى جَعَلَ لَكُمُ ٱلَّيْلَ لِبَاسًا وَٱلنَّوْمَ سُبَاتًا وَجَعَلَ ٱلنَّهَارَ نُشُورًا ۝

48. And it is He Who sends forth the winds as a herald before His mercy: and We send down from the sky pure water;

وَهُوَ ٱلَّذِىٓ أَرْسَلَ ٱلرِّيَٰحَ بُشْرًۢا بَيْنَ يَدَىْ رَحْمَتِهِۦ ۚ وَأَنزَلْنَا مِنَ ٱلسَّمَآءِ مَآءً طَهُورًا ۝

49. That We quicken thereby a dead land, and We may give drink from it to what We have created of the cattle and human beings many.

لِّنُحْۦِىَ بِهِۦ بَلْدَةً مَّيْتًا وَنُسْقِيَهُۥ مِمَّا خَلَقْنَآ أَنْعَٰمًا وَأَنَاسِىَّ كَثِيرًا ۝

50. And We set it forth among them that they may be admonished, but most men begrudge anything save infidelity.

وَلَقَدْ صَرَّفْنَٰهُ بَيْنَهُمْ لِيَذَّكَّرُوا۟ فَأَبَىٰٓ أَكْثَرُ ٱلنَّاسِ إِلَّا كُفُورًا ۝

51. And had We willed, We would have raised a warner in every town.

وَلَوْ شِئْنَا لَبَعَثْنَا فِى كُلِّ قَرْيَةٍ نَّذِيرًا ۝

52. So obey not you the infidels, but strive against them with a great striving.

فَلَا تُطِعِ ٱلْكَٰفِرِينَ وَجَٰهِدْهُم بِهِۦ جِهَادًا كَبِيرًا ۝

53. And it is He Who has mixed the two oceans; this sweet and thirst-quenching; that, saltish and bitter; and has placed between the two a barrier and a partition complete.

وَهُوَ ٱلَّذِى مَرَجَ ٱلْبَحْرَيْنِ هَٰذَا عَذْبٌ فُرَاتٌ وَهَٰذَا مِلْحٌ أُجَاجٌ وَجَعَلَ بَيْنَهُمَا بَرْزَخًا وَحِجْرًا مَّحْجُورًا ۝

---

564. In other words, We contract the shadows. The main point is that it is God Who effects all these physical changes; none of them are brought about automatically, independent of Divine will.

54. And it is He Who has created man from water, and then made kinship for him by blood and wedlock. And your Lord is ever Potent.

وَهُوَ ٱلَّذِي خَلَقَ مِنَ ٱلْمَاءِ بَشَرًا فَجَعَلَهُۥ نَسَبًا وَصِهْرًا وَكَانَ رَبُّكَ قَدِيرًا ۝

55. And yet they worship besides Allah, what can neither benefit them nor hurt them; and the infidel is ever an aider of the devil against his Lord.

وَيَعْبُدُونَ مِن دُونِ ٱللَّهِ مَا لَا يَنفَعُهُمْ وَلَا يَضُرُّهُمْ وَكَانَ ٱلْكَافِرُ عَلَىٰ رَبِّهِۦ ظَهِيرًا ۝

56. And We sent you but as a bearer of glad tidings and a warner.

وَمَآ أَرْسَلْنَٰكَ إِلَّا مُبَشِّرًا وَنَذِيرًا ۝

57. Say: 'I ask of you no wage for this, save that whosoever wills may take a way unto his Lord.'

قُلْ مَآ أَسْـَٔلُكُمْ عَلَيْهِ مِنْ أَجْرٍ إِلَّا مَن شَآءَ أَن يَتَّخِذَ إِلَىٰ رَبِّهِۦ سَبِيلًا ۝

58. And trust in the Living One Who dies not, and hallow His praise. It suffices that He is Aware of the sins of His bondsmen,

وَتَوَكَّلْ عَلَى ٱلْحَيِّ ٱلَّذِي لَا يَمُوتُ وَسَبِّحْ بِحَمْدِهِۦ وَكَفَىٰ بِهِۦ بِذُنُوبِ عِبَادِهِۦ خَبِيرًا ۝

59. Who created the heavens and the earth and whatsoever is in between them in six days, then He established Himself on the Throne - the Compassionate! So concerning Him, ask anyone informed.

ٱلَّذِي خَلَقَ ٱلسَّمَٰوَٰتِ وَٱلْأَرْضَ وَمَا بَيْنَهُمَا فِي سِتَّةِ أَيَّامٍ ثُمَّ ٱسْتَوَىٰ عَلَى ٱلْعَرْشِ ٱلرَّحْمَٰنُ فَسْـَٔلْ بِهِۦ خَبِيرًا ۝

60. And when it is said to them: 'Prostrate yourselves before the Compassionate', they say: 'What is the Compassionate? Shall we prostrate ourselves unto what you command us?' And it increases in them only aversion.

وَإِذَا قِيلَ لَهُمُ ٱسْجُدُوا۟ لِلرَّحْمَٰنِ قَالُوا۟ وَمَا ٱلرَّحْمَٰنُ أَنَسْجُدُ لِمَا تَأْمُرُنَا وَزَادَهُمْ نُفُورًا ۩ ۝

Section 6

61. Blessed be He Who has placed big stars in the sky and has placed therein a lamp and a moon enlightening.

تَبَارَكَ الَّذِى جَعَلَ فِى السَّمَاءِ بُرُوجًا وَجَعَلَ فِيهَا سِرَاجًا وَقَمَرًا مُّنِيرًا ۝٦١

62. And it is He Who has assigned the night and the day a succession, for him who wishes to consider or who wishes to be grateful.

وَهُوَ الَّذِى جَعَلَ الَّيْلَ وَالنَّهَارَ خِلْفَةً لِّمَنْ أَرَادَ أَن يَذَّكَّرَ أَوْ أَرَادَ شُكُورًا ۝٦٢

63. And the servants of the Compassionate are those who walk upon the earth meekly, and when the ignorant address them, they say: 'Peace';

وَعِبَادُ الرَّحْمَٰنِ الَّذِينَ يَمْشُونَ عَلَى الْأَرْضِ هَوْنًا وَإِذَا خَاطَبَهُمُ الْجَاهِلُونَ قَالُوا سَلَامًا ۝٦٣

64. And those who pass the night before their Lord prostrate and standing up;

وَالَّذِينَ يَبِيتُونَ لِرَبِّهِمْ سُجَّدًا وَقِيَامًا ۝٦٤

65. And those who say: 'Our Lord! Avert from us the torment of Hell;[565] verily its torment is perishment;

وَالَّذِينَ يَقُولُونَ رَبَّنَا اصْرِفْ عَنَّا عَذَابَ جَهَنَّمَ إِنَّ عَذَابَهَا كَانَ غَرَامًا ۝٦٥

565. Mark the miraculous change for the better that the Prophet of Islam almost immediately brought about in his erstwhile ferocious, dissolute and irreligious countrymen. 'From time beyond memory, Mecca and the whole peninsula had been steeped in spiritual torpor. The people were sunk in superstition, cruelty, and vice. Thirteen years before the Hijrat, Mecca lay lifeless in this debased state. What a change had those thirteen years now produced! A band of several hundred persons had rejected idolatry, adopted the worship of One God, and surrendered themselves implicitly to the guidance of what they believed a Revelation from Him; praying to the Almighty with frequency and fervour, looking for pardon through His mercy, and striving to follow after good works, almsgiving, purity and justice. They now lived under a constant sense of the omnipotent power of God, and of His providential care over the minutes of their concerns. In all the gifts of nature, in every relation of life, at each turn of their affair, individual or public, they saw His hand. Mohammad was the minister of life to them, the source under God of their new born hopes; and to him they yielded an implicit submission' (Muir, *Life of Muhammad*, p. 161-62). 'Wine, women and war were the only three objects which claimed the love and devotion of the Arab' (Kremer, *Contribution to the History of Islamic Civilization*, p. 156). 'A few years prior to this they were sunk in superstition and practised all sorts of vice, but they now prostrated themselves five times a day in prayer to an invisible Allah, whom they had before known only imperfectly at best, and were honestly trying to follow the precepts that they believed had been sent directly from Him to them' (Gilman, *The Saracens*, p. 135).

66. Verily ill it is as an abode and as a station.'

إِنَّهَا سَآءَتْ مُسْتَقَرًّا وَمُقَامًا ﴿٦٦﴾

67. And those who when they expend are neither extravagant nor stingy; and it is a medium in between;

وَالَّذِينَ إِذَآ أَنفَقُواْ لَمْ يُسْرِفُواْ وَلَمْ يَقْتُرُواْ وَكَانَ بَيْنَ ذَٰلِكَ قَوَامًا ﴿٦٧﴾

68. And those who do not call on other gods along with Allah, and do not slay any soul which Allah has forbidden, save in justification; and do not commit adultery. And whosoever will do this, shall incur the meed.

وَالَّذِينَ لَا يَدْعُونَ مَعَ اللَّهِ إِلَٰهًا ءَاخَرَ وَلَا يَقْتُلُونَ النَّفْسَ الَّتِي حَرَّمَ اللَّهُ إِلَّا بِالْحَقِّ وَلَا يَزْنُونَ وَمَن يَفْعَلْ ذَٰلِكَ يَلْقَ أَثَامًا ﴿٦٨﴾

69. Multiplied for him shall be the torment on the Day of Resurrection, and he shall abide therein disgraced;

يُضَٰعَفْ لَهُ الْعَذَابُ يَوْمَ الْقِيَٰمَةِ وَيَخْلُدْ فِيهِ مُهَانًا ﴿٦٩﴾

70. Save he who repents and believes and works righteous works. Then these! For them Allah shall change their vices into virtues. Verily Allah is ever Forgiving, Merciful.

إِلَّا مَن تَابَ وَءَامَنَ وَعَمِلَ عَمَلًا صَٰلِحًا فَأُوْلَٰئِكَ يُبَدِّلُ اللَّهُ سَيِّئَاتِهِمْ حَسَنَٰتٍ وَكَانَ اللَّهُ غَفُورًا رَّحِيمًا ﴿٧٠﴾

71. And whosoever repents and works righteously, then surely he repents toward Him with a true repentance.

وَمَن تَابَ وَعَمِلَ صَٰلِحًا فَإِنَّهُ يَتُوبُ إِلَى اللَّهِ مَتَابًا ﴿٧١﴾

72. And also those who do not witness falsehood, and when they pass by some vanity pass by with dignity.

وَالَّذِينَ لَا يَشْهَدُونَ الزُّورَ وَإِذَا مَرُّواْ بِاللَّغْوِ مَرُّواْ كِرَامًا ﴿٧٢﴾

73. And also those who are admonished by the command of Allah, do not fall down thereat, deaf and blind.

وَالَّذِينَ إِذَا ذُكِّرُواْ بِـَٔايَٰتِ رَبِّهِمْ لَمْ يَخِرُّواْ عَلَيْهَا صُمًّا وَعُمْيَانًا ﴿٧٣﴾

74. And who say: 'Say; O our Lord! Bestow on us the coolness of eyes from our wives and our offspring,[566] and make us a pattern unto the God-fearing.'

75. Those shall be rewarded with the highest apartment, because of their fortitude; and there they shall be met with a greeting and salutation,

76. Abiders therein; excellent it is as an abode and as a station.

77. Say: 'My Lord does not care for you were it not for your prayer whereas you have ever belied, so presently this denial shall come as cleaving punishment.'

وَالَّذِينَ يَقُولُونَ رَبَّنَا هَبْ لَنَا مِنْ أَزْوَٰجِنَا وَذُرِّيَّـٰتِنَا قُرَّةَ أَعْيُنٍ وَٱجْعَلْنَا لِلْمُتَّقِينَ إِمَامًا ۝

أُو۟لَـٰٓئِكَ يُجْزَوْنَ ٱلْغُرْفَةَ بِمَا صَبَرُوا۟ وَيُلَقَّوْنَ فِيهَا تَحِيَّةً وَسَلَـٰمًا ۝

خَـٰلِدِينَ فِيهَا حَسُنَتْ مُسْتَقَرًّا وَمُقَامًا ۝

قُلْ مَا يَعْبَؤُا۟ بِكُمْ رَبِّي لَوْلَا دُعَآؤُكُمْ فَقَدْ كَذَّبْتُمْ فَسَوْفَ يَكُونُ لِزَامًا ۝

---

566. This once more reasserts the doctrine that Islam, unlike Christianity, does not regard this world as inherently bad, and does not reject family ties as an impediment to the service of God. Celibacy far from being a handmaid of believers is rather an impediment in his way.

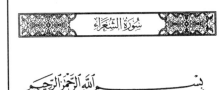

Sūrah 26

al-Shu'arā'

(Makkan, 11 Sections, 227 Verses)

In the name of Allah, the Compassionate, the Merciful.

Section 1

1. *Ṭā, Sīn, Mīm.*

2. These are the verses of a luminous Book.

3. Perhaps you shall kill yourself with grief because they do not become believers.

4. If We will, We can send down to them a sign from the heavens so that their necks would become submissive to it.

5. And there comes not to them any fresh admonition from the Compassionate but they are wont to be turning away therefrom.

6. So they have surely belied; so presently there shall appear to them the Truth of what they have been mocking at.

7. Do they not observe the earth – how We cause to grow therein every manner of fruit?

8. Verily therein is a sign, but most of them are not believers.

إِنَّ فِى ذَٰلِكَ لَأَيَةً وَمَا كَانَ أَكۡثَرُهُم مُّؤۡمِنِينَ ﴿٨﴾

9. And verily your Lord! He is the Mighty, the Merciful.

وَإِنَّ رَبَّكَ لَهُوَ ٱلۡعَزِيزُ ٱلرَّحِيمُ ﴿٩﴾

Section 2

10. And recall when your Lord said to Moses: 'Go you to an ungodly people,

وَإِذۡ نَادَىٰ رَبُّكَ مُوسَىٰٓ أَنِ ٱئۡتِ ٱلۡقَوۡمَ ٱلظَّٰلِمِينَ ﴿١٠﴾

11. The people of Pharaoh; they fear Me not?'

قَوۡمَ فِرۡعَوۡنَ أَلَا يَتَّقُونَ ﴿١١﴾

12. Moses said: 'Lord! I fear he will belie me;

قَالَ رَبِّ إِنِّى أَخَافُ أَن يُكَذِّبُونِ ﴿١٢﴾

13. And my breast straiten and my tongue move not quickly: so send for Aaron;

وَيَضِيقُ صَدۡرِى وَلَا يَنطَلِقُ لِسَانِى فَأَرۡسِلۡ إِلَىٰ هَٰرُونَ ﴿١٣﴾

14. And they have a crime against me; so I fear they shall slay me.'

وَلَهُمۡ عَلَىَّ ذَنۢبٌ فَأَخَافُ أَن يَقۡتُلُونِ ﴿١٤﴾

15. Allah said: 'By no means! So go both of you with Our signs; I shall be with you listening.

قَالَ كَلَّا فَٱذۡهَبَا بِـَٔايَٰتِنَآ إِنَّا مَعَكُم مُّسۡتَمِعُونَ ﴿١٥﴾

16. So go both of you to Pharaoh and say: 'We are the Messengers of the Lord of the worlds;

فَأۡتِيَا فِرۡعَوۡنَ فَقُولَآ إِنَّا رَسُولُ رَبِّ ٱلۡعَٰلَمِينَ ﴿١٦﴾

17. Send with us the children of Israel.'

أَنۡ أَرۡسِلۡ مَعَنَا بَنِىٓ إِسۡرَٰٓءِيلَ ﴿١٧﴾

18. Pharaoh said: 'Did we not bring you up among us as a child, and you stayed with us many years of your life?

قَالَ أَلَمۡ نُرَبِّكَ فِينَا وَلِيدًا وَلَبِثۡتَ فِينَا مِنۡ عُمُرِكَ سِنِينَ ﴿١٨﴾

19. And you did the deed you did; and you are of the ingrates.'

وَفَعَلْتَ فَعْلَتَكَ ٱلَّتِي فَعَلْتَ وَأَنتَ مِنَ ٱلْكَفِرِينَ ﴿١٩﴾

20. Moses said: 'I did the deed when I was mistaken.

قَالَ فَعَلْتُهَآ إِذًا وَأَنَا۠ مِنَ ٱلضَّآلِّينَ ﴿٢٠﴾

21. Then I fled from you when I feared you, and my Lord bestowed on me judgement and made me one of the envoys.

فَفَرَرْتُ مِنكُمْ لَمَّا خِفْتُكُمْ فَوَهَبَ لِى رَبِّى حُكْمًا وَجَعَلَنِى مِنَ ٱلْمُرْسَلِينَ ﴿٢١﴾

22. And the favour with which you did oblige me was that you had enslaved the children of Israel.'

وَتِلْكَ نِعْمَةٌ تَمُنُّهَا عَلَىَّ أَنْ عَبَّدتَّ بَنِىٓ إِسْرَٰٓءِيلَ ﴿٢٢﴾

23. Pharaoh said: 'And what is this: Lord of the worlds?'

قَالَ فِرْعَوْنُ وَمَا رَبُّ ٱلْعَٰلَمِينَ ﴿٢٣﴾

24. Moses said: 'Lord of the heavens and the earth and whatever is in-between, if you seek to be convinced.'

قَالَ رَبُّ ٱلسَّمَٰوَٰتِ وَٱلْأَرْضِ وَمَا بَيْنَهُمَآ إِن كُنتُم مُّوقِنِينَ ﴿٢٤﴾

25. Pharaoh said to those around him in amazement: 'Do you not hear?'

قَالَ لِمَنْ حَوْلَهُۥٓ أَلَا تَسْتَمِعُونَ ﴿٢٥﴾

26. Moses said: 'Your Lord and Lord of your ancestors.'

قَالَ رَبُّكُمْ وَرَبُّ ءَابَآئِكُمُ ٱلْأَوَّلِينَ ﴿٢٦﴾

27. Pharaoh said: 'The Messenger sent to you is mad indeed.'

قَالَ إِنَّ رَسُولَكُمُ ٱلَّذِىٓ أُرْسِلَ إِلَيْكُمْ لَمَجْنُونٌ ﴿٢٧﴾

28. Moses said: 'Lord of the east and the west and whatever is in-between, if you care to understand'.

قَالَ رَبُّ ٱلْمَشْرِقِ وَٱلْمَغْرِبِ وَمَا بَيْنَهُمَآ إِن كُنتُمْ تَعْقِلُونَ ﴿٢٨﴾

29. Pharaoh said: 'If you will take a god other than me, I shall surely place you among the prisoners.'

قَالَ لَئِنِ ٱتَّخَذتَ إِلَٰهًا غَيْرِى لَأَجْعَلَنَّكَ مِنَ ٱلْمَسْجُونِينَ ﴿٢٩﴾

30. Moses said: 'What, even if I bring to you something evident?'

قَالَ أَوَلَوْ جِئْتُكَ بِشَيْءٍ مُّبِيْنٍ ۝

31. Pharaoh said: 'Forth with it then, if you are of the truth-tellers.'

قَالَ فَأْتِ بِهٖۤ إِنْ كُنْتَ مِنَ الصّٰدِقِيْنَ ۝

32. Then he cast down his rod, and it was a serpent manifest.

فَأَلْقٰى عَصَاهُ فَإِذَا هِيَ ثُعْبَانٌ مُّبِيْنٌ ۝

33. And he drew forth his hand, and it was white unto the beholders.

وَنَزَعَ يَدَهُ فَإِذَا هِيَ بَيْضَآءُ لِلنّٰظِرِيْنَ ۝

Section 3

34. Pharaoh said to the chiefs around him: 'Verily he is a magician knowing;

قَالَ لِلْمَلَإِ حَوْلَهٗۤ إِنَّ هٰذَا لَسٰحِرٌ عَلِيْمٌ ۝

35. He would drive you out of your land through his magic, what is it then that you command?'

يُرِيْدُ أَنْ يُّخْرِجَكُمْ مِّنْ أَرْضِكُمْ بِسِحْرِهٖ فَمَاذَا تَأْمُرُوْنَ ۝

36. They said: 'Put him off and his brother, and send callers to the cities;

قَالُوۤا أَرْجِهْ وَأَخَاهُ وَابْعَثْ فِي الْمَدَآئِنِ حٰشِرِيْنَ ۝

37. That they may bring to you every magician knowing.'

يَأْتُوْكَ بِكُلِّ سَحَّارٍ عَلِيْمٍ ۝

38. So the magicians were assembled at a set time on a day made known.

فَجُمِعَ السَّحَرَةُ لِمِيْقَاتِ يَوْمٍ مَّعْلُوْمٍ ۝

39. And it was said to the people: 'Are you are going to assemble?

وَقِيْلَ لِلنَّاسِ هَلْ أَنْتُمْ مُّجْتَمِعُوْنَ ۝

40. Likely we are to follow the magicians, if they are the winners.'

لَعَلَّنَا نَتَّبِعُ السَّحَرَةَ إِنْ كَانُوْا هُمُ الْغٰلِبِيْنَ ۝

41. Then when the magicians came they said to Pharaoh: 'Will there be a big reward for us if we are the winners?'

42. He said: 'Yea; and you shall be of those brought nigh.'

43. Moses said to them: 'Cast down what you have to cast.'

44. Then they cast their ropes and their staves, and said: 'By the might of Pharaoh we shall be victors.'

45. Then Moses cast his rod, and lo! It swallowed up what they had invented.

46. Then the magicians flung themselves prostrate.

47. They said: 'We now believe in the Lord of the worlds,

48. The Lord of Moses and Aaron.'

49. Pharaoh said: 'You believed ere I gave you leave. Surely he is your chief who taught you magic; so you shall surely come to know I shall certainly cut off your hands and feet on opposite sides, and certainly I shall crucify you all.'

50. They said: 'No harm! Verily to our Lord we are to return;

51. We long that our Lord shall forgive us our faults as we have been the first of believers.'

فَلَمَّا جَآءَ السَّحَرَةُ قَالُوا لِفِرْعَوْنَ أَئِنَّ لَنَا لَأَجْرًا إِن كُنَّا نَحْنُ الْغَالِبِينَ ﴿٤١﴾

قَالَ نَعَمْ وَإِنَّكُمْ إِذًا لَّمِنَ الْمُقَرَّبِينَ ﴿٤٢﴾

قَالَ لَهُم مُّوسَىٰ أَلْقُوا مَآ أَنتُم مُّلْقُونَ ﴿٤٣﴾

فَأَلْقَوْا حِبَالَهُمْ وَعِصِيَّهُمْ وَقَالُوا بِعِزَّةِ فِرْعَوْنَ إِنَّا لَنَحْنُ الْغَالِبُونَ ﴿٤٤﴾

فَأَلْقَىٰ مُوسَىٰ عَصَاهُ فَإِذَا هِيَ تَلْقَفُ مَا يَأْفِكُونَ ﴿٤٥﴾

فَأُلْقِيَ السَّحَرَةُ سَاجِدِينَ ﴿٤٦﴾

قَالُوا ءَامَنَّا بِرَبِّ الْعَالَمِينَ ﴿٤٧﴾

رَبِّ مُوسَىٰ وَهَارُونَ ﴿٤٨﴾

قَالَ ءَامَنتُمْ لَهُۥ قَبْلَ أَنْ ءَاذَنَ لَكُمْ إِنَّهُۥ لَكَبِيرُكُمُ الَّذِى عَلَّمَكُمُ السِّحْرَ فَلَسَوْفَ تَعْلَمُونَ لَأُقَطِّعَنَّ أَيْدِيَكُمْ وَأَرْجُلَكُم مِّنْ خِلَفٍ وَلَأُصَلِّبَنَّكُمْ أَجْمَعِينَ ﴿٤٩﴾

قَالُوا لَا ضَيْرَ إِنَّا إِلَىٰ رَبِّنَا مُنقَلِبُونَ ﴿٥٠﴾

إِنَّا نَطْمَعُ أَن يَغْفِرَ لَنَا رَبُّنَا خَطَايَانَا أَن كُنَّا أَوَّلَ الْمُؤْمِنِينَ ﴿٥١﴾

Section 4

52. And We revealed to Moses: 'Depart by night with My bondsmen; certainly you will be pursued.'

وَأَوْحَيْنَا إِلَىٰ مُوسَىٰ أَنْ أَسْرِ بِعِبَادِي إِنَّكُم مُّتَّبَعُونَ ﴿٥٢﴾

53. Then Pharaoh sent callers to the cities:

فَأَرْسَلَ فِرْعَوْنُ فِي الْمَدَائِنِ حَاشِرِينَ ﴿٥٣﴾

54. 'Verily these are but a small band;

إِنَّ هَٰؤُلَاءِ لَشِرْذِمَةٌ قَلِيلُونَ ﴿٥٤﴾

55. And verily they have enraged us;

وَإِنَّهُمْ لَنَا لَغَائِظُونَ ﴿٥٥﴾

56. And we are the host well-provided.'

وَإِنَّا لَجَمِيعٌ حَاذِرُونَ ﴿٥٦﴾

57. Then We drove them from gardens and streams;

فَأَخْرَجْنَاهُم مِّن جَنَّاتٍ وَعُيُونٍ ﴿٥٧﴾

58. And treasures and a noble station,

وَكُنُوزٍ وَمَقَامٍ كَرِيمٍ ﴿٥٨﴾

59. Even so. And We caused the children of Israel to inherit them.

كَذَٰلِكَ وَأَوْرَثْنَاهَا بَنِي إِسْرَائِيلَ ﴿٥٩﴾

60. And they pursued them at sunrise.

فَأَتْبَعُوهُم مُّشْرِقِينَ ﴿٦٠﴾

61. And when the two parties saw each other the companions of Moses said: 'Verily we are overtaken.'

فَلَمَّا تَرَاءَى الْجَمْعَانِ قَالَ أَصْحَابُ مُوسَىٰ إِنَّا لَمُدْرَكُونَ ﴿٦١﴾

62. Moses said: 'By no means! With me is my Lord; He shall guide me.'

قَالَ كَلَّا إِنَّ مَعِيَ رَبِّي سَيَهْدِينِ ﴿٦٢﴾

63. Then We revealed to Moses: 'Smite you the sea with your rod.' So it became separated, and each part was like a mighty mount.

فَأَوْحَيْنَا إِلَىٰ مُوسَىٰ أَنِ اضْرِب بِّعَصَاكَ الْبَحْرَ فَانفَلَقَ فَكَانَ كُلُّ فِرْقٍ كَالطَّوْدِ الْعَظِيمِ ﴿٦٣﴾

64. And near We brought there the others on.

وَأَزْلَفْنَا ثَمَّ ٱلْأَخَرِينَ ﴿٦٤﴾

65. And We delivered Moses and those with him together.

وَأَنجَيْنَا مُوسَىٰ وَمَن مَّعَهُۥٓ أَجْمَعِينَ ﴿٦٥﴾

66. Then We drowned the others.

ثُمَّ أَغْرَقْنَا ٱلْأَخَرِينَ ﴿٦٦﴾

67. Verily herein is a sign, yet most of them are not believers.

إِنَّ فِى ذَٰلِكَ لَأَيَةً وَمَا كَانَ أَكْثَرُهُم مُّؤْمِنِينَ ﴿٦٧﴾

68. And verily your Lord! He is the Mighty, the Merciful.

وَإِنَّ رَبَّكَ لَهُوَ ٱلْعَزِيزُ ٱلرَّحِيمُ ﴿٦٨﴾

Section 5

69. And recite to them the story of Abraham;

وَٱتْلُ عَلَيْهِمْ نَبَأَ إِبْرَٰهِيمَ ﴿٦٩﴾

70. When he said to his father and his people: 'What do you worship?'

إِذْ قَالَ لِأَبِيهِ وَقَوْمِهِۦ مَا تَعْبُدُونَ ﴿٧٠﴾

71. They said: 'We worship idols, and to them we are ever devoted.'

قَالُوا۟ نَعْبُدُ أَصْنَامًا فَنَظَلُّ لَهَا عَٰكِفِينَ ﴿٧١﴾

72. He said: 'Do they hear you when you cry?

قَالَ هَلْ يَسْمَعُونَكُمْ إِذْ تَدْعُونَ ﴿٧٢﴾

73. Or, do they benefit you, or do they hurt you?'

أَوْ يَنفَعُونَكُمْ أَوْ يَضُرُّونَ ﴿٧٣﴾

74. They said: 'Nay: but we found our fathers doing in this wise.'

قَالُوا۟ بَلْ وَجَدْنَآ ءَابَآءَنَا كَذَٰلِكَ يَفْعَلُونَ ﴿٧٤﴾

75. He said: 'Have you observed what you have been worshipping,

قَالَ أَفَرَءَيْتُم مَّا كُنتُمْ تَعْبُدُونَ ﴿٧٥﴾

76. You and your forefathers?

أَنتُمْ وَءَابَآؤُكُمُ ٱلْأَقْدَمُونَ ﴿٧٦﴾

77. Verily they are an enemy to me, save the Lord of the worlds;

فَإِنَّهُمْ عَدُوٌّ لِّىٓ إِلَّا رَبَّ ٱلْعَٰلَمِينَ ﴿٧٧﴾

78. Who has created me, and He guides me;

اَلَّذِى خَلَقَنِى فَهُوَ يَهْدِينِ ۝

79. He Who feeds me and gives me to drink;

وَالَّذِى هُوَ يُطْعِمُنِى وَيَسْقِينِ ۝

80. And when I sicken, then He heals me.

وَإِذَا مَرِضْتُ فَهُوَ يَشْفِينِ ۝

81. And He Who will cause me to die, then will quicken me.

وَالَّذِى يُمِيتُنِى ثُمَّ يُحْيِينِ ۝

82. And He Who, I long for, will forgive me my faults on the Day of Requital.

وَالَّذِىٓ أَطْمَعُ أَن يَغْفِرَ لِى خَطِيٓئَتِى يَوْمَ الدِّينِ ۝

83. Lord! Bestow on me wisdom, and join me with the righteous.

رَبِّ هَبْ لِى حُكْمًا وَأَلْحِقْنِى بِالصَّالِحِينَ ۝

84. And assign to me an honourable mention among the posterity.

وَاجْعَل لِّى لِسَانَ صِدْقٍ فِى الْأَخِرِينَ ۝

85. And make me of the inheritors of the Garden of Delight.

وَاجْعَلْنِى مِن وَرَثَةِ جَنَّةِ النَّعِيمِ ۝

86. And forgive my father; verily he is of the erring.

وَاغْفِرْ لِأَبِىٓ إِنَّهُۥ كَانَ مِنَ الضَّآلِّينَ ۝

87. And do not humiliate me on the Day when mankind will be raised,

وَلَا تُخْزِنِى يَوْمَ يُبْعَثُونَ ۝

88. The Day whereon neither riches nor sons will be of any avail;

يَوْمَ لَا يَنفَعُ مَالٌ وَلَا بَنُونَ ۝

89. Unless it be he, who shall bring to Allah a whole heart;

إِلَّا مَنْ أَتَى اللَّهَ بِقَلْبٍ سَلِيمٍ ۝

90. And the Garden will be brought nigh of the God-fearing;

وَأُزْلِفَتِ الْجَنَّةُ لِلْمُتَّقِينَ ۝

91. And the fierce Fire will be made apparent to the seduced ones.

وَبُرِّزَتِ ٱلْجَحِيمُ لِلْغَاوِينَ ۝

92. And it will be said to them, where is that which you were wont to worship,

وَقِيلَ لَهُمْ أَيْنَ مَا كُنتُمْ تَعْبُدُونَ ۝

93. Besides Allah? Can they succour you or succour even themselves?'

مِن دُونِ ٱللَّهِ هَلْ يَنصُرُونَكُمْ أَوْ يَنتَصِرُونَ ۝

94. Then they will be hurled therein, they and those seduced.

فَكُبْكِبُوا۟ فِيهَا هُمْ وَٱلْغَاوُۥنَ ۝

95. And the hosts of Iblis together.

وَجُنُودُ إِبْلِيسَ أَجْمَعُونَ ۝

96. And they while contending therein, will say:

قَالُوا۟ وَهُمْ فِيهَا يَخْتَصِمُونَ ۝

97. 'By Allah, we have indeed been in error manifest,

تَٱللَّهِ إِن كُنَّا لَفِى ضَلَٰلٍ مُّبِينٍ ۝

98. When we equalled you with the Lord of the worlds.

إِذْ نُسَوِّيكُم بِرَبِّ ٱلْعَٰلَمِينَ ۝

99. And none led us astray except the culprits.

وَمَآ أَضَلَّنَآ إِلَّا ٱلْمُجْرِمُونَ ۝

100. So none we have as intercessors;

فَمَا لَنَا مِن شَٰفِعِينَ ۝

101. Nor any loving friend.

وَلَا صَدِيقٍ حَمِيمٍ ۝

102. Were there for us a return, we would be of the believers.'

فَلَوْ أَنَّ لَنَا كَرَّةً فَنَكُونَ مِنَ ٱلْمُؤْمِنِينَ ۝

103. Verily in this story is a sign, yet most of them are not believers.

إِنَّ فِى ذَٰلِكَ لَءَايَةً وَمَا كَانَ أَكْثَرُهُم مُّؤْمِنِينَ ۝

104. And truly your Lord! He is the Mighty, the Merciful.

وَإِنَّ رَبَّكَ لَهُوَ ٱلْعَزِيزُ ٱلرَّحِيمُ ۝

Section 6

105. And Noah's people belied Our envoys;

كَذَّبَتۡ قَوۡمُ نُوحٍ ٱلۡمُرۡسَلِينَ ۝

106. When their brother Noah said to them: 'Fear you not?

إِذۡ قَالَ لَهُمۡ أَخُوهُمۡ نُوحٌ أَلَا تَتَّقُونَ ۝

107. Verily I am unto you a trusted Messenger;

إِنِّي لَكُمۡ رَسُولٌ أَمِينٌ ۝

108. So fear Allah and obey me.

فَٱتَّقُوا۟ ٱللَّهَ وَأَطِيعُونِ ۝

109. And I ask of you no wage for it; my wage is but with the Lord of the worlds.

وَمَآ أَسۡـَٔلُكُمۡ عَلَيۡهِ مِنۡ أَجۡرٍ إِنۡ أَجۡرِيَ إِلَّا عَلَىٰ رَبِّ ٱلۡعَٰلَمِينَ ۝

110. So fear Allah and obey me.'

فَٱتَّقُوا۟ ٱللَّهَ وَأَطِيعُونِ ۝

111. They said: 'Shall we believe in you when the meanest of us are your followers?'

قَالُوٓا۟ أَنُؤۡمِنُ لَكَ وَٱتَّبَعَكَ ٱلۡأَرۡذَلُونَ ۝

112. He said: 'I have no knowledge of what they have been working;

قَالَ وَمَا عِلۡمِي بِمَا كَانُوا۟ يَعۡمَلُونَ ۝

113. Their reckoning is upon my Lord, if you but know;

إِنۡ حِسَابُهُمۡ إِلَّا عَلَىٰ رَبِّي لَوۡ تَشۡعُرُونَ ۝

114. And I am not to drive away the Believers.

وَمَآ أَنَا۠ بِطَارِدِ ٱلۡمُؤۡمِنِينَ ۝

115. I am not but a manifest warner.'

إِنۡ أَنَا۠ إِلَّا نَذِيرٌ مُّبِينٌ ۝

116. They said: 'If you desist not, you shall be of those stoned.'

قَالُوا۟ لَئِن لَّمۡ تَنتَهِ يَٰنُوحُ لَتَكُونَنَّ مِنَ ٱلۡمَرۡجُومِينَ ۝

117. He said: 'Lord! My people have belied me.

قَالَ رَبِّ إِنَّ قَوۡمِي كَذَّبُونِ ۝

118. So decide between us and them, and deliver me and those who are with me of the believers.'

فَٱفْتَحْ بَيْنِي وَبَيْنَهُمْ فَتْحًا وَنَجِّنِي وَمَن مَّعِيَ مِنَ ٱلْمُؤْمِنِينَ ﴿١١٨﴾

119. Therefore We delivered him and those with him in a laden ark.

فَأَنجَيْنَٰهُ وَمَن مَّعَهُۥ فِي ٱلْفُلْكِ ٱلْمَشْحُونِ ﴿١١٩﴾

120. Then We drowned the rest thereafter.

ثُمَّ أَغْرَقْنَا بَعْدُ ٱلْبَاقِينَ ﴿١٢٠﴾

121. Verily in this story is a sign: yet most of them are not Believers.

إِنَّ فِي ذَٰلِكَ لَأَيَةً وَمَا كَانَ أَكْثَرُهُم مُّؤْمِنِينَ ﴿١٢١﴾

122. And your Lord! He is the Mighty, the Merciful.

وَإِنَّ رَبَّكَ لَهُوَ ٱلْعَزِيزُ ٱلرَّحِيمُ ﴿١٢٢﴾

Section 7

123. The 'Ad belied Our envoys;

كَذَّبَتْ عَادٌ ٱلْمُرْسَلِينَ ﴿١٢٣﴾

124. When their brother Hud said to them: 'Fear you not?

إِذْ قَالَ لَهُمْ أَخُوهُمْ هُودٌ أَلَا تَتَّقُونَ ﴿١٢٤﴾

125. Verily I am unto you a trusted Messenger;

إِنِّي لَكُمْ رَسُولٌ أَمِينٌ ﴿١٢٥﴾

126. So fear Allah and obey me;

فَٱتَّقُوا ٱللَّهَ وَأَطِيعُونِ ﴿١٢٦﴾

127. And I ask of you no wage for it; my wage is but with the Lord of the worlds.

وَمَا أَسْـَٔلُكُمْ عَلَيْهِ مِنْ أَجْرٍ إِنْ أَجْرِيَ إِلَّا عَلَىٰ رَبِّ ٱلْعَٰلَمِينَ ﴿١٢٧﴾

128. Do you build on every eminence a landmark in vanity?

أَتَبْنُونَ بِكُلِّ رِيعٍ ءَايَةً تَعْبَثُونَ ﴿١٢٨﴾

129. And do you take for yourselves castles that perhaps you may abide?

وَتَتَّخِذُونَ مَصَانِعَ لَعَلَّكُمْ تَخْلُدُونَ ﴿١٢٩﴾

130. And when you seize you seize like unto tyrant.

وَإِذَا بَطَشْتُم بَطَشْتُمْ جَبَّارِينَ ﴿١٣٠﴾

131. So fear Allah and obey me.

فَٱتَّقُوا۟ ٱللَّهَ وَأَطِيعُونِ ﴿١٣١﴾

132. And fear Him Who has aided you with all that you know.

وَٱتَّقُوا۟ ٱلَّذِىٓ أَمَدَّكُم بِمَا تَعْلَمُونَ ﴿١٣٢﴾

133. He has aided you with the cattle and sons;

أَمَدَّكُم بِأَنْعَٰمٍ وَبَنِينَ ﴿١٣٣﴾

134. And gardens and springs.

وَجَنَّٰتٍ وَعُيُونٍ ﴿١٣٤﴾

135. Verily I fear for you the torment of a mighty Day.'

إِنِّىٓ أَخَافُ عَلَيْكُمْ عَذَابَ يَوْمٍ عَظِيمٍ ﴿١٣٥﴾

136. They said: 'It is equal to us whether you admonish or are you not of the admonishers.

قَالُوا۟ سَوَآءٌ عَلَيْنَآ أَوَعَظْتَ أَمْ لَمْ تَكُن مِّنَ ٱلْوَٰعِظِينَ ﴿١٣٦﴾

137. This is but a custom of the ancients;

إِنْ هَٰذَآ إِلَّا خُلُقُ ٱلْأَوَّلِينَ ﴿١٣٧﴾

138. And we are not going to be tormented.'

وَمَا نَحْنُ بِمُعَذَّبِينَ ﴿١٣٨﴾

139. And they belied him; so We destroyed them. Verily in this story is a sign; yet most of them are not believers.

فَكَذَّبُوهُ فَأَهْلَكْنَٰهُمْ إِنَّ فِى ذَٰلِكَ لَآيَةً وَمَا كَانَ أَكْثَرُهُم مُّؤْمِنِينَ ﴿١٣٩﴾

140. And verily your Lord! He is the Mighty, the Merciful.

وَإِنَّ رَبَّكَ لَهُوَ ٱلْعَزِيزُ ٱلرَّحِيمُ ﴿١٤٠﴾

Section 8

141. The Thamūd belied Our envoys;

كَذَّبَتْ ثَمُودُ ٱلْمُرْسَلِينَ ﴿١٤١﴾

142. When their brother Ṣāliḥ said unto them: 'Fear you not?

إِذْ قَالَ لَهُمْ أَخُوهُمْ صَٰلِحٌ أَلَا تَتَّقُونَ ﴿١٤٢﴾

143. Verily I am unto you a trusted Messenger.

إِنِّى لَكُمْ رَسُولٌ أَمِينٌ ﴿١٤٣﴾

144. So fear Allah and obey me.

فَٱتَّقُوا۟ ٱللَّهَ وَأَطِيعُونِ ﴿١٤٤﴾

145. And I ask you no wage for it, my wage is but with the Lord of the worlds.

وَمَآ أَسْـَٔلُكُمْ عَلَيْهِ مِنْ أَجْرٍ إِنْ أَجْرِىَ إِلَّا عَلَىٰ رَبِّ ٱلْعَٰلَمِينَ ﴿١٤٥﴾

146. Will ye be left secure in what is before us;

أَتُتْرَكُونَ فِى مَا هَٰهُنَآ ءَامِنِينَ ﴿١٤٦﴾

147. In gardens and springs;

فِى جَنَّٰتٍ وَعُيُونٍ ﴿١٤٧﴾

148. And cornfields and palm trees of which the spathes are fine?

وَزُرُوعٍ وَنَخْلٍ طَلْعُهَا هَضِيمٌ ﴿١٤٨﴾

149. And do you hew out in the rocks houses skilfully?

وَتَنْحِتُونَ مِنَ ٱلْجِبَالِ بُيُوتًا فَٰرِهِينَ ﴿١٤٩﴾

150. So fear Allah and obey me.

فَٱتَّقُوا۟ ٱللَّهَ وَأَطِيعُونِ ﴿١٥٠﴾

151. And do not follow the bidding of the extravagant.

وَلَا تُطِيعُوٓا۟ أَمْرَ ٱلْمُسْرِفِينَ ﴿١٥١﴾

152. Who act corruptly in the land and do not rectify.'

ٱلَّذِينَ يُفْسِدُونَ فِى ٱلْأَرْضِ وَلَا يُصْلِحُونَ ﴿١٥٢﴾

153. They said: 'You are but one of the bewitched.

قَالُوٓا۟ إِنَّمَآ أَنتَ مِنَ ٱلْمُسَحَّرِينَ ﴿١٥٣﴾

154. You are but a human being like us. So bring you a sign if you are of the truthful.'

مَآ أَنتَ إِلَّا بَشَرٌ مِّثْلُنَا فَأْتِ بِـَٔايَةٍ إِن كُنتَ مِنَ ٱلصَّٰدِقِينَ ﴿١٥٤﴾

155. He said: 'This is a she-camel; to her is a drink, and to you is a drink, each on a day known.

قَالَ هَٰذِهِۦ نَاقَةٌ لَّهَا شِرْبٌ وَلَكُمْ شِرْبُ يَوْمٍ مَّعْلُومٍ ﴿١٥٥﴾

156. And do not touch her with an evil, lest there take hold of you the torment of a mighty Day.'

وَلَا تَمَسُّوهَا بِسُوٓءٍ فَيَأْخُذَكُمْ عَذَابُ يَوْمٍ عَظِيمٍ ﴿١٥٦﴾

157. Then they hamstrung her; then they became regretful.

فَعَقَرُوهَا فَأَصْبَحُوا نَـٰدِمِينَ ۝

158. So the chastisement overtook them. Verily in this story is a sign, yet most of them are not believers.

فَأَخَذَهُمُ الْعَذَابُ إِنَّ فِي ذَٰلِكَ لَآيَةً وَمَا كَانَ أَكْثَرُهُم مُّؤْمِنِينَ ۝

159. And verily your Lord! He is the Mighty, the Merciful.

وَإِنَّ رَبَّكَ لَهُوَ الْعَزِيزُ الرَّحِيمُ ۝

Section 9

160. Then the people of Lot belied Our envoys;

كَذَّبَتْ قَوْمُ لُوطٍ الْمُرْسَلِينَ ۝

161. When their brother Lot said to them: 'Fear you not?

إِذْ قَالَ لَهُمْ أَخُوهُمْ لُوطٌ أَلَا تَتَّقُونَ ۝

162. Verily I am unto you a trusted Messenger.

إِنِّي لَكُمْ رَسُولٌ أَمِينٌ ۝

163. So fear Allah and obey me.

فَاتَّقُوا اللَّهَ وَأَطِيعُونِ ۝

164. And I ask of you no wage for it; my wage is but with the Lord of the worlds.

وَمَا أَسْأَلُكُمْ عَلَيْهِ مِنْ أَجْرٍ إِنْ أَجْرِيَ إِلَّا عَلَىٰ رَبِّ الْعَالَمِينَ ۝

165. Do you go in, of all creatures, unto the males?

أَتَأْتُونَ الذُّكْرَانَ مِنَ الْعَالَمِينَ ۝

166. And do you leave your spouses your Lord has created for you? Aye! You are a people trespassing.'

وَتَذَرُونَ مَا خَلَقَ لَكُمْ رَبُّكُم مِّنْ أَزْوَاجِكُم بَلْ أَنتُمْ قَوْمٌ عَادُونَ ۝

167. They said: 'If you desist not, O Lot! You shall be of those driven forth.'

قَالُوا لَئِن لَّمْ تَنتَهِ يَٰلُوطُ لَتَكُونَنَّ مِنَ الْمُخْرَجِينَ ۝

168. He said: 'Verily I am of those who abhor what you do.

قَالَ إِنِّى لِعَمَلِكُم مِّنَ ٱلۡقَالِينَ ﴿١٦٨﴾

169. Lord! Deliver me and my household from what they work.'

رَبِّ نَجِّنِى وَأَهۡلِى مِمَّا يَعۡمَلُونَ ﴿١٦٩﴾

170. So We delivered him and his household all;

فَنَجَّيۡنَٰهُ وَأَهۡلَهُۥٓ أَجۡمَعِينَ ﴿١٧٠﴾

171. Save an old woman among the lingers.

إِلَّا عَجُوزًا فِى ٱلۡغَٰبِرِينَ ﴿١٧١﴾

172. Thereafter We annihilated the rest.

ثُمَّ دَمَّرۡنَا ٱلۡأٓخَرِينَ ﴿١٧٢﴾

173. And We rained on them a rain – ill was the rain on those warned.

وَأَمۡطَرۡنَا عَلَيۡهِم مَّطَرًا فَسَآءَ مَطَرُ ٱلۡمُنذَرِينَ ﴿١٧٣﴾

174. Verily in this story is a sign, yet most of them are not believers.

إِنَّ فِى ذَٰلِكَ لَأٓيَةً وَمَا كَانَ أَكۡثَرُهُم مُّؤۡمِنِينَ ﴿١٧٤﴾

175. And verily your Lord! He is the Mighty, the Merciful.

وَإِنَّ رَبَّكَ لَهُوَ ٱلۡعَزِيزُ ٱلرَّحِيمُ ﴿١٧٥﴾

Section 10

176. The dwellers of the wood belied Our envoys.

كَذَّبَ أَصۡحَٰبُ لۡئَيۡكَةِ ٱلۡمُرۡسَلِينَ ﴿١٧٦﴾

177. When their brother Shu'ayb said to them: 'Fear you not?

إِذۡ قَالَ لَهُمۡ شُعَيۡبٌ أَلَا تَتَّقُونَ ﴿١٧٧﴾

178. Verily I am unto you a trusted Messenger;

إِنِّى لَكُمۡ رَسُولٌ أَمِينٌ ﴿١٧٨﴾

179. So fear Allah and obey me.

فَٱتَّقُوا ٱللَّهَ وَأَطِيعُونِ ﴿١٧٩﴾

180. And I ask you no wage; my wage is but with the Lord of the worlds.

وَمَآ أَسۡـَٔلُكُمۡ عَلَيۡهِ مِنۡ أَجۡرٍ إِنۡ أَجۡرِىَ إِلَّا عَلَىٰ رَبِّ ٱلۡعَٰلَمِينَ ﴿١٨٠﴾

181. Give full measure, and be not of those who cause others to lose.

أَوْفُوا۟ ٱلْكَيْلَ وَلَا تَكُونُوا۟ مِنَ ٱلْمُخْسِرِينَ ﴿١٨١﴾

182. And weigh with a straight balance.

وَزِنُوا۟ بِٱلْقِسْطَاسِ ٱلْمُسْتَقِيمِ ﴿١٨٢﴾

183. And defraud not people of their things, and commit not corruption on the earth.

وَلَا تَبْخَسُوا۟ ٱلنَّاسَ أَشْيَآءَهُمْ وَلَا تَعْثَوْا۟ فِى ٱلْأَرْضِ مُفْسِدِينَ ﴿١٨٣﴾

184. So fear Him Who has created you and the former generations.’

وَٱتَّقُوا۟ ٱلَّذِى خَلَقَكُمْ وَٱلْجِبِلَّةَ ٱلْأَوَّلِينَ ﴿١٨٤﴾

185. They said: ‘You are but of the bewitched.

قَالُوٓا۟ إِنَّمَآ أَنتَ مِنَ ٱلْمُسَحَّرِينَ ﴿١٨٥﴾

186. And you are but a human being like us, and we consider you to be of the liars,

وَمَآ أَنتَ إِلَّا بَشَرٌ مِّثْلُنَا وَإِن نَّظُنُّكَ لَمِنَ ٱلْكَٰذِبِينَ ﴿١٨٦﴾

187. So cause you a fragment of the sky to fall upon us, if you are of the truthful.’

فَأَسْقِطْ عَلَيْنَا كِسَفًا مِّنَ ٱلسَّمَآءِ إِن كُنتَ مِنَ ٱلصَّٰدِقِينَ ﴿١٨٧﴾

188. He said: ‘My Lord is the Best Knower of what you work.’

قَالَ رَبِّىٓ أَعْلَمُ بِمَا تَعْمَلُونَ ﴿١٨٨﴾

189. Then they belied him. Wherefore there seized them the torment of the Day of Shadow. Verily it was the torment of a Mighty Day.

فَكَذَّبُوهُ فَأَخَذَهُمْ عَذَابُ يَوْمِ ٱلظُّلَّةِ إِنَّهُۥ كَانَ عَذَابَ يَوْمٍ عَظِيمٍ ﴿١٨٩﴾

190. Verily in this story is a sign; yet most of them are not believers.

إِنَّ فِى ذَٰلِكَ لَءَايَةً وَمَا كَانَ أَكْثَرُهُم مُّؤْمِنِينَ ﴿١٩٠﴾

191. And verily your Lord! He is the Mighty, the Merciful.

وَإِنَّ رَبَّكَ لَهُوَ ٱلْعَزِيزُ ٱلرَّحِيمُ ﴿١٩١﴾

Section 11

192. Verily it is a revelation of the Lord of the worlds.

وَإِنَّهُۥ لَتَنزِيلُ رَبِّ ٱلۡعَٰلَمِينَ ۝

193. The trusted spirit has brought it down;

نَزَلَ بِهِ ٱلرُّوحُ ٱلۡأَمِينُ ۝

194. Upon your heart, that you may be of the warners.

عَلَىٰ قَلۡبِكَ لِتَكُونَ مِنَ ٱلۡمُنذِرِينَ ۝

195. In plain Arabic speech.

بِلِسَانٍ عَرَبِيٍّ مُّبِينٍ ۝

196. And verily it is in the Scriptures of the ancients.

وَإِنَّهُۥ لَفِى زُبُرِ ٱلۡأَوَّلِينَ ۝

197. Is it not an evidence with them that the learned among the children of Israel know it?

أَوَلَمۡ يَكُن لَّهُمۡ ءَايَةً أَن يَعۡلَمَهُۥ عُلَمَٰٓؤُاْ بَنِىٓ إِسۡرَٰٓءِيلَ ۝

198. And had We revealed it to any of the non-Arabs,

وَلَوۡ نَزَّلۡنَٰهُ عَلَىٰ بَعۡضِ ٱلۡأَعۡجَمِينَ ۝

199. And he had read it unto them, even then they would not have been believers in it.

فَقَرَأَهُۥ عَلَيۡهِم مَّا كَانُواْ بِهِۦ مُؤۡمِنِينَ ۝

200. In this wise We have made way for it into the hearts of the culprits.

كَذَٰلِكَ سَلَكۡنَٰهُ فِى قُلُوبِ ٱلۡمُجۡرِمِينَ ۝

201. They will not believe in it until they see the afflictive torment.

لَا يُؤۡمِنُونَ بِهِۦ حَتَّىٰ يَرَوُاْ ٱلۡعَذَابَ ٱلۡأَلِيمَ ۝

202. It shall come unto them suddenly, and they will not perceive.

فَيَأۡتِيَهُم بَغۡتَةً وَهُمۡ لَا يَشۡعُرُونَ ۝

203. Then they will say: 'Are we to be respited?'

فَيَقُولُواْ هَلۡ نَحۡنُ مُنظَرُونَ ۝

204. Do they then wish to hurry Our chastisement?

أَفَبِعَذَابِنَا يَسۡتَعۡجِلُونَ ۝

205. Think! If We let them enjoy for years;

أَفَرَءَيْتَ إِن مَّتَّعْنَـٰهُمْ سِنِينَ ۝

206. And then there comes to them what they had been promised;

ثُمَّ جَآءَهُم مَّا كَانُوا يُوعَدُونَ ۝

207. Those shall not avail them what they enjoyed.

مَآ أَغْنَىٰ عَنْهُم مَّا كَانُوا يُمَتَّعُونَ ۝

208. Not a city We destroyed but it had its warners;

وَمَآ أَهْلَكْنَا مِن قَرْيَةٍ إِلَّا لَهَا مُنذِرُونَ ۝

209. By way of admonition, and We have never been unjust.

ذِكْرَىٰ وَمَا كُنَّا ظَـٰلِمِينَ ۝

210. And it is not the devils who have brought it down.

وَمَا تَنَزَّلَتْ بِهِ الشَّيَـٰطِينُ ۝

211. Neither it behoves them, nor can they.[567]

وَمَا يَنۢبَغِى لَهُمْ وَمَا يَسْتَطِيعُونَ ۝

212. Verily very far from its hearing are they removed.

إِنَّهُمْ عَنِ السَّمْعِ لَمَعْزُولُونَ ۝

213. So call not you upon another god along with Allah lest you be doomed.

فَلَا تَدْعُ مَعَ اللَّهِ إِلَـٰهًا ءَاخَرَ فَتَكُونَ مِنَ الْمُعَذَّبِينَ ۝

214. And warn you your clan, the nearest ones.

وَأَنذِرْ عَشِيرَتَكَ الْأَقْرَبِينَ ۝

215. And behave you with meekness towards those who follow you as believers.

وَاخْفِضْ جَنَاحَكَ لِمَنِ اتَّبَعَكَ مِنَ الْمُؤْمِنِينَ ۝

216. And if they disobey you, say: 'I am quit of what you do.'

فَإِنْ عَصَوْكَ فَقُلْ إِنِّى بَرِىٓءٌ مِّمَّا تَعْمَلُونَ ۝

---

567. They could not produce such a Book even if they willed. The pagans maintained that the Qurʾān was prompted by the devils. The Qurʾān answers, that, in the first place, it was preposterous to assume that the propagators of darkness would prompt a Book that is Light in its entirety; and, secondly, it was beyond their powers, even if they willed. Neither is it meet for them, nor is it within their power.

217. And rely you upon the Mighty, the Merciful;

وَتَوَكَّلْ عَلَى ٱلْعَزِيزِ ٱلرَّحِيمِ ۞

218. Who sees you when you stand up;

ٱلَّذِى يَرَىٰكَ حِينَ تَقُومُ ۞

219. And your movement among those who fall prostrate.

وَتَقَلُّبَكَ فِى ٱلسَّٰجِدِينَ ۞

220. Verily He! He is the Hearer, the Knower.

إِنَّهُۥ هُوَ ٱلسَّمِيعُ ٱلْعَلِيمُ ۞

221. Shall I declare to you upon whom the devils descend?

هَلْ أُنَبِّئُكُمْ عَلَىٰ مَن تَنَزَّلُ ٱلشَّيَٰطِينُ ۞

222. They descend upon every calumniator, sinner;

تَنَزَّلُ عَلَىٰ كُلِّ أَفَّاكٍ أَثِيمٍ ۞

223. Who give ear, and most of them are liars.

يُلْقُونَ ٱلسَّمْعَ وَأَكْثَرُهُمْ كَٰذِبُونَ ۞

224. As for the poets. It is the deluded who follow them.

وَٱلشُّعَرَآءُ يَتَّبِعُهُمُ ٱلْغَاوُۥنَ ۞

225. Do you not see, that they wander aimlessly in every vale?

أَلَمْ تَرَ أَنَّهُمْ فِى كُلِّ وَادٍ يَهِيمُونَ ۞

226. And that they say, what they do not act.

وَأَنَّهُمْ يَقُولُونَ مَا لَا يَفْعَلُونَ ۞

227. Save those who believe and work righteous deeds and[568] remember Allah much and vindicate themselves after they have been wronged. And those who do wrong, shall presently come to know by what overturning they are being overturned.

إِلَّا ٱلَّذِينَ ءَامَنُواْ وَعَمِلُواْ ٱلصَّٰلِحَٰتِ وَذَكَرُواْ ٱللَّهَ كَثِيرًا وَٱنتَصَرُواْ مِنۢ بَعْدِ مَا ظُلِمُواْ وَسَيَعْلَمُ ٱلَّذِينَ ظَلَمُوٓاْ أَىَّ مُنقَلَبٍ يَنقَلِبُونَ ۞

---

568. Even in their satirical invectives when overpowered by grave provocation. Poetry, with its usual concomitant of imagination running riot, is condemned outright. An exception however is made in favour of such poets as enjoin the true faith and piety and vindicate and promulgate the Religion of God.

Sūrah 27

al-Naml

(Makkan, 7 Sections, 93 Verses)

In the name of Allah, the Compassionate, the Merciful.

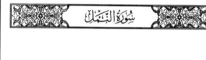

Section 1

1. *Ṭā, Sīn.* These are the verses of the Qur'ān and a Book luminous,

2. A guidance and glad tidings to the believers;

3. Who establish the prayer and pay the poor-rate, and of the Hereafter they are convinced.

4. Verily those who do not believe in the Hereafter, fair-seeming to them We have made their works, so that they wander perplexed.

5. Those are they for whom there will be an ill chastisement, and in the Hereafter they will be the greatest losers.

6. And surely you are receiving the Qur'an from before the Wise, the Knowing.

7. Recall when Moses came to his household and said: 'Verily I see a fire afar; I shall forthwith bring you tidings thereof, or bring you a brand lighted therefrom, haply you may warm yourselves.'

8. Then when he came to it, he was cried unto thus: 'Blessed is whosoever is in the fire and whosoever is around it, and hallowed be Allah, the Lord of the worlds.

فَلَمَّا جَآءَهَا نُودِيَ أَنۢ بُورِكَ مَن فِي ٱلنَّارِ وَمَنۡ حَوۡلَهَا وَسُبۡحَٰنَ ٱللَّهِ رَبِّ ٱلۡعَٰلَمِينَ ﴿٨﴾

9. 'O Moses! It is really I, Allah, the Mighty, the Wise.

يَٰمُوسَىٰٓ إِنَّهُۥٓ أَنَا ٱللَّهُ ٱلۡعَزِيزُ ٱلۡحَكِيمُ ﴿٩﴾

10. And cast down your rod.' Then when he saw it wriggling as though it was a serpent, he turned in flight and did not look back. 'Moses! Do not be alarmed, in My presence the sent ones do not fear;

وَأَلۡقِ عَصَاكَ فَلَمَّا رَءَاهَا تَهۡتَزُّ كَأَنَّهَا جَآنٌّ وَلَّىٰ مُدۡبِرًا وَلَمۡ يُعَقِّبۡ يَٰمُوسَىٰ لَا تَخَفۡ إِنِّي لَا يَخَافُ لَدَيَّ ٱلۡمُرۡسَلُونَ ﴿١٠﴾

11. Excepting any who may have done wrong and thereafter changes evil for good; then verily I am forgiving, Merciful.

إِلَّا مَن ظَلَمَ ثُمَّ بَدَّلَ حُسۡنًۢا بَعۡدَ سُوٓءٍ فَإِنِّي غَفُورٌ رَّحِيمٌ ﴿١١﴾

12. And put your hand into your bosom, it shall come forth white, without any hurt: among nine signs to Pharaoh and his people. Verily they have been a people transgressing.'

وَأَدۡخِلۡ يَدَكَ فِي جَيۡبِكَ تَخۡرُجۡ بَيۡضَآءَ مِنۡ غَيۡرِ سُوٓءٍ فِي تِسۡعِ ءَايَٰتٍ إِلَىٰ فِرۡعَوۡنَ وَقَوۡمِهِۦٓ إِنَّهُمۡ كَانُوا۟ قَوۡمًا فَٰسِقِينَ ﴿١٢﴾

13. Then when Our signs came to them illuminating, they said: 'This is a magic manifest.'

فَلَمَّا جَآءَتۡهُمۡ ءَايَٰتُنَا مُبۡصِرَةً قَالُوا۟ هَٰذَا سِحۡرٌ مُّبِينٌ ﴿١٣﴾

14. And they gainsaid them, out of spite and arrogance, although their souls were convinced thereof. So behold! What has been the end of the corrupters?.

وَجَحَدُوا۟ بِهَا وَٱسۡتَيۡقَنَتۡهَآ أَنفُسُهُمۡ ظُلۡمًا وَعُلُوًّا فَٱنظُرۡ كَيۡفَ كَانَ عَٰقِبَةُ ٱلۡمُفۡسِدِينَ ﴿١٤﴾

Section 2

15. And assuredly We vouchsafed to David and Solomon, a knowledge, and the two said: 'Praise be to Allah Who has preferred us to many of His believing bondsmen!'

وَلَقَدْ ءَاتَيْنَا دَاوُدَ وَسُلَيْمَنَ عِلْمًا وَقَالَا الْحَمْدُ لِلَّهِ الَّذِي فَضَّلَنَا عَلَىٰ كَثِيرٍ مِّنْ عِبَادِهِ الْمُؤْمِنِينَ ﴿١٥﴾

16. And Solomon inherited from David, and he said: 'O mankind! We have been taught the language of birds, and we have been vouchsafed of everything, and surely this is an evident grace.'

وَوَرِثَ سُلَيْمَنُ دَاوُدَ وَقَالَ يَـٰٓأَيُّهَا النَّاسُ عُلِّمْنَا مَنطِقَ الطَّيْرِ وَأُوتِينَا مِن كُلِّ شَىْءٍ إِنَّ هَـٰذَا لَهُوَ الْفَضْلُ الْمُبِينُ ﴿١٦﴾

17. And there were gathered unto Solomon his hosts of *jinns* and mankind and birds, and they were set in bands.

وَحُشِرَ لِسُلَيْمَنَ جُنُودُهُ مِنَ الْجِنِّ وَالْإِنسِ وَالطَّيْرِ فَهُمْ يُوزَعُونَ ﴿١٧﴾

18. And when they came to the valley of the ants, an ant said: 'Ants! Enter your habitations lest Solomon and his hosts may crush you while they perceive not.'

حَتَّىٰٓ إِذَآ أَتَوْا عَلَىٰ وَادِ النَّمْلِ قَالَتْ نَمْلَةٌ يَـٰٓأَيُّهَا النَّمْلُ ادْخُلُوا مَسَـٰكِنَكُمْ لَا يَحْطِمَنَّكُمْ سُلَيْمَنُ وَجُنُودُهُ وَهُمْ لَا يَشْعُرُونَ ﴿١٨﴾

19. So, amused at her speech, he smiled and said: 'Lord! Dispose me that I should be grateful for the favour wherewith You have favoured me and my parents, and that I should work righteously pleasing You; and out of Your mercy enter me among Your righteous bondsmen.'[569]

فَتَبَسَّمَ ضَاحِكًا مِّن قَوْلِهَا وَقَالَ رَبِّ أَوْزِعْنِىٓ أَنْ أَشْكُرَ نِعْمَتَكَ الَّتِىٓ أَنْعَمْتَ عَلَىَّ وَعَلَىٰ وَٰلِدَىَّ وَأَنْ أَعْمَلَ صَـٰلِحًا تَرْضَىٰهُ وَأَدْخِلْنِى بِرَحْمَتِكَ فِى عِبَادِكَ الصَّـٰلِحِينَ ﴿١٩﴾

---

569. In other words, the prophets and the saints. So that Solomon remained a true Muslim and a Prophet of God till the end of his time. This is expressly to refute the Christian charge that he had become ungodly in the later part of his life.

20. And he sought after the birds and said: 'What is the matter that I do not see the hoopoe, is he among the absentees?[569]

وَتَفَقَّدَ ٱلطَّيْرَ فَقَالَ مَالِيَ لَآ أَرَى ٱلْهُدْهُدَ أَمْ كَانَ مِنَ ٱلْغَآئِبِينَ ۝

21. I shall chastise him surely or I shall slaughter him unless he offers me good explanation.'

لَأُعَذِّبَنَّهُۥ عَذَابًا شَدِيدًا أَوْ لَأَاْذْبَحَنَّهُۥٓ أَوْ لَيَأْتِيَنِّي بِسُلْطَٰنٍ مُّبِينٍ ۝

22. But he tarried not long, and said: 'I have comprehended what you have not yet comprehended, and I came to you from Sabā' with a sure tiding.

فَمَكَثَ غَيْرَ بَعِيدٍ فَقَالَ أَحَطتُ بِمَا لَمْ تُحِطْ بِهِۦ وَجِئْتُكَ مِن سَبَإٍ بِنَبَإٍ يَقِينٍ ۝

23. I have found a woman ruling over them, and she has been vouchsafed of everything, and hers is a mighty throne.

إِنِّي وَجَدتُّ ٱمْرَأَةً تَمْلِكُهُمْ وَأُوتِيَتْ مِن كُلِّ شَىْءٍ وَلَهَا عَرْشٌ عَظِيمٌ ۝

24. 'I have found her and her people adoring the sun instead of Allah, and Satan has made their work fair-seeming to them and has barred them from the way, as they are not guided;

وَجَدتُّهَا وَقَوْمَهَا يَسْجُدُونَ لِلشَّمْسِ مِن دُونِ ٱللَّهِ وَزَيَّنَ لَهُمُ ٱلشَّيْطَٰنُ أَعْمَٰلَهُمْ فَصَدَّهُمْ عَنِ ٱلسَّبِيلِ فَهُمْ لَا يَهْتَدُونَ ۝

25. So that they adore not Allah Who brings forth the hidden in the heavens and the earth, and knows what you conceal and what you declare.

أَلَّا يَسْجُدُوا۟ لِلَّهِ ٱلَّذِى يُخْرِجُ ٱلْخَبْءَ فِى ٱلسَّمَٰوَٰتِ وَٱلْأَرْضِ وَيَعْلَمُ مَا تُخْفُونَ وَمَا تُعْلِنُونَ ۝

26. Allah! There is no god but He! The Lord of the magnificent throne.'

ٱللَّهُ لَآ إِلَٰهَ إِلَّا هُوَ رَبُّ ٱلْعَرْشِ ٱلْعَظِيمِ ۩ ۝

27. Solomon said: 'We shall now see whether you have spoken the truth or whether you are of the liars.

قَالَ سَنَنظُرُ أَصَدَقْتَ أَمْ كُنتَ مِنَ ٱلْكَٰذِبِينَ ۝

28. 'Go you with this letter of mine, and cast it down unto them and turn aside from them, and see what they return.'

اذْهَب بِّكِتَـٰبِى هَـٰذَا فَأَلْقِهْ إِلَيْهِمْ ثُمَّ تَوَلَّ عَنْهُمْ فَٱنظُرْ مَاذَا يَرْجِعُونَ ﴿٢٨﴾

29. She said: 'O Chiefs! There has been cast to us an honourable epistle.

قَالَتْ يَـٰٓأَيُّهَا ٱلْمَلَؤُا۟ إِنِّىٓ أُلْقِىَ إِلَىَّ كِتَـٰبٌ كَرِيمٌ ﴿٢٩﴾

30. It is from Solomon, and it runs: "In the name of Allah, the Compassionate, the Merciful."'

إِنَّهُۥ مِن سُلَيْمَـٰنَ وَإِنَّهُۥ بِسْمِ ٱللَّهِ ٱلرَّحْمَـٰنِ ٱلرَّحِيمِ ﴿٣٠﴾

31. Saying: "rise not against me, and come to me submissive."'

أَلَّا تَعْلُوا۟ عَلَىَّ وَأْتُونِى مُسْلِمِينَ ﴿٣١﴾

Section 3

32. She said: 'O Chiefs! Counsel me in the affair. I do not resolve on any affair until you counsel me.'

قَالَتْ يَـٰٓأَيُّهَا ٱلْمَلَؤُا۟ أَفْتُونِى فِىٓ أَمْرِى مَا كُنتُ قَاطِعَةً أَمْرًا حَتَّىٰ تَشْهَدُونِ ﴿٣٢﴾

33. They said: 'We possess great force and great might; but yours is the command, we shall see what you command.'

قَالُوا۟ نَحْنُ أُو۟لُوا۟ قُوَّةٍ وَأُو۟لُوا۟ بَأْسٍ شَدِيدٍ وَٱلْأَمْرُ إِلَيْكِ فَٱنظُرِى مَاذَا تَأْمُرِينَ ﴿٣٣﴾

34. She said: 'Verily the kings when they enter a city, despoil it and make its most powerful inhabitants the most abased; so they also will do.

قَالَتْ إِنَّ ٱلْمُلُوكَ إِذَا دَخَلُوا۟ قَرْيَةً أَفْسَدُوهَا وَجَعَلُوٓا۟ أَعِزَّةَ أَهْلِهَآ أَذِلَّةً وَكَذَٰلِكَ يَفْعَلُونَ ﴿٣٤﴾

35. Therefore I am going to send them a present, and see with what answer the envoys come back.'

وَإِنِّى مُرْسِلَةٌ إِلَيْهِم بِهَدِيَّةٍ فَنَاظِرَةٌۢ بِمَ يَرْجِعُ ٱلْمُرْسَلُونَ ﴿٣٥﴾

سُوۡرَةُ النَّمۡل

36. Then when he came to Solomon, he said: 'Are you going to add riches to me – while what Allah has vouchsafed to me is better than what He has vouchsafed to you. Aye! It is you who exult in your present.

فَلَمَّا جَآءَ سُلَيۡمَٰنَ قَالَ أَتُمِدُّونَنِ بِمَالٍ فَمَآ ءَاتَٰىٰنَ ٱللَّهُ خَيۡرٌ مِّمَّآ ءَاتَٰىٰكُم بَلۡ أَنتُم بِهَدِيَّتِكُمۡ تَفۡرَحُونَ ﴿٣٦﴾

37. 'Go you back to them. Surely we shall come upon them with hosts which they cannot withstand and we shall drive them forth from their place abased and they will be humbled.'

ٱرۡجِعۡ إِلَيۡهِمۡ فَلَنَأۡتِيَنَّهُم بِجُنُودٍ لَّا قِبَلَ لَهُم بِهَا وَلَنُخۡرِجَنَّهُم مِّنۡهَآ أَذِلَّةً وَهُمۡ صَٰغِرُونَ ﴿٣٧﴾

38. Solomon said: 'Chiefs! Which of you will bring me her throne before they came to me surrendering themselves.'

قَالَ يَٰٓأَيُّهَا ٱلۡمَلَؤُاْ أَيُّكُمۡ يَأۡتِينِي بِعَرۡشِهَا قَبۡلَ أَن يَأۡتُونِي مُسۡلِمِينَ ﴿٣٨﴾

39. A giant from the *jinn* said: 'I shall bring it to you before you arise from your seat; surely I am strong enough for test and am reliable.'

قَالَ عِفۡرِيتٌ مِّنَ ٱلۡجِنِّ أَنَا۠ ءَاتِيكَ بِهِۦ قَبۡلَ أَن تَقُومَ مِن مَّقَامِكَ وَإِنِّي عَلَيۡهِ لَقَوِيٌّ أَمِينٌ ﴿٣٩﴾

40. But one who had some knowledge of the Book said: 'I shall bring it to you before your eye twinkles.' Then when Solomon saw it placed before him, he said: 'This is of the grace of my Lord that He may test me whether I thank Him or am ungrateful. Whosoever gives thanks only gives thanks for his own soul, and whosoever is ungrateful, then my Lord is the Self-Sufficient, the Munificent.'

قَالَ ٱلَّذِي عِندَهُۥ عِلۡمٌ مِّنَ ٱلۡكِتَٰبِ أَنَا۠ ءَاتِيكَ بِهِۦ قَبۡلَ أَن يَرۡتَدَّ إِلَيۡكَ طَرۡفُكَ فَلَمَّا رَءَاهُ مُسۡتَقِرًّا عِندَهُۥ قَالَ هَٰذَا مِن فَضۡلِ رَبِّي لِيَبۡلُوَنِيٓ ءَأَشۡكُرُ أَمۡ أَكۡفُرُ وَمَن شَكَرَ فَإِنَّمَا يَشۡكُرُ لِنَفۡسِهِۦ وَمَن كَفَرَ فَإِنَّ رَبِّي غَنِيٌّ كَرِيمٌ ﴿٤٠﴾

41. He said: 'Disguise her throne, so that we may see whether she is guided or of those who are not guided.'[570]

قَالَ نَكِّرُوا لَهَا عَرْشَهَا نَنظُرْ أَتَهْتَدِىٰٓ أَمْ تَكُونُ مِنَ ٱلَّذِينَ لَا يَهْتَدُونَ ۝

42. Then when she arrived,[571] it was said: 'Is your throne like this?' She said: 'It is as though it were it; and we have been vouchsafed the knowledge before this, and we have been Muslims.'

فَلَمَّا جَآءَتْ قِيلَ أَهَٰكَذَا عَرْشُكِ قَالَتْ كَأَنَّهُۥ هُوَ وَأُوتِينَا ٱلْعِلْمَ مِن قَبْلِهَا وَكُنَّا مُسْلِمِينَ ۝

43. And there hindered her what she worshipped instead of Allah; indeed she was of an infidel people.

وَصَدَّهَا مَا كَانَت تَّعْبُدُ مِن دُونِ ٱللَّهِ إِنَّهَا كَانَتْ مِن قَوْمٍ كَٰفِرِينَ ۝

44. It was said to her: 'Enter the palace', then when she saw it she imagined it a pool and bared her shanks. He said: 'It is a pavilion smoothed of crystal.' She said: 'Lord! I have wronged my soul, and I surrender myself together with Solomon to Allah, the Lord of the worlds.'

قِيلَ لَهَا ٱدْخُلِي ٱلصَّرْحَ فَلَمَّا رَأَتْهُ حَسِبَتْهُ لُجَّةً وَكَشَفَتْ عَن سَاقَيْهَا قَالَ إِنَّهُۥ صَرْحٌ مُّمَرَّدٌ مِّن قَوَارِيرَ قَالَتْ رَبِّ إِنِّى ظَلَمْتُ نَفْسِى وَأَسْلَمْتُ مَعَ سُلَيْمَٰنَ لِلَّهِ رَبِّ ٱلْعَٰلَمِينَ ۝

---

570. Solomon (peace and blessings be upon him) intended thereby to test the intelligence of the Queen. If intelligent and of good common–sense she was more likely to see her way to the Truth.

571. For a very different account of the visit of the Queen of Sheba to Solomon in the Bible, see: 1 Ki. 10 : 1–13.

Section 4

45. And assuredly We sent to Thamud their brother Salih, saying: 'Worship Allah.' Then lo! They became two parties contending.

وَلَقَدۡ أَرۡسَلۡنَآ إِلَىٰ ثَمُودَ أَخَاهُمۡ صَٰلِحًا أَنِ ٱعۡبُدُواْ ٱللَّهَ فَإِذَا هُمۡ فَرِيقَانِ يَخۡتَصِمُونَ ﴿٤٥﴾

46. He said: 'My people! Why do you seek to hasten the evil before the good? Why do you not seek the forgiveness of Allah, that haply you may be shown mercy?'

قَالَ يَٰقَوۡمِ لِمَ تَسۡتَعۡجِلُونَ بِٱلسَّيِّئَةِ قَبۡلَ ٱلۡحَسَنَةِ لَوۡلَا تَسۡتَغۡفِرُونَ ٱللَّهَ لَعَلَّكُمۡ تُرۡحَمُونَ ﴿٤٦﴾

47. They said: 'We augur ill of you and of those who are with you.' He said: 'Your augury is with Allah. Aye! You are a people being tempted.'

قَالُواْ ٱطَّيَّرۡنَا بِكَ وَبِمَن مَّعَكَ قَالَ طَٰٓئِرُكُمۡ عِندَ ٱللَّهِ بَلۡ أَنتُمۡ قَوۡمٌ تُفۡتَنُونَ ﴿٤٧﴾

48. And there were nine of a group in the city, who spread corruption in the land and did not rectify.

وَكَانَ فِي ٱلۡمَدِينَةِ تِسۡعَةُ رَهۡطٍ يُفۡسِدُونَ فِي ٱلۡأَرۡضِ وَلَا يُصۡلِحُونَ ﴿٤٨﴾

49. They said: 'Swear by God one to another that we shall surely fall upon him and his household by night; and thereafter we shall tell his heir: "We did not see the destruction of his household, and we are truthful." '

قَالُواْ تَقَاسَمُواْ بِٱللَّهِ لَنُبَيِّتَنَّهُۥ وَأَهۡلَهُۥ ثُمَّ لَنَقُولَنَّ لِوَلِيِّهِۦ مَا شَهِدۡنَا مَهۡلِكَ أَهۡلِهِۦ وَإِنَّا لَصَٰدِقُونَ ﴿٤٩﴾

50. And they plotted a plot, and We plotted a plot, and they perceived it not.

وَمَكَرُواْ مَكۡرًا وَمَكَرۡنَا مَكۡرًا وَهُمۡ لَا يَشۡعُرُونَ ﴿٥٠﴾

51. So behold you how was the end of their plot. Verily, We annihilated them and their nation all together.

فَٱنظُرۡ كَيۡفَ كَانَ عَٰقِبَةُ مَكۡرِهِمۡ أَنَّا دَمَّرۡنَٰهُمۡ وَقَوۡمَهُمۡ أَجۡمَعِينَ ﴿٥١﴾

52. These are their houses overturned, for they did wrong. Verily, herein is a Sign for a people who know.

فَتِلْكَ بُيُوْتُهُمْ خَاوِيَةً بِمَا ظَلَمُوْا ۚ إِنَّ فِيْ ذٰلِكَ لَأٰيَةً لِّقَوْمٍ يَّعْلَمُوْنَ ۞

53. And We rescued them who believed and were wont to be God-fearing.

وَأَنْجَيْنَا الَّذِيْنَ ءَامَنُوْا وَكَانُوْا يَتَّقُوْنَ ۞

54. And recall Lot! When he said to his people: 'Do you commit indecency while you see its enormity.[572]

وَلُوْطًا إِذْ قَالَ لِقَوْمِهِ أَتَأْتُوْنَ الْفَاحِشَةَ وَأَنْتُمْ تُبْصِرُوْنَ ۞

55. Would you go in lustfully to men instead of women? Aye! You are a people addicted to pagan ways?'

أَئِنَّكُمْ لَتَأْتُوْنَ الرِّجَالَ شَهْوَةً مِّنْ دُوْنِ النِّسَاءِ ۚ بَلْ أَنْتُمْ قَوْمٌ تَجْهَلُوْنَ ۞

56. There was no answer of his people save that they said: 'Drive forth the family of Lot from your city. They are a people clean indeed.'

فَمَا كَانَ جَوَابَ قَوْمِهِ إِلَّا أَنْ قَالُوْا أَخْرِجُوْا ءَالَ لُوْطٍ مِّنْ قَرْيَتِكُمْ ۖ إِنَّهُمْ أُنَاسٌ يَّتَطَهَّرُوْنَ ۞

57. Then We rescued Lot and his family except his wife. Her we destined to be of the lingerers.

فَأَنْجَيْنَاهُ وَأَهْلَهُ إِلَّا امْرَأَتَهُ قَدَّرْنَاهَا مِنَ الْغٰبِرِيْنَ ۞

58. And We rained upon them a rain, ill was that rain upon the warned.

وَأَمْطَرْنَا عَلَيْهِمْ مَّطَرًا ۖ فَسَاءَ مَطَرُ الْمُنْذَرِيْنَ ۞

59. Say: 'All praise to Allah, and peace upon His bondsmen whom He has chosen. Is Allah Best, or what they associate with Him?'

قُلِ الْحَمْدُ لِلّٰهِ وَسَلٰمٌ عَلٰى عِبَادِهِ الَّذِيْنَ اصْطَفٰى ۗ ءَاللّٰهُ خَيْرٌ أَمَّا يُشْرِكُوْنَ ۞

---

572. In other words, while you fully recognize its enormity? Observe and compare the increasingly complacent attitude of modern civilization towards sexual inverts and perverts and the growing tendency among contemporary physicians and legislators to condone and make light of even the most atrocious homosexual practices.

Section 5

60. Is not He best. Who has created the heavens and the earth, and Who sends down water for you from the sky whereby We cause beautiful orchards to grow up and the trees of which it was not possible for you to cause to grow up? Is there any other god along with Allah? Nay! Yet they are a people who equalize.

أَمَّنۡ خَلَقَ السَّمٰوٰتِ وَالۡأَرۡضَ وَأَنزَلَ لَكُم مِّنَ السَّمَآءِ مَآءً فَأَنۢبَتۡنَا بِهِۦ حَدَآئِقَ ذَاتَ بَهۡجَةٍ مَّا كَانَ لَكُمۡ أَن تُنۢبِتُوۡا شَجَرَهَآ أَءِلٰهٌ مَّعَ اللّٰهِ بَلۡ هُمۡ قَوۡمٌ يَعۡدِلُوۡنَ ۝

61. Is not He best Who has made the earth a fixed abode and has placed the rivers in its midst and has placed firm mountains on it, and has placed a barrier between the two seas? Is there any other god along with Allah? Nay! Yet most of them do not know.

أَمَّنۡ جَعَلَ الۡأَرۡضَ قَرَارًا وَجَعَلَ خِلٰلَهَآ أَنۡهَٰرًا وَجَعَلَ لَهَا رَوَاسِيَ وَجَعَلَ بَيۡنَ الۡبَحۡرَيۡنِ حَاجِزًا أَءِلٰهٌ مَّعَ اللّٰهِ بَلۡ أَكۡثَرُهُمۡ لَا يَعۡلَمُوۡنَ ۝

62. Is not He best Who answers the distressed when he calls unto Him and averts the evil, and has made you the successors in the earth? Is there any other god along with Allah? Little do you reflect.

أَمَّنۡ يُّجِيۡبُ الۡمُضۡطَرَّ إِذَا دَعَاهُ وَيَكۡشِفُ السُّوۡٓءَ وَيَجۡعَلُكُمۡ خُلَفَآءَ الۡأَرۡضِ أَءِلٰهٌ مَّعَ اللّٰهِ قَلِيۡلًا مَّا تَذَكَّرُوۡنَ ۝

63. Is not He the best Who guides you in the darknesses of the land and the sea and Who sends the winds as heralds before His mercy? Is there any other god along with Allah? Exalted be Allah above what they associate with Him.

أَمَّنۡ يَّهۡدِيۡكُمۡ فِيۡ ظُلُمٰتِ الۡبَرِّ وَالۡبَحۡرِ وَمَنۡ يُّرۡسِلُ الرِّيَٰحَ بُشۡرًۢا بَيۡنَ يَدَيۡ رَحۡمَتِهِۦٓ أَءِلٰهٌ مَّعَ اللّٰهِ تَعٰلَى اللّٰهُ عَمَّا يُشۡرِكُوۡنَ ۝

64. Is not He the best Who originates creation[573], and shall thereafter restore it, and Who provides for you from the heavens and the earth? Is there any other god along with Allah? Say: 'Bring you proof if you are truthful.'

أَمَّن يَبْدَؤُاْ الْخَلْقَ ثُمَّ يُعِيدُهُۥ وَمَن يَرْزُقُكُم مِّنَ السَّمَآءِ وَالْأَرْضِ أَءِلَٰهٌ مَّعَ اللَّهِ قُلْ هَاتُوا بُرْهَٰنَكُمْ إِن كُنتُمْ صَٰدِقِينَ ٦٤

65. Say: 'None in the heavens and the earth knows the Unseen save Allah, nor can they perceive when they will be raised.'

قُل لَّا يَعْلَمُ مَن فِى السَّمَٰوَٰتِ وَالْأَرْضِ الْغَيْبَ إِلَّا اللَّهُ وَمَا يَشْعُرُونَ أَيَّانَ يُبْعَثُونَ ٦٥

66. Aye! Their knowledge does not attain to the Hereafter. Aye! They are in doubt about it. Aye! They are blind to it.

بَلِ ادَّٰرَكَ عِلْمُهُمْ فِى الْآخِرَةِ بَلْ هُمْ فِى شَكٍّ مِّنْهَا بَلْ هُم مِّنْهَا عَمُونَ ٦٦

Section 6

67. Those who disbelieve say: 'When we have become dust, we and our forefathers; shall we, in truth, be brought forth?

وَقَالَ الَّذِينَ كَفَرُوٓا أَءِذَا كُنَّا تُرَٰبًا وَءَابَآؤُنَآ أَئِنَّا لَمُخْرَجُونَ ٦٧

68. Assuredly we have been promised this before, we and our forefathers. Naught is this, but the fables of the ancients.'

لَقَدْ وُعِدْنَا هَٰذَا نَحْنُ وَءَابَآؤُنَا مِن قَبْلُ إِنْ هَٰذَآ إِلَّآ أَسَٰطِيرُ الْأَوَّلِينَ ٦٨

---

573. Contrast this with the openly polytheistic teaching of the NT. 'Giving thanks unto the Father hath translated us into the kingdom of his dear Son. Who is the image of the invisible God, the first born of every creature: for by him were all things created, that are in heaven, and that are in earth, visible and invisible, whether they be thrones, or dominions, or principalities, or powers: all things were created by him, and for him: and he is before all things, and by him all things consist. For it pleased the Father that in him should all fullness dwell' (Col. 1: 12–19).

69. Say: 'Travel in the land and behold how has been the end of the culprits.

قُلْ سِيرُوا۟ فِى ٱلْأَرْضِ فَٱنظُرُوا۟ كَيْفَ كَانَ عَٰقِبَةُ ٱلْمُجْرِمِينَ ﴿٦٩﴾

70. Grieve you not over them, nor be straitened on what they plot.'

وَلَا تَحْزَنْ عَلَيْهِمْ وَلَا تَكُن فِى ضَيْقٍ مِّمَّا يَمْكُرُونَ ﴿٧٠﴾

71. And they say: 'When will this promise be fulfilled, if you say sooth?'

وَيَقُولُونَ مَتَىٰ هَٰذَا ٱلْوَعْدُ إِن كُنتُمْ صَٰدِقِينَ ﴿٧١﴾

72. Say: 'Perhaps close behind you may be what you would hasten on.'

قُلْ عَسَىٰٓ أَن يَكُونَ رَدِفَ لَكُم بَعْضُ ٱلَّذِى تَسْتَعْجِلُونَ ﴿٧٢﴾

73. Verily your Lord is full of grace for mankind, yet most of them give not thanks.

وَإِنَّ رَبَّكَ لَذُو فَضْلٍ عَلَى ٱلنَّاسِ وَلَٰكِنَّ أَكْثَرَهُمْ لَا يَشْكُرُونَ ﴿٧٣﴾

74. Verily your Lord knows what their breasts conceal and what they disclose.

وَإِنَّ رَبَّكَ لَيَعْلَمُ مَا تُكِنُّ صُدُورُهُمْ وَمَا يُعْلِنُونَ ﴿٧٤﴾

75. And naught there is hidden in the heaven and the earth but it is in a Book manifest.

وَمَا مِنْ غَآئِبَةٍ فِى ٱلسَّمَآءِ وَٱلْأَرْضِ إِلَّا فِى كِتَٰبٍ مُّبِينٍ ﴿٧٥﴾

76. Verily this Qur'ān recounts with truth to the children of Israel much of what they contend with.[574]

إِنَّ هَٰذَا ٱلْقُرْءَانَ يَقُصُّ عَلَىٰ بَنِىٓ إِسْرَٰٓءِيلَ أَكْثَرَ ٱلَّذِى هُمْ فِيهِ يَخْتَلِفُونَ ﴿٧٦﴾

77. And verily it is a guidance and a mercy to the believers.

وَإِنَّهُۥ لَهُدًى وَرَحْمَةٌ لِّلْمُؤْمِنِينَ ﴿٧٧﴾

---

574. They contend among themselves. The Holy Qur'an corrects many of the Jews' misconceptions and pronounces final judgement on many of their controversies.

78. And verily your Lord shall decide between them by His Judgement and He is the Mighty, the Knowing.

إِنَّ رَبَّكَ يَقْضِى بَيْنَهُم بِحُكْمِهِ وَهُوَ ٱلْعَزِيزُ ٱلْعَلِيمُ ۝

79. So put your trust in Allah; verily you are on manifest truth.

فَتَوَكَّلْ عَلَى ٱللَّهِ إِنَّكَ عَلَى ٱلْحَقِّ ٱلْمُبِينِ ۝

80. Surely you cannot make the dead hear, nor can you make the deaf hear the call when they flee turning their backs.

إِنَّكَ لَا تُسْمِعُ ٱلْمَوْتَىٰ وَلَا تُسْمِعُ ٱلصُّمَّ ٱلدُّعَآءَ إِذَا وَلَّوْا مُدْبِرِينَ ۝

81. Nor can you lead the blind out of their error. You can make none hear save those who believe in Our signs and who have submitted themselves.

وَمَآ أَنتَ بِهَـٰدِى ٱلْعُمْىِ عَن ضَلَٰلَتِهِمْ إِن تُسْمِعُ إِلَّا مَن يُؤْمِنُ بِـَٔايَٰتِنَا فَهُم مُّسْلِمُونَ ۝

82. And when the word concerning them shall come to be fulfilled, We shall bring forth a beast of the earth speaking to them, that of Our signs the people have not been convinced.

وَإِذَا وَقَعَ ٱلْقَوْلُ عَلَيْهِمْ أَخْرَجْنَا لَهُمْ دَآبَّةً مِّنَ ٱلْأَرْضِ تُكَلِّمُهُمْ أَنَّ ٱلنَّاسَ كَانُوا بِـَٔايَٰتِنَا لَا يُوقِنُونَ ۝

Section 7

83. And remind them of the Day on which We shall gather from every community a troop of those who belied Our signs, and they will be held in order;

وَيَوْمَ نَحْشُرُ مِن كُلِّ أُمَّةٍ فَوْجًا مِّمَّن يُكَذِّبُ بِـَٔايَٰتِنَا فَهُمْ يُوزَعُونَ ۝

84. Until when they will have come, He will say: 'Did you belie My signs when you could not comprehend them in your knowledge; nay, what else was it that you have been working?'

حَتَّىٰ إِذَا جَآءُو قَالَ أَكَذَّبْتُم بِـَٔايَٰتِى وَلَمْ تُحِيطُوا بِهَا عِلْمًا أَمَّاذَا كُنتُمْ تَعْمَلُونَ ۝

85. And the word concerning them shall be fulfilled because they did wrong and they shall not be able to speak.

86. Do they not consider that We have made the night that they may repose in it, and the day sight-giving. Verily in them are signs for those who believe.

87. And remind them of the Day on which the trumpet shall be blown, and terrified shall be those who are in the heavens and the earth, save him whom Allah wills. And all shall come to Him lowly.

88. And you shall see the mountains you deem solid passing away as the passing away of the clouds, the handiwork of Allah Who has perfected everything. Verily He is Aware of all that you do.

89. Whosoever will bring good shall have better than its worth; and they will be secure from the terror of that Day.

90. And whosoever will bring evil their faces shall be cast down in the Fire. Are you being requited aught save what you have been working?

91. I am commanded only to worship the Lord of this city which He has sanctified, and His is everything, and I am commanded to be of the Muslims;

وَوَقَعَ ٱلْقَوْلُ عَلَيْهِم بِمَا ظَلَمُوا فَهُمْ لَا يَنطِقُونَ ۝

أَلَمْ يَرَوْا أَنَّا جَعَلْنَا ٱلَّيْلَ لِيَسْكُنُوا فِيهِ وَٱلنَّهَارَ مُبْصِرًا إِنَّ فِي ذَٰلِكَ لَأَيَـٰتٍ لِّقَوْمٍ يُؤْمِنُونَ ۝

وَيَوْمَ يُنفَخُ فِي ٱلصُّورِ فَفَزِعَ مَن فِي ٱلسَّمَـٰوَٰتِ وَمَن فِي ٱلْأَرْضِ إِلَّا مَن شَآءَ ٱللَّهُ وَكُلٌّ أَتَوْهُ دَٰخِرِينَ ۝

وَتَرَى ٱلْجِبَالَ تَحْسَبُهَا جَامِدَةً وَهِيَ تَمُرُّ مَرَّ ٱلسَّحَابِ صُنْعَ ٱللَّهِ ٱلَّذِىٓ أَتْقَنَ كُلَّ شَىْءٍ إِنَّهُۥ خَبِيرٌ بِمَا تَفْعَلُونَ ۝

مَن جَآءَ بِٱلْحَسَنَةِ فَلَهُۥ خَيْرٌ مِّنْهَا وَهُم مِّن فَزَعٍ يَوْمَئِذٍ ءَامِنُونَ ۝

وَمَن جَآءَ بِٱلسَّيِّئَةِ فَكُبَّتْ وُجُوهُهُمْ فِي ٱلنَّارِ هَلْ تُجْزَوْنَ إِلَّا مَا كُنتُمْ تَعْمَلُونَ ۝

إِنَّمَآ أُمِرْتُ أَنْ أَعْبُدَ رَبَّ هَـٰذِهِ ٱلْبَلْدَةِ ٱلَّذِى حَرَّمَهَا وَلَهُۥ كُلُّ شَىْءٍ وَأُمِرْتُ أَنْ أَكُونَ مِنَ ٱلْمُسْلِمِينَ ۝

92. And that I should recite the Qur'ān, and whosoever receives guidance, receives it for his own soul, and as for him who strays, say: 'I am only of the warners.'

وَأَنۡ أَتۡلُوَاْ ٱلۡقُرۡءَانَّ فَمَنِ ٱهۡتَدَىٰ فَإِنَّمَا يَهۡتَدِى لِنَفۡسِهِۦۖ وَمَن ضَلَّ فَقُلۡ إِنَّمَآ أَنَا۠ مِنَ ٱلۡمُنذِرِينَ ﴿٩٢﴾

93. And say: 'All praise to Allah. Presently He will show you His signs, so that you will recognise them. And your Lord is not heedless of what you do.'

وَقُلِ ٱلۡحَمۡدُ لِلَّهِ سَيُرِيكُمۡ ءَايَٰتِهِۦ فَتَعۡرِفُونَهَاۚ وَمَا رَبُّكَ بِغَٰفِلٍ عَمَّا تَعۡمَلُونَ ﴿٩٣﴾

Surah 28

al-Qaṣaṣ

(Makkan, 9 Sections, 88 Verses)

In the name of Allah, the Compassionate, the Merciful.

Section 1

1. *Ṭā, Sīn, Mīm.*

2. These are verses of the manifest Book.

3. We recite to you of the story of Moses and Pharaoh with truth, for a people who believe.

4. Verily Pharaoh exalted himself in the land and made its people in sects, weakening a party among them, slaying their sons and letting their women live. Verily he was of the corrupters.

5. And We intended that We should be gracious to those who were weakened in the land, and We should make them leaders, and We should make them the inheritors.

6. And We should establish them in the land, and We should let Pharaoh and Haman and their hosts receive from them what they dreaded.

7. And We inspired the mother of Moses, saying: 'Suckle him, then when you fear for him, cast him into the river and have no fear or sorrow; verily We are going to restore him to you, and shall make him one of Our envoys.'

وَأَوْحَيْنَا إِلَىٰٓ أُمِّ مُوسَىٰٓ أَنْ أَرْضِعِيهِ فَإِذَا خِفْتِ عَلَيْهِ فَأَلْقِيهِ فِى الْيَمِّ وَلَا تَخَافِى وَلَا تَحْزَنِىٓ إِنَّا رَآدُّوهُ إِلَيْكِ وَ جَاعِلُوهُ مِنَ الْمُرْسَلِينَ ۝

8. And the household of Pharaoh picked him up, that he may ultimately prove for them an enemy and a grief. Verily Pharaoh and Haman and their hosts were sinners.

فَالْتَقَطَهُۥٓ ءَالُ فِرْعَوْنَ لِيَكُونَ لَهُمْ عَدُوًّا وَحَزَنًا إِنَّ فِرْعَوْنَ وَهَـٰمَـٰنَ وَ جُنُودَهُمَا كَانُوا خَـٰطِـِٔينَ ۝

9. And the wife of Pharoah said: 'A comfort to me and you! Slay him not, perhaps he may be of benefit to us or we may take him for a son.' And they did not perceive.

وَقَالَتِ امْرَأَتُ فِرْعَوْنَ قُرَّتُ عَيْنٍ لِّى وَلَكَ لَا تَقْتُلُوهُ عَسَىٰٓ أَن يَنفَعَنَا أَوْ نَتَّخِذَهُۥ وَلَدًا وَهُمْ لَا يَشْعُرُونَ ۝

10. And the heart of Moses's mother became void, and she had almost given up the secret, had We not fortified her heart, that she might remain one of the believers.

وَأَصْبَحَ فُؤَادُ أُمِّ مُوسَىٰ فَـٰرِغًا إِن كَادَتْ لَتُبْدِى بِهِۦ لَوْلَآ أَن رَّبَطْنَا عَلَىٰ قَلْبِهَا لِتَكُونَ مِنَ الْمُؤْمِنِينَ ۝

11. And she said to his sister: 'Follow him you.' So she watched him from afar, and they perceived not.

وَقَالَتْ لِأُخْتِهِۦ قُصِّيهِ فَبَصُرَتْ بِهِۦ عَن جُنُبٍ وَهُمْ لَا يَشْعُرُونَ ۝

12. And We had already forbidden other foster mothers for him, so she said: 'Shall I direct you to a household who will rear him for you and who would be to him good counsellors?'

وَحَرَّمْنَا عَلَيْهِ الْمَرَاضِعَ مِن قَبْلُ فَقَالَتْ هَلْ أَدُلُّكُمْ عَلَىٰٓ أَهْلِ بَيْتٍ يَكْفُلُونَهُۥ لَكُمْ وَهُمْ لَهُۥ نَـٰصِحُونَ ۝

13. So We restored him to his mother that she might be comforted and not grieve, and that she might know that the promise of Allah is true. Yet most of them know not.

فَرَدَدْنَاهُ إِلَىٰ أُمِّهِ كَىْ تَقَرَّ عَيْنُهَا وَلَا تَحْزَنَ وَلِتَعْلَمَ أَنَّ وَعْدَ اللّٰهِ حَقٌّ وَلَـٰكِنَّ أَكْثَرَهُمْ لَا يَعْلَمُونَ ۝

Section 2

14. And when he attained his full strength and became firm, We vouchsafed to him wisdom and knowledge, and thus We reward the well-doers.

وَلَمَّا بَلَغَ أَشُدَّهُ وَاسْتَوَىٰ ءَاتَيْنَاهُ حُكْمًا وَعِلْمًا وَكَذَٰلِكَ نَجْزِى الْمُحْسِنِينَ ۝

15. And he entered the city at a time of the unawareness of its inhabitants, and he found two men fighting therein, one being of his own party, and the other of his enemies. And he who was of his party called him for help against the one who was of his enemies. So Moses struck him with his fist, and put an end to him. Moses said: 'This is of the work of Satan, verily he is an enemy, a misleader manifest.'

وَدَخَلَ الْمَدِينَةَ عَلَىٰ حِينِ غَفْلَةٍ مِّنْ أَهْلِهَا فَوَجَدَ فِيهَا رَجُلَيْنِ يَقْتَتِلَانِ هَـٰذَا مِن شِيعَتِهِ وَهَـٰذَا مِنْ عَدُوِّهِ فَاسْتَغَاثَهُ الَّذِى مِن شِيعَتِهِ عَلَى الَّذِى مِنْ عَدُوِّهِ فَوَكَزَهُ مُوسَىٰ فَقَضَىٰ عَلَيْهِ قَالَ هَـٰذَا مِنْ عَمَلِ الشَّيْطَانِ إِنَّهُ عَدُوٌّ مُّضِلٌّ مُّبِينٌ ۝

16. Moses said: 'Lord! Verily I have wronged my soul, so forgive.' So He forgave him. Verily He! He is Forgiving, the Owner of Mercy.

قَالَ رَبِّ إِنِّى ظَلَمْتُ نَفْسِى فَاغْفِرْ لِى فَغَفَرَ لَهُ إِنَّهُ هُوَ الْغَفُورُ الرَّحِيمُ ۝

17. Moses said: 'Lord! Whereas You have favoured me, I shall never more be a supporter of the culprits.'

قَالَ رَبِّ بِمَا أَنْعَمْتَ عَلَىَّ فَلَنْ أَكُونَ ظَهِيرًا لِّلْمُجْرِمِينَ ۝

18. And in the morning he was fearing and looking about in the city when lo! He who had asked his succour yesterday was crying out to him. Moses said: 'You are a manifest seducer.'

فَأَصْبَحَ فِي الْمَدِينَةِ خَآئِفًا يَتَرَقَّبُ فَإِذَا الَّذِي اسْتَنصَرَهُ بِالْأَمْسِ يَسْتَصْرِخُهُ قَالَ لَهُ مُوسَىٰ إِنَّكَ لَغَوِيٌّ مُّبِينٌ ۝

19. And when Moses sought to seize him who was an enemy to them both, he said: 'O Moses! Would you slay me as you did slay a person yesterday? You seek to be a tyrant in the land, and not to be of the reconcilers.'

فَلَمَّا أَنْ أَرَادَ أَن يَبْطِشَ بِالَّذِي هُوَ عَدُوٌّ لَّهُمَا قَالَ يَمُوسَىٰ أَتُرِيدُ أَن تَقْتُلَنِي كَمَا قَتَلْتَ نَفْسًا بِالْأَمْسِ إِن تُرِيدُ إِلَّا أَن تَكُونَ جَبَّارًا فِي الْأَرْضِ وَمَا تُرِيدُ أَن تَكُونَ مِنَ الْمُصْلِحِينَ ۝

20. And there came a man running from the farthest part of the city. He said: 'O Moses, the chiefs are counselling together regarding you, that they might slay you; so depart you, verily I am to you of the advisors.'

وَجَاءَ رَجُلٌ مِّنْ أَقْصَا الْمَدِينَةِ يَسْعَىٰ قَالَ يَمُوسَىٰ إِنَّ الْمَلَأَ يَأْتَمِرُونَ بِكَ لِيَقْتُلُوكَ فَاخْرُجْ إِنِّي لَكَ مِنَ النَّصِحِينَ ۝

21. So he went forth from there fearing, looking about. He said: 'Lord! Deliver me from the ungodly people.'

فَخَرَجَ مِنْهَا خَآئِفًا يَتَرَقَّبُ قَالَ رَبِّ نَجِّنِي مِنَ الْقَوْمِ الظَّالِمِينَ ۝

Section 3

22. And when he betook himself towards Madyan, he said: 'Perchance my Lord will guide me to an even way.'

وَلَمَّا تَوَجَّهَ تِلْقَاءَ مَدْيَنَ قَالَ عَسَىٰ رَبِّي أَن يَهْدِيَنِي سَوَاءَ السَّبِيلِ ۝

23. Then when he arrived at the waters of Madyan he found there a community of people watering. And he found, apart from them, two women, keeping back their flocks. He said: 'What is the matter with you two?' They said: 'We do not draw water until the shepherds have driven away their flocks, and our father is a very old man.'

وَلَمَّا وَرَدَ مَآءَ مَدۡيَنَ وَجَدَ عَلَيۡهِ أُمَّةً مِّنَ ٱلنَّاسِ يَسۡقُونَ وَوَجَدَ مِن دُونِهِمُ ٱمۡرَأَتَيۡنِ تَذُودَانِۖ قَالَ مَا خَطۡبُكُمَاۖ قَالَتَا لَا نَسۡقِى حَتَّىٰ يُصۡدِرَ ٱلرِّعَآءُۖ وَأَبُونَا شَيۡخٌ كَبِيرٌ ﴿٢٣﴾

24. Then he watered their flocks for the two. Then he turned aside into the shade, and said: 'Lord, I have need of the good which You may send down for me.'

فَسَقَىٰ لَهُمَا ثُمَّ تَوَلَّىٰٓ إِلَى ٱلظِّلِّ فَقَالَ رَبِّ إِنِّى لِمَآ أَنزَلۡتَ إِلَىَّ مِنۡ خَيۡرٍ فَقِيرٌ ﴿٢٤﴾

25. Then one of the two came to him walking bashfully, and said: 'My father invites you that he may recompense you with a wage for that you did water the flocks for us.' Then when he had come to him and recounted to him the whole story, he said: 'Have no fear; you have escaped from the wrongdoing people.'

فَجَآءَتۡهُ إِحۡدَىٰهُمَا تَمۡشِى عَلَى ٱسۡتِحۡيَآءٍ قَالَتۡ إِنَّ أَبِى يَدۡعُوكَ لِيَجۡزِيَكَ أَجۡرَ مَا سَقَيۡتَ لَنَاۚ فَلَمَّا جَآءَهُۥ وَقَصَّ عَلَيۡهِ ٱلۡقَصَصَ قَالَ لَا تَخَفۡۖ نَجَوۡتَ مِنَ ٱلۡقَوۡمِ ٱلظَّـٰلِمِينَ ﴿٢٥﴾

26. And said one of them: 'Father hire him, for the best that you can hire is a strong and reliable person.'

قَالَتۡ إِحۡدَىٰهُمَا يَـٰٓأَبَتِ ٱسۡتَـٔۡجِرۡهُۖ إِنَّ خَيۡرَ مَنِ ٱسۡتَـٔۡجَرۡتَ ٱلۡقَوِىُّ ٱلۡأَمِينُ ﴿٢٦﴾

27. He said: 'I wish I would marry one of these two daughters of mine, provided that you hire yourself to me for eight years, then if you complete ten it will be of your own accord, and I would not make it hard for you; you shall find me, Allah willing, of the righteous.'

قَالَ إِنِّىٓ أُرِيدُ أَنۡ أُنكِحَكَ إِحۡدَى ٱبۡنَتَىَّ هَٰتَيۡنِ عَلَىٰٓ أَن تَأۡجُرَنِى ثَمَٰنِىَ حِجَجٍ ۖ فَإِنۡ أَتۡمَمۡتَ عَشۡرًا فَمِنۡ عِندِكَ ۖ وَمَآ أُرِيدُ أَنۡ أَشُقَّ عَلَيۡكَ ۚ سَتَجِدُنِىٓ إِن شَآءَ ٱللَّهُ مِنَ ٱلصَّٰلِحِينَ ۝

28. Moses said: 'Be it then between me and you; whichever of the two terms I fulfil, it shall be no harshness to me; and Allah is witness of what we say.'

قَالَ ذَٰلِكَ بَيۡنِى وَبَيۡنَكَ ۖ أَيَّمَا ٱلۡأَجَلَيۡنِ قَضَيۡتُ فَلَا عُدۡوَٰنَ عَلَىَّ ۖ وَٱللَّهُ عَلَىٰ مَا نَقُولُ وَكِيلٌ ۝

Section 4

29. Then when Moses had fulfilled the term and was journeying with his family, he saw a fire on the side of Ṭūr, and said to his family: 'Bide you here; I see a fire afar, haply I may bring to you news of it, or a brand out of the fire, haply you may warm yourselves.'

فَلَمَّا قَضَىٰ مُوسَى ٱلۡأَجَلَ وَسَارَ بِأَهۡلِهِۦٓ ءَانَسَ مِن جَانِبِ ٱلطُّورِ نَارًا قَالَ لِأَهۡلِهِ ٱمۡكُثُوٓاْ إِنِّىٓ ءَانَسۡتُ نَارًا لَّعَلِّىٓ ءَاتِيكُم مِّنۡهَا بِخَبَرٍ أَوۡ جَذۡوَةٍ مِّنَ ٱلنَّارِ لَعَلَّكُمۡ تَصۡطَلُونَ ۝

30. Then when he had arrived thereto, he was called from the right side of the valley in the ground blessed with the tree: 'Moses! Verily! I am Allah, the Lord of the worlds;575

فَلَمَّآ أَتَىٰهَا نُودِىَ مِن شَٰطِئِ ٱلۡوَادِ ٱلۡأَيۡمَنِ فِى ٱلۡبُقۡعَةِ ٱلۡمُبَٰرَكَةِ مِنَ ٱلشَّجَرَةِ أَن يَٰمُوسَىٰٓ إِنِّىٓ أَنَا ٱللَّهُ رَبُّ ٱلۡعَٰلَمِينَ ۝

---

575. The epithet 'Lord of the worlds' is added to emphasize the fact that God is not to be located to any particular spot, much less to a 'burning bush'. He is beyond all space, transcending all objects.

31. And cast down your rod.' And when he saw it stirring as though it were a serpent, he turned in flight and looked not back. 'Moses! Draw nigh, and fear not; you are of the secure ones.

وَأَنْ أَلْقِ عَصَاكَ فَلَمَّا رَآهَا تَهْتَزُّ كَأَنَّهَا جَآنٌّ وَلَّى مُدْبِرًا وَلَمْ يُعَقِّبْ يَٰمُوسَىٰ أَقْبِلْ وَلَا تَخَفْ إِنَّكَ مِنَ ٱلْآمِنِينَ ﴿٣١﴾

32. Slip your hand in your bosom, it will come forth white without hurt and draw back the arm to you for fear. These will be two bits of evidence from your Lord for Pharaoh and his chiefs; verily they have been a people given to transgression.'

ٱسْلُكْ يَدَكَ فِى جَيْبِكَ تَخْرُجْ بَيْضَآءَ مِنْ غَيْرِ سُوٓءٍ وَٱضْمُمْ إِلَيْكَ جَنَاحَكَ مِنَ ٱلرَّهْبِ فَذَٰنِكَ بُرْهَٰنَانِ مِن رَّبِّكَ إِلَىٰ فِرْعَوْنَ وَمَلَإِيْهِ إِنَّهُمْ كَانُوا۟ قَوْمًا فَٰسِقِينَ ﴿٣٢﴾

33. He said: 'Lord! I have slain a man among them, and I fear they may slay me;

قَالَ رَبِّ إِنِّى قَتَلْتُ مِنْهُمْ نَفْسًا فَأَخَافُ أَن يَقْتُلُونِ ﴿٣٣﴾

34. And my brother Aaron! He is more eloquent than I am in speech. So send him with me as a support to corroborate me, verily I fear they will belie me.'

وَأَخِى هَٰرُونُ هُوَ أَفْصَحُ مِنِّى لِسَانًا فَأَرْسِلْهُ مَعِىَ رِدْءًا يُصَدِّقُنِى إِنِّى أَخَافُ أَن يُكَذِّبُونِ ﴿٣٤﴾

35. Allah said: 'We shall indeed strengthen your arm with your brother, and We shall give to you authority, so that they shall not be able to come up to you. Go forth with Our signs! You two and those who follow you shall be the victors.'

قَالَ سَنَشُدُّ عَضُدَكَ بِأَخِيكَ وَنَجْعَلُ لَكُمَا سُلْطَٰنًا فَلَا يَصِلُونَ إِلَيْكُمَا بِـَٔايَٰتِنَآ أَنتُمَا وَمَنِ ٱتَّبَعَكُمَا ٱلْغَٰلِبُونَ ﴿٣٥﴾

36. Then when Moses came to them with Our manifest signs, they said: 'This is nothing but magic fabricated, and we heard not of this in our fathers of old.'

فَلَمَّا جَآءَهُم مُّوسَىٰ بِـَٔايَٰتِنَا بَيِّنَٰتٍ قَالُوا۟ مَا هَٰذَآ إِلَّا سِحْرٌ مُّفْتَرًى وَمَا سَمِعْنَا بِهَٰذَا فِىٓ ءَابَآئِنَا ٱلْأَوَّلِينَ ﴿٣٦﴾

37. And Moses said: 'My Lord best knows him who brings guidance from before the Lord, and him whose will be the happy end of the abode, verily the ungodly shall not thrive.'

وَقَالَ مُوسَىٰ رَبِّيٓ أَعْلَمُ بِمَن جَآءَ بِالْهُدَىٰ مِنْ عِندِهِۦ وَمَن تَكُونُ لَهُۥ عَٰقِبَةُ ٱلدَّارِ إِنَّهُۥ لَا يُفْلِحُ ٱلظَّٰلِمُونَ ٣٧

38. And Pharaoh said: 'O chiefs! I know not of a god for you except me. So light you for me, Hāmān, clay, and make for me a lofty tower that I may ascend to the god of Moses; and surely I imagine him to be of liars.'

وَقَالَ فِرْعَوْنُ يَٰٓأَيُّهَا ٱلْمَلَأُ مَا عَلِمْتُ لَكُم مِّنْ إِلَٰهٍ غَيْرِى فَأَوْقِدْ لِى يَٰهَٰمَٰنُ عَلَى ٱلطِّينِ فَٱجْعَل لِّى صَرْحًا لَّعَلِّىٓ أَطَّلِعُ إِلَىٰٓ إِلَٰهِ مُوسَىٰ وَإِنِّى لَأَظُنُّهُۥ مِنَ ٱلْكَٰذِبِينَ ٣٨

39. And he and his hosts were stiff-necked in the land unjustifiably and imagined that they would not be brought back to Us.

وَٱسْتَكْبَرَ هُوَ وَجُنُودُهُۥ فِى ٱلْأَرْضِ بِغَيْرِ ٱلْحَقِّ وَظَنُّوٓا۟ أَنَّهُمْ إِلَيْنَا لَا يُرْجَعُونَ ٣٩

40. So We seized him and his hosts and flung them into the sea. So behold you what has been the end of the ungodly!

فَأَخَذْنَٰهُ وَجُنُودَهُۥ فَنَبَذْنَٰهُمْ فِى ٱلْيَمِّ فَٱنظُرْ كَيْفَ كَانَ عَٰقِبَةُ ٱلظَّٰلِمِينَ ٤٠

41. We have made them leaders calling to the Fire, and they shall not be succoured on the Day of Resurrection.

وَجَعَلْنَٰهُمْ أَئِمَّةً يَدْعُونَ إِلَى ٱلنَّارِ وَيَوْمَ ٱلْقِيَٰمَةِ لَا يُنصَرُونَ ٤١

42. And We caused a curse to pursue them in this world and on the Day of Resurrection they will be of the castaway.

وَأَتْبَعْنَٰهُمْ فِى هَٰذِهِ ٱلدُّنْيَا لَعْنَةً وَيَوْمَ ٱلْقِيَٰمَةِ هُم مِّنَ ٱلْمَقْبُوحِينَ ٤٢

Section 5

43. And assuredly We vouch-safed to Moses, after We had destroyed the generations of old, the Scripture, enlightenment to mankind and a guidance and a mercy, that haply they be admonished.

وَلَقَدْ ءَاتَيْنَا مُوسَى ٱلْكِتَبَ مِنْ بَعْدِ مَآ أَهْلَكْنَا ٱلْقُرُونَ ٱلْأُولَىٰ بَصَآئِرَ لِلنَّاسِ وَهُدًى وَرَحْمَةً لَّعَلَّهُمْ يَتَذَكَّرُونَ ﴿٤٣﴾

44. And you were not on the western side when We decreed the affair to Moses, and you were not of the witnesses.

وَمَا كُنتَ بِجَانِبِ ٱلْغَرْبِيِّ إِذْ قَضَيْنَآ إِلَىٰ مُوسَى ٱلْأَمْرَ وَمَا كُنتَ مِنَ ٱلشَّهِدِينَ ﴿٤٤﴾

45. And We produced genera-tions and life was prolonged unto them, nor were you a dweller among the people of Madyan, reciting to them Our revelations; but it is We Who were to send.

وَلَكِنَّآ أَنشَأْنَا قُرُونًا فَتَطَاوَلَ عَلَيْهِمُ ٱلْعُمُرُ وَمَا كُنتَ ثَاوِيًا فِىٓ أَهْلِ مَدْيَنَ تَتْلُوا۟ عَلَيْهِمْ ءَايَتِنَا وَلَكِنَّا كُنَّا مُرْسِلِينَ ﴿٤٥﴾

46. Nor were you beside the Tur when We called, but you are sent as a mercy from your Lord that you may warn a people to whom no warner came before you, that haply they might be admonished.

وَمَا كُنتَ بِجَانِبِ ٱلطُّورِ إِذْ نَادَيْنَا وَلَكِن رَّحْمَةً مِّن رَّبِّكَ لِتُنذِرَ قَوْمًا مَّآ أَتَهُم مِّن نَّذِيرٍ مِّن قَبْلِكَ لَعَلَّهُمْ يَتَذَكَّرُونَ ﴿٤٦﴾

47. And lest an affliction had visited them for what their hands had sent before, they should have said: 'Our Lord! Why did not You send a Messenger unto us, so that we might have followed Your revelations and been of the believers.'

وَلَوْلَآ أَن تُصِيبَهُم مُّصِيبَةٌ بِمَا قَدَّمَتْ أَيْدِيهِمْ فَيَقُولُوا۟ رَبَّنَا لَوْلَآ أَرْسَلْتَ إِلَيْنَا رَسُولًا فَنَتَّبِعَ ءَايَتِكَ وَنَكُونَ مِنَ ٱلْمُؤْمِنِينَ ﴿٤٧﴾

48. Yet when the truth is come to them from before Us, they say: 'Why has he not been vouchsafed the like to what was given to Moses?' Did they not disbelieve in what was given to Moses before?' They say: 'Two magics supporting each other.' And they say: 'We are disbelievers in all such things.'

فَلَمَّا جَاءَهُمُ الْحَقُّ مِنْ عِندِنَا قَالُواْ لَوْلَا أُوتِيَ مِثْلَ مَا أُوتِيَ مُوسَىٰٓ أَوَلَمْ يَكْفُرُواْ بِمَا أُوتِيَ مُوسَىٰ مِن قَبْلُ قَالُواْ سِحْرَانِ تَظَٰهَرَا وَقَالُوٓاْ إِنَّا بِكُلٍّ كَٰفِرُونَ ٤٨

49. Say: 'Then bring a Book from before Allah that is better in guidance than these two, and I shall follow it – if you are truthful.

قُلْ فَأْتُواْ بِكِتَٰبٍ مِّنْ عِندِ اللَّهِ هُوَ أَهْدَىٰ مِنْهُمَآ أَتَّبِعْهُ إِن كُنتُمْ صَٰدِقِينَ ٤٩

50. Then if they do not answer you, know you that they only follow their own desires; and who is farther astray than he who follows his own desire without a guidance from Allah? Verily Allah does not guide a wrong-doing people.'

فَإِن لَّمْ يَسْتَجِيبُواْ لَكَ فَاعْلَمْ أَنَّمَا يَتَّبِعُونَ أَهْوَآءَهُمْ وَمَنْ أَضَلُّ مِمَّنِ اتَّبَعَ هَوَىٰهُ بِغَيْرِ هُدًى مِّنَ اللَّهِ إِنَّ اللَّهَ لَا يَهْدِي الْقَوْمَ الظَّٰلِمِينَ ٥٠

Section 6

51. And assuredly We have caused the Word to reach them in succession, that haply they may be admonished.

وَلَقَدْ وَصَّلْنَا لَهُمُ الْقَوْلَ لَعَلَّهُمْ يَتَذَكَّرُونَ ٥١

52. Those unto who We vouchsafed the Book before it – they believe therein.

الَّذِينَ ءَاتَيْنَٰهُمُ الْكِتَٰبَ مِن قَبْلِهِۦ هُم بِهِۦ يُؤْمِنُونَ ٥٢

53. And when it is rehearsed to them, they say: 'We believe therein, verily this is the Truth from our Lord;' verily We have been even before it of those who submit themselves.

وَإِذَا يُتْلَىٰ عَلَيْهِمْ قَالُوٓاْ ءَامَنَّا بِهِۦٓ إِنَّهُ الْحَقُّ مِن رَّبِّنَآ إِنَّا كُنَّا مِن قَبْلِهِۦ مُسْلِمِينَ ٥٣

54. These shall be vouchsafed their wage twice over, because they have persevered, and they repel evil with good, and expend of what We have provided them.

أُوْلَٰٓئِكَ يُؤْتَوْنَ أَجْرَهُم مَّرَّتَيْنِ بِمَا صَبَرُواْ وَيَدْرَءُونَ بِٱلْحَسَنَةِ ٱلسَّيِّئَةَ وَمِمَّا رَزَقْنَٰهُمْ يُنفِقُونَ ﴿٥٤﴾

55. And when they hear a vain discourse, they withdraw therefrom and say: 'To us our works, and to you your works; peace be to you; and we do not seek ignorant ones.'

وَإِذَا سَمِعُواْ ٱللَّغْوَ أَعْرَضُواْ عَنْهُ وَقَالُواْ لَنَآ أَعْمَٰلُنَا وَلَكُمْ أَعْمَٰلُكُمْ سَلَٰمٌ عَلَيْكُمْ لَا نَبْتَغِي ٱلْجَٰهِلِينَ ﴿٥٥﴾

56. Verily you cannot guide whomsoever you like but it is Allah Who shall guide whomsoever He will.576 And He knows best who are the guided.577

إِنَّكَ لَا تَهْدِى مَنْ أَحْبَبْتَ وَلَٰكِنَّ ٱللَّهَ يَهْدِى مَن يَشَآءُ وَهُوَ أَعْلَمُ بِٱلْمُهْتَدِينَ ﴿٥٦﴾

57. And they say: 'Were we to follow the guidance with you, we shall be snatched away from our land.' Have We not established for them an inviolable sanctuary to which are brought all manner of fruits! A provision from Our presence? Yet most of them know not.

وَقَالُوٓاْ إِن نَّتَّبِعِ ٱلْهُدَىٰ مَعَكَ نُتَخَطَّفْ مِنْ أَرْضِنَآ أَوَلَمْ نُمَكِّن لَّهُمْ حَرَمًا ءَامِنًا يُجْبَىٰٓ إِلَيْهِ ثَمَرَٰتُ كُلِّ شَىْءٍ رِّزْقًا مِّن لَّدُنَّا وَلَٰكِنَّ أَكْثَرَهُمْ لَا يَعْلَمُونَ ﴿٥٧﴾

---

576. It is beyond the power of man, even of the greatest man, to make anyone see the right path. It is God alone Who can, and does guide in accordance with His infinite wisdom.

577. Far from having the power to show the path of guidance to others, no mortal has even the knowledge of those who shall be guided.

58. And how many a city have We destroyed that exulted in their living, and there are their dwellings which have not been inhabited after them unless for a little while; and verily We have been the inheritors.

وَكَمْ أَهْلَكْنَا مِن قَرْيَةٍ بَطِرَتْ مَعِيشَتَهَا فَتِلْكَ مَسَٰكِنُهُمْ لَمْ تُسْكَن مِّنۢ بَعْدِهِمْ إِلَّا قَلِيلًا وَكُنَّا نَحْنُ ٱلْوَٰرِثِينَ ۝

59. Nor was your Lord to destroy the cities until He had raised up in their mother city a Messenger reciting to them Our revelations. Nor were We to destroy the cities unless their inhabitants had been ungodly.

وَمَا كَانَ رَبُّكَ مُهْلِكَ ٱلْقُرَىٰ حَتَّىٰ يَبْعَثَ فِىٓ أُمِّهَا رَسُولًا يَتْلُوا۟ عَلَيْهِمْ ءَايَٰتِنَا وَمَا كُنَّا مُهْلِكِى ٱلْقُرَىٰٓ إِلَّا وَأَهْلُهَا ظَٰلِمُونَ ۝

60. And whatever you are vouchsafed is an enjoyment of the life of this world and its adornment; and what is with Allah is better and more lasting. Will you not then reflect?

وَمَآ أُوتِيتُم مِّن شَىْءٍ فَمَتَٰعُ ٱلْحَيَوٰةِ ٱلدُّنْيَا وَزِينَتُهَا وَمَا عِندَ ٱللَّهِ خَيْرٌ وَأَبْقَىٰٓ أَفَلَا تَعْقِلُونَ ۝

Section 7

61. Is he, then, whom We have promised an excellent promise which he is going to meet like him whom We have allowed the enjoyment of this world awhile, then on the Day of Resurrection he shall be of those arraigned?

أَفَمَن وَعَدْنَٰهُ وَعْدًا حَسَنًا فَهُوَ لَٰقِيهِ كَمَن مَّتَّعْنَٰهُ مَتَٰعَ ٱلْحَيَوٰةِ ٱلدُّنْيَا ثُمَّ هُوَ يَوْمَ ٱلْقِيَٰمَةِ مِنَ ٱلْمُحْضَرِينَ ۝

62. And on the Day when He will call unto them and say: 'Where are My partners whom you were wont to assert?'

وَيَوْمَ يُنَادِيهِمْ فَيَقُولُ أَيْنَ شُرَكَآءِىَ ٱلَّذِينَ كُنتُمْ تَزْعُمُونَ ۝

63. Those on whom the sentence will be pronounced will say: 'Our Lord; these are they whom we seduced; we seduced them even as we ourselves were seduced; we declare ourselves quit of them before You; not ourselves they were wont to worship.'

قَالَ الَّذِينَ حَقَّ عَلَيْهِمُ الْقَوْلُ رَبَّنَا هَٰؤُلَآءِ الَّذِينَ أَغْوَيْنَا أَغْوَيْنَٰهُمْ كَمَا غَوَيْنَا ۖ تَبَرَّأْنَآ إِلَيْكَ ۖ مَا كَانُوٓا إِيَّانَا يَعْبُدُونَ ۝

64. And it shall be said: 'Call upon your associate-gods.' And they will call upon them, and they shall not be answered, and they shall see the torment. Would that they had received the guidance!

وَقِيلَ ادْعُوا شُرَكَآءَكُمْ فَدَعَوْهُمْ فَلَمْ يَسْتَجِيبُوا لَهُمْ وَرَأَوُا الْعَذَابَ ۚ لَوْ أَنَّهُمْ كَانُوا يَهْتَدُونَ ۝

65. And on the Day when He shall call unto them and say: 'What answer did you give to Our envoys?'

وَيَوْمَ يُنَادِيهِمْ فَيَقُولُ مَاذَآ أَجَبْتُمُ الْمُرْسَلِينَ ۝

66. Bedimmed unto them on that Day shall be all excuses, and so they shall not be able to ask one of another.

فَعَمِيَتْ عَلَيْهِمُ الْأَنْبَآءُ يَوْمَئِذٍ فَهُمْ لَا يَتَسَآءَلُونَ ۝

67. However, whoso will repent and believe and work righteous deeds – perchance he will be of the thrivers.

فَأَمَّا مَنْ تَابَ وَءَامَنَ وَعَمِلَ صَٰلِحًا فَعَسَىٰٓ أَن يَكُونَ مِنَ الْمُفْلِحِينَ ۝

68. And your Lord creates whatsoever He wills and chooses; no choice is to be for them. Hallowed be Allah and exalted above what they associate![578]

وَرَبُّكَ يَخْلُقُ مَا يَشَآءُ وَيَخْتَارُ ۗ مَا كَانَ لَهُمُ الْخِيَرَةُ ۚ سُبْحَٰنَ اللَّهِ وَتَعَٰلَىٰ عَمَّا يُشْرِكُونَ ۝

---

578. With what they associate with Him. He is above all restrictions and limitations that the ignorant philosophers of Greece and other polytheists have sought to impose on His illimitable, infinite power, potency, and majesty.

69. And your Lord knows what their hearts conceal and what they disclose.

وَرَبُّكَ يَعْلَمُ مَا تُكِنُّ صُدُورُهُمْ وَمَا يُعْلِنُونَ ۝

70. He is Allah! There is no god but He! His is all praise in the first and in the last; and His is the command, and to Him you shall be returned.[579]

وَهُوَ اللَّهُ لَا إِلَٰهَ إِلَّا هُوَ لَهُ الْحَمْدُ فِي الْأُولَىٰ وَالْآخِرَةِ وَلَهُ الْحُكْمُ وَإِلَيْهِ تُرْجَعُونَ ۝

71. Say: 'Think you, if Allah made night continuous for you till the Day of Resurrection, what god is there besides Allah, who would bring you light? Do you not hear?'

قُلْ أَرَأَيْتُمْ إِن جَعَلَ اللَّهُ عَلَيْكُمُ اللَّيْلَ سَرْمَدًا إِلَىٰ يَوْمِ الْقِيَامَةِ مَنْ إِلَٰهٌ غَيْرُ اللَّهِ يَأْتِيكُم بِضِيَاءٍ أَفَلَا تَسْمَعُونَ ۝

72. Say: 'Think you, if Allah made for you day continuous till the Day of Resurrection, what god is there, besides Allah, who would bring you night in which you have repose? Do you not see?'

قُلْ أَرَأَيْتُمْ إِن جَعَلَ اللَّهُ عَلَيْكُمُ النَّهَارَ سَرْمَدًا إِلَىٰ يَوْمِ الْقِيَامَةِ مَنْ إِلَٰهٌ غَيْرُ اللَّهِ يَأْتِيكُم بِلَيْلٍ تَسْكُنُونَ فِيهِ أَفَلَا تُبْصِرُونَ ۝

73. It is of His mercy that He has made for you night and day, that in them you may have repose and that you may seek of His Grace, and that haply you may give thanks.

وَمِن رَّحْمَتِهِ جَعَلَ لَكُمُ اللَّيْلَ وَالنَّهَارَ لِتَسْكُنُوا فِيهِ وَلِتَبْتَغُوا مِن فَضْلِهِ وَلَعَلَّكُمْ تَشْكُرُونَ ۝

74. And on the Day when He shall call unto them, and say: 'Where are My associates whom you were wont to assert?'

وَيَوْمَ يُنَادِيهِمْ فَيَقُولُ أَيْنَ شُرَكَاءِيَ الَّذِينَ كُنتُمْ تَزْعُمُونَ ۝

---

579. He is Supreme, All-Pervading, Omniscient, not one of the gods but the Sole God.

75. We shall take out from every community a witness, and We shall say: 'Come forth with your proof'; then they will know that the truth was Allah's, and astray will go from them what they were wont to fabricate.

وَنَزَعْنَا مِن كُلِّ أُمَّةٍ شَهِيدًا فَقُلْنَا هَاتُوا بُرْهَانَكُمْ فَعَلِمُوا أَنَّ الْحَقَّ لِلَّهِ وَضَلَّ عَنْهُم مَّا كَانُوا يَفْتَرُونَ ۝

Section 8

76. Verily Qārūn was of the people of Moses; then he behaved arrogantly towards them. And We had vouchsafed him of the treasures that of which the keys would have weighed down a band of strong men. Recall when his people said to him: 'Exult not; verily Allah does not like the exultant.

إِنَّ قَارُونَ كَانَ مِن قَوْمِ مُوسَىٰ فَبَغَىٰ عَلَيْهِمْ وَآتَيْنَاهُ مِنَ الْكُنُوزِ مَا إِنَّ مَفَاتِحَهُ لَتَنُوءُ بِالْعُصْبَةِ أُولِي الْقُوَّةِ إِذْ قَالَ لَهُ قَوْمُهُ لَا تَفْرَحْ إِنَّ اللَّهَ لَا يُحِبُّ الْفَرِحِينَ ۝

77. And seek the abode of the Hereafter with what Allah has vouchsafed you, and forget not your portion in the world[580], and be generous and Allah has been generous to you, and seek not corruption in the land, verily Allah approves not corrupters.'

وَابْتَغِ فِيمَا آتَاكَ اللَّهُ الدَّارَ الْآخِرَةَ وَلَا تَنسَ نَصِيبَكَ مِنَ الدُّنْيَا وَأَحْسِن كَمَا أَحْسَنَ اللَّهُ إِلَيْكَ وَلَا تَبْغِ الْفَسَادَ فِي الْأَرْضِ إِنَّ اللَّهَ لَا يُحِبُّ الْمُفْسِدِينَ ۝

---

580. In other words work towards the Next world. Wealth, in Islam, is not to be regarded as an excuse for vanity and luxury, but is to be held as an opportunity for giving freely to the service of God and humanity.

78. He said: 'I have achieved all this because of the knowledge I possess.' Did he not know that Allah had destroyed before him, of the generations, who were stronger than he in might and larger in respect of following? And the culprits will not be (immediately) questioned of their sins.

قَالَ إِنَّمَآ أُوتِيتُهُۥ عَلَىٰ عِلْمٍ عِندِىٓ أَوَلَمْ يَعْلَمْ أَنَّ ٱللَّهَ قَدْ أَهْلَكَ مِن قَبْلِهِۦ مِنَ ٱلْقُرُونِ مَنْ هُوَ أَشَدُّ مِنْهُ قُوَّةً وَأَكْثَرُ جَمْعًا وَلَا يُسْـَٔلُ عَن ذُنُوبِهِمُ ٱلْمُجْرِمُونَ ﴿٧٨﴾

79. Then he went forth before his people in his pomp. Then those who sought the life of this world said: 'Would that we had the like of what has been vouchsafed to Qārūn? Surely he is the owner of a great fortune.'

فَخَرَجَ عَلَىٰ قَوْمِهِۦ فِى زِينَتِهِۦ قَالَ ٱلَّذِينَ يُرِيدُونَ ٱلْحَيَوٰةَ ٱلدُّنْيَا يَٰلَيْتَ لَنَا مِثْلَ مَآ أُوتِىَ قَٰرُونُ إِنَّهُۥ لَذُو حَظٍّ عَظِيمٍ ﴿٧٩﴾

80. And those who were given the knowledge said: 'Woe be to you! The reward of Allah is best for him who believes and works righteously, and none shall attain it except the steadfast.'

وَقَالَ ٱلَّذِينَ أُوتُوا۟ ٱلْعِلْمَ وَيْلَكُمْ ثَوَابُ ٱللَّهِ خَيْرٌ لِّمَنْ ءَامَنَ وَعَمِلَ صَٰلِحًا وَلَا يُلَقَّىٰهَآ إِلَّا ٱلصَّٰبِرُونَ ﴿٨٠﴾

81. Then We sank the earth with him and his dwelling place. And he had no host to defend him against Allah, nor was he of those who could defend themselves.

فَخَسَفْنَا بِهِۦ وَبِدَارِهِ ٱلْأَرْضَ فَمَا كَانَ لَهُۥ مِن فِئَةٍ يَنصُرُونَهُۥ مِن دُونِ ٱللَّهِ وَمَا كَانَ مِنَ ٱلْمُنتَصِرِينَ ﴿٨١﴾

82. And those who had coveted his lot the day before now began to say: 'Ah! Allah expands the provision for whomsoever of His bondsmen He wills, and also stints. Had not Allah been gracious to us, He would have sunk the earth with us also. Ah! The infidels do not thrive.'

وَأَصْبَحَ ٱلَّذِينَ تَمَنَّوْا۟ مَكَانَهُۥ بِٱلْأَمْسِ يَقُولُونَ وَيْكَأَنَّ ٱللَّهَ يَبْسُطُ ٱلرِّزْقَ لِمَن يَشَآءُ مِنْ عِبَادِهِۦ وَيَقْدِرُ لَوْلَآ أَن مَّنَّ ٱللَّهُ عَلَيْنَا لَخَسَفَ بِنَا وَيْكَأَنَّهُۥ لَا يُفْلِحُ ٱلْكَٰفِرُونَ ﴿٨٢﴾

Section 9

83. This is the abode of the Hereafter; We assign it to those only who do not seek exaltation or corruption in the land; and the happy end is for the God-fearing.

تِلْكَ الدَّارُ الْأَخِرَةُ نَجْعَلُهَا لِلَّذِينَ لَا يُرِيدُونَ عُلُوًّا فِي الْأَرْضِ وَلَا فَسَادًا وَالْعَاقِبَةُ لِلْمُتَّقِينَ ﴿٨٣﴾

84. Whosoever brings good shall have better than it, and whosoever brings evil, then those who work evil deeds shall only be rewarded for what they have been working.

مَن جَآءَ بِالْحَسَنَةِ فَلَهُ خَيْرٌ مِّنْهَا وَمَن جَآءَ بِالسَّيِّئَةِ فَلَا يُجْزَى الَّذِينَ عَمِلُوا السَّيِّئَاتِ إِلَّا مَا كَانُوا يَعْمَلُونَ ﴿٨٤﴾

85. Verily He who has imposed the Qur'ān on you is surely to bring you back home. Say: 'My Lord knows best as to who brings guidance and who is in error manifest.'

إِنَّ الَّذِي فَرَضَ عَلَيْكَ الْقُرْءَانَ لَرَآدُّكَ إِلَى مَعَادٍ قُل رَّبِّي أَعْلَمُ مَن جَآءَ بِالْهُدَىٰ وَمَنْ هُوَ فِي ضَلَالٍ مُّبِينٍ ﴿٨٥﴾

86. And you were not expecting that the Book would be inspired in you, but it is a mercy from your Lord; so do not be you a supporter of the infidels.

وَمَا كُنتَ تَرْجُوا أَن يُلْقَىٰ إِلَيْكَ الْكِتَابُ إِلَّا رَحْمَةً مِّن رَّبِّكَ فَلَا تَكُونَنَّ ظَهِيرًا لِّلْكَافِرِينَ ﴿٨٦﴾

87. And let them not turn you aside from the signs of Allah after they have been sent down unto you. And call you mankind to your Lord, and do not be you of the associators.

وَلَا يَصُدُّنَّكَ عَنْ ءَايَاتِ اللَّهِ بَعْدَ إِذْ أُنزِلَتْ إِلَيْكَ وَادْعُ إِلَى رَبِّكَ وَلَا تَكُونَنَّ مِنَ الْمُشْرِكِينَ ﴿٨٧﴾

88. And do not invoke you any other god along with Allah.[581] There is no god but He. Perishable is everything save His Face.[582] His is the Judgement, and to Him you all shall be returned.

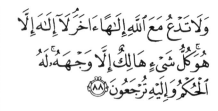

---

581. Many of the Arabian pagans fondly hoped that the Prophet acting on a policy of 'give and take' might be persuaded to make a compromise with them at least in some matters of Faith. This verse puts an end to all such fancies and delusions.

582. He alone is Immortal, Ever-living; all else is perishable. In the whole of the universe everything is slippery, doubtful; death alone is certain. This also negates the immortality of the soul, matter or anything except God.

Sūrah 29

al-'Ankabūt

(Makkan, 7 Sections, 69 Verses)

In the name of Allah, the Compassionate, the Merciful.

Section 1

1. *Alif, Lām, Mīm.*

2. Do people think that they shall be left alone because they say: 'We believe'; and that they shall not be tested?

3. And assuredly We have tested those who were before them. So Allah will surely know those who are true and will surely know the liars.

4. Or do those who work ill-deeds think that they will outstrip Us? Ill do they judge!

5. Whosoever hopes for the meeting with Allah, then Allah's term is surely coming, and He is the Hearer, the Knower.

6. And whosoever strives, strives only for himself, verily Allah is Independent of the worlds.

7. And whosoever believes and works righteous deeds, We shall purge away the evil deeds from them, and shall recompense them the best of what they have been working.

8. And We have enjoined on man kindness to parents, but if they strive to make you associate with Me that of which you have no knowledge, do not obey them; to Me is your return, and I shall declare to you what you have been doing.

وَوَصَّيْنَا الْإِنسَنَ بِوَلِدَيْهِ حُسْنًا وَإِن جَهَدَاكَ لِتُشْرِكَ بِى مَا لَيْسَ لَكَ بِهِ عِلْمٌ فَلَا تُطِعْهُمَا إِلَى مَرْجِعُكُمْ فَأُنَبِّئُكُم بِمَا كُنتُمْ تَعْمَلُونَ ۞

9. And those who believe and work righteous deeds We shall surely make them enter among the righteous.

وَالَّذِينَ ءَامَنُوا وَعَمِلُوا الصَّلِحَتِ لَنُدْخِلَنَّهُمْ فِى الصَّلِحِينَ ۞

10. Of mankind are some who say, 'we believe in Allah,' then if they are afflicted in the way of Allah, they take the persecution of men as the torment of Allah, and then, if succour comes from your Lord they say, 'verily we have been with you.' Is not Allah the best Knower of what is in the breasts of the creatures?

وَمِنَ النَّاسِ مَن يَقُولُ ءَامَنَّا بِاللَّهِ فَإِذَآ أُوذِىَ فِى اللَّهِ جَعَلَ فِتْنَةَ النَّاسِ كَعَذَابِ اللَّهِ وَلَئِن جَاءَ نَصْرٌ مِّن رَّبِّكَ لَيَقُولُنَّ إِنَّا كُنَّا مَعَكُمْ أَوَلَيْسَ اللَّهُ بِأَعْلَمَ بِمَا فِى صُدُورِ الْعَلَمِينَ ۞

11. And surely Allah will come to know those who believe, and surely He will come to know the hypocrites.[583]

وَلَيَعْلَمَنَّ اللَّهُ الَّذِينَ ءَامَنُوا وَلَيَعْلَمَنَّ الْمُنَفِقِينَ ۞

12. And those who disbelieve say to those who believe: 'Follow our way, and we shall surely bear your sins;' whereas they shall not bear aught of their sins; verily they are the liars.

وَقَالَ الَّذِينَ كَفَرُوا لِلَّذِينَ ءَامَنُوا اتَّبِعُوا سَبِيلَنَا وَلْنَحْمِلْ خَطَيَكُمْ وَمَا هُم بِحَمِلِينَ مِنْ خَطَيَهُم مِّن شَىْءٍ إِنَّهُمْ لَكَذِبُونَ ۞

---

583. Of course this does not mean that there will be an addition to His knowledge, or that He will come to know something of which He was previously ignorant. The only meaning is that He will test, He will demonstrate.

13. And assuredly they shall bear their loads and other loads besides their own loads, and surely they shall be questioned on the Day of Resurrection concerning what they were wont to fabricate.

وَلَيَحْمِلُنَّ أَثْقَالَهُمْ وَأَثْقَالًا مَّعَ أَثْقَالِهِمْ ۖ وَلَيُسْـَٔلُنَّ يَوْمَ الْقِيَٰمَةِ عَمَّا كَانُوا۟ يَفْتَرُونَ ۝

Section 2

14. And assuredly We sent Noah to his people. Then he stayed among them for a thousand years, less fifty years; and then the deluge overtook them, while they were wrongdoers.

وَلَقَدْ أَرْسَلْنَا نُوحًا إِلَىٰ قَوْمِهِۦ فَلَبِثَ فِيهِمْ أَلْفَ سَنَةٍ إِلَّا خَمْسِينَ عَامًا فَأَخَذَهُمُ الطُّوفَانُ وَهُمْ ظَٰلِمُونَ ۝

15. Then We delivered him and those with him in the ark, and made it a sign to the worlds.

فَأَنجَيْنَٰهُ وَأَصْحَٰبَ السَّفِينَةِ وَجَعَلْنَٰهَآ ءَايَةً لِّلْعَٰلَمِينَ ۝

16. And We sent Abraham. Recall when he said to his people: 'Worship Allah and fear Him; that is best for you if you but know.

وَإِبْرَٰهِيمَ إِذْ قَالَ لِقَوْمِهِ ٱعْبُدُوا۟ اللَّهَ وَاتَّقُوهُ ۖ ذَٰلِكُمْ خَيْرٌ لَّكُمْ إِن كُنتُمْ تَعْلَمُونَ ۝

17. You worship only images instead of Allah, and it is a fiction you have created. Verily those whom you worship instead of Allah own no provision for you. So seek provision with Allah and worship Him, and to Him give thanks; to Him you shall be returned.

إِنَّمَا تَعْبُدُونَ مِن دُونِ اللَّهِ أَوْثَٰنًا وَتَخْلُقُونَ إِفْكًا ۚ إِنَّ الَّذِينَ تَعْبُدُونَ مِن دُونِ اللَّهِ لَا يَمْلِكُونَ لَكُمْ رِزْقًا فَابْتَغُوا۟ عِندَ اللَّهِ الرِّزْقَ وَاعْبُدُوهُ وَاشْكُرُوا۟ لَهُۥٓ ۖ إِلَيْهِ تُرْجَعُونَ ۝

18. And if you belie me, then communities before you have belied; and naught is upon the Messenger but a manifest preaching.'

وَإِن تُكَذِّبُوا فَقَدْ كَذَّبَ أُمَمٌ مِّن قَبْلِكُمْ وَمَا عَلَى ٱلرَّسُولِ إِلَّا ٱلْبَلَٰغُ ٱلْمُبِينُ ﴿١٨﴾

19. Do they not see how Allah originates creation? And then He shall restore it; surely that is easy for Allah.

أَوَلَمْ يَرَوْا كَيْفَ يُبْدِئُ ٱللَّهُ ٱلْخَلْقَ ثُمَّ يُعِيدُهُۥٓ إِنَّ ذَٰلِكَ عَلَى ٱللَّهِ يَسِيرٌ ﴿١٩﴾

20. Say: 'Go about in the land, and see how He originated creation, and then Allah will bring another production; verily Allah is Potent over everything.

قُلْ سِيرُوا فِي ٱلْأَرْضِ فَٱنظُرُوا كَيْفَ بَدَأَ ٱلْخَلْقَ ثُمَّ ٱللَّهُ يُنشِئُ ٱلنَّشْأَةَ ٱلْأَخِرَةَ إِنَّ ٱللَّهَ عَلَىٰ كُلِّ شَيْءٍ قَدِيرٌ ﴿٢٠﴾

21. He shall chastise whom He will, and shall show mercy to whom He will; and to Him you shall be returned.

يُعَذِّبُ مَن يَشَآءُ وَيَرْحَمُ مَن يَشَآءُ وَإِلَيْهِ تُقْلَبُونَ ﴿٢١﴾

22. And you cannot escape in the earth nor in the heaven, and for you there is no friend and helper besides Allah.'

وَمَا أَنتُم بِمُعْجِزِينَ فِي ٱلْأَرْضِ وَلَا فِي ٱلسَّمَآءِ وَمَا لَكُم مِّن دُونِ ٱللَّهِ مِن وَلِيٍّ وَلَا نَصِيرٍ ﴿٢٢﴾

Section 3

23. Those who disbelieve in the signs of Allah and in their meeting with Him, they shall despair of My mercy, and they! Theirs shall be an afflictive torment.

وَٱلَّذِينَ كَفَرُوا بِـَٔايَٰتِ ٱللَّهِ وَلِقَآئِهِۦٓ أُوْلَٰٓئِكَ يَئِسُوا مِن رَّحْمَتِي وَأُوْلَٰٓئِكَ لَهُمْ عَذَابٌ أَلِيمٌ ﴿٢٣﴾

24. Then the answer of his people was naught but that they said: 'Slay him, or burn him.' Then Allah rescued him from the fire; herein are signs for a people who believe.

فَمَا كَانَ جَوَابَ قَوْمِهِۦٓ إِلَّآ أَن قَالُوا ٱقْتُلُوهُ أَوْ حَرِّقُوهُ فَأَنجَىٰهُ ٱللَّهُ مِنَ ٱلنَّارِ إِنَّ فِي ذَٰلِكَ لَـَٔايَٰتٍ لِّقَوْمٍ يُؤْمِنُونَ ﴿٢٤﴾

25. And he said: 'You have taken images instead of Allah out of affection between you in the life of this world; but on the Day of Resurrection you will deny each other and you shall curse each other; and your resort shall be the Fire, and you shall have no helpers.'

وَقَالَ إِنَّمَا ٱتَّخَذْتُم مِّن دُونِ ٱللَّهِ أَوْثَـٰنًا مَّوَدَّةَ بَيْنِكُمْ فِى ٱلْحَيَوٰةِ ٱلدُّنْيَا ثُمَّ يَوْمَ ٱلْقِيَـٰمَةِ يَكْفُرُ بَعْضُكُم بِبَعْضٍ وَيَلْعَنُ بَعْضُكُم بَعْضًا وَمَأْوَىٰكُمُ ٱلنَّارُ وَمَا لَكُم مِّن نَّـٰصِرِينَ ﴿٢٥﴾

26. And Lot believed in him. And he said: 'Verily I will flee to my Lord; verily He is the Mighty, the Wise.'

فَـَٔامَنَ لَهُۥ لُوطٌ وَقَالَ إِنِّى مُهَاجِرٌ إِلَىٰ رَبِّىٓ إِنَّهُۥ هُوَ ٱلْعَزِيزُ ٱلْحَكِيمُ ﴿٢٦﴾

27. And We bestowed on him Isaac and Jacob, and We assigned prophecy and the Book to be among his posterity, and We vouchsafed to him his reward in this world, and in the Hereafter he shall be of the righteous.

وَوَهَبْنَا لَهُۥٓ إِسْحَـٰقَ وَيَعْقُوبَ وَجَعَلْنَا فِى ذُرِّيَّتِهِ ٱلنُّبُوَّةَ وَٱلْكِتَـٰبَ وَءَاتَيْنَـٰهُ أَجْرَهُۥ فِى ٱلدُّنْيَا وَإِنَّهُۥ فِى ٱلْـَٔاخِرَةِ لَمِنَ ٱلصَّـٰلِحِينَ ﴿٢٧﴾

28. And Lot! Recall when he said to his people: 'You commit an indecency in which none has preceded you in the worlds.

وَلُوطًا إِذْ قَالَ لِقَوْمِهِۦٓ إِنَّكُمْ لَتَأْتُونَ ٱلْفَـٰحِشَةَ مَا سَبَقَكُم بِهَا مِنْ أَحَدٍ مِّنَ ٱلْعَـٰلَمِينَ ﴿٢٨﴾

29. You go in indeed to males, and you rob on the highway, and you commit what is disreputable in your assembly.' The answer of his people was nothing but that they said: 'Bring Allah's chastisement on us, if you are of the truthful.'

أَئِنَّكُمْ لَتَأْتُونَ ٱلرِّجَالَ وَتَقْطَعُونَ ٱلسَّبِيلَ وَتَأْتُونَ فِى نَادِيكُمُ ٱلْمُنكَرَ فَمَا كَانَ جَوَابَ قَوْمِهِۦٓ إِلَّآ أَن قَالُوا۟ ٱئْتِنَا بِعَذَابِ ٱللَّهِ إِن كُنتَ مِنَ ٱلصَّـٰدِقِينَ ﴿٢٩﴾

30. He said: 'Lord! Give me victory over the corrupt people.'

قَالَ رَبِّ ٱنصُرْنِى عَلَى ٱلْقَوْمِ ٱلْمُفْسِدِينَ ﴿٣٠﴾

Section 4

31. And when Our envoys came to Abraham with the glad tidings, they said: 'we are about to destroy the inhabitants of that city; verily its inhabitants have become wrongdoers.'

وَلَمَّا جَآءَتْ رُسُلُنَآ إِبْرَٰهِيمَ بِالْبُشْرَىٰ قَالُوٓاْ إِنَّا مُهْلِكُوٓاْ أَهْلِ هَٰذِهِ ٱلْقَرْيَةِ إِنَّ أَهْلَهَا كَانُواْ ظَٰلِمِينَ ﴿٣١﴾

32. He said but there is Lot. They said: 'We know very well who is therein; we are to deliver him and his household, save his wife; she is to be of the lingerers.'

قَالَ إِنَّ فِيهَا لُوطًا قَالُواْ نَحْنُ أَعْلَمُ بِمَن فِيهَا لَنُنَجِّيَنَّهُۥ وَأَهْلَهُۥٓ إِلَّا ٱمْرَأَتَهُۥ كَانَتْ مِنَ ٱلْغَٰبِرِينَ ﴿٣٢﴾

33. And when Our envoys came to Lot, he was distressed on their account and felt straitened on their account. They said: 'Have no fear and do not grieve; verily we are to deliver you and your household save your wife; she is to be of the lingerers.'

وَلَمَّآ أَن جَآءَتْ رُسُلُنَا لُوطًا سِيٓءَ بِهِمْ وَضَاقَ بِهِمْ ذَرْعًا وَقَالُواْ لَا تَخَفْ وَلَا تَحْزَنْ إِنَّا مُنَجُّوكَ وَأَهْلَكَ إِلَّا ٱمْرَأَتَكَ كَانَتْ مِنَ ٱلْغَٰبِرِينَ ﴿٣٣﴾

34. Verily we are about to bring down upon the inhabitants of this city a scourge from the heaven, for they have been transgressing.

إِنَّا مُنزِلُونَ عَلَىٰٓ أَهْلِ هَٰذِهِ ٱلْقَرْيَةِ رِجْزًا مِّنَ ٱلسَّمَآءِ بِمَا كَانُواْ يَفْسُقُونَ ﴿٣٤﴾

35. And assuredly We have left of that a manifest sign for a people who reflect.

وَلَقَد تَّرَكْنَا مِنْهَآ ءَايَةًۢ بَيِّنَةً لِّقَوْمٍ يَعْقِلُونَ ﴿٣٥﴾

36. And to Madyan We sent their brother Shu'ayb. He said: 'My people, worship Allah and fear the Last Day, and do not commit evil on the land as corrupters.'

وَإِلَىٰ مَدْيَنَ أَخَاهُمْ شُعَيْبًا فَقَالَ يَٰقَوْمِ ٱعْبُدُواْ ٱللَّهَ وَٱرْجُواْ ٱلْيَوْمَ ٱلْأَخِرَ وَلَا تَعْثَوْاْ فِي ٱلْأَرْضِ مُفْسِدِينَ ﴿٣٦﴾

37. Then they belied him, so an earthquake seized them and they lay in their dwellings, crouching.

فَكَذَّبُوهُ فَأَخَذَتْهُمُ ٱلرَّجْفَةُ فَأَصْبَحُواْ فِي دَارِهِمْ جَٰثِمِينَ ﴿٣٧﴾

38. And the 'Ād and the Thamūd! Of a surety their destruction is apparent to you from their dwellings. Satan made their works fair-seeming to them, and so kept them off from the path, while they were endued with sight.

وَعَادًا وَثَمُودَا۟ وَقَد تَّبَيَّنَ لَكُم مِّن مَّسَٰكِنِهِمْ وَزَيَّنَ لَهُمُ ٱلشَّيْطَٰنُ أَعْمَٰلَهُمْ فَصَدَّهُمْ عَنِ ٱلسَّبِيلِ وَكَانُوا۟ مُسْتَبْصِرِينَ ﴿٣٨﴾

39. And Qārūn and Pharaoh and Hāmān! And assuredly there came to them Moses with evidence, yet they were stiff-necked in the land, And they could not outstrip Us.

وَقَٰرُونَ وَفِرْعَوْنَ وَهَٰمَٰنَ وَلَقَدْ جَآءَهُم مُّوسَىٰ بِٱلْبَيِّنَٰتِ فَٱسْتَكْبَرُوا۟ فِي ٱلْأَرْضِ وَمَا كَانُوا۟ سَٰبِقِينَ ﴿٣٩﴾

40. Each of them We laid hold of for his sin. Of them were some on whom We sent a violent wind; and of them were some who were overtaken by a shout; and of them were some with whom we sank the earth; and of them were some whom We drowned. Allah was not such as to wrong them, but themselves they were wont to wrong.

فَكُلًّا أَخَذْنَا بِذَنۢبِهِۦ فَمِنْهُم مَّنْ أَرْسَلْنَا عَلَيْهِ حَاصِبًا وَمِنْهُم مَّنْ أَخَذَتْهُ ٱلصَّيْحَةُ وَمِنْهُم مَّنْ خَسَفْنَا بِهِ ٱلْأَرْضَ وَمِنْهُم مَّنْ أَغْرَقْنَا وَمَا كَانَ ٱللَّهُ لِيَظْلِمَهُمْ وَلَٰكِن كَانُوا۟ أَنفُسَهُمْ يَظْلِمُونَ ﴿٤٠﴾

41. The likeness of those who take other patrons than Allah is as the likeness of the spider which takes to herself a house. And the frailest of all houses is the spider's house, if they but knew.

مَثَلُ ٱلَّذِينَ ٱتَّخَذُوا۟ مِن دُونِ ٱللَّهِ أَوْلِيَآءَ كَمَثَلِ ٱلْعَنكَبُوتِ ٱتَّخَذَتْ بَيْتًا وَإِنَّ أَوْهَنَ ٱلْبُيُوتِ لَبَيْتُ ٱلْعَنكَبُوتِ لَوْ كَانُوا۟ يَعْلَمُونَ ﴿٤١﴾

42. Verily Allah knows whatsoever they invoke beside Him, and He is the Mighty, the Wise.

إِنَّ ٱللَّهَ يَعْلَمُ مَا يَدْعُونَ مِن دُونِهِۦ مِن شَىْءٍ وَهُوَ ٱلْعَزِيزُ ٱلْحَكِيمُ ﴿٤٢﴾

43. And these similitudes! We propound them for mankind and none understands them save men of learning.

وَتِلْكَ ٱلْأَمْثَـٰلُ نَضْرِبُهَا لِلنَّاسِ وَمَا يَعْقِلُهَآ إِلَّا ٱلْعَـٰلِمُونَ ﴿٤٣﴾

44. Allah has created the heavens and the earth with a purpose, verily in them is a sign for the believers.

خَلَقَ ٱللَّهُ ٱلسَّمَـٰوَٰتِ وَٱلْأَرْضَ بِٱلْحَقِّ إِنَّ فِى ذَٰلِكَ لَآيَةً لِّلْمُؤْمِنِينَ ﴿٤٤﴾

Section 5

45. Recite you what has been revealed to you of the Book and establish you the prayer; verily prayer forbids indecency[584] and dishonour,[585] and remembrance of Allah is the highest. And Allah knows what you perform.

ٱتْلُ مَآ أُوحِىَ إِلَيْكَ مِنَ ٱلْكِتَـٰبِ وَأَقِمِ ٱلصَّلَوٰةَ إِنَّ ٱلصَّلَوٰةَ تَنْهَىٰ عَنِ ٱلْفَحْشَآءِ وَٱلْمُنكَرِ وَلَذِكْرُ ٱللَّهِ أَكْبَرُ وَٱللَّهُ يَعْلَمُ مَا تَصْنَعُونَ ﴿٤٥﴾

---

584. This brings to mind, by way of contrast, the strong connection that has frequently existed between obscenity and the acts of worship as ordained by the so–called religions of the world. In many of them even prostitution appears to have been not merely tolerated but rather encouraged. 'The Kedeshoth mentioned in the Bible were prostitutes attached to the Canaanite temples, and were held in the highest reverence by the worshippers. Temple prostitutes, in all countries, and at all times, have been highly thought of' (Scott, *History of Prostitution*, p. 10). 'In its earlier phases prostitution was always associated with religion; and there seem strong grounds for the assumption that the first brothels were run by priests' (Ibid., p. 59).

585. That the Islamic prayer is a powerful means of moral elevation and a means of purifying the heart has been recognized at all times, and is almost a truism. But its value in other spheres is also well – merited. 'Von Kremer rightly sees in the salat', says Noeldeke, 'a substitute, to some extent, for military drill. In the ceremony the Arabs, hitherto wholly unaccustomed to discipline, were obliged en masse to repeat the formulae with strict exactitude after their leader and to copy every one of his

movements, and any man who was unable to perform the salat with the congregation was none the less bound to strict compliance with the form of prayer in which he had been instructed' (*HHW*. VIII. p. 14). And in the words of a distinguished American psychologist: 'All historians declare that the amazing success of Islam in dominating the world lay in the astounding coherence or sense of unity in the group, but they do not explain how this miracle was worked. There can be little doubt that one of the most effective means was prayer. The five daily prayers, when all the faithful wherever they were, alone in the grim solitude of the desert or in vast assemblies in the crowded city, knelt and prostrated themselves towards Mecca, uttering the same words of adoration for the one true God and of loyalty to His Prophet, produce an overwhelming effect upon the spectator, and the psychological effect of thus fusing the minds of the worshippers in a common adoration and expression of loyalty is certainly stupendous' (Denison, *Emotion as the Basis of Civilization*, pp. 274–275).

46. Do not dispute with the people of the Book unless in the best manner, save with those of them who do wrong; and say: 'We believe in what has been sent down to us and in what has been sent down to you, our God and your God is One, and to Him we are submissive.'

وَلَا تُجَـٰدِلُوٓا۟ أَهْلَ ٱلْكِــتَـٰبِ إِلَّا بِٱلَّتِى هِىَ أَحْسَنُ إِلَّا ٱلَّذِينَ ظَلَمُوا۟ مِنْهُمْ وَقُولُوٓا۟ ءَامَنَّا بِٱلَّذِىٓ أُنزِلَ إِلَيْنَا وَأُنزِلَ إِلَيْكُمْ وَإِلَـٰهُنَا وَإِلَـٰهُكُمْ وَٰحِدٌ وَنَحْنُ لَهُۥ مُسْلِمُونَ ﴿٤٦﴾

47. Likewise We have sent down the Book to you, so those to whom we vouchsafed the Book believe in it, and some of these also believe in it. And none belie Our signs except the infidels.

وَكَذَٰلِكَ أَنزَلْنَآ إِلَيْكَ ٱلْكِــتَـٰبَ فَٱلَّذِينَ ءَاتَيْنَـٰهُمُ ٱلْكِتَـٰبَ يُؤْمِنُونَ بِهِۦ وَمِنْ هَـٰٓؤُلَآءِ مَن يُؤْمِنُ بِهِۦ وَمَا يَجْحَدُ بِـَٔايَـٰتِنَآ إِلَّا ٱلْكَـٰفِرُونَ ﴿٤٧﴾

48. And before It you have not been reading any Book[586] nor have you been inscribing it with your right hand, for then followers of falsehood might have doubted.

وَمَا كُنتَ تَتْلُوا۟ مِن قَبْلِهِۦ مِن كِتَـٰبٍ وَلَا تَخُطُّهُۥ بِيَمِينِكَ إِذًا لَّٱرْتَابَ ٱلْمُبْطِلُونَ ﴿٤٨﴾

49. Aye! It is itself a manifest sign in the breasts of those who have been vouchsafed knowledge; and none belie Our signs except the wrong-doers.

بَلْ هُوَ ءَايَـٰتٌۢ بَيِّنَـٰتٌ فِى صُدُورِ ٱلَّذِينَ أُوتُوا۟ ٱلْعِلْمَ وَمَا يَجْحَدُ بِـَٔايَـٰتِنَآ إِلَّا ٱلظَّـٰلِمُونَ ﴿٤٩﴾

---

586. That is before the Revelation of the Qur'ān. That the Holy Prophet was illiterate, and could neither read nor write is an admitted historical fact, questioned only by a few modern traducers of Islam.

50. And they say: 'Why are not signs sent down unto him from his Lord?' Say: 'Signs are with Allah only and I am but a manifest warner.'

وَقَالُوا۟ لَوْلَآ أُنزِلَ عَلَيْهِ ءَايَٰتٌ مِّن رَّبِّهِۦ ۖ قُلْ إِنَّمَا ٱلْأَيَٰتُ عِندَ ٱللَّهِ وَإِنَّمَآ أَنَا۠ نَذِيرٌ مُّبِينٌ ﴿٥٠﴾

51. Does it not suffice with them that We have sent down to you the Book to be recited to them? Verily herein is a mercy and an admonition to a people who believe.

أَوَلَمْ يَكْفِهِمْ أَنَّآ أَنزَلْنَا عَلَيْكَ ٱلْكِتَٰبَ يُتْلَىٰ عَلَيْهِمْ ۚ إِنَّ فِى ذَٰلِكَ لَرَحْمَةً وَذِكْرَىٰ لِقَوْمٍ يُؤْمِنُونَ ﴿٥١﴾

Section 6

52. Say: 'Allah suffices as a witness between me and you. He knows whatever is in the heavens and the earth; and they who believe in falsehood and dis-believe in Allah, these! They shall be the losers.'

قُلْ كَفَىٰ بِٱللَّهِ بَيْنِى وَبَيْنَكُمْ شَهِيدًا ۖ يَعْلَمُ مَا فِى ٱلسَّمَٰوَٰتِ وَٱلْأَرْضِ ۗ وَٱلَّذِينَ ءَامَنُوا۟ بِٱلْبَٰطِلِ وَكَفَرُوا۟ بِٱللَّهِ أُو۟لَٰٓئِكَ هُمُ ٱلْخَٰسِرُونَ ﴿٥٢﴾

53. And they ask you to hasten on the torment. And had there not been a term appointed, the torment would surely have come to them. And surely it shall come upon them while they perceive not.

وَيَسْتَعْجِلُونَكَ بِٱلْعَذَابِ ۚ وَلَوْلَآ أَجَلٌ مُّسَمًّى لَّجَآءَهُمُ ٱلْعَذَابُ وَلَيَأْتِيَنَّهُم بَغْتَةً وَهُمْ لَا يَشْعُرُونَ ﴿٥٣﴾

54. They ask you to hasten on the torment; and verily Hell is about to encompass the infidels.

يَسْتَعْجِلُونَكَ بِٱلْعَذَابِ وَإِنَّ جَهَنَّمَ لَمُحِيطَةٌ بِٱلْكَٰفِرِينَ ﴿٥٤﴾

55. On the Day whereon the torment shall cover them from above them and from underneath their feet, and He shall say: 'Taste what you have been working!'

يَوْمَ يَغْشَىٰهُمُ ٱلْعَذَابُ مِن فَوْقِهِمْ وَمِن تَحْتِ أَرْجُلِهِمْ وَيَقُولُ ذُوقُوا۟ مَا كُنتُمْ تَعْمَلُونَ ﴿٥٥﴾

56.　O My bondsmen who believe! Verily My earth is wide, so worship Me alone.'[587]

يَـٰعِبَادِىَ ٱلَّذِينَ ءَامَنُوٓاْ إِنَّ أَرْضِى وَٰسِعَةٌ فَإِيَّـٰىَ فَٱعْبُدُونِ ۝

57.　Every soul shall taste of death, then unto Us you shall be returned.

كُلُّ نَفْسٍ ذَآئِقَةُ ٱلْمَوْتِ ثُمَّ إِلَيْنَا تُرْجَعُونَ ۝

58.　And those who believe and work righteous deeds – them We will surely settle in lofty dwellings of the Garden whereunder rivers flow; they shall be abiders therein. Excellent is the reward of the workers.

وَٱلَّذِينَ ءَامَنُواْ وَعَمِلُواْ ٱلصَّـٰلِحَـٰتِ لَنُبَوِّئَنَّهُم مِّنَ ٱلْجَنَّةِ غُرَفًا تَجْرِى مِن تَحْتِهَا ٱلْأَنْهَـٰرُ خَـٰلِدِينَ فِيهَا نِعْمَ أَجْرُ ٱلْعَـٰمِلِينَ ۝

59.　Who persevere and trust in their Lord.

ٱلَّذِينَ صَبَرُواْ وَعَلَىٰ رَبِّهِمْ يَتَوَكَّلُونَ ۝

60.　And how many a moving creature there is that bears not its provision. Allah provides for it and for you and He is the Hearer, the Knower.

وَكَأَيِّن مِّن دَآبَّةٍ لَّا تَحْمِلُ رِزْقَهَا ٱللَّهُ يَرْزُقُهَا وَإِيَّاكُمْ وَهُوَ ٱلسَّمِيعُ ٱلْعَلِيمُ ۝

61.　And were you to ask them: who has created the heavens and the earth and has subjected the sun and the moon? They would surely say: 'Allah.' How then are they deviating?

وَلَئِن سَأَلْتَهُم مَّنْ خَلَقَ ٱلسَّمَـٰوَٰتِ وَٱلْأَرْضَ وَسَخَّرَ ٱلشَّمْسَ وَٱلْقَمَرَ لَيَقُولُنَّ ٱللَّهُ فَأَنَّىٰ يُؤْفَكُونَ ۝

62.　Allah expands provision for whom He will of His bondsmen and stints it for him also. Verily Allah is the Knower of everything.

ٱللَّهُ يَبْسُطُ ٱلرِّزْقَ لِمَن يَشَآءُ مِنْ عِبَادِهِۦ وَيَقْدِرُ لَهُۥٓ إِنَّ ٱللَّهَ بِكُلِّ شَىْءٍ عَلِيمٌ ۝

---

587. If you cannot practise the true religion in one particular city or country, emigrate into another, where you may serve God properly; for the earth is wide enough and you can easily find a place of refuge.

63. And were you to ask them: 'Who sends down water from the sky, and therewith revives the earth after its death?', they would surely say: 'Allah.' Say: 'All praise to Allah!' Aye! Most of them reflect not.

وَلَئِن سَأَلْتَهُم مَّن نَّزَّلَ مِنَ ٱلسَّمَآءِ مَآءً فَأَحْيَا بِهِ ٱلْأَرْضَ مِنۢ بَعْدِ مَوْتِهَا لَيَقُولُنَّ ٱللَّهُ قُلِ ٱلْحَمْدُ لِلَّهِ بَلْ أَكْثَرُهُمْ لَا يَعْقِلُونَ ٦٣

Section 7

64. And this life of the world is but sport and play. Verily the home of the Hereafter – that is life indeed, if they but know!

وَمَا هَذِهِ ٱلْحَيَوٰةُ ٱلدُّنْيَا إِلَّا لَهْوٌ وَلَعِبٌ وَإِنَّ ٱلدَّارَ ٱلْأَخِرَةَ لَهِيَ ٱلْحَيَوَانُ لَوْ كَانُوا يَعْلَمُونَ ٦٤

65. So when they mount upon the ship they call on Allah, making faith pure for Him; then when He delivers them safely on the land, lo! They associate.

فَإِذَا رَكِبُوا فِي ٱلْفُلْكِ دَعَوُا ٱللَّهَ مُخْلِصِينَ لَهُ ٱلدِّينَ فَلَمَّا نَجَّىٰهُمْ إِلَى ٱلْبَرِّ إِذَا هُمْ يُشْرِكُونَ ٦٥

66. So that they become ungrateful for what We have vouchsafed to them, and that they enjoy themselves; but presently they shall know.

لِيَكْفُرُوا بِمَآ ءَاتَيْنَاهُمْ وَلِيَتَمَتَّعُوا فَسَوْفَ يَعْلَمُونَ ٦٦

67. Do they not see that We have appointed an inviolable sanctuary, while men are being snatched away round about them? In falsehood would then they believe, and unto favours of Allah would they be ungrateful?

أَوَلَمْ يَرَوْا أَنَّا جَعَلْنَا حَرَمًا ءَامِنًا وَيُتَخَطَّفُ ٱلنَّاسُ مِنْ حَوْلِهِمْ أَفَبِٱلْبَطِلِ يُؤْمِنُونَ وَبِنِعْمَةِ ٱللَّهِ يَكْفُرُونَ ٦٧

68. And who is a greater wrong-doer than he who forges a lie against Allah or belies the truth when it comes to him? Will there not be in the Hell an abiding-place of the infidels?

وَمَنْ أَظْلَمُ مِمَّنِ افْتَرَى عَلَى اللَّهِ كَذِبًا أَوْ كَذَّبَ بِالْحَقِّ لَمَّا جَاءَهُ أَلَيْسَ فِي جَهَنَّمَ مَثْوًى لِّلْكَافِرِينَ ۞

69. And those who strive hard in us, We shall surely guide them in Our paths;[588] verily Allah is with the well-doers.

وَالَّذِينَ جَاهَدُوا فِينَا لَنَهْدِيَنَّهُمْ سُبُلَنَا وَإِنَّ اللَّهَ لَمَعَ الْمُحْسِنِينَ ۞

---

588. Note that the mere sincere search after God and His Truths, apart from all consequences, entails promised reward. Sincerity of purpose is the main thing, good results will follow of themselves.

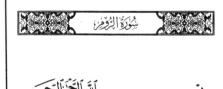

Sūrah 30

al-Rūm

(Makkan, 6 Sections, 60 Verses)

In the name of Allah, the Compassionate, the Merciful.

Section 1

1. *Alif, Lām, Mīm.*

2. The Byzantines have been overcome,

3. In a nearer land, and they, after being overcome shall soon overcome

4. In a few years. Allah's is the command, before and after, and on that day the believers shall rejoice

5.   In Allah's succour, He succours whom He will. And He is the Mighty, the Merciful.

6.   This is Allah's promise and Allah does not fail His promise. Yet most men know not.

7. They only know the outside appearance of the life of the world, and of the Hereafter they are neglectful.

8. Do they not ponder in their minds? Allah has not created the heavens and the earth and what is in between except with a purpose and for an appointed term? And verily many men are unbelievers in the meeting of their Lord.

أَوَلَمْ يَتَفَكَّرُوا فِى أَنفُسِهِم مَّا خَلَقَ اللَّهُ ٱلسَّمَٰوَٰتِ وَٱلْأَرْضَ وَمَا بَيْنَهُمَآ إِلَّا بِٱلْحَقِّ وَأَجَلٍ مُّسَمًّى وَإِنَّ كَثِيرًا مِّنَ ٱلنَّاسِ بِلِقَآئِ رَبِّهِمْ لَكَٰفِرُونَ ﴿٨﴾

9. Have they not journeyed in the land and observed how has been the end of those before them? Those were stronger than these in power and they broke up the earth and they inhabited it with greater affluence than these have inhabited it, and their Messengers came to them with evidence And Allah was not the One to wrong them, but themselves they were wont to wrong.

أَوَلَمْ يَسِيرُوا فِى ٱلْأَرْضِ فَيَنظُرُوا كَيْفَ كَانَ عَٰقِبَةُ ٱلَّذِينَ مِن قَبْلِهِمْ كَانُوٓا أَشَدَّ مِنْهُمْ قُوَّةً وَأَثَارُوا ٱلْأَرْضَ وَعَمَرُوهَآ أَكْثَرَ مِمَّا عَمَرُوهَا وَجَآءَتْهُمْ رُسُلُهُم بِٱلْبَيِّنَٰتِ فَمَا كَانَ ٱللَّهُ لِيَظْلِمَهُمْ وَلَٰكِن كَانُوٓا أَنفُسَهُمْ يَظْلِمُونَ ﴿٩﴾

10. Then the end of those who committed evil was evil, for they belied the signs of Allah, and they were wont to mock at them.

ثُمَّ كَانَ عَٰقِبَةَ ٱلَّذِينَ أَسَٰٓـُٔوا ٱلسُّوٓأَىٰٓ أَن كَذَّبُوا بِـَٔايَٰتِ ٱللَّهِ وَكَانُوا بِهَا يَسْتَهْزِءُونَ ﴿١٠﴾

Section 2

11. Allah originates the creation, then He shall restore it, then to Him you shall be returned.

ٱللَّهُ يَبْدَؤُا ٱلْخَلْقَ ثُمَّ يُعِيدُهُۥ ثُمَّ إِلَيْهِ تُرْجَعُونَ ﴿١١﴾

12. And on the Day whereon the Hour arrives, the culprits will be dumb-struck.

وَيَوْمَ تَقُومُ ٱلسَّاعَةُ يُبْلِسُ ٱلْمُجْرِمُونَ ﴿١٢﴾

13. And not from their associate-gods there will be intercessors for them, and they will be unbelievers to their associate-gods.

وَلَمْ يَكُن لَّهُم مِّن شُرَكَآئِهِمْ شُفَعَـٰٓؤُاْ وَكَانُواْ بِشُرَكَآئِهِمْ كَـٰفِرِينَ ﴿١٣﴾

14. On the Day whereon the Hour arrives, that day they will be separated.

وَيَوْمَ تَقُومُ ٱلسَّاعَةُ يَوْمَئِذٍ يَتَفَرَّقُونَ ﴿١٤﴾

15. Then as for those who believed and worked righteous deeds, they shall be in a meadow made happy.

فَأَمَّا ٱلَّذِينَ ءَامَنُواْ وَعَمِلُواْ ٱلصَّـٰلِحَـٰتِ فَهُمْ فِى رَوْضَةٍ يُحْبَرُونَ ﴿١٥﴾

16. And as for those who disbelieved and belied Our signs and the meeting of the Hereafter – these shall be brought to the torment.

وَأَمَّا ٱلَّذِينَ كَفَرُواْ وَكَذَّبُواْ بِـَٔايَـٰتِنَا وَلِقَآئِ ٱلْأَخِرَةِ فَأُوْلَـٰٓئِكَ فِى ٱلْعَذَابِ مُحْضَرُونَ ﴿١٦﴾

17. So hallow Allah when you enter the night and when you enter the morning.

فَسُبْحَـٰنَ ٱللَّهِ حِينَ تُمْسُونَ وَحِينَ تُصْبِحُونَ ﴿١٧﴾

18. And His is all praise in the heavens and the earth, and at the sun's setting and decline and when you enter the noon.

وَلَهُ ٱلْحَمْدُ فِى ٱلسَّمَـٰوَٰتِ وَٱلْأَرْضِ وَعَشِيًّا وَحِينَ تُظْهِرُونَ ﴿١٨﴾

19. He brings forth the living from the lifeless, and He brings forth the lifeless from the living, and He revives the earth after its death, and thus you too, will be brought forth.

يُخْرِجُ ٱلْحَىَّ مِنَ ٱلْمَيِّتِ وَيُخْرِجُ ٱلْمَيِّتَ مِنَ ٱلْحَىِّ وَيُحْىِ ٱلْأَرْضَ بَعْدَ مَوْتِهَا وَكَذَٰلِكَ تُخْرَجُونَ ﴿١٩﴾

Section 3

20. Of His signs is that He created you of dust, and then lo! You are humankind spreading yourselves.

وَمِنْ ءَايَتِهِ أَنْ خَلَقَكُم مِّن تُرَابٍ ثُمَّ إِذَآ أَنتُم بَشَرٌ تَنتَشِرُونَ ﴿٢٠﴾

21. And of His signs is, that He created for you from yourselves mates that you may find repose in them,[589] and He set between you affection and mercy,[590] verily in this are signs for a people who ponder.

وَمِنْ ءَايَتِهِ أَنْ خَلَقَ لَكُم مِّنْ أَنفُسِكُمْ أَزْوَاجًا لِّتَسْكُنُوٓا إِلَيْهَا وَجَعَلَ بَيْنَكُم مَّوَدَّةً وَرَحْمَةً إِنَّ فِى ذَٰلِكَ لَءَايَتٍ لِّقَوْمٍ يَتَفَكَّرُونَ ﴿٢١﴾

589. The word connotes companionship and mutual love, which is distinct from mere sexual pleasure. This determines the proper status of the wife in Islam. She is not a handmaid, but a lifelong companion of her husband, his consort. Her function is to be, by her words, acts, or by her mere presence, a source of comfort and solace to him. She must constitute the chief consoling, soothing element of his life. And a relation of affection, harmony, and mutual happiness and goodwill ought to subsist between man and wife. Contrast this with the attitude of the early Church. 'We cannot but notice, even in the greatest of the Christian fathers, a lamentably low estimate of women, and consequently of the marriage relationship. Even St. Augustine can see no justification for marriage, except in a grave desire deliberately adopted of having children; and in accordance with this view, all married intercourse, except for this single purpose, is honestly condemned. This idea of the mutual society, help, and comfort that the one ought to have of the other, both in prosperity and adversity, hardly existed, and hardly yet exists' (*DCA*. II. p. 1909).

590. Which ought to be the even truer and deeper motives of marriage than mere sexual harmony. 'Marriage, we must never forget as too often happens is more than an erotic union. To the truly ideal marriage there goes not only an erotic harmony but a union of many-sided and ever-deepening non-erotic affection, or community of tastes and feelings and interests, a life in common, a probability of shared parenthood, and often an economic unity' (Ellis, *Psychology of Sex*, p. 284). 'Complete sex relationship demands relationship of the whole personality of the man, his intelligence, imagination, emotions, will, interest, sentiments and all the rest that go to make up his personality with all those things in the woman. That is intercourse can never be a complete sex relationship. To be complete, a sex-relationship must fulfill these conditions; it must involve the whole personality of both persons; it must not impede but assist the growth of both partners; and thirdly it must give security and permanence of relationship' (Livia–Noble, *The School Psychologist*, p. 103).

22. And of His signs are the creation of the heavens and the earth, and the variation of your languages and complexions.[591] Verily in this are signs for men of knowledge.

وَمِنْ ءَايَٰتِهِۦ خَلْقُ ٱلسَّمَٰوَٰتِ وَٱلْأَرْضِ وَٱخْتِلَٰفُ أَلْسِنَتِكُمْ وَأَلْوَٰنِكُمْ إِنَّ فِى ذَٰلِكَ لَءَايَٰتٍ لِّلْعَٰلِمِينَ ۝

23. And of His signs are your sleeping by night and day, and your seeking of His grace? Verily in this are signs for a people who listen.

وَمِنْ ءَايَٰتِهِۦ مَنَامُكُم بِٱلَّيْلِ وَٱلنَّهَارِ وَٱبْتِغَآؤُكُم مِّن فَضْلِهِۦٓ إِنَّ فِى ذَٰلِكَ لَءَايَٰتٍ لِّقَوْمٍ يَسْمَعُونَ ۝

24. And of His signs is that He shows you lightning for a fear and for a hope, and sends down from the sky water, and therewith revives the earth after its death; verily in this are signs for a people who reflect.

وَمِنْ ءَايَٰتِهِۦ يُرِيكُمُ ٱلْبَرْقَ خَوْفًا وَطَمَعًا وَيُنَزِّلُ مِنَ ٱلسَّمَآءِ مَآءً فَيُحْىِۦ بِهِ ٱلْأَرْضَ بَعْدَ مَوْتِهَآ إِنَّ فِى ذَٰلِكَ لَءَايَٰتٍ لِّقَوْمٍ يَعْقِلُونَ ۝

25. And of His Signs is that the heavens and the earth stand fast by His command, and thereafter when He calls you, a call from the earth, lo! You shall come forth.

وَمِنْ ءَايَٰتِهِۦٓ أَن تَقُومَ ٱلسَّمَآءُ وَٱلْأَرْضُ بِأَمْرِهِۦ ثُمَّ إِذَا دَعَاكُمْ دَعْوَةً مِّنَ ٱلْأَرْضِ إِذَآ أَنتُمْ تَخْرُجُونَ ۝

26. His is whosoever is in the heavens and the earth; all are obedient to Him.

وَلَهُۥ مَن فِى ٱلسَّمَٰوَٰتِ وَٱلْأَرْضِ كُلٌّ لَّهُۥ قَٰنِتُونَ ۝

591. This diversity of human language and complexions has been, in the case of pagan nations both old and new, one of the most potent causes of racial ill – feeling, communal jealousy, and international animosity.

27. And He it is Who originates the creation, then shall restore it, and this is for Him very easy. His is the most exalted similitude in the heavens and the earth, and He is the Mighty, the Wise.[592]

وَهُوَ الَّذِى يَبْدَؤُا الْخَلْقَ ثُمَّ يُعِيدُهُ وَهُوَ أَهْوَنُ عَلَيْهِ وَلَهُ الْمَثَلُ الْأَعْلَى فِى السَّمَوَتِ وَالْأَرْضِ وَهُوَ الْعَزِيزُ الْحَكِيمُ ۝

Section 4

28. He propounds to you a similitude taken from yourselves: have you, from among those whom your right hand possess, partners in that which We have provided, so that you are equal in respect thereof and you fear them as you fear each other? Thus do We detail the signs for a people who reflect.

ضَرَبَ لَكُم مَّثَلًا مِّنْ أَنفُسِكُمْ هَل لَّكُم مِّن مَّا مَلَكَتْ أَيْمَنُكُم مِّن شُرَكَآءَ فِى مَا رَزَقْنَكُمْ فَأَنتُمْ فِيهِ سَوَآءٌ تَخَافُونَهُمْ كَخِيفَتِكُمْ أَنفُسَكُمْ كَذَلِكَ نُفَصِّلُ الْأَيَتِ لِقَوْمٍ يَعْقِلُونَ ۝

29. Aye! Those who do wrong follow their own lusts without knowledge. Who, then, will guide them whom Allah has sent astray? And for them there will be no helpers.

بَلِ اتَّبَعَ الَّذِينَ ظَلَمُوٓا أَهْوَآءَهُم بِغَيْرِ عِلْمٍ فَمَن يَهْدِى مَنْ أَضَلَّ اللَّهُ وَمَا لَهُم مِّن نَّصِرِينَ ۝

---

592. Nothing in heaven or on the earth is comparable to Him, seeing He is the Creator of all. In speaking of Him and His attributes we must make use of the most noble and magnificent expressions we can possibly desire and even then we shall fall far short of the actual reality.

30. So set you your face towards the true faith uprightly. And follow you the constitution of Allah according to which He has constituted mankind[593] and let there be no alteration in Allah's creation.[594] That is the right religion, but most men know not.

فَأَقِمْ وَجْهَكَ لِلدِّينِ حَنِيفًا ۚ فِطْرَتَ اللَّهِ الَّتِي فَطَرَ النَّاسَ عَلَيْهَا ۚ لَا تَبْدِيلَ لِخَلْقِ اللَّهِ ۚ ذَٰلِكَ الدِّينُ الْقَيِّمُ وَلَٰكِنَّ أَكْثَرَ النَّاسِ لَا يَعْلَمُونَ ﴿٣٠﴾

31. And remain turning penitently to Him, and fear Him, and establish prayer, and be not of the associators.

مُنِيبِينَ إِلَيْهِ وَاتَّقُوهُ وَأَقِيمُوا الصَّلَوٰةَ وَلَا تَكُونُوا مِنَ الْمُشْرِكِينَ ﴿٣١﴾

32. Of those who split their religion and become sects, each band is exulting in what is with it.

مِنَ الَّذِينَ فَرَّقُوا دِينَهُمْ وَكَانُوا شِيَعًا ۖ كُلُّ حِزْبٍ بِمَا لَدَيْهِمْ فَرِحُونَ ﴿٣٢﴾

33. And when any hurt visits mankind, they cry to their Lord, turning penitently to Him; then when He causes them to taste of His mercy, lo! A part of them joins others with their Lord,

وَإِذَا مَسَّ النَّاسَ ضُرٌّ دَعَوْا رَبَّهُم مُّنِيبِينَ إِلَيْهِ ثُمَّ إِذَا أَذَاقَهُم مِّنْهُ رَحْمَةً إِذَا فَرِيقٌ مِّنْهُم بِرَبِّهِمْ يُشْرِكُونَ ﴿٣٣﴾

34. So that they may be ungrateful for that which We have vouchsafed to them. So enjoy awhile; presently you shall come to know.

لِيَكْفُرُوا بِمَا آتَيْنَاهُمْ ۚ فَتَمَتَّعُوا فَسَوْفَ تَعْلَمُونَ ﴿٣٤﴾

---

593. In this way you are sure to remain guided. The Unity of God is an intuitive truth, plain to every man of commonsense, unless he perverts himself by the prejudices of education. 'Islam is the natural religion that a child left to itself would develop. Indeed, as a Western critic once described it, "Islam is the religion of commonsenses" ' (Lady Cobbold, *Pilgrimage to Mecca*, p. XIII).

594. Man is naturally disposed to become a Muslim. It is only false teaching that corrupts his moral and spiritual lookout, and leads him to infidelity. The Prophet, according to an authentic report, has said: 'Every infant is born in a state of conformity to the natural disposition with which he is created in his mother's womb; it is his parents that make him a Jew, a Christian, and a Magian.'

35. Or, have We sent to them any authority, so that it speaks of what they have been associating with Him?

أَمْ أَنزَلْنَا عَلَيْهِمْ سُلْطَانًا فَهُوَ يَتَكَلَّمُ بِمَا كَانُوا بِهِ يُشْرِكُونَ ﴿٣٥﴾

36. And when We cause mankind to taste of mercy, they exult at it; then if an evil befalls them because of what their hands have sent forth; lo! They despair.

وَإِذَا أَذَقْنَا النَّاسَ رَحْمَةً فَرِحُوا بِهَا وَإِن تُصِبْهُمْ سَيِّئَةٌ بِمَا قَدَّمَتْ أَيْدِيهِمْ إِذَا هُمْ يَقْنَطُونَ ﴿٣٦﴾

37. Do they not see that Allah expands the provision for whomsoever He will, and stints? Verily in that is a sign for a people who believe.

أَوَلَمْ يَرَوْا أَنَّ اللَّهَ يَبْسُطُ الرِّزْقَ لِمَن يَشَاءُ وَيَقْدِرُ إِنَّ فِي ذَلِكَ لَآيَاتٍ لِقَوْمٍ يُؤْمِنُونَ ﴿٣٧﴾

38. So give you to the kinsman his due and to the needy and to the wayfarer. That is best for those who seek Allah's pleasure, and those are the blissful ones.

فَآتِ ذَا الْقُرْبَى حَقَّهُ وَالْمِسْكِينَ وَابْنَ السَّبِيلِ ذَلِكَ خَيْرٌ لِّلَّذِينَ يُرِيدُونَ وَجْهَ اللَّهِ وَأُوْلَئِكَ هُمُ الْمُفْلِحُونَ ﴿٣٨﴾

39. And whatever you give in gift in order that it may increase among the substance of men does not increase with Allah, and what you pay in poor-rate, seeking the favour of Allah, then these! They shall have manifold increase.

وَمَا آتَيْتُم مِّن رِّبًا لِّيَرْبُوَ فِي أَمْوَالِ النَّاسِ فَلَا يَرْبُو عِندَ اللَّهِ وَمَا آتَيْتُم مِّن زَكَوةٍ تُرِيدُونَ وَجْهَ اللَّهِ فَأُوْلَئِكَ هُمُ الْمُضْعِفُونَ ﴿٣٩﴾

40. Allah is He Who created you and provided food for you, then He causes you to die, and then He shall quicken you. Is there any of your associate-gods that does anything of that? Hallowed and exalted be He above what they associate!

اللَّهُ الَّذِي خَلَقَكُمْ ثُمَّ رَزَقَكُمْ ثُمَّ يُمِيتُكُمْ ثُمَّ يُحْيِيكُمْ هَلْ مِن شُرَكَائِكُم مَّن يَفْعَلُ مِن ذَلِكُم مِّن شَيْءٍ سُبْحَانَهُ وَتَعَالَى عَمَّا يُشْرِكُونَ ﴿٤٠﴾

Section 5

41. Corruptness has prevailed on land and sea because of what men's hands have earned, so that He may make them taste a part of what they have worked, in order that haply they may turn.

ظَهَرَ الْفَسَادُ فِى الْبَرِّ وَالْبَحْرِ بِمَا كَسَبَتْ أَيْدِى النَّاسِ لِيُذِيقَهُم بَعْضَ الَّذِى عَمِلُوا لَعَلَّهُمْ يَرْجِعُونَ ۝

42. Say: 'Go forth in the land and see what has been the end of those aforetime?' And most of them were associators.

قُلْ سِيرُوا فِى الْأَرْضِ فَانظُرُوا كَيْفَ كَانَ عَٰقِبَةُ الَّذِينَ مِن قَبْلُ كَانَ أَكْثَرُهُم مُّشْرِكِينَ ۝

43. So set your face towards the right religion before the Day arrives from which there is no averting from Allah. On that Day they shall be sundered.

فَأَقِمْ وَجْهَكَ لِلدِّينِ الْقَيِّمِ مِن قَبْلِ أَن يَأْتِىَ يَوْمٌ لَّا مَرَدَّ لَهُۥ مِنَ اللَّهِ يَوْمَئِذٍ يَصَّدَّعُونَ ۝

44. Whoever disbelieves, on him is his infidelity, and those who work righteously are preparing themselves.

مَن كَفَرَ فَعَلَيْهِ كُفْرُهُۥ وَمَنْ عَمِلَ صَٰلِحًا فَلِأَنفُسِهِمْ يَمْهَدُونَ ۝

45. So that He shall recompense out of His grace those who believe and work righteous deeds; verily He does not approve the infidels.

لِيَجْزِىَ الَّذِينَ ءَامَنُوا وَعَمِلُوا الصَّٰلِحَٰتِ مِن فَضْلِهِ إِنَّهُۥ لَا يُحِبُّ الْكَٰفِرِينَ ۝

46. And of His signs is that He sends winds heralding rain and that He may make you taste of His mercy, and that the ships may sail at His command, and that you seek His grace, and that haply you may return thanks.

وَمِنْ ءَايَٰتِهِ أَن يُرْسِلَ الرِّيَاحَ مُبَشِّرَٰتٍ وَلِيُذِيقَكُم مِّن رَّحْمَتِهِ وَلِتَجْرِىَ الْفُلْكُ بِأَمْرِهِ وَلِتَبْتَغُوا مِن فَضْلِهِ وَلَعَلَّكُمْ تَشْكُرُونَ ۝

47.   And assuredly We sent Messengers before you to their people. They brought them manifest signs. Then We requited them who transgressed. And incumbent upon Us was the avenging of the believers.

وَلَقَدۡ أَرۡسَلۡنَا مِن قَبۡلِكَ رُسُلًا إِلَىٰ قَوۡمِهِمۡ فَجَآءُوهُم بِٱلۡبَيِّنَٰتِ فَٱنتَقَمۡنَا مِنَ ٱلَّذِينَ أَجۡرَمُوا۟ۖ وَكَانَ حَقًّا عَلَيۡنَا نَصۡرُ ٱلۡمُؤۡمِنِينَ ۝

48.   Allah is He Who sends the winds so that they raise a cloud and then spreads it along the sky as He will, and then breaks it into fragments, and you see the rain come forth from its midst. Then when He makes it fall upon such of His bondsmen as He will lo! They rejoice,

ٱللَّهُ ٱلَّذِى يُرۡسِلُ ٱلرِّيَٰحَ فَتُثِيرُ سَحَابًا فَيَبۡسُطُهُۥ فِى ٱلسَّمَآءِ كَيۡفَ يَشَآءُ وَيَجۡعَلُهُۥ كِسَفًا فَتَرَى ٱلۡوَدۡقَ يَخۡرُجُ مِنۡ خِلَٰلِهِۦۖ فَإِذَآ أَصَابَ بِهِۦ مَن يَشَآءُ مِنۡ عِبَادِهِۦٓ إِذَا هُمۡ يَسۡتَبۡشِرُونَ ۝

49.   Even though before it was sent down upon them, they were surely despairing before that.

وَإِن كَانُوا۟ مِن قَبۡلِ أَن يُنَزَّلَ عَلَيۡهِم مِّن قَبۡلِهِۦ لَمُبۡلِسِينَ ۝

50.   Look then at the effects of Allah's mercy: how He revives the earth after its death, verily He is the Quickener of the dead, and He is Potent over everything.

فَٱنظُرۡ إِلَىٰٓ ءَاثَٰرِ رَحۡمَتِ ٱللَّهِ كَيۡفَ يُحۡىِ ٱلۡأَرۡضَ بَعۡدَ مَوۡتِهَآۚ إِنَّ ذَٰلِكَ لَمُحۡىِ ٱلۡمَوۡتَىٰۖ وَهُوَ عَلَىٰ كُلِّ شَىۡءٍ قَدِيرٌ ۝

51.   And if We send a wind and they should see their tilth yellow, then they would thereafter remain disbelieving.

وَلَئِنۡ أَرۡسَلۡنَا رِيحًا فَرَأَوۡهُ مُصۡفَرًّا لَّظَلُّوا۟ مِنۢ بَعۡدِهِۦ يَكۡفُرُونَ ۝

52.   Surely you cannot make the dead hear, nor can you make the deaf hear the call when they turn away in flight.

فَإِنَّكَ لَا تُسۡمِعُ ٱلۡمَوۡتَىٰ وَلَا تُسۡمِعُ ٱلصُّمَّ ٱلدُّعَآءَ إِذَا وَلَّوۡا۟ مُدۡبِرِينَ ۝

53. Nor can you be a guide to the blind out of their error; you can make none to hear save those who believe in Our signs, and who have surrendered.

وَمَآ أَنتَ بِهَادِ ٱلْعُمْىِ عَن ضَلَٰلَتِهِمْ إِن تُسْمِعُ إِلَّا مَن يُؤْمِنُ بِـَٔايَٰتِنَا فَهُم مُّسْلِمُونَ ٥٣

Section 6

54. Allah is He Who created you in weakness, then He assigned strength after weakness, then after strength weakness and grey hair. He creates what He will, and He is the Knower, the Potent.

ٱللَّهُ ٱلَّذِى خَلَقَكُم مِّن ضَعْفٍ ثُمَّ جَعَلَ مِنۢ بَعْدِ ضَعْفٍ قُوَّةً ثُمَّ جَعَلَ مِنۢ بَعْدِ قُوَّةٍ ضَعْفًا وَشَيْبَةً يَخْلُقُ مَا يَشَآءُ وَهُوَ ٱلْعَلِيمُ ٱلْقَدِيرُ ٥٤

55. And on the Day when the Hour arrives the culprits will swear that they tarried not but an hour, thus were they ever deluded.

وَيَوْمَ تَقُومُ ٱلسَّاعَةُ يُقْسِمُ ٱلْمُجْرِمُونَ مَا لَبِثُوا۟ غَيْرَ سَاعَةٍ كَذَٰلِكَ كَانُوا۟ يُؤْفَكُونَ ٥٥

56. And those who have been vouchsafed knowledge and faith will say: 'Assuredly you have tarried according to the decree of Allah until the Day of Upraising;' so this is the Day of Upraising, but you were wont not to know.

وَقَالَ ٱلَّذِينَ أُوتُوا۟ ٱلْعِلْمَ وَٱلْإِيمَٰنَ لَقَدْ لَبِثْتُمْ فِى كِتَٰبِ ٱللَّهِ إِلَىٰ يَوْمِ ٱلْبَعْثِ فَهَٰذَا يَوْمُ ٱلْبَعْثِ وَلَٰكِنَّكُمْ كُنتُمْ لَا تَعْلَمُونَ ٥٦

57. On that Day the excusing of themselves will not profit them who did wrong, nor shall they be allowed to please Allah.

فَيَوْمَئِذٍ لَّا يَنفَعُ ٱلَّذِينَ ظَلَمُوا۟ مَعْذِرَتُهُمْ وَلَا هُمْ يُسْتَعْتَبُونَ ٥٧

58. And assuredly We have in this Qur'ān propounded all means of similitude for mankind and if you bring them a sign those who disbelieve are sure to say: you are but deluded.

وَلَقَدْ ضَرَبْنَا لِلنَّاسِ فِى هَٰذَا ٱلْقُرْءَانِ مِن كُلِّ مَثَلٍ وَلَئِن جِئْتَهُم بِـَٔايَةٍ لَّيَقُولَنَّ ٱلَّذِينَ كَفَرُوٓا۟ إِنْ أَنتُمْ إِلَّا مُبْطِلُونَ ٥٨

59. Thus does Allah seal the hearts of those who do not believe.

كَذَٰلِكَ يَطۡبَعُ ٱللَّهُ عَلَىٰ قُلُوبِ ٱلَّذِينَ لَا يَعۡلَمُونَ ﴿٥٩﴾

60. Have you patience?; verily Allah's promise is true. And let not those who have no conviction make you unsteady.

فَٱصۡبِرۡ إِنَّ وَعۡدَ ٱللَّهِ حَقٌّ وَلَا يَسۡتَخِفَّنَّكَ ٱلَّذِينَ لَا يُوقِنُونَ ﴿٦٠﴾

Sūrah 31

Luqmān

(Makkan, 4 Sections, 34 Verses)

In the name of Allah, the
Compassionate, the Merciful.

Section 1

1.   *Alif, Lām, Mīm.*

2.   These are verses of the Wise
Book.

3.   A guidance and a mercy for
the well-doers.

4.   Those who establish the
prayer and pay the poor-rate and
are convinced of the Hereafter.

5.   These are on guidance from
their Lord, and these! They are
the blissful.

6.   And of man is he who
purchases an idle discourse that he
may mislead from Allah's way
without knowledge, and takes it
by way of mockery. These! For
them shall be an ignominious
chastisement.

7.   And when Our revelations are
recited to him, he turns away in
pride as though he did not hear
that at all: as though there was a
heaviness in his ears. Announce
you to him an afflictive torment.

8. Verily those who believe and work righteous deeds, theirs shall be Gardens of Delight.

إِنَّ ٱلَّذِينَ ءَامَنُوا۟ وَعَمِلُوا۟ ٱلصَّٰلِحَٰتِ لَهُمْ جَنَّٰتُ ٱلنَّعِيمِ ۝

9. Abiders they will be therein; a true promise of Allah. And He is the Mighty, the Wise.

خَٰلِدِينَ فِيهَا وَعْدَ ٱللَّهِ حَقًّا وَهُوَ ٱلْعَزِيزُ ٱلْحَكِيمُ ۝

10. He has created the heavens that you see without pillars and has cast firm mountains in the earth lest it move away with you, and He has scattered thereon every kind of animal. And We send down water from the sky and We make all manner of goodly growth therein.

خَلَقَ ٱلسَّمَٰوَٰتِ بِغَيْرِ عَمَدٍ تَرَوْنَهَا وَأَلْقَىٰ فِى ٱلْأَرْضِ رَوَٰسِىَ أَن تَمِيدَ بِكُمْ وَبَثَّ فِيهَا مِن كُلِّ دَابَّةٍ وَأَنزَلْنَا مِنَ ٱلسَّمَآءِ مَآءً فَأَنۢبَتْنَا فِيهَا مِن كُلِّ زَوْجٍ كَرِيمٍ ۝

11. This is the creation of Allah. Show me what those besides Allah have created. Aye! The ungodly are in manifest error.

هَٰذَا خَلْقُ ٱللَّهِ فَأَرُونِى مَاذَا خَلَقَ ٱلَّذِينَ مِن دُونِهِۦ بَلِ ٱلظَّٰلِمُونَ فِى ضَلَٰلٍ مُّبِينٍ ۝

Section 2

12. And assuredly We vouchsafed wisdom to Luqmān saying: 'Give thanks to Allah', and whoever gives thanks, gives thanks for his soul; and whosoever is unthankful then verily Allah is the Self-Sufficient, the Praiseworthy.

وَلَقَدْ ءَاتَيْنَا لُقْمَٰنَ ٱلْحِكْمَةَ أَنِ ٱشْكُرْ لِلَّهِ وَمَن يَشْكُرْ فَإِنَّمَا يَشْكُرُ لِنَفْسِهِۦ وَمَن كَفَرَ فَإِنَّ ٱللَّهَ غَنِىٌّ حَمِيدٌ ۝

13. And recall when Luqmān said to his son, while he was exhorting him: 'O my son: associate not anyone with Allah; verily this associating is a tremendous wrong.'

وَإِذْ قَالَ لُقْمَٰنُ لِٱبْنِهِۦ وَهُوَ يَعِظُهُۥ يَٰبُنَىَّ لَا تُشْرِكْ بِٱللَّهِ إِنَّ ٱلشِّرْكَ لَظُلْمٌ عَظِيمٌ ۝

14. And We have enjoined upon man concerning his parents, his mother bears him in hardship upon hardship, and his weaning is in two years, give thanks to Me and your parents; unto Me is the goal.

15. And if the two strive to make you associate with Me that whereof you have no knowledge, then obey them not. And keep them honourable company in this world reputably and follow you the path of him who turns to Me penitently. Then to Me is your return, and I shall declare to you what you have been working.

16. Son! Though it be but of the weight of a grain of mustard-seed, and though it be in a rock, or in the heavens, or in the earth. Allah shall bring if forth, verily Allah is the Subtle, the Aware.

17. Son! Establish the prayer and do what is reputable and forbid iniquity, and bear patiently whatever may befall you; verily that is of the firmness of the affairs.

18. And turn not your cheek from men, nor walk on the earth struttingly; verily Allah does not approve any vainglorious boaster.

19. And be you modest in your gait and lower your voice; verily the most abominable of voices is the voice of the ass.'

وَوَصَّيۡنَا ٱلۡإِنسَٰنَ بِوَٰلِدَيۡهِ حَمَلَتۡهُ أُمُّهُۥ وَهۡنًا عَلَىٰ وَهۡنٍ وَفِصَٰلُهُۥ فِي عَامَيۡنِ أَنِ ٱشۡكُرۡ لِي وَلِوَٰلِدَيۡكَ إِلَيَّ ٱلۡمَصِيرُ ﴿١٤﴾

وَإِن جَٰهَدَاكَ عَلَىٰٓ أَن تُشۡرِكَ بِي مَا لَيۡسَ لَكَ بِهِۦ عِلۡمٌ فَلَا تُطِعۡهُمَا وَصَاحِبۡهُمَا فِي ٱلدُّنۡيَا مَعۡرُوفًا وَٱتَّبِعۡ سَبِيلَ مَنۡ أَنَابَ إِلَيَّ ثُمَّ إِلَيَّ مَرۡجِعُكُمۡ فَأُنَبِّئُكُم بِمَا كُنتُمۡ تَعۡمَلُونَ ﴿١٥﴾

يَٰبُنَيَّ إِنَّهَآ إِن تَكُ مِثۡقَالَ حَبَّةٍ مِّنۡ خَرۡدَلٍ فَتَكُن فِي صَخۡرَةٍ أَوۡ فِي ٱلسَّمَٰوَٰتِ أَوۡ فِي ٱلۡأَرۡضِ يَأۡتِ بِهَا ٱللَّهُ إِنَّ ٱللَّهَ لَطِيفٌ خَبِيرٌ ﴿١٦﴾

يَٰبُنَيَّ أَقِمِ ٱلصَّلَوٰةَ وَأۡمُرۡ بِٱلۡمَعۡرُوفِ وَٱنۡهَ عَنِ ٱلۡمُنكَرِ وَٱصۡبِرۡ عَلَىٰ مَآ أَصَابَكَ إِنَّ ذَٰلِكَ مِنۡ عَزۡمِ ٱلۡأُمُورِ ﴿١٧﴾

وَلَا تُصَعِّرۡ خَدَّكَ لِلنَّاسِ وَلَا تَمۡشِ فِي ٱلۡأَرۡضِ مَرَحًا إِنَّ ٱللَّهَ لَا يُحِبُّ كُلَّ مُخۡتَالٍ فَخُورٍ ﴿١٨﴾

وَٱقۡصِدۡ فِي مَشۡيِكَ وَٱغۡضُضۡ مِن صَوۡتِكَ إِنَّ أَنكَرَ ٱلۡأَصۡوَٰتِ لَصَوۡتُ ٱلۡحَمِيرِ ﴿١٩﴾

Section 3

20. Do you not see that Allah has subjected for you whatever is in the heavens and whatever is in the earth,[595] and has completed His favours on you outwardly and inwardly. And yet of mankind is one who disputes concerning Allah without knowledge and with neither guidance nor a luminous Book.

اَلَمْ تَرَوْا اَنَّ اللّٰهَ سَخَّرَ لَكُمْ مَّا فِي السَّمٰوٰتِ وَمَا فِي الْاَرْضِ وَاَسْبَغَ عَلَيْكُمْ نِعَمَهٗ ظَاهِرَةً وَّبَاطِنَةً ۗ وَمِنَ النَّاسِ مَنْ يُّجَادِلُ فِي اللّٰهِ بِغَيْرِ عِلْمٍ وَّلَا هُدًى وَّلَا كِتٰبٍ مُّنِيْرٍ ۝

21. And when it is said to them: 'Follow what Allah has sent down, they say; nay! We shall follow what we found our fathers upon.' What! Even though Satan had been calling on them to the torment of the Blaze.

وَاِذَا قِيْلَ لَهُمُ اتَّبِعُوْا مَا اَنْزَلَ اللّٰهُ قَالُوْا بَلْ نَتَّبِعُ مَا وَجَدْنَا عَلَيْهِ اٰبَآءَنَا ۗ اَوَلَوْ كَانَ الشَّيْطٰنُ يَدْعُوْهُمْ اِلٰى عَذَابِ السَّعِيْرِ ۝

22. And whoso submits his face to Allah and he is a well-doer, he has of a surety got hold of a firm cable. Unto Allah is the end of all affairs.

وَمَنْ يُّسْلِمْ وَجْهَهٗۤ اِلَى اللّٰهِ وَهُوَ مُحْسِنٌ فَقَدِ اسْتَمْسَكَ بِالْعُرْوَةِ الْوُثْقٰى ۗ وَاِلَى اللّٰهِ عَاقِبَةُ الْاُمُوْرِ ۝

---

595. This lays down distinctly that everything created, however huge or vast to look at, is subservient to man, directly or indirectly. How foolish, then, it is for man to bow down to these objects of nature in worship, and to treat as his masters what are in reality his servants. Compare the ways of the polytheists: 'In the pantheon of classic mythology not all, but the principal figures belong to strict Nature-worship. They are Heaven and Earth, Rain and Thunder, Water and Sea, Fire and Sun and Moon, worshipped either directly for themselves, or as animated by their special deities' (*PC*. II. pp. 254-255).

23. And whoso disbelieves, let not his infidelity grieve you, to Us is their return, and We shall declare to them what they have worked. Verily Allah is the Knower of what is in their breasts.

ومَن كَفَرَ فَلَا يَحْزُنكَ كُفْرُهُۥ إِلَيْنَا مَرْجِعُهُمْ فَنُنَبِّئُهُم بِمَا عَمِلُوٓا۟ إِنَّ ٱللَّهَ عَلِيمٌۢ بِذَاتِ ٱلصُّدُورِ ﴿٢٣﴾

24. We let them enjoy for a while, and then We shall drive them to a rough torment.

نُمَتِّعُهُمْ قَلِيلًا ثُمَّ نَضْطَرُّهُمْ إِلَىٰ عَذَابٍ غَلِيظٍ ﴿٢٤﴾

25. And were you to ask them who has created the heavens and the earth, they will surely say; 'Allah'. Say: 'All praise to Allah!' But most of them know not.

وَلَئِن سَأَلْتَهُم مَّنْ خَلَقَ ٱلسَّمَٰوَٰتِ وَٱلْأَرْضَ لَيَقُولُنَّ ٱللَّهُ قُلِ ٱلْحَمْدُ لِلَّهِ بَلْ أَكْثَرُهُمْ لَا يَعْلَمُونَ ﴿٢٥﴾

26. Allah's is whatsoever is in the heavens and the earth. Verily Allah, He is the Self-Sufficient, the Laudable.

لِلَّهِ مَا فِى ٱلسَّمَٰوَٰتِ وَٱلْأَرْضِ إِنَّ ٱللَّهَ هُوَ ٱلْغَنِىُّ ٱلْحَمِيدُ ﴿٢٦﴾

27. And if whatever trees are on the earth were pens, and sea were ink, with seven more seas to help it, the words of Allah could not be exhausted; verily Allah is the Mighty, the Wise.

وَلَوْ أَنَّمَا فِى ٱلْأَرْضِ مِن شَجَرَةٍ أَقْلَٰمٌ وَٱلْبَحْرُ يَمُدُّهُۥ مِنۢ بَعْدِهِۦ سَبْعَةُ أَبْحُرٍ مَّا نَفِدَتْ كَلِمَٰتُ ٱللَّهِ إِنَّ ٱللَّهَ عَزِيزٌ حَكِيمٌ ﴿٢٧﴾

28. And the creation of you all and the upraising of you all are as though of one soul,[596] verily Allah is the Hearing, the Beholding.

مَّا خَلْقُكُمْ وَلَا بَعْثُكُمْ إِلَّا كَنَفْسٍ وَٰحِدَةٍ إِنَّ ٱللَّهَ سَمِيعٌۢ بَصِيرٌ ﴿٢٨﴾

---

596. God Almighty being Infinite, the raising of all mankind is as easy with Him as that of a single soul.

29. Do you not see that Allah plunges the day into the night and the night into the day and has subjected the sun and the moon, each running to an appointed term, and that Allah is Aware of what you do?

أَلَمْ تَرَ أَنَّ ٱللَّهَ يُولِجُ ٱلَّيْلَ فِى ٱلنَّهَارِ وَيُولِجُ ٱلنَّهَارَ فِى ٱلَّيْلِ وَسَخَّرَ ٱلشَّمْسَ وَٱلْقَمَرَ كُلٌّ يَجْرِىٓ إِلَىٰٓ أَجَلٍ مُّسَمًّى وَأَنَّ ٱللَّهَ بِمَا تَعْمَلُونَ خَبِيرٌ ۝

30. That is because Allah! He is the Truth, because whatsoever they call upon beside Allah is falsehood, and because He is the Exalted, the Great.

ذَٰلِكَ بِأَنَّ ٱللَّهَ هُوَ ٱلْحَقُّ وَأَنَّ مَا يَدْعُونَ مِن دُونِهِ ٱلْبَٰطِلُ وَأَنَّ ٱللَّهَ هُوَ ٱلْعَلِىُّ ٱلْكَبِيرُ ۝

Section 4

31. Do you not see that the ship sails into the sea by the favour of Allah, that He might show you of His signs? Verily therein are Signs for every persevering, grateful heart.

أَلَمْ تَرَ أَنَّ ٱلْفُلْكَ تَجْرِى فِى ٱلْبَحْرِ بِنِعْمَتِ ٱللَّهِ لِيُرِيَكُم مِّنْ ءَايَٰتِهِ إِنَّ فِى ذَٰلِكَ لَءَايَٰتٍ لِّكُلِّ صَبَّارٍ شَكُورٍ ۝

32. And when a wave covers them like awnings, they call upon Allah making their faith pure for Him. Then when He delivers them on the land, only some of them keep to the middle course. And none disputes Our signs save each perfidious, ungrateful one.

وَإِذَا غَشِيَهُم مَّوْجٌ كَٱلظُّلَلِ دَعَوُا ٱللَّهَ مُخْلِصِينَ لَهُ ٱلدِّينَ فَلَمَّا نَجَّىٰهُمْ إِلَى ٱلْبَرِّ فَمِنْهُم مُّقْتَصِدٌ وَمَا يَجْحَدُ بِـَٔايَٰتِنَآ إِلَّا كُلُّ خَتَّارٍ كَفُورٍ ۝

33. O mankind, fear your Lord and dread the Day whereon no father will atone for his son and no son will atone for his father at all. Verily the promise of Allah is true. Let not the life of this world beguile you, and let not the great beguiler beguile you in regard to Allah.

يَٰٓأَيُّهَا ٱلنَّاسُ ٱتَّقُوا رَبَّكُمْ وَٱخْشَوْا يَوْمًا لَّا يَجْزِى وَالِدٌ عَن وَلَدِهِ وَلَا مَوْلُودٌ هُوَ جَازٍ عَن وَالِدِهِ شَيْئًا إِنَّ وَعْدَ ٱللَّهِ حَقٌّ فَلَا تَغُرَّنَّكُمُ ٱلْحَيَوٰةُ ٱلدُّنْيَا وَلَا يَغُرَّنَّكُم بِٱللَّهِ ٱلْغَرُورُ ۝

34. Verily Allah! With Him alone is the knowledge of the Hour, and He it is Who sends down the rain, and knows what is in the wombs. And no person knows what he will earn on the morrow; and a person does not know in what land he will die. Verily Allah is the Knowing, the Aware.

إِنَّ ٱللَّهَ عِندَهُۥ عِلْمُ ٱلسَّاعَةِ وَيُنَزِّلُ ٱلْغَيْثَ وَيَعْلَمُ مَا فِى ٱلْأَرْحَامِ وَمَا تَدْرِى نَفْسٌ مَّاذَا تَكْسِبُ غَدًا وَمَا تَدْرِى نَفْسٌ بِأَىِّ أَرْضٍ تَمُوتُ إِنَّ ٱللَّهَ عَلِيمٌ خَبِيرٌ ۩

Sūrah 32

al-Sajdah

(Makkan, 3 Sections, 30 Verses)

In the name of Allah, the
Compassionate, the Merciful.

Section 1

1. *Alif, Lām, Mīm.*

2. The revelation of this Book of which[597] there is no doubt, is from the Lord of the worlds.

3. Will they say: 'He has fabricated it'? Aye! It is the Truth from your Lord that you may warn therewith a people to whom no warner came before you, that haply they may be guided.

4. Allah it is Who has created the heavens and the earth and whatsoever is in between in six days, and then He established Himself on the throne. No patron have you nor an intercessor, besides Him. Will you not then be admonished?

---

597. Or 'wherein'. The phrase may mean either that there is no doubt about this Qur'ān being the Word of God, or that there is no sort of doubt or uncertainty in the teaching of the Qur'ān. This also clearly enunciates that there is in the Qur'ān, unlike the Bible and other Sacred writings, no inexplicable 'mysteries'. Every doctrine, every article of Faith, clearly conforms with commonsense.

5. He disposes every affair from the heaven to the earth; thereafter it shall ascend unto Him on a Day whereof the measure is one thousand years of what you compute.

يُدَبِّرُ ٱلْأَمْرَ مِنَ ٱلسَّمَآءِ إِلَى ٱلْأَرْضِ ثُمَّ يَعْرُجُ إِلَيْهِ فِى يَوْمٍ كَانَ مِقْدَارُهُۥٓ أَلْفَ سَنَةٍ مِّمَّا تَعُدُّونَ ۞

6. Such is the knower of the unseen and the seen, the Mighty, the Merciful,

ذَٰلِكَ عَٰلِمُ ٱلْغَيْبِ وَٱلشَّهَٰدَةِ ٱلْعَزِيزُ ٱلرَّحِيمُ ۞

7. Who has made everything good which He has created. And He originated the creation of man from clay.

ٱلَّذِىٓ أَحْسَنَ كُلَّ شَىْءٍ خَلَقَهُۥ وَبَدَأَ خَلْقَ ٱلْإِنسَٰنِ مِن طِينٍ ۞

8. Then He made his progeny from an extract of mean water.

ثُمَّ جَعَلَ نَسْلَهُۥ مِن سُلَٰلَةٍ مِّن مَّآءٍ مَّهِينٍ ۞

9. Then He fashioned him and breathed into him something of a spirit from Him; and He ordained for you hearing and sight and hearts. Little is the thanks you return.

ثُمَّ سَوَّىٰهُ وَنَفَخَ فِيهِ مِن رُّوحِهِۦ وَجَعَلَ لَكُمُ ٱلسَّمْعَ وَٱلْأَبْصَٰرَ وَٱلْأَفْـِٔدَةَ قَلِيلًا مَّا تَشْكُرُونَ ۞

10. And they say: 'When we are vanished in the earth, shall we be raised in a new creation?' Aye! They are disbelieving in the meeting with their Lord.

وَقَالُوٓا۟ أَءِذَا ضَلَلْنَا فِى ٱلْأَرْضِ أَءِنَّا لَفِى خَلْقٍ جَدِيدٍ بَلْ هُم بِلِقَآءِ رَبِّهِمْ كَٰفِرُونَ ۞

11. Say: 'The angel of death who is set over you shall cause you to die, thereafter you shall be returned to your Lord.'

قُلْ يَتَوَفَّىٰكُم مَّلَكُ ٱلْمَوْتِ ٱلَّذِى وُكِّلَ بِكُمْ ثُمَّ إِلَىٰ رَبِّكُمْ تُرْجَعُونَ ۞

Section 2

12. Could you but see when the culprits shall hang their heads before their Lord saying: 'Lord! We have now seen and heard; so send us back; we shall now work righteously, verily we are convinced.'

وَلَوْ تَرَىٰٓ إِذِ ٱلۡمُجۡرِمُونَ نَاكِسُوا۟ رُءُوسِهِمْ عِندَ رَبِّهِمْ رَبَّنَآ أَبْصَرْنَا وَسَمِعْنَا فَٱرْجِعْنَا نَعْمَلْ صَٰلِحًا إِنَّا مُوقِنُونَ ﴿١٢﴾

13. And had We willed, surely We would have given every soul its guidance, but true must be the word from Me; I shall surely fill Hell with the *jinn* and mankind together.

وَلَوْ شِئۡنَا لَءَاتَيۡنَا كُلَّ نَفْسٍ هُدَىٰهَا وَلَٰكِنْ حَقَّ ٱلْقَوْلُ مِنِّى لَأَمْلَأَنَّ جَهَنَّمَ مِنَ ٱلْجِنَّةِ وَٱلنَّاسِ أَجْمَعِينَ ﴿١٣﴾

14. So taste you the sequel for as much as you forgot the meeting of this Day, verily We have forgotten you. Taste the abiding torment for what you have been working.

فَذُوقُوا۟ بِمَا نَسِيتُمْ لِقَآءَ يَوْمِكُمْ هَٰذَآ إِنَّا نَسِينَٰكُمْ وَذُوقُوا۟ عَذَابَ ٱلْخُلْدِ بِمَا كُنتُمْ تَعْمَلُونَ ﴿١٤﴾

15. They alone believe in Our revelations who, when they are reminded thereof, fall down prostrate and hallow the praise of their Lord, and they are not proud.

إِنَّمَا يُؤْمِنُ بِـَٔايَٰتِنَا ٱلَّذِينَ إِذَا ذُكِّرُوا۟ بِهَا خَرُّوا۟ سُجَّدًا وَسَبَّحُوا۟ بِحَمْدِ رَبِّهِمْ وَهُمْ لَا يَسْتَكْبِرُونَ ۩ ﴿١٥﴾

16. Their sides leave off the couches, calling upon their Lord in fear and in desire, and they expend of that with which We have provided them.

تَتَجَافَىٰ جُنُوبُهُمْ عَنِ ٱلْمَضَاجِعِ يَدْعُونَ رَبَّهُمْ خَوْفًا وَطَمَعًا وَمِمَّا رَزَقْنَٰهُمْ يُنفِقُونَ ﴿١٦﴾

17. No soul knows what is kept hidden from them of perfect comfort as a recompense for what they have been working.

فَلَا تَعْلَمُ نَفْسٌ مَّآ أُخْفِىَ لَهُم مِّن قُرَّةِ أَعْيُنٍ جَزَآءً بِمَا كَانُوا۟ يَعْمَلُونَ ﴿١٧﴾

18. Shall he, therefore, who is a believer be like him who is a transgressor? Equal they are not.

أَفَمَن كَانَ مُؤْمِنًا كَمَن كَانَ فَاسِقًا لَّا يَسْتَوُوْنَ ۝

19. As for those who believe and work righteous deeds for them are Gardens of Abode: an entertainment for what they had been working.

أَمَّا ٱلَّذِينَ ءَامَنُوا۟ وَعَمِلُوا۟ ٱلصَّٰلِحَٰتِ فَلَهُمْ جَنَّٰتُ ٱلْمَأْوَىٰ نُزُلًا بِمَا كَانُوا۟ يَعْمَلُونَ ۝

20. And as for those who transgress – their abode is the Fire. Whenever they will desire to get thereout, they shall be drawn back thereto, and it will be said to them: 'Taste the torment of the Fire which you were wont to belie.'

وَأَمَّا ٱلَّذِينَ فَسَقُوا۟ فَمَأْوَىٰهُمُ ٱلنَّارُ كُلَّمَا أَرَادُوٓا۟ أَن يَخْرُجُوا۟ مِنْهَآ أُعِيدُوا۟ فِيهَا وَقِيلَ لَهُمْ ذُوقُوا۟ عَذَابَ ٱلنَّارِ ٱلَّذِى كُنتُم بِهِۦ تُكَذِّبُونَ ۝

21. And surely We shall make them taste of the smaller torment before the greater that haply they may yet return.

وَلَنُذِيقَنَّهُم مِّنَ ٱلْعَذَابِ ٱلْأَدْنَىٰ دُونَ ٱلْعَذَابِ ٱلْأَكْبَرِ لَعَلَّهُمْ يَرْجِعُونَ ۝

22. And who is a greater wrong-doer than he who is reminded of His signs, and he turns aside therefrom? Verily We are going to be the Avenger unto the culprits.

وَمَنْ أَظْلَمُ مِمَّن ذُكِّرَ بِـَٔايَٰتِ رَبِّهِۦ ثُمَّ أَعْرَضَ عَنْهَآ إِنَّا مِنَ ٱلْمُجْرِمِينَ مُنتَقِمُونَ ۝

Section 3

23. Assuredly We vouchsafed the Book to Moses; so be you not in doubt in receiving it. And We assigned it to be a guidance to the children of Israel.

وَلَقَدْ ءَاتَيْنَا مُوسَى ٱلْكِتَٰبَ فَلَا تَكُن فِى مِرْيَةٍ مِّن لِّقَآئِهِۦ وَجَعَلْنَٰهُ هُدًى لِّبَنِىٓ إِسْرَٰٓءِيلَ ۝

24. And We appointed from amongst them leaders, guiding others by Our command, when they had persevered, and of Our signs they were convinced.

وَجَعَلْنَا مِنْهُمْ أَئِمَّةً يَهْدُونَ بِأَمْرِنَا لَمَّا صَبَرُواْ وَكَانُواْ بِآيَـٰتِنَا يُوقِنُونَ ۝

25. Verily your Lord; He shall decide between them on the Judgement Day concerning that wherein they have been differing.

إِنَّ رَبَّكَ هُوَ يَفْصِلُ بَيْنَهُمْ يَوْمَ الْقِيَـٰمَةِ فِيمَا كَانُواْ فِيهِ يَخْتَلِفُونَ ۝

26. Has this not guided them; how many a generation We have destroyed before them amidst whose dwellings they walk? Surely therein are signs; will they not listen?

أَوَلَمْ يَهْدِ لَهُمْ كَمْ أَهْلَكْنَا مِن قَبْلِهِم مِّنَ الْقُرُونِ يَمْشُونَ فِى مَسَـٰكِنِهِمْ إِنَّ فِى ذَٰلِكَ لَآيَـٰتٍ أَفَلَا يَسْمَعُونَ ۝

27. Do they not see that We drive water to a bare land, and bring forth therewith crops of which their cattle and they themselves eat? Will they not therefore be enlightened?

أَوَلَمْ يَرَوْاْ أَنَّا نَسُوقُ الْمَآءَ إِلَى الْأَرْضِ الْجُرُزِ فَنُخْرِجُ بِهِۦ زَرْعًا تَأْكُلُ مِنْهُ أَنْعَـٰمُهُمْ وَأَنفُسُهُمْ أَفَلَا يُبْصِرُونَ ۝

28. And they say: 'When will this decision arrive, if you speak truth?'

وَيَقُولُونَ مَتَىٰ هَـٰذَا الْفَتْحُ إِن كُنتُمْ صَـٰدِقِينَ ۝

29. Say: 'On the day of the decision their belief will not profit those who have disbelieved; nor will they be respited.'

قُلْ يَوْمَ الْفَتْحِ لَا يَنفَعُ الَّذِينَ كَفَرُواْ إِيمَـٰنُهُمْ وَلَا هُمْ يُنظَرُونَ ۝

30. So turn aside you from them, and await, verily they are awaiting.

فَأَعْرِضْ عَنْهُمْ وَانتَظِرْ إِنَّهُم مُّنتَظِرُونَ ۝

Sūrah 33
al-Aḥzāb

(Madinan, 9 Sections, 73 Verses)

In the name of Allah, the Compassionate, the Merciful.

Section 1

1. O Prophet, fear Allah, and do not yield to the infidels and the hypocrites; verily Allah is ever Knowing, Wise.

2. And follow that which is revealed to you from your Lord; verily Allah is Aware of what you do.

3. And put your trust in Allah, and Allah suffices as a Trustee.

4. Allah has not placed two hearts in any man, in his inside. Neither has He made your wives whom you pronounce to be your mother's back your real mothers,[598] nor has He made your adopted sons your

---

598. Ẓihār was a pagan formula of divorce. When the pagan husband wanted to get rid of his wife without leaving her free to remarry, he simply said to her: 'You are to me as the back of my mother'. By pronouncing these words he deprived her of all conjugal rights and yet retained control over her. The Qur'ān prohibited this barbaric form of divorce, and thereby effected a great reform in the status of Arab women.

own sons.[599] This is only your saying by your mouths, whereas Allah says the truth and He guides the way.

5. Call them after their fathers; that will be more equitable in the sight of Allah. And if you do not know their fathers then they are your brethren in faith and your friends. And there is no fault in you in regard to the mistake you have made therein, except in regard to what your hearts deliberately intend, and Allah is ever Forgiving, Merciful.

6. The Prophet is nearer to believers than themselves, and his wives are their mothers. And kinsmen are nearer one to another than other believers and the emigrants in the ordinance of Allah, except that you may act humbly to your friends. This has been inscribed in the Book.

7. And recall when We took a bond from the Prophets and from you, and from Noah and Abraham and Moses and Jesus, son of Maryam. And We took from them a solemn bond;

ذَٰلِكُمْ قَوْلُكُم بِأَفْوَٰهِكُمْ وَٱللَّهُ يَقُولُ ٱلْحَقَّ وَهُوَ يَهْدِى ٱلسَّبِيلَ ﴿٤﴾

ٱدْعُوهُمْ لِءَابَآئِهِمْ هُوَ أَقْسَطُ عِندَ ٱللَّهِ فَإِن لَّمْ تَعْلَمُوٓا۟ ءَابَآءَهُمْ فَإِخْوَٰنُكُمْ فِى ٱلدِّينِ وَمَوَٰلِيكُمْ وَلَيْسَ عَلَيْكُمْ جُنَاحٌ فِيمَآ أَخْطَأْتُم بِهِۦ وَلَٰكِن مَّا تَعَمَّدَتْ قُلُوبُكُمْ وَكَانَ ٱللَّهُ غَفُورًا رَّحِيمًا ﴿٥﴾

ٱلنَّبِىُّ أَوْلَىٰ بِٱلْمُؤْمِنِينَ مِنْ أَنفُسِهِمْ وَأَزْوَٰجُهُۥٓ أُمَّهَٰتُهُمْ وَأُو۟لُوا۟ ٱلْأَرْحَامِ بَعْضُهُمْ أَوْلَىٰ بِبَعْضٍ فِى كِتَٰبِ ٱللَّهِ مِنَ ٱلْمُؤْمِنِينَ وَٱلْمُهَٰجِرِينَ إِلَّآ أَن تَفْعَلُوٓا۟ إِلَىٰٓ أَوْلِيَآئِكُم مَّعْرُوفًا كَانَ ذَٰلِكَ فِى ٱلْكِتَٰبِ مَسْطُورًا ﴿٦﴾

وَإِذْ أَخَذْنَا مِنَ ٱلنَّبِيِّۦنَ مِيثَٰقَهُمْ وَمِنكَ وَمِن نُّوحٍ وَإِبْرَٰهِيمَ وَمُوسَىٰ وَعِيسَى ٱبْنِ مَرْيَمَ وَأَخَذْنَا مِنْهُم مِّيثَٰقًا غَلِيظًا ﴿٧﴾

---

599. This repudiates both pagan and Christian (Catholic) notions according to which an adopted son was treated as a natural son so that the same impediments of marriage arose from this supposed relation in the prohibited degrees as it would have done in the case of a genuine son. Strangely enough, the heathen Arabs, while they had no scruples in marrying the wives (excluding of course their own mothers) of a deceased father, considered it awfully wrong to marry the divorced wife of an adopted son. It was this crudity of pagan morals that, upon the Prophet's marrying the divorced wife of his freedman Zaid, who was also his adopted son, gave rise to a great deal of hostile and scandalous gossip and criticism.

8.   That He may question the truthful of their truth, and for the infidels He has prepared an afflictive torment.

لِّيَسْـَٔلَ الصَّٰدِقِينَ عَن صِدْقِهِمْ ۚ وَأَعَدَّ لِلْكَٰفِرِينَ عَذَابًا أَلِيمًا ۝

Section 2

9.   O you who believe! Remember Allah's favour to you when there came unto you hosts, and We sent against them a wind and hosts which you did not see, and Allah was the Beholder of what you were working.

يَـٰٓأَيُّهَا الَّذِينَ ءَامَنُوا اذْكُرُوا نِعْمَةَ اللَّهِ عَلَيْكُمْ إِذْ جَآءَتْكُمْ جُنُودٌ فَأَرْسَلْنَا عَلَيْهِمْ رِيحًا وَجُنُودًا لَّمْ تَرَوْهَا ۚ وَكَانَ اللَّهُ بِمَا تَعْمَلُونَ بَصِيرًا ۝

10.   When they came upon you from above you and from below you, and when eyes turned aside and hearts reached to the gullets in terror, and of Allah you were imagining various things.

إِذْ جَآءُوكُم مِّن فَوْقِكُمْ وَمِنْ أَسْفَلَ مِنكُمْ وَإِذْ زَاغَتِ الْأَبْصَٰرُ وَبَلَغَتِ الْقُلُوبُ الْحَنَاجِرَ وَتَظُنُّونَ بِاللَّهِ الظُّنُونَا ۝

11.   Then were the faithful turned and shaken with a mighty shaking.

هُنَالِكَ ابْتُلِيَ الْمُؤْمِنُونَ وَزُلْزِلُوا زِلْزَالًا شَدِيدًا ۝

12.   And when the hypocrites and those in whose hearts is disease were saying: 'Allah and his Messenger have promised us nothing but delusion.'

وَإِذْ يَقُولُ الْمُنَٰفِقُونَ وَالَّذِينَ فِى قُلُوبِهِم مَّرَضٌ مَّا وَعَدَنَا اللَّهُ وَرَسُولُهُۥٓ إِلَّا غُرُورًا ۝

13.   And when a party of them said: 'O people of Yathrib! There is no place for you; so retire.' And a party of them asked leave of the Messenger saying: 'Verily our houses stand exposed,' whereas they stood not exposed; they only wished to flee.

وَإِذْ قَالَت طَّآئِفَةٌ مِّنْهُمْ يَـٰٓأَهْلَ يَثْرِبَ لَا مُقَامَ لَكُمْ فَارْجِعُوا ۚ وَيَسْتَـْٔذِنُ فَرِيقٌ مِّنْهُمُ النَّبِىَّ يَقُولُونَ إِنَّ بُيُوتَنَا عَوْرَةٌ وَمَا هِىَ بِعَوْرَةٍ ۖ إِن يُرِيدُونَ إِلَّا فِرَارًا ۝

14. And if they were to be entered upon from the sides thereof and they were asked to sedition, they would surely have committed it, and they would have stayed therein but slightly.

وَلَوْ دُخِلَتْ عَلَيْهِم مِّنْ أَقْطَارِهَا ثُمَّ سُئِلُوا الْفِتْنَةَ لَآتَوْهَا وَمَا تَلَبَّثُوا بِهَا إِلَّا يَسِيرًا ﴿١٤﴾

15. And assuredly they had already covenanted with Allah that they would not turn their backs; verily the covenant with Allah must be questioned about.

وَلَقَدْ كَانُوا عَاهَدُوا اللَّهَ مِن قَبْلُ لَا يُوَلُّونَ الْأَدْبَارَ وَكَانَ عَهْدُ اللَّهِ مَسْئُولًا ﴿١٥﴾

16. Say: 'Flight will not avail you if you flee from death or slaughter, and lo! You will not enjoy life except for a little.'

قُل لَّن يَنفَعَكُمُ الْفِرَارُ إِن فَرَرْتُم مِّنَ الْمَوْتِ أَوِ الْقَتْلِ وَإِذًا لَّا تُمَتَّعُونَ إِلَّا قَلِيلًا ﴿١٦﴾

17. Say: 'Who is there that will protect you from Allah, if He intends to bring evil on you or intends mercy for you?' And they shall not find, besides Allah, for themselves a patron or helper.

قُلْ مَن ذَا الَّذِي يَعْصِمُكُم مِّنَ اللَّهِ إِنْ أَرَادَ بِكُمْ سُوءًا أَوْ أَرَادَ بِكُمْ رَحْمَةً وَلَا يَجِدُونَ لَهُم مِّن دُونِ اللَّهِ وَلِيًّا وَلَا نَصِيرًا ﴿١٧﴾

18. Surely Allah knows those amongst you who hinder others and those who say to their brethren: 'Come here to us', while they themselves come not to the battle save a little.

قَدْ يَعْلَمُ اللَّهُ الْمُعَوِّقِينَ مِنكُمْ وَالْقَائِلِينَ لِإِخْوَانِهِمْ هَلُمَّ إِلَيْنَا وَلَا يَأْتُونَ الْبَأْسَ إِلَّا قَلِيلًا ﴿١٨﴾

19. Being niggardly towards you, when fighting comes you behold them to look to you, their eyes rolling like the eyes of him who faints unto death. Then when the fighting is over, they inveigh against you with sharp tongues, being deprived of good things. These have not believed, so Allah has made their works of no avail; and that is with Allah ever easy.

أَشِحَّةً عَلَيْكُمْ فَإِذَا جَاءَ الْخَوْفُ رَأَيْتَهُمْ يَنظُرُونَ إِلَيْكَ تَدُورُ أَعْيُنُهُمْ كَالَّذِي يُغْشَى عَلَيْهِ مِنَ الْمَوْتِ فَإِذَا ذَهَبَ الْخَوْفُ سَلَقُوكُم بِأَلْسِنَةٍ حِدَادٍ أَشِحَّةً عَلَى الْخَيْرِ أُولَٰئِكَ لَمْ يُؤْمِنُوا فَأَحْبَطَ اللَّهُ أَعْمَالَهُمْ وَكَانَ ذَٰلِكَ عَلَى اللَّهِ يَسِيرًا ﴿١٩﴾

20. They imagine that the confederates have not yet departed; and if the confederates should come, they would rather be in the desert with the wandering Arabs asking for news of you. And if they happen to be among you, they would fight but little.

يَحْسَبُونَ الأَحْزَابَ لَمْ يَذْهَبُوا وَإِنْ يَأْتِ الأَحْزَابُ يَوَدُّوا لَوْ أَنَّهُمْ بَادُونَ فِي الأَعْرَابِ يَسْأَلُونَ عَنْ أَنْبَائِكُمْ وَلَوْ كَانُوا فِيكُمْ مَّا قَاتَلُوا إِلَّا قَلِيلًا ۝

Section 3

21. Assuredly there has been an excellent pattern for you in the Messenger of Allah,[600] for him who hopes in Allah and the Last Day and remembers Allah much.[601]

لَّقَدْ كَانَ لَكُمْ فِي رَسُولِ اللَّهِ أُسْوَةٌ حَسَنَةٌ لِّمَن كَانَ يَرْجُوا اللَّهَ وَالْيَوْمَ الْآخِرَ وَذَكَرَ اللَّهَ كَثِيرًا ۝

22. And when the faithful saw the confederates, they said: 'This is what Allah and His Messenger had promised us, and Allah and His Messenger had spoken the truth.' It only increases in the faithful belief and self-surrender.

وَلَمَّا رَءَا الْمُؤْمِنُونَ الأَحْزَابَ قَالُوا هَذَا مَا وَعَدَنَا اللَّهُ وَرَسُولُهُ وَصَدَقَ اللَّهُ وَرَسُولُهُ وَمَا زَادَهُمْ إِلَّا إِيمَانًا وَتَسْلِيمًا ۝

---

600. As he combines in himself all types of virtue. Note that it is a personality, a living personality, rather than abstract copy book maxims that is, in Islam, held up as the object of imitation. The Prophet of Islam is the great example, his daily behaviour has instituted a course which millions observe to this day with conscious mimicry. 'No one regarded by any section of the human race as Perfect Man has been imitated so minutely' (Hogarth, *Arabia*, p. 52).

601. 'The example the Prophet has set' before us in his actions and sayings. His wonderful life was a living illustration and explanation of the Qur'ān, and we can do no greater justice to this Holy Book than by following him who was the mouthpiece of its revelation' (Asad, *Islam at the Crossroads*, p. 91).

23. Of the faithful are men who have fulfilled their covenant with Allah. Some of them have performed their vow, and some of them are waiting, and they have not changed in the least.

مِّنَ ٱلْمُؤْمِنِينَ رِجَالٌ صَدَقُوا مَا عَٰهَدُوا ٱللَّهَ عَلَيْهِ فَمِنْهُم مَّن قَضَىٰ نَحْبَهُۥ وَمِنْهُم مَّن يَنتَظِرُ وَمَا بَدَّلُوا تَبْدِيلًا ۞

24. All this happened in order that Allah may recompense the truthful for their truth, and may punish the hypocrites if He may relent towards them. Verily, Allah is the Forgiving, the Merciful.

لِّيَجْزِيَ ٱللَّهُ ٱلصَّٰدِقِينَ بِصِدْقِهِمْ وَيُعَذِّبَ ٱلْمُنَٰفِقِينَ إِن شَآءَ أَوْ يَتُوبَ عَلَيْهِمْ إِنَّ ٱللَّهَ كَانَ غَفُورًا رَّحِيمًا ۞

25. Allah drove back those who disbelieved in their rage, they obtained no advantage; and Allah sufficed for the faithful in the fighting. Allah is ever Strong, Mighty.

وَرَدَّ ٱللَّهُ ٱلَّذِينَ كَفَرُوا بِغَيْظِهِمْ لَمْ يَنَالُوا خَيْرًا وَكَفَى ٱللَّهُ ٱلْمُؤْمِنِينَ ٱلْقِتَالَ وَكَانَ ٱللَّهُ قَوِيًّا عَزِيزًا ۞

26. He brought those of the people of the Book who backed them down from their fortresses and cast terror in their hearts, a part of them you slew, and a part you made captives.

وَأَنزَلَ ٱلَّذِينَ ظَٰهَرُوهُم مِّنْ أَهْلِ ٱلْكِتَٰبِ مِن صَيَاصِيهِمْ وَقَذَفَ فِي قُلُوبِهِمُ ٱلرُّعْبَ فَرِيقًا تَقْتُلُونَ وَتَأْسِرُونَ فَرِيقًا ۞

27. And He caused you to inherit their land and their houses and their riches, and the land which you have not trodden, and Allah is Potent over everything.

وَأَوْرَثَكُمْ أَرْضَهُمْ وَدِيَٰرَهُمْ وَأَمْوَٰلَهُمْ وَأَرْضًا لَّمْ تَطَئُوهَا وَكَانَ ٱللَّهُ عَلَىٰ كُلِّ شَيْءٍ قَدِيرًا ۞

Section 4

28. O Prophet! Say to your wives: 'If it be that you seek the life of the world and its adornment, then come, I shall make a provision for you, and shall release you with a handsome release.

يَـٰٓأَيُّهَا ٱلنَّبِيُّ قُل لِّأَزْوَٰجِكَ إِن كُنتُنَّ تُرِدْنَ ٱلْحَيَوٰةَ ٱلدُّنْيَا وَزِينَتَهَا فَتَعَالَيْنَ أُمَتِّعْكُنَّ وَأُسَرِّحْكُنَّ سَرَاحًا جَمِيلًا ۝

29. And if you seek Allah and His Messenger and the abode of the Hereafter then verily Allah has prepared of the well-doers among you a mighty reward.'

وَإِن كُنتُنَّ تُرِدْنَ ٱللَّهَ وَرَسُولَهُ وَٱلدَّارَ ٱلْءَاخِرَةَ فَإِنَّ ٱللَّهَ أَعَدَّ لِلْمُحْسِنَـٰتِ مِنكُنَّ أَجْرًا عَظِيمًا ۝

30. O wives of the Prophet! Whosoever of you commits a flagrant indecency, doubled for her would be the punishment twice over; and with Allah that is easy.

يَـٰنِسَآءَ ٱلنَّبِيِّ مَن يَأْتِ مِنكُنَّ بِفَـٰحِشَةٍ مُّبَيِّنَةٍ يُضَـٰعَفْ لَهَا ٱلْعَذَابُ ضِعْفَيْنِ وَكَانَ ذَٰلِكَ عَلَى ٱللَّهِ يَسِيرًا ۝

31. Whosoever of you is obedient to Allah and His Messenger and works righteously, her reward We shall give her twice over and We have prepared for her a generous provision.

وَمَن يَقْنُتْ مِنكُنَّ لِلَّهِ وَرَسُولِهِ وَتَعْمَلْ صَـٰلِحًا نُّؤْتِهَآ أَجْرَهَا مَرَّتَيْنِ وَأَعْتَدْنَا لَهَا رِزْقًا كَرِيمًا ۝

32. O wives of the Prophet! You are not like any other women if you are God-fearing. So do not be soft in speech, lest in whose heart is disease, should be moved with desire, but make an honourable speech.

يَـٰنِسَآءَ ٱلنَّبِيِّ لَسْتُنَّ كَأَحَدٍ مِّنَ ٱلنِّسَآءِ إِنِ ٱتَّقَيْتُنَّ فَلَا تَخْضَعْنَ بِٱلْقَوْلِ فَيَطْمَعَ ٱلَّذِى فِى قَلْبِهِ مَرَضٌ وَقُلْنَ قَوْلًا مَّعْرُوفًا ۝

33. And stay in your houses.[602] And do not display yourselves[603] as did the pagans of old.[604] And establish the prayer and pay the poor-rate and obey Allah and His Messenger. Allah only desires to remove uncleanliness from you, and to purify you with a thorough purification, O people of the household of the Prophet.

وَقَرْنَ فِي بُيُوتِكُنَّ وَلَا تَبَرَّجْنَ تَبَرُّجَ الْجَاهِلِيَّةِ الْأُولَىٰ وَأَقِمْنَ الصَّلَوٰةَ وَءَاتِينَ الزَّكَوٰةَ وَأَطِعْنَ اللَّهَ وَرَسُولَهُ إِنَّمَا يُرِيدُ اللَّهُ لِيُذْهِبَ عَنكُمُ الرِّجْسَ أَهْلَ الْبَيْتِ وَيُطَهِّرَكُمْ تَطْهِيرًا ۝

34. And bear in mind what is rehearsed in your homes of the Revelations of Allah and the wisdom, Verily Allah is ever Subtle, Aware.

وَاذْكُرْنَ مَا يُتْلَىٰ فِي بُيُوتِكُنَّ مِنْ ءَايَٰتِ اللَّهِ وَالْحِكْمَةِ إِنَّ اللَّهَ كَانَ لَطِيفًا خَبِيرًا ۝

---

602. This does not pertain to menfolk. Islam enjoins strict isolation upon its womenfolk, which is not without parallel or precedent in the teachings of the ancient Prophets of Israel. 'The women had indeed in the innermost part of the house their own apartments to which access was not permitted to men, or, in the case of wealthy people or people of rank, they had a separate house to themselves' (*EBi.* c. 2946). The rule was also observed, at any rate, in regard to public worship, by the Jews and early Christians. 'In the early church the women were always separated from the men in public worship. The practice may probably have come into the Christian church without any formal enactment from the usage of Jewish worship, in which the women were (and are to this day) separated from the men' (*DCA.* II. p. 1891).

603. Muslim women are strictly warned against adorning themselves with their finery and going abroad into the streets to show themselves to men.

604. Note that the condition of woman in pagan Arabia closely resembled that of her sister in the West today. Indecent exposure of parts of her body was as common in the streets of Makka and Madina as it is today in the electrified centres of modern civilization. '*Jāhiliyyah*' denotes the time or state of paganism that preceded the advent of the Holy Prophet – a way of life that is reasserting itself in the West. And there can be little doubt that this new paganism is far more licentious than its ancient variety.

Section 5

35. Surely the Muslim men and women, and the believing men and women, and the devout men and women, and the men and women of veracity, and the persevering men and women, and the men and women of humility, and the almsgiving men and women, and the fasting men and women, and the men and women who guard their private parts, and Allah remembering men and women – for them Allah has got ready forgiveness and a mighty reward.

إِنَّ ٱلْمُسْلِمِينَ وَٱلْمُسْلِمَٰتِ وَ ٱلْمُؤْمِنِينَ وَٱلْمُؤْمِنَٰتِ وَٱلْقَٰنِتِينَ وَٱلْقَٰنِتَٰتِ وَٱلصَّٰدِقِينَ وَٱلصَّٰدِقَٰتِ وَٱلصَّٰبِرِينَ وَٱلصَّٰبِرَٰتِ وَٱلْخَٰشِعِينَ وَٱلْخَٰشِعَٰتِ وَٱلْمُتَصَدِّقِينَ وَٱلْمُتَصَدِّقَٰتِ وَٱلصَّٰئِمِينَ وَ ٱلصَّٰئِمَٰتِ وَٱلْحَٰفِظِينَ فُرُوجَهُمْ وَٱلْحَٰفِظَٰتِ وَٱلذَّٰكِرِينَ ٱللَّهَ كَثِيرًا وَٱلذَّٰكِرَٰتِ أَعَدَّ ٱللَّهُ لَهُم مَّغْفِرَةً وَ أَجْرًا عَظِيمًا ۝

36. And it is not for believing men or women, when Allah and His Messenger have decreed an affair, that they should have any choice in their affair. And whoso disobeys Allah and His Messenger has strayed manifestly.

وَمَا كَانَ لِمُؤْمِنٍ وَلَا مُؤْمِنَةٍ إِذَا قَضَى ٱللَّهُ وَرَسُولُهُۥٓ أَمْرًا أَن يَكُونَ لَهُمُ ٱلْخِيَرَةُ مِنْ أَمْرِهِمْ وَمَن يَعْصِ ٱللَّهَ وَرَسُولَهُۥ فَقَدْ ضَلَّ ضَلَٰلًا مُّبِينًا ۝

37. And recall when you were saying to him on whom Allah has conferred a favour and you have conferred a favour: 'Keep your wife to yourself and fear Allah', and you were concealing within you what Allah was going to disclose, and you were fearing mankind, while Allah had a greater right that Him you should fear. Then when Zaid had accomplished his purpose regarding her, We wedded her to you so that there should be no blame on the believers in respect of wives of their adopted sons, when they have accomplished their purpose with regard to them. And the ordinance of Allah was to be fulfilled.

وَإِذْ تَقُولُ لِلَّذِىٓ أَنْعَمَ ٱللَّهُ عَلَيْهِ وَأَنْعَمْتَ عَلَيْهِ أَمْسِكْ عَلَيْكَ زَوْجَكَ وَٱتَّقِ ٱللَّهَ وَتُخْفِى فِى نَفْسِكَ مَا ٱللَّهُ مُبْدِيهِ وَتَخْشَى ٱلنَّاسَ وَٱللَّهُ أَحَقُّ أَن تَخْشَىٰهُ فَلَمَّا قَضَىٰ زَيْدٌ مِّنْهَا وَطَرًا زَوَّجْنَٰكَهَا لِكَىْ لَا يَكُونَ عَلَى ٱلْمُؤْمِنِينَ حَرَجٌ فِىٓ أَزْوَٰجِ أَدْعِيَآئِهِمْ إِذَا قَضَوْا۟ مِنْهُنَّ وَطَرًا وَكَانَ أَمْرُ ٱللَّهِ مَفْعُولًا ۝

38. No blame there is on the Prophet in what Allah has decreed for him. That has been Allah's dispensation with those who have passed away before and the ordinance of Allah has been a destiny determined,

مَّا كَانَ عَلَى ٱلنَّبِيِّ مِنْ حَرَجٍ فِيمَا فَرَضَ ٱللَّهُ لَهُ ۖ سُنَّةَ ٱللَّهِ فِى ٱلَّذِينَ خَلَوْا۟ مِن قَبْلُ ۚ وَكَانَ أَمْرُ ٱللَّهِ قَدَرًا مَّقْدُورًا ﴿٣٨﴾

39. Those who preached the messages of Allah, and feared Him, and none save Allah. And Allah suffices as the Reckoner.

ٱلَّذِينَ يُبَلِّغُونَ رِسَٰلَٰتِ ٱللَّهِ وَيَخْشَوْنَهُ ۥ وَلَا يَخْشَوْنَ أَحَدًا إِلَّا ٱللَّهَ ۗ وَكَفَىٰ بِٱللَّهِ حَسِيبًا ﴿٣٩﴾

40. Muḥammad is not the father of any of your males, but a Messenger of Allah and the seal of the Prophets,[605] and Allah is the Knower of everything.

مَّا كَانَ مُحَمَّدٌ أَبَآ أَحَدٍ مِّن رِّجَالِكُمْ وَلَٰكِن رَّسُولَ ٱللَّهِ وَخَاتَمَ ٱلنَّبِيِّـۧنَ ۗ وَكَانَ ٱللَّهُ بِكُلِّ شَىْءٍ عَلِيمًا ﴿٤٠﴾

Section 6

41. O you who believe! Remember Allah oft.

يَٰٓأَيُّهَا ٱلَّذِينَ ءَامَنُوا۟ ٱذْكُرُوا۟ ٱللَّهَ ذِكْرًا كَثِيرًا ﴿٤١﴾

---

605. In this way closing the long line of Messengers. He is not 'a Prophet', but the Final Prophet. 'The last of a company of men whence the last of the prophets.' 'This idea of finality is perhaps the most original idea in the cultural history of mankind; its true significance can be understood only by those who carefully study the history of the pre – Islamic Magian culture in Western and Middle Asia. The concept of Magian culture, according to modern research, includes culture associated with Zoroastrianism, Judaism, Christianity, Chaldean and Sabean religions. To these creed – communities the idea of the continuity of prophethood was essential, and consequently they lived in a sate of constant expectation. The result of the Magian attitude was the disintegration of the old communities and the constant formation of fresh ones by all sorts of religious adventurers. It is obvious that Islam that claims to weld all the various communities of the world into one single community cannot reconcile itself to a movement which threatens its present solidarity and holds forth the promise of further rifts in human society' (Iqbal, *Reconstruction of Religious Thought in Islam*).

42. And hallow Him morning and evening.

وَسَبِّحُوهُ بُكْرَةً وَأَصِيلًا ۝

43. He it is Who sends His benedictions to you, and His angels also,[606] that He may bring you forth from darkness into light, and to the faithful He is ever Merciful.

هُوَ الَّذِي يُصَلِّي عَلَيْكُمْ وَمَلَٰئِكَتُهُ لِيُخْرِجَكُم مِّنَ الظُّلُمَٰتِ إِلَى النُّورِ وَكَانَ بِالْمُؤْمِنِينَ رَحِيمًا ۝

44. Their greeting on the Day when they meet Him will be: 'Peace!' And He has got ready for them a generous reward.

تَحِيَّتُهُمْ يَوْمَ يَلْقَوْنَهُ سَلَٰمٌ وَأَعَدَّ لَهُمْ أَجْرًا كَرِيمًا ۝

45. O Prophet! We have verily sent you as a witness and a bearer of glad tidings and a warner.

يَٰٓأَيُّهَا النَّبِيُّ إِنَّآ أَرْسَلْنَٰكَ شَٰهِدًا وَمُبَشِّرًا وَنَذِيرًا ۝

46. And a summoner unto Allah by His command, and a luminous lamp.

وَدَاعِيًا إِلَى اللَّهِ بِإِذْنِهِ وَسِرَاجًا مُّنِيرًا ۝

47. And bear to the faithful the glad tidings that there is for them a great grace from Allah.

وَبَشِّرِ الْمُؤْمِنِينَ بِأَنَّ لَهُم مِّنَ اللَّهِ فَضْلًا كَبِيرًا ۝

48. Do not yield you to the infidels and the hypocrites and disregard their insolence, and trust in Allah, and Allah suffices as the Trustee.

وَلَا تُطِعِ الْكَٰفِرِينَ وَالْمُنَٰفِقِينَ وَدَعْ أَذَىٰهُمْ وَتَوَكَّلْ عَلَى اللَّهِ وَكَفَىٰ بِاللَّهِ وَكِيلًا ۝

---

606. This by means of prayer. Angels' sending their benedictions to mankind in so far as they pray for God's blessings to mankind.

49. O you who believe! When you marry believing women and divorce them before you have touched them, then there is no waiting-period incumbent upon them from you, that you should count. So make a provision for them and release them with a seemly release.

يَـٰٓأَيُّهَا ٱلَّذِينَ ءَامَنُوٓاْ إِذَا نَكَحْتُمُ ٱلْمُؤْمِنَـٰتِ ثُمَّ طَلَّقْتُمُوهُنَّ مِن قَبْلِ أَن تَمَسُّوهُنَّ فَمَا لَكُمْ عَلَيْهِنَّ مِنْ عِدَّةٍ تَعْتَدُّونَهَا فَمَتِّعُوهُنَّ وَسَرِّحُوهُنَّ سَرَاحًا جَمِيلًا ٤٩

50. O Prophet! He has allowed to you your wives to whom you have paid their wages, also those whom your right hand owns of those whom Allah has given you as spoils of war and the daughters of your paternal uncle and the daughters of your paternal aunts and the daughters of your maternal uncles and the daughters of your maternal aunts, who migrated with you, and the believing women, when she offers herself to the Prophet, if the Prophet desires to wed her – this provision is exclusively for you, above the rest of the believers. Surely, We know what We have ordained to them concerning their wives and those whom their right hands possess, in order that there may be no blame upon you, and Allah is ever Forgiving, Merciful.

يَـٰٓأَيُّهَا ٱلنَّبِيُّ إِنَّآ أَحْلَلْنَا لَكَ أَزْوَٰجَكَ ٱلَّـٰتِىٓ ءَاتَيْتَ أُجُورَهُنَّ وَمَا مَلَكَتْ يَمِينُكَ مِمَّآ أَفَآءَ ٱللَّهُ عَلَيْكَ وَبَنَاتِ عَمِّكَ وَبَنَاتِ عَمَّـٰتِكَ وَبَنَاتِ خَالِكَ وَبَنَاتِ خَـٰلَـٰتِكَ ٱلَّـٰتِى هَاجَرْنَ مَعَكَ وَٱمْرَأَةً مُّؤْمِنَةً إِن وَهَبَتْ نَفْسَهَا لِلنَّبِيِّ إِنْ أَرَادَ ٱلنَّبِيُّ أَن يَسْتَنكِحَهَا خَالِصَةً لَّكَ مِن دُونِ ٱلْمُؤْمِنِينَ قَدْ عَلِمْنَا مَا فَرَضْنَا عَلَيْهِمْ فِىٓ أَزْوَٰجِهِمْ وَمَا مَلَكَتْ أَيْمَـٰنُهُمْ لِكَيْلَا يَكُونَ عَلَيْكَ حَرَجٌ وَكَانَ ٱللَّهُ غَفُورًا رَّحِيمًا ٥٠

51. You may put off such of them as you will, and you may take unto you such of them as you will; and when you desire such as you had set aside there is no blame upon you. This is likelier to cool their eyes and let them not grieve and to keep them pleased with what you shall give everyone of them. Allah knows what is in your hearts, and Allah is ever Knowing, Forbearing.

تَرۡجِي مَن تَشَآءُ مِنۡهُنَّ وَتُـٔۡوِىٓ إِلَيۡكَ مَن تَشَآءُۖ وَمَنِ ابۡتَغَيۡتَ مِمَّنۡ عَزَلۡتَ فَلَا جُنَاحَ عَلَيۡكَۚ ذَٰلِكَ أَدۡنَىٰٓ أَن تَقَرَّ أَعۡيُنُهُنَّ وَلَا يَحۡزَنَّ وَيَرۡضَيۡنَ بِمَآ ءَاتَيۡتَهُنَّ كُلُّهُنَّۚ وَاللَّهُ يَعۡلَمُ مَا فِي قُلُوبِكُمۡۚ وَكَانَ اللَّهُ عَلِيمًا حَلِيمًا ۝

52. Henceforth women are not allowed to you, nor may you change them for other wives, although their beauty please you save those whom your right hand shall own, and Allah is ever Watcher over everything.

لَّا يَحِلُّ لَكَ النِّسَآءُ مِنۢ بَعۡدُ وَلَآ أَن تَبَدَّلَ بِهِنَّ مِنۡ أَزۡوَٰجٍ وَلَوۡ أَعۡجَبَكَ حُسۡنُهُنَّ إِلَّا مَا مَلَكَتۡ يَمِينُكَۗ وَكَانَ اللَّهُ عَلَىٰ كُلِّ شَيۡءٍ رَّقِيبًا ۝

Section 7

53. O you who believe! Enter not the houses of the Prophet, except when leave is given you, for a meal and at a time that you will have to wait for its preparation; but when you are invited, then enter, and when you have had the meal, then disperse, without lingering to enter into familiar discourse. Verily this inaccommodates the Prophet, and he is shy of asking you to depart, but Allah is not shy of the truth. And when you ask of them aught, ask it of them from behind a curtain. That shall be purer for your hearts and for their hearts. And it is not lawful for you that you should cause annoyance to the Messenger of Allah, nor that you should ever marry his wives after him; verily that shall be an enormity in the sight of Allah.

يَـٰٓأَيُّهَا الَّذِينَ ءَامَنُوا لَا تَدۡخُلُوا بُيُوتَ النَّبِيِّ إِلَّآ أَن يُؤۡذَنَ لَكُمۡ إِلَىٰ طَعَامٍ غَيۡرَ نَٰظِرِينَ إِنَىٰهُ وَلَٰكِنۡ إِذَا دُعِيتُمۡ فَادۡخُلُوا فَإِذَا طَعِمۡتُمۡ فَانتَشِرُوا وَلَا مُسۡتَـٔۡنِسِينَ لِحَدِيثٍۚ إِنَّ ذَٰلِكُمۡ كَانَ يُؤۡذِي النَّبِيَّ فَيَسۡتَحۡيِۦ مِنكُمۡۖ وَاللَّهُ لَا يَسۡتَحۡيِۦ مِنَ الۡحَقِّۚ وَإِذَا سَأَلۡتُمُوهُنَّ مَتَٰعًا فَسۡـَٔلُوهُنَّ مِن وَرَآءِ حِجَابٍۚ ذَٰلِكُمۡ أَطۡهَرُ لِقُلُوبِكُمۡ وَقُلُوبِهِنَّۚ وَمَا كَانَ لَكُمۡ أَن تُؤۡذُوا رَسُولَ اللَّهِ وَلَآ أَن تَنكِحُوٓا أَزۡوَٰجَهُۥ مِنۢ بَعۡدِهِۦٓ أَبَدًاۚ إِنَّ ذَٰلِكُمۡ كَانَ عِندَ اللَّهِ عَظِيمًا ۝

54. Whether you disclose a thing or conceal it, verily Allah is ever Knower of everything.

إِن تُبْدُوا شَيْئًا أَوْ تُخْفُوهُ فَإِنَّ ٱللَّهَ كَانَ بِكُلِّ شَىْءٍ عَلِيمًا ﴿٥٤﴾

55. It is no sin for them in respect of their fathers or brothers, or their brother's sons or their sister's sons or their own women, or those whom their right hands own; and fear Allah, verily Allah is ever a Witness of everything.

لَّا جُنَاحَ عَلَيْهِنَّ فِىٓ ءَابَآئِهِنَّ وَلَآ أَبْنَآئِهِنَّ وَلَآ إِخْوَٰنِهِنَّ وَلَآ أَبْنَآءِ إِخْوَٰنِهِنَّ وَلَآ أَبْنَآءِ أَخَوَٰتِهِنَّ وَلَا نِسَآئِهِنَّ وَلَا مَا مَلَكَتْ أَيْمَٰنُهُنَّ وَٱتَّقِينَ ٱللَّهَ إِنَّ ٱللَّهَ كَانَ عَلَىٰ كُلِّ شَىْءٍ شَهِيدًا ﴿٥٥﴾

56. Verily Allah and His angels send their benedictions upon the Prophet.[607] O you who believe! Send your benedictions also upon him and salute him with a goodly salutation.[608]

إِنَّ ٱللَّهَ وَمَلَٰٓئِكَتَهُۥ يُصَلُّونَ عَلَى ٱلنَّبِىِّ يَٰٓأَيُّهَا ٱلَّذِينَ ءَامَنُوا صَلُّوا عَلَيْهِ وَسَلِّمُوا تَسْلِيمًا ﴿٥٦﴾

57. Surely those who annoy Allah and His Messenger, Allah has cursed them in this world and the Hereafter, and has prepared for them an ignominious torment.

إِنَّ ٱلَّذِينَ يُؤْذُونَ ٱللَّهَ وَرَسُولَهُۥ لَعَنَهُمُ ٱللَّهُ فِى ٱلدُّنْيَا وَٱلْأَخِرَةِ وَأَعَدَّ لَهُمْ عَذَابًا مُّهِينًا ﴿٥٧﴾

58. And those who annoy the believing men and women without their deserving it, shall surely bear the guilt of calumny and evident sin.

وَٱلَّذِينَ يُؤْذُونَ ٱلْمُؤْمِنِينَ وَٱلْمُؤْمِنَٰتِ بِغَيْرِ مَا ٱكْتَسَبُوا فَقَدِ ٱحْتَمَلُوا بُهْتَٰنًا وَإِثْمًا مُّبِينًا ﴿٥٨﴾

---

607. God's benediction upon His Prophet is clear enough. The angels' benediction means that they pray to God for His blessings on the Prophet.

608. In other words, honour his memory. Hence the practice among Muslims of adding the words 'on whom be the blessing of Allah and peace' to his name.

Section 8

59. O Prophet! Say to your wives and your daughters and women of the believers that they should let down upon them their wrapping garments. That would be more likely to distinguish them, so that they will not be affronted, and Allah is ever Forgiving, Merciful.

يَـٰٓأَيُّهَا ٱلنَّبِىُّ قُل لِّأَزۡوَٰجِكَ وَبَنَاتِكَ وَنِسَآءِ ٱلۡمُؤۡمِنِينَ يُدۡنِينَ عَلَيۡهِنَّ مِن جَلَـٰبِيبِهِنَّ ذَٰلِكَ أَدۡنَىٰٓ أَن يُعۡرَفۡنَ فَلَا يُؤۡذَيۡنَ وَكَانَ ٱللَّهُ غَفُورًا رَّحِيمًا ﴿٥٩﴾

60. If the hypocrites and those in whose heart is a disease and the raisers of commotion in Madina do not desist, We shall certainly set you up against them. Now onwards they shall not be allowed to neighbour you therein, except for a little while.

لَّئِن لَّمۡ يَنتَهِ ٱلۡمُنَٰفِقُونَ وَٱلَّذِينَ فِى قُلُوبِهِم مَّرَضٌ وَٱلۡمُرۡجِفُونَ فِى ٱلۡمَدِينَةِ لَنُغۡرِيَنَّكَ بِهِمۡ ثُمَّ لَا يُجَاوِرُونَكَ فِيهَآ إِلَّا قَلِيلًا ﴿٦٠﴾

61. Accursed, wherever found, they shall be seized and slain with a relentless slaughter.

مَّلۡعُونِينَ أَيۡنَمَا ثُقِفُوٓاْ أُخِذُواْ وَقُتِّلُواْ تَقۡتِيلًا ﴿٦١﴾

62. That has been the dispensation of Allah with those who have passed away before, and you shall not find any change in the dispensation of Allah.

سُنَّةَ ٱللَّهِ فِى ٱلَّذِينَ خَلَوۡاْ مِن قَبۡلُ وَلَن تَجِدَ لِسُنَّةِ ٱللَّهِ تَبۡدِيلًا ﴿٦٢﴾

63. People question you concerning the Hour. Say: 'Its knowledge is with Allah only, and what do you know? Perhaps the Hour may be nigh.'

يَسۡـَٔلُكَ ٱلنَّاسُ عَنِ ٱلسَّاعَةِ قُلۡ إِنَّمَا عِلۡمُهَا عِندَ ٱللَّهِ وَمَا يُدۡرِيكَ لَعَلَّ ٱلسَّاعَةَ تَكُونُ قَرِيبًا ﴿٦٣﴾

64. Verily Allah has cursed the infidels, and has prepared for them a Blaze.

إِنَّ ٱللَّهَ لَعَنَ ٱلۡكَٰفِرِينَ وَأَعَدَّ لَهُمۡ سَعِيرًا ﴿٦٤﴾

65. Abiders therein they shall be for ever, and they will find neither a protecting friend nor a helper.

خَٰلِدِينَ فِيهَآ أَبَدٗاۖ لَّا يَجِدُونَ وَلِيّٗا وَلَا نَصِيرٗا ٦٥

66. On the Day when their faces shall be rolled in Fire, they will say: 'Ah! That we had obeyed Allah and had obeyed the Messenger!'

يَوۡمَ تُقَلَّبُ وُجُوهُهُمۡ فِي ٱلنَّارِ يَقُولُونَ يَٰلَيۡتَنَآ أَطَعۡنَا ٱللَّهَ وَأَطَعۡنَا ٱلرَّسُولَا۠ ٦٦

67. And they will say: 'Our Lord! We obeyed our chiefs and our elders and they led us astray from the way.

وَقَالُواْ رَبَّنَآ إِنَّآ أَطَعۡنَا سَادَتَنَا وَكُبَرَآءَنَا فَأَضَلُّونَا ٱلسَّبِيلَا۠ ٦٧

68. 'Our Lord! Give them Punishment twofold, and curse them with a great curse.'

رَبَّنَآ ءَاتِهِمۡ ضِعۡفَيۡنِ مِنَ ٱلۡعَذَابِ وَٱلۡعَنۡهُمۡ لَعۡنٗا كَبِيرٗا ٦٨

Section 9

69. O you who believe! Do not be like those who annoyed Moses, but Allah cleared him of what they said; and he was illustrious with Allah.

يَٰٓأَيُّهَا ٱلَّذِينَ ءَامَنُواْ لَا تَكُونُواْ كَٱلَّذِينَ ءَاذَوۡاْ مُوسَىٰ فَبَرَّأَهُ ٱللَّهُ مِمَّا قَالُواْۚ وَكَانَ عِندَ ٱللَّهِ وَجِيهٗا ٦٩

70. O you who believe! Fear Allah, and speak a straight speech.

يَٰٓأَيُّهَا ٱلَّذِينَ ءَامَنُواْ ٱتَّقُواْ ٱللَّهَ وَقُولُواْ قَوۡلٗا سَدِيدٗا ٧٠

71. He will amend your works for you and forgive you your sins, and whoso obeys Allah and His Messenger, he has indeed accomplished a great achievement.

يُصۡلِحۡ لَكُمۡ أَعۡمَٰلَكُمۡ وَيَغۡفِرۡ لَكُمۡ ذُنُوبَكُمۡۗ وَمَن يُطِعِ ٱللَّهَ وَرَسُولَهُۥ فَقَدۡ فَازَ فَوۡزًا عَظِيمًا ٧١

72. Verily We! We offered the trust to the heavens and the earth and the mountains, but they declined to bear it and shrank from it. But man undertook it; surely he was very sinful, very foolish.

إِنَّا عَرَضْنَا الْأَمَانَةَ عَلَى السَّمَوَتِ وَالْأَرْضِ وَالْجِبَالِ فَأَبَيْنَ أَن يَحْمِلْنَهَا وَأَشْفَقْنَ مِنْهَا وَحَمَلَهَا الْإِنسَنُ إِنَّهُ كَانَ ظَلُومًا جَهُولًا ۝

73. So that Allah will chastise the hypocritical men and women and the associators and the associatoresses. And Allah will relent towards the believing men and women, and Allah is ever Forgiving, Merciful.

لِّيُعَذِّبَ اللَّهُ الْمُنَفِقِينَ وَالْمُنَفِقَتِ وَالْمُشْرِكِينَ وَالْمُشْرِكَتِ وَيَتُوبَ اللَّهُ عَلَى الْمُؤْمِنِينَ وَالْمُؤْمِنَتِ وَكَانَ اللَّهُ غَفُورًا رَّحِيمًا ۝

Sūrah 34

Sabā'

(Makkan, 6 Sections, 54 Verses)

In the name of Allah, the Compassionate, the Merciful.

Section 1

1. All praise to Allah Whose is what is in the heavens and what is in the earth; and His is the praise in the Hereafter. And He is the Wise, the Aware.

2. He knows what penetrates into the earth and what comes forth from it, and what descends from the heaven and what ascends to it. And He is the Merciful, the Forgiving.

3. Those who disbelieve say: 'The Hour will not come unto us.' Say: 'Yea! By my Lord, the Knower of the Unseen, it will surely come unto you. Not an atom's weight escapes Him in the heavens or in the earth, nor is there anything smaller than it or greater but it is inscribed in a luminous Book,

4. That He may recompense those who believed and worked righteous deeds. Those! Theirs shall be forgiveness and a generous provision.'

5. And those who attempted to frustrate Our signs – those! Theirs shall be a chastisement of afflictive calamity.

وَٱلَّذِينَ سَعَوْ فِىٓ ءَايَٰتِنَا مُعَٰجِزِينَ أُوْلَٰٓئِكَ لَهُمْ عَذَابٌ مِّن رِّجْزٍ أَلِيمٌ ۝

6. And those who have been vouchsafed knowledge behold that the Book revealed to you from your Lord – it is the truth and it guides to the path of the Mighty, the Laudable.

وَيَرَى ٱلَّذِينَ أُوتُوا ٱلْعِلْمَ ٱلَّذِىٓ أُنزِلَ إِلَيْكَ مِن رَّبِّكَ هُوَ ٱلْحَقَّ وَيَهْدِىٓ إِلَىٰ صِرَٰطِ ٱلْعَزِيزِ ٱلْحَمِيدِ ۝

7. And those who disbelieve say: 'Shall we direct you to a man declaring to you that when you have dispersed with full dispersion, then you will be raised unto a new creation?'[609]

وَقَالَ ٱلَّذِينَ كَفَرُوٓا هَلْ نَدُلُّكُمْ عَلَىٰ رَجُلٍ يُنَبِّئُكُمْ إِذَا مُزِّقْتُمْ كُلَّ مُمَزَّقٍ إِنَّكُمْ لَفِى خَلْقٍ جَدِيدٍ ۝

8. Has he fabricated a lie against Allah, or is there a madness in him? Nay, but those who disbelieve in the Hereafter are themselves in a torment and error far-reaching.

أَفْتَرَىٰ عَلَى ٱللَّهِ كَذِبًا أَم بِهِۦ جِنَّةٌۢ بَلِ ٱلَّذِينَ لَا يُؤْمِنُونَ بِٱلْءَاخِرَةِ فِى ٱلْعَذَابِ وَٱلضَّلَٰلِ ٱلْبَعِيدِ ۝

9. Do they not see what is before them and what is behind them of the heavens and the earth?[610] If We will, We shall sink the earth with them, or cause a fragment of the sky to fall on them. Verily there is a sign therein unto every penitent bondsman.

أَفَلَمْ يَرَوْا إِلَىٰ مَا بَيْنَ أَيْدِيهِمْ وَمَا خَلْفَهُم مِّنَ ٱلسَّمَآءِ وَٱلْأَرْضِ إِن نَّشَأْ نَخْسِفْ بِهِمُ ٱلْأَرْضَ أَوْ نُسْقِطْ عَلَيْهِمْ كِسَفًا مِّنَ ٱلسَّمَآءِ إِنَّ فِى ذَٰلِكَ لَءَايَةً لِّكُلِّ عَبْدٍ مُّنِيبٍ ۝

---

609. The pagan Arab denied Resurrection altogether, and looked askance at the Messenger who preached such a 'preposterous' doctrine.

610. Do they not think that so powerful a Creator and Preserver is able to bring about a new creation?

Section 2

10. And assuredly We vouch-safed to David grace from Us and said: 'O mountains! Repeat Our praise with him, and birds you also!' And We softened for him iron.

وَلَقَدْ ءَاتَيْنَا دَاوُدَ مِنَّا فَضْلًا يَٰجِبَالُ أَوِّبِى مَعَهُۥ وَالطَّيْرَ وَأَلَنَّا لَهُ ٱلْحَدِيدَ ۝

11. Saying: 'Make complete coats of mail and rightly dispose the links, and work righteously. Verily I am of that which you work the Beholder.'

أَنِ ٱعْمَلْ سَٰبِغَٰتٍ وَقَدِّرْ فِى ٱلسَّرْدِ وَٱعْمَلُوا۟ صَٰلِحًا إِنِّى بِمَا تَعْمَلُونَ بَصِيرٌ ۝

12. And to Solomon We subjected the wind, of which the morning journeying was a month and the evening journeying a month. And We made the fount of brass flow for him. And of the *Jinn* were who worked be-fore him by the will of His Lord. And whosoever of them swerved from Our command, him We shall cause to taste the torment of the Blaze.

وَلِسُلَيْمَٰنَ ٱلرِّيحَ غُدُوُّهَا شَهْرٌ وَرَوَاحُهَا شَهْرٌ وَأَسَلْنَا لَهُۥ عَيْنَ ٱلْقِطْرِ وَمِنَ ٱلْجِنِّ مَن يَعْمَلُ بَيْنَ يَدَيْهِ بِإِذْنِ رَبِّهِ وَمَن يَزِغْ مِنْهُمْ عَنْ أَمْرِنَا نُذِقْهُ مِنْ عَذَابِ ٱلسَّعِيرِ ۝

13. They fashioned for him whatsoever he wished, of lofty halls and statues and basins like cisterns and cauldrons standing firm. O house of David, work with gratitude; few of My bondsmen are grateful.

يَعْمَلُونَ لَهُۥ مَا يَشَآءُ مِن مَّحَٰرِيبَ وَتَمَٰثِيلَ وَجِفَانٍ كَٱلْجَوَابِ وَقُدُورٍ رَّاسِيَٰتٍ ٱعْمَلُوٓا۟ ءَالَ دَاوُدَ شُكْرًا وَقَلِيلٌ مِّنْ عِبَادِىَ ٱلشَّكُورُ ۝

14. Then when We decreed death for him, naught discovered his death to them, save a moving creature of the earth, which gnawed away his staff. Then when he fell, the *jinn* clearly perceived that, if they had known the Unseen they would not have tarried in the ignominious torment.

فَلَمَّا قَضَيْنَا عَلَيْهِ ٱلْمَوْتَ مَا دَلَّهُمْ عَلَىٰ مَوْتِهِۦٓ إِلَّا دَآبَّةُ ٱلْأَرْضِ تَأْكُلُ مِنسَأَتَهُۥۖ فَلَمَّا خَرَّ تَبَيَّنَتِ ٱلْجِنُّ أَن لَّوْ كَانُوا۟ يَعْلَمُونَ ٱلْغَيْبَ مَا لَبِثُوا۟ فِى ٱلْعَذَابِ ٱلْمُهِينِ ﴿١٤﴾

15. Assuredly for Sabā' a sign in their own dwelling place; two gardens on the right hand and on the left. Eat you of the provision of your Lord, and give thanks to Him: a fair land and a Forgiving Lord!

لَقَدْ كَانَ لِسَبَإٍ فِى مَسْكَنِهِمْ ءَايَةٌ ۖ جَنَّتَانِ عَن يَمِينٍ وَشِمَالٍ ۖ كُلُوا۟ مِن رِّزْقِ رَبِّكُمْ وَٱشْكُرُوا۟ لَهُۥ ۚ بَلْدَةٌ طَيِّبَةٌ وَرَبٌّ غَفُورٌ ﴿١٥﴾

16. But they turned away. So We sent upon them the inundation of the dam and We exchanged their two gardens for two gardens bearing bitter fruit, and tamarisk and few lote-trees.

فَأَعْرَضُوا۟ فَأَرْسَلْنَا عَلَيْهِمْ سَيْلَ ٱلْعَرِمِ وَبَدَّلْنَٰهُم بِجَنَّتَيْهِمْ جَنَّتَيْنِ ذَوَاتَىْ أُكُلٍ خَمْطٍ وَأَثْلٍ وَشَىْءٍ مِّن سِدْرٍ قَلِيلٍ ﴿١٦﴾

17. In this way We requited them, as they were ungrateful. And We do not requite thus any save the ungrateful ones.

ذَٰلِكَ جَزَيْنَٰهُم بِمَا كَفَرُوا۟ ۖ وَهَلْ نُجَٰزِىٓ إِلَّا ٱلْكَفُورَ ﴿١٧﴾

18. And We had placed between them and the cities which We had blessed, cities easy to be seen, and We had made the stages of the journey between them easy: travel in them nights and days secure.

وَجَعَلْنَا بَيْنَهُمْ وَبَيْنَ ٱلْقُرَى ٱلَّتِى بَٰرَكْنَا فِيهَا قُرًى ظَٰهِرَةً وَقَدَّرْنَا فِيهَا ٱلسَّيْرَ ۖ سِيرُوا۟ فِيهَا لَيَالِىَ وَأَيَّامًا ءَامِنِينَ ﴿١٨﴾

19. And they said: 'Our Lord! Make the distance between our journeys longer'; and they wronged themselves. So We made them bywords and dispersed them totally. Surely herein are signs for every persevering, grateful person.

فَقَالُوۡا رَبَّنَا بَـٰعِدۡ بَيۡنَ أَسۡفَارِنَا وَظَلَمُوۡٓا أَنفُسَهُمۡ فَجَعَلۡنَـٰهُمۡ أَحَادِيثَ وَمَزَّقۡنَـٰهُمۡ كُلَّ مُمَزَّقٍۚ إِنَّ فِى ذَٰلِكَ لَأٓيَـٰتٍ لِّكُلِّ صَبَّارٍ شَكُورٍ ۝

20. And assuredly Iblīs found his conjecture regarding them true; and they followed him, all save a party of the believers.

وَلَقَدۡ صَدَّقَ عَلَيۡهِمۡ إِبۡلِيسُ ظَنَّهُۥ فَاتَّبَعُوهُ إِلَّا فَرِيقًا مِّنَ ٱلۡمُؤۡمِنِينَ ۝

21. And he has no authority over them, except that We would know him who believes in the Hereafter from him who is in doubt thereof. And your Lord is the Warden over everything.

وَمَا كَانَ لَهُۥ عَلَيۡهِم مِّن سُلۡطَـٰنٍ إِلَّا لِنَعۡلَمَ مَن يُؤۡمِنُ بِٱلۡأٓخِرَةِ مِمَّنۡ هُوَ مِنۡهَا فِى شَكٍّۗ وَرَبُّكَ عَلَىٰ كُلِّ شَىۡءٍ حَفِيظٌ ۝

Section 3

22. Say: 'Call upon those whom you assert besides Allah. They do not own an atom's weight either in the heavens or in the earth, nor have they any partnership in either. Nor is there for Him any supporter from among them.

قُلِ ٱدۡعُوا۟ ٱلَّذِينَ زَعَمۡتُم مِّن دُونِ ٱللَّهِۖ لَا يَمۡلِكُونَ مِثۡقَالَ ذَرَّةٍ فِى ٱلسَّمَـٰوَٰتِ وَلَا فِى ٱلۡأَرۡضِ وَمَا لَهُمۡ فِيهِمَا مِن شِرۡكٍ وَمَا لَهُۥ مِنۡهُم مِّن ظَهِيرٍ ۝

23. Intercession with Him profits not save the intercession of him whom He gives leave. They hold their peace until when fright is taken off from their hearts, they say: "What is it that your Lord has said?" They say: "The very Truth." And He is the Exalted, the Great.'

وَلَا تَنفَعُ ٱلشَّفَـٰعَةُ عِندَهُۥٓ إِلَّا لِمَنۡ أَذِنَ لَهُۥۚ حَتَّىٰٓ إِذَا فُزِّعَ عَن قُلُوبِهِمۡ قَالُوا۟ مَاذَا قَالَ رَبُّكُمۡۖ قَالُوا۟ ٱلۡحَقَّۖ وَهُوَ ٱلۡعَلِىُّ ٱلۡكَبِيرُ ۝

24. Say: 'Who does provide food for you from the heavens and the earth?' Say: 'Allah; verily either we or you are on the guidance, or in clear error.'

قُلْ مَنْ يَرْزُقُكُمْ مِّنَ السَّمَوَاتِ وَالْأَرْضِ قُلِ اللَّهُ وَإِنَّا أَوْ إِيَّاكُمْ لَعَلَى هُدًى أَوْ فِى ضَلَالٍ مُّبِينٍ ﴿٢٤﴾

25. Say: 'You will not be questioned about what we have committed. Nor will we be questioned about what you work.'

قُلْ لَّا تُسْئَلُونَ عَمَّا أَجْرَمْنَا وَلَا نُسْئَلُ عَمَّا تَعْمَلُونَ ﴿٢٥﴾

26. Say: 'Our Lord shall assemble us together, then He shall judge between us with truth; and He is the great Judge, the Knower.'

قُلْ يَجْمَعُ بَيْنَنَا رَبُّنَا ثُمَّ يَفْتَحُ بَيْنَنَا بِالْحَقِّ وَهُوَ الْفَتَّاحُ الْعَلِيمُ ﴿٢٦﴾

27. Say: 'Show me those whom you have joined with Him as associates. By no means! Aye! He is Allah, the Mighty, the Wise.'

قُلْ أَرُونِىَ الَّذِينَ أَلْحَقْتُمْ بِهِ شُرَكَاءَ كَلَّا بَلْ هُوَ اللَّهُ الْعَزِيزُ الْحَكِيمُ ﴿٢٧﴾

28. And We have not sent you save as a bearer of glad tiding and a warner to all mankind;[611] yet most mankind do not know.

وَمَا أَرْسَلْنَاكَ إِلَّا كَافَّةً لِّلنَّاسِ بَشِيرًا وَنَذِيرًا وَلَكِنَّ أَكْثَرَ النَّاسِ لَا يَعْلَمُونَ ﴿٢٨﴾

29. And they say: 'When is the promise to come, if you speak truth?'

وَيَقُولُونَ مَتَى هَذَا الْوَعْدُ إِن كُنْتُمْ صَادِقِينَ ﴿٢٩﴾

30. Say: 'The assignment to you is for a Day which you cannot put back for an hour nor can you anticipate.'

قُلْ لَّكُمْ مِيعَادُ يَوْمٍ لَّا تَسْتَأْخِرُونَ عَنْهُ سَاعَةً وَلَا تَسْتَقْدِمُونَ ﴿٣٠﴾

---

611. This brings into strong relief the essentially cosmopolitan character of Islam. Its Message is extended to the whole world, and is not confined to a particular race or people.

Section 4

31. And those who disbelieve say: 'We shall by no means believe in the Qur'ān nor in what has been before it.' Would that you could see when the ungodly shall be made to stand before their Lord. They shall cast back the word one to another. Those who were deemed weak will say to those who were proud: 'Had it not been for you, we should surely have been believers.'

وَقَالَ ٱلَّذِينَ كَفَرُواْ لَن نُّؤْمِنَ بِهَٰذَا ٱلْقُرْءَانِ وَلَا بِٱلَّذِى بَيْنَ يَدَيْهِ وَلَوْ تَرَىٰٓ إِذِ ٱلظَّٰلِمُونَ مَوْقُوفُونَ عِندَ رَبِّهِمْ يَرْجِعُ بَعْضُهُمْ إِلَىٰ بَعْضٍ ٱلْقَوْلَ يَقُولُ ٱلَّذِينَ ٱسْتُضْعِفُواْ لِلَّذِينَ ٱسْتَكْبَرُوٓاْ لَوْلَآ أَنتُمْ لَكُنَّا مُؤْمِنِينَ ﴿٣١﴾

32. Those who were proud will say to those who were deemed weak: 'Was it we who prevented you from the guidance after it had come to you? Aye! You have been guilty yourselves.'

قَالَ ٱلَّذِينَ ٱسْتَكْبَرُواْ لِلَّذِينَ ٱسْتُضْعِفُوٓاْ أَنَحْنُ صَدَدْنَٰكُمْ عَنِ ٱلْهُدَىٰ بَعْدَ إِذْ جَآءَكُم بَلْ كُنتُم مُّجْرِمِينَ ﴿٣٢﴾

33. And those who were deemed weak will say to those who were proud: 'Aye! It was your plotting night and day, when you were commanding us that we should disbelieve in Allah and set up peers unto Him.' And they will keep secret their shame when they behold the torment. And We shall place shackles on the necks of those who disbelieved. They shall be requited not save according to what they had been working.

وَقَالَ ٱلَّذِينَ ٱسْتُضْعِفُواْ لِلَّذِينَ ٱسْتَكْبَرُواْ بَلْ مَكْرُ ٱلَّيْلِ وَٱلنَّهَارِ إِذْ تَأْمُرُونَنَآ أَن نَّكْفُرَ بِٱللَّهِ وَنَجْعَلَ لَهُۥٓ أَندَادًا وَأَسَرُّواْ ٱلنَّدَامَةَ لَمَّا رَأَوُاْ ٱلْعَذَابَ وَجَعَلْنَا ٱلْأَغْلَٰلَ فِىٓ أَعْنَاقِ ٱلَّذِينَ كَفَرُواْ هَلْ يُجْزَوْنَ إِلَّا مَا كَانُواْ يَعْمَلُونَ ﴿٣٣﴾

34. And We sent not a warner to a town but the affluent thereof said: 'We are disbelievers in that with which you have been sent.'

وَمَآ أَرْسَلْنَا فِى قَرْيَةٍ مِّن نَّذِيرٍ إِلَّا قَالَ مُتْرَفُوهَآ إِنَّا بِمَآ أُرْسِلْتُم بِهِۦ كَٰفِرُونَ ﴿٣٤﴾

35. And they said: 'We are greater in riches and children, and we are not going to be chastised.'

وَقَالُوا نَحْنُ أَكْثَرُ أَمْوَالًا وَأَوْلَادًا وَمَا نَحْنُ بِمُعَذَّبِينَ ﴿٣٥﴾

36. Say: 'Verily my Lord expands the provision for whom He will and stints it likewise, but most of mankind know not.'

قُلْ إِنَّ رَبِّي يَبْسُطُ الرِّزْقَ لِمَن يَشَاءُ وَيَقْدِرُ وَلَكِنَّ أَكْثَرَ النَّاسِ لَا يَعْلَمُونَ ﴿٣٦﴾

Section 5

37. It is not your riches nor your children that will draw you nigh unto Us with a near approach, but whoso believes and works righteously then those! Theirs will be a twofold meed for what they will have worked, and they will be in upper apartments secure.

وَمَا أَمْوَالُكُمْ وَلَا أَوْلَادُكُم بِالَّتِي تُقَرِّبُكُمْ عِندَنَا زُلْفَى إِلَّا مَنْ ءَامَنَ وَعَمِلَ صَلِحًا فَأُوْلَئِكَ لَهُمْ جَزَاءُ الضِّعْفِ بِمَا عَمِلُوا وَهُمْ فِي الْغُرُفَتِ ءَامِنُونَ ﴿٣٧﴾

38. And those who endeavour to frustrate Our signs, torment will be brought to them.

وَالَّذِينَ يَسْعَوْنَ فِي ءَايَتِنَا مُعَجِزِينَ أُوْلَئِكَ فِي الْعَذَابِ مُحْضَرُونَ ﴿٣٨﴾

39. Say you: 'My Lord expands the provision for whom He will of His bondsmen and also stints it for him, and what you expend of aught, He will replace it. And He is the Best of Providers.

قُلْ إِنَّ رَبِّي يَبْسُطُ الرِّزْقَ لِمَن يَشَاءُ مِنْ عِبَادِهِ وَيَقْدِرُ لَهُ وَمَا أَنفَقْتُم مِّن شَيْءٍ فَهُوَ يُخْلِفُهُ وَهُوَ خَيْرُ الرَّازِقِينَ ﴿٣٩﴾

40. And on the Day when He gathers them together, He will say to the angels: 'Was it you that these polytheists were wont to worship?'

وَيَوْمَ يَحْشُرُهُمْ جَمِيعًا ثُمَّ يَقُولُ لِلْمَلَئِكَةِ أَهَؤُلَاءِ إِيَّاكُمْ كَانُوا يَعْبُدُونَ ﴿٤٠﴾

41. They will say: 'Hallowed be You! You are our Protector, not they. Aye! They have been worshipping the *jinn*; in them most of them were believers.'

قَالُوا۟ سُبْحَٰنَكَ أَنتَ وَلِيُّنَا مِن دُونِهِم
بَلْ كَانُوا۟ يَعْبُدُونَ ٱلْجِنَّ أَكْثَرُهُم
بِهِم مُّؤْمِنُونَ ﴿٤١﴾

42. Today you cannot benefit or hurt one another. And We shall say to those who did wrong: 'Taste the torment of the Fire which you were wont to belie.'

فَٱلْيَوْمَ لَا يَمْلِكُ بَعْضُكُمْ لِبَعْضٍ نَّفْعًا وَلَا
ضَرًّا وَنَقُولُ لِلَّذِينَ ظَلَمُوا۟ ذُوقُوا۟ عَذَابَ
ٱلنَّارِ ٱلَّتِى كُنتُم بِهَا تُكَذِّبُونَ ﴿٤٢﴾

43. And when there are rehearsed to them Our plain revelations they say: 'This Messenger is nothing but a man, who seeks to prevent you from what your fathers have been worshipping.' And they say: 'This Message is nothing but a fraud fabricated. And those who disbelieve say of the Truth, when it is come unto them, this is nothing but manifest magic.'

وَإِذَا تُتْلَىٰ عَلَيْهِمْ ءَايَٰتُنَا بَيِّنَٰتٍ قَالُوا۟ مَا هَٰذَآ
إِلَّا رَجُلٌ يُرِيدُ أَن يَصُدَّكُمْ عَمَّا كَانَ يَعْبُدُ
ءَابَآؤُكُمْ وَقَالُوا۟ مَا هَٰذَآ إِلَّآ إِفْكٌ مُّفْتَرًى
وَقَالَ ٱلَّذِينَ كَفَرُوا۟ لِلْحَقِّ لَمَّا جَآءَهُمْ إِنْ
هَٰذَآ إِلَّا سِحْرٌ مُّبِينٌ ﴿٤٣﴾

44. And We had not vouchsafed to them Books they should have been studying. Nor had We sent to them any warner before you.

وَمَآ ءَاتَيْنَٰهُم مِّن كُتُبٍ يَدْرُسُونَهَا وَمَآ
أَرْسَلْنَآ إِلَيْهِمْ قَبْلَكَ مِن نَّذِيرٍ ﴿٤٤﴾

45. And those before them belied, and these have not arrived to a tithe of which We had vouchsafed them. But they belied My Messengers. So how terrible was My disapproval!

وَكَذَّبَ ٱلَّذِينَ مِن قَبْلِهِمْ وَمَا بَلَغُوا۟
مِعْشَارَ مَآ ءَاتَيْنَٰهُمْ فَكَذَّبُوا۟ رُسُلِى
فَكَيْفَ كَانَ نَكِيرِ ﴿٤٥﴾

Section 6

46. Say: 'I but exhort you to one thing; that you stand, for Allah's sake, by twos and singly, and then ponder; in your companion there is no madness, he is naught but a warner to you of a severe torment.'

قُلۡ إِنَّمَاۤ أَعِظُكُم بِوَٰحِدَةٍ أَن تَقُومُواْ لِلَّهِ مَثۡنَىٰ وَفُرَٰدَىٰ ثُمَّ تَتَفَكَّرُواْ مَا بِصَاحِبِكُم مِّن جِنَّةٍ إِنۡ هُوَ إِلَّا نَذِيرٌ لَّكُم بَيۡنَ يَدَىۡ عَذَابٍ شَدِيدٍ ﴿٤٦﴾

47. Say: 'Whatever wage I might have asked of you is yours; my reward is with Allah;[612] and He is a Witness of everything.'

قُلۡ مَا سَأَلۡتُكُم مِّنۡ أَجۡرٍ فَهُوَ لَكُمۡ إِنۡ أَجۡرِىَ إِلَّا عَلَى اللَّهِ وَهُوَ عَلَىٰ كُلِّ شَىۡءٍ شَهِيدٌ ﴿٤٧﴾

48. Say: 'My Lord hurls the Truth; the Knower of things hidden.'

قُلۡ إِنَّ رَبِّى يَقۡذِفُ بِالۡحَقِّ عَلَّٰمُ الۡغُيُوبِ ﴿٤٨﴾

49. Say: 'The Truth is come, and falsehood shall neither originate nor be restored.'

قُلۡ جَاۤءَ الۡحَقُّ وَمَا يُبۡدِئُ الۡبَٰطِلُ وَمَا يُعِيدُ ﴿٤٩﴾

50. Say: 'If ever I go astray, I shall stray only against myself; and if I remain guided it is because of what My Lord has revealed to me. Verily He is the Hearing, the Near.'

قُلۡ إِن ضَلَلۡتُ فَإِنَّمَاۤ أَضِلُّ عَلَىٰ نَفۡسِى وَإِنِ اهۡتَدَيۡتُ فَبِمَا يُوحِىٓ إِلَىَّ رَبِّىٓ إِنَّهُۥ سَمِيعٌ قَرِيبٌ ﴿٥٠﴾

51. Could you see the time when they shall be terrified. Then there shall be no escaping, and they shall be seized from a place quite near.

وَلَوۡ تَرَىٰٓ إِذۡ فَزِعُواْ فَلَا فَوۡتَ وَأُخِذُواْ مِن مَّكَانٍ قَرِيبٍ ﴿٥١﴾

---

612. The Qur'ān, first by appealing to the sanity of the Arabs, refuted the charge of mental weakness hurled against the Prophet, and now it proceeds to say that his claim to Prophethood is not due to any worldly gain either.

52. And then they will say: 'We believe in it.' But whence can there be the attainment of faith from a place so afar?

وَقَالُوٓاْ ءَامَنَّا بِهِۦ وَأَنَّىٰ لَهُمُ ٱلتَّنَاوُشُ مِن مَّكَانٍ بَعِيدٍ ۝

53. Whereas they disbelieved in it before, and conjectured about the Unseen from a place so afar.

وَقَدۡ كَفَرُواْ بِهِۦ مِن قَبۡلُ وَيَقۡذِفُونَ بِٱلۡغَيۡبِ مِن مَّكَانٍ بَعِيدٍ ۝

54. And they will be shut off from what they shall ardently desire, as shall be done with the likes of them of yore. Verily they have been in doubt perplexing.

وَحِيلَ بَيۡنَهُمۡ وَبَيۡنَ مَا يَشۡتَهُونَ كَمَا فُعِلَ بِأَشۡيَاعِهِم مِّن قَبۡلُ إِنَّهُمۡ كَانُواْ فِي شَكٍّ مُّرِيبٍ ۝

Sūrah 35

Fāṭir

(Makkan, 5 Sections, 45 Verses)

In the name of Allah, the Compassionate, the Merciful.

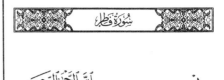

Section 1

1. All praise to Allah, the Creator of the heavens and the earth, the appointer of the angels as His Messengers with wings of twos and threes and fours. He adds in creation what He wills. Verily Allah is Potent over everything.

2. Whatsoever of mercy Allah may grant to mankind none there is to withhold it, and whatsoever He may withhold none there is to release it thereafter. And He is the Mighty, the Wise.

3. O mankind! Remember the favour of Allah towards you. Is there any creator other than Allah who provides for you from the heaven and the earth?[613] There is no god but He. Whither then are you deviating?

---

613. He is the Sole Creator and the Sole Preserver. Contrast with this the grossly polytheistic teaching of the NT. Speaking of Christ, 'the image of the invisible God, the firstborn of every creature', it says: 'By him were all things created, that are in heaven, and that are in earth, visible and invisible, whether they be thrones, or dominions, or principalities, or powers: all things were created by him, and for him' (Col. 1: 15, 16). And again: 'All things were made by him; and without him was not anything made that was made' (Jn. 1: 3). And yet again: 'To us there is one Lord,

Jesus Christ, by whom are all things, and we by him' (1 Cor. 8: 6). 'The profound and enduring impression which Jesus made upon His followers even constrained them to associate Him with the Father in the work of creation. It was He who had brought redemption from sin, and given them a glad new sense of sonship with God. But Lordship in the spiritual world must and did ultimately involve equal Lordship in the material world and in the whole realm of the Divine activity. This idea was early expressed by St. Paul confirmed a development which had been in progress for several decades, by which Jesus as the Son was definitely classed with God, the Father, and associated with Him in the creation and government of both the visible and invisible world' (*ERE.* IV. pp. 141 – 142).

4. And if they belie you, then Messengers have been belied before you, and to Allah shall be brought back all affairs.

وَإِن يُكَذِّبُوكَ فَقَدۡ كُذِّبَتۡ رُسُلٌ مِّن قَبۡلِكَ ۚ وَإِلَى ٱللَّهِ تُرۡجَعُ ٱلۡأُمُورُ ﴿٤﴾

5. O mankind! Verily the promise of Allah is true, so let not the life of this world beguile you, and with respect to Allah let not the great beguiler beguile you.

يَٰٓأَيُّهَا ٱلنَّاسُ إِنَّ وَعۡدَ ٱللَّهِ حَقٌّ ۖ فَلَا تَغُرَّنَّكُمُ ٱلۡحَيَوٰةُ ٱلدُّنۡيَا ۖ وَلَا يَغُرَّنَّكُم بِٱللَّهِ ٱلۡغَرُورُ ﴿٥﴾

6. Verily Satan is an enemy to you; so take him for an enemy, he only tempts his confederates that they become the inmates of the Blaze.

إِنَّ ٱلشَّيۡطَٰنَ لَكُمۡ عَدُوٌّ فَٱتَّخِذُوهُ عَدُوًّا ۚ إِنَّمَا يَدۡعُواْ حِزۡبَهُۥ لِيَكُونُواْ مِنۡ أَصۡحَٰبِ ٱلسَّعِيرِ ﴿٦﴾

7. Those who disbelieve, theirs shall be a severe torment. And those who believe and work righteous deeds, theirs shall be forgiveness and a great reward.

ٱلَّذِينَ كَفَرُواْ لَهُمۡ عَذَابٌ شَدِيدٌ ۖ وَٱلَّذِينَ ءَامَنُواْ وَعَمِلُواْ ٱلصَّٰلِحَٰتِ لَهُم مَّغۡفِرَةٌ وَأَجۡرٌ كَبِيرٌ ﴿٧﴾

Section 2

8. Can he whose evil work has been made fair-seeming to him, so that he considers it good be as he who rightly perceives the Truth? Verily Allah sends astray whom He will and guides whom He will, so let not your souls expire after them in sighings. Verily Allah is the Knower of what they perform.

أَفَمَن زُيِّنَ لَهُۥ سُوٓءُ عَمَلِهِۦ فَرَءَاهُ حَسَنًا ۖ فَإِنَّ ٱللَّهَ يُضِلُّ مَن يَشَآءُ وَيَهۡدِى مَن يَشَآءُ ۖ فَلَا تَذۡهَبۡ نَفۡسُكَ عَلَيۡهِمۡ حَسَرَٰتٍ ۚ إِنَّ ٱللَّهَ عَلِيمٌۢ بِمَا يَصۡنَعُونَ ﴿٨﴾

9. And it is Allah Who sends the winds, and they raise a cloud, and then We drive it into a dead land and We raise thereby the earth after its death. Even so shall be the Resurrection.

وَٱللَّهُ ٱلَّذِىٓ أَرْسَلَ ٱلرِّيَٰحَ فَتُثِيرُ سَحَابًا فَسُقْنَٰهُ إِلَىٰ بَلَدٍ مَّيِّتٍ فَأَحْيَيْنَا بِهِ ٱلْأَرْضَ بَعْدَ مَوْتِهَا ۚ كَذَٰلِكَ ٱلنُّشُورُ ﴿٩﴾

10. Whosoever desires glory, then all glory is Allah's; to Him mount up goodly words, and the righteous work exalts it. And those who plot evils, theirs shall be a severe torment, and the plotting of those! It shall perish.

مَن كَانَ يُرِيدُ ٱلْعِزَّةَ فَلِلَّهِ ٱلْعِزَّةُ جَمِيعًا ۚ إِلَيْهِ يَصْعَدُ ٱلْكَلِمُ ٱلطَّيِّبُ وَٱلْعَمَلُ ٱلصَّٰلِحُ يَرْفَعُهُۥ ۚ وَٱلَّذِينَ يَمْكُرُونَ ٱلسَّيِّئَاتِ لَهُمْ عَذَابٌ شَدِيدٌ ۖ وَمَكْرُ أُو۟لَٰٓئِكَ هُوَ يَبُورُ ﴿١٠﴾

11. And Allah created you of dust, then of seed; then He made you pairs, no female bears or brings forth but with His Knowledge.[614] And no aged man grows old, nor is aught diminished of his life, but it is in a Book; verily for Allah that is easy.

وَٱللَّهُ خَلَقَكُم مِّن تُرَابٍ ثُمَّ مِن نُّطْفَةٍ ثُمَّ جَعَلَكُمْ أَزْوَٰجًا ۚ وَمَا تَحْمِلُ مِنْ أُنثَىٰ وَلَا تَضَعُ إِلَّا بِعِلْمِهِۦ ۚ وَمَا يُعَمَّرُ مِن مُّعَمَّرٍ وَلَا يُنقَصُ مِنْ عُمُرِهِۦٓ إِلَّا فِى كِتَٰبٍ ۚ إِنَّ ذَٰلِكَ عَلَى ٱللَّهِ يَسِيرٌ ﴿١١﴾

12. And the two seas are not alike: this, sweet, thirst-quenching and pleasant to drink, and that, saltish and bitter. And yet from each you eat fresh flesh and bring forth the ornaments that you wear. And you see therein the ships cleaving water, that you may seek of His grace, and that haply you may give thanks.

وَمَا يَسْتَوِى ٱلْبَحْرَانِ هَٰذَا عَذْبٌ فُرَاتٌ سَآئِغٌ شَرَابُهُۥ وَهَٰذَا مِلْحٌ أُجَاجٌ ۖ وَمِن كُلٍّ تَأْكُلُونَ لَحْمًا طَرِيًّا وَتَسْتَخْرِجُونَ حِلْيَةً تَلْبَسُونَهَا ۖ وَتَرَى ٱلْفُلْكَ فِيهِ مَوَاخِرَ لِتَبْتَغُوا۟ مِن فَضْلِهِۦ وَلَعَلَّكُمْ تَشْكُرُونَ ﴿١٢﴾

---

614. He is Omniscient, and He knows every event beforehand; unlike the heathen gods of very limited and partial knowledge.

13. He plunges the night into the day and plunges the day into the night; and He has subjected the sun and moon, each running till an appointed term. Such is Allah, your Lord; His is the dominion; and those whom you call upon beside Him do not own even the husk of a date-stone.

يُوْلِجُ الَّيْلَ فِى النَّهَارِ وَيُوْلِجُ النَّهَارَ فِى الَّيْلِ وَسَخَّرَ الشَّمْسَ وَالْقَمَرَ كُلٌّ يَجْرِىْ لِأَجَلٍ مُّسَمًّى ذٰلِكُمُ اللّٰهُ رَبُّكُمْ لَهُ الْمُلْكُ وَالَّذِيْنَ تَدْعُوْنَ مِنْ دُوْنِهٖ مَا يَمْلِكُوْنَ مِنْ قِطْمِيْرٍ ۝

14. If you call unto them, they hear not your calling, and even if they heard they could not answer you. On the Day of Judgement they will deny your associating. And none can declare to you the truth like Him Who is Aware.

إِنْ تَدْعُوْهُمْ لَا يَسْمَعُوْا دُعَاءَكُمْ وَلَوْ سَمِعُوْا مَا اسْتَجَابُوْا لَكُمْ وَيَوْمَ الْقِيٰمَةِ يَكْفُرُوْنَ بِشِرْكِكُمْ وَلَا يُنَبِّئُكَ مِثْلُ خَبِيْرٍ ۝

Section 3

15. O mankind! You are the ones that stand in need of Allah, and Allah! He is the Self-Sufficient, the Praiseworthy.

يٰأَيُّهَا النَّاسُ أَنْتُمُ الْفُقَرَاءُ إِلَى اللّٰهِ وَاللّٰهُ هُوَ الْغَنِيُّ الْحَمِيْدُ ۝

16. If He will, He can take you away, and bring about a new creation.

إِنْ يَشَأْ يُذْهِبْكُمْ وَيَأْتِ بِخَلْقٍ جَدِيْدٍ ۝

17. And with Allah that shall not be hard.

وَمَا ذٰلِكَ عَلَى اللّٰهِ بِعَزِيْزٍ ۝

18. And no bearer of a burden shall bear another's burden, and if one heavy laden calls for his load nothing of it shall be borne, although he be of kin. You can warn only those who fear their Lord, Unseen, and establish prayer. And whosoever becomes clean, becomes clean only for himself; and to Allah is the return.

وَلَا تَزِرُ وَازِرَةٌ وِزْرَ أُخْرٰى وَإِنْ تَدْعُ مُثْقَلَةٌ إِلَى حِمْلِهَا لَا يُحْمَلْ مِنْهُ شَيْءٌ وَلَوْ كَانَ ذَا قُرْبٰى إِنَّمَا تُنْذِرُ الَّذِيْنَ يَخْشَوْنَ رَبَّهُمْ بِالْغَيْبِ وَأَقَامُوا الصَّلٰوةَ وَمَنْ تَزَكّٰى فَإِنَّمَا يَتَزَكّٰى لِنَفْسِهٖ وَإِلَى اللّٰهِ الْمَصِيْرُ ۝

19. No alike are the blind and the seeing,

وَمَا يَسۡتَوِى ٱلۡأَعۡمَىٰ وَٱلۡبَصِيرُ ﴿١٩﴾

20. Neither darkness and light,

وَلَا ٱلظُّلُمَٰتُ وَلَا ٱلنُّورُ ﴿٢٠﴾

21. Nor the shade and the sun's heat.

وَلَا ٱلظِّلُّ وَلَا ٱلۡحَرُورُ ﴿٢١﴾

22. Nor alike are the living and the dead. Verily Allah makes whosoever He will, to hear and you can not make them hear who are in the graves.

وَمَا يَسۡتَوِى ٱلۡأَحۡيَآءُ وَلَا ٱلۡأَمۡوَٰتُ إِنَّ ٱللَّهَ يُسۡمِعُ مَن يَشَآءُ وَمَآ أَنتَ بِمُسۡمِعٖ مَّن فِى ٱلۡقُبُورِ ﴿٢٢﴾

23. You are but a warner.

إِنۡ أَنتَ إِلَّا نَذِيرٌ ﴿٢٣﴾

24. Verily We! We have sent you with the Truth, as a bearer of glad tidings and as a warner; and there is not a community but there has passed away among them of a warner.

إِنَّآ أَرۡسَلۡنَٰكَ بِٱلۡحَقِّ بَشِيرٗا وَنَذِيرٗا وَإِن مِّنۡ أُمَّةٍ إِلَّا خَلَا فِيهَا نَذِيرٌ ﴿٢٤﴾

25. And if they belie you, then surely those before them have also belied. Their Messengers came to them with evidence and Scriptures and a luminous Book.

وَإِن يُكَذِّبُوكَ فَقَدۡ كَذَّبَ ٱلَّذِينَ مِن قَبۡلِهِمۡ جَآءَتۡهُمۡ رُسُلُهُم بِٱلۡبَيِّنَٰتِ وَبِٱلزُّبُرِ وَبِٱلۡكِتَٰبِ ٱلۡمُنِيرِ ﴿٢٥﴾

26. Then I took hold of those who disbelieved. So how terrible was My disapproval!

ثُمَّ أَخَذۡتُ ٱلَّذِينَ كَفَرُواْ فَكَيۡفَ كَانَ نَكِيرِ ﴿٢٦﴾

Section 4

27. Do you not see that Allah sends down water from the sky, and then We thereby bring fruit of diverse hues? And in the mountains are streaks white and red, of diverse hues, and also intensely black.

أَلَمۡ تَرَ أَنَّ ٱللَّهَ أَنزَلَ مِنَ ٱلسَّمَآءِ مَآءٗ فَأَخۡرَجۡنَا بِهِۦ ثَمَرَٰتٖ مُّخۡتَلِفًا أَلۡوَٰنُهَا وَمِنَ ٱلۡجِبَالِ جُدَدُۢ بِيضٞ وَحُمۡرٞ مُّخۡتَلِفٌ أَلۡوَٰنُهَا وَغَرَابِيبُ سُودٌ ﴿٢٧﴾

28. And of men and beasts and cattle, likewise of diverse colours. Those of His bondsmen fear Allah who have knowledge. Verily, Allah is the Mighty, the Forgiving.

وَمِنَ ٱلنَّاسِ وَٱلدَّوَآبِّ وَٱلْأَنْعَمِ مُخْتَلِفٌ أَلْوَٰنُهُ كَذَٰلِكَ إِنَّمَا يَخْشَى ٱللَّهَ مِنْ عِبَادِهِ ٱلْعُلَمَٰٓؤُاْ إِنَّ ٱللَّهَ عَزِيزٌ غَفُورٌ ﴿٢٨﴾

29. Verily those who read the Book of Allah and establish prayer and expend of that with which We have provided them, secretly and in open, look for a commerce that will not perish,

إِنَّ ٱلَّذِينَ يَتْلُونَ كِتَٰبَ ٱللَّهِ وَأَقَامُواْ ٱلصَّلَوٰةَ وَأَنفَقُواْ مِمَّا رَزَقْنَٰهُمْ سِرًّا وَعَلَانِيَةً يَرْجُونَ تِجَٰرَةً لَّن تَبُورَ ﴿٢٩﴾

30. That He may pay them their reward in full and increase to them of His grace; surely He is the Forgiving, the Appreciative.

لِيُوَفِّيَهُمْ أُجُورَهُمْ وَيَزِيدَهُم مِّن فَضْلِهِ إِنَّهُ غَفُورٌ شَكُورٌ ﴿٣٠﴾

31. And what We have revealed to you of the Book it is the very Truth confirming what has been before it. Verily Allah is unto His bondsmen the Aware, the Beholder.

وَٱلَّذِىٓ أَوْحَيْنَآ إِلَيْكَ مِنَ ٱلْكِتَٰبِ هُوَ ٱلْحَقُّ مُصَدِّقًا لِّمَا بَيْنَ يَدَيْهِ إِنَّ ٱللَّهَ بِعِبَادِهِ لَخَبِيرٌ بَصِيرٌ ﴿٣١﴾

32. Afterwards We made those We chose of Our bondsmen the inheritors of the Book. Then of them are some who wrong themselves, and of them are some who keep the middle way, and of them are some who go ahead, by Allah's leave, in virtues. That! That is indeed a great grace.

ثُمَّ أَوْرَثْنَا ٱلْكِتَٰبَ ٱلَّذِينَ ٱصْطَفَيْنَا مِنْ عِبَادِنَا فَمِنْهُمْ ظَالِمٌ لِّنَفْسِهِ وَمِنْهُم مُّقْتَصِدٌ وَمِنْهُمْ سَابِقٌ بِٱلْخَيْرَٰتِ بِإِذْنِ ٱللَّهِ ذَٰلِكَ هُوَ ٱلْفَضْلُ ٱلْكَبِيرُ ﴿٣٢﴾

33. Gardens everlasting! These they shall enter wearing therein bracelets of gold and pearls, and their apparel therein shall be of silk.

جَنَّٰتُ عَدْنٍ يَدْخُلُونَهَا يُحَلَّوْنَ فِيهَا مِنْ أَسَاوِرَ مِن ذَهَبٍ وَلُؤْلُؤًا وَلِبَاسُهُمْ فِيهَا حَرِيرٌ ﴿٣٣﴾

34. And they will say; all praise to Allah Who has taken away grief from us, verily Our Lord is the Forgiving, the Appreciative.

وَقَالُوا۟ ٱلْحَمْدُ لِلَّهِ ٱلَّذِىٓ أَذْهَبَ عَنَّا ٱلْحَزَنَ إِنَّ رَبَّنَا لَغَفُورٌ شَكُورٌ ﴿٣٤﴾

35. Who has through His grace, lodged us in the everlasting abode, wherein there will not touch us toil and wherein there will not touch us weariness.

ٱلَّذِىٓ أَحَلَّنَا دَارَ ٱلْمُقَامَةِ مِن فَضْلِهِۦ لَا يَمَسُّنَا فِيهَا نَصَبٌ وَلَا يَمَسُّنَا فِيهَا لُغُوبٌ ﴿٣٥﴾

36. And those who disbelieve, for them shall be the Fire. It shall not be decreed to them that they should die, nor shall its torment be lightened for them. Thus do We requite every ungrateful person.

وَٱلَّذِينَ كَفَرُوا۟ لَهُمْ نَارُ جَهَنَّمَ لَا يُقْضَىٰ عَلَيْهِمْ فَيَمُوتُوا۟ وَلَا يُخَفَّفُ عَنْهُم مِّنْ عَذَابِهَا كَذَٰلِكَ نَجْزِى كُلَّ كَفُورٍ ﴿٣٦﴾

37. And they shall be shouting therein: 'Our Lord! Take us out; we will work righteously, not what we have been working.' Did We not give you lives long enough so that whosoever would receive admonition could receive it therein? And there came to you a warner; taste therefore. And for the ungodly there will be no helper.

وَهُمْ يَصْطَرِخُونَ فِيهَا رَبَّنَآ أَخْرِجْنَا نَعْمَلْ صَٰلِحًا غَيْرَ ٱلَّذِى كُنَّا نَعْمَلُ أَوَلَمْ نُعَمِّرْكُم مَّا يَتَذَكَّرُ فِيهِ مَن تَذَكَّرَ وَجَآءَكُمُ ٱلنَّذِيرُ فَذُوقُوا۟ فَمَا لِلظَّٰلِمِينَ مِن نَّصِيرٍ ﴿٣٧﴾

Section 5

38. Verily Allah is the Knower of the Unseen of the heavens and the earth. Verily He is the Knower of what is in the breasts.

إِنَّ ٱللَّهَ عَٰلِمُ غَيْبِ ٱلسَّمَٰوَٰتِ وَٱلْأَرْضِ إِنَّهُۥ عَلِيمٌۢ بِذَاتِ ٱلصُّدُورِ ﴿٣٨﴾

39. He it is Who had made you successors in the earth. So whosoever disbelieves, on him will befall his infidelity. And for the infidels their infidelity increases naught with their Lord save abhorrence. And for the infidels their infidelity increases nothing save loss.

هُوَ ٱلَّذِى جَعَلَكُمْ خَلَـٰٓئِفَ فِى ٱلْأَرْضِ فَمَن كَفَرَ فَعَلَيْهِ كُفْرُهُۥ وَلَا يَزِيدُ ٱلْكَـٰفِرِينَ كُفْرُهُمْ عِندَ رَبِّهِمْ إِلَّا مَقْتًا وَلَا يَزِيدُ ٱلْكَـٰفِرِينَ كُفْرُهُمْ إِلَّا خَسَارًا ﴿٣٩﴾

40. Say: 'What do you consider of your associate gods upon which you call besides Allah? Show me whatsoever they have created of the earth. Or, have they any partnership in the heavens? Or, have We vouchsafed to them a Book so that they stand upon an evidence from it? Nay! The ungodly promise to each other only delusions.'615

قُلْ أَرَءَيْتُمْ شُرَكَآءَكُمُ ٱلَّذِينَ تَدْعُونَ مِن دُونِ ٱللَّهِ أَرُونِى مَاذَا خَلَقُوا مِنَ ٱلْأَرْضِ أَمْ لَهُمْ شِرْكٌ فِى ٱلسَّمَـٰوَٰتِ أَمْ ءَاتَيْنَـٰهُمْ كِتَـٰبًا فَهُمْ عَلَىٰ بَيِّنَتٍ مِّنْهُ بَلْ إِن يَعِدُ ٱلظَّـٰلِمُونَ بَعْضُهُم بَعْضًا إِلَّا غُرُورًا ﴿٤٠﴾

41. Verily Allah withholds the heavens and the earth lest they cease;616 and should they cease, not anyone could withhold them after Him. Verily He is ever Forbearing, Forgiving.

إِنَّ ٱللَّهَ يُمْسِكُ ٱلسَّمَـٰوَٰتِ وَٱلْأَرْضَ أَن تَزُولَا وَلَئِن زَالَتَا إِنْ أَمْسَكَهُمَا مِنْ أَحَدٍ مِّنۢ بَعْدِهِۦٓ إِنَّهُۥ كَانَ حَلِيمًا غَفُورًا ﴿٤١﴾

---

615. The purport is: the 'traditional' religion of polytheism has no basis whatsoever either in reason or in the Scriptures.

616. Lest they cease to function. God is not only the Creator or Originator of the universe but also its constant Regulator, Sustainer, and Preserver.

42. And they swore by Allah with a most solemn oath, that if there came a warner unto them, they would surely be better guided than any of the other communities. Then when there did come to them a warner, it increased in them nothing save aversion,

وَأَقْسَمُوا۟ بِٱللَّهِ جَهْدَ أَيْمَٰنِهِمْ لَئِن جَآءَهُمْ نَذِيرٌ لَّيَكُونُنَّ أَهْدَىٰ مِنْ إِحْدَى ٱلْأُمَمِ فَلَمَّا جَآءَهُمْ نَذِيرٌ مَّا زَادَهُمْ إِلَّا نُفُورًا ﴿٤٢﴾

43. Through their stiff-neckedness in the land and their plotting of evil. And the plotting of evil only enfolds its author. Do they then wait only the dispensation of the ancients? And you will not find in the dispensation of Allah a change, nor will you find in the dispensation of Allah a turning off.

ٱسْتِكْبَارًا فِى ٱلْأَرْضِ وَمَكْرَ ٱلسَّيِّئِ وَلَا يَحِيقُ ٱلْمَكْرُ ٱلسَّيِّئُ إِلَّا بِأَهْلِهِ فَهَلْ يَنظُرُونَ إِلَّا سُنَّتَ ٱلْأَوَّلِينَ فَلَن تَجِدَ لِسُنَّتِ ٱللَّهِ تَبْدِيلًا وَلَن تَجِدَ لِسُنَّتِ ٱللَّهِ تَحْوِيلًا ﴿٤٣﴾

44. Have they not journeyed on the earth, so that they might see how has been the end of those before them, although they were stronger in power than these? Allah is not such that nothing in the heavens and the earth can frustrate Him. Verily, He is ever Knowing, Potent.

أَوَلَمْ يَسِيرُوا۟ فِى ٱلْأَرْضِ فَيَنظُرُوا۟ كَيْفَ كَانَ عَٰقِبَةُ ٱلَّذِينَ مِن قَبْلِهِمْ وَكَانُوٓا۟ أَشَدَّ مِنْهُمْ قُوَّةً وَمَا كَانَ ٱللَّهُ لِيُعْجِزَهُۥ مِن شَىْءٍ فِى ٱلسَّمَٰوَٰتِ وَلَا فِى ٱلْأَرْضِ إِنَّهُۥ كَانَ عَلِيمًا قَدِيرًا ﴿٤٤﴾

45. Were Allah to take mankind to task for what they earn, He would not leave a moving creature on its back;[617] but He puts them off till a term assigned, then when that term arrives then, verily, Allah is ever a Beholder of His bondsmen.

وَلَوْ يُؤَاخِذُ اللّٰهُ النَّاسَ بِمَا كَسَبُوا مَا تَرَكَ عَلَى ظَهْرِهَا مِن دَآبَّةٍ وَلَـٰكِن يُؤَخِّرُهُمْ إِلَىٰ أَجَلٍ مُّسَمًّى فَإِذَا جَآءَ أَجَلُهُمْ فَإِنَّ اللّٰهَ كَانَ بِعِبَادِهِ بَصِيرًا ۝

---

617. Even the believers would then have been removed, for in the universal scheme of God, there is no meaning in populating the world with the obedient alone. The world, as it is constituted, demands that good, without its counterpart evil, should have no sense.

Sūrah 36

Yā Sīn

(Makkan, 5 Sections, 83 Verses)

*In the name of Allah, the
Compassionate, the Merciful.*

Section 1

1.　*Yā, Sīn.*[618]

2.　By the Qur'ān, full of wisdom.

3.　Verily you are of the sent ones,

4.　Upon the straight path.

5.　This is a revelation of the
Mighty, the Merciful,

6.　That you may warn a people
whose fathers were not warned,
so they are neglectful.

7.　Assuredly the word has been
justified against most of them, so
they shall not believe.

8.　Surely We have placed on
their necks shackles which are up
to the chins; so that their heads are
forced up.

---

618. This Chapter is regarded with special reverence by the faithful, and is usually
recited loudly on the approach of death.

9. And We have placed before them a barrier and behind them a barrier, so We have covered them; so that they do not see.[619]

وَجَعَلْنَا مِنْ بَيْنِ أَيْدِيهِمْ سَدًّا وَمِنْ خَلْفِهِمْ سَدًّا فَأَغْشَيْنَاهُمْ فَهُمْ لَا يُبْصِرُونَ ۝

10. It is alike to them, whether you warn them or warn them not; they will never have faith.

وَسَوَآءٌ عَلَيْهِمْ ءَأَنذَرْتَهُمْ أَمْ لَمْ تُنذِرْهُمْ لَا يُؤْمِنُونَ ۝

11. You can warn him only who follows the admonition and fears the Compassionate, Unseen. Bear you to him the glad tidings of forgiveness and a generous reward.

إِنَّمَا تُنذِرُ مَنِ ٱتَّبَعَ ٱلذِّكْرَ وَخَشِيَ ٱلرَّحْمَٰنَ بِٱلْغَيْبِ فَبَشِّرْهُ بِمَغْفِرَةٍ وَأَجْرٍ كَرِيمٍ ۝

12. Verily We! We shall raise the dead; and We write down what they have forwarded and what they have left behind. And everything We have counted up in a luminous record.

إِنَّا نَحْنُ نُحْيِ ٱلْمَوْتَىٰ وَنَكْتُبُ مَا قَدَّمُوا وَءَاثَارَهُمْ وَكُلَّ شَىْءٍ أَحْصَيْنَاهُ فِىٓ إِمَامٍ مُّبِينٍ ۝

Section 2

13. And recount you to them the similitude of the residents of a town, when there came thereto the sent ones.

وَٱضْرِبْ لَهُم مَّثَلًا أَصْحَابَ ٱلْقَرْيَةِ إِذْ جَآءَهَا ٱلْمُرْسَلُونَ ۝

14. When We sent to them two. Then they belied the two; so We strengthened them with a third, and they said: 'We are envoys unto you.'

إِذْ أَرْسَلْنَآ إِلَيْهِمُ ٱثْنَيْنِ فَكَذَّبُوهُمَا فَعَزَّزْنَا بِثَالِثٍ فَقَالُوٓا إِنَّآ إِلَيْكُم مُّرْسَلُونَ ۝

---

619. The whole passage is a vivid description of utter blindness and unshakeable obstinacy on the part of the perverse and willful opponents of Truth and Light.

15. They said: 'You are but human beings like ourselves. The Compassionate has not sent down aught, you are only lying.'

قَالُوا مَا أَنتُمْ إِلَّا بَشَرٌ مِّثْلُنَا وَمَا أَنزَلَ الرَّحْمَٰنُ مِن شَيْءٍ إِنْ أَنتُمْ إِلَّا تَكْذِبُونَ ﴿١٥﴾

16. The envoys said: 'Our Lord knows that surely we are envoys to you.

قَالُوا رَبُّنَا يَعْلَمُ إِنَّا إِلَيْكُمْ لَمُرْسَلُونَ ﴿١٦﴾

17. And on us is nothing but manifest preaching.'

وَمَا عَلَيْنَا إِلَّا الْبَلَٰغُ الْمُبِينُ ﴿١٧﴾

18. They said: 'Surely we augur ill of you; and if you do not desist, we shall certainly stone you, and there will befall you from us an afflictive chastisement.'

قَالُوا إِنَّا تَطَيَّرْنَا بِكُمْ لَئِن لَّمْ تَنتَهُوا لَنَرْجُمَنَّكُمْ وَلَيَمَسَّنَّكُم مِّنَّا عَذَابٌ أَلِيمٌ ﴿١٨﴾

19. The envoys said: 'Evil augury be with you. What! Do you call it ill luck because you are admonished? Aye! You are a people extravagant.'

قَالُوا طَائِرُكُم مَّعَكُمْ أَئِن ذُكِّرْتُم بَلْ أَنتُمْ قَوْمٌ مُّسْرِفُونَ ﴿١٩﴾

20. And there came a man running from the end of the town. He said: 'My people, follow the envoys.

وَجَاءَ مِنْ أَقْصَا الْمَدِينَةِ رَجُلٌ يَسْعَىٰ قَالَ يَٰقَوْمِ اتَّبِعُوا الْمُرْسَلِينَ ﴿٢٠﴾

21. Follow those who do not ask any wage of you, and who are the guided ones.

اتَّبِعُوا مَن لَّا يَسْأَلُكُمْ أَجْرًا وَهُم مُّهْتَدُونَ ﴿٢١﴾

22. And why should I not worship Him alone Who has originated me, and to whom you shall be returned?

وَمَا لِيَ لَا أَعْبُدُ الَّذِي فَطَرَنِي وَإِلَيْهِ تُرْجَعُونَ ﴿٢٢﴾

23. Shall I take, besides Him gods when, if the Compassionate intends me any harm, their intercession will not avail me at all, nor would they save me?

أَأَتَّخِذُ مِن دُونِهِ آلِهَةً إِن يُرِدْنِ الرَّحْمَٰنُ بِضُرٍّ لَّا تُغْنِ عَنِّي شَفَٰعَتُهُمْ شَيْئًا وَلَا يُنقِذُونِ ﴿٢٣﴾

24. Verily then I should be in clear error.

إِنِّىٓ إِذًا لَّفِى ضَلَلٍ مُّبِينٍ ۝

25. Verily now I believe in your Lord, so listen to me.'

إِنِّىٓ ءَامَنتُ بِرَبِّكُمْ فَٱسْمَعُونِ ۝

26. It was said: 'Enter you the Garden.' He said: 'Would that my people knew.

قِيلَ ٱدْخُلِ ٱلْجَنَّةَ قَالَ يَٰلَيْتَ قَوْمِى يَعْلَمُونَ ۝

27. That my Lord has forgiven me, and has made me of the honoured ones.'

بِمَا غَفَرَ لِى رَبِّى وَجَعَلَنِى مِنَ ٱلْمُكْرَمِينَ ۝

28. And We sent not against his people after him, a host from heaven, and We have not been sending down any such.

وَمَآ أَنزَلْنَا عَلَىٰ قَوْمِهِۦ مِنۢ بَعْدِهِۦ مِن جُندٍ مِّنَ ٱلسَّمَآءِ وَمَا كُنَّا مُنزِلِينَ ۝

29. It was but one shout, and lo! They were extinct.

إِن كَانَتْ إِلَّا صَيْحَةً وَٰحِدَةً فَإِذَا هُمْ خَٰمِدُونَ ۝

30. Ah the misery of Our bondsmen! There comes not to them any Messenger of Ours but him they have been mocking.

يَٰحَسْرَةً عَلَى ٱلْعِبَادِ مَا يَأْتِيهِم مِّن رَّسُولٍ إِلَّا كَانُوا۟ بِهِۦ يَسْتَهْزِءُونَ ۝

31. Do they not see how many of the generations before them We have destroyed? Surely to them they shall not return.

أَلَمْ يَرَوْا۟ كَمْ أَهْلَكْنَا قَبْلَهُم مِّنَ ٱلْقُرُونِ أَنَّهُمْ إِلَيْهِمْ لَا يَرْجِعُونَ ۝

32. And surely all, everyone of them, shall be brought to Us.

وَإِن كُلٌّ لَّمَّا جَمِيعٌ لَّدَيْنَا مُحْضَرُونَ ۝

Section 3

33. And a sign unto them is dead land. We revive it and thereout We bring forth grain, so that they eat of it.

وَءَايَةٌ لَّهُمُ ٱلْأَرْضُ ٱلْمَيْتَةُ أَحْيَيْنَٰهَا وَأَخْرَجْنَا مِنْهَا حَبًّا فَمِنْهُ يَأْكُلُونَ ۝

34. And We place therein the gardens of date-palms and vines, and therein We cause springs to gush forth,

وَجَعَلْنَا فِيهَا جَنّٰتٍ مِّن نَّخِيلٍ وَأَعْنَابٍ وَفَجَّرْنَا فِيهَا مِنَ الْعُيُونِ ﴿٣٤﴾

35. That they may eat the fruit thereof, and their hands worked it not. Will they not, therefore, give thanks?

لِيَأْكُلُوا مِن ثَمَرِهِ وَمَا عَمِلَتْهُ أَيْدِيهِمْ أَفَلَا يَشْكُرُونَ ﴿٣٥﴾

36. Hallowed be He, Who has created all the pairs[620] of what the earth grows and of themselves, and of what they know not.

سُبْحَانَ الَّذِي خَلَقَ الْأَزْوَاجَ كُلَّهَا مِمَّا تُنبِتُ الْأَرْضُ وَمِنْ أَنفُسِهِمْ وَمِمَّا لَا يَعْلَمُونَ ﴿٣٦﴾

37. And a sign with them is night, We draw off the day therefrom, and lo! They are darkened.

وَءَايَةٌ لَّهُمُ الَّيْلُ نَسْلَخُ مِنْهُ النَّهَارَ فَإِذَا هُم مُّظْلِمُونَ ﴿٣٧﴾

38. And the sun runs to its assigned term; that is the disposition of the Mighty, the Knowing.

وَالشَّمْسُ تَجْرِي لِمُسْتَقَرٍّ لَّهَا ذَلِكَ تَقْدِيرُ الْعَزِيزِ الْعَلِيمِ ﴿٣٨﴾

39. And the moon! For it We have decreed mansions till it reverts like the old branch of a palm tree.

وَالْقَمَرَ قَدَّرْنَاهُ مَنَازِلَ حَتَّى عَادَ كَالْعُرْجُونِ الْقَدِيمِ ﴿٣٩﴾

40. It is not permitted to the sun to overtake the moon, nor can the night outstrip the day, each in an orbit, they float.

لَا الشَّمْسُ يَنبَغِي لَهَا أَن تُدْرِكَ الْقَمَرَ وَلَا الَّيْلُ سَابِقُ النَّهَارِ وَكُلٌّ فِي فَلَكٍ يَسْبَحُونَ ﴿٤٠﴾

41. And a sign unto them is that We bear their off-spring in a laden ship.

وَءَايَةٌ لَّهُمْ أَنَّا حَمَلْنَا ذُرِّيَّتَهُمْ فِي الْفُلْكِ الْمَشْحُونِ ﴿٤١﴾

---

620. One of the recent scientific discoveries is that everything in nature exists in pairs as male and female. Not only does this pertain to vegetable and animal life but even rock crystals and electricity have their sets of opposites.

42. And We have created for them of the like there unto. So on them they ride.

وَخَلَقۡنَا لَهُمۡ مِّن مِّثۡلِهٖ مَا يَرۡكَبُونَ ﴿٤٢﴾

43. And if We will, We shall drown them, and there will be no shout for them, nor will they be saved,

وَإِن نَّشَأۡ نُغۡرِقۡهُمۡ فَلَا صَرِيخَ لَهُمۡ وَلَا هُمۡ يُنقَذُونَ ﴿٤٣﴾

44. Unless it be a mercy from Us, and as an enjoyment for a season.

إِلَّا رَحۡمَةً مِّنَّا وَمَتَٰعًا إِلَىٰ حِينٍ ﴿٤٤﴾

45. And when it is said to them: 'Fear what is before you and what is behind you, that perchance you may find mercy,' they withdraw.

وَإِذَا قِيلَ لَهُمُ ٱتَّقُواۡ مَا بَيۡنَ أَيۡدِيكُمۡ وَمَا خَلۡفَكُمۡ لَعَلَّكُمۡ تُرۡحَمُونَ ﴿٤٥﴾

46. And not a sign of the signs of their Lord comes to them, but they are backsliders therefrom.

وَمَا تَأۡتِيهِم مِّنۡ ءَايَةٍ مِّنۡ ءَايَٰتِ رَبِّهِمۡ إِلَّا كَانُواۡ عَنۡهَا مُعۡرِضِينَ ﴿٤٦﴾

47. And when it is said to them: 'Expend of that with which Allah has provided you, those who disbelieve say to the faithful; shall we feed those whom Allah Himself would have fed, had He willed? You are but in manifest error.'

وَإِذَا قِيلَ لَهُمۡ أَنفِقُواۡ مِمَّا رَزَقَكُمُ ٱللَّهُ قَالَ ٱلَّذِينَ كَفَرُواۡ لِلَّذِينَ ءَامَنُواۡ أَنُطۡعِمُ مَن لَّوۡ يَشَآءُ ٱللَّهُ أَطۡعَمَهُۥ إِنۡ أَنتُمۡ إِلَّا فِي ضَلَٰلٍ مُّبِينٍ ﴿٤٧﴾

48. And they say: 'When will the promise be fulfilled, if you speak truth?'

وَيَقُولُونَ مَتَىٰ هَٰذَا ٱلۡوَعۡدُ إِن كُنتُمۡ صَٰدِقِينَ ﴿٤٨﴾

49. They await not but a single shout which shall seize them while they are yet wrangling.

مَا يَنظُرُونَ إِلَّا صَيۡحَةً وَٰحِدَةً تَأۡخُذُهُمۡ وَهُمۡ يَخِصِّمُونَ ﴿٤٩﴾

50. And they will not be able to make a disposition, nor to their family will they return.

فَلَا يَسۡتَطِيعُونَ تَوۡصِيَةً وَلَا إِلَىٰ أَهۡلِهِمۡ يَرۡجِعُونَ ﴿٥٠﴾

Section 4

51.   And the Trumpet will be blown, and lo! From their tombs they shall be hastening to their Lord.

وَنُفِخَ فِى ٱلصُّورِ فَإِذَا هُم مِّنَ ٱلۡأَجۡدَاثِ إِلَىٰ رَبِّهِمۡ يَنسِلُونَ ۝

52.   They will say: 'Ah woe to us! Who has roused us from our sleeping-place?' This is what the Compassionate had promised, and truly spake the sent ones.

قَالُوا۟ يَٰوَيۡلَنَا مَنۢ بَعَثَنَا مِن مَّرۡقَدِنَاۗ هَٰذَا مَا وَعَدَ ٱلرَّحۡمَٰنُ وَصَدَقَ ٱلۡمُرۡسَلُونَ ۝

53.   It shall be but one shout; and lo! They shall all be brought together before Us.[621]

إِن كَانَتۡ إِلَّا صَيۡحَةً وَٰحِدَةً فَإِذَا هُمۡ جَمِيعٌ لَّدَيۡنَا مُحۡضَرُونَ ۝

54.   Today no soul shall be wronged at all; nor shall you be requited but for what you have been doing.

فَٱلۡيَوۡمَ لَا تُظۡلَمُ نَفۡسٌ شَيۡـًٔا وَلَا تُجۡزَوۡنَ إِلَّا مَا كُنتُمۡ تَعۡمَلُونَ ۝

55.   Verily the dwellers of the Garden today shall be happily employed.

إِنَّ أَصۡحَٰبَ ٱلۡجَنَّةِ ٱلۡيَوۡمَ فِى شُغُلٍ فَٰكِهُونَ ۝

56.   They and their mates shall be reclining on couches in shade.

هُمۡ وَأَزۡوَٰجُهُمۡ فِى ظِلَٰلٍ عَلَى ٱلۡأَرَآئِكِ مُتَّكِـُٔونَ ۝

57.   Theirs shall be fruit therein, and theirs shall be whatsoever they ask for.

لَهُمۡ فِيهَا فَٰكِهَةٌ وَلَهُم مَّا يَدَّعُونَ ۝

58.   Peace shall be the word from the Lord Merciful.

سَلَٰمٌ قَوۡلًا مِّن رَّبٍّ رَّحِيمٍ ۝

59.   And separate yourselves, this Day, O you culprits!

وَٱمۡتَٰزُوا۟ ٱلۡيَوۡمَ أَيُّهَا ٱلۡمُجۡرِمُونَ ۝

---

621. So that no merit shall go unawarded, nor shall any penalty be exacted unmerited.

60. Children of Adam! Did I not enjoin you, that you shall not serve Satan; verily he is your manifest foe?

أَلَمۡ أَعۡهَدۡ إِلَيۡكُمۡ يَٰبَنِيۤ ءَادَمَ أَن لَّا تَعۡبُدُوا۟ الشَّيۡطَٰنَ إِنَّهُۥ لَكُمۡ عَدُوٌّ مُّبِينٌ ۝

61. And that, you shall worship Me! This is the straight path.

وَأَنِ اعۡبُدُونِي هَٰذَا صِرَٰطٌ مُّسۡتَقِيمٌ ۝

62. And yet he has assuredly led astray a great multitude of you. Why do you not reflect?

وَلَقَدۡ أَضَلَّ مِنكُمۡ جِبِلًّا كَثِيرًا أَفَلَمۡ تَكُونُوا۟ تَعۡقِلُونَ ۝

63. There is Hell which you were promised.

هَٰذِهِۦ جَهَنَّمُ الَّتِي كُنتُمۡ تُوعَدُونَ ۝

64. Roast therein today for that you have been disbelieving.

اصۡلَوۡهَا الۡيَوۡمَ بِمَا كُنتُمۡ تَكۡفُرُونَ ۝

65. Today We will seal up their mouths, and their hands shall speak to Us and their feet shall bear witness to what they have been earning.

الۡيَوۡمَ نَخۡتِمُ عَلَىٰٓ أَفۡوَٰهِهِمۡ وَتُكَلِّمُنَآ أَيۡدِيهِمۡ وَتَشۡهَدُ أَرۡجُلُهُم بِمَا كَانُوا۟ يَكۡسِبُونَ ۝

66. And if We willed. We would surely wipe out their eyes so that they would struggle for the way; how then would they see?

وَلَوۡ نَشَآءُ لَطَمَسۡنَا عَلَىٰٓ أَعۡيُنِهِمۡ فَاسۡتَبَقُوا۟ الصِّرَٰطَ فَأَنَّىٰ يُبۡصِرُونَ ۝

67. And if We willed, We would surely transform them in their places, so that they would be able neither to go forward nor to return.

وَلَوۡ نَشَآءُ لَمَسَخۡنَٰهُمۡ عَلَىٰ مَكَانَتِهِمۡ فَمَا اسۡتَطَٰعُوا۟ مُضِيًّا وَلَا يَرۡجِعُونَ ۝

Section 5

68. And to whom We grant long life, We reverse him in creation; why do then they not reflect?

وَمَن نُّعَمِّرۡهُ نُنَكِّسۡهُ فِي الۡخَلۡقِ أَفَلَا يَعۡقِلُونَ ۝

69. And We have not taught him poetry, nor does it become him.[622] This is but an admonition and a luminous recital.

وَمَا عَلَّمۡنٰهُ الشِّعۡرَ وَمَا یَنۡۢبَغِیۡ لَهٗ ؕ اِنۡ هُوَ اِلَّا ذِكۡرٌ وَّقُرۡاٰنٌ مُّبِیۡنٌ ۙ ۶۹

70. In order that it may warn him who is alive, and that the sentence may be justified on the infidels.

لِّیُنۡذِرَ مَنۡ كَانَ حَیًّا وَّیَحِقَّ الۡقَوۡلُ عَلَی الۡكٰفِرِیۡنَ ۷۰

71. Do they not see that We have created for them, of what Our hands have created, cattle, so that they are their owners.

اَوَلَمۡ یَرَوۡا اَنَّا خَلَقۡنَا لَهُمۡ مِّمَّا عَمِلَتۡ اَیۡدِیۡنَاۤ اَنۡعَامًا فَهُمۡ لَهَا مٰلِكُوۡنَ ۷۱

72. And to them We have subdued them so that some of them they have for riding and on some of them they feed?

وَذَلَّلۡنٰهَا لَهُمۡ فَمِنۡهَا رَكُوۡبُهُمۡ وَمِنۡهَا یَاۡكُلُوۡنَ ۷۲

73. And they have therefrom other benefits and drinks. Will they not then give thanks?

وَلَهُمۡ فِیۡهَا مَنَافِعُ وَمَشَارِبُ ؕ اَفَلَا یَشۡكُرُوۡنَ ۷۳

74. And they have taken besides Allah gods, hoping that they may haply be succoured.

وَاتَّخَذُوۡا مِنۡ دُوۡنِ اللّٰهِ اٰلِهَةً لَّعَلَّهُمۡ یُنۡصَرُوۡنَ ۷۴

---

622. The thing is much beneath him. This is said in answer to the pagan Arabs who held the Prophet to be a poet. A poet in their parlance did not mean a versifier. Poetry according to them, as according to most primitive peoples, was not a fine art, but a sort of magical utterance, inspired by powers from the Unseen; and the poet in their estimation was more allied to a soothsayer than to a literary composer. 'The Arabian poet (Shā'ir), as the name indicates, was originally one endowed with knowledge hidden from the common man, which knowledge he received from a demon, his special shaytān (Satan). As a poet he was in league with the unseen powers and could by his curses bring evil upon the enemy. Satire (hija') was therefore a very early form of Arabic poetry' (Hitti, History of the Arabs, p. 94). This disavowal does not refer primarily to the poetic art, but rather to the person and character of the poets themselves. He the divinely inspired Prophet could have nothing to do with men who owed their inspiration to demons and gloried in the ideals of paganism which he was striving to overthrow' (Nicholson, Literary History of the Arabs, p. 159).

75. They are not able to give them succour, whereas they shall be against them a host brought forward.

لَا يَسْتَطِيعُونَ نَصْرَهُمْ وَهُمْ لَهُمْ جُنْدٌ مُحْضَرُونَ ۝

76. So let not their speech grieve you. Verily We! We know what they conceal and what they disclose.

فَلَا يَحْزُنْكَ قَوْلُهُمْ إِنَّا نَعْلَمُ مَا يُسِرُّونَ وَمَا يُعْلِنُونَ ۝

77. Does not man see that We have created him of sperm? Yet lo! He is a manifest opponent.

أَوَلَمْ يَرَ الْإِنسَٰنُ أَنَّا خَلَقْنَٰهُ مِن نُّطْفَةٍ فَإِذَا هُوَ خَصِيمٌ مُّبِينٌ ۝

78. And he recounts for Us a similitude and forgets his creation. He says: 'Who shall quicken the bones after they are decayed?'

وَضَرَبَ لَنَا مَثَلًا وَنَسِيَ خَلْقَهُ قَالَ مَن يُحْيِ الْعِظَٰمَ وَهِيَ رَمِيمٌ ۝

79. Say: 'He shall quicken them Who brought forth them for the first time. And He is the Knower of every manner of creation.

قُلْ يُحْيِيهَا الَّذِي أَنشَأَهَا أَوَّلَ مَرَّةٍ وَهُوَ بِكُلِّ خَلْقٍ عَلِيمٌ ۝

80. Who gives you fire out of the green tree? And lo! You kindle therewith.

الَّذِي جَعَلَ لَكُم مِّنَ الشَّجَرِ الْأَخْضَرِ نَارًا فَإِذَا أَنتُم مِّنْهُ تُوقِدُونَ ۝

81. Is not He Who created the heavens and earth for the first time able to create the like of them? Yes! He is the Supreme Creator, the Knower.

أَوَلَيْسَ الَّذِي خَلَقَ السَّمَٰوَٰتِ وَالْأَرْضَ بِقَٰدِرٍ عَلَىٰ أَن يَخْلُقَ مِثْلَهُم بَلَىٰ وَهُوَ الْخَلَّٰقُ الْعَلِيمُ ۝

82. His affair, when He intends a thing, is only that He says to it, 'Be', and it becomes.[623]

إِنَّمَا أَمْرُهُ إِذَا أَرَادَ شَيْئًا أَن يَقُولَ لَهُ كُن فَيَكُونُ ۝

---

623. This by a single act of His all-powerful will. His Word of command is all that is needed to bring it into existence according to His plan; and this is the clearest evidence of His absolute Omnipotence.

83. Wherefore Hallowed be He, in Whose hand is the governance of everything, and to Whom you shall be returned.

فَسُبْحَنَ ٱلَّذِى بِيَدِهِ مَلَكُوتُ كُلِّ شَىْءٍ وَإِلَيْهِ تُرْجَعُونَ ﴿٨٣﴾

Sūrah 37

al-Ṣāffāt

(Makkan, 5 Sections, 182 Verses)

In the name of Allah, the Compassionate, the Merciful.

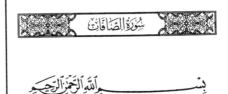

Section 1

1. By the angels ranged in ranks.

2. By the angels driving away,

3. By the angels reciting the praise.

4. Verily your God is One.

5. Lord of the heavens and the earth, and what is in between,[624] and Lord of the easts.

6. Verily We! We have adorned the nearest heaven with adornment in the stars,

7. And have placed therein a guard against any devil forward.

8. They cannot listen to the exalted assembly and they are darted at from every side,

9. With a driving fusillade, and theirs shall be a perpetual torment!

624.　Which completely uproots the three fold division of Vedic gods into the Celestial gods (such as Dyaus, Varuna and Surya), Atmospheric gods (such as Indra, Vayu and Apah), and Terrestrial deities (such as Agni, Prithivi and Sarasvati). Cf. *ERE.* XII. pp. 603 ff.

10. Except him who snatches away a word by stealth and then pursues him a glowing flame.

إِلَّا مَنْ خَطِفَ الْخَطْفَةَ فَأَتْبَعَهُ شِهَابٌ ثَاقِبٌ ۝

11. Ask them you: 'Are they stronger in structure or those others whom We have created?' Verily We! We have created them of a sticky clay.

فَاسْتَفْتِهِمْ أَهُمْ أَشَدُّ خَلْقًا أَم مَّنْ خَلَقْنَا إِنَّا خَلَقْنَهُم مِّن طِينٍ لَّازِبٍ ۝

12. Verily you marvel, and they scoff.

بَلْ عَجِبْتَ وَيَسْخَرُونَ ۝

13. And when they are admonished, they receive no admonition.

وَإِذَا ذُكِّرُوا لَا يَذْكُرُونَ ۝

14. And when they see a sign, they turn to scoffing.

وَإِذَا رَأَوْا ءَايَةً يَسْتَسْخِرُونَ ۝

15. And they say: 'This Qur'ān is naught but a manifest magic.

وَقَالُوا إِنْ هَذَا إِلَّا سِحْرٌ مُّبِينٌ ۝

16. When we have become dead and become dust and bones, shall we then verily be raised?

أَءِذَا مِتْنَا وَكُنَّا تُرَابًا وَعِظَامًا أَءِنَّا لَمَبْعُوثُونَ ۝

17. And also our forefathers?'

أَوَءَابَاؤُنَا الْأَوَّلُونَ ۝

18. Say: 'Yea; and verily then you shall be despicable.'

قُلْ نَعَمْ وَأَنتُمْ دَاخِرُونَ ۝

19. It shall be a single shout, and lo! They shall be staring.

فَإِنَّمَا هِيَ زَجْرَةٌ وَاحِدَةٌ فَإِذَا هُمْ يَنظُرُونَ ۝

20. And they will say: 'Woe unto us! This is the Day of Requital.'

وَقَالُوا يَوَيْلَنَا هَذَا يَوْمُ الدِّينِ ۝

21. This is the Day of Judgement, which you were wont to belie.

هَذَا يَوْمُ الْفَصْلِ الَّذِي كُنتُم بِهِ تُكَذِّبُونَ ۝

Section 2

22. Gather together those who did wrong and their companions and what they were wont to worship,

اَحْشُرُوا الَّذِيْنَ ظَلَمُوْا وَاَزْوَاجَهُمْ وَمَا كَانُوْا يَعْبُدُوْنَ ﴿٢٢﴾

23. Besides Allah, and lead them on to the path of the Flaming Fire;

مِنْ دُوْنِ اللّٰهِ فَاهْدُوْهُمْ اِلٰى صِرَاطِ الْجَحِيْمِ ﴿٢٣﴾

24. And stop them, verily they are to be questioned:

وَقِفُوْهُمْ اِنَّهُمْ مَّسْئُوْلُوْنَ ﴿٢٤﴾

25. 'What is the matter with you that you do not succour one another?'

مَا لَكُمْ لَا تَنَاصَرُوْنَ ﴿٢٥﴾

26. Nay! That Day they will be entirely submissive.

بَلْ هُمُ الْيَوْمَ مُسْتَسْلِمُوْنَ ﴿٢٦﴾

27. And they will advance towards each other mutually questioning.

وَاَقْبَلَ بَعْضُهُمْ عَلٰى بَعْضٍ يَّتَسَآءَلُوْنَ ﴿٢٧﴾

28. They will say: 'Verily you! You were wont to come to us imposing.'

قَالُوْا اِنَّكُمْ كُنْتُمْ تَأْتُوْنَنَا عَنِ الْيَمِيْنِ ﴿٢٨﴾

29. They will say: 'Nay! You yourselves were unbelievers;

قَالُوْا بَلْ لَّمْ تَكُوْنُوْا مُؤْمِنِيْنَ ﴿٢٩﴾

30. And we had over you no authority but you were a people exorbitant.

وَمَا كَانَ لَنَا عَلَيْكُمْ مِّنْ سُلْطٰنٍ بَلْ كُنْتُمْ قَوْمًا طٰغِيْنَ ﴿٣٠﴾

31. So on us has been justified the sentence of our Lord: surely we are to taste.

فَحَقَّ عَلَيْنَا قَوْلُ رَبِّنَا اِنَّا لَذَآئِقُوْنَ ﴿٣١﴾

32. We seduced you astray; verily we were ourselves the seduced ones.'

فَاَغْوَيْنٰكُمْ اِنَّا كُنَّا غٰوِيْنَ ﴿٣٢﴾

33. So on the Day they all will be sharers in the torment.

فَإِنَّهُمْ يَوْمَئِذٍ فِى ٱلْعَذَابِ مُشْتَرِكُونَ ۝

34. Verily We, We in this way deal with the culprits.

إِنَّا كَذَٰلِكَ نَفْعَلُ بِٱلْمُجْرِمِينَ ۝

35. Of a surety, when it was said to them: 'There is no god but Allah,' they ever grew stiff-necked,

إِنَّهُمْ كَانُوٓاْ إِذَا قِيلَ لَهُمْ لَآ إِلَٰهَ إِلَّا ٱللَّهُ يَسْتَكْبِرُونَ ۝

36. And said: 'Are we going to abandon our gods on account of a poet distracted?'

وَيَقُولُونَ أَئِنَّا لَتَارِكُوٓاْ ءَالِهَتِنَا لِشَاعِرٍ مَّجْنُونٍ ۝

37. Aye! He has come with the Truth and he confirms the sent ones.

بَلْ جَآءَ بِٱلْحَقِّ وَصَدَّقَ ٱلْمُرْسَلِينَ ۝

38. Verily you are going to taste an afflictive torment.

إِنَّكُمْ لَذَآئِقُواْ ٱلْعَذَابِ ٱلْأَلِيمِ ۝

39. And you shall be requited not except for what you have been working.

وَمَا تُجْزَوْنَ إِلَّا مَا كُنتُمْ تَعْمَلُونَ ۝

40. But the bondsmen of Allah, the sincere ones.

إِلَّا عِبَادَ ٱللَّهِ ٱلْمُخْلَصِينَ ۝

41. Those! Theirs shall be a provision known.

أُوْلَٰٓئِكَ لَهُمْ رِزْقٌ مَّعْلُومٌ ۝

42. Fruits; and they shall be honoured,

فَوَٰكِهُ وَهُم مُّكْرَمُونَ ۝

43. In the Gardens of Delight,

فِى جَنَّٰتِ ٱلنَّعِيمِ ۝

44. On couches, facing one another.

عَلَىٰ سُرُرٍ مُّتَقَٰبِلِينَ ۝

45. Round shall be passed a cup unto them, filled with limpid drink,

يُطَافُ عَلَيْهِم بِكَأْسٍ مِّن مَّعِينٍ ۝

46. White; a pleasure to the drinkers.

بَيْضَآءَ لَذَّةٍ لِّلشَّـٰرِبِينَ ۞

47. No headiness there shall be in it, nor shall they be inebriated with it.

لَا فِيهَا غَوْلٌ وَّلَا هُمْ عَنْهَا يُنزَفُونَ ۞

48. And with them shall be damsels of refraining looks, large-eyed,

وَعِنْدَهُمْ قَـٰصِرَٰتُ ٱلطَّرْفِ عِينٌ ۞

49. As though they were eggs preserved.

كَأَنَّهُنَّ بَيْضٌ مَّكْنُونٌ ۞

50. Then they will advance towards one another, mutually questioning.

فَأَقْبَلَ بَعْضُهُمْ عَلَىٰ بَعْضٍ يَتَسَآءَلُونَ ۞

51. And a speaker from among them will say: 'Verily there was a friend of mine,

قَالَ قَآئِلٌ مِّنْهُمْ إِنِّى كَانَ لِى قَرِينٌ ۞

52. Who said: 'Are you of them who confess to the doctrine of Resurrection:

يَقُولُ أَءِنَّكَ لَمِنَ ٱلْمُصَدِّقِينَ ۞

53. Are we, when we are dead and have become dust and bones, going to be requited?'

أَءِذَا مِتْنَا وَكُنَّا تُرَابًا وَعِظَـٰمًا أَءِنَّا لَمَدِينُونَ ۞

54. Allah will say: 'Will you look down?'

قَالَ هَلْ أَنتُم مُّطَّلِعُونَ ۞

55. Then he will look down and see him in the midst of the Flaming Fire.

فَٱطَّلَعَ فَرَءَاهُ فِى سَوَآءِ ٱلْجَحِيمِ ۞

56. And he will say: 'By Allah, you had what caused me to perish,

قَالَ تَٱللَّهِ إِن كِدتَّ لَتُرْدِينِ ۞

57. And but for the favour of my Lord, I would have been of those brought forward.

وَلَوْلَا نِعْمَةُ رَبِّى لَكُنتُ مِنَ ٱلْمُحْضَرِينَ ۞

58. Are we then not to die any more?

59. Save our first death, and are we not to be chastised?'

60. Verily this! This is the supreme achievement.

61. For the like of it let the workers work.

62. Is this better as an entertainment or the tree of Zaqqūm?

63. Verily We! We have made it a temptation for the ungodly.

64. Verily it is a tree that springs forth in the bottom of the Flaming Fire.

65. The fruit of it is as though it were the hoods of the serpents.

66. And verily they must eat of it and must fill their bellies from it.

67. And on the top of it thereafter they shall have a drought of boiling water.

68. And thereafter their return is verily to the Flaming Fire.

69. Verily they found their fathers gone astray;

70. So they are rushing in their footsteps.

71. And assuredly many of the ancients went astray before them.

أَفَمَا نَحۡنُ بِمَيِّتِينَ ۝

إِلَّا مَوۡتَتَنَا ٱلۡأُولَىٰ وَمَا نَحۡنُ بِمُعَذَّبِينَ ۝

إِنَّ هَٰذَا لَهُوَ ٱلۡفَوۡزُ ٱلۡعَظِيمُ ۝

لِمِثۡلِ هَٰذَا فَلۡيَعۡمَلِ ٱلۡعَٰمِلُونَ ۝

أَذَٰلِكَ خَيۡرٌ نُّزُلًا أَمۡ شَجَرَةُ ٱلزَّقُّومِ ۝

إِنَّا جَعَلۡنَٰهَا فِتۡنَةً لِّلظَّٰلِمِينَ ۝

إِنَّهَا شَجَرَةٌ تَخۡرُجُ فِىٓ أَصۡلِ ٱلۡجَحِيمِ ۝

طَلۡعُهَا كَأَنَّهُۥ رُءُوسُ ٱلشَّيَٰطِينِ ۝

فَإِنَّهُمۡ لَءَاكِلُونَ مِنۡهَا فَمَالِـُٔونَ مِنۡهَا ٱلۡبُطُونَ ۝

ثُمَّ إِنَّ لَهُمۡ عَلَيۡهَا لَشَوۡبًا مِّنۡ حَمِيمٍ ۝

ثُمَّ إِنَّ مَرۡجِعَهُمۡ لَإِلَى ٱلۡجَحِيمِ ۝

إِنَّهُمۡ أَلۡفَوۡاْ ءَابَآءَهُمۡ ضَآلِّينَ ۝

فَهُمۡ عَلَىٰٓ ءَاثَٰرِهِمۡ يُهۡرَعُونَ ۝

وَلَقَدۡ ضَلَّ قَبۡلَهُمۡ أَكۡثَرُ ٱلۡأَوَّلِينَ ۝

72. And assuredly We sent warners among them.

وَلَقَدۡ أَرۡسَلۡنَا فِيهِم مُّنذِرِينَ ﴿٧٢﴾

73. So behold, what has been the end of those who had been warned,

فَٱنظُرۡ كَيۡفَ كَانَ عَٰقِبَةُ ٱلۡمُنذَرِينَ ﴿٧٣﴾

74. Save the sincere bondsmen of Allah?

إِلَّا عِبَادَ ٱللَّهِ ٱلۡمُخۡلَصِينَ ﴿٧٤﴾

Section 3

75. And assuredly Noah cried unto Us and We are the Best of the answerers.

وَلَقَدۡ نَادَىٰنَا نُوحٌ فَلَنِعۡمَ ٱلۡمُجِيبُونَ ﴿٧٥﴾

76. And We rescued him and his people from the great affliction.

وَنَجَّيۡنَٰهُ وَأَهۡلَهُۥ مِنَ ٱلۡكَرۡبِ ٱلۡعَظِيمِ ﴿٧٦﴾

77. And his offspring! Them We made the survivors.

وَجَعَلۡنَا ذُرِّيَّتَهُۥ هُمُ ٱلۡبَاقِينَ ﴿٧٧﴾

78. And for him We left among the posterity.

وَتَرَكۡنَا عَلَيۡهِ فِي ٱلۡأَخِرِينَ ﴿٧٨﴾

79. Peace be upon Noah, among the worlds.

سَلَٰمٌ عَلَىٰ نُوحٍ فِي ٱلۡعَٰلَمِينَ ﴿٧٩﴾

80. Verily We! We thus recompense the well-doers.

إِنَّا كَذَٰلِكَ نَجۡزِى ٱلۡمُحۡسِنِينَ ﴿٨٠﴾

81. Verily he was of Our believing bondsmen.

إِنَّهُۥ مِنۡ عِبَادِنَا ٱلۡمُؤۡمِنِينَ ﴿٨١﴾

82. Then We drowned the others.

ثُمَّ أَغۡرَقۡنَا ٱلۡأَخَرِينَ ﴿٨٢﴾

83. And of his sect was Abraham.

وَإِنَّ مِن شِيعَتِهِۦ لَإِبۡرَٰهِيمَ ﴿٨٣﴾

84. Recall when he came to his Lord with a whole heart.

إِذۡ جَآءَ رَبَّهُۥ بِقَلۡبٍ سَلِيمٍ ﴿٨٤﴾

85. Recall when he said to his father and his people: 'What is it that you worship?

إِذْ قَالَ لِأَبِيهِ وَقَوْمِهِ مَاذَا تَعْبُدُونَ ﴿٨٥﴾

86. Is it a falsehood, gods besides Allah that you seek?

أَئِفْكًا ءَالِهَةً دُونَ ٱللَّهِ تُرِيدُونَ ﴿٨٦﴾

87. What then, is your opinion of the Lord of the worlds?'

فَمَا ظَنُّكُم بِرَبِّ ٱلْعَٰلَمِينَ ﴿٨٧﴾

88. Then he cast a glance at the stars.

فَنَظَرَ نَظْرَةً فِى ٱلنُّجُومِ ﴿٨٨﴾

89. And he said: 'I am about to be sick.'

فَقَالَ إِنِّى سَقِيمٌ ﴿٨٩﴾

90. Then they departed from him, turning their backs.

فَتَوَلَّوْا۟ عَنْهُ مُدْبِرِينَ ﴿٩٠﴾

91. Then he slipped to their gods and said: 'Do you not eat?

فَرَاغَ إِلَىٰٓ ءَالِهَتِهِمْ فَقَالَ أَلَا تَأْكُلُونَ ﴿٩١﴾

92. What is the matter that you do not speak?'

مَا لَكُمْ لَا تَنطِقُونَ ﴿٩٢﴾

93. Then he slipped to them, striking them with his right hand.

فَرَاغَ عَلَيْهِمْ ضَرْبًۢا بِٱلْيَمِينِ ﴿٩٣﴾

94. Then they advanced toward him, hastening.

فَأَقْبَلُوٓا۟ إِلَيْهِ يَزِفُّونَ ﴿٩٤﴾

95. He said: 'Do you worship what you carve?

قَالَ أَتَعْبُدُونَ مَا تَنْحِتُونَ ﴿٩٥﴾

96. Whereas Allah has created you and what you make.'

وَٱللَّهُ خَلَقَكُمْ وَمَا تَعْمَلُونَ ﴿٩٦﴾

97. They said: 'Build for him a building and cast him into the Flaming Fire.'

قَالُوا۟ ٱبْنُوا۟ لَهُۥ بُنْيَٰنًا فَأَلْقُوهُ فِى ٱلْجَحِيمِ ﴿٩٧﴾

98. And they devised a plot for him, but We made them the humble.

فَأَرَادُوا۟ بِهِۦ كَيْدًا فَجَعَلْنَٰهُمُ ٱلْأَسْفَلِينَ ﴿٩٨﴾

99. And he said: 'Verily I am going to my Lord Who will guide me.

وَقَالَ إِنِّى ذَاهِبٌ إِلَىٰ رَبِّى سَيَهْدِينِ ۝

100. Lord! Bestow on me a son who will be of the righteous.'⁶²⁵

رَبِّ هَبۡ لِى مِنَ ٱلصَّٰلِحِينَ ۝

101. Wherefore We gave him the glad tidings of a gentle boy,⁶²⁶

فَبَشَّرۡنَٰهُ بِغُلَٰمٍ حَلِيمٍ ۝

102. And when the boy attained the age of running with him, he said: 'Son! I have seen in a dream that I am slaughtering you; so look, what do you consider?' He said: 'Father! Do what you are commanded; you will find me, Allah willing, of the patient.'

فَلَمَّا بَلَغَ مَعَهُ ٱلسَّعۡىَ قَالَ يَٰبُنَىَّ إِنِّىٓ أَرَىٰ فِى ٱلۡمَنَامِ أَنِّىٓ أَذۡبَحُكَ فَٱنظُرۡ مَاذَا تَرَىٰ قَالَ يَٰٓأَبَتِ ٱفۡعَلۡ مَا تُؤۡمَرُ سَتَجِدُنِىٓ إِن شَآءَ ٱللَّهُ مِنَ ٱلصَّٰبِرِينَ ۝

103. Then when the two submitted themselves, and he had prostrated him on the temple.

فَلَمَّآ أَسۡلَمَا وَتَلَّهُۥ لِلۡجَبِينِ ۝

104. We cried to him: 'Abraham!

وَنَٰدَيۡنَٰهُ أَن يَٰٓإِبۡرَٰهِيمُ ۝

105. Of a surety you have fulfilled the vision. Verily We! Thus do We recompense the well-doers.'

قَدۡ صَدَّقۡتَ ٱلرُّءۡيَآ إِنَّا كَذَٰلِكَ نَجۡزِى ٱلۡمُحۡسِنِينَ ۝

106. Verily that! That was a manifest trial.

إِنَّ هَٰذَا لَهُوَ ٱلۡبَلَٰٓؤُاْ ٱلۡمُبِينُ ۝

107. And We ransomed him with a mighty victim.

وَفَدَيۡنَٰهُ بِذِبۡحٍ عَظِيمٍ ۝

---

625. Notice that Abraham prays not only for a son but for a son who would grow up in righteousness and piety; and the great Prophet's prayer was sure to be granted.

626. The epithet contradicts the ferocity of temperament attributed to Ishmael by the Jews and Christians.

108. And for him We left among the posterity;

وَتَرَكۡنَا عَلَیۡهِ فِی ٱلۡأٓخِرِینَ ۝

109. Peace be upon Abraham.

سَلَـٰمٌ عَلَىٰۤ إِبۡرَٰهِیمَ ۝

110. Verily We! Thus do We recompense the well-doers.

كَذَٰلِكَ نَجۡزِی ٱلۡمُحۡسِنِینَ ۝

111. Verily he was of Our believing bondsmen.

إِنَّهُۥ مِنۡ عِبَادِنَا ٱلۡمُؤۡمِنِینَ ۝

112. And We gave him the glad tidings of Isaac, a Prophet, and of the righteous.

وَبَشَّرۡنَـٰهُ بِإِسۡحَٰقَ نَبِیًّا مِّنَ ٱلصَّـٰلِحِینَ ۝

113. And We blessed him and Isaac; and of their offspring some are well-doers, and some who wrong themselves manifestly.

وَبَٰرَكۡنَا عَلَیۡهِ وَعَلَىٰۤ إِسۡحَٰقَ وَمِن ذُرِّیَّتِهِمَا مُحۡسِنٌ وَظَالِمٌ لِّنَفۡسِهِۦ مُبِینٌ ۝

Section 4

114. And assuredly We gave grace to Moses and Aaron.

وَلَقَدۡ مَنَنَّا عَلَىٰ مُوسَىٰ وَهَٰرُونَ ۝

115. And delivered them and their people from the great affliction.

وَنَجَّیۡنَٰهُمَا وَقَوۡمَهُمَا مِنَ ٱلۡكَرۡبِ ٱلۡعَظِیمِ ۝

116. And We succoured them, so they became the victors.

وَنَصَرۡنَٰهُمۡ فَكَانُوا۟ هُمُ ٱلۡغَٰلِبِینَ ۝

117. And We vouchsafed to the two a luminous Book.

وَءَاتَیۡنَٰهُمَا ٱلۡكِتَٰبَ ٱلۡمُسۡتَبِینَ ۝

118. And We led the two on to the straight path.

وَهَدَیۡنَٰهُمَا ٱلصِّرَٰطَ ٱلۡمُسۡتَقِیمَ ۝

119. And We left for the two among the posterity.

وَتَرَكۡنَا عَلَیۡهِمَا فِی ٱلۡأٓخِرِینَ ۝

120. Peace be unto Moses and Aaron.

سَلَـٰمٌ عَلَىٰ مُوسَىٰ وَهَٰرُونَ ۝

121. Verily We! Thus do We recompense the well-doers.

إِنَّا كَذَلِكَ نَجْزِى الْمُحْسِنِينَ ﴿١٢١﴾

122. Verily the two were of Our believing bondsmen.

إِنَّهُمَا مِنْ عِبَادِنَا الْمُؤْمِنِينَ ﴿١٢٢﴾

123. And verily, Ilyas was of the sent ones.

وَإِنَّ إِلْيَاسَ لَمِنَ الْمُرْسَلِينَ ﴿١٢٣﴾

124. Recall when he said to his people: 'Do you not fear?

إِذْ قَالَ لِقَوْمِهِ أَلَا تَتَّقُونَ ﴿١٢٤﴾

125. Do you call upon Baal, and forsake the Best of creators?

أَتَدْعُونَ بَعْلًا وَتَذَرُونَ أَحْسَنَ الْخَالِقِينَ ﴿١٢٥﴾

126. Allah, your Lord, and the Lord of your forefathers?'

اللَّهَ رَبَّكُمْ وَرَبَّ ءَابَآئِكُمُ الْأَوَّلِينَ ﴿١٢٦﴾

127. Then they belied him, so verily they are to be brought up,

فَكَذَّبُوهُ فَإِنَّهُمْ لَمُحْضَرُونَ ﴿١٢٧﴾

128. Except the sincere bondsmen of Allah.

إِلَّا عِبَادَ اللَّهِ الْمُخْلَصِينَ ﴿١٢٨﴾

129. And We left for him among the posterity.

وَتَرَكْنَا عَلَيْهِ فِى الْآخِرِينَ ﴿١٢٩﴾

130. Peace be on Ilyasin.

سَلَامٌ عَلَى إِلْ يَاسِينَ ﴿١٣٠﴾

131. Verily We! Thus do We recompense the well-doers.

إِنَّا كَذَلِكَ نَجْزِى الْمُحْسِنِينَ ﴿١٣١﴾

132. Verily he was of Our believing bondsmen.

إِنَّهُ مِنْ عِبَادِنَا الْمُؤْمِنِينَ ﴿١٣٢﴾

133. And verily Lot was among the sent ones.

وَإِنَّ لُوطًا لَمِنَ الْمُرْسَلِينَ ﴿١٣٣﴾

134. Recall when We delivered him and his household all,

إِذْ نَجَّيْنَاهُ وَأَهْلَهُ أَجْمَعِينَ ﴿١٣٤﴾

135. Save an old woman among the lingerers.

إِلَّا عَجُوزًا فِى الْغَابِرِينَ ﴿١٣٥﴾

136. Then We annihilated the others.

ثُمَّ دَمَّرْنَا الْآخَرِينَ ﴿١٣٦﴾

137. And surely you pass by them in the morning.

وَإِنَّكُمْ لَتَمُرُّونَ عَلَيْهِم مُّصْبِحِينَ ﴿١٣٧﴾

138. And at night; will you not then reflect?

وَبِٱلَّيْلِ أَفَلَا تَعْقِلُونَ ﴿١٣٨﴾

Section 5

139. And verily Jonah was of the sent ones.

وَإِنَّ يُونُسَ لَمِنَ ٱلْمُرْسَلِينَ ﴿١٣٩﴾

140. Recall when he ran away to a laden ship.

إِذْ أَبَقَ إِلَى ٱلْفُلْكِ ٱلْمَشْحُونِ ﴿١٤٠﴾

141. Then he joined the lots and was of the condemned.

فَسَاهَمَ فَكَانَ مِنَ ٱلْمُدْحَضِينَ ﴿١٤١﴾

142. And fish swallowed him, while he was reproaching himself.

فَٱلْتَقَمَهُ ٱلْحُوتُ وَهُوَ مُلِيمٌ ﴿١٤٢﴾

143. And had he not been of them who hallow Him,

فَلَوْلَآ أَنَّهُۥ كَانَ مِنَ ٱلْمُسَبِّحِينَ ﴿١٤٣﴾

144. He would have tarried in its belly till the Day when they are raised.

لَلَبِثَ فِى بَطْنِهِۦٓ إِلَىٰ يَوْمِ يُبْعَثُونَ ﴿١٤٤﴾

145. Then We cast him on a bare desert while he was sick.

فَنَبَذْنَٰهُ بِٱلْعَرَآءِ وَهُوَ سَقِيمٌ ﴿١٤٥﴾

146. And We caused to grow over him a tree, a gourd.

وَأَنۢبَتْنَا عَلَيْهِ شَجَرَةً مِّن يَقْطِينٍ ﴿١٤٦﴾

147. And We had sent him to a hundred thousand: rather they exceeded.

وَأَرْسَلْنَٰهُ إِلَىٰ مِائَةِ أَلْفٍ أَوْ يَزِيدُونَ ﴿١٤٧﴾

148. And they believed; so We let them enjoy life for a season.

فَـَٔامَنُوا۟ فَمَتَّعْنَٰهُمْ إِلَىٰ حِينٍ ﴿١٤٨﴾

149. Now ask you them: 'Are there daughters for your Lord and sons for them?'

فَٱسْتَفْتِهِمْ أَلِرَبِّكَ ٱلْبَنَاتُ وَلَهُمُ ٱلْبَنُونَ ﴿١٤٩﴾

150. Or, did We create angels female while they were witnesses?

أَمْ خَلَقْنَا ٱلْمَلَـٰٓئِكَةَ إِنَـٰثًا وَهُمْ شَـٰهِدُونَ ﴿١٥٠﴾

151. Lo! Verily it is of their falsehood that they say.

أَلَآ إِنَّهُم مِّنْ إِفْكِهِمْ لَيَقُولُونَ ﴿١٥١﴾

152. Allah has begotten. Verily they are the liars.

وَلَدَ ٱللَّهُ وَإِنَّهُمْ لَكَـٰذِبُونَ ﴿١٥٢﴾

153. Has He chosen daughters above sons?

أَصْطَفَى ٱلْبَنَاتِ عَلَى ٱلْبَنِينَ ﴿١٥٣﴾

154. What ails you? How do you judge?

مَا لَكُمْ كَيْفَ تَحْكُمُونَ ﴿١٥٤﴾

155. Will you not then be admonished?

أَفَلَا تَذَكَّرُونَ ﴿١٥٥﴾

156. Or, is there for you a clear authority?

أَمْ لَكُمْ سُلْطَـٰنٌ مُّبِينٌ ﴿١٥٦﴾

157. Then bring your Book, if you speak truth.

فَأْتُوا بِكِتَـٰبِكُمْ إِن كُنتُمْ صَـٰدِقِينَ ﴿١٥٧﴾

158. And they have made a kinship between Him and the *jinn*, whereas the *jinn* assuredly know that they are to be brought up.

وَجَعَلُوا بَيْنَهُۥ وَبَيْنَ ٱلْجِنَّةِ نَسَبًا وَلَقَدْ عَلِمَتِ ٱلْجِنَّةُ إِنَّهُمْ لَمُحْضَرُونَ ﴿١٥٨﴾

159. Hallowed be Allah from what they associate to Him.

سُبْحَـٰنَ ٱللَّهِ عَمَّا يَصِفُونَ ﴿١٥٩﴾

160. Except the sincere bondsmen of Allah.

إِلَّا عِبَادَ ٱللَّهِ ٱلْمُخْلَصِينَ ﴿١٦٠﴾

161. So neither you nor what you worship,

فَإِنَّكُمْ وَمَا تَعْبُدُونَ ﴿١٦١﴾

162. Can tempt anyone to rebel against Him,

مَآ أَنتُمْ عَلَيْهِ بِفَـٰتِنِينَ ﴿١٦٢﴾

163. Save him who is to roast in the Flaming Fire.

إِلَّا مَنْ هُوَ صَالِ ٱلْجَحِيمِ ﴿١٦٣﴾

164. None of us there is but has a station assigned.

وَمَا مِنَّا إِلَّا لَهُ مَقَامٌ مَّعْلُومٌ ۝

165. And verily we! We are ranged in ranks.

وَإِنَّا لَنَحْنُ الصَّآفُّونَ ۝

166. And verily we! We hallow.

وَإِنَّا لَنَحْنُ الْمُسَبِّحُونَ ۝

167. And they surely were wont to say;

وَإِن كَانُوا لَيَقُولُونَ ۝

168. 'Had we an admonition as had the ancients,

لَوْ أَنَّ عِندَنَا ذِكْرًا مِّنَ الْأَوَّلِينَ ۝

169. Surely we would have been the sincere bondsmen of Allah.'

لَكُنَّا عِبَادَ اللَّهِ الْمُخْلَصِينَ ۝

170. Yet they as believe therein; presently they shall come to know.

فَكَفَرُوا بِهِ فَسَوْفَ يَعْلَمُونَ ۝

171. And assuredly Our word has gone forth for Our bondsmen, the sent ones,

وَلَقَدْ سَبَقَتْ كَلِمَتُنَا لِعِبَادِنَا الْمُرْسَلِينَ ۝

172. That verily they shall be made triumphant.

إِنَّهُمْ لَهُمُ الْمَنصُورُونَ ۝

173. And verily Our host! They are to overcome.

وَإِنَّ جُندَنَا لَهُمُ الْغَالِبُونَ ۝

174. So turn you aside from them for a season.

فَتَوَلَّ عَنْهُمْ حَتَّىٰ حِينٍ ۝

175. And see them you, how they themselves shall presently fare.

وَأَبْصِرْهُمْ فَسَوْفَ يُبْصِرُونَ ۝

176. Do they seek Our torment to hasten on?

أَفَبِعَذَابِنَا يَسْتَعْجِلُونَ ۝

177. Then when it descends to them, face to face, a helpless morn that shall be for those who had been warned.

فَإِذَا نَزَلَ بِسَاحَتِهِمْ فَسَآءَ صَبَاحُ الْمُنذَرِينَ ۝

178. And turn you aside from them for a season.

وَتَوَلَّ عَنْهُمْ حَتَّىٰ حِينٍ ۝

179. And see you; they themselves shall presently see.

وَأَبْصِرْ فَسَوْفَ يُبْصِرُونَ ۝

180. Hallowed be your Lord, the Lord of majesty, from what they associate to Him!

سُبْحَٰنَ رَبِّكَ رَبِّ ٱلْعِزَّةِ عَمَّا يَصِفُونَ ۝

181. And peace be unto the sent ones.

وَسَلَٰمٌ عَلَى ٱلْمُرْسَلِينَ ۝

182. And all praise to Allah, the Lord of the worlds!

وَٱلْحَمْدُ لِلَّهِ رَبِّ ٱلْعَٰلَمِينَ ۝

Sūrah 38

Ṣād

(Makkan, 5 Sections, 88 Verses)

In the name of Allah, the Compassionate, the Merciful.

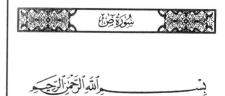

Section 1

1. *Ṣād.* By the Qur'ān, full of admonition.

2. Verily those who disbelieve are in vainglory and schism.

3. How many a generation We have destroyed before them and they cried, but the time to flee was past.

4. And they marvel that there should come to them a warner from amongst them. And the infidels say: 'This is a magic and a lie.

5. Does he make the gods, One God?[627] Surely that is a thing extraordinary.'

6. The chiefs among them departed saying: 'Go and persevere in your gods; surely this is a thing designed.

7. We have not heard of it in the later faith; this is nothing but an invention.

---

627. So that was the only real 'offence' of the Prophet of God, his preaching of the One True God in place of so many separate godlings!

8. What, has out of us, upon him been sent down the admonition?' Yea! They are in doubt concerning My admonition. Yea! They have not yet tasted My chastisement.

أَءُنزِلَ عَلَيْهِ ٱلذِّكْرُ مِنۢ بَيْنِنَا ۚ بَلْ هُمْ فِى شَكٍّ مِّن ذِكْرِى ۚ بَل لَّمَّا يَذُوقُواْ عَذَابِ ۸

9. Or is it that with them there are treasures of the mercy of your Lord, the Bestower?

أَمْ عِندَهُمْ خَزَآئِنُ رَحْمَةِ رَبِّكَ ٱلْعَزِيزِ ٱلْوَهَّابِ ۹

10. Or is it that theirs is the dominion of the heavens and the earth and what is in between? If so, let them ascend by steps.

أَمْ لَهُم مُّلْكُ ٱلسَّمَٰوَٰتِ وَٱلْأَرْضِ وَمَا بَيْنَهُمَا ۖ فَلْيَرْتَقُواْ فِى ٱلْأَسْبَٰبِ ۱۰

11. Here there is a host of the confederates only to be defeated.

جُندٌ مَّا هُنَالِكَ مَهْزُومٌ مِّنَ ٱلْأَحْزَابِ ۱۱

12. Before them there belied the people of Noah and the 'Ād and Pharaoh, the owner of the stakes.

كَذَّبَتْ قَبْلَهُمْ قَوْمُ نُوحٍ وَعَادٌ وَفِرْعَوْنُ ذُو ٱلْأَوْتَادِ ۱۲

13. And the Thamūd, and the people of Lot, and the dwellers of the wood, these were the confederates.

وَثَمُودُ وَقَوْمُ لُوطٍ وَأَصْحَٰبُ لْـَٔيْكَةِ ۚ أُوْلَٰٓئِكَ ٱلْأَحْزَابُ ۱۳

14. There was not one but did not belie the Messengers; so My wrath was just.

إِن كُلٌّ إِلَّا كَذَّبَ ٱلرُّسُلَ فَحَقَّ عِقَابِ ۱۴

Section 2

15. And these wait but for one cry which will not be deferred.

وَمَا يَنظُرُ هَٰٓؤُلَآءِ إِلَّا صَيْحَةً وَٰحِدَةً مَّا لَهَا مِن فَوَاقٍ ۱۵

16. And they say: 'Our Lord! Hasten our portion to us before the Day of Reckoning.'

وَقَالُواْ رَبَّنَا عَجِّل لَّنَا قِطَّنَا قَبْلَ يَوْمِ ٱلْحِسَابِ ۱۶

17. Bear you with what they say, and remember Our bondsman, David, endued with strength; verily he was oft-returning to Us.

أَصْبِرْ عَلَىٰ مَا يَقُولُونَ وَاذْكُرْ عَبْدَنَا دَاوُدَ ذَا الْأَيْدِ إِنَّهُۥ أَوَّابٌ ۝

18. Verily We so subjected the mountains that they hallowed Us with him at nightfall and sunrise.

إِنَّا سَخَّرْنَا الْجِبَالَ مَعَهُۥ يُسَبِّحْنَ بِالْعَشِيِّ وَالْإِشْرَاقِ ۝

19. And so did the birds also, gathering; all oft-returning to him on his account.

وَالطَّيْرَ مَحْشُورَةً كُلٌّ لَّهُۥ أَوَّابٌ ۝

20. And We strengthened his dominion and vouchsafed to him wisdom and decisive speech.

وَشَدَدْنَا مُلْكَهُۥ وَءَاتَيْنَاهُ الْحِكْمَةَ وَفَصْلَ الْخِطَابِ ۝

21. And has the news of the contending parties reached you, when they walled his apartment?

وَهَلْ أَتَىٰكَ نَبَؤُاْ الْخَصْمِ إِذْ تَسَوَّرُواْ الْمِحْرَابَ ۝

22. When they went into David, he was frightened at them. They said: 'Have no fear; we are two contending parties. One of us has oppressed the other; so judge between us with truth, and be not iniquitous, and guide us to the even path.

إِذْ دَخَلُواْ عَلَىٰ دَاوُدَ فَفَزِعَ مِنْهُمْ قَالُواْ لَا تَخَفْ خَصْمَانِ بَغَىٰ بَعْضُنَا عَلَىٰ بَعْضٍ فَاحْكُم بَيْنَنَا بِالْحَقِّ وَلَا تُشْطِطْ وَاهْدِنَا إِلَىٰ سَوَاءِ الصِّرَاطِ ۝

23. Verily this my brother has ninety-nine ewes while I have a solitary ewe, and he says; entrust it to me, and he has overcome me in argument.'

إِنَّ هَٰذَا أَخِى لَهُۥ تِسْعٌ وَتِسْعُونَ نَعْجَةً وَلِيَ نَعْجَةٌ وَاحِدَةٌ فَقَالَ أَكْفِلْنِيهَا وَعَزَّنِى فِي الْخِطَابِ ۝

24. David said: 'Assuredly he has wronged you in demanding your ewe in addition to his ewes and surely many of the partners oppress each other save such as believe and work righteous deeds, and few are they.' And David imagined that We had tried him. So he asked forgiveness of his Lord, and he fell down bowing and turned in penitence.

قَالَ لَقَدْ ظَلَمَكَ بِسُؤَالِ نَعْجَتِكَ إِلَىٰ نِعَاجِهِ ۖ وَإِنَّ كَثِيرًا مِّنَ الْخُلَطَآءِ لَيَبْغِى بَعْضُهُمْ عَلَىٰ بَعْضٍ إِلَّا الَّذِينَ ءَامَنُوا وَعَمِلُوا الصَّٰلِحَٰتِ وَقَلِيلٌ مَّا هُمْ ۗ وَظَنَّ دَاوُدُ أَنَّمَا فَتَنَّٰهُ فَاسْتَغْفَرَ رَبَّهُ وَخَرَّ رَاكِعًا وَأَنَابَ ۩ ۝

25. So We forgave him that; and verily for him is an access to Us and a happy retreat.

فَغَفَرْنَا لَهُ ذَٰلِكَ ۖ وَإِنَّ لَهُ عِندَنَا لَزُلْفَىٰ وَحُسْنَ مَـَٔابٍ ۝

26. O David! We have appointed you a vicegerent in the earth; so judge between mankind with truth, and do not follow your desire, lest it cause you to err from the path of Allah. Verily those who err from the path of Allah, to them shall be a severe torment for they ignored the Day of Resurrection.

يَٰدَاوُدُ إِنَّا جَعَلْنَٰكَ خَلِيفَةً فِى الْأَرْضِ فَاحْكُم بَيْنَ النَّاسِ بِالْحَقِّ وَلَا تَتَّبِعِ الْهَوَىٰ فَيُضِلَّكَ عَن سَبِيلِ اللَّهِ ۚ إِنَّ الَّذِينَ يَضِلُّونَ عَن سَبِيلِ اللَّهِ لَهُمْ عَذَابٌ شَدِيدٌ بِمَا نَسُوا يَوْمَ الْحِسَابِ ۝

Section 3

27. And We have not created the heavens and the earth and what is in between in vain. That is the conjecture of those who disbelieve. And woe unto those who disbelieve the Fire!

وَمَا خَلَقْنَا السَّمَآءَ وَالْأَرْضَ وَمَا بَيْنَهُمَا بَٰطِلًا ۚ ذَٰلِكَ ظَنُّ الَّذِينَ كَفَرُوا ۚ فَوَيْلٌ لِّلَّذِينَ كَفَرُوا مِنَ النَّارِ ۝

28. Shall We make those who believe and work righteous deeds like unto the corrupters in the earth? Or shall We make the pious like unto the ungodly?

أَمْ نَجْعَلُ الَّذِينَ ءَامَنُوا وَعَمِلُوا الصَّٰلِحَٰتِ كَالْمُفْسِدِينَ فِى الْأَرْضِ أَمْ نَجْعَلُ الْمُتَّقِينَ كَالْفُجَّارِ ۝

29. This is a Book blessed, We have sent down unto you that they may ponder the revelations thereof, and that there may be admonished the men of understanding.

كِتَبٌ أَنزَلْنَهُ إِلَيْكَ مُبَرَكٌ لِيَدَّبَّرُوٓاْ ءَايَتِهِۦ وَلِيَتَذَكَّرَ أُوْلُواْ الْأَلْبَبِ ٢٩

30. And We vouchsafed to David, Solomon. An excellent bondsman! He was oft-returning.

وَوَهَبْنَا لِدَاوُۥدَ سُلَيْمَنَ نِعْمَ الْعَبْدُ إِنَّهُۥٓ أَوَّابٌ ٣٠

31. Recall when there were presented to him at eventide coursers swift-footed.

إِذْ عُرِضَ عَلَيْهِ بِالْعَشِيِّ الصَّفِنَتُ الْجِيَادُ ٣١

32. He said: 'Verily I have loved earthly good above the remembrance of my Lord until the sun has disappeared behind the veil.

فَقَالَ إِنِّىٓ أَحْبَبْتُ حُبَّ الْخَيْرِ عَن ذِكْرِ رَبِّى حَتَّىٰ تَوَارَتْ بِالْحِجَابِ ٣٢

33. Bring them back to me,' and he set about slashing their legs and necks.

رُدُّوهَا عَلَىَّ فَطَفِقَ مَسْحًا بِالسُّوقِ وَالْأَعْنَاقِ ٣٣

34. And assuredly We tried Solomon, and set upon his throne a mere body. And then he was penitent.

وَلَقَدْ فَتَنَّا سُلَيْمَنَ وَأَلْقَيْنَا عَلَىٰ كُرْسِيِّهِۦ جَسَدًا ثُمَّ أَنَابَ ٣٤

35. He said: 'Lord! Forgive me, and bestow on me a dominion which no one may obtain besides me. Verily You! You are the Bestower.'

قَالَ رَبِّ اغْفِرْ لِى وَهَبْ لِى مُلْكًا لَّا يَنۢبَغِى لِأَحَدٍ مِّنۢ بَعْدِىٓ إِنَّكَ أَنتَ الْوَهَّابُ ٣٥

36. Then We subjected to him the wind; it ran gently by his command witherward he directed.

فَسَخَّرْنَا لَهُ الرِّيحَ تَجْرِى بِأَمْرِهِۦ رُخَآءً حَيْثُ أَصَابَ ٣٦

37. And We subjected to him the evil ones: every builder and diver.

وَالشَّيَـٰطِينَ كُلَّ بَنَّآءٍ وَغَوَّاصٍ ۝

38. And others bound in fetters.

وَءَاخَرِينَ مُقَرَّنِينَ فِى ٱلْأَصْفَادِ ۝

39. This is Our gift, so spend you or withhold, without rendering an account.

هَـٰذَا عَطَآؤُنَا فَٱمْنُنْ أَوْ أَمْسِكْ بِغَيْرِ حِسَابٍ ۝

40. And verily for him is an approach to Us, and a happy end.

وَإِنَّ لَهُۥ عِندَنَا لَزُلْفَىٰ وَحُسْنَ مَـَٔابٍ ۝

Section 4

41. And remember Our bondsman Job when he cried to his Lord: 'Verily Satan has touched me with affliction and suffering.'

وَٱذْكُرْ عَبْدَنَآ أَيُّوبَ إِذْ نَادَىٰ رَبَّهُۥٓ أَنِّى مَسَّنِىَ ٱلشَّيْطَـٰنُ بِنُصْبٍ وَعَذَابٍ ۝

42. 'Stamp you the ground with your foot; there is water, to wash in, cool, and to drink.'

ٱرْكُضْ بِرِجْلِكَ هَـٰذَا مُغْتَسَلٌۢ بَارِدٌ وَشَرَابٌ ۝

43. And We bestowed on him his household and along with them the like thereof, out of mercy from Us, and a remembrance to men of understanding.

وَوَهَبْنَا لَهُۥٓ أَهْلَهُۥ وَمِثْلَهُم مَّعَهُمْ رَحْمَةً مِّنَّا وَذِكْرَىٰ لِأُو۟لِى ٱلْأَلْبَـٰبِ ۝

44. 'And take in your hand a handful of twigs, and strike with it and break not your oath.' Verily We! We found him patient. An excellent bondsman! Verily he was oft-returning.

وَخُذْ بِيَدِكَ ضِغْثًا فَٱضْرِب بِّهِۦ وَلَا تَحْنَثْ إِنَّا وَجَدْنَـٰهُ صَابِرًا نِّعْمَ ٱلْعَبْدُ إِنَّهُۥٓ أَوَّابٌ ۝

45. And remember Our bondsmen, Abraham and Isaac and Jacob, all owners of might and vision.

وَٱذْكُرْ عِبَـٰدَنَآ إِبْرَٰهِيمَ وَإِسْحَـٰقَ وَيَعْقُوبَ أُو۟لِى ٱلْأَيْدِى وَٱلْأَبْصَـٰرِ ۝

46. Verily We! We distinguished them with a distinct quality: the remembrance of the Abode.

إِنَّآ أَخۡلَصۡنَٰهُم بِخَالِصَةٖ ذِكۡرَى ٱلدَّارِ ﴿٤٦﴾

47. And verily they are of the elect of the excellent ones with Us.

وَإِنَّهُمۡ عِندَنَا لَمِنَ ٱلۡمُصۡطَفَيۡنَ ٱلۡأَخۡيَارِ ﴿٤٧﴾

48. And remember Ishmael and al-Yasaʿ and Dhū al-Kifl, all of the excellent ones.

وَٱذۡكُرۡ إِسۡمَٰعِيلَ وَٱلۡيَسَعَ وَذَا ٱلۡكِفۡلِۖ وَكُلّٞ مِّنَ ٱلۡأَخۡيَارِ ﴿٤٨﴾

49. This is an admonition. And verily for the pious is a happy retreat.

هَٰذَا ذِكۡرٞۚ وَإِنَّ لِلۡمُتَّقِينَ لَحُسۡنَ مَـَٔابٖ ﴿٤٩﴾

50. Gardens everlasting, the portals of which remain opened for them.

جَنَّٰتِ عَدۡنٖ مُّفَتَّحَةٗ لَّهُمُ ٱلۡأَبۡوَٰبُ ﴿٥٠﴾

51. Therein they will recline; therein they will call for plenteous fruit and drink.

مُتَّكِـِٔينَ فِيهَا يَدۡعُونَ فِيهَا بِفَٰكِهَةٖ كَثِيرَةٖ وَشَرَابٖ ﴿٥١﴾

52. And with them will be virgins of refraining looks and of equal age.

وَعِندَهُمۡ قَٰصِرَٰتُ ٱلطَّرۡفِ أَتۡرَابٌ ﴿٥٢﴾

53. This it is which you are promised for the Day of Resurrection.

هَٰذَا مَا تُوعَدُونَ لِيَوۡمِ ٱلۡحِسَابِ ﴿٥٣﴾

54. Verily this is of Our provision; there will be no ceasing of it.

إِنَّ هَٰذَا لَرِزۡقُنَا مَا لَهُۥ مِن نَّفَادٍ ﴿٥٤﴾

55. This for the righteous. And verily for the exorbitant there shall be an evil retreat.

هَٰذَاۚ وَإِنَّ لِلطَّٰغِينَ لَشَرَّ مَـَٔابٖ ﴿٥٥﴾

56. Hell, wherein they roast, a wretched couch.

جَهَنَّمَ يَصْلَوْنَهَا فَبِئْسَ الْمِهَادُ ﴿٥٦﴾

57. This let them taste it, scalding water and corruption.

هَٰذَا فَلْيَذُوقُوهُ حَمِيمٌ وَغَسَّاقٌ ﴿٥٧﴾

58. And other torments, like them conjoined.

وَءَاخَرُ مِن شَكْلِهِۦٓ أَزْوَٰجٌ ﴿٥٨﴾

59. This is a crowd, rushing in along with you; no welcome for them; they are to roast in the Fire.

هَٰذَا فَوْجٌ مُّقْتَحِمٌ مَّعَكُمْ لَا مَرْحَبًۢا بِهِمْ إِنَّهُمْ صَالُوا۟ النَّارِ ﴿٥٩﴾

60. They will say: 'Nay! It is you for whom there is no welcome; it is you who have brought it upon us.' Ill shall be their resting-place.

قَالُوا۟ بَلْ أَنتُمْ لَا مَرْحَبًۢا بِكُمْ أَنتُمْ قَدَّمْتُمُوهُ لَنَا فَبِئْسَ الْقَرَارُ ﴿٦٠﴾

61. They will say: 'Our Lord! Whomsoever has brought this upon us, to him increase doubly the torment of the Fire.'

قَالُوا۟ رَبَّنَا مَن قَدَّمَ لَنَا هَٰذَا فَزِدْهُ عَذَابًا ضِعْفًا فِى النَّارِ ﴿٦١﴾

62. And they will say: 'What is the matter that we do not see the men whom we counted among the evil ones?

وَقَالُوا۟ مَا لَنَا لَا نَرَىٰ رِجَالًا كُنَّا نَعُدُّهُم مِّنَ الْأَشْرَارِ ﴿٦٢﴾

63. Did we take them for a butt of mockery, so unjustly, or are they deluding our eyes?'

أَتَّخَذْنَٰهُمْ سِخْرِيًّا أَمْ زَاغَتْ عَنْهُمُ الْأَبْصَٰرُ ﴿٦٣﴾

64. Verily this is very Truth; this wrangling of the inmates of the Fire.

إِنَّ ذَٰلِكَ لَحَقٌّ تَخَاصُمُ أَهْلِ النَّارِ ﴿٦٤﴾

Section 5

65. Say: 'I am but a warner, and there is no god but Allah, the One, the Subduer.

قُلْ إِنَّمَا أَنَا۟ مُنذِرٌ وَمَا مِنْ إِلَٰهٍ إِلَّا اللَّهُ الْوَٰحِدُ الْقَهَّارُ ﴿٦٥﴾

66. Lord of the heavens and the earth and whatsoever is in between them, the Mighty, the Forgiver.'

رَبُّ ٱلسَّمَوَٰتِ وَٱلْأَرْضِ وَمَا بَيْنَهُمَا ٱلْعَزِيزُ ٱلْغَفَّٰرُ ﴿٦٦﴾

67. Say: 'It is a great news.

قُلْ هُوَ نَبَؤٌاْ عَظِيمٌ ﴿٦٧﴾

68. You are averting therefrom.

أَنتُمْ عَنْهُ مُعْرِضُونَ ﴿٦٨﴾

69. I had no knowledge of the chiefs on high when they were disputing.

مَا كَانَ لِيَ مِنْ عِلْمٍ بِٱلْمَلَإِ ٱلْأَعْلَىٰٓ إِذْ يَخْتَصِمُونَ ﴿٦٩﴾

70. Nothing is revealed to me except that I am a manifest warner.'

إِن يُوحَىٰٓ إِلَيَّ إِلَّآ أَنَّمَآ أَنَا۠ نَذِيرٌ مُّبِينٌ ﴿٧٠﴾

71. Recall when your Lord said to the angels: 'I am about to create a human being from clay;

إِذْ قَالَ رَبُّكَ لِلْمَلَٰٓئِكَةِ إِنِّي خَٰلِقٌۢ بَشَرًا مِّن طِينٍ ﴿٧١﴾

72. Then when I have created him and breathed into him of My Spirit, fall down before him prostrate.'

فَإِذَا سَوَّيْتُهُۥ وَنَفَخْتُ فِيهِ مِن رُّوحِي فَقَعُواْ لَهُۥ سَٰجِدِينَ ﴿٧٢﴾

73. The angels fell prostrate; all of them.

فَسَجَدَ ٱلْمَلَٰٓئِكَةُ كُلُّهُمْ أَجْمَعُونَ ﴿٧٣﴾

74. Not so Iblīs. He grew stiff-necked, and became of the infidels.

إِلَّآ إِبْلِيسَ ٱسْتَكْبَرَ وَكَانَ مِنَ ٱلْكَٰفِرِينَ ﴿٧٤﴾

75. Allah said: 'Iblis! What does prevent you from prostrating yourself before what I have created with My hands? Have you been stiff-necked, or are you of the exalted ones?'

قَالَ يَٰٓإِبْلِيسُ مَا مَنَعَكَ أَن تَسْجُدَ لِمَا خَلَقْتُ بِيَدَيَّ أَسْتَكْبَرْتَ أَمْ كُنتَ مِنَ ٱلْعَالِينَ ﴿٧٥﴾

76. Iblis said: 'I am better than he; me You have created of fire, and him You have created of clay.'

قَالَ أَنَا۠ خَيْرٌ مِّنْهُ خَلَقْتَنِي مِن نَّارٍ وَخَلَقْتَهُۥ مِن طِينٍ ﴿٧٦﴾

77. Allah said: 'Get you forth from here, verily you are driven away.

قَالَ فَاخۡرُجۡ مِنۡهَا فَإِنَّكَ رَجِيمٌ ۝

78. And verily My curse shall be on you till the Day of Requital.'

وَإِنَّ عَلَيۡكَ لَعۡنَتِىٓ إِلَىٰ يَوۡمِ ٱلدِّينِ ۝

79. Iblis said: 'Lord! Respite me till the Day whereon they are raised up.'

قَالَ رَبِّ فَأَنظِرۡنِىٓ إِلَىٰ يَوۡمِ يُبۡعَثُونَ ۝

80. Allah said: 'Verily, you are of those respited.

قَالَ فَإِنَّكَ مِنَ ٱلۡمُنظَرِينَ ۝

81. Till the Day of the time appointed.'

إِلَىٰ يَوۡمِ ٱلۡوَقۡتِ ٱلۡمَعۡلُومِ ۝

82. Iblīs said: 'By Your Majesty, then I shall surely seduce them, all,

قَالَ فَبِعِزَّتِكَ لَأُغۡوِيَنَّهُمۡ أَجۡمَعِينَ ۝

83. Save Your sincere bondsmen among them.'

إِلَّا عِبَادَكَ مِنۡهُمُ ٱلۡمُخۡلَصِينَ ۝

84. Allah said: 'The Truth is, and it is the Truth I always say,

قَالَ فَٱلۡحَقُّ وَٱلۡحَقَّ أَقُولُ ۝

85. That I shall fill Hell with you and such of them as shall follow you, all together.'

لَأَمۡلَأَنَّ جَهَنَّمَ مِنكَ وَمِمَّن تَبِعَكَ مِنۡهُمۡ أَجۡمَعِينَ ۝

86. Say: 'I ask of you no wage for it nor am I of the affecters.

قُلۡ مَآ أَسۡـَٔلُكُمۡ عَلَيۡهِ مِنۡ أَجۡرٍ وَمَآ أَنَا۠ مِنَ ٱلۡمُتَكَلِّفِينَ ۝

87. It is nothing but an admonition to the worlds.

إِنۡ هُوَ إِلَّا ذِكۡرٌ لِّلۡعَٰلَمِينَ ۝

88. And you shall surely come to know of its truth after a season.'

وَلَتَعۡلَمُنَّ نَبَأَهُ بَعۡدَ حِينٍ ۝

Sūrah 39

al-Zumar

(Makkan, 8 Sections, 75 Verses)

*In the name of Allah, the
Compassionate, the Merciful.*

Section 1

1.　The revelation of this Book is
from Allah, the Mighty, the Wise.

2.　Verily We! We have sent
down the Book to you with truth;
so worship Allah, making
exclusion for Him in religion.

3.　Lo! For Allah is the Religion
exclusive. And those who take
patrons besides Him, saying: 'We
do not worship them save in order
that they may bring us nigh unto
Allah.'[628] Verily Allah will judge
between them concerning that
wherein they differ. Verily Allah
does not guide him who is a liar
and ungrateful.

628.　This being the ever-recurring plea of polytheistic peoples. Compare and
contrast with this absolute, pure, and unadulterated monotheism of Islam the
palpably polytheistic attitude of Christianity. 'The faithful who belong to the Church
militant upon earth, in offering their prayers to God, call at the same time to their aid
the saints who belong to the Church in heaven; and these, standing on the highest
steps of approach to God, by their prayers and intercessions purify, strengthen,
and offer before God the prayers of the faithful living upon earth, and by the will of
God work graciously and beneficently upon them' (Longer Orthodox Catechism,
quoted in the *ERE*. XI. p. 51). 'We ask God to grant blessings, we ask the saints to
be our advocates. To God we say: "Have mercy on us"; to the saints we commonly
say: "Pray for us". We beg of them, as they are pitiful, to take compassion on us
and interpose in our behalf' (Roman Catechism quoted in the *ERE*. XI. p. 51). This
mentality, perhaps is at the root of the primitive man's worship and the Christian
cults of the dead. 'A crowd of saints, who were once men and women, now form
an order of inferior deities, active in the affairs of men and receiving from them
reverence and prayer' (*PC*. II. p. 120).

4. Had Allah willed to take a son, He would have chosen whomsoever He pleased out of what He has created. Hallowed be He! He is Allah, the One, the Subduer.

لَوْ أَرَادَ اللَّهُ أَن يَتَّخِذَ وَلَدًا لَّاصْطَفَىٰ مِمَّا يَخْلُقُ مَا يَشَآءُ سُبْحَـٰنَهُ هُوَ اللَّهُ الْوَٰحِدُ الْقَهَّارُ ٤

5. He has created the heavens and the earth with a purpose. He rolls the night around the day, and He rolls the day around the night and He has subjected the sun and the moon, each running on for a term appointed. Lo! He is the Mighty, the Forgiving.

خَلَقَ السَّمَـٰوَٰتِ وَالْأَرْضَ بِالْحَقِّ يُكَوِّرُ الَّيْلَ عَلَى النَّهَارِ وَيُكَوِّرُ النَّهَارَ عَلَى الَّيْلِ وَسَخَّرَ الشَّمْسَ وَالْقَمَرَ كُلٌّ يَجْرِى لِأَجَلٍ مُّسَمًّى أَلَا هُوَ الْعَزِيزُ الْغَفَّـٰرُ ٥

6. He created you of a single soul[629] and made his spouse therefrom; and of the cattle He sent down unto you eight kinds. He creates you in the bellies of your mothers, one creation after creation, in threefold darkness.[630] Such is Allah, your Lord. His is the dominion, there is no god but He. Whither then turn you away?

خَلَقَكُم مِّن نَّفْسٍ وَٰحِدَةٍ ثُمَّ جَعَلَ مِنْهَا زَوْجَهَا وَأَنزَلَ لَكُم مِّنَ الْأَنْعَامِ ثَمَـٰنِيَةَ أَزْوَٰجٍ يَخْلُقُكُمْ فِى بُطُونِ أُمَّهَـٰتِكُمْ خَلْقًا مِّنۢ بَعْدِ خَلْقٍ فِى ظُلُمَـٰتٍ ثَلَـٰثٍ ذَٰلِكُمُ اللَّهُ رَبُّكُمْ لَهُ الْمُلْكُ لَآ إِلَـٰهَ إِلَّا هُوَ فَأَنَّىٰ تُصْرَفُونَ ٦

---

629. A soul which He originated. The Qur'ān makes it absolutely plain that all varieties of mankind have descended from a single undivided stock, and that the white, the black, and the red-skinned people of today, have sprung from one common ancestor. 'Specific unity of mankind is shown, in the words of a recent authority on anthropology, in the prevailing physical and mental uniformity of all peoples. According to E.B. Tylor, all tribes of men, from the blackest to the whitest, the most savage to the most cultured, have such general likeness, in the structure of their bodies and the working of their minds, as is easiest and best accounted for by their being descended from a common ancestry, however, distant" (*ERE*. V. p. 522). The Qur'ān is clear and emphatic in asserting the basic unity of mankind and in proclaiming that man is of one kind.

630. The embryo is covered by a membrane which is in the womb, which again is in the belly; hence the three veils of darkness.

7. If you disbelieve, then verily Allah is independent of you. And He does not approve of infidelity in His bondsmen. And if you return thanks, He approves of that in you. No burdened soul shall have another's burden. Your return is thereafter to your Lord, and He shall declare to you what you have been doing, verily He is the Knower of innumerate secrets.

إِن تَكۡفُرُوا۟ فَإِنَّ ٱللَّهَ غَنِيٌّ عَنكُمۡ وَلَا يَرۡضَىٰ لِعِبَادِهِ ٱلۡكُفۡرَ وَإِن تَشۡكُرُوا۟ يَرۡضَهُ لَكُمۡ وَلَا تَزِرُ وَازِرَةٌ وِزۡرَ أُخۡرَىٰ ثُمَّ إِلَىٰ رَبِّكُم مَّرۡجِعُكُمۡ فَيُنَبِّئُكُم بِمَا كُنتُمۡ تَعۡمَلُونَ إِنَّهُۥ عَلِيمٌۢ بِذَاتِ ٱلصُّدُورِ ۝

8. And when some hurt touches man, he calls upon his Lord, turning to Him in penitence. Then when He bestows upon him a favour from Himself, he forgets that for which he had called on Him before, and sets up peers to Allah that he may lead astray others from His path. Say: 'Enjoy you life in your infidelity for a while, verily you are of the inmates of the Fire.'

وَإِذَا مَسَّ ٱلۡإِنسَٰنَ ضُرٌّ دَعَا رَبَّهُۥ مُنِيبًا إِلَيۡهِ ثُمَّ إِذَا خَوَّلَهُۥ نِعۡمَةً مِّنۡهُ نَسِيَ مَا كَانَ يَدۡعُوٓا۟ إِلَيۡهِ مِن قَبۡلُ وَجَعَلَ لِلَّهِ أَندَادًا لِّيُضِلَّ عَن سَبِيلِهِۦ قُلۡ تَمَتَّعۡ بِكُفۡرِكَ قَلِيلًا إِنَّكَ مِنۡ أَصۡحَٰبِ ٱلنَّارِ ۝

9. Is he who is devout in the watches of the night prostrating himself and standing, bewaring of the Hereafter and hoping for the mercy of His Lord to be dealt with like a wicked infidel? Say: 'Shall they who know and those who know not be held equal?' It is only men of understanding who receive admonition.

أَمَّنۡ هُوَ قَٰنِتٌ ءَانَآءَ ٱلَّيۡلِ سَاجِدًا وَقَآئِمًا يَحۡذَرُ ٱلۡءَاخِرَةَ وَيَرۡجُوا۟ رَحۡمَةَ رَبِّهِۦ قُلۡ هَلۡ يَسۡتَوِى ٱلَّذِينَ يَعۡلَمُونَ وَٱلَّذِينَ لَا يَعۡلَمُونَ إِنَّمَا يَتَذَكَّرُ أُو۟لُوا۟ ٱلۡأَلۡبَٰبِ ۝

Section 2

10. Say: 'My faithful bondsmen! Fear your Lord.' For those who do good in this world there is good; and Allah's earth is spacious. Surely the steadfast will be given their reward in full without reckoning.

11. Say: 'Verily I am bidden to worship Allah, making religion exclusive for Him.

12. And I am bidden this, in order that I may be the first of those who submit.'

13. Say: 'I fear, if I disobeyed my Lord, chastisement of an awful Day.'

14. Say: 'It is Allah I worship, making faith for Him exclusive.

15. So worship whatever you will besides Him O pagans.' Say: 'The real losers are those who shall have lost themselves and their household on the Day of Judgement.' Lo! That will be a manifest loss.

16. For them! Coverings of the Fire will be above them and beneath them. With this Allah frightens His bondsmen. My bondsmen, therefore fear Me.

قُلْ يَـٰعِبَادِ ٱلَّذِينَ ءَامَنُواْ ٱتَّقُواْ رَبَّكُمْ لِلَّذِينَ أَحْسَنُواْ فِى هَـٰذِهِ ٱلدُّنْيَا حَسَنَةٌ وَأَرْضُ ٱللَّهِ وَٰسِعَةٌ إِنَّمَا يُوَفَّى ٱلصَّـٰبِرُونَ أَجْرَهُم بِغَيْرِ حِسَابٍ ﴿١٠﴾

قُلْ إِنِّىٓ أُمِرْتُ أَنْ أَعْبُدَ ٱللَّهَ مُخْلِصًا لَّهُ ٱلدِّينَ ﴿١١﴾

وَأُمِرْتُ لِأَنْ أَكُونَ أَوَّلَ ٱلْمُسْلِمِينَ ﴿١٢﴾

قُلْ إِنِّىٓ أَخَافُ إِنْ عَصَيْتُ رَبِّى عَذَابَ يَوْمٍ عَظِيمٍ ﴿١٣﴾

قُلِ ٱللَّهَ أَعْبُدُ مُخْلِصًا لَّهُ دِينِى ﴿١٤﴾

فَٱعْبُدُواْ مَا شِئْتُم مِّن دُونِهِ قُلْ إِنَّ ٱلْخَـٰسِرِينَ ٱلَّذِينَ خَسِرُوٓاْ أَنفُسَهُمْ وَأَهْلِيهِمْ يَوْمَ ٱلْقِيَـٰمَةِ أَلَا ذَٰلِكَ هُوَ ٱلْخُسْرَانُ ٱلْمُبِينُ ﴿١٥﴾

لَهُم مِّن فَوْقِهِمْ ظُلَلٌ مِّنَ ٱلنَّارِ وَمِن تَحْتِهِمْ ظُلَلٌ ذَٰلِكَ يُخَوِّفُ ٱللَّهُ بِهِ عِبَادَهُ يَـٰعِبَادِ فَٱتَّقُونِ ﴿١٦﴾

17. And those who shun the devils lest they should worship them and turn to Allah in penitence, for them are glad tidings. So give you glad tidings to My bondsmen,

وَٱلَّذِينَ ٱجْتَنَبُوا ٱلطَّـٰغُوتَ أَن يَعْبُدُوهَا وَأَنَابُوٓا إِلَى ٱللَّهِ لَهُمُ ٱلْبُشْرَىٰ فَبَشِّرْ عِبَادِ ١٧

18. Who listen to the Word and follow the excellent thereof. Those are they whom Allah has guided, and those are men of understanding.

ٱلَّذِينَ يَسْتَمِعُونَ ٱلْقَوْلَ فَيَتَّبِعُونَ أَحْسَنَهُ أُوْلَـٰٓئِكَ ٱلَّذِينَ هَدَىٰهُمُ ٱللَّهُ وَأُوْلَـٰٓئِكَ هُمْ أُوْلُوا ٱلْأَلْبَـٰبِ ١٨

19. Is he then on whom is justified the decree of torment; will you rescue him who is in the Fire?

أَفَمَنْ حَقَّ عَلَيْهِ كَلِمَةُ ٱلْعَذَابِ أَفَأَنتَ تُنقِذُ مَن فِى ٱلنَّارِ ١٩

20. But those who fear their Lord, for them are lofty chambers with lofty chambers above them, built, where under rivers flow; the promise of Allah, and Allah fails not His appointment.

لَـٰكِنِ ٱلَّذِينَ ٱتَّقَوْا رَبَّهُمْ لَهُمْ غُرَفٌ مِّن فَوْقِهَا غُرَفٌ مَّبْنِيَّةٌ تَجْرِى مِن تَحْتِهَا ٱلْأَنْهَـٰرُ وَعْدَ ٱللَّهِ لَا يُخْلِفُ ٱللَّهُ ٱلْمِيعَادَ ٢٠

21. Do you not see that Allah sends down water from the sky, and causes it to enter springs in the earth, and thereby produces corn various-coloured? Thereafter it withers and you see it turn yellow; then He makes it chaff. Verily herein is admonition for men of understanding.

أَلَمْ تَرَ أَنَّ ٱللَّهَ أَنزَلَ مِنَ ٱلسَّمَآءِ مَآءً فَسَلَكَهُ يَنَـٰبِيعَ فِى ٱلْأَرْضِ ثُمَّ يُخْرِجُ بِهِۦ زَرْعًا مُّخْتَلِفًا أَلْوَٰنُهُ ثُمَّ يَهِيجُ فَتَرَىٰهُ مُصْفَرًّا ثُمَّ يَجْعَلُهُۥ حُطَـٰمًا إِنَّ فِى ذَٰلِكَ لَذِكْرَىٰ لِأُوْلِى ٱلْأَلْبَـٰبِ ٢١

Section 3

22. Shall there, then, be one whose breast Allah has expanded for Islam, so that he follows a light from His Lord, be as he whose heart is hardened? Then woe to those who hearts are hardened against the remembrance of Allah. They are in manifest error.

أَفَمَن شَرَحَ ٱللَّهُ صَدْرَهُۥ لِلْإِسْلَٰمِ فَهُوَ عَلَىٰ نُورٍ مِّن رَّبِّهِۦ فَوَيْلٌ لِّلْقَٰسِيَةِ قُلُوبُهُم مِّن ذِكْرِ ٱللَّهِ أُوْلَٰٓئِكَ فِى ضَلَٰلٍ مُّبِينٍ ﴿٢٢﴾

23. Allah has revealed the most excellent discourse, a Book consimilar,[631] oft-repeated, at which trembles the skin; of those who fear their Lord; then their skin and heart soften to the remembrance of Allah. This is Allah's guidance to which He guides whom He will; and whom Allah sends astray, for him there is no guide.

ٱللَّهُ نَزَّلَ أَحْسَنَ ٱلْحَدِيثِ كِتَٰبًا مُّتَشَٰبِهًا مَّثَانِيَ تَقْشَعِرُّ مِنْهُ جُلُودُ ٱلَّذِينَ يَخْشَوْنَ رَبَّهُمْ ثُمَّ تَلِينُ جُلُودُهُمْ وَقُلُوبُهُمْ إِلَىٰ ذِكْرِ ٱللَّهِ ذَٰلِكَ هُدَى ٱللَّهِ يَهْدِى بِهِۦ مَن يَشَآءُ وَمَن يُضْلِلِ ٱللَّهُ فَمَا لَهُۥ مِنْ هَادٍ ﴿٢٣﴾

24. Is he, then, who will shield himself with his face from the evils of torment on the Day of Resurrection be as he who is secure therefrom? And it will be said to the ungodly: 'Taste what you have been earning.'

أَفَمَن يَتَّقِى بِوَجْهِهِۦ سُوٓءَ ٱلْعَذَابِ يَوْمَ ٱلْقِيَٰمَةِ وَقِيلَ لِلظَّٰلِمِينَ ذُوقُواْ مَا كُنتُمْ تَكْسِبُونَ ﴿٢٤﴾

25. Those who belied before them, on them came the torment from whence they knew not.

كَذَّبَ ٱلَّذِينَ مِن قَبْلِهِمْ فَأَتَىٰهُمُ ٱلْعَذَابُ مِنْ حَيْثُ لَا يَشْعُرُونَ ﴿٢٥﴾

---

631. Or 'self-resembling' alike throughout the excellence of its contents. The whole of the Qur'ān, although revealed piecemeal and during a long interval of about 23 years and dealing with facts and events far removed from each other is nonetheless a Book consistent with itself, and conformable in all its various parts.

26. Allah made them taste humiliation in this world; and surely the torment of the Hereafter is greater, if they but know.

فَأَذَاقَهُمُ اللَّهُ الْخِزْيَ فِي الْحَيَوةِ الدُّنْيَا وَلَعَذَابُ الْأَخِرَةِ أَكْبَرُ لَوْكَانُوا يَعْلَمُونَ ۝

27. And assuredly We have propounded in this Qur'ān every manner of similitudes for mankind, that haply they may be admonished.

وَلَقَدْ ضَرَبْنَا لِلنَّاسِ فِي هَذَا الْقُرْءَانِ مِن كُلِّ مَثَلٍ لَّعَلَّهُمْ يَتَذَكَّرُونَ ۝

28. And the Arabic Qur'ān, without any crookedness, that haply they may fear.

قُرْءَانًا عَرَبِيًّا غَيْرَ ذِى عِوَجٍ لَّعَلَّهُمْ يَتَّقُونَ ۝

29. Allah propounds a similitude; a man has several partners, quarrelling, and a man, the property of one man. Are the two equal in likeness? Praise be to Allah! But most of them know not.

ضَرَبَ اللَّهُ مَثَلًا رَّجُلًا فِيهِ شُرَكَاءُ مُتَشَاكِسُونَ وَرَجُلًا سَلَمًا لِّرَجُلٍ هَلْ يَسْتَوِيَانِ مَثَلًا الْحَمْدُ لِلَّهِ بَلْ أَكْثَرُهُمْ لَا يَعْلَمُونَ ۝

30. Verily you are mortal and they are mortals.

إِنَّكَ مَيِّتٌ وَإِنَّهُم مَّيِّتُونَ ۝

31. Then on the Day of Resurrection you shall be contending before your Lord.

ثُمَّ إِنَّكُمْ يَوْمَ الْقِيَمَةِ عِندَ رَبِّكُمْ تَخْتَصِمُونَ ۝

Section 4

32. And who is a greater wrong-doer than he who fabricates a lie against Allah, and belies the Truth when it comes to him? Will there not be the abode in Hell for the infidels?

فَمَنْ أَظْلَمُ مِمَّن كَذَبَ عَلَى اللَّهِ وَكَذَّبَ بِالصِّدْقِ إِذْ جَاءَهُ أَلَيْسَ فِي جَهَنَّمَ مَثْوًى لِّلْكَفِرِينَ ۝

33. And whosoever brings the Truth and whosoever gives credence to it, these! They are the pious.

وَٱلَّذِى جَآءَ بِٱلصِّدۡقِ وَصَدَّقَ بِهِۦٓ أُوْلَٰٓئِكَ هُمُ ٱلۡمُتَّقُونَ ﴿٣٣﴾

34. Theirs shall be whatever they will desire with their Lord: that is the reward of the well-doers.

لَهُم مَّا يَشَآءُونَ عِندَ رَبِّهِمۡۚ ذَٰلِكَ جَزَآءُ ٱلۡمُحۡسِنِينَ ﴿٣٤﴾

35. This will be in order that Allah may expiate from them the evil of what they may have worked, and may recompense them their wage for the best of what they have been working.

لِيُكَفِّرَ ٱللَّهُ عَنۡهُمۡ أَسۡوَأَ ٱلَّذِى عَمِلُواْ وَيَجۡزِيَهُمۡ أَجۡرَهُم بِأَحۡسَنِ ٱلَّذِى كَانُواْ يَعۡمَلُونَ ﴿٣٥﴾

36. Is Allah not sufficient for His bondsmen? Yet they would frighten you with those besides Him. And whom Allah sends astray, for him there will be no guide.

أَلَيۡسَ ٱللَّهُ بِكَافٍ عَبۡدَهُۥۖ وَيُخَوِّفُونَكَ بِٱلَّذِينَ مِن دُونِهِۦۚ وَمَن يُضۡلِلِ ٱللَّهُ فَمَا لَهُۥ مِنۡ هَادٍ ﴿٣٦﴾

37. And whom Allah guides, for him there will be no misleader. Is not Allah the Mighty and the Lord of Retribution?

وَمَن يَهۡدِ ٱللَّهُ فَمَا لَهُۥ مِن مُّضِلٍّ أَلَيۡسَ ٱللَّهُ بِعَزِيزٍ ذِى ٱنتِقَامٍ ﴿٣٧﴾

38. Were you to ask them: 'Who has created the heavens and the earth?,' they will surely say: 'Allah'. Say: 'Consider you then that those whom you call upon besides Allah, could they, if Allah intended some hurt for me, remove His hurt? Or if He intended some mercy for me, could they withhold His mercy?' Say: 'Enough for me is Allah; in Him the trusting put their trust.'

وَلَئِن سَأَلۡتَهُم مَّنۡ خَلَقَ ٱلسَّمَٰوَٰتِ وَٱلۡأَرۡضَ لَيَقُولُنَّ ٱللَّهُۚ قُلۡ أَفَرَءَيۡتُم مَّا تَدۡعُونَ مِن دُونِ ٱللَّهِ إِنۡ أَرَادَنِىَ ٱللَّهُ بِضُرٍّ هَلۡ هُنَّ كَٰشِفَٰتُ ضُرِّهِۦٓ أَوۡ أَرَادَنِى بِرَحۡمَةٍ هَلۡ هُنَّ مُمۡسِكَٰتُ رَحۡمَتِهِۦۚ قُلۡ حَسۡبِىَ ٱللَّهُۖ عَلَيۡهِ يَتَوَكَّلُ ٱلۡمُتَوَكِّلُونَ ﴿٣٨﴾

39. Say: 'O my people act according to your station; I am going to act in my way; presently you shall come to know,

قُلْ يَقَوْمِ اعْمَلُوا عَلَىٰ مَكَانَتِكُمْ إِنِّى عَامِلٌ فَسَوْفَ تَعْلَمُونَ ۝

40. On whom comes a humiliating torment and on whom alights a lasting torment.'

مَن يَأْتِيهِ عَذَابٌ يُخْزِيهِ وَيَحِلُّ عَلَيْهِ عَذَابٌ مُّقِيمٌ ۝

41. Verily We! We have sent down to you the Book for mankind with truth. Then whoever receives guidance it is for his own soul, and whoever strays, strays only to his hurt; and you are not a guardian over them.

إِنَّآ أَنزَلْنَا عَلَيْكَ ٱلْكِتَـٰبَ لِلنَّاسِ بِٱلْحَقِّ فَمَنِ ٱهْتَدَىٰ فَلِنَفْسِهِۦ وَمَن ضَلَّ فَإِنَّمَا يَضِلُّ عَلَيْهَا وَمَآ أَنتَ عَلَيْهِم بِوَكِيلٍ ۝

Section 5

42. Allah it is Who takes away the souls at the time of their death and those who do not die in their sleep; then He withholds those on whom He has decreed death, then sends back the rest for an appointed term. Verily herein are signs for those who ponder.

ٱللَّهُ يَتَوَفَّى ٱلْأَنفُسَ حِينَ مَوْتِهَا وَٱلَّتِى لَمْ تَمُتْ فِى مَنَامِهَا فَيُمْسِكُ ٱلَّتِى قَضَىٰ عَلَيْهَا ٱلْمَوْتَ وَيُرْسِلُ ٱلْأُخْرَىٰ إِلَىٰ أَجَلٍ مُّسَمًّى إِنَّ فِى ذَٰلِكَ لَآيَـٰتٍ لِّقَوْمٍ يَتَفَكَّرُونَ ۝

43. Have they taken others for intercessors besides Allah? Say: 'What! Even you they own not aught and understand not?'

أَمِ ٱتَّخَذُوا مِن دُونِ ٱللَّهِ شُفَعَآءَ قُلْ أَوَلَوْ كَانُوا لَا يَمْلِكُونَ شَيْئًا وَلَا يَعْقِلُونَ ۝

44. Say: 'Allah's is intercession altogether.[632] His is the dominion of the heavens and the earth; then to Him you shall be returned.'

45. When mention is made of Allah alone, the hearts of those who believe not in the Hereafter shrink with aversion; and when mention is made of those besides Him, lo! They rejoice.

46. Say: 'Allah! Creator of the heavens and the earth! Knower of the hidden and the open! You shall judge between them concerning what they have been differing in.'

47. And were the ungodly to own all that is on the earth, and with it as much again, they will seek surely to ransom therewith from the torment of the Day of Judgement, and there will become apparent to them from Allah what they had not been reckoning.

قُل لِّلَّهِ ٱلشَّفَٰعَةُ جَمِيعًا لَّهُ مُلْكُ ٱلسَّمَٰوَٰتِ وَٱلْأَرْضِ ثُمَّ إِلَيْهِ تُرْجَعُونَ ﴿٤٤﴾

وَإِذَا ذُكِرَ ٱللَّهُ وَحْدَهُ ٱشْمَأَزَّتْ قُلُوبُ ٱلَّذِينَ لَا يُؤْمِنُونَ بِٱلْأَخِرَةِ وَإِذَا ذُكِرَ ٱلَّذِينَ مِن دُونِهِۦ إِذَا هُمْ يَسْتَبْشِرُونَ ﴿٤٥﴾

قُلِ ٱللَّهُمَّ فَاطِرَ ٱلسَّمَٰوَٰتِ وَٱلْأَرْضِ عَٰلِمَ ٱلْغَيْبِ وَٱلشَّهَٰدَةِ أَنتَ تَحْكُمُ بَيْنَ عِبَادِكَ فِى مَا كَانُوا۟ فِيهِ يَخْتَلِفُونَ ﴿٤٦﴾

وَلَوْ أَنَّ لِلَّذِينَ ظَلَمُوا۟ مَا فِى ٱلْأَرْضِ جَمِيعًا وَمِثْلَهُۥ مَعَهُۥ لَٱفْتَدَوْا۟ بِهِۦ مِن سُوٓءِ ٱلْعَذَابِ يَوْمَ ٱلْقِيَٰمَةِ وَبَدَا لَهُم مِّنَ ٱللَّهِ مَا لَمْ يَكُونُوا۟ يَحْتَسِبُونَ ﴿٤٧﴾

632. None can presume to intercede with Him, unless by His permission. This strikes at the very root of Saviourhood and the mediation of Christ and others. Referring to four passages in the NT, says a modern spokesman of Christianity: 'In all these passages Christ is represented as mediating between God and man. God and man have been estranged. The relation which normally subsists between them has been destroyed, and the work of the mediator is to restore it. In Timothy this work is explicitly connected with the redemptive death of Christ; there is one mediator between God and men, Himself man, Christ Jesus, who gave Himself a ransom for all' (*ERE*. VIII. p. 516). The Christians pride themselves on calling this faith the religion of mediation. 'While the word "mediator" is rarely met with, the idea contained in it is one of the most vital and influential thoughts in religion. Nearly every religion bears witness to it (It) is found more clearly and forcibly expressed in Christianity than in any other type of religion. So prominent and characteristic is the idea that we might define Christianity in the abstract as Theism plus Mediation for it is this idea that most distinguishes the religion of the New Testament from pure Theism' (*DB*, III. p. 311 – 312).

48. And there will become apparent to them the evils of what they earned, and there will surround them what they had been mocking at.

وَبَدَا لَهُمْ سَيِّئَاتُ مَا كَسَبُواْ وَحَاقَ بِهِم مَّا كَانُواْ بِهِۦ يَسْتَهْزِءُونَ ۝

49. When hurt touches a man he calls on Us, and afterwards when We have changed it into a favour from Us, he says: 'I have obtained it by force of my knowledge.' Aye! It is a trial, but most of them know not.

فَإِذَا مَسَّ ٱلْإِنسَٰنَ ضُرٌّ دَعَانَا ثُمَّ إِذَا خَوَّلْنَٰهُ نِعْمَةً مِّنَّا قَالَ إِنَّمَآ أُوتِيتُهُۥ عَلَىٰ عِلْمٍ بَلْ هِىَ فِتْنَةٌ وَلَٰكِنَّ أَكْثَرَهُمْ لَا يَعْلَمُونَ ۝

50. Surely said it those before them, yet there did not avail them what they have been earning.

قَدْ قَالَهَا ٱلَّذِينَ مِن قَبْلِهِمْ فَمَآ أَغْنَىٰ عَنْهُم مَّا كَانُواْ يَكْسِبُونَ ۝

51. And there befell them the evils of what they had earned. And of them they who go wrong presently will befall them the evil of what they earn; nor can they frustrate .

فَأَصَابَهُمْ سَيِّئَاتُ مَا كَسَبُواْ وَٱلَّذِينَ ظَلَمُواْ مِنْ هَٰٓؤُلَآءِ سَيُصِيبُهُمْ سَيِّئَاتُ مَا كَسَبُواْ وَمَا هُم بِمُعْجِزِينَ ۝

52. Do they not know that Allah expands provision for whom He will, and stints it for whom He will? Verily herein are signs for those who believe.

أَوَلَمْ يَعْلَمُوٓاْ أَنَّ ٱللَّهَ يَبْسُطُ ٱلرِّزْقَ لِمَن يَشَآءُ وَيَقْدِرُ إِنَّ فِى ذَٰلِكَ لَآيَٰتٍ لِّقَوْمٍ يُؤْمِنُونَ ۝

Section 6

53. Say: 'My bondsmen who have committed extravagance against themselves; despair not of the mercy of Allah;' verily Allah will forgive the sins altogether. Verily He! He is the Forgiving, the Merciful.

قُلْ يَٰعِبَادِىَ ٱلَّذِينَ أَسْرَفُواْ عَلَىٰٓ أَنفُسِهِمْ لَا تَقْنَطُواْ مِن رَّحْمَةِ ٱللَّهِ إِنَّ ٱللَّهَ يَغْفِرُ ٱلذُّنُوبَ جَمِيعًا إِنَّهُۥ هُوَ ٱلْغَفُورُ ٱلرَّحِيمُ ۝

54. Turn penitently to your Lord, and submit to Him, before there comes to you the torment, and then you shall not be succoured.

وَأَنِيبُوٓاْ إِلَىٰ رَبِّكُمْ وَأَسْلِمُواْ لَهُۥ مِن قَبْلِ أَن يَأْتِيَكُمُ ٱلْعَذَابُ ثُمَّ لَا تُنصَرُونَ ﴿٥٤﴾

55. And follow the best of what has been sent down to you from your Lord before there comes to you the torment of a sudden, while you perceive not?

وَٱتَّبِعُوٓاْ أَحْسَنَ مَآ أُنزِلَ إِلَيْكُم مِّن رَّبِّكُم مِّن قَبْلِ أَن يَأْتِيَكُمُ ٱلْعَذَابُ بَغْتَةً وَأَنتُمْ لَا تَشْعُرُونَ ﴿٥٥﴾

56. Lest a soul should say: 'Alas! For that I have been remiss in respect of Allah, and I was but of the scoffers!'

أَن تَقُولَ نَفْسٌ يَٰحَسْرَتَىٰ عَلَىٰ مَا فَرَّطتُ فِى جَنۢبِ ٱللَّهِ وَإِن كُنتُ لَمِنَ ٱلسَّٰخِرِينَ ﴿٥٦﴾

57. Or, lest it should say: 'Had Allah but guided me, I would surely have been of the pious.'

أَوْ تَقُولَ لَوْ أَنَّ ٱللَّهَ هَدَىٰنِى لَكُنتُ مِنَ ٱلْمُتَّقِينَ ﴿٥٧﴾

58. Or, lest it should say when it beholds the torment: 'Were there for me a return I would be of the well-doers.'

أَوْ تَقُولَ حِينَ تَرَى ٱلْعَذَابَ لَوْ أَنَّ لِى كَرَّةً فَأَكُونَ مِنَ ٱلْمُحْسِنِينَ ﴿٥٨﴾

59. Yea! Surely there came to you My revelations, but you belied them and were stiff-necked and of the infidels.

بَلَىٰ قَدْ جَآءَتْكَ ءَايَٰتِى فَكَذَّبْتَ بِهَا وَٱسْتَكْبَرْتَ وَكُنتَ مِنَ ٱلْكَٰفِرِينَ ﴿٥٩﴾

60. And on the Day of Judgement you shall see those who lied against Allah, their faces blackened. Is there not the abode of the stiff-necked in Hell?

وَيَوْمَ ٱلْقِيَٰمَةِ تَرَى ٱلَّذِينَ كَذَبُواْ عَلَى ٱللَّهِ وُجُوهُهُم مُّسْوَدَّةٌ أَلَيْسَ فِى جَهَنَّمَ مَثْوًى لِّلْمُتَكَبِّرِينَ ﴿٦٠﴾

61. And Allah will deliver them who feared Him to their place of safety. Evil will not touch them. Nor will they grieve.

وَيُنَجِّى ٱللَّهُ ٱلَّذِينَ ٱتَّقَوْاْ بِمَفَازَتِهِمْ لَا يَمَسُّهُمُ ٱلسُّوٓءُ وَلَا هُمْ يَحْزَنُونَ ﴿٦١﴾

62. Allah is the Creator of everything. And He is a Trustee over everything.

اللّٰهُ خَالِقُ كُلِّ شَىْءٍ وَهُوَ عَلَىٰ كُلِّ شَىْءٍ وَكِيْلٌ ۝

63. His are the keys of the heavens and the earth; and those who disbelieve in the revelation of Allah, those! They are losers.

لَّهُ مَقَالِيْدُ السَّمٰوٰتِ وَالْأَرْضِ وَالَّذِيْنَ كَفَرُوْا بِاٰيٰتِ اللّٰهِ أُولٰٓئِكَ هُمُ الْخَاسِرُوْنَ ۝

Section 7

64. Say: 'Is it other than Allah that you call me to worship, O you pagans!'

قُلْ أَفَغَيْرَ اللّٰهِ تَأْمُرُوْنِّيْ أَعْبُدُ أَيُّهَا الْجَاهِلُوْنَ ۝

65. And assuredly it has been revealed to you and to those before you; if you join surely of no effect shall be made your work, and you shall surely be of the losers.

وَلَقَدْ أُوْحِيَ إِلَيْكَ وَإِلَى الَّذِيْنَ مِنْ قَبْلِكَ لَئِنْ أَشْرَكْتَ لَيَحْبَطَنَّ عَمَلُكَ وَلَتَكُوْنَنَّ مِنَ الْخَاسِرِيْنَ ۝

66. Aye! Allah must you worship, and be among the thankful.

بَلِ اللّٰهَ فَاعْبُدْ وَكُنْ مِّنَ الشَّاكِرِيْنَ ۝

67. And they do not estimate Allah with an estimation due to Him, whereas the whole earth shall be His handful on the Day of Judgement, and the heavens shall be rolled in His right hand. Hallowed be He and Exalted above what they associate

وَمَا قَدَرُوا اللّٰهَ حَقَّ قَدْرِهٖ وَالْأَرْضُ جَمِيْعًا قَبْضَتُهٗ يَوْمَ الْقِيٰمَةِ وَالسَّمٰوٰتُ مَطْوِيّٰتٌ بِيَمِيْنِهٖ سُبْحٰنَهٗ وَتَعٰلٰى عَمَّا يُشْرِكُوْنَ ۝

68. And the trumpet shall be blown, when all who are in the heavens and all who are on the earth shall swoon away, save whom Allah wills. Then it shall be blown again, and lo! They shall be standing, looking on.

وَنُفِخَ فِى الصُّوْرِ فَصَعِقَ مَنْ فِى السَّمٰوٰتِ وَمَنْ فِى الْأَرْضِ إِلَّا مَنْ شَاءَ اللّٰهُ ثُمَّ نُفِخَ فِيْهِ أُخْرَىٰ فَإِذَا هُمْ قِيَامٌ يَنْظُرُوْنَ ۝

69. And the earth will gleam with the light of the Lord and the record will be set up, and the Prophets and the witnesses will be brought, and the Judgement between them will be given with truth, and they will not be wronged.

وَأَشْرَقَتِ ٱلْأَرْضُ بِنُورِ رَبِّهَا وَوُضِعَ ٱلْكِتَبُ وَجِأْىَٰءَ بِٱلنَّبِيِّنَ وَٱلشُّهَدَآءِ وَقُضِىَ بَيْنَهُم بِٱلْحَقِّ وَهُمْ لَا يُظْلَمُونَ ۝

70. Every soul will be paid in full what it has worked; and He is the Best Knower of what they do.[633]

وَوُفِّيَتْ كُلُّ نَفْسٍ مَّا عَمِلَتْ وَهُوَ أَعْلَمُ بِمَا يَفْعَلُونَ ۝

Section 8

71. And those who disbelieve will be driven to Hell in troops till, when they arrive thereto, its portals will be opened, and its keepers will say to them; did not there come to you Messengers from amongst you, rehearsing to you the revelations of your Lord and warning you of the meeting of this your Day? They will say, 'Yea!', but the word of chastisement has been justified on the infidels.

وَسِيقَ ٱلَّذِينَ كَفَرُوٓا۟ إِلَىٰ جَهَنَّمَ زُمَرًا حَتَّىٰٓ إِذَا جَآءُوهَا فُتِحَتْ أَبْوَٰبُهَا وَقَالَ لَهُمْ خَزَنَتُهَآ أَلَمْ يَأْتِكُمْ رُسُلٌ مِّنكُمْ يَتْلُونَ عَلَيْكُمْ ءَايَٰتِ رَبِّكُمْ وَيُنذِرُونَكُمْ لِقَآءَ يَوْمِكُمْ هَٰذَا قَالُوا۟ بَلَىٰ وَلَٰكِنْ حَقَّتْ كَلِمَةُ ٱلْعَذَابِ عَلَى ٱلْكَٰفِرِينَ ۝

72. It will be said: 'Enter the portals of Hell to be abiders therein. How ill, then is the abode of the stiff-necked!'

قِيلَ ٱدْخُلُوٓا۟ أَبْوَٰبَ جَهَنَّمَ خَٰلِدِينَ فِيهَا فَبِئْسَ مَثْوَى ٱلْمُتَكَبِّرِينَ ۝

---

633. Compare this highly monotheistic description of Judgement Day with a similar but, essentially polytheistic one in the NT, Mt. 25: 31 ff.

73. And those who feared their Lord will be driven to the Garden in troops till, when they arrive thereto, and its portals will be opened, and its keepers will say to them: 'Peace be to you! Excellent are you, enter it as abiders.'

وَسِيقَ ٱلَّذِينَ ٱتَّقَوْاْ رَبَّهُمْ إِلَى ٱلْجَنَّةِ زُمَرًا حَتَّىٰٓ إِذَا جَآءُوهَا وَفُتِحَتْ أَبْوَٰبُهَا وَقَالَ لَهُمْ خَزَنَتُهَا سَلَٰمٌ عَلَيْكُمْ طِبْتُمْ فَٱدْخُلُوهَا خَٰلِدِينَ ۝

74. And they will say: 'All praise to Allah, Who had made good His promise to us, and made us inherit this land, so that we may dwell in the Garden wherever we will!' Excellent, then, is the reward of the workers!

وَقَالُواْ ٱلْحَمْدُ لِلَّهِ ٱلَّذِى صَدَقَنَا وَعْدَهُۥ وَأَوْرَثَنَا ٱلْأَرْضَ نَتَبَوَّأُ مِنَ ٱلْجَنَّةِ حَيْثُ نَشَآءُ فَنِعْمَ أَجْرُ ٱلْعَٰمِلِينَ ۝

75. And you will see the angels thronging round the throne, hallowing the praise of their Lord. And Judgement will be given between them with truth; and it will be said: 'All praise to Allah, the Lord of the worlds.'

وَتَرَى ٱلْمَلَٰٓئِكَةَ حَآفِّينَ مِنْ حَوْلِ ٱلْعَرْشِ يُسَبِّحُونَ بِحَمْدِ رَبِّهِمْ وَقُضِىَ بَيْنَهُم بِٱلْحَقِّ وَقِيلَ ٱلْحَمْدُ لِلَّهِ رَبِّ ٱلْعَٰلَمِينَ ۝

Sūrah 40

Ghāfir

(Makkan, 9 Sections, 85 Verses)

*In the name of Allah, the
Compassionate, the Merciful.*

Section 1

1. *Ḥā, Mīm.*

2. The revelation of the Book is
from Allah, the Mighty, the
Knower.

3. The Forgiver of sin, Acceptor
of repentance,[634] Severe in
chastisement, Lord of Power, no
god is there but He; to Him is the
journeying.

4. None disputes concerning the
revelation of Allah save those who
disbelieve; so let not their going
about in the cities beguile you.

5. The people of Noah and the
confederates after them, belied
their Messengers before them, and
every disbelieving community
advanced towards their
Messenger that they may seize
him, and disputed with vain talk,
that they may confute the Truth
thereby. So I seized them, and
how terrible was My
chastisement!

---

634. Note once more that the expiation of sin in Islam rests entirely, on the one hand,
on the repentance of the sinner and, on the other on the forgiving and merciful
nature of God.

6. And thus the word of your Lord has been justified on them who disbelieve, that they shall be the inmates of the Fire.

وَكَذَٰلِكَ حَقَّتْ كَلِمَتُ رَبِّكَ عَلَى ٱلَّذِينَ كَفَرُوٓا۟ أَنَّهُمْ أَصْحَٰبُ ٱلنَّارِ ۝

7. Those who bear the throne, and those who are round about it, hallow the praise of their Lord and believe in Him and ask forgiveness for the faithful, saying: 'Our Lord! You comprehend everything in mercy and knowledge, so forgive those who repent and follow Your path, and protect them from the torment of the Flaming Fire.

ٱلَّذِينَ يَحْمِلُونَ ٱلْعَرْشَ وَمَنْ حَوْلَهُۥ يُسَبِّحُونَ بِحَمْدِ رَبِّهِمْ وَيُؤْمِنُونَ بِهِۦ وَيَسْتَغْفِرُونَ لِلَّذِينَ ءَامَنُوا۟ رَبَّنَا وَسِعْتَ كُلَّ شَىْءٍ رَّحْمَةً وَعِلْمًا فَٱغْفِرْ لِلَّذِينَ تَابُوا۟ وَٱتَّبَعُوا۟ سَبِيلَكَ وَقِهِمْ عَذَابَ ٱلْجَحِيمِ ۝

8. Our Lord! Make them enter the everlasting Gardens which You have promised them, and also such of their fathers and their wives and their offspring as are fit. Verily You! You are the Mighty, the Wise.

رَبَّنَا وَأَدْخِلْهُمْ جَنَّٰتِ عَدْنٍ ٱلَّتِى وَعَدتَّهُمْ وَمَن صَلَحَ مِنْ ءَابَآئِهِمْ وَأَزْوَٰجِهِمْ وَذُرِّيَّٰتِهِمْ إِنَّكَ أَنتَ ٱلْعَزِيزُ ٱلْحَكِيمُ ۝

9. And guard them against evil. And whom You shall protect from evil on the Day, him You have certainly taken into mercy; and that; it is a mighty achievement.'

وَقِهِمُ ٱلسَّيِّـَٔاتِ وَمَن تَقِ ٱلسَّيِّـَٔاتِ يَوْمَئِذٍ فَقَدْ رَحِمْتَهُۥ وَذَٰلِكَ هُوَ ٱلْفَوْزُ ٱلْعَظِيمُ ۝

Section 2

10. Verily those who disbelieve they will be cried unto: 'Surely Allah's abhorrence was greater than is your abhorrence toward yourselves, when you were called to belief, and you rejected.'

إِنَّ ٱلَّذِينَ كَفَرُوا۟ يُنَادَوْنَ لَمَقْتُ ٱللَّهِ أَكْبَرُ مِن مَّقْتِكُمْ أَنفُسَكُمْ إِذْ تُدْعَوْنَ إِلَى ٱلْإِيمَٰنِ فَتَكْفُرُونَ ۝

11. They will say: 'Our Lord! You have made us die twice, and You have made us live twice, now we confess our sins, is there no getting out any way?'

قَالُوا رَبَّنَا أَمَتَّنَا اثْنَتَيْنِ وَأَحْيَيْتَنَا اثْنَتَيْنِ فَاعْتَرَفْنَا بِذُنُوبِنَا فَهَلْ إِلَىٰ خُرُوجٍ مِّن سَبِيلٍ ۝

12. That is because when Allah alone was called upon you denied; and when someone was associated with Him you believed. So the judgement is of Allah, the Exalted, the Great.

ذَٰلِكُم بِأَنَّهُ إِذَا دُعِيَ اللَّهُ وَحْدَهُ كَفَرْتُمْ وَإِن يُشْرَكْ بِهِ تُؤْمِنُوا فَالْحُكْمُ لِلَّهِ الْعَلِيِّ الْكَبِيرِ ۝

13. He it is Who shows you His signs and sends down provision for you from the heaven, and none receives admonition save him who turns in penitence.

هُوَ الَّذِي يُرِيكُمْ آيَاتِهِ وَيُنَزِّلُ لَكُم مِّنَ السَّمَاءِ رِزْقًا وَمَا يَتَذَكَّرُ إِلَّا مَن يُنِيبُ ۝

14. Therefore call to Allah, making faith pure for Him, averse as the infidels may be.

فَادْعُوا اللَّهَ مُخْلِصِينَ لَهُ الدِّينَ وَلَوْ كَرِهَ الْكَافِرُونَ ۝

15. He is Lofty in degrees, Lord of the Throne, He casts the Spirit of His command upon whomsoever He will of His bondsmen, that He may warn the people of the Day of Meeting.

رَفِيعُ الدَّرَجَاتِ ذُو الْعَرْشِ يُلْقِي الرُّوحَ مِنْ أَمْرِهِ عَلَىٰ مَن يَشَاءُ مِنْ عِبَادِهِ لِيُنذِرَ يَوْمَ التَّلَاقِ ۝

16. The Day whereon they will appear; nothing of them will be concealed from Allah. Whose is the dominion today? It is of Allah, the One, the Subduer.

يَوْمَ هُم بَارِزُونَ لَا يَخْفَىٰ عَلَى اللَّهِ مِنْهُمْ شَيْءٌ لِّمَنِ الْمُلْكُ الْيَوْمَ لِلَّهِ الْوَاحِدِ الْقَهَّارِ ۝

17. Today every soul will be recompensed for what it has earned, no wrong-doing today; verily Allah is Swift at reckoning.

الْيَوْمَ تُجْزَىٰ كُلُّ نَفْسٍ بِمَا كَسَبَتْ لَا ظُلْمَ الْيَوْمَ إِنَّ اللَّهَ سَرِيعُ الْحِسَابِ ۝

18. Warn them of the Day of Portending whereon their hearts will be in their throats, choking; then for the ungodly there will be no ardent friend nor an intercessor to be given heed to.

وَأَنذِرْهُمْ يَوْمَ ٱلْأَزِفَةِ إِذِ ٱلْقُلُوبُ لَدَى ٱلْحَنَاجِرِ كَظِمِينَ مَا لِلظَّٰلِمِينَ مِنْ حَمِيمٍ وَلَا شَفِيعٍ يُطَاعُ ﴿١٨﴾

19. He knows the fraud of the eyes, and what the breasts conceal.

يَعْلَمُ خَائِنَةَ ٱلْأَعْيُنِ وَمَا تُخْفِي ٱلصُّدُورُ ﴿١٩﴾

20. Allah decrees with truth, while those whom they call upon beside Allah cannot decree anything.[635] Verily Allah: He is the Hearer, the Beholder!

وَٱللَّهُ يَقْضِى بِٱلْحَقِّ وَٱلَّذِينَ يَدْعُونَ مِن دُونِهِ لَا يَقْضُونَ بِشَىْءٍ إِنَّ ٱللَّهَ هُوَ ٱلسَّمِيعُ ٱلْبَصِيرُ ﴿٢٠﴾

Section 3

21. Have they not travelled about in the land so that they may see how has been the end of those who were before them? They were mightier than these in strength and in the traces in the land. Yet Allah seized them for their sins, and from Allah they had none as protector.

أَوَلَمْ يَسِيرُوا۟ فِى ٱلْأَرْضِ فَيَنظُرُوا۟ كَيْفَ كَانَ عَٰقِبَةُ ٱلَّذِينَ كَانُوا۟ مِن قَبْلِهِمْ كَانُوا۟ هُمْ أَشَدَّ مِنْهُمْ قُوَّةً وَءَاثَارًا فِى ٱلْأَرْضِ فَأَخَذَهُمُ ٱللَّهُ بِذُنُوبِهِمْ وَمَا كَانَ لَهُم مِّنَ ٱللَّهِ مِن وَاقٍ ﴿٢١﴾

---

635. God is and shall be the Sole Judge. This repudiates the Christian doctrine of Jesus being the Judge and Arbiter. Cf. the NT: 'For the Son of man shall come in the glory of his Father with his angels; and then he shall reward every man according to his works' (Mt. 16: 27). 'When the Son of man shall come in his glory, and all the holy angels with him, then shall he sit upon the throne of his glory: and before him shall be gathered all nations: and he shall separate them one from another, as a shepherd divideth his sheep from the goats: and he shall set the sheep on his right hand but the goats on the left. Then shall the king say unto them on his right hand, Come, ye blessed of my Father, inherit the kingdom prepared for you from the foundation of the world' (Mt. 25: 31–34).

22. This, because their Messengers were wont to bring them evidence, but they disbelieved; so Allah seized them. Verily He is the Strong, the Severe in chastisement.

ذَٰلِكَ بِأَنَّهُمْ كَانَت تَّأْتِيهِمْ رُسُلُهُم بِالْبَيِّنَٰتِ فَكَفَرُوا فَأَخَذَهُمُ اللَّهُ إِنَّهُۥ قَوِيٌّ شَدِيدُ الْعِقَابِ ﴿٢٢﴾

23. And assuredly We sent Moses with Our signs; and a clear authority;

وَلَقَدْ أَرْسَلْنَا مُوسَىٰ بِـَٔايَٰتِنَا وَسُلْطَٰنٍ مُّبِينٍ ﴿٢٣﴾

24. To Pharaoh, Hāmān and Qārūn, but they said: 'A magician, a liar.'

إِلَىٰ فِرْعَوْنَ وَهَٰمَٰنَ وَقَٰرُونَ فَقَالُوا سَٰحِرٌ كَذَّابٌ ﴿٢٤﴾

25. And when he came to them with truth from before Us they said: 'Slay the sons of those who have believed with him and let their women live.' And the plot of the infidels was nothing but vain.

فَلَمَّا جَاءَهُم بِالْحَقِّ مِنْ عِندِنَا قَالُوا اقْتُلُوا أَبْنَاءَ الَّذِينَ ءَامَنُوا مَعَهُۥ وَاسْتَحْيُوا نِسَاءَهُمْ وَمَا كَيْدُ الْكَٰفِرِينَ إِلَّا فِى ضَلَٰلٍ ﴿٢٥﴾

26. And said Pharaoh: 'Leave me alone, that I may slay Moses and let him call upon his Lord. I fear that he may change your religion or that he may cause disruption in the land.'

وَقَالَ فِرْعَوْنُ ذَرُونِى أَقْتُلْ مُوسَىٰ وَلْيَدْعُ رَبَّهُۥ إِنِّى أَخَافُ أَن يُبَدِّلَ دِينَكُمْ أَوْ أَن يُظْهِرَ فِى الْأَرْضِ الْفَسَادَ ﴿٢٦﴾

27. And said Moses: 'Verily I seek refuge in my Lord and your Lord from every stiff-necked person who does not believe in the Day of Reckoning'.

وَقَالَ مُوسَىٰ إِنِّى عُذْتُ بِرَبِّى وَرَبِّكُم مِّن كُلِّ مُتَكَبِّرٍ لَّا يُؤْمِنُ بِيَوْمِ الْحِسَابِ ﴿٢٧﴾

Section 4

28. And a believing man of Pharaoh's household, hiding his faith, said: 'Would you slay a man because he says, my Lord is Allah, and has come to you with evidence from your Lord? If he is an impostor, upon him will be his imposture, but if he is truthful, then shall befall you some of what he threatens you with. Verily Allah does not guide anyone extravagant or a liar.

وَقَالَ رَجُلٌ مُّؤْمِنٌ مِّنْ ءَالِ فِرْعَوْنَ يَكْتُمُ إِيمَٰنَهُۥٓ أَتَقْتُلُونَ رَجُلًا أَن يَقُولَ رَبِّىَ ٱللَّهُ وَقَدْ جَآءَكُم بِٱلْبَيِّنَٰتِ مِن رَّبِّكُمْ وَإِن يَكُ كَٰذِبًا فَعَلَيْهِ كَذِبُهُۥ وَإِن يَكُ صَادِقًا يُصِبْكُم بَعْضُ ٱلَّذِى يَعِدُكُمْ إِنَّ ٱللَّهَ لَا يَهْدِى مَنْ هُوَ مُسْرِفٌ كَذَّابٌ ٢٨

29. 'My people! Yours is the kingdom today, you are being triumphant in the land; but who will succour us against the scourge of Allah if it comes to us?' Pharaoh said: 'I show you only what I see; and I guide you to the path of rectitude.'

يَٰقَوْمِ لَكُمُ ٱلْمُلْكُ ٱلْيَوْمَ ظَٰهِرِينَ فِى ٱلْأَرْضِ فَمَن يَنصُرُنَا مِنۢ بَأْسِ ٱللَّهِ إِن جَآءَنَا قَالَ فِرْعَوْنُ مَآ أُرِيكُمْ إِلَّا مَآ أَرَىٰ وَمَآ أَهْدِيكُمْ إِلَّا سَبِيلَ ٱلرَّشَادِ ٢٩

30. And he who believed said: 'My people! I fear for you a fate like that of the factions of the old.

وَقَالَ ٱلَّذِىٓ ءَامَنَ يَٰقَوْمِ إِنِّىٓ أَخَافُ عَلَيْكُم مِّثْلَ يَوْمِ ٱلْأَحْزَابِ ٣٠

31. Like the fate of the people of Noah and the 'Ād and the Thamūd and those after them; and Allah does not intend any wrong to His bondsmen.

مِثْلَ دَأْبِ قَوْمِ نُوحٍ وَعَادٍ وَثَمُودَ وَٱلَّذِينَ مِنۢ بَعْدِهِمْ وَمَا ٱللَّهُ يُرِيدُ ظُلْمًا لِّلْعِبَادِ ٣١

32. And, my people! I fear for you a day of Mutual Calling.

وَيَٰقَوْمِ إِنِّىٓ أَخَافُ عَلَيْكُمْ يَوْمَ ٱلتَّنَادِ ٣٢

33. A Day whereon you shall turn away retreating; for you there will be no protector from Allah, and he whom Allah sends astray, for him there is no guide.'

يَوْمَ تُوَلُّونَ مُدْبِرِينَ مَا لَكُم مِّنَ ٱللَّهِ مِنْ عَاصِمٍ وَمَن يُضْلِلِ ٱللَّهُ فَمَا لَهُۥ مِنْ هَادٍ ٣٣

34. And assuredly earlier there came to you Joseph with evidence, yet you ceased not to be in doubt concerning what he brought to you, until he died, and you said: 'Allah will by no means raise a Messenger after him.' Thus does Allah keep astray one who is extravagant and a doubter,

وَلَقَدْ جَآءَكُمْ يُوسُفُ مِن قَبْلُ بِالْبَيِّنَتِ فَمَا زِلْتُمْ فِى شَكٍّ مِّمَّا جَآءَكُم بِهِ ۖ حَتَّىٰٓ إِذَا هَلَكَ قُلْتُمْ لَن يَبْعَثَ اللَّهُ مِنۢ بَعْدِهِۦ رَسُولًا ۚ كَذَٰلِكَ يُضِلُّ اللَّهُ مَنْ هُوَ مُسْرِفٌ مُّرْتَابٌ ۝

35. Those who wrangle concerning the signs of Allah without any authority that has come to them. It is greatly abhorrent to Allah and to those who believe. Thus Allah seals up the heart of every stiff-necked, high-handed person.

ٱلَّذِينَ يُجَٰدِلُونَ فِىٓ ءَايَٰتِ ٱللَّهِ بِغَيْرِ سُلْطَٰنٍ أَتَىٰهُمْ ۖ كَبُرَ مَقْتًا عِندَ ٱللَّهِ وَعِندَ ٱلَّذِينَ ءَامَنُوا ۚ كَذَٰلِكَ يَطْبَعُ ٱللَّهُ عَلَىٰ كُلِّ قَلْبِ مُتَكَبِّرٍ جَبَّارٍ ۝

36. And Pharaoh said: 'Haman! Build for me a tower that I may reach the roads.

وَقَالَ فِرْعَوْنُ يَٰهَٰمَٰنُ ٱبْنِ لِى صَرْحًا لَّعَلِّىٓ أَبْلُغُ ٱلْأَسْبَٰبَ ۝

37. The roads of the heavens so that I may mount up to the God of Moses, and surely I believe him to be a liar.' And thus fair-seeming to Pharaoh was made the evil of his work, and he was hindered from the path. And the plot of Pharaoh was made the evil of his work, and he was hindered from the path, and the plot of Pharaoh ended only in perdition.

أَسْبَٰبَ ٱلسَّمَٰوَٰتِ فَأَطَّلِعَ إِلَىٰٓ إِلَٰهِ مُوسَىٰ وَإِنِّى لَأَظُنُّهُۥ كَٰذِبًا ۚ وَكَذَٰلِكَ زُيِّنَ لِفِرْعَوْنَ سُوٓءُ عَمَلِهِۦ وَصُدَّ عَنِ ٱلسَّبِيلِ ۚ وَمَا كَيْدُ فِرْعَوْنَ إِلَّا فِى تَبَابٍ ۝

Section 5

38. And he who had believed said: 'My people! Follow me, and I shall guide you to the path of rectitude.

وَقَالَ الَّذِىٓ ءَامَنَ يَٰقَوْمِ اتَّبِعُونِ أَهْدِكُمْ سَبِيلَ الرَّشَادِ ﴿٣٨﴾

39. My people ! The life of this world is only a passing enjoyment, and verily the Hereafter! That is the Abode of rest.

يَٰقَوْمِ إِنَّمَا هَٰذِهِ الْحَيَوٰةُ الدُّنْيَا مَتَٰعٌ وَإِنَّ الْأَخِرَةَ هِىَ دَارُ الْقَرَارِ ﴿٣٩﴾

40. Whosoever works an evil, he shall not be requited except the like thereof; and whosoever, male or female, works righteously, and is a believer they will enter a Garden wherein they shall be provided for without measure.

مَنْ عَمِلَ سَيِّئَةً فَلَا يُجْزَىٰٓ إِلَّا مِثْلَهَا وَمَنْ عَمِلَ صَٰلِحًا مِّن ذَكَرٍ أَوْ أُنثَىٰ وَهُوَ مُؤْمِنٌ فَأُوْلَٰٓئِكَ يَدْخُلُونَ الْجَنَّةَ يُرْزَقُونَ فِيهَا بِغَيْرِ حِسَابٍ ﴿٤٠﴾

41. And, my people! How is it that I call you unto salvation, while you call me to the Fire?

وَيَٰقَوْمِ مَا لِىٓ أَدْعُوكُمْ إِلَى النَّجَوٰةِ وَتَدْعُونَنِىٓ إِلَى النَّارِ ﴿٤١﴾

42. You call me for this, that I should blaspheme against Allah, and associate with Him that of which I have no knowledge, while I call you to the Mighty, the Forgiver.

تَدْعُونَنِى لِأَكْفُرَ بِاللَّهِ وَأُشْرِكَ بِهِۦ مَا لَيْسَ لِى بِهِۦ عِلْمٌ وَأَنَا أَدْعُوكُمْ إِلَى الْعَزِيزِ الْغَفَّٰرِ ﴿٤٢﴾

43. Undoubtedly you only call me to what is not to be invoked in this world nor in the Hereafter; and verily our return shall be to Allah; and the extravagant! They shall be the inmates of the Fire.

لَا جَرَمَ أَنَّمَا تَدْعُونَنِىٓ إِلَيْهِ لَيْسَ لَهُۥ دَعْوَةٌ فِى الدُّنْيَا وَلَا فِى الْأَخِرَةِ وَأَنَّ مَرَدَّنَآ إِلَى اللَّهِ وَأَنَّ الْمُسْرِفِينَ هُمْ أَصْحَٰبُ النَّارِ ﴿٤٣﴾

44. And soon you shall remember what I am telling you. I confide my affair to Allah, verily Allah is the Beholder of His bondsmen.'

فَسَتَذْكُرُونَ مَاۤ أَقُولُ لَكُمْ وَأُفَوِّضُ أَمْرِىۤ إِلَى اللَّهِۚ إِنَّ اللَّهَ بَصِيرٌۢ بِالْعِبَادِ ۝

45. So Allah protected him from the ills which they plotted, and the evil of the torment surrounded the household of Pharaoh.

فَوَقَىٰهُ اللَّهُ سَيِّئَاتِ مَا مَكَرُواْ وَحَاقَ بِآلِ فِرْعَوْنَ سُوۤءُ الْعَذَابِ ۝

46. The Fire! They are exposed thereto morning and evening. And on the day whereon the Hour will uprise, it will be said: 'Cause the household of Pharaoh to enter the most grievous torment.'

النَّارُ يُعْرَضُونَ عَلَيْهَا غُدُوًّا وَعَشِيًّا ۖ وَيَوْمَ تَقُومُ السَّاعَةُ أَدْخِلُوۤاْ ءَالَ فِرْعَوْنَ أَشَدَّ الْعَذَابِ ۝

47. And consider what time they will wrangle in the Fire together, and the oppressed will say to the stiff-necked: 'Verily we have been unto you a following; are you going to avail us against a portion of the Fire?'

وَإِذْ يَتَحَاۤجُّونَ فِى النَّارِ فَيَقُولُ الضُّعَفَٰۤؤُاْ لِلَّذِينَ اسْتَكْبَرُوۤاْ إِنَّا كُنَّا لَكُمْ تَبَعًا فَهَلْ أَنتُم مُّغْنُونَ عَنَّا نَصِيبًا مِّنَ النَّارِ ۝

48. Those who were stiff-necked will say: 'Verily we are all in it; verily Allah has judged between His bondsmen.'

قَالَ الَّذِينَ اسْتَكْبَرُوۤاْ إِنَّا كُلٌّ فِيهَاۤ إِنَّ اللَّهَ قَدْ حَكَمَ بَيْنَ الْعِبَادِ ۝

49. And those in the Fire will say to the keepers of Hell: 'Pray to your Lord that He may lighten for us a day of torment.'

وَقَالَ الَّذِينَ فِى النَّارِ لِخَزَنَةِ جَهَنَّمَ ادْعُواْ رَبَّكُمْ يُخَفِّفْ عَنَّا يَوْمًا مِّنَ الْعَذَابِ ۝

50. They will say: 'Did not there come to you your Messengers with evidence?' They will say: 'Yea!' They will say: 'Pray then yourselves.' And the praying of the infidels is but in wandering.

قَالُوۤاْ أَوَلَمْ تَكُ تَأْتِيكُمْ رُسُلُكُم بِالْبَيِّنَٰتِۖ قَالُواْ بَلَىٰۚ قَالُواْ فَادْعُواْۗ وَمَا دُعَٰۤؤُاْ الْكَٰفِرِينَ إِلَّا فِى ضَلَٰلٍ ۝

Section 6

51. Verily We! We shall surely succour Our Messengers and those who believe, both in the life of this world and on a Day whereon the witnesses will stand forth.

إِنَّا لَنَنصُرُ رُسُلَنَا وَالَّذِينَ ءَامَنُوا فِي الْحَيَوٰةِ الدُّنْيَا وَيَوْمَ يَقُومُ الْأَشْهَٰدُ ۝

52. A Day whereon their excuse will not profit the ungodly. Theirs will be the curse and theirs the evil abode.

يَوْمَ لَا يَنفَعُ الظَّٰلِمِينَ مَعْذِرَتُهُمْ وَلَهُمُ اللَّعْنَةُ وَلَهُمْ سُوٓءُ الدَّارِ ۝

53. And assuredly We vouch-safed to Moses the guidance and We caused the children of Israel to inherit the Book.

وَلَقَدْ ءَاتَيْنَا مُوسَى الْهُدَىٰ وَأَوْرَثْنَا بَنِىٓ إِسْرَٰٓءِيلَ الْكِتَٰبَ ۝

54. A guidance and an admonition to men of understanding.

هُدًى وَذِكْرَىٰ لِأُوْلِى الْأَلْبَٰبِ ۝

55. Wherefore you be steadfast. The promise of Allah is true; and ask forgiveness for your fault;[636] and hallow the praise of your Lord at evening and dawn.

فَاصْبِرْ إِنَّ وَعْدَ اللَّهِ حَقٌّ وَاسْتَغْفِرْ لِذَنۢبِكَ وَسَبِّحْ بِحَمْدِ رَبِّكَ بِالْعَشِىِّ وَالْإِبْكَٰرِ ۝

56. Verily those who wrangle concerning the revelations of Allah without an authority having come to them naught is there in their breasts save ambitions which they shall not achieve. Seek refuge you then in Allah; verily He! He is the Hearer, the Beholder.

إِنَّ الَّذِينَ يُجَٰدِلُونَ فِى ءَايَٰتِ اللَّهِ بِغَيْرِ سُلْطَٰنٍ أَتَىٰهُمْ إِن فِى صُدُورِهِمْ إِلَّا كِبْرٌ مَّا هُم بِبَٰلِغِيهِ فَاسْتَعِذْ بِاللَّهِ إِنَّهُ هُوَ السَّمِيعُ الْبَصِيرُ ۝

---

636. When spoken of in reference to the Prophets this means an act of inadvertence, 'not blamable in itself, but only unworthy of their high rank' (Th.). Mere erring, or error of judgement with no moral delinquency, of course, does not constitute a sin.

57. The creation of the heavens and the earth is indeed greater than the creation of mankind; yet most of mankind know not.

لَخَلْقُ ٱلسَّمَوَاتِ وَٱلْأَرْضِ أَكْبَرُ مِنْ خَلْقِ ٱلنَّاسِ وَلَكِنَّ أَكْثَرَ ٱلنَّاسِ لَا يَعْلَمُونَ ۝

58. Not equal are the blind and the seeing, nor those who believe and work righteous deeds and the wicked. Little are you admonished.

وَمَا يَسْتَوِى ٱلْأَعْمَىٰ وَٱلْبَصِيرُ وَٱلَّذِينَ ءَامَنُوا۟ وَعَمِلُوا۟ ٱلصَّٰلِحَٰتِ وَلَا ٱلْمُسِىٓءُ قَلِيلًا مَّا تَتَذَكَّرُونَ ۝

59. Verily the Hour is coming; there is no doubt thereof, yet most of mankind believe not.

إِنَّ ٱلسَّاعَةَ لَآتِيَةٌ لَّا رَيْبَ فِيهَا وَلَكِنَّ أَكْثَرَ ٱلنَّاسِ لَا يُؤْمِنُونَ ۝

60. And your Lord has said: 'Call upon Me, and I shall answer you.' Verily those who are stiff-necked against My worship, now they will enter Hell abject.

وَقَالَ رَبُّكُمُ ٱدْعُونِىٓ أَسْتَجِبْ لَكُمْ إِنَّ ٱلَّذِينَ يَسْتَكْبِرُونَ عَنْ عِبَادَتِى سَيَدْخُلُونَ جَهَنَّمَ دَاخِرِينَ ۝

Section 7

61. Allah it is Who has made the night that you may repose therein, and the day enlightening. Verily Allah is the Lord of grace for mankind; yet most of mankind return not thanks.

ٱللَّهُ ٱلَّذِى جَعَلَ لَكُمُ ٱلَّيْلَ لِتَسْكُنُوا۟ فِيهِ وَٱلنَّهَارَ مُبْصِرًا إِنَّ ٱللَّهَ لَذُو فَضْلٍ عَلَى ٱلنَّاسِ وَلَكِنَّ أَكْثَرَ ٱلنَّاسِ لَا يَشْكُرُونَ ۝

62. Such is Allah, your Lord, the Creator of everything;[637] there is no god but He. Whither then are you straying away?

ذَٰلِكُمُ ٱللَّهُ رَبُّكُمْ خَٰلِقُ كُلِّ شَىْءٍ لَّآ إِلَٰهَ إِلَّا هُوَ فَأَنَّىٰ تُؤْفَكُونَ ﴿٦٢﴾

63. In this wise those who were wont to gainsay the signs of Allah have strayed away.

كَذَٰلِكَ يُؤْفَكُ ٱلَّذِينَ كَانُوا۟ بِـَٔايَٰتِ ٱللَّهِ يَجْحَدُونَ ﴿٦٣﴾

64. Allah it is Who has made the earth for you a resting-place and the sky a structure; and fashioned you and fashioned well, and provided for you goodly things. Such is Allah, your Lord! So blessed be Allah, the Lord of the worlds.

ٱللَّهُ ٱلَّذِى جَعَلَ لَكُمُ ٱلْأَرْضَ قَرَارًا وَٱلسَّمَآءَ بِنَآءً وَصَوَّرَكُمْ فَأَحْسَنَ صُوَرَكُمْ وَرَزَقَكُم مِّنَ ٱلطَّيِّبَٰتِ ذَٰلِكُمُ ٱللَّهُ رَبُّكُمْ فَتَبَارَكَ ٱللَّهُ رَبُّ ٱلْعَٰلَمِينَ ﴿٦٤﴾

65. He is the Living; no god there is but He. So call upon Him, making faith pure for Him. All praise for Allah, the Lord of the worlds.

هُوَ ٱلْحَىُّ لَآ إِلَٰهَ إِلَّا هُوَ فَٱدْعُوهُ مُخْلِصِينَ لَهُ ٱلدِّينَ ٱلْحَمْدُ لِلَّهِ رَبِّ ٱلْعَٰلَمِينَ ﴿٦٥﴾

---

637. This strikes at the godless, childish and materialistic cosmogonies of the Greek philosophers. According to Plato, 'fire and water and earth and air all exist by Nature and chance' and none of them by an action of mind, and 'the bodies which come next in order – the earth, sun, moon and stars – have been created by means of these absolutely inanimate existences. The various elements are moved by chance, and also by inherent forces according to certain affinities amongst them. After this fashion has been created the whole of heaven and all that is therein, as well as all animals and plants and all the seasons. These come from these elements, not by any action of mind or of any god or from art but by Nature and chance only' (*EMK.* I. p. 3). And, according to an Aristotelian dictum, 'nothing comes into existence out of that which is not, but everything out of that which is'; so that 'there can have been no process of creation, merely a redistribution of four elements and their four qualities' (Ibid.).

66. Say you: 'Verily I am forbidden that I should worship those whom you call upon besides Allah when evidence has come to me from my Lord, and I am commanded that I should submit to the Lord of the worlds.

قُلْ إِنِّى نُهِيتُ أَنْ أَعْبُدَ الَّذِينَ تَدْعُونَ مِن دُونِ اللَّهِ لَمَّا جَآءَنِىَ الْبَيِّنَتُ مِن رَّبِّى وَأُمِرْتُ أَنْ أُسْلِمَ لِرَبِّ الْعَلَمِينَ ﴿٦٦﴾

67. He it is Who created you of dust, and then of a drop, and then of a clot, and then He brings you forth as an infant, and then He ordains that you attain your full strength, and then that you become old men though some of you die earlier and that you attain the appointed term; and that haply you may reflect.

هُوَ الَّذِى خَلَقَكُم مِّن تُرَابٍ ثُمَّ مِن نُّطْفَةٍ ثُمَّ مِنْ عَلَقَةٍ ثُمَّ يُخْرِجُكُمْ طِفْلاً ثُمَّ لِتَبْلُغُوٓا أَشُدَّكُمْ ثُمَّ لِتَكُونُوا شُيُوخًا وَمِنكُم مَّن يُتَوَفَّى مِن قَبْلُ وَلِتَبْلُغُوٓا أَجَلاً مُّسَمًّى وَلَعَلَّكُمْ تَعْقِلُونَ ﴿٦٧﴾

68. He it is Who causes life and death;[638] and whence He decrees an affair He only says to it, "Be", and it becomes.'

هُوَ الَّذِى يُحْيِۦ وَيُمِيتُ فَإِذَا قَضَىٰٓ أَمْرًا فَإِنَّمَا يَقُولُ لَهُۥ كُن فَيَكُونُ ﴿٦٨﴾

Section 8

69. Do you not see those who wrangle concerning the revelations of Allah, whither are they turning away?

أَلَمْ تَرَ إِلَى الَّذِينَ يُجَٰدِلُونَ فِىٓ ءَايَٰتِ اللَّهِ أَنَّىٰ يُصْرَفُونَ ﴿٦٩﴾

70. Those who belie the Book and the Message with which We sent Our Messengers, presently they will come to know,

الَّذِينَ كَذَّبُوا بِالْكِتَٰبِ وَبِمَآ أَرْسَلْنَا بِهِۦ رُسُلَنَا فَسَوْفَ يَعْلَمُونَ ﴿٧٠﴾

---

638. He is the real, Ultimate Source of all life and death, and there is no sense in the myth that there is one god the creator and another god the destroyer.

71. When shackles will be on their necks and also chains; they will be dragged

إِذِ ٱلْأَغْلَٰلُ فِىٓ أَعْنَٰقِهِمْ وَٱلسَّلَٰسِلُ يُسْحَبُونَ ﴿٧١﴾

72. Into the boiling water; then into the Fire they will be stoked.

فِى ٱلْحَمِيمِ ثُمَّ فِى ٱلنَّارِ يُسْجَرُونَ ﴿٧٢﴾

73. Then it will be said to them: 'Where are those whom you have been associating,

ثُمَّ قِيلَ لَهُمْ أَيْنَ مَا كُنتُمْ تُشْرِكُونَ ﴿٧٣﴾

74. Besides Allah?' They will say: 'They have failed us; aye! We have not been calling on aught before.' Thus does Allah lead the infidels astray.

مِن دُونِ ٱللَّهِ قَالُوا۟ ضَلُّوا۟ عَنَّا بَل لَّمْ نَكُن نَّدْعُوا۟ مِن قَبْلُ شَيْـًٔا كَذَٰلِكَ يُضِلُّ ٱللَّهُ ٱلْكَٰفِرِينَ ﴿٧٤﴾

75. That is because you had been exulting in the earth without any right, and because you had been strutting.

ذَٰلِكُم بِمَا كُنتُمْ تَفْرَحُونَ فِى ٱلْأَرْضِ بِغَيْرِ ٱلْحَقِّ وَبِمَا كُنتُمْ تَمْرَحُونَ ﴿٧٥﴾

76. Enter ye the gates of Hell, as abiders therein, Hapless is the abode of the stiff-necked.

ٱدْخُلُوٓا۟ أَبْوَٰبَ جَهَنَّمَ خَٰلِدِينَ فِيهَا فَبِئْسَ مَثْوَى ٱلْمُتَكَبِّرِينَ ﴿٧٦﴾

77. Wherefore be steadfast; verily the promise of Allah is true. Then whether We let you see a portion of what We have promised them, or whether We cause them to die, to Us they all will be returned.

فَٱصْبِرْ إِنَّ وَعْدَ ٱللَّهِ حَقٌّ فَإِمَّا نُرِيَنَّكَ بَعْضَ ٱلَّذِى نَعِدُهُمْ أَوْ نَتَوَفَّيَنَّكَ فَإِلَيْنَا يُرْجَعُونَ ﴿٧٧﴾

78. Assuredly We have sent Messengers before you; of them are some whose story We have recounted to you and those whose story We have not recounted to you. And it was not possible for any Messenger to bring a sign save by Allah's leave. So when comes the command of Allah, Judgement will be given with truth, and then the followers of falsehood will lose.

وَلَقَدْ أَرْسَلْنَا رُسُلًا مِّن قَبْلِكَ مِنْهُم مَّن قَصَصْنَا عَلَيْكَ وَمِنْهُم مَّن لَّمْ نَقْصُصْ عَلَيْكَ وَمَا كَانَ لِرَسُولٍ أَن يَأْتِىَ بِـَٔايَةٍ إِلَّا بِإِذْنِ ٱللَّهِ فَإِذَا جَآءَ أَمْرُ ٱللَّهِ قُضِىَ بِٱلْحَقِّ وَخَسِرَ هُنَالِكَ ٱلْمُبْطِلُونَ ﴿٧٨﴾

Section 9

79.　Allah it is Who has made cattle for you, that you may ride on some of them, and of others you eat.

80.　And for you there are other benefits in them, and that you may attain through them any desire that is in your breasts; and upon them and upon the ships you are borne.

81.　And He shows you His sign, which, then, of the signs of Allah will you deny?

82.　Have they not travelled on the earth that they may behold how has been the end of those before them? They were more numerous than these, and mightier in strength and the traces in the land. But nothing availed them of what they had been earning.

83.　And when their Messengers came to them with evidence, they exulted in the knowledge they had with them, and there surrounded them what they had been mocking.

84.　Then when they beheld Our prowess they said: 'We believe in Allah alone, and we disbelieve in what we have been associating with Him.'

اللّٰهُ الَّذِى جَعَلَ لَكُمُ الْأَنْعَامَ لِتَرْكَبُوْا مِنْهَا وَمِنْهَا تَأْكُلُوْنَ ۟ ۷۹

وَلَكُمْ فِيْهَا مَنَافِعُ وَلِتَبْلُغُوْا عَلَيْهَا حَاجَةً فِىْ صُدُوْرِكُمْ وَعَلَيْهَا وَعَلَى الْفُلْكِ تُحْمَلُوْنَ ۟ ۸۰

وَيُرِيْكُمْ اٰيَاتِهٖ ۖ فَأَىَّ اٰيَاتِ اللّٰهِ تُنْكِرُوْنَ ۸۱

أَفَلَمْ يَسِيْرُوْا فِى الْأَرْضِ فَيَنْظُرُوْا كَيْفَ كَانَ عَاقِبَةُ الَّذِيْنَ مِنْ قَبْلِهِمْ ۚ كَانُوْا أَكْثَرَ مِنْهُمْ وَأَشَدَّ قُوَّةً وَّاٰثَارًا فِى الْأَرْضِ فَمَا أَغْنٰى عَنْهُمْ مَّا كَانُوْا يَكْسِبُوْنَ ۸۲

فَلَمَّا جَاءَتْهُمْ رُسُلُهُمْ بِالْبَيِّنٰتِ فَرِحُوْا بِمَا عِنْدَهُمْ مِّنَ الْعِلْمِ وَحَاقَ بِهِمْ مَّا كَانُوْا بِهٖ يَسْتَهْزِءُوْنَ ۸۳

فَلَمَّا رَأَوْا بَأْسَنَا قَالُوْا اٰمَنَّا بِاللّٰهِ وَحْدَهٗ وَكَفَرْنَا بِمَا كُنَّا بِهٖ مُشْرِكِيْنَ ۸۴

85. But their belief profited them not when they had seen Our prowess. This is Allah's dispensation that has been in regard to His bondsmen. And lost were the infidels then and there.

فَلَمْ يَكُ يَنفَعُهُمْ إِيمَنُهُمْ لَمَّا رَأَوْا بَأْسَنَا سُنَّتَ ٱللَّهِ ٱلَّتِى قَدْ خَلَتْ فِى عِبَادِهِۦ وَخَسِرَ هُنَالِكَ ٱلْكَفِرُونَ ۞

Sūrah 41

Fuṣṣilat

(Makkan, 6 Sections, 54 Verses)

In the name of Allah, the Compassionate, the Merciful.

Section 1

1. *Ḥā, Mīm.*

2. This is a revelation from Allah, the Compassionate, the Merciful.

3. A Book whereof the verses are detailed an Arabic Qur'ān, for a people who know.

4. A bearer of glad tidings and a warner. Yet most of them turn aside, so that they listen not.

5. And they say: 'Our hearts are under a veil from what you call us to, and in our ears is heaviness, and there is a curtain between us and you; so work you, we are also working.'

6. Say: 'I am only a human being like you; only it is revealed to me that your God is but One God, so take the straight path to Him, and seek forgiveness of Him, and woe be to the associators,

7. Who pay not the poor-rate, and they! Disbelievers they are in the Hereafter!'

8. Verily those who believe and work righteous deeds to them shall be a reward unceasing.

إِنَّ ٱلَّذِينَ ءَامَنُواْ وَعَمِلُواْ ٱلصَّٰلِحَٰتِ لَهُمۡ أَجۡرٌ غَيۡرُ مَمۡنُونٍ ۝

Section 2

9. Say: 'Are you indeed those who disbelieve in Him Who has created the earth in two days, and set up peers unto Him?' That is the Lord of the worlds.

قُلۡ أَئِنَّكُمۡ لَتَكۡفُرُونَ بِٱلَّذِى خَلَقَ ٱلۡأَرۡضَ فِى يَوۡمَيۡنِ وَتَجۡعَلُونَ لَهُۥٓ أَندَادًا ذَٰلِكَ رَبُّ ٱلۡعَٰلَمِينَ ۝

10. And He placed therein mountains firmly rooted rising above it, and He blessed it, and ordained therein the sustenance thereof, all this in four days, complete; this for the inquirers.

وَجَعَلَ فِيهَا رَوَٰسِىَ مِن فَوۡقِهَا وَبَٰرَكَ فِيهَا وَقَدَّرَ فِيهَآ أَقۡوَٰتَهَا فِىٓ أَرۡبَعَةِ أَيَّامٍ سَوَآءً لِّلسَّآئِلِينَ ۝

11. He thereafter turned to the heaven, and it was as smoke, and said to it and to the earth: 'Do you two come willingly or loth?', they said, 'we come willingly'.

ثُمَّ ٱسۡتَوَىٰٓ إِلَى ٱلسَّمَآءِ وَهِىَ دُخَانٌ فَقَالَ لَهَا وَلِلۡأَرۡضِ ٱئۡتِيَا طَوۡعًا أَوۡ كَرۡهًا قَالَتَآ أَتَيۡنَا طَآئِعِينَ ۝

12. Then He decreed them as seven heavens in two days, and revealed to each heaven the command thereof. And We bedecked the nether heaven with lamps and placed therein a guard. That is the ordinance of the Mighty, the Knower.

فَقَضَىٰهُنَّ سَبۡعَ سَمَٰوَاتٍ فِى يَوۡمَيۡنِ وَأَوۡحَىٰ فِى كُلِّ سَمَآءٍ أَمۡرَهَا وَزَيَّنَّا ٱلسَّمَآءَ ٱلدُّنۡيَا بِمَصَٰبِيحَ وَحِفۡظًا ذَٰلِكَ تَقۡدِيرُ ٱلۡعَزِيزِ ٱلۡعَلِيمِ ۝

13. Then if they still turn away, say: 'I warn you of a calamity of the 'Ād, and the Thamūd.'

فَإِنۡ أَعۡرَضُواْ فَقُلۡ أَنذَرۡتُكُمۡ صَٰعِقَةً مِّثۡلَ صَٰعِقَةِ عَادٍ وَثَمُودَ ۝

14. Recall when the Messengers came to them from before them and behind them saying: 'Worship none save Allah.' They said: 'Had our Lord willed, He would have sent down angels,[639] so verily we disbelieve altogether in what you have been sent with.'

إِذْ جَآءَتْهُمُ ٱلرُّسُلُ مِنۢ بَيْنِ أَيْدِيهِمْ وَمِنْ خَلْفِهِمْ أَلَّا تَعْبُدُوٓاْ إِلَّا ٱللَّهَ قَالُواْ لَوْ شَآءَ رَبُّنَا لَأَنزَلَ مَلَٰٓئِكَةً فَإِنَّا بِمَآ أُرْسِلْتُم بِهِۦ كَٰفِرُونَ ﴿١٤﴾

15. As for the 'Ad, they grew stiff-necked on the earth without justification, and said: 'Who is mightier in strength than we?' Did they not see that Allah, Who created them, He was mightier in strength than they? And they used to gainsay Our signs.

فَأَمَّا عَادٌ فَٱسْتَكْبَرُواْ فِي ٱلْأَرْضِ بِغَيْرِ ٱلْحَقِّ وَقَالُواْ مَنْ أَشَدُّ مِنَّا قُوَّةً أَوَلَمْ يَرَوْاْ أَنَّ ٱللَّهَ ٱلَّذِي خَلَقَهُمْ هُوَ أَشَدُّ مِنْهُمْ قُوَّةً وَكَانُواْ بِـَٔايَٰتِنَا يَجْحَدُونَ ﴿١٥﴾

16. Wherefore We sent upon them a raging wind in inauspicious days, so that We might make them taste the torment of humiliation in the life of this world, and surely the torment of the Hereafter will be more humiliating, nor will they be succoured.

فَأَرْسَلْنَا عَلَيْهِمْ رِيحًا صَرْصَرًا فِيٓ أَيَّامٍ نَّحِسَاتٍ لِّنُذِيقَهُمْ عَذَابَ ٱلْخِزْيِ فِي ٱلْحَيَوٰةِ ٱلدُّنْيَا وَلَعَذَابُ ٱلْأَخِرَةِ أَخْزَىٰ وَهُمْ لَا يُنصَرُونَ ﴿١٦﴾

17. And as for the Thamūd, We guided them, but they preferred blindness to guidance, wherefore the bolt of the torment of abjection struck them because of what they had been earning.

وَأَمَّا ثَمُودُ فَهَدَيْنَٰهُمْ فَٱسْتَحَبُّواْ ٱلْعَمَىٰ عَلَى ٱلْهُدَىٰ فَأَخَذَتْهُمْ صَٰعِقَةُ ٱلْعَذَابِ ٱلْهُونِ بِمَا كَانُواْ يَكْسِبُونَ ﴿١٧﴾

18. And We delivered those who believed and were God-fearing.

وَنَجَّيْنَا ٱلَّذِينَ ءَامَنُواْ وَكَانُواْ يَتَّقُونَ ﴿١٨﴾

---

639. Not mere human beings like yourselves. The fact of the Prophets being mortal and mere human beings has always proved a stumbling block to pagan nations.

Section 3

19. And on the Day when the enemies of Allah will be gathered towards the Fire, they will be set in bands;

وَيَوۡمَ يُحۡشَرُ أَعۡدَآءُ ٱللَّهِ إِلَى ٱلنَّارِ فَهُمۡ يُوزَعُونَ ۝

20. Until when they come to it their ears and their sights and their skins will bear witness against them of what they had been working.⁶⁴⁰

حَتَّىٰٓ إِذَا مَا جَآءُوهَا شَهِدَ عَلَيۡهِمۡ سَمۡعُهُمۡ وَأَبۡصَٰرُهُمۡ وَجُلُودُهُم بِمَا كَانُواْ يَعۡمَلُونَ ۝

21. And they will say to their skins: 'Why do you bear witness against us?' They will say: 'Allah has caused us to speak, as He causes everything to speak, and Who created you the first time, and to Whom you are now caused to return.

وَقَالُواْ لِجُلُودِهِمۡ لِمَ شَهِدتُّمۡ عَلَيۡنَا قَالُوٓاْ أَنطَقَنَا ٱللَّهُ ٱلَّذِىٓ أَنطَقَ كُلَّ شَىۡءٍ وَهُوَ خَلَقَكُمۡ أَوَّلَ مَرَّةٍ وَإِلَيۡهِ تُرۡجَعُونَ ۝

22. And you have not been taking cover against yourselves, lest your ears and your eyes and your skins should bear witness against you,⁶⁴¹ and you imagined that Allah did not know much of what you were working.

وَمَا كُنتُمۡ تَسۡتَتِرُونَ أَن يَشۡهَدَ عَلَيۡكُمۡ سَمۡعُكُمۡ وَلَآ أَبۡصَٰرُكُمۡ وَلَا جُلُودُكُمۡ وَلَٰكِن ظَنَنتُمۡ أَنَّ ٱللَّهَ لَا يَعۡلَمُ كَثِيرٗا مِّمَّا تَعۡمَلُونَ ۝

---

640. If we bear in mind, in this context, the modern development of palm and finger–print proofing , i.e., the evidence of one's own limbs, would be interesting as well as instructive.

641. In other words you are powerless from hiding your sins from your very own limbs and members and even though it is difficult to imagine ever they will rise up against you as hostile witnesses.

23. That concept of yours which you formed of your Lord has ruined you, and you have become of the losers.'

وَذَٰلِكُمْ ظَنُّكُمُ الَّذِى ظَنَنتُم بِرَبِّكُمْ أَرْدَىٰكُمْ فَأَصْبَحْتُم مِّنَ الْخَٰسِرِينَ ﴿٢٣﴾

24. Then if they are patient, the Fire is their very home, and if they seek terms to please Allah, then they will not be of those who are allowed to please Allah.

فَإِن يَصْبِرُوا فَالنَّارُ مَثْوًى لَّهُمْ وَإِن يَسْتَعْتِبُوا فَمَا هُم مِّنَ الْمُعْتَبِينَ ﴿٢٤﴾

25. And We have assigned to them companions who had bedecked to them what was before them and what was behind them. Justified upon them was the Word pronounced on the communities of *jinn* and mankind who passed away before them. Verily they were the losers.

وَقَيَّضْنَا لَهُمْ قُرَنَآءَ فَزَيَّنُوا لَهُم مَّا بَيْنَ أَيْدِيهِمْ وَمَا خَلْفَهُمْ وَحَقَّ عَلَيْهِمُ الْقَوْلُ فِى أُمَمٍ قَدْ خَلَتْ مِن قَبْلِهِم مِّنَ الْجِنِّ وَالْإِنسِ إِنَّهُمْ كَانُوا خَٰسِرِينَ ﴿٢٥﴾

Section 4

26. And those who disbelieve say: 'Listen not to this Qur'ān and babble therein, haply you may overcome.'

وَقَالَ الَّذِينَ كَفَرُوا لَا تَسْمَعُوا لِهَٰذَا الْقُرْءَانِ وَالْغَوْا فِيهِ لَعَلَّكُمْ تَغْلِبُونَ ﴿٢٦﴾

27. So We will cause those who disbelieve to taste a severe torment, and We will surely requite them the worst of what they have been working.

فَلَنُذِيقَنَّ الَّذِينَ كَفَرُوا عَذَابًا شَدِيدًا وَلَنَجْزِيَنَّهُمْ أَسْوَأَ الَّذِى كَانُوا يَعْمَلُونَ ﴿٢٧﴾

28. That is the meed of the enemies of Allah – the Fire. Therein is their home of abidance, a meed for their gainsaying of Our signs.

ذَٰلِكَ جَزَآءُ أَعْدَآءِ اللَّهِ النَّارُ لَهُمْ فِيهَا دَارُ الْخُلْدِ جَزَآءً بِمَا كَانُوا بِآيَٰتِنَا يَجْحَدُونَ ﴿٢٨﴾

29. And those who disbelieve will say: 'Our Lord! Show us those of *jinn* and mankind who led us astray and we will place them under our feet that they may be of the nethermost.'

وَقَالَ ٱلَّذِينَ كَفَرُوا۟ رَبَّنَآ أَرِنَا ٱلَّذَيْنِ أَضَلَّانَا مِنَ ٱلْجِنِّ وَٱلْإِنسِ نَجْعَلْهُمَا تَحْتَ أَقْدَامِنَا لِيَكُونَا مِنَ ٱلْأَسْفَلِينَ ﴿٢٩﴾

30. Verily those who said: 'Our Lord is Allah', and have thereafter stood by it on them will descend the angels saying: 'Fear not, nor grieve, and rejoice at the glad-tidings of the Garden which you have been promised.'

إِنَّ ٱلَّذِينَ قَالُوا۟ رَبُّنَا ٱللَّهُ ثُمَّ ٱسْتَقَٰمُوا۟ تَتَنَزَّلُ عَلَيْهِمُ ٱلْمَلَٰٓئِكَةُ أَلَّا تَخَافُوا۟ وَلَا تَحْزَنُوا۟ وَأَبْشِرُوا۟ بِٱلْجَنَّةِ ٱلَّتِى كُنتُمْ تُوعَدُونَ ﴿٣٠﴾

31. We have been your friends in the life of the world, and are such in the Hereafter; herein whatsoever you desire shall be yours and whatsoever you call for shall be yours.

نَحْنُ أَوْلِيَآؤُكُمْ فِى ٱلْحَيَوٰةِ ٱلدُّنْيَا وَفِى ٱلْءَاخِرَةِ وَلَكُمْ فِيهَا مَا تَشْتَهِىٓ أَنفُسُكُمْ وَلَكُمْ فِيهَا مَا تَدَّعُونَ ﴿٣١﴾

32. An entertainment for you from your Lord, the Forgiving, the Merciful.'

نُزُلًا مِّنْ غَفُورٍ رَّحِيمٍ ﴿٣٢﴾

Section 5

33. And who is better in speech than he who summons unto Allah and works righteously, and says: 'Verily I am of the Muslims?'

وَمَنْ أَحْسَنُ قَوْلًا مِّمَّن دَعَآ إِلَى ٱللَّهِ وَعَمِلَ صَٰلِحًا وَقَالَ إِنَّنِى مِنَ ٱلْمُسْلِمِينَ ﴿٣٣﴾

34. Good and evil cannot be equal. Repeal evil with what is goodly, then behold! He, between whom and you was enmity, will be as though he was a warm friend.

وَلَا تَسْتَوِى ٱلْحَسَنَةُ وَلَا ٱلسَّيِّئَةُ ٱدْفَعْ بِٱلَّتِى هِىَ أَحْسَنُ فَإِذَا ٱلَّذِى بَيْنَكَ وَبَيْنَهُۥ عَدَٰوَةٌ كَأَنَّهُۥ وَلِىٌّ حَمِيمٌ ﴿٣٤﴾

35. And none attains that except those who are patient; and none attains that except the owner of mighty good fortune.

وَمَا يُلَقَّىٰهَآ إِلَّا ٱلَّذِينَ صَبَرُوا۟ وَمَا يُلَقَّىٰهَآ إِلَّا ذُو حَظٍّ عَظِيمٍ ۝

36. And if there stirs you an incitement from Satan, then seek refuge in Allah. Verily He! He is the Hearer, the Knower.

وَإِمَّا يَنزَغَنَّكَ مِنَ ٱلشَّيْطَٰنِ نَزْغٌ فَٱسْتَعِذْ بِٱللَّهِ إِنَّهُۥ هُوَ ٱلسَّمِيعُ ٱلْعَلِيمُ ۝

37. And of His signs are the night and the day and the sun and the moon. So do not prostrate yourselves to the sun and the moon, but prostrate yourselves to Allah Who has created them, if it is Allah alone Whom you are worshipping.

وَمِنْ ءَايَٰتِهِ ٱلَّيْلُ وَٱلنَّهَارُ وَٱلشَّمْسُ وَٱلْقَمَرُ لَا تَسْجُدُوا۟ لِلشَّمْسِ وَلَا لِلْقَمَرِ وَٱسْجُدُوا۟ لِلَّهِ ٱلَّذِى خَلَقَهُنَّ إِن كُنتُمْ إِيَّاهُ تَعْبُدُونَ ۝

38. And if they grew stiff-necked, then those who are with your Lord, hallow Him night and day, and they weary not.

فَإِنِ ٱسْتَكْبَرُوا۟ فَٱلَّذِينَ عِندَ رَبِّكَ يُسَبِّحُونَ لَهُۥ بِٱلَّيْلِ وَٱلنَّهَارِ وَهُمْ لَا يَسْـَٔمُونَ ۩ ۝

39. And of his signs is that you see the earth lowly, and when We send down water on it, it stirs to life and grows. Verily He Who quickens it, is the Quickener of the dead. Verily He is Potent over everything.

وَمِنْ ءَايَٰتِهِۦٓ أَنَّكَ تَرَى ٱلْأَرْضَ خَٰشِعَةً فَإِذَآ أَنزَلْنَا عَلَيْهَا ٱلْمَآءَ ٱهْتَزَّتْ وَرَبَتْ إِنَّ ٱلَّذِىٓ أَحْيَاهَا لَمُحْىِ ٱلْمَوْتَىٰٓ إِنَّهُۥ عَلَىٰ كُلِّ شَىْءٍ قَدِيرٌ ۝

40. Verily those who blaspheme Our revelations are not hidden from Us. Is he then who will be cast into the Fire better or he who comes secure on the Day of Resurrection? Do what you will, verily He is the Beholder of what you do.

إِنَّ ٱلَّذِينَ يُلْحِدُونَ فِىٓ ءَايَٰتِنَا لَا يَخْفَوْنَ عَلَيْنَآ أَفَمَن يُلْقَىٰ فِى ٱلنَّارِ خَيْرٌ أَم مَّن يَأْتِىٓ ءَامِنًا يَوْمَ ٱلْقِيَٰمَةِ ٱعْمَلُوا۟ مَا شِئْتُمْ إِنَّهُۥ بِمَا تَعْمَلُونَ بَصِيرٌ ۝

41. Verily those who disbelieve in the admonition when it comes to them are themselves at fault; verily it is a mighty Book.

إِنَّ ٱلَّذِينَ كَفَرُواْ بِٱلذِّكْرِ لَمَّا جَآءَهُمۡ وَإِنَّهُۥ لَكِتَٰبٌ عَزِيزٌ ۝

42. Falsehood cannot come to it from before it or from behind it. It is a revelation from the One, the Wise and the Praiseworthy.

لَّا يَأْتِيهِ ٱلْبَٰطِلُ مِنۢ بَيْنِ يَدَيْهِ وَلَا مِنْ خَلْفِهِۦ تَنزِيلٌ مِّنْ حَكِيمٍ حَمِيدٍ ۝

43. Naught is said to you save what was said to the Messengers before you. Your Lord is the Owner of forgiveness and the Owner of afflictive chastisement.

مَّا يُقَالُ لَكَ إِلَّا مَا قَدْ قِيلَ لِلرُّسُلِ مِن قَبْلِكَ إِنَّ رَبَّكَ لَذُو مَغْفِرَةٍ وَذُو عِقَابٍ أَلِيمٍ ۝

44. And had We made it a recital into a foreign tongue, they would certainly have said: 'Why are not the verses thereof explained to us? A foreign tongue and an Arab!' Say to those who believe in it: 'It is a guidance and a healing'; and those who do not believe, in their ears is a heaviness and to them it is blindness. These are they who are cried unto from a place far-off.

وَلَوْ جَعَلْنَٰهُ قُرْءَانًا أَعْجَمِيًّا لَّقَالُواْ لَوْلَا فُصِّلَتْ ءَايَٰتُهُۥٓ ءَا۬عْجَمِيٌّ وَعَرَبِيٌّ قُلْ هُوَ لِلَّذِينَ ءَامَنُواْ هُدًى وَشِفَآءٌ وَٱلَّذِينَ لَا يُؤْمِنُونَ فِيٓ ءَاذَانِهِمْ وَقْرٌ وَهُوَ عَلَيْهِمْ عَمًى أُوْلَٰٓئِكَ يُنَادَوْنَ مِن مَّكَانٍۭ بَعِيدٍ ۝

Section 6

45. And assuredly We vouchsafed the Book to Moses and there arose differences concerning it. And had not a word gone forth from your Lord, the affair would have been decreed between them. And verily they are in regard thereto in doubt and dubitable.

وَلَقَدْ ءَاتَيْنَا مُوسَى ٱلْكِتَٰبَ فَٱخْتُلِفَ فِيهِ وَلَوْلَا كَلِمَةٌ سَبَقَتْ مِن رَّبِّكَ لَقُضِيَ بَيْنَهُمْ وَإِنَّهُمْ لَفِى شَكٍّ مِّنْهُ مُرِيبٍ ۝

46. Whosoever works righteously it is for his own soul, and whosoever works evil it is against it. And your Lord is not an oppressor to His bondsmen.[642]

47. To Him alone is referred the knowledge of the Hour. And not a fruit comes forth from its sheath, nor does a female conceive or bring forth but with His knowledge. And on the Day when He will call unto them: 'Where are My associates?', they will say: 'We assure You, none of us is a witness thereof.'

48. And those whom they had been calling upon before will fail them, and they will perceive that there is no refuge for them.

49. Man is never wearied of praying for his worldly good, and if an evil visits him, he is despondent, despairing.

50. And if, after an affliction has visited him, We cause him to taste of Our mercy, he is sure to say: 'This is my own and I do not think that the Hour will ever arise, and were I to be brought back to my Lord, surely there will be for me an excellent reward from Him.' But We shall surely declare to those who disbelieve what they have worked, and make them taste a rough torment.

مَنْ عَمِلَ صَٰلِحًا فَلِنَفْسِهِۦ وَمَنْ أَسَآءَ فَعَلَيْهَا وَمَا رَبُّكَ بِظَلَّٰمٍ لِّلْعَبِيدِ ﴿٤٦﴾

إِلَيْهِ يُرَدُّ عِلْمُ ٱلسَّاعَةِ وَمَا تَخْرُجُ مِن ثَمَرَٰتٍ مِّنْ أَكْمَامِهَا وَمَا تَحْمِلُ مِنْ أُنثَىٰ وَلَا تَضَعُ إِلَّا بِعِلْمِهِۦ وَيَوْمَ يُنَادِيهِمْ أَيْنَ شُرَكَآءِى قَالُوٓا۟ ءَاذَنَّٰكَ مَا مِنَّا مِن شَهِيدٍ ﴿٤٧﴾

وَضَلَّ عَنْهُم مَّا كَانُوا۟ يَدْعُونَ مِن قَبْلُ وَظَنُّوا۟ مَا لَهُم مِّن مَّحِيصٍ ﴿٤٨﴾

لَّا يَسْـَٔمُ ٱلْإِنسَٰنُ مِن دُعَآءِ ٱلْخَيْرِ وَإِن مَّسَّهُ ٱلشَّرُّ فَيَـُٔوسٌ قَنُوطٌ ﴿٤٩﴾

وَلَئِنْ أَذَقْنَٰهُ رَحْمَةً مِّنَّا مِنۢ بَعْدِ ضَرَّآءَ مَسَّتْهُ لَيَقُولَنَّ هَٰذَا لِى وَمَآ أَظُنُّ ٱلسَّاعَةَ قَآئِمَةً وَلَئِن رُّجِعْتُ إِلَىٰ رَبِّىٓ إِنَّ لِى عِندَهُۥ لَلْحُسْنَىٰ فَلَنُنَبِّئَنَّ ٱلَّذِينَ كَفَرُوا۟ بِمَا عَمِلُوا۟ وَلَنُذِيقَنَّهُم مِّنْ عَذَابٍ غَلِيظٍ ﴿٥٠﴾

---

642. The God of Islam, as contradistinguished from tribal or national gods of other communities, is perfectly Just and absolutely Benevolent; not vindictive or malevolent.

51. And when We show favour to man, he turns aside and withdraws on his side, and when evil touches him, he is full of prolonged prayer.

وَإِذَآ أَنْعَمْنَا عَلَى الْإِنسَنِ أَعْرَضَ وَنَأَ بِجَانِبِهِۦ وَإِذَا مَسَّهُ الشَّرُّ فَذُو دُعَآءٍ عَرِيضٍ ۝

52. Say: 'Think! If it is really from Allah and you reject it, who is further astray than one who is in a far-off schism?'

قُلْ أَرَءَيْتُمْ إِن كَانَ مِنْ عِندِ اللَّهِ ثُمَّ كَفَرْتُم بِهِۦ مَنْ أَضَلُّ مِمَّنْ هُوَ فِى شِقَاقٍ بَعِيدٍ ۝

53. Soon We shall show them Our signs in the universe and in their own selves until it becomes manifest to them that it is the truth. Does it not suffice in regard to your Lord, that He is a Witness over everything?

سَنُرِيهِمْ ءَايَتِنَا فِى الْأَفَاقِ وَفِىٓ أَنفُسِهِمْ حَتَّىٰ يَتَبَيَّنَ لَهُمْ أَنَّهُ الْحَقُّ أَوَلَمْ يَكْفِ بِرَبِّكَ أَنَّهُۥ عَلَىٰ كُلِّ شَىْءٍ شَهِيدٌ ۝

54. Lo! They are in doubt concerning their meeting with their Lord. Lo! He is the Encompassor of everything.

أَلَآ إِنَّهُمْ فِى مِرْيَةٍ مِّن لِّقَآءِ رَبِّهِمْ أَلَآ إِنَّهُۥ بِكُلِّ شَىْءٍ مُّحِيطٌ ۝

Sūrah 42

al-Shūrā

(Makkan, 5 Sections, 53 Verses)

In the name of Allah, the Compassionate, the Merciful.

Section 1

1. *Ḥā, Mīm.*

2. *'Ayn, Sīn, Qāf.*

3. Thus reveals to you and to those before you Allah, the Mighty, the Wise.

4. His is whatever is in the heavens and whatever is in the earth, and He is the Exalted, the Grand.

5. Soon might be rent the heavens from above them. And the angels hallow the praise of their Lord and ask His forgiveness for those on the earth. Lo! Verily Allah; He is the Forgiver, the Merciful.

6. And those who take patrons besides Him Allah is a Warden over them, and you are not guardian over them.

7. And thus We have revealed to you the Qur'ān in Arabic, that you may warn thereby the mother-town[643] and those around it, and that you may warn them of a Day of Assembling whereof there is no doubt. And of mankind a party will be in the Garden, and a party in the Blaze.

وَكَذَٰلِكَ أَوْحَيْنَا إِلَيْكَ قُرْءَانًا عَرَبِيًّا لِّتُنذِرَ أُمَّ الْقُرَىٰ وَمَنْ حَوْلَهَا وَتُنذِرَ يَوْمَ الْجَمْعِ لَا رَيْبَ فِيهِ فَرِيقٌ فِي الْجَنَّةِ وَفَرِيقٌ فِي السَّعِيرِ ۝

8. And had Allah willed, He would have made them all a single community. But He causes whom He will to enter into His mercy, And the ungodly! For them there shall be no patron or helper.

وَلَوْ شَآءَ اللَّهُ لَجَعَلَهُمْ أُمَّةً وَاحِدَةً وَلَٰكِن يُدْخِلُ مَن يَشَآءُ فِي رَحْمَتِهِ وَالظَّالِمُونَ مَا لَهُم مِّن وَلِيٍّ وَلَا نَصِيرٍ ۝

9. Have they taken patrons besides Him? But Allah! He is the Patron. He quickens the dead, and He is Potent over everything.

أَمِ اتَّخَذُوا مِن دُونِهِ أَوْلِيَآءَ فَاللَّهُ هُوَ الْوَلِيُّ وَهُوَ يُحْيِ الْمَوْتَىٰ وَهُوَ عَلَىٰ كُلِّ شَىْءٍ قَدِيرٌ ۝

Section 2

10. And whatsoever it be in which you differ, the decision thereof is with Allah; such is Allah, my Lord. In Him I put my trust, and to Him I turn in penitence.

وَمَا اخْتَلَفْتُمْ فِيهِ مِن شَىْءٍ فَحُكْمُهُ إِلَى اللَّهِ ذَٰلِكُمُ اللَّهُ رَبِّي عَلَيْهِ تَوَكَّلْتُ وَإِلَيْهِ أُنِيبُ ۝

---

643. This primarily, and in the first instance. The 'mother of towns' is the city of Makka, so called because it is the greatest of towns in dignity, where all the believing peoples on the earth repair, and also because it was held by ancient geographers to be in the centre of the earth. The inter-continental location of Arabia, and its central position in the midst of the three continents of the old world are facts of very great significance. 'The wide diffusion of Islam is an instance in point. This religion has been singularly fortunate in the land of its birth. The central position of its birth place has been a powerful geographical factor in its wide dissemination to the remotest corners of the world, the importance of which factor has rarely been recognized, much less emphasized, by investigators' (Inayatullah, *Geographical Factors in Arabic Life and History*, p. 37).

11. The Originator of the heavens and the earth. He has made for you mates of yourselves, and for the cattle also mates, whereby He diffuses you. Not like Him[644] is anyone,[645] and He is the Hearer, the Beholder.

فَاطِرُ ٱلسَّمَوَٰتِ وَٱلْأَرْضِ جَعَلَ لَكُم مِّنْ أَنفُسِكُمْ أَزْوَٰجًا وَمِنَ ٱلْأَنْعَٰمِ أَزْوَٰجًا يَذْرَؤُكُمْ فِيهِ لَيْسَ كَمِثْلِهِۦ شَىْءٌ وَهُوَ ٱلسَّمِيعُ ٱلْبَصِيرُ ۝

12. His are the keys of the heavens and the earth, He expands the provision for whomsoever He will and also straitens. He is the Knower of everything.

لَهُۥ مَقَالِيدُ ٱلسَّمَوَٰتِ وَٱلْأَرْضِ يَبْسُطُ ٱلرِّزْقَ لِمَن يَشَآءُ وَيَقْدِرُ إِنَّهُۥ بِكُلِّ شَىْءٍ عَلِيمٌ ۝

13. He has ordained for you in the faith what He had enjoined upon Noah[646] and what We have revealed to you, and what We had enjoined upon Abraham and Moses and Jesus, saying: 'Establish the faith, and be not divided in it. Grievous unto the polytheists is that to which you call them. Allah chooses for Himself whom He will, and Allah guides to Himself him who turns in penitence.'

شَرَعَ لَكُم مِّنَ ٱلدِّينِ مَا وَصَّىٰ بِهِۦ نُوحًا وَٱلَّذِىٓ أَوْحَيْنَآ إِلَيْكَ وَمَا وَصَّيْنَا بِهِۦٓ إِبْرَٰهِيمَ وَمُوسَىٰ وَعِيسَىٰٓ أَنْ أَقِيمُوا ٱلدِّينَ وَلَا تَتَفَرَّقُوا فِيهِ كَبُرَ عَلَى ٱلْمُشْرِكِينَ مَا تَدْعُوهُمْ إِلَيْهِ ٱللَّهُ يَجْتَبِىٓ إِلَيْهِ مَن يَشَآءُ وَيَهْدِىٓ إِلَيْهِ مَن يُنِيبُ ۝

---

644. Nothing has any affinity with Him. The God of Islam, though intimately concerned with all things that are, is Himself absolutely distinct from them as their Creator.

645. Whether in person, nature or attributes, i.e. He is the Unique, the Absolute, the Incomparable. This rules out anthropomorphism and all forms of polytheism, overt or covert.

646. Namely the one True Religion revealed from the beginning to all true Prophets, the religion of monotheism, the oldest religion known to humanity. 'Ethnological investigation into cultural history shows that the first religion of mankind was monotheistic, and that the ethical and moral level of the oldest jungle-tribe-civilizations (though very poor materially) has been an extremely high one' (Ehrenfels, *The Islamic Culture* (October 1940), p. 446).

14. And they divided not till knowledge had come to them, through spite among themselves. And had not a word gone forth from your Lord for an appointed term, the affair would surely have been judged between them. And verily those who have been made the heirs of the Book after them are those in doubt thereof, dubitable.

وَمَا تَفَرَّقُوٓا إِلَّا مِنۢ بَعْدِ مَا جَآءَهُمُ ٱلْعِلْمُ بَغْيًۢا بَيْنَهُمْ ۚ وَلَوْلَا كَلِمَةٌ سَبَقَتْ مِن رَّبِّكَ إِلَىٰٓ أَجَلٍ مُّسَمًّى لَّقُضِىَ بَيْنَهُمْ ۚ وَإِنَّ ٱلَّذِينَ أُورِثُوا ٱلْكِتَـٰبَ مِنۢ بَعْدِهِمْ لَفِى شَكٍّ مِّنْهُ مُرِيبٍ ﴿١٤﴾

15. Summon therefore to that, and be steadfast as you have been commanded, and follow not their desires. And say: 'I believe in whatsoever Allah has sent down of the Book, and I am commanded that I should do justice between you; Allah is our Lord and your Lord. Unto us our works and unto you your works; let there be no contention between us and you. Allah will assemble us all, and to Him is the return.'

فَلِذَٰلِكَ فَٱدْعُ ۖ وَٱسْتَقِمْ كَمَآ أُمِرْتَ ۖ وَلَا تَتَّبِعْ أَهْوَآءَهُمْ ۖ وَقُلْ ءَامَنتُ بِمَآ أَنزَلَ ٱللَّهُ مِن كِتَـٰبٍ ۖ وَأُمِرْتُ لِأَعْدِلَ بَيْنَكُمُ ٱللَّهُ رَبُّنَا وَرَبُّكُمْ ۖ لَنَآ أَعْمَـٰلُنَا وَلَكُمْ أَعْمَـٰلُكُمْ ۖ لَا حُجَّةَ بَيْنَنَا وَبَيْنَكُمُ ٱللَّهُ يَجْمَعُ بَيْنَنَا ۖ وَإِلَيْهِ ٱلْمَصِيرُ ﴿١٥﴾

16. And those who contend in respect of the religion of Allah after it has been acknowledged; their contention is void in the sight of their Lord, and upon them shall befall His wrath and theirs shall be a severe chastisement.

وَٱلَّذِينَ يُحَآجُّونَ فِى ٱللَّهِ مِنۢ بَعْدِ مَا ٱسْتُجِيبَ لَهُۥ حُجَّتُهُمْ دَاحِضَةٌ عِندَ رَبِّهِمْ وَعَلَيْهِمْ غَضَبٌ وَلَهُمْ عَذَابٌ شَدِيدٌ ﴿١٦﴾

17. Allah it is Who has sent down the Book with the truth and the balance. And what shall make you know? Haply the hour may be nigh.

ٱللَّهُ ٱلَّذِىٓ أَنزَلَ ٱلْكِتَـٰبَ بِٱلْحَقِّ وَٱلْمِيزَانَ ۗ وَمَا يُدْرِيكَ لَعَلَّ ٱلسَّاعَةَ قَرِيبٌ ﴿١٧﴾

18. It is only those who do not believe therein who seek to hasten it, and those who believe therein are fearful thereof, and know that it is the Truth. Lo! Verily those who debate concerning the Hour are in far-off error.

19. Allah is Gentle to His bondsmen. He provides for whomsoever He will, and He is the Strong, the Mighty.

Section 3

20. Whosoever seeks the tillage of the Hereafter, to him We shall give increase in his tillage; and whosoever seeks the tillage of this world, We shall give him somewhat thereof, and in the Hereafter his shall be no portion.

21. Have they associate-gods who have instituted for them a religion which Allah has not approved? And had there not been a decisive word, the affair would have been judged between them. And verily the ungodly! Theirs shall be an afflictive torment.

22. You shall see the ungodly fearful on account of what they have earned, and it is sure to befall them. And those who believe and work righteous deeds will be in meadows of the Gardens. Theirs will be whatsoever they desire with their Lord. That! That is the supreme grace.

يَسْتَعْجِلُ بِهَا الَّذِيْنَ لَا يُؤْمِنُوْنَ بِهَا ۖ وَالَّذِيْنَ ءَامَنُوْا مُشْفِقُوْنَ مِنْهَا ۖ وَيَعْلَمُوْنَ أَنَّهَا الْحَقُّ ۗ أَلَا إِنَّ الَّذِيْنَ يُمَارُوْنَ فِى السَّاعَةِ لَفِىْ ضَلَلٍ بَعِيْدٍ ۝

اللّٰهُ لَطِيْفٌ بِعِبَادِهٖ يَرْزُقُ مَنْ يَشَاءُ ۖ وَهُوَ الْقَوِيُّ الْعَزِيْزُ ۝

مَنْ كَانَ يُرِيْدُ حَرْثَ الْأَخِرَةِ نَزِدْ لَهُ فِىْ حَرْثِهٖ ۖ وَمَنْ كَانَ يُرِيْدُ حَرْثَ الدُّنْيَا نُؤْتِهٖ مِنْهَا وَمَا لَهُ فِى الْأَخِرَةِ مِنْ نَّصِيْبٍ ۝

أَمْ لَهُمْ شُرَكَؤُا شَرَعُوْا لَهُمْ مِّنَ الدِّيْنِ مَا لَمْ يَأْذَنْ بِهِ اللّٰهُ ۚ وَلَوْلَا كَلِمَةُ الْفَصْلِ لَقُضِىَ بَيْنَهُمْ ۗ وَإِنَّ الظّٰلِمِيْنَ لَهُمْ عَذَابٌ أَلِيْمٌ ۝

تَرَى الظّٰلِمِيْنَ مُشْفِقِيْنَ مِمَّا كَسَبُوْا وَهُوَ وَاقِعٌ بِهِمْ ۗ وَالَّذِيْنَ ءَامَنُوْا وَعَمِلُوا الصّٰلِحٰتِ فِىْ رَوْضَاتِ الْجَنّٰتِ ۖ لَهُمْ مَّا يَشَاءُوْنَ عِنْدَ رَبِّهِمْ ۚ ذٰلِكَ هُوَ الْفَضْلُ الْكَبِيْرُ ۝

23. That is the glad tidings Allah gives to His bondsmen who believe and work righteous deeds. Say: 'I ask of you no wage for that save affection in respect of kinship.' And whosoever does a good deed We shall increase to him good in respect thereof; verily Allah is the Forgiving, the Appreciative.

ذَٰلِكَ ٱلَّذِى يُبَشِّرُ ٱللَّهُ عِبَادَهُ ٱلَّذِينَ ءَامَنُوا۟ وَعَمِلُوا۟ ٱلصَّٰلِحَٰتِ قُل لَّآ أَسْـَٔلُكُمْ عَلَيْهِ أَجْرًا إِلَّا ٱلْمَوَدَّةَ فِى ٱلْقُرْبَىٰ وَمَن يَقْتَرِفْ حَسَنَةً نَّزِدْ لَهُۥ فِيهَا حُسْنًا إِنَّ ٱللَّهَ غَفُورٌ شَكُورٌ ۝

24. So they say: 'He has fabricated a lie concerning Allah?' Now if Allah willed He could seal your heart; and Allah abolishes falsehood and establishes Truth by His word. Verily He is the Knower of what is in the breasts.

أَمْ يَقُولُونَ ٱفْتَرَىٰ عَلَى ٱللَّهِ كَذِبًا فَإِن يَشَإِ ٱللَّهُ يَخْتِمْ عَلَىٰ قَلْبِكَ وَيَمْحُ ٱللَّهُ ٱلْبَٰطِلَ وَيُحِقُّ ٱلْحَقَّ بِكَلِمَٰتِهِۦ إِنَّهُۥ عَلِيمٌۢ بِذَاتِ ٱلصُّدُورِ ۝

25. And He it is Who accepts repentance from His bondsmen, and pardons evil deeds and knows what you do.

وَهُوَ ٱلَّذِى يَقْبَلُ ٱلتَّوْبَةَ عَنْ عِبَادِهِۦ وَيَعْفُوا۟ عَنِ ٱلسَّيِّـَٔاتِ وَيَعْلَمُ مَا تَفْعَلُونَ ۝

26. He answers those who believe and work righteous deeds and increases to them of His grace. And the infidels! Theirs shall be a severe torment.

وَيَسْتَجِيبُ ٱلَّذِينَ ءَامَنُوا۟ وَعَمِلُوا۟ ٱلصَّٰلِحَٰتِ وَيَزِيدُهُم مِّن فَضْلِهِۦ وَٱلْكَٰفِرُونَ لَهُمْ عَذَابٌ شَدِيدٌ ۝

27. And had Allah expanded the provision for His bondsmen they surely would have rebelled in the earth, but He sends down by measure as He wills. Verily He is in respect of His bondsmen, the Aware, the Beholder.

وَلَوْ بَسَطَ ٱللَّهُ ٱلرِّزْقَ لِعِبَادِهِۦ لَبَغَوْا۟ فِى ٱلْأَرْضِ وَلَٰكِن يُنَزِّلُ بِقَدَرٍ مَّا يَشَآءُ إِنَّهُۥ بِعِبَادِهِۦ خَبِيرٌۢ بَصِيرٌ ۝

28. And He it is Who sends down the rain after men have despaired, and spreads abroad His mercy and He is the Patron, the Praiseworthy.

وَهُوَ ٱلَّذِى يُنَزِّلُ ٱلْغَيْثَ مِنۢ بَعْدِ مَا قَنَطُوا۟ وَيَنشُرُ رَحْمَتَهُۥ وَهُوَ ٱلْوَلِىُّ ٱلْحَمِيدُ ۝

29. And of His signs is the creation of the heavens and the earth and of the moving creatures which He has dispersed in both. And He is Potent over their assembling whenever He will.

وَمِنۡ ءَايَٰتِهِۦ خَلۡقُ ٱلسَّمَٰوَٰتِ وَٱلۡأَرۡضِ وَمَا بَثَّ فِيهِمَا مِن دَآبَّةٍۚ وَهُوَ عَلَىٰ جَمۡعِهِمۡ إِذَا يَشَآءُ قَدِيرٞ ٢٩

Section 4

30. And whatever of affliction befalls you is owing to what your hands have earned; and He pardons much.

وَمَآ أَصَٰبَكُم مِّن مُّصِيبَةٖ فَبِمَا كَسَبَتۡ أَيۡدِيكُمۡ وَيَعۡفُوا۟ عَن كَثِيرٖ ٣٠

31. And you cannot frustrate Him in the earth; and you have, besides Allah, neither a protector nor a helper.

وَمَآ أَنتُم بِمُعۡجِزِينَ فِي ٱلۡأَرۡضِۖ وَمَا لَكُم مِّن دُونِ ٱللَّهِ مِن وَلِيّٖ وَلَا نَصِيرٖ ٣١

32. And of His signs are ships in the sea like high mountains.

وَمِنۡ ءَايَٰتِهِ ٱلۡجَوَارِ فِي ٱلۡبَحۡرِ كَٱلۡأَعۡلَٰمِ ٣٢

33. If He wills He causes the wind to cease, so that they stand still on the back thereof; verily therein are signs for everyone patient and grateful.

إِن يَشَأۡ يُسۡكِنِ ٱلرِّيحَ فَيَظۡلَلۡنَ رَوَاكِدَ عَلَىٰ ظَهۡرِهِۦٓۚ إِنَّ فِي ذَٰلِكَ لَأٓيَٰتٖ لِّكُلِّ صَبَّارٖ شَكُورٍ ٣٣

34. Or He may destroy them for what the people have earned; and He pardons many of them.

أَوۡ يُوبِقۡهُنَّ بِمَا كَسَبُوا۟ وَيَعۡفُ عَن كَثِيرٖ ٣٤

35. And those who dispute in respect of Our revelations may know that there is for them no place of shelter.

وَيَعۡلَمَ ٱلَّذِينَ يُجَٰدِلُونَ فِيٓ ءَايَٰتِنَا مَا لَهُم مِّن مَّحِيصٖ ٣٥

36. So whatsoever things are vouchsafed to you are but a passing enjoyment for the life of this world; and what is with Allah, better and more lasting is for those who believe and put their trust in Allah;

فَمَآ أُوتِيتُم مِّن شَىْءٍ فَمَتَٰعُ الْحَيَوٰةِ الدُّنْيَا وَمَا عِندَ اللَّهِ خَيْرٌ وَأَبْقَىٰ لِلَّذِينَ ءَامَنُوا وَعَلَىٰ رَبِّهِمْ يَتَوَكَّلُونَ ﴿٣٦﴾

37. And those who avoid heinous sins and indecencies and forgive when they are wrathful;

وَالَّذِينَ يَجْتَنِبُونَ كَبَٰٓئِرَ الْإِثْمِ وَالْفَوَٰحِشَ وَإِذَا مَا غَضِبُوا هُمْ يَغْفِرُونَ ﴿٣٧﴾

38. And those who answer the call of their Lord and establish prayer and whose affair being a matter of counsel among themselves and who spend of that wherewith We have provided them;

وَالَّذِينَ اسْتَجَابُوا لِرَبِّهِمْ وَأَقَامُوا الصَّلَوٰةَ وَأَمْرُهُمْ شُورَىٰ بَيْنَهُمْ وَمِمَّا رَزَقْنَٰهُمْ يُنفِقُونَ ﴿٣٨﴾

39. And those who vindicate themselves when they are oppressed.

وَالَّذِينَ إِذَآ أَصَابَهُمُ الْبَغْىُ هُمْ يَنتَصِرُونَ ﴿٣٩﴾

40. The meed of an ill deed is an ill like thereunto, but whosoever pardons and is reconciled, his reward is on Allah; verily He does not approve the wrong-doers.

وَجَزَٰٓؤُا۟ سَيِّئَةٍ سَيِّئَةٌ مِّثْلُهَا فَمَنْ عَفَا وَأَصْلَحَ فَأَجْرُهُۥ عَلَى اللَّهِ إِنَّهُۥ لَا يُحِبُّ الظَّٰلِمِينَ ﴿٤٠﴾

41. And whosoever vindicates himself after wrong done to him; these! Against them there is no way of blame.

وَلَمَنِ انتَصَرَ بَعْدَ ظُلْمِهِۦ فَأُو۟لَٰٓئِكَ مَا عَلَيْهِم مِّن سَبِيلٍ ﴿٤١﴾

42. The way of blame is only against those who wrong mankind, and rebel on the earth without justification; these, for them is an afflictive torment.

إِنَّمَا السَّبِيلُ عَلَى الَّذِينَ يَظْلِمُونَ النَّاسَ وَيَبْغُونَ فِى الْأَرْضِ بِغَيْرِ الْحَقِّ أُو۟لَٰٓئِكَ لَهُمْ عَذَابٌ أَلِيمٌ ﴿٤٢﴾

43. And whosoever forgives and forbears, that verily is of the firmness of affairs.

وَلَمَن صَبَرَ وَغَفَرَ إِنَّ ذَٰلِكَ لَمِنْ عَزْمِ الْأُمُورِ ﴿٤٣﴾

Section 5

44. And whomsoever Allah sends astray, for him there will be no protecting friend to take His place. And you will see the ungodly when they will face the torment, saying: 'Is there any way to return?'

وَمَن يُضْلِلِ اللَّهُ فَمَا لَهُ مِن وَلِيٍّ مِّنۢ بَعْدِهِۦ وَتَرَى الظَّالِمِينَ لَمَّا رَأَوُا الْعَذَابَ يَقُولُونَ هَلْ إِلَىٰ مَرَدٍّ مِّن سَبِيلٍ ﴿٤٤﴾

45. And you will see them set up before it, down cast with ignominy, looking with stealthy glance. And those who believe will say: 'Surely the losers are those who have lost themselves and their housefolk on the Day of Resurrection.' Lo! The ungodly will be in a lasting torment.

وَتَرَىٰهُمْ يُعْرَضُونَ عَلَيْهَا خَٰشِعِينَ مِنَ الذُّلِّ يَنظُرُونَ مِن طَرْفٍ خَفِيٍّ وَقَالَ الَّذِينَ ءَامَنُوٓا إِنَّ الْخَٰسِرِينَ الَّذِينَ خَسِرُوٓا أَنفُسَهُمْ وَأَهْلِيهِمْ يَوْمَ الْقِيَٰمَةِ أَلَآ إِنَّ الظَّٰلِمِينَ فِي عَذَابٍ مُّقِيمٍ ﴿٤٥﴾

46. And they will have no patrons succouring them besides Allah. Whosoever Allah sends astray, there will be for him no way.

وَمَا كَانَ لَهُم مِّنْ أَوْلِيَآءَ يَنصُرُونَهُم مِّن دُونِ اللَّهِ وَمَن يُضْلِلِ اللَّهُ فَمَا لَهُ مِن سَبِيلٍ ﴿٤٦﴾

47. Answer the call of your Lord before there comes to you a Day on which there is no averting from Allah. You will have no place of refuge on that Day, nor will there be for you any denying of your guilt.

اسْتَجِيبُوا لِرَبِّكُم مِّن قَبْلِ أَن يَأْتِيَ يَوْمٌ لَّا مَرَدَّ لَهُۥ مِنَ اللَّهِ مَا لَكُم مِّن مَّلْجَإٍ يَوْمَئِذٍ وَمَا لَكُم مِّن نَّكِيرٍ ﴿٤٧﴾

48. If they turn away, then We have not sent you as a warden over them; on you is nothing but preaching. And verily We! When We cause man to taste of mercy from Us, he exults at it; and if an ill befalls them for what their hands have sent on, then man becomes ungrateful.

فَإِنْ أَعْرَضُوا فَمَآ أَرْسَلْنَاكَ عَلَيْهِمْ حَفِيظًا ۖ إِنْ عَلَيْكَ إِلَّا ٱلْبَلَغُ ۚ وَإِنَّآ إِذَآ أَذَقْنَا ٱلْإِنسَنَ مِنَّا رَحْمَةً فَرِحَ بِهَا ۖ وَإِن تُصِبْهُمْ سَيِّئَةٌ بِمَا قَدَّمَتْ أَيْدِيهِمْ فَإِنَّ ٱلْإِنسَنَ كَفُورٌ ﴿٤٨﴾

49. Allah's is the dominion of the heavens and the earth. He creates whatsoever He will. He bestows females on whomsoever He will, and bestows males on whomsoever He will.

لِّلَّهِ مُلْكُ ٱلسَّمَوَتِ وَٱلْأَرْضِ ۚ يَخْلُقُ مَا يَشَآءُ ۚ يَهَبُ لِمَن يَشَآءُ إِنَثًا وَيَهَبُ لِمَن يَشَآءُ ٱلذُّكُورَ ﴿٤٩﴾

50. Or, He conjoins them males and females; and He makes barren whomsoever He will. Verily He is the Knower, the Potent.

أَوْ يُزَوِّجُهُمْ ذُكْرَانًا وَإِنَثًا ۖ وَيَجْعَلُ مَن يَشَآءُ عَقِيمًا ۚ إِنَّهُ عَلِيمٌ قَدِيرٌ ﴿٥٠﴾

51. And it is not possible for any human being that Allah should speak to him otherwise than by revelation[647] or from behind a veil, or that He sends a Messenger, so that the Messenger may reveal, by His command whatsoever He will. Verily He is the Exalted, the Wise.

وَمَا كَانَ لِبَشَرٍ أَن يُكَلِّمَهُ ٱللَّهُ إِلَّا وَحْيًا أَوْ مِن وَرَآئِ حِجَابٍ أَوْ يُرْسِلَ رَسُولًا فَيُوحِيَ بِإِذْنِهِ مَا يَشَآءُ ۚ إِنَّهُ عَلِىٌّ حَكِيمٌ ﴿٥١﴾

---

647. Revelation is a direct Message from God to a Prophet which, to the exclusion of all others, the receiver alone can perceive.

52.   In this manner We have revealed unto you a Spirit of Our command; you know not what the Book was, nor what the Faith. Yet we have made it a Light wherewith We guide whomsoever We will of Our bondsmen. And verily you guide to a straight path.

53.   The path of Allah, Whose is whatsoever is in the heavens and whatsoever is in the earth. Lo! To Allah tend all affairs.

وَكَذَٰلِكَ أَوْحَيْنَآ إِلَيْكَ رُوحًا مِّنْ أَمْرِنَا ۚ مَا كُنتَ تَدْرِى مَا ٱلْكِتَـٰبُ وَلَا ٱلْإِيمَـٰنُ وَلَـٰكِن جَعَلْنَـٰهُ نُورًا نَّهْدِى بِهِۦ مَن نَّشَآءُ مِنْ عِبَادِنَا ۚ وَإِنَّكَ لَتَهْدِىٓ إِلَىٰ صِرَٰطٍ مُّسْتَقِيمٍ ﴿٥٢﴾

صِرَٰطِ ٱللَّهِ ٱلَّذِى لَهُۥ مَا فِى ٱلسَّمَـٰوَٰتِ وَمَا فِى ٱلْأَرْضِ ۗ أَلَآ إِلَى ٱللَّهِ تَصِيرُ ٱلْأُمُورُ ﴿٥٣﴾

Sūrah 43

al-Zukhruf

(Makkan, 7 Sections, 89 Verses)

In the name of Allah, the Compassionate, the Merciful.

Section 1

1. *Ḥā, Mīm.*

2. By this luminous Book.

3. Verily We! We have made it an Arabic Qur'ān that haply you may reflect.

4. And verily it is in the Original Book before Us, indeed exalted, full of wisdom.

5. Shall We take away from you the admonition because you are a people extravagant?

6. And how many a Prophet We have sent among the ancients.

7. And not a Prophet came to them but him they used to mock.

8. Therefore We destroyed peoples mightier than these in prowess; and there has gone forth the example of the ancients.

9. And if you question them, 'who has created the heavens and the earth?', they will surely say: 'Created them the Mighty, the Knower.'

10. Who has made the earth a bed for you and has made therein paths for you that haply you may be directed?

اَلَّذِى جَعَلَ لَكُمُ الْأَرْضَ مَهْدًا وَجَعَلَ لَكُمْ فِيهَا سُبُلًا لَّعَلَّكُمْ تَهْتَدُونَ ۝

11. And who sends down water from the heaven in measure? Then We quicken a dead land therewith and even so you will be brought forth.

وَالَّذِى نَزَّلَ مِنَ السَّمَاءِ مَاءً بِقَدَرٍ فَأَنشَرْنَا بِهِ بَلْدَةً مَّيْتًا كَذَٰلِكَ تُخْرَجُونَ ۝

12. And who has created the pairs, all of them, and appointed for you from ships and cattle on which you ride,

وَالَّذِى خَلَقَ الْأَزْوَاجَ كُلَّهَا وَجَعَلَ لَكُم مِّنَ الْفُلْكِ وَالْأَنْعَامِ مَا تَرْكَبُونَ ۝

13. That you may mount firmly on their backs, and then may remember the favour of your Lord when you mount thereon, and may say: 'Hallowed be He Who has subjected this to us, and we could have it not.

لِتَسْتَوُۥا عَلَىٰ ظُهُورِهِ ثُمَّ تَذْكُرُوا نِعْمَةَ رَبِّكُمْ إِذَا اسْتَوَيْتُمْ عَلَيْهِ وَتَقُولُوا سُبْحَٰنَ الَّذِى سَخَّرَ لَنَا هَٰذَا وَمَا كُنَّا لَهُ مُقْرِنِينَ ۝

14. And verily to Our Lord we are to return.'

وَإِنَّا إِلَىٰ رَبِّنَا لَمُنقَلِبُونَ ۝

15. And they assign out of His bondsmen co-partners. Verily man is manifestly ungrateful.

وَجَعَلُوا لَهُ مِنْ عِبَادِهِ جُزْءًا إِنَّ الْإِنسَٰنَ لَكَفُورٌ مُّبِينٌ ۝

Section 2

16. Has He taken, from His creatures, daughters for Himself, and honoured you with sons?

أَمِ اتَّخَذَ مِمَّا يَخْلُقُ بَنَاتٍ وَأَصْفَىٰكُم بِالْبَنِينَ ۝

17. And when there is announced to any of them the birth of what he likens to the Compassionate, his countenance remains darkened the whole day, and he is indignant inwardly.

وَإِذَا بُشِّرَ أَحَدُهُم بِمَا ضَرَبَ لِلرَّحْمَٰنِ مَثَلًا ظَلَّ وَجْهُهُۥ مُسْوَدًّا وَهُوَ كَظِيمٌ ۝

18. Has He taken to Himself what is reared in ornaments, and is not clear in contention?

أَوَمَن يُنَشَّؤُاْ فِي ٱلْحِلْيَةِ وَهُوَ فِي ٱلْخِصَامِ غَيْرُ مُبِينٍ ۝

19. And they make the angels who are the bondsmen of the Compassionate females. Have they witnessed their creation? Their testimony will be written down and they will be questioned.

وَجَعَلُواْ ٱلْمَلَٰٓئِكَةَ ٱلَّذِينَ هُمْ عِبَٰدُ ٱلرَّحْمَٰنِ إِنَٰثًا أَشَهِدُواْ خَلْقَهُمْ سَتُكْتَبُ شَهَٰدَتُهُمْ وَيُسْـَٔلُونَ ۝

20. And they say: 'Had the Compassionate willed, we would not have worshipped them.' No knowledge they have of it, they are only guessing.

وَقَالُواْ لَوْ شَآءَ ٱلرَّحْمَٰنُ مَا عَبَدْنَٰهُم مَّا لَهُم بِذَٰلِكَ مِنْ عِلْمٍ إِنْ هُمْ إِلَّا يَخْرُصُونَ ۝

21. Have We vouchsafed them any Book before this, so that they are clinging to it?

أَمْ ءَاتَيْنَٰهُمْ كِتَٰبًا مِّن قَبْلِهِۦ فَهُم بِهِۦ مُسْتَمْسِكُونَ ۝

22. Nay! They say: 'We have found our fathers on a certain way, and by their footsteps we are guided.'[648]

بَلْ قَالُوٓاْ إِنَّا وَجَدْنَآ ءَابَآءَنَا عَلَىٰٓ أُمَّةٍ وَإِنَّا عَلَىٰٓ ءَاثَٰرِهِم مُّهْتَدُونَ ۝

---

648. In the pre-Islamic society of Arabia, as in most primitive societies, 'a man did not choose his religion or frame it for himself; it came to him as part of the general scheme of social obligations and ordinances laid upon him, as a matter of course, by his position in the family and in the nation. Religion did not exist for the saving of souls but for the preservation and welfare of society, and all that was necessary to this end every man had to take his part, or break with the domestic and political community to which he belonged. Thus a man was born with a fixed relation to certain gods as surely as he was born into relation to his fellow-men; and his religion, that is, the part of conduct which was determined by his relation to the gods, was simply one side of the general scheme of conduct prescribed for him by his position as a member of society' (Robertson-Smith, *Religion of the Semites*, pp. 28 – 30).

23. And in this wise We sent not a warner before you in any city but the affluent thereof said: 'Verily we found our fathers on a certain way and verily their footsteps we are following.'

وَكَذَلِكَ مَآ أَرْسَلْنَا مِن قَبْلِكَ فِى قَرْيَةٍ مِّن نَّذِيرٍ إِلَّا قَالَ مُتْرَفُوهَآ إِنَّا وَجَدْنَآ ءَابَآءَنَا عَلَىٰٓ أُمَّةٍ وَإِنَّا عَلَىٰٓ ءَاثَٰرِهِم مُّقْتَدُونَ ۝

24. The warner therefore said: 'What! Even if I bring you a better guidance than what you found your fathers upon?' They said: 'We deny that wherewith you are sent.'

قَٰلَ أَوَلَوْ جِئْتُكُم بِأَهْدَىٰ مِمَّا وَجَدتُّمْ عَلَيْهِ ءَابَآءَكُمْ قَالُوٓاْ إِنَّا بِمَآ أُرْسِلْتُم بِهِۦ كَٰفِرُونَ ۝

25. Therefore We took revenge on them. Behold then how has been the end of the beliers!

فَٱنتَقَمْنَا مِنْهُمْ فَٱنظُرْ كَيْفَ كَانَ عَٰقِبَةُ ٱلْمُكَذِّبِينَ ۝

Section 3

26. And recall when Abraham said to his father and his people: 'Verily I am quit of what you worship;

وَإِذْ قَالَ إِبْرَٰهِيمُ لِأَبِيهِ وَقَوْمِهِۦٓ إِنَّنِى بَرَآءٌ مِّمَّا تَعْبُدُونَ ۝

27. Save Him, Who has created me and then He would guide me.'

إِلَّا ٱلَّذِى فَطَرَنِى فَإِنَّهُۥ سَيَهْدِينِ ۝

28. And Abraham made it a word lasting among his posterity that haply they should return.

وَجَعَلَهَا كَلِمَةًۢ بَاقِيَةً فِى عَقِبِهِۦ لَعَلَّهُمْ يَرْجِعُونَ ۝

29. Aye! I let these and their fathers enjoy life, until there came unto them the Truth, and a plain Messenger.

بَلْ مَتَّعْتُ هَٰٓؤُلَآءِ وَءَابَآءَهُمْ حَتَّىٰ جَآءَهُمُ ٱلْحَقُّ وَرَسُولٌ مُّبِينٌ ۝

30. And when the Truth came to them, they say: 'This is magic, and verily we are therein disbelievers.'

وَلَمَّا جَآءَهُمُ ٱلْحَقُّ قَالُواْ هَٰذَا سِحْرٌ وَإِنَّا بِهِۦ كَٰفِرُونَ ۝

31. And they say: 'Why has not this Qur'ān been revealed to a leading man in the two cities?'

وَقَالُوا۟ لَوۡلَا نُزِّلَ هَٰذَا ٱلۡقُرۡءَانُ عَلَىٰ رَجُلٍ مِّنَ ٱلۡقَرۡيَتَيۡنِ عَظِيمٍ ۝

32. Shall they apportion their Lord's mercy? It is We Who have apportioned among them their livelihood in the life of the world, and have raised some of them over others in degrees,[649] so that one of them may take another as a serf, and the mercy of your Lord is better than what they amass.

أَهُمۡ يَقۡسِمُونَ رَحۡمَتَ رَبِّكَ نَحۡنُ قَسَمۡنَا بَيۡنَهُم مَّعِيشَتَهُمۡ فِى ٱلۡحَيَوٰةِ ٱلدُّنۡيَا وَرَفَعۡنَا بَعۡضَهُمۡ فَوۡقَ بَعۡضٍ دَرَجَٰتٍ لِّيَتَّخِذَ بَعۡضُهُم بَعۡضًا سُخۡرِيًّا وَرَحۡمَتُ رَبِّكَ خَيۡرٌ مِّمَّا يَجۡمَعُونَ ۝

33. And were it not that mankind would have become one community; We could make for those who disbelieve in the Compassionate roofs of silver for their houses and silver stairways whereby they ascend,

وَلَوۡلَا أَن يَكُونَ ٱلنَّاسُ أُمَّةً وَٰحِدَةً لَّجَعَلۡنَا لِمَن يَكۡفُرُ بِٱلرَّحۡمَٰنِ لِبُيُوتِهِمۡ سُقُفًا مِّن فِضَّةٍ وَمَعَارِجَ عَلَيۡهَا يَظۡهَرُونَ ۝

34. And silver doors for their houses and silver couches whereon they recline?

وَلِبُيُوتِهِمۡ أَبۡوَٰبًا وَسُرُرًا عَلَيۡهَا يَتَّكِـُٔونَ ۝

35. And ornaments of gold. And yet all that would have been but a provision of the life of this world; and the Hereafter with your Lord is for the God-fearing.

وَزُخۡرُفًا وَإِن كُلُّ ذَٰلِكَ لَمَّا مَتَٰعُ ٱلۡحَيَوٰةِ ٱلدُّنۡيَا وَٱلۡأَخِرَةُ عِندَ رَبِّكَ لِلۡمُتَّقِينَ ۝

---

649. In degrees of wealth, rank, or station. This does away with all the socialistic and communistic utopian theories of the 'equal distribution of wealth and property.'

Section 4

36. And whosoever blinds himself to the admonition of the Compassionate, We assign to him a devil, and he becomes his companion.

وَمَن يَعْشُ عَن ذِكْرِ ٱلرَّحْمَٰنِ نُقَيِّضْ لَهُۥ شَيْطَٰنًا فَهُوَ لَهُۥ قَرِينٌ ﴿٣٦﴾

37. And verily they hinder them from the way, while they imagine that they are rightly guided.

وَإِنَّهُمْ لَيَصُدُّونَهُمْ عَنِ ٱلسَّبِيلِ وَيَحْسَبُونَ أَنَّهُم مُّهْتَدُونَ ﴿٣٧﴾

38. Until when he comes to Us, he will say: 'Ah! Would that there had been between me and you the distance of the two orients, an evil companion!'

حَتَّىٰٓ إِذَا جَآءَنَا قَالَ يَٰلَيْتَ بَيْنِى وَبَيْنَكَ بُعْدَ ٱلْمَشْرِقَيْنِ فَبِئْسَ ٱلْقَرِينُ ﴿٣٨﴾

39. And because you have done wrong, today it will profit you not, that you are sharers in the torment.

وَلَن يَنفَعَكُمُ ٱلْيَوْمَ إِذ ظَّلَمْتُمْ أَنَّكُمْ فِى ٱلْعَذَابِ مُشْتَرِكُونَ ﴿٣٩﴾

40. So can you make the deaf hear or can you guide the blind or him who is in manifest error?

أَفَأَنتَ تُسْمِعُ ٱلصُّمَّ أَوْ تَهْدِى ٱلْعُمْىَ وَمَن كَانَ فِى ضَلَٰلٍ مُّبِينٍ ﴿٤٠﴾

41. And even though We take you away, We shall surely take vengeance on them.

فَإِمَّا نَذْهَبَنَّ بِكَ فَإِنَّا مِنْهُم مُّنتَقِمُونَ ﴿٤١﴾

42. Or if We show you that with which We threaten them; verily We are going to prevail over them.

أَوْ نُرِيَنَّكَ ٱلَّذِى وَعَدْنَٰهُمْ فَإِنَّا عَلَيْهِم مُّقْتَدِرُونَ ﴿٤٢﴾

43. Hold you fast to what We have revealed to you; verily you are on the straight path.

فَٱسْتَمْسِكْ بِٱلَّذِىٓ أُوحِىَ إِلَيْكَ إِنَّكَ عَلَىٰ صِرَٰطٍ مُّسْتَقِيمٍ ﴿٤٣﴾

44. And verily it is an admonition to you and your people, and presently you will be questioned.

وَإِنَّهُۥ لَذِكْرٌ لَّكَ وَلِقَوْمِكَ وَسَوْفَ تُسْـَٔلُونَ ﴿٤٤﴾

45. And ask you Our Messengers whom We sent before you; did We appoint gods, besides the Compassionate, to be worshipped?

وَسْـَٔلْ مَنْ أَرْسَلْنَا مِن قَبْلِكَ مِن رُّسُلِنَآ أَجَعَلْنَا مِن دُونِ الرَّحْمَٰنِ ءَالِهَةً يُعْبَدُونَ ﴿٤٥﴾

Section 5

46. And assuredly We sent Moses with Our signs to Pharaoh and his chiefs, and he said: 'Verily I am a Messenger of the Lord of the worlds.'

وَلَقَدْ أَرْسَلْنَا مُوسَىٰ بِـَٔايَٰتِنَآ إِلَىٰ فِرْعَوْنَ وَمَلَإِيْهِۦ فَقَالَ إِنِّى رَسُولُ رَبِّ ٱلْعَٰلَمِينَ ﴿٤٦﴾

47. Then when he came to them with Our signs, lo! They were laughing at those signs.

فَلَمَّا جَآءَهُم بِـَٔايَٰتِنَآ إِذَا هُم مِّنْهَا يَضْحَكُونَ ﴿٤٧﴾

48. And not a sign We showed them but it was greater than its like, and We seized them with chastisement that haply they might turn.

وَمَا نُرِيهِم مِّنْ ءَايَةٍ إِلَّا هِىَ أَكْبَرُ مِنْ أُخْتِهَا وَأَخَذْنَٰهُم بِالْعَذَابِ لَعَلَّهُمْ يَرْجِعُونَ ﴿٤٨﴾

49. And they said: 'Magician! Supplicate your Lord for us for what He has covenanted with you, verily we shall let ourselves be directed.'

وَقَالُوا يَٰٓأَيُّهَ السَّاحِرُ ادْعُ لَنَا رَبَّكَ بِمَا عَهِدَ عِندَكَ إِنَّنَا لَمُهْتَدُونَ ﴿٤٩﴾

50. Then when We had removed from them the chastisement, lo! They were breaking their promise.

فَلَمَّا كَشَفْنَا عَنْهُمُ الْعَذَابَ إِذَا هُمْ يَنكُثُونَ ﴿٥٠﴾

51. And Pharaoh proclaimed among his people saying: 'My people! Is not mine the kingdom of Egypt and the rivers flowing underneath me? Do you not see?

وَنَادَىٰ فِرْعَوْنُ فِي قَوْمِهِۦ قَالَ يَـٰقَوْمِ أَلَيْسَ لِي مُلْكُ مِصْرَ وَهَـٰذِهِ ٱلْأَنْهَـٰرُ تَجْرِي مِن تَحْتِيٓ أَفَلَا تُبْصِرُونَ ﴿٥١﴾

52. Aye! I am better than this one who is contemptible, and unable even to make his speech plain.

أَمْ أَنَا۠ خَيْرٌ مِّنْ هَـٰذَا ٱلَّذِي هُوَ مَهِينٌ وَلَا يَكَادُ يُبِينُ ﴿٥٢﴾

53. Why, then, have the bracelets of gold not been set upon him, and why have the angels not come accompanying him?'

فَلَوْلَآ أُلْقِيَ عَلَيْهِ أَسْوِرَةٌ مِّن ذَهَبٍ أَوْ جَآءَ مَعَهُ ٱلْمَلَـٰٓئِكَةُ مُقْتَرِنِينَ ﴿٥٣﴾

54. Then he incited his people and they obeyed him; they were ever a transgressing people.

فَٱسْتَخَفَّ قَوْمَهُۥ فَأَطَاعُوهُ إِنَّهُمْ كَانُوا۟ قَوْمًا فَـٰسِقِينَ ﴿٥٤﴾

55. So when they angered Us, We took vengeance on them,[650] and We drowned them all.

فَلَمَّآ ءَاسَفُونَا ٱنتَقَمْنَا مِنْهُمْ فَأَغْرَقْنَـٰهُمْ أَجْمَعِينَ ﴿٥٥﴾

56. And We made them a precedent, and an example to those after.

فَجَعَلْنَـٰهُمْ سَلَفًا وَمَثَلًا لِّلْـَٔاخِرِينَ ﴿٥٦﴾

Section 6

57. And when the son of Maryam is held up as an example, lo! Your people cry out at that.

وَلَمَّا ضُرِبَ ٱبْنُ مَرْيَمَ مَثَلًا إِذَا قَوْمُكَ مِنْهُ يَصِدُّونَ ﴿٥٧﴾

---

650. Western writers in their dread of anthropomorphism have often gone to the other extreme of conceiving Almighty God as a Buddha on a grand scale, a Being of purely passionless repose, able to punish none, to forgive none and to reward none, unmoved at the sight of unspeakable enormities. The God of Islam is Just, Powerful and Holy, Able to execute His laws to vindicate His Majesty and to punish the culprit.

58. And they say: 'Are not our gods better, or is he?' They mention him not to you save for disputation. Aye! They are a people contentious.

وَقَالُوٓا۟ ءَأَلِهَتُنَا خَيْرٌ أَمْ هُوَ مَا ضَرَبُوهُ لَكَ إِلَّا جَدَلًۢا بَلْ هُمْ قَوْمٌ خَصِمُونَ ۝

59. He is naught but a bondsman; him We favoured, and him We made an example to the children of Israel.

إِنْ هُوَ إِلَّا عَبْدٌ أَنْعَمْنَا عَلَيْهِ وَجَعَلْنَٰهُ مَثَلًا لِّبَنِىٓ إِسْرَٰٓءِيلَ ۝

60. And had We willed We would have appointed angels among you in the earth to succeed each other.

وَلَوْ نَشَآءُ لَجَعَلْنَا مِنكُم مَّلَٰٓئِكَةً فِى ٱلْأَرْضِ يَخْلُفُونَ ۝

61. And verily he is a sign of the Hour,[651] so do not be in doubt concerning it and follow Me; this is the straight path.

وَإِنَّهُۥ لَعِلْمٌ لِّلسَّاعَةِ فَلَا تَمْتَرُنَّ بِهَا وَٱتَّبِعُونِ هَٰذَا صِرَٰطٌ مُّسْتَقِيمٌ ۝

62. And let not Satan hinder you; verily he is to you a manifest enemy.

وَلَا يَصُدَّنَّكُمُ ٱلشَّيْطَٰنُ إِنَّهُۥ لَكُمْ عَدُوٌّ مُّبِينٌ ۝

63. And when Jesus came with evidence, he said; 'Surely I have come to you with wisdom, to expound to you some of that wherein you differ, so fear Allah and obey me.

وَلَمَّا جَآءَ عِيسَىٰ بِٱلْبَيِّنَٰتِ قَالَ قَدْ جِئْتُكُم بِٱلْحِكْمَةِ وَلِأُبَيِّنَ لَكُم بَعْضَ ٱلَّذِى تَخْتَلِفُونَ فِيهِ فَٱتَّقُوا۟ ٱللَّهَ وَأَطِيعُونِ ۝

64. And verily Allah! He is my Lord and your Lord;[652] so worship Him; this is the straight path.'

إِنَّ ٱللَّهَ هُوَ رَبِّى وَرَبُّكُمْ فَٱعْبُدُوهُ هَٰذَا صِرَٰطٌ مُّسْتَقِيمٌ ۝

---

651. Which shall be known by his descending. The reference is to 'the second coming of Jesus in the Last Days just before the Resurrection, when he will destroy the false doctrines that pass under his name, and prepare the way for the universal acceptance of Islam, the Gospel of Unity and Peace, the Straight Way of the Quran' (AYA.).

652. This emphatically repudiates the teaching of the Gospels: 'I my Father are one' (Jn. 10: 30), and the teaching of the Christian Church: 'The Son is as Divine as the Father and therefore can be worshipped without idolatry and bestow Divine life, because it is His to bestow' (*EBr.* II. p. 599).

65. Then the sects differed among themselves.[653] Woe to those who do wrong, because of the torment of the Afflictive Day.

فَٱخْتَلَفَ ٱلْأَحْزَابُ مِنۢ بَيْنِهِمْ ۖ فَوَيْلٌ لِّلَّذِينَ ظَلَمُواْ مِنْ عَذَابِ يَوْمٍ أَلِيمٍ ۝

66. They await but the Hour; that it should come upon them of a sudden while they perceive not.

هَلْ يَنظُرُونَ إِلَّا ٱلسَّاعَةَ أَن تَأْتِيَهُم بَغْتَةً وَهُمْ لَا يَشْعُرُونَ ۝

67. The intimate friends will be on that Day hostile one to another, save the God-fearing.

ٱلْأَخِلَّآءُ يَوْمَئِذٍۭ بَعْضُهُمْ لِبَعْضٍ عَدُوٌّ إِلَّا ٱلْمُتَّقِينَ ۝

Section 7

68. My bondsmen, there shall be no fear upon you today, nor shall you grieve.

يَـٰعِبَادِ لَا خَوْفٌ عَلَيْكُمُ ٱلْيَوْمَ وَلَآ أَنتُمْ تَحْزَنُونَ ۝

69. You who believed in Our revelations and were Muslims.

ٱلَّذِينَ ءَامَنُواْ بِـَٔايَـٰتِنَا وَكَانُواْ مُسْلِمِينَ ۝

70. Enter the Garden, you and your spouses, joyfully.

ٱدْخُلُواْ ٱلْجَنَّةَ أَنتُمْ وَأَزْوَٰجُكُمْ تُحْبَرُونَ ۝

---

653. In this way the pure Religion of 'Isā degenerated into gross idolatry. 'During the fifth century the practice of introducing images into churches increased and in the sixth it had become prevalent. The common people, who had never been able to comprehend doctrinal mysteries, found their religious wants satisfied in turning to these effigies. With singular obtuseness, they believed that the saint is present in his image, though hundreds of the same kind were in existence, each having an equal and exclusive right to the spiritual presence. The doctrine of invocation of the departed saints, which assumed prominence in the fifth century, was greatly strengthened by these graphic forms. Pagan idolatry had reappeared' (Draper, *History of the Intellectual Development of Europe*, I. p. 413).

71. Passed around among them will be dishes of gold and goblets, and therein will be whatsoever souls desire and eyes delight in; and you will be therein[654] abiders.

يُطَافُ عَلَيْهِم بِصِحَافٍ مِّن ذَهَبٍ وَأَكْوَابٍ ۖ وَفِيهَا مَا تَشْتَهِيهِ ٱلْأَنفُسُ وَتَلَذُّ ٱلْأَعْيُنُ ۖ وَأَنتُمْ فِيهَا خَٰلِدُونَ ﴿٧١﴾

72. This is the Garden which you have been made to inherit for what you have been working.

وَتِلْكَ ٱلْجَنَّةُ ٱلَّتِىٓ أُورِثْتُمُوهَا بِمَا كُنتُمْ تَعْمَلُونَ ﴿٧٢﴾

73. For you there will be fruits in plenty which you will eat.

لَكُمْ فِيهَا فَٰكِهَةٌ كَثِيرَةٌ مِّنْهَا تَأْكُلُونَ ﴿٧٣﴾

74. Verily the culprits will be abiders in Hell's torment.

إِنَّ ٱلْمُجْرِمِينَ فِى عَذَابِ جَهَنَّمَ خَٰلِدُونَ ﴿٧٤﴾

75. It shall not be abated from off them, and therein they will become despondent.

لَا يُفَتَّرُ عَنْهُمْ وَهُمْ فِيهِ مُبْلِسُونَ ﴿٧٥﴾

76. And We wronged them not, but they have been the wrong-doers themselves.

وَمَا ظَلَمْنَٰهُمْ وَلَٰكِن كَانُوا۟ هُمُ ٱلظَّٰلِمِينَ ﴿٧٦﴾

77. And they will cry: 'O keeper! Let your Lord make an end of us.' He will say: 'Verily you shall abide for ever.'

وَنَادَوْا۟ يَٰمَٰلِكُ لِيَقْضِ عَلَيْنَا رَبُّكَ ۖ قَالَ إِنَّكُم مَّٰكِثُونَ ﴿٧٧﴾

78. Assuredly We brought the Truth to you, but most of you are averse to the Truth.

لَقَدْ جِئْنَٰكُم بِٱلْحَقِّ وَلَٰكِنَّ أَكْثَرَكُمْ لِلْحَقِّ كَٰرِهُونَ ﴿٧٨﴾

79. Have they determined an affair? Then We also are determining.

أَمْ أَبْرَمُوٓا۟ أَمْرًا فَإِنَّا مُبْرِمُونَ ﴿٧٩﴾

---

654. The delight of the soul and body in Paradise shall be not only full and complete but also eternal and unending.

80. Do they think that We hear not their secrets and their whispers? Yea! We do, and Our envoys present with them write it down.

أَمْ يَحْسَبُونَ أَنَّا لَا نَسْمَعُ سِرَّهُمْ وَنَجْوَىٰهُم بَلَىٰ وَرُسُلُنَا لَدَيْهِمْ يَكْتُبُونَ ﴿٨٠﴾

81. Say: 'Had the Compassionate a son, I should have been the first of his worshippers.'

قُلْ إِن كَانَ لِلرَّحْمَٰنِ وَلَدٌ فَأَنَا۠ أَوَّلُ ٱلْعَٰبِدِينَ ﴿٨١﴾

82. Hallowed be the Lord of the heavens and the earth, the Lord of the throne from what they ascribe.

سُبْحَٰنَ رَبِّ ٱلسَّمَٰوَٰتِ وَٱلْأَرْضِ رَبِّ ٱلْعَرْشِ عَمَّا يَصِفُونَ ﴿٨٢﴾

83. So let them you alone wading and sporting till they meet the Day which they are promised.

فَذَرْهُمْ يَخُوضُوا۟ وَيَلْعَبُوا۟ حَتَّىٰ يُلَٰقُوا۟ يَوْمَهُمُ ٱلَّذِى يُوعَدُونَ ﴿٨٣﴾

84. And He it is Who is God in the sky and God on the earth,[655] and He is the Wise, the Knower.

وَهُوَ ٱلَّذِى فِى ٱلسَّمَآءِ إِلَٰهٌ وَفِى ٱلْأَرْضِ إِلَٰهٌ وَهُوَ ٱلْحَكِيمُ ٱلْعَلِيمُ ﴿٨٤﴾

85. And blessed be He Whose is the dominion of the heavens and the earth and what is in between, and with Him is the knowledge of the Hour and to Him you will be made to return.

وَتَبَارَكَ ٱلَّذِى لَهُ مُلْكُ ٱلسَّمَٰوَٰتِ وَٱلْأَرْضِ وَمَا بَيْنَهُمَا وَعِندَهُ عِلْمُ ٱلسَّاعَةِ وَإِلَيْهِ تُرْجَعُونَ ﴿٨٥﴾

---

655. This repudiates the religion of many a polytheistic people who believe the heaven and the earth to be ruled over by separate deities. In the religion of Babylonia, Anu rules in heaven, Enlil on earth and in the air, and Ea in the waters. The Vedic gods are also divided into three classes, gods of the sky, gods of the air, and gods of earth' (*ERE*. X. p. 114). 'The Vedic gods may most conveniently be classified as deities of heaven, air, and earth, according to the three-fold divisions suggested by the Rigveda itself' (Ibid., XII. p. 603).

86. And whom they call upon besides Him, they do not own the power of intercession, save those who bear witness to the Truth and who know.

وَلَا يَمْلِكُ ٱلَّذِينَ يَدْعُونَ مِن دُونِهِ ٱلشَّفَعَةَ إِلَّا مَن شَهِدَ بِٱلْحَقِّ وَهُمْ يَعْلَمُونَ ﴿٨٦﴾

87. And were you to ask them who created them, they will surely say, 'Allah'. Then whither are they deviating?

وَلَئِن سَأَلْتَهُم مَّنْ خَلَقَهُمْ لَيَقُولُنَّ ٱللَّهُ فَأَنَّىٰ يُؤْفَكُونَ ﴿٨٧﴾

88. And We hear his saying: 'Lord! Verily they are a people who do not believe.'

وَقِيلِهِۦ يَٰرَبِّ إِنَّ هَٰٓؤُلَآءِ قَوْمٌ لَّا يُؤْمِنُونَ ﴿٨٨﴾

89. So turn you aside from them, and say, 'peace'. Presently they shall come to know.

فَٱصْفَحْ عَنْهُمْ وَقُلْ سَلَٰمٌ فَسَوْفَ يَعْلَمُونَ ﴿٨٩﴾

Sūrah 44

al-Dukhān

(Makkan, 3 Sections, 59 Verses)

In the name of Allah, the Compassionate, the Merciful.

Section 1

1. *Ḥā, Mīm.*

2. By the luminous Book.

3. We have sent it down on a blessed night;[656] verily We were to become warners.

4. Therein is decreed every affair of wisdom,

5. As a command from before Us. Verily We were to become senders,

6. A mercy from the Lord. Verily He! He is the Hearer, the Knower.

7. Lord of the heavens and the earth and whatsoever is in between, if only you would be convinced.

8. There is no god but He. He quickens and causes to die; your Lord and the Lord of your forefathers.

---

656. Which is one of the odd nights in the last ten days of the month of Ramaḍān.

9. Aye! They are in doubt sporting.

بَلْ هُمْ فِي شَكٍّ يَلْعَبُونَ ۝

10. So wait you for a day when the sky will bring forth a manifest smoke,

فَارْتَقِبْ يَوْمَ تَأْتِي السَّمَاءُ بِدُخَانٍ مُّبِينٍ ۝

11. Covering the people. This shall be a dreadful scourge.

يَغْشَى النَّاسَ هَـٰذَا عَذَابٌ أَلِيمٌ ۝

12. Our Lord! Lift up from us this scourge; verily we shall become believers.'

رَّبَّنَا اكْشِفْ عَنَّا الْعَذَابَ إِنَّا مُؤْمِنُونَ ۝

13. How can there be an admonition unto them when there came to them a clear Messenger?

أَنَّىٰ لَهُمُ الذِّكْرَىٰ وَقَدْ جَاءَهُمْ رَسُولٌ مُّبِينٌ ۝

14. Yet they turned away from him and said: 'One tutored one, distracted!'

ثُمَّ تَوَلَّوْا عَنْهُ وَقَالُوا مُعَلَّمٌ مَّجْنُونٌ ۝

15. Verily We shall remove the chastisement for a while; but verily you shall revert.

إِنَّا كَاشِفُو الْعَذَابِ قَلِيلًا إِنَّكُمْ عَائِدُونَ ۝

16. On the Day when We assault them with the greatest assault, verily We shall take vengeance.

يَوْمَ نَبْطِشُ الْبَطْشَةَ الْكُبْرَىٰ إِنَّا مُنْتَقِمُونَ ۝

17. And assuredly before them We tried Pharaoh's people, and there came to them an honoured Messenger, saying:

وَلَقَدْ فَتَنَّا قَبْلَهُمْ قَوْمَ فِرْعَوْنَ وَجَاءَهُمْ رَسُولٌ كَرِيمٌ ۝

18. 'Restore to me the bondsmen of Allah, I am unto you a trusted Messenger.'

أَنْ أَدُّوا إِلَيَّ عِبَادَ اللَّهِ إِنِّي لَكُمْ رَسُولٌ أَمِينٌ ۝

19. And saying: 'Exalt not yourselves against Allah, verily I have come to you with a manifest authority,

وَأَن لَّا تَعْلُوا عَلَى اللَّهِ إِنِّي ءَاتِيكُم بِسُلْطَٰنٍ مُّبِينٍ ۝

20. And verily I have sought refuge in my Lord and your Lord lest you stone me.

وَإِنِّي عُذْتُ بِرَبِّي وَرَبِّكُمْ أَن تَرْجُمُونِ ۝

21. And if you will not believe in me, then let me alone.'

وَإِن لَّمْ تُؤْمِنُوا لِي فَاعْتَزِلُونِ ۝

22. Then he called upon his Lord: 'These are a guilty people.'

فَدَعَا رَبَّهُۥٓ أَنَّ هَٰٓؤُلَآءِ قَوْمٌ مُّجْرِمُونَ ۝

23. Allah said: 'So depart you with My bondsmen by night; surely you will be pursued.

فَأَسْرِ بِعِبَادِى لَيْلًا إِنَّكُم مُّتَّبَعُونَ ۝

24. And leave you the sea parted; verily they are a host to be drowned.'

وَاتْرُكِ الْبَحْرَ رَهْوًا إِنَّهُمْ جُندٌ مُّغْرَقُونَ ۝

25. They left how many of gardens and springs,

كَمْ تَرَكُوا مِن جَنَّٰتٍ وَعُيُونٍ ۝

26. And cornfields and goodly positions.

وَزُرُوعٍ وَمَقَامٍ كَرِيمٍ ۝

27. And the delights which they had been enjoying!

وَنَعْمَةٍ كَانُوا فِيهَا فَٰكِهِينَ ۝

28. Even so. And We caused another people to inherit them.

كَذَٰلِكَ وَأَوْرَثْنَٰهَا قَوْمًا ءَاخَرِينَ ۝

29. And the heavens and the earth did not shed tears for them! Nor were they reprieved.

فَمَا بَكَتْ عَلَيْهِمُ السَّمَآءُ وَالْأَرْضُ وَمَا كَانُوا مُنظَرِينَ ۝

Section 2

30.   Assuredly We saved the children of Israel from a degrading scourge,

وَلَقَدْ نَجَّيْنَا بَنِيٓ إِسْرَٰٓءِيلَ مِنَ ٱلْعَذَابِ ٱلْمُهِينِ ﴿٣٠﴾

31.   From Pharaoh; verily he was haughty and of the extravagant.

مِن فِرْعَوْنَ إِنَّهُۥ كَانَ عَالِيًا مِّنَ ٱلْمُسْرِفِينَ ﴿٣١﴾

32.   And assuredly We chose them with knowledge advisedly above the worlds.

وَلَقَدِ ٱخْتَرْنَٰهُمْ عَلَىٰ عِلْمٍ عَلَى ٱلْعَٰلَمِينَ ﴿٣٢﴾

33.   And We vouchsafed to them signs in which was a manifest favour from Us.

وَءَاتَيْنَٰهُم مِّنَ ٱلْءَايَٰتِ مَا فِيهِ بَلَٰٓؤٌاْ مُّبِينٌ ﴿٣٣﴾

34.   Verily these! They say:

إِنَّ هَٰٓؤُلَآءِ لَيَقُولُونَ ﴿٣٤﴾

35.   'Nothing is there but our first death, and we shall not be raised again;

إِنْ هِىَ إِلَّا مَوْتَتُنَا ٱلْأُولَىٰ وَمَا نَحْنُ بِمُنشَرِينَ ﴿٣٥﴾

36.   Bring back then our fathers, if you speak truth.'

فَأْتُواْ بِـَٔابَآئِنَآ إِن كُنتُمْ صَٰدِقِينَ ﴿٣٦﴾

37.   Are these better or the people of Tubba' and those before them? We destroyed them. They were culprits.

أَهُمْ خَيْرٌ أَمْ قَوْمُ تُبَّعٍ وَٱلَّذِينَ مِن قَبْلِهِمْ أَهْلَكْنَٰهُمْ إِنَّهُمْ كَانُواْ مُجْرِمِينَ ﴿٣٧﴾

38.   And We did not create the heavens and the earth and what is in between in sport.

وَمَا خَلَقْنَا ٱلسَّمَٰوَٰتِ وَٱلْأَرْضَ وَمَا بَيْنَهُمَا لَٰعِبِينَ ﴿٣٨﴾

39.   We did not create them save with a purpose, yet most of them know not.

مَا خَلَقْنَٰهُمَآ إِلَّا بِٱلْحَقِّ وَلَٰكِنَّ أَكْثَرَهُمْ لَا يَعْلَمُونَ ﴿٣٩﴾

40.   Verily the Day of Distinction is the term appointed for all of them.

إِنَّ يَوْمَ ٱلْفَصْلِ مِيقَٰتُهُمْ أَجْمَعِينَ ﴿٤٠﴾

41. A Day whereon a friend shall not avail a friend at all. Nor shall they be succoured,

يَوْمَ لَا يُغْنِى مَوْلًى عَن مَّوْلًى شَيْئًا وَلَا هُمْ يُنصَرُونَ ﴿٤١﴾

42. Save those on whom Allah will have Mercy. Verily He! He is the Mighty, the Merciful.

إِلَّا مَن رَّحِمَ اللَّهُ إِنَّهُۥ هُوَ الْعَزِيزُ الرَّحِيمُ ﴿٤٢﴾

Section 3

43. Verily the tree of Zaqqūm,

إِنَّ شَجَرَتَ الزَّقُّومِ ﴿٤٣﴾

44. Food of the sinners.

طَعَامُ الْأَثِيمِ ﴿٤٤﴾

45. Like the dregs of oil; it shall seethe in the bellies,

كَالْمُهْلِ يَغْلِى فِى الْبُطُونِ ﴿٤٥﴾

46. As the seething of boiling water.

كَغَلْىِ الْحَمِيمِ ﴿٤٦﴾

47. Seize him and drag him to the midst of the Flaming Fire.

خُذُوهُ فَاعْتِلُوهُ إِلَىٰ سَوَاءِ الْجَحِيمِ ﴿٤٧﴾

48. Then pour upon his head the torment of boiling water.

ثُمَّ صُبُّوا فَوْقَ رَأْسِهِۦ مِنْ عَذَابِ الْحَمِيمِ ﴿٤٨﴾

49. Taste you! You are indeed mighty, honoured!

ذُقْ إِنَّكَ أَنتَ الْعَزِيزُ الْكَرِيمُ ﴿٤٩﴾

50. Verily this is what you were used to doubt.[657]

إِنَّ هَٰذَا مَا كُنتُم بِهِۦ تَمْتَرُونَ ﴿٥٠﴾

51. Verily the God-fearing ones will be in a station secure,

إِنَّ الْمُتَّقِينَ فِى مَقَامٍ أَمِينٍ ﴿٥١﴾

52. Amidst gardens and springs,

فِى جَنَّٰتٍ وَعُيُونٍ ﴿٥٢﴾

53. Attired in fine silk and brocade, facing each other.

يَلْبَسُونَ مِن سُندُسٍ وَإِسْتَبْرَقٍ مُّتَقَٰبِلِينَ ﴿٥٣﴾

---

657. All this will be said by the angels to the damned to add to their mental anguish.

54. Even so. And We shall mate them with fair damsels large-eyed.

كَذَٰلِكَ وَزَوَّجْنَٰهُم بِحُورٍ عِينٍ ﴿٥٤﴾

55. They will call therein for every manner of fruit in security.

يَدْعُونَ فِيهَا بِكُلِّ فَٰكِهَةٍ ءَامِنِينَ ﴿٥٥﴾

56. They will not taste of death therein, except the first death, and He will guard them against the chastisement of the Flaming Fire.

لَا يَذُوقُونَ فِيهَا ٱلْمَوْتَ إِلَّا ٱلْمَوْتَةَ ٱلْأُولَىٰ وَوَقَىٰهُمْ عَذَابَ ٱلْجَحِيمِ ﴿٥٦﴾

57. A bounty from your Lord! That! That is the supreme achievement.

فَضْلًا مِّن رَّبِّكَ ذَٰلِكَ هُوَ ٱلْفَوْزُ ٱلْعَظِيمُ ﴿٥٧﴾

58. And We have made it easy in your language haply they might be admonished.

فَإِنَّمَا يَسَّرْنَٰهُ بِلِسَانِكَ لَعَلَّهُمْ يَتَذَكَّرُونَ ﴿٥٨﴾

59. Wait you then, they are also waiting.

فَٱرْتَقِبْ إِنَّهُم مُّرْتَقِبُونَ ﴿٥٩﴾

Sūrah 45

al-Jāthiyah

(Makkan, 4 Sections, 37 Verses).

In the name of Allah, the Compassionate, the Merciful.

Section 1

1. *Ḥā, Mīm.*

2. The revelation of the Book is from Allah, the Mighty, the Wise.

3. Verily in the heavens and the earth are signs for the faithful.

4. And in the creation of yourselves and the beasts that He has scattered over the earth are signs for a people who are convinced.

5. And in the alternation of night and day what Allah sends down of provision from the heaven and thereby quickens the earth after its death and in the turning about of the winds, are signs for a people who reflect.

6. These are the revelations of Allah which We rehearse to you with truth. In what discourse, then, after Allah and His revelations, will they believe?

7. Woe unto every liar, sinner!

8. Who hears the revelations of Allah rehearsed to him, and yet persists with stiff-neckedness as though he heard them not. Announce you to him, then, an afflictive torment.

9. And he comes to know aught of Our revelations, he takes it scoffingly. These! Theirs shall be an ignominious torment.

10. Before them is Hell. Nothing will avail them of what they have earned nor those whom they took for patrons besides Allah. Theirs shall be a mighty torment.

11. This Book is a guidance; and those who disbelieve in the revelations of their Lord, theirs shall be a torment of afflictive calamity.

Section 2

12. Allah it is Who has subjected the sea to you that ships may run on it by His command, and that you may seek of His grace, and that haply you may return thanks.

13. And He has subjected to you whatsoever is in the heavens and whatsoever is on the earth, the whole from Himself. Verily herein are signs for a people who ponder.

يَسۡمَعُ ءَايَٰتِ ٱللَّهِ تُتۡلَىٰ عَلَيۡهِ ثُمَّ يُصِرُّ مُسۡتَكۡبِرًا كَأَن لَّمۡ يَسۡمَعۡهَا فَبَشِّرۡهُ بِعَذَابٍ أَلِيمٍ ۝

وَإِذَا عَلِمَ مِنۡ ءَايَٰتِنَا شَيۡـًٔا ٱتَّخَذَهَا هُزُوًا أُوْلَٰٓئِكَ لَهُمۡ عَذَابٌ مُّهِينٌ ۝

مِّن وَرَآئِهِمۡ جَهَنَّمُ وَلَا يُغۡنِى عَنۡهُم مَّا كَسَبُوا۟ شَيۡـًٔا وَلَا مَا ٱتَّخَذُوا۟ مِن دُونِ ٱللَّهِ أَوۡلِيَآءَ وَلَهُمۡ عَذَابٌ عَظِيمٌ ۝

هَٰذَا هُدًى وَٱلَّذِينَ كَفَرُوا۟ بِـَٔايَٰتِ رَبِّهِمۡ لَهُمۡ عَذَابٌ مِّن رِّجۡزٍ أَلِيمٌ ۝

ٱللَّهُ ٱلَّذِى سَخَّرَ لَكُمُ ٱلۡبَحۡرَ لِتَجۡرِىَ ٱلۡفُلۡكُ فِيهِ بِأَمۡرِهِۦ وَلِتَبۡتَغُوا۟ مِن فَضۡلِهِۦ وَلَعَلَّكُمۡ تَشۡكُرُونَ ۝

وَسَخَّرَ لَكُم مَّا فِى ٱلسَّمَٰوَٰتِ وَمَا فِى ٱلۡأَرۡضِ جَمِيعًا مِّنۡهُ إِنَّ فِى ذَٰلِكَ لَءَايَٰتٍ لِّقَوۡمٍ يَتَفَكَّرُونَ ۝

14. Say to the faithful, let them forgive those who hope not for the days of Allah, that He may recompense a community for what they have been working.

قُل لِّلَّذِينَ ءَامَنُوا يَغْفِرُوا لِلَّذِينَ لَا يَرْجُونَ أَيَّامَ اللَّهِ لِيَجْزِىَ قَوْمًا بِمَا كَانُوا يَكْسِبُونَ ١٤

15. Whosoever works righteously, works for himself, and whosoever does evil, does against himself; then to your Lord you will be made to return.

مَنْ عَمِلَ صَٰلِحًا فَلِنَفْسِهِ ۖ وَمَنْ أَسَآءَ فَعَلَيْهَا ثُمَّ إِلَىٰ رَبِّكُمْ تُرْجَعُونَ ١٥

16. And assuredly We vouchsafed to the children of Israel the Book and wisdom and the prophet-hood, and We provided them with good things, and preferred them above the worlds.

وَلَقَدْ ءَاتَيْنَا بَنِىٓ إِسْرَٰٓءِيلَ الْكِتَٰبَ وَالْحُكْمَ وَالنُّبُوَّةَ وَرَزَقْنَٰهُم مِّنَ الطَّيِّبَٰتِ وَفَضَّلْنَٰهُمْ عَلَى الْعَٰلَمِينَ ١٦

17. And We vouchsafed to them the evidence of the affairs. And they differed not except through spite among themselves after the knowledge had come to them. Verily the Lord will decide between them on the Day of Judgement concerning what they have been differing in.

وَءَاتَيْنَٰهُم بَيِّنَٰتٍ مِّنَ الْأَمْرِ فَمَا اخْتَلَفُوٓا إِلَّا مِنْ بَعْدِ مَا جَآءَهُمُ الْعِلْمُ بَغْيًۢا بَيْنَهُمْ إِنَّ رَبَّكَ يَقْضِى بَيْنَهُمْ يَوْمَ الْقِيَٰمَةِ فِيمَا كَانُوا فِيهِ يَخْتَلِفُونَ ١٧

18. And thereafter We have placed you upon the law of the religion;[658] so follow it you, and follow not the vain desires of those who do not know.

ثُمَّ جَعَلْنَٰكَ عَلَىٰ شَرِيعَةٍ مِّنَ الْأَمْرِ فَاتَّبِعْهَا وَلَا تَتَّبِعْ أَهْوَآءَ الَّذِينَ لَا يَعْلَمُونَ ١٨

---

658. The *Sharī'ah* is not only a law or ordinance but also a religion, or way of belief and practice in respect of religion (*LL.*).

19. Verily they cannot avail you at all against Allah. And the wicked! Friends are they one to another, and Allah is the friend of the God-fearing.

إِنَّهُمْ لَن يُغْنُواْ عَنكَ مِنَ ٱللَّهِ شَيْئًا وَإِنَّ ٱلظَّٰلِمِينَ بَعْضُهُمْ أَوْلِيَآءُ بَعْضٍ وَٱللَّهُ وَلِىُّ ٱلْمُتَّقِينَ ۝

20. This Book is an enlightenment and a guidance to mankind, and a mercy to people who are convinced.

هَٰذَا بَصَٰٓئِرُ لِلنَّاسِ وَهُدًى وَرَحْمَةٌ لِّقَوْمٍ يُوقِنُونَ ۝

21. Do those who commit ill-deeds imagine that We shall place them as those who believed and worked righteous works? Equal is their life and death. How ill they judge!

أَمْ حَسِبَ ٱلَّذِينَ ٱجْتَرَحُواْ ٱلسَّيِّئَاتِ أَن نَّجْعَلَهُمْ كَٱلَّذِينَ ءَامَنُواْ وَعَمِلُواْ ٱلصَّٰلِحَٰتِ سَوَآءً مَّحْيَاهُمْ وَمَمَاتُهُمْ سَآءَ مَا يَحْكُمُونَ ۝

Section 3

22. Allah has created the heavens and the earth with purpose, and that every soul may be recompensed for what it has earned. And they will not be wronged.

وَخَلَقَ ٱللَّهُ ٱلسَّمَٰوَٰتِ وَٱلْأَرْضَ بِٱلْحَقِّ وَلِتُجْزَىٰ كُلُّ نَفْسٍ بِمَا كَسَبَتْ وَهُمْ لَا يُظْلَمُونَ ۝

23. Have you seen him who takes for his god his own vain desire, and Allah has sent him astray despite his knowledge, and has sealed up his hearing and his heart and has set up a covering on his sight? Who will guide him after Allah? Will you not then be admonished?

أَفَرَءَيْتَ مَنِ ٱتَّخَذَ إِلَٰهَهُ هَوَىٰهُ وَأَضَلَّهُ ٱللَّهُ عَلَىٰ عِلْمٍ وَخَتَمَ عَلَىٰ سَمْعِهِ وَقَلْبِهِ وَجَعَلَ عَلَىٰ بَصَرِهِ غِشَٰوَةً فَمَن يَهْدِيهِ مِنۢ بَعْدِ ٱللَّهِ أَفَلَا تَذَكَّرُونَ ۝

24. And they say: 'Nothing is there but the life of this world, we die and we live; and none kills us save time.'[659] And they have no true knowledge of it,[660] only conjecture.

وَقَالُوا مَا هِيَ إِلَّا حَيَاتُنَا الدُّنْيَا نَمُوتُ وَنَحْيَا وَمَا يُهْلِكُنَا إِلَّا الدَّهْرُ وَمَا لَهُم بِذَٰلِكَ مِنْ عِلْمٍ إِنْ هُمْ إِلَّا يَظُنُّونَ ۩

25. And when Our manifest revelations are rehearsed to them, their argument is no other than that they say: 'Bring back our fathers, if you speak truth.'

وَإِذَا تُتْلَىٰ عَلَيْهِمْ ءَايَٰتُنَا بَيِّنَٰتٍ مَّا كَانَ حُجَّتَهُمْ إِلَّا أَن قَالُوا ائْتُوا بِآبَائِنَا إِن كُنتُمْ صَٰدِقِينَ ۩

26. Say: 'Allah keeps you alive, then He will cause you to die; then He will assemble you on the Day of Resurrection, of which there is no doubt; but most of mankind do not know.'

قُلِ اللَّهُ يُحْيِيكُمْ ثُمَّ يُمِيتُكُمْ ثُمَّ يَجْمَعُكُمْ إِلَىٰ يَوْمِ الْقِيَٰمَةِ لَا رَيْبَ فِيهِ وَلَٰكِنَّ أَكْثَرَ النَّاسِ لَا يَعْلَمُونَ ۩

---

659. Or Fortune. *al-Dahr* is, literally, 'Time from the beginning of the world to its end. Hence because, in one sense, time brings to pass events, good and evil, was applied by the Arabs to fortune, or fate; and they used to blame or revile it' (LL.). 'Time as an abstract deity was personified by the Arabs, and formed perhaps a regular part of their pantheon. Time in the abstract was popularly imagined to be the cause of all earthly happiness and especially of all earthly misery... The poets are continually alluding to the action of Time (*Dahr, Zamān*), for which they often substitute "the days", or the nights. Time is represented as bringing misfortune, causing perpetual change etc' (*ERE*. I. pp. 661, 662). 'The people of Central Arabia, to judge from the poetical and other remains, were indifferent to religious ideas. The utmost they could attain to was a vague deism or belief in Fate' (*EI*. I. p. 999).

660. They have no real, true knowledge; no proof, either in reason or of fact, to support them; their denial of Resurrection and Final Judgement is based on sheer ignorance and superstition, and not on any canons of reason; logic or knowledge. The idea of responsibility to his Creator is perhaps, next to monotheism, the greatest gift that Islam has bestowed on a negligent and forgetful humanity. Its importance in the history of human beliefs and morals cannot be overestimated.

Section 4

27. Allah's is the dominion of the heavens and the earth; and on the Day when the Hour arrives, the followers of falsehood shall lose.

وَلِلَّهِ مُلْكُ ٱلسَّمَوَٰتِ وَٱلْأَرْضِ وَيَوْمَ تَقُومُ ٱلسَّاعَةُ يَوْمَئِذٍ يَخْسَرُ ٱلْمُبْطِلُونَ ﴿٢٧﴾

28. And you shall behold every community kneeling; every community shall be summoned to its Book. This Day you shall be recompensed for what you had been working.

وَتَرَىٰ كُلَّ أُمَّةٍ جَاثِيَةً كُلُّ أُمَّةٍ تُدْعَىٰ إِلَىٰ كِتَٰبِهَا ٱلْيَوْمَ تُجْزَوْنَ مَا كُنتُمْ تَعْمَلُونَ ﴿٢٨﴾

29. This Book of Ours speaks against you with truth; verily We have been setting down whatsoever you had been working.

هَٰذَا كِتَٰبُنَا يَنطِقُ عَلَيْكُم بِٱلْحَقِّ إِنَّا كُنَّا نَسْتَنسِخُ مَا كُنتُمْ تَعْمَلُونَ ﴿٢٩﴾

30. Then, as for those who believed and worked righteous deeds, their Lord will cause them to enter into His Mercy; that is a manifest achievement.

فَأَمَّا ٱلَّذِينَ ءَامَنُوا۟ وَعَمِلُوا۟ ٱلصَّٰلِحَٰتِ فَيُدْخِلُهُمْ رَبُّهُمْ فِى رَحْمَتِهِ ذَٰلِكَ هُوَ ٱلْفَوْزُ ٱلْمُبِينُ ﴿٣٠﴾

31. And as for those who disbelieved; were not My revelations rehearsed to you? But you were stiff-necked and you were a people guilty.

وَأَمَّا ٱلَّذِينَ كَفَرُوٓا۟ أَفَلَمْ تَكُنْ ءَايَٰتِى تُتْلَىٰ عَلَيْكُمْ فَٱسْتَكْبَرْتُمْ وَكُنتُمْ قَوْمًا مُّجْرِمِينَ ﴿٣١﴾

32. And when it was said: 'Verily Allah's promise is true, and no doubt is there about the Hour,' you said: 'We do not know what the Hour is; we do not imagine it but as a conjecture, and we have no faith therein.'

وَإِذَا قِيلَ إِنَّ وَعْدَ ٱللَّهِ حَقٌّ وَٱلسَّاعَةُ لَا رَيْبَ فِيهَا قُلْتُم مَّا نَدْرِى مَا ٱلسَّاعَةُ إِن نَّظُنُّ إِلَّا ظَنًّا وَمَا نَحْنُ بِمُسْتَيْقِنِينَ ﴿٣٢﴾

33. And the evils of what they had worked shall become apparent to them, and there will surround them that at which they had been mocking.

وَبَدَا لَهُمْ سَيِّئَاتُ مَا عَمِلُوا وَحَاقَ بِهِم مَّا كَانُوا بِهِ يَسْتَهْزِءُونَ ﴿٣٣﴾

34. And it will be said: 'This Day We shall ignore you as you ignored the meeting of this Day; your abode will be the Fire, and none you will have as helpers.'

وَقِيلَ الْيَوْمَ نَنسَاكُمْ كَمَا نَسِيتُمْ لِقَاءَ يَوْمِكُمْ هَٰذَا وَمَأْوَاكُمُ النَّارُ وَمَا لَكُم مِّن نَّاصِرِينَ ﴿٣٤﴾

35. That is because you took the revelations of Allah in mockery, and there deluded you the life of this world. Today therefore they will not be taken forth therefrom, and nor will they be allowed to please Allah.

ذَٰلِكُم بِأَنَّكُمُ اتَّخَذْتُمْ ءَايَٰتِ اللَّهِ هُزُوًا وَغَرَّتْكُمُ الْحَيَوٰةُ الدُّنْيَا فَالْيَوْمَ لَا يُخْرَجُونَ مِنْهَا وَلَا هُمْ يُسْتَعْتَبُونَ ﴿٣٥﴾

36. All praise, then, to Allah, the Lord of the heavens and the Lord of the earth,661 the Lord of the worlds.

فَلِلَّهِ الْحَمْدُ رَبِّ السَّمَٰوَٰتِ وَرَبِّ الْأَرْضِ رَبِّ الْعَٰلَمِينَ ﴿٣٦﴾

37. And His alone is the majesty in the heavens and the earth, and He is the Mighty, the Wise.662

وَلَهُ الْكِبْرِيَاءُ فِي السَّمَٰوَٰتِ وَالْأَرْضِ وَهُوَ الْعَزِيزُ الْحَكِيمُ ﴿٣٧﴾

---

661. He is its Creator and Preserver. Even so simple a truth as that the earth is a created being stood in need of special emphasis in view of the widely-spread worship of the 'Mother-World'. The significant fact, says a distinguished archaeologist, about the ancient Indus civilization is that 'it was based on a religion precisely characteristic of present-day Hinduism. Numerous effigies of the great Mother-goddess have been found. That same devotion which Indians are now showing to Mother India they have for at least 5000 years shown to the Mother-World, the Mother Universe — which has brought both Mother India and themselves into existence and sustained and inspired them through life. This Mother-World they personified in the time of the ancient Indus civilization as the mother Goddess, and in more recent times as Kali'.

662. This unqualified and unreserved assertion of God's sole Sovereignty in Islam has been noted and admirably commented upon by many a non-Muslim observer. Contrast with God's absolute Sovereignty and Majesty the helplessness of man. From the very beginning the slave of nature and fighting for his own preservation, he finds himself still, after his creation of 'culture', 'nations', 'states', and 'sciences', enslaved by his own creations.

Sūrah 46

al-Aḥqāf

(Makkan, 4 Sections, 35 Verses)

In the name of Allah, the Compassionate, the Merciful.

Section 1

1. *Ḥā, Mīm.*

حـمٓ ۝

2. The revelation of the Book is from Allah, the Mighty, the Wise.

تَنزِيلُ ٱلْكِتَٰبِ مِنَ ٱللَّهِ ٱلْعَزِيزِ ٱلْحَكِيمِ ۝

3. We created not the heavens and the earth and what is in between save with a purpose and for a term determined. And those who disbelieve backslide from what they are warned of.

مَا خَلَقْنَا ٱلسَّمَٰوَٰتِ وَٱلْأَرْضَ وَمَا بَيْنَهُمَآ إِلَّا بِٱلْحَقِّ وَأَجَلٍ مُّسَمًّى ۚ وَٱلَّذِينَ كَفَرُوا۟ عَمَّآ أُنذِرُوا۟ مُعْرِضُونَ ۝

4. Say: 'Think! Whatsoever you call upon besides Allah, show me what they have created of the earth? Or, have they any share in the creation of the heavens? Bring me a Book before this or some trace of knowledge, if you speak truth.'

قُلْ أَرَءَيْتُم مَّا تَدْعُونَ مِن دُونِ ٱللَّهِ أَرُونِي مَاذَا خَلَقُوا۟ مِنَ ٱلْأَرْضِ أَمْ لَهُمْ شِرْكٌ فِي ٱلسَّمَٰوَٰتِ ۖ ٱئْتُونِي بِكِتَٰبٍ مِّن قَبْلِ هَٰذَآ أَوْ أَثَٰرَةٍ مِّنْ عِلْمٍ إِن كُنتُمْ صَٰدِقِينَ ۝

5. And who is more misguided than he who calls besides Allah such as will not answer him till the Day of Resurrection, and who are even unaware of their call?

وَمَنْ أَضَلُّ مِمَّن يَدْعُوا۟ مِن دُونِ ٱللَّهِ مَن لَّا يَسْتَجِيبُ لَهُۥٓ إِلَىٰ يَوْمِ ٱلْقِيَٰمَةِ وَهُمْ عَن دُعَآئِهِمْ غَٰفِلُونَ ۝

6. And when mankind are gathered, they will become enemies unto them, and will become deniers of their worship.

وَإِذَا حُشِرَ ٱلنَّاسُ كَانُوا۟ لَهُمْ أَعْدَآءً وَكَانُوا۟ بِعِبَادَتِهِمْ كَٰفِرِينَ ۝

7. And when Our manifest revelations are rehearsed to them, those who disbelieve say of the Truth when it is come to them: 'This is magic manifest.'

وَإِذَا تُتْلَىٰ عَلَيْهِمْ ءَايَٰتُنَا بَيِّنَٰتٍ قَالَ ٱلَّذِينَ كَفَرُوا لِلْحَقِّ لَمَّا جَآءَهُمْ هَٰذَا سِحْرٌ مُّبِينٌ ٧

8. Do they say: 'He has fabricated it?' Say: 'If I have fabricated it, you cannot avail me against Allah in any way. He is the Knower of what you utter respecting it. He suffices as a Witness between me and you and He is the Forgiving, the Merciful.'

أَمْ يَقُولُونَ ٱفْتَرَىٰهُ قُلْ إِنِ ٱفْتَرَيْتُهُۥ فَلَا تَمْلِكُونَ لِي مِنَ ٱللَّهِ شَيْئًا هُوَ أَعْلَمُ بِمَا تُفِيضُونَ فِيهِ كَفَىٰ بِهِۦ شَهِيدًۢا بَيْنِى وَبَيْنَكُمْ وَهُوَ ٱلْغَفُورُ ٱلرَّحِيمُ ٨

9. Say: 'I am not an innovator among the Messengers. Nor do I know what will be done with me or with you;[663] I only follow what is revealed to me, and I am but a manifest warner.'

قُلْ مَا كُنتُ بِدْعًا مِّنَ ٱلرُّسُلِ وَمَآ أَدْرِى مَا يُفْعَلُ بِى وَلَا بِكُمْ إِنْ أَتَّبِعُ إِلَّا مَا يُوحَىٰ إِلَىَّ وَمَآ أَنَا۠ إِلَّا نَذِيرٌ مُّبِينٌ ٩

10. Say: 'Think! If it is from Allah while you disbelieve in it, and a witness from the children of Israel bears witness to the like thereof and believes, while you are still stiff-necked, then who is further astray than you? Verily Allah does not guide a wicked people.'

قُلْ أَرَءَيْتُمْ إِن كَانَ مِنْ عِندِ ٱللَّهِ وَكَفَرْتُم بِهِۦ وَشَهِدَ شَاهِدٌ مِّنۢ بَنِىٓ إِسْرَٰٓءِيلَ عَلَىٰ مِثْلِهِۦ فَـَٔامَنَ وَٱسْتَكْبَرْتُمْ إِنَّ ٱللَّهَ لَا يَهْدِى ٱلْقَوْمَ ٱلظَّٰلِمِينَ ١٠

---

663. The Prophet here states that he lays no claim to omniscience at all; in fact he is not even sure of his own future.

Section 2

11. And they who disbelieve say of those who believe:[664] 'Had it been good, they would not have preceded us thereto.' And when they have not let themselves be guided by it, they say: 'This is an ancient falsehood.'

وَقَالَ الَّذِينَ كَفَرُوا لِلَّذِينَ ءَامَنُوا لَوْ كَانَ خَيْرًا مَّا سَبَقُونَا إِلَيْهِ وَإِذْ لَمْ يَهْتَدُوا بِهِ فَسَيَقُولُونَ هَٰذَآ إِفْكٌ قَدِيمٌ ﴿١١﴾

12. And prior to it there has been the Book of Moses, a guidance and a mercy. And this is a Book confirming it in Arabic speech, that it may warn those who have done wrong and as glad tidings to the well-doers.

وَمِن قَبْلِهِ كِتَٰبُ مُوسَىٰٓ إِمَامًا وَرَحْمَةً وَهَٰذَا كِتَٰبٌ مُّصَدِّقٌ لِّسَانًا عَرَبِيًّا لِّيُنذِرَ الَّذِينَ ظَلَمُوا وَبُشْرَىٰ لِلْمُحْسِنِينَ ﴿١٢﴾

13. Verily those who say: 'Our Lord is Allah', and then stand fast to it, no fear shall come upon them, nor shall they grieve.

إِنَّ الَّذِينَ قَالُوا رَبُّنَا اللَّهُ ثُمَّ اسْتَقَٰمُوا فَلَا خَوْفٌ عَلَيْهِمْ وَلَا هُمْ يَحْزَنُونَ ﴿١٣﴾

14. Those are the inmates of the Garden, abiders therein; a recompense for what they have been working.

أُولَٰٓئِكَ أَصْحَٰبُ الْجَنَّةِ خَٰلِدِينَ فِيهَا جَزَآءً بِمَا كَانُوا يَعْمَلُونَ ﴿١٤﴾

---

664. This refers to the arrogant Quraish who held the believers in contempt. The first converts to Islam were mostly found among the poor.

15. And We have enjoined upon man kindness to the parents, with hardship bears him his mother, and with hardship she brings him forth, and the bearing of him and the weaning of him is thirty months, until, when he attains his full strength and attains the age of forty years, he says: 'Lord! Grant me that I may give thanks for the favour which You have done me and my parents and that I may work righteously such as You may approve. And be You good in my progeny, verily I have turned to You penitent; verily I am of those who submit.'

وَوَصَّيۡنَا ٱلۡإِنسَٰنَ بِوَٰلِدَيۡهِ إِحۡسَٰنًا حَمَلَتۡهُ أُمُّهُۥ كُرۡهًا وَوَضَعَتۡهُ كُرۡهًا وَحَمۡلُهُۥ وَفِصَٰلُهُۥ ثَلَٰثُونَ شَهۡرًا حَتَّىٰٓ إِذَا بَلَغَ أَشُدَّهُۥ وَبَلَغَ أَرۡبَعِينَ سَنَةً قَالَ رَبِّ أَوۡزِعۡنِىٓ أَنۡ أَشۡكُرَ نِعۡمَتَكَ ٱلَّتِىٓ أَنۡعَمۡتَ عَلَىَّ وَعَلَىٰ وَٰلِدَىَّ وَأَنۡ أَعۡمَلَ صَٰلِحًا تَرۡضَىٰهُ وَأَصۡلِحۡ لِى فِى ذُرِّيَّتِىٓ إِنِّى تُبۡتُ إِلَيۡكَ وَإِنِّى مِنَ ٱلۡمُسۡلِمِينَ ﴿١٥﴾

16. Those are they from whom We shall accept the best of what they have worked, and their misdeeds We shall pass by. They will be among the inmates of the Garden, a true promise this, and what they have been promised.

أُوْلَٰٓئِكَ ٱلَّذِينَ نَتَقَبَّلُ عَنۡهُمۡ أَحۡسَنَ مَا عَمِلُوا۟ وَنَتَجَاوَزُ عَن سَيِّـَٔاتِهِمۡ فِىٓ أَصۡحَٰبِ ٱلۡجَنَّةِ وَعۡدَ ٱلصِّدۡقِ ٱلَّذِى كَانُوا۟ يُوعَدُونَ ﴿١٦﴾

17. And he who says to his parents: 'Fie upon you both! Do you threaten me that I shall be taken forth, whereas generations have passed away before me?' And the two implore Allah's assistance. 'Woe to you! Come to believe, verily the promise of Allah is true.' Yet he says: 'This is nothing but the fables of the ancients.'

وَٱلَّذِى قَالَ لِوَٰلِدَيۡهِ أُفٍّ لَّكُمَآ أَتَعِدَانِنِىٓ أَنۡ أُخۡرَجَ وَقَدۡ خَلَتِ ٱلۡقُرُونُ مِن قَبۡلِى وَهُمَا يَسۡتَغِيثَانِ ٱللَّهَ وَيۡلَكَ ءَامِنۡ إِنَّ وَعۡدَ ٱللَّهِ حَقٌّ فَيَقُولُ مَا هَٰذَآ إِلَّآ أَسَٰطِيرُ ٱلۡأَوَّلِينَ ﴿١٧﴾

18. Those are they upon whom has been justified the saying about the communities of *jinn* and mankind who have passed away before them; verily they are ever the losers.

أُوْلَٰٓئِكَ ٱلَّذِينَ حَقَّ عَلَيْهِمُ ٱلْقَوْلُ فِىٓ أُمَمٍ قَدْ خَلَتْ مِن قَبْلِهِم مِّنَ ٱلْجِنِّ وَٱلْإِنسِ إِنَّهُمْ كَانُوا۟ خَٰسِرِينَ ۝

19. And for all are ranks according to what they have worked, that He may repay them in full for their work, and they shall not be wronged.

وَلِكُلٍّ دَرَجَٰتٌ مِّمَّا عَمِلُوا۟ وَلِيُوَفِّيَهُمْ أَعْمَٰلَهُمْ وَهُمْ لَا يُظْلَمُونَ ۝

20. And on the Day when those who disbelieve shall be placed before the Fire; you made away with your good things in your life of the world, and you enjoyed yourselves therewith, so today you shall be requited with the torment of ignominy because you have been growing stiff-necked on the earth without justification, and because you have been transgressing.

وَيَوْمَ يُعْرَضُ ٱلَّذِينَ كَفَرُوا۟ عَلَى ٱلنَّارِ أَذْهَبْتُمْ طَيِّبَٰتِكُمْ فِى حَيَاتِكُمُ ٱلدُّنْيَا وَٱسْتَمْتَعْتُم بِهَا فَٱلْيَوْمَ تُجْزَوْنَ عَذَابَ ٱلْهُونِ بِمَا كُنتُمْ تَسْتَكْبِرُونَ فِى ٱلْأَرْضِ بِغَيْرِ ٱلْحَقِّ وَبِمَا كُنتُمْ تَفْسُقُونَ ۝

Section 3

21. And remember you the brother of the 'Ād when he warned his people in the sand-hills and surely there have passed away warners before him and after him saying: 'Worship none save Allah, verily I fear for you the chastisement of an awful Day.'

وَٱذْكُرْ أَخَا عَادٍ إِذْ أَنذَرَ قَوْمَهُۥ بِٱلْأَحْقَافِ وَقَدْ خَلَتِ ٱلنُّذُرُ مِنۢ بَيْنِ يَدَيْهِ وَمِنْ خَلْفِهِۦٓ أَلَّا تَعْبُدُوٓا۟ إِلَّا ٱللَّهَ إِنِّىٓ أَخَافُ عَلَيْكُمْ عَذَابَ يَوْمٍ عَظِيمٍ ۝

22. They said: 'Have you come to us that you may turn us aside from our gods? Then bring you upon us that with which you threaten us, if you are truthful.'

قَالُوٓاْ أَجِئۡتَنَا لِتَأۡفِكَنَا عَنۡ ءَالِهَتِنَا فَأۡتِنَا بِمَا تَعِدُنَآ إِن كُنتَ مِنَ ٱلصَّٰدِقِينَ ﴿٢٢﴾

23. He said: 'The knowledge is only with Allah, and I preach to you that wherewith I am sent,[665] but I see you are a people given to ignorance.'

قَالَ إِنَّمَا ٱلۡعِلۡمُ عِندَ ٱللَّهِ وَأُبَلِّغُكُم مَّآ أُرۡسِلۡتُ بِهِۦ وَلَٰكِنِّيٓ أَرَىٰكُمۡ قَوۡمٗا تَجۡهَلُونَ ﴿٢٣﴾

24. And when they saw it as an overpeering cloud tending towards their valleys they said: 'That is an overpeering cloud bringing us rain.' Nay! It is what you sought to be hastened; a wind wherein is an afflictive torment.

فَلَمَّا رَأَوۡهُ عَارِضٗا مُّسۡتَقۡبِلَ أَوۡدِيَتِهِمۡ قَالُواْ هَٰذَا عَارِضٞ مُّمۡطِرُنَاۚ بَلۡ هُوَ مَا ٱسۡتَعۡجَلۡتُم بِهِۦۖ رِيحٞ فِيهَا عَذَابٌ أَلِيمٞ ﴿٢٤﴾

25. It shall annihilate everything by the command of its Lord. Therefore they became such that nothing could be seen of them save their dwellings. We thus requite a nation of the guilty.

تُدَمِّرُ كُلَّ شَيۡءِۭ بِأَمۡرِ رَبِّهَا فَأَصۡبَحُواْ لَا يُرَىٰٓ إِلَّا مَسَٰكِنُهُمۡۚ كَذَٰلِكَ نَجۡزِى ٱلۡقَوۡمَ ٱلۡمُجۡرِمِينَ ﴿٢٥﴾

26. And them We had assuredly established in that flourishing condition wherein We have not established you and We had assigned for them hearing and sight and hearts; yet their hearing and sight and hearts availed them not at all. They used to gainsay the revelations of Allah, and then encompassed them what they had been mocking at.

وَلَقَدۡ مَكَّنَّٰهُمۡ فِيمَآ إِن مَّكَّنَّٰكُمۡ فِيهِ وَجَعَلۡنَا لَهُمۡ سَمۡعٗا وَأَبۡصَٰرٗا وَأَفۡـِٔدَةٗ فَمَآ أَغۡنَىٰ عَنۡهُمۡ سَمۡعُهُمۡ وَلَآ أَبۡصَٰرُهُمۡ وَلَآ أَفۡـِٔدَتُهُم مِّن شَيۡءٍ إِذۡ كَانُواْ يَجۡحَدُونَ بِـَٔايَٰتِ ٱللَّهِ وَحَاقَ بِهِم مَّا كَانُواْ بِهِۦ يَسۡتَهۡزِءُونَ ﴿٢٦﴾

---

665. In other words, I only know that punishment is sure to visit you, but I cannot tell at what particular time it will come.

Section 4

27. And assuredly We have destroyed the cities round about you,⁶⁶⁶ and we have variously propounded Our signs that haply they might return.

ولَقَدْ أَهْلَكْنَا مَا حَوْلَكُم مِّنَ ٱلْقُرَىٰ وَصَرَّفْنَا ٱلْآيَـٰتِ لَعَلَّهُمْ يَرْجِعُونَ ۝

28. Then why succoured them not those whom they had taken for gods beside Allah, as a means of approach? Aye! They failed them. And that was their lie which they had been fabricating.

فَلَوْلَا نَصَرَهُمُ ٱلَّذِينَ ٱتَّخَذُوا مِن دُونِ ٱللَّهِ قُرْبَانًا ءَالِهَةً بَلْ ضَلُّوا عَنْهُمْ وَذَٰلِكَ إِفْكُهُمْ وَمَا كَانُوا يَفْتَرُونَ ۝

29. And recall when We sent towards you a company of the *jinn*⁶⁶⁷ listening to the Qur'ān. So when they came in the presence thereof they said, 'give ears'. Then when it was ended, they returned back to their people as warners.

وَإِذْ صَرَفْنَا إِلَيْكَ نَفَرًا مِّنَ ٱلْجِنِّ يَسْتَمِعُونَ ٱلْقُرْءَانَ فَلَمَّا حَضَرُوهُ قَالُوا أَنصِتُوا فَلَمَّا قُضِيَ وَلَّوْا إِلَىٰ قَوْمِهِم مُّنذِرِينَ ۝

30. They said: 'O our people; verily we have hearkened to a Book sent down after Moses, confirming what was before it, guiding to the Truth and a straight path.

قَالُوا يَـٰقَوْمَنَا إِنَّا سَمِعْنَا كِتَـٰبًا أُنزِلَ مِنۢ بَعْدِ مُوسَىٰ مُصَدِّقًا لِّمَا بَيْنَ يَدَيْهِ يَهْدِي إِلَى ٱلْحَقِّ وَإِلَىٰ طَرِيقٍ مُّسْتَقِيمٍ ۝

---

666. Such as the settlements of the Thamūdites, Midyanites, and the cities of Sodom and Gomorrah.

667. It was at Nakhlah on the Prophet's return journey from Taif to Makka in the early days of his ministry that he was visited, while reciting the Qur'ān in his night prayer, by several *jinns*.

31. O our people! Answer Allah's summoner, and believe in him; He shall forgive you your sins and shall shield you from an afflictive chastisement.'

يَٰقَوۡمَنَآ أَجِيبُواْ دَاعِىَ ٱللَّهِ وَءَامِنُواْ بِهِۦ يَغۡفِرۡ لَكُم مِّن ذُنُوبِكُمۡ وَيُجِرۡكُم مِّنۡ عَذَابٍ أَلِيمٍ ٣١

32. And whoso does not answer Allah's summoner, he cannot frustrate His vengeance on the earth, and there will be no patrons for him, besides Him. Those are in manifest error.

وَمَن لَّا يُجِبۡ دَاعِىَ ٱللَّهِ فَلَيۡسَ بِمُعۡجِزٍ فِى ٱلۡأَرۡضِ وَلَيۡسَ لَهُۥ مِن دُونِهِۦٓ أَوۡلِيَآءُۚ أُوْلَٰٓئِكَ فِى ضَلَٰلٍ مُّبِينٍ ٣٢

33. Do they not think that Allah Who created the heavens and the earth and was not fatigued with the creation thereof,[668] is able to quicken the dead? Aye! Verily He is Potent over everything.

أَوَلَمۡ يَرَوۡاْ أَنَّ ٱللَّهَ ٱلَّذِى خَلَقَ ٱلسَّمَٰوَٰتِ وَٱلۡأَرۡضَ وَلَمۡ يَعۡىَ بِخَلۡقِهِنَّ بِقَٰدِرٍ عَلَىٰٓ أَن يُحۡيِۦَ ٱلۡمَوۡتَىٰۚ بَلَىٰٓ إِنَّهُۥ عَلَىٰ كُلِّ شَىۡءٍ قَدِيرٌ ٣٣

34. And on the Day when those who disbelieve will be placed before the Fire, 'is this not real?' They will say: 'Yes! By our Lord!' He will say: 'Taste therefore the torment for you have been disbelieving.'

وَيَوۡمَ يُعۡرَضُ ٱلَّذِينَ كَفَرُواْ عَلَى ٱلنَّارِ أَلَيۡسَ هَٰذَا بِٱلۡحَقِّۖ قَالُواْ بَلَىٰ وَرَبِّنَاۚ قَالَ فَذُوقُواْ ٱلۡعَذَابَ بِمَا كُنتُمۡ تَكۡفُرُونَ ٣٤

---

668. This is to emphatically deny the idea of fatigue and weariness to God as implied in the Bible. Cf. the OT: 'And on the seventh day God ended his work which he had made; and he rested on the seventh day from all his work which he had made. And God blessed the seventh day and sanctified it; because that in it he had rested from all his work which God created and made' (Ge. 2: 2, 3). 'For in six days the Lord made heaven and earth, and on the seventh day he rested, and was refreshed' (Ex. 31: 17). 'For in six days the Lord made heaven and earth, the sea, and all that in them is, and rested the seventh day' (Ex. 20: 11). And the NT: 'And God did rest the seventh day from all his works' (He. 4: 4). The idea of God needing rest at the end of His creative activity, as if the Creator were worn out with worrying toils and struggled under burdens too heavy for Him, is preposterous to the Muslim mind, but the fact remains that the Bible clearly inculcates so curious a doctrine.

35. Bear you then with patience, as did the Messengers, endued with resolution bear with patience and seek not to hasten on for them. On the Day when they will behold that with which they are threatened, it will seem to them as though they had tarried but for an hour of a day. A proclamation this; so none will be destroyed but the nation of transgressors.

فَٱصۡبِرۡ كَمَا صَبَرَ أُوۡلُوا۟ ٱلۡعَزۡمِ مِنَ ٱلرُّسُلِ وَلَا تَسۡتَعۡجِل لَّهُمۡ كَأَنَّهُمۡ يَوۡمَ يَرَوۡنَ مَا يُوعَدُونَ لَمۡ يَلۡبَثُوٓا۟ إِلَّا سَاعَةً مِّن نَّهَارٍ بَلَـٰغٌ فَهَلۡ يُهۡلَكُ إِلَّا ٱلۡقَوۡمُ ٱلۡفَـٰسِقُونَ ٣٥

Sūrah 47

Muḥammad

(Madinan, 4 Sections, 38 Verses)

In the name of Allah, the Compassionate, the Merciful.

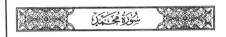

Section 1

1. Those who disbelieve and hinder others from the path of Allah – their works He shall send astray.

2. And those who believe and work righteous deeds and believe in what has been revealed to Muḥammad and it is the Truth from their Lord their misdeeds He shall expiate from them and shall make good their state.

3. That is because those who disbelieve follow falsehood and those who believe follow the Truth from their Lord. And thus does Allah propound to mankind their similitudes.

4. Now when you meet those who disbelieve smite their necks until when you have slain them greatly, then make fast the bonds, then thereafter let them off freely or by ransom, until the war lays off its burden. That you shall do. And had Allah willed He would have vindicated Himself against them. But He ordained fighting in order that He may test you one by the other. And those who are slain in the cause of Allah, He shall not let their works go astray.

5. Soon He will guide them and make good their state.

سَيَهْدِيهِمْ وَيُصْلِحُ بَالَهُمْ ۝

6. And He will make them enter the Garden and will make it known to them.

وَيُدْخِلُهُمُ الْجَنَّةَ عَرَّفَهَا لَهُمْ ۝

7. O you who believe! If you succour Allah, He will succour you and make your feet firm.

يَا أَيُّهَا الَّذِينَ ءَامَنُوا إِن تَنصُرُوا اللَّهَ يَنصُرْكُمْ وَيُثَبِّتْ أَقْدَامَكُمْ ۝

8. And those who disbelieve, theirs shall be the downfall, and their work He will send astray.

وَالَّذِينَ كَفَرُوا فَتَعْسًا لَهُمْ وَأَضَلَّ أَعْمَالَهُمْ ۝

9. That is because they detest what Allah has sent down and so He will make their works of non-effect.

ذَلِكَ بِأَنَّهُمْ كَرِهُوا مَا أَنزَلَ اللَّهُ فَأَحْبَطَ أَعْمَالَهُمْ ۝

10. Have they not journeyed on the earth so that they might see how has been the end of those before them? Allah annihilated them: and for the infidels theirs shall be the like fate therefor.

أَفَلَمْ يَسِيرُوا فِي الْأَرْضِ فَيَنظُرُوا كَيْفَ كَانَ عَاقِبَةُ الَّذِينَ مِن قَبْلِهِمْ دَمَّرَ اللَّهُ عَلَيْهِمْ وَلِلْكَافِرِينَ أَمْثَالُهَا ۝

11. That is because Allah is the Patron of those who believe, and the infidels! No patron is theirs!

ذَلِكَ بِأَنَّ اللَّهَ مَوْلَى الَّذِينَ ءَامَنُوا وَأَنَّ الْكَافِرِينَ لَا مَوْلَى لَهُمْ ۝

Section 2

12. Verily Allah will cause those who believe and work righteous deeds to enter the Garden whereunder rivers flow. And those who disbelieve enjoy themselves and eat even as the cattle eat and the Fire shall be the abode for them.

إِنَّ اللَّهَ يُدْخِلُ الَّذِينَ ءَامَنُوا وَعَمِلُوا الصَّالِحَاتِ جَنَّاتٍ تَجْرِي مِن تَحْتِهَا الْأَنْهَارُ وَالَّذِينَ كَفَرُوا يَتَمَتَّعُونَ وَيَأْكُلُونَ كَمَا تَأْكُلُ الْأَنْعَامُ وَالنَّارُ مَثْوًى لَهُمْ ۝

13. And many a city, mightier in strength than the city which drove you forth, We destroyed and there was no helper of theirs.

وَكَأَيِّن مِّن قَرۡيَةٍ هِىَ أَشَدُّ قُوَّةً مِّن قَرۡيَتِكَ الَّتِىٓ أَخۡرَجَتۡكَ أَهۡلَكۡنَٰهُمۡ فَلَا نَاصِرَ لَهُمۡ ﴿١٣﴾

14. Is he then who stands on an evidence from his Lord like him whose evil of work is bedecked to him, and those who follow their lusts?

أَفَمَن كَانَ عَلَىٰ بَيِّنَةٍ مِّن رَّبِّهِۦ كَمَن زُيِّنَ لَهُۥ سُوٓءُ عَمَلِهِۦ وَاتَّبَعُوٓاْ أَهۡوَآءَهُم ﴿١٤﴾

15. A likeness of the Garden which has been promised to the God-fearing is this, therein are rivers of water incorruptible, rivers of milk of unchangeable flavour, rivers of wine, a joy to the drinkers; and rivers of honey clarified; therein theirs shall be every manner of fruit, and forgiveness from their Lord. Shall persons enjoying such bliss be like those who are abiders in the Fire, and are given to drinking boiling water so that it mangles their entrails?

مَّثَلُ ٱلۡجَنَّةِ ٱلَّتِى وُعِدَ ٱلۡمُتَّقُونَ فِيهَآ أَنۡهَٰرٌ مِّن مَّآءٍ غَيۡرِ ءَاسِنٍ وَأَنۡهَٰرٌ مِّن لَّبَنٍ لَّمۡ يَتَغَيَّرۡ طَعۡمُهُۥ وَأَنۡهَٰرٌ مِّنۡ خَمۡرٍ لَّذَّةٍ لِّلشَّٰرِبِينَ وَأَنۡهَٰرٌ مِّنۡ عَسَلٍ مُّصَفًّى وَلَهُمۡ فِيهَا مِن كُلِّ ٱلثَّمَرَٰتِ وَمَغۡفِرَةٌ مِّن رَّبِّهِمۡ كَمَنۡ هُوَ خَٰلِدٌ فِى ٱلنَّارِ وَسُقُواْ مَآءً حَمِيمًا فَقَطَّعَ أَمۡعَآءَهُمۡ ﴿١٥﴾

16. Of them are some who listen to you, until, when they go forth from before you, they say to those who are vouchsafed knowledge: 'What is that he said just now?' Those are they whose hearts Allah has sealed up, and they follow their lusts.

وَمِنۡهُم مَّن يَسۡتَمِعُ إِلَيۡكَ حَتَّىٰٓ إِذَا خَرَجُواْ مِنۡ عِندِكَ قَالُواْ لِلَّذِينَ أُوتُواْ ٱلۡعِلۡمَ مَاذَا قَالَ ءَانِفًا أُوْلَٰٓئِكَ ٱلَّذِينَ طَبَعَ ٱللَّهُ عَلَىٰ قُلُوبِهِمۡ وَٱتَّبَعُوٓاْ أَهۡوَآءَهُمۡ ﴿١٦﴾

17. And those who are guided, He adds their guidance and gives them protection against evil.

وَٱلَّذِينَ ٱهۡتَدَوۡاْ زَادَهُمۡ هُدًى وَءَاتَىٰهُمۡ تَقۡوَىٰهُمۡ ﴿١٧﴾

18. Do they only await the Hour, that it should come upon them of a sudden? Portents thereof are already come, so how will it be with them when there comes to them their admonition?

فَهَلۡ يَنظُرُونَ إِلَّا ٱلسَّاعَةَ أَن تَأۡتِيَهُم بَغۡتَةً فَقَدۡ جَآءَ أَشۡرَاطُهَا فَأَنَّىٰ لَهُمۡ إِذَا جَآءَتۡهُمۡ ذِكۡرَىٰهُمۡ ۝

19. So know you that there is no god save Allah, and ask forgiveness for your fault and for the believing men and women. And Allah knows well your moving about and your place of rest.

فَٱعۡلَمۡ أَنَّهُۥ لَآ إِلَٰهَ إِلَّا ٱللَّهُ وَٱسۡتَغۡفِرۡ لِذَنۢبِكَ وَلِلۡمُؤۡمِنِينَ وَٱلۡمُؤۡمِنَٰتِ وَٱللَّهُ يَعۡلَمُ مُتَقَلَّبَكُمۡ وَمَثۡوَىٰكُمۡ ۝

Section 3

20. And those who believe say: 'Why has a Surah not been revealed?' Then when there is revealed a *Sūrah* firmly-constructed and fighting is prescribed therein, you see those in whose heart is a disease looking at you with a look of one who is fainting unto death: so alas for them!

وَيَقُولُ ٱلَّذِينَ ءَامَنُوا۟ لَوۡلَا نُزِّلَتۡ سُورَةٌ فَإِذَآ أُنزِلَتۡ سُورَةٌ مُّحۡكَمَةٌ وَذُكِرَ فِيهَا ٱلۡقِتَالُ رَأَيۡتَ ٱلَّذِينَ فِي قُلُوبِهِم مَّرَضٌ يَنظُرُونَ إِلَيۡكَ نَظَرَ ٱلۡمَغۡشِيِّ عَلَيۡهِ مِنَ ٱلۡمَوۡتِ فَأَوۡلَىٰ لَهُمۡ ۝

21. The hypocrites' obedience and speech are known. Then when the affair is resolved, if even then they gave credence to Allah, it would have been better for them.

طَاعَةٌ وَقَوۡلٌ مَّعۡرُوفٌ فَإِذَا عَزَمَ ٱلۡأَمۡرُ فَلَوۡ صَدَقُوا۟ ٱللَّهَ لَكَانَ خَيۡرًا لَّهُمۡ ۝

22. Then if you turn away, you are likely to cause corruption on the earth and to sever your kinship.

فَهَلۡ عَسَيۡتُمۡ إِن تَوَلَّيۡتُمۡ أَن تُفۡسِدُوا۟ فِي ٱلۡأَرۡضِ وَتُقَطِّعُوٓا۟ أَرۡحَامَكُمۡ ۝

23. Those are they whom Allah has cursed and then has deafened them and blinded their sights.

أُوْلَٰٓئِكَ ٱلَّذِينَ لَعَنَهُمُ ٱللَّهُ فَأَصَمَّهُمْ وَأَعْمَىٰٓ أَبْصَٰرَهُمْ ٢٣

24. Do they not ponder over the Qur'ān, or are there locks upon their hearts?

أَفَلَا يَتَدَبَّرُونَ ٱلْقُرْءَانَ أَمْ عَلَىٰ قُلُوبٍ أَقْفَالُهَآ ٢٤

25. Verily those who have apostated on their backs after the guidance had become manifest to them, Satan has embellished this apostasy to them, and has given them false hopes.

إِنَّ ٱلَّذِينَ ٱرْتَدُّوا۟ عَلَىٰٓ أَدْبَٰرِهِم مِّنۢ بَعْدِ مَا تَبَيَّنَ لَهُمُ ٱلْهُدَى ٱلشَّيْطَٰنُ سَوَّلَ لَهُمْ وَأَمْلَىٰ لَهُمْ ٢٥

26. That is because they said to those who abhor what Allah has revealed; we shall obey in part of the affair; and Allah knows their talking in secret.

ذَٰلِكَ بِأَنَّهُمْ قَالُوا۟ لِلَّذِينَ كَرِهُوا۟ مَا نَزَّلَ ٱللَّهُ سَنُطِيعُكُمْ فِى بَعْضِ ٱلْأَمْرِ وَٱللَّهُ يَعْلَمُ إِسْرَارَهُمْ ٢٦

27. How then shall it be, when the angels shall take them away at death, their faces and their backs?

فَكَيْفَ إِذَا تَوَفَّتْهُمُ ٱلْمَلَٰٓئِكَةُ يَضْرِبُونَ وُجُوهَهُمْ وَأَدْبَٰرَهُمْ ٢٧

28. That is because they followed what incensed Allah and abhorred His good will. So He made their works of non-effect.

ذَٰلِكَ بِأَنَّهُمُ ٱتَّبَعُوا۟ مَآ أَسْخَطَ ٱللَّهَ وَكَرِهُوا۟ رِضْوَٰنَهُۥ فَأَحْبَطَ أَعْمَٰلَهُمْ ٢٨

Section 4

29. Do then in whose hearts is a disease imagine that Allah will never bring to light their rancour?

أَمْ حَسِبَ ٱلَّذِينَ فِى قُلُوبِهِم مَّرَضٌ أَن لَّن يُخْرِجَ ٱللَّهُ أَضْغَٰنَهُمْ ٢٩

30. And if We willed, We would surely show them to you so that you should know them by their marks. And you shall surely know them by mode of their speech. And Allah knows your works.

وَلَوْ نَشَآءُ لَأَرَيْنَٰكَهُمْ فَلَعَرَفْتَهُم بِسِيمَٰهُمْ وَلَتَعْرِفَنَّهُمْ فِى لَحْنِ ٱلْقَوْلِ وَٱللَّهُ يَعْلَمُ أَعْمَٰلَكُمْ ٣٠

31. And of a surety We shall put you to the proof till We know the valiant among you and the steadfast, and We shall know your different states.

وَلَنَبْلُوَنَّكُمْ حَتَّىٰ نَعْلَمَ ٱلْمُجَٰهِدِينَ مِنكُمْ وَٱلصَّٰبِرِينَ وَنَبْلُوَا۟ أَخْبَارَكُمْ ۞

32. Verily those who have disbelieved and have hindered others from the path of Allah and have opposed the Messengers after the guidance has become manifest to them shall not hurt Allah at all, and soon He shall make their works fruitless.

إِنَّ ٱلَّذِينَ كَفَرُوا۟ وَصَدُّوا۟ عَن سَبِيلِ ٱللَّهِ وَشَآقُّوا۟ ٱلرَّسُولَ مِنۢ بَعْدِ مَا تَبَيَّنَ لَهُمُ ٱلْهُدَىٰ لَن يَضُرُّوا۟ ٱللَّهَ شَيْـًٔا وَسَيُحْبِطُ أَعْمَٰلَهُمْ ۞

33. O you who believe! Obey Allah and obey the Messenger, and do not render your works vain.

يَٰٓأَيُّهَا ٱلَّذِينَ ءَامَنُوٓا۟ أَطِيعُوا۟ ٱللَّهَ وَأَطِيعُوا۟ ٱلرَّسُولَ وَلَا تُبْطِلُوٓا۟ أَعْمَٰلَكُمْ ۞

34. Verily those who disbelieve and hinder others from the path of Allah die as infidels; Allah shall by no means forgive them.

إِنَّ ٱلَّذِينَ كَفَرُوا۟ وَصَدُّوا۟ عَن سَبِيلِ ٱللَّهِ ثُمَّ مَاتُوا۟ وَهُمْ كُفَّارٌ فَلَن يَغْفِرَ ٱللَّهُ لَهُمْ ۞

35. So do not faint, nor cry out for peace; and you shall be triumphant. And Allah is with you, and He will not defraud you of your works.

فَلَا تَهِنُوا۟ وَتَدْعُوٓا۟ إِلَى ٱلسَّلْمِ وَأَنتُمُ ٱلْأَعْلَوْنَ وَٱللَّهُ مَعَكُمْ وَلَن يَتِرَكُمْ أَعْمَٰلَكُمْ ۞

36. The life of this world is but a sport and a pastime. And if you believe and shun evil, He will give you reward and will not require of you your substance.

إِنَّمَا ٱلْحَيَوٰةُ ٱلدُّنْيَا لَعِبٌ وَلَهْوٌ وَإِن تُؤْمِنُوا۟ وَتَتَّقُوا۟ يُؤْتِكُمْ أُجُورَكُمْ وَلَا يَسْـَٔلْكُمْ أَمْوَٰلَكُمْ ۞

37. If He required it of you and importuned you, you would be niggardly, and He will bring to light your secret malevolence.

إِن يَسْـَٔلْكُمُوهَا فَيُحْفِكُمْ تَبْخَلُوا۟ وَيُخْرِجْ أَضْغَٰنَكُمْ ۞

38. Look here! You are those who are called to expend in the cause of Allah; then of you there are some who are niggardly. And whosoever is niggardly is only niggardly to his soul. Allah is Self-Sufficient and you are the needy.[669] And if you turn away, He will substitute for you another people, and then they will not be your likeness.

هَٰٓأَنتُمۡ هَٰٓؤُلَآءِ تُدۡعَوۡنَ لِتُنفِقُوۡا فِىۡ سَبِيۡلِ ٱللَّهِ فَمِنكُم مَّن يَبۡخَلُ وَمَن يَبۡخَلۡ فَإِنَّمَا يَبۡخَلُ عَن نَّفۡسِهِۦ وَٱللَّهُ ٱلۡغَنِىُّ وَأَنتُمُ ٱلۡفُقَرَآءُ وَإِن تَتَوَلَّوۡا يَسۡتَبۡدِلۡ قَوۡمًا غَيۡرَكُمۡ ثُمَّ لَا يَكُوۡنُوۡٓا أَمۡثَٰلَكُمۡ ۝

---

669. God is the real owner of everything; man is only a dispenser, who will have to render account of every gift. Wealth is but a trust and a test.

Sūrah 48

al-Fatḥ

(Madinan, 4 Sections, 29 Verses)

*In the name of Allah, the
Compassionate, the Merciful.*

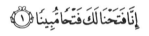

Section 1

1. Verily We! A victory, We have
given you a manifest victory.[670]

اِنَّا فَتَحْنَا لَكَ فَتْحًا مُّبِيْنًا ۝

---

670. The reference is to the truce of Ḥudaybiyah, 'which, though at the time it
seemed a set-back to the Muslims, proved in fact the greatest victory for al-
Islam. In the sixth year of the Hijrah, the Prophet set out with some 1400
Muslims from al-Madīnah and the country round, in the garb of pilgrims, not
for war but to visit the Ka'bah. When they draw near Mecca, they were warned
that Qureysh had gathered their allies against them, and that their cavalry
under Khālid ibn al-Walīd was on the road before them. Making a detour
through gullies of the hills, they escaped the cavalry and coming into the
valley of Mecca, encamped at al-Ḥudeybiyeh below the city. The Prophet
resolutely refused to give battle and persisted in attempts to parley with Qureysh
who had sworn not to let him reach the Ka'bah. Qureysh at length agreed to a
truce of which the terms were favourable to them. The Prophet and his multitude
were to give up the project of visiting the sanctuary for that year, but were to
make the pilgrimage the following year when the idolaters undertook to evacuate
Mecca for three days to allow them to do so. Fugitives from Qureysh to the
Muslims were to be returned, but not fugitives from the Muslims to Qureysh;
and there was not to be hostility between the parties for ten years' (Pickthall,
Meaning of the Glorious Qur'an). 'The people, led by vision to anticipate an
unopposed visit to the Ka'ba, were crest – fallen at the abortive result of
their long journey. But, in truth, a great step had been gained by Mohammad.
His political status, as an equal and independent power, was acknowledged
by the treaty; the ten years' truce would afford opportunity and time for the
new religion to expand, and to force its claims upon the conviction of Koreish;
while conquest material as well spiritual, might be pursued on every other
side. Above all, it was a great and manifest success that free permission was
conceded to visit Mecca in the following year, and for three days to occupy
the city undisturbed'. (Muir, *Life of Muhammad*, p. 360). This was for the
first time that the Muslims were treated on equal terms by the Makkans, and
the Treaty practically ended the Makkan wars.

2. That He may forgive you of your sins, past and future, and may accomplish all the more His favour on you and may keep you guided on the straight path.

لِيَغۡفِرَ لَكَ ٱللَّهُ مَا تَقَدَّمَ مِن ذَنۢبِكَ وَمَا تَأَخَّرَ وَيُتِمَّ نِعۡمَتَهُۥ عَلَيۡكَ وَيَهۡدِيَكَ صِرَٰطٗا مُّسۡتَقِيمٗا ٢

3. And that Allah may succour you with a mighty succour.

وَيَنصُرَكَ ٱللَّهُ نَصۡرًا عَزِيزًا ٣

4. He it is Who has sent down tranquillity into the hearts of the believers that they might increase belief to their belief. And Allah's are the hosts of the heavens and the earth, Allah is Ever Knowing, Wise.

هُوَ ٱلَّذِىٓ أَنزَلَ ٱلسَّكِينَةَ فِى قُلُوبِ ٱلۡمُؤۡمِنِينَ لِيَزۡدَادُوٓاْ إِيمَٰنٗا مَّعَ إِيمَٰنِهِمۡۗ وَلِلَّهِ جُنُودُ ٱلسَّمَٰوَٰتِ وَٱلۡأَرۡضِۚ وَكَانَ ٱللَّهُ عَلِيمًا حَكِيمٗا ٤

5. He has prescribed war in order that He may admit the believing men and women into Gardens, whereunder rivers flow as abiders therein and that He may expiate from them their misdeeds. And that is with Allah ever a mighty achievement.

لِيُدۡخِلَ ٱلۡمُؤۡمِنِينَ وَٱلۡمُؤۡمِنَٰتِ جَنَّٰتٖ تَجۡرِى مِن تَحۡتِهَا ٱلۡأَنۡهَٰرُ خَٰلِدِينَ فِيهَا وَيُكَفِّرَ عَنۡهُمۡ سَيِّـَٔاتِهِمۡۚ وَكَانَ ذَٰلِكَ عِندَ ٱللَّهِ فَوۡزًا عَظِيمٗا ٥

6. And that He may chastise the hypocritical men and women and the polytheist men and women, and the thinkers of evil thought concerning Allah. To them shall befall the evil turn of fortune and Allah shall be indignant with them, and shall curse them and He has prepared for them Hell, an ill-destination!

وَيُعَذِّبَ ٱلۡمُنَٰفِقِينَ وَٱلۡمُنَٰفِقَٰتِ وَٱلۡمُشۡرِكِينَ وَٱلۡمُشۡرِكَٰتِ ٱلظَّآنِّينَ بِٱللَّهِ ظَنَّ ٱلسَّوۡءِۚ عَلَيۡهِمۡ دَآئِرَةُ ٱلسَّوۡءِۖ وَغَضِبَ ٱللَّهُ عَلَيۡهِمۡ وَلَعَنَهُمۡ وَأَعَدَّ لَهُمۡ جَهَنَّمَۖ وَسَآءَتۡ مَصِيرٗا ٦

7. And Allah's are the legions of the heavens and the earth. And Allah is ever Mighty, Wise.

وَلِلَّهِ جُنُودُ السَّمَوَاتِ وَالْأَرْضِ وَكَانَ اللَّهُ عَزِيزًا حَكِيمًا ۝

8. Verily We! We have sent you as a witness and a bearer of glad tidings and a warner.

إِنَّا أَرْسَلْنَاكَ شَاهِدًا وَمُبَشِّرًا وَنَذِيرًا ۝

9. That you may believe in Allah and His Messenger and may assist Him and honour Him and may hallow Him morning and evening.

لِتُؤْمِنُوا بِاللَّهِ وَرَسُولِهِ وَتُعَزِّرُوهُ وَتُوَقِّرُوهُ وَتُسَبِّحُوهُ بُكْرَةً وَأَصِيلًا ۝

10. Verily those who swear fealty to you indeed swear fealty to Allah; the hand of Allah is over their hands.[671] So whosoever breaks his oath breaks it only to his soul's hurt; and whosoever fulfils his covenant with Allah, him He shall soon give a great reward.

إِنَّ الَّذِينَ يُبَايِعُونَكَ إِنَّمَا يُبَايِعُونَ اللَّهَ يَدُ اللَّهِ فَوْقَ أَيْدِيهِمْ فَمَن نَّكَثَ فَإِنَّمَا يَنكُثُ عَلَى نَفْسِهِ وَمَنْ أَوْفَى بِمَا عَاهَدَ عَلَيْهُ اللَّهَ فَسَيُؤْتِيهِ أَجْرًا عَظِيمًا ۝

Section 2

11. Those of the desert Arabs who lagged behind will presently say to you: 'Our properties and our families kept us occupied, so ask you forgiveness for us.' They say with their tongues what is not in their hearts. Say: 'Who can avail you in anything against Allah, if He intended you hurt or intended you benefit?' Yea! Allah is ever Aware of what you do.

سَيَقُولُ لَكَ الْمُخَلَّفُونَ مِنَ الْأَعْرَابِ شَغَلَتْنَا أَمْوَالُنَا وَأَهْلُونَا فَاسْتَغْفِرْ لَنَا يَقُولُونَ بِأَلْسِنَتِهِم مَّا لَيْسَ فِي قُلُوبِهِمْ قُلْ فَمَن يَمْلِكُ لَكُم مِّنَ اللَّهِ شَيْئًا إِنْ أَرَادَ بِكُمْ ضَرًّا أَوْ أَرَادَ بِكُمْ نَفْعًا بَلْ كَانَ اللَّهُ بِمَا تَعْمَلُونَ خَبِيرًا ۝

---

671. The Believers, according to Arab custom, placed hand on hand when solemnly affirming fidelity.

12. Yea! You imagined that the Messenger and the believers would never return to their families, and that became bedecked in your hearts, and you bethought an evil thought, and you became a people doomed.

بَلْ ظَنَنتُمْ أَن لَّن يَنقَلِبَ الرَّسُولُ وَ الْمُؤْمِنُونَ إِلَىٰٓ أَهْلِيهِمْ أَبَدًا وَزُيِّنَ ذَٰلِكَ فِى قُلُوبِكُمْ وَظَنَنتُمْ ظَنَّ السَّوْءِ وَكُنتُمْ قَوْمًا بُورًا ۝

13. And whosoever does not believe in Allah and His Messenger – then verily We have prepared the Blaze for the infidels.

وَمَن لَّمْ يُؤْمِن بِاللَّهِ وَرَسُولِهِۦ فَإِنَّآ أَعْتَدْنَا لِلْكَٰفِرِينَ سَعِيرًا ۝

14. And Allah's is the dominion of the heavens and the earth. He forgives whomsoever He will, and chastizes whomsoever He will; and Allah is ever Forgiving, Merciful.

وَلِلَّهِ مُلْكُ السَّمَٰوَٰتِ وَالْأَرْضِ يَغْفِرُ لِمَن يَشَآءُ وَيُعَذِّبُ مَن يَشَآءُ وَكَانَ اللَّهُ غَفُورًا رَّحِيمًا ۝

15. Those who lagged behind will when you march forth to take the spoils presently say: 'Leave us, we shall follow you.' They were to change the word of Allah. Say: 'You shall by no means follow us; thus has Allah said before.' Then they will say: 'Aye! You envy us. Aye! Little it is you are wont to understand.'

سَيَقُولُ الْمُخَلَّفُونَ إِذَا انطَلَقْتُمْ إِلَىٰ مَغَانِمَ لِتَأْخُذُوهَا ذَرُونَا نَتَّبِعْكُمْ يُرِيدُونَ أَن يُبَدِّلُوا كَلَٰمَ اللَّهِ قُل لَّن تَتَّبِعُونَا كَذَٰلِكُمْ قَالَ اللَّهُ مِن قَبْلُ فَسَيَقُولُونَ بَلْ تَحْسُدُونَنَا بَلْ كَانُوا لَا يَفْقَهُونَ إِلَّا قَلِيلًا ۝

16. Say to those of the desert Arabs who lagged behind: 'Surely you shall be summoned to fight against a people endued with exceeding violence, then you will fight them or they will surrender. Then if you obey, Allah will give you a goodly reward; but if you turn away, as you turned away before, He will chastise you with an afflictive chastisement.'

قُل لِّلْمُخَلَّفِينَ مِنَ الْأَعْرَابِ سَتُدْعَوْنَ إِلَىٰ قَوْمٍ أُوْلِى بَأْسٍ شَدِيدٍ تُقَٰتِلُونَهُمْ أَوْ يُسْلِمُونَ فَإِن تُطِيعُوا يُؤْتِكُمُ اللَّهُ أَجْرًا حَسَنًا وَإِن تَتَوَلَّوْا كَمَا تَوَلَّيْتُم مِّن قَبْلُ يُعَذِّبْكُمْ عَذَابًا أَلِيمًا ۝

17. No blame there is upon the blind and no blame upon the lame and no blame upon the sick. And whosoever obeys Allah and His Messenger, He will admit him into Gardens whereunder rivers flow; and whosoever turns away, him He shall torment with an afflictive torment.

Section 3

18. Assuredly well-pleased was Allah with the faithful when they swore fealty to you under the tree, and He knew what was in their hearts; so He sent down on them tranquillity, and rewarded them with a victory near at hand,

19. And abundant spoils that they are taking. And Allah is ever Mighty, Wise.

20. Allah has promised you abundant spoils that you shall take, and these He has hastened to you and has restrained the hands of the people from you, that it may be a sign to the believers, and that He may guide you to a straight path.

21. And another victory He promised, over which as yet you have no power; Allah has surely encompassed it, and Allah is ever Potent over everything.

لَيْسَ عَلَى الْأَعْمَى حَرَجٌ وَلَا عَلَى الْأَعْرَجِ حَرَجٌ وَلَا عَلَى الْمَرِيضِ حَرَجٌ وَمَن يُطِعِ اللَّهَ وَرَسُولَهُ يُدْخِلْهُ جَنَّتٍ تَجْرِى مِن تَحْتِهَا الْأَنْهَرُ وَمَن يَتَوَلَّ يُعَذِّبْهُ عَذَابًا أَلِيمًا ﴿١٧﴾

لَقَدْ رَضِىَ اللَّهُ عَنِ الْمُؤْمِنِينَ إِذْ يُبَايِعُونَكَ تَحْتَ الشَّجَرَةِ فَعَلِمَ مَا فِى قُلُوبِهِمْ فَأَنزَلَ السَّكِينَةَ عَلَيْهِمْ وَأَثَابَهُمْ فَتْحًا قَرِيبًا ﴿١٨﴾

وَمَغَانِمَ كَثِيرَةً يَأْخُذُونَهَا وَكَانَ اللَّهُ عَزِيزًا حَكِيمًا ﴿١٩﴾

وَعَدَكُمُ اللَّهُ مَغَانِمَ كَثِيرَةً تَأْخُذُونَهَا فَعَجَّلَ لَكُمْ هَذِهِ وَكَفَّ أَيْدِىَ النَّاسِ عَنكُمْ وَلِتَكُونَ ءَايَةً لِّلْمُؤْمِنِينَ وَيَهْدِيَكُمْ صِرَاطًا مُّسْتَقِيمًا ﴿٢٠﴾

وَأُخْرَى لَمْ تَقْدِرُوا عَلَيْهَا قَدْ أَحَاطَ اللَّهُ بِهَا وَكَانَ اللَّهُ عَلَى كُلِّ شَىْءٍ قَدِيرًا ﴿٢١﴾

22. And had those who disbelieve fought against you, surely they would have turned their backs and then they would have found no patron nor helper.

وَلَوْ قَاتَلَكُمُ الَّذِينَ كَفَرُوا لَوَلَّوُا الْأَدْبَارَ ثُمَّ لَا يَجِدُونَ وَلِيًّا وَلَا نَصِيرًا ۝

23. That has been the dispensation of Allah with those who passed away before; and you shall not find any change in the dispensation of Allah.

سُنَّةَ اللَّهِ الَّتِي قَدْ خَلَتْ مِن قَبْلُ وَلَن تَجِدَ لِسُنَّةِ اللَّهِ تَبْدِيلًا ۝

24. And He it is Who restrained their hands from you and restrained your hands from them, in the vale of Makka after He had made you victorious over them, and Allah is ever a Beholder of what you do.

وَهُوَ الَّذِي كَفَّ أَيْدِيَهُمْ عَنكُمْ وَأَيْدِيَكُمْ عَنْهُم بِبَطْنِ مَكَّةَ مِنْ بَعْدِ أَنْ أَظْفَرَكُمْ عَلَيْهِمْ وَكَانَ اللَّهُ بِمَا تَعْمَلُونَ بَصِيرًا ۝

25. They were those who disbelieved and debarred you from the Sacred Mosque, and prevented the detained offering, that it should arrive at its goal. And had it not been for the believing men and women you know not and whom you might have trampled on and been guilty on their account unknowingly. This He did that He might abide with His mercy whomsoever He will. Had they been distinguished one from another, surely We had chastized those who disbelieved among them with a painful chastisement.

هُمُ الَّذِينَ كَفَرُوا وَصَدُّوكُمْ عَنِ الْمَسْجِدِ الْحَرَامِ وَالْهَدْيَ مَعْكُوفًا أَن يَبْلُغَ مَحِلَّهُ وَلَوْلَا رِجَالٌ مُّؤْمِنُونَ وَنِسَاءٌ مُّؤْمِنَاتٌ لَّمْ تَعْلَمُوهُمْ أَن تَطَئُوهُمْ فَتُصِيبَكُم مِّنْهُم مَّعَرَّةٌ بِغَيْرِ عِلْمٍ لِيُدْخِلَ اللَّهُ فِي رَحْمَتِهِ مَن يَشَاءُ لَوْ تَزَيَّلُوا لَعَذَّبْنَا الَّذِينَ كَفَرُوا مِنْهُمْ عَذَابًا أَلِيمًا ۝

26. When those who disbelieve had put in their hearts a zeal, the goal of paganism, then Allah sent down a tranquillity upon His Messenger and the believers and kept them fixed on the way of piety, and they were worthy of it and meet for it; and Allah is ever the Knower of everything.

إِذْ جَعَلَ ٱلَّذِينَ كَفَرُوا۟ فِى قُلُوبِهِمُ ٱلْحَمِيَّةَ حَمِيَّةَ ٱلْجَٰهِلِيَّةِ فَأَنزَلَ ٱللَّهُ سَكِينَتَهُۥ عَلَىٰ رَسُولِهِۦ وَعَلَى ٱلْمُؤْمِنِينَ وَأَلْزَمَهُمْ كَلِمَةَ ٱلتَّقْوَىٰ وَكَانُوٓا۟ أَحَقَّ بِهَا وَأَهْلَهَا ۚ وَكَانَ ٱللَّهُ بِكُلِّ شَىْءٍ عَلِيمًا ۝

Section 4

27. Assuredly did Allah show a true vision to His Messenger in very truth; Allah willing, you shall surely enter the Sacred Mosque, secure, with your head shaven and your hair cropped, and you shall have no fear. He knows what you do not know. So He has assigned, besides that, a victory nigh.

لَّقَدْ صَدَقَ ٱللَّهُ رَسُولَهُ ٱلرُّءْيَا بِٱلْحَقِّ ۖ لَتَدْخُلُنَّ ٱلْمَسْجِدَ ٱلْحَرَامَ إِن شَآءَ ٱللَّهُ ءَامِنِينَ مُحَلِّقِينَ رُءُوسَكُمْ وَمُقَصِّرِينَ لَا تَخَافُونَ ۖ فَعَلِمَ مَا لَمْ تَعْلَمُوا۟ فَجَعَلَ مِن دُونِ ذَٰلِكَ فَتْحًا قَرِيبًا ۝

28. He it is Who has sent His Messenger with guidance and true faith that He may make it prevail over all faiths, and Allah suffices as a Witness.

هُوَ ٱلَّذِىٓ أَرْسَلَ رَسُولَهُۥ بِٱلْهُدَىٰ وَدِينِ ٱلْحَقِّ لِيُظْهِرَهُۥ عَلَى ٱلدِّينِ كُلِّهِ ۚ وَكَفَىٰ بِٱللَّهِ شَهِيدًا ۝

29. Muhammad is the Messenger of Allah. And those who are with him[672] are stern against the infidels and merciful among them-

مُّحَمَّدٌ رَّسُولُ ٱللَّهِ ۚ وَٱلَّذِينَ مَعَهُۥٓ أَشِدَّآءُ عَلَى ٱلْكُفَّارِ رُحَمَآءُ بَيْنَهُمْ ۖ تَرَىٰهُمْ رُكَّعًا سُجَّدًا

---

672. Namelys, his companions in general, and those who accompanied him on the Ḥudaybiyah expedition in particular.

selves.[673] You see them bowing down and falling prostrate, and seeking grace from Allah and His goodwill.[674] This mark is on their faces, a trace in the Gospel; like a seed that puts forth its shoot and strengthens it, and grows and rises straight upon its stalk delighting the sowers.[675] Such are the early Muslims described that He may enrage the infidels with them. To those among them who believe and work righteous deeds, Allah has promised forgiveness and a splendid reward.

يَبْتَغُونَ فَضْلًا مِّنَ ٱللَّهِ وَرِضْوَٰنًا سِيمَاهُمْ فِى وُجُوهِهِم مِّنْ أَثَرِ ٱلسُّجُودِ ذَٰلِكَ مَثَلُهُمْ فِى ٱلتَّوْرَىٰةِ وَمَثَلُهُمْ فِى ٱلْإِنجِيلِ كَزَرْعٍ أَخْرَجَ شَطْـَٔهُۥ فَـَٔازَرَهُۥ فَٱسْتَغْلَظَ فَٱسْتَوَىٰ عَلَىٰ سُوقِهِۦ يُعْجِبُ ٱلزُّرَّاعَ لِيَغِيظَ بِهِمُ ٱلْكُفَّارَ وَعَدَ ٱللَّهُ ٱلَّذِينَ ءَامَنُوا۟ وَعَمِلُوا۟ ٱلصَّٰلِحَٰتِ مِنْهُم مَّغْفِرَةً وَأَجْرًا عَظِيمًۢا ﴿٢٩﴾

---

673. Merciful toward each other; to their brethren in faith. Formidable to the enemies of God they were meekness itself to His friends.

674. 'These men were the true moral heirs of the Prophet, the faithful trustees of all that Muhammad taught unto the men of God. They had really changed for the better from every point of view, and later on as statesmen and generals, in the most difficult moments of the war of conquest they gave magnificent and undeniable proof that the ideas and the doctrines of Muhammad had been cast on fruitful soil, and had produced a body of men of the very highest worth. They were the depositories of the sacred test of the Quran, which they alone knew by heart; they were the jealous guardians of the memory of every word and bidding of the Prophet, the trustees of the moral heritage of Muhammad'. (Caetani, quoted in Arnold's *Preaching of Islam*, pp. 41 – 2).

675. The seed in the parable is, of course, the religion of Islam, the growth of which, both in strength and numbers, simply amazed its onlookers; and by sowers are meant the Prophet and his Companions

Sūrah 49

al-Ḥujurāt

(Madinan, 2 Sections, 18 Verses)

*In the name of Allah, the
Compassionate, the Merciful.*

Section 1

1. O you who believe! Do not be
forward in the presence of Allah
and His Messenger, and fear
Allah. Verily Allah is the Hearing,
the Knowing.

2. O you who believe! Do not
raise your voice above the voice
of the Prophet, nor shout loud to
him in discourse, as you do to one
another, lest your works may be
rendered fruitless, while you
perceive not.

3. Verily those who lower their
voices in the presence of the
Messenger of Allah! Those are
they whose hearts Allah has
disposed towards piety; theirs will
be forgiveness and splendid
reward.

4. Verily these who call aloud to
you from without the inner
apartments, most of them are
foolish.

5. And had they waited till you
had come out unto them, it had
surely been better for them; and
Allah is the Forgiving, the Merciful.

6. O you who believe! If a mischief-maker comes to you with a report, then make a strict inquiry, lest you may hurt a people unknowingly and thereafter repent of what you have done.

يَـٰٓأَيُّهَا ٱلَّذِينَ ءَامَنُوٓاْ إِن جَآءَكُمۡ فَاسِقُۢ بِنَبَإٍ فَتَبَيَّنُوٓاْ أَن تُصِيبُواْ قَوۡمَۢا بِجَهَٰلَةٖ فَتُصۡبِحُواْ عَلَىٰ مَا فَعَلۡتُمۡ نَٰدِمِينَ ٦

7. And know that verily among you there is the Messenger of Allah. If he were to obey you, you would surely be in trouble, but Allah has endeared faith to you and has bedecked it in your hearts and has made infidelity and wickedness and disobedience abhorrent to you. These! They are the men of rectitude,

وَٱعۡلَمُوٓاْ أَنَّ فِيكُمۡ رَسُولَ ٱللَّهِۚ لَوۡ يُطِيعُكُمۡ فِي كَثِيرٖ مِّنَ ٱلۡأَمۡرِ لَعَنِتُّمۡ وَلَٰكِنَّ ٱللَّهَ حَبَّبَ إِلَيۡكُمُ ٱلۡإِيمَٰنَ وَزَيَّنَهُۥ فِي قُلُوبِكُمۡ وَكَرَّهَ إِلَيۡكُمُ ٱلۡكُفۡرَ وَٱلۡفُسُوقَ وَٱلۡعِصۡيَانَۚ أُوْلَـٰٓئِكَ هُمُ ٱلرَّٰشِدُونَ ٧

8. Through grace from Allah and His favour, and Allah is the Knowing, the Wise.

فَضۡلٗا مِّنَ ٱللَّهِ وَنِعۡمَةٗۚ وَٱللَّهُ عَلِيمٌ حَكِيمٌ ٨

9. And if two parties of the believers fall to mutual fighting, then affect reconciliation between them. But if one of them rebels against the other, then fight the party which rebels till it reverts to the commandment of Allah. Then if it reverts, affect reconciliation between them justly and be equitable, Allah loves the equitable.

وَإِن طَآئِفَتَانِ مِنَ ٱلۡمُؤۡمِنِينَ ٱقۡتَتَلُواْ فَأَصۡلِحُواْ بَيۡنَهُمَاۖ فَإِنۢ بَغَتۡ إِحۡدَىٰهُمَا عَلَى ٱلۡأُخۡرَىٰ فَقَٰتِلُواْ ٱلَّتِي تَبۡغِي حَتَّىٰ تَفِيٓءَ إِلَىٰٓ أَمۡرِ ٱللَّهِۚ فَإِن فَآءَتۡ فَأَصۡلِحُواْ بَيۡنَهُمَا بِٱلۡعَدۡلِ وَأَقۡسِطُوٓاْۖ إِنَّ ٱللَّهَ يُحِبُّ ٱلۡمُقۡسِطِينَ ٩

10. The believers are but brethren;[676] so affect reconciliation between your brethren[677] and fear Allah that haply mercy may be shown to you.[678]

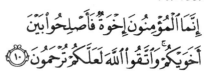

إِنَّمَا الْمُؤْمِنُوْنَ إِخْوَةٌ فَأَصْلِحُوْا بَيْنَ أَخَوَيْكُمْ وَاتَّقُوا اللّٰهَ لَعَلَّكُمْ تُرْحَمُوْنَ ۝

676. Brethren, however different they may be from one another in other respects. This is neither nationalization nor Arabicization but humanization in the true sense of the word. It means that the community of believers as a bond of union is superior to, and more fundamental than, any other bond at all, merging all colours, ranks and races in the consciousness of a common brotherhood. 'This was the first attempt in the history of Arabia at a social orgnization with religion, rather than blood, as its basis. Thus by one stroke the most vital bond of Arab relationship, that of tribal kinship, was replaced by a new bond, that of faith; a sort of *Pan-Islamica* was instituted for Arabia'. (Hitti, *History of the Arabs,* pp. 120–1). 'It must be admitted that Mohammedans have, from whatever causes, acted up to their creed in this respect more fully than have Christians' (Bosworth Smith, *Mohammed and Mohammedanism,* p. 246). 'A Muslim is Muslim first and a Turk, an Afghan, or an Arab afterwards, and this is no mere formula or figure of speech, Instead, that vast assemblage of peoples and of tongues to whom the Prophet of Arabia, by teaching them to worship the one true God, has given a bond of union stronger than any tie of blood or nation.' (Ibid., p. 306). 'A religious theory that is very strikingly realised in Muhammadan society and seldom fails to express itself in acts of kindness towards the new convert. Whatever be his race, colour or antecedents he is received into the brotherhood of believers and takes his place as an equal among equals.' (Arnold, *Preaching of Islam,* p. 416).

677. The Prophet said: 'None of you has faith until he desires for his brother what he desires for himself' (Bukhari, 2 : 6). 'To abuse a Muslim is an evil deed, and to fight him, an act of unbelief'. (Ibid., 2 : 36)

678. 'The equality in Islam of all believers and the common brotherhood, of all Muslims, which suffered no distinctions between Arab and non-Arab, between free and slave, to exist among the faithful, was an idea that ran directly counter to the proud clan-feeling of the Arab, who grounded his claims to personal consideration on the fame of his ancestors, and in the strength of the same carried on the endless blood-feuds in which his soul delighted'. (Arnold, *Preaching of Islam,* pp. 42–3). 'In India Mohammedans make converts by hundreds from among the Hindus, while Christians with difficulty make ten, and this partly at least because they receive their converts on terms of entire social equality, while Europeans, in spite of all the efforts of missionaries to the contrary, seem either unwilling or unable to treat their converts as other than inferiors.' (Bosworth Smith, *Mohammed and Mohammedanism,* p. 247). Canon Isaac Taylor uttered the following words at a meeting of the Church Congress, England: 'Islam preaches a practical brotherhood, the social equality of all Muslims. The convert is admitted at once to an exclusive social caste; he becomes a member of a vast confraternity of 105,000,000. A Christian convert is not regarded as a social equal, but the Muslims brotherhood is a reality.'

Section 2

11. O you who believe! Let not one group scoff at another group; perchance they may be better than they are, nor let some women scoff at other women, perchance the latter may be better than they are. And do not traduce one another, nor revile one another by odious appellations; ill is the name of sin after belief. And whosoever will not repent, then those are the wicked.

يَـٰٓأَيُّهَا ٱلَّذِينَ ءَامَنُوا۟ لَا يَسْخَرْ قَوْمٌ مِّن قَوْمٍ عَسَىٰٓ أَن يَكُونُوا۟ خَيْرًا مِّنْهُمْ وَلَا نِسَآءٌ مِّن نِّسَآءٍ عَسَىٰٓ أَن يَكُنَّ خَيْرًا مِّنْهُنَّ وَلَا تَلْمِزُوٓا۟ أَنفُسَكُمْ وَلَا تَنَابَزُوا۟ بِٱلْأَلْقَـٰبِ بِئْسَ ٱلِٱسْمُ ٱلْفُسُوقُ بَعْدَ ٱلْإِيمَـٰنِ وَمَن لَّمْ يَتُبْ فَأُو۟لَـٰٓئِكَ هُمُ ٱلظَّـٰلِمُونَ ۝

12. O you who believe! Avoid much suspicion; indeed some suspicion is a sin. And spy not, nor backbite one another.[679] Would any of you relish to eat the flesh of his dead brother? You detest that. And fear Allah; verily Allah is the Relenting, the Merciful.

يَـٰٓأَيُّهَا ٱلَّذِينَ ءَامَنُوا۟ ٱجْتَنِبُوا۟ كَثِيرًا مِّنَ ٱلظَّنِّ إِنَّ بَعْضَ ٱلظَّنِّ إِثْمٌ وَلَا تَجَسَّسُوا۟ وَلَا يَغْتَب بَّعْضُكُم بَعْضًا أَيُحِبُّ أَحَدُكُمْ أَن يَأْكُلَ لَحْمَ أَخِيهِ مَيْتًا فَكَرِهْتُمُوهُ وَٱتَّقُوا۟ ٱللَّهَ إِنَّ ٱللَّهَ تَوَّابٌ رَّحِيمٌ ۝

13. Mankind! Verily We! We have created you[680] of a male[681]

يَـٰٓأَيُّهَا ٱلنَّاسُ إِنَّا خَلَقْنَـٰكُم مِّن ذَكَرٍ وَأُنثَىٰ

---

679. This even though the imputations made may be true. The essence of which is to speak of a person in such a way as would grieve him. When it is false, it is termed slander. It is this great social vice, the habit of slandering an absent person that has caused untold misery in the world and has poisoned the atmosphere of almost every household.

680. Created all of you; the entirety of mankind, which means, in plain speech, all races of men: European, Asiatic and African, white, brown and black are equally His creations. He has made them vary in colour, language and mode of life, and has placed them in different lands, but He takes thought for all alike.

681. None of us are begotten by different ancestors. Thus the Holy Book of Islam directly preaches the specific unity of mankind, and favours what in the language of anthropology is called monogenism, man being one genus with one species, as

apposed to the rival theory of 'polygenism' which affirms different groups as originating independently in different geographical areas as separate units. 'Although the existing races of man differ in many respects, yet if their whole structure be taken into consideration they are found to resemble each other closely in a multitude of points. Now when naturalists observe a close agreement in numerous small details of habits, tastes, and dispositions between two or more domestic races or between nearly-allied natural forms, they use this fact as an argument that they are descended from a common progenitor who has thus endowed; and consequently that all should be classed under the same species. The same argument may be applied with much force to the races of man' (Darwin, *Descent of Man*, pp. 276–8).

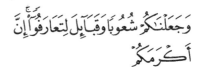

and a female,[682] and We have made you nations and tribes[683] that you might know one another.[684] Verily the noble of you

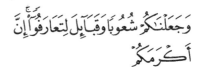

---

682. Referring to the Christian habit of attributing the inferior status of woman to the religion of Islam or to the Prophet a modern Christian writer says: 'Mohammad is supposed to have inspired her docile acquiescence to faith, to have denied her self-expression in competition with men, and to have closed to her all doors which made spiritual and mental development possible. But this idea is contrary to fact. On the advent of Mohammad the position of woman was not enviable. He found her to be little more than a chattel – a condition which was due in large part to the teaching of the Hebrew rabbis. The Hebrew religion, which was practised throughout the area into which Mohammad carried his teaching, had placed a decided stamp of inferiority upon her. She was inherited like any piece of furniture, and the heir could do with her as he pleased. She had no protection, no recourse to law, no right of inheritance. That to the Prophet was a state of affairs no longer to be tolerated. He believed woman to be the "equal sister of man" and determined to strengthen the Moslem State by forcing a recognition of her equality. He limited polygamy and abolished infanticide. He instituted the marriage contract, inheritance right, and the privilege of divorce for woman, while he discouraged divorce at the behest of one or the other where differences could reasonably be dissolved. He established the principle of dowry and provided for the inviolable maintenance of part of it for the woman's protection. He safeguarded her further by decreeing religious favour to those who would assist in the support of widows and orphans. He recognized woman's earlier as well as contemporary contribution to civilization, and urged her highest development spiritually and morally as an asset to the State. This was indeed a signal advance in the thinking of that period, and a transformation in social custom which would be remarkable in any age.' (Flory, *The Moslem World*, (January 1940), pp. 16–17).

683. This strikes at the root of the caste system which maintains that mankind are not born equal, but in different stages of spiritual development. 'The orthodox Hindu holds that his gods have ordained a social state at whose top everlasting sits the Brahmin, endowed with all privilege; below the Brahmin descend by steps some three to four thousand inferior castes and sub-castes, each inescapably fettered as to every concern in life, within its own compartment; whilst beneath them all wallow helpless and hopeless millions of outcasts – humanly born so low that they possess no rights of any sort and their very shadow defiles whatever it falls upon.' In the words of a modern non-Muslim philosopher, '(In Islam) the colour of the skin is of no consequence; the quality of the heart is of every consequence. The racial or national label matters nothing; the character matters everything.'

The verse rendered here equally demolishes the myth of a Master Race, and completely supports the scientific finding that racial discrimination has no foundation in the biological fact.

with Allah is the most pious of you.[685] Verily Allah is the Knowing, the Wise.

عِندَ ٱللَّهِ أَنقَىٰكُمۡ إِنَّ ٱللَّهَ عَلِيمٌ خَبِيرٌ ۝

14. The desert Arabs say, 'we have believed'. Say: 'You have not believed, rather say, "we have submitted to Islam" while faith has not yet entered your hearts.[686] And if you obey Allah and His Messenger, He shall not diminish any of your works. Verily Allah is the Forgiving, the Merciful.'

قَالَتِ ٱلۡأَعۡرَابُ ءَامَنَّا قُل لَّمۡ تُؤۡمِنُوا۟ وَلَٰكِن قُولُوٓا۟ أَسۡلَمۡنَا وَلَمَّا يَدۡخُلِ ٱلۡإِيمَٰنُ فِى قُلُوبِكُمۡ وَإِن تُطِيعُوا۟ ٱللَّهَ وَرَسُولَهُۥ لَا يَلِتۡكُم مِّنۡ أَعۡمَٰلِكُمۡ شَيۡئًا إِنَّ ٱللَّهَ غَفُورٌ رَّحِيمٌ ۝

---

684. So the doctrine of a biologically chosen people, as a race apart, designed by nature to rule the world is not only positively mischievous but also mythical. And this puts an end to the vast pseudo-science of racial biology seeking to justify political ambitions, economic ends and class prejudices.

685. Most pious in the conduct of his daily affairs, and not the high-born of you. Here indeed is a re-classification of humanity – a promulgation of a new order of nobility – the division of mankind not between princes and peasants, nor between touchables and untouchables, but between the more moral and the less moral. 'It is this absence of class prejudices which constitutes the real strength of Islam in India and enables it to win so many converts from Hinduism.' (Arnold, *Preaching of Islam*, p. 291). 'The equality of all men before God was a principle which Mohammad everywhere maintained, and which, taking, as it did, all caste feeling from slavery, took away also its chief sting' (Bosworth Smith, *Mohammed and Mohammedanism*, p. 246). 'No considerations of birth, or race, or colour, or money, have prevented a man rising to the post for which it had been recognised that he was best fitted. Zaid, the Prophet's freedman led his armies in war. A dynasty of Circassian slaves ruled Egypt for a century before its conquest by the Ottoman Turks, and it is said that Christians from the Caucasus were glad to be carried off as slaves to Egypt because each one felt that he might rise to be sultan' (Ibid., p. 250).

686. Mere conformity with, and obedience to, certain formal rules is not Faith. It is only when sincerity is joined to it, that a man becomes a true believer.

15. The believers are those only who have faith in Allah and His Messenger, and have not doubted thereafter, and have striven hard with their riches and their lives in the cause of Allah. Those; they are the truthful.

إِنَّمَا ٱلۡمُؤۡمِنُونَ ٱلَّذِينَ ءَامَنُواْ بِٱللَّهِ وَرَسُولِهِۦ ثُمَّ لَمۡ يَرۡتَابُواْ وَجَٰهَدُواْ بِأَمۡوَٰلِهِمۡ وَأَنفُسِهِمۡ فِى سَبِيلِ ٱللَّهِ أُوْلَٰٓئِكَ هُمُ ٱلصَّٰدِقُونَ ﴿١٥﴾

16. Say: 'What! Will you instruct Allah about your religion? Whereas Allah knows whatsoever is in the heavens and whatsoever is in the earth, and Allah is Aware of everything.'

قُلۡ أَتُعَلِّمُونَ ٱللَّهَ بِدِينِكُمۡ وَٱللَّهُ يَعۡلَمُ مَا فِى ٱلسَّمَٰوَٰتِ وَمَا فِى ٱلۡأَرۡضِ وَٱللَّهُ بِكُلِّ شَىۡءٍ عَلِيمٌ ﴿١٦﴾

17. They regard it as a favour to you that they have embraced Islam. Say: 'Deem not your surrender a favour to me'; nay! Allah has conferred a favour upon you as He has guided you to the faith, if you are sincere.

يَمُنُّونَ عَلَيۡكَ أَنۡ أَسۡلَمُواْ قُل لَّا تَمُنُّواْ عَلَىَّ إِسۡلَٰمَكُم بَلِ ٱللَّهُ يَمُنُّ عَلَيۡكُمۡ أَنۡ هَدَىٰكُمۡ لِلۡإِيمَٰنِ إِن كُنتُمۡ صَٰدِقِينَ ﴿١٧﴾

18. Allah knows the hidden in the heavens and the earth, and Allah is the Beholder of what you do.

إِنَّ ٱللَّهَ يَعۡلَمُ غَيۡبَ ٱلسَّمَٰوَٰتِ وَٱلۡأَرۡضِ وَٱللَّهُ بَصِيرٌۢ بِمَا تَعۡمَلُونَ ﴿١٨﴾

Sūrah 50

Qāf

(Makkan, 3 Sections, 45 Verses)

*In the name of Allah, the
Compassionate, the Merciful.*

Section 1

1. *Qāf.* By the glorious Qur'ān,
We have sent you as a warner.

2. Aye! They marvel that a
warner has come to them from
among themselves, and so the
infidels say: 'This is a thing
wonderful;

3. Shall we be brought back
when we are dead and have
become dust? That is a return
remote!'

4. Surely We know what the
earth consumes of them, and with
Us is a Book preserved.

5. Aye! They denied the Truth
when it came to them; so they are
confused in the matter.

6. Have they not looked up to
the sky above them; how We
have constructed it, and adorned
it and that there is no rift therein?

7. And the earth! We have
spread it forth, and have cast
upon it firm mountains, and have
caused to grow in it every manner
of beautiful plant.

8. An insight and admonition for every penitent bondsman.

تَبْصِرَةً وَذِكْرَىٰ لِكُلِّ عَبْدٍ مُّنِيبٍ ۝

9. And We have sent down water from the heaven and blessed with it. We have caused the gardens to grow, and the grain reaped,

وَنَزَّلْنَا مِنَ ٱلسَّمَآءِ مَآءً مُّبَٰرَكًا فَأَنۢبَتْنَا بِهِۦ جَنَّٰتٍ وَحَبَّ ٱلْحَصِيدِ ۝

10. And tall date-palms laden with ranged clusters.

وَٱلنَّخْلَ بَاسِقَٰتٍ لَّهَا طَلْعٌ نَّضِيدٌ ۝

11. As a provision for Our bondsman; and with it We made the dead land alive. Such will be the coming forth.

رِّزْقًا لِّلْعِبَادِ وَأَحْيَيْنَا بِهِۦ بَلْدَةً مَّيْتًا كَذَٰلِكَ ٱلْخُرُوجُ ۝

12. Denied before them the people of Noah and the dwellers of Rass and the Thamūd,

كَذَّبَتْ قَبْلَهُمْ قَوْمُ نُوحٍ وَأَصْحَٰبُ ٱلرَّسِّ وَثَمُودُ ۝

13. And the 'Ād, and Pharoah and the brethren of Lot,

وَعَادٌ وَفِرْعَوْنُ وَإِخْوَٰنُ لُوطٍ ۝

14. And the dwellers of the wood, and the people of Tubba'. Each one belied the Messengers, and so My Judgement was fulfilled.

وَأَصْحَٰبُ ٱلْأَيْكَةِ وَقَوْمُ تُبَّعٍ كُلٌّ كَذَّبَ ٱلرُّسُلَ فَحَقَّ وَعِيدِ ۝

15. Are We then wearied with the first creation? Aye! They are in doubt regarding a new creation.

أَفَعَيِينَا بِٱلْخَلْقِ ٱلْأَوَّلِ بَلْ هُمْ فِى لَبْسٍ مِّنْ خَلْقٍ جَدِيدٍ ۝

Section 2

16. Assuredly We have created man, and We know his soul whispers within him, We are nearer to him than his jugular vein.[687]

وَلَقَدْ خَلَقْنَا ٱلْإِنسَٰنَ وَنَعْلَمُ مَا تُوَسْوِسُ بِهِۦ نَفْسُهُۥ وَنَحْنُ أَقْرَبُ إِلَيْهِ مِنْ حَبْلِ ٱلْوَرِيدِ ۝

---

687. Allah is even more minutely conscious of his innermost feelings than is his own self. That is the exact relationship, in Islam, between God and man. Of course there is no identity between the two; we remain ourselves, and He the great Other. Yet His communion with us is of an even more intimate nature than is that of ourselves with ourselves. The verse also does away entirely with the idea of God being remote and unapproachable, and stresses His all-pervading character and His intimacy with all His creatures.

17. Behold! When the two receivers receive one on the right hand and the other, on the left, a sitter.

إِذْ يَتَلَقَّى الْمُتَلَقِّيَانِ عَنِ الْيَمِينِ وَعَنِ الشِّمَالِ قَعِيدٌ ۝

18. Not a word he utters but there is a watcher ready.[688]

مَّا يَلْفِظُ مِن قَوْلٍ إِلَّا لَدَيْهِ رَقِيبٌ عَتِيدٌ ۝

19. And the stupor of death will come in truth, this is what you have been avoiding.

وَجَآءَتْ سَكْرَةُ الْمَوْتِ بِالْحَقِّ ذَٰلِكَ مَا كُنتَ مِنْهُ تَحِيدُ ۝

20. And the trumpet will be blown; this is the Day of Threat.

وَنُفِخَ فِي الصُّورِ ذَٰلِكَ يَوْمُ الْوَعِيدِ ۝

21. And there shall come every soul, with whom will be a driver and a witness.

وَجَآءَتْ كُلُّ نَفْسٍ مَّعَهَا سَآئِقٌ وَشَهِيدٌ ۝

22. Assuredly you have been heedless thereof; now we have lifted off from you your veil, so your sight today is piercing.

لَّقَدْ كُنتَ فِي غَفْلَةٍ مِّنْ هَٰذَا فَكَشَفْنَا عَنكَ غِطَآءَكَ فَبَصَرُكَ الْيَوْمَ حَدِيدٌ ۝

23. And his companion will say: 'This is what with me is ready.'

وَقَالَ قَرِينُهُ هَٰذَا مَا لَدَيَّ عَتِيدٌ ۝

24. Cast you both into Hell every person, rebellious, contumacious,

أَلْقِيَا فِي جَهَنَّمَ كُلَّ كَفَّارٍ عَنِيدٍ ۝

25. Hinderer of good, trespasser, doubter;

مَّنَّاعٍ لِّلْخَيْرِ مُعْتَدٍ مُّرِيبٍ ۝

26. Who set up with Allah another god, so cast him in the severe torment.

الَّذِي جَعَلَ مَعَ اللَّهِ إِلَٰهًا ءَاخَرَ فَأَلْقِيَاهُ فِي الْعَذَابِ الشَّدِيدِ ۝

---

688. A watcher ready to note it. Every little word uttered by the human mouth is noted by the recording angels. The angelic records are full and complete.

27. His Companion will say: 'Lord! I did not cause him to transgress, he was himself in error far-off.'

قَالَ قَرِينُهُۥ رَبَّنَا مَآ أَطْغَيْتُهُۥ وَلَٰكِن كَانَ فِي ضَلَٰلٍ بَعِيدٍ ﴿٢٧﴾

28. Allah will say: 'Do not wrangle in My presence, and I had already proffered you the warning.

قَالَ لَا تَخْتَصِمُوا لَدَيَّ وَقَدْ قَدَّمْتُ إِلَيْكُم بِالْوَعِيدِ ﴿٢٨﴾

29. The Word shall not be changed in My presence, nor am I an oppressor at all to My bondsmen.'

مَا يُبَدَّلُ الْقَوْلُ لَدَيَّ وَمَآ أَنَا۠ بِظَلَّٰمٍ لِّلْعَبِيدِ ﴿٢٩﴾

Section 3

30. Mention you the Day when We shall say to Hell: 'Are you filled?', and it will say: 'Is there yet any addition?'

يَوْمَ نَقُولُ لِجَهَنَّمَ هَلِ امْتَلَأْتِ وَتَقُولُ هَلْ مِن مَّزِيدٍ ﴿٣٠﴾

31. And to the godly the Garden will be brought near, not far-off!

وَأُزْلِفَتِ الْجَنَّةُ لِلْمُتَّقِينَ غَيْرَ بَعِيدٍ ﴿٣١﴾

32. This is what you were promised: for every oft-returning heedful one,

هَٰذَا مَا تُوعَدُونَ لِكُلِّ أَوَّابٍ حَفِيظٍ ﴿٣٢﴾

33. Who fears the Compassionate, in the Unseen and comes to Him with a penitent heart;

مَّنْ خَشِيَ الرَّحْمَٰنَ بِالْغَيْبِ وَجَآءَ بِقَلْبٍ مُّنِيبٍ ﴿٣٣﴾

34. Enter it in peace. This is the Day of Abidance.

ادْخُلُوهَا بِسَلَٰمٍ ذَٰلِكَ يَوْمُ الْخُلُودِ ﴿٣٤﴾

35. Theirs therein will be whatever they wish and with Us will be yet more.

لَهُم مَّا يَشَآءُونَ فِيهَا وَلَدَيْنَا مَزِيدٌ ﴿٣٥﴾

36. And how many a generation We destroyed before them who were mightier in power than they, and they traversed the cities! And no place of refuge could they find.

وَكَمْ أَهْلَكْنَا قَبْلَهُم مِّن قَرْنٍ هُمْ أَشَدُّ مِنْهُم بَطْشًا فَنَقَّبُوا۟ فِى ٱلْبِلَٰدِ هَلْ مِن مَّحِيصٍ ﴿٣٦﴾

37. Verily herein is an admonition to him who has a heart, or gives ear while he is heedful.

إِنَّ فِى ذَٰلِكَ لَذِكْرَىٰ لِمَن كَانَ لَهُۥ قَلْبٌ أَوْ أَلْقَى ٱلسَّمْعَ وَهُوَ شَهِيدٌ ﴿٣٧﴾

38. And assuredly We created the heavens and the earth and what is in between in six days, and nothing touched Us of weariness.

وَلَقَدْ خَلَقْنَا ٱلسَّمَٰوَٰتِ وَٱلْأَرْضَ وَمَا بَيْنَهُمَا فِى سِتَّةِ أَيَّامٍ وَمَا مَسَّنَا مِن لُّغُوبٍ ﴿٣٨﴾

39. So bear you patiently with what they say, and hallow the praise of your Lord before the rising of the sun and before its setting.

فَٱصْبِرْ عَلَىٰ مَا يَقُولُونَ وَسَبِّحْ بِحَمْدِ رَبِّكَ قَبْلَ طُلُوعِ ٱلشَّمْسِ وَقَبْلَ ٱلْغُرُوبِ ﴿٣٩﴾

40. And hallow Him in the night-time, and also after the prescribed prostration.[689]

وَمِنَ ٱلَّيْلِ فَسَبِّحْهُ وَأَدْبَٰرَ ٱلسُّجُودِ ﴿٤٠﴾

41. And hearken you: the Day when the caller will call from a place quite near –

وَٱسْتَمِعْ يَوْمَ يُنَادِ ٱلْمُنَادِ مِن مَّكَانٍ قَرِيبٍ ﴿٤١﴾

42. The Day, when they will surely hear the shout that is the Day of Coming Forth.

يَوْمَ يَسْمَعُونَ ٱلصَّيْحَةَ بِٱلْحَقِّ ذَٰلِكَ يَوْمُ ٱلْخُرُوجِ ﴿٤٢﴾

43. Verily We! It is We Who give life and cause death, and to Us is the journeying.

إِنَّا نَحْنُ نُحْىِۦ وَنُمِيتُ وَإِلَيْنَا ٱلْمَصِيرُ ﴿٤٣﴾

---

689. The reference is to the supererogatory prayer after the prescribed ones, and to the exercise of contemplation and remembrance of God.

937 سُوْرَةُ ق

44. That shall be the Day when the earth shall be cleft from off them, as they hasten forth. That shall be a gathering unto Us easy.

يَوْمَ تَشَقَّقُ الْأَرْضُ عَنْهُمْ سِرَاعًا ذَلِكَ حَشْرٌ عَلَيْنَا يَسِيرٌ ﴿٤٤﴾

45. We are the best Knower of what they say; and you are not a tyrant over them. So admonish you by the Qur'ān him who fears My warning.[690]

نَحْنُ أَعْلَمُ بِمَا يَقُولُونَ وَمَا أَنتَ عَلَيْهِم بِجَبَّارٍ فَذَكِّرْ بِالْقُرْآنِ مَن يَخَافُ وَعِيدِ ﴿٤٥﴾

690. They alone receive admonition from the Qur'ān who have the will to receive it.

Sūrah 51

al-Dhāriyāt

(Makkan, 3 Sections, 60 Verses)

In the name of Allah, the Compassionate, the Merciful.

Section 1

1. By the dispersing winds that disperse,

2. And the clouds bearing a load,

3. And the ships that glide with ease,

4. And the envoys who distribute the affair,

5. What you are threatened with is surely true.

6. And the Requital is sure to happen.

7. By the sky full of paths,

8. Verily you are in divided opinion.

9. Turned aside therefrom, is he who is turned.

10. Perish the conjecturers,

11. Who are in heedlessness, neglectful.

12. They ask: 'When is the Day of Requital coming?'

وَٱلذَّٰرِيَٰتِ ذَرْوًا ۝١

فَٱلْحَٰمِلَٰتِ وِقْرًا ۝٢

فَٱلْجَٰرِيَٰتِ يُسْرًا ۝٣

فَٱلْمُقَسِّمَٰتِ أَمْرًا ۝٤

إِنَّمَا تُوعَدُونَ لَصَادِقٌ ۝٥

وَإِنَّ ٱلدِّينَ لَوَٰقِعٌ ۝٦

وَٱلسَّمَآءِ ذَاتِ ٱلْحُبُكِ ۝٧

إِنَّكُمْ لَفِى قَوْلٍ مُّخْتَلِفٍ ۝٨

يُؤْفَكُ عَنْهُ مَنْ أُفِكَ ۝٩

قُتِلَ ٱلْخَرَّٰصُونَ ۝١٠

ٱلَّذِينَ هُمْ فِى غَمْرَةٍ سَاهُونَ ۝١١

يَسْـَٔلُونَ أَيَّانَ يَوْمُ ٱلدِّينِ ۝١٢

13. It will be the Day whereon they will be burned in the Fire.

يَوْمَ هُمْ عَلَى النَّارِ يُفْتَنُوْنَ ﴿١٣﴾

14. Taste your burning. This is what you sought to be hastened.

ذُوْقُوْا فِتْنَتَكُمْ هٰذَا الَّذِىْ كُنْتُمْ بِهٖ تَسْتَعْجِلُوْنَ ﴿١٤﴾

15. Verily the God-fearing will be in the Gardens and water-springs,

إِنَّ الْمُتَّقِيْنَ فِىْ جَنّٰتٍ وَّعُيُوْنٍ ﴿١٥﴾

16. Taking whatsoever their Lord will vouchsafe to them. Verily they have been well-doers before that.

ءَاخِذِيْنَ مَآ اٰتٰهُمْ رَبُّهُمْ إِنَّهُمْ كَانُوْا قَبْلَ ذٰلِكَ مُحْسِنِيْنَ ﴿١٦﴾

17. Little of the night they were wont to slumber.

كَانُوْا قَلِيْلًا مِّنَ الَّيْلِ مَا يَهْجَعُوْنَ ﴿١٧﴾

18. And in the dawns they used to pray for forgiveness.

وَبِالْأَسْحَارِهُمْ يَسْتَغْفِرُوْنَ ﴿١٨﴾

19. And in their substance there was the right of the beggar and non-beggar.

وَفِىْ أَمْوَالِهِمْ حَقٌّ لِّلسَّآئِلِ وَالْمَحْرُوْمِ ﴿١٩﴾

20. And on the earth there are signs for those who would be convinced,

وَفِى الْأَرْضِ اٰيٰتٌ لِّلْمُوْقِنِيْنَ ﴿٢٠﴾

21. And also in your own selves. Behold you not?

وَفِىْ أَنْفُسِكُمْ أَفَلَا تُبْصِرُوْنَ ﴿٢١﴾

22. And in the heaven is your provision and what you are promised.

وَفِى السَّمَآءِ رِزْقُكُمْ وَمَا تُوْعَدُوْنَ ﴿٢٢﴾

23. By the Lord of the heaven and the earth is certain, even as it is a fact that you are speaking.

فَوَرَبِّ السَّمَآءِ وَالْأَرْضِ إِنَّهُ لَحَقٌّ مِّثْلَ مَا أَنَّكُمْ تَنْطِقُوْنَ ﴿٢٣﴾

Section 2

24. Has there come to you the story of Abraham's honoured guests?

هَلْ أَتَىٰكَ حَدِيثُ ضَيْفِ إِبْرَٰهِيمَ الْمُكْرَمِينَ ۝

25. When they went in to him and said: 'Peace!' He said: 'Peace!' They were a people unknown.

إِذْ دَخَلُوا عَلَيْهِ فَقَالُوا سَلَـٰمًا قَالَ سَلَـٰمٌ قَوْمٌ مُّنكَرُونَ ۝

26. Then he turned away into his household and brought a calf fatted.

فَرَاغَ إِلَىٰ أَهْلِهِ فَجَآءَ بِعِجْلٍ سَمِينٍ ۝

27. And he set it before them and said: 'Why do you not eat?'

فَقَرَّبَهُۥ إِلَيْهِمْ قَالَ أَلَا تَأْكُلُونَ ۝

28. Then he conceived a fear of them. They said: 'Have no fear.' And they gave him the glad tidings of a knowing son.

فَأَوْجَسَ مِنْهُمْ خِيفَةً قَالُوا لَا تَخَفْ وَبَشَّرُوهُ بِغُلَـٰمٍ عَلِيمٍ ۝

29. Then his wife drew near, vociferating and smote her face and said: 'An old barren woman?'

فَأَقْبَلَتِ ٱمْرَأَتُهُۥ فِى صَرَّةٍ فَصَكَّتْ وَجْهَهَا وَقَالَتْ عَجُوزٌ عَقِيمٌ ۝

30. They said: 'Even so, says your Lord. Verily He! He is the Wise, the Knower.'

قَالُوا كَذَٰلِكِ قَالَ رَبُّكِ إِنَّهُۥ هُوَ ٱلْحَكِيمُ ٱلْعَلِيمُ ۝

31. And he said: 'What is your errand, O envoys?'

قَالَ فَمَا خَطْبُكُمْ أَيُّهَا ٱلْمُرْسَلُونَ ۝

32. They said: 'We are sent to a guilty people,

قَالُوا إِنَّا أُرْسِلْنَا إِلَىٰ قَوْمٍ مُّجْرِمِينَ ۝

33. That we may send down upon them stones of baked clay,

لِنُرْسِلَ عَلَيْهِمْ حِجَارَةً مِّن طِينٍ ۝

34. Marked from before your Lord for the extravagant.'

مُّسَوَّمَةً عِندَ رَبِّكَ لِلْمُسْرِفِينَ ۝

35. Thus We brought forth from herein the believers.

فَأَخْرَجْنَا مَن كَانَ فِيهَا مِنَ ٱلْمُؤْمِنِينَ ﴿٣٥﴾

36. But We found not there but one household of Muslims.

فَمَا وَجَدْنَا فِيهَا غَيْرَ بَيْتٍ مِّنَ ٱلْمُسْلِمِينَ ﴿٣٦﴾

37. And We left therein a sign for those who fear an awful chastisement.

وَتَرَكْنَا فِيهَآ ءَايَةً لِّلَّذِينَ يَخَافُونَ ٱلْعَذَابَ ٱلْأَلِيمَ ﴿٣٧﴾

38. And in Moses also was a lesson, when We sent him to Pharaoh with manifest authority.

وَفِي مُوسَىٰٓ إِذْ أَرْسَلْنَٰهُ إِلَىٰ فِرْعَوْنَ بِسُلْطَٰنٍ مُّبِينٍ ﴿٣٨﴾

39. He turned away with his court, and said: 'A magician or a mad man!'

فَتَوَلَّىٰ بِرُكْنِهِۦ وَقَالَ سَٰحِرٌ أَوْ مَجْنُونٌ ﴿٣٩﴾

40. Then we seized him and flung him and his hosts into the sea and he was reproachable.[691]

فَأَخَذْنَٰهُ وَجُنُودَهُۥ فَنَبَذْنَٰهُمْ فِي ٱلْيَمِّ وَهُوَ مُلِيمٌ ﴿٤٠﴾

41. And in the ʿĀd also was a lesson when We let loose on them a blighting wind.

وَفِي عَادٍ إِذْ أَرْسَلْنَا عَلَيْهِمُ ٱلرِّيحَ ٱلْعَقِيمَ ﴿٤١﴾

42. It left nothing. It came upon but blew it into spreads.

مَا تَذَرُ مِن شَىْءٍ أَتَتْ عَلَيْهِ إِلَّا جَعَلَتْهُ كَٱلرَّمِيمِ ﴿٤٢﴾

43. And in the Thamūd also was a lesson, when it was said to them 'enjoy yourselves for a while.'

وَفِي ثَمُودَ إِذْ قِيلَ لَهُمْ تَمَتَّعُوا۟ حَتَّىٰ حِينٍ ﴿٤٣﴾

44. They disdained the command of their Lord; so the bolt laid hold of them while they looked on.

فَعَتَوْا۟ عَنْ أَمْرِ رَبِّهِمْ فَأَخَذَتْهُمُ ٱلصَّٰعِقَةُ وَهُمْ يَنظُرُونَ ﴿٤٤﴾

45. So they were neither able to stand, nor could they help themselves.

فَمَا ٱسْتَطَٰعُوا۟ مِن قِيَامٍ وَمَا كَانُوا۟ مُنتَصِرِينَ ﴿٤٥﴾

---

691. Justice was only meted out to Pharaoh after he had been given many chances to repent.

46. And the people of Noah We destroyed before; verily they were a sinful people.

Section 3

47. And the heaven! We have built it with might, and verily We are Powerful.

48. And the earth! We have stretched it forth; an excellent Spreader are We!

49. And of everything We have created pairs,[692] that haply you might remember.

50. Then flee to Allah; verily I am a manifest warner to you from Him.

51. And do not set up another god with Allah; verily I am a manifest warner to you from Him.

52. Likewise, there came not a Messenger to those before them but they said: 'A magician or a mad man!'

53. Have they handed over this to one another? Nay! They are a people contumacious.

54. So turn away you from them; for you are not blameworthy.

وَقَوْمَ نُوحٍ مِّن قَبْلُ إِنَّهُمْ كَانُوا قَوْمًا فَٰسِقِينَ ۝

وَٱلسَّمَآءَ بَنَيْنَٰهَا بِأَيْدٍ وَإِنَّا لَمُوسِعُونَ ۝

وَٱلْأَرْضَ فَرَشْنَٰهَا فَنِعْمَ ٱلْمَٰهِدُونَ ۝

وَمِن كُلِّ شَيْءٍ خَلَقْنَا زَوْجَيْنِ لَعَلَّكُمْ تَذَكَّرُونَ ۝

فَفِرُّوٓا إِلَى ٱللَّهِ إِنِّى لَكُم مِّنْهُ نَذِيرٌ مُّبِينٌ ۝

وَلَا تَجْعَلُوا مَعَ ٱللَّهِ إِلَٰهًا ءَاخَرَ إِنِّى لَكُم مِّنْهُ نَذِيرٌ مُّبِينٌ ۝

كَذَٰلِكَ مَآ أَتَى ٱلَّذِينَ مِن قَبْلِهِم مِّن رَّسُولٍ إِلَّا قَالُوا سَاحِرٌ أَوْ مَجْنُونٌ ۝

أَتَوَاصَوْا بِهِۦ بَلْ هُمْ قَوْمٌ طَاغُونَ ۝

فَتَوَلَّ عَنْهُمْ فَمَآ أَنتَ بِمَلُومٍ ۝

---

692. Such as light and darkness, subject and object, wet and dry, active and passive, male and female, the living and the non-living. This verse may also well hint at the universality of the law of sex.

55. And admonish, for admonition benefits the believers.

وَذَكِّرْ فَإِنَّ الذِّكْرَىٰ تَنفَعُ الْمُؤْمِنِينَ ۝

56. And I have not created the *jinn* and mankind but that they should worship Me,

وَمَا خَلَقْتُ الْجِنَّ وَالْإِنسَ إِلَّا لِيَعْبُدُونِ ۝

57. I seek not any provision from them, nor do I desire that they should feed Me.

مَا أُرِيدُ مِنْهُم مِّن رِّزْقٍ وَمَا أُرِيدُ أَن يُطْعِمُونِ ۝

58. Verily Allah! He is the Provider, the Owner of Power, the Firm.

إِنَّ اللَّهَ هُوَ الرَّزَّاقُ ذُو الْقُوَّةِ الْمَتِينُ ۝

59. So verily unto those who do wrong, there is a portion of their fellows; so let them not ask Me to hasten on.

فَإِنَّ لِلَّذِينَ ظَلَمُوا ذَنُوبًا مِّثْلَ ذَنُوبِ أَصْحَٰبِهِمْ فَلَا يَسْتَعْجِلُونِ ۝

60. Woe, then, to those who disbelieve when their threatened Day arrives.

فَوَيْلٌ لِّلَّذِينَ كَفَرُوا مِن يَوْمِهِمُ الَّذِي يُوعَدُونَ ۝

Sūrah 52

al-Ṭūr

(Makkan, 2 Sections, 49 Verses)

In the name of Allah, the Compassionate, the Merciful.

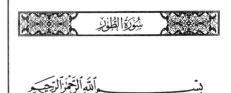

Section 1

1. By the Mount.

2. By the Book inscribed,

3. In parchment unrolled.

4. By the House frequented.

5. By the roof elevated.

6. By the sea overflowing.

7. Verily the chastisement of your Lord is sure to overtake.

8. Of it there is no averter,

9. On the Day when the heaven will shake with awful shaking.

10. And the mountains will move away with an awful movement.

11. Woe, then, it will be on that Day to the beliers,

12. Who sport themselves in wading.

13. On the Day when they will be pushed into Hell Fire with a dreadful pushing.

وَٱلطُّورِ ﴿١﴾

وَكِتَٰبٍ مَّسْطُورٍ ﴿٢﴾

فِى رَقٍّ مَّنشُورٍ ﴿٣﴾

وَٱلْبَيْتِ ٱلْمَعْمُورِ ﴿٤﴾

وَٱلسَّقْفِ ٱلْمَرْفُوعِ ﴿٥﴾

وَٱلْبَحْرِ ٱلْمَسْجُورِ ﴿٦﴾

إِنَّ عَذَابَ رَبِّكَ لَوَٰقِعٌ ﴿٧﴾

مَّا لَهُۥ مِن دَافِعٍ ﴿٨﴾

يَوْمَ تَمُورُ ٱلسَّمَآءُ مَوْرًا ﴿٩﴾

وَتَسِيرُ ٱلْجِبَالُ سَيْرًا ﴿١٠﴾

فَوَيْلٌ يَوْمَئِذٍ لِّلْمُكَذِّبِينَ ﴿١١﴾

ٱلَّذِينَ هُمْ فِى خَوْضٍ يَلْعَبُونَ ﴿١٢﴾

يَوْمَ يُدَعُّونَ إِلَىٰ نَارِ جَهَنَّمَ دَعًّا ﴿١٣﴾

14. This is the Fire you used to belie.

هَـٰذِهِ ٱلنَّارُ ٱلَّتِي كُنتُم بِهَا تُكَذِّبُونَ ﴿١٤﴾

15. Is this magic? Or are you still unable to see?

أَفَسِحْرٌ هَـٰذَآ أَمْ أَنتُمْ لَا تُبْصِرُونَ ﴿١٥﴾

16. Roast therein. Endure it or endure it not, all is equal to you. You are being requited for what you have been working.

ٱصْلَوْهَا فَٱصْبِرُوٓاْ أَوْ لَا تَصْبِرُواْ سَوَآءٌ عَلَيْكُمْ إِنَّمَا تُجْزَوْنَ مَا كُنتُمْ تَعْمَلُونَ ﴿١٦﴾

17. Verily the godly will be in the Gardens and delight,

إِنَّ ٱلْمُتَّقِينَ فِي جَنَّٰتٍ وَنَعِيمٍ ﴿١٧﴾

18. Rejoicing in what their Lord has vouchsafed to them, and their Lord will shield them from the torment of the Flame.

فَـٰكِهِينَ بِمَآ ءَاتَىٰهُمْ رَبُّهُمْ وَوَقَىٰهُمْ رَبُّهُمْ عَذَابَ ٱلْجَحِيمِ ﴿١٨﴾

19. Eat and drink with relish for what you have been working.

كُلُواْ وَٱشْرَبُواْ هَنِيٓـًٔا بِمَا كُنتُمْ تَعْمَلُونَ ﴿١٩﴾

20. Reclining on couches ranged. And We shall couple them with damsels wide-eyed.

مُتَّكِئِينَ عَلَىٰ سُرُرٍ مَّصْفُوفَةٍ وَزَوَّجْنَـٰهُم بِحُورٍ عِينٍ ﴿٢٠﴾

21. And those who believe and whose progeny follow them in faith – We shall cause their progeny to join them, and We shall not diminish any of their own work. Every man is a pledge for what he has worked.

وَٱلَّذِينَ ءَامَنُواْ وَٱتَّبَعَتْهُمْ ذُرِّيَّتُهُم بِإِيمَـٰنٍ أَلْحَقْنَا بِهِمْ ذُرِّيَّتَهُمْ وَمَآ أَلَتْنَـٰهُم مِّنْ عَمَلِهِم مِّن شَيْءٍ كُلُّ ٱمْرِئٍ بِمَا كَسَبَ رَهِينٌ ﴿٢١﴾

22. And We shall increasingly give them fruit and meat as they desire.

وَأَمْدَدْنَـٰهُم بِفَـٰكِهَةٍ وَلَحْمٍ مِّمَّا يَشْتَهُونَ ﴿٢٢﴾

23. Therein they will snatch a cup from one another; therein there will be neither vain babble nor sin.

يَتَنَـٰزَعُونَ فِيهَا كَأْسًا لَّا لَغْوٌ فِيهَا وَلَا تَأْثِيمٌ ﴿٢٣﴾

24. And there will go round on them youths appointed to attend them as if they were pearls concealed.

وَيَطُوفُ عَلَيْهِمْ غِلْمَانٌ لَّهُمْ كَأَنَّهُمْ لُؤْلُؤٌ مَّكْنُونٌ ﴿٢٤﴾

25. And they will advance to each other, asking questions.

وَأَقْبَلَ بَعْضُهُمْ عَلَىٰ بَعْضٍ يَتَسَآءَلُونَ ﴿٢٥﴾

26. They will say: 'we were aforetime in the midst of our household, ever in dread.

قَالُوٓا إِنَّا كُنَّا قَبْلُ فِىٓ أَهْلِنَا مُشْفِقِينَ ﴿٢٦﴾

27. Therefore Allah obliged us, and has protected us from the torment of the Scorch.

فَمَنَّ اللَّهُ عَلَيْنَا وَوَقَىٰنَا عَذَابَ السَّمُومِ ﴿٢٧﴾

28. We used to pray to Him aforetime. Verily He! It is He, the Benign, the Merciful.

إِنَّا كُنَّا مِن قَبْلُ نَدْعُوهُ إِنَّهُ هُوَ الْبَرُّ الرَّحِيمُ ﴿٢٨﴾

Section 2

29. Therefore admonish! By the grace of your Lord, you are neither a soothsayer nor a mad man.

فَذَكِّرْ فَمَآ أَنتَ بِنِعْمَتِ رَبِّكَ بِكَاهِنٍ وَلَا مَجْنُونٍ ﴿٢٩﴾

30. Do they say: 'A poet, for whom we wait only some adverse turn of fortune?'

أَمْ يَقُولُونَ شَاعِرٌ نَّتَرَبَّصُ بِهِ رَيْبَ الْمَنُونِ ﴿٣٠﴾

31. Say: 'Wait; verily I am with you, among the waiters.'

قُلْ تَرَبَّصُوا فَإِنِّى مَعَكُم مِّنَ الْمُتَرَبِّصِينَ ﴿٣١﴾

32. Does their reason enjoin them to this? Or, are they a people contumacious?

أَمْ تَأْمُرُهُمْ أَحْلَامُهُم بِهَٰذَآ أَمْ هُمْ قَوْمٌ طَاغُونَ ﴿٣٢﴾

33. Do they say: 'He has forged it?' Aye! They will not believe.

أَمْ يَقُولُونَ تَقَوَّلَهُ بَل لَّا يُؤْمِنُونَ ﴿٣٣﴾

34. Let them bring a discourse like thereunto, if they speak truth.

فَلْيَأْتُوا بِحَدِيثٍ مِّثْلِهِ إِن كَانُوا صَدِقِينَ ﴿٣٤﴾

35. Have they not been created by anyone? Or are they the creators?

أَمْ خُلِقُوا مِنْ غَيْرِ شَيْءٍ أَمْ هُمُ الْخَلِقُونَ ﴿٣٥﴾

36. Did they create the heavens and the earth? Aye! They will not be convinced.

أَمْ خَلَقُوا السَّمَوَتِ وَالْأَرْضَ بَل لَّا يُوقِنُونَ ﴿٣٦﴾

37. Are with them the treasures of your Lord? Or are they the dispensers?

أَمْ عِندَهُمْ خَزَآئِنُ رَبِّكَ أَمْ هُمُ الْمُصَيْطِرُونَ ﴿٣٧﴾

38. Have they a stairway whereby they overhear? Then let their listener bring a clear authority.

أَمْ لَهُمْ سُلَّمٌ يَسْتَمِعُونَ فِيهِ فَلْيَأْتِ مُسْتَمِعُهُم بِسُلْطَنٍ مُّبِينٍ ﴿٣٨﴾

39. Has He daughters and you sons?

أَمْ لَهُ الْبَنَتُ وَلَكُمُ الْبَنُونَ ﴿٣٩﴾

40. Or ask you a wage from them, so that they are laden with debt?

أَمْ تَسْئَلُهُمْ أَجْرًا فَهُم مِّن مَّغْرَمٍ مُّثْقَلُونَ ﴿٤٠﴾

41. Is with them the Unseen, and they write it down?

أَمْ عِندَهُمُ الْغَيْبُ فَهُمْ يَكْتُبُونَ ﴿٤١﴾

42. Do they seek to lay a plot? Then those who disbelieve — it is they who shall be plotted against.

أَمْ يُرِيدُونَ كَيْدًا فَالَّذِينَ كَفَرُوا هُمُ الْمَكِيدُونَ ﴿٤٢﴾

43. Is theirs a god beside Allah? Hallowed be Allah from what they associate!

أَمْ لَهُمْ إِلَهٌ غَيْرُ اللَّهِ سُبْحَنَ اللَّهِ عَمَّا يُشْرِكُونَ ﴿٤٣﴾

44. And even if they should see a fragment of the sky falling down they would say: it is only clouds amassed.

وَإِن يَرَوْا كِسْفًا مِّنَ السَّمَاءِ سَاقِطًا يَقُولُوا سَحَابٌ مَّرْكُومٌ ﴿٤٤﴾

45. So let you them alone, till they meet their Day whereon they shall swoon –

46. A Day when their plotting shall not avail them at all. Nor will they be succoured.

47. And for those who are ungodly, there is a chastisement before that but most of them know not.

48. And wait the judgement of your Lord patiently; verily you are ever before Our eyes. And hallow the praise of your Lord before you arise.

49. And hallow Him in the night and at the declining of the stars.

فَذَرْهُمْ حَتَّىٰ يُلَـٰقُواْ يَوْمَهُمُ ٱلَّذِى فِيهِ يُصْعَقُونَ ﴿٤٥﴾

يَوْمَ لَا يُغْنِى عَنْهُمْ كَيْدُهُمْ شَيْئًا وَلَا هُمْ يُنصَرُونَ ﴿٤٦﴾

وَإِنَّ لِلَّذِينَ ظَلَمُواْ عَذَابًا دُونَ ذَٰلِكَ وَلَـٰكِنَّ أَكْثَرَهُمْ لَا يَعْلَمُونَ ﴿٤٧﴾

وَٱصْبِرْ لِحُكْمِ رَبِّكَ فَإِنَّكَ بِأَعْيُنِنَا وَسَبِّحْ بِحَمْدِ رَبِّكَ حِينَ تَقُومُ ﴿٤٨﴾

وَمِنَ ٱلَّيْلِ فَسَبِّحْهُ وَإِدْبَـٰرَ ٱلنُّجُومِ ﴿٤٩﴾

Sūrah 53

al-Najm

(Makkan, 3 Sections, 62 Verses)

In the name of Allah, the Compassionate, the Merciful.

Section 1

1. By the star when it goes down.

وَالنَّجْمِ إِذَا هَوَىٰ ﴿١﴾

2. Your companion has not gone astray. Nor has he erred.

مَا ضَلَّ صَاحِبُكُمْ وَمَا غَوَىٰ ﴿٢﴾

3. And he speaks not of his own desire.[693]

وَمَا يَنطِقُ عَنِ الْهَوَىٰ ﴿٣﴾

4. It is but a revelation revealed.[694]

إِنْ هُوَ إِلَّا وَحْىٌ يُوحَىٰ ﴿٤﴾

5. One of mighty powers has taught it to him.

عَلَّمَهُ شَدِيدُ الْقُوَىٰ ﴿٥﴾

6. One of mighty make. Then he stood straight;

ذُو مِرَّةٍ فَاسْتَوَىٰ ﴿٦﴾

7. While he was on the uppermost horizon.

وَهُوَ بِالْأُفُقِ الْأَعْلَىٰ ﴿٧﴾

8. Thereafter he drew nigh then he let himself down.

ثُمَّ دَنَا فَتَدَلَّىٰ ﴿٨﴾

---

693. In other words, while uttering God's Truth. He only speaks when God commands him to do so; and therefore both the Qur'ān and the Prophet's *Sūnnah* are to be followed.

694. Revelation as distinguished from mere inspiration, always comes from outside, and is never evolved from within – an outcome of the seer's own spiritual awakening. And in order to receive the revelation, the Prophet must be a purely passive, receptive, instrument of God, eliminating his own personality altogether.

9. Till he was two bows length off or yet nearer.

فَكَانَ قَابَ قَوْسَيْنِ أَوْ أَدْنَىٰ ۝

10. Thus He revealed to this His bondsman whatever he revealed.

فَأَوْحَىٰٓ إِلَىٰ عَبْدِهِۦ مَآ أَوْحَىٰ ۝

11. The heart lied not in what he saw.

مَا كَذَبَ ٱلْفُؤَادُ مَا رَأَىٰٓ ۝

12. Will you then dispute with him concerning what he saw?

أَفَتُمَٰرُونَهُۥ عَلَىٰ مَا يَرَىٰ ۝

13. And assuredly he saw him at another descent,

وَلَقَدْ رَءَاهُ نَزْلَةً أُخْرَىٰ ۝

14. Nigh unto the lote-tree at the boundary.

عِندَ سِدْرَةِ ٱلْمُنتَهَىٰ ۝

15. Nigh thereto is the Garden of Abode.

عِندَهَا جَنَّةُ ٱلْمَأْوَىٰٓ ۝

16. When that covered the lote-tree which covered it.

إِذْ يَغْشَى ٱلسِّدْرَةَ مَا يَغْشَىٰ ۝

17. The eye did not wander, nor did it turn aside.

مَا زَاغَ ٱلْبَصَرُ وَمَا طَغَىٰ ۝

18. Assuredly he beheld of the greatest signs of his Lord.

لَقَدْ رَأَىٰ مِنْ ءَايَٰتِ رَبِّهِ ٱلْكُبْرَىٰٓ ۝

19. Have you then considered Lāt and 'Uzzā?

أَفَرَءَيْتُمُ ٱللَّٰتَ وَٱلْعُزَّىٰ ۝

20. And Manāt, the other third?

وَمَنَوٰةَ ٱلثَّالِثَةَ ٱلْأُخْرَىٰٓ ۝

21. What! For you the males and for Him the females?

أَلَكُمُ ٱلذَّكَرُ وَلَهُ ٱلْأُنثَىٰ ۝

22. That indeed is an unfair division!

تِلْكَ إِذًا قِسْمَةٌ ضِيزَىٰ ۝

23. They are but names which you have named, you and your fathers, for which Allah has sent down no authority. They follow but their fancy and what pleases their souls, whereas there has come to them assuredly the guidance from their Lord.

إِنْ هِيَ إِلَّا أَسْمَاءٌ سَمَّيْتُمُوهَا أَنتُمْ وَءَابَآؤُكُم مَّآ أَنزَلَ ٱللَّهُ بِهَا مِن سُلْطَنٍ إِن يَتَّبِعُونَ إِلَّا ٱلظَّنَّ وَمَا تَهْوَى ٱلْأَنفُسُ وَلَقَدْ جَآءَهُم مِّن رَّبِّهِمُ ٱلْهُدَىٰ ﴿٢٣﴾

24. Shall man have whatsoever he wishes?

أَمْ لِلْإِنسَٰنِ مَا تَمَنَّىٰ ﴿٢٤﴾

25. Allah's is the last and the first.

فَلِلَّهِ ٱلْءَاخِرَةُ وَٱلْأُولَىٰ ﴿٢٥﴾

Section 2

26. And many an angel there is in the heavens whose intercession will not avail at all save after Allah's leave for whomsoever He wills and is well-pleased.

وَكَم مِّن مَّلَكٍ فِى ٱلسَّمَٰوَٰتِ لَا تُغْنِى شَفَٰعَتُهُمْ شَيْئًا إِلَّا مِنۢ بَعْدِ أَن يَأْذَنَ ٱللَّهُ لِمَن يَشَآءُ وَيَرْضَىٰ ﴿٢٦﴾

27. Verily those who believe not in the Hereafter name the angels with female names.695

إِنَّ ٱلَّذِينَ لَا يُؤْمِنُونَ بِٱلْءَاخِرَةِ لَيُسَمُّونَ ٱلْمَلَٰٓئِكَةَ تَسْمِيَةَ ٱلْأُنثَىٰ ﴿٢٧﴾

28. Verily they have no true knowledge thereof; they follow but a conjecture and conjecture is no substitute for the Truth.

وَمَا لَهُم بِهِۦ مِنْ عِلْمٍ إِن يَتَّبِعُونَ إِلَّا ٱلظَّنَّ وَإِنَّ ٱلظَّنَّ لَا يُغْنِى مِنَ ٱلْحَقِّ شَيْئًا ﴿٢٨﴾

29. So withdraw you from him who turns away from Our admonition and seeks only the life of the world.

فَأَعْرِضْ عَن مَّن تَوَلَّىٰ عَن ذِكْرِنَا وَلَمْ يُرِدْ إِلَّا ٱلْحَيَوٰةَ ٱلدُّنْيَا ﴿٢٩﴾

---

695. In the religious imagination and devotion of the Arabs, the angels were females, and daughters of God.

30. That is their highest point of knowledge. Verily your Lord! It is He Who is the Best Knower of him who strays from His way, and He is the Best Knower of him who lets himself be guided.

ذَلِكَ مَبْلَغُهُم مِّنَ ٱلْعِلْمِ إِنَّ رَبَّكَ هُوَ أَعْلَمُ بِمَن ضَلَّ عَن سَبِيلِهِ وَهُوَ أَعْلَمُ بِمَنِ ٱهْتَدَىٰ ٣٠

31. And Allah's is whatsoever is in the heavens and whatsoever is in the earth, that He may recompense the evil-doers for what they worked and reward those who do good with goodness.

وَلِلَّهِ مَا فِى ٱلسَّمَوَاتِ وَمَا فِى ٱلْأَرْضِ لِيَجْزِىَ ٱلَّذِينَ أَسَاءُوا بِمَا عَمِلُوا وَيَجْزِىَ ٱلَّذِينَ أَحْسَنُوا بِٱلْحُسْنَى ٣١

32. The are those who shun heinous sins and indecencies save the minor offences. Verily your Lord is of vast forgiveness; He is the Best Knower of you when He produced you out of the earth, and when you were embryos in the bellies of your mothers. So do not ascribe purity to yourselves. He is the Best Knower of him who fears Him.[696]

ٱلَّذِينَ يَجْتَنِبُونَ كَبَائِرَ ٱلْإِثْمِ وَٱلْفَوَاحِشَ إِلَّا ٱللَّمَمَ إِنَّ رَبَّكَ وَاسِعُ ٱلْمَغْفِرَةِ هُوَ أَعْلَمُ بِكُمْ إِذْ أَنشَأَكُم مِّنَ ٱلْأَرْضِ وَإِذْ أَنتُمْ أَجِنَّةٌ فِى بُطُونِ أُمَّهَاتِكُمْ فَلَا تُزَكُّوٓا أَنفُسَكُمْ هُوَ أَعْلَمُ بِمَنِ ٱتَّقَىٰ ٣٢

Section 3

33. Did you observe him who turned away,

أَفَرَءَيْتَ ٱلَّذِى تَوَلَّىٰ ٣٣

34. And give a little, and then stopped?

وَأَعْطَىٰ قَلِيلًا وَأَكْدَىٰ ٣٤

---

696. So He Alone is the true Judge of men's merits and demerits – even better than man himself. This curbs one's morbid appetite for fame, honour, and self-laudation.

35. Is with him the knowledge of the Unseen so that he sees?

أَعِندَهُۥ عِلْمُ ٱلْغَيْبِ فَهُوَ يَرَىٰ ۝

36. Has he not been told of what is in the Scriptures of Moses,

أَمْ لَمْ يُنَبَّأْ بِمَا فِى صُحُفِ مُوسَىٰ ۝

37. And of Abraham who faithfully fulfilled?

وَإِبْرَٰهِيمَ ٱلَّذِى وَفَّىٰٓ ۝

38. To wit, that a burdened soul shall not bear the burden of another,

أَلَّا تَزِرُ وَازِرَةٌ وِزْرَ أُخْرَىٰ ۝

39. And that there shall be for man nothing except what he endeavours.[697]

وَأَن لَّيْسَ لِلْإِنسَٰنِ إِلَّا مَا سَعَىٰ ۝

40. And that his endeavour shall soon be seen;

وَأَنَّ سَعْيَهُۥ سَوْفَ يُرَىٰ ۝

41. Thereafter he shall be recompensed with the fullest recompense.

ثُمَّ يُجْزَىٰهُ ٱلْجَزَآءَ ٱلْأَوْفَىٰ ۝

42. And that unto your Lord is the goal,

وَأَنَّ إِلَىٰ رَبِّكَ ٱلْمُنتَهَىٰ ۝

43. And that it is He Who causes one to laugh and causes one to weep.

وَأَنَّهُۥ هُوَ أَضْحَكَ وَأَبْكَىٰ ۝

44. And that it is He Who causes death and causes life,

وَأَنَّهُۥ هُوَ أَمَاتَ وَأَحْيَا ۝

45. And that He creates the pair, the male and female.

وَأَنَّهُۥ خَلَقَ ٱلزَّوْجَيْنِ ٱلذَّكَرَ وَٱلْأُنثَىٰ ۝

46. From a seed when it is emitted.

مِن نُّطْفَةٍ إِذَا تُمْنَىٰ ۝

---

697. This in the realm of faith. This hits hard at the Christian idea of redemption and damnation, and establishes once and for all that every believer is his own redeemer.

47. And that upon Him is another bringing forth.

وَأَنَّ عَلَيْهِ النَّشْأَةَ الْأُخْرَىٰ ﴿٤٧﴾

48. And that it is He Who enriches and preserves property.

وَأَنَّهُ هُوَ أَغْنَىٰ وَأَقْنَىٰ ﴿٤٨﴾

49. And that it is He Who is the Lord of Sirius.

وَأَنَّهُ هُوَ رَبُّ الشِّعْرَىٰ ﴿٤٩﴾

50. And that He destroyed the former 'Ad,

وَأَنَّهُ أَهْلَكَ عَادًا الْأُولَىٰ ﴿٥٠﴾

51. And that He left not the Thamud,

وَثَمُودَا فَمَا أَبْقَىٰ ﴿٥١﴾

52. And also the people of Noah before. Verily they were even greater wrong-doers and more contumacious.

وَقَوْمَ نُوحٍ مِّن قَبْلُ إِنَّهُمْ كَانُوا هُمْ أَظْلَمَ وَأَطْغَىٰ ﴿٥٢﴾

53. And He overthrew the subverted cities.

وَالْمُؤْتَفِكَةَ أَهْوَىٰ ﴿٥٣﴾

54. Then covered them with what covered them.

فَغَشَّاهَا مَا غَشَّىٰ ﴿٥٤﴾

55. Which then of your Lord's benefits will you doubt?

فَبِأَيِّ آلَاءِ رَبِّكَ تَتَمَارَىٰ ﴿٥٥﴾

56. This Messenger is a warner among the warners of old.

هَٰذَا نَذِيرٌ مِّنَ النُّذُرِ الْأُولَىٰ ﴿٥٦﴾

57. There has approached the approaching Hour.

أَزِفَتِ الْآزِفَةُ ﴿٥٧﴾

58. None can avert it, except Allah.

لَيْسَ لَهَا مِن دُونِ اللَّهِ كَاشِفَةٌ ﴿٥٨﴾

59. Do you marvel then at this discourse?

أَفَمِنْ هَٰذَا الْحَدِيثِ تَعْجَبُونَ ﴿٥٩﴾

60. And laugh light-heartedly and not weep!

وَتَضْحَكُونَ وَلَا تَبْكُونَ ﴿٦٠﴾

61. And you are being impatient,

وَأَنتُمْ سَامِدُونَ ﴿٦١﴾

62. So prostrate yourselves before Allah and worship.

فَاسْجُدُوا لِلَّهِ وَاعْبُدُوا ۩ ﴿٦٢﴾

Sūrah 54

al-Qamar

(Makkan, 3 Sections, 55 Verses)

In the name of Allah, the Compassionate, the Merciful.

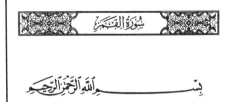

Section 1

1. The Hour has drawn nigh, and the moon has been rent asunder.[698]

2. And if they behold a sign, they turn away, and say, 'magic continuous.'

3. And they belied, and they followed their lusts, and every affair comes to a final goal.

4. And assuredly there has come to them tidings wherein is a deterrent.

5. Wisdom consummate. But warnings avail not.

6. So withdraw you from them. The Day when the summoner will summon mankind to a thing unpleasant.

7. They will come forth with the downcast looks from the tomb as if they were locusts scattered.

---

698. This as a sign of the Hour's approach. The allusion is to a famous miracle of the Prophet recorded in several authentic traditions of the Companions and performed at the insistent demand of the pagans for a sign in the early days of his ministry.

8. Hastening towards the summoner. The infidels will say: 'A hard Day this!'

مُّهْطِعِينَ إِلَى الدَّاعِ يَقُولُ الْكَٰفِرُونَ هَٰذَا يَوْمٌ عَسِرٌ ۝

9. There belied before them the people of Noah. So they belied Our bondsman Noah, and said: 'A mad man,' and he was reproved.

كَذَّبَتْ قَبْلَهُمْ قَوْمُ نُوحٍ فَكَذَّبُوا عَبْدَنَا وَقَالُوا مَجْنُونٌ وَازْدُجِرَ ۝

10. Thereupon he prayed to his Lord: 'Verily I am overcome, so vindicate me.'

فَدَعَا رَبَّهُ أَنِّي مَغْلُوبٌ فَانْتَصِرْ ۝

11. Then We opened the portals of heaven with water poured out.

فَفَتَحْنَا أَبْوَٰبَ السَّمَاءِ بِمَاءٍ مُّنْهَمِرٍ ۝

12. And We made the earth gush forth with springs, that the water met after an affair already decreed.

وَفَجَّرْنَا الْأَرْضَ عُيُونًا فَالْتَقَى الْمَاءُ عَلَىٰ أَمْرٍ قَدْ قُدِرَ ۝

13. And We bore him on a thing of planks and nails.

وَحَمَلْنَٰهُ عَلَىٰ ذَاتِ أَلْوَٰحٍ وَدُسُرٍ ۝

14. Moving forward under Our eyes: a vindication of him who had been rejected.

تَجْرِي بِأَعْيُنِنَا جَزَاءً لِّمَن كَانَ كُفِرَ ۝

15. And assuredly We left it for a sign. Is there, then anyone who would be admonished?

وَلَقَدْ تَرَكْنَٰهَا آيَةً فَهَلْ مِن مُّدَّكِرٍ ۝

16. So how dreadful have been My chastisement and My warnings?

فَكَيْفَ كَانَ عَذَابِي وَنُذُرِ ۝

17. And assuredly We have made the Qur'ān easy for admonition. So is there, then, anyone who would be admonished?

وَلَقَدْ يَسَّرْنَا الْقُرْءَانَ لِلذِّكْرِ فَهَلْ مِن مُّدَّكِرٍ ۝

18. And there belied the 'Ād, So how dreadful have been My chastisement and My warnings!

كَذَّبَتْ عَادٌ فَكَيْفَ كَانَ عَذَابِي وَنُذُرِ ﴿١٨﴾

19. Verily We! We sent against them a raging wind on a day of continuous calamity.

إِنَّا أَرْسَلْنَا عَلَيْهِمْ رِيحًا صَرْصَرًا فِي يَوْمِ نَحْسٍ مُّسْتَمِرٍّ ﴿١٩﴾

20. Carrying men away, as if they were trunks of uprooted palm trees.

تَنزِعُ النَّاسَ كَأَنَّهُمْ أَعْجَازُ نَخْلٍ مُّنقَعِرٍ ﴿٢٠﴾

21. So how dreadful have been My chastisement and My warnings.

فَكَيْفَ كَانَ عَذَابِي وَنُذُرِ ﴿٢١﴾

22. And assuredly We have made the Qur'ān easy for admonition. Is there, then, anyone who would be admonished?

وَلَقَدْ يَسَّرْنَا الْقُرْءَانَ لِلذِّكْرِ فَهَلْ مِن مُّدَّكِرٍ ﴿٢٢﴾

Section 2

23. And the Thamūd belied the warnings.

كَذَّبَتْ ثَمُودُ بِالنُّذُرِ ﴿٢٣﴾

24. And they said: 'A mere human being from amongst us and alone shall we follow him? Then indeed we should be in error and madness.

فَقَالُوٓا أَبَشَرًا مِّنَّا وَاحِدًا نَّتَّبِعُهُ إِنَّا إِذًا لَّفِي ضَلَلٍ وَسُعُرٍ ﴿٢٤﴾

25. Has the admonition been laid upon him from amongst us? Aye: he is an insolent liar!'

أَءُلْقِيَ الذِّكْرُ عَلَيْهِ مِنْ بَيْنِنَا بَلْ هُوَ كَذَّابٌ أَشِرٌ ﴿٢٥﴾

26. They shall learn tomorrow who is an insolent liar!

سَيَعْلَمُونَ غَدًا مَّنِ الْكَذَّابُ الْأَشِرُ ﴿٢٦﴾

27. Verily We are sending a she-camel as a test for them, so watch them and have patience.

إِنَّا مُرْسِلُوا النَّاقَةِ فِتْنَةً لَّهُمْ فَارْتَقِبْهُمْ وَاصْطَبِرْ ﴿٢٧﴾

28. And declare to them that water has been divided between them, every drinking shall be by turns.

وَنَبِّئْهُمْ أَنَّ ٱلْمَآءَ قِسْمَةٌۢ بَيْنَهُمْ كُلُّ شِرْبٍ مُّحْتَضَرٌ ۝

29. Then they called their comrade, and took the sword, and hamstrung her.

فَنَادَوْا۟ صَاحِبَهُمْ فَتَعَاطَىٰ فَعَقَرَ ۝

30. So how dreadful have been My chastisement and My warnings!

فَكَيْفَ كَانَ عَذَابِى وَنُذُرِ ۝

31. Verily We! We sent upon one shout, and they became as the stubble of a fold-builder.

إِنَّآ أَرْسَلْنَا عَلَيْهِمْ صَيْحَةً وَٰحِدَةً فَكَانُوا۟ كَهَشِيمِ ٱلْمُحْتَظِرِ ۝

32. And assuredly We have made the Qur'ān easy for admonition. Is there anyone who would be admonished?

وَلَقَدْ يَسَّرْنَا ٱلْقُرْءَانَ لِلذِّكْرِ فَهَلْ مِن مُّدَّكِرٍ ۝

33. Then belied the warnings the people of Lot.

كَذَّبَتْ قَوْمُ لُوطٍۭ بِٱلنُّذُرِ ۝

34. Verily We! We sent upon them a gravel storm save the family of Lot. Them We delivered at early dawn,

إِنَّآ أَرْسَلْنَا عَلَيْهِمْ حَاصِبًا إِلَّآ ءَالَ لُوطٍ نَّجَّيْنَٰهُم بِسَحَرٍ ۝

35. As a favour from Us. Thus do We recompense him who gives thanks.

نِّعْمَةً مِّنْ عِندِنَا كَذَٰلِكَ نَجْزِى مَن شَكَرَ ۝

36. And assuredly he had warned them of Our punishment but they doubted the warnings.

وَلَقَدْ أَنذَرَهُم بَطْشَتَنَا فَتَمَارَوْا۟ بِٱلنُّذُرِ ۝

37. And they solicited him for his guests; then We deprived them of their sight, taste then My chastisement and My warnings.

وَلَقَدْ رَٰوَدُوهُ عَن ضَيْفِهِۦ فَطَمَسْنَآ أَعْيُنَهُمْ فَذُوقُوا۟ عَذَابِى وَنُذُرِ ۝

38. And thus met them early in the morning a settled chastisement.

وَلَقَدْ صَبَّحَهُم بُكْرَةً عَذَابٌ مُّسْتَقِرٌّ ﴿٣٨﴾

39. Taste then My chastisement and My warnings.

فَذُوقُوا۟ عَذَابِى وَنُذُرِ ﴿٣٩﴾

40. And assuredly We have made the Qur'ān easy for admonition. Is there, then, anyone who would be admonished?

وَلَقَدْ يَسَّرْنَا الْقُرْءَانَ لِلذِّكْرِ فَهَلْ مِن مُّدَّكِرٍ ﴿٤٠﴾

Section 3

41. And assuredly there came the warning unto the household of Pharaoh.

وَلَقَدْ جَآءَ ءَالَ فِرْعَوْنَ النُّذُرُ ﴿٤١﴾

42. They belied Our signs, everyone thereof. Then We seized them with the grip of the Mighty, the Powerful.

كَذَّبُوا۟ بِـَٔايَٰتِنَا كُلِّهَا فَأَخَذْنَٰهُمْ أَخْذَ عَزِيزٍ مُّقْتَدِرٍ ﴿٤٢﴾

43. Are you infidels better than those? Or, is there an immunity for you in the Writs?

أَكُفَّارُكُمْ خَيْرٌ مِّنْ أُو۟لَٰٓئِكُمْ أَمْ لَكُم بَرَآءَةٌ فِى الزُّبُرِ ﴿٤٣﴾

44. Or is it that they say: 'We are a people prevailing?'

أَمْ يَقُولُونَ نَحْنُ جَمِيعٌ مُّنتَصِرٌ ﴿٤٤﴾

45. Soon will this multitude be vanquished, and they will turn their backs.

سَيُهْزَمُ الْجَمْعُ وَيُوَلُّونَ الدُّبُرَ ﴿٤٥﴾

46. Aye! The Hour is their appointed term and the Hour will be far more grievous and far more bitter.

بَلِ السَّاعَةُ مَوْعِدُهُمْ وَالسَّاعَةُ أَدْهَىٰ وَأَمَرُّ ﴿٤٦﴾

47. Verily the culprits are in great error and madness.

إِنَّ الْمُجْرِمِينَ فِى ضَلَٰلٍ وَسُعُرٍ ﴿٤٧﴾

48. On the Day when they shall be dragged on their faces into the Fire, it will be said to them: 'Taste the touch of the Scorching.'

يَوۡمَ يُسۡحَبُونَ فِى ٱلنَّارِ عَلَىٰ وُجُوهِهِمۡ ذُوقُواْ مَسَّ سَقَرَ ﴿٤٨﴾

49. Verily We have created everything by a measure.

إِنَّا كُلَّ شَىۡءٍ خَلَقۡنَٰهُ بِقَدَرٍ ﴿٤٩﴾

50. And Our commandment is but one as the twinkling of an eye.

وَمَآ أَمۡرُنَآ إِلَّا وَٰحِدَةٌ كَلَمۡحِۭ بِٱلۡبَصَرِ ﴿٥٠﴾

51. And assuredly We have destroyed your likes. Is there, then, any one who would be admonished?

وَلَقَدۡ أَهۡلَكۡنَآ أَشۡيَاعَكُمۡ فَهَلۡ مِن مُّدَّكِرٍ ﴿٥١﴾

52. And everything they have done is in the Writs.

وَكُلُّ شَىۡءٍ فَعَلُوهُ فِى ٱلزُّبُرِ ﴿٥٢﴾

53. And everything, small or big, has been written down.

وَكُلُّ صَغِيرٍ وَكَبِيرٍ مُّسۡتَطَرٌ ﴿٥٣﴾

54. Verily the pious will be amid Gardens and rivers,

إِنَّ ٱلۡمُتَّقِينَ فِى جَنَّٰتٍ وَنَهَرٍ ﴿٥٤﴾

55. In a good seat, near the Sovereign, the Omnipotent.

فِى مَقۡعَدِ صِدۡقٍ عِندَ مَلِيكٍ مُّقۡتَدِرٍۭ ﴿٥٥﴾

Sūrah 55

al-Raḥmān

(Madinan, 3 Sections, 78 Verses)

In the name of Allah, the Compassionate, the Merciful.

Section 1

1. The Compassionate.

2. He taught the Qur'ān.

3. He created man.

4. He taught him distinctness.

5. The sun and the moon are in the reckoning.

6. And herbs and trees do obeisance.[699]

7. And the sky! He has elevated it and set the balance,

8. That you should not trespass in respect of the balance.

9. And observe the weight with equity, and do not make the balance deficient.

---

699. Obeisance to His will and disposition. This strikes at the root of the universally prevalent plant – lore and tree – cult. 'Trees have been objects of worship in all parts of the world. They were worshipped among the Semites and the Hebrews were no exception to this'. (*JE.* XII. p. 239). 'The worship of sacred trees is one of the most widely rife religious phenomena in the early Greek world' (*DB.* V. p. 113). 'There is abundant evidence that in all parts of the Semitic area trees were adored as divine' (Robertson–Smith, *Religion of the Semites*, p. 185). 'In fact, the evidence of tree–worship is almost unmanageably large' (*EBr.* XXVII. p. 236, 11th Ed)

10. And the earth: He has laid it for the creatures.

وَٱلْأَرْضَ وَضَعَهَا لِلْأَنَامِ ۝

11. Therein are fruit and palm trees sheathed,

فِيهَا فَاكِهَةٌ وَٱلنَّخْلُ ذَاتُ ٱلْأَكْمَامِ ۝

12. And grain chaffed and other food.

وَٱلْحَبُّ ذُو ٱلْعَصْفِ وَٱلرَّيْحَانُ ۝

13. Which, then, of the benefits of your Lord will you twain deny?

فَبِأَيِّ ءَالَآءِ رَبِّكُمَا تُكَذِّبَانِ ۝

14. He created man from potter's clay.

خَلَقَ ٱلْإِنسَٰنَ مِن صَلْصَٰلٍ كَٱلْفَخَّارِ ۝

15. And has created the *jinn* from a flame of fire.

وَخَلَقَ ٱلْجَآنَّ مِن مَّارِجٍ مِّن نَّارٍ ۝

16. Which, then, of the benefits of your Lord will you twain deny?

فَبِأَيِّ ءَالَآءِ رَبِّكُمَا تُكَذِّبَانِ ۝

17. He is the Lord of the two easts and the two wests.

رَبُّ ٱلْمَشْرِقَيْنِ وَرَبُّ ٱلْمَغْرِبَيْنِ ۝

18. Which, then, of the benefits of your Lord will you twain deny?

فَبِأَيِّ ءَالَآءِ رَبِّكُمَا تُكَذِّبَانِ ۝

19. He has let loose the two oceans.

مَرَجَ ٱلْبَحْرَيْنِ يَلْتَقِيَانِ ۝

20. In between them is a barrier they cannot pass.

بَيْنَهُمَا بَرْزَخٌ لَّا يَبْغِيَانِ ۝

21. Which, then, of the benefits of your Lord will you twain deny?

فَبِأَيِّ ءَالَآءِ رَبِّكُمَا تُكَذِّبَانِ ۝

22. There come forth from the two the pearl and the coral.

يَخْرُجُ مِنْهُمَا ٱللُّؤْلُؤُ وَٱلْمَرْجَانُ ۝

23. Which, then, of the benefits of your Lord will you twain deny?

فَبِأَيِّ ءَالَآءِ رَبِّكُمَا تُكَذِّبَانِ ۝

24. His are the ships slanted like mountains in the sea.

وَلَهُ ٱلْجَوَارِ ٱلْمُنشَئَاتُ فِي ٱلْبَحْرِ كَٱلْأَعْلَٰمِ ۝

25. Which, then, of the benefits of your Lord will you twain deny?

فَبِأَيِّ ءَالَآءِ رَبِّكُمَا تُكَذِّبَانِ ﴿٢٥﴾

Section 2

26. Everyone who is thereon is mortal.

كُلُّ مَنْ عَلَيْهَا فَانٍ ﴿٢٦﴾

27. And there will remain the Face of your Lord, the Owner of majesty and beneficence.

وَيَبْقَىٰ وَجْهُ رَبِّكَ ذُو الْجَلَالِ وَالْإِكْرَامِ ﴿٢٧﴾

28. Which, then, of the benefits of your Lord will you twain deny?

فَبِأَيِّ ءَالَآءِ رَبِّكُمَا تُكَذِّبَانِ ﴿٢٨﴾

29. Of Him begs whosoever is in the heavens and the earth. Every day He is in a new state.[700]

يَسْـَٔلُهُ مَن فِى السَّمَٰوَٰتِ وَالْأَرْضِ كُلَّ يَوْمٍ هُوَ فِى شَأْنٍ ﴿٢٩﴾

30. Which, then, of the benefits of your Lord will you twain deny?

فَبِأَيِّ ءَالَآءِ رَبِّكُمَا تُكَذِّبَانِ ﴿٣٠﴾

---

700. Creating and re-creating the world and ever renewing His activities. God is thus not only the Creator of the universe but also its Sustainer at every moment of its existence. The entire cosmic order is ever dependent on His will, incapable of sustaining and developing itself and performing its work, without His aid, in virtue of its own inherent energies, and hence creation is not an act of the past combining automatically; His creative activity is incessant. This refutes the Hindu doctrine that Brahma, 'having performed his legitimate part in the mundane evolution by his original creation of the universe, has retired into the background' (*EBr.* XI. p. 577). This also repudiates the mechanistic concept of deism, which limits Divine activity to creation of the world and denies to Him any direct contact with His creation and also the Greek idea that God is static, and aloof from the world. A Christian scholar sums up the position of the orthodox Muslim theologian thus: 'He regards the world and all the events in the world as a perpetual miracle — always and constantly going on. It is not only that, by a creative miracle, the world was brought into existence; but all through the existence of the world from moment to moment there is this miraculous creation going on. When fire burns or when a knife cuts, that is not by any nature in the fire or quality in the knife. The cutting and the being cut, the burning and the being burned are all by Allah' (McDonald, *Aspects of Islam*, pp. 137–139).

31. Soon We shall direct Ourselves to you, O two classes!

سَنَفۡرُغُ لَكُمۡ أَيُّهَ ٱلثَّقَلَانِ ﴿٣١﴾

32. Which, then, of the benefits of your Lord will you twain deny?

فَبِأَيِّ ءَالَآءِ رَبِّكُمَا تُكَذِّبَانِ ﴿٣٢﴾

33. O assembly of *jinn* and mankind! If you are able to pass out of the regions of the heavens and the earth, then do pass out, but you cannot pass out except with an authority.

يَٰمَعۡشَرَ ٱلۡجِنِّ وَٱلۡإِنسِ إِنِ ٱسۡتَطَعۡتُمۡ أَن تَنفُذُوا۟ مِنۡ أَقۡطَارِ ٱلسَّمَٰوَٰتِ وَٱلۡأَرۡضِ فَٱنفُذُوا۟ لَا تَنفُذُونَ إِلَّا بِسُلۡطَٰنٍ ﴿٣٣﴾

34. Which, then, of the benefits of your Lord will you twain deny?

فَبِأَيِّ ءَالَآءِ رَبِّكُمَا تُكَذِّبَانِ ﴿٣٤﴾

35. There shall be sent against both of you a flame of fire, and smoke, and you will not be able to defend yourselves.

يُرۡسَلُ عَلَيۡكُمَا شُوَاظٌ مِّن نَّارٍ وَنُحَاسٌ فَلَا تَنتَصِرَانِ ﴿٣٥﴾

36. Which, then, of the benefits of your Lord will you twain deny?

فَبِأَيِّ ءَالَآءِ رَبِّكُمَا تُكَذِّبَانِ ﴿٣٦﴾

37. And when the heaven will be rent asunder and will become rosy like red hide.

فَإِذَا ٱنشَقَّتِ ٱلسَّمَآءُ فَكَانَتۡ وَرۡدَةً كَٱلدِّهَانِ ﴿٣٧﴾

38. Which, then, of the benefits of your Lord will you twain deny?

فَبِأَيِّ ءَالَآءِ رَبِّكُمَا تُكَذِّبَانِ ﴿٣٨﴾

39. Neither man nor *jinn* will be questioned of his sin that Day.

فَيَوۡمَئِذٍ لَّا يُسۡـَٔلُ عَن ذَنۢبِهِۦٓ إِنسٌ وَلَا جَآنٌّ ﴿٣٩﴾

40. Which, then, of the benefits of your Lord will you twain deny?

فَبِأَيِّ ءَالَآءِ رَبِّكُمَا تُكَذِّبَانِ ﴿٤٠﴾

41. The culprits will be known from their marks and will be seized by their fore-locks and their feet.

يُعۡرَفُ ٱلۡمُجۡرِمُونَ بِسِيمَٰهُمۡ فَيُؤۡخَذُ بِٱلنَّوَٰصِي وَٱلۡأَقۡدَامِ ﴿٤١﴾

42. Which, then, of the benefits of your Lord will you twain deny?

فَبِأَيِّ ءَالَآءِ رَبِّكُمَا تُكَذِّبَانِ ۝

43. This is Hell which the culprits denied.

هٰذِهٖ جَهَنَّمُ الَّتِيْ يُكَذِّبُ بِهَا الْمُجْرِمُوْنَ ۝

44. They shall go round between it and boiling hot water.

يَطُوْفُوْنَ بَيْنَهَا وَبَيْنَ حَمِيْمٍ ءَانٍ ۝

45. Which, then, of the benefits of your Lord will you twain deny?

فَبِأَيِّ ءَالَآءِ رَبِّكُمَا تُكَذِّبَانِ ۝

Section 3

46. And for him who dreads the standing before his Lord will be two Gardens.

وَلِمَنْ خَافَ مَقَامَ رَبِّهٖ جَنَّتَانِ ۝

47. Which, then, of the benefits of your Lord will you twain deny?

فَبِأَيِّ ءَالَآءِ رَبِّكُمَا تُكَذِّبَانِ ۝

48. With spreading branches.

ذَوَاتَآ أَفْنَانٍ ۝

49. Which, then, of the benefits of your Lord will you twain deny?

فَبِأَيِّ ءَالَآءِ رَبِّكُمَا تُكَذِّبَانِ ۝

50. In them will be two fountains running.

فِيْهِمَا عَيْنَانِ تَجْرِيَانِ ۝

51. Which, then, of the benefits of your Lord will you twain deny?

فَبِأَيِّ ءَالَآءِ رَبِّكُمَا تُكَذِّبَانِ ۝

52. In them will be every kind of fruit in pairs.

فِيْهِمَا مِنْ كُلِّ فَاكِهَةٍ زَوْجَانِ ۝

53. Which, then, of the benefits of your Lord will you twain deny?

فَبِأَيِّ ءَالَآءِ رَبِّكُمَا تُكَذِّبَانِ ۝

54. Reclining on the carpets lined with rich brocade: and the fruits of the two Gardens will be near at hand.

مُتَّكِئِيْنَ عَلٰى فُرُشٍ بَطَائِنُهَا مِنْ إِسْتَبْرَقٍ وَجَنَى الْجَنَّتَيْنِ دَانٍ ۝

55. Which, then, of the benefits of your Lord will you twain deny?

فَبِأَيِّ ءَالَآءِ رَبِّكُمَا تُكَذِّبَانِ ﴿٥٥﴾

56. Therein shall be damsels of refraining looks touched by neither men nor *jinn*.[701]

فِيْهِنَّ قَاصِرَاتُ الطَّرْفِ لَمْ يَطْمِثْهُنَّ إِنْسٌ قَبْلَهُمْ وَلَا جَانٌّ ﴿٥٦﴾

57. Which, then, of the benefits of your Lord will you twain deny?

فَبِأَيِّ ءَالَآءِ رَبِّكُمَا تُكَذِّبَانِ ﴿٥٧﴾

58. Like rubies and coral.

كَأَنَّهُنَّ الْيَاقُوْتُ وَالْمَرْجَانُ ﴿٥٨﴾

59. Which, then, of the benefits of your Lord will you twain deny?

فَبِأَيِّ ءَالَآءِ رَبِّكُمَا تُكَذِّبَانِ ﴿٥٩﴾

60. Is the recompense for good other than good?

هَلْ جَزَآءُ الْإِحْسَانِ إِلَّا الْإِحْسَانُ ﴿٦٠﴾

61. Which, then, of the benefits of your Lord will you twain deny?

فَبِأَيِّ ءَالَآءِ رَبِّكُمَا تُكَذِّبَانِ ﴿٦١﴾

62. And below the two there will be two other Gardens.

وَمِنْ دُوْنِهِمَا جَنَّتَانِ ﴿٦٢﴾

63. Which, then, of the benefits of your Lord will you twain deny?

فَبِأَيِّ ءَالَآءِ رَبِّكُمَا تُكَذِّبَانِ ﴿٦٣﴾

64. Dark-green.

مُدْهَآمَّتَانِ ﴿٦٤﴾

65. Which, then, of the benefits of your Lord will you twain deny?

فَبِأَيِّ ءَالَآءِ رَبِّكُمَا تُكَذِّبَانِ ﴿٦٥﴾

---

701. In other words, there, before their destined spouses. Christian writers look askance, and almost in horror, at passages like this. And quite naturally. For in the system of Christian morality, sexual relations are conceived of as something inherently evil, at best only to be tolerated. This morbid attitude to life has appeared only with the advent of the black Christian era. 'Islam has reversed this diseased outlook. It holds, freely and frankly, with modern scientific knowledge that sexual life is the source of the highest joys for which there is no substitute. It is the supreme and incomparable physiological happiness, which should be nursed and treasured, and not persecuted. Sex life is not at all a tolerated evil, difficult to escape, but a great blessing, without which life is colourless. The sexual element in human existence must be valued and treasured' (Nemilov, *Biological Tragedy of Woman*, pp. 200–201).

66. In them will be two fountains gushing forth.

فِيهِمَا عَيۡنَانِ نَضَّاخَتَانِ ۝

67. Which, then, of the benefits of your Lord will you twain deny?

فَبِأَيِّ ءَالَآءِ رَبِّكُمَا تُكَذِّبَانِ ۝

68. In them will be the fruit, date-palms and pomegranates.

فِيهِمَا فَاكِهَةٌ وَنَخۡلٌ وَرُمَّانٌ ۝

69. Which, then, of the benefits of your Lord will you twain deny?

فَبِأَيِّ ءَالَآءِ رَبِّكُمَا تُكَذِّبَانِ ۝

70. Therein will be damsels comely and beautiful.

فِيهِنَّ خَيۡرَٰتٌ حِسَانٌ ۝

71. Which, then, of the benefits of your Lord will you twain deny?

فَبِأَيِّ ءَالَآءِ رَبِّكُمَا تُكَذِّبَانِ ۝

72. Fair ones, cloistered in tents.[702]

حُورٌ مَّقۡصُورَٰتٌ فِي ٱلۡخِيَامِ ۝

73. Which, then, of the benefits of your Lord will you twain deny?

فَبِأَيِّ ءَالَآءِ رَبِّكُمَا تُكَذِّبَانِ ۝

74. Untouched by men and *jinn*.

لَمۡ يَطۡمِثۡهُنَّ إِنسٌ قَبۡلَهُمۡ وَلَا جَآنٌّ ۝

75. Which, then, of the benefits of your Lord will you twain deny?

فَبِأَيِّ ءَالَآءِ رَبِّكُمَا تُكَذِّبَانِ ۝

76. Reclining upon green cushions and rich carpets.

مُتَّكِئِينَ عَلَىٰ رَفۡرَفٍ خُضۡرٍ وَعَبۡقَرِيٍّ حِسَانٍ ۝

77. Which, then, of the benefits of your Lord will you twain deny?

فَبِأَيِّ ءَالَآءِ رَبِّكُمَا تُكَذِّبَانِ ۝

78. Blessed be the name of your Lord, the Owner of majesty and beneficence.

تَبَٰرَكَ ٱسۡمُ رَبِّكَ ذِي ٱلۡجَلَٰلِ وَٱلۡإِكۡرَامِ ۝

---

702. In other words, as respectable, modest maidens closely guarded from public view.

Sūrah 56

al-Wāqi'ah

(Makkan, 3 Sections, 96 Verses)

In the name of Allah, the Compassionate, the Merciful.

بِسْمِ اللهِ الرَّحْمَنِ الرَّحِيمِ

Section 1

1. When the Event happens,

إِذَا وَقَعَتِ الْوَاقِعَةُ ۝

2. And there can be no denial of its happening.

لَيْسَ لِوَقْعَتِهَا كَاذِبَةٌ ۝

3. Abasing one, exalting others.

خَافِضَةٌ رَّافِعَةٌ ۝

4. This will be when the earth is shaken and shaken.

إِذَا رُجَّتِ الْأَرْضُ رَجًّا ۝

5. And the mountains are crumbled and crumbled.

وَبُسَّتِ الْجِبَالُ بَسًّا ۝

6. So that they become scattered dust.

فَكَانَتْ هَبَاءً مُّنْبَثًّا ۝

7. And you are in three groups.

وَكُنْتُمْ أَزْوَاجًا ثَلَاثَةً ۝

8. Those on the right hand, how happy shall those on the right hand be!

فَأَصْحَابُ الْمَيْمَنَةِ مَا أَصْحَابُ الْمَيْمَنَةِ ۝

9. Those on the left hand; how miserable shall those on the left hand be!

وَأَصْحَابُ الْمَشْئَمَةِ مَا أَصْحَابُ الْمَشْئَمَةِ ۝

10. And the preceders are the preceders.

وَالسَّابِقُونَ السَّابِقُونَ ۝

11. Those shall be brought near.

أُولَئِكَ الْمُقَرَّبُونَ ۝

12. In the Gardens of Delight.

فِي جَنَّاتِ النَّعِيمِ ۝

13. A multitude from the ancients.

ثُلَّةٌ مِّنَ الْأَوَّلِينَ ﴿١٣﴾

14. And a few from the later generations.

وَقَلِيلٌ مِّنَ الْآخِرِينَ ﴿١٤﴾

15. On couches lined with gold.

عَلَىٰ سُرُرٍ مَّوْضُونَةٍ ﴿١٥﴾

16. Reclining on them facing each other.

مُتَّكِئِينَ عَلَيْهَا مُتَقَابِلِينَ ﴿١٦﴾

17. Youths ever-young will go around them.[703]

يَطُوفُ عَلَيْهِمْ وِلْدَانٌ مُّخَلَّدُونَ ﴿١٧﴾

18. With goblets and ewers and cups of limpid drink.

بِأَكْوَابٍ وَأَبَارِيقَ وَكَأْسٍ مِّن مَّعِينٍ ﴿١٨﴾

19. Theirs will be no headiness. Nor will they be inebriated.[704]

لَّا يُصَدَّعُونَ عَنْهَا وَلَا يُنزِفُونَ ﴿١٩﴾

20. And with the fruit of their choice.

وَفَاكِهَةٍ مِّمَّا يَتَخَيَّرُونَ ﴿٢٠﴾

21. And with fowl flesh of their desire.

وَلَحْمِ طَيْرٍ مِّمَّا يَشْتَهُونَ ﴿٢١﴾

22. And there will be fair ones large-eyed.

وَحُورٌ عِينٌ ﴿٢٢﴾

23. The like unto pearls well-guarded.

كَأَمْثَالِ اللُّؤْلُؤِ الْمَكْنُونِ ﴿٢٣﴾

24. A recompense for what they had been doing.

جَزَاءً بِمَا كَانُوا يَعْمَلُونَ ﴿٢٤﴾

25. No vain or sinful talk will they hear therein.

لَا يَسْمَعُونَ فِيهَا لَغْوًا وَلَا تَأْثِيمًا ﴿٢٥﴾

---

703. Those destined to continue in boyhood for ever. 'Always of the same age; never altering in age; or, endowed with perpetual vigour; that never becomes decrepit' (*LL.*).

704. All pagan mythologies, even the most refined of them, are full of the amours of gods and goddesses and their jealousies and bickerings. Note that the Islamic Heaven knows no such thing.

26. Only the saying: 'Peace! peace.'

إِلَّا قِيلًا سَلَامًا سَلَامًا ﴿٢٦﴾

27. And the fellows on the right hand; how happy shall the fellows on the right hand be!

وَأَصْحَابُ ٱلْيَمِينِ مَآ أَصْحَابُ ٱلْيَمِينِ ﴿٢٧﴾

28. Midst thornless lote-trees.

فِى سِدْرٍ مَّخْضُودٍ ﴿٢٨﴾

29. And plantains laden with fruits,

وَطَلْحٍ مَّنضُودٍ ﴿٢٩﴾

30. And the shade overspread.

وَظِلٍّ مَّمْدُودٍ ﴿٣٠﴾

31. And water overflowing,

وَمَآءٍ مَّسْكُوبٍ ﴿٣١﴾

32. And fruits abundant,

وَفَٰكِهَةٍ كَثِيرَةٍ ﴿٣٢﴾

33. Neither ending nor forbidden.

لَّا مَقْطُوعَةٍ وَلَا مَمْنُوعَةٍ ﴿٣٣﴾

34. And couches raised.

وَفُرُشٍ مَّرْفُوعَةٍ ﴿٣٤﴾

35. Verily We! We have created those maidens by a special creation.

إِنَّآ أَنشَأْنَٰهُنَّ إِنشَآءً ﴿٣٥﴾

36. And have made them perpetual virgins.

فَجَعَلْنَٰهُنَّ أَبْكَارًا ﴿٣٦﴾

37. Loving, of equal age.

عُرُبًا أَتْرَابًا ﴿٣٧﴾

38. For the fellows on the right hand.

لِّأَصْحَٰبِ ٱلْيَمِينِ ﴿٣٨﴾

Section 2

39. A multitude from the ancients,

ثُلَّةٌ مِّنَ ٱلْأَوَّلِينَ ﴿٣٩﴾

40. And a multitude from the later generations.

وَثُلَّةٌ مِّنَ ٱلْآخِرِينَ ﴿٤٠﴾

41. And the fellows on the left hand! How miserable shall the fellows on the left hand be!

وَأَصْحَابُ ٱلشِّمَالِ مَآ أَصْحَابُ ٱلشِّمَالِ ﴿٤١﴾

42. Amidst scorching wind and scalding water.

فِى سَمُوْمٍ وَّحَمِيْمٍ ﴿٤٢﴾

43. And the shade of dark smoke.

وَظِلٍّ مِّنْ يَّحْمُوْمٍ ﴿٤٣﴾

44. Neither cool nor pleasant.

لَّا بَارِدٍ وَّلَا كَرِيْمٍ ﴿٤٤﴾

45. Verily they had been affluent before.

إِنَّهُمْ كَانُوْا قَبْلَ ذٰلِكَ مُتْرَفِيْنَ ﴿٤٥﴾

46. And they had been persisting in heinous offences.

وَكَانُوْا يُصِرُّوْنَ عَلَى الْحِنْثِ الْعَظِيْمِ ﴿٤٦﴾

47. And they used to say: 'When we are dead and have become dust and bones, shall we indeed be raised?

وَكَانُوْا يَقُوْلُوْنَ أَئِذَا مِتْنَا وَكُنَّا تُرَابًا وَّعِظَامًا أَءِنَّا لَمَبْعُوْثُوْنَ ﴿٤٧﴾

48. We and our fathers of old?'

أَوَ اٰبَاؤُنَا الْأَوَّلُوْنَ ﴿٤٨﴾

49. Say: 'Verily the ancients and those of the later generations,

قُلْ إِنَّ الْأَوَّلِيْنَ وَالْآخِرِيْنَ ﴿٤٩﴾

50. Are all going to be assembled on the assigned time of a Day known.

لَمَجْمُوْعُوْنَ إِلَى مِيْقَاتِ يَوْمٍ مَّعْلُوْمٍ ﴿٥٠﴾

51. Then verily you, you erring, denying people.

ثُمَّ إِنَّكُمْ أَيُّهَا الضَّالُّوْنَ الْمُكَذِّبُوْنَ ﴿٥١﴾

52. Shall surely eat of the tree of Zaqqūm,

لَآكِلُوْنَ مِنْ شَجَرٍ مِّنْ زَقُّوْمٍ ﴿٥٢﴾

53. And shall fill your bellies with it.

فَمَالِئُوْنَ مِنْهَا الْبُطُوْنَ ﴿٥٣﴾

54. And shall drink of boiling water,

فَشَارِبُوْنَ عَلَيْهِ مِنَ الْحَمِيْمِ ﴿٥٤﴾

55. Drinking as the drinking of thirsty camels raging with thirst.'

فَشَارِبُوْنَ شُرْبَ الْهِيْمِ ﴿٥٥﴾

56. This shall be their entertainment on the Day of Requital.

هٰذَا نُزُلُهُمْ يَوْمَ الدِّيْنِ ﴿٥٦﴾

57. Verily We! It is We, Who created you, why do you not confess?

نَحۡنُ خَلَقۡنَٰكُمۡ فَلَوۡلَا تُصَدِّقُونَ ۝

58. Do you behold what you emit?

أَفَرَءَيۡتُم مَّا تُمۡنُونَ ۝

59. Then is it you who create him, or are We the creator?

ءَأَنتُمۡ تَخۡلُقُونَهُۥٓ أَمۡ نَحۡنُ ٱلۡخَٰلِقُونَ ۝

60. We! It is We, Who have decreed death unto you all and We are not to be outstripped,[705]

نَحۡنُ قَدَّرۡنَا بَيۡنَكُمُ ٱلۡمَوۡتَ وَمَا نَحۡنُ بِمَسۡبُوقِينَ ۝

61. In that We may substitute others like you and may produce you into what you know not.

عَلَىٰٓ أَن نُّبَدِّلَ أَمۡثَٰلَكُمۡ وَنُنشِئَكُمۡ فِى مَا لَا تَعۡلَمُونَ ۝

62. And assuredly you have fully known the first production. Why do you not heed?

وَلَقَدۡ عَلِمۡتُمُ ٱلنَّشۡأَةَ ٱلۡأُولَىٰ فَلَوۡلَا تَذَكَّرُونَ ۝

63. Do you behold what you sow?

أَفَرَءَيۡتُم مَّا تَحۡرُثُونَ ۝

64. Do you cause it to grow, or are We the grower?

ءَأَنتُمۡ تَزۡرَعُونَهُۥٓ أَمۡ نَحۡنُ ٱلزَّٰرِعُونَ ۝

65. If We willed, We would surely make it chaff, so that you would be left wondering:

لَوۡ نَشَآءُ لَجَعَلۡنَٰهُ حُطَٰمًا فَظَلۡتُمۡ تَفَكَّهُونَ ۝

---

705. Not be outstripped in Our purpose, i.e., none can frustrate Divine decrees. Death is not in the nature of punishment; it is not the result of some initial disobedience on the part of man. It is a cardinal condition of existence. This lends no support whatsoever to the Biblical concept of death, that it is the result of an act of disobedience. 'But of the tree of the knowledge of good and evil thou shalt not eat of it: for in the day that thou eatest thereof thou shalt surely die' (Ge. 2: 17). 'Wherefore, as by one man sin entered into the world, and death by sin; and so death passed upon all men for that all have sinned' (Ro. 5: 12). For the wages of sin is death' (Ro. 6: 23). And sin, when it is finished, bringeth forth death' (Ja. 1: 15).

سُوۡرَةُ الوَاقِعَة

66. 'We are undone indeed.

إِنَّا لَمُغۡرَمُونَ ﴿٦٦﴾

67. Aye! We are deprived altogether.'

بَلۡ نَحۡنُ مَحۡرُومُونَ ﴿٦٧﴾

68. Do you behold the water which you drink?

أَفَرَءَيۡتُمُ ٱلۡمَآءَ ٱلَّذِى تَشۡرَبُونَ ﴿٦٨﴾

69. Is it you who sends it down from the rain-cloud, or are We the sender down?

ءَأَنتُمۡ أَنزَلۡتُمُوهُ مِنَ ٱلۡمُزۡنِ أَمۡ نَحۡنُ ٱلۡمُنزِلُونَ ﴿٦٩﴾

70. If We willed, We would surely make it brackish. Why do you not give thanks?

لَوۡ نَشَآءُ جَعَلۡنَٰهُ أُجَاجًا فَلَوۡلَا تَشۡكُرُونَ ﴿٧٠﴾

71. Do you behold the fire you strike out?

أَفَرَءَيۡتُمُ ٱلنَّارَ ٱلَّتِى تُورُونَ ﴿٧١﴾

72. Is it you who produce the tree thereof, or are We the producer?

ءَأَنتُمۡ أَنشَأۡتُمۡ شَجَرَتَهَآ أَمۡ نَحۡنُ ٱلۡمُنشِـُٔونَ ﴿٧٢﴾

73. We! It is We, Who made it a reminder, and a provision for the campers.

نَحۡنُ جَعَلۡنَٰهَا تَذۡكِرَةً وَمَتَٰعًا لِّلۡمُقۡوِينَ ﴿٧٣﴾

74. So hallow you the name of your Lord, the Mighty.

فَسَبِّحۡ بِٱسۡمِ رَبِّكَ ٱلۡعَظِيمِ ﴿٧٤﴾

Section 3

75. I swear by the setting of the stars.

فَلَآ أُقۡسِمُ بِمَوَٰقِعِ ٱلنُّجُومِ ﴿٧٥﴾

76. And that is a mighty oath, if you but knew,

وَإِنَّهُۥ لَقَسَمٌ لَّوۡ تَعۡلَمُونَ عَظِيمٌ ﴿٧٦﴾

77. That it is an honoured recitation.

إِنَّهُۥ لَقُرۡءَانٌ كَرِيمٌ ﴿٧٧﴾

78. In the Book well-guarded.

فِى كِتَٰبٍ مَّكۡنُونٍ ﴿٧٨﴾

79. Which none can touch except the purified.

لَّا يَمَسُّهُۥٓ إِلَّا ٱلۡمُطَهَّرُونَ ﴿٧٩﴾

80. It is a revelation from the Lord of the worlds.

تَنزِيلٌ مِّن رَّبِّ الْعَالَمِينَ ۝

81. Is this the discourse that you hold so lightly?

أَفَبِهَٰذَا الْحَدِيثِ أَنتُم مُّدْهِنُونَ ۝

82. And make it your provision that you should deny it?

وَتَجْعَلُونَ رِزْقَكُمْ أَنَّكُمْ تُكَذِّبُونَ ۝

83. Wherefore then, when the soul comes up to the wind-pipe,

فَلَوْلَا إِذَا بَلَغَتِ الْحُلْقُومَ ۝

84. And you are looking on.

وَأَنتُمْ حِينَئِذٍ تَنظُرُونَ ۝

85. We are nearer to him than you are, but you behold not.

وَنَحْنُ أَقْرَبُ إِلَيْهِ مِنكُمْ وَلَٰكِن لَّا تُبْصِرُونَ ۝

86. Wherefore then, if you are not to be requited.

فَلَوْلَا إِن كُنتُمْ غَيْرَ مَدِينِينَ ۝

87. Can you cause it not to return, if you speak truth?

تَرْجِعُونَهَا إِن كُنتُمْ صَادِقِينَ ۝

88. Then if he be of the brought near.

فَأَمَّا إِن كَانَ مِنَ الْمُقَرَّبِينَ ۝

89. For him shall be repose and fragrance and a Garden of Delight.

فَرَوْحٌ وَرَيْحَانٌ وَجَنَّتُ نَعِيمٍ ۝

90. And if he be of the fellows on the right hand,

وَأَمَّا إِن كَانَ مِنْ أَصْحَابِ الْيَمِينِ ۝

91. Then: peace unto you, for you are of those on the right hand.

فَسَلَامٌ لَّكَ مِنْ أَصْحَابِ الْيَمِينِ ۝

92. And if he be of the rejecters, the erring,

وَأَمَّا إِن كَانَ مِنَ الْمُكَذِّبِينَ الضَّالِّينَ ۝

93. Then: an entertainment of the boiling water,

فَنُزُلٌ مِّنْ حَمِيمٍ ۝

94. And roasting in the Blaze.

وَتَصْلِيَةُ جَحِيمٍ ۝

95. Verily this! This is the very Truth.

إِنَّ هَٰذَا لَهُوَ حَقُّ الۡيَقِينِ ۝

96. So hallow you the name of your Lord, the Mighty.

فَسَبِّحۡ بِاسۡمِ رَبِّكَ الۡعَظِيمِ ۝

Sūrah 57

al-Ḥadīd

(Madinan, 4 Sections, 29 Verses)

In the name of Allah, the Compassionate, the Merciful.

Section 1

1. Hallows Allah whatsoever is in the heavens and the earth, and He is the Mighty, the Wise.

2. His is the dominion of the heavens and the earth; He gives life and causes death; and He is Potent over everything.

3. He is the First and the Last, and the Evident and the Imminent and He is the Knower of everything.

4. He it is Who created the heavens and the earth in six days; then He established Himself on the throne. He knows[706] whatsoever plunges into the earth, and whatsoever comes forth therefrom, and whatsoever descends from the heaven, and whatsoever ascends thereto; and He is with you wheresoever you be; and Allah is the Beholder of whatever you do.

---

706. Although He Himself is only partly known, His Own knowledge is not in the least degree imperfect. His knowledge is absolutely perfect and all-encompassing.

5. His is the dominion of the heavens and the earth, and to Allah will all affairs be brought back.

لَهُۥمُلْكُ ٱلسَّمَـٰوَٰتِ وَٱلْأَرْضِ وَإِلَى ٱللَّهِ تُرْجَعُ ٱلْأُمُورُ ۝

6. He plunges the night into the day, and plunges the day into the night, and He is the Knower of whatsoever is in the breasts.

يُولِجُ ٱلَّيْلَ فِى ٱلنَّهَارِ وَيُولِجُ ٱلنَّهَارَ فِى ٱلَّيْلِ وَهُوَ عَلِيمٌ بِذَاتِ ٱلصُّدُورِ ۝

7. Believe in Allah and His Messenger and spend of that whereof He has made you successors to.[707] Those of you who believe and spend, theirs shall be a great reward.

ءَامِنُوا بِٱللَّهِ وَرَسُولِهِۦ وَأَنفِقُوا مِمَّا جَعَلَكُم مُّسْتَخْلَفِينَ فِيهِ فَٱلَّذِينَ ءَامَنُوا مِنكُمْ وَأَنفَقُوا لَهُمْ أَجْرٌ كَبِيرٌ ۝

8. And why is it that you believe not in Allah whereas the Messenger is calling you to believe in your Lord, and He has already taken your bond, if you are going to be believers?

وَمَا لَكُمْ لَا تُؤْمِنُونَ بِٱللَّهِ وَٱلرَّسُولُ يَدْعُوكُمْ لِتُؤْمِنُوا بِرَبِّكُمْ وَقَدْ أَخَذَ مِيثَٰقَكُمْ إِن كُنتُم مُّؤْمِنِينَ ۝

9. He it is Who sends down to His bondsman clear signs that He may bring you forth from darkness into the light, and verily Allah is to you the Tender, the Merciful.

هُوَ ٱلَّذِى يُنَزِّلُ عَلَىٰ عَبْدِهِۦ ءَايَٰتٍ بَيِّنَٰتٍ لِّيُخْرِجَكُم مِّنَ ٱلظُّلُمَٰتِ إِلَى ٱلنُّورِ وَإِنَّ ٱللَّهَ بِكُمْ لَرَءُوفٌ رَّحِيمٌ ۝

---

707. Notice the essential impermanence of wealth implied in the words 'successors to'. All wealth really belongs to God; men are only stewards or trustees, succeeding one another.

10. And how is it that you spend not in the cause of Allah when Allah's shall be the inheritance of the heavens and the earth? Those of you who spent and fought before the victory shall not be held equal. They are greater in rank than those who spend and fought afterwards; unto each, Allah has promised good; and He is Aware of whatsoever you do.

وَمَا لَكُمْ أَلَّا تُنفِقُوا فِي سَبِيلِ اللَّهِ وَلِلَّهِ مِيرَٰثُ السَّمَٰوَٰتِ وَالْأَرْضِ لَا يَسْتَوِي مِنكُم مَّنْ أَنفَقَ مِن قَبْلِ الْفَتْحِ وَقَٰتَلَ أُو۟لَٰٓئِكَ أَعْظَمُ دَرَجَةً مِّنَ الَّذِينَ أَنفَقُوا۟ مِنۢ بَعْدُ وَقَٰتَلُوا۟ وَكُلًّا وَعَدَ اللَّهُ الْحُسْنَىٰ وَاللَّهُ بِمَا تَعْمَلُونَ خَبِيرٌ ۝

Section 2

11. Who is he that will lend Allah a goodly loan, so that He may multiply it for him? And his will be an honourable reward.

مَّن ذَا الَّذِي يُقْرِضُ اللَّهَ قَرْضًا حَسَنًا فَيُضَٰعِفَهُۥ لَهُۥ وَلَهُۥٓ أَجْرٌ كَرِيمٌ ۝

12. Mention the Day whereon you shall see the believing men and women, their light running before them and on their right hands;[708] glad tidings to you today; Gardens with running water beneath them, they will abide therein. That; that is a mighty achievement.

يَوْمَ تَرَى الْمُؤْمِنِينَ وَالْمُؤْمِنَٰتِ يَسْعَىٰ نُورُهُم بَيْنَ أَيْدِيهِمْ وَبِأَيْمَٰنِهِم بُشْرَىٰكُمُ الْيَوْمَ جَنَّٰتٌ تَجْرِي مِن تَحْتِهَا الْأَنْهَٰرُ خَٰلِدِينَ فِيهَا ذَٰلِكَ هُوَ الْفَوْزُ الْعَظِيمُ ۝

---

708. This light will emanate from the Book wherein their actions are recorded and which they will hold in their right hand.

13. It shall be the Day whereon the hypocrites, men and women, will say to the faithful: 'Wait for us that we may borrow some light from you.' It will be said: 'Go back and seek a light elsewhere.' A high wall, will then be set up between them, wherein will be a door, of which the inside has mercy and the outside of which is towards the torment.

يَوْمَ يَقُولُ ٱلْمُنَـٰفِقُونَ وَٱلْمُنَـٰفِقَـٰتُ لِلَّذِينَ ءَامَنُوا ٱنظُرُونَا نَقْتَبِسْ مِن نُّورِكُمْ قِيلَ ٱرْجِعُوا وَرَآءَكُمْ فَٱلْتَمِسُوا نُورًا فَضُرِبَ بَيْنَهُم بِسُورٍ لَّهُۥ بَابٌ بَاطِنُهُۥ فِيهِ ٱلرَّحْمَةُ وَظَـٰهِرُهُۥ مِن قِبَلِهِ ٱلْعَذَابُ ﴿١٣﴾

14. They will call to them: 'Have we not been with you?' They will say: 'Yes, but you tempted your souls and you waited and you doubted and your vain desires beguiled you until there came the affair of Allah, and in respect of Allah, the beguiler beguiled you.'

يُنَادُونَهُمْ أَلَمْ نَكُن مَّعَكُمْ قَالُوا بَلَىٰ وَلَـٰكِنَّكُمْ فَتَنتُمْ أَنفُسَكُمْ وَتَرَبَّصْتُمْ وَٱرْتَبْتُمْ وَغَرَّتْكُمُ ٱلْأَمَانِىُّ حَتَّىٰ جَآءَ أَمْرُ ٱللَّهِ وَغَرَّكُم بِٱللَّهِ ٱلْغَرُورُ ﴿١٤﴾

15. Today thereof will no ransom be accepted of you, nor of those who openly disbelieved; your abode is the Fire; that is your companion, a hapless destination.

فَٱلْيَوْمَ لَا يُؤْخَذُ مِنكُمْ فِدْيَةٌ وَلَا مِنَ ٱلَّذِينَ كَفَرُوا مَأْوَىٰكُمُ ٱلنَّارُ هِىَ مَوْلَىٰكُمْ وَبِئْسَ ٱلْمَصِيرُ ﴿١٥﴾

16. Has not the time yet come for those who believe, that their hearts would humble themselves to Allah's admonition and to the Truth which has been revealed, and that they do not become as those who were given the Book before, and the time was extended to them, and so their hearts were hardened? And many of them were ungodly.

أَلَمْ يَأْنِ لِلَّذِينَ ءَامَنُوا أَن تَخْشَعَ قُلُوبُهُمْ لِذِكْرِ ٱللَّهِ وَمَا نَزَلَ مِنَ ٱلْحَقِّ وَلَا يَكُونُوا كَٱلَّذِينَ أُوتُوا ٱلْكِتَـٰبَ مِن قَبْلُ فَطَالَ عَلَيْهِمُ ٱلْأَمَدُ فَقَسَتْ قُلُوبُهُمْ وَكَثِيرٌ مِّنْهُمْ فَـٰسِقُونَ ﴿١٦﴾

17. Know that Allah quickens the earth after its death. Surely We have propounded to you the signs that haply you may reflect.

اَعْلَمُوۡۤا اَنَّ اللّٰهَ يُحۡىِ الۡاَرۡضَ بَعۡدَ مَوۡتِهَا ۚ قَدۡ بَيَّنَّا لَكُمُ الۡاٰيٰتِ لَعَلَّكُمۡ تَعۡقِلُوۡنَ ۞

18. Verily the alms-giving men and women and they are lending a goodly loan to Allah and it shall be multiplied for them and theirs shall be an honourable reward.

اِنَّ الۡمُصَّدِّقِيۡنَ وَالۡمُصَّدِّقٰتِ وَاَقۡرَضُوا اللّٰهَ قَرۡضًا حَسَنًا يُّضٰعَفُ لَهُمۡ وَلَهُمۡ اَجۡرٌ كَرِيۡمٌ ۞

19. And those who believe in Allah and His Messengers, they are the saints and martyrs in the sight of their Lord; theirs shall be their full wage and their light, and those who disbelieved and belied Our signs they shall be the fellows of the Blaze.

وَالَّذِيۡنَ اٰمَنُوۡا بِاللّٰهِ وَرُسُلِهٖۤ اُولٰٓئِكَ هُمُ الصِّدِّيۡقُوۡنَ ۖ وَالشُّهَدَآءُ عِنۡدَ رَبِّهِمۡ ۚ لَهُمۡ اَجۡرُهُمۡ وَنُوۡرُهُمۡ ۚ وَالَّذِيۡنَ كَفَرُوۡا وَكَذَّبُوۡا بِاٰيٰتِنَآ اُولٰٓئِكَ اَصۡحٰبُ الۡجَحِيۡمِ ۞

Section 3

20. Know that the life of this world is but a sport and a play, and an adornment and a self-glorification among you and a rivalry in riches and children. It is as the vegetation after rains the growth of which pleases the husbandmen, then it withers and you see it becoming yellow, then it becomes chaff. And in the Hereafter there is both a grievous torment and forgiveness from Allah and His pleasure; and the life of this world is but a vain bauble.

اِعۡلَمُوۡۤا اَنَّمَا الۡحَيٰوةُ الدُّنۡيَا لَعِبٌ وَّلَهۡوٌ وَّزِيۡنَةٌ وَّتَفَاخُرٌۢ بَيۡنَكُمۡ وَتَكَاثُرٌ فِى الۡاَمۡوَالِ وَالۡاَوۡلَادِ ۚ كَمَثَلِ غَيۡثٍ اَعۡجَبَ الۡكُفَّارَ نَبَاتُهٗ ثُمَّ يَهِيۡجُ فَتَرٰىهُ مُصۡفَرًّا ثُمَّ يَكُوۡنُ حُطَامًا ۚ وَفِى الۡاٰخِرَةِ عَذَابٌ شَدِيۡدٌ ۙ وَّمَغۡفِرَةٌ مِّنَ اللّٰهِ وَرِضۡوَانٌ ۚ وَمَا الۡحَيٰوةُ الدُّنۡيَاۤ اِلَّا مَتَاعُ الۡغُرُوۡرِ ۞

21.　Strive with one another in hastening towards forgiveness from your Lord and towards a Garden of which the width is as the width of the heavens and the earth, prepared for those who believe in Allah and His Messengers. This is the grace of Allah! He vouchsafes it to whomsoever He will; and Allah is the Owner of mighty grace.

سَابِقُوٓاْ إِلَىٰ مَغْفِرَةٍ مِّن رَّبِّكُمْ وَجَنَّةٍ عَرْضُهَا كَعَرْضِ ٱلسَّمَآءِ وَٱلْأَرْضِ أُعِدَّتْ لِلَّذِينَ ءَامَنُواْ بِٱللَّهِ وَرُسُلِهِۦ ذَٰلِكَ فَضْلُ ٱللَّهِ يُؤْتِيهِ مَن يَشَآءُ وَٱللَّهُ ذُو ٱلْفَضْلِ ٱلْعَظِيمِ ﴿٢١﴾

22.　Naught of affliction befalls the earth or your persons but it is inscribed in the Book, even before We have created them. Verily that is easy with Allah.

مَآ أَصَابَ مِن مُّصِيبَةٍ فِى ٱلْأَرْضِ وَلَا فِىٓ أَنفُسِكُمْ إِلَّا فِى كِتَٰبٍ مِّن قَبْلِ أَن نَّبْرَأَهَآ إِنَّ ذَٰلِكَ عَلَى ٱللَّهِ يَسِيرٌ ﴿٢٢﴾

23.　This is announced lest you feel sorry for what you miss, or exult over what He has vouchsafed to you, and Allah loves not any vainglorious boaster.

لِّكَيْلَا تَأْسَوْاْ عَلَىٰ مَا فَاتَكُمْ وَلَا تَفْرَحُواْ بِمَآ ءَاتَىٰكُمْ وَٱللَّهُ لَا يُحِبُّ كُلَّ مُخْتَالٍ فَخُورٍ ﴿٢٣﴾

24.　They who are niggardly and enjoin others to be niggardly. And whosoever turns away, then verily Allah! He is the Self-Sufficient, the Praiseworthy.

ٱلَّذِينَ يَبْخَلُونَ وَيَأْمُرُونَ ٱلنَّاسَ بِٱلْبُخْلِ وَمَن يَتَوَلَّ فَإِنَّ ٱللَّهَ هُوَ ٱلْغَنِىُّ ٱلْحَمِيدُ ﴿٢٤﴾

25.　Assuredly We sent Our Messengers with evidence and We sent down with them the Book and the balance that the people might observe equity. And We sent down iron in which is great violence and also advantages to mankind, and that Allah may know him who succours Allah, Unseen, and His Messengers. Verily Allah is the Strong, the Mighty.

لَقَدْ أَرْسَلْنَا رُسُلَنَا بِٱلْبَيِّنَٰتِ وَأَنزَلْنَا مَعَهُمُ ٱلْكِتَٰبَ وَٱلْمِيزَانَ لِيَقُومَ ٱلنَّاسُ بِٱلْقِسْطِ وَأَنزَلْنَا ٱلْحَدِيدَ فِيهِ بَأْسٌ شَدِيدٌ وَمَنَٰفِعُ لِلنَّاسِ وَلِيَعْلَمَ ٱللَّهُ مَن يَنصُرُهُۥ وَرُسُلَهُۥ بِٱلْغَيْبِ إِنَّ ٱللَّهَ قَوِىٌّ عَزِيزٌ ﴿٢٥﴾

Section 4

26. Assuredly We sent Noah and Abraham, and placed in the posterity of the two prophethood and the Book. Then of them are some guided ones, and many of them are ungodly.

وَلَقَدۡ أَرۡسَلۡنَا نُوحًا وَإِبۡرَٰهِيمَ وَجَعَلۡنَا فِي ذُرِّيَّتِهِمَا ٱلنُّبُوَّةَ وَٱلۡكِتَٰبَ فَمِنۡهُم مُّهۡتَدٍ وَكَثِيرٌ مِّنۡهُمۡ فَٰسِقُونَ ﴿٢٦﴾

27. And thereafter We caused Our Messengers to follow in their footsteps, and We caused Jesus, son of Maryam, to follow them, and We vouchsafed to him the Gospel, and We placed in the hearts of those who truly followed him, tenderness and compassion. And asceticism. We did not prescribe it for them; they innovated it,[709] only seeking Allah's goodwill, but they tended it not with the tendence due to it. So we vouchsafed to such of them as believed their reward; and many of them are ungodly.

ثُمَّ قَفَّيۡنَا عَلَىٰٓ ءَاثَٰرِهِم بِرُسُلِنَا وَقَفَّيۡنَا بِعِيسَى ٱبۡنِ مَرۡيَمَ وَءَاتَيۡنَٰهُ ٱلۡإِنجِيلَ وَجَعَلۡنَا فِي قُلُوبِ ٱلَّذِينَ ٱتَّبَعُوهُ رَأۡفَةً وَرَحۡمَةً وَرَهۡبَانِيَّةً ٱبۡتَدَعُوهَا مَا كَتَبۡنَٰهَا عَلَيۡهِمۡ إِلَّا ٱبۡتِغَآءَ رِضۡوَٰنِ ٱللَّهِ فَمَا رَعَوۡهَا حَقَّ رِعَايَتِهَا فَـَٔاتَيۡنَا ٱلَّذِينَ ءَامَنُوا مِنۡهُمۡ أَجۡرَهُمۡ وَكَثِيرٌ مِّنۡهُمۡ فَٰسِقُونَ ﴿٢٧﴾

---

709. Islam unlike Christian and many pagan philosophies, does not base its system of religio–moral perfection on the concept of the wickedness and sinfulness of the human body; and the law of Islam does not repudiate the earthly life *in toto* as intrinsically impure. It does not demand the suppression of fleshly impulses; it only requires that they should be curbed and controlled in accordance with the norm supplied by itself. Celibacy on a large scale is designed to defeat the very aim and purpose of nature and the replenishment of the earth.

28. O Believers! Fear Allah and believe in His Messenger, He will vouchsafe to you twofold portions of His mercy and will assign to you a light with which you will walk, and He will forgive you. And Allah is the Forgiving, the Merciful.

29. This He will award that the people of the Book may know that they control nothing of the grace of Allah, and that the grace is in Allah's hand. He vouchsafes it to whom He will, and Allah is the Owner of mighty grace.

يَـٰٓأَيُّهَا ٱلَّذِينَ ءَامَنُوا۟ ٱتَّقُوا۟ ٱللَّهَ وَءَامِنُوا۟ بِرَسُولِهِۦ يُؤۡتِكُمۡ كِفۡلَيۡنِ مِن رَّحۡمَتِهِۦ وَيَجۡعَل لَّكُمۡ نُورًا تَمۡشُونَ بِهِۦ وَيَغۡفِرۡ لَكُمۡ وَٱللَّهُ غَفُورٌ رَّحِيمٌ ۝

لِّئَلَّا يَعۡلَمَ أَهۡلُ ٱلۡكِتَـٰبِ أَلَّا يَقۡدِرُونَ عَلَىٰ شَىۡءٍ مِّن فَضۡلِ ٱللَّهِ وَأَنَّ ٱلۡفَضۡلَ بِيَدِ ٱللَّهِ يُؤۡتِيهِ مَن يَشَآءُ وَٱللَّهُ ذُو ٱلۡفَضۡلِ ٱلۡعَظِيمِ ۝

Sūrah 58

al-Mujādalah

(Madinan, 3 Sections, 22 Verses)

In the name of Allah, the Compassionate, the Merciful.

Section 1

1. Surely has Allah heard the saying of her who pleaded with you concerning her husband and made her complaint to Allah, and Allah has heard your mutual conversation. Verily Allah is the Hearing, the Beholding.

2. As to those among you who put away their wives by pronouncing *Zihār*, their mothers they are not. Their mothers are only those who gave them birth; and they utter a word disreputable and false. Verily Allah is the Pardoning, the Forgiving.

3. Those who put away their wives by pronouncing *Zihār* and thereafter would retract what they have said, then upon them is the freeing of a slave before they touch each other. You are exhorted to that; and Allah is Aware of whatsoever you do.

4. And whoso does not find a slave to free, on him is the fasting for two months consecutively before they touch each other, and on him who is unable to do so is the feeding of sixty indigent ones. That is in order that you may believe in Allah and His Messenger. These are the ordinances of Allah, and for the infidels is an afflictive chastisement.

فَمَن لَّمْ يَجِدْ فَصِيَامُ شَهْرَيْنِ مُتَتَابِعَيْنِ مِن قَبْلِ أَن يَتَمَاسَّا فَمَن لَّمْ يَسْتَطِعْ فَإِطْعَامُ سِتِّينَ مِسْكِينًا ذَٰلِكَ لِتُؤْمِنُوا بِٱللَّهِ وَرَسُولِهِۦ وَتِلْكَ حُدُودُ ٱللَّهِ وَلِلْكَٰفِرِينَ عَذَابٌ أَلِيمٌ ٤

5. Verily those who oppose Allah and His Messenger shall be abased even as those before them were abased; and surely we have sent down manifest signs. And for the infidels is an ignominious chastisement.

إِنَّ ٱلَّذِينَ يُحَادُّونَ ٱللَّهَ وَرَسُولَهُۥ كُبِتُوا كَمَا كُبِتَ ٱلَّذِينَ مِن قَبْلِهِمْ وَقَدْ أَنزَلْنَآ ءَايَٰتٍۭ بَيِّنَٰتٍ وَلِلْكَٰفِرِينَ عَذَابٌ مُّهِينٌ ٥

6. On the Day when Allah will raise them all together and declare to them what they have worked. Allah has taken count thereof, while they forget it. And Allah is a Witness over everything.

يَوْمَ يَبْعَثُهُمُ ٱللَّهُ جَمِيعًا فَيُنَبِّئُهُم بِمَا عَمِلُوا أَحْصَىٰهُ ٱللَّهُ وَنَسُوهُ وَٱللَّهُ عَلَىٰ كُلِّ شَىْءٍ شَهِيدٌ ٦

Section 2

7. Have you not seen that Allah knows whatsoever is in the heavens and whatsoever is in the earth? There is no whispering among three but He is their fourth, nor among five but He is their sixth, nor fewer nor more, but He is with them wheresoever they may be. And thereafter He will declare to them, on the Day of Judgement what they have worked. Verily Allah is the Knower of everything.

أَلَمْ تَرَ أَنَّ ٱللَّهَ يَعْلَمُ مَا فِى ٱلسَّمَٰوَٰتِ وَمَا فِى ٱلْأَرْضِ مَا يَكُونُ مِن نَّجْوَىٰ ثَلَٰثَةٍ إِلَّا هُوَ رَابِعُهُمْ وَلَا خَمْسَةٍ إِلَّا هُوَ سَادِسُهُمْ وَلَآ أَدْنَىٰ مِن ذَٰلِكَ وَلَآ أَكْثَرَ إِلَّا هُوَ مَعَهُمْ أَيْنَ مَا كَانُوا ثُمَّ يُنَبِّئُهُم بِمَا عَمِلُوا يَوْمَ ٱلْقِيَٰمَةِ إِنَّ ٱللَّهَ بِكُلِّ شَىْءٍ عَلِيمٌ ٧

8.　Have you not seen those who were forbidden whispering, and they returned afterwards to what they had been forbidden? And they whisper among themselves of sin, and transgression and disobedience to the Messenger. And when they come to you, they do not greet you with that with which Allah greets you, and say within themselves: 'Why does Allah not punish us for what we utter?' Sufficient unto them is Hell, wherein they will roast, a hapless destination!

أَلَمْ تَرَ إِلَى ٱلَّذِينَ نُهُوا عَنِ ٱلنَّجْوَىٰ ثُمَّ يَعُودُونَ لِمَا نُهُوا عَنْهُ وَيَتَنَـٰجَوْنَ بِٱلْإِثْمِ وَٱلْعُدْوَٰنِ وَمَعْصِيَتِ ٱلرَّسُولِ وَإِذَا جَآءُوكَ حَيَّوْكَ بِمَا لَمْ يُحَيِّكَ بِهِ ٱللَّهُ وَيَقُولُونَ فِىٓ أَنفُسِهِمْ لَوْلَا يُعَذِّبُنَا ٱللَّهُ بِمَا نَقُولُ ۚ حَسْبُهُمْ جَهَنَّمُ يَصْلَوْنَهَا ۖ فَبِئْسَ ٱلْمَصِيرُ ۝

9. O Believers! When you whisper together, do not whisper of sin and transgression and disobedience to the Messenger, but whisper for virtue and piety. And fear Allah unto Whom you will be gathered.

يَـٰٓأَيُّهَا ٱلَّذِينَ ءَامَنُوٓا إِذَا تَنَـٰجَيْتُمْ فَلَا تَتَنَـٰجَوْا بِٱلْإِثْمِ وَٱلْعُدْوَٰنِ وَمَعْصِيَتِ ٱلرَّسُولِ وَتَنَـٰجَوْا بِٱلْبِرِّ وَٱلتَّقْوَىٰ ۖ وَٱتَّقُوا ٱللَّهَ ٱلَّذِىٓ إِلَيْهِ تُحْشَرُونَ ۝

10.　Whispering is only from Satan that he may grieve the believers; and he cannot harm them at all save with the leave of Allah. So in Allah let the believers trust.

إِنَّمَا ٱلنَّجْوَىٰ مِنَ ٱلشَّيْطَـٰنِ لِيَحْزُنَ ٱلَّذِينَ ءَامَنُوا وَلَيْسَ بِضَآرِّهِمْ شَيْـًٔا إِلَّا بِإِذْنِ ٱللَّهِ ۚ وَعَلَى ٱللَّهِ فَلْيَتَوَكَّلِ ٱلْمُؤْمِنُونَ ۝

11.　O Believers! When it is said to you; make room in your assemblies, then make room; Allah will make room for you. And when it is said; rise up, then rise up. Allah will exalt, in degree, those of you who believe and those who are endowed with knowledge. Allah is aware of whatsoever you work.

يَـٰٓأَيُّهَا ٱلَّذِينَ ءَامَنُوٓا إِذَا قِيلَ لَكُمْ تَفَسَّحُوا فِى ٱلْمَجَـٰلِسِ فَٱفْسَحُوا يَفْسَحِ ٱللَّهُ لَكُمْ ۖ وَإِذَا قِيلَ ٱنشُزُوا فَٱنشُزُوا يَرْفَعِ ٱللَّهُ ٱلَّذِينَ ءَامَنُوا مِنكُمْ وَٱلَّذِينَ أُوتُوا ٱلْعِلْمَ دَرَجَـٰتٍ ۚ وَٱللَّهُ بِمَا تَعْمَلُونَ خَبِيرٌ ۝

12. O Believers! When you come to the Messenger for private consultation, offer alms before your whispering. That is better for you and purer. Then if you do not find the wherewithal, Allah is the Forgiving, the Merciful.

يَـٰٓأَيُّهَا ٱلَّذِينَ ءَامَنُوٓا۟ إِذَا نَـٰجَيْتُمُ ٱلرَّسُولَ فَقَدِّمُوا۟ بَيْنَ يَدَىْ نَجْوَىٰكُمْ صَدَقَةً ذَٰلِكَ خَيْرٌ لَّكُمْ وَأَطْهَرُ فَإِن لَّمْ تَجِدُوا۟ فَإِنَّ ٱللَّهَ غَفُورٌ رَّحِيمٌ ۝١٢

13. Do you shrink at your spending something in charity before your whispering? Then, when you could not do it, and Allah relented towards you, establish prayer and pay the poor-rate, and obey Allah and His Messenger. And Allah is aware of what you do.

ءَأَشْفَقْتُمْ أَن تُقَدِّمُوا۟ بَيْنَ يَدَىْ نَجْوَىٰكُمْ صَدَقَـٰتٍ فَإِذْ لَمْ تَفْعَلُوا۟ وَتَابَ ٱللَّهُ عَلَيْكُمْ فَأَقِيمُوا۟ ٱلصَّلَوٰةَ وَءَاتُوا۟ ٱلزَّكَوٰةَ وَأَطِيعُوا۟ ٱللَّهَ وَرَسُولَهُۥ وَٱللَّهُ خَبِيرٌ بِمَا تَعْمَلُونَ ۝١٣

Section 3

14. Do you not see those who take for friends a people with whom Allah is angered? They are neither of you nor of them, and they swear to a lie while they know.

أَلَمْ تَرَ إِلَى ٱلَّذِينَ تَوَلَّوْا۟ قَوْمًا غَضِبَ ٱللَّهُ عَلَيْهِم مَّا هُم مِّنكُمْ وَلَا مِنْهُمْ وَيَحْلِفُونَ عَلَى ٱلْكَذِبِ وَهُمْ يَعْلَمُونَ ۝١٤

15. Allah has prepared for them a grievous torment; verily vile is what they have been working.

أَعَدَّ ٱللَّهُ لَهُمْ عَذَابًا شَدِيدًا إِنَّهُمْ سَآءَ مَا كَانُوا۟ يَعْمَلُونَ ۝١٥

16. They have taken their oaths as a shield, and they have hindered others from the way of Allah, and theirs shall be a debasing torment.

ٱتَّخَذُوٓا۟ أَيْمَـٰنَهُمْ جُنَّةً فَصَدُّوا۟ عَن سَبِيلِ ٱللَّهِ فَلَهُمْ عَذَابٌ مُّهِينٌ ۝١٦

17. Their riches or their progeny will not avail them against Allah at all. They are the fellows of the Fire; there they shall abide.

لَّن تُغْنِىَ عَنْهُمْ أَمْوَٰلُهُمْ وَلَآ أَوْلَـٰدُهُم مِّنَ ٱللَّهِ شَيْـًٔا أُو۟لَـٰٓئِكَ أَصْحَـٰبُ ٱلنَّارِ هُمْ فِيهَا خَـٰلِدُونَ ۝١٧

18. This will happen on a Day when Allah will raise all together; then they will swear to Allah, as they swear to you today; imagining that they rest upon something, lo! Verily they are liars.

يَوْمَ يَبْعَثُهُمُ اللَّهُ جَمِيعًا فَيَحْلِفُونَ لَهُ كَمَا يَحْلِفُونَ لَكُمْ وَيَحْسَبُونَ أَنَّهُمْ عَلَى شَىْءٍ أَلَا إِنَّهُمْ هُمُ الْكَذِبُونَ ۝

19. Satan has overpowered them and has caused them to forget the remembrance of Allah. These are the band of Satan. Lo! Verily it is the band of Satan that shall be the losers.

اسْتَحْوَذَ عَلَيْهِمُ الشَّيْطَنُ فَأَنسَهُمْ ذِكْرَ اللَّهِ أُولَئِكَ حِزْبُ الشَّيْطَنِ أَلَا إِنَّ حِزْبَ الشَّيْطَنِ هُمُ الْخَسِرُونَ ۝

20. Verily those who resist Allah and His Messenger, they are among the lowest.

إِنَّ الَّذِينَ يُحَادُّونَ اللَّهَ وَرَسُولَهُ أُولَئِكَ فِى الْأَذَلِينَ ۝

21. Allah has prescribed: 'Surely I will overcome: I and My Messengers.' Verily Allah is the Strong, the Mighty.

كَتَبَ اللَّهُ لَأَغْلِبَنَّ أَنَا وَرُسُلِى إِنَّ اللَّهَ قَوِىٌّ عَزِيزٌ ۝

22. You shall not find a people who believe in Allah and the last Day befriending those who oppose Allah and His Messenger even though they be their fathers of their sons or their brethren or their kindred. These! He has inscribed faith on their hearts and has strengthened them with a spirit from Him; and He shall make them enter Gardens whereunder rivers flow as abiders therein. Well pleased is Allah with them, and well-pleased are they with Him; these are Allah's band, lo! Verily it is Allah's band that are the blissful.

لَا تَجِدُ قَوْمًا يُؤْمِنُونَ بِاللَّهِ وَالْيَوْمِ الْآخِرِ يُوَادُّونَ مَنْ حَادَّ اللَّهَ وَرَسُولَهُ وَلَوْ كَانُوا آبَاءَهُمْ أَوْ أَبْنَاءَهُمْ أَوْ إِخْوَنَهُمْ أَوْ عَشِيرَتَهُمْ أُولَئِكَ كَتَبَ فِى قُلُوبِهِمُ الْإِيمَنَ وَأَيَّدَهُم بِرُوحٍ مِّنْهُ وَيُدْخِلُهُمْ جَنَّتٍ تَجْرِى مِن تَحْتِهَا الْأَنْهَرُ خَلِدِينَ فِيهَا رَضِىَ اللَّهُ عَنْهُمْ وَرَضُوا عَنْهُ أُولَئِكَ حِزْبُ اللَّهِ أَلَا إِنَّ حِزْبَ اللَّهِ هُمُ الْمُفْلِحُونَ ۝

Sūrah 59

al-Ḥashr

(Madinan, 3 Sections, 24 Verses)

In the name of Allah, the Compassionate, the Merciful.

Section 1

1. Whatsoever is in the heavens and whatsoever is in the earth hallows Allah, and He is the Mighty, the Wise.

2. He it is Who drove forth the people of the Book who disbelieved from their homes at the first meeting. You did not imagine that they would go forth; and they imagined that their strongholds would defend them against Allah. Then Allah came upon them from where they reckoned not, cast terror in their hearts so that they made their houses desolate by their own hands as well as the hands of the believers. Take warning, therefore, O you with eyes!

3. And had not Allah ordained banishment for them, surely He would have chastised them in this world, and in the Hereafter theirs is a chastisement of the Fire.

4. This, because they opposed Allah and His Messenger, and whoso opposes Allah, then, Allah is stern in chastising.

ذَٰلِكَ بِأَنَّهُمۡ شَآقُّواْ ٱللَّهَ وَرَسُولَهُۥ وَمَن يُشَآقِّ ٱللَّهَ فَإِنَّ ٱللَّهَ شَدِيدُ ٱلۡعِقَابِ ﴿٤﴾

5. Whatever fine palms you cut down or left standing on their roots, it was by Allah's leave and in order that He might abase the transgressors.

مَا قَطَعۡتُم مِّن لِّينَةٍ أَوۡ تَرَكۡتُمُوهَا قَآئِمَةً عَلَىٰٓ أُصُولِهَا فَبِإِذۡنِ ٱللَّهِ وَلِيُخۡزِيَ ٱلۡفَٰسِقِينَ ﴿٥﴾

6. And as to what He restored to His Messenger, you rushed neither horse nor camel upon it, but Allah gives mastery to His Messenger over whomsoever He will. And Allah is potent over everything.

وَمَآ أَفَآءَ ٱللَّهُ عَلَىٰ رَسُولِهِۦ مِنۡهُمۡ فَمَآ أَوۡجَفۡتُمۡ عَلَيۡهِ مِنۡ خَيۡلٍ وَلَا رِكَابٍ وَلَٰكِنَّ ٱللَّهَ يُسَلِّطُ رُسُلَهُۥ عَلَىٰ مَن يَشَآءُ وَٱللَّهُ عَلَىٰ كُلِّ شَىۡءٍ قَدِيرٌ ﴿٦﴾

7. Whatsoever Allah may restore to His Messenger from the people of the cities is due unto Allah and the Messenger and his kinsmen, and the orphans and the indigent and the wayfarer, so that it may not be confined to the rich among you. Take whatsoever the Messenger gives you, and refrain from[710] whatsoever he forbids you. And fear Allah; verily Allah is Stern in chastising.

مَّآ أَفَآءَ ٱللَّهُ عَلَىٰ رَسُولِهِۦ مِنۡ أَهۡلِ ٱلۡقُرَىٰ فَلِلَّهِ وَلِلرَّسُولِ وَلِذِى ٱلۡقُرۡبَىٰ وَٱلۡيَتَٰمَىٰ وَٱلۡمَسَٰكِينِ وَٱبۡنِ ٱلسَّبِيلِ كَىۡ لَا يَكُونَ دُولَةًۢ بَيۡنَ ٱلۡأَغۡنِيَآءِ مِنكُمۡ وَمَآ ءَاتَىٰكُمُ ٱلرَّسُولُ فَخُذُوهُ وَمَا نَهَىٰكُمۡ عَنۡهُ فَٱنتَهُواْ وَٱتَّقُواْ ٱللَّهَ إِنَّ ٱللَّهَ شَدِيدُ ٱلۡعِقَابِ ﴿٧﴾

---

710. The Prophet's 'wonderful life was a living illustration and explanation of the Qur'ān, and we can do no greater justice to the Holy Book than by following him who was the mouthpiece of its revelation' (Asad, *Islam at the Crossroads*, p. 91). His life serves as the infallible model, in every little detail, to every true believer.

8.   And it is due to the poor *Muhājirūn* who have been driven forth from their homes and their substance, seeking grace and goodwill from Allah and succouring Allah and His Messenger. These! They are the sincere.

9.   And it is also due to those who are settled in the dwelling and the faith before them, loving those who have migrated to them and finding in their breasts no desire for what has been given them, preferring them above themselves even though there was want among them and whosoever is preserved from the greed of his soul, then these!, they are the blissful.

10.   And it is also due to those who came after them, saying: 'Lord! Forgive us and our brethren who have preceded us in faith and put not in our hearts any rancour toward those who have already believed, Lord! You are the Tender, the Merciful.

Section 2

11.   See you not those who dissemble saying to their brethren who disbelieve among the people of the Book: if you are banished we too, will go forth with you and we will not listen to anyone in respect of you, and if you are attacked, we will succour you. Allah bears witness that they are certainly liars.

لِلْفُقَرَاءِ ٱلْمُهَٰجِرِينَ ٱلَّذِينَ أُخْرِجُوا۟ مِن دِيَٰرِهِمْ وَأَمْوَٰلِهِمْ يَبْتَغُونَ فَضْلًا مِّنَ ٱللَّهِ وَرِضْوَٰنًا وَيَنصُرُونَ ٱللَّهَ وَرَسُولَهُۥٓ أُو۟لَٰٓئِكَ هُمُ ٱلصَّٰدِقُونَ ۝

وَٱلَّذِينَ تَبَوَّءُو ٱلدَّارَ وَٱلْإِيمَٰنَ مِن قَبْلِهِمْ يُحِبُّونَ مَنْ هَاجَرَ إِلَيْهِمْ وَلَا يَجِدُونَ فِى صُدُورِهِمْ حَاجَةً مِّمَّآ أُوتُوا۟ وَيُؤْثِرُونَ عَلَىٰٓ أَنفُسِهِمْ وَلَوْ كَانَ بِهِمْ خَصَاصَةٌ وَمَن يُوقَ شُحَّ نَفْسِهِۦ فَأُو۟لَٰٓئِكَ هُمُ ٱلْمُفْلِحُونَ ۝

وَٱلَّذِينَ جَآءُو مِنۢ بَعْدِهِمْ يَقُولُونَ رَبَّنَا ٱغْفِرْ لَنَا وَلِإِخْوَٰنِنَا ٱلَّذِينَ سَبَقُونَا بِٱلْإِيمَٰنِ وَلَا تَجْعَلْ فِى قُلُوبِنَا غِلًّا لِّلَّذِينَ ءَامَنُوا۟ رَبَّنَآ إِنَّكَ رَءُوفٌ رَّحِيمٌ ۝

أَلَمْ تَرَ إِلَى ٱلَّذِينَ نَافَقُوا۟ يَقُولُونَ لِإِخْوَٰنِهِمُ ٱلَّذِينَ كَفَرُوا۟ مِنْ أَهْلِ ٱلْكِتَٰبِ لَئِنْ أُخْرِجْتُمْ لَنَخْرُجَنَّ مَعَكُمْ وَلَا نُطِيعُ فِيكُمْ أَحَدًا أَبَدًا وَإِن قُوتِلْتُمْ لَنَنصُرَنَّكُمْ وَٱللَّهُ يَشْهَدُ إِنَّهُمْ لَكَٰذِبُونَ ۝

12. To be sure, if they are banished, they will not go forth with them, and if they are attacked, they will not succour them and even if they did succour them they would turn their backs, and then they should not be succoured.

لَّئِنْ أُخْرِجُوا لَا يَخْرُجُونَ مَعَهُمْ وَلَئِن قُوتِلُوا لَا يَنصُرُونَهُمْ وَلَئِن نَّصَرُوهُمْ لَيُوَلُّنَّ ٱلْأَدْبَارَ ثُمَّ لَا يُنصَرُونَ ۝

13. Surely in their breasts you are more awful than Allah. That is because they are a people who have no understanding.

لَأَنتُمْ أَشَدُّ رَهْبَةً فِى صُدُورِهِم مِّنَ ٱللَّهِ ذَٰلِكَ بِأَنَّهُمْ قَوْمٌ لَّا يَفْقَهُونَ ۝

14. They shall not fight against you, not even together, except in fenced townships or from behind walls. Their violence among themselves is great; you deem them united while their hearts are diverse. That is because they are a people who do not reflect.

لَا يُقَٰتِلُونَكُمْ جَمِيعًا إِلَّا فِى قُرًى مُّحَصَّنَةٍ أَوْ مِن وَرَآءِ جُدُرٍ بَأْسُهُم بَيْنَهُمْ شَدِيدٌ تَحْسَبُهُمْ جَمِيعًا وَقُلُوبُهُمْ شَتَّىٰ ذَٰلِكَ بِأَنَّهُمْ قَوْمٌ لَّا يَعْقِلُونَ ۝

15. They are like those a little before them; they tasted the ill-effect of their affairs, and theirs will be an afflictive torment.

كَمَثَلِ ٱلَّذِينَ مِن قَبْلِهِمْ قَرِيبًا ذَاقُوا وَبَالَ أَمْرِهِمْ وَلَهُمْ عَذَابٌ أَلِيمٌ ۝

16. They are like Satan when he says to man: 'Disbelieve;' and then when he disbelieves, says: 'I am quit of you. I verily fear Allah, Lord of the worlds.'

كَمَثَلِ ٱلشَّيْطَٰنِ إِذْ قَالَ لِلْإِنسَٰنِ ٱكْفُرْ فَلَمَّا كَفَرَ قَالَ إِنِّى بَرِىٓءٌ مِّنكَ إِنِّىٓ أَخَافُ ٱللَّهَ رَبَّ ٱلْعَٰلَمِينَ ۝

17. The end of both, however, will be that they will be in the Fire, abiding therein; that is the recompense of the ungodly.

فَكَانَ عَٰقِبَتَهُمَآ أَنَّهُمَا فِى ٱلنَّارِ خَٰلِدَيْنِ فِيهَا وَذَٰلِكَ جَزَٰٓؤُا ٱلظَّٰلِمِينَ ۝

Section 3

18. O you who believe! Fear Allah, and let every soul look to what it sends forward for the morrow. And fear Allah; Allah is aware of what you do.

يَـٰٓأَيُّهَا ٱلَّذِينَ ءَامَنُوا۟ ٱتَّقُوا۟ ٱللَّهَ وَلْتَنظُرْ نَفْسٌ مَّا قَدَّمَتْ لِغَدٍ وَٱتَّقُوا۟ ٱللَّهَ إِنَّ ٱللَّهَ خَبِيرٌۢ بِمَا تَعْمَلُونَ ۱۸

19. And be not as those who forgot Allah, so He caused them to forget their own souls. These! they are the transgressors.

وَلَا تَكُونُوا۟ كَٱلَّذِينَ نَسُوا۟ ٱللَّهَ فَأَنسَىٰهُمْ أَنفُسَهُمْ أُو۟لَـٰٓئِكَ هُمُ ٱلْفَـٰسِقُونَ ۱۹

20. Not alike are the fellows of the Fire and the fellows of the Garden. Fellows of the Garden are the achievers.

لَا يَسْتَوِىٓ أَصْحَـٰبُ ٱلنَّارِ وَأَصْحَـٰبُ ٱلْجَنَّةِ أَصْحَـٰبُ ٱلْجَنَّةِ هُمُ ٱلْفَآئِزُونَ ۲۰

21. Had We sent down this Qur'ān on a mountain, you would surely have seen it humbling itself and cleaving in sunder in awe of Allah. Such similitudes We propound to mankind that haply they may reflect.

لَوْ أَنزَلْنَا هَـٰذَا ٱلْقُرْءَانَ عَلَىٰ جَبَلٍ لَّرَأَيْتَهُۥ خَـٰشِعًا مُّتَصَدِّعًا مِّنْ خَشْيَةِ ٱللَّهِ وَتِلْكَ ٱلْأَمْثَـٰلُ نَضْرِبُهَا لِلنَّاسِ لَعَلَّهُمْ يَتَفَكَّرُونَ ۲۱

22. He is Allah, there is no god but He, the Knower of the unseen and the seen, He is the Compassionate, the Merciful.

هُوَ ٱللَّهُ ٱلَّذِى لَآ إِلَـٰهَ إِلَّا هُوَ عَـٰلِمُ ٱلْغَيْبِ وَٱلشَّهَـٰدَةِ هُوَ ٱلرَّحْمَـٰنُ ٱلرَّحِيمُ ۲۲

23. He is Allah, there is no god but He, the Sovereign, the Holy, the Author of Safety, the Giver of Peace, the Protector, the Mighty, the Mender, the Majestic. Hallowed be Allah from what they associate.

هُوَ ٱللَّهُ ٱلَّذِى لَآ إِلَـٰهَ إِلَّا هُوَ ٱلْمَلِكُ ٱلْقُدُّوسُ ٱلسَّلَـٰمُ ٱلْمُؤْمِنُ ٱلْمُهَيْمِنُ ٱلْعَزِيزُ ٱلْجَبَّارُ ٱلْمُتَكَبِّرُ سُبْحَـٰنَ ٱللَّهِ عَمَّا يُشْرِكُونَ ۲۳

24. He is Allah, the Creator, the Maker, The Fashioner; His are the excellent names. Him hallows whatsoever is in the heavens and the earth, and He is the Mighty, the Wise.

هُوَ ٱللَّهُ ٱلۡخَٰلِقُ ٱلۡبَارِئُ ٱلۡمُصَوِّرُ لَهُ ٱلۡأَسۡمَآءُ ٱلۡحُسۡنَىٰ يُسَبِّحُ لَهُۥ مَا فِى ٱلسَّمَٰوَٰتِ وَٱلۡأَرۡضِ وَهُوَ ٱلۡعَزِيزُ ٱلۡحَكِيمُ ﴿٢٤﴾

Sūrah 60

al-Mumtaḥanah

(Madinan, 2 Sections, 13 Verses)

In the name of Allah, the Compassionate, the Merciful.

Section 1

1. O you who believe! Do not make friends with those who are My enemies and yours, showing affection towards them, while of a surety they deny what has come to you of the Truth, and have driven forth the Messenger and yourselves because you believe in Allah, your Lord, if you have come forth to strive in My cause, and to seek My goodwill. You show them affection in secret, while I know very well what you conceal and what you disclose. And whosoever of you does this, he has surely strayed from the straight path.

2. Should they come upon you, they will be your enemies and will stretch out their hands against you and also their tongues with evil, and would like that you should disbelieve.

3.   Neither your kindred nor your children will profit you on the Day of Judgement. He will decide between you; and Allah is the Beholder of what you do.

4.   Surely an excellent pattern has been for you in Abraham and those with him, when they said to their people: 'verily we are quit of you and what you worship beside Allah, and we renounce you; and there has appeared between us and you hostility and hatred for evermore until you believe in Allah alone, except the saying of Abraham to his father: 'Surely I shall seek forgiveness for you, and surely I have no power for you with Allah at all.' Our Lord! In You we put our trust and to You we turn and to You is our journeying.

5.   Our Lord! Make us not a trial for those who disbelieve, and forgive us our Lord. Verily You are the Mighty, the Wise.'

6.   Assuredly there has been an excellent pattern for you in them for him who hopes for Allah and the Last Day. And whosoever turns away, then verily Allah! He is the Self-Sufficient, the Laudable.

لَن تَنفَعَكُمْ أَرْحَامُكُمْ وَلَآ أَوْلَٰدُكُمْ يَوْمَ ٱلْقِيَٰمَةِ يَفْصِلُ بَيْنَكُمْ وَٱللَّهُ بِمَا تَعْمَلُونَ بَصِيرٌ ﴿٣﴾

قَدْ كَانَتْ لَكُمْ أُسْوَةٌ حَسَنَةٌ فِىٓ إِبْرَٰهِيمَ وَٱلَّذِينَ مَعَهُۥٓ إِذْ قَالُوا۟ لِقَوْمِهِمْ إِنَّا بُرَءَٰٓؤُا۟ مِنكُمْ وَمِمَّا تَعْبُدُونَ مِن دُونِ ٱللَّهِ كَفَرْنَا بِكُمْ وَبَدَا بَيْنَنَا وَبَيْنَكُمُ ٱلْعَدَٰوَةُ وَٱلْبَغْضَآءُ أَبَدًا حَتَّىٰ تُؤْمِنُوا۟ بِٱللَّهِ وَحْدَهُۥٓ إِلَّا قَوْلَ إِبْرَٰهِيمَ لِأَبِيهِ لَأَسْتَغْفِرَنَّ لَكَ وَمَآ أَمْلِكُ لَكَ مِنَ ٱللَّهِ مِن شَىْءٍ رَّبَّنَا عَلَيْكَ تَوَكَّلْنَا وَإِلَيْكَ أَنَبْنَا وَإِلَيْكَ ٱلْمَصِيرُ ﴿٤﴾

رَبَّنَا لَا تَجْعَلْنَا فِتْنَةً لِّلَّذِينَ كَفَرُوا۟ وَٱغْفِرْ لَنَا رَبَّنَآ إِنَّكَ أَنتَ ٱلْعَزِيزُ ٱلْحَكِيمُ ﴿٥﴾

لَقَدْ كَانَ لَكُمْ فِيهِمْ أُسْوَةٌ حَسَنَةٌ لِّمَن كَانَ يَرْجُوا۟ ٱللَّهَ وَٱلْيَوْمَ ٱلْءَاخِرَ وَمَن يَتَوَلَّ فَإِنَّ ٱللَّهَ هُوَ ٱلْغَنِىُّ ٱلْحَمِيدُ ﴿٦﴾

Section 2

7. Allah may perhaps place affection between you and those whom you hold as enemies.[711] And Allah is the Potent, and Allah is the Forgiving, the Merciful.

عَسَى اللَّهُ أَن يَجْعَلَ بَيْنَكُمْ وَبَيْنَ الَّذِينَ عَادَيْتُم مِّنْهُم مَّوَدَّةً وَاللَّهُ قَدِيرٌ وَاللَّهُ غَفُورٌ رَّحِيمٌ ۝

8. Allah does not forbid you to deal benevolently and equitably with those who did not fight against you on account of religion nor drove you out from homes; verily Allah loves the equitable.

لَّا يَنْهَاكُمُ اللَّهُ عَنِ الَّذِينَ لَمْ يُقَاتِلُوكُمْ فِي الدِّينِ وَلَمْ يُخْرِجُوكُم مِّن دِيَارِكُمْ أَن تَبَرُّوهُمْ وَتُقْسِطُوا إِلَيْهِمْ إِنَّ اللَّهَ يُحِبُّ الْمُقْسِطِينَ ۝

9. It is only concerning those who fought against you on account of religion and drove you out from your homes and helped in driving you out, that Allah forbids you to befriend them. And whosoever will befriend them, then these are the wrongdoers.

إِنَّمَا يَنْهَاكُمُ اللَّهُ عَنِ الَّذِينَ قَاتَلُوكُمْ فِي الدِّينِ وَأَخْرَجُوكُم مِّن دِيَارِكُمْ وَظَاهَرُوا عَلَىٰ إِخْرَاجِكُمْ أَن تَوَلَّوْهُمْ وَمَن يَتَوَلَّهُمْ فَأُولَٰئِكَ هُمُ الظَّالِمُونَ ۝

10. O you who believe! When believing women come to you as emigrants, examine them. Allah is the Best Knower of their faith. Then if you ascertain that they are believers, then do not send them back to the infidels; they are not lawful to them, nor are they lawful to them, and give them what they

يَا أَيُّهَا الَّذِينَ آمَنُوا إِذَا جَاءَكُمُ الْمُؤْمِنَاتُ مُهَاجِرَاتٍ فَامْتَحِنُوهُنَّ اللَّهُ أَعْلَمُ بِإِيمَانِهِنَّ فَإِنْ عَلِمْتُمُوهُنَّ مُؤْمِنَاتٍ فَلَا تَرْجِعُوهُنَّ إِلَى الْكُفَّارِ لَا هُنَّ حِلٌّ لَّهُمْ وَلَا هُمْ يَحِلُّونَ لَهُنَّ

---

711. This by inclining their hearts to Islam. This is exactly what happened on the taking of Makka, when the leading Quraish, who had till then been inveterate enemies of Islam, embraced faith and became friends and brethren of Muslims.

have spent. Nor is it a crime if you wed them when you have paid their wages. And do not hold to the ties of the infidel women, and ask back what you have spent, and let them ask back what they have spent. That is the judgement of Allah, He judges between you. And Allah is the Knowing, the Wise.

وَءَاتُوهُم مَّآ أَنفَقُوا ۚ وَلَا جُنَاحَ عَلَيْكُمْ أَن تَنكِحُوهُنَّ إِذَآ ءَاتَيْتُمُوهُنَّ أُجُورَهُنَّ ۚ وَلَا تُمْسِكُوا بِعِصَمِ ٱلْكَوَافِرِ وَسْـَٔلُوا مَآ أَنفَقْتُمْ وَلْيَسْـَٔلُوا مَآ أَنفَقُوا ۚ ذَٰلِكُمْ حُكْمُ ٱللَّهِ ۖ يَحْكُمُ بَيْنَكُمْ ۚ وَٱللَّهُ عَلِيمٌ حَكِيمٌ ﴿١٠﴾

11. And if any of your wives have been left with the infidels and you have retaliated, then give to those whose wives have gone away the like of what they have expended, and fear Allah in Whom you believe.

وَإِن فَاتَكُمْ شَىْءٌ مِّنْ أَزْوَٰجِكُمْ إِلَى ٱلْكُفَّارِ فَعَاقَبْتُمْ فَـَٔاتُوا ٱلَّذِينَ ذَهَبَتْ أَزْوَٰجُهُم مِّثْلَ مَآ أَنفَقُوا ۚ وَٱتَّقُوا ٱللَّهَ ٱلَّذِىٓ أَنتُم بِهِۦ مُؤْمِنُونَ ﴿١١﴾

12. O Prophet! When believing women come to you swearing fealty, that they shall not associate anyone with Allah, nor shall they steal, nor shall they commit fornication, nor shall they slay their children, nor shall they produce any falsehood that they have fabricated between their hands and feet, nor shall they disobey you in anything reputable, then accept you their fealty, and pray to Allah for their forgiveness, Verily Allah is the Forgiving, the Merciful.

يَٰٓأَيُّهَا ٱلنَّبِىُّ إِذَا جَآءَكَ ٱلْمُؤْمِنَٰتُ يُبَايِعْنَكَ عَلَىٰٓ أَن لَّا يُشْرِكْنَ بِٱللَّهِ شَيْـًٔا وَلَا يَسْرِقْنَ وَلَا يَزْنِينَ وَلَا يَقْتُلْنَ أَوْلَٰدَهُنَّ وَلَا يَأْتِينَ بِبُهْتَٰنٍ يَفْتَرِينَهُۥ بَيْنَ أَيْدِيهِنَّ وَأَرْجُلِهِنَّ وَلَا يَعْصِينَكَ فِى مَعْرُوفٍ فَبَايِعْهُنَّ وَٱسْتَغْفِرْ لَهُنَّ ٱللَّهَ ۖ إِنَّ ٱللَّهَ غَفُورٌ رَّحِيمٌ ﴿١٢﴾

13. O you who believe! Do not make friends with a people who have incurred the wrath of Allah. Surely they have despaired of the Hereafter, as despaired are the infidels buried dead.

يَٰٓأَيُّهَا ٱلَّذِينَ ءَامَنُوا۟ لَا تَتَوَلَّوْا۟ قَوْمًا غَضِبَ ٱللَّهُ عَلَيْهِمْ قَدْ يَئِسُوا۟ مِنَ ٱلْءَاخِرَةِ كَمَا يَئِسَ ٱلْكُفَّارُ مِنْ أَصْحَٰبِ ٱلْقُبُورِ ۝١٣

Sūrah 61

al-Ṣaff

(Madinan, 2 Sections, 14 Verses)

In the name of Allah, the Compassionate, the Merciful.

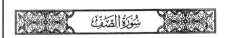

Section 1

1. Hallows Allah whatsoever is in the heavens and whatsoever is in the earth. And He is the Mighty, the Wise.

2. O Believers! Why do you say what you do not act?

3. Most odious it is to Allah that you should say what you do not act.

4. Verily Allah loves those who fight in His cause, drawn up in ranks, as though they were a structure well-compacted.

5. And recall when Moses said to his people: 'My people! Why do you hurt me when you know surely that I am Allah's Messenger to you?' Then when they swerved, Allah made their hearts swerve; and Allah does not guide a transgressing people.

6. And recall when Jesus, son of Maryam, said: 'O children of Israel! Verily I am Allah's Messenger to you, confirming the Torah before me and conveying the glad news of a Messenger coming after me;[712] his name will be Ahmad.[713] Then when he came to them with evidence, they said: 'This is manifest magic.'

وَإِذْ قَالَ عِيسَى ابْنُ مَرْيَمَ يَٰبَنِىٓ إِسْرَٰٓءِيلَ إِنِّى رَسُولُ ٱللَّهِ إِلَيْكُم مُّصَدِّقًا لِّمَا بَيْنَ يَدَىَّ مِنَ ٱلتَّوْرَىٰةِ وَمُبَشِّرًۢا بِرَسُولٍ يَأْتِى مِنۢ بَعْدِى ٱسْمُهُۥٓ أَحْمَدُ فَلَمَّا جَآءَهُم بِٱلْبَيِّنَٰتِ قَالُواْ هَٰذَا سِحْرٌ مُّبِينٌ ﴿٦﴾

7. And who is a greater wrong-doer than he who, when he is summoned to Islam, fabricates a lie against Allah? And Allah does not guide an ungodly people.

وَمَنْ أَظْلَمُ مِمَّنِ ٱفْتَرَىٰ عَلَى ٱللَّهِ ٱلْكَذِبَ وَهُوَ يُدْعَىٰٓ إِلَى ٱلْإِسْلَٰمِ وَٱللَّهُ لَا يَهْدِى ٱلْقَوْمَ ٱلظَّٰلِمِينَ ﴿٧﴾

---

712. That the teaching of Jesus (on him be peace), as a universal code of conduct, was singularly inadequate and incomplete, and necessitated the advent of another teacher is admitted by the Christian apologists themselves, and accounted for in ways that are more amusing than convincing. 'The Saviour refrained from all attempt to guide His followers by rules, but gradually taught them that their lives were to be quickened by the Holy Spirit whose indwelling was to them their strength and inspiration for all times. In view of this prospect, we can understand why His ethical teaching was so suggestive but so paradoxical, so figurative, and incomplete. It was designed, not to save us from the trouble of thinking but to turn our thoughts to the Comforter whom He promised to send' (*ERE*, XII. p. 621).

713. Which word was employed as a translation of the *periclytos* in old Arabic versions of the NT. See Muir and Sale. 'Ahmad or Muhammad the praised One is almost a translation of the Greek word, *periclytos*. In the present Gospel of John, 14: 16, 15: 26 and 16: 7, the word "Comforter" in the English version is for the Greek word, *percolates*, which means "Advocate", "one called to the help of another, a kind friend," rather than "Comforter". Our doctors contend that Paracletos is a corrupt reading for Periclytos, and that in the original saying of Jesus there was a prophecy of our holy Prophet Ahmad by name. Even if we read Paraclete, it would apply to the holy Prophet, who is "a Mercy for all creatures" (AYA. LXI : 107), and "most kind and merciful to the believers' (AYA. IX : 128). Similar references in the non-canonical Gospel of Barnabas are almost too numerous and too explicit to be passed over.

8.　They intend to extinguish the light of Allah with their mouths, and Allah is going to accomplish His light, though the infidels may be averse.

يُرِيدُونَ لِيُطْفِئُوا نُورَ اللَّهِ بِأَفْوَاهِهِمْ وَاللَّهُ مُتِمُّ نُورِهِ وَلَوْ كَرِهَ الْكَافِرُونَ ﴿٨﴾

9.　He it is Who has sent His Messenger with guidance and true faith, that He may make it triumph over every other faith, though the associates may be averse.

هُوَ الَّذِى أَرْسَلَ رَسُولَهُ بِالْهُدَىٰ وَدِينِ الْحَقِّ لِيُظْهِرَهُ عَلَى الدِّينِ كُلِّهِ وَلَوْ كَرِهَ الْمُشْرِكُونَ ﴿٩﴾

Section 2

10.　O you who believe! Shall I direct you to a trade which will deliver you from an afflictive torment?

يَا أَيُّهَا الَّذِينَ ءَامَنُوا هَلْ أَدُلُّكُمْ عَلَىٰ تِجَٰرَةٍ تُنجِيكُم مِّنْ عَذَابٍ أَلِيمٍ ﴿١٠﴾

11.　It is; believe in Allah and His Messenger and strive in the cause of Allah with your riches and lives. That is best for you if you only know!

تُؤْمِنُونَ بِاللَّهِ وَرَسُولِهِ وَتُجَٰهِدُونَ فِى سَبِيلِ اللَّهِ بِأَمْوَٰلِكُمْ وَأَنفُسِكُمْ ذَٰلِكُمْ خَيْرٌ لَّكُمْ إِن كُنتُمْ تَعْلَمُونَ ﴿١١﴾

12.　He will forgive you your sins, and make you enter the Gardens with running rivers, and happy abodes in the Everlasting Gardens. That is a great achievement.

يَغْفِرْ لَكُمْ ذُنُوبَكُمْ وَيُدْخِلْكُمْ جَنَّٰتٍ تَجْرِى مِن تَحْتِهَا الْأَنْهَٰرُ وَمَسَٰكِنَ طَيِّبَةً فِى جَنَّٰتِ عَدْنٍ ذَٰلِكَ الْفَوْزُ الْعَظِيمُ ﴿١٢﴾

13.　And also another bliss which you love: succour from Allah and a swift victory. And bear the glad tidings to the believers.

وَأُخْرَىٰ تُحِبُّونَهَا نَصْرٌ مِّنَ اللَّهِ وَفَتْحٌ قَرِيبٌ وَبَشِّرِ الْمُؤْمِنِينَ ﴿١٣﴾

14. O you who believe! Be Allah's helpers, even as Jesus, son of Maryam, said to the disciples: 'Who shall be my helpers for Allah?' The disciples said: 'We are Allah's helpers.' Then a party of the children of Israel believed, and another party disbelieved. Then We strengthened those who believed against their foe; so they became triumphant.

يَٰٓأَيُّهَا ٱلَّذِينَ ءَامَنُوا۟ كُونُوٓا۟ أَنصَارَ ٱللَّهِ كَمَا قَالَ عِيسَى ٱبْنُ مَرْيَمَ لِلْحَوَارِيِّۦنَ مَنْ أَنصَارِىٓ إِلَى ٱللَّهِ ۖ قَالَ ٱلْحَوَارِيُّونَ نَحْنُ أَنصَارُ ٱللَّهِ ۖ فَـَٔامَنَت طَّآئِفَةٌ مِّنۢ بَنِىٓ إِسْرَٰٓءِيلَ وَكَفَرَت طَّآئِفَةٌ ۖ فَأَيَّدْنَا ٱلَّذِينَ ءَامَنُوا۟ عَلَىٰ عَدُوِّهِمْ فَأَصْبَحُوا۟ ظَٰهِرِينَ ۝

Sūrah 62

al-Jumu'ah

(Madinan, 2 Sections, 11 Verses)

In the name of Allah, the
Compassionate, the Merciful.

Section 1

1. Hallows whatsoever is in the heavens and whatsoever is in the earth Allah, the Sovereign, the Holy, the Mighty, the Wise.

2. He it is Who has raised amidst the unlettered ones a Messenger from among themselves, rehearsing to them His revelations and purifying them and teaching them the Book and wisdom, though they have been before in gross error.

3. And also others of them who have not yet joined them. And He is the Mighty, the Wise.

4. That is the grace of Allah; He vouchsafes it to whomsoever He will; and Allah is the Owner of mighty grace.

5. The case of those who were laden with the Torah but who bore it not is as the case of an ass bearing tomes. Hapless is the case of those who belie the signs of Allah, and Allah does not guide a wrong-doing people.

يُسَبِّحُ لِلَّهِ مَا فِي السَّمَوَاتِ وَمَا فِي الْأَرْضِ الْمَلِكِ الْقُدُّوسِ الْعَزِيزِ الْحَكِيمِ ﴿١﴾

هُوَ الَّذِى بَعَثَ فِي الْأُمِّيِّنَ رَسُولًا مِّنْهُمْ يَتْلُواْ عَلَيْهِمْ ءَايَٰتِهِ وَيُزَكِّيهِمْ وَيُعَلِّمُهُمُ الْكِتَٰبَ وَالْحِكْمَةَ وَإِن كَانُواْ مِن قَبْلُ لَفِى ضَلَٰلٍ مُّبِينٍ ﴿٢﴾

وَءَاخَرِينَ مِنْهُمْ لَمَّا يَلْحَقُواْ بِهِمْ وَهُوَ الْعَزِيزُ الْحَكِيمُ ﴿٣﴾

ذَٰلِكَ فَضْلُ اللَّهِ يُؤْتِيهِ مَن يَشَآءُ وَاللَّهُ ذُو الْفَضْلِ الْعَظِيمِ ﴿٤﴾

مَثَلُ الَّذِينَ حُمِّلُواْ التَّوْرَىٰةَ ثُمَّ لَمْ يَحْمِلُوهَا كَمَثَلِ الْحِمَارِ يَحْمِلُ أَسْفَارًا بِئْسَ مَثَلُ الْقَوْمِ الَّذِينَ كَذَّبُواْ بِـَٔايَٰتِ اللَّهِ وَاللَّهُ لَا يَهْدِى الْقَوْمَ الظَّٰلِمِينَ ﴿٥﴾

6. Say: 'O those who are Judaised; if you think you are the friends of Allah above mankind, then wish for death, if you speak truth.'

قُل يَـٰٓأَيُّهَا ٱلَّذِينَ هَادُوٓا۟ إِن زَعَمْتُمْ أَنَّكُمْ أَوْلِيَآءُ لِلَّهِ مِن دُونِ ٱلنَّاسِ فَتَمَنَّوُا۟ ٱلْمَوْتَ إِن كُنتُمْ صَـٰدِقِينَ ٦

7. And they will never wish for it, because of what their hands have sent forward. And Allah is the Knower of the wrong-doers.

وَلَا يَتَمَنَّوْنَهُۥٓ أَبَدًۢا بِمَا قَدَّمَتْ أَيْدِيهِمْ وَٱللَّهُ عَلِيمٌۢ بِٱلظَّـٰلِمِينَ ٧

8. Say you: 'The death which you flee from will certainly meet you, and thereafter you will be brought back to the Knower of the Unseen and the seen, and He will declare to you what you have been working.'

قُلْ إِنَّ ٱلْمَوْتَ ٱلَّذِى تَفِرُّونَ مِنْهُ فَإِنَّهُۥ مُلَـٰقِيكُمْ ثُمَّ تُرَدُّونَ إِلَىٰ عَـٰلِمِ ٱلْغَيْبِ وَٱلشَّهَـٰدَةِ فَيُنَبِّئُكُم بِمَا كُنتُمْ تَعْمَلُونَ ٨

Section 2

9. O you who believe! When the call is made to the prayer on Friday[714] hasten to the remembrance of Allah and leave off bargaining. That is better for you, if you know.

يَـٰٓأَيُّهَا ٱلَّذِينَ ءَامَنُوٓا۟ إِذَا نُودِىَ لِلصَّلَوٰةِ مِن يَوْمِ ٱلْجُمُعَةِ فَٱسْعَوْا۟ إِلَىٰ ذِكْرِ ٱللَّهِ وَذَرُوا۟ ٱلْبَيْعَ ذَٰلِكُمْ خَيْرٌ لَّكُمْ إِن كُنتُمْ تَعْلَمُونَ ٩

---

714. Literally, 'the day of Congregation'. Friday to the Muslims is a day of religious joy, not at all like the Sabbath of the Jews and the Sunday of the Christians, a day of idleness and of abstinence from all work. To the superstitious Christians, Friday is an inauspicious day. Pope Nicholas I even declared abstinence from meat on Fridays to be obligatory throughout the Church. 'Brides have shunned Friday (and still do!) owing to superstition. Christian people have always considered it an unlucky day for weddings because our Lord was crucified on that day and tradition says that it was on Friday that Adam and Eve ate the forbidden fruit' (*CD.* p. 384).

10. Then when the prayer is ended,[715] disperse on the land and seek of the grace of Allah, and remember Allah, and remember Allah much; haply you may thrive.

فَإِذَا قُضِيَتِ ٱلصَّلَوٰةُ فَٱنتَشِرُواْ فِي ٱلْأَرْضِ وَٱبْتَغُواْ مِن فَضْلِ ٱللَّهِ وَٱذْكُرُواْ ٱللَّهَ كَثِيرًا لَّعَلَّكُمْ تُفْلِحُونَ ﴿١٠﴾

11. And when they beheld merchandise or sport, they flocked thereto, and left you standing. Say: 'What is with Allah is far better than sport and merchandize, and Allah is the Best of providers.'

وَإِذَا رَأَوْاْ تِجَٰرَةً أَوْ لَهْوًا ٱنفَضُّوٓاْ إِلَيْهَا وَتَرَكُوكَ قَآئِمًا قُلْ مَا عِندَ ٱللَّهِ خَيْرٌ مِّنَ ٱللَّهْوِ وَمِنَ ٱلتِّجَٰرَةِ وَٱللَّهُ خَيْرُ ٱلرَّٰزِقِينَ ﴿١١﴾

---

715. 'The Friday prayer is obligatory upon all adult males. It is held at the mosque at noon with a congregation of at least forty of the Faithful and under the direction of an imam. Before the prayer the imam delivers from the pulpit two addresses (*Khutba*) in Arabic. He then performs two rakats with the congregation. Friday is not regarded as a weekly day of rest, this observance being unknown in Islam' (Lammens, *Islam: Beliefs and Institutions*, pp. 59 and 60).

Sūrah 63

al-Munāfiqūn

(Madinan, 2 Sections, 11 Verses)

*In the name of Allah, the
Compassionate, the Merciful.*

Section 1

1. When the hypocrites come to
you, they say: 'We bear witness
that you are Allah's Messenger.'
Allah knows well that you are His
Messenger, but Allah also bears
witness that the hypocrites are
liars indeed.

2. They have made their oaths a
shield; and they turn men away
from the path of Allah. Vile indeed
is what they have been working.

3. This, because they first
believed and then disbelieved,
their hearts are therefore sealed,
so that they do not understand.

4. And when you look at them,
their persons please you, and if
they speak, you listen to their
discourse; they look as though
they are blocks of wood propped
up. They imagine every shout to
be at them. They are the foe; so
beware of them. Perish them
Allah! Whither are they deviating.

إِذَا جَآءَكَ ٱلْمُنَافِقُونَ قَالُواْ نَشْهَدُ إِنَّكَ
لَرَسُولُ ٱللَّهِ ۗ وَٱللَّهُ يَعْلَمُ إِنَّكَ لَرَسُولُهُۥ وَ
ٱللَّهُ يَشْهَدُ إِنَّ ٱلْمُنَافِقِينَ لَكَاذِبُونَ ۝

ٱتَّخَذُوٓاْ أَيْمَانَهُمْ جُنَّةً فَصَدُّواْ عَن سَبِيلِ
ٱللَّهِ ۚ إِنَّهُمْ سَآءَ مَا كَانُواْ يَعْمَلُونَ ۝

ذَٰلِكَ بِأَنَّهُمْ ءَامَنُواْ ثُمَّ كَفَرُواْ فَطُبِعَ عَلَىٰ
قُلُوبِهِمْ فَهُمْ لَا يَفْقَهُونَ ۝

وَإِذَا رَأَيْتَهُمْ تُعْجِبُكَ أَجْسَامُهُمْ ۖ وَإِن
يَقُولُواْ تَسْمَعْ لِقَوْلِهِمْ ۖ كَأَنَّهُمْ خُشُبٌ مُّسَنَّدَةٌ ۖ
يَحْسَبُونَ كُلَّ صَيْحَةٍ عَلَيْهِمْ ۚ هُمُ ٱلْعَدُوُّ
فَٱحْذَرْهُمْ ۚ قَاتَلَهُمُ ٱللَّهُ ۖ أَنَّىٰ يُؤْفَكُونَ ۝

5. And when it is said to them: 'Come! So that the Messenger of Allah may ask forgiveness for you', they twist their heads, and you see them retire. While they are stiff-necked.

وَإِذَا قِيلَ لَهُمْ تَعَالَوْا يَسْتَغْفِرْ لَكُمْ رَسُولُ اللَّهِ لَوَّوْا رُءُوسَهُمْ وَرَأَيْتَهُمْ يَصُدُّونَ وَهُم مُّسْتَكْبِرُونَ ۝

6. It is alike to them whether you ask forgiveness for them or not; Allah shall not forgive them. Allah does not guide a transgressing people.

سَوَآءٌ عَلَيْهِمْ أَسْتَغْفَرْتَ لَهُمْ أَمْ لَمْ تَسْتَغْفِرْ لَهُمْ لَن يَغْفِرَ اللَّهُ لَهُمْ إِنَّ اللَّهَ لَا يَهْدِى الْقَوْمَ الْفَاسِقِينَ ۝

7. They are the ones who say: 'Spend not on those who are with Allah's Messenger, so that they may desert him,' whereas Allah's are the treasures of the heavens and the earth. Yet the hypocrites do not understand.

هُمُ الَّذِينَ يَقُولُونَ لَا تُنفِقُوا عَلَىٰ مَنْ عِندَ رَسُولِ اللَّهِ حَتَّىٰ يَنفَضُّوا وَلِلَّهِ خَزَآئِنُ السَّمَـٰوَٰتِ وَالْأَرْضِ وَلَـٰكِنَّ الْمُنَافِقِينَ لَا يَفْقَهُونَ ۝

8. They say: 'Surely if we return to Madina, the mightier shall drive out the meaner thence, whereas the might belongs to Allah, and His Messenger and the faithful. Yet the hypocrites do not know.

يَقُولُونَ لَئِن رَّجَعْنَا إِلَى الْمَدِينَةِ لَيُخْرِجَنَّ الْأَعَزُّ مِنْهَا الْأَذَلَّ وَلِلَّهِ الْعِزَّةُ وَلِرَسُولِهِ وَلِلْمُؤْمِنِينَ وَلَـٰكِنَّ الْمُنَافِقِينَ لَا يَعْلَمُونَ ۝

Section 2

9. O you who believe; let not your riches or your children divert you from the remembrance of Allah. And whoso does that, verily they are the losers.

يَـٰٓأَيُّهَا الَّذِينَ ءَامَنُوا لَا تُلْهِكُمْ أَمْوَٰلُكُمْ وَلَآ أَوْلَـٰدُكُمْ عَن ذِكْرِ اللَّهِ وَمَن يَفْعَلْ ذَٰلِكَ فَأُوْلَـٰٓئِكَ هُمُ الْخَـٰسِرُونَ ۝

10. And spend of that with which We have provided you before death comes to one of you, and he says: 'Lord would You not respite me for a short time, so that I would spend in charity and become of the righteous.'

وَأَنفِقُوا۟ مِن مَّا رَزَقْنَـٰكُم مِّن قَبْلِ أَن يَأْتِىَ أَحَدَكُمُ ٱلْمَوْتُ فَيَقُولَ رَبِّ لَوْلَآ أَخَّرْتَنِىٓ إِلَىٰٓ أَجَلٍ قَرِيبٍ فَأَصَّدَّقَ وَأَكُن مِّنَ ٱلصَّـٰلِحِينَ ۝

11. And Allah does not respite a soul when its term has arrived, and Allah is Aware of what you do.

وَلَن يُؤَخِّرَ ٱللَّهُ نَفْسًا إِذَا جَآءَ أَجَلُهَا وَٱللَّهُ خَبِيرٌۢ بِمَا تَعْمَلُونَ ۝

Sūrah 64

al-Taghābun

(Madinan, 2 Sections, 18 Verses)

In the name of Allah, the Compassionate, the Merciful.

Section 1

1. Hallows Allah whatsoever is in the heavens and whatsoever is on the earth. His is the kingdom, His is the praise, and He is Potent over everything.

2. He it is Who has created you, so of you some are infidels and some are believers, and Allah is the Beholder of what you do.

3. He has created the heavens and the earth with truth, and has fashioned you, and has fashioned you in a comely shape, and to Him is the return.

4. He knows whatsoever is in the heavens and the earth; and He knows whatsoever you conceal and whatsoever you disclose; and Allah is the Knower of whatsoever is in the breasts.

5. Has not the news reached you of those who disbelieved aforetime, and so tasted of the ill consequences of their affair, and theirs will be an afflictive torment.

يُسَبِّحُ لِلَّهِ مَا فِي السَّمَوَاتِ وَمَا فِي الْأَرْضِ لَهُ الْمُلْكُ وَلَهُ الْحَمْدُ وَهُوَ عَلَى كُلِّ شَيْءٍ قَدِيرٌ ﴿١﴾

هُوَ الَّذِي خَلَقَكُمْ فَمِنكُمْ كَافِرٌ وَمِنكُم مُّؤْمِنٌ وَاللَّهُ بِمَا تَعْمَلُونَ بَصِيرٌ ﴿٢﴾

خَلَقَ السَّمَوَاتِ وَالْأَرْضَ بِالْحَقِّ وَصَوَّرَكُمْ فَأَحْسَنَ صُوَرَكُمْ وَإِلَيْهِ الْمَصِيرُ ﴿٣﴾

يَعْلَمُ مَا فِي السَّمَوَاتِ وَالْأَرْضِ وَيَعْلَمُ مَا تُسِرُّونَ وَمَا تُعْلِنُونَ وَاللَّهُ عَلِيمٌ بِذَاتِ الصُّدُورِ ﴿٤﴾

أَلَمْ يَأْتِكُمْ نَبَؤُا الَّذِينَ كَفَرُوا مِن قَبْلُ فَذَاقُوا وَبَالَ أَمْرِهِمْ وَلَهُمْ عَذَابٌ أَلِيمٌ ﴿٥﴾

6. That was because their Messengers came to them with evidence but they said: 'Will there guide us a mere human being?'⁷¹⁶ So they disbelieved and turned away. And Allah did not need them. Allah is the Self-Sufficient, the Praiseworthy.

7. Those who disbelieved asserted that they would not be raised. Say: 'By my Lord, you shall surely be raised, and to you shall be declared what you worked. And that is easy for Allah.'

8. So believe in Allah and His Messenger and the light which We have sent down. And Allah is Aware of what you work.

9. Remember the Day when He will assemble you on the Day of Assembly; that will be the Day of mutual loss and gain. Then whosoever believes in Allah and acts righteously He will expiate from him his misdeeds and will make him enter the Gardens whereunder rivers flow, as abiders therein for ever. That is a great achievement.

---

716. This 'humanity' of the Divine Messenger has always been the stumbling-block of polytheistic peoples. It is incomprehensible to them that a mere servant of God, who is neither a demi-God nor an Incarnation, nor even an angel, should receive and publish His Divine Message. To them, the barriers between the human and the Divine have always seemed impossible to pass.

10. And they who disbelieve and belie Our signs!, those will be the fellows of the Fire as abiders therein – a hapless destination!

وَٱلَّذِينَ كَفَرُوا وَكَذَّبُوا بِـَٔايَٰتِنَآ أُوْلَٰٓئِكَ أَصْحَٰبُ ٱلنَّارِ خَٰلِدِينَ فِيهَا وَبِئْسَ ٱلْمَصِيرُ ۝

Section 2

11. No calamity befalls man save by Allah's leave. And whoso believes in Allah, his heart He guides, and Allah is the Knower of everything.

مَآ أَصَابَ مِن مُّصِيبَةٍ إِلَّا بِإِذْنِ ٱللَّهِ وَمَن يُؤْمِنۢ بِٱللَّهِ يَهْدِ قَلْبَهُۥ وَٱللَّهُ بِكُلِّ شَىْءٍ عَلِيمٌ ۝

12. Obey Allah and obey the Messenger; then if you turn away, on Our Messenger there is only the clear preaching.

وَأَطِيعُوا ٱللَّهَ وَأَطِيعُوا ٱلرَّسُولَ فَإِن تَوَلَّيْتُمْ فَإِنَّمَا عَلَىٰ رَسُولِنَا ٱلْبَلَٰغُ ٱلْمُبِينُ ۝

13. Allah! There is no god but He! In Allah therefore let the believers put their trust.

ٱللَّهُ لَآ إِلَٰهَ إِلَّا هُوَ وَعَلَى ٱللَّهِ فَلْيَتَوَكَّلِ ٱلْمُؤْمِنُونَ ۝

14. O you who believe! Verily you have an enemy among your wives and your children; so beware of them. And if you pardon and pass over and forgive, then surely Allah is the Forgiving, the Merciful.

يَٰٓأَيُّهَا ٱلَّذِينَ ءَامَنُوٓا إِنَّ مِنْ أَزْوَٰجِكُمْ وَأَوْلَٰدِكُمْ عَدُوًّا لَّكُمْ فَٱحْذَرُوهُمْ وَإِن تَعْفُوا وَتَصْفَحُوا وَتَغْفِرُوا فَإِنَّ ٱللَّهَ غَفُورٌ رَّحِيمٌ ۝

15. Your riches and your children are but a trial, and Allah! With Him is a mighty reward.

إِنَّمَآ أَمْوَٰلُكُمْ وَأَوْلَٰدُكُمْ فِتْنَةٌ وَٱللَّهُ عِندَهُۥٓ أَجْرٌ عَظِيمٌ ۝

16. Therefore fear Allah as far as you are able, and listen and obey and spend, for the benefit of your souls. And whoso is

فَٱتَّقُوا ٱللَّهَ مَا ٱسْتَطَعْتُمْ وَٱسْمَعُوا وَأَطِيعُوا وَأَنفِقُوا خَيْرًا لِّأَنفُسِكُمْ

guarded against the avarice of his soul, those!, they are blissful.

17. If you lend to Allah a goodly loan, He will multiply it to you and will forgive you, and Allah is the Appreciative, the Forbearing.

18. Knower of the Unseen and the seen, the Mighty, the Wise.

وَمَن يُوقَ شُحَّ نَفْسِهِۦ فَأُوْلَٰٓئِكَ هُمُ ٱلْمُفْلِحُونَ ۝

إِن تُقْرِضُوا۟ ٱللَّهَ قَرْضًا حَسَنًا يُضَٰعِفْهُ لَكُمْ وَيَغْفِرْ لَكُمْ ۚ وَٱللَّهُ شَكُورٌ حَلِيمٌ ۝

عَٰلِمُ ٱلْغَيْبِ وَٱلشَّهَٰدَةِ ٱلْعَزِيزُ ٱلْحَكِيمُ ۝

Sūrah 65

al-Ṭalāq

(Madinan, 2 Sections, 12 Verses)

In the name of Allah, the
Compassionate, the Merciful.

Section 1

1. O Prophet! When you divorce women, divorce them before their waiting period, and count their waiting period; and fear Allah, your Lord.[717] And do not drive them out of their houses, nor should they themselves go forth, unless they commit a flagrant indecency. These are the bounds of Allah, and he who trespasses the bounds of Allah has surely wronged himself. You know not that after this Allah may bring something new to pass.

2. Then when they have attained their term, either retain them reputably, or part with them reputably, and take as witnesses two honest men from among you, and set up your testimony for Allah. Thus is exhorted he who believes in Allah and the Last Day. And whoso fears Allah He makes an outlet for him.

يَـٰٓأَيُّهَا ٱلنَّبِىُّ إِذَا طَلَّقْتُمُ ٱلنِّسَآءَ فَطَلِّقُوهُنَّ لِعِدَّتِهِنَّ وَأَحْصُوا ٱلْعِدَّةَ وَٱتَّقُوا ٱللَّهَ رَبَّكُمْ لَا تُخْرِجُوهُنَّ مِنۢ بُيُوتِهِنَّ وَلَا يَخْرُجْنَ إِلَّآ أَن يَأْتِينَ بِفَٰحِشَةٍ مُّبَيِّنَةٍ وَتِلْكَ حُدُودُ ٱللَّهِ وَمَن يَتَعَدَّ حُدُودَ ٱللَّهِ فَقَدْ ظَلَمَ نَفْسَهُ لَا تَدْرِى لَعَلَّ ٱللَّهَ يُحْدِثُ بَعْدَ ذَٰلِكَ أَمْرًا ١

فَإِذَا بَلَغْنَ أَجَلَهُنَّ فَأَمْسِكُوهُنَّ بِمَعْرُوفٍ أَوْ فَارِقُوهُنَّ بِمَعْرُوفٍ وَأَشْهِدُوا ذَوَىْ عَدْلٍ مِّنكُمْ وَأَقِيمُوا ٱلشَّهَٰدَةَ لِلَّهِ ذَٰلِكُمْ يُوعَظُ بِهِۦ مَن كَانَ يُؤْمِنُ بِٱللَّهِ وَٱلْيَوْمِ ٱلْأَخِرِ وَمَن يَتَّقِ ٱللَّهَ يَجْعَل لَّهُۥ مَخْرَجًا ٢

---

717. Who in His wisdom and providence has ordained all these laws for your benefit. This emphasizes that matters of marital relations are not to be treated lightly.

3. And He provides for him from where he never reckons. And whoso puts his trust in Allah, He will suffice him. Verily Allah is sure to attain His purpose, and has assigned to everything a measure.

وَيَرْزُقْهُ مِنْ حَيْثُ لَا يَحْتَسِبُ وَمَن يَتَوَكَّلْ عَلَى ٱللَّهِ فَهُوَ حَسْبُهُۥٓ إِنَّ ٱللَّهَ بَٰلِغُ أَمْرِهِۦ قَدْ جَعَلَ ٱللَّهُ لِكُلِّ شَىْءٍ قَدْرًا ۝

4. And as to such of your women as have despaired of menstruation, if you be in doubt thereof, their waiting-period is three months, as also of those who have not yet menstruated. And as to those with burdens, their term is when they have laid down their burden. And whoso fears Allah, He has made his affair easy unto himself.

وَٱلَّٰٓـِٔى يَئِسْنَ مِنَ ٱلْمَحِيضِ مِن نِّسَآئِكُمْ إِنِ ٱرْتَبْتُمْ فَعِدَّتُهُنَّ ثَلَٰثَةُ أَشْهُرٍ وَٱلَّٰٓـِٔى لَمْ يَحِضْنَ وَأُولَٰتُ ٱلْأَحْمَالِ أَجَلُهُنَّ أَن يَضَعْنَ حَمْلَهُنَّ وَمَن يَتَّقِ ٱللَّهَ يَجْعَل لَّهُۥ مِنْ أَمْرِهِۦ يُسْرًا ۝

5. That is the commandment of Allah which He has sent down unto you. And whoso fears Allah, He will expiate his misdeeds from him, and will magnify his reward for him.

ذَٰلِكَ أَمْرُ ٱللَّهِ أَنزَلَهُۥٓ إِلَيْكُمْ وَمَن يَتَّقِ ٱللَّهَ يُكَفِّرْ عَنْهُ سَيِّـَٔاتِهِۦ وَيُعْظِمْ لَهُۥٓ أَجْرًا ۝

6. Lodge them wheresoever you are lodging according to your means, and do not hurt them so as to straiten them. And if they are with burden, spend on them until they lay down their burden. Then if they suckle their children for you, give them their wage, and take counsel together reputably. And if you make hardship for each other, then another woman shall suckle for him.

أَسْكِنُوهُنَّ مِنْ حَيْثُ سَكَنتُم مِّن وُجْدِكُمْ وَلَا تُضَآرُّوهُنَّ لِتُضَيِّقُوا عَلَيْهِنَّ وَإِن كُنَّ أُولَٰتِ حَمْلٍ فَأَنفِقُوا عَلَيْهِنَّ حَتَّىٰ يَضَعْنَ حَمْلَهُنَّ فَإِنْ أَرْضَعْنَ لَكُمْ فَـَٔاتُوهُنَّ أُجُورَهُنَّ وَأْتَمِرُوا بَيْنَكُم بِمَعْرُوفٍ وَإِن تَعَاسَرْتُمْ فَسَتُرْضِعُ لَهُۥٓ أُخْرَىٰ ۝

7. Let the affluent spend according to his means, and whoso is stinted in his subsistence, let him spend of what Allah has given him. Allah does not task any soul except according to what He has vouchsafed it. Allah will soon appoint ease for hardship.

لِيُنفِقْ ذُو سَعَةٍ مِّن سَعَتِهِ ۖ وَمَن قُدِرَ عَلَيْهِ رِزْقُهُ فَلْيُنفِقْ مِمَّا ءَاتَىٰهُ ٱللَّهُ ۚ لَا يُكَلِّفُ ٱللَّهُ نَفْسًا إِلَّا مَا ءَاتَىٰهَا ۚ سَيَجْعَلُ ٱللَّهُ بَعْدَ عُسْرٍ يُسْرًا ۝

Section 2

8. And how many a city trespassed the commandment of its Lord and His Messenger. We therefore reckoned with them sternly and inflicted on them a chastizement unheard of.

وَكَأَيِّن مِّن قَرْيَةٍ عَتَتْ عَنْ أَمْرِ رَبِّهَا وَرُسُلِهِ فَحَاسَبْنَٰهَا حِسَابًا شَدِيدًا وَعَذَّبْنَٰهَا عَذَابًا نُّكْرًا ۝

9. So they tasted the ill consequence of their affairs, and loss was the end of their affair.

فَذَاقَتْ وَبَالَ أَمْرِهَا وَكَانَ عَٰقِبَةُ أَمْرِهَا خُسْرًا ۝

10. Allah has prepared for them a grievous punishment; so fear Allah, O men of understanding! Those who have believed. Surely, He has sent down unto you an admonition.

أَعَدَّ ٱللَّهُ لَهُمْ عَذَابًا شَدِيدًا ۖ فَٱتَّقُوا ٱللَّهَ يَٰٓأُو۟لِى ٱلْأَلْبَٰبِ ٱلَّذِينَ ءَامَنُوا ۚ قَدْ أَنزَلَ ٱللَّهُ إِلَيْكُمْ ذِكْرًا ۝

11. A Messenger reciting to you the revelations of Allah as evidence, that he may bring forth those who believe and work righteous works from darkness unto light. And whoso believes in Allah and works righteously, him He shall cause to enter the Gardens whereunder rivers flow as abiders therein for ever. Surely Allah has made for such an excellent provision.

رَّسُولًا يَتْلُوا عَلَيْكُمْ ءَايَٰتِ ٱللَّهِ مُبَيِّنَٰتٍ لِّيُخْرِجَ ٱلَّذِينَ ءَامَنُوا وَعَمِلُوا ٱلصَّٰلِحَٰتِ مِنَ ٱلظُّلُمَٰتِ إِلَى ٱلنُّورِ ۚ وَمَن يُؤْمِن بِٱللَّهِ وَيَعْمَلْ صَٰلِحًا يُدْخِلْهُ جَنَّٰتٍ تَجْرِى مِن تَحْتِهَا ٱلْأَنْهَٰرُ خَٰلِدِينَ فِيهَآ أَبَدًا ۖ قَدْ أَحْسَنَ ٱللَّهُ لَهُ رِزْقًا ۝

12. Allah it is Who has created seven heavens and of the earth the like thereof: His Commandment comes down between them; so that you may know that Allah is Potent over everything, and that Allah does encompass everything in His knowledge.

ٱللَّهُ ٱلَّذِى خَلَقَ سَبْعَ سَمَوَاتٍ وَمِنَ ٱلْأَرْضِ مِثْلَهُنَّ يَتَنَزَّلُ ٱلْأَمْرُ بَيْنَهُنَّ لِتَعْلَمُوٓاْ أَنَّ ٱللَّهَ عَلَىٰ كُلِّ شَىْءٍ قَدِيرٌ وَأَنَّ ٱللَّهَ قَدْ أَحَاطَ بِكُلِّ شَىْءٍ عِلْمًۢا ﴿١٢﴾

Sūrah 66

al-Taḥrīm

(Madinan, 2 Sections, 12 Verses)

*In the name of Allah, the
Compassionate, the Merciful.*

Section 1

1. O Prophet! Why do you forbid for you what Allah has allowed to you, seeking the goodwill of your wives? And Allah is the Forgiving, the Merciful.

2. Surely Allah has ordained for you absolution from you oaths and Allah is your Patron, and He is the Knower, the Wise.

3. And recall when the Prophet confided a story to one of his spouses, then she disclosed it. Allah apprised him of it; he made known a part of it, and a part he withheld. Then when he had apprised her of it, she said: 'Who has told you of it?' He said: 'The Knower, the Aware has told me.

4. Then if you turn to Allah repentant, it is well, surely your hearts are so inclined. But if you support each other against him, then verily Allah! His friend is He and Gabriel, and so are the righteous believers, and furthermore angels are his aiders.

5. If he divorces you, perchance his Lord will give him in exchange better wives than you; Muslims, believers, devout, penitent, worshippers, given to fasting, both non-virgins and virgins.

6. O you who believe! Guard yourselves and your households against the Fire the fuel whereof is mankind and stones. Over it are angels, stern, strong; they do not disobey Allah in what He commands them, and they do what they are commanded.[718]

7. O you who disbelieve! Excuse not yourselves today; you are only being requited for what you have been working.

Section 2

8. O you who believe! Turn to Allah with a sincere repentance. Perchance your Lord will expiate from you your misdeeds and cause you to the enter the Gardens whereunder rivers flow; on the Day whereon Allah will not humiliate the Prophet and those who believe with him. Their light will be

عَسَىٰ رَبُّهُۥٓ إِن طَلَّقَكُنَّ أَن يُبْدِلَهُۥٓ أَزْوَٰجًا خَيْرًا مِّنكُنَّ مُسْلِمَٰتٍ مُّؤْمِنَٰتٍ قَٰنِتَٰتٍ تَٰٓئِبَٰتٍ عَٰبِدَٰتٍ سَٰٓئِحَٰتٍ ثَيِّبَٰتٍ وَأَبْكَارًا ۝

يَٰٓأَيُّهَا ٱلَّذِينَ ءَامَنُواْ قُوٓاْ أَنفُسَكُمْ وَأَهْلِيكُمْ نَارًا وَقُودُهَا ٱلنَّاسُ وَٱلْحِجَارَةُ عَلَيْهَا مَلَٰٓئِكَةٌ غِلَاظٌ شِدَادٌ لَّا يَعْصُونَ ٱللَّهَ مَآ أَمَرَهُمْ وَيَفْعَلُونَ مَا يُؤْمَرُونَ ۝

يَٰٓأَيُّهَا ٱلَّذِينَ كَفَرُواْ لَا تَعْتَذِرُواْ ٱلْيَوْمَ إِنَّمَا تُجْزَوْنَ مَا كُنتُمْ تَعْمَلُونَ ۝

يَٰٓأَيُّهَا ٱلَّذِينَ ءَامَنُواْ تُوبُوٓاْ إِلَى ٱللَّهِ تَوْبَةً نَّصُوحًا عَسَىٰ رَبُّكُمْ أَن يُكَفِّرَ عَنكُمْ سَيِّـَٔاتِكُمْ وَيُدْخِلَكُمْ جَنَّٰتٍ تَجْرِى مِن تَحْتِهَا ٱلْأَنْهَٰرُ يَوْمَ لَا يُخْزِى ٱللَّهُ ٱلنَّبِىَّ وَٱلَّذِينَ ءَامَنُواْ مَعَهُۥ نُورُهُمْ

---

718. The angels, in Islam, possess like all living sentient beings distinct personalities, and are neither degraded gods nor mere attributes and abstractions personified. They are perfectly obedient servants of God. This does away with the Jewish and Christian misconceptions of angels. 'The OT nowhere lays stress on the moral character of angels. Consequently, angels were divided not into good and bad, but into those who worked wholly and those who worked only partly, in obedience to God. This latter division still seems to hold its own in NT alongside of the former' (*EBi.* c. 168).

running before them and on their right hands, and they will say: 'Our Lord! Perfect for us our light, and forgive us; verily You are over everything Potent.'

9. O Prophet! Strive hard against the infidels and the hypocrites, and be stern to them. And their abode is Hell; a hapless destination.

10. Allah propounds for those who disbelieve the similitude of the wife of Noah and the wife of Lot. They were under two of Our righteous bondsmen, then they defrauded them. Therefore nothing availed them against Allah, and it was said: 'Enter you the Fire with those who enter.'

11. And Allah propounds for those who believe the similitude of the wife of Pharaoh, when she said: 'My Lord! Build me in Your presence a house in the Garden and deliver me from Pharaoh and his handiwork, and deliver me from the transgressing people.'

12. And the similitude of Maryam, daughter of 'Imran, who preserved her chastity, wherefore we breathed in it of Our spirit. And she testified to the words of her Lord and His Books and she was of the devout.[719]

يَسْعَىٰ بَيْنَ أَيْدِيهِمْ وَبِأَيْمَٰنِهِم يَقُولُونَ رَبَّنَآ أَتْمِمْ لَنَا نُورَنَا وَٱغْفِرْ لَنَآ إِنَّكَ عَلَىٰ كُلِّ شَىْءٍ قَدِيرٌ ۝

يَٰٓأَيُّهَا ٱلنَّبِىُّ جَٰهِدِ ٱلْكُفَّارَ وَٱلْمُنَٰفِقِينَ وَٱغْلُظْ عَلَيْهِمْ وَمَأْوَىٰهُمْ جَهَنَّمُ وَبِئْسَ ٱلْمَصِيرُ ۝

ضَرَبَ ٱللَّهُ مَثَلًا لِّلَّذِينَ كَفَرُوا۟ ٱمْرَأَتَ نُوحٍ وَٱمْرَأَتَ لُوطٍ كَانَتَا تَحْتَ عَبْدَيْنِ مِنْ عِبَادِنَا صَٰلِحَيْنِ فَخَانَتَاهُمَا فَلَمْ يُغْنِيَا عَنْهُمَا مِنَ ٱللَّهِ شَيْـًٔا وَقِيلَ ٱدْخُلَا ٱلنَّارَ مَعَ ٱلدَّٰخِلِينَ ۝

وَضَرَبَ ٱللَّهُ مَثَلًا لِّلَّذِينَ ءَامَنُوا۟ ٱمْرَأَتَ فِرْعَوْنَ إِذْ قَالَتْ رَبِّ ٱبْنِ لِى عِندَكَ بَيْتًا فِى ٱلْجَنَّةِ وَنَجِّنِى مِن فِرْعَوْنَ وَعَمَلِهِ وَنَجِّنِى مِنَ ٱلْقَوْمِ ٱلظَّٰلِمِينَ ۝

وَمَرْيَمَ ٱبْنَتَ عِمْرَٰنَ ٱلَّتِىٓ أَحْصَنَتْ فَرْجَهَا فَنَفَخْنَا فِيهِ مِن رُّوحِنَا وَصَدَّقَتْ بِكَلِمَٰتِ رَبِّهَا وَكُتُبِهِ وَكَانَتْ مِنَ ٱلْقَٰنِتِينَ ۝

---

719. Neither a Divine Being to be adored as imagined by the Christians, nor an immoral woman as supposed by her Jewish calumniators.

Sūrah 67

al-Mulk

(Makkan, 2 Sections, 30 Verses)

In the name of Allah, the Compassionate, the Merciful.

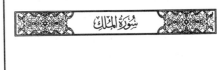

Section 1

1. Blessed be He in Whose hand is sovereignty, and He is Potent over everything,

2. Who has created death and life,[720] that He might test you as to which of you is excellent in work. And He is the Mighty, the Forgiver.

3. Who has created the seven heavens in storeys. You shall not find any oversight in the creation of the Compassionate. Then repeat your look, do you find any crack?

4. Then repeat your look twice over and your look will return to you dim and drowsy.[721]

تَبَارَكَ الَّذِى بِيَدِهِ الْمُلْكُ وَهُوَ عَلَىٰ كُلِّ شَىْءٍ قَدِيرٌ ۝

اَلَّذِى خَلَقَ الْمَوْتَ وَالْحَيَوٰةَ لِيَبْلُوَكُمْ اَيُّكُمْ اَحْسَنُ عَمَلًا وَهُوَ الْعَزِيزُ الْغَفُورُ ۝

اَلَّذِى خَلَقَ سَبْعَ سَمٰوٰتٍ طِبَاقًا مَّا تَرَىٰ فِى خَلْقِ الرَّحْمٰنِ مِنْ تَفٰوُتٍ فَارْجِعِ الْبَصَرَ هَلْ تَرَىٰ مِنْ فُطُورٍ ۝

ثُمَّ ارْجِعِ الْبَصَرَ كَرَّتَيْنِ يَنْقَلِبْ اِلَيْكَ الْبَصَرُ خَاسِئًا وَهُوَ حَسِيرٌ ۝

---

720. This corrects and contradicts the Jewish views: 'God created man to be immortal... nevertheless through the envy of the devil came death into the world. For God made not death.' *(JE, IV, 483).*

721. The more we observe Nature, the more we realize that it is a vast, huge unity, every part in the substantial fabric of the universe being bound to every other part, with no rift, no lacuna whatsoever.

5. And assuredly We have bedecked the nearest sky with lamps and We have made them missiles for pelting devils, and We have prepared for them the torment of the Blaze.

وَلَقَدْ زَيَّنَّا ٱلسَّمَآءَ ٱلدُّنْيَا بِمَصَٰبِيحَ وَجَعَلْنَٰهَا رُجُومًا لِّلشَّيَٰطِينِ وَأَعْتَدْنَا لَهُمْ عَذَابَ ٱلسَّعِيرِ ۝

6. And for those who disbelieve in their Lord will be the torment of Hell; a hapless destination!

وَلِلَّذِينَ كَفَرُوا بِرَبِّهِمْ عَذَابُ جَهَنَّمَ وَبِئْسَ ٱلْمَصِيرُ ۝

7. When they will be cast in it, they will hear a braying as it boils up;

إِذَآ أُلْقُوا فِيهَا سَمِعُوا لَهَا شَهِيقًا وَهِىَ تَفُورُ ۝

8. It almost bursts up with rage. So often as company is cast in it, its keepers will ask them: 'Did not a warner come to you?'

تَكَادُ تَمَيَّزُ مِنَ ٱلْغَيْظِ كُلَّمَآ أُلْقِىَ فِيهَا فَوْجٌ سَأَلَهُمْ خَزَنَتُهَآ أَلَمْ يَأْتِكُمْ نَذِيرٌ ۝

9. They will say: 'Surely a warner did come to us but we belied him and said: "God has not sent down anyone; you are but in a great error."'

قَالُوا بَلَىٰ قَدْ جَآءَنَا نَذِيرٌ فَكَذَّبْنَا وَقُلْنَا مَا نَزَّلَ ٱللَّهُ مِن شَىْءٍ إِنْ أَنتُمْ إِلَّا فِى ضَلَٰلٍ كَبِيرٍ ۝

10. And they will say: 'Had we been wont to listen or to reflect,[722] we would not have been among the fellows of the Blaze.'

وَقَالُوا لَوْ كُنَّا نَسْمَعُ أَوْ نَعْقِلُ مَا كُنَّا فِىٓ أَصْحَٰبِ ٱلسَّعِيرِ ۝

11. So they will confess their sin. Far away be they, the fellows of the Blaze!

فَٱعْتَرَفُوا بِذَنۢبِهِمْ فَسُحْقًا لِّأَصْحَٰبِ ٱلسَّعِيرِ ۝

---

722. In other words, to use our own intelligence. Apart from glittering light of revelation, there is in all the nature around us and in our own conscience enough manifest Signs of God and His unity.

12. Those Who are in awe of their Lord Unseen, theirs shall be forgiveness and a great reward.

إِنَّ ٱلَّذِينَ يَخْشَوْنَ رَبَّهُم بِٱلْغَيْبِ لَهُم مَّغْفِرَةٌ وَأَجْرٌ كَبِيرٌ ۝

13. And whether you keep your discourse secret or disclose it, verily He is the Knower of what is in the breasts.

وَأَسِرُّوا۟ قَوْلَكُمْ أَوِ ٱجْهَرُوا۟ بِهِۦٓ إِنَّهُۥ عَلِيمٌۢ بِذَاتِ ٱلصُّدُورِ ۝

14. Will not He Who has created know? He is the Subtle, the Aware.

أَلَا يَعْلَمُ مَنْ خَلَقَ وَهُوَ ٱللَّطِيفُ ٱلْخَبِيرُ ۝

Section 2

15. He it is Who has made the earth subservient[723] to you; so go forth in the tracts thereof, and eat of His provision. And to Him is the Resurrection.

هُوَ ٱلَّذِى جَعَلَ لَكُمُ ٱلْأَرْضَ ذَلُولًا فَٱمْشُوا۟ فِى مَنَاكِبِهَا وَكُلُوا۟ مِن رِّزْقِهِۦ وَإِلَيْهِ ٱلنُّشُورُ ۝

16. Are you secure that He Who is in the heaven will not sink the earth with you, and then it should quake?

ءَأَمِنتُم مَّن فِى ٱلسَّمَآءِ أَن يَخْسِفَ بِكُمُ ٱلْأَرْضَ فَإِذَا هِىَ تَمُورُ ۝

17. Or are you secure that He Who is in the heaven will not send against you a whirlwind? Soon you shall know how has been My warning.

أَمْ أَمِنتُم مَّن فِى ٱلسَّمَآءِ أَن يُرْسِلَ عَلَيْكُمْ حَاصِبًا فَسَتَعْلَمُونَ كَيْفَ نَذِيرِ ۝

18. And assuredly those before them have belied, then how has been My wrath?

وَلَقَدْ كَذَّبَ ٱلَّذِينَ مِن قَبْلِهِمْ فَكَيْفَ كَانَ نَكِيرِ ۝

---

723. It is the earth that is made for man, and not man for the earth. The enunciation of this simple doctrine demolishes the polytheistic concept of Earth-goddess and Mother-Earth.

19. Do they not see the birds above them outstretching their wings and also closing them? None sustains them except the Compassionate. Verily He is the Beholder of everything.

أَوَلَمۡ يَرَوۡا إِلَى ٱلطَّيۡرِ فَوۡقَهُمۡ صَٰٓفَّٰتٍ وَيَقۡبِضۡنَ مَا يُمۡسِكُهُنَّ إِلَّا ٱلرَّحۡمَٰنُ إِنَّهُۥ بِكُلِّ شَىۡءٍ بَصِيرٌ ۝١٩

20. Who is he, besides the Compassionate, that can be an army unto you and succour you? The infidels are but in delusion.

أَمَّنۡ هَٰذَا ٱلَّذِى هُوَ جُندٌ لَّكُمۡ يَنصُرُكُم مِّن دُونِ ٱلرَّحۡمَٰنِ إِنِ ٱلۡكَٰفِرُونَ إِلَّا فِى غُرُورٍ ۝٢٠

21. Should He withhold His provision, who is he that can provide for you? Aye! They persist in perversity and aversion.

أَمَّنۡ هَٰذَا ٱلَّذِى يَرۡزُقُكُمۡ إِنۡ أَمۡسَكَ رِزۡقَهُۥ بَل لَّجُّوا فِى عُتُوٍّ وَنُفُورٍ ۝٢١

22. Is he, then, who goes about grovelling upon his face better directed or he who walks evenly on a straight path?

أَفَمَن يَمۡشِى مُكِبًّا عَلَىٰ وَجۡهِهِۦٓ أَهۡدَىٰٓ أَمَّن يَمۡشِى سَوِيًّا عَلَىٰ صِرَٰطٍ مُّسۡتَقِيمٍ ۝٢٢

23. Say: 'He it is Who has brought you forth and has endowed you with hearing and sights and hearts. Little thanks it is you give!'

قُلۡ هُوَ ٱلَّذِىٓ أَنشَأَكُمۡ وَجَعَلَ لَكُمُ ٱلسَّمۡعَ وَٱلۡأَبۡصَٰرَ وَٱلۡأَفۡـِٔدَةَ قَلِيلًا مَّا تَشۡكُرُونَ ۝٢٣

24. Say: 'He it is Who has spread you over the earth, and to Him you shall be gathered.'

قُلۡ هُوَ ٱلَّذِى ذَرَأَكُمۡ فِى ٱلۡأَرۡضِ وَإِلَيۡهِ تُحۡشَرُونَ ۝٢٤

25. And they say: 'When will this promise come to pass, if you speak truth.'

وَيَقُولُونَ مَتَىٰ هَٰذَا ٱلۡوَعۡدُ إِن كُنتُمۡ صَٰدِقِينَ ۝٢٥

26. Say: 'The knowledge thereof is only with Allah, and I am but a manifest warner.'

قُلۡ إِنَّمَا ٱلۡعِلۡمُ عِندَ ٱللَّهِ وَإِنَّمَآ أَنَا۠ نَذِيرٌ مُّبِينٌ ۝٢٦

27. But when they will see it proximating, sad will be the countenances of those who disbelieve, and it will be said: 'This is what you have been calling for.'

فَلَمَّا رَأَوْهُ زُلْفَةً سِيْئَتْ وُجُوْهُ الَّذِيْنَ كَفَرُوْا وَقِيْلَ هَذَا الَّذِيْ كُنْتُمْ بِهِ تَدَّعُوْنَ ۝

28. Say: 'Think! If Allah destroys me and those with me, or has mercy on us, who will protect the infidels from an afflictive torment?'

قُلْ أَرَءَيْتُمْ إِنْ أَهْلَكَنِيَ اللَّهُ وَمَنْ مَّعِيَ أَوْ رَحِمَنَا فَمَنْ يُجِيْرُ الْكَفِرِيْنَ مِنْ عَذَابٍ أَلِيْمٍ ۝

29. Say: 'He is the Compassionate; in Him we have believed, and in Him we have put our trust. And soon you will know who it is that is in manifest error.'

قُلْ هُوَ الرَّحْمَنُ ءَامَنَّا بِهِ وَعَلَيْهِ تَوَكَّلْنَا فَسَتَعْلَمُوْنَ مَنْ هُوَ فِيْ ضَلَلٍ مُّبِيْنٍ ۝

30. Say: 'Think! Were your water to be sunk away, who then could bring you water welling-up?'

قُلْ أَرَءَيْتُمْ إِنْ أَصْبَحَ مَاؤُكُمْ غَوْرًا فَمَنْ يَأْتِيْكُمْ بِمَاءٍ مَّعِيْنٍ ۝

Sūrah 68

al-Qalam

(Makkan, 2 Sections, 52 Verses)

In the name of Allah, the Compassionate, the Merciful.

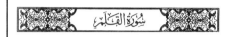

Section 1

1. Nun. By the pen and by what they inscribe.

2. Through the grace of your Lord. You are not mad.

3. And verily for you will be an unending reward.

4. And verily you are of a high and noble disposition.

5. Soon you will see and they will see,

6. Which of you is afflicted with madness.

7. Verily your Lord is the best Knower of him who has strayed from the path and the best Knower of him who is the guided one.

8. So do not obey the beliers.

9. They would like that you should be a pliant, so that they also will be a pliant.

10. And do not obey any ignominious swearer,

وَلَا تُطِعْ كُلَّ حَلَّافٍ مَّهِينٍ ۝

11. Defamer, spreader abroad of slander,

هَمَّازٍ مَّشَّاءٍ بِنَمِيمٍ ۝

12. Hinderer of the good, trespasser, sinner.

مَّنَّاعٍ لِّلْخَيْرِ مُعْتَدٍ أَثِيمٍ ۝

13. Gross, and moreover ignoble,

عُتُلٍّ بَعْدَ ذَٰلِكَ زَنِيمٍ ۝

14. And thus, because he is the owner of riches and children.

أَن كَانَ ذَا مَالٍ وَبَنِينَ ۝

15. When Our revelations are rehearsed to him he says: 'Fables of the ancients.'

إِذَا تُتْلَىٰ عَلَيْهِ ءَايَٰتُنَا قَالَ أَسَٰطِيرُ الْأَوَّلِينَ ۝

16. Soon We shall brand him on the snout.

سَنَسِمُهُ عَلَى الْخُرْطُومِ ۝

17. Verily We! We have tried them even as We tried the men of a garden when they swore that they would surely pluck it in the morning.

إِنَّا بَلَوْنَٰهُمْ كَمَا بَلَوْنَا أَصْحَٰبَ الْجَنَّةِ إِذْ أَقْسَمُوا لَيَصْرِمُنَّهَا مُصْبِحِينَ ۝

18. And they made in the assertion no reservation.

وَلَا يَسْتَثْنُونَ ۝

19. Therefore there visited it from your Lord an encircling visitation while they slept.

فَطَافَ عَلَيْهَا طَآئِفٌ مِّن رَّبِّكَ وَهُمْ نَآئِمُونَ ۝

20. Then in the morning it became as if it had been plucked.

فَأَصْبَحَتْ كَالصَّرِيمِ ۝

21. Then in the morning they cried out to each other.

فَتَنَادَوْا مُصْبِحِينَ ۝

22. Saying: 'Go out early to your tilth if you would pluck.'

أَنِ اغْدُوا عَلَىٰ حَرْثِكُمْ إِن كُنتُمْ صَٰرِمِينَ ۝

23. Then they went off, speaking to each other in a low voice;

فَانطَلَقُوا وَهُمْ يَتَخَفَّتُونَ ۝

24. 'Let there enter upon you no needy man today.'

أَن لَّا يَدْخُلَنَّهَا الْيَوْمَ عَلَيْكُم مِّسْكِينٌ ۝

25. And they went out early determined in purpose.

وَغَدَوْا عَلَىٰ حَرْدٍ قَدِرِينَ ۝

26. Then when they saw it, they said: 'Indeed we are gone astray.'

فَلَمَّا رَأَوْهَا قَالُوا إِنَّا لَضَآلُّونَ ۝

27. 'Alas! It is we who have been robbed!'

بَلْ نَحْنُ مَحْرُومُونَ ۝

28. And the more moderate of them said: 'Did I not tell you: why do you not hallow Him?'

قَالَ أَوْسَطُهُمْ أَلَمْ أَقُل لَّكُمْ لَوْلَا تُسَبِّحُونَ ۝

29. They said now in repentance: 'Hallowed be Our Lord! Verily we have been wrong-doers.'

قَالُوا سُبْحَٰنَ رَبِّنَا إِنَّا كُنَّا ظَٰلِمِينَ ۝

30. Then they turned to each other reproaching.

فَأَقْبَلَ بَعْضُهُمْ عَلَىٰ بَعْضٍ يَتَلَٰوَمُونَ ۝

31. They said: 'Woe to us! Surely we have been arrogant.

قَالُوا يَٰوَيْلَنَا إِنَّا كُنَّا طَٰغِينَ ۝

32. Perhaps our Lord may exchange for us a better garden than this, verily we are beseechers to our Lord.'

عَسَىٰ رَبُّنَا أَن يُبْدِلَنَا خَيْرًا مِّنْهَا إِنَّا إِلَىٰ رَبِّنَا رَٰغِبُونَ ۝

33. Such is the chastisement, and the chastisement of the Hereafter is far greater, if they but knew.

كَذَٰلِكَ الْعَذَابُ وَلَعَذَابُ الْآخِرَةِ أَكْبَرُ لَوْ كَانُوا يَعْلَمُونَ ۝

Section 2

34. Verily for the pious there are Gardens of Delight with their Lord.

إِنَّ لِلْمُتَّقِينَ عِندَ رَبِّهِمْ جَنَّتِ ٱلنَّعِيمِ ﴿٣٤﴾

35. Shall We make the Muslims like the culprits?

أَفَنَجْعَلُ ٱلْمُسْلِمِينَ كَٱلْمُجْرِمِينَ ﴿٣٥﴾

36. How it is with you! How ill do you judge!

مَا لَكُمْ كَيْفَ تَحْكُمُونَ ﴿٣٦﴾

37. Is there with you a Book wherein you study,

أَمْ لَكُمْ كِتَٰبٌ فِيهِ تَدْرُسُونَ ﴿٣٧﴾

38. That therein is for you what you may choose?

إِنَّ لَكُمْ فِيهِ لَمَا تَخَيَّرُونَ ﴿٣٨﴾

39. Or, have you oaths from Us, reaching to the Day of Resurrection, that yours will be what you judge?

أَمْ لَكُمْ أَيْمَٰنٌ عَلَيْنَا بَٰلِغَةٌ إِلَىٰ يَوْمِ ٱلْقِيَٰمَةِ إِنَّ لَكُمْ لَمَا تَحْكُمُونَ ﴿٣٩﴾

40. Ask them, which of them will stand thereof as a guarantee?

سَلْهُمْ أَيُّهُم بِذَٰلِكَ زَعِيمٌ ﴿٤٠﴾

41. Have they associate-gods? Let them produce their associate-gods if they speak truth!

أَمْ لَهُمْ شُرَكَآءُ فَلْيَأْتُوا بِشُرَكَآئِهِمْ إِن كَانُوا صَٰدِقِينَ ﴿٤١﴾

42. Remember the Day when the shank shall be bared and they shall be called upon to prostrate themselves, but they shall not be able.

يَوْمَ يُكْشَفُ عَن سَاقٍ وَيُدْعَوْنَ إِلَى ٱلسُّجُودِ فَلَا يَسْتَطِيعُونَ ﴿٤٢﴾

43. Downcast will be their looks; abjectness will overspread them. Surely they had been called upon to prostrate themselves, while yet they were whole (in full possession of judgement and will).

خَٰشِعَةً أَبْصَٰرُهُمْ تَرْهَقُهُمْ ذِلَّةٌ وَقَدْ كَانُوا يُدْعَوْنَ إِلَى ٱلسُّجُودِ وَهُمْ سَٰلِمُونَ ﴿٤٣﴾

44. Let Me alone with him who belies this discourse. We lead them on by steps which they perceive not.

فَذَرْنِى وَمَن يُكَذِّبُ بِهَذَا الْحَدِيثِ سَنَسْتَدْرِجُهُم مِّنْ حَيْثُ لَا يَعْلَمُونَ ۝

45. And I bear with them. Verily My contrivance is sure.

وَأُمْلِى لَهُمْ إِنَّ كَيْدِى مَتِينٌ ۝

46. Do you ask them a wage, so that they are laden with debt?

أَمْ تَسْـَٔلُهُمْ أَجْرًا فَهُم مِّن مَّغْرَمٍ مُّثْقَلُونَ ۝

47. Is with them the Unseen, so that they write down Allah's decrees?

أَمْ عِندَهُمُ الْغَيْبُ فَهُمْ يَكْتُبُونَ ۝

48. Be you patient, then, with your Lord's judgement, and do not be you like him of the fish, when he cried out, while, he was in anguish.

فَاصْبِرْ لِحُكْمِ رَبِّكَ وَلَا تَكُن كَصَاحِبِ الْحُوتِ إِذْ نَادَىٰ وَهُوَ مَكْظُومٌ ۝

49. Had there not reached him the grace from his Lord, he would surely have been cast into the wilderness in a plight.

لَّوْلَا أَن تَدَارَكَهُ نِعْمَةٌ مِّن رَّبِّهِ لَنُبِذَ بِالْعَرَاءِ وَهُوَ مَذْمُومٌ ۝

50. Then his Lord chose him, and made him of the righteous.

فَاجْتَبَاهُ رَبُّهُ فَجَعَلَهُ مِنَ الصَّالِحِينَ ۝

51. And when those who disbelieve hear the admonition; they shall cause you to stumble with the stern looks, and they say: 'Indeed he is mad.'

وَإِن يَكَادُ الَّذِينَ كَفَرُوا لَيُزْلِقُونَكَ بِأَبْصَارِهِمْ لَمَّا سَمِعُوا الذِّكْرَ وَيَقُولُونَ إِنَّهُ لَمَجْنُونٌ ۝

52. While it is nothing but an admonition to the worlds.

وَمَا هُوَ إِلَّا ذِكْرٌ لِّلْعَالَمِينَ ۝

Sūrah 69

al-Ḥāqqah

(Makkan, 2 Sections, 52 Verses)

In the name of Allah, the Compassionate, the Merciful.

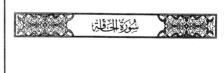

Section 1

1. The Inevitable calamity!

2. What is the inevitable calamity?

3. And what will make you know what the inevitable calamity is?

4. The tribes of the Thamūd and 'Ād belied the striking Day.

5. As for the Thamūd, they were destroyed by an outburst.

6. And as for the 'Ād, they were destroyed by a wind, furious and roaring,

7. To which He subjected them for seven nights and eight days in succession so that you might have seen men during it lying prostrate, as though they were stumps of palm ruined.

8. Do you see any remnant of them?

9. And Pharaoh and those before him and the overturned cities committed sins.

10. And they disbelieved their Lord's Messenger, so He seized them with an increasing grip.

فَعَصَوْا رَسُولَ رَبِّهِمْ فَأَخَذَهُمْ أَخْذَةً رَّابِيَةً ۝

11. Verily We bore you, when the water rose, upon a traversing ark.

إِنَّا لَمَّا طَغَا الْمَاءُ حَمَلْنَاكُمْ فِي الْجَارِيَةِ ۝

12. That We might make it an admonition unto you and that it might be retained by the retaining ears.

لِنَجْعَلَهَا لَكُمْ تَذْكِرَةً وَتَعِيَهَا أُذُنٌ وَاعِيَةٌ ۝

13. And when the trumpet will sound a single blast,

فَإِذَا نُفِخَ فِي الصُّورِ نَفْخَةٌ وَاحِدَةٌ ۝

14. And the earth and the mountains will be borne, and they will be crushed with a single crushing.

وَحُمِلَتِ الْأَرْضُ وَالْجِبَالُ فَدُكَّتَا دَكَّةً وَاحِدَةً ۝

15. On that Day will happen the event.

فَيَوْمَئِذٍ وَقَعَتِ الْوَاقِعَةُ ۝

16. And the heaven will be rent asunder; frail it will be on that Day.

وَانْشَقَّتِ السَّمَاءُ فَهِيَ يَوْمَئِذٍ وَاهِيَةٌ ۝

17. And the angels will be on its borders, and eight of them will on that Day bear the throne of your Lord over them.

وَالْمَلَكُ عَلَى أَرْجَائِهَا وَيَحْمِلُ عَرْشَ رَبِّكَ فَوْقَهُمْ يَوْمَئِذٍ ثَمَانِيَةٌ ۝

18. The Day whereon you will be mustered, nothing hidden by you will be hidden.

يَوْمَئِذٍ تُعْرَضُونَ لَا تَخْفَى مِنكُمْ خَافِيَةٌ ۝

19. Then as to him, whose book will be vouchsafed to him in his right hand, he will say: 'Here! Read my record;

فَأَمَّا مَنْ أُوتِيَ كِتَابَهُ بِيَمِينِهِ فَيَقُولُ هَاؤُمُ اقْرَءُوا كِتَابِيَهْ ۝

20. Verily I was sure that I would have to face my reckoning.'

إِنِّى ظَنَنتُ أَنِّى مُلَٰقٍ حِسَابِيَهۡ ۝

21. Then he shall be in a life well-pleasing.

فَهُوَ فِى عِيشَةٍ رَّاضِيَةٍ ۝

22. In a lofty Garden,

فِى جَنَّةٍ عَالِيَةٍ ۝

23. Of which the clusters will be near at hand.

قُطُوفُهَا دَانِيَةٌ ۝

24. Eat and drink with benefit for what you sent on beforehand in days past.

كُلُوا۟ وَٱشۡرَبُوا۟ هَنِيٓـًٔۢا بِمَآ أَسۡلَفۡتُمۡ فِى ٱلۡأَيَّامِ ٱلۡخَالِيَةِ ۝

25. Then as to him whose record will be vouchsafed to him in his left hand, he will say: 'Oh! Would that I had not been given my record at all,

وَأَمَّا مَنۡ أُوتِىَ كِتَٰبَهُۥ بِشِمَالِهِۦ فَيَقُولُ يَٰلَيۡتَنِى لَمۡ أُوتَ كِتَٰبِيَهۡ ۝

26. Nor known what was my reckoning.

وَلَمۡ أَدۡرِ مَا حِسَابِيَهۡ ۝

27. Oh! Would that it would have been the ending.

يَٰلَيۡتَهَا كَانَتِ ٱلۡقَاضِيَةَ ۝

28. My riches have availed me not;

مَآ أَغۡنَىٰ عَنِّى مَالِيَهۡ ۝

29. My authority has perished for me.'

هَلَكَ عَنِّى سُلۡطَٰنِيَهۡ ۝

30. Seize him, and chain him;

خُذُوهُ فَغُلُّوهُ ۝

31. Then roast him in the Scorch;

ثُمَّ ٱلۡجَحِيمَ صَلُّوهُ ۝

32. Then fasten him with a chain, seventy cubits long.

ثُمَّ فِى سِلۡسِلَةٍ ذَرۡعُهَا سَبۡعُونَ ذِرَاعًا فَٱسۡلُكُوهُ ۝

33. Verily he was wont not to believe in Allah, the Great;

إِنَّهُۥ كَانَ لَا يُؤۡمِنُ بِٱللَّهِ ٱلۡعَظِيمِ ۝

34. Nor he urged on others the feeding of the poor.

وَلَا يَحُضُّ عَلَىٰ طَعَامِ ٱلۡمِسۡكِينِ ۝

35. No friend is therefore for him here this Day,

فَلَيْسَ لَهُ الْيَوْمَ هَهُنَا حَمِيمٌ ﴿٣٥﴾

36. Nor any food except the filthy corruption.

وَلَا طَعَامٌ إِلَّا مِنْ غِسْلِينٍ ﴿٣٦﴾

37. None will eat it except the sinners.

لَا يَأْكُلُهُ إِلَّا الْخَاطِئُونَ ﴿٣٧﴾

Section 2

38. I swear by what you see,

فَلَا أُقْسِمُ بِمَا تُبْصِرُونَ ﴿٣٨﴾

39. And by what you do not see,

وَمَا لَا تُبْصِرُونَ ﴿٣٩﴾

40. That it is the speech brought by an honourable envoy.

إِنَّهُ لَقَوْلُ رَسُولٍ كَرِيمٍ ﴿٤٠﴾

41. And it is not the speech of a poet. Little it is that you believe.

وَمَا هُوَ بِقَوْلِ شَاعِرٍ قَلِيلًا مَّا تُؤْمِنُونَ ﴿٤١﴾

42. Nor it is the speech of a soothsayer. Little are you admonished.

وَلَا بِقَوْلِ كَاهِنٍ قَلِيلًا مَّا تَذَكَّرُونَ ﴿٤٢﴾

43. It is a revelation from the Lord of the worlds.

تَنزِيلٌ مِّن رَّبِّ الْعَالَمِينَ ﴿٤٣﴾

44. And if he had forged concerning Us some discourses,

وَلَوْ تَقَوَّلَ عَلَيْنَا بَعْضَ الْأَقَاوِيلِ ﴿٤٤﴾

45. We surely would have seized him by the right hand,

لَأَخَذْنَا مِنْهُ بِالْيَمِينِ ﴿٤٥﴾

46. And then severed his life vein.

ثُمَّ لَقَطَعْنَا مِنْهُ الْوَتِينَ ﴿٤٦﴾

47. And not one of you would have withheld Us from punishing him.

فَمَا مِنكُم مِّنْ أَحَدٍ عَنْهُ حَاجِزِينَ ﴿٤٧﴾

48. And surely it is an admonition to the God-fearing.

وَإِنَّهُ لَتَذْكِرَةٌ لِّلْمُتَّقِينَ ﴿٤٨﴾

49. And verily We know that some among you belie.

وَإِنَّا لَنَعْلَمُ أَنَّ مِنكُم مُّكَذِّبِينَ ۝

50. And verily it shall be an occasion of anguish to the infidels.

وَإِنَّهُ لَحَسْرَةٌ عَلَى ٱلْكَٰفِرِينَ ۝

51. And verily it is the Truth of absolute certainty.

وَإِنَّهُ لَحَقُّ ٱلْيَقِينِ ۝

52. So hallow you the name of your Lord, the Great.

فَسَبِّحْ بِٱسْمِ رَبِّكَ ٱلْعَظِيمِ ۝

Sūrah 70

al-Ma'ārij

(Makkan, 2 Sections, 44 Verses)

*In the name of Allah, the
Compassionate, the Merciful.*

Section 1

1. A questioner has questioned
about the chastisement about to
befall

سَأَلَ سَآئِلٌ بِعَذَابٍ وَاقِعٍ ﴿١﴾

2. The infidels which is not to be
averted,

لِّلْكَفِرِينَ لَيْسَ لَهُ دَافِعٌ ﴿٢﴾

3. From Allah, the Owner of the
ascending steps.

مِّنَ اللَّهِ ذِى الْمَعَارِجِ ﴿٣﴾

4. Thereby the angels ascend to
Him and also the spirit; on a Day
whose space is fifty thousand
years.

تَعْرُجُ الْمَلَئِكَةُ وَالرُّوحُ إِلَيْهِ فِى يَوْمٍ كَانَ مِقْدَارُهُ خَمْسِينَ أَلْفَ سَنَةٍ ﴿٤﴾

5. Be you patient with a
becoming patience.

فَاصْبِرْ صَبْرًا جَمِيلًا ﴿٥﴾

6. Verily they see it afar off.

إِنَّهُمْ يَرَوْنَهُ بَعِيدًا ﴿٦﴾

7. And We see it near.

وَنَرَاهُ قَرِيبًا ﴿٧﴾

8. It shall befall on a Day whereon
the sky will become like dregs of
oil.

يَوْمَ تَكُونُ السَّمَآءُ كَالْمُهْلِ ﴿٨﴾

9. And the mountains will become
like dyed wool,

وَتَكُونُ الْجِبَالُ كَالْعِهْنِ ﴿٩﴾

10. And not a friend shall ask a
friend,

وَلَا يَسْئَلُ حَمِيمٌ حَمِيمًا ﴿١٠﴾

11. Though they shall be made to see one another. The guilty would like to ransom himself from the torment of that Day by his children,

يُبَصَّرُونَهُمْ يَوَدُّ الْمُجْرِمُ لَوْ يَفْتَدِى مِنْ عَذَابِ يَوْمِئِذٍ بِبَنِيهِ ﴿١١﴾

12. And his wife and his brother,

وَصَاحِبَتِهِ وَأَخِيهِ ﴿١٢﴾

13. And his kin that sheltered him,

وَفَصِيلَتِهِ الَّتِى تُؤْوِيهِ ﴿١٣﴾

14. And all those on the earth; so that this might deliver him.

وَمَن فِى الْأَرْضِ جَمِيعًا ثُمَّ يُنجِيهِ ﴿١٤﴾

15. By no means! It is a Flame,

كَلَّا إِنَّهَا لَظَى ﴿١٥﴾

16. Flying off the scalp-skin.

نَزَّاعَةً لِّلشَّوَى ﴿١٦﴾

17. It shall call him who turns away and back-slides,

تَدْعُوا مَنْ أَدْبَرَ وَتَوَلَّى ﴿١٧﴾

18. And who amasses and hoards.

وَجَمَعَ فَأَوْعَى ﴿١٨﴾

19. Verily man is formed impatient,

إِنَّ الْإِنسَانَ خُلِقَ هَلُوعًا ﴿١٩﴾

20. Bewailing when evil touches him,

إِذَا مَسَّهُ الشَّرُّ جَزُوعًا ﴿٢٠﴾

21. And begrudging, when good visits him.

وَإِذَا مَسَّهُ الْخَيْرُ مَنُوعًا ﴿٢١﴾

22. Not so are the prayerful,

إِلَّا الْمُصَلِّينَ ﴿٢٢﴾

23. Who are constant at their prayer,

الَّذِينَ هُمْ عَلَى صَلَاتِهِمْ دَائِمُونَ ﴿٢٣﴾

24. And in whose riches is a recognized right,

وَالَّذِينَ فِى أَمْوَالِهِمْ حَقٌّ مَّعْلُومٌ ﴿٢٤﴾

25. For the beggar and the destitute,

لِّلسَّائِلِ وَالْمَحْرُومِ ﴿٢٥﴾

26. And who testify to the Day of Requital,

وَالَّذِينَ يُصَدِّقُونَ بِيَوْمِ الدِّينِ ﴿٢٦﴾

27. And who are fearful of their Lord's torment.

وَالَّذِينَ هُم مِّنۡ عَذَابِ رَبِّهِم مُّشۡفِقُونَ ۝

28. Verily from the torment of their Lord none can feel secure.

إِنَّ عَذَابَ رَبِّهِمۡ غَيۡرُ مَأۡمُونٍ ۝

29. As also those who guard their private parts,

وَالَّذِينَ هُمۡ لِفُرُوجِهِمۡ حَافِظُونَ ۝

30. Save in regard to their women and those whom their right hands own. So they are not reproachable.

إِلَّا عَلَىٰٓ أَزۡوَاجِهِمۡ أَوۡ مَا مَلَكَتۡ أَيۡمَانُهُمۡ فَإِنَّهُمۡ غَيۡرُ مَلُومِينَ ۝

31. Add whoso seeks beyond that, then it is those who are the trespassers.

فَمَنِ ابۡتَغَىٰ وَرَآءَ ذَٰلِكَ فَأُوْلَٰٓئِكَ هُمُ الۡعَادُونَ ۝

32. As also those who keep their trusts and their covenant,[724]

وَالَّذِينَ هُمۡ لِأَمَٰنَٰتِهِمۡ وَعَهۡدِهِمۡ رَاعُونَ ۝

33. And who stand firm in their testimonies.

وَالَّذِينَ هُم بِشَهَٰدَٰتِهِمۡ قَآئِمُونَ ۝

34. And who are observant of their prayer.

وَالَّذِينَ هُمۡ عَلَىٰ صَلَاتِهِمۡ يُحَافِظُونَ ۝

35. Honoured, they shall dwell in Gardens.

أُوْلَٰٓئِكَ فِي جَنَّٰتٍ مُّكۡرَمُونَ ۝

Section 2

36. What ails those who disbelieve, hastening towards you,

فَمَالِ الَّذِينَ كَفَرُواۡ قِبَلَكَ مُهۡطِعِينَ ۝

---

724. Those who fulfill all their obligations, whether financial or otherwise. The sacredness attached to everyday trusts and convenants in Islam is very remarkable.

عَنِ ٱلۡيَمِينِ وَعَنِ ٱلشِّمَالِ عِزِينَ ﴿٣٧﴾

37. On the right and on the left, in companies?

أَيَطۡمَعُ كُلُّ ٱمۡرِيٍّ مِّنۡهُمۡ أَن يُدۡخَلَ جَنَّةَ نَعِيمٍ ﴿٣٨﴾

38. Does everyone of them covet that he shall enter the Garden of Delight?

كَلَّآ إِنَّا خَلَقۡنَٰهُم مِّمَّا يَعۡلَمُونَ ﴿٣٩﴾

39. By no means! We have created them from what they know.

فَلَآ أُقۡسِمُ بِرَبِّ ٱلۡمَشَٰرِقِ وَٱلۡمَغَٰرِبِ إِنَّا لَقَٰدِرُونَ ﴿٤٠﴾

40. I swear by the Lord of the easts and wests[725] that We are able,

عَلَىٰٓ أَن نُّبَدِّلَ خَيۡرٗا مِّنۡهُمۡ وَمَا نَحۡنُ بِمَسۡبُوقِينَ ﴿٤١﴾

41. To replace them by others better than they, and We are not to be frustrated.

فَذَرۡهُمۡ يَخُوضُواْ وَيَلۡعَبُواْ حَتَّىٰ يُلَٰقُواْ يَوۡمَهُمُ ٱلَّذِي يُوعَدُونَ ﴿٤٢﴾

42. So let you them alone plunging in vanity and sporting until they meet their Day which they are promised.

يَوۡمَ يَخۡرُجُونَ مِنَ ٱلۡأَجۡدَاثِ سِرَاعٗا كَأَنَّهُمۡ إِلَىٰ نُصُبٍ يُوفِضُونَ ﴿٤٣﴾

43. The Day whereon they will come forth from the sepulchres hurrying as if they were hastening to an altar.

خَٰشِعَةً أَبۡصَٰرُهُمۡ تَرۡهَقُهُمۡ ذِلَّةٌ ذَٰلِكَ ٱلۡيَوۡمُ ٱلَّذِي كَانُواْ يُوعَدُونَ ﴿٤٤﴾

44. Downcast shall be their looks, abjectness shall overspread them. Such is the Day they were promised.

---

725. In the plural these signify the different points of the horizon at which the sun rises and sets in the course of the year. This completely repudiates the polytheistic idea of *Loka palas* or guardians of the world, presiding over the four cardinal and the intermediate points of the compass. Among the Hindus, for instance, 'Indra, the chief of the gods, was regarded as the regent of the east; Agni the fire, was in the same way associated with the south-east; Yama with the south; Surya, the sun, with the south-west; Varuna originally the representative of the all-embracing heaven or atmosphere, now the god of the ocean, with the west; Vayu, the wind, with the north-west, Kubera, the god of wealth, with the north; and Soma, with the north-east' (*EBr*. III. p. 1016). Tibetan mythology also has a parallel set of deities for each of the four cardinal points. See *ERE*. VIII. p. 76.

Sūrah 71

Nūḥ

(Makkan, 2 Sections, 28 Verses)

*In the name of Allah, the
Compassionate, the Merciful.*

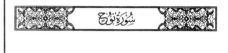

Section 1

1. Verily We! We sent forth Noah
to his people saying: 'Warn your
people before there comes to
them an afflictive chastisement.'

2. He said: 'My people! I am to
you a manifest warner.

3. Worship Allah, and fear Him,
and obey me.

4. He will forgive you your sins,
and will defer you to an appointed
term. Verily the term of Allah,
when it comes, shall not be
deferred, if you but know.'

5. He said: 'Lord! Verily I have
called my people night and day.

6. And my calling has only
increased their aversion.

7. Verily whenever I call them,
that You may forgive them, they
place their fingers in their ears,
and wrap themselves with their
garments, and persist in their
denial, and are stiff-necked.

إِنَّآ أَرْسَلْنَا نُوحًا إِلَىٰ قَوْمِهِۦٓ أَنْ أَنذِرْ قَوْمَكَ مِن قَبْلِ أَن يَأْتِيَهُمْ عَذَابٌ أَلِيمٌ ۞

قَالَ يَٰقَوْمِ إِنِّى لَكُمْ نَذِيرٌ مُّبِينٌ ۞

أَنِ ٱعْبُدُوا۟ ٱللَّهَ وَٱتَّقُوهُ وَأَطِيعُونِ ۞

يَغْفِرْ لَكُم مِّن ذُنُوبِكُمْ وَيُؤَخِّرْكُمْ إِلَىٰٓ أَجَلٍ مُّسَمًّى إِنَّ أَجَلَ ٱللَّهِ إِذَا جَآءَ لَا يُؤَخَّرُ لَوْ كُنتُمْ تَعْلَمُونَ ۞

قَالَ رَبِّ إِنِّى دَعَوْتُ قَوْمِى لَيْلًا وَنَهَارًا ۞

فَلَمْ يَزِدْهُمْ دُعَآءِىٓ إِلَّا فِرَارًا ۞

وَإِنِّى كُلَّمَا دَعَوْتُهُمْ لِتَغْفِرَ لَهُمْ جَعَلُوٓا۟ أَصَٰبِعَهُمْ فِىٓ ءَاذَانِهِمْ وَٱسْتَغْشَوْا۟ ثِيَابَهُمْ وَأَصَرُّوا۟ وَٱسْتَكْبَرُوا۟ ٱسْتِكْبَارًا ۞

8. Then I have called them aloud.

ثُمَّ إِنِّيٓ دَعَوۡتُهُمۡ جِهَارًا ۝

9. Then I spoke to them in public and in private I addressed them.'

ثُمَّ إِنِّيٓ أَعۡلَنۡتُ لَهُمۡ وَأَسۡرَرۡتُ لَهُمۡ إِسۡرَارًا ۝

10. And I said: 'Beg forgiveness of your Lord; He is ever Most Forgiving.

فَقُلۡتُ ٱسۡتَغۡفِرُوا۟ رَبَّكُمۡ إِنَّهُۥ كَانَ غَفَّارًا ۝

11. He will send down upon you rains copiously.

يُرۡسِلِ ٱلسَّمَآءَ عَلَيۡكُم مِّدۡرَارًا ۝

12. And He will increase you in riches and children and will assign to you Gardens and will assign to you rivers.

وَيُمۡدِدۡكُم بِأَمۡوَٰلٍ وَبَنِينَ وَيَجۡعَل لَّكُمۡ جَنَّٰتٍ وَيَجۡعَل لَّكُمۡ أَنۡهَٰرًا ۝

13. What ails you that you look not for majesty in Allah,

مَّا لَكُمۡ لَا تَرۡجُونَ لِلَّهِ وَقَارًا ۝

14. While He has created you by stages?

وَقَدۡ خَلَقَكُمۡ أَطۡوَارًا ۝

15. Do you not see how Allah has created the seven heavens in storeys?

أَلَمۡ تَرَوۡا۟ كَيۡفَ خَلَقَ ٱللَّهُ سَبۡعَ سَمَٰوَٰتٍ طِبَاقًا ۝

16. And He has placed the moon therein for a light and has made the sun for a lamp?

وَجَعَلَ ٱلۡقَمَرَ فِيهِنَّ نُورًا وَجَعَلَ ٱلشَّمۡسَ سِرَاجًا ۝

17. And Allah has caused you to grow from the earth as a growth.

وَٱللَّهُ أَنۢبَتَكُم مِّنَ ٱلۡأَرۡضِ نَبَاتًا ۝

18. And hence He will cause you to return to it and He will bring you forth completely.

ثُمَّ يُعِيدُكُمۡ فِيهَا وَيُخۡرِجُكُمۡ إِخۡرَاجًا ۝

19. And Allah has made for you the earth an expanse.

وَٱللَّهُ جَعَلَ لَكُمُ ٱلۡأَرۡضَ بِسَاطًا ۝

20. That of it you may traverse the open ways.'"

لِّتَسْلُكُوْا مِنْهَا سُبُلًا فِجَاجًا ۟

Section 2

21. Noah said: 'Lord! Verily they have denied me and have followed him whose riches and children have only increased him in loss.

قَالَ نُوْحٌ رَّبِّ إِنَّهُمْ عَصَوْنِيْ وَاتَّبَعُوْا مَنْ لَّمْ يَزِدْهُ مَالُهُ وَوَلَدُهُ إِلَّا خَسَارًا ۟

22. And they have plotted a tremendous plot.'

وَمَكَرُوْا مَكْرًا كُبَّارًا ۟

23. And they have said: 'You shall not leave[726] your gods, nor shall you leave Wadd nor Suwā' nor Yaghūth nor Ya'ūq nor Nasr.'

وَقَالُوْا لَا تَذَرُنَّ ءَالِهَتَكُمْ وَلَا تَذَرُنَّ وَدًّا وَّلَا سُوَاعًا وَّلَا يَغُوْثَ وَيَعُوْقَ وَنَسْرًا ۟

24. And surely they have led many astray. Increase these wrong-doers in naught save error.

وَقَدْ أَضَلُّوْا كَثِيْرًا وَلَا تَزِدِ الظّٰلِمِيْنَ إِلَّا ضَلٰلًا ۟

25. And because of their misdeeds they were drowned, and then made to enter the Fire. Then they did not find for themselves any helpers besides Allah.

مِّمَّا خَطِيْئَاتِهِمْ أُغْرِقُوْا فَأُدْخِلُوْا نَارًا فَلَمْ يَجِدُوْا لَهُمْ مِّنْ دُوْنِ اللّٰهِ أَنْصَارًا ۟

---

726. The names of the five oldest false Pagan gods and the symbols under which they were represented are as follows:

Pagan god	Shape	The Quality represented
1. Wadd	Man	Manly power
2. Suwā'	Woman	Mutability, Beauty
3. Yaghūth	Lion (or Bull)	Brute strength
4. Ya'uq	Horse	Swiftness
5. Nasr	Eagle, or Vulture or Falcon	Sharp sight, Insight.

(AYA.).

26. And Noah said: 'Lord! Leave not of the infidels any inhabitant upon the earth.

وَقَالَ نُوحٌ رَّبِّ لَا تَذَرْ عَلَى ٱلْأَرْضِ مِنَ ٱلْكَٰفِرِينَ دَيَّارًا ٢٦

27. For should You leave them, they will lead astray Your bondsmen and will surely beget sinning infidels.

إِنَّكَ إِن تَذَرْهُمْ يُضِلُّوا۟ عِبَادَكَ وَلَا يَلِدُوٓا۟ إِلَّا فَاجِرًا كَفَّارًا ٢٧

28. Lord! Forgive me and my parents and him who enters my house as a believer, and all the faithful men and women, and increase not the ungodly save in perdition.'

رَّبِّ ٱغْفِرْ لِى وَلِوَٰلِدَىَّ وَلِمَن دَخَلَ بَيْتِىَ مُؤْمِنًا وَلِلْمُؤْمِنِينَ وَٱلْمُؤْمِنَٰتِ وَلَا تَزِدِ ٱلظَّٰلِمِينَ إِلَّا تَبَارًا ٢٨

Sūrah 72

al-Jinn

(Makkan, 2 Sections, 28 Verses)

In the name of Allah, the Compassionate, the Merciful.

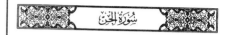

Section 1

1. Say: 'It has been revealed to me that a company of the jinn listened and said: "Verily we have listened to a recitation wondrous.

2. Guiding to rectitude; so we have believed in it, and we shall not by any means associate any one with our Lord.'"

3. And He, exalted be the majesty of our Lord, has taken neither a wife nor a son.

4. And the foolish among us were wont to forge a lie against Allah exceedingly.

5. And verily we believed that neither man nor *jinn* could ever forge a lie against Allah.

6. And persons among mankind have been seeking refuge with persons of the *jinn*, so that they increased them in evil.

7. And indeed they imagined, as you too imagined, that Allah will not raise anyone.

8. And we sought to reach the heaven, then we found it filled with a strong guard and darting meteors.

وَأَنَّا لَمَسْنَا ٱلسَّمَآءَ فَوَجَدْنَٰهَا مُلِئَتْ حَرَسًا شَدِيدًا وَشُهُبًا ۝

9. And we were wont to sit on seats therein to listen; but whosoever listens now finds for him a darting meteor in wait.

وَأَنَّا كُنَّا نَقْعُدُ مِنْهَا مَقَٰعِدَ لِلسَّمْعِ فَمَن يَسْتَمِعِ ٱلْءَانَ يَجِدْ لَهُۥ شِهَابًا رَّصَدًا ۝

10. And we do not know whether evil is boded for those on the earth, or their Lord intends for them a right direction.

وَأَنَّا لَا نَدْرِىٓ أَشَرٌّ أُرِيدَ بِمَن فِى ٱلْأَرْضِ أَمْ أَرَادَ بِهِمْ رَبُّهُمْ رَشَدًا ۝

11. And of us there are some righteous and of us are some otherwise; we have been following very diverse paths.

وَأَنَّا مِنَّا ٱلصَّٰلِحُونَ وَمِنَّا دُونَ ذَٰلِكَ كُنَّا طَرَآئِقَ قِدَدًا ۝

12. And we know that we cannot frustrate Allah in the earth. Nor can we elude Him by flight.

وَأَنَّا ظَنَنَّآ أَن لَّن نُّعْجِزَ ٱللَّهَ فِى ٱلْأَرْضِ وَلَن نُّعْجِزَهُۥ هَرَبًا ۝

13. And when we heard the message of guidance we believed in it, and whoso believes in his Lord, he shall fear neither diminution nor wrong.

وَأَنَّا لَمَّا سَمِعْنَا ٱلْهُدَىٰٓ ءَامَنَّا بِهِۦ فَمَن يُؤْمِنۢ بِرَبِّهِۦ فَلَا يَخَافُ بَخْسًا وَلَا رَهَقًا ۝

14. And of us some are Muslims, and some are deviators. Then whoso has embraced Islam, such have endeavoured after a path of rectitude.

وَأَنَّا مِنَّا ٱلْمُسْلِمُونَ وَمِنَّا ٱلْقَٰسِطُونَ فَمَنْ أَسْلَمَ فَأُو۟لَٰٓئِكَ تَحَرَّوْا۟ رَشَدًا ۝

15. And as to the deviators, they shall be firewood for Hell.

وَأَمَّا ٱلْقَٰسِطُونَ فَكَانُوا۟ لِجَهَنَّمَ حَطَبًا ۝

16. And had they kept to the right path, surely We would have watered them with plentiful rains.

وَأَلَّوِ ٱسْتَقَٰمُوا۟ عَلَى ٱلطَّرِيقَةِ لَأَسْقَيْنَٰهُم مَّآءً غَدَقًا ۝

17. That We might try them thereby. And whoso turns aside from the remembrance of his Lord, him He shall thrust into a vehement torment.

لِنَفْتِنَهُمْ فِيهِ وَمَن يُعْرِضْ عَن ذِكْرِ رَبِّهِ يَسْلُكْهُ عَذَابًا صَعَدًا ﴿١٧﴾

18. And prostrations are for Allah, so do not call along with Allah anyone.

وَأَنَّ ٱلْمَسَاجِدَ لِلَّهِ فَلَا تَدْعُوا مَعَ ٱللَّهِ أَحَدًا ﴿١٨﴾

19. And when the bondsman of Allah stood calling upon Him, they almost pressed upon him stifling.[727]

وَأَنَّهُ لَمَّا قَامَ عَبْدُ ٱللَّهِ يَدْعُوهُ كَادُوا يَكُونُونَ عَلَيْهِ لِبَدًا ﴿١٩﴾

Section 2

20. Say you: 'I simply call upon Allah, and do not associate anyone with Him.'

قُلْ إِنَّمَا أَدْعُوا رَبِّي وَلَا أُشْرِكُ بِهِ أَحَدًا ﴿٢٠﴾

21. Say: 'I do not own for you power of hurt nor of benefit.'

قُلْ إِنِّي لَا أَمْلِكُ لَكُمْ ضَرًّا وَلَا رَشَدًا ﴿٢١﴾

22. Say: 'None can protect me from Allah, nor can I find besides Him any refuge.

قُلْ إِنِّي لَن يُجِيرَنِي مِنَ ٱللَّهِ أَحَدٌ وَلَنْ أَجِدَ مِن دُونِهِ مُلْتَحَدًا ﴿٢٢﴾

---

727. The allusion is to the rough treatment which the Prophet received at the hands of the crowd at Ṭā'if. His attitude and behaviour on the occasion have won the admiration of even some of his hostile critics. 'Stirred up to hasten the departure of the unwelcome visitor, the people hooted him through the streets, pelted him with stones, and at last obliged him to flee the city, pursued by a relentless rabble. Blood flowed from both his legs. The mob did not desist until they had chased him two or three miles across the sandy plain to the foot of the surrounding hill. There is something lofty and heroic in this journey of Mohammed to al-Taif; a solitary man, despised and rejected by his own people, going boldly forth in the name of God, like Jonah to Nineveh, and summoning an idolatrous city to repent and support his mission. It sheds a strong light on the intensity of his belief in the divine origin of his calling' (Muir, *Life of Muhammad*, pp. 109 – 113).

23. Mine is but preaching from Allah and His Messengers; and whosoever disobeys Allah and His Messenger, his portion is the Hell-fire abiding there for ever.'

إِلَّا بَلَٰغًا مِّنَ ٱللَّهِ وَرِسَٰلَٰتِهِۦ ۚ وَمَن يَعْصِ ٱللَّهَ وَرَسُولَهُۥ فَإِنَّ لَهُۥ نَارَ جَهَنَّمَ خَٰلِدِينَ فِيهَآ أَبَدًا ۝

24. They will go on denying until they see what they are promised. Then they will know who is weaker in protectors and fewer in number.

حَتَّىٰٓ إِذَا رَأَوْا۟ مَا يُوعَدُونَ فَسَيَعْلَمُونَ مَنْ أَضْعَفُ نَاصِرًا وَأَقَلُّ عَدَدًا ۝

25. Say: 'I do not know whether what you are promised is near, or whether my Lord has appointed it for a distant term.

قُلْ إِنْ أَدْرِىٓ أَقَرِيبٌ مَّا تُوعَدُونَ أَمْ يَجْعَلُ لَهُۥ رَبِّىٓ أَمَدًا ۝

26. He is the Knower of the Unseen and He does not disclose His Unseen to anyone,

عَٰلِمُ ٱلْغَيْبِ فَلَا يُظْهِرُ عَلَىٰ غَيْبِهِۦٓ أَحَدًا ۝

27. Save to a Messenger chosen. And then He causes to go before him and behind him a guard.

إِلَّا مَنِ ٱرْتَضَىٰ مِن رَّسُولٍ فَإِنَّهُۥ يَسْلُكُ مِنۢ بَيْنِ يَدَيْهِ وَمِنْ خَلْفِهِۦ رَصَدًا ۝

28. That He may know that they have delivered the message of their Lord. And He comprehends whatever is with them and He keeps count of everything numbered.'

لِّيَعْلَمَ أَن قَدْ أَبْلَغُوا۟ رِسَٰلَٰتِ رَبِّهِمْ وَأَحَاطَ بِمَا لَدَيْهِمْ وَأَحْصَىٰ كُلَّ شَىْءٍ عَدَدًا ۝

Sūrah 73

al-Muzzammil

(Makkan, 2 Sections, 20 Verses)

*In the name of Allah, the
Compassionate, the Merciful.*

Section 1

1. O you enwrapped!

2. Keep vigil all night save a little.

3. Half of it, or a little less of it,

4. Or a little more. And intone the Qur'ān with a measured intonation.

5. Verily We soon shall be casting on you a weighty word.

6. Verily the rising by night is most curbing and most conducive to right speech.

7. Verily for you is the day a prolonged occupation.

8. And remember the name of your Lord and devote yourself to Him exclusively.

9. Lord of the east and the west! No god is there but He! So take Him for your trustee.

10. And bear patiently with what they say, and depart from them with a becoming departure.

11. And let Me alone with the beliers, owners of comfort and respite them a little.

وَذَرۡنِى وَالۡمُكَذِّبِيۡنَ أُولِى النَّعۡمَةِ وَمَهِّلۡهُمۡ قَلِيۡلًا ۝

12. Verily with Us are heavy fetters and scorch,

إِنَّ لَدَيۡنَا أَنۡكَالًا وَّجَحِيۡمًا ۝

13. And a food that chokes and a painful torment,

وَطَعَامًا ذَا غُصَّةٍ وَّعَذَابًا أَلِيۡمًا ۝

14. On a Day when the earth and mountains shall quake, and the mountains shall become a sand heap poured forth.

يَوۡمَ تَرۡجُفُ الۡأَرۡضُ وَالۡجِبَالُ وَكَانَتِ الۡجِبَالُ كَثِيۡبًا مَّهِيۡلًا ۝

15. Verily We! We have sent to you a Messenger, a witness over you, as We sent to Pharaoh a Messenger.

إِنَّا أَرۡسَلۡنَا إِلَيۡكُمۡ رَسُوۡلًا شَاهِدًا عَلَيۡكُمۡ كَمَا أَرۡسَلۡنَا إِلَى فِرۡعَوۡنَ رَسُوۡلًا ۝

16. Then Pharaoh denied the Messenger, therefore We seized him with a painful grip.

فَعَصَى فِرۡعَوۡنُ الرَّسُوۡلَ فَأَخَذۡنَهُ أَخۡذًا وَّبِيۡلًا ۝

17. How then, if you deny, shall you escape, on a Day that will make children grey-headed,

فَكَيۡفَ تَتَّقُوۡنَ إِنۡ كَفَرۡتُمۡ يَوۡمًا يَّجۡعَلُ الۡوِلۡدَانَ شِيۡبًا ۝

18. And the sky will be split therein. His promise is certainly to be accomplished.

السَّمَاءُ مُنۡفَطِرٌ بِهِ كَانَ وَعۡدُهُ مَفۡعُوۡلًا ۝

19. Verily this is an admonition; let him therefore, who will, choose a way unto his Lord.

إِنَّ هَذِهِ تَذۡكِرَةٌ فَمَنۡ شَاءَ اتَّخَذَ إِلَى رَبِّهِ سَبِيۡلًا ۝

Section 2

20. Verily your Lord knows that you stay up near two-thirds of the night, or a half of it, or a third of it, and also a party of those who are with you. And Allah measures the night and the day. He knows that you cannot compute it; so He has relented towards you. Recite now of the Qur'ān so much as is easy. He knows that there will be among you some sick, and others shall be travelling in the land, seeking the grace of Allah, and some others shall be fighting in the cause of Allah. Recite of it, therefore, so much as is easy, and establish the prayer, and pay the poor-rate, and lend unto Allah a goodly loan. Whatsoever good you will send on for your souls, you will find it with Allah better and greater in reward. And beg the forgiveness of Allah; verily Allah is the Forgiving, the Merciful.

إِنَّ رَبَّكَ يَعْلَمُ أَنَّكَ تَقُومُ أَدْنَىٰ مِن ثُلُثَيِ ٱلَّيْلِ وَنِصْفَهُۥ وَثُلُثَهُۥ وَطَآئِفَةٌ مِّنَ ٱلَّذِينَ مَعَكَ وَٱللَّهُ يُقَدِّرُ ٱلَّيْلَ وَٱلنَّهَارَ عَلِمَ أَن لَّن تُحْصُوهُ فَتَابَ عَلَيْكُمْ فَٱقْرَءُوا۟ مَا تَيَسَّرَ مِنَ ٱلْقُرْءَانِ عَلِمَ أَن سَيَكُونُ مِنكُم مَّرْضَىٰ وَءَاخَرُونَ يَضْرِبُونَ فِى ٱلْأَرْضِ يَبْتَغُونَ مِن فَضْلِ ٱللَّهِ وَءَاخَرُونَ يُقَـٰتِلُونَ فِى سَبِيلِ ٱللَّهِ فَٱقْرَءُوا۟ مَا تَيَسَّرَ مِنْهُ وَأَقِيمُوا۟ ٱلصَّلَوٰةَ وَءَاتُوا۟ ٱلزَّكَوٰةَ وَأَقْرِضُوا۟ ٱللَّهَ قَرْضًا حَسَنًا وَمَا تُقَدِّمُوا۟ لِأَنفُسِكُم مِّنْ خَيْرٍ تَجِدُوهُ عِندَ ٱللَّهِ هُوَ خَيْرًا وَأَعْظَمَ أَجْرًا وَٱسْتَغْفِرُوا۟ ٱللَّهَ إِنَّ ٱللَّهَ غَفُورٌ رَّحِيمٌ ﴿٢٠﴾

Sūrah 74

al-Muddaththir

(Makkan, 2 Sections, 56 Verses)

In the name of Allah, the Compassionate, the Merciful.

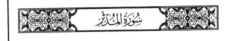

Section 1

1. O you enveloped,

2. Arise, and warn.

3. And magnify your Lord.

4. And purify your raiment.

5. And shun pollution.

6. And do not bestow your favour in order to obtain more from them.

7. And be patient for the goodwill of your Lord.

8. Then when the horn sounds.

9. That shall be that Day, a day of anguish.

10. For the infidels, not easy.

11. Let Me alone with him whom I created lonely.

12. And for whom[728] I assigned extended wealth.

---

728. This without any merits on his part. All the blessings a man enjoys are gifts from God, not an outcome of his own merit.

13. And sons present by his side. وَبَنِينَ شُهُودًا ۝

14. And for whom I smoothed everything. وَمَهَّدتُّ لَهُ تَمْهِيدًا ۝

15. And who yet covets that I shall increase. ثُمَّ يَطْمَعُ أَنْ أَزِيدَ ۝

16. Certainly he has not been a foe to Our signs. كَلَّا إِنَّهُ كَانَ لِآيَاتِنَا عَنِيدًا ۝

17. Soon I shall afflict him with a fearful woe. سَأُرْهِقُهُ صَعُودًا ۝

18. Surely he considered and devised. إِنَّهُ فَكَّرَ وَقَدَّرَ ۝

19. Perish he; how maliciously he schemed. فَقُتِلَ كَيْفَ قَدَّرَ ۝

20. And again perish he! How maliciously he schemed! ثُمَّ قُتِلَ كَيْفَ قَدَّرَ ۝

21. Then he looked. ثُمَّ نَظَرَ ۝

22. Then he frowned, and scowled. ثُمَّ عَبَسَ وَبَسَرَ ۝

23. Then he turned back, and grew stiff-necked. ثُمَّ أَدْبَرَ وَاسْتَكْبَرَ ۝

24. Then he said: 'Naught is this but magic from of old. فَقَالَ إِنْ هَذَا إِلَّا سِحْرٌ يُؤْثَرُ ۝

25. Naught is this but the word of man.' إِنْ هَذَا إِلَّا قَوْلُ الْبَشَرِ ۝

26. Soon I shall roast him in the Scorching Fire. سَأُصْلِيهِ سَقَرَ ۝

27. And how do you know what the Scorching Fire is? وَمَا أَدْرَاكَ مَا سَقَرُ ۝

28. It shall not spare anyone guilty, nor leave. لَا تُبْقِي وَلَا تَذَرُ ۝

29. Scorching the skin.

لَوَّاحَةٌ لِّلۡبَشَرِ ۩

30. Over it are appointed nineteen angels.

عَلَيۡهَا تِسۡعَةَ عَشَرَ ۩

31. And We have appointed none but the angels to be wardens of the Fire, and We have made this number only a trial for them who disbelieve, so that those who are vouchsafed the Book may be convinced and that the believers may increase in faith, and that those who are vouchsafed the Book and the believers may not be in doubt, and that those in whose hearts is a disease and the infidels may utter: 'What does Allah mean by this description?' Thus does Allah send astray whom He will, and guide whom He will. And none knows the hosts of your Lord but He. And this is not but an admonition to man.

وَمَا جَعَلۡنَآ أَصۡحَٰبَ ٱلنَّارِ إِلَّا مَلَٰٓئِكَةً ۖ وَمَا جَعَلۡنَا عِدَّتَهُمۡ إِلَّا فِتۡنَةً لِّلَّذِينَ كَفَرُوا۟ لِيَسۡتَيۡقِنَ ٱلَّذِينَ أُوتُوا۟ ٱلۡكِتَٰبَ وَيَزۡدَادَ ٱلَّذِينَ ءَامَنُوٓا۟ إِيمَٰنًا ۙ وَلَا يَرۡتَابَ ٱلَّذِينَ أُوتُوا۟ ٱلۡكِتَٰبَ وَٱلۡمُؤۡمِنُونَ ۙ وَلِيَقُولَ ٱلَّذِينَ فِى قُلُوبِهِم مَّرَضٌ وَٱلۡكَٰفِرُونَ مَاذَآ أَرَادَ ٱللَّهُ بِهَٰذَا مَثَلًا ۚ كَذَٰلِكَ يُضِلُّ ٱللَّهُ مَن يَشَآءُ وَيَهۡدِى مَن يَشَآءُ ۚ وَمَا يَعۡلَمُ جُنُودَ رَبِّكَ إِلَّا هُوَ ۚ وَمَا هِىَ إِلَّا ذِكۡرَىٰ لِلۡبَشَرِ ۩

Section 2

32. Nay! And by the moon.

كَلَّا وَٱلۡقَمَرِ ۩

33. And by the night when it withdraws.

وَٱلَّيۡلِ إِذۡ أَدۡبَرَ ۩

34. And by the morning when it brightens.

وَٱلصُّبۡحِ إِذَآ أَسۡفَرَ ۩

35. Surely it is one of the greatest woes,

إِنَّهَا لَإِحۡدَى ٱلۡكُبَرِ ۩

36. A warning to mankind.

نَذِيرًا لِّلۡبَشَرِ ۩

37. A warning to him of you who shall go forward or who chooses to lag behind.

لِمَن شَآءَ مِنكُمْ أَن يَتَقَدَّمَ أَوْ يَتَأَخَّرَ ۝

38. Every soul will be a pledge for what it has worked,

كُلُّ نَفْسٍ بِمَا كَسَبَتْ رَهِينَةٌ ۝

39. Save the fellows of the right.

إِلَّآ أَصْحَٰبَ ٱلْيَمِينِ ۝

40. In the Gardens. They shall be questioning,

فِى جَنَّٰتٍ يَتَسَآءَلُونَ ۝

41. Concerning the culprits.

عَنِ ٱلْمُجْرِمِينَ ۝

42. What did lead you to the Scorching Fire?

مَا سَلَكَكُمْ فِى سَقَرَ ۝

43. They will say: 'We have not been of those who prayed.

قَالُوا۟ لَمْ نَكُ مِنَ ٱلْمُصَلِّينَ ۝

44. And we have not been feeding the poor,

وَلَمْ نَكُ نُطْعِمُ ٱلْمِسْكِينَ ۝

45. And we have been wading with waders.

وَكُنَّا نَخُوضُ مَعَ ٱلْخَآئِضِينَ ۝

46. And we have been denying the Day of Requital,

وَكُنَّا نُكَذِّبُ بِيَوْمِ ٱلدِّينِ ۝

47. Until there came to us the certainty.'

حَتَّىٰٓ أَتَىٰنَا ٱلْيَقِينُ ۝

48. Then there will not profit them the intercession of the interceders.

فَمَا تَنفَعُهُمْ شَفَٰعَةُ ٱلشَّٰفِعِينَ ۝

49. What ails them then that they are turning away from the admonition,

فَمَا لَهُمْ عَنِ ٱلتَّذْكِرَةِ مُعْرِضِينَ ۝

50. As though they were startled donkeys,

كَأَنَّهُمْ حُمُرٌ مُّسْتَنفِرَةٌ ۝

51. Fleeing away from a lion.

فَرَّتْ مِن قَسْوَرَةٍ ۝

52. Aye! Everyone of them desires that he may be vouchsafed expanded scrolls.

بَلْ يُرِيدُ كُلُّ ٱمْرِئٍ مِّنْهُمْ أَن يُؤْتَىٰ صُحُفًا مُّنَشَّرَةً ۝

53. Certainly not! Aye! They do not fear the Hereafter.

كَلَّا بَل لَّا يَخَافُونَ ٱلْآخِرَةَ ۝

54. Certainly not! Surely this Qur'ān is an admonition.

كَلَّا إِنَّهُ تَذْكِرَةٌ ۝

55. So let him who will take heed.

فَمَن شَاءَ ذَكَرَهُ ۝

56. And none shall heed it, unless with Allah's will. He is the Lord of piety, the Lord of forgiveness.

وَمَا يَذْكُرُونَ إِلَّا أَن يَشَاءَ ٱللَّهُ هُوَ أَهْلُ ٱلتَّقْوَىٰ وَأَهْلُ ٱلْمَغْفِرَةِ ۝

Sūrah 75

al-Qiyāmah

(Makkan, 2 Sections, 40 Verses)

In the name of Allah, the Compassionate, the Merciful.

بِسْمِ اللَّهِ الرَّحْمَنِ الرَّحِيمِ

Section 1

1. I swear by the Day of Resurrection.

لَآ أُقْسِمُ بِيَوْمِ الْقِيَمَةِ ۝

2. And I swear by the self-reproaching soul.

وَلَآ أُقْسِمُ بِالنَّفْسِ اللَّوَّامَةِ ۝

3. Does man imagine that We shall not gather his bones?

أَيَحْسَبُ الْإِنسَنُ أَلَّن نَّجْمَعَ عِظَامَهُ ۝

4. Yes! We are able to put together evenly his very fingertips.

بَلَىٰ قَدِرِينَ عَلَىٰٓ أَن نُّسَوِّىَ بَنَانَهُ ۝

5. Aye! Man desires that he may go on sinning.

بَلْ يُرِيدُ الْإِنسَنُ لِيَفْجُرَ أَمَامَهُ ۝

6. He questions, when will be the Day of Resurrection?

يَسْئَلُ أَيَّانَ يَوْمُ الْقِيَمَةِ ۝

7. When, then, the sight shall be dazed.

فَإِذَا بَرِقَ الْبَصَرُ ۝

8. And the moon shall be eclipsed,

وَخَسَفَ الْقَمَرُ ۝

9. And the sun and the moon shall be joined.

وَجُمِعَ الشَّمْسُ وَالْقَمَرُ ۝

10. Man, on that Day, shall say: 'Where to flee?'

يَقُولُ الْإِنسَنُ يَوْمَئِذٍ أَيْنَ الْمَفَرُّ ۝

11. Certainly no refuge on that Day.

كَلَّا لَا وَزَرَ ۝

12. To your Lord that Day shall be the recourse.

إِلَىٰ رَبِّكَ يَوْمَئِذٍ الْمُسْتَقَرُّ ۝

13. To man shall be declared that Day what he has sent on and left behind?

يُنَبَّؤُا الْإِنْسَانُ يَوْمَئِذٍ بِمَا قَدَّمَ وَأَخَّرَ ۝

14. Aye! Man shall be an evidence against himself.

بَلِ الْإِنْسَانُ عَلَىٰ نَفْسِهِ بَصِيرَةٌ ۝

15. Though he may put forth pleas.729

وَلَوْ أَلْقَىٰ مَعَاذِيرَهُ ۝

16. Move not your tongue therewith that you may hasten.

لَا تُحَرِّكْ بِهِ لِسَانَكَ لِتَعْجَلَ بِهِ ۝

17. Verily upon Us is the collecting of it and the reciting of it.

إِنَّ عَلَيْنَا جَمْعَهُ وَقُرْآنَهُ ۝

18. So when We recite it, follow the reciting thereof.

فَإِذَا قَرَأْنَاهُ فَاتَّبِعْ قُرْآنَهُ ۝

19. And thereafter upon Us is the expounding of it.

ثُمَّ إِنَّ عَلَيْنَا بَيَانَهُ ۝

20. By no means! Verily you love the herein.

كَلَّا بَلْ تُحِبُّونَ الْعَاجِلَةَ ۝

21. And leave the Hereafter.

وَتَذَرُونَ الْآخِرَةَ ۝

22. Faces on that Day shall be radiant.

وُجُوهٌ يَوْمَئِذٍ نَاضِرَةٌ ۝

23. Looking towards their Lord.

إِلَىٰ رَبِّهَا نَاظِرَةٌ ۝

---

729. So as falsely to excuse himself. It is the Qur'ān which, with all the lustre and brilliance of a newly discovered Truth, awakened in man the idea of his accountability to God, and inculcated in mankind the doctrine of man being a moral agent.

24. And faces on that Day shall be scowling,

وَوُجُوهٌ يَوْمَئِذٍ بَاسِرَةٌ ﴿٢٤﴾

25. Apprehending that there will befall them a calamity waist-breaking.

تَظُنُّ أَن يُفْعَلَ بِهَا فَاقِرَةٌ ﴿٢٥﴾

26. By no means! When it comes up to the collar-bone,

كَلَّا إِذَا بَلَغَتِ التَّرَاقِيَ ﴿٢٦﴾

27. And it is cried aloud: 'Where is the enchanter?'

وَقِيلَ مَنْ رَاقٍ ﴿٢٧﴾

28. And he thinks that it is the time of parting.

وَظَنَّ أَنَّهُ الْفِرَاقُ ﴿٢٨﴾

29. And shank is entangled with shank.

وَالْتَفَّتِ السَّاقُ بِالسَّاقِ ﴿٢٩﴾

30. The drive that Day is unto your Lord.

إِلَىٰ رَبِّكَ يَوْمَئِذٍ الْمَسَاقُ ﴿٣٠﴾

Section 2

31. He neither believed nor prayed.

فَلَا صَدَّقَ وَلَا صَلَّىٰ ﴿٣١﴾

32. Indeed, he belied and turned away.

وَلَٰكِن كَذَّبَ وَتَوَلَّىٰ ﴿٣٢﴾

33. Then he departed to his family conceitedly.

ثُمَّ ذَهَبَ إِلَىٰ أَهْلِهِ يَتَمَطَّىٰ ﴿٣٣﴾

34. Woe to you, woe!

أَوْلَىٰ لَكَ فَأَوْلَىٰ ﴿٣٤﴾

35. And again woe to you, woe!

ثُمَّ أَوْلَىٰ لَكَ فَأَوْلَىٰ ﴿٣٥﴾

36. Does man imagine that he is to be left uncontrolled?

أَيَحْسَبُ الْإِنسَٰنُ أَن يُتْرَكَ سُدًى ﴿٣٦﴾

37. Was he not a sperm of emission emitted?

أَلَمْ يَكُ نُطْفَةً مِّن مَّنِيٍّ يُمْنَىٰ ﴿٣٧﴾

38. Then he became a clot; then Allah created him and formed him.

ثُمَّ كَانَ عَلَقَةً فَخَلَقَ فَسَوَّىٰ ۝

39. And He made of him the two sexes, male and female,

فَجَعَلَ مِنْهُ الزَّوْجَيْنِ الذَّكَرَ وَالْأُنثَىٰ ۝

40. Is not that One then able to quicken the dead?

أَلَيْسَ ذَٰلِكَ بِقَادِرٍ عَلَىٰ أَن يُحْيِۦَ الْمَوْتَىٰ ۝

Sūrah 76

al-Insān

(Makkan, 2 Sections, 31 Verses)

In the name of Allah, the Compassionate, the Merciful.

Section 1

1. Surely there has come upon man a space of time when he was not a thing worth mentioning.

2. Verily We created man from a sperm drop, a mixture, that We might test him, wherefore We made him hearing, seeing.

3. Verily We showed him the way; then he becomes either thankful or ungrateful.

4. Verily We have prepared for the infidels chains and collars and the Blaze.

5. Verily the pious shall drink of a cup whereof the admixture is camphor.

6. It will be from a fountain, where the bondsmen of Allāh will drink, causing it to gush abundantly.

7. They are those who fulfil their vow, and dread the Day, the evil of which shall be wide-spreading.

8. And they feed, for love of Him, with food the destitute, the orphan and the captive.

وَيُطْعِمُونَ الطَّعَامَ عَلَى حُبِّهِ مِسْكِينًا وَيَتِيمًا وَأَسِيرًا ۝

9. Saying: 'We feed you only for the sake of Allah; we desire not from you any recompense or thanks.

إِنَّمَا نُطْعِمُكُمْ لِوَجْهِ اللَّهِ لَا نُرِيدُ مِنكُمْ جَزَآءً وَلَا شُكُورًا ۝

10. Verily we dread from our Lord a Day, grim and distressful.'

إِنَّا نَخَافُ مِن رَّبِّنَا يَوْمًا عَبُوسًا قَمْطَرِيرًا ۝

11. Therefore Allah shall protect them from the evil of that Day, and shall cause them to enjoy radiance and pleasure.

فَوَقَىٰهُمُ اللَّهُ شَرَّ ذَٰلِكَ الْيَوْمِ وَلَقَّىٰهُمْ نَضْرَةً وَسُرُورًا ۝

12. And their recompense shall be for they bear patiently, the Garden and silken raiment.

وَجَزَىٰهُم بِمَا صَبَرُوا جَنَّةً وَحَرِيرًا ۝

13. They shall recline therein on couches and shall feel neither scorching sun nor exceeding cold.

مُّتَّكِئِينَ فِيهَا عَلَى الْأَرَآئِكِ لَا يَرَوْنَ فِيهَا شَمْسًا وَلَا زَمْهَرِيرًا ۝

14. And close upon them will be the shades thereof, and low will hang the clusters thereof greatly.

وَدَانِيَةً عَلَيْهِمْ ظِلَٰلُهَا وَذُلِّلَتْ قُطُوفُهَا تَذْلِيلًا ۝

15. And brought round amongst them will be vessels of silver and also goblets of glass.

وَيُطَافُ عَلَيْهِم بِآنِيَةٍ مِّن فِضَّةٍ وَأَكْوَابٍ كَانَتْ قَوَارِيرَا۟ ۝

16. Goblets of silver, they shall have filled them to exact measure.

قَوَارِيرَا۟ مِن فِضَّةٍ قَدَّرُوهَا تَقْدِيرًا ۝

17. And therein they shall drink of a cup whose admixture will be ginger.

وَيُسْقَوْنَ فِيهَا كَأْسًا كَانَ مِزَاجُهَا زَنجَبِيلًا ۝

18. And this from a fountain therein, named Salsabīl.

عَيْنًا فِيهَا تُسَمَّىٰ سَلْسَبِيلًا ۝

19. And there shall go round unto them youths ever-young. When you see them you would deem them pearls unstrung.

وَيَطُوفُ عَلَيْهِمْ وِلْدَانٌ مُّخَلَّدُونَ إِذَا رَأَيْتَهُمْ حَسِبْتَهُمْ لُؤْلُؤًا مَّنثُورًا ﴿١٩﴾

20. And when you look them you behold delight and a magnificent dominion.

وَإِذَا رَأَيْتَ ثَمَّ رَأَيْتَ نَعِيمًا وَمُلْكًا كَبِيرًا ﴿٢٠﴾

21. On them shall be garments of fine green silk and of brocades. And adorned they shall be with bracelets of silver; and their Lord shall give them a drink of pure beverage.

عَالِيَهُمْ ثِيَابُ سُندُسٍ خُضْرٌ وَإِسْتَبْرَقٌ وَحُلُّوا أَسَاوِرَ مِن فِضَّةٍ وَسَقَاهُمْ رَبُّهُمْ شَرَابًا طَهُورًا ﴿٢١﴾

22. Verily this is for you by way of recompense, and your endeavour has been accepted.

إِنَّ هَذَا كَانَ لَكُمْ جَزَاءً وَكَانَ سَعْيُكُم مَّشْكُورًا ﴿٢٢﴾

Section 2

23. Verily it is We Who have revealed to you the Qur'ān, a gradual revelation.

إِنَّا نَحْنُ نَزَّلْنَا عَلَيْكَ الْقُرْءَانَ تَنزِيلًا ﴿٢٣﴾

24. So preserve with the command of your Lord, and obey not them, any sinner or ungrateful person.

فَاصْبِرْ لِحُكْمِ رَبِّكَ وَلَا تُطِعْ مِنْهُمْ ءَاثِمًا أَوْ كَفُورًا ﴿٢٤﴾

25. And remember the name of your Lord, every morning and evening.

وَاذْكُرِ اسْمَ رَبِّكَ بُكْرَةً وَأَصِيلًا ﴿٢٥﴾

26. And during night worship Him; and hallow Him throughout the long night.

وَمِنَ الَّيْلِ فَاسْجُدْ لَهُ وَسَبِّحْهُ لَيْلًا طَوِيلًا ﴿٢٦﴾

27. Verily those love the Herein, and leave in front of them a heavy Day.

إِنَّ هَـٰٓؤُلَآءِ يُحِبُّونَ ٱلۡعَاجِلَةَ وَيَذَرُونَ وَرَآءَهُمۡ يَوۡمٗا ثَقِيلًا ۝

28. It is We Who created them and made them firm of make and whenever We will, We can replace them with others like them.

نَّحۡنُ خَلَقۡنَٰهُمۡ وَشَدَدۡنَآ أَسۡرَهُمۡۖ وَإِذَا شِئۡنَا بَدَّلۡنَآ أَمۡثَٰلَهُمۡ تَبۡدِيلًا ۝

29. Verily this is an admonition, then whosoever will may choose a way unto his Lord.

إِنَّ هَٰذِهِۦ تَذۡكِرَةٌۖ فَمَن شَآءَ ٱتَّخَذَ إِلَىٰ رَبِّهِۦ سَبِيلًا ۝

30. And you cannot will, unless Allah wills. Verily Allah is the Knowing, the Wise.

وَمَا تَشَآءُونَ إِلَّآ أَن يَشَآءَ ٱللَّهُۚ إِنَّ ٱللَّهَ كَانَ عَلِيمًا حَكِيمًا ۝

31. He makes whomsoever He wills enter His mercy; and as for the ungodly, He has prepared for them an afflictive torment.

يُدۡخِلُ مَن يَشَآءُ فِي رَحۡمَتِهِۦۚ وَٱلظَّٰلِمِينَ أَعَدَّ لَهُمۡ عَذَابًا أَلِيمًۢا ۝

Sūrah 77

al-Mursalāt

(Makkan, 2 Sections, 50 Verses)

In the name of Allah, the Compassionate, the Merciful.

Section 1

1. By the winds sent forth with beneficence,

2. And those raging swiftly,

3. By the spreading winds spreading,

4. And the scattering winds scattering.

5. And the winds that bring down the remembrance,

6. By way of excuse or warning,

7. Verily what you are promised is about to befall.

8. So when the stars are effaced.

9. And when the sky is cleft asunder,

10. And when the mountains are carried away by wind,

11. And when the Messengers are assembled at the appointed time.

12. For what day is it timed?

وَٱلْمُرْسَلَٰتِ عُرْفًا ۝

فَٱلْعَٰصِفَٰتِ عَصْفًا ۝

وَٱلنَّٰشِرَٰتِ نَشْرًا ۝

فَٱلْفَٰرِقَٰتِ فَرْقًا ۝

فَٱلْمُلْقِيَٰتِ ذِكْرًا ۝

عُذْرًا أَوْ نُذْرًا ۝

إِنَّمَا تُوعَدُونَ لَوَٰقِعٌ ۝

فَإِذَا ٱلنُّجُومُ طُمِسَتْ ۝

وَإِذَا ٱلسَّمَاءُ فُرِجَتْ ۝

وَإِذَا ٱلْجِبَالُ نُسِفَتْ ۝

وَإِذَا ٱلرُّسُلُ أُقِّتَتْ ۝

لِأَيِّ يَوْمٍ أُجِّلَتْ ۝

13. For the Day of Decision.

لِيَوۡمِ الۡفَصۡلِ ۝

14. And do you know what the Day of Decision is?

وَمَاۤ اَدۡرٰىكَ مَا يَوۡمُ الۡفَصۡلِ ۝

15. Woe on that Day to the beliers.

وَيۡلٌ يَّوۡمَئِذٍ لِّلۡمُكَذِّبِيۡنَ ۝

16. Have We not destroyed the ancients?

اَلَمۡ نُهۡلِكِ الۡاَوَّلِيۡنَ ۝

17. And then We shall cause the latter ones to follow them.

ثُمَّ نُتۡبِعُهُمُ الۡاٰخِرِيۡنَ ۝

18. Thus We do with the culprits.

كَذٰلِكَ نَفۡعَلُ بِالۡمُجۡرِمِيۡنَ ۝

19. Woe on that Day to the beliers!

وَيۡلٌ يَّوۡمَئِذٍ لِّلۡمُكَذِّبِيۡنَ ۝

20. Did We not create you of despicable water,

اَلَمۡ نَخۡلُقۡكُّمۡ مِّنۡ مَّآءٍ مَّهِيۡنٍ ۝

21. Which We placed in a safe depository,

فَجَعَلۡنٰهُ فِيۡ قَرَارٍ مَّكِيۡنٍ ۝

22. Till a time limited?

اِلٰى قَدَرٍ مَّعۡلُوۡمٍ ۝

23. So We decreed. How excellent are We as decreer!

فَقَدَرۡنَا فَنِعۡمَ الۡقٰدِرُوۡنَ ۝

24. Woe on that Day to the beliers!

وَيۡلٌ يَّوۡمَئِذٍ لِّلۡمُكَذِّبِيۡنَ ۝

25. Have We not made earth a receptacle,

اَلَمۡ نَجۡعَلِ الۡاَرۡضَ كِفَاتًا ۝

26. Both for the living and the dead,

اَحۡيَآءً وَّاَمۡوَاتًا ۝

27. And have placed therein firm and tall mountains and given you to drink of fresh water?

وَجَعَلۡنَا فِيۡهَا رَوَاسِيَ شٰمِخٰتٍ وَّاَسۡقَيۡنٰكُمۡ مَّآءً فُرَاتًا ۝

28. Woe on that Day to the beliers!

وَيۡلٌ يَّوۡمَئِذٍ لِّلۡمُكَذِّبِيۡنَ ۝

29. Depart unto what you were used to belie.

أَنطَلِقُوٓاْ إِلَىٰ مَا كُنتُم بِهِۦ تُكَذِّبُونَ ۝

30. Depart unto the shadows three branched.[730]

أَنطَلِقُوٓاْ إِلَىٰ ظِلٍّ ذِى ثَلَٰثِ شُعَبٍ ۝

31. Neither shading nor availing against the flame.

لَّا ظَلِيلٍ وَلَا يُغْنِى مِنَ ٱللَّهَبِ ۝

32. Verily it shall cast forth sparks like unto a castle.

إِنَّهَا تَرْمِى بِشَرَرٍ كَٱلْقَصْرِ ۝

33. As though they were camels yellow, tawny.

كَأَنَّهُۥ جِمَٰلَتٌ صُفْرٌ ۝

34. Woe on that Day to the beliers!

وَيْلٌ يَوْمَئِذٍ لِّلْمُكَذِّبِينَ ۝

35. This is the Day when they shall not be able to speak.

هَٰذَا يَوْمُ لَا يَنطِقُونَ ۝

36. Nor shall they be permitted, so that they might excuse themselves.

وَلَا يُؤْذَنُ لَهُمْ فَيَعْتَذِرُونَ ۝

37. Woe on that Day to the beliers!

وَيْلٌ يَوْمَئِذٍ لِّلْمُكَذِّبِينَ ۝

38. This is the Day of Decision. We have assembled you and the ancients.

هَٰذَا يَوْمُ ٱلْفَصْلِ جَمَعْنَٰكُمْ وَٱلْأَوَّلِينَ ۝

39. If now you have any craft, try that craft upon Me.

فَإِن كَانَ لَكُمْ كَيْدٌ فَكِيدُونِ ۝

40. Woe on that Day to the beliers!

وَيْلٌ يَوْمَئِذٍ لِّلْمُكَذِّبِينَ ۝

Section 2

41. Verily the God-fearing shall be amid shades and springs,

إِنَّ ٱلْمُتَّقِينَ فِى ظِلَٰلٍ وَعُيُونٍ ۝

---

730. The fire of Hell on the Day of Resurrection will divide into three parts, and whenever the infidels will attempt to go to a place of safety it will repel them.

42. And fruits such as they desire.

وَفَوَٰكِهَ مِمَّا يَشْتَهُونَ ﴿٤٢﴾

43. Eat and drink with relish for what you have been working.

كُلُواْ وَاشْرَبُواْ هَنِيٓـًٔا بِمَا كُنتُمْ تَعْمَلُونَ ﴿٤٣﴾

44. Verily We! In this way We recompense the well-doers.

إِنَّا كَذَٰلِكَ نَجْزِى ٱلْمُحْسِنِينَ ﴿٤٤﴾

45. Woe on that Day to the beliers!

وَيْلٌ يَوْمَئِذٍ لِّلْمُكَذِّبِينَ ﴿٤٥﴾

46. Eat and drink but little; you are culprits.

كُلُواْ وَتَمَتَّعُواْ قَلِيلًا إِنَّكُم مُّجْرِمُونَ ﴿٤٦﴾

47. Woe on that Day to the beliers!

وَيْلٌ يَوْمَئِذٍ لِّلْمُكَذِّبِينَ ﴿٤٧﴾

48. And when it is said: 'Bow down', they do not bow down.

وَإِذَا قِيلَ لَهُمُ ٱرْكَعُواْ لَا يَرْكَعُونَ ﴿٤٨﴾

49. Woe on that Day to the beliers!

وَيْلٌ يَوْمَئِذٍ لِّلْمُكَذِّبِينَ ﴿٤٩﴾

50. In what discourse then, after it,[731] will they believe?

فَبِأَىِّ حَدِيثٍۭ بَعْدَهُۥ يُؤْمِنُونَ ﴿٥٠﴾

731. What will they believe after a Message so plain and so effective as the Qur'ān?

Sūrah 78

al-Nabā'

(Makkan, 2 Sections, 40 Verses)

In the name of Allah, the Compassionate, the Merciful.

Section 1

1. Of what are they asking?

2. Of the fateful announcement,

3. Concerning which they differ.

4. No, indeed they shall soon know the Truth.

5. Again, no indeed, they shall soon know the Truth.

6. Have We not made the earth an expanse.

7. And the mountains as stakes?

8. And We have created you in pairs.

9. And We have made your sleep a rest.

10. And We have made the night a covering.

11. And We have made the day for seeking livelihood.

12. And We have built over you seven strong heavens.

13. And We have set therein a lamp glowing.

وَجَعَلۡنَا سِرَاجًا وَهَّاجًا ۝

14. And We have sent down from the rain-clouds abundant water.

وَأَنزَلۡنَا مِنَ الۡمُعۡصِرَٰتِ مَآءً ثَجَّاجًا ۝

15. So that We bring forth from them corn and vegetation.

لِّنُخۡرِجَ بِهِۦ حَبًّا وَنَبَاتًا ۝

16. And gardens thick with trees.

وَجَنَّٰتٍ أَلۡفَافًا ۝

17. Verily the Day of Decision is an appointed time.

إِنَّ يَوۡمَ الۡفَصۡلِ كَانَ مِيقَٰتًا ۝

18. A Day whereon the trumpet will be blown, and you will come in multitudes.

يَوۡمَ يُنفَخُ فِي الصُّورِ فَتَأۡتُونَ أَفۡوَاجًا ۝

19. And the sky will have been opened and it will have become as doors.

وَفُتِحَتِ السَّمَآءُ فَكَانَتۡ أَبۡوَٰبًا ۝

20. And the mountains will have been removed away, and they will have become as a mirage.

وَسُيِّرَتِ الۡجِبَالُ فَكَانَتۡ سَرَابًا ۝

21. Verily Hell is an ambuscade.

إِنَّ جَهَنَّمَ كَانَتۡ مِرۡصَادًا ۝

22. A receptacle for the exorbitant.

لِّلطَّٰغِينَ مَئَابًا ۝

23. For ages they will tarry therein.

لَّٰبِثِينَ فِيهَآ أَحۡقَابًا ۝

24. They will not taste therein cool or any drink,

لَّا يَذُوقُونَ فِيهَا بَرۡدًا وَلَا شَرَابًا ۝

25. Save scalding water and corruption,

إِلَّا حَمِيمًا وَغَسَّاقًا ۝

26. Recompense fitted,

جَزَآءً وِفَاقًا ۝

27. Verily they were wont not to look for a reckoning,

إِنَّهُمۡ كَانُوا۟ لَا يَرۡجُونَ حِسَابًا ۝

28. And they belied Our signs totally.

وَكَذَّبُوا بِاٰيٰتِنَا كِذَّابًا ۝

29. And We have recorded everything in a Book.

وَكُلَّ شَىْءٍ أَحْصَيْنٰهُ كِتٰبًا ۝

30. Taste therefore. We shall only increase you in torment.

فَذُوقُوا فَلَنْ نَّزِيدَكُمْ إِلَّا عَذَابًا ۝

Section 2

31. Verily for the pious is an achievement.

إِنَّ لِلْمُتَّقِيْنَ مَفَازًا ۝

32. Gardens enclosed and vine-yards,

حَدَائِقَ وَأَعْنٰبًا ۝

33. And full-breasted maidens of equal age,

وَكَوَاعِبَ أَتْرَابًا ۝

34. And an overflowing cup.

وَكَأْسًا دِهَاقًا ۝

35. They will hear therein no babble or falsehood.

لَّا يَسْمَعُوْنَ فِيْهَا لَغْوًا وَّلَا كِذَّابًا ۝

36. A recompense from your Lord, a gift sufficient,

جَزَاءً مِّنْ رَّبِّكَ عَطَاءً حِسَابًا ۝

37. From the Lord of the heavens and the earth and of what is in-between,[732] the Compassionate with whom they cannot demand audience.

رَّبِّ السَّمٰوٰتِ وَالْأَرْضِ وَمَا بَيْنَهُمَا الرَّحْمٰنِ لَا يَمْلِكُوْنَ مِنْهُ خِطَابًا ۝

---

732. Even the atmosphere separating sky and earth has been held sacred, by several polytheistic communities, and worshipped either directly for itself or as animated by some special deity. The 'invisible beings who are supposed to hover between heaven and earth, that is, whose proper abode is the circumambient atmosphere are called Air-Gods, and are described at length in the pages of *ERE*. (I. p. 222 ff.), 'Amulets of Shu' (the atmosphere in Egypt), were made in the XIIth dynasty and were common' (Petrie, *Religious Life in Ancient Egypt*, p. 3).

38. The Day whereon the souls and the angels will stand arrayed, they will not be able to speak, except whom the Compassionate gives leave and who speaks aright.

يَوْمَ يَقُومُ الرُّوحُ وَالْمَلَئِكَةُ صَفًّا لَّا يَتَكَلَّمُونَ إِلَّا مَنْ أَذِنَ لَهُ الرَّحْمَنُ وَقَالَ صَوَابًا ۝

39. That is the sure Day. Let him who wills, seek a way back to his Lord.

ذَلِكَ الْيَوْمُ الْحَقُّ فَمَن شَآءَ اتَّخَذَ إِلَى رَبِّهِ مَـَابًا ۝

40. Verily We have warned you of an imminent chastisement, a Day whereon man will see what he has sent forth, and the infidel will say: 'Would that I had been dust!'

إِنَّآ أَنذَرْنَكُمْ عَذَابًا قَرِيبًا يَوْمَ يَنظُرُ الْمَرْءُ مَا قَدَّمَتْ يَدَاهُ وَيَقُولُ الْكَافِرُ يَلَيْتَنِي كُنتُ تُرَابًا ۝

Sūrah 79

al-Nāzi'āt

(Makkan, 2 Sections, 46 Verses)

In the name of Allah, the Compassionate, the Merciful.

Section 1

1. By the angels who drag forth vehemently.[733]

وَٱلنَّزِعَٰتِ غَرْقًا ۝

2. By the angels who release most gently.

وَٱلنَّٰشِطَٰتِ نَشْطًا ۝

3. By the angels who glide swimmingly,

وَٱلسَّٰبِحَٰتِ سَبْحًا ۝

4. And who then speed with foremost speed.

فَٱلسَّٰبِقَٰتِ سَبْقًا ۝

5. And who then manage the affair decreed.

فَٱلْمُدَبِّرَٰتِ أَمْرًا ۝

6. A Day shall come when the quaking will quake.

يَوْمَ تَرْجُفُ ٱلرَّاجِفَةُ ۝

7. And there will follow it the next blast.

تَتْبَعُهَا ٱلرَّادِفَةُ ۝

8. Hearts that Day will be throbbing.

قُلُوبٌ يَوْمَئِذٍ وَاجِفَةٌ ۝

9. Their looks will be downcast.

أَبْصَٰرُهَا خَٰشِعَةٌ ۝

---

733. The angel of death, with his assistants, will pull the souls of the wicked from the inmost part of their bodies in a most rough and cruel manner.

10. They are saying: 'Shall we indeed be restored to our former state.

يَقُولُونَ أَءِنَّا لَمَرْدُودُونَ فِي ٱلْحَافِرَةِ ﴿١٠﴾

11. After we have become decayed bones?'

أَءِذَا كُنَّا عِظَٰمًا نَّخِرَةً ﴿١١﴾

12. They are saying: 'That indeed shall be a losing return?'

قَالُوا۟ تِلْكَ إِذًا كَرَّةٌ خَاسِرَةٌ ﴿١٢﴾

13. In fact, it will be only a scaring shout.

فَإِنَّمَا هِيَ زَجْرَةٌ وَٰحِدَةٌ ﴿١٣﴾

14. And lo! They all shall appear on the surface.

فَإِذَا هُم بِٱلسَّاهِرَةِ ﴿١٤﴾

15. Has there come to you the story of Moses?

هَلْ أَتَىٰكَ حَدِيثُ مُوسَىٰ ﴿١٥﴾

16. Recall when your Lord called to him in the holy vale of Ṭuwā.

إِذْ نَادَىٰهُ رَبُّهُۥ بِٱلْوَادِ ٱلْمُقَدَّسِ طُوًى ﴿١٦﴾

17. 'Go you to Pharaoh; verily he has waxed exorbitant.'

ٱذْهَبْ إِلَىٰ فِرْعَوْنَ إِنَّهُۥ طَغَىٰ ﴿١٧﴾

18. Then say you: 'Would you be purified?

فَقُلْ هَل لَّكَ إِلَىٰٓ أَن تَزَكَّىٰ ﴿١٨﴾

19. I shall guide you to your Lord, so that you shall fear.'

وَأَهْدِيَكَ إِلَىٰ رَبِّكَ فَتَخْشَىٰ ﴿١٩﴾

20. Then he showed him the great sign.

فَأَرَىٰهُ ٱلْءَايَةَ ٱلْكُبْرَىٰ ﴿٢٠﴾

21. Yet he belied and rebelled.

فَكَذَّبَ وَعَصَىٰ ﴿٢١﴾

22. Then he turned back, striving.

ثُمَّ أَدْبَرَ يَسْعَىٰ ﴿٢٢﴾

23. Then he gathered his people and cried aloud.

فَحَشَرَ فَنَادَىٰ ﴿٢٣﴾

24. And he said: 'I am your Lord, most high.'[734]

فَقَالَ أَنَا۟ رَبُّكُمُ الْأَعْلَىٰ ۝

25. Thereupon Allah seized him with the chastisement of the Hereafter and the present.

فَأَخَذَهُ اللَّهُ نَكَالَ الْآخِرَةِ وَالْأُولَىٰ ۝

26. Surely herein is a lesson for him who fears.

إِنَّ فِي ذَٰلِكَ لَعِبْرَةً لِّمَن يَخْشَىٰ ۝

Section 2

27. Are you harder to create or the sky He has built?

ءَأَنتُمْ أَشَدُّ خَلْقًا أَمِ السَّمَاءُ بَنَاهَا ۝

28. He raised its height and perfected it.

رَفَعَ سَمْكَهَا فَسَوَّاهَا ۝

29. And He has made its night dark and its sunshine bright.

وَأَغْطَشَ لَيْلَهَا وَأَخْرَجَ ضُحَاهَا ۝

30. And thereafter, he stretched out the earth.

وَالْأَرْضَ بَعْدَ ذَٰلِكَ دَحَاهَا ۝

31. And He brought forth therefrom its water and its pasture.

أَخْرَجَ مِنْهَا مَاءَهَا وَمَرْعَاهَا ۝

32. And He set firm the mountains.

وَالْجِبَالَ أَرْسَاهَا ۝

---

734. The Pharaohs believed themselves to be the visible gods, begotten by God, and themselves the divine begetters of their wives' children. Each of the Pharaohs, so long as he reigned, was considered to be the living image of and vicegerent of the sun-god, invested with the attributes of divinity, and presumed to be of like nature with the gods. 'While it easily happened that conspicuous individuals after death came to be regarded by a later generation as effective gods, the cult of the actually living king prevailed in both Babylonia and Egypt and royal statues were objects of worship. In the Amarna Letters (about 1400 BC) the petty princes of Syria and Palestine address the reigning Pharaoh as "my sun-god" or "my god", (*EMK*.II p.106).

33. A provision for you and your cattle.

مَتَـٰعًا لَّكُمْ وَلِأَنْعَـٰمِكُمْ ۝

34. Then when the grand calamity comes.

فَإِذَا جَآءَتِ ٱلطَّآمَّةُ ٱلْكُبْرَىٰ ۝

35. The Day whereon man will remember what he has striven for.

يَوْمَ يَتَذَكَّرُ ٱلْإِنسَـٰنُ مَا سَعَىٰ ۝

36. And the Scorch will be made apparent to anyone who sees.

وَبُرِّزَتِ ٱلْجَحِيمُ لِمَن يَرَىٰ ۝

37. Then as for him who waxed exorbitant,

فَأَمَّا مَن طَغَىٰ ۝

38. And who chose the life of this world.

وَءَاثَرَ ٱلْحَيَوٰةَ ٱلدُّنْيَا ۝

39. Verily the Scorch shall be his resort.

فَإِنَّ ٱلْجَحِيمَ هِيَ ٱلْمَأْوَىٰ ۝

40. And as for him who dreaded standing before his Lord, and restrained his soul from desires.

وَأَمَّا مَنْ خَافَ مَقَامَ رَبِّهِۦ وَنَهَى ٱلنَّفْسَ عَنِ ٱلْهَوَىٰ ۝

41. Verily the Garden shall be his resort.

فَإِنَّ ٱلْجَنَّةَ هِيَ ٱلْمَأْوَىٰ ۝

42. They question you regarding the Hour: 'When will its arrival be?'

يَسْـَٔلُونَكَ عَنِ ٱلسَّاعَةِ أَيَّانَ مُرْسَىٰهَا ۝

43. By no reason are you concerned with the declaration thereof?[735]

فِيمَ أَنتَ مِن ذِكْرَىٰهَآ ۝

44. Unto your Lord is the knowledge of the limit fixed thereof.

إِلَىٰ رَبِّكَ مُنتَهَىٰهَآ ۝

---

735. It is not the business of any of His Prophets to announce the exact Hour and date of the Resurrection.

45. You are but a warner to him who fears it.

إِنَّمَآ أَنتَ مُنذِرُ مَن يَخۡشَىٰهَا ۝

46. On the Day whereon they see it, it will appear to them as though they had not tarried save an evening or the morning.

كَأَنَّهُمۡ يَوۡمَ يَرَوۡنَهَا لَمۡ يَلۡبَثُوٓاْ إِلَّا عَشِيَّةً أَوۡ ضُحَىٰهَا ۝

Sūrah 80

'Abasa

(Makkan, 1 Section, 42 Verses)

In the name of Allah, the
Compassionate, the Merciful.

Section 1

1. He frowned and turned away,

2. Because there came to him a
blind man.[736]

3. How can you know, whether
he might be cleansed,

4. Or be admonished, so that the
admonition might have profited
him?

5. As for him who regards himself
self-sufficient,

6. To him you attend;

7. Whereas it is not on you that
he is not cleansed.

عَبَسَ وَتَوَلَّى ۞

أَن جَآءَهُ ٱلْأَعْمَىٰ ۞

وَمَا يُدْرِيكَ لَعَلَّهُۥ يَزَّكَّىٰ ۞

أَوْ يَذَّكَّرُ فَتَنفَعَهُ ٱلذِّكْرَىٰ ۞

أَمَّا مَنِ ٱسْتَغْنَىٰ ۞

فَأَنتَ لَهُۥ تَصَدَّىٰ ۞

وَمَا عَلَيْكَ أَلَّا يَزَّكَّىٰ ۞

---

736. A certain believer, named 'Abdullāh ibn Umm Maktūm, a man 'of little
consideration' (Muir, *Life of Mahomet*, p. 66). This refers to an occasion when the
Holy Prophet, engrossed in earnest discourse with some of the principal Quraysh
whose conversion he had long cherished, was interrupted by a blind Muslim. The
Prophet, habitually so solicitous of the poor and lowly, apprehended that at that
moment the haughty Quraysh would take umbrage at this importunity of a 'commoner'
and would use it as a pretext for their immediately leaving his company, and hence
in the interest of Islam ignored the intruder and turned his face away from him.

8. And as for him who comes to you running,

9. And he fears.

10. Him you neglect.

11. No Indeed![737] Verily it is an admonition.[738]

12. So whosoever wills, let him be admonished with it,

13. Inscribed in honoured Writs,

14. Exalted, purified,

15. By the hands of scribes,

16. Honourable, virtuous.

17. Perish man! How ungrateful he is!

18. Of what has He created him?

وَأَمَّا مَن جَآءَكَ يَسْعَىٰ ۝

وَهُوَ يَخْشَىٰ ۝

فَأَنتَ عَنْهُ تَلَهَّىٰ ۝

كَلَّآ إِنَّهَا تَذْكِرَةٌ ۝

فَمَن شَآءَ ذَكَرَهُ ۝

فِى صُحُفٍ مُّكَرَّمَةٍ ۝

مَّرْفُوعَةٍ مُّطَهَّرَةٍ ۝

بِأَيْدِى سَفَرَةٍ ۝

كِرَامٍ بَرَرَةٍ ۝

قُتِلَ ٱلْإِنسَٰنُ مَآ أَكْفَرَهُ ۝

مِنْ أَيِّ شَىْءٍ خَلَقَهُ ۝

---

737. 'This incident shows the tender and ready perception by Mohammad of the slight he had offered, and the magnanimity with which he could confess his fault' (Muir, p. 66). 'Mohammad is justly praised for the magnanimous spirit shown in this passage. Throughout his career we rarely find him courting after the favour of the rich or the great, and he was ever ready to recognize merit in the poorest of his followers' (Wherry, *Commentary on the Koran*). Such then is the verdict of anti-Muslims and Christians.

738. In other words, it is open to everybody. 'This is the Book which today is accepted by nearly four hundred million human beings as containing the Creator's final message to mankind. Its influence on the course of history has obviously been immense, and will as obviously continue to be extremely great. The Koran was the prime inspiration of a religious movement which gave rise to a civilization of wide extent, vast power, and profound vitality. No man seeking to live in the same world as Islam, and to understand the affairs of Islam, can afford to regard lightly or to judge ignorantly, the Book that is called the Koran. It is among the greatest movements of mankind. It surely deserves and demands to be more widely known and better comprehended in the West' (Arberry, *The Koran Interpreted*, p. 33)

19. Of a drop of seed. He created him and set him in a proper form.

مِن نُّطۡفَةٍ خَلَقَهُۥ فَقَدَّرَهُۥ ۝

20. Then He made easy the way.

ثُمَّ ٱلسَّبِيلَ يَسَّرَهُۥ ۝

21. Then He caused him to die and be buried.

ثُمَّ أَمَاتَهُۥ فَأَقۡبَرَهُۥ ۝

22. Then when He wills, He shall raise him to life.

ثُمَّ إِذَا شَآءَ أَنشَرَهُۥ ۝

23. No indeed! Man performed not what He had commanded him.

كَلَّا لَمَّا يَقۡضِ مَآ أَمَرَهُۥ ۝

24. Let man look at his food.

فَلۡيَنظُرِ ٱلۡإِنسَٰنُ إِلَىٰ طَعَامِهِۦٓ ۝

25. It is We Who pour forth water in abundance.

أَنَّا صَبَبۡنَا ٱلۡمَآءَ صَبًّا ۝

26. Then We cleave the earth in clefts.

ثُمَّ شَقَقۡنَا ٱلۡأَرۡضَ شَقًّا ۝

27. Then We cause therein the grain to grow,

فَأَنۢبَتۡنَا فِيهَا حَبًّا ۝

28. And vines and vegetables,

وَعِنَبًا وَقَضۡبًا ۝

29. And olives and palms,

وَزَيۡتُونًا وَنَخۡلًا ۝

30. And luxuriant enclosed gardens,

وَحَدَآئِقَ غُلۡبًا ۝

31. And fruits and herbage.

وَفَٰكِهَةً وَأَبًّا ۝

32. A provision for you and your cattle.

مَّتَٰعًا لَّكُمۡ وَلِأَنۡعَٰمِكُمۡ ۝

33. Then when comes the deafening cry.

فَإِذَا جَآءَتِ ٱلصَّآخَّةُ ۝

34. On the Day when man shall flee from his brother,

يَوۡمَ يَفِرُّ ٱلۡمَرۡءُ مِنۡ أَخِيهِ ۝

35. And his mother and father,

وَأُمِّهِۦ وَأَبِيهِ ۝

36. And his wife and sons.

وَصَاحِبَتِهِۦ وَبَنِيهِ ﴿٣٦﴾

37. For everyone on that Day shall have business enough to occupy him.

لِكُلِّ ٱمْرِئٍ مِّنْهُمْ يَوْمَئِذٍ شَأْنٌ يُغْنِيهِ ﴿٣٧﴾

38. Faces of some on that Day shall be beaming,

وُجُوهٌ يَوْمَئِذٍ مُّسْفِرَةٌ ﴿٣٨﴾

39. Laughing, rejoicing.

ضَاحِكَةٌ مُّسْتَبْشِرَةٌ ﴿٣٩﴾

40. And faces of others on that Day shall be gloomy.

وَوُجُوهٌ يَوْمَئِذٍ عَلَيْهَا غَبَرَةٌ ﴿٤٠﴾

41. Dust-covered,

تَرْهَقُهَا قَتَرَةٌ ﴿٤١﴾

42. Those! They shall be the infidels, the ungodly.

أُوْلَٰٓئِكَ هُمُ ٱلْكَفَرَةُ ٱلْفَجَرَةُ ﴿٤٢﴾

Sūrah 81

al-Takwīr

(Makkan, 1 Section, 29 Verses)

In the name of Allah, the Compassionate, the Merciful.

Section 1

1. When the sun shall be wound round,

إِذَا الشَّمْسُ كُوِّرَتْ ۝١

2. And the stars shall dart down,

وَإِذَا النُّجُومُ انكَدَرَتْ ۝٢

3. And when the mountains shall be made to pass away.

وَإِذَا الْجِبَالُ سُيِّرَتْ ۝٣

4. And when the she-camels, big with young shall be abandoned,

وَإِذَا الْعِشَارُ عُطِّلَتْ ۝٤

5. And when the wild beasts shall be gathered together,

وَإِذَا الْوُحُوشُ حُشِرَتْ ۝٥

6. And when the seas shall be filled,[739]

وَإِذَا الْبِحَارُ سُجِّرَتْ ۝٦

7. And[740] when the souls shall be paired.[741]

وَإِذَا النُّفُوسُ زُوِّجَتْ ۝٧

---

739. Filled with fire. At the first blast of the Trumpet all seas shall flow forth one into another, and thus become one sea, and then they shall be kindled and become fire.

740. Now begin the happenings at the second blast of the Trumpet.

741. In other words, united with their fellows; like will be joined with like; each sect or party shall be united with those whom it has followed.

8. And when the girl buried alive[742] shall be questioned:

وَإِذَا الْمَوْءُ دَةُ سُئِلَتْ ۝۸

9. For what sin she was slain,

بِأَيِّ ذَنۢبٍ قُتِلَتْ ۝۹

10. And when the Writs shall be laid open.

وَإِذَا الصُّحُفُ نُشِرَتْ ۝۱۰

11. And when the sky shall be stripped off,

وَإِذَا السَّمَاءُ كُشِطَتْ ۝۱۱

12. And when the Scorch shall be set ablaze.

وَإِذَا الْجَحِيْمُ سُعِّرَتْ ۝۱۲

---

742. 'It was customary among the ancient Arabs to bury their daughters alive as soon as they were born for the fear that they should be impoverished by providing for them, or should suffer disgrace on their account' (Sale). 'At that time there were many survivals of barbarism among the inhabitants of central Arabia. For instance, the practice of burying newborn daughters alive was very general' (*HHW*. VIII. p. 8). 'Amongst the Arabs before Mohammad. sons were preserved, but daughters were usually buried alive' (*ERE*. I. p. 3 : 4). 'At any rate in some places and sometimes, there was a strong pressure of public opinion against sparing any daughter, even though she were the only child of her parents' (Robertson-Smith, *Kinship and Marriage in Early Arabia*, pp. 129-30). In India, this practice continued as late as the mid-nineteenth century. 'Among all the races of India; there is none more noble than the Rajput; and among the Rajputs, the first rank belongs to the Chuhans. These people are numerous in the United Provinces. In the district of Mainpuri there are more than 30,000 of them, and not about sixty years ago it was discovered that among them was not a single girl. Every daughter that was born was killed. The higher the rank of the family the more constant and systematic was the crime. This is not rhetoric but the statement of a fact. In 1856 special inquiries were instituted. It was found that this practice of infanticide although especially prevalent among the Rajputs, was by no means confined to them, and it was common not only in the Agra province but in Oudh, the Punjab, and in parts of the Bombay Presidency. Numbers of villages were visited where there was not a single girl and where there had never been one within the memory of man. In 1869 another investigation showed that there was little change for the better' (Strachey, *India*, 4th Ed., pp. 433-4). 'Infanticide of female infants has been practised in India from unknown times amongst the ancient Gakkhar race in the Punjab, and it has been constant custom, and continued in several parts of India down to the later third of the 19th century' (*EI*. II. p. 397). As a matter of fact, wherever polyandry is in existence baby-girls are killed in large numbers.

13. And when the Garden shall be brought near,

وَإِذَا الْجَنَّةُ أُزْلِفَتْ ۝

14. Then every soul shall know what it has presented.

عَلِمَتْ نَفْسٌ مَّا أَحْضَرَتْ ۝

15. I swear by the receding stars,

فَلَا أُقْسِمُ بِالْخُنَّسِ ۝

16. Moving swiftly and hiding themselves.

الْجَوَارِ الْكُنَّسِ ۝

17. And by the night when it departs,

وَالَّيْلِ إِذَا عَسْعَسَ ۝

18. And by the morning when it shines forth.

وَالصُّبْحِ إِذَا تَنَفَّسَ ۝

19. Verily it is a word brought by an honoured Messenger,

إِنَّهُ لَقَوْلُ رَسُولٍ كَرِيمٍ ۝

20. The owner of strength, and of established dignity with the Lord of the Throne,

ذِي قُوَّةٍ عِنْدَ ذِي الْعَرْشِ مَكِينٍ ۝

21. Obeyed one there, as also trusty.

مُطَاعٍ ثَمَّ أَمِينٍ ۝

22. Nor is your companion distracted,

وَمَا صَاحِبُكُم بِمَجْنُونٍ ۝

23. Assuredly he has seen him in open horizon.

وَلَقَدْ رَآهُ بِالْأُفُقِ الْمُبِينِ ۝

24. And he is not a tenacious concealer of the Unseen.

وَمَا هُوَ عَلَى الْغَيْبِ بِضَنِينٍ ۝

25. Nor is it the word of the accursed Satan.

وَمَا هُوَ بِقَوْلِ شَيْطَانٍ رَّجِيمٍ ۝

26. Where then are you going?

فَأَيْنَ تَذْهَبُونَ ۝

27. This is not but an admonition to the worlds.[743]

28. To whomsoever of you who wills to walk straight.[744]

29. And you cannot will unless it be that Allah, the Lord of the worlds, wills.[745]

---

743. And as such is not directed at a particular race or class. Notice once more the universality of the message of Islam.

744. Only those will profit by it. This repudiates the doctrine of *Karma* and determinism, in all its forms and varieties.

745. This refutes the doctrine of free-will and liberty, in all its forms and varieties.

Sūrah 82

al-Infiṭār

(Makkan, 1 Section, 19 Verses)

In the name of Allah, the Compassionate, the Merciful.

بِسْمِ اللّٰهِ الرَّحْمٰنِ الرَّحِيمِ

Section 1

1. When the sky is cleft,

إِذَا السَّمَاءُ انفَطَرَتْ ۝

2. And when the stars are scattered,

وَإِذَا الْكَوَاكِبُ انتَثَرَتْ ۝

3. And when the seas are flowed out,

وَإِذَا الْبِحَارُ فُجِّرَتْ ۝

4. And when the graves are ransacked,

وَإِذَا الْقُبُورُ بُعْثِرَتْ ۝

5. Each soul shall know what it sent afore and what it left behind.

عَلِمَتْ نَفْسٌ مَّا قَدَّمَتْ وَأَخَّرَتْ ۝

6. O man! What has deluded you concerning your Lord, the Bountiful.

يَٰأَيُّهَا الْإِنسَٰنُ مَا غَرَّكَ بِرَبِّكَ الْكَرِيمِ ۝

7. Who created you, then moulded you, then proportioned you?

الَّذِي خَلَقَكَ فَسَوَّىٰكَ فَعَدَلَكَ ۝

8. He constructed you in whatsoever form He willed.

فِي أَيِّ صُورَةٍ مَّا شَاءَ رَكَّبَكَ ۝

9. No indeed! Aye! You deny the Requital!

كَلَّا بَلْ تُكَذِّبُونَ بِالدِّينِ ۝

10. Verily guardians there are for you;

وَإِنَّ عَلَيْكُمْ لَحَٰفِظِينَ ۝

11. Honourable scribes.

كِرَامًا كَٰتِبِينَ ۝

12. They know whatsoever you do.

يَعۡلَمُوۡنَ مَا تَفۡعَلُوۡنَ ۝

13. Verily the pious will be in delight.

إِنَّ ٱلۡأَبۡرَارَ لَفِى نَعِيمٍ ۝

14. And the ungodly in the Scorch.

وَإِنَّ ٱلۡفُجَّارَ لَفِى جَحِيمٍ ۝

15. Roasted they will be therein on the Day of Requital.

يَصۡلَوۡنَهَا يَوۡمَ ٱلدِّينِ ۝

16. And from there they will not be allowed to be absent.

وَمَا هُمۡ عَنۡهَا بِغَآئِبِينَ ۝

17. And what will make you understand what the Day of Requital is?

وَمَآ أَدۡرَىٰكَ مَا يَوۡمُ ٱلدِّينِ ۝

18. Again, what will make you understand what the Day of Requital is?[746]

ثُمَّ مَآ أَدۡرَىٰكَ مَا يَوۡمُ ٱلدِّينِ ۝

19. A Day whereon no soul will own aught of power for any other soul, and the command will be wholly Allah's.[747]

يَوۡمَ لَا تَمۡلِكُ نَفۡسٌ لِّنَفۡسٍ شَيۡئًا وَٱلۡأَمۡرُ يَوۡمَئِذٍ لِّلَّهِ ۝

---

746. The interrogation is repeated for magnifying the importance.

747. This rejects the doctrine of Mediation or Intercession, whatever be its form.

Sūrah 83

al-Muṭaffifīn

(Makkan, 1 Section, 36 Verses)

In the name of Allah, the
Compassionate, the Merciful.

Section 1

1. Woe to the scrimpers.

2. Who when they take from others, exact the full measure.

3. And when they measure to them or weigh for them, diminish.

4. Do not such men imagine that they shall be raised up?

5. On a fateful Day![748]

6. A Day when mankind shall stand before the Lord of the worlds.

7. By no means! The record of the ungodly is in Sijjīn.

8. And what will make you understand what the Sijjīn is?

9. A record of misdeeds written.

---

748. The Day of Account, when they shall have to answer for every act of theirs. 'This passage, as well as many others in this portion of the Qur'an, illustrates the character of the instruction given by the reformer of Makka. It has a genuine ring about it. A pure morality is insisted on, and enforced by the doctrine of a final judgment' (Wherry, *Commentary on the Koran*).

10. Woe be on that Day to the beliers,

وَيْلٌ يَوْمَئِذٍ لِّلْمُكَذِّبِيْنَ ﴿١٠﴾

11. Who belie the Day of Requital.

اَلَّذِيْنَ يُكَذِّبُوْنَ بِيَوْمِ الدِّيْنِ ﴿١١﴾

12. And none belies it save a trespasser, sinner.

وَمَا يُكَذِّبُ بِهٖ إِلَّا كُلُّ مُعْتَدٍ أَثِيْمٍ ﴿١٢﴾

13. And when Our revelations are read to him, he says: 'Fables of the ancients!'

إِذَا تُتْلٰى عَلَيْهِ ءَايٰتُنَا قَالَ أَسٰطِيْرُ الْأَوَّلِيْنَ ﴿١٣﴾

14. By no means! Aye! Encrusted upon their hearts is what they have been earning.749

كَلَّا بَلْ رَانَ عَلٰى قُلُوْبِهِمْ مَّا كَانُوْا يَكْسِبُوْنَ ﴿١٤﴾

15. By no means! Verily on the Day they will be shut out from their Lord.

كَلَّا إِنَّهُمْ عَنْ رَّبِّهِمْ يَوْمَئِذٍ لَّمَحْجُوْبُوْنَ ﴿١٥﴾

16. Then verily they will be roasted into the Scorch.

ثُمَّ إِنَّهُمْ لَصَالُوا الْجَحِيْمِ ﴿١٦﴾

17. Then it will be said: 'This is what you were used to belie.'

ثُمَّ يُقَالُ هٰذَا الَّذِيْ كُنْتُمْ بِهٖ تُكَذِّبُوْنَ ﴿١٧﴾

18. By no means! The record of the virtuous will be in 'Illīyīn.750

كَلَّا إِنَّ كِتٰبَ الْأَبْرَارِ لَفِيْ عِلِّيِّيْنَ ﴿١٨﴾

19. And what will make you understand what 'Illīyūn is?

وَمَا أَدْرٰىكَ مَا عِلِّيُّوْنَ ﴿١٩﴾

20. A record of good deeds written,

كِتٰبٌ مَّرْقُوْمٌ ﴿٢٠﴾

---

749. The purport being that this persistence in wickedness has blackened their hearts and rendered them incapable of receiving God's truths.

750. 'A place in the Seventh Heaven, to which ascend the souls of the believers, or the highest of the places; or a certain thing above another thing or loftiness above loftiness' (LL.).

21. To which will bear witness those placed near.

يَشْهَدُهُ الْمُقَرَّبُونَ ۞

22. Verily the virtuous will be in delight,

إِنَّ الْأَبْرَارَ لَفِى نَعِيمٍ ۞

23. Reclining on couches, looking on.

عَلَى الْأَرَآئِكِ يَنظُرُونَ ۞

24. You will perceive the brightness of delight in their faces.

تَعْرِفُ فِى وُجُوهِهِمْ نَضْرَةَ النَّعِيمِ ۞

25. They will be given to drink of pure wine, sealed;

يُسْقَوْنَ مِن رَّحِيقٍ مَّخْتُومٍ ۞

26. The seal of which will be of musk. To this end let the aspirers aspire.

خِتَمُهُ مِسْكٌ وَفِى ذَلِكَ فَلْيَتَنَافَسِ الْمُتَنَافِسُونَ ۞

27. And mixed therewith will be the water of Tasnīm;

وَمِزَاجُهُ مِن تَسْنِيمٍ ۞

28. A spring whereof will drink those brought near.[751]

عَيْنًا يَشْرَبُ بِهَا الْمُقَرَّبُونَ ۞

29. Verily the culprits were wont to laugh at those who believed.

إِنَّ الَّذِينَ أَجْرَمُوا كَانُوا مِنَ الَّذِينَ ءَامَنُوا يَضْحَكُونَ ۞

30. And, when they passed by, to wink at each other.

وَإِذَا مَرُّوا بِهِمْ يَتَغَامَزُونَ ۞

31. And when they returned to their household, they returned jesting.

وَإِذَا انقَلَبُوا إِلَى أَهْلِهِمُ انقَلَبُوا فَكِهِينَ ۞

32. And when they saw them, they said scornfully: 'Certainly these are the strayed ones.'

وَإِذَا رَأَوْهُمْ قَالُوا إِنَّ هَؤُلَاءِ لَضَآلُّونَ ۞

---

751. Those of the highest grade in Paradise will continually drink of this water pure and unmixed, which will be superior even to pure wine.

33. Whereas they were not sent over them as watchers.

وَمَآ أُرۡسِلُوا۟ عَلَيۡهِمۡ حَٰفِظِينَ ۝

34. So today the faithful are laughing at the infidels,

فَٱلۡيَوۡمَ ٱلَّذِينَ ءَامَنُوا۟ مِنَ ٱلۡكُفَّارِ يَضۡحَكُونَ ۝

35. Reclining on couches, looking on.

عَلَى ٱلۡأَرَآئِكِ يَنظُرُونَ ۝

36. The infidels have indeed been rewarded for what they have been doing.

هَلۡ ثُوِّبَ ٱلۡكُفَّارُ مَا كَانُوا۟ يَفۡعَلُونَ ۝

Sūrah 84

al-Inshiqāq

(Makkan, 1 Section, 25 Verses)

*In the name of Allah, the
Compassionate, the Merciful.*

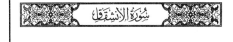

Section 1

1. When the sky will be rent asunder,

2. And hearkens to its Lord, and is dutiful.

3. And when the earth will be stretched forth,

4. And will cast out all that is within it, and will void itself,

5. And it hearkens to its Lord, and is dutiful.

6. O man! Verily you are toiling towards your Lord, a painful toiling, and are about to meet Him.

7. Then as to him who will be given his book in his right hand,

8. His account will presently be taken by an easy reckoning.

9. And he shall return to his people[752] joyfully.

---

752. Those nearest and dearest to him, who themselves are true believers, shall be waiting to receive him.

10. And as to him who will be given his book from behind his back.

وَأَمَّا مَنۡ أُوتِيَ كِتَٰبَهُۥ وَرَآءَ ظَهۡرِهِۦ ۝

11. He will presently call for death

فَسَوۡفَ يَدۡعُواْ ثُبُورًا ۝

12. And he shall roast in the Blaze.

وَيَصۡلَىٰ سَعِيرًا ۝

13. Verily he was in this world joyful among his people.

إِنَّهُۥ كَانَ فِىٓ أَهۡلِهِۦ مَسۡرُورًا ۝

14. Certainly he imagined that he would not revert.

إِنَّهُۥ ظَنَّ أَن لَّن يَحُورَ ۝

15. Yea! His Lord had been ever beholding him.

بَلَىٰٓ إِنَّ رَبَّهُۥ كَانَ بِهِۦ بَصِيرًا ۝

16. I swear by the afterglow of the sunset,

فَلَآ أُقۡسِمُ بِٱلشَّفَقِ ۝

17. And by the night and what it brings together,

وَٱلَّيۡلِ وَمَا وَسَقَ ۝

18. And by the moon when it is at the full,

وَٱلۡقَمَرِ إِذَا ٱتَّسَقَ ۝

19. Surely you will march on from stage to stage.

لَتَرۡكَبُنَّ طَبَقًا عَن طَبَقٍ ۝

20. What ails them, that they do not care to believe?

فَمَا لَهُمۡ لَا يُؤۡمِنُونَ ۝

21. And that when the Qur'ān is read to them, they do not prostrate themselves?

وَإِذَا قُرِئَ عَلَيۡهِمُ ٱلۡقُرۡءَانُ لَا يَسۡجُدُونَ ۝

22. Yea! The infidels belie.

بَلِ ٱلَّذِينَ كَفَرُواْ يُكَذِّبُونَ ۝

23. Whereas Allah knows best what they cherish.

وَٱللَّهُ أَعۡلَمُ بِمَا يُوعُونَ ۝

24. So announce to them an afflictive torment,

فَبَشِّرۡهُم بِعَذَابٍ أَلِيمٍ ۝

25. But those who believe and work righteously, unending will be their reward.

إِلَّا ٱلَّذِينَ ءَامَنُواْ وَعَمِلُواْ ٱلصَّٰلِحَٰتِ لَهُمۡ أَجۡرٌ غَيۡرُ مَمۡنُونٍ ۝

Sūrah 85

al-Burūj

(Makkan, 1 Section, 22 Verses)

*In the name of Allah, the
Compassionate, the Merciful.*

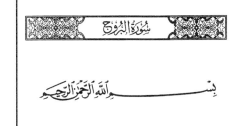

Section 1

1. By the sky adorned with big
stars.

2. And by the Promised Day,[753]

3. And by the witnessing day and
the witnessed day,

4. Perish the fellows of the ditch,

5. Of the fuel-fed fire,[754]

---

753. Of Judgement and Requital. The occurrence of that Day is not a matter of
opinion, but a definite promise on the part of God.

754. The allusion is to a frightful persecution of the Christians by a Jewish king in
Yemen. 'In 523 A.D. the throne was seized by a bigoted and dissolute usurper. A
proselyte to Judaism, he perpetrated frightful cruelties on the Christians of the
neighbouring provinces of Najran who refused to embrace his faith. Trenches filled
with combustible materials were lighted, and the martyrs cast into the flames.
Tradition gives the number thus miserably burned, or slain by the sword, at twenty
thousand' (Muir, *Life of Muhammad*, p. xciii). In the early part of the sixth century
the Hebrew religion had such a hold upon al – Yemen that the last Himyarite King
Dhu – Nuwas was a Jew ... Rivalry between the South Arabian converts of the two
newly introduced monotheistic religions led to active hostility. Evidently Dhu Nuwas
representing the nationalistic spirit, associated the native Christians with the hated
rule of the Christian Abyssinians. To this Jewish monarch is ascribed the famous
massacre of the Christians of Najran in October 523' (Hitti, op. cit., p. 62). The event
is of great historical importance, since it led to the intervention of the Negus of
Ethiopia, at the instance of the Emperor Justinian, in the Yemen and its capture by
him. The Jews too, have a tradition of their own fiery persecution by an idolatrous
king (*JE*. II. p. 363).

6. When they sat by it,

إِذۡ هُمۡ عَلَيۡهَا قُعُودٌ ۝٦

7. And were witnesses to what they did with the faithful.

وَهُمۡ عَلَىٰ مَا يَفۡعَلُونَ بِالۡمُؤۡمِنِينَ شُهُودٌ ۝٧

8. And they persecuted them for nothing save that they believed in Allah, the Mighty, the Laudable.

وَمَا نَقَمُوا مِنۡهُمۡ إِلَّآ أَن يُؤۡمِنُوا بِاللَّهِ الۡعَزِيزِ الۡحَمِيدِ ۝٨

9. Him, Whose domain is the heavens and the earth. And Allah is a Witness over everything.

الَّذِى لَهُ مُلۡكُ السَّمَٰوَٰتِ وَالۡأَرۡضِ وَاللَّهُ عَلَىٰ كُلِّ شَىۡءٍ شَهِيدٌ ۝٩

10. Verily those who persecuted the believing men and women, and then repented not, for them shall be the torment of Hell, and for them shall be the torment of burning.

إِنَّ الَّذِينَ فَتَنُوا الۡمُؤۡمِنِينَ وَالۡمُؤۡمِنَٰتِ ثُمَّ لَمۡ يَتُوبُوا فَلَهُمۡ عَذَابُ جَهَنَّمَ وَلَهُمۡ عَذَابُ الۡحَرِيقِ ۝١٠

11. Those who believed and worked righteous works for them shall be the Gardens where under rivers flow; that is the supreme achievement.

إِنَّ الَّذِينَ ءَامَنُوا وَعَمِلُوا الصَّٰلِحَٰتِ لَهُمۡ جَنَّٰتٌ تَجۡرِى مِن تَحۡتِهَا الۡأَنۡهَٰرُ ذَٰلِكَ الۡفَوۡزُ الۡكَبِيرُ ۝١١

12. Verify the grip of your Lord is terrible.

إِنَّ بَطۡشَ رَبِّكَ لَشَدِيدٌ ۝١٢

13. Verily He! It is He, Who begins and repeats.

إِنَّهُ هُوَ يُبۡدِئُ وَيُعِيدُ ۝١٣

14. And He is the Forgiving, the Loving.

وَهُوَ الۡغَفُورُ الۡوَدُودُ ۝١٤

15. Lord of the Throne, the Glorious.[755]

ذُو الۡعَرۡشِ الۡمَجِيدُ ۝١٥

---

755. He without let or hindrance. His is the absolutely sovereign will, unfettered by any conditions or restrictions. Nothing can come between His will and its execution. Unlike the head of many a pantheon, who is surrounded by fellow deities and whose will frequently clashes with theirs and who must at times bow to the over-ruling fate, the God of Islam is all-in-all, Sovereign in the absolute sense of the word.

16. Doer of whatsoever He intends.

فَعَّالٌ لِّمَا يُرِيدُ ﴿١٦﴾

17. Has there come unto you the story of the hosts,

هَلْ أَتَىٰكَ حَدِيثُ الْجُنُودِ ﴿١٧﴾

18. Of Pharaoh and the Thamūd?

فِرْعَوْنَ وَثَمُودَ ﴿١٨﴾

19. Aye! Those who disbelieve are engaged in denial.

بَلِ الَّذِينَ كَفَرُوا فِي تَكْذِيبٍ ﴿١٩﴾

20. While Allah is encompassing from behind them.

وَاللَّهُ مِن وَرَائِهِم مُّحِيطٌ ﴿٢٠﴾

21. Aye! It is a glorious recitation,

بَلْ هُوَ قُرْآنٌ مَّجِيدٌ ﴿٢١﴾

22. Inscribed in the preserved tablet.

فِي لَوْحٍ مَّحْفُوظٍ ﴿٢٢﴾

Sūrah 86

al-Ṭāriq

(Makkan, 1 Section, 17 Verses)

In the name of Allah, the Compassionate, the Merciful.

Section 1

1. By the sky and the night-comer.

2. And what will make you understand what the night-comer is?

3. It is the star shining brightly.

4. No soul is there but has a watcher over it.

5. So let man look; from what is he created?

6. Created from a water dripping,

7. That issues from between the loins and the breast bones.

8. Surely He is able to restore him,

9. On the Day when secrets shall be out.

10. Then man shall have no power nor any helper.

11. By the sky which returns,

12. And by the earth which splits,

وَٱلْأَرْضِ ذَاتِ ٱلصَّدْعِ ۝

13. Verily it is a discourse decisive.

إِنَّهُ لَقَوْلٌ فَصْلٌ ۝

14. And it is not a frivolity.

وَمَا هُوَ بِٱلْهَزْلِ ۝

15. Verily they are plotting a plot.

إِنَّهُمْ يَكِيدُونَ كَيْدًا ۝

16. And I am plotting a plot.

وَأَكِيدُ كَيْدًا ۝

17. So respite the infidels a gentle respite.

فَمَهِّلِ ٱلْكَٰفِرِينَ أَمْهِلْهُمْ رُوَيْدًا ۝

Sūrah 87

al-A'lā

(Makkan, 1 Section, 19 Verses)

In the name of Allah, the Compassionate, the Merciful.

Section 1

1. Hallow the name of your Lord, the Most High,

سَبِّحِ اسْمَ رَبِّكَ الْأَعْلَى ﴿١﴾

2. Who has created the universe and then proportioned it,

الَّذِى خَلَقَ فَسَوَّى ﴿٢﴾

3. And Who has disposed and then guided it,

وَالَّذِى قَدَّرَ فَهَدَى ﴿٣﴾

4. And Who brings forth pasturage.

وَالَّذِى أَخْرَجَ الْمَرْعَى ﴿٤﴾

5. Then He makes it dusky stubble.

فَجَعَلَهُ غُثَاءً أَحْوَى ﴿٥﴾

6. We shall enable you to recite, and then you shall not forget it,

سَنُقْرِئُكَ فَلَا تَنْسَى ﴿٦﴾

7. Save what Allah may will. Surely He knows the public and what is hidden.[756]

إِلَّا مَا شَاءَ اللَّهُ إِنَّهُ يَعْلَمُ الْجَهْرَ وَمَا يَخْفَى ﴿٧﴾

8. And We make easy unto you the easy way.

وَنُيَسِّرُكَ لِلْيُسْرَى ﴿٨﴾

9. So admonish you; surely has admonition profited.

فَذَكِّرْ إِنْ نَفَعَتِ الذِّكْرَى ﴿٩﴾

---

756. So whatever He does is in accordance with His universal knowledge and wisdom.

10. Admonished is he indeed who fears,

سَيَذَّكَّرُ مَن يَخۡشٰی ۝

11. And the wretched shuns it.

وَيَتَجَنَّبُهَا الۡاَشۡقَی ۝

12. He who shall roast into the Great Fire,

اَلَّذِی يَصۡلَی النَّارَ الۡكُبۡرٰی ۝

13. Wherein he shall neither die nor live.

ثُمَّ لَا يَمُوۡتُ فِيۡهَا وَلَا يَحۡیٰی ۝

14. He indeed has attained bliss who has cleansed himself,

قَدۡ اَفۡلَحَ مَن تَزَكّٰی ۝

15. And who remembers the name of his Lord, and then prays.

وَذَكَرَ اسۡمَ رَبِّهٖ فَصَلّٰی ۝

16. Aye; you prefer the life of this world,

بَلۡ تُؤۡثِرُوۡنَ الۡحَيٰوةَ الدُّنۡيَا ۝

17. Whereas the Hereafter is far better and more lasting.

وَالۡاٰخِرَةُ خَيۡرٌ وَّاَبۡقٰی ۝

18. Verily this is in ancient Writs.

اِنَّ هٰذَا لَفِی الصُّحُفِ الۡاُوۡلٰی ۝

19. Writs of Abraham and Moses.[757]

صُحُفِ اِبۡرٰهِيۡمَ وَمُوۡسٰی ۝

---

757. There must have been some Testament of Abraham, which like so many other Hebrew Scriptures is now lost to the world. A book said to be 'apocryphal', entitled the *Testament of Abraham* was translated from the Greek original and published for the first time in 1892, at Cambridge, by M. R. James. 'Ethiopic, Salvonic and Rumanian versions also have been found, and some of them published' (*JE*.I. p. 93).

Sūrah 88

al-Ghāshiyah

(Makkan, 1 Section, 26 Verses)

In the name of Allah, the Compassionate, the Merciful.

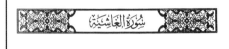

Section 1

1. Has there come to you the story of the Enveloping Event?

2. Faces on that Day shall be downcast,

3. Travailing, worn.

4. They shall roast in the scalding Fire.

5. Given to drink of a spring fiercely boiling.

6. No food shall be for them save bitter thorns,

7. Which shall neither nourish nor avail against hunger.

8. Faces on that Day shall be delighted,

9. Well-pleased with their endeavour,

10. In a lofty Garden,

11. No vain discourse they shall hear therein,

12. Therein shall be a spring running!

13. Therein shall be elevated couches!

فِیۡهَا سُرُرٌ مَّرۡفُوۡعَةٌ ۙ﴿۱۳﴾

14. And ready placed goblets!

وَّاَکۡوَابٌ مَّوۡضُوۡعَةٌ ۙ﴿۱۴﴾

15. And ranged cushions!

وَّنَمَارِقُ مَصۡفُوۡفَةٌ ۙ﴿۱۵﴾

16. And ready-spread carpets!

وَّزَرَابِیُّ مَبۡثُوۡثَةٌ ؕ﴿۱۶﴾

17. Do they not look at the camels, how they are created?

اَفَلَا یَنۡظُرُوۡنَ اِلَی الۡاِبِلِ کَیۡفَ خُلِقَتۡ ۙ﴿۱۷﴾

18. And at the sky, how it is raised?

وَاِلَی السَّمَآءِ کَیۡفَ رُفِعَتۡ ۙ﴿۱۸﴾

19. And at the mountains, how they are rooted?[758]

وَاِلَی الۡجِبَالِ کَیۡفَ نُصِبَتۡ ۙ﴿۱۹﴾

20. And at the earth, how it is outspread.

وَاِلَی الۡاَرۡضِ کَیۡفَ سُطِحَتۡ ﴿۲۰﴾

21. Admonish then; you are but an admonisher.

فَذَکِّرۡ ؕ اِنَّمَاۤ اَنۡتَ مُذَکِّرٌ ؕ﴿۲۱﴾

22. You are not over them a warden.

لَسۡتَ عَلَیۡهِمۡ بِمُصَیۡطِرٍ ۙ﴿۲۲﴾

23. So whoever will turn back and disbelieve,

اِلَّا مَنۡ تَوَلّٰی وَکَفَرَ ۙ﴿۲۳﴾

24. Allah shall torment him with the greatest torment.

فَیُعَذِّبُهُ اللّٰهُ الۡعَذَابَ الۡاَکۡبَرَ ؕ﴿۲۴﴾

25. Verily unto Us is their return,

اِنَّ اِلَیۡنَاۤ اِیَابَهُمۡ ۙ﴿۲۵﴾

26. Then unto Us is their reckoning.

ثُمَّ اِنَّ عَلَیۡنَا حِسَابَهُمۡ ﴿۲۶﴾

---

758. Note that it is only the quality of firmness and the stability of mountains that the Holy Qur'ān makes mention of. Compare and contrast this with the attitude of fetishistic religions towards mountains, worshipping them and regarding them as god. Parvats (mountains) in the Indian religions are well-known deities.

Sūrah 89

al-Fajr

(Makkan, 1 Section, 30 Verses)

In the name of Allah, the Compassionate, the Merciful.

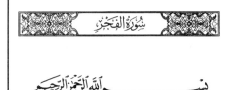

Section 1

1. By the dawn,

2. And by the ten nights,

3. And by the even and the odd,

4. And by the night when it departs,

5. Indeed in them is an oath for men of sense.

6. Did you not see how your Lord dealt with the ʿĀd,

7. And the people of many columned Iram,[759]

8. The like of which was not built in the cities,

9. And with the Thamūd who hewed out rocks in the vale?

10. And with Pharaoh, the owner of the stakes,[760]

---

759. The reference is to the earthly paradise built by Shaddād, son of ʿĀd, and one of the greatest kings of his dynasty.

760. The epithet, in Arabic idiom, is expressive of power, arrogance and obstinacy. The stakes may also refer to those to which the tyrant bound his victims.

11. Who all waxed exorbitant in the cities;

اَلَّذِينَ طَغَوْا فِي الْبِلَادِ ۝

12. So they multiplied corruption therein,

فَأَكْثَرُوا فِيهَا الْفَسَادَ ۝

13. So your Lord inflicted on them the scourge of His chastisement.

فَصَبَّ عَلَيْهِمْ رَبُّكَ سَوْطَ عَذَابٍ ۝

14. Verily your Lord is in an ambuscade.

إِنَّ رَبَّكَ لَبِالْمِرْصَادِ ۝

15. As for man when his Lord tries him and honours him, and is bountiful to him, he says: 'My Lord has honoured me.'

فَأَمَّا الْإِنْسَانُ إِذَا مَا ابْتَلَاهُ رَبُّهُ فَأَكْرَمَهُ وَنَعَّمَهُ فَيَقُولُ رَبِّيَ أَكْرَمَنِ ۝

16. And when his Lord tries him and stints unto him his provision, he says: 'My Lord has despised me.'

وَأَمَّا إِذَا مَا ابْتَلَاهُ فَقَدَرَ عَلَيْهِ رِزْقَهُ فَيَقُولُ رَبِّيَ أَهَانَنِ ۝

17. No indeed! But you do not honour the orphan,

كَلَّا بَل لَّا تُكْرِمُونَ الْيَتِيمَ ۝

18. Nor urge upon each other the feeding of the poor,

وَلَا تَحَاضُّونَ عَلَى طَعَامِ الْمِسْكِينِ ۝

19. And you devour the inheritance greedily,

وَتَأْكُلُونَ التُّرَاثَ أَكْلًا لَّمًّا ۝

20. And you love riches with exceeding love.

وَتُحِبُّونَ الْمَالَ حُبًّا جَمًّا ۝

21. No indeed! When the earth is ground with exceeding grinding.

كَلَّا إِذَا دُكَّتِ الْأَرْضُ دَكًّا دَكًّا ۝

22. And comes your Lord and the angels, rank on rank,

وَجَاءَ رَبُّكَ وَالْمَلَكُ صَفًّا صَفًّا ۝

23. And Hell that Day is brought near, man on that Day shall remember, but how can remembrance avail him then?

وَجِآئَ يَوْمَئِذٍ بِجَهَنَّمَ يَوْمَئِذٍ يَّتَذَكَّرُ الْإِنسَٰنُ وَأَنَّىٰ لَهُ الذِّكْرَىٰ ﴿٢٣﴾

24. Man will say: 'Would that I had sent before for this life of mine.'

يَقُولُ يَٰلَيْتَنِى قَدَّمْتُ لِحَيَاتِى ﴿٢٤﴾

25. So on that Day none shall torment any like His torment.

فَيَوْمَئِذٍ لَّا يُعَذِّبُ عَذَابَهُۥٓ أَحَدٌ ﴿٢٥﴾

26. Nor shall bind any like His bond.

وَلَا يُوثِقُ وَثَاقَهُۥٓ أَحَدٌ ﴿٢٦﴾

27. O you peaceful soul!

يَٰٓأَيَّتُهَا النَّفْسُ الْمُطْمَئِنَّةُ ﴿٢٧﴾

28. Return unto your Lord, well-pleased and well-pleasing.

ارْجِعِىٓ إِلَىٰ رَبِّكِ رَاضِيَةً مَّرْضِيَّةً ﴿٢٨﴾

29. Enter among My righteous bondsmen,[761]

فَادْخُلِى فِى عِبَٰدِى ﴿٢٩﴾

30. And enter My Garden.

وَادْخُلِى جَنَّتِى ﴿٣٠﴾

---

761. In other words, devotees. The saintly soul will find himself in the company of other excellent souls, thus making his life still more pleasant, and not lonely or isolated.

Sūrah 90

al-Balad

(Makkan, 1 Section, 20 Verses)

In the name of Allah, the
Compassionate, the Merciful.

Section 1

1. I swear by this city,

لَا أُقْسِمُ بِهَٰذَا الْبَلَدِ ﴿١﴾

2. And you shall be allowed in this city,

وَأَنتَ حِلٌّ بِهَٰذَا الْبَلَدِ ﴿٢﴾

3. And by the begetter and what he begat.

وَوَالِدٍ وَمَا وَلَدَ ﴿٣﴾

4. Assuredly We have created man in toil,

لَقَدْ خَلَقْنَا الْإِنسَٰنَ فِى كَبَدٍ ﴿٤﴾

5. Does he think that none can overcome him?

أَيَحْسَبُ أَن لَّن يَقْدِرَ عَلَيْهِ أَحَدٌ ﴿٥﴾

6. He says: 'I have squandered abundant riches.'

يَقُولُ أَهْلَكْتُ مَالًا لُّبَدًا ﴿٦﴾

7. Does he suppose that no one has seen him?

أَيَحْسَبُ أَن لَّمْ يَرَهُۥ أَحَدٌ ﴿٧﴾

8. Have We not made for him two eyes,

أَلَمْ نَجْعَل لَّهُۥ عَيْنَيْنِ ﴿٨﴾

9. And a tongue and two lips,

وَلِسَانًا وَشَفَتَيْنِ ﴿٩﴾

10. And shown to him the two highways?

وَهَدَيْنَٰهُ النَّجْدَيْنِ ﴿١٠﴾

11. Yet he does not attempt the steep.

فَلَا اقْتَحَمَ الْعَقَبَةَ ﴿١١﴾

12. And what shall make you understand what the steep is?

وَمَا أَدْرَىٰكَ مَا الْعَقَبَةُ ﴿١٢﴾

13. It is freeing the neck,

فَكُّ رَقَبَةٍ ۝

14. Or, feeding in a day of privation,

أَوۡ إِطۡعَٰمٌ فِىۡ يَوۡمٍ ذِىۡ مَسۡغَبَةٍ ۝

15. An orphan of kin,

يَتِيۡمًا ذَا مَقۡرَبَةٍ ۝

16. Or a poor man, cleaving to the dust.

أَوۡ مِسۡكِيۡنًا ذَا مَتۡرَبَةٍ ۝

17. Then he became one of those who believed and enjoined on each other steadfastness and enjoined on each other compassion.

ثُمَّ كَانَ مِنَ الَّذِيۡنَ ءَامَنُوۡا وَتَوَاصَوۡا بِالصَّبۡرِ وَتَوَاصَوۡا بِالۡمَرۡحَمَةِ ۝

18. These are the fellows of the right-hand.

أُولَٰئِكَ أَصۡحَٰبُ الۡمَيۡمَنَةِ ۝

19. And those who disbelieved in Our signs they are the fellows of the left-hand.

وَالَّذِيۡنَ كَفَرُوۡا بِئَايَٰتِنَا هُمۡ أَصۡحَٰبُ الۡمَشۡئَمَةِ ۝

20. Over them shall be the Fire closing round.

عَلَيۡهِمۡ نَارٌ مُّؤۡصَدَةٌ ۝

Sūrah 91

al-Shams

(Makkan, 1 Section, 15 Verses)

In the name of Allah, the Compassionate, the Merciful.

Section 1

1. By the sun and its morning brightness,

وَالشَّمْسِ وَضُحَىٰهَا ۚ ﴿١﴾

2. And by the moon when it follows it,

وَالْقَمَرِ إِذَا تَلَىٰهَا ۚ ﴿٢﴾

3. By the day when it glorifies the sun,

وَالنَّهَارِ إِذَا جَلَّىٰهَا ۚ ﴿٣﴾

4. By the night when it envelops the sun,

وَالَّيْلِ إِذَا يَغْشَىٰهَا ۚ ﴿٤﴾

5. By the sky and Him Who built it,

وَالسَّمَآءِ وَمَا بَنَىٰهَا ۚ ﴿٥﴾

6. By the earth and Him Who stretched it forth,

وَالْأَرْضِ وَمَا طَحَىٰهَا ۚ ﴿٦﴾

7. By the soul and Him Who proportioned it,

وَنَفْسٍ وَمَا سَوَّىٰهَا ۚ ﴿٧﴾

8. And inspired it with its impurity and purity,

فَأَلْهَمَهَا فُجُورَهَا وَتَقْوَىٰهَا ۚ ﴿٨﴾

9. Surely blissful is he who has cleansed his soul,

قَدْ أَفْلَحَ مَن زَكَّىٰهَا ۚ ﴿٩﴾

10. And miserable is he who has buried it.[762]

وَقَدْ خَابَ مَن دَسَّىٰهَا ۚ ﴿١٠﴾

---

762. Buried it under evil works, in the exercise of his free-will. All this clearly repudiates, on the one hand, the Pauline doctrine of an original, hereditary sin, and, on the other, the Hindu and Buddhist determinism known as *Karma*. Sin is nothing more, nothing less, and nothing else than a man's wrong use of his free-will, just as merit is its right use.

11. The Thamūd belied in their exorbitance,

كَذَّبَتْ ثَمُودُ بِطَغْوَىٰهَآ ۞

12. When the greatest wretch of them rose up.

إِذِ انْبَعَثَ أَشْقَىٰهَا ۞

13. Then the Messenger of Allah said to them: 'Beware of the she-camel of Allah and her drink.'

فَقَالَ لَهُمْ رَسُولُ اللَّهِ نَاقَةَ اللَّهِ وَسُقْيَىٰهَا ۞

14. Then they belied him and hamstrung her; then their Lord overwhelmed them for their crime, and made it common.

فَكَذَّبُوهُ فَعَقَرُوهَا فَدَمْدَمَ عَلَيْهِمْ رَبُّهُم بِذَنۢبِهِمْ فَسَوَّىٰهَا ۞

15. And He feared not the consequences thereof.[763]

وَلَا يَخَافُ عُقْبَىٰهَا ۞

---

763. Islam knows no such thing as the repentance of God and His grief over His own actions, as portrayed by the Bible: 'And it repented the Lord that he had made men on the earth, and it grieved him at his heart' (Ge. 6: 6).

Sūrah 92

al-Layl

(Makkan, 1 Section, 21 Verses)

*In the name of Allah, the
Compassionate, the Merciful.*

Section 1

1. By the night when it envelopes,

وَٱلَّيۡلِ إِذَا يَغۡشَىٰ ﴿١﴾

2. By the day when it appears in glory,

وَٱلنَّهَارِ إِذَا تَجَلَّىٰ ﴿٢﴾

3. By Him Who has created the male and the female,

وَمَا خَلَقَ ٱلذَّكَرَ وَٱلۡأُنثَىٰٓ ﴿٣﴾

4. Verily your endeavours are diverse.

إِنَّ سَعۡيَكُمۡ لَشَتَّىٰ ﴿٤﴾

5. Then as for him who gives and fears Him,

فَأَمَّا مَنۡ أَعۡطَىٰ وَٱتَّقَىٰ ﴿٥﴾

6. And testifies to the good,

وَصَدَّقَ بِٱلۡحُسۡنَىٰ ﴿٦﴾

7. To him We shall indeed make easy the path to ease.

فَسَنُيَسِّرُهُۥ لِلۡيُسۡرَىٰ ﴿٧﴾

8. And as for him who stints and is unheeding,

وَأَمَّا مَنۢ بَخِلَ وَٱسۡتَغۡنَىٰ ﴿٨﴾

9. And who belies the good,

وَكَذَّبَ بِٱلۡحُسۡنَىٰ ﴿٩﴾

10. To him We shall indeed make easy the path to hardship,

فَسَنُيَسِّرُهُۥ لِلۡعُسۡرَىٰ ﴿١٠﴾

11. And when he perishes, his substance will not avail him.

وَمَا يُغۡنِى عَنۡهُ مَالُهُۥٓ إِذَا تَرَدَّىٰٓ ﴿١١﴾

12. Verily on Us is the guidance,

إِنَّ عَلَيۡنَا لَلۡهُدَىٰ ﴿١٢﴾

13. And verily Ours is both the Hereafter and the present life.

وَإِنَّ لَنَا لَلۡءَاخِرَةَ وَالۡأُوۡلَىٰ ۞

14. Therefore I have warned you of the Flaming Fire.

فَأَنۡذَرۡتُكُمۡ نَارًا تَلَظَّىٰ ۞

15. None shall roast therein except the most wretched,

لَا يَصۡلَىٰهَآ إِلَّا الۡأَشۡقَى ۞

16. Who denies and turns away.

الَّذِى كَذَّبَ وَتَوَلَّىٰ ۞

17. And the pious shall avoid it altogether,

وَسَيُجَنَّبُهَا الۡأَتۡقَى ۞

18. He who spends his substance that he may be cleansed,

الَّذِى يُؤۡتِى مَالَهُۥ يَتَزَكَّىٰ ۞

19. And who has no favour from any one to pay back,[764]

وَمَا لِأَحَدٍ عِنۡدَهُۥ مِنۡ نِّعۡمَةٍ تُجۡزَىٰٓ ۞

20. But only seeks the goodwill of his Lord, the Most High.

إِلَّا ابۡتِغَآءَ وَجۡهِ رَبِّهِ الۡأَعۡلَىٰ ۞

21. And soon he shall be well-pleased.

وَلَسَوۡفَ يَرۡضَىٰ ۞

---

764. The giving of his wealth is absolutely in the way of God, not in return for some past favour from someone or in expectation of some future reward.

Sūrah 93

al-Ḍuḥā

(Makkan, 1 Section, 11 Verses)

In the name of Allah, the Compassionate, the Merciful.

Section 1

1. By the morning brightness,

2. By the night, when it darkens.

3. Your Lord has not forsaken you,[765] nor is He displeased.

4. And the Hereafter is indeed better unto you than the present life.

5. And soon shall your Lord give unto you so that you shall be well-pleased.

6. Did He not find you an orphan? So He sheltered you.

7. And He found you wandering.[766] So He guided you.

---

765. This is addressed to the Prophet. The implication is that God never forsakes His devoted servants, much less His true Prophets. And thus the verse contradicts the reported cry of the agony of 'Isa Jesus: 'My God, My God, why hast Thou forsaken me' (Mk. 15: 34; Mt. 27: 46).

766. Wandering in the way of God, born as you were in the midst of the worst idolatry, i.e., struggling to find thy way; in search of the true light. That the character of the Prophet was even in his youth exemplary and exceptional in the most tempting environment of Makka is borne out by hostile biographers. 'It is quite in keeping with the character of Mohammed that he should have shrunk from the coarse and licentious practices of his youthful friends. Endowed with a refined mind and delicate taste, reserved and meditative, he lived much within himself, and the ponderings of his heart no doubt supplied occupation for leisure hours spent by others of a lower stamp in rude sports and profligacy. The fair character and honorable bearing of the unobtrusive youth won the approbation of his fellow-citizens; and he received the title, by common consent, of al-Amin, the faithful' (Muir, *Life of Muhammad*, pp. 19–20).

8.　And He found you destitute.
So He enriched you.

وَوَجَدَكَ عَآئِلًا فَأَغۡنٰی ۸

9.　Therefore as to the orphan
be not overbearing unto him;

فَأَمَّا الۡیَتِیۡمَ فَلَا تَقۡهَرۡ ۹

10.　And as to the beggar, chide
him not;

وَأَمَّا السَّآئِلَ فَلَا تَنۡهَرۡ ۱۰

11.　And as to the favours of your
Lord, discourse you thereof.[767]

وَأَمَّا بِنِعۡمَةِ رَبِّكَ فَحَدِّثۡ ۱۱

---

767. Compare a remarkable tribute paid to the spiritual genius and constructive greatness of the Prophet made by an unfriendly Christian: 'Muhammad's career is a wonderful instance of the force and life that resides in him who possesses an intense faith in God and the unseen world he will always be regarded as one of those who have had that influence over the faith, morals, and whole earthly life of their fellow-men, which none but a really great man ever did, or can exercise, and as one of those whose efforts to propagate a great verity will prosper' (Rodwell, *The Koran*, pp. 14–15).

Sūrah 94

al-Sharḥ

(Makkan, 1 Section, 8 Verses)

In the name of Allah, the Compassionate, the Merciful.

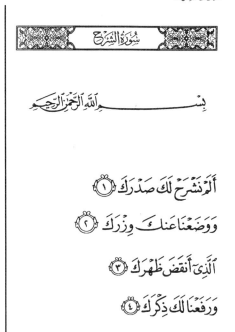

Section 1

1. Have We not opened for you your breast?[768]

2. And We have taken off from you your burden,[769]

3. Which weighed down your back.

4. And We have exalted your fame.[770]

---

768. This by disposing and expanding it to receive the Truth and wisdom, and by freeing it from ignorance and uneasiness. Again this is addressed to the Prophet.

769. By making your soul fully illumined.

770. So much so that even anti-Muslim Christian scholars have to acknowledge the greatness, almost super-human, nature of the Holy Prophet. 'One of the most remarkable men in the history of the world' (Drinkwater, *Outline of Literature*, I, p. 146). To mention another tribute, Charles Issawi of New York City, writing under the heading 'Muhammad's Historical Role', says at the end of his article. 'It does not seem too much to say that if any one man changed the course of history that man was Muhammad' (*The Muslim World*, April 1950, p. 95). 'The Man', says Draper, who 'of all men, has exercised the greatest influence upon the human race.' (*History of the Intellectual Development of Europe*, I, p. 329). The same verdict is endorsed in one of the recent editions of the *Encyclopedia Britannica* which refers to him as 'that most successful of all prophets and religious personalities' (*EBr.* XV. p. 898). In the words of yet another Christian: 'Compare Mohammed with the long roll of men whom the world by common consent has called "Great". Take him all in all, what he was and what he did, and what those inspired by him have done, he seems to me to stand alone above and beyond them all' (Bosworth Smith, *Mohammed and Mohammedanism*, pp. 339 – 340). 'Within a brief span of mortal life Muhammad called forth out of unpromising material a nation never united before, in a country that was hitherto but a geographical expression; established a religion which in vast areas superseded Christianity and Judaism and still claims the adherence of a goodly portion of the human race; and laid the basis of an empire that was soon to embrace within its far-flung boundaries the fairest provinces of the then civilized world' (Hitti, *History of the Arabs*, pp. 121 – 122).

5. Verily then along with every hardship is ease.

فَإِنَّ مَعَ الۡعُسۡرِ يُسۡرًا ۞

6. Verily along with every hardship is ease.

إِنَّ مَعَ الۡعُسۡرِ يُسۡرًا ۞

7. Toil then when you are relieved.

فَإِذَا فَرَغۡتَ فَانۡصَبۡ ۞

8. And attend to your Lord.

وَإِلَىٰ رَبِّكَ فَارۡغَبۡ ۞

Sūrah 95

al-Tīn

(Makkan, 1 Section, 8 Verses)

*In the name of Allah, the
Compassionate, the Merciful.*

Section 1

1. By the fig, by the olive,

2. By Mount Sinai,

3. By this secure city,

4. Assuredly We have created man in the best mould.[771]

5. Thereafter We revert him to the lowest of the low.[772]

6. Save those who believe and work righteous deeds.[773] Theirs shall be the reward unending.

7. What will make you deny the Requital?

8. Is not Allah the Greatest of rulers?

---

771. Man as the comeliest specimen of God's handiwork is born pure and individually perfect, with no chain of reincarnation to stagger through and certainly with no stigma of original sin.

772. Or 'the vilest of the vile'. Sinners destroy their original perfection by their own hands.

773. Man's original, innate, purity can be retained by realizing God's unity and submitting to His laws.

Sūrah 96

al-ʿAlaq

(Makkan, 1 Section, 19 Verses)

In the name of Allah, the Compassionate, the Merciful.

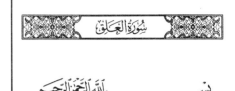

Section 1

1. Recite in the name of your Lord Who has created everything,

2. Has created man from a clot.

3. Recite and your Lord is the Most Bountiful.

4. Who has taught man the pen.

5. Has taught man what he knew not.[774]

6. No indeed: Verily man exorbitates,

7. As he considers himself self-sufficient.

8. Truly to your Lord is the return.

9. Have you considered him who forbids,

10. A bondsman of Ours when he prays?

---

774. The first five verses of this Chapter are the first revelation of the Qurʾān, which took place in the month of Ramaḍān – probably during the last ten nights of it corresponding to July or August 610 CE.

11. Have you considered if he is himself guided,

أَرَءَيْتَ إِن كَانَ عَلَى الْهُدَىٰٓ ﴿١١﴾

12. Or, he commands piety?

أَوْ أَمَرَ بِالتَّقْوَىٰٓ ﴿١٢﴾

13. Have you considered, if he denies and turns away?

أَرَءَيْتَ إِن كَذَّبَ وَتَوَلَّىٰٓ ﴿١٣﴾

14. Does he not know that Allah sees?

أَلَمْ يَعْلَم بِأَنَّ اللَّهَ يَرَىٰ ﴿١٤﴾

15. No indeed: If he desists not, We shall seize and deal him by the forelock.

كَلَّا لَئِن لَّمْ يَنتَهِ لَنَسْفَعًا بِالنَّاصِيَةِ ﴿١٥﴾

16. A forelock, lying, sinning.

نَاصِيَةٍ كَاذِبَةٍ خَاطِئَةٍ ﴿١٦﴾

17. Well, then, let him call his assembly.[775]

فَلْيَدْعُ نَادِيَهُۥ ﴿١٧﴾

18. We also shall call the infernal guards.

سَنَدْعُ الزَّبَانِيَةَ ﴿١٨﴾

19. No indeed! Do not obey him. Continue to adore, and continue to draw near.

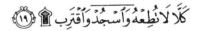 كَلَّا لَا تُطِعْهُ وَاسْجُدْ وَاقْتَرِب ﴿١٩﴾

---

775. Call the assembly for assistance. The allusion is to the principal Makkans, the greater part of whom were adherents of Abu Jahl.

Sūrah 97

al-Qadr

(Makkan, 1 Section, 5 Verses)

In the name of Allah, the Compassionate, the Merciful.

Section 1

1. Verily We have sent it down on the night of power.

إِنَّآ أَنزَلْنَٰهُ فِى لَيْلَةِ ٱلْقَدْرِ ﴿١﴾

2. And what will make you know what the night of power is?

وَمَآ أَدْرَىٰكَ مَا لَيْلَةُ ٱلْقَدْرِ ﴿٢﴾

3. The night of power is better than a thousand months.[776]

لَيْلَةُ ٱلْقَدْرِ خَيْرٌ مِّنْ أَلْفِ شَهْرٍ ﴿٣﴾

4. The angels and the spirit descend therein by the command of their Lord with His decrees for every affair.

تَنَزَّلُ ٱلْمَلَٰٓئِكَةُ وَٱلرُّوحُ فِيهَا بِإِذْنِ رَبِّهِم مِّن كُلِّ أَمْرٍ ﴿٤﴾

5. It is all peace till the rising of the dawn.

سَلَٰمٌ هِىَ حَتَّىٰ مَطْلَعِ ٱلْفَجْرِ ﴿٥﴾

---

776. To pray in that single night is even more meritorious than to pray during these long months. The Messenger of Allah said: 'Whosoever keeps awake during the night of Qadr with faith and in view of God, shall be forgiven that which is past of his sin' (Bdh. I. 15: 35).

Sūrah 98

al-Bayyinah

(Makkan, 1 Section, 8 Verses)

In the name of Allah, the Compassionate, the Merciful

Section 1

1. Those who have disbelieved from among the People of the Book and the associators, could not break off until there came unto them evidence.

2. A Messenger from Allah, rehearsing Writs cleansed,

3. Wherein there are eternal discourses.

4. And those who are vouch-safed the Book differed not save after there had come unto them evidence.

5. And they were commanded not but they should worship Allah keeping religion pure for Him, as upright men and that they should establish the prayer and pay the poor-rate. That is the right religion.[777]

---

777. 'A creed so precise, so stripped of all theological complexities and consequently so accessible to the ordinary understanding, might be expected to possess and does indeed possess a marvellous power of winning its way into the conscience of men', (Edward Montent, quoted in Arnold's *Preaching of Islam*, p. 414).

6. Verily those who disbelieved from among the People of the Book and the associators shall be cast unto Hell-fire as abiders therein. These are the worst of creatures.

إِنَّ ٱلَّذِينَ كَفَرُواْ مِنۡ أَهۡلِ ٱلۡكِتَٰبِ وَٱلۡمُشۡرِكِينَ فِى نَارِ جَهَنَّمَ خَٰلِدِينَ فِيهَآ أُوْلَٰٓئِكَ هُمۡ شَرُّ ٱلۡبَرِيَّةِ ۝

7. Verily those who believe and work righteous works. These, they are the best of creatures.

إِنَّ ٱلَّذِينَ ءَامَنُواْ وَعَمِلُواْ ٱلصَّٰلِحَٰتِ أُوْلَٰٓئِكَ هُمۡ خَيۡرُ ٱلۡبَرِيَّةِ ۝

8. Their recompense with their Lord shall be Gardens everlasting with running waters, as abiders therein for ever. Well-pleased will Allah be with them and well-pleased will they be with Allah. That is for him who fears his Lord.

جَزَآؤُهُمۡ عِندَ رَبِّهِمۡ جَنَّٰتُ عَدۡنٍ تَجۡرِى مِن تَحۡتِهَا ٱلۡأَنۡهَٰرُ خَٰلِدِينَ فِيهَآ أَبَدًا رَّضِىَ ٱللَّهُ عَنۡهُمۡ وَرَضُواْ عَنۡهُ ذَٰلِكَ لِمَنۡ خَشِىَ رَبَّهُ ۝

Sūrah 99

al-Zalzalah

(Madinan, 1 Section, 8 Verses)

In the name of Allah, the Compassionate, the Merciful.

Section 1

1. When the earth is shaken by her full shaking,

2. And the earth shakes off her burdens,

3. And man says: 'What ails her',

4. On that Day will she relate what happened to it,

5. Since your Lord will inspire it.

6. On that Day will mankind proceed in bands, that they may be shown their works.

7. Then whosoever has worked good of an atom's weight shall see it.

8. And whosoever has worked ill of an atom's weight shall see it.

Sūrah 100

al-'Ādiyāt

(Makkan, 1 Section, 11 Verses)

In the name of Allah, the Compassionate, the Merciful.

Section 1

1. By the chargers panting,

2. And the striking sparks of fire by dashing their hoofs,

3. And raiding at dawn,

4. And therein raising dust,

5. And cleaving therein their way unto the host,

6. Verily man is ungrateful to his Lord.

7. And to that he is a witness.

8. And he is vehement in the love of wealth.

9. Does he not know – when what is in the graves shall be ransacked?

10. And what is in the breasts shall be brought to light?

11. Verily their Lord that Day shall be well-apprised of them.

وَٱلْعَٰدِيَٰتِ ضَبْحًا ﴿١﴾

فَٱلْمُورِيَٰتِ قَدْحًا ﴿٢﴾

فَٱلْمُغِيرَٰتِ صُبْحًا ﴿٣﴾

فَأَثَرْنَ بِهِۦ نَقْعًا ﴿٤﴾

فَوَسَطْنَ بِهِۦ جَمْعًا ﴿٥﴾

إِنَّ ٱلْإِنسَٰنَ لِرَبِّهِۦ لَكَنُودٌ ﴿٦﴾

وَإِنَّهُۥ عَلَىٰ ذَٰلِكَ لَشَهِيدٌ ﴿٧﴾

وَإِنَّهُۥ لِحُبِّ ٱلْخَيْرِ لَشَدِيدٌ ﴿٨﴾

أَفَلَا يَعْلَمُ إِذَا بُعْثِرَ مَا فِي ٱلْقُبُورِ ﴿٩﴾

وَحُصِّلَ مَا فِي ٱلصُّدُورِ ﴿١٠﴾

إِنَّ رَبَّهُم بِهِمْ يَوْمَئِذٍ لَّخَبِيرٌ ﴿١١﴾

Sūrah 101

al-Qāri'ah

(Makkan, 1 Section, 11 Verses)

In the name of Allah, the Compassionate, the Merciful.

Section 1

1. The clatterer!

اَلْقَارِعَةُ ۝

2. What is the clatterer?

مَا الْقَارِعَةُ ۝

3. And what will make you understand what the clatterer is?

وَمَآ اَدْرٰىكَ مَا الْقَارِعَةُ ۝

4. A Day when mankind shall become as moths scattered.[778]

يَوْمَ يَكُوْنُ النَّاسُ كَالْفَرَاشِ الْمَبْثُوْثِ ۝

5. And mountains shall become as wool carded.

وَتَكُوْنُ الْجِبَالُ كَالْعِهْنِ الْمَنْفُوْشِ ۝

6. Then as for him whose balances are heavy,

فَاَمَّا مَنْ ثَقُلَتْ مَوَازِيْنُهٗ ۝

7. He shall be in a life well-pleasing.

فَهُوَ فِيْ عِيْشَةٍ رَّاضِيَةٍ ۝

8. And as for him whose balances are light,[779]

وَاَمَّا مَنْ خَفَّتْ مَوَازِيْنُهٗ ۝

9. His abode shall be the Abyss.

فَاُمُّهٗ هَاوِيَةٌ ۝

10. And what shall make you understand what this is?

وَمَآ اَدْرٰىكَ مَا هِيَهْ ۝

11. A Fire exceedingly hot.

نَارٌ حَامِيَةٌ ۝

---

778. Scattered in a violent storm. The phrase conveys the idea of the confusion, distress and helplessness with which men will find themselves overwhelmed on the Judgement Day.

779. Whose good works do not counterbalance his evil ones, and who is devoid of true belief and faith. Of course any creed that promises bliss as the reward for faith and good works must also threaten damnation as the penalty for infidelity and evil-doing.

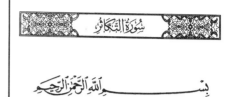

Sūrah 102

al-Takāthur

(Makkan, 1 Section, 8 Verses)

*In the name of Allah, the
Compassionate, the Merciful.*

Section 1

1. The emulous desire of abundance engrosses you,[780]

2. Until you visit the graves.

3. Lo! You shall soon know,

4. Again lo! You shall soon know.

5. Lo! Would that you knew now with sure knowledge!

6. Surely you shall behold the Scorch.

7. Then you shall behold with sure vision.

8. Then on that Day, you shall be questioned about the delights.

---

780. Thus it keeps you heedless of the Hereafter, you having no time for things spiritual. The address may as well be to nations as it is to individuals.

Sūrah 103

al-'Aṣr

(Makkan, 1 Section, 3 Verses)

In the name of Allah, the Compassionate, the Merciful.

Section 1

1. By the time,

2. Verily man is in loss.

3. But not those who believe and work righteous deeds, and enjoin upon each other truth and enjoin upon each other steadfastness.

وَٱلْعَصْرِ ۝

إِنَّ ٱلْإِنسَٰنَ لَفِى خُسْرٍ ۝

إِلَّا ٱلَّذِينَ ءَامَنُوا۟ وَعَمِلُوا۟ ٱلصَّٰلِحَٰتِ وَتَوَاصَوْا۟ بِٱلْحَقِّ وَتَوَاصَوْا۟ بِٱلصَّبْرِ ۝

Sūrah 104

al-Humazah

(Makkan, 1 Section, 9 Verses)

In the name of Allah, the
Compassionate, the Merciful.

Section 1

1. Woe be to every slanderer, traducer,

وَيْلٌ لِّكُلِّ هُمَزَةٍ لُّمَزَةٍ ۝١

2. Who amasses wealth and counts it.

الَّذِى جَمَعَ مَالًا وَعَدَّدَهُ ۝٢

3. He thinks that his wealth shall abide for him.

يَحْسَبُ أَنَّ مَالَهُ أَخْلَدَهُ ۝٣

4. Lo! He shall surely be cast into the crushing Fire.

كَلَّا لَيُنْبَذَنَّ فِى الْحُطَمَةِ ۝٤

5. And what shall make you understand what the crushing Fire is?

وَمَا أَدْرَىٰكَ مَا الْحُطَمَةُ ۝٥

6. Fire of Allah, kindled,

نَارُ اللَّهِ الْمُوقَدَةُ ۝٦

7. Which mounts up to the hearts.

الَّتِى تَطَّلِعُ عَلَى الْأَفْئِدَةِ ۝٧

8. Verily it shall close upon them,

إِنَّهَا عَلَيْهِم مُّؤْصَدَةٌ ۝٨

9. In pillars stretched forth.

فِى عَمَدٍ مُّمَدَّدَةٍ ۝٩

Sūrah 105

al-Fīl

(Makkan, 1 Section, 5 Verses)

In the name of Allah, the Compassionate, the Merciful.

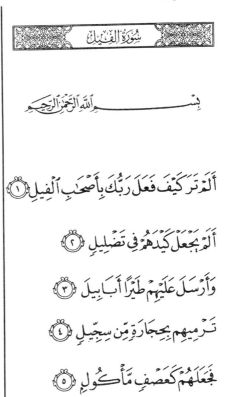

Section 1

1. Have you not seen how your Lord dealt with the fellows of the elephant?[781]

2. Did He not set their stratagem at naught?

3. And He sent against them birds in flocks.

4. They hurled upon them clay stones.

5. Then He rendered them as stubble devoured.

---

781. This *Surah* is remarkable for its allusion to an incident in the history of Makka, as an example of how God deals with those who oppose His will. About 50 days before the birth of the Prophet, Abrahah, the Abyssinian viceroy of Yemen, Christian by religion, proceeded against Makka, at the head of a large army, with the object of destroying the Ka'bah. He had with him, one or more elephants, and the invading army was deemed invincible. The Makkans in their despondency retired to the neighbouring hills, leaving the Lord of the Ka'bah to protect it. Suddenly a large flock of birds, like swallows, came flying from the sea-coast and pelted the invading army with stones. Panic-stricken they made a hasty retreat in disorder and dismay, and there was an outbreak of smallpox in the camp. Scattered among the valleys, and forsaken by their guides, everyone of these perished, including Abrahah himself, and the Holy Ka'bah was miraculously saved from destruction. 'The incident is said to have taken place in the year of the birth of the Prophet (570 or 571), which year has been dubbed 'Ām al-fil' the year of the elephant, after the elephants, which accompanied Abraha on his northward march and which greatly impressed the Arabians of al-Ḥijāz, where elephants had never been seen. The Abyssinian army was destroyed by smallpox, "the small pebbles" (sijjīl) of the Koran.' (Hitti, *History of the Arabs*, p. 64). This Abrahah had 'built in Ṣan'ā', now the capital, one of the most magnificent cathedrals of the age, called by the Arabian writers al-Qalis. The cathedral, of which little is left today but the site, was built from the ruins of ancient Ma'rib' (Ibid., pp. 62–63).

Sūrah 106

Quraysh

(Makkan, 1 Section, 4 Verses)

*In the name of Allah, the
Compassionate, the Merciful.*

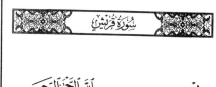

Section 1

1. For the protection of the Quraysh,[782]

لِإِيلَٰفِ قُرَيْشٍ ۝١

2. For certain protection for the journey in the winter and the summer –

إِۦلَٰفِهِمْ رِحْلَةَ ٱلشِّتَآءِ وَٱلصَّيْفِ ۝٢

3. Let them worship the Lord of this House,

فَلْيَعْبُدُوا۟ رَبَّ هَٰذَا ٱلْبَيْتِ ۝٣

4. Who has fed them against hunger, and has rendered them secure from fear of being waylaid.[783]

ٱلَّذِىٓ أَطْعَمَهُم مِّن جُوعٍ وَءَامَنَهُم مِّنْ خَوْفٍۭ ۝٤

---

782. The Quraysh, among whom the Prophet was born, was a tribe held in great esteem by the Arabs as the guardians of the Ka'bah. The tribe, a branch of the northern Arabs, was of the purest stock, and formed the aristocracy of Hijaz.

783. This in the course of their journeyings, by making them respectable and esteemed in the eyes of others as guardians of the Holy House. The blessings of satiety and security, welcome everywhere, were particularly more so in a country so poor in natural resources as Arabia.

Sūrah 107

al-Mā'ūn

(Makkan, 1 Section, 7 Verses)

In the name of Allah, the
Compassionate, the Merciful.

Section 1

1.　Have you seen him who denies the Requital?

2.　It is he who pushes away the orphan,

3.　And does not urge the feeding of the poor.

4.　So woe be to such performers of prayers,

5.　As　are heedless of their prayers –

6.　They who would be seen;

7.　And who withhold even the common necessaries from others.

Sūrah 108

al-Kawthar

(Makkan, 1 Section, 3 Verses)

In the name of Allah, the Compassionate, the Merciful.

Section 1

1. Verily We have bestowed on you Kawthar.

إِنَّا أَعْطَيْنَاكَ ٱلْكَوْثَرَ ۝

2. So pray to your Lord, and sacrifice.

فَصَلِّ لِرَبِّكَ وَٱنْحَرْ ۝

3. Truly it is your traducer who shall be childless.

إِنَّ شَانِئَكَ هُوَ ٱلْأَبْتَرُ ۝

Sūrah 109

al-Kāfirūn

(Makkan, 1 Section, 6 Verses)

In the name of Allah, the Compassionate, the Merciful.

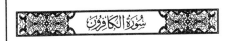

Section 1

1. Say: Infidels![784]

2. I worship not what you worship,

3. Nor are you the worshippers of what I worship,

4. And I shall not be a worshipper of what you have worshipped.

5. Nor will you be the worshipper of what I worship.

6. Your requital shall be yours, and my requital shall be mine.

---

784. Some of the leading pagans of Makka had proposed to the Prophet a compromise between Islam and the ancient faith such as they conceived it, whereby he would concede to their gods an honourable place. This *Sūrah* indignantly repudiates all such suggestions. And this *Sūrah* 'breathes a spirit of uncompromising hostility to idolatry' (Muir, *Life of Muhammad*, p. 74).

Sūrah 110

al-Naṣr

(Makkan, 1 Section, 3 Verses)

In the name of Allah, the Compassionate, the Merciful.

Section 1

1. When there come the succour of Allah and victory,

2. And you find mankind entering the religion of Allah in crowds,

3. Then hallow the praise of your Lord, and ask forgiveness of Allah. Verily He is Ever-Relenting.

إِذَا جَاءَ نَصْرُ اللَّهِ وَالْفَتْحُ ۝

وَرَأَيْتَ النَّاسَ يَدْخُلُونَ فِي دِينِ اللَّهِ أَفْوَاجًا ۝

فَسَبِّحْ بِحَمْدِ رَبِّكَ وَاسْتَغْفِرْهُ إِنَّهُ كَانَ تَوَّابًا ۝

Sūrah 111

al-Masad

(Makkan, 1 Section, 5 Verses)

*In the name of Allah, the
Compassionate, the Merciful.*

Section 1

1. Perish the two hands of Abū
Lahab,[785] and perish he!

2. His riches availed him not, nor
what he earned.

3. Soon he shall roast in a Fire
flame,

4. And his wife also;[786] a fuel
carrier.

5. Around her neck shall be a cord
of twisted palm-fibers.

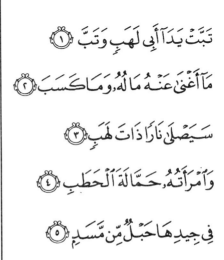

---

785. Abū Lahab (literally, 'The Father of Flame') was the nickname of 'Abdul
'Uzzā, one of the Prophet's uncles, and a bitter and powerful opponent of
Islam. 'He made it his business to torment the Prophet, and his wife took a
pleasure in carrying thorn bushes and strewing them in the sand where she
knew that the Prophet was sure to walk' (Pickthall, *Meaning of the Glorious
Qur'an*). 'Until his death he sided with the most resolute adversaries of
Muhammad in Makka' (*EI.* I. p. 97). The two hands of Abū Lahab may mean his
hopes both in this world and the Next.

786. Known as Umm Jamīl, a daughter of Ḥarb and a sister of Abū Sufyān, she
was the miserable creature who had often strewn thorns on the Prophet's
path. 'She showed much hostility to the Prophet and stirred against him her
husband's antagonism' (*EI.* I. p. 97). 'She used to tie bundles of thorns with
ropes of twisted palm-leaf fibre and carry them and strew them about on dark
nights in the paths which the Prophet was expected to take, in order to cause
him bodily injury' (AYA.).

Sūrah 112

al-Ikhlāṣ

(Makkan, 1 Section, 4 Verses)

In the name of Allah, the Compassionate, the Merciful.

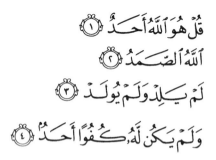

Section 1

1. Say: He is Allah, the One.

2. Allah, the Independent.

3. He begets not,[787] nor was He begotten.

4. And never has there been anyone co-equal with Him.[788]

---

787. This refutes the belief of the Christians and many polytheistic peoples. Compare and contrast the Christian creed: 'God the Father, the First Person of the Blessed Trinity is truly Father as He begets a co-eternal and co-equal Son, to whom He imparts the plenitude of His nature and in Whom He contemplates His own perfect image' (*CD*. p. 360). According to popular Hinduism, the creation was brought about by Brahma's incest with his daughter. See *ERE*. II. p. 811.

788. Either in nature, person, or attributes, i.e., least of all He is an anthropomorphic God. 'In this uncompromising monotheism, with its simple, enthusiastic faith in the supreme rule of a transcendent being, lies the chief strength of Islam as a religion' (Hitti, *History of the Arabs*, p. 129). 'The Vedic pantheon was peopled with gods that lived in the heavens or in the atmosphere or upon earth, their number was reckoned as thirty-three, but those to whom the greatest number of hymns were devoted were Indra, Agni, and Soma. Later Siva and Visnu attained the predominant position and joined with Brahma formed the great Trinity' (Tara Chand, p. 5).

Sūrah 113

al-Falaq

(Makkan, 1 Section, 5 Verses)

In the name of Allah, the Compassionate, the Merciful.

Section 1

1. Say: I seek refuge with the Lord of the daybreak,[789]

2. From the evil of what He has created,[790]

3. And from the mischief of the darkening when it comes,

4. And from the mischief of the women blowers upon the knots,

5. And from the mischief of the envier when he envies.

قُلْ أَعُوذُ بِرَبِّ الْفَلَقِ ﴿١﴾

مِن شَرِّ مَا خَلَقَ ﴿٢﴾

وَمِن شَرِّ غَاسِقٍ إِذَا وَقَبَ ﴿٣﴾

وَمِن شَرِّ النَّفَّاثَاتِ فِي الْعُقَدِ ﴿٤﴾

وَمِن شَرِّ حَاسِدٍ إِذَا حَسَدَ ﴿٥﴾

---

789. The *Sūrah* is really a prayer for protection, teaching mankind the way to ask for protection from fears proceeding from the unknown.

790. So that He may deliver me from its mischief. The verse implies that everything is a creation of God the Almighty, and nothing, neither the devil nor anything else, has the power to hurt anyone.

Sūrah 114

al-Nās

(Makkan, 1 Section, 6 Verses)

In the name of Allah, the Compassionate, the Merciful.

Section 1

1. Say: I seek refuge with the Lord of mankind.

2. The King of mankind,

3. The God of mankind,

4. From the mischief of the sneaking whisperer,

5. Who whispers into the breasts of mankind,

6. Whether of *jinn* or of mankind.

قُلۡ أَعُوذُ بِرَبِّ ٱلنَّاسِ ﴿١﴾

مَلِكِ ٱلنَّاسِ ﴿٢﴾

إِلَٰهِ ٱلنَّاسِ ﴿٣﴾

مِن شَرِّ ٱلۡوَسۡوَاسِ ٱلۡخَنَّاسِ ﴿٤﴾

ٱلَّذِى يُوَسۡوِسُ فِى صُدُورِ ٱلنَّاسِ ﴿٥﴾

مِنَ ٱلۡجِنَّةِ وَٱلنَّاسِ ﴿٦﴾

BIBLIOGRAPHY

I. General Works of Reference

The Encyclopedia Britannica. 11th edition.

J.A. Hammerton, *The Encyclopedia of Modern Knowledge* (London, 1936).

The Columbia Encyclopedia.

II. Works on Religion

James Hastings, *Encyclopedia of Religion and Ethics* (London, 1921).

A. Menzies, *History of Religion* (London, 1895).

C.G.B. Allen, *The Evolution of the Idea of God* (London, 1897).

S.H. Longdon, *The Mythology of All Races* (Boston, 1931).

W. Robertson Smith, *Lectures on the Religion of the Semites* (London, 1894).

W.M.F. Petrie, *Religious Life in Ancient Egypt* (London, 1924).

J.R. Dummelow, *Commentary on the Holy Bible* (London, 1909).

W. Butler, *Catechism* (Allahabad, n.d.).

E. Swedenborg, *The True Christian Religion* (London, 1890).

De Bunsen, *Islam or True Christianity* (London, 1905).

J.E. Renan, *The Life of Jesus* (London, 1864).

A.T. Innes, *Trial of Jesus Christ* (Edinburgh, 1899).

G. Rosadi, *The Trial of Jesus* (London, 1905).

J.W. Draper, *History of the Conflict Between Religion and Science* (London, 1927).

C. Marston, *The Bible is True* (London, 1934).

C. Marston, *The Bible Comes Alive* (London, 1910).

F.W. Newman, *Phases of Faith* (London, 1850).

Friedlander, *The Jewish Religion* (London, 1953).

M. Joseph, *Judaism as Creed and Life* (London, 1903).

H.J. Schonfield, *According to the Hebrews* (London, 1956).

H. Polano, *The Talmudic Selections* (London, 1877).

A. Ptoserpie, *The Council of Ephesus and the Divine Motherhood* (London, 1902).

L. Ragg, *The Gospel of St. Barnabas* (London, 1907).

Islam

W.H. Macnaghten, *Principles and Precedents of Mohammedan Law* (Lahore, 1870).

Mahmuddullah, *The Muslim Law of Inheritance* (Delhi, 1895).

M. Iqbal, *Reconstruction of Religious Thought in Islam* (Lahore, 1940).

E. Dermingham, *The Life of Mahomet* (London, 1930).

R.A. Nicholson, *A Literary History of the Arabs* (London, 1952).

D.B. MacDonald, *Aspects of Islam* (New York, 1911).

A.J. Arberry, *The Koran Interpreted* (London, 1955).

M.M. Pickthall, *The Meaning of the Glorious Qur'an* (London, 1930).

E.H. Palmer, *The Qur'an* (Oxford, 1880).

J.M. Rodwell, *The Koran* (London, 1861).

E.M. Wherry, *A Comprehensive Commentary on the Koran* (London, 1882-86).

Muhammad Asad, *Islam at the Crossroads* (Gibraltar, 1934).

T.W. Arnold, *Preaching of Islam* (London, 1896).

T.W. Arnold, *Islamic Faith* (Lahore, 1910).

W. Muir, *The Life of Muhammad* (London, 1856-81).

Syed Ahmad Khan, *Essays on the Life of Muhammad* (London, 1870).

D.S. Margoliouth, *Mohammed* (London, 1939).

T. Andrae, *Mohammed: The Man and His Faith* (London, 1936).

Bosworth Smith, *Mohammed and Mohammedanism* (London, 1874).

C.S. Hurgronje, *Mohammadanism* (New York, 1916).

Abdur Rahim, *Muhammadan Jurisprudence* (Lahore, 1938).

R. Levy, *Sociology of Islam* (Cambridge, 1957).

Lady Cobbold, *Pilgrimage to Mecca* (London, 1910).

Robert Roberts, *The Social Laws of the Qur'an* (London, 1911).

Henry Stubbe, *An Account of the Rise and Progress of Mahometanism* (London, 1911).

Philip K. Hitti, *History of the Arabs* (London, 1948).

Inayatullah, *Geographical Factors in Arabic Life and History* (Lahore, 1942).

H. Lammens, *Islam: Beliefs and Institutions* (London, 1907).

D.B. McDonald, *The Religious Attitude and Life in Islam* (New York, 1957).

C.C. Torrey, *The Jewish Foundations of Islam* (New York, 1937).

F.A. Klein, *The Religion of Islam* (Lahore, n.d.).

Kremer, *Contribution to the History of Islamic Civilization.*

III. Works on History and other Subjects

G. Finlay, *Greece Under the Romans* (Edinburgh, 1844).

Z.A. Ragozin, *The Story of Chaldea* (New York, 1886).

L. Woolley, *Abraham* (London, 1935).

L. Woolley, *Ur of the Chaldees* (London, 1938).

A. Gilman, *The Saracens* (London, 1885).

J.W. Draper, *History of the Intellectual Development of Europe* (London, 1864).

P.M. Sykes, *A History of Persia* (London, 1915).

G. Rawlinson, *Moses: His Life and Times* (London, 1887).

A.H. Layard, *Ninevah and Babylon* (Leipzig, 1856).

C. Huart, *Ancient Persia and Iranian Civilization* (London, 1927).

W. James, *The Varieties of Religious Experience* (London, 1903).

W.E.H. Lecky, *History of European Morals* (London, 1862).

H. Maine, *Lectures on the Early History of Institutions* (London, 1890).

J.H. Denison, *Emotion as the Basis of Civilization* (New York, 1928).

Westermarck, *Short History of Marriage* (London, n.d.).

C.J.M. Letourneau, *The Evolution of Marriage and of the Family* (New York. 1911).

H. Ellis, *Man and Woman* (London, 1904).

Andre Maurois, *Art of Living* (New York, 1940).

A.M. Ludovici, *The Woman: A Vindication* (London, 1923

W. Robertson Smith, *Kinship and Marriage in Early Arabia* (Cambridge, 1885).

C.A. Mercier, *Conduct and its Disorders Biologically Considered* (London, 1911).

E.R. Seligman, *Encyclopaedia of the Social Sciences* (New York, 1930).

J.F. Stephen, *A History of the Criminal Law of England* (London, 1883).

C. Darwin, *The Descent of Man* (London, 1890).

A. Nemilov, *The Biological Tragedy of Woman* (London, 1832).

B.A. Bauer, *Woman and Love* (London, 1927).

Julian Huxley, *Essays in Popular Science* (London, 1937).

E.B. Tylor, *Anthropology* (London, 1881).

A. Forbath (ed.)., *Love, Marriage, Jealousy* (London, 1939).

I. Bloch, *Sexual Life in England: Past and Present* (London, 1938).

H. Ellis, *Psychology of Sex* (London, 1933).

Kisch, *Sexual Life of Woman.*

Reader, Maxim, *Currents in Modern Science.*

Haeckel, *Riddle of the Universe.*

Russell, *Marriage and Morals.*

Scott, *History of Prostitution.*

Index

Imprimé en France. - JOUVE, 11 bd de Sébastopol, 75001 PARIS
N° 312835S. - Dépôt légal : Novembre 2002